T0137155

Human–Computer Interaction Series

Editors-in-Chief

Desney Tan
Microsoft Research, Redmond, WA, USA

Jean Vanderdonckt
Louvain School of Management, Université catholique de Louvain,
Louvain-La-Neuve, Belgium

The Human-Computer Interaction Series, launched in 2004, publishes books that advance the science and technology of developing systems which are effective and satisfying for people in a wide variety of contexts. Titles focus on theoretical perspectives (such as formal approaches drawn from a variety of behavioural sciences), practical approaches (such as techniques for effectively integrating user needs in system development), and social issues (such as the determinants of utility, usability and acceptability).

HCI is a multidisciplinary field and focuses on the human aspects in the development of computer technology. As technology becomes increasingly more pervasive the need to take a human-centred approach in the design and development of computer-based systems becomes ever more important.

Titles published within the Human–Computer Interaction Series are included in Thomson Reuters' Book Citation Index, The DBLP Computer Science Bibliography and The HCI Bibliography.

More information about this series at http://www.springer.com/series/6033

Yeliz Yesilada · Simon Harper
Editors

Web Accessibility

A Foundation for Research

Second Edition

 Springer

Editors
Yeliz Yesilada
Middle East Technical University
Northern Cyprus Campus
Güzelyurt, Turkey

Simon Harper
School of Computer Science
University of Manchester
Manchester, UK

ISSN 1571-5035   ISSN 2524-4477   (electronic)
Human–Computer Interaction Series
ISBN 978-1-4471-7442-4   ISBN 978-1-4471-7440-0   (eBook)
https://doi.org/10.1007/978-1-4471-7440-0

This Springer imprint is published by the registered company Springer-Verlag London Ltd. part of Springer Nature.
The registered company address is: The Campus, 4 Crinan Street, London, N1 9XW, United Kingdom

Foreword

I am excited to see the second edition of *Web Accessibility* come out 10 years since the first edition that I participated in as a chapter author. This edition is very different with many new authors and topics. Although many accessibility topics have persisted over the past 10 years, there are many new ones as well. New ones include understanding situationally-induced and speech-language related disabilities, new approaches to conducting accessibility research, the impact of policy and law, and ubiquitous computing topics such as wearables, tangible interfaces, fabrication and the Internet of things. There has been significant progress on the old topics with new research and development. This wonderful book highlights the progress on old topics and the excitement and potential of new topics. This unique book covers all the major topics in web accessibility research. For any student, faculty member or industry employee who wants to learn the field of accessibility, this volume is a must read with chapters written by leaders in the field. A theme that permeates accessibility research and is reflected in this book is that accessibility is becoming mainstream. Accessibility research has become a major topic in mainstream conferences like the ACM CHI Conference on Human Factors in Computing Systems. Universities around the world take pride in their accessibility research innovations by faculty members and students. More and more universities and colleges are including accessibility in their courses. Major companies like Apple, Google and Microsoft include as part of their user interfaces ways to access their computing systems by people who are blind, deaf, or have mobility-related disabilities. This book is not just for accessibility researchers and practitioners, but for anyone who wants to learn about accessibility and its impact on society.

Seattle, WA, USA
March 2019

Richard E. Ladner
Professor Emeritus
University of Washington

Preface

Web accessibility conjures the vision of designers, technologists and researchers valiantly making the World Wide Web (Web) open to disabled users. While this maybe true in part, the reality is a little different. Indeed, Web accessibility is actually about achieving two complementary objectives: (1) reverse engineering and design rediscovery—correcting our past mistakes by making the current Web fulfil the original Web vision of access for all; and (2) the discovery and understanding of factors which influence the accessibility of the Web within the context of the human interaction. It just so happens that in the process of trying to achieve these objectives, which have for the most part been ignored, we may understand and even solve, a number of 'larger–scale' usability issues faced by every Web user. Indeed, by understanding disabled–user's interaction we enhance our understanding of all users operating in constrained modalities where the user is disabled by both environment and technology. It is for this reason that Web accessibility is a natural preface to wider Web usability and universal accessibility; it is also why 'mainstream' human factors researchers take it so seriously and understand its cross-cutting benefits.

> Humans are variously skilled and part of assuring the accessibility of technology consists of seeing that an individual's skills match up well with the requirements for operating the technology. There are two components to this; training the human to accommodate the needs of the technology and designing the technology to meet the needs of the human. The better we do the latter, the less we need of the former. One of the non-trivial tasks given to a designer of human–machine interfaces is to minimize the need for training. Because computer-based technology is relatively new, we have concentrated primarily on the learnability aspects of interface design, but efficiency of use once learning has occurred and automaticity achieved has not received its due attention. In addition, we have focused largely on the ergonomic problems of users, sometimes not asking if the software is causing cognetic problems. In the area of accessibility, efficiency and cognetics can be of primary concern. For example, users who must operate a keyboard with a pointer held in their mouths benefit from specially designed keyboards and well-shaped pointers. However well-made the pointer, however refined the keyboard layout, and however comfortable the physical environment we have made for this user, if the software requires more keystrokes than absolutely necessary, we are not delivering an optimal interface for that user. When we

study interface design, we usually think in terms of accommodating higher mental activities, the human capabilities of conscious thought and ratiocination. Working with these areas of thought bring us to questions of culture and learning, and the problems of localizing and customizing interface designs. These efforts are essential, but it is almost paradoxical that most interface designs fail to first assure that the interfaces are compatible with the universal traits of the human nervous system in particular those traits that are sub-cortical and that we share with other animals. These characteristics are independent of culture and learning, and often are unaffected by disabilities. Most interfaces, whether designed to accommodate accessibility issues or not, fail to satisfy the more general and lower-level needs of the human nervous system. In the future, designers should make sure that an interface satisfies the universal properties of the human brain as a first step to assuring usability at cognitive levels.

Jef Raskin—'The Humane Interface'

We may imagine that there are many reasons for the Web to be accessible ranging from moral necessity, through ethical requirement, to legal obligation. However, the two most compelling are solid mainstream considerations: the business case and the 'über–use case'.

The business case for Web accessibility is strong on three fronts. First, one in five people over the age of 65 are disabled. Population demographics indicate that our populations are ageing across the board. As the population ages, the financial requirement to work longer is increased, but the ability to work longer is reduced because disability becomes a bar to employment. Second, an ageing and disabled, but Web literate, population indicates a large market for online shopping and services especially when mobility is a problem for the shopper. A final benefit for business, keeping in mind that disability does not equal unskilled, is a highly motivated and skill-rich workforce. With the growth of the knowledge economy through many developed countries, and a move from manual work to more thought and communication-based activities, there is the very real possibility of disabled Web users being able to finding productive, fulfilling and social empowering employment; if only technology, and specifically the Web, where available to them. *Web accessibility means commercial success.*

Web accessibility is really just an 'über–use case' because in the end we will all be disabled by the technology or the environment. Work on Web accessibility is helping us address many other domains including those centred around user mobility. For instance, work on physical disability and the Web is helping to solve problems of the usability of mobile technology. By applying the same technology, used to counter physically disabled users tremors and jerky movements, to the mobile Web, the operational problems of mobile interaction in moving environments are being solved. Similarly, mobile Web access suffers from the interoperability and usability problems that make the Web as difficult to interact with for mainstream users as it is for visually impaired users. Again, solutions proposed 3–4 years ago in the Web accessibility community are now being applied to mainstream mobile devices. Indeed, a fact often forgotten is that we are all unique. The disabled user serves as a reminder that Web accessibility is a truly individual experience and that by understanding the flexible and personalisation required by disabled users we can understand that at some point this same flexibility and personalisation will be required by all. *To understand the needs of disabled users is to understand the needs of everyone.*

An important route to achieve Web accessibility is to improve our knowledge and understanding of it through research and innovation. Although many books have been published on Web accessibility, unfortunately they have been mostly written from a technical perspective. They do not really tell the whole story—What about research on Web accessibility? How did it all start? How did it evolve? Which sub-areas have been developed? What is the current state-of-the-art? What are the missing pieces? If we want to take Web accessibility to the next level, we need to answer these questions and this book aims to do that. We have invited experts from different specialised areas of Web accessibility to give us an overview of their area, discuss the limitations and strengths, and present their thoughts on the future directions of that area. As one famous research scientist said *research is to see what everybody else has seen and to think what nobody else has thought.* This book aims to help research scientists who are new in the area to see what everybody else has seen and help them think what nobody else thought.

Keep in Mind that to understand accessibility the researcher must take account a number of truths: (1) there is never just one solution; (2) solutions are not simple; (3) a single solution will never work, instead, combinations of solutions are required; (4) you do not know the user or their requirements at the granularity required to make assumptions; and finally, (5) the Web accessibility work is not only for disabled people; organisations and people without disabilities can also benefit.

To build applications and content that allows for heterogeneity, flexibility and device independence is incredibly difficult, incredibly challenging and incredibly necessary.

With this in mind, we will split this book into six main parts. First, we will examine the intersection between accessibility and disability in effort to understand the differing needs of users, and the technology provided to fulfil those needs; you could consider this to be a Disability Primer. In parts two and three, we will describe how to conduct accessibility research, and how that research links to society and standards in general. We will next set out the technical foundations of accessibility research and outline the tools, techniques and technologies in current use to help design, build, check and transform Web pages into accessible forms, and look at web technology off the desktop into real world. Finally, we will present an analysis of the future direction of Web accessibility based on an investigation of emergent technologies and techniques.

Güzelyurt, Turkey   Yeliz Yesilada
Manchester, UK   Simon Harper
January 2019

Acknowledgements

We would like to thank the many people who have contributed to the successful completion of this book. Especially to our web accessibility research community and the Web4All conference for being the best home for us! On a more personal note, we would individually like to thank the special people in our lives:

Yeliz: "I would like to thank my husband, Nihat, for always being an endless source of encouragement. This project like others would not be completed without his love and support. I would like to dedicate this book to my kids: Rüya and Arda, who constantly remind me that there is more to life than work!".

Simon: "I would like to thank my wife, Rina and son Yoseph, along with my family and my extended family of friends for all their love and support over the years. I'd like to dedicate this book to my Granddaughter Lydia. She symbolises, as does our research, all of our futures".

Güzelyurt, Turkey   Yeliz Yesilada
Manchester, UK   Simon Harper
January 2019

About This Book

New and fully updated to cover the last 10 years of accessibility research published since the first edition, this book covers key areas of evaluation and methodology, client-side applications, specialist and novel technologies, along with initial appraisals of disabilities. It provides comprehensive coverage of Web accessibility research. Building on the first, this second edition places more focus on Mobile Web technologies, Web applications, the Internet of Things and future developments where the Web as we know it is blending into infrastructure, and where Web-based interface design has become predominant, Written by leading experts in the field, it provides an overview of existing research and also looks at future developments, providing a much deeper insight than can be obtained through existing research libraries, aggregations or search engines. In tackling the subject from a research rather than a practitioner standpoint, scientists, engineers and postgraduate students will find a definitive and foundational text that includes field overviews, references, issues, new research, problems and solutions, and opinions from industrial experts and renowned academics, from leading international institutions.

Contents

Contributors

Julio Abascal Egokituz Laboratory of Human-Computer Interaction for Special Needs, Informatics School, University of the Basque Country/Euskal Herriko Unibertsitatea, Donostia, Spain

Shadi Abou-Zahra Web Accessibility Initiative (WAI) of the World Wide Web Consortium (W3C), Sophia Antipolis, France

Dragan Ahmetovic Università degli Studi di Torino, Turin, Italy

Humberto Lidio Antonelli Federal Institute of Education, Science and Technology of São Paulo, São Carlos, SP, Brazil

Andrew Arch Intopia, Parramatta, NSW, Australia;
Intopia Digital, Woodned, VIC, Australia

Myriam Arrue Egokituz Laboratory of Human-Computer Interaction for Special Needs, Informatics School, University of the Basque Country/Euskal Herriko Unibertsitatea, Donostia, Spain

Chieko Asakawa IBM Thomas J. Watson Research Center, New York, USA;
IBM T. J. Watson Research Center, Pittsburgh, USA

Vikas Ashok Department of Computer Science, Stony Brook University, New York, NY, USA

Tom Babinszki IBM Research, Cleveland, OH, USA

Ricardo Baeza–Yates Universitat Pompeu Fabra, Barcelon, Spain

Chris Bailey Enabling Insights Ltd., London, UK

Mark S. Baldwin University of California, Irvine, CA, USA

Armando Barreto Electrical & Computer Engineering Department, Florida International University, Miami, FL, USA

Cristian Bernareggi Università degli Studi di, Turin, Italy

Syed Masum Billah Department of Computer Science, Stony Brook University, New York, NY, USA

Giorgio Brajnik Department of Mathematics, Informatics and Physics, University of Udine, Udine, Italy

Judy Brewer Web Accessibility Initiative (WAI) of the World Wide Web Consortium (W3C), Sophia Antipolis, France

Sheryl Burgstahler The University of Washington, Seattle, WA, USA

Marina Buzzi IIT-CNR, Pisa, Italy

Luís Carriço LASIGE, Faculdade de Ciências da Universidade de Lisboa, Lisboa, Portugal

Anna Cavender Google, Mountain View, CA, USA

Federica Cena University of Torino, Turin, Italy

Colin Clark Inclusive Design Research Centre, OCAD University, Toronto, ON, USA

Vivienne Conway Web Key IT Pty Ltd, Wanneroo, WA, Australia

Renata Pontin de Mattos Fortes University of São Paulo, São Carlos, SP, Brazil

Carlos Duarte LASIGE, Departamento de Informática, Faculdade de Ciências, Universidade de Lisboa, Lisbon, Portugal

C. Edler Technical University Dortmund, Dortmund, Germany

Sukru Eraslan Middle East Technical University, Northern Cyprus Campus, Kalkanlı, Güzelyurt, Mersin 10, Turkey

Sergio Firmenich LIFIA, Facultad de Informática, Universidad Nacional de La Plata and CONICET, La Plata, Argentina

Björn Fisseler FernUniversitÄt in Hagen, Hagen, Germany

James Fogarty University of Washington, Seattle, WA, USA

Manuel J. Fonseca LASIGE, Departamento de Informática, Faculdade de Ciências, Universidade de Lisboa, Lisbon, Portugal

Kentarou Fukuda IBM Research, Tokyo, Japan

John Gardner ViewPlus Inc., Corvallis, OR, USA

Alejandra Garrido LIFIA, Facultad de Informática, Universidad Nacional de La Plata and CONICET, La Plata, Argentina

Michael Gower IBM Research, Cleveland, OH, USA

Tiago Guerreiro LASIGE, Faculdade de Ciências da Universidade de Lisboa, Lisboa, Portugal

Robert Haines Research IT, University of Manchester, Manchester, UK

Simon Harper University of Manchester, Manchester, UK

Gillian R. Hayes University of California, Irvine, CA, USA

P. Heumader Johannes Kepler University Linz, Linz, Austria

Jeffery Hoehl Google, Mountain View, CA, USA

Scott Hollier Edith Cowan University, Perth, WA, Australia

Sarah Horton The Paciello Group, Clearwater, FL, USA

Amy Hurst New York University (NYU), New York City, USA

Caroline Jay School of Computer Science, University of Manchester, Manchester, UK

Shaun K. Kane Department of Computer Science, University of Colorado Boulder, Boulder, CO, USA

Rushil Khurana Carnegie Mellon University, Pittsburgh, PA, USA

Sri Kurniawan University of California Santa Cruz, Santa Cruz, USA

Raja Kushalnagar Gallaudet University, Washington, DC, USA

Jonathan Lazar College of Information Studies, University of Maryland, College Park, MD, USA

Barbara Leporini ISTI-CNR, Pisa, Italy

Clayton Lewis Department of Computer Science, University of Colorado Boulder, Boulder, USA

Darcy Lima Google, Mountain View, CA, USA

Amanda Mace Web Key IT Pty Ltd, Wanneroo, WA, Australia

Jennifer Mankoff University of Washington, Seattle, WA, USA

Erich Manser IBM Research, Littleton, MA, USA

Jane Marshall Division of Language and Communication Science, City, University of London, London, UK

Duncan McIsaac Carnegie Mellon University, Pittsburgh, PA, USA

K. Miesenberger Johannes Kepler University Linz, Linz, Austria

Kyle Montague Open Lab, School of Computing, Newcastle University, Newcastle upon Tyne, England

Timothy Neate Centre for Human Computer Interaction Design, City, University of London, London, UK

Hugo Nicolau Department of Computer Science and Engineering, Instituto Superior Técnico, INESC-ID, Porto Salvo, Portugal

Steve Noble University of Louisville, Louisville, KY, USA

Fabio Paternò CNR-ISTI, HIIS Laboratory, Pisa, Italy

Helen Petrie Department of Computer Science, University of York, York, UK

A. Petz Johannes Kepler University Linz, Linz, Austria

Christopher Power Department of Computer Science, University of York, York, UK

Sarah Pulis Intopia, Parramatta, NSW, Australia

I. V. Ramakrishnan Department of Computer Science, Stony Brook University, New York, NY, USA

Amon Rapp University of Torino, Turin, Italy

Maria Rauschenberger Universitat Pompeu Fabra, Barcelon, Spain

Luz Rello IE Business School, IE University, Madrid, Spain

Jan Richards Inclusive Design Research Centre, Metrolinx, Toronto, ON, USA

André Rodrigues LASIGE, Faculdade de Ciências da Universidade de Lisboa, Lisboa, Portugal

Abi Roper Centre for Human Computer Interaction Design & Division of Language and Communication Science, City, University of London, London, UK

Gustavo Rossi LIFIA, Facultad de Informática, Universidad Nacional de La Plata and CONICET, La Plata, Argentina

Daisuke Sato IBM Research, Tokyo, Japan

Jane Seale The Open University, Milton Keynes, UK

Lisa Seeman Athena ICT, Jerusalem, Israel; Athena ICT, Beit Shemesh, Israel

Cynthia C. Shelly Starbucks Coffee Company, Seattle, WA, USA

Glenda Sims Deque Systems, Inc., Austin, TX, USA

David Sloan The Paciello Group, Clearwater, FL, USA

Sean-Ryan Smith University of California Santa Cruz, Santa Cruz, USA

Neil Soiffer Talking Cat Software, Portland, OR, USA

Volker Sorge University of Birmingham, Birmingham, UK

Yuqian Sun University of Washington, Seattle, WA, USA

Hironobu Takagi IBM Research, Tokyo, Japan

Ilaria Torre University of Genoa, Genoa, Italy

Tracy Tran University of Washington, Seattle, WA, USA

Jutta Treviranus Inclusive Design Research Centre, OCAD University, Toronto, ON, USA

Shari Trewin IBM Research, Yorktown Heights, NY, USA

Xabier Valencia Egokituz Laboratory of Human-Computer Interaction for Special Needs, Informatics School, University of the Basque Country/Euskal Herriko Unibertsitatea, Donostia, Spain

Markel Vigo School of Computer Science, University of Manchester, Manchester, UK

Willian Massami Watanabe Federal University of Technology – Paraná, Cornélio Procópio, PR, Brazil

Stephanie Wilson Centre for Human Computer Interaction Design, City, University of London, London, UK

Jacob O. Wobbrock The Information School, DUB Group, University of Washington, Seattle, WA, USA

Yeliz Yesilada Middle East Technical University, Kalkanlı, Güzelyurt, Mersin 10, Turkey

Xiaoyi Zhang University of Washington, Seattle, WA, USA

Part I
Understanding Disabilities

Chapter 1
Visual Disabilities

Armando Barreto and Scott Hollier

Abstract This chapter presents a summary of the physiological processes that support key visual functional capabilities such as visual acuity, contrast sensitivity, and field of view. The chapter also considers some of the most common causes of visual dysfunction and their impact on the visual capabilities that are necessary for successful interaction with contemporary computer systems, particularly for access to the World Wide Web (the Web). The chapter then outlines some of the key steps that have been taken in the last few years to promote the appropriate access to the World Wide Web by users who might have restrictions in their visual functionalities, as described.

1.1 Introduction: The Physiological Basis of Visual Perception

In the analysis of the processes at play during the performance of human–computer interactions, it is common to consider that there are at least three types of human subsystems involved. Card et al. (1983) proposed that successful human–computer interaction would require the involvement of a perceptual system, receiving sensory messages from the computer, a motor system, controlling the actions that the user performs to provide input to the computer and a cognitive system, connecting the other two systems, by integrating the sensory input received to determine appropriate user actions. Given the pervasiveness of Graphic User Interfaces (GUIs) in most contemporary computing systems, and certainly in the majority of websites, the demands placed on the visual channel of the user's perceptual system have been raised beyond the capabilities of a significant portion of potential Web users.

A. Barreto (✉)
Electrical & Computer Engineering Department, Florida International University, 10555 W. Flagler St., EC-3981, Miami, FL 33174, USA
e-mail: barretoa@fiu.edu

S. Hollier
Edith Cowan University, Perth, WA, Australia
e-mail: scott.hollier@ecu.edu.au

© Springer-Verlag London Ltd., part of Springer Nature 2019
Y. Yesilada and S. Harper (eds.), *Web Accessibility*, Human–Computer Interaction Series, https://doi.org/10.1007/978-1-4471-7440-0_1

Typically, a computer system utilizes the user's visual channel by presenting, on a surface (computer screen), patterns of light point sources (pixels) emitting light made up of the mixture of three basic colors: red, green, and blue. If all three colors are fully present, the resulting mixture will be perceived as a white pixel. If none of the colors is present, at all, the pixel will be perceived as "black" or "off". Partial mixtures of red, green, and blue will yield the perception of a pixel with a specific color (e.g., purple). Effective human–computer interaction requires that the light patterns formed on the computer screen be successfully processed through a two-stage sequence: the physical reception of the stimulus (e.g., a desktop icon) and then the interpretation of that stimulus by the user (Dix et al. 1998).

Unfortunately, even the reception of the stimulus may be hindered if the visual system of the user is not performing its expected functions at its full capacity. One could consider the process needed to receive visual information from a computer interface as involving two necessary stages. First, the refraction system of the eye must create a proper distribution of light on the retina, to represent the graphical element being viewed. In addition to this requirement, the neural function of the retina must be operative to translate the retinal image into a proper set of neural signals that will be carried to the brain, where they will be ultimately interpreted. This is shown as a simplified diagram in Fig. 1.1.

1.1.1   Formation of the Retinal Image

The process of visual perception begins in the eye, where the distribution of point light sources that make up a pattern in the computer display (e.g., an icon), must be faithfully projected onto the retina, the layer at the back of the inside of the eyeball where photoreceptors known as cones and rods will trigger electrical signals called action potentials when stimulated by light. The eye is often compared to a digital camera, and the analogy is indeed attractive, since, just as for the camera, the image of an external object must be appropriately formed on the imaging device of the camera (commonly an array of charge-coupled devices, or CCDs), where the images would also be converted to electrical signals. Ideally, each point source of light in the computer display should be projected onto the retina in a single location, to achieve a one-to-one correspondence between the points of light that make up a pattern (e.g., an icon) and a corresponding distribution of illuminated points on the retina (albeit

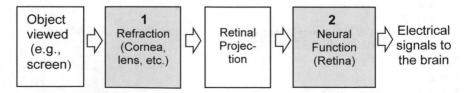

Fig. 1.1 Two stages of functionality required for reception of visual information

scaled-down, upside down and reverted left-to-right). However, this requires that the rays of light emanating from each pixel, which naturally diverge, be bent back into a single point of the retina. If this bending of the rays from a single external point source did not take place, each point source in the scene being viewed (e.g., each pixel on the computer screen) would result in the illumination of a relatively widespread area on the retina, which would be perceived as a blur, instead of a point. Overall, this would result in the perception of a defocused or distorted image. The eye performs the necessary bending of the light or refraction primarily in two stages. Refraction first occurs when the light passes from the air to the cornea, the transparent portion of the outer layer of the eye, in front of the opening of the eye, known as the pupil. Ideally, the cornea should have a hemispheric shape, which would cause it to introduce a fixed and uniform amount of refraction. One more stage of significant refraction occurs as the light passes from the aqueous humor (filling the space between the cornea and the lens) into the denser lens (Martini et al. 2014). Furthermore, the lens provides a variable level of refraction, depending on its shape. If the lens is allowed to take its intrinsically spherical shape, it will perform a stronger bending of the rays of light. This is needed to focus the image from a nearby point source, whose rays are clearly divergent when they reach the observer's eye. On the other hand, focusing the light from a distant point source will require less refraction, as the rays in this case arrive at the eye in an almost parallel configuration. In this case, the refraction provided by the lens is decreased by pulling on it radially, which flattens it. This process of reshaping of the lens to achieve the right amount of overall refraction in the eye that will map a point light source (located at different distances from the observer) to an illuminated point in the retina is called accommodation, and is controlled by the ciliary muscle of the eye. If a computer user is unable to accommodate properly, in order to focus images displayed on the computer screen, each pixel will be perceived as a blur, instead of a point, and the pattern displayed may be perceived as blurred or distorted, compromising its role in the use of a GUI. In addition to deficiencies in the accommodation, irregularities in the refraction introduced by the cornea (from simple lack of radial symmetry, such as astigmatism, to some more complex irregularities, such as keratoconus) may result in the distortion of the retinal representation of each pixel, and therefore in a distorted retinal image.

The formation of a properly focused and undistorted retinal image will produce a distribution of light on the retina that will be sampled by visual receptors, rods, and cones, which cover the posterior inner wall of the eyeball. Each of these receptors triggers electrical signals, known as action potentials, when enough light impinges on it. The rods are very sensitive, triggering action potentials even if very low levels of illumination act on them, and respond to any of the light frequencies or colors. They are somewhat scattered on the whole retinal surface. Because of these characteristics, the rods are key to our peripheral vision and support vision under dimly lit conditions, but are not capable of providing perception of details. On the other hand, there are three types of cone receptors, classified according to the color which each perceives: red, green, and blue. Most of the roughly 6 million cones are found densely packed in a central region within the retina, called the fovea (Martini et al. 2014). The high density of cones in the fovea implies that we normally are capable to perceive higher levels of detail in objects that lie in our central vision, i.e., near the visual axis of the eye, which is an imaginary straight-line crossing through the fovea and the center of the pupil.

1.1.2 Neurological Function in the Retina

The retina does more than just sampling the light distribution defined by the objects we view. Cones and rods transmit their action potentials to the second layer of excitable cells, the bipolar cells, which in turn transmit their impulses to a layer of ganglion cells, whose axons collectively leave the eye globe at a single location (the optic disc), to constitute the optic nerve. However, the transmission of visual information from receptors to bipolar cells and from these to ganglion cells is not a simple relay. Instead, neural processing takes place in the retina, which also includes horizontal cells and amacrine cells, which interconnect cells present in the same layer. This retinal neural processing is suspected to be responsible for an additional increase in our net contrast sensitivity. Further, while the transmission of neural information from the cones to their corresponding ganglion cells (P cells) is approximately in a proportion of 1:1, the neural activity in each of the ganglion cells associated with rods (M cells) may be defined by as many as a thousand rods, making our low-illumination vision less capable of perceiving detail.

About half of the fibers of the optic nerve of each eye project to a structure in the brain called the lateral geniculate nucleus (LGN) on the same side as the originating eye, while the remaining fibers cross over to the lateral geniculate nucleus of the opposite side. From each LGN, neural activity associated with visual input is relayed to the occipital area of the corresponding brain hemisphere, i.e., to the visual cortex, where the interpretative phase of visual perception commences.

Hopefully, the previous sketch of the process by which we sense visual information will provide some background for the following sections, in which some key functional capabilities of our visual system will be considered, as well as their potential disruption and the impact that it may have on human–computer interaction.

1.2 Overview: Functional Requirements for Visual Perception

Proper function of the visual system of a computer user would endow the user with visual capabilities that may be considered in terms of specific visual functions. Four critical visual functions that can be considered and assessed for each given individual are visual acuity, contrast sensitivity, visual field, and color perception (Jacko et al. 2002).

Visual acuity refers to the capability of the eye to resolve two point sources of light that may be located close to each other. As mentioned before, a single point source of light should ideally result in a very small illuminated region of the retina. In practice, even without visual dysfunction, the retinal spot corresponding to a distant point source of light may be as wide as 11 micrometers in diameter (Guyton and Hall 1996). Therefore, two distant point light sources might be perceived as a single source if the physical separation between them is smaller than a certain threshold. The normal visual acuity of the human eye for discriminating between point sources of light is about 25 s of arc (Guyton and Hall 1996). Clinically, visual acuity is assessed through the identification of letters of decreasing size, which will therefore have features that are progressively harder to resolve. With the use of an eye chart, such as the Snellen chart, acuity assessments are expressed by comparison to a norm. So, 20/20 acuity indicates that a specific subject can see details at a distance of 20 feet as clearly as would an individual with normal vision, whereas 20/30 indicates a decreased visual acuity, by which the subject must be at 20 feet from an object to discern details that a person with normal vision could distinguish at 30 feet (Martini et al. 2014). Clearly, accommodation impairments or refractive errors due to imperfections of the cornea or the lens will result in decreased visual acuity.

Contrast sensitivity describes the ability of a subject to discern subtle differences in shades of gray present in an image (Ginsburg and Hendee 1993). Clinically, contrast sensitivity may be assessed with the use of the Pelli-Robson chart, in which letters at different levels of contrast are presented to the subject (Pelli et al. 1988).

The field of vision is the visual area seen by an eye at a given instant. The extent of the field of vision may be assessed through a method called perimetry, which requires the subject to look toward a central fixation point, directly in front of the eye. Under those circumstances, a small illumination source is gradually brought into the field of view along a meridian trajectory, and the subject is asked to report when it is first perceived, therefore providing an approximate location for the edge of the field of view along that meridian (Guyton and Hall 1996).

The color perception capability of the human eye is based on the fact that there are three populations of cones in the retina: red, green, and blue, which are sensitive only to electromagnetic radiation in the corresponding spectral regions (around 450 nm wavelength for blue cones, around 575 nm wavelength for green cones, and around 600 nm wavelength for red cones). Proper color perception can be tested with pseudoisochromatic color plates, which will fail to reveal the expected numerical patterns if the viewer has specific color perception deficiencies. Color perception can also be tested with Farnsworth ordering tests.

1.3 Discussion: Functionality Restrictions in Visual Disorders

The significant human capabilities in terms of visual acuity, contrast sensitivity, field of view, and color vision, along with the continuous increasing performance characteristics of computer displays, have encouraged the designers of graphic interfaces and web pages to fully exploit the resolution, size, and color available to them. However, this has, indirectly, set the demands on the user's visual system very high. Unfortunately, there is a wide variety of conditions that may result in diminishing visual functionality.

It is not uncommon at all to find individuals for whom the refraction implemented by the cornea and the lens is imperfect. This leads to an inability to accommodate images from objects located far away (myopia) or at close range (hyperopia). The inability to focus objects at a close range is, in fact, expected as the individual becomes older, since aging tends to make the lens less elastic (presbyopia). A young adult can usually focus on objects 15–20 cm away, but as aging proceeds this near point of vision shifts gradually. The near point at age 60 is typically 83 cm (Martini et al. 2014). Further, a corneal shape that departs from a hemisphere implies that the effective refraction implemented by the eye is not the same along different axes of the field of view (e.g., horizontal versus vertical). This lack of symmetry in the refraction, or astigmatism, will produce distorted retinal projections of the external objects viewed. Similarly, other more severe refraction imperfections, such as keratoconus, produced by an abnormal shaping of the cornea which approximates a conical shape, will produce retinal images that do not faithfully reflect the external objects being viewed. All of these circumstances will deteriorate the effective visual acuity and contrast sensitivity of the individual, reducing them to levels that may be insufficient to meet the high demands imposed by high-resolution graphic interfaces.

The formation of a proper retinal image may also be impeded by the abnormal presence of opacities in the lens or "cataracts" which may result from drug reactions or simply from aging (Martini et al. 2014). The intervening opacities may result in deteriorated visual acuity and restricted field of view.

Beyond the formation of a properly focused retinal image representing the external object being viewed (e.g., an icon on a computer screen), adequate perception of the image requires that all the elements that support the neural function of the retina be present and fully functional. For example, a subject with a congenital lack of red cones (protanopia) will not be able to distinguish red from green. Similarly, there can be a lack of green cones (deuteranopia) or a lack or underrepresentation of blue cones (tritanopia) (Guyton and Hall 1996). These conditions clearly constrain the typical color vision capabilities of the individual and may compromise the understanding of graphic user interfaces that rely heavily on color to communicate their message to the user.

In addition to congenital deficiencies in the neural function of the retina, there are several diseases that may result in deterioration of that neural function. So, for example, in the United States, the most common causes of decreased vision are diabetic retinopathy, glaucoma, and age-related macular degeneration (AMD) (Jacko et al. 2002).

Diabetic retinopathy develops in many individuals with diabetes mellitus, which affects approximately 16 million Americans (Jacko et al. 2002), although the damage to the retina may not be noticeable for years. Diabetic retinopathy develops over a period of years due to the circulatory effects of diabetes, which may include degeneration and rupture of blood vessels in the retina. Visual acuity is lost, and over time the photoreceptors are destroyed due to the lack of proper oxygenation (Martini et al. 2014).

Glaucoma is a relatively common condition, with over 2 million cases reported in the United States alone (Martini et al. 2014), and it is one of the most common causes of blindness. Glaucoma is characterized by a pathological increase of the intraocular pressure (normally varying between 12 and 20 mm Hg), rising acutely as high as 60–70 mm Hg, sometimes due to inappropriate drainage of the aqueous humor (which fills the space between the cornea and the lens). As pressure rises, the axons of the optic nerve are compressed where they leave the eyeball, at the optic disc. This compression is believed to block axonal flow of cytoplasm, resulting in a lack of appropriate nutrition to the fibers, which eventually causes the death of the cells affected (Guyton and Hall 1996). Glaucoma may result in progressive loss of peripheral vision, with the central vision typically being affected only late in the disease. If the condition is not corrected, blindness may result.

Age-related macular degeneration is the leading cause of irreversible visual loss in the Western world, in individuals over 60 years of age. The most common form of the disease is characterized by the deposition of abnormal material beneath the retina and degeneration and atrophy of the central retina in the area known as the "macula lutea," which contains the fovea. The less common AMD variant ("wet") is characterized by the growth of abnormal blood vessels beneath the central retina, which elevate and distort the retina, and may leak fluid and blood beneath or into the retina. AMD can cause profound loss of central vision but generally does not affect peripheral vision (Jacko et al. 2002). It should be noted that, since AMD commonly affects elderly individuals, it may be accompanied by other forms of visual limitations (e.g., refractive errors) that are also common in that age group.

1.4 Approaches to Enhance Human–Computer Interaction

This section considers an overview of the approaches that have been proposed to facilitate the access of individuals with different levels of visual impairment to graphic interfaces, such as those used in web pages.

Clearly, the most desirable solution for an individual experiencing visual impairment would be a clinical intervention capable of restoring, as much as possible, standard visual functionality, which would, therefore, allow the individual to access information presented by a computer in an unimpeded fashion. Such clinical interventions are many times available, and may range in complexity from the simple use of spectacles or contact lenses to complex surgical procedures, such as the replacement of the eye's lens with an artificial lens to overcome cataracts. The following paragraphs consider the situation in which full restoration of visual function is not possible and alternative solutions are sought to specifically aid an individual in his or her interaction with computer systems. Approaches suggested to aid individuals who are completely blind are different to those suggested for individuals who have "low vision," i.e., individuals who have significantly diminished visual capabilities (such as visual acuity, contrast sensitivity, or field of vision), and therefore encounter difficulty in interacting with computers.

Most approaches aimed at facilitating the access of blind users to computers focus on the presentation of information through alternative sensory channels. In particular, significant efforts have been directed to the presentation of output information from the computer through the auditory channel and through tactile devices. A class of alternative computer output systems that use the auditory channel is the "screen readers." One of these systems, which has become very popular, is the Job Access With Speech (JAWS) system (Supalo et al. 2007). It presents the information that would be displayed to a sighted user as synthesized speech, providing a number of features for speeding and simplifying the search of relevant information in the source being explored. Currently, many blind individuals are able to interact with personal computers using this type of system. However, screen readers provide to their users only the textual contents of the interfaces. This is particularly troublesome for users attempting to interact with web pages, as a screen reader will only be able to substitute the information associated with any picture or graphic element to the extent that the creator of the web page included helpful descriptors (e.g., "alt" text in the HTML source code for the web page). Further, the (often important) information coded in the layout of web pages is poorly represented by standard screen readers (Donker et al. 2002). Similar limitations apply to refreshable Braille displays, which, in addition, have a limited character capacity and require the user to be proficient at reading Braille.

In contrast, most approaches suggested to facilitate the access of individuals with low vision to graphic interfaces revolve around magnification of the graphical elements. This certainly reduces the functional demand on the user, in terms of visual acuity, as each of the features of the graphical elements will be assigned larger extents in terms of visual angle. On the other hand, for a given finite display surface, magnification of graphical elements must establish a trade-off with the ability to present the complete interface to the user at once. In addition, the limitations in visual field of users with conditions such as glaucoma or AMD may further constrain the usefulness of indiscriminate magnification, forcing the users to inspect different portions of the interface in a sequential manner and adding to the cognitive load involved in interacting with the computer. Jacko et al. (2001) studied the interaction styles of AMD patients and concluded that a solution based on simply enlarging the graphic elements of the interface fails to recognize the different ways in which the visual capability of these users is affected. These authors suggested that multiple factors, such as size of graphic elements, background color, number and arrangement of the graphical elements, etc., must be considered comprehensively in proposing interface enhancements for AMD users.

Another school of thought, which has been proposed by Peli and his colleagues, focuses primarily on the contrast sensitivity losses suffered by many individuals with low vision. As such, these proponents model the visual deficiency as a generic low-pass spatial filter that is implicitly operating in the eye of the low-vision computer user. The associated display enhancement consists of the implementation of a generic high-pass spatial filtering process, termed "pre-emphasis" on the images to be displayed (Peli et al. 1986).

It should be noted that the "accessibility options" of contemporary operating systems for personal computers address both of the trends discussed above, by including screen magnification facilities and the ability to select high-contrast representations for the operating system windows and text messages. Further details on these and other technological approaches to aid users in their interaction with computers are discussed in the chapter on "Assistive Technologies."

1.5 Recent and Future Directions: Access to the World Wide Web

For a person with a vision disability, access to the Web represents far more than the sum of its parts—it offers the promise of independence. In order for this to be realized, two fundamental things need to occur. First, the person with a vision disability must be able to use the assistive technologies they need on their device of choice. The second is that the content must be created in an accessible manner to work with such technologies (Hollier and Brown 2014).

At the time of the first edition of this book, both of these access requirements remained elusive. While many websites and apps remain inaccessible, the first part of this equation has been largely addressed due to improvements to the assistive technologies available, the provision of multiple interfaces for engagements, and significant reductions in cost. The continuing evolution in web standards and their adoption has also seen some inroads into broader web accessibility challenges. This section focuses on the important milestones that have led to improvements in web accessibility for people with vision disabilities and highlights some of the emerging technologies likely to provide continued support.

The 1998 inclusion of Section 508 to the US Rehabilitation Act of 1973, based in part on a draft version of the World Wide Web Consortium (W3C) Web Content Accessibility Guidelines (WCAG) 1.0, saw the addition of a procurement requirement in which accessibility features needed to be added to popular operating systems to ensure the products could be purchased by the US Federal government. While the use of screen readers such as JAWS (Supalo et al. 2007) for blind users and Zoom-Text (Su and Uslan 1998) for people with low vision was commonplace at this time, the legislative change led to an inclusion of similar software tools but with limited functionality such as the introduction of the Narrator screen reader being introduced into Windows in 2000 (Microsoft 2014; Jaeger 2002; Lazzaro and American Library Association 2001).

Although Narrator was not considered an effective screen reader for daily use with a warning message confirming this when the application was launched (Hollier 2006), for people with vision disabilities it began a notable shift in the expectations for the provision of assistive technologies. The VoiceOver screen reader (Leporini et al. 2012) in Mac OS X in 2005, a fully functional screen reader, further cemented the expectation around affordability given that the price of a Mac minicomputer containing the VoiceOver screen reader was significantly more affordable at this time than just purchasing JAWS for Windows. A similar path for people with low vision had followed with Windows featuring a screen magnification tool with limited functionality in the form of Magnifier while by contrast Mac Os introduced a fully featured zoom magnification application (Brunsell and Horejsi 2011; González et al. 2007).

While the question of affordable assistive technology was starting to evolve at this time, it was still generally accepted that most people who were blind would use a third-party screen reader application which relied on the use of a keyboard, and people with low vision would use a commercially available screen magnification software that relied on a combination of keyboard and mouse to navigate around the field of view, zooming in and out as required. However, where there were shortcomings in the operating system such as Narrator at this time, projects such as the Nonvisual Desktop Access (NVDA) screen reader were created with the specific intent to bring a screen reader that operated in a similar way to the popular JAWS to Windows but as a free open-source application. The initial 2006 release attracted significant interest and continues to be a popular free option for blind computer users (GitHub 2018; NV Access 2018).

While catalysts of legislation and affordability concerns ultimately led to significant improvements for blind and low-vision users, an important development related to web accessibility was the ability for developers of websites and related web content to use the built-in or open-source tools to assess the accessibility of their work. The inclusion of accessibility features not only moved the consideration of accessibility from a specialist need to a mainstream consideration, but it also meant that ability to test content became readily available.

Due to the use of screen readers at this time being largely limited to the use of a keyboard interface and screen magnification tools being reliant on the use of a traditional mouse and keyboard, the arrival of the WCAG 2.0 standard in 2008 placed a significant weight on the need to address vision-related accessibility issues and that the focus would particularly highlight the issues faced by screen reader users along with color contrast requirements (World Wide Web Consortium 2008). Indeed, of the 12 guidelines in WCAG 2.0, 10 are directly relevant to addressing web accessibility issues faced by people with vision disabilities.

Specifically, Guideline 1.1 focuses on the provision of text alternatives for non-text content which enables screen reader users to hear explanatory text about images. Guideline 1.2 includes the provision of audio descriptions so that multimedia content can support descriptive narration, while Guideline 1.3 focuses on ensuring that assistive technologies such as screen readers can perceive the same representation of information as is presented in a visual context. Guideline 1.4 is also focused on addressing vision-related issues by providing guidance on color contrast, while Guideline 2.1 requires that all functionality is available from a keyboard given that this was the primary interaction method for desktop computer users at the time (World Wide Web Consortium 2008).

Other WCAG 2.0 guidelines that were relevant to web accessibility for people who are blind or have low vision include Guideline 2.2 which factored in the need for additional time to complete tasks, Guideline 2.4 that provided information on where a user was located in a website, Guideline 3.2 which ensured that content worked in predictable ways, Guideline 3.3 which focused on providing form labels and error messages to assistive technologies such as screen readers, and Guideline 4.1 which required code validation so that assistive technologies such as screen readers did not perform erratically (World Wide Web Consortium 2008).

The gradual integration of WCAG 2.0 into policy and legislative frameworks, with such a significant focus on vision-related web accessibility issues, raised hopes that the use of traditional interfaces would be made accessible. While web accessibility issues still remain prevalent, changes to the mechanisms for accessing digital content have provided additional options for people with vision disabilities when navigating the Web (Abou-Zahra 2008; Pedlow 2002; Raman 2008). This is particularly highlighted by the introduction of touchscreen-based smartphones and tablets.

The arrival of the Apple iPhone in 2008 saw a swift innovation in support for people with vision disabilities with the introduction of the first mainstream accessible touchscreen device 1 year later in the form of the 2009 Apple iPhone 3GS. Additional platforms followed with the more affordable Google Android in 2011, and the touch-enabled Windows 8 in 2012 (Hollier 2013). Prior to the release of the iPhone 3GS with its VoiceOver touch-enabled screen reader, there was significant concern that the arrival of touch-enabled devices would be to the detriment of people with vision disabilities and create a greater divide in access to web content. However, the innovative use of touch and gesture commands combined with haptic feedback through vibrations of the mobile device resulted in the opposite effect. In essence, the iPhone 3GS demonstrated that what had been considered a critical part of the screen reader interface—the keyboard—was no longer required for input and navigation, resulting in both accessibility and portability (Gonçalves et al. 2011; Kalpana and Arvinder 2013; Nicolau et al. 2014).

While the high-end cost of Apple products made it prohibitive for some, the price was competitive with commercial screen reader software and was generally more affordable than specialist hardware products that had less functionality (de Jonge 2014). The arrival of Google Android and its Talkback screen reader continued the trend by introducing accessibility features in more affordable devices (Hollier 2013). In addition, the integration of touchscreen support in Windows 8 provided the first significant opportunity for people with vision disabilities to have a choice of interface for accessibility features. The operating system completely rebuilt its limited Narrator and Magnifier features to enable both the screen reader and magnifier to be available via traditional keyboard and mouse commands or by touchscreen. While mobile operating systems did provide some limited keyboard support, Windows 8 endeavored to ensure that all functionality could be achieved by multiple input devices. In addition to significant interface improvements, it also led to an upgrade in the quality of the built-in accessibility features.

1.6   Authors' Opinion of the Field

The perception of web accessibility for people with vision disabilities today has seen a continued evolution of accessibility improvements. It is now assumed that the four major consumer operating systems of Windows, Mac OS, iOS, and Android, all have high-quality and built-in accessibility features and the need to purchase additional software is the exception rather than the rule.

For people with vision disabilities, there are a wealth of integrated features including effective screen readers, screen magnification tools, color correction filters, high-contrast themes, and scalable text sizes. There is also the ability to seamlessly combine multiple features such as the use of a screen reader in combination with a full-screen zoom feature and a high-contrast theme (Microsoft 2018; Apple 2018; Google 2018).

Instead of third-party applications filling an essential accessibility requirement, mobile apps are now using web content to provide additional support such as real-world navigation functionality in Google Maps and vision-specific apps such as Seeing AI app on the iPhone (Microsoft 2017) and the Eye-D app on Android (Gingermind Technologies 2017).

However, with the touchscreen interface now been a popular choice for people with vision disabilities, there was growing concern that the WCAG standard, which was largely based on the assumption that people with vision disabilities would use a keyboard for assistive technologies, was rapidly becoming outdated. As such, in 2018, W3C released the WCAG 2.1 standard (World Wide Web Consortium 2018). This saw the addition of Guideline 2.5 which focused on making it easier to use inputs other than keyboard. The inclusion of this guideline along with additional mobile-specific updates to other guidelines has again provided support to developers in their ability to make web content accessible on different platforms using different assistive technology interfaces.

Yet in a similar way to the rapid growth of touchscreen devices, another disruptive interface has arrived which also has implications for people with vision disabilities in providing another mechanism to gain access to web content. The use of digital assistants, both as software on mobile devices and as standalone digital assistants such as the Amazon Echo and Google home, represents another potentially accessible mechanism to use web functionality. Given that such technologies are reliant on the web and can also provide access to big data and the Internet of Things (IoT) by connecting to mechanisms that can directly assist people with vision disabilities based on human limitations, it can be argued that this type of interface interaction is, in principle, a form of assistive technology in itself (Hennig 2016).

Popular standalone "smartspeaker" product families of digital assistants in this category include the Amazon Echo, Google Home, and the Apple Home Pod. While the smart speaker itself does not contain much in the way of assistive technology tools, the conversational nature of its interface, which can now rival human comprehension, makes it ideal for people with vision disabilities to find information and request actions such as asking for a specific radio station to be streamed instead of using a physical radio or searching an inaccessible website or app for the feature (Mitchell 2016; Dores et al. 2014; Hollier et al. 2017). While a standalone digital assistant is unlikely to replace the use of a desktop or mobile device, its audio-based interaction can provide a complementary service in specific scenarios (Hollier et al. 2017).

Given the ongoing changes to technology and their potential impact on people with vision disabilities, the W3C has decided to take a more pro-active approach for the development of its next web standard to avoid delays such as the release of the WCAG 2.1 standard nearly a decade after the release of an accessible smartphone. The new initiative, code-named Silver (AG) is endeavoring to combine several current standards including WCAG to provide one set of overarching guidelines and associated testable success criteria to support current and emerging technologies (World Wide Web Consortium 2017). While the project is ambitious, its success would ensure that as innovative industry developments are created, applicable accessibility standards will already be available for guidance on how best to meet the needs of people with a vision disability.

1.7   Conclusions

The brief summary presented here of the basic physiological processes, the expected functional capabilities, and the most common afflictions of the human visual system may prove useful in trying to understand how visual impairments introduce critical barriers in the process of human–computer interaction.

Similarly, the linkages presented between the physiological processes involved in visual function and the most important visual capabilities required for efficient interaction with computers may provide a guide for future exploration of mechanisms by which new technologies might be able to adapt the visual output of the computer for a better assimilation by individuals whose visual system may not be fully functional.

It is encouraging, therefore, that emerging trends associated with digital access support for people with vision disabilities appear to be improving. This includes a recent focus in the provision of assistive technology cross-compatibility such as the use of a screen reader, screen magnifier, and high-contrast themes simultaneously along with the ability to choose from multiple accessible interfaces including keyboard, haptic touchscreens, and conversational digital assistants.

However, despite such improvements, accessibility issues within web content remain prevalent. Thankfully, significant efforts are now focused on some of the most critical challenges. Recent improvements to web standards such as WCAG 2.1 endeavor to address some of these issues by providing specific guidance for the mobile web. Further, the pro-active approach of the emerging W3C Silver standard, while ambitious, may help break the cat-and-mouse pursuit of technological innovation and the accessibility support that follows it. As the web continues to transform, it is hoped that industry will continue to evolve with it to ensure that the issues faced by people with vision disabilities will achieve equality as part of an open and accessible web.

References

Abou-Zahra S (2008) Web accessibility evaluation web accessibility: a foundation for research. Springer, pp 79–106

Apple (2018) Accessibility. https://www.apple.com/accessibility/. Accessed 12 June 2018

Brunsell E, Horejsi M (2011) Personalizing the PC for accessibility. Sci Teach 78(3):10

Card SK, Moran TP, Newell A (1983) The psychology of human computer interaction. Lawrence Erlbaum Associates, Hillsdale, NJ

de Jonge D (2014) Beyond adaptation: getting smarter with assistive technology. Int J Ther Rehabil 21(12):556–557. https://doi.org/10.12968/ijtr.2014.21.12.556

Dix A, Finlay J, Abowd G, Beale R (1998) Human–computer interaction, 2nd edn. Prentice-Hall

Donker H, Klante P, Gorny P (2002) The design of auditory interfaces for blind users. In: Proceedings of the second Nordic conference on human–computer interaction, pp 149–156

Dores C, Reis L, Paulo S, Vasco Lopes N (2014) Internet of things and cloud computing, pp 1–4

Gingermind Technologies (2017) Eye-D vision impairment should pose no challenge for easy access to information or opportunities. https://eye-d.in/. Accessed 12 Dec 2017

Ginsburg AP, Hendeee WR (1993) Quantification of visual capability. In: Hendee WR, Wells PNT (eds) The perception of visual information. Springer, New York

GitHub (2018) NVDA, the free and open source screen reader for microsoft windows. https://github.com/nvaccess/nvda. Accessed 11 June 2018

Gonçalves D, Carriço L, Vigo M (2011) Mobile accessibility workshop, vol. 6949. Springer, Berlin, Heidelberg, pp 734–735

González ÁL, Mariscal G, Martínez L, Ruiz C (2007) Comparative analysis of the accessibility of desktop operating systems. In: Stephanidis C (ed) Universal access in human computer interaction. Coping with Diversity. UAHCI 2007. Lecture notes in computer science, vol 4554. Springer, Berlin, Heidelberg

Google (2018) Accessibility. https://www.google.com/accessibility/. Accessed 10 June 2018

Guyton AC, Hall JE (1996) Textbook of medical physiology, 9th edn. W.B. Saunders Company, Philadelphia, PA

Hennig N (2016) Natural user interfaces and accessibility. Libr Technol Rep 52(3):5–17, 12

Hollier S (2006) The disability divide: a study into the impact of computing and internet-related technologies on people who are blind or vision impaired/Scott Emery Hollier. Ph.D. thesis, Curtin University of Technology

Hollier S (2013) The android accessibility journey: a vision impaired user perspective. Media access Australia. http://www.mediaaccess.org.au/latest_news/general/the-android-accessibility-journey-a-vision-impaired-user-perspective. Accessed 29 Sept 2013

Hollier S, Brown J (2014) Web accessibility implications and responsibilities: an Australian election case study. In: Proceedings of the Australian and New Zealand communication association annual conference, Swinburne University, Victoria, 9–11 July

Hollier S, McRae L, Ellis K, Kent M (2017) Internet of things (IoT) education: implications for students with disabilities. Curtin University. Note: this version of the report was specifically prepared for the support W3C processes. https://www.w3.org/WAI/APA/wiki/Web_of_Things. Accessed 11 June 2018

Jacko JA, Scott IU, Barreto AB, Bautsch HS, Chu JYM, Fain WB (2001) Iconic visual search strategies: a comparison of computer users with AMD versus computer users with normal vision. In: Proceedings of the 9th international conference on human–computer interaction. HCI International, New Orleans, LA

Jacko JA, Vittense HS, Scott IU (2002) Perceptual impairments and computing technologies. In: Jacko JA, Sears A (eds) The human–computer interaction handbook: fundamentals, evolving technologies and emerging applications. Lawrence Erlbaum Associates Inc., Mahwah, NJ, pp 504–522

Jaeger P (2002) Section 508 goes to the library: complying with federal legal standards to produce accessible electronic and information technology in libraries. Inf Technol Disabil 8(2)

Kalpana J, Arvinder K (2013) Mobile metrics: measuring the accessibility of web contents on mobile handsets. Softw Qual Prof 15(2):16

Lazzaro J, American Library Association (2001) Adaptive technologies for learning & work environments. American Library Association, Chicago

Leporini B, Buzzi MC, Buzzi M (2012) Interacting with mobile devices via voiceOver: usability and accessibility issues. In: Proceedings of the 24th Australian computer–human interaction conference (OzCHI'12), pp 339–348

Martini FH, Nath JL, Bartholomew EF (2014) Fundamentals of anatomy & physiology, 10th edn. Pearson, Upper Saddle River, NJ

Microsoft (2014) Windows 2000 accessibility tutorials. http://www.microsoft.com/enable/training/windows2000/

Microsoft (2017) Seeing AI app. https://www.microsoft.com/en-us/sccing-ai. Accessed 13 Dec 2017

Microsoft (2018) Microsoft accessibility. https://www.microsoft.com/en-us/accessibility. Accessed 13 June

Mitchell N (2016) The 2016 state of the speech technology industry. Speech Technol 21(1):29–41

Nicolau H, Guerreiro J, Guerreiro T (2014) Stressing the boundaries of mobile accessibility

NV Access (2018) Download NVDA. https://www.nvaccess.org/download/. Accessed 11 June 2018

Pedlow R (2002) Who benefits from accessible web content? Why Australian organisations should make their web presence accessible to all. Telecommun J Aust 53(4)

Peli E, Arend LE, Timberlake GT (1986) Computerized image enhancement for low vision: new technology, new possibilities. J Vis Impair Blind 80:849–854

Pelli DG, Robson JG, Wilkins AJ (1988) The design of a new letter chart for measuring contrast sensitivity. Clin Vis Sci 2(3):187–199

Raman TV (2008) Cloud computing and equal access for all. In: Paper presented at the W4A 2008. Beijing, China, 21–22 April 2008

Su JC, Uslan MM (1998) A review of ZoomText Xtra screen magnification program for Windows 95. J Vis Impair Blind (JVIB) 92(2):116–119

Supalo CA, Mallouk TE, Amorosi C, Rankel L, Wohlers HD, Roth A, Greenberg A (2007) Talking tools to assist students who are blind in laboratory courses. J Sci Educ Stud Disabil 12(1, Winter):27–32

World Wide Web Consortium (2017) Silver talk force. https://www.w3.org/WAI/GL/task-forces/silver/. Accessed 12 Dec 2017

World Wide Web Consortium (2008) Web content accessibility guidelines (WCAG) 2.0. http://www.w3.org/TR/WCAG20/. Accessed 17 Dec 2013

World Wide Web Consortium (2018) Web content accessibility guidelines (WCAG) 2.1. http://www.w3.org/TR/WCAG21/. Accessed 14 June 2018

Chapter 2
Physical Disabilities

Shari Trewin

Abstract Physical actions are a fundamental aspect of using the Web. Physical disabilities can impact these actions in many ways. This chapter reviews physical disabilities affecting dexterity, the different ways people physically access the Web, and the impact of these disabilities on physical access. Although voice control is an increasingly popular alternate input method, the underlying health conditions that lead to physical impairment can often also impair an individual's speech or sensory and cognitive abilities. Consequently, easy to use, intuitive physical controls are essential to a Web that is usable by everyone.

2.1 Introduction

Today, people use a wide variety of devices for Web access, from traditional desktop computers with keyboards and mice to smartphones, voice-controlled assistants, and wearable devices. This chapter focuses on the physical aspects of accessing and using the Web, such as tapping and performing gestures on a touch screen, using a mouse or trackpad, and typing on a keyboard. When an individual's ability to physically perform these actions is impaired, a physical Web access disability arises. This chapter will describe the health conditions and forms of physical impairment leading to physical disability in accessing the Web, the resulting access barriers, and solutions to reduce or eliminate these barriers. For more depth on assistive technologies used by people with physical disabilities, refer to Chap. 18.

Not all physical disability is caused by an underlying impairment. Situational disabilities, such as operating a smartphone in a coach on a bumpy road, or while walking, can also cause physical access challenges. These situational disabilities are described by Wobbrock in Part 1 of this volume and are not further discussed in this chapter.

S. Trewin (✉)
IBM Research, Yorktown Heights, NY 10598, USA
e-mail: trewin@us.ibm.com

© Springer-Verlag London Ltd., part of Springer Nature 2019   19
Y. Yesilada and S. Harper (eds.), *Web Accessibility*, Human–Computer
Interaction Series, https://doi.org/10.1007/978-1-4471-7440-0_2

2.2   Terminology and Context

The World Health Organization's International Classification of Disability, Function-ing and Health (WHO 2001) sets out a useful model of the complex relationships between health, impairment, environment, and disability, which will be adopted throughout this chapter. In this model, the term *functioning* covers body functions, activities, and participation, while *disability* is an umbrella term that covers impair-ments, activity limitations, or restrictions. *Impairment* refers to a loss or abnormality of body structure or of a physiological or psychological function. Impairment is the result of a *health condition*, such as diabetes or spinal cord injury. It may or may not lead to disability, depending on an individual's ability to perform their desired activity in a given context.

A *physical disability* is the result of an impairment or limitation in performing a desired physical activity. For the purposes of this discussion, the desired activities are the actions of Web browsing. The context includes the device being used, its placement and mounting, and any assistive technologies used with it, or accessibility settings active on the device. *Physical impairments* of importance in this context are typically those affecting the arms and hands. They include partial or complete paral-ysis, muscle weakness or loss of control, loss of limbs, and reduced joint mobility. Although some individuals operate their devices using other methods, this chapter will focus on disabilities arising from hand and arm impairments.

2.3   Physical Disabilities and Web Access

Many people with physical disabilities rely heavily on the Web to provide access to services and opportunities they would otherwise be unable to use independently. As more and more enterprises move to the cloud, the Web browser is fast becoming the preferred entry point to critical applications. Through their browser, an individual can manage their own finances, run a business, do their own shopping, access education, find work, perform work, and socialize on an equal basis.

With the increasing sophistication of Web application capabilities, using the Web is not simply about clicking on links and typing into form fields. Through a Web browser, we can control players in virtual worlds, explore visualizations of vast data repositories, build structures, "walk" the streets of distant cities, and perform many complex actions. This is achieved by touching and manipulating input devices with precision. On desktop devices, mice and keyboards still dominate, requiring users to reach out to precise locations, make controlled press and release actions, and sometimes sustain those actions while moving to a new location (e.g., when dragging with the mouse). Laptops provide a physical keyboard and a trackpad for cursor control, with similar physical demands plus more sophisticated trackpad gestures such as two-finger scrolling or pinch and spread to zoom in and out. Some laptops also have a touch screen. On smartphones and tablets, gestures such as tapping, swiping, dragging, pinching, and rotating, made with one or more digits, are used directly on the screen. The screen is sensitive to all touches, and accurate timing and touch location are needed. Due to the small size of some mobile devices, touch targets can sometimes be physically small relative to the size of a fingertip.

The following section describes some of the physical impairments that can impact an individual's ability to perform the actions of Web use.

2.4 Physical Impairments and Health Conditions

Significant numbers of people have health conditions that can lead to physical impairment. One large British survey (Grundy et al. 1999) estimated that 14.3% of the adult population of the United Kingdom has some (self-reported) mobility impairment, where mobility includes locomotion (the ability to walk), reaching and stretching, and dexterity.

Physical impairments are often not static—some are associated with progressive diseases and worsen over time. Others are temporary or curable. Still others may follow an unpredictable pattern of progression and remission. The severity of impairment also varies from mild disruption that affects only the most delicate tasks to severe impairment in which movement is lost entirely. Some people's position on this spectrum varies on a daily or hourly basis.

Dexterity impairments are those that specifically affect the use of the hands and arms. These have the greatest impact on technology and Web access, since the vast majority of computer input mechanisms are manual. The following sections present the more prevalent musculoskeletal and movement disorders that impair dexterity.

2.4.1 Musculoskeletal Impairments

Musculoskeletal impairments are those arising in the muscle or skeletal system, or specifically the interaction between those two systems. They can be caused by deformity, injury, or disease.

Impairments that limit an individual's range of movement may make it difficult to reach a key, grasp a mouse, or touch a part of a screen. If both hands are lost or affected, then it may be necessary to control technology with some other body part, such as a foot or elbow, or by using a stick held in the mouth.

Stiff swollen joints are a primary symptom of arthritis and can affect dexterity even in early stages of the disease. In the United States, 27% of adults report chronic joint pain or stiffness (Lethbridge-Çejku et al. 2006). Hands are particularly prone to the development of both osteoarthritis and rheumatoid arthritis, which are the most common forms.

Movement can also be restricted by health conditions such as carpal tunnel syndrome or cumulative trauma disorder, in which repetitive motions cause injury to the muscles, nerves, and tendons. Further repetition of the overused movements can aggravate the injury and may be extremely painful, or simply impossible.

Worldwide, studies of musculoskeletal disorders, including carpal tunnel syndrome and cumulative trauma disorder, have reported prevalence rates based on medical examination ranging from 9.3 to 26.9% (Huisstede et al. 2006). Self-reported prevalence rates are much higher, at 30–53%, with the highest rates being reported by studies of textile workers and students in the USA (Huisstede et al. 2006).

2.4.2   Movement Disorders

Damage to the nervous system or neuromuscular system leads to movement disorders, a very different class of impairments. One major source of such damage is stroke, which is the second leading cause of death, globally, and the third leading cause of disability (WHO 2016; Johnson et al. 2016). 75% of those who survive a stroke are left with paresis (partial paralysis) in their arms, and 55% in their face, which may affect speech (Rathore et al. 2002). Stroke may impact muscle power and tone, reflexes, and coordination. Other common health conditions leading to movement disorders include spinal cord injury, multiple sclerosis, cerebral palsy, and Parkinson's disease.

The most common movement disorders are as follows:

- **Ataxia** is a loss of gross coordination of muscle movements leading to unsteady and clumsy motion. This is often due to atrophy of cells in the central nervous system. It can be caused by many health conditions including stroke, multiple sclerosis, cerebral palsy, and tumors.
- **Chorea** is characterized by brief, irregular contractions that occur without conscious effort, caused by overactivity of the neurotransmitter dopamine. It is seen in Huntington's disease, and as a side effect of certain drugs (e.g., for Parkinson's treatment), or a complication of rheumatic fever.
- **Dystonia** produces involuntary sustained muscle contractions, due to damage in the basal ganglia. The muscle contractions cause repetitive movements or abnormal postures, and can be very painful.
- **Myoclonus** is involuntary twitching of a muscle or group of muscles, due to lesions of the brain or spinal cord. It is found in multiple sclerosis, Parkinson's disease, and Alzheimer's disease.
- Partial (paresis) or complete (paralysis) **loss of muscle function** for one or more muscle groups is most often caused by damage to the brain or spinal cord. It is not strictly a disorder of movement, but a loss.
- **Parkinsonism** is a combined term covering the Parkinson's Disease symptoms of tremor, rigidity (increase in muscle tone resulting in resistance to movement), bradykinesia (slow execution of movements), and akinesia (inability to initiate movements). Parkinsonism is produced by Parkinson's disease, Huntington's disease, and other disorders of the basal ganglia.

- **Spasm** is a sudden involuntary contraction of a muscle, due to imbalance of signals between the nervous system and the muscles. Common causes of spasticity are cerebral palsy, brain or spinal cord injury, and stroke. Spasticity may range from slight muscle stiffness to contracture—permanent shortening of the muscle that causes the joint to become misshapen.
- **Tremors** are unintentional, somewhat rhythmic muscle movements involving oscillations, stemming from problems in the brain. Essential tremor is by far the most common form, and the hands are involved in 90% of cases (Lou and Jankovic 1991). Tremor also occurs in multiple sclerosis, Parkinson's Disease, traumatic brain injury, and stroke, and can also be triggered by some medications. Stress or fatigue can exacerbate tremor. There are many different types of tremor. Essential tremor generally occurs when trying to maintain a fixed posture, or make a movement, and is estimated to affect 2% of people (6–7 million) in the United States (Louis and Ottman 2014). Parkinsonian tremor occurs when the muscles are at rest.

2.5 Relation to Other Impairments

Physical impairment can often occur alongside sensory or cognitive impairments, depending on the underlying health condition. The British survey described previously (Grundy et al. 1999) estimated that while 6.2% of the adult population had mobility as their only loss of function, 3.9% had both mobility and sensory losses, 1.7% had mobility and cognitive loss, and 2.5% had mobility, sensory, and cognitive loss. In other words, most adults with a mobility impairment also had a cognitive or sensory impairment.

Physical impairments associated with aging can co-occur with age-related changes in vision and cognition. Perhaps more significantly, many health conditions that cause physical impairment can also cause sensory or cognitive impairment. For example, the damage caused to the brain by stroke or traumatic brain injury can have a wide range of effects, depending on the area affected. A large proportion of individuals with cerebral palsy also have some cognitive impairment with estimates ranging from 25% to two-thirds (Krigger 2006; Odding et al. 2006).

Disabilities that affect movement can also affect the muscles of the eye, and a person's ability to focus on a screen. For example, cerebral palsy is a neurological disorder affecting motor function. This can include the muscles of the eye, making it difficult to focus or to change focus. 25–39% of adults with cerebral palsy also have some visual impairment (Krigger 2006). For this group, it is important to consider the visual aspects of access in combination with the physical.

Movement disabilities can also impact speech: one study of stroke events reported a 24% incidence of speech deficits (Rathore et al. 2002). This means that voice control is not always a viable alternative to using physical devices.

Multiple sclerosis can affect vision, attention, speech, and concentration. People with multiple sclerosis may find that controlling their movements is very fatiguing, and fatigue tends to magnify any visual and cognitive difficulties.

This has important implications for the access solutions that individuals choose to adopt. Solutions that compensate for physical impairment by placing additional cognitive and/or visual load on the user are not always suitable. For example, keyboard shortcuts must be memorized. Word prediction systems require additional reading and decision-making by the user. Conversely, strategies intended to compensate for visual or cognitive impairments sometimes assume a high level of dexterity, excluding users with co-occurring physical impairment (Trewin et al. 2013). There will always be a need for enormous variety in the assistive solutions available to individuals with physical impairments, to allow everyone to choose an approach that fits their strengths.

2.6 The Rise of Touch Screen Devices

Today, people use a wide range of devices to access the Web, most notably smartphones, tablets, laptops, and desktop computers. Growing numbers of people in both developed and emerging countries use smartphones for Internet access (Poushter 2016). In 2016 in the United States, a Pew Research Center study found that 12% of U.S. adults were "smartphone only" Internet users, especially among lower income groups (Anderson 2017). 77% of Americans with disabilities report using the Internet, with 61% owning a desktop or laptop computer, 58% owning a smartphone, and 36% owning a tablet device (Anderson and Perrin 2017).

Touch screen devices offer a number of advantages over traditional computers. Their operation is cognitively simpler than using a mouse, because the user directly touches what they are looking at. This also eliminates the need to shift focus between a display and an input device, which can be difficult for some people. Touch screens are suitable for people with very low muscle strength, as no force is needed to activate buttons. They can be placed in a variety of locations, and at different angles, for the most comfortable operation. Another important advantage for many people is that they can be operated using body parts other than a fingertip, such as a knuckle, or by using a stylus gripped in the hand.

Standard touch screen interactions include taps, swipes, slides, multi-finger taps, repeated taps, and multi-touch gestures like pinch and spread. These complex actions may represent access barriers for people with impaired dexterity. Anthony et al. (2013) used online videos as a resource to investigate touch screen use by people with dexterity impairments. Through analysis of 187 videos showing a person with a dexterity impairment using a touch screen, they found that the devices were often empowering, but also identified a number of accessibility issues. Other studies of people with dexterity impairment using smartphones and tablets (Trewin et al. 2013) found a similar mix of benefits and challenges in using touch screens.

2.7   Web Access Barriers

Sears et al. (2008) provide an overview of physical impairments and their effects on access to computing, and review research in this field. Studies have suggested that advanced age and disabilities make keyboard and mouse use and movement slower and less accurate (Riviere and Thakor 1996; Trewin and Pain 1999). With today's shifts in device ownership, the physical actions commonly used to access the Web are coming to be dominated by touch screen interactions.

Whatever input mechanisms are used, the fundamental actions of Web browsing can be significantly affected by dexterity impairments. Access and physical control issues can be exacerbated by fatigue and pain, which is commonly associated with many health conditions, including arthritis, cumulative trauma disorders, and cerebral palsy. In the remainder of this section, we consider common control actions and their relation to physical impairment.

2.7.1   Pointing to a Target

Pointing to a target is perhaps the most fundamental Web action. Targets on the Web vary enormously in size, with scroll bars, check boxes, and radio buttons being among the smallest. The reasons for difficulty in pointing to these small targets will depend on the specific impairment. Arthritis may affect an individual's ability to make the necessary movements. Ataxia or tremor may make it difficult to move along the desired path to the target. Akinesia and bradykinesia, in contrast, make it hard to start and stop the movement accurately. Quite different issues are caused by myoclonus, chorea, tremor, and spasms, where unwanted diversions, taps, or mouse clicks can occur during pointing movements. This may leave the finger or cursor far from the intended target, or activate unwanted functions. Spasticity or dystonia can force an individual into an extreme body position that makes it difficult for them to see the screen and use a mouse at the same time. In compensating for such difficulties, older adults, and people with physical impairments sometimes use very different movement strategies to those without impairments, with multiple small sub-movements, especially when close to the target (Keates and Trewin 2005).

2.7.2   Clicking on a Target

Clicking on a target is another fundamental Web operation for mouse and trackpad users. A click will fail if the cursor moves off the target during the click. On some pages, this may even cause an item to be dragged instead of selected. Tremor can make it very difficult for an individual to keep the mouse on target while clicking. With Parkinsonism, a user also clicks more slowly, giving even greater opportunity for slippage. Numbness in the fingers (for example, in multiple sclerosis) makes it difficult for a user to tell if their finger is on top of a mouse button. If their finger slips, they may press multiple buttons, or the wrong button. Again, users may adopt a "move then check before clicking" strategy. Dystonia and contractures can also make it necessary to use a device in an unusual way, for example, to move a mouse by pushing it with the wrist of one hand, and then click with a knuckle of the other hand. Again, this makes it difficult to keep the device stable while clicking. Some users, who cannot click a button, use software that generates a click when they dwell on a target for a period of time. Users of dwell-based selection have similar challenges in maintaining the cursor over the target until the click is generated.

2.7.3 Typing on a Physical Keyboard

In addition to pointing and clicking, accurate text entry is also a fundamental requirement. Many forms of physical impairment affect typing accuracy for users of standard keyboards. Again, the effects of specific impairments can be very different. For example, ataxia may make it difficult to release a key, causing long key presses and requiring adjustment to the key repeat delay on the keyboard. Tremor may cause a key to be pressed multiple times. In general, movement disorders may cause users to press unwanted keys, or miss the keys they intended to press (Trewin and Pain 1999). Typing passwords accurately can be a particular challenge, since there is no feedback indicating what has been typed. Web sites that lock users out of their accounts after several incorrect password attempts can be very frustrating to use.

2.7.4 Tapping and Typing on a Touch screen

Sesto et al. (2012) have examined touch screen tapping, contrasting touch characteristics of people with and without dexterity impairment. They used a large touch surface mounted at an angle, and a simple tapping task, finding that people with fine and gross motor control impairment had significantly longer dwell times than a control group, where dwell time is the time the finger was in contact with the surface. Those with gross motor control impairment had dwell times 1.6–2.3 times greater than the other groups, combined with significantly more total force applied (2.0–2.7 times that of the other participants). Some mobile devices use long dwell times to trigger actions.

Nicolau and Jorge (2012) studied typing errors in older adults with varying degrees of hand tremor, on both mobile phone and tablet touch screens. Error rates were strongly correlated with tremor, but different errors related to different aspects of tremor. They reported errors in a copy-typing task including substitution errors (aiming errors and slips) and insertion errors (bounce errors and accidental touches). Bounce errors and accidental touches were shorter in duration than normal taps.

Slip errors and accidental touches were correlated with hand oscillation, while the common error of poor aiming correlated with task-specific tremor (a subjective measure). They calculated that introducing a debounce time, similar to that available in the keyboard accessibility settings of desktop computers, would have reduced errors significantly. They also noted consistent offsets in participants' tap locations and calculated that taking these personal patterns into account could have significantly reduced errors, especially on the phone.

To support touch screen users with dexterity impairments, researchers have explored alternative keyboards with larger keys (Condado et al. 2011). Older adults with tremor positively evaluated an alternative tapping technique in which users slide their finger over the screen and raise it when they are on their target (Wacharamanotham et al. 2011). The method reduced tremor oscillation and errors.

2.7.5 Multi-Touch Gestures

A study of publicly available video of people with physical disabilities using touch screen devices (Anthony et al. 2013) identified several specific usability problems caused by lack of fine or gross motor control. Gestures such as pinch and swipe were described as being problematic, and none of the videos depicted users performing multi-touch gestures. Apple's iOS 11 (Apple 2017) provides an *Assistive Touch* feature that can be used to perform gestures with single taps, but in a follow-up survey of 12 users in the videos, only 50% were aware of it, and only 25% used it regularly. One reported "it's not too intuitive." In addition to difficulty with gestures, the videos showed problems caused by unintended screen touches, a problem echoed in other anecdotal reports (Hager 2010). Anthony et al. (2013) suggest that an assistance feature that ignores long, stationary screen touches would be useful. One user also reported that it was difficult to tap quickly enough, and suggested a feature that extended the length of touch that is recognized as a tap. Finally, users also reported that the physical buttons on their mobile devices were difficult to activate. Again, the iOS *Assistive Touch* feature (Apple 2017) provides a way to activate the same functions, though it is not known whether it was used for this purpose by the individuals in the videos.

2.7.6 Sustained Actions

Sustaining an action over a period of time can be difficult, not only for people with movement disorders but also for those with muscle weakness or paresis. In addition, the longer the action must be sustained, the more opportunity for it to be disrupted by an involuntary movement. Dragging with a mouse (e.g., on a scroll bar) is a common example, where the mouse button must be held down as the mouse is moved. Another sustained action is following a path through a cascading menu, where any deviation from the correct path will cause the user to lose the menu.

2.7.7 Time-Dependent Actions

Some Web pages, particularly those involving forms and financial transactions, will timeout if the user does not complete and submit the form within a set time period. For people with very limited movement control, typing rates may be just a few words per minute (Trnka et al. 2009). Bradykinesia will cause typing rates on a physical keyboard to be greatly reduced. It may be impossible to complete the form in time without assistance.

2.7.8 Keyboard Access

Finally, some users do not have a pointing device and control the computer through keystrokes alone, either from a physical keyboard or generated by software such as a scanning system. It is essential that these users be able to access all the functions that a mouse/touch screen user could access. The standard way to accommodate diverse input mechanisms is to ensure that browsers and targets on Web pages can be accessed and controlled via keystrokes. However, even when this is done, significant usability issues often remain (Mankoff et al. 2002; Schrepp 2006).

2.8 Physical Access Solutions

People with dexterity impairments use a variety of creative solutions for controlling technology. These options are discussed in more detail in Chap. 18, and include alternative keyboards and pointing devices, speech input, keyboard-based pointing methods, and pointing-based typing methods (e.g., use of eye gaze tracking with an on-screen keyboard and selection by dwelling on an item). Some users operate keyboards and pointing devices with their feet, elbows, or head. Users with very limited motion can use one or two binary signals generated by a physical switch, tongue switch, EMG sensor, or other devices, and can control a computer, tablet, or phone by scanning through the available options (manually or automatically) and selecting the items of interest.

In the study of Anthony et al.'s more iPad devices than phones were depicted, usually used flat or in a stand. The videos showed many different interaction styles, and physical adaptations such as the addition of physical guides, barriers and screen protectors, or the use of slings for arm support. The use of barriers supports earlier research highlighting the value of raised edges in touch screen interaction for this population. For example, Froehlich et al. (2007) examined touch screen mobile devices operated with a stylus, experimenting with the use of the raised screen edge as a stabilizing barrier to aid pointing accuracy for people with dexterity impairment. Earlier work on EdgeWrite (Wobbrock et al. 2003) also leveraged raised screen edges, demonstrating benefits for people with dexterity impairment.

Perhaps inspired by this research, and user feedback, mobile device manufacturers continue to extend the range of physical access features built into their operating systems. For example, Apple's iOS 11 (Apple 2017) includes built-in, configurable switch control across multiple devices from a single set of switches, assistive touch to enable users to perform multi-touch actions with a single finger, and the ability to control some aspects of the timing of actions, such as double taps and long taps. These features, combined with word prediction, keyboard shortcuts, voice control, and support for external keyboards, offer a powerful set of controls for people to configure their iOS devices to suit their physical abilities and reduce physical effort. For more information on these and other assistive technologies, see Chap. 18.

2.9 Discussion

Research continues to explore ways to improve the physical accessibility of devices used to access the Web (e.g., Valencia et al. 2017). As manufacturers move to build new adaptive capabilities into their devices and browsers, more people with physical disabilities will be able to enjoy all that the Web has to offer from mainstream devices. Device adaptations and assistive technologies are an essential piece of the puzzle, helping to improve the comfort, accuracy, and speed of using devices.

Nevertheless, physical disabilities can mean lower touch accuracy, accidental actions, slower input, and more laborious, indirect methods of controlling devices. Web designers and developers play an important role in physical accessibility of the Web. Being aware of the physical demands of a design and reducing these demands as much as possible can have an enormous impact. For example, designs with larger, more separated targets are physically easier to use. Alternatives to sustained actions (e.g., dragging) and multipoint actions (e.g., two-finger gestures) are beneficial for many users and essential for some. Some users will be accessing the Web using very limited bandwidth, perhaps a single button to select items as they are scanned, so it is important to provide an intuitive scanning order and ensure that all controls are included and reachable. Designs with good error recovery help users to reduce the effects of unintended actions. In interactions with a time limit, some users may find it difficult to complete the required actions in time, and a method for extending the time period or requesting additional time is essential. These and other accessible design features are part of WCAG 2.1, the latest Web Content Accessibility Guidelines from W3C (Kirkpatrick et al. 2018), described in more detail in Chap. 13. Many of the W3C's Mobile Web Best Practices (Rabin and McCathieNeville 2008) are also beneficial for physical usability of Web pages (Trewin 2006).

2.10 Future Directions

The demographics of disability are changing, as new medical advances and treatments become available. For instance, some Parkinsonian and essential tremors can now be controlled by deep brain stimulation, a procedure in which electrodes are implanted into the brain and deliver a small electric current that blocks the tremors. However, medical advances do not necessarily mean that physical impairment or disability is becoming less prevalent. For example, the prevalence of cerebral palsy is rising. This trend is attributed to improvements in antenatal care that have enabled more low birthweight babies to survive (Odding et al. 2006; Krigger 2006). More people are surviving stroke or traumatic brain injury, but they may be left with severe physical impairments. Technology is available to extend the lives of individuals with advanced neuromuscular diseases, who cannot breathe for themselves. The changing demographic of society in many countries, with more older citizens, will also lead to a likely increase in the number of people with impairments.

New assistive technologies, such as brain–computer interfaces, hold great promise in enabling people with very severe impairments to access and control technology. People with disabilities are often pioneers of novel user interface technologies like these at a time when they are not robust or reliable enough to become generally popular.

Voice control is also emerging as a mainstream access method, with the rise of personal home assistants such as Amazon's Alexa (Amazon 2018) and device-based voice assistants like Siri (Apple 2018). These systems provide voice control of simple Web services, for example, accessing a weather forecast. As machine understanding of natural language improves, such assistants will perform increasingly complex tasks. APIs are also available for visual Web applications to support speech control, and speech recognition quality has now improved to the point where vendors claim near parity with human abilities. Voice control is likely to become much more widely available, to the benefit of those who have a physical disability but no difficulty with speech. Nevertheless, speech-based control does not offer a solution for all users, given that health conditions affecting the muscles and control of movement can also affect the muscles that control speech. Coexisting cognitive impairments can also impact speech production and fluency (Chap. 7).

As described in Part 6 of this volume, the Internet is becoming more and more tightly integrated with the physical world and our daily activities. New, wearable control devices (Chap. 35) combined with augmented reality or holographic displays will introduce new physical access challenges that have yet to be fully understood and explored.

2.11   Author's Opinion of the Field

People with physical impairments comprise the second largest accessibility group, after those with cognitive impairments. They are a very diverse group, using a wide variety of different access strategies, as well as standard devices. Consequently, physical access is a very important aspect of Web accessibility.

Touch screen devices have been a boon for many people with physical disabilities in making access to the Web easier. However, the very qualities that make them so attractive—direct interaction, device mobility, screen sensitivity, and small size—also introduce challenges for people with dexterity impairments, when the screen is sensitive to every contact, and touch targets are often very small. There is a need for devices to better understand the intentions of their users, in the way a human observer often can, and to better adapt to their users' capabilities. The use of artificial intelligence (AI) techniques to interpret user input is an exciting and largely untapped area. AI solutions could be applied to interpretation of input from touch screens and other devices, and when systems are able to combine such techniques with knowledge of Web interaction patterns, and user intentions, this could revolutionize physical access.

2.12   Conclusions

Information technology, and especially the Internet, is transforming the lives of many people with physical impairments. Users of both standard and specialized input devices can find that dexterity impairments adversely impact both speed and accuracy of Web navigation and text entry. As a result, physical accessibility remains an important area in the field of Web accessibility as a whole.

Physical Web access requires solutions at many levels: the input devices used, the configuration of those devices and operating system parameters, the configuration of the browser, and the user's ability to apply their preferences to a specific Web page. Basic research is still needed to find interaction techniques that support physical Web access without imposing excessive cognitive or visual burden on users.

References

Amazon, Inc (2018) Amazon Alexa. https://developer.amazon.com/alexa. Accessed 31 Aug 2018

Anderson M (2017) Digital divide persists even as lower-income Americans make gains in tech adoption. Pew Research Center. http://www.pewresearch.org/fact-tank/2017/03/22/digital-divide-persists-even-as-lower-income-americans-make-gains-in-tech-adoption/. Accessed 28 June 2018

Anderson M, Perrin A (2017) Disabled Americans are less likely to use technology. Pew Research Center. http://www.pewresearch.org/fact-tank/2017/04/07/disabled-americans-are-less-likely-to-use-technology/. Accessed 28 June 2018

Anthony L, Kim Y, Findlater L (2013) Analyzing user-generated YouTube videos to understand touchscreen use by people with motor impairments. Proc CHI 2013:1223–1232

Apple, Inc (2017) iOS 11. https://www.apple.com/ios/ios-11/. Accessed 31 Aug 2018

Apple, Inc (2018) Siri. https://www.apple.com/ios/siri/. Accessed 31 Aug 2018

Condado A, Godinho R, Zacaries M, Lobo F (2011) EasyWrite: a touch-based entry method for mobile devices. In: Proceedings of INTERACT 2011 workshop on mobile accessibility (MOBACC 2011), Lisbon, Portugal, 1–8

Froehlich J, Wobbrock JO, Kane SK (2007) Barrier pointing: using physical edges to assist target acquisition on mobile device touch screens. In: Proceedings of the 9th international ACM SIGACCESS conference on computers and accessibility (ASSETS '07). ACM, New York, NY, USA, 19–26. https://doi.org/10.1145/1296843.1296849

Grundy E, Ahlburg D, Ali M, Breeze E, Sloggett A (1999) Disability in Great Britain: results from the 1996/97 disability follow-up to the family resources survey. Charlesworth Group, Huddersfield, UK

Hager E (2010) iPad opens world to a disabled boy. New York Times, October 29, 2010. https://www.nytimes.com/2010/10/31/nyregion/31owen.html. Accessed 31 Aug 2018

Huisstede B, Bierma-Zeinstra S, Koes B, Verhaar J (2006) Incidence and prevalence of upper-extremity musculoskeletal disorders. A systematic appraisal of the literature. BMC Musculoskelet Disord 7(7). https://doi.org/10.1186/1471-2474-7-7

Johnson W, Onuma O, Owolabi M, Sanchdev S (2016) Stroke. A global response is needed. Bull World Health Organ 94:634–634A. https://doi.org/10.2471/blt.16.181636

Keates S, Trewin S (2005) Effect of age and Parkinson's disease on cursor positioning using a mouse. In: Proceedings of ASSETS 2005: 7th international ACM SIGACCESS conference on computers and accessibility, Baltimore, MD, USA, October 2005, pp 68–75. ACM Press

Kirkpatrick A, O'Connor J, Cooper M (2018) Web content accessibility guidelines (WCAG) 2.1. W3C recommendation 5 June 2018. https://www.w3.org/TR/WCAG21/. Accessed 1 July 2018

Krigger K (2006) Cerebral palsy: an overview. Am Fam Physician 73(1):91–100. American Academy of Family Physicians. https://www.aafp.org/afp/2006/0101/p91.html. Accessed 31 Aug 2018

Lethbridge-Çejku M, Rose D, Vickerie J (2006) Summary health statistics for U.S. adults: National health interview survey, 2004. Vital Health Stat 10(228). National Center for Health Statistics.

Lou J, Jankovic J (1991) Essential tremor: clinical correlates in 350 patients. Neurology 41:234–238

Louis ED, Ottman R (2014) How many people in the USA have essential tremor? Deriving a population estimate based on epidemiological data. Tremor Other Hyperkinetic Mov 4. https://doi.org/10.7916/d8tt4p4b

Mankoff J, Dey A, Batra B, Moore M (2002) Web accessibility for low bandwidth input. In: Proceedings of the fifth international ACM conference on Assistive technologies, 08–10 July 2002, Edinburgh, Scotland. ACM Press

Nicolau H, Jorge J (2012) Elderly text-entry performance on touchscreens. In: Proceedings of the 14th International ACM SIGACCESS conference on computers and accessibility (ASSETS '12). ACM, New York, NY, USA, 127–134

Odding E, Roebroeck M, Stam H (2006) The epidemiology of cerebral palsy: incidence, impairments and risk factors. Disabil Rehabil 28(4):183–191

Poushter J (2016) Smartphone ownership and internet usage continues to climb in emerging economies. Pew Research Center, February 2016

Rabin J, McCathieNevile C (2008) Mobile web best practices 1.0. W3C recommendation 29 July 2008. http://www.w3.org/TR/mobile-bp/. Accessed July 2018

Rathore SS, Hinn AR, Cooper LS, Tyroler HA, Rosamond WD (2002) Characterization of incident stroke signs and symptoms. findings from the atherosclerosis risk in communities study. Stroke 33:2718–2721. https://doi.org/10.1161/01.STR.0000035286.87503.31

Riviere C, Thakor N (1996) Effects of age and disability on tracking tasks with a computer mouse: accuracy and linearity. J Rehabil Res Dev 33:6–15

Schrepp M (2006) On the efficiency of keyboard navigation in Web sites. Univers Access Inf Soc 5:180–188

Sears A, Young M, Feng J (2008) Physical disabilities and computing technology: an analysis of impairments. In: Jacko J, Sears A (eds) The human-computer interaction handbook: fundamentals, evolving technologies and emerging applications, 2nd edn. Lawrence Erlbaum, New Jersey, USA, pp 829–852

Sesto ME, Irwin CB, Chen KB, Chourasia AO, Wiegmann DA (2012) Effect of touch screen button size and spacing on touch characteristics of users with and without disabilities. Hum Factors J Hum Factors Ergon Soc 54:425

Trnka K, McCaw J, Yarrington D, McCoy KF, Pennington C (2009) User interaction with word prediction: the effects of prediction quality. ACM Trans. Access. Comput. 1, 3, Article 17 (February 2009), 34 pp. https://doi.org/10.1145/1497302.1497307

Trewin S (2006) Physical usability and the mobile web. In: Proceedings of the WWW 2006 international cross-disciplinary workshop on Web accessibility (W4A): Building the mobile web: rediscovering accessibility? Edinburgh, Scotland, May 2006, pp 109–112, ACM Press

Trewin S, Swart C, Pettick D (2013) Physical accessibility of touchscreen smartphones. In: Proceedings of ASSETS 2013: 15th international ACM SIGACCESS conference on computers and accessibility, ACM

Trewin S, Pain H (1999) Keyboard and mouse errors due to motor disabilities. Int J Hum Comput Stud 50(2):109–144

Valencia X, Perez E, Arrue M, Abascal J, Duarte C, Moreno L (2017) Adapting the web for people with upper body motor impairments using touch screen tablets. Interact Comput 29(6)

Wacharamanotham C, Hurtmanns J, Mertens A, Kronenbuerger M, Schlick C, Borchers J (2011) Evaluating swabbing: a touchscreen input method for elderly users with tremor. Proc CHI 2011:623–626

Wobbrock JO, Myers BA, Kembel JA (2003) EdgeWrite: a stylus-based text entry method designed for high accuracy and stability of motion. In: Proceedings of the 16th annual ACM symposium on user interface software and technology (UIST '03). ACM, New York, NY, USA, 61–70

World Health Organization (2001) International classification of functioning, disability and health (ICF). WHO. ISBN: 9789241545426. Accessed online 28 July 2018 at http://www.who.int/classifications/icf/en/

World Health Organization (2018) Global health estimates 2016: deaths by cause, age, sex, by country and by region, 2000–2016. Geneva. http://www.who.int/healthinfo/global_burden_disease/estimates/en/. Accessed 27 June 2018

Chapter 3
Deafness and Hearing Loss

Raja Kushalnagar

Abstract People with hearing loss tend to use assistive and accessible technology differently from most other groups of people with disabilities, primarily due to the fact that their hearing loss influences their communication. As a result, their degree of hearing loss is but one of many aspects of their disability, which influences their preferred assistive or accessible technology. For example, for television programs, some viewers with hearing loss may prefer to turn up the volume, while others may prefer to read verbatim captions, and others prefer to follow the program with a sign language interpreter overlay. Because of these differences, designers and providers should strive to provide accessibility for people with hearing loss across multiple dimensions—hearing loss, legal requirements, communication and cultural preferences.

3.1 Introduction

Hearing loss affects social, language, and communication fluency. These skills develop most rapidly in childhood. The term "hearing impaired" was originally used to describe people with any degree of hearing loss, from mild to profound, including those who are deaf and those who are hard of hearing. Many individuals who are deaf or hard of hearing prefer the terms "deaf" or "hard of hearing," as it has a more positive connotation than the term "hearing impaired," which implies a deficit or that something is wrong that makes a person less than whole.

3.1.1 Demographics

When hearing loss goes undetected, the individual's development of communication skills is likely to be delayed. The World Health Organization estimates that there were

R. Kushalnagar (✉)
Gallaudet University, 800 Florida Ave, Washington, DC, USA
e-mail: raja.kushalnagar@gallaudet.edu

© Springer-Verlag London Ltd., part of Springer Nature 2019
Y. Yesilada and S. Harper (eds.), *Web Accessibility*, Human–Computer
Interaction Series, https://doi.org/10.1007/978-1-4471-7440-0_3

360 million people with disabling hearing loss (World Health Organization, 2015). In the United States, there are about 30 million people who are hard of hearing and about 500,000 people who use American Sign Language (Mitchell et al. 2006). Most people with hearing loss are elderly people who have lost some or all of their hearing.

Deafness is low incidence and random among children but is more prevalent among senior citizens. The percentage of people who are deaf or hard of hearing varies from 0.2 percent for those under 18 to 50 percent for senior citizens over age 75 (Erickson et al. 2013). This is attributable to the fact that most senior citizens progressively lose functionality in hearing as they age. It is a predictable and widespread phenomenon. Many senior citizens also relocate to retirement communities creating population concentrations. As a result, the needs of and solutions for social interaction and learning challenges differ for each group.

The fact that deafness is low incidence and thinly dispersed has several subtle implications. For example, more than half of all deaf students have no classmates with similar challenges. Without appropriate support accommodations to facilitate inclusion by peers or to encourage interaction or group communication, they face participation barriers in informal social and formal learning communities. Older people, on the other hand, often live close to and interact frequently with each other but face difficulties in communicating with loved ones or in adapting to multimedia that is gradually becoming less accessible to them.

3.1.2   Deaf or Hard of Hearing Dimensions

People who are deaf or hard of hearing are shaped by diverse experiences and social forces in terms of hearing loss, physical accessibility, multimodal accessibility, communication, knowledge, language, and legal dimensions. These dimensions are commonly encapsulated into three models: the medical model, the social model, and the cultural model (Ladd 2005) which can shape the development of accessible and assistive technologies.

In the medical model, deafness is viewed as an undesirable condition, to be so treated. Within the social model, the design of the deaf person's environment is viewed as the major disabling factor. In the cultural model, deaf individuals belong to a culture in which they are neither infirm nor disabled.

Regardless of age and experience, deaf or hard of hearing people are at risk for becoming less included in national society. They remain underrepresented in school, college, employment and retirement. Societal and attitudinal barriers, such as stereotype threat, can interfere directly with learning and social interaction. The cumulative impact of less interaction and information has negative consequences for their representation and retention in educational, workplace, and social life.

Thus, increased adoption and use of accessibility features not only increases inclusion in everyday life but also enhances social, legal, and technical acceptance. Ongoing dissonance is likely to reduce participation and growth, and trigger disillusionment from society. Deaf and hard of hearing individuals are likely to thrive and grow when paired with others sharing similar struggles along with people seeking to provide support. The goal is not to merely increase inclusion for a few individuals, but to encourage them to thrive and grow.

3.1.3 Hearing Loss Dimension

People have a wide range of hearing losses—some may have a hearing loss so severe that there is very little or no functional hearing, while others may have enough residual hearing that an auditory device, such as a hearing aid or FM system, provides adequate assistance to process speech. They may choose to use hearing aids, cochlear implants, and/or other assistive listening devices to boost available hearing. Alternatively, or in addition, they may read lips, use sign language, sign language interpreters, and/or captioning.

Hearing loss is generally described as slight, mild, moderate, severe, or profound, depending upon how well a person can hear the frequencies most strongly associated with speech. Impairments in hearing can occur in either or both areas and may exist in only one ear or in both ears. Generally, only children whose hearing loss is greater than 90 decibels (dB) are considered deaf. There are two kinds of hearing losses—conductive or sensorineural hearing loss.

Conductive hearing losses are caused by diseases or obstructions in the outer or middle ear (the pathways for sound to reach the inner ear). Conductive hearing losses usually affect all frequencies of hearing evenly and do not result in severe losses. A person with a conductive hearing loss usually is able to use a hearing aid well or can be helped medically or surgically.

Sensorineural hearing losses result from damage to the delicate sensory hair cells of the inner ear or the nerves that supply it. These hearing losses can range from mild to profound. They often affect the person's ability to hear certain frequencies more than others. Thus, even with amplification to increase the sound level, a person with a sensorineural hearing loss may perceive distorted sounds, sometimes making the successful use of a hearing aid impossible.

A mixed hearing loss refers to a combination of conductive and sensorineural loss and means that a problem occurs in both the outer or middle and the inner ears. A central hearing loss results from damage or impairment to the nerves or nuclei of the central nervous system, either in the pathways to the brain or in the brain itself.

3.1.4 Physical and Multimodal Accessibility

For physical environments, evolving social compacts and legal mandates have led to the widespread development and deployment of universal access interfaces. These interfaces have evolved over time to serve the full continuum of abilities and differences among people with a broad range of disabilities. For example, the implementation of sidewalk ramps and curb cuts for people with mobility disabilities has evolved, not only to serve people with a range of mobility disabilities but also those with visual disabilities. Curb cuts now have gentle slopes, tread, and striped markers that serve people with a range of mobility, visual, and tactile abilities. Similarly, digital and computing interfaces have emerged, such as captions for people with hearing disabilities, and auditory descriptions for people with visual disabilities.

These universal accessibility interfaces aid not only people with disabilities but also the general public, including those with situational needs. For example, a physical universal accessibility interface, such as a sidewalk ramp, benefits not only people with a permanent ambulatory disability (e.g., paraplegic), or those with temporary ambulatory disabilities (e.g., broken leg), but people with situational needs (e.g., worker delivering a heavy package with the help of a trolley or a bicyclist). Similarly, a digital universal accessibility feature, such as closed captioning, has proved to be useful across a wide range of settings, such as bars, restaurants, and airports, and to aid in various activities, such as improving literacy skills in children and in people learning English as a Second Language. Increased adoption and use of universal accessibility features increase not only inclusion in everyday life of individuals with disabilities, but social, legal, and technical acceptance, which are often intertwined. For example, the U.S. Supreme Court held in 1979 that a university nursing program could deny admission to a prospective student who was deaf based on safety reasons. The court concluded that the student would not be able to lip-read when her and her colleagues' mouths were covered by surgical masks. The court commented that its decision was largely influenced by the fact that existing technology was insufficient to meet the student's academic needs, but added that, in the future, its ruling might change if conditions made it possible to overcome this obstacle. The court pointed out, "Technological advances can be expected to enhance opportunities to rehabilitate the handicapped or otherwise to qualify them for some useful employment. Such advances also may enable attainment of these goals without imposing undue financial and administrative burdens upon a state. Thus, situations may arise where a refusal to modify an existing program might become unreasonable and discriminatory."

More than 30 years later, social and technological advances have indeed changed the technological landscape: several doctors and nurses with sensory disabilities have attended and graduated from medical and nursing schools and gone on to pursue highly successful careers in both private and hospital settings (Moreland et al. 2013). Many new or existing methods of accommodating deaf individuals, such as real-time captioning or sign language interpreting, have emerged or become widespread. For example, at the time of the Supreme Court case, real-time captioning was simply not possible, but is now widespread. Similarly, remote video relay services and interpreting did not exist at that time.

3.1.5 Multimodal Accessibility

Physical communication and learning are not wholly contained in a single communication modality (i.e., sight, sound, taste, touch, and smell). Comprehensive meaning in communication is conveyed through the synthesis of information and associated meaning from each modality. The absence of one or more of the five senses not only impacts brain plasticity but also shapes the brain's development and a person's contextual knowledge of the world.

The transformation of information from one format to another in learning and communication can reduce the shared understanding of the world and interfere with the personal connection between deaf and hearing peers. It also reduces their direct interaction with their social or learning environment, which in turn can limit learning and socialization. The lack of shared understanding and interaction can be frustrating and isolating and lead to low graduation rates and underemployment. Fewer than 30 percent of individuals with visual or aural disabilities are employed (Erickson et al. 2013).

Before the advent of multimodal communication options, most services used a single method of communication. This can severely disrupt a deaf individual's perception and understanding. Deaf people have full access while interacting over Internet text-based chat or watching silent movies, while, without assistance, blind people have no access and people with low vision struggled to access the visual information. The evolution from communication by using a single method (telegraph or telephone) to one that incorporates multiple platforms (audiovisual conferencing) can enhance accessibility because they offer at least one format that is accessible to someone. For example, audio-only conference calls would be completely inaccessible to deaf individuals, while an audio–video conference call can support aural and visual accommodation services such as automatic speech-to-text service for deaf individuals.

Universal design for multimodal access is hard to provide because preferences can vary depending on how the information is presented. For example, early silent movies featured a very different presentation style compared with that offered in today's movies. The early movies presented dialogue and action separately, unlike today's movies, which present speech (in sound and in captions) and action simultaneously.

The silent movie era, which spanned 1900 to 1930, was a fully accessible form of entertainment for deaf and hard of hearing moviegoers. Speech- and non-speech-based information were conveyed through pantomime or partially synchronized "intertitles" that were spliced between scenes; they paraphrased dialogue and other bare-bones information about the story that was not apparent from visual clues. Although these intertitles did not present speech simultaneously with action, moviegoers liked the seamless alternation between dialogue and action. Producers later tried to use subtitles, in which the spoken text is overlaid on the video, but these subtitled movies were unpopular and remained rare in comparison with inter-titled movies.

Beginning with the early 1930s, movies offered both video and audio, ushering in the "talkies" era; this format completely replaced silent movies. Deaf viewers mourned the loss of access to this form of entertainment and hoped to regain access to talkies via subtitles that were being introduced for foreign movies. However, deaf and hard of hearing moviegoers who had watched both inter-titled silent movies and subtitled talkies, realized that subtitled talkies were not fully accessible in comparison with silent movies as evidenced in an essay by a deaf high school student who grew up with silent movies and then lost access to movies after the talkies became universal:

> Perhaps, in time, an invention will be perfected that will enable the deaf to hear the "talkies," or an invention which will throw the words spoken directly under the screen as well as being spoken at the same time. The real solution, I believe, is to have a silent theater in every city where there are a large number of deaf people.
>
> — Emil S. Ladner, a deaf high school senior, in an essay that won in a nationwide competition sponsored by the Atlantic Magazine (Ladner, 1931).

Technology evolution has increased fidelity, availability, and interactivity of multimodal interfaces (e.g., high-definition interfaces on interactive portable devices). The goal is to mirror human physical and social interaction to leverage existing human interactive knowledge. However, human interaction, such as gesture and speech, is conducted in many different ways and such communication can be difficult for users with different abilities and education and who are from different cultures. Many new technology services, such as online customer service and government services, are becoming pervasive, but are not fully accessible. To comply with accessibility mandates, these services retrofit accessibility, which is usually expensive and not scalable enough to provide universal access. The ability to go beyond basic accessibility mandates that enable full participation by relatively small segments of the population, including deaf or hard of hearing individuals to meet the needs of a much larger segment of people with situational disabilities (universal design), is vital.

Conversely, there is a danger that new services will completely supplant rather than supplement legacy services. If these services are not fully accessible, deaf or hard of hearing consumers can actually become more isolated. For example, a deaf consumer can converse with a hearing consumer if both have text telephones (TTY), but a deaf consumer may not find it easy to converse with a hearing consumer if both have videophones, because the audiovisual quality rarely approaches that of face-to-face audiovisual communication. Similarly, the growth of videophones at the expense of legacy TTYs has had an adverse impact on 911 services. A deaf consumer using a TTY can call 911 directly and communicate with the operator and the caller's address and location can be accurately identified. A deaf consumer who uses video relay service over a mobile phone cannot call 911 directly to communicate with the responder and the address and location cannot accurately pinpointed.

Over time, as deaf consumers replaced their TTYs with videophones, most providers ceased offering TTY-compatible networks and service because they would no longer be cost effective.

Videophones offer a closer approximation of a face-to-face meeting, by providing multimodal information. These users can enhance their access by using appropriate accommodations. A deaf signer can use a sign language interpreter to translate audio to video or audio to text. Many current initiatives, such as Next-Generation 911, expand on this multimodal accessibility concept of total conversation through which a user can choose the most accessible combination of audio, video, and text media. If all three media are available, multimodal applications of this type do not reduce accessibility; they enhance and extend legacy services.

3.1.6 Language Dimension

Language is too often taken as equivalent to speech. Language is a cognitive faculty that can be realized in two modalities: oral–aural, realized as speech, and manual–visual, realized as sign.

Deaf individuals who are raised using only spoken language do not receive enough access to auditory information to develop language; they are deprived of early language development with increasing cognitive delay as time goes by during the critical period between birth and 3 or 4 years old (Humphries et al. 2013; 2014). Many of these cases fall near the extreme end of the spectrum of disorders or harms in that these children never become entirely fluent in a language and have cognitive deficits associated with those faculties that require a firm foundation in a first language (Mayberry et al. 2002). Yet, public policy does not reflect the view that these harms are preventable or avoidable to the extent of placing the responsibility for avoiding them on anyone. As long as treatments, therapies, and interventions established by the hearing sciences are employed with deaf children, it is assumed that what can be done is being done, and if the deaf child has deficits, these are due to the condition of deafness rather than being anyone's fault.

With their increased exposure to incidental learning through to their language abilities, they have enough knowledge fund to be capable of comprehending preventive healthcare information as presented to hearing audience. With their fund of knowledge, they only require full visual accessibility of information in order to be able to apply it to their lives. Deaf or hard of hearing people have varying levels of language ability due to the lack of consistent exposure to accessible language from birth. While the average reading level has been found to be at fourth grade, approximately 8–15% have been identified as performing at or beyond their reading grade level (Qi and Mitchell 2012).

There are different levels of issues with basic accessibility and comprehension of online information (Kushalnagar et al. 2016). With a wide variety of language abilities and knowledge among deaf or hard of hearing individuals, it is not possible to provide readers with a single information version that fits all. It is likely that multiple versions will be needed for providing effective comprehension and comfortable reading experience to the wide range of deaf and hard of hearing readers.

3.1.6.1 Knowledge Fund Dimension

A person's knowledge fund is their accumulated environmental information, also known as incidental learning, which can occur through media, word of mouth, or even dinner table conversation with families (Hall et al. 2017). Those minor bits of information accumulate through life, leading to general understanding of many aspects of society. With many avenues for fund of knowledge accumulation being inaccessible to deaf community, this causes a deficit in the fund of knowledge in deaf community when compared to hearing community (Antia et al. 2011). Gaps in knowledge lead to difficulty in comprehending information that assumes a certain level of knowledge fund in their readers. Thus, to ensure full access to information through technology, this factor, along with language abilities, has to be taken into consideration.

Deaf or hard of hearing individuals with knowledge funds comparable to their hearing peers may be able to use information that is directly transformed into a visual modality. For example, auditory information can be transformed directly to verbatim captions that they can follow even with occasional spelling or syntactic errors that they can correct in real time. On the other hand, if their knowledge fund is less compared with their hearing peers, information may have to be transformed both visually and in terms of content. For example, auditory information should be transformed into simple English captions that can be supplemented with pictures or other visual cues for unfamiliar words.

3.1.7 Legal Dimension

In the legal system, disabilities including deafness have been usually defined in terms of functional impact on daily life activities. Worldwide, accessibility has consistently been regarded as a public good the market cannot provide, and that the cost of providing accessibility must be borne by the entities providing the products and services, including the government. Those costs, in turn, might ultimately be passed through to other consumers in the form of higher prices, or to the public at large, through taxes.

In the United States, the Americans with Disabilities Act (United States Congress, 1990) is a federal law that prohibits discrimination against qualified individuals with disabilities. Individuals with disabilities include those who have impairments that substantially limit a major life activity, have a record (or history) of a substantially limiting impairment, or are regarded as having a disability. Furthermore, under the amendments, a determination of disability must ignore the positive effects of any mitigating measure that is used. For example, a mitigating measure may include the use of a hearing aid or cochlear implant.

The ADA requires employers to provide adjustments or modifications—called reasonable accommodations—to enable applicants and employees with disabilities to enjoy equal employment opportunities unless doing so would be an undue hardship (that is, a significant difficulty or expense). Accommodations vary depending on the needs of the individual with a disability. Not all employees with a hearing disability will need an accommodation or require the same accommodations. For example, a deaf employee, depending on their communication preference, may request video relay interpreting, real-time captions, or an Assistive Listening Device (ALD). The deaf employee simply has to tell the employer that she needs an adjustment or change at work because of her hearing loss. An employer only may exclude an individual with a hearing impairment from a job for safety reasons when the individual poses a direct threat.

The laws recognize that disability can be a product of the environment. For example, if deaf people could not hear a fire alarm, it was not because of their inability to hear, but rather was the fault of an architect with too narrow an imagination of the building's potential users.

Post ADA, public buildings are required to provide audiovisual fire alarms. And yet, technology's patterns force people to fit in and exclude people from participation when they do not fit. Only in a few explicit cases—such as emergencies—does accessibility design get incorporated. While audiovisual alarms are required, audiovisual elevator notifications to alert that elevator door has opened are not.

And the problem only becomes more complex when the relationship between technology and its users is more than simply physical. Technology designs can require cognitive skills as well as physical abilities to achieve optimal performance. A computer interface that presents information textually may fail to communicate effectively, for example, to people who learn visually or spatially or by working with their hands. We are used to thinking of such challenges as capable of being overcome through training, but that perspective may underestimate the scope of the barriers design poses to the integration of diverse people into technological systems.

3.1.8 Social Dimension

Social isolation is a complex, multidimensional phenomenon that is caused by the relative lack of social interaction and leisure opportunities deaf individuals enjoy compared with their peers. The resulting loneliness can result in poor physical and emotional outcomes in terms of feelings of stigma, anxiety, and poor academic performance.

Social peers are vital to people's lives: they promote interaction, learning, teaching, and nurturing. While families are able to nurture and support learning, it is equally important to promote socialization with same-age peers to broaden the individual's experiences. However, when the deaf individual and same-age peers do not share the same language, communication difficulties arise and can interfere with the development of friendships.

Unfortunately, many peers in society tend to focus on the deficits. When others do not understand these types of disabilities or feel helpless around deaf individuals, they may conclude that interaction is not worth the effort. But those peers who draw this conclusion fail to understand that deaf individuals do not learn or interact the same way. The peers may not understand the importance of adopting alternative interaction approaches. For example, a deaf student may prefer to communicate in sign language but may find it much easier to directly communicate by writing to peers who do not know sign language. The student may have better interaction with other peers who prefer spontaneous texting to spontaneous verbal communication.

Without technology, peers are limited in their interaction. Accessible technology, on the other hand, exposes people to and encourages interaction among a vast community of peers. With a larger social network of peers, deaf individuals have access to a greater number who share similar interests.

Technologies also do not stand by themselves, isolated from other facets of society. Rather, they are integrated into larger, more complex socio-technical arrangements that distribute their benefits, costs, and risks across different groups. These arrangements can require financial, social, or even political abilities in order to gain access to and use new technologies. Human variation in cognitive, financial, and sociopolitical abilities is, of course, just as wide as in physical abilities. The failure to design for that variability is just as disabling.

3.1.9   Discussion

Deaf or hard of hearing people can benefit from learning how to adapt aural information to visual information and in strengthening connections with peers. However, these people are likely to face hindrances from nondisabled peers, teachers, or mentors who do not have incentives to understand and adapt. Since much learning is conveyed peer-to-peer, this can be a serious hindrance to their knowledge acquisition. The ongoing dissonance is likely to reduce their participation and growth and trigger disillusionment and withdrawal from society. They are likely to thrive and grow when paired with others with whom they can identify and from whom they can find support using accessible technology. The minimum number of others who can form a support system can be in the single digits. It is sufficient that the support system peers have answers for most of the issues and challenges for everyday life. The goal is not to merely increase inclusion for a few individuals with sensory disabilities, but to encourage them to thrive and grow.

3.2   Future Discussion

The cumulative impact of less interaction with peers and information that can be accessed by deaf individuals takes a toll on their representation and retention in the classroom, workplace, and social settings. For example, individuals with disabilities decline from 14% of the school-aged population, to 11% in undergraduate education, and 1% in Ph.D. programs (Thurgood et al. 2006). In addition to encountering a deficit of information and interaction, they are commonly discouraged from pursuing further education. When they do enroll, many do not have full access to and are not fully included in more rigorous learning activities such as laboratory activities, diminishing their engagement and success.

For information that does not have augmented content for students with sensory disabilities, accessible technologies may help, but do not guarantee accessibility. A survey (Fichten et al. 2009) revealed that none of 18 e-learning applications evaluated were completely accessible to the blind participants. Similarly, the percentage of captioned or described videos on commercial video services remains small due to content-creation companies' failure to add a workflow for universal captioning.

3.3 Author's Opinion

A holistic approach can broaden horizons for deaf or hard of hearing individuals. They do not want to be defined by their needs; nor do they want their unique experiences to be ignored. Mentors and peers should approach the individual, not in terms of disability, but as an individual with a unique experience and secondarily as a person with a disability. Then they are more likely to socialize and interact freely.

Deaf or hard of hearing individuals also benefit from the pooled experience and wisdom of a community of similar peers and knowledgeable mentors. It is also worth noting that a community of peers is likely to have access to far more available resources than would a single person operating independently.

3.4 Conclusions

It is important to engage deaf or hard of hearing people on their own terms, and letting them take the lead, and recognize that technology powerfully shapes human outcomes. Technology design is an ongoing process that remains sensitive to the evolution of technology and of consumers' changing needs and desires. It is fairly common for developers to focus on features that are relatively unimportant to deaf individuals even when explicitly designing accessibility into communications programs. Investigation of a specific issue in collaboration with a deaf or low-vision individual offers a unique teaching opportunity for peers to consider complex, real-world issues as a balancing act between the technology, interface and cognitive and perceptual capabilities.

Properly designed tools have the potential to create a new educational and social paradigm for deaf individuals. Integrating accessibility in core infrastructure can lower the difficulty of providing accessible applications, which can in turn be scaled to address the needs of deaf individuals and increase inclusiveness of communities.

While much accessibility progress has been made, there are specific areas needing intensive attention. Deaf individuals should have access to services in centers that accumulate a pool of expertise. These centers can also offer an opportunity to meet others and receive multidisciplinary services from qualified personnel. Further, these services can facilitate the collection and measurement of qualitative and quantitative data. This could include demographics, language access and acquisition, literacy and academic benchmarks, cognitive ability, social/emotional development, post-school outcomes, and developmental indicators. Such data retention can assess the efficacy of programs at the local, state, and national level.

Given trends in education and accessibility, we recommend the following actions. Accessible technology should be funded as a social and public good to enhance affordability. Accessibility has seen incremental gains for many years but integrating accessibility in everyday technology has the potential to be a game-changing, transformative tool, capable of improving lifelong outcomes for deaf or hard of hearing individuals.

References

Antia SD, Jones P, Luckner J, Kreimeyer KH, Reed S (2011) Social outcomes of students who are deaf and hard of hearing in general education classrooms. Except Child 77(4): 489–504. Retrieved from http://search.proquest.com/docview/877027156?accountid=108

Erickson W, Lee C, Von Schrader S (2013). Disability statistics from the 2011 american community survey (ACS)

Fichten CS, Asuncion JV, Barile M, Ferraro V, Wolforth J (2009) Accessibility of e-learning and computer and information technologies for students with visual impairments in postsecondary education. J Vis Impair Blind 103(9):543–557

Hall WC, Levin LL, Anderson ML (2017) Language deprivation syndrome: a possible neurodevelopmental disorder with sociocultural origins. Soc Psychiatry Psychiatr Epidemiol 52(6):761–776. https://doi.org/10.1007/s00127-017-1351-7

Humphries T, Kushalnagar P, Mathur G, Napoli DJ, Padden C, Rathmann C (2014) Ensuring language acquisition for deaf children: What linguists can do. Language, 90(2). https://doi.org/10.1353/lan.2014.0036

Humphries T, Kushalnagar R, Mathur G, Napoli DJDJ, Padden C, Rathmann C, Smith S (2013) The right to language. J Law Med Ethics J Am Soc Law Med Ethics 41(4):872–884. https://doi.org/10.1111/jlme.12097

Kushalnagar P, Smith S, Hopper M, Ryan C, Rinkevich M, Kushalnagar RS (2016) Making cancer health text on the internet easier to read for deaf people who use american sign language. J Cancer Educ, 1–7. https://doi.org/10.1007/s13187-016-1059-5

Ladd P (2005) Deafhood: a concept stressing possibilities, not deficits. Scand J Public Health 33(66_suppl):12–17. https://doi.org/10.1080/14034950510033318

Mayberry RI, Lock E, Kazmi H (2002) Linguistic ability and early language exposure. Nature 417:38. Retrieved from http://dx.doi.org/10.1038/417038a

Mitchell RE, Young TA, Bachleda B, Karchmer MA (2006) How many people use ASL in the United States? why estimates need updating. Sign Lang Stud 6(3):306–335. https://doi.org/10.1353/sls.2006.0019

Moreland CJ, Latimore D, Sen A, Arato N, Zazove P (2013) Deafness among physicians and trainees: a national survey. Acad Med J Assoc Am Med Coll 88(2):224–232. https://doi.org/10.1097/ACM.0b013e31827c0d60

Qi S, Mitchell RE (2012) Large-Scale Academic Achievement Testing of Deaf and Hard-of-Hearing Students: Past, Present, and Future. J Deaf Stud Deaf Educ 17(1):1–18. https://doi.org/10.1093/deafed/enr028

Thurgood L, Golladay MJ, Hill ST (2006) U.S. Doctorates in the 20th Century

United States Congress. Americans with Disabilities Act, Pub. L. No. 101-336, 104 Stat. 328, Pub. L. No. 104–328 (1990). United States of America

World Health Organization (2015) Deafness and Hearing Loss. *N 5*

Chapter 4
Cognitive and Learning Disabilities

Lisa Seeman and Clayton Lewis

Abstract People with cognitive disabilities are gaining in a long struggle for recognition of their right to control their lives. In the information society, access to the Web is essential to this control. Cognitive barriers to this access are diverse, reflecting the complexity of human cognitive faculties. Advances in supporting configurable presentation and interaction methods, and in representing the meaning as well as the form of information, will yield progress. This progress is being accelerated by increasing international awareness of the importance of cognitive access.

4.1 Introduction

People with cognitive disabilities are gaining in a long struggle for recognition of their right to control their lives. Not long ago it was common for people with cognitive disabilities to be institutionalized, and restricted to segregated educational and employment programs (Braddock and Parish 2001). Due in significant part to the rise of self-advocacy organizations (Roth 1983; Dybwad and Bersani 1996), in which people with cognitive disabilities speak out in defense of their right to independence, most people with cognitive disabilities now live outside of institutions and attend schools for the general public. In the USA, nearly 200,000 people with cognitive disabilities lived in institutions in 1967, while fewer than 20,000 were in institutions in 2017 (Braddock et al. 2017). Access to employment continues to be an issue, with low levels of employment. In the USA, fewer than 27% of people with cognitive disabilities were employed in 2016, compared to more than 76% of people without disabilities https://disabilitycompendium.org/sites/default/files/user-uploads/Compendium_2017_Final.pdf. Data on employment of people with

L. Seeman
Athena ICT, Beit Shemesh, Israel
e-mail: Lisa.seeman@zoho.com
URL: http://accessibility.athena-ict.com/

C. Lewis (✉)
Department of Computer Science, University of Colorado Boulder, Boulder, USA
e-mail: clayton.lewis@colorado.edu

© Springer-Verlag London Ltd., part of Springer Nature 2019   49
Y. Yesilada and S. Harper (eds.), *Web Accessibility*, Human–Computer
Interaction Series, https://doi.org/10.1007/978-1-4471-7440-0_4

cognitive disabilities elsewhere are not reported separately from those for people with disabilities generally, but the World Report on Disability (http://www.who.int/disabilities/world_report/2011/report.pdf) suggests that the rate of employment is lower than that for people with disabilities generally, which in turn is substantially lower than for people generally.

In the information society, access to the Web is essential to full, independent participation. Information of all kinds, addressing such vital concerns as health, employment, and civic participation, as well as entertainment and personal enrichment, is now commonly available on the Web. For example, in 2013, 72% of Internet users in the USA looked for health information online (http://www.pewinternet.org/2013/07/26/e-patients-and-their-hunt-for-health-information-2/). Access to goods and services also increasingly comes via the Web. In 2015, 80% of people in the USA shopped online. A participant in a focus group of people with traumatic brain injury, when asked about the importance of the Web for him, said, "Well, how else would I buy my health insurance?" Unfortunately, people with cognitive and learning limitations face barriers to effective Web access, when the content and structure of Web sites are not matched to their abilities.

4.2 Overview

Cognitive and learning impairments are extremely diverse, both in origin and impact. This is because the human cognitive apparatus is extremely complex and multi-faceted, so that there are many different cognitive functions whose operation can be impaired, and many possible causes of such impairments.

Starting on the functional side, the Cognitive and Learning Disabilities Accessibility Task Force of the W3C Web Accessibility Initiative identifies these challenges (see Cognitive Accessibility User Research, online at https://w3c.github.io/coga/user-research/; see also Francik 1999):

Memory—Working Memory, Short-Term Memory, Long-Term Memory, Visual Memory, Visuospatial Memory, Auditory Memory (memory for sound patterns and others).
Executive Functions—Emotional Control and Self-Monitoring; Planning/Organization and Execution; and Judgment.
Reasoning—Fluid Reasoning (logical reasoning), Mathematical Intelligence, Seriation, Crystallized Intelligence, and Abstraction.
Attention—Selective Attention and Sustained Attention.
Language—Speech Perception, Auditory Discrimination, Naming Skills, and Morphosyntax.
Understanding Figurative Language—similes, personification, oxymorons, idioms, and puns.

Literacy depends upon functions including Speech Perception, Visual Perception, Phoneme Processing, and Cross-Modal Association (association of sign and concept).
Other Perception—Motor Perception, Psychomotor Perception.
Knowledge—Cultural Knowledge, Jargon (subject matter); Web Jargon and Technology; Metaphors and Idioms; Symbols Knowledge (such as icons); and Mathematical Knowledge.
Behavioral—Understanding Social Cues.

Each of these functional categories has many additional aspects. For example, memory includes encoding of new information, as well as retrieval; delayed retrieval is a different function from immediate retrieval; recognition is different from recall; skill learning is different from learning of facts; and so on. Language function includes comprehension as well as production, reading as well speech processing, issues with vocabulary as well as syntax, and so on.

The typical operation of any of these functions can be interfered with in many ways. Chromosomal abnormalities, as in Down syndrome, injuries to the brain from external impact or from stroke, effects of aging, diseases like Alzheimer's or Parkinson's, or severe mental illness, can all cause cognitive impairments. Many people have cognitive impairments for which no cause can be identified.

Historically, much emphasis was given to classifying cognitive disabilities by these different origins rather than cognitive functions. Under this "medical model," a disability was seen as a medical condition, centered in an individual; the response to a disability was based on identifying that condition, just as treating a disease is based on identifying it (Areheart 2008). Over time, the medical model has largely been replaced by functional models, accompanied by the recognition that it is the interaction between the environment and a person's functional capabilities, not the functional capabilities themselves, that lead to success or failure in people's activities. The World Health Organization's International Classification of Functioning, Disability and Health (ICF), first approved in 2001, reflects this new view: "The ICF includes environmental factors in recognition of the important role of environment in people's functioning. These factors range from physical factors (such as climate, terrain or building design) to social factors (such as attitudes, institutions, and laws). Interaction with environmental factors is an essential aspect of the scientific understanding of 'functioning and disability'" (https://www.cdc.gov/nchs/data/icd/icfoverview_finalforwho10sept.pdf).

While one still often encounters medical classifications, they contribute little if anything to accessibility work. It is often not known what classification a particular user belongs to, and, even if it were, the variability of function within the classifications is very large. For example, some people with Down syndrome are nonliterate, while others earn college degrees; more on this below. Further, preoccupation with classification can contribute to a tendency to view people with disabilities as if the disabilities, and not the people, are important. What is important is recognizing that people can have difficulty in any of the many functional areas listed above, and to consider how Web access can be facilitated in the presence of these difficulties. That is, the focus should be on how to improve access, not on impairments (Backenroth 2001; Roth 1983; see also Rapley 2004).

A common misconception, one actually associated with earlier research approaches in the field, is that cognitive disabilities can be understood in terms of IQ. IQ is still sometimes used administratively in classifying people, or in determining eligibility for support programs (for critical discussion see "Assessment and Identification" in President's Commission 2002; see also discussion of policies in European countries in European Commission 2002). But, consistent with the functional view presented above, it is increasingly recognized that IQ measures only some aspects of cognitive function. Thus, a person with high IQ can have severe cognitive or learning impairments (Sternberg and Grigorenko 2004; Stanovich 2005). It is also true that a person with low IQ can function very effectively in some areas. Research suggests that variation in IQ accounts for only about 10% of objective success in life, assessed by various criteria, with some scientists arguing that even that figure is an overestimate (Sternberg 2000).

Demographic data, not plentiful to begin with, are often organized by disability classifications, not around function. There are also methodological problems in the demographics (see, e.g., Hendershot et al. 2005). Nevertheless, these data have some value in establishing that large numbers of people encounter cognitive and learning barriers, certainly enough to justify substantial attention to increasing accessibility, though the data are not useful for prioritizing attention to particular functions.

Numbers differ, but all show significant sized groups. For example, estimates in the United States range from 5 to 17% for dyslexia of school-aged children, and 14% of all individuals have a learning disability (http://www.ncsall.net/index.html@id= 278.html). According to the National Center for Education Statistics of the U.S. Department of Education, 11% of school children required services for educational disabilities (compared to 0.1% for Visual impairments) (http://nces.ed.gov/fastfacts/ display.asp?id=64). These numbers seem typical; in England, an estimated 10% of children are affected by a learning disability (http://www.sciencedaily.com/releases/ 2013/04/130418142309.htm). In the U.S., statistics for the percentage of adults aged 18–49 years with perceived cognitive impairment range from approximately 4–8%, with percentages for adults aged 50 or older ranging from approximately 9–15% (http://www.cdc.gov/aging/pdf/cognitive_impairment/cogimp_poilicy_final.pdf). It can be assumed that age-related cognitive impairments will grow as the population ages. Today, the people aged 65 and older represent roughly 7% of the world population; by 2030 that will increase to 19–20% and by 2050 to 40%. People 65 and older are expected to be 19% of the US population by 2030 (http://www. census.gov/prod/2014pubs/p25-1140.pdf, http://www.aoa.acl.gov/Aging_Statistics/ index.aspx). There are 47.5 million people with dementia worldwide, and this figure is also expected to grow (http://www.smart4md.eu/).

People who are unfamiliar with cognitive disabilities sometimes assume that people with these impairments cannot use computers, or could not be represented in the professional, administrative, or managerial workforce. While it is true that there are people who cannot use computers, a survey commissioned by Microsoft (n.d.) produced the estimate that 16% of working-age computer users in the USA have a cognitive or learning impairment. Lazar et al. (2011; see also Kumin et al. 2012) report on the computer skills of a sample of people with Down syndrome who use computers every day in the workplace. Data on employees of the federal government of the USA in 2015 (United States Equal Employment Opportunity Commission 2015) show 484 people with "severe intellectual disability," a subcategory of the larger group with cognitive and learning impairments of all kinds, holding "white-collar" jobs. People with learning disabilities are often successful, with cognitive strengths in fields that are not affected by the disability. For example, an estimated 40% of successful business people have a learning disability (https://www.noodle.com/articles/strengths-of-people-with-learning-disabilities) or up to 25% of CEOs (https://chiefexecutive.net/quarter-ceos-dyslexic-says-ciscos-john-chambers/).

4.3 Discussion

The history of attitudes toward and treatment of people with cognitive disabilities is a sad one (Braddock and Parish 2001). As mentioned earlier, assumptions about what they could and could not do led to widespread institutionalization (for UK history see Henley 2001), and to restrictions on access to education and other opportunities. Hunt (1967) recounts the struggle of a person with Down syndrome, and his family, for literacy education: in the mid-twentieth century, the authoritative view in England was that a person with Down syndrome could not be literate. Today, while some people with Down syndrome are not literate, most are, or could be with appropriate education (Buckley n.d.), some have completed secondary school, and some have earned postsecondary degrees, illustrating the range of functional impact of the condition. See Grigal et al. (2012) for a review of postsecondary educational programs in the USA for people with cognitive disabilities.

The range of functional impact also means that while many people with cognitive impairments live completely independently, some need help with some aspects of daily life (theArc 1997; Prouty et al. 2006). As mentioned earlier, the employment rate for people with disabilities of all kinds is low in the USA and Europe. The shift in the labor market to jobs requiring higher levels of skill and education is a serious challenge.

In meeting this and other challenges, a very positive development is the emergence around the world of the self-advocacy movement. Maintaining the principle, "nothing about us without us," self-advocates play an active role in policy change and development, with notable success in deinstitutionalization in particular. Self-advocates are continuing to press for reforms in the treatment of benefit payments and access to employment.

As mentioned earlier, the Web is a key channel of access for information, services, and participation. But people with cognitive and learning impairments are not well supported by current Web accessibility efforts. For example, Hoehl (2016) found that people with cognitive disabilities were not comfortable making purchases online, while online shopping has become typical for people generally.

While there have not been many studies of Web use by people with cognitive disabilities (WebAIM 2013b), there are data that indicate that the problems encountered by many people with cognitive disabilities are, broadly, the same usability problems that affect all users, but the impact on people with cognitive disabilities is more severe (Small et al. 2005; Harrysson et al. 2004; Freeman et al. 2005). For example, all users have trouble when the back button fails to work, but a user with a cognitive impairment may have more trouble recovering from the problem. All users have trouble processing large amounts of text, but people who cannot read well have more trouble. Pirolli (2005) presents simulation results showing that a small decrease in how well cues (like link labels) are interpreted can lead to an enormous increase in time needed to search a website, suggesting that search problems that are bad for good readers may be terrible for poor readers.

This relationship between accessibility for people with cognitive disability and usability for a general audience suggests a difference between cognitive accessibility and other aspects of accessibility, at least given current approaches. Current approaches embody the hope that reasonable support for accessibility for people with visual impairment, for example, can be secured by requiring design features that can easily be checked, like inclusion of text descriptions for images (W3C 2018, Success Criterion 1.1.1, Non-text Content). But it has long been argued (Gould and Lewis 1985) that promoting usability requires user testing, not feature checking. Redish (2000) makes this same argument for comprehensibility, perhaps the key component of cognitive accessibility. This need for user testing makes cognitive accessibility a challenge for regulatory frameworks and guidelines with enforcement concerns, settings in which easy compliance checking is wanted. The matters are discussed further in Chap. 16.

Leaving aside questions of compliance checking, there are approaches to increasing cognitive accessibility that show promise. Guidelines on presentation and organization of text, navigation, and other matters can be found in WebAim (2013a, b, c); see also Hudson et al. (2005). While much of this material concentrates on text, some people with cognitive difficulties do better with non-textual presentation of information, or with non-textual supplements (Seeman 2002). As Seeman argues, the different roles of text for some people with cognitive disabilities are another source of mismatch between the needs of cognitive accessibility and existing accessibility approaches. The concept coding framework[1] and Symbered projects[2] address the development of information presentations using pictorial symbols. As part of its Immersive Reader program, Microsoft includes access to a dictionary of pictures to supplement text by illustrating key concepts (https://www.onenote.com/learningtools).

---

[1]http://www.conceptcoding.org/
[2]http://www.symbolnet.org/en/index.html

4.4 Future Directions

Self-advocacy has an important role to play in the future development of Web accessibility. While people with visual and auditory impairments have commonly been included in technical advisory bodies on accessibility, people with cognitive impairments have not. Not least among the benefits of increased inclusion will be greater recognition that people with cognitive disabilities have a wide range of capabilities, and that there really is an audience for increased cognitive accessibility.

The wide variation in capabilities, and limitations, will lead to greater emphasis on configurability in technology. In this approach, the view a user will have of a Web page will be shaped by a profile that represents his or her information presentation preferences. The WAI Personalization Taskforce of the W3C is standardizing semantics and vocabularies to enable better adaption to the individual needs of the user, focusing on cognitive accessibility scenarios (see https://www.w3.org/TR/personalization-semantics-1.0/). This group has active participation from leading technology providers such as IBM and Google. They are also maintaining a wiki of implementations (https://github.com/w3c/personalization-semantics/wiki/Implementations-of-Semantics). The international Global Public Inclusive Infrastructure project (Vanderheiden et al. 2014; see also Jordan et al. 2018) is aimed directly at this goal. Relatedly, the Fluid project (fluidproject.org) is developing swappable user interface components to provide tailored user experiences for Web applications generally. Rather than requiring the development of different versions of Web content for different audiences, an approach with well-understood drawbacks in unequal access to up-to-date content, the configuration approach separates content from presentation, so that all users receive a view of the same underlying content. Configurability is one aspect of the *ability-based design* approach, a strategic conception of accessibility with potential for people with cognitive disabilities as well as other audiences (Wobbrock et al. 2011). In ability-based design, systems are shaped to fit the abilities of individual users, rather than users being required to adapt to systems, for example, by using assistive technology.

As long as most systems are not designed to be configurable, or otherwise to fit the abilities of people with cognitive disabilities, tools to improve access of Web content will be needed. Many people with cognitive disabilities benefit from text to speech tools for reading Web pages; features like those of Microsoft's Immersive Reader, mentioned earlier, provide further assistance.

Advances in natural language processing, based on machine learning, may also make it possible to transform textual content so as to make it easier to understand (Djamasbi 2017). Currently, however, these techniques fall well short of what human editors can do, especially where understanding of the underlying meaning of text is involved. For example, human editors on the Medicaid Reference Desk project (see Lewis and Ward 2011) replaced this description of a support program by the much shorter description that follows:

Original: Occupational therapy services involve the treatment prescribed by a physician to develop, restore, or improve functional abilities related to self-help, adaptive behavior and sensory, motor, postural, and emotional development that have been limited by a physical injury, illness, or other dysfunctional condition. It involves the use of purposeful activity interventions and adaptations to enhance functional performance.

As revised: Occupational therapy services help with day-to-day activities and testing to see if you need special tools to help you eat, work, and live in the community.

Current automated tools cannot make all of the changes reflected here. They can replace rare words like "dysfunctional", but they cannot recognize that "testing", which is not mentioned in the original passage, is part of the process of prescribing a treatment. We can expect progress here, however, as machine learning techniques capable of recognizing and learning more complex relationships in text continue to develop, as in Trinh and Le (2018).

4.5   Authors' Opinion of the Field

Recent years have seen much more attention to technology access for people with disabilities than formerly. The UN Convention on the Rights of Persons with Disabilities, issued in 2006 and now adopted by 177 countries, requires access to "information and communication services," including "electronic services." Intellectual impairments are explicitly within the scope of the convention. More generally, attention to cognitive access has also increased, but, as discussed further in Chap. 16, current accessibility guidelines lack strong support for cognitive access. Seeking to promote progress in cognitive access to technology of all kinds, a group of advocacy organizations in the USA have issued a Declaration of The Rights of People With Cognitive Disabilities to Technology and Information Access (Braddock et al. 2013), now endorsed by many other organizations, political entities, and individuals (see https://www.colemaninstitute.org/declaration-tools-2/). The current authors expect that the ideals expressed in this declaration, and in the UN Convention, will increasingly be realized in the evolving reality of the Web; however, old misconceptions, although less prevalent, may still stand in the way of practical progress. As the use of Web content and mobile apps become more ubiquities, the lack of digital inclusion may be a risk for the autonomy of people with cognitive and learning disabilities and must be addressed.

Acknowledgements The second author thanks the Coleman Institute for Cognitive Disabilities for support.

References

Areheart B (2008) When disability isn't just right: the entrenchment of the medical model of disability and the goldilocks dilemma. Ind LJ 83:181

Backenroth GAM (2001) People with disabilities and the changing labor market: Some challenges for counseling practice and research on workplace counseling. Int J Adv Couns 23:21–30

Braddock DL, Hemp R, Tanis ES, Wu J, Haffer L (2017). State of the states in intellectual and developmental disabilities: 2017. American Association on Intellectual and Developmental Disabilities

Braddock D, Hoehl J, Tanis S, Ablowitz E, Haffer L (2013) The rights of people with cognitive disabilities to technology and information access. Inclusion 1(2):95–102

Braddock D, Parish S (2001) An institutional history of disability. In: Albrecht GL, Seelman KD, Bury M (eds) Handbook of disability studies. Sage, Thousand Oaks, CA, pp 11–68

Buckley SJ (n.d.) Reading and writing for individuals with down syndrome—an overview. Down syndrome information network. http://information.downsed.org/library/dsii/07/01/

Djamasbi S (2017) Improving manual and automated text simplification, Doctoral dissertation, UMass Medical School

Dybwad G, Bersani H (eds) (1996) New voices: self-advocacy by people with disabilities. Brookline Books, Cambridge, MA

European Commission Directorate-General for Employment and Social Affairs (2002) Definitions of disability in Europe: a comparative analysis. ec.europa.eu/employment_social/index/complete_report_en.pdf

Francik E (1999) Telecommunications problems and design strategies for people with cognitive disabilities. http://www.wid.org/archives/telecom/

Freeman E, Clare L, Savitch N, Royan L, Litherland R, Lindsay M (2005) Improving website accessibility for people with early-stage dementia: a preliminary investigation. Aging Ment Health 9:442–448

Gould JD, Lewis C (1985) Designing for usability: key principles and what designers think. Commun ACM 28(3):300–311

Grigal M, Hart D, Weir C (2012) A survey of postsecondary education programs for students with intellectual disabilities in the United States. J Policy Pract Intellect Disabil 9(4):223–233

Harrysson B, Svensk A, Johansson GI (2004) How people with developmental disabilities navigate the internet. Br J Spec Educ 31:138–142

Hendershot GE, Larson SA, Lakin KC, Doljanac R (2005) Problems in defining mental retardation and developmental disability: using the national health interview survey. DD Data Brief 7. http://rtc.umn.edu/misc/pubcount.asp?publicationid=131

Henley CA (2001) Good intentions-unpredictable consequences. Disabil Soc 16:933–947

Hoehl J (2016) Exploring Web simplification for people with cognitive disabilities. Dissertation. https://scholar.colorado.edu/cgi/viewcontent.cgi?article=1114&context=csci_gradetds

Hudson R, Weakley R, Firminger P (2005) An accessibility frontier: cognitive disabilities and learning difficulties. In: Originally presented at OZeWAI 2004 conference, La Trobe University, Melbourne, Australia, http://usability.com.au/2004/12/an-accessibility-frontier-cognitive-disabilities-and-learning-difficulties-2004/, 2 Dec 2004

Hunt N (1967) The world of Nigel hunt. Garrett Publications, New York

Jordan JB, Vanderheiden GC, Kaine-Krolak M, Roberts V (2018) A pilot study of computer auto-personalization at American job centers. J Technol Pers Disabil. http://scholarworks.csun.edu/bitstream/handle/10211.3/202999/JTPD-2018-ID29-p247-260.pdf?sequence=1

Kumin L, Lazar J, Feng JH, Wentz B, Ekedebe N (2012) A usability evaluation of workplace-related tasks on a multi-touch tablet computer by adults with Down syndrome. J Usability Stud 7(4):118–142

Lazar J, Kumin L, Feng JH (2011) Understanding the computer skills of adult expert users with down syndrome: an exploratory study. In: The proceedings of the 13th international ACM SIGACCESS conference on computers and accessibility. ACM, pp 51–58

Lewis C, Ward N (2011) Opportunities in cloud computing for people with cognitive disabilities: designer and user perspective. In: Constantine Stephanidis (ed) Proceedings of the 6th international conference on Universal access in human-computer interaction: users diversity (UAHCI'11), vol 6766, Part II. Springer, Berlin, Heidelberg, pp 326–331

Microsoft (n.d.) The market for accessible technology—the wide range of abilities and its impact on computer use. https://www.microsoft.com/en-us/download/details.aspx?id=18446

Pirolli P (2005) Rational analyses of information foraging on the Web. Cogn Sci 29:343–373

President's Commission on Excellence in Special Education (2002) A new era: revitalizing special education for children and their families. http://ectacenter.org/~pdfs/calls/2010/earlypartc/revitalizing_special_education.pdf

Prouty RW, Smith, G, Lakin KC (2006) Residential services for persons with developmental disabilities: status and trends through 2005. Res Train Cent Commun Living. http://rtc.umn.edu/risp05

Rapley M (2004) The social construction of intellectual disability. Cambridge University Press, Cambridge

Redish J (2000) Readability formulas have even more limitations than Klare discusses. ACM J Comput Doc 24:132–137

Roth W (1983) Handicap as a social construct. Society 20(3): 56–61

Seeman L (2002) Inclusion of cognitive disabilities in the Web accessibility movement. In: WWW2002, Eleventh international World Wide Web conference (Honolulu, Hawaii, USA, 7–11 May 2002). http://www2002.org/CDROM/alternate/689/

Small J, Schallau P, Brown K, Appleyard R (2005) Web accessibility for people with cognitive disabilities. In: CHI '05 extended abstracts on human factors in computing systems (Portland, OR, USA, 02–07 Apr 2005). CHI '05. ACM Press, New York, NY, pp 1793–1796

Stanovich KE (2005) The future of a mistake: will discrepancy measurement continue to make the learning disabilities field a pseudoscience? Learn Disabil Quart 28:103–106

Sternberg RJ (2000) The ability is not general, and neither are the conclusions. Behav Brain Sci 23(5):697–698

Sternberg RJ, Grigorenko EL (2004) Learning disabilities, giftedness, and gifted/LD. In: Newman TM, Sternberg RJ (eds) Students with both gifts and learning disabilities. Kluwer, New York, pp 17–31

theARC (1997) Community living. http://www.thearc.org/faqs/comliv.html

Trinh TH, Le QV (2018) A simple method for commonsense reasoning. arXiv preprint arXiv:1806.02847

United States Equal Employment Opportunity Commission (2015) Annual report on the federal work force: fiscal year 2015. https://www.eeoc.gov/federal/reports/fsp2015/index.cfm#_bookmark37

Vanderheiden GC, Treviranus J, Ortega-Moral M, Peissner M, de Lera E (2014) Creating a global public inclusive infrastructure (GPII). In: International conference on universal access in human-computer interaction pp 506–515

W3C (2018) Web content accessibility guidelines (WCAG) 2.1. https://www.w3.org/TR/WCAG21

WebAIM (2013a) Cognitive disabilities. https://webaim.org/articles/cognitive/

WebAIM (2013b) Cognitive disabilities Part 1: we still know too little, and we do even less. https://webaim.org/articles/cognitive/cognitive_too_little/

WebAIM (2013c) Cognitive disabilities Part 2: conceptualizing design considerations. https://webaim.org/articles/cognitive/conceptualize/

Wobbrock JO, Kane SK, Gajos KZ, Harada S, Froehlich J (2011) Ability-based design: concept, principles and examples. ACM Trans Access Comput (TACCESS) 3(3):9

Chapter 5
Situationally-Induced Impairments and Disabilities

Jacob O. Wobbrock

Abstract This chapter presents an overview of situationally-induced impairments and disabilities, or SIIDs, which are caused by situations, contexts, or environments that negatively affect the abilities of people interacting with technology, especially when they are on-the-go. Although the lived experience of SIIDs is, of course, unlike that of health-induced impairments and disabilities, both can be approached from an accessibility point-of-view, as both benefit from improving access and use in view of constraints on ability. This chapter motivates the need for the conception of SIIDs, relates the history of this conception, and places SIIDs within a larger framework of Wobbrock et al.'s ability-based design (ACM Trans Access Comput 3(3), 2011, Commun ACM 61(6):62–71, 2018). Various SIIDs are named, categorized, and linked to prior research that investigates them. They are also illustrated with examples in a space defined by two dimensions, LOCATION and DURATION, which describe the source of the impairing forces and the length of those forces' persistence, respectively. Results from empirical studies are offered, which show how situational factors affect technology use and to what extent. Finally, specific projects undertaken by this chapter's author and his collaborators show how some situational factors can be addressed in interactive computing through advanced sensing, modeling, and adapting to users and situations. As interactive computing continues to move beyond the desktop and into the larger dynamic world, SIIDs will continue to affect all users, with implications for human attention, action, autonomy, and safety.

5.1 Introduction

The computer user of today would be quite unrecognizable to the computer user of 30 years ago. Most likely, that user sat comfortably at a desk, typed with two hands, and was not distracted or bothered by outside people, noises, forces, or situations. He would have enjoyed ample lighting, a dry environment, moderate ambient tem-

J. O. Wobbrock (✉)
The Information School, DUB Group, University of Washington,
Seattle, WA 98195-2840, USA
e-mail: wobbrock@uw.edu

© Springer-Verlag London Ltd., part of Springer Nature 2019   59
Y. Yesilada and S. Harper (eds.), *Web Accessibility*, Human–Computer
Interaction Series, https://doi.org/10.1007/978-1-4471-7440-0_5

peratures, and a physically safe environment. Of course, these conditions describe most of today's office computing environments as well. But the computer user of today can also be described quite differently (Kristoffersen and Ljungberg 1999). Today, such a user might be walking through an outdoor space, her attention repeatedly diverted to her surroundings as she navigates among people, along sidewalks, through doors, up and down stairs, and amidst moving vehicles. She might be in the rain, her screen getting wet. Her hands might be cold so that her fingers feel stiff and clumsy. She might only be able to hold her computer in one hand, as her other arm carries groceries, luggage, or an infant. She might be doing all of this at night, when lighting is dim and uneven, or in the blazing heat of a sunny day, with sweat and glare making it difficult to use her screen.

The computer in the above scenario is not much like the desktop computer of 30 years ago. Today's mobile and wearable computers, especially smartphones, tablets, and smartwatches, enable us to interact with computers in a variety of situations, contexts, and environments. But the flexibility of computing in these settings does not come for free—it comes at a cost to our cognitive, perceptual, motor, and social abilities. These abilities are taxed all the more in mobile, dynamic settings, where we must attend to more than just a computer on our desk.

The notion that situations, contexts, and environments can negatively affect our abilities, particularly when it comes to our use of computers, has been framed in terms of disability (Gajos et al. 2012; Newell 1995; Sears et al. 2003; Sears and Young 2003; Vanderheiden 1997; Wobbrock 2006). When disability is conceptualized as limits on ability, then a notion of "situational disabilities" is meaningful, because situations of many kinds clearly limit the expression of our abilities. In recent years, an increasing number of studies show how various situations, contexts, and environments negatively affect people's abilities to interact with computing systems (e.g., Dobbelstein et al. 2017; Lin et al. 2007; Ng et al. 2014a; Sarsenbayeva et al. 2016, 2018). Also, researchers in human–computer interaction have developed working prototypes to demonstrate the feasibility of sensing and overcoming situational disabilities (e.g., Goel et al. 2012a; Mariakakis et al. 2015; Qian et al. 2013b; Sarsenbayeva et al. 2017a), often employing smartphone sensors and machine learning to adapt interfaces to better suit their users in given contexts.

Despite a trend in framing certain challenges as arising from situational disabilities, the concept of situational disabilities is not without controversy. One might argue that calling a "disability" that which can be alleviated by a change in circumstances diminishes the lived experiences of those with lifelong disabilities. A person experiencing a situational disability suffers neither the sting of stigma nor the exile of exclusion. Modern social scientists acknowledge that disability is as much a cultural identifier as it is a personal ascription (Mankoff et al. 2010; Reid-Cunningham 2009; Sinclair 2010), and nondisabled people experiencing a situational disability take no part in, and make no contribution to, a "disability culture." In fact, neither a person experiencing a situational disability, nor anyone observing him or her, regards that person as having a disability at all. No accommodations are required; no laws must be enacted; no rights must be protected or enshrined. Perhaps, therefore, the notion of SIIDs is not only wrong, but also misguided and offensive.

Indeed, the aforementioned arguments have merit. There should be no confusing situational disabilities with sensory, cognitive, or health-related disabilities. And yet, many researchers today find that the notion of situational disabilities offers a useful perspective, providing at least three benefits:

First, the notion of situational disabilities highlights that *everyone* experiences limits to their abilities, sometimes drastic ones (Saulynas et al. 2017; Saulynas and Kuber 2018), when interacting with technology in dynamic situations, contexts, or environments. The notion is a reminder that disability is not just "about others" but about people generally, and accessibility is for everyone to varying degrees. Perhaps, this perspective simply redefines the term "disability" to be synonymous with "inability," in which case, one could promote the phrase "situational inabilities"; but thus far, the field has adopted a disability lens and viewed situational challenges to ability in terms of accessibility.

Second, the notion of situational disabilities is about finding design solutions that benefit multiple people. Of course, the experience of a person holding a bag of groceries is nothing like the experience of a person with one arm; but a smartphone capable of being operated easily by one hand might be usable by and beneficial to both people. In this sense, when one allows for situational disabilities in one's design thinking, one approaches designing for all users and their abilities—for what they *can* do in a given situation, and not what they *cannot* do (Bowe 1987; Chickowski 2004; Newell 1995; Wobbrock et al. 2011, 2018).

Third, situational disabilities have real, even life or death, consequences because people's abilities *are* significantly diminished by them. For example, the popular press has reported regularly on walking "smartphone zombies" who have hit and been hit by other people, objects, and vehicles (Brody 2015; Haberman 2018; Richtel 2010). In 2009–2010, The New York Times ran an entire series on the negative impacts on human attention due to texting while driving (Richtel et al. 2009). Frighteningly, the Federal Communications Commission estimates that at any given daylight moment in the United States, 481,000 drivers are texting while driving.[1]

Cities around the world are attempting to remedy these dangers. In Stockholm, Sweden, traffic signs alert drivers to oblivious walking texters.[2] In Chongqing, China, city officials have divided their sidewalks into two lanes, one for people fixated on their smartphones and one for people promising to refrain.[3] London, England experimented with padded lampposts along some of its lanes after injurious collisions by texting walkers.[4] In Bodegraven, near Amsterdam, red lights at busy intersections illuminate the sidewalks at people's feet so that smartphone users looking down halt before entering crosswalks prematurely.[5] The Utah Transit Authority fines people

---

[1] https://www.fcc.gov/consumers/guides/dangers-texting-while-driving.

[2] https://www.telegraph.co.uk/news/worldnews/europe/sweden/12139462/Road-signs-warn-pedestrians-not-to-use-smartphones.html.

[3] http://www.newsweek.com/chinese-city-creates-cell-phone-lane-walkers-271102.

[4] https://www.independent.co.uk/news/world/americas/honolulu-texting-walking-hawaii-city-distracted-pedestrian-law-a8018686.html.

[5] https://www.nytimes.com/2017/10/23/business/honolulu-walking-and-texting-fine.html.

$50 USD for distracted walking near light rail tracks, which includes texting while walking.[6] In Honolulu, Hawaii and Montclair, California, recent distracted walking laws make it illegal to text while crossing the street (Haberman 2018).[7]

When faced with the challenges and consequences of situational disabilities, creators of interactive technologies must ask what they can do to better understand these negative effects and how to design solutions to address them. This chapter is devoted to furthering these aims.

5.2 Background

Andrew Sears and Mark Young first joined the words "situational" and "disabilities" together in 2003. The full phrase for their concept was "situationally-induced impairments and disabilities (SIIDs)" (Sears and Young 2003) (p. 488). Their key observation was:

> Both the environment in which an individual is working and the current context (e.g., the activities in which the person is engaged) can contribute to the existence of impairments, disabilities, and handicaps (p. 488).

In a paper that same year, Sears et al. (2003) focused on the relevance of SIIDs to ubiquitous computing:

> As computers are embedded into everyday things, the situations users encounter become more variable. As a result, situationally-induced impairment and disabilities (SIID) [sic] will become more common and user interfaces will play an even more important role. ... Both the work environment and the activities the individual is engaged in can lead to SIID (pp. 1298, 1300).

In both papers, the authors borrowed from the World Health Organization (WHO) (World Health Organization 2000) when distinguishing among impairments, disabilities, and handicaps. This chapter will generally use the acronym SIIDs, and it is worth noting the distinctions between impairments, disabilities, and handicaps. According to Sears and Young (2003), who paraphrase the WHO classification:

- *Impairments* are "a loss or abnormality of body structure or function." Impairments generally manifest as limitations to perception, action, or cognition; they occur at a functional level. Impairments can be caused by health conditions. For example, arthritis (a health condition) might cause stiffness in the fingers (an impairment). Impairments can also be caused by a user's environment. For example, stiffness in the fingers might also be caused by cold temperatures from prolonged outdoor exposure.

---

[6]http://www.businessinsider.com/apps-and-street-signs-to-get-people-to-stop-texting-and-walking-2016-2/#salt-lake-city-utah-a-50-fine-6.

[7]https://www.nytimes.com/2017/10/23/business/honolulu-walking-and-texting-fine.html.

- *Disabilities* are "difficulties an individual may have in executing a task or action." Disabilities are generally activity limitations; they occur at a task level. They might be caused by impairments. For example, stiffness in the fingers (an impairment) might lead to the inability to use a smartphone keyboard (a disability). Disabilities might also be caused by the user's context. For example, walking might cause enough extraneous body motion that using a smartphone keyboard is too difficult without stopping.
- *Handicaps* are "problems an individual may experience in involvement in life situations." Handicaps are generally restrictions on participation in society; they occur at a social level. They are often caused by disabilities. For example, difficulty using a computer keyboard (a disability) might result in the inability to search for and apply to jobs online (a handicap). Handicaps might also be caused by a user's situation. For example, the distraction caused by incoming text messages might make it difficult for a user to participate in face-to-face conversations at a meeting or cocktail party.

Although this chapter will refer to SIIDs as encompassing both "situational impairments" and "situational disabilities," it is useful to consider their difference. For the purpose of technology design, "situational disabilities" is a helpful notion because it is at the level of tasks and activities that design opportunities present themselves—i.e., how to make a certain task or activity more achievable for users. In contrast, "situational impairments" says nothing about the specific tasks or activities being attempted. For example, addressing stiff fingers due to cold temperatures (a situational impairment) says nothing about the task being attempted or the technology being used; a remedy might simply be to wear gloves. But if the intended activity is "texting on a small smartphone keyboard," then stiff fingers *and* gloves are both likely to be a problem. In considering how to design technologies to be more usable and accessible in the presence of SIIDs, we consider how we can better enable accomplishing specific tasks and activities.

Sears and Young (2003) were not the first to observe that situations, contexts, and environments can give rise to disabling conditions. In 1995, eight years prior, Alan F. Newell began his edited volume on *Extra-Ordinary Human-Computer Interaction* with a chapter containing a subsection entitled, "People are handicapped by their environments" (Newell 1995) (pp. 8-9). In it, he described a soldier on a battlefield:

> *He or she can be blinded by smoke, be deafened by gunfire, be mobility impaired by being up to the waist in mud, have poor tactile sensitivity and dexterity because of wearing a chemical warfare suit, and be cognitively impaired because of being scared stiff of being killed—and this is before the solider is wounded! If one were to measure the effective abilities of a person in such an environment, they would be poor enough over a number of dimensions for him or her to be classified as severely disabled in a more normal environment (p. 9).*

Newell went on to argue that everyone has a certain set of abilities and degrees of those abilities, and situations, contexts, and environments play a major role in affecting the expression of abilities in all people.

Two years after Newell, in 1997, Gregg C. Vanderheiden (1997) articulated the benefits of designing for people in disabling situations, arguing that when done successfully, it creates more accessible interfaces for people with disabilities also:

If we design systems which are truly ubiquitous and nomadic; that we can use whether we are walking down the hall, driving the car, sitting at our workstation, or sitting in a meeting; that we can use when we're under stress or distracted; and that make it easy for us to locate and use new services—we will have created systems which are accessible to almost anyone with a physical or sensory disability (p. 1439).

Vanderheiden (1997) further emphasized:

[D]ifferent environments will put constraints on the type of physical and sensory input and output techniques that will work (e.g., it is difficult to use a keyboard when walking; it is difficult and dangerous to use visual displays when driving a car; and speech input and output, which work great in a car, may not be usable in a shared environment, in a noisy mall, in the midst of a meeting, or while in the library). ... [M]ost all of the issues around providing access to people with disabilities will be addressed if we simply address the issues raised by [this] "range of environments" (p. 1440).

Two years later, in 1999, Steinar Kristoffersen and Fredrik Ljungberg (1999) published a seminal study of mobile group work, observing in the process that the impediments to successful interaction are not only due to deficiencies in mobile platform design, but due to the situations in which such platforms are used. In studying telecommunications engineers and maritime consultants, they observed:

The context in which these people use computers is very different from the office ... Four important features of the work contexts studied are: (1) Tasks external to operating the mobile computer are the most important, as opposed to tasks taking place "in the computer" (e.g., a spreadsheet for an office worker); (2) Users' hands are often used to manipulate physical objects, as opposed to users in the traditional office setting, whose hands are safely and ergonomically placed on the keyboard; (3) Users may be involved in tasks ("outside the computer") that demand a high level of visual attention (to avoid danger as well as monitor progress), as opposed to the traditional office setting where a large degree of visual attention is usually directed at the computer; (4) Users may be highly mobile during the task, as opposed to in the office, where doing and typing are often separated (p. 276) (emphasis theirs).

In 2006, three years after Sears and Young coined their "SIIDs" acronym, and still prior to the advent of the Apple iPhone in 2007, Wobbrock (2006) identified four trends in mobile computing, one of which was the need to make mobile devices more usable in the presence of situational impairments. Wobbrock wrote:

As mobile devices permeate our lives, greater opportunities exist for interacting with computers away from the desktop. But the contexts of mobile device use are far more varied, and potentially compromised, than the contexts in which we interact with desktop computers. For example, a person using a mobile device on the beach in San Diego may struggle to read the device's screen due to glare caused by bright sunlight, while a user on an icy sidewalk in Pittsburgh may have gloves on and be unable to accurately press keys or extract a stylus (p. 132).

Wobbrock (2006) went on to suggest design opportunities that could help reduce the negative impacts of SIIDs:

Ultimately, it should be feasible to construct devices and interfaces that automatically adjust themselves to better accommodate situational impairments. ... A device could sense environmental factors like glare, light levels, temperature, walking speed, gloves, ambient noise—perhaps even user attention and distraction—and adjust its displays and input mechanisms accordingly. For example, imagine a device that is aware of cold temperatures, low light levels, and a user who is walking and wearing gloves. The device could automatically adjust its contrast, turn on its backlight, and enlarge its font and soft buttons so as to make the use of a stylus unnecessary. If it detects street noise it could raise the volume of its speakers or go into vibration mode. In short, understanding situational impairments presents us with opportunities for better user models, improved accessibility, and adaptive user interfaces (p. 132).

Although more than a dozen years have passed since these ideas were proposed, and in that time we have seen an explosion of "smart" and wearable devices, these devices still remain largely oblivious to their users' situations, contexts, and environments. Even in the research literature, only a handful of projects demonstrate the sensing, modeling, and adaptive capabilities necessary to approach the kind of accommodations proposed above.[8] Clearly, more progress in developing "situationally aware" and "situationally accessible" technologies is needed.

The early writings by Sears et al. (2003), Sears and Young (2003), Newell (1995), Vanderheiden (1997), Kristoffersen and Ljungberg (1999), Wobbrock (2006), and others clearly established the link between situation, accessibility, and disability that underlies the notion of SIIDs today. Most recently, Wobbrock et al. (2011, 2018) developed ability-based design as a holistic design approach that takes both ability and situation into account, unifying "designing for people with disabilities" and "designing for people in disabling situations." Although a full treatment of ability-based design is beyond the current scope, it represents the most unified conception of SIIDs and their relation to accessible design to date. What seems necessary going forward are more technological breakthroughs and infrastructure to enable designers and engineers to sense the presence of (or potential for) SIIDs and overcome them.

5.3 Situations, Contexts, and Environments

This chapter has, thus far, used the words "situation," "context," and "environment" rather loosely and interchangeably. Here is neither the first place to do so nor the first place to attempt a more formal separation of these terms. In the abstract of their highly cited article on context-aware computing, Dey et al. (2001) utilize all three of these words within their one-sentence definition:

By <u>context</u>, we refer to any information that characterizes a <u>situation</u> related to the interaction between humans, applications, and the surrounding <u>environment</u> (p. 97) (emphasis ours).

The precise meanings of these terms in computing have not reached consensus despite being discussed for decades (see, e.g., Bristow et al. 2004; Dey et al. 2001;

---

[8]Some of the author's projects are offered as examples near the end of this chapter.

Dourish 2004; Pascoe 1998; Schmidt et al. 1999; Sears et al. 2003). Nonetheless, the terms present relevant differences that are useful when discussing SIIDs. For our purposes, we employ the following distinctions, which we admit are not always in keeping with definitions from prior work since those, too, are mixed:

- *Situation* refers to the specific circumstance in which the user finds him- or herself. The situation encompasses the "immediate now" of the user.
- *Context* refers to the current activities in which the user is generally engaged, including the user's purpose, goals, and motivations for those activities, and the user's physical, mental, and emotional state while doing those activities.
- *Environment* refers to the larger setting the user is in, including both the physical and social setting.

The three terms above, progressing from situation to context to environment, increase scope in time and space. A *situation* is highly specific, immediate, and local. A *context* is broader, as activities have a narrative arc to them, including what came before and what comes next; moreover, users undergo a process of doing, feeling, and experiencing along this arc. An *environment* is broader still, encompassing physical and social dimensions beyond the user's immediate locale but that influence the user nonetheless.

An example helps make the above distinctions clear. Consider a worker in a factory (the environment) welding metal parts while wearing a dark welder's mask (the context). A red light on a nearby wall suddenly illuminates (the situation), but is not visible through the welder's dark mask (an impairment), causing the welder to remain unaware of a potential safety hazard (a disability), thereby violating company protocol by failing to evacuate the building (a handicap).

The above distinctions make clear, then, that the term "situational impairment" refers to *a functional limitation experienced by a user in a specific circumstance*; similarly, the term "situational disability" refers to *the task or activity limitation experienced by a user in a specific circumstance*. These two notions are therefore combined in "situationally-induced impairments and disabilities," or SIIDs (Sears et al. 2003; Sears and Young 2003).

5.4   A Categorized List of Factors That Can Cause SIIDs

The expanse of potential impairing or disabling factors that can arise for users of interactive computing technologies is vast indeed. Table 5.1 offers a list of such factors, assembled in part from prior sources (Abdolrahmani et al. 2016; Kane et al. 2008; Newell 1995; Sarsenbayeva et al. 2017b; Saulynas et al. 2017; Sears et al. 2003; Sears and Young 2003; Vanderheiden 1997; Wobbrock et al. 2018) and categorized here in an original scheme (behavioral, environmental, attentional, affective, social, and technological). References to empirical studies that have explored each factor are listed, along with technological inventions that have attempted to sense or accommodate that factor. The references assembled are not comprehensive, but they give the interested reader plenty to peruse.

5.5 A Two-Dimensional Space of Impairing and Disabling Factors

Within the framework of ability-based design, Wobbrock et al. (2018) defined a two-dimensional space in which examples of impairing and disabling factors can be arranged. Portraying this space allows one to consider a broad range of factors, both health-induced and situationally-induced. Specifically, one axis for this space is LOCATION, which refers to whether the potentially disabling factor comes from within the user ("intrinsic"), arises external to the user ("extrinsic"), or is a mix of both. Another axis is DURATION, a spectrum for indicating whether the potentially disabling factor ranges from very short-lived to very long-lived. SIIDs tend to arise from short-lived extrinsic factors, but they are not limited to this zone. Table 5.2, adapted from prior work (Wobbrock et al. 2018, p. 67), shows an example in each zone of the two-dimensional space.

5.6 Some Empirical Results of SIIDs in Mobile Human–Computer Interaction

This section highlights some empirical results from studies of situational factors found in Table 5.1. Three factors that can affect people's interactions with mobile devices and services are discussed: walking, cold temperatures, and divided attention. Each is addressed in turn.

5.6.1 The Effects of Walking

Perhaps unsurprisingly, walking has received the most attention by researchers wishing to understand the effects of SIIDs on mobile computing, especially on the use of smartphones. It is not only users' abilities that are affected by walking—it is walking *itself* that is also affected by interacting when mobile. For example, walking speed slows by about 30–40% when interacting with a handheld touch screen device (Barnard et al. 2005; Bergstrom-Lehtovirta et al. 2011; Brewster et al. 2003; Lin et al. 2007; Marentakis and Brewster 2006; Mizobuchi et al. 2005; Oulasvirta et al. 2005; Schedlbauer et al. 2006; Schildbach and Rukzio 2010; Vadas et al. 2006). Here, we report specifically on target acquisition (i.e., pointing), text entry, and text readability while walking.

Table 5.1 Potentially disabling situational, contextual, and environmental factors that can negatively affect a user's ability to interact with computing technologies and services. Studies of these factors' effects on use, and technology inventions to sense or accommodate them, are referenced

Disabling factors	Empirical studies	Sensing and accommodating
Behavioral		
Walking	Abdolrahmani et al. (2016), Barnard et al. (2005, 2007), Bergstrom-Lehtovirta et al. (2011), Brewster (2002), Chamberlain and Kalawsky (2004), Clawson et al. (2014), Dobbelstein et al. (2017), Kane et al. (2009), Lin et al. (2005, 2007), Lu and Lo (2018), Mizobuchi et al. (2005), Mustonen et al. (2004), Ng et al. (2014a, 2015), Nicolau and Jorge (2012), Oulasvirta et al. (2005), Perry and Hourcade (2008), Price et al. (2004), Schedlbauer and Heines (2007), Schedlbauer et al. (2006), Schildbach and Rukzio (2010), Vadas et al. (2006), Zucco et al. (2006)	Brewster et al. (2003), Goel et al. (2012a) Hincapié-Ramos and Irani (2013), Kane et al. (2008), Lu and Lo (2018), MacKay et al. (2005), Marentakis and Brewster (2006), Mott and Wobbrock (2019), Qian et al. (2013a, b), Vertanen and Kristensson (2009), Yamabe and Takahashi (2007), Yang et al. (2012), Yatani and Truong (2007, 2009), Zhou et al. (2016)
Riding (e.g., in a car, bus, etc.)	Abdolrahmani et al. (2016), Brewster et al. (2007), Kane et al. (2009), Naftali and Findlater (2014)	Brewster et al. (2007)
Driving	Alm and Nilsson (1994, 1995), Brookhuis et al. (1991), Brown et al. (1969), Brumby et al. (2009), Fridman et al. (2018), Fussell et al. (2002), Goodman et al. (1999), Haigney et al. (2000), McKnight and McKnight (1993), Redelmeier and Tibshirani (1997), Reed and Green (1999), Schneider and Kiesler (2005), Strayer and Johnston (2001)	Manalavan et al. (2002), Paredes et al. (2018), Qian et al. (2013b)
Operating machinery (e.g., in a factory)		
Navigating obstacles	Abdolrahmani et al. (2016), Barnard et al. (2007), Lin et al. (2007), Vadas et al. (2006)	Hincapié-Ramos and Irani (2013)

(continued)

Table 5.1 (continued)

Disabling factors	Empirical studies	Sensing and accommodating
Various postures or grips	Azenkot and Zhai (2012), Le et al. (2018), Ng et al. (2014a), Nicolau and Jorge (2012), Schedlbauer et al. (2006), Wobbrock et al. (2008)	Cheng et al. (2012a, b), Goel et al. (2012b), Lim et al. (2016), Yin et al. (2013)
One-handed use, hands-busy/free use	Abdolrahmani et al. (2016), Karlson et al. (2008), Le et al. (2018), Parhi et al. (2006), Perry and Hourcade (2008), Price et al. (2004)	Boring et al. (2012), Goel et al. (2012b, 2013), Huot and Lecolinet (2006), Karlson and Bederson (2007), Karlson et al. (2005), Miyaki and Rekimoto (2009), Pascoe et al. (2000), Sawhney and Schmandt (2000), Yang et al. (2012)
Encumbrance (e.g., carrying luggage)	Abdolrahmani et al. (2016), Dobbelstein et al. (2017), Ng et al. (2014a, b, 2015), Wolf et al. (2017)	
Device out of reach	Naftali and Findlater (2014)	
Wearing impeding clothing (e.g., gloves)	Naftali and Findlater (2014)	
Environmental		
Vibration		
Cold temperatures	Blomkvist and Gard (2000), Goncalves et al. (2017), Halvey et al. (2012), Sarsenbayeva et al. (2016), Ylipulli et al. (2014)	Sarsenbayeva et al. (2017a)
Ambient noise	Abdolrahmani et al. (2016), Sarsenbayeva et al. (2018), Wolf et al. (2017)	Qian et al. (2013b), Reis et al. (2009), Zamora et al. (2017)
Rainwater, humidity	Halvey et al. (2012), Naftali and Findlater (2014), Ylipulli et al. (2014)	Tung et al. (2018)
Dim light, darkness	Barnard et al. (2005, 2007), Kane et al. (2009), Ylipulli et al. (2014)	
Bright light, glare	Fisher and Christie (1965), Fry and Alpern (1953), Kane et al. (2009), Macpherson et al. (2018), Tigwell et al. (2018a, b)	LiKamWa and Zhong (2011)
Coloration	Flatla and Gutwin (2010)	Flatla and Gutwin (2012a, b)

(continued)

Table 5.1 (continued)

Disabling factors	Empirical studies	Sensing and accommodating
Smoke, fog, smog, haze	Wolf et al. (2017)	
Difficult terrain (e.g., ice, mud, stairs)		
Confinement, constraining spaces		
Extraneous forces (e.g., G-forces)		
Attentional		
Divided attention, distraction	Abdolrahmani et al. (2016), Bragdon et al. (2011), Lu and Lo (2018), Oulasvirta (2005), Oulasvirta et al. (2005)	van Dantzich et al. (2002), Horvitz et al. (2003), Kern et al. (2010), Mariakakis et al. (2015), Pascoe et al. (2000)
Diverted gaze, eyes-busy, eyes-free use	Fussell et al. (2002), Price et al. (2004)	Azenkot et al. (2013), Brewster et al. (2003), Chen et al. (2014), Ghosh et al. (2018), Hincapié-Ramos and Irani (2013), Li et al. (2008), Lumsden and Brewster (2003), MacKenzie and Castellucci (2012), Mariakakis et al. (2015), Pielot et al. (2012), Saponas et al. (2011), Sawhney and Schmandt (2000), Tinwala and MacKenzie (2009, 2010), Zhao et al. (2007)
Interruptions	Adamczyk and Bailey (2004), Czerwinski et al. (2004), Iqbal and Horvitz (2007), Kane et al. (2009), Karlson et al. (2010), Mark et al. (2005, 2008), McFarlane (2002), Salvucci (2010)	Fischer et al. (2011), Fogarty et al. (2005), Horvitz et al. (1999), Parnin and DeLine (2010)
Multitasking	Abdolrahmani et al. (2016), Brumby et al. (2009), Czerwinski et al. (2004), Gonzalez and Mark (2004), Levy et al. (2011, 2012), Salvucci and Bogunovich (2010), Su and Mark (2008), Zhang and Hornof (2014)	Smith et al. (2003), Vizer and Sears (2017), Wang and Chang (2010)

(continued)

Table 5.1 (continued)

Disabling factors	Empirical studies	Sensing and accommodating
Information overload	Fussell et al. (2002), Levy et al. (2011, 2012)	
High cognitive workload	Salvucci and Bogunovich (2010), Schildbach and Rukzio (2010)	Fridman et al. (2018), Kosch et al. (2018)
Affective		
Stress, anxiety	Levy et al. (2011, 2012)	Ciman and Wac (2018), Ciman et al. (2015), Costa et al. (2016), Ghandeharioun and Picard (2017), Hernandez et al. (2014), Maehr (2008), Moraveji et al. (2011, 2012), Paredes et al. (2018), Sun et al. (2014)
Fear		
Fatigue, exhaustion	Kane et al. (2009), Williamson and Feyer (2000)	Dinges and Powell (1985)
Haste		
Elation		
Intoxication	Peterson et al. (1990), Vuchinich and Sobell (1978)	Mariakakis et al. (2018)
Social		
Conversation, multiple conversations	Mayer et al. (2018)	
Crowds	Kane et al. (2009)	
Social norms or expectations	Abdolrahmani et al. (2016)	Qian et al. (2013b)
Laws, policies, or procedures		
Privacy or security concerns	Naftali and Findlater (2014)	
Technological		
Small output displays (e.g., tiny fonts)	Brewster (2002), Christie et al. (2004), Kim and Albers (2001), Yesilada et al. (2010)	Baudisch and Chu (2009), Baudisch et al. (2004), Wobbrock et al. (2002)
Small input areas (e.g., tiny keys)	Brewster et al. (2007), Clarkson et al. (2005), Clawson et al. (2014), Yesilada et al. (2010)	Brewster et al. (2007), Chen et al. (2014), Miniotas et al. (2003), Oney et al. (2013), Shibata et al. (2016)
Lack of power (e.g., dead battery)		
Lack of connectivity (e.g., Wi-Fi out)		

Table 5.2 Examples of impairing or disabling factors, many of which are situational in nature, categorized on a two-dimensional space defined by LOCATION and DURATION. The former distinguishes factors that come primarily from within people or from outside them. The latter indicates how long-lived factors are. Accessibility research and practice applies not just to long-lived health-induced impairments and disabilities, but also to SIIDs, which are found largely, but not exclusively, in the rightmost column

	LOCATION		
Duration	From within ("intrinsic")	Mixed, both	From without ("extrinsic")
Seconds	Double vision from watery eyes	Sneezing from allergies due to pollen	Loud truck passing
Minutes	Out of breath from sprinting	Wheelchair users encountering stairs	Arms full of groceries
Hours	Sleeping	Intoxication	Prisoner's straightjacket during prison transfer
Days	Soreness from exercise	Illness from common cold	Walking over difficult terrain while hiking
Weeks	Ankle sprain	Injured arm in a hard cast	Solitary confinement
Months	Insomnia	Seasonal affective disorder	Darkness in Alaskan winter
Years	Young children's psychomotor development	Addiction	Incarceration
Decades or more	Muscular dystrophy	Color vision deficiency	Heavy water, air, or soil pollution

Target Acquisition. Prior studies have shown that walking reduces human motor performance. In a stylus-based target-tapping task modeled with Fitts' law (Fitts 1954; MacKenzie 1992; Soukoreff and MacKenzie 2004), Lin et al. (2005, 2007) demonstrated the appropriateness of that law and showed that Fitts' throughput, a combined speed–accuracy measure of pointing efficiency, was 18.2% higher when seated than when walking. Schedlbauer and Heines (2007) also confirmed the suitability of Fitts' law for modeling pointing performance while walking, and measured standing to have 8.9% higher throughput than walking. They also observed a 2.4× increase in stylus-tapping errors while walking. Chamberlain and Kalawsky (2004) conducted a stylus-tapping test, finding a 19.3% increase in target acquisition time when walking than when standing.

Today's handheld mobile devices operate more often with fingers than with styli. Schildbach and Rukzio (2010) evaluated finger-based target acquisition while walking, finding a 31.4% increase in time and 30.4% increase in errors when walking compared to standing for small targets (6.74 sq. mm).[9] Bergstrom-Lehtovirta et al.

---

[9]This target size was based on the Apple iPhone Human Interface Guidelines of 2009.

(2011) also examined finger touch, but across a range of walking speeds, finding selection accuracy to be 100% while standing, 85% while walking at 50% of one's preferred walking speed (PWS), 80% at full PWS, and degrading quickly thereafter to only 60% at 140% of PWS.

Human performance with wearable computers is also subject to the adverse effects of walking. Zucco et al. (2006) evaluated four handheld input devices in pointing tasks with a heads-up display. While standing, the gyroscope had the fastest selection time at 32.2 s, but while walking, it was the slowest at 120.1 s. The trackball, which had been second while standing at 36.6 s, was the fastest while walking at 37.6 s. Error rates were lowest for the gyroscope when standing and the touchpad when walking. More recently, Dobbelstein et al. (2017) evaluated targeting on a smartwatch while standing and walking, seeing a standing error rate of 2.9% more than triple to 9.7% when walking.

Text Entry. Prior studies of walking with a mobile device have also focused a great deal on text entry, a fundamental task in mobile computing. Mizobuchi et al. (2005) tested stylus keyboards with users who were standing or walking, finding that text entry speed was slower for walking for all but the largest key size. Text entry error rates were also generally higher when walking.[10] For thumb-based, rather than stylus-based, touch screen text entry, Nicolau and Jorge (2012) found that when text entry and walking speeds were maintained from standing to walking, insertion errors increased from 4.3 to 7.0%, substitution errors increased from 3.8 to 5.5%, and omission errors increased from 1.7 to 3.0%. Clawson et al. (2014) studied the effects of walking on text entry with hardware keys, such as the mini-QWERTY keyboards found on BlackBerry devices. After training each of 36 participants for 300 minutes to become expert mini-QWERTY typists, their study showed that seated and standing text entry rates were about 56.7 words per minute (WPM), while walking entry rates were about 52.5 WPM, a statistically significant reduction. Error rates, however, did not exhibit a difference for the experts tested.

Using keys, whether "soft" or "hard," to enter text while walking is a difficult task, and other input modalities might be better suited. Price et al. (2004) investigated speech-based text entry while walking, finding that walking increases speech recognition error rates by about 18.3% with an IBM Via Voice Pro system; however, first training the recognizer while walking improves recognition for both walking *and* seated scenarios. Along similar lines, Vertanen and Kristensson (2009) evaluated *Parakeet*, a novel mobile user interface atop the PocketSphinx speech recognizer (Huggins-Daines et al. 2006). Entry rates for Parakeet were 18.4 WPM indoors and 12.8 WPM outdoors. Speech recognition error rates were 16.2% indoors and 25.6% outdoors. The authors noted the influence of other situational impairments besides walking, including wind and sunlight glare, adding further difficulty to the outdoor tasks.

Text Readability. Input while walking is only half the challenge; output is affected by walking, too. For example, studies have examined users' ability to read and com-

---

[10]Unfortunately, specific numeric results are not reported directly in the paper. They are graphed but only support visual estimation.

prehend text while on-the-go. Early work on this topic by Mustonen et al. (2004) found that reading speed, visual search speed, and visual search accuracy significantly decreased with increasing walking speed. Similarly, Barnard et al. (2007) conducted a reading comprehension task on a personal digital assistant (PDA) with sitting and walking participants, finding that walking increased reading time by about 14.0% over sitting, and was about 10.0% less accurate. Vadas et al. (2006) obtained a similar result: reading comprehension was 17.1% more accurate for seated participants than walking participants. Similarly, Schildbach and Rukzio (2010) saw an 18.6% decrease in reading speed due to walking in a mobile reading task.

Although much more could be said about the effects of walking on mobile human–computer interaction, this brief review makes it clear that walking imposes a significant hindrance on users' motor performance, text comprehension, and visual search. Of course, walking imposes additional constraints on people's abilities, too, such as generating body movement, dividing attention, causing fatigue, and so on. Such effects could be isolated and studied further.

5.6.2   The Effects of Cold Temperatures

In many parts of the world and for many activities, mobile devices are used out of doors. Capacitive touch screens usually function best when bare fingers are used to operate them, raising the possibility that ambient temperature could be an issue. Two recent investigations have examined the effects of cold temperatures on mobile human–computer interaction. Sarsenbayeva et al. (2016) investigated the effects of cold temperatures on both fine motor performance and visual search time, finding the former was reduced significantly by cold but not the latter. Specifically, after about 10 min of standing in a −10 °C room, touch screen target acquisition in cold temperatures was 2.5% slower, and 4.7% less accurate, than in warm temperatures (a 20 °C room). The authors report that 16 of 24 participants "felt they were less precise in cold rather than in warm [temperatures] … [because of a] sense of cold and numb fingers" (p. 92).

A follow-up study by Goncalves et al. (2017) produced findings from a formal Fitts' law-style target acquisition task using index fingers and thumbs on a smartphone. They found that Fitts' throughput was higher in warm temperatures (a 24 °C room) than in cold temperatures (a −10 °C room) for index fingers and thumbs. Interestingly, speed was slower in cold temperatures, but accuracy was lower only for the thumb, not for the index finger. As the authors observed:

> One potential reason why this effect was stronger in one-handed operation (i.e. using the thumb) is that [...] [the task] required thumb movement and dexterity, whereas when completing the task with the index finger, no finger dexterity was required since the task required more of the wrist movement, than finger movement (p. 362).

Commendably, the authors of these studies did not stop with their empirical findings, but proceeded to take initial steps to sense ambient cold using temperature effects on a smartphone's battery Sarsenbayeva et al. (2017a). Perhaps future mobile devices and interfaces used for prolonged periods in cold weather will automatically adapt to such environments.

5.6.3 The Effects of Divided Attention and Distraction

In 1971, Herb Simon famously wrote (Simon 1971):

> *In an information-rich world, the wealth of information means a dearth of something else: a scarcity of whatever it is that information consumes. What information consumes is rather obvious: it consumes the attention of its recipients. Hence a wealth of information creates a poverty of attention and a need to allocate that attention efficiently among the overabundance of information sources that might consume it (pp. 40–41).*

Today, nigh on 50 years after Simon's quote, it is even more relevant in the context of mobile human–computer interaction, where situational, contextual, and environmental factors can contribute to regular and repeated distractions, resulting in highly fragmented and divided attention.

Oulasvirta (2005) and Oulasvirta et al. (2005) were pioneers in quantifying just how fragmented our attention is when computing on-the-go. Specifically, they studied attention fragmentation arising from participants moving through urban settings: walking down quiet and busy streets, riding escalators, riding buses, and eating at cafés. Findings indicate that on a mobile Web browsing task, depending on the situation, participants' attention focused on the device for only about 6–16 s before switching away for about 4–8 s and then returning. Clearly, the fragmentation of our attention during mobile interactions is very different from that during focused desktop work (Kristoffersen and Ljungberg 1999).

Bragdon et al. (2011) studied three different levels of distraction, with a particular interest in how touch screen gestures compare to soft buttons. Distractions were operationalized using situation awareness tasks, with three levels: sitting with no distractions, treadmill walking with a moderate situation awareness task, and sitting with an attention-saturating task. They found that *bezel marks* (Roth and Turner 2009)—swipe gestures that begin off-screen on a device's bezel and come onto the screen to form a specific shape (e.g., an "L")—were 13.4–18.7% faster with slightly better accuracy than conventional soft buttons for the distraction tasks. The time taken to use soft buttons degraded with increasing levels of distraction, but not so with bezel marks. Also, the number of glances at the screen with soft buttons was over 10× as much than for bezel marks, occurring on 98.8% of trials compared to just 3.5% for bezel marks! These results show that conventional touch screen soft buttons demand much more time and attention than do touch screen gestures.

People with health-induced impairments and disabilities also experience SIIDs (Kane et al. 2009). Abdolrahmani et al. (2016) conducted interviews with eight blind participants about their experiences of SIIDs. Problems that emerged included the challenges of one-handed device use while using a cane; the inability to hear auditory feedback in noisy or crowded settings; an unwillingness to use a device on buses or trains due to privacy and security concerns; difficulties entering text when riding public transportation due to vibration and ambient noise; cold and windy weather affecting device use; the inability to use a device while encumbered (e.g., while carrying shopping bags); the demands of attending to the environment (e.g., curbs, steps, cars, etc.) while also interacting with a device; and the challenge of covertly and quickly interacting with a device without violating social norms (e.g., when in a meeting). Thus, the SIIDs experienced by blind users are much the same as, but more intrusive than, the SIIDs experienced by sighted users. Although challenging to design, interfaces that enable blind users to overcome SIIDs undoubtedly would be more usable interfaces for sighted people, too.

5.7 Some Example Projects Addressing SIIDs in Mobile Human–Computer Interaction

General context-aware computing infrastructures have been pursued for many years (e.g., Dey et al. 2001; Mäntyjärvi and Seppänen 2003; Pascoe 1998; Schmidt et al. 1999a, b), but as shown in Table 5.1, *specific* technological innovations have also been pursued to sense or accommodate certain SIIDs. In this section, six specific projects by the author and his collaborators are reviewed. These projects attempt to sense, model, and in some cases, ameliorate, the impairing or disabling effects of walking, one-handed grips, diverted gaze, and even intoxication. In every project, only commodity devices are used without any custom or add-on sensors. Here, only brief descriptions of each project are given; for more in-depth treatments, the reader is directed to the original sources.

Walking User Interfaces. Kane et al. (2008) explored walking user interfaces (WUIs), which adapt their screen elements to whether the user is walking or standing. Specifically, in their prototype, buttons, list items, and fonts all increased 2–3× in size when moving from standing to walking. Study results showed that walking with a nonadaptive interface increased task time by 18%, but with an adaptive WUI, task time was not increased.

WalkType. Goel et al. (2012a) addressed the challenge of two-thumb touch screen typing while walking. Their prototype utilized machine learning to detect systematic inward rotations of the thumbs during walking. Specifically, features including finger location, touch duration, and travel distance were combined with accelerometer readings to train decision trees for classifying keypresses. In a study, WalkType was about 50% more accurate and 12% faster than an equivalent conventional keyboard, making mobile text entry much more accurate while walking.

GripSense. WalkType assumed a hand posture of two-thumb typing using two hands, common for mobile text entry. To detect hand posture in the first place, Goel et al. (2012b) created GripSense, which detected one- or two-handed interaction, thumb or index finger use, use on a table, and even screen pressure (without using a pressure-sensitive screen). GripSense worked by using interaction signals (e.g., touch down/up, thumb/finger swipe arc, etc.) as well as tilt inference from the accelerometers. For pressure sensing, it measured the dampening of the gyroscope when the vibration motor was "pulsed" in a short burst during a long-press on the screen. GripSense could also detect when a device was squeezed (e.g., to silence an incoming call without removing the device from a pocket). GripSense's classification accuracy was about 99.7% for device in-hand versus on-the-table, 84.3% for distinguishing three hand postures within five taps or swipes, and 95.1% for distinguishing three levels of pressure.

ContextType. In something of a blend of WalkType and GripSense, Goel et al. (2013) created ContextType, a system that improved touch screen typing by inferring hand posture to employ different underlying keypress classification models. Specifically, ContextType differentiated between typing with two thumbs, the left or right thumb only, and the index finger. ContextType combined a user's personalized touch model with a language model to classify touch events as keypresses, improving text entry accuracy by 20.6%.

SwitchBack. In light of Oulasvirta's (2005) and Oulasvirta et al.'s (2005) findings about fragmented and divided attention, Mariakakis et al. (2015) created SwitchBack, which aided users returning their gaze to a screen after looking away. Specifically, SwitchBack tracked a user's gaze position using the front-facing smartphone camera. When the user looked away from the screen, SwitchBack noted the last viewed screen position; when the user returned her gaze, SwitchBack highlighted the last viewed screen area. The SwitchBack prototype was implemented primarily for screens full of text, such as newspaper articles, where "finding one's place" in a sea of words and letters can be a significant challenge when reading on-the-go. In their study, Mariakakis et al. found that SwitchBack had an error rate of only 3.9% and improved mobile reading speeds by 7.7%.

Drunk User Interfaces. Mariakakis et al. (2018) showed how to detect blood alcohol level (BAL) using nothing more than a commodity smartphone. They termed a set of user interfaces for administering a quick battery of human performance tasks "drunk user interfaces," and these included interfaces for (1) touch screen typing, (2) swiping, (3) holding a smartphone flat and still while also obtaining heart rate measurements through the phone's camera covered by the index finger (Han et al. 2015), (4) simple reaction time, and (5) choice reaction time. The DUI app, which combined these tasks, used random forest machine learning to create personalized models of task performance for each user. In their longitudinal study, which progressively intoxicated participants over subsequent days, Mariakakis et al. showed that DUI estimated a person's BAL as measured by a breathalyzer with an absolute mean error of $0.004\% \pm 0.005\%$, and a Pearson correlation of $r = 0.96$. This high level of accuracy was achievable in the DUI app in just over four minutes of use!

5.8 Future Directions

This chapter has provided an overview of SIIDs. Collectively, the topic of SIIDs covers a large space concerning both science and invention, ranging from studying the effects of certain activities (like walking or driving) on mobile interaction, to devising ways of sensing, modeling, and adapting to environmental factors and their effects on users, like cold temperatures. Even though we are approaching 20 years since Sears and Young coined the term "situationally-induced impairments and disabilities" (Sears and Young 2003), we have only begun to understand and overcome SIIDs.

Future work should continue to pursue a deeper, quantitative, and qualitative understanding of SIIDs and their effects on users, especially during mobile human-computer interaction. This improved understanding can then guide the development of better methods of sensing, modeling, and adapting to SIIDs. The example projects by the author and his collaborators, described above, show how much can be done with commodity smartphone sensors, including detecting gait, grip, gaze point, and even blood alcohol level. Custom sensors included on future devices ought to be able to do much more, and motivation for them to do so might come from compelling studies showing how SIIDs affect users and usage. Clever adaptive strategies can then improve devices' interfaces for mobile users in just the right ways, at just the right times.

For researchers and developers, software and sensor toolkits to support the rapid development and deployment of platform-independent context-aware applications and services would be a welcome priority for future work. Ideally, such toolkits must take full advantage of each mobile platform on which they are deployed, while allowing developers to remain above the gritty details of specific hardware and software configurations. Simplifying the development and deployment of context-aware applications and services will enable the greater proliferation of context-awareness, with benefits to all.

5.9 Author's Opinion of the Field

Including a chapter on situationally-induced impairments and disabilities (SIIDs) in a book on Web and computer accessibility is admittedly controversial, and perhaps to some readers, objectionable. At the outset of this chapter, I presented my arguments for why SIIDs are real, relevant, and even potentially dangerous—in my view, they are worthy of our research and development attention. But SIIDs do sit apart from sensory, cognitive, motor, and mobility impairments and disabilities, and they should indeed be regarded differently. To date, researchers within the fields of assistive technology and accessible computing have not widely embraced SIIDs as a research topic. For example, the ACM's flagship accessible computing conference, ASSETS, has published very few papers devoted to the topic thus far. This lack of embrace is, I think, less due to a rejection of SIIDs as worthy of study and more due to a lack of awareness of SIIDs as accessibility challenges. Furthermore, as a research topic, SIIDs sit at the intersection of accessible computing and ubiquitous computing, subfields that share few researchers between them. Where research into SIIDs does appear, it tends to be published at mainstream conferences in human–computer interaction, mobile computing, or ubiquitous computing. Publications tend to present scientific studies about the effects of SIIDs more often than technological solutions for ameliorating those effects. The predominance of studies over inventions betrays a relatively immature topic of inquiry, one whose scientific foundations are still being established. Ultimately, the range of issues raised by SIIDs is vast, and solutions to SIIDs will come both from within and beyond the field of accessible computing. That is a good thing, as SIIDs have the potential to broaden the conversation about accessibility and its relevance not just to people with disabilities, but to all users of technology.

5.10 Conclusion

This chapter has presented situationally-induced impairments and disabilities, or SIIDs—what they are; their origins; how they relate to health-induced impairments, disabilities, and handicaps; the distinctions between situations, contexts, and environments; a categorization of many situational factors and prior research on them; a two-dimensional space of SIIDs with examples; some empirical findings about SIIDs as they relate to mobile human–computer interaction; and a series of technological innovations by the author and his collaborators for sensing and overcoming them.

It is the author's hope that the reader will be convinced that SIIDs, however, momentary, are real. They matter, because successful interactions with technologies are key to enjoying the advantages, privileges, and responsibilities that those technologies bring. SIIDs deserve our attention, because we can do more to make technologies respect human situations, contexts, and environments and better serve their users. In the end, more than just usability is at stake: safety, health, engagement with others, participation in society, and a sense that we control our devices, rather than our devices controlling us, depends on getting this right.

Acknowledgements The author thanks Anne Marie Piper and Darren Gergle for recent conversations about this chapter. He also thanks his co-authors on the research projects presented herein. This work was funded in part by a Google Faculty Award. In addition, many of the projects by the author and his collaborators described in this chapter were funded by the National Science Foundation under grant IIS-1217627. Any opinions, findings, conclusions, or recommendations expressed in our work are those of the author and do not necessarily reflect those of Google or the National Science Foundation.

References

Abdolrahmani A, Kuber R, Hurst A (2016) An empirical investigation of the situationally-induced impairments experienced by blind mobile device users. In: Proceedings of the ACM web for all conference (W4A'16). ACM Press, New York. Article No. 21. https://doi.org/10.1145/2899475. 2899482

Adamczyk PD, Bailey BP (2004) If not now, when?: the effects of interruption at different moments within task execution. In: Proceedings of the ACM conference on human factors in computing systems (CHI'04). ACM Press, New York, pp 271–278. https://doi.org/10.1145/985692.985727

Alm H, Nilsson L (1994) Changes in driver behaviour as a function of handsfree mobile phones—a simulator study. Accid Anal Prev 26(4):441–451. https://doi.org/10.1016/0001-4575(94)90035-3

Alm H, Nilsson L (1995) The effects of a mobile telephone task on driver behaviour in a car following situation. Accid Anal Prev 27(5):707–715. https://doi.org/10.1016/0001-4575(95)00026-V

Azenkot S, Zhai S (2012) Touch behavior with different postures on soft smartphone keyboards. In: Proceedings of the ACM conference on human-computer interaction with mobile devices and services (MobileHCI'14). ACM Press, New York, pp 251–260. https://doi.org/10.1145/2371574. 2371612

Azenkot S, Bennett CL, Ladner RE (2013) DigiTaps: eyes-free number entry on touchscreens with minimal audio feedback. In: Proceedings of the ACM symposium on user interface software and technology (UIST'13). ACM Press, New York, pp 85–90. https://doi.org/10.1145/2501988. 2502056

Barnard L, Yi JS, Jacko JA, Sears A (2005) An empirical comparison of use-in-motion evaluation scenarios for mobile computing devices. Int J Hum-Comput Stud 62(4):487–520. https://doi.org/ 10.1016/j.ijhcs.2004.12.002

Barnard L, Yi JS, Jacko JA, Sears A (2007) Capturing the effects of context on human performance in mobile computing systems. Pers Ubiquitous Comput 11(2):81–96. https://doi.org/10.1007/ s00779-006-0063-x

Baudisch P, Chu G (2009) Back-of-device interaction allows creating very small touch devices. In: Proceedings of the ACM conference on human factors in computing systems (CHI'09). ACM Press, New York, pp 1923–1932. https://doi.org/10.1145/1518701.1518995

Baudisch P, Xie X, Wang C, Ma W-Y (2004) Collapse-to-zoom: viewing web pages on small screen devices by interactively removing irrelevant content. In: Proceedings of the ACM symposium on user interface software and technology (UIST'04). ACM Press, New York, pp 91–94. https://doi. org/10.1145/1029632.1029647

Bergstrom-Lehtovirta J, Oulasvirta A, Brewster S (2011) The effects of walking speed on target acquisition on a touchscreen interface. In: Proceedings of the ACM conference on human-computer interaction with mobile devices and services (MobileHCI'11). ACM Press, New York, pp 143–146. https://doi.org/10.1145/2037373.2037396

Blomkvist A-C, Gard G (2000) Computer usage with cold hands; an experiment with pointing devices. Int J Occup Saf Ergon 6(4):429–450. https://doi.org/10.1080/10803548.2000.11076466

Boring S, Ledo D, Chen XA, Marquardt N, Tang A, Greenberg S (2012) The fat thumb: using the thumb's contact size for single-handed mobile interaction. In: Proceedings of the ACM conference on human-computer interaction with mobile devices and services (MobileHCI'12). ACM Press, New York, pp 39–48. https://doi.org/10.1145/2371574.2371582

Bowe F (1987) Making computers accessible to disabled people. M.I.T. Technol Rev 90:52–59, 72

Bragdon A, Nelson E, Li Y, Hinckley K (2011) Experimental analysis of touch-screen gesture designs in mobile environments. In: Proceedings of the ACM conference on human factors in computing systems (CHI'11). ACM Press, New York, pp 403–412. https://doi.org/10.1145/1978942. 1979000

Brewster S (2002) Overcoming the lack of screen space on mobile computers. Pers Ubiquitous Comput 6(3):188–205. https://doi.org/10.1007/s007790200019

Brewster S, Lumsden J, Bell M, Hall M, Tasker S (2003) Multimodal "eyes-free" interaction techniques for wearable devices. In: Proceedings of the ACM conference on human factors in computing systems (CHI'03). ACM Press, New York, pp 473–480. https://doi.org/10.1145/642611.
642694
Brewster S, Chohan F, Brown L (2007). Tactile feedback for mobile interactions. In: Proceedings of
the ACM conference on human factors in computing systems (CHI'07). ACM Press, New York,
pp 159–162. https://doi.org/10.1145/1240624.1240649
Bristow HW, Baber C, Cross J, Knight JF, Woolley SI (2004) Defining and evaluating context for
wearable computing. Int J Hum-Comput Stud 60(5–6):798–819. https://doi.org/10.1016/j.ijhcs.
2003.11.009
Brody JE (2015) Not just drivers driven to distraction. The New York Times, p D5. https://well.
blogs.nytimes.com/2015/12/07/its-not-just-drivers-being-driven-to-distraction/
Brookhuis KA, de Vries G, de Waard D (1991) The effects of mobile telephoning on driving
performance. Accid Anal Prev 23(4):309–316. https://doi.org/10.1016/0001-4575(91)90008-S
Brown ID, Tickner AH, Simmonds DCV (1969) Interference between concurrent tasks of driving
and telephoning. J Appl Psychol 53(5):419–424. https://doi.org/10.1037/h0028103
Brumby DP, Salvucci DD, Howes A (2009) Focus on driving: how cognitive constraints shape the
adaptation of strategy when dialing while driving. In: Proceedings of the ACM conference on
human factors in computing systems (CHI'09). ACM Press, New York, pp 1629–1638. https://
doi.org/10.1145/1518701.1518950
Chamberlain A, Kalawsky R (2004) A comparative investigation into two pointing systems for use
with wearable computers while mobile. In: Proceedings of the IEEE international symposium
on wearable computers (ISWC'04). IEEE Computer Society, Los Alamitos, pp 110–117. https://
doi.org/10.1109/ISWC.2004.1
Chen XA, Grossman T, Fitzmaurice G (2014) Swipeboard: a text entry technique for ultra-small
interfaces that supports novice to expert transitions. In: Proceedings of the ACM symposium on
user interface software and technology (UIST'14). ACM Press, New York, pp 615–620. https://
doi.org/10.1145/2642918.2647354
Cheng L-P, Hsiao F-I, Liu Y-T, Chen MY (2012a) iRotate: automatic screen rotation based on face
orientation. In: Proceedings of the ACM conference on human factors in computing systems
(CHI'12). ACM Press, New York, pp 2203–2210. https://doi.org/10.1145/2207676.2208374
Cheng L-P, Hsiao F-I, Liu Y-T, Chen MY (2012b) iRotate grasp: automatic screen rotation based
on grasp of mobile devices. In: Adjunct proceedings of the ACM symposium on user interface
software and technology (UIST'12). ACM Press, New York, pp 15–16. https://doi.org/10.1145/
2380296.2380305
Chickowski E (2004) It's all about access. Alsk Airl Mag 28(12):26–31, 80–82
Christie J, Klein RM, Watters C (2004) A comparison of simple hierarchy and grid metaphors for
option layouts on small-size screens. Int J Hum-Comput Stud 60(5–6):564–584. https://doi.org/
10.1016/j.ijhcs.2003.10.003
Ciman M, Wac K (2018) Individuals' stress assessment using human-smartphone interaction analysis. IEEE Trans Affect Comput 9(1):51–65. https://doi.org/10.1109/TAFFC.2016.2592504
Ciman M, Wac K, Gaggi O (2015) iSenseStress: assessing stress through human-smartphone interaction analysis. In: Proceedings of the 9th international conference on pervasive computing
technologies for healthcare (PervasiveHealth'15). ICST, Brussels, pp 84–91. https://dl.acm.org/
citation.cfm?id=2826178
Clarkson E, Clawson J, Lyons K, Starner T (2005) An empirical study of typing rates on mini-
QWERTY keyboards. In: Extended abstracts of the ACM conference on human factors in computing systems (CHI'05). ACM Press, New York, pp 1288–1291. https://doi.org/10.1145/1056808.
1056898
Clawson J, Starner T, Kohlsdorf D, Quigley DP, Gilliland S (2014) Texting while walking: an
evaluation of mini-qwerty text input while on-the-go. In: Proceedings of the ACM conference
on human-computer interaction with mobile devices and services (MobileHCI'14). ACM Press,
New York, pp 339–348. https://doi.org/10.1145/2628363.2628408

Costa J, Adams AT, Jung MF, Guimbretière F, Choudhury T (2016) EmotionCheck: leveraging bodily signals and false feedback to regulate our emotions. In: Proceedings of the ACM conference on pervasive and ubiquitous computing (UbiComp'16). ACM Press, New York, pp 758–769. https://doi.org/10.1145/2971648.2971752

Czerwinski M, Horvitz E, Wilhite S (2004) A diary study of task switching and interruptions. In: Proceedings of the ACM conference on human factors in computing systems (CHI'04). ACM Press, New York, pp 175–182. https://doi.org/10.1145/985692.985715

Dey AK, Abowd GD, Salber D (2001) A conceptual framework and a toolkit for supporting the rapid prototyping of context-aware applications. Hum-Comput Interact 16(2):97–166. https://doi.org/10.1207/S15327051HCI16234_02

Dinges DF, Powell JW (1985) Microcomputer analyses of performance on a portable, simple visual RT task during sustained operations. Behav Res Methods Instrum Comput 17(6):652–655. https://doi.org/10.3758/BF03200977

Dobbelstein D, Haas G, Rukzio E (2017) The effects of mobility, encumbrance, and (non-)dominant hand on interaction with smartwatches. In: Proceedings of the ACM international symposium on wearable computers (ISWC'17). ACM Press, New York, pp 90–93. https://doi.org/10.1145/3123021.3123033

Dourish P (2004) What we talk about when we talk about context. Pers Ubiquitous Comput 8(1):19–30. https://doi.org/10.1007/s00779-003-0253-8

Fisher AJ, Christie AW (1965) A note on disability glare. Vis Res 5(10–11):565–571. https://doi.org/10.1016/0042-6989(65)90089-1

Fischer JE, Greenhalgh C, Benford S (2011) Investigating episodes of mobile phone activity as indicators of opportune moments to deliver notifications. In: Proceedings of the ACM conference on human-computer interaction with mobile devices and services (MobileHCI'11). ACM Press, New York, pp 181–190. https://doi.org/10.1145/2037373.2037402

Fitts PM (1954) The information capacity of the human motor system in controlling the amplitude of movement. J Exp Psychol 47(6):381–391

Flatla DR, Gutwin C (2010) Individual models of color differentiation to improve interpretability of information visualization. In: Proceedings of the ACM conference on human factors in computing systems (CHI'10). ACM Press, New York, pp 2563–2572. https://doi.org/10.1145/1753326.1753715

Flatla DR, Gutwin C (2012a) SSMRecolor: improving recoloring tools with situation-specific models of color differentiation. In: Proceedings of the ACM conference on human factors in computing systems (CHI'12). ACM Press, New York, pp 2297–2306. https://doi.org/10.1145/2207676.2208388

Flatla DR, Gutwin C (2012b) Situation-specific models of color differentiation. ACM Trans Access Comput 4(3). Article No. 13. https://doi.org/10.1145/2399193.2399197

Fogarty J, Hudson SE, Atkeson CG, Avrahami D, Forlizzi J, Kiesler S, Lee JC, Yang J (2005) Predicting human interruptibility with sensors. ACM Trans Comput-Hum Interact 12(1):119–146. https://doi.org/10.1145/1057237.1057243

Fridman L, Reimer B, Mehler B, Freeman WT (2018) Cognitive load estimation in the wild. In: Proceedings of the ACM conference on human factors in computing systems (CHI'18). ACM Press, New York. Paper No. 652. https://doi.org/10.1145/3173574.3174226

Fry GA, Alpern M (1953) The effect of a peripheral glare source upon the apparent brightness of an object. J Opt Soc Am 43(3):189–195. https://doi.org/10.1364/JOSA.43.000189

Fussell SR, Grenville D, Kiesler S, Forlizzi J, Wichansky AM (2002) Accessing multi-modal information on cell phones while sitting and driving. In: Proceedings of the human factors and ergonomics society 46th annual meeting (HFES'02). Human Factors and Ergonomics Society, Santa Monica, pp 1809–1813. https://doi.org/10.1177/154193120204602207

Gajos KZ, Hurst A, Findlater L (2012) Personalized dynamic accessibility. Interactions 19(2):69–73. https://doi.org/10.1145/2090150.2090167

Ghandeharioun A, Picard R (2017) BrightBeat: effortlessly influencing breathing for cultivating calmness and focus. In: Extended abstracts of the ACM conference on human factors in computing systems (CHI'17). ACM Press, New York, pp 1624–1631. https://doi.org/10.1145/3027063. 3053164

Ghosh D, Foong PS, Zhao S, Chen D, Fjeld M (2018) EDITalk: towards designing eyes-free interactions for mobile word processing. In: Proceedings of the ACM conference on human factors in computing systems (CHI'18). ACM Press, New York. Paper No. 403. https://doi.org/10.1145/3173574.3173977

Goel M, Findlater L, Wobbrock JO (2012a) WalkType: using accelerometer data to accommodate situational impairments in mobile touch screen text entry. In: Proceedings of the ACM conference on human factors in computing systems (CHI'12). ACM Press, New York, pp 2687–2696. https://doi.org/10.1145/2207676.2208662

Goel M, Wobbrock JO, Patel SN (2012b) GripSense: using built-in sensors to detect hand posture and pressure on commodity mobile phones. In: Proceedings of the ACM symposium on user interface software and technology (UIST'12). ACM Press, New York, pp 545–554. https://doi.org/10.1145/2380116.2380184

Goel M, Jansen A, Mandel T, Patel SN, Wobbrock JO (2013) ContextType: using hand posture information to improve mobile touch screen text entry. In: Proceedings of the ACM conference on human factors in computing systems (CHI'13). ACM Press, New York, pp 2795–2798. https://doi.org/10.1145/2470654.2481386

Goncalves J, Sarsenbayeva Z, van Berkel N, Luo C, Hosio S, Risanen S, Rintamäki H, Kostakos V (2017) Tapping task performance on smartphones in cold temperature. Interact Comput 29(3):355–367. https://doi.org/10.1093/iwc/iww029

Gonzalez VM, Mark G (2004) Constant, constant, multi-tasking craziness: managing multiple working spheres. In: Proceedings of the ACM conference on human factors in computing systems (CHI'04). ACM Press, New York, pp 113–120. https://doi.org/10.1145/985692.985707

Goodman MJ, Tijerina L, Bents FD, Wierwille WW (1999) Using cellular telephones in vehicles: safe or unsafe? Transp Hum Factors 1(1):3–42. https://doi.org/10.1207/sthf0101_2

Haberman C (2018) The dangers of walking while texting. The New York Times, p SR10. https://www.nytimes.com/2018/03/17/opinion/do-not-read-this-editorial-while-walking.html

Haigney DE, Taylor RG, Westerman SJ (2000) Concurrent mobile (cellular) phone use and driving performance: task demand characteristics and compensatory processes. Transp Res Part F 3(3):113–121. https://doi.org/10.1016/S1369-8478(00)00020-6

Halvey M, Wilson G, Brewster S, Hughes S (2012) Baby it's cold outside: the influence of ambient temperature and humidity on thermal feedback. In: Proceedings of the ACM conference on human factors in computing systems (CHI'12). ACM Press, New York, pp 715–724. https://doi.org/10.1145/2207676.2207779

Han T, Xiao X, Shi L, Canny J, Wang J (2015) Balancing accuracy and fun: designing camera based mobile games for implicit heart rate monitoring. In: Proceedings of the ACM conference on human factors in computing systems (CHI'15). ACM Press, New York, pp 847–856. https://doi.org/10.1145/2702123.2702502

Hernandez J, Paredes P, Roseway A, Czerwinski M (2014) Under pressure: sensing stress of computer users. In: Proceedings of the ACM conference on human factors in computing systems (CHI'14). ACM Press, New York, pp 51–60. https://doi.org/10.1145/2556288.2557165

Hincapié-Ramos JD, Irani P (2013) CrashAlert: enhancing peripheral alertness for eyes-busy mobile interaction while walking. In: Proceedings of the ACM conference on human factors in computing systems (CHI'13). ACM Press, New York, pp 3385–3388. https://doi.org/10.1145/2470654.2466463

Horvitz E, Jacobs A, Hovel D (1999) Attention-sensitive alerting. In: Proceedings of the conference on uncertainty in artificial intelligence (UAI'99). Morgan Kaufmann, San Francisco, pp 305–313. https://dl.acm.org/citation.cfm?id=2073831

Horvitz E, Kadie C, Paek T, Hovel D (2003) Models of attention in computing and communication: from principles to applications. Commun ACM 46(3):52–59. https://doi.org/10.1145/636772.636798

Huggins-Daines D, Kumar M, Chan A, Black AW, Ravishankar M, Rudnicky AI (2006) Pocket-sphinx: a free, real-time continuous speech recognition system for hand-held devices. In: Proceedings of the IEEE international conference on acoustics speech and signal processing (ICASSP'06). IEEE Signal Processing Society, Piscataway, pp 185–188. https://doi.org/10.1109/ICASSP.2006. 1659988

Huot S, Lecolinet E (2006) SpiraList: a compact visualization technique for one-handed interaction with large lists on mobile devices. In: Proceedings of the Nordic conference on human-computer interaction (NordiCHI'06). ACM Press, New York, pp 445–448. https://doi.org/10. 1145/1182475.1182533

Iqbal ST, Horvitz E (2007) Disruption and recovery of computing tasks: field study, analysis, and directions. In: Proceedings of the ACM conference on human factors in computing systems (CHI'07). ACM Press, New York, pp 677–686. https://doi.org/10.1145/1240624.1240730

Kane SK, Wobbrock JO, Smith IE (2008) Getting off the treadmill: evaluating walking user interfaces for mobile devices in public spaces. In: Proceedings of the ACM conference on human-computer interaction with mobile devices and services (MobileHCI'08). ACM Press, New York, pp 109–118. https://doi.org/10.1145/1409240.1409253

Kane SK, Jayant C, Wobbrock JO, Ladner RE (2009) Freedom to roam: a study of mobile device adoption and accessibility for people with visual and motor disabilities. In: Proceedings of the ACM SIGACCESS conference on computers and accessibility (ASSETS'09). ACM Press, New York, pp 115–122. https://doi.org/10.1145/1639642.1639663

Karlson AK, Bederson BB (2007) ThumbSpace: generalized one-handed input for touchscreen-based mobile devices. In: Proceedings of the IFIP TC13 11th international conference on human-computer interaction (INTERACT'07). Lecture notes in computer science, vol 4662. Springer, Berlin, pp 324–338. https://doi.org/10.1007/978-3-540-74796-3_30

Karlson AK, Bederson BB, SanGiovanni J (2005) AppLens and LaunchTile: two designs for one-handed thumb use on small devices. In: Proceedings of the ACM conference on human factors in computing systems (CHI'05). ACM Press, New York, pp 201–210. https://doi.org/10.1145/ 1054972.1055001

Karlson AK, Bederson BB, Contreras-Vidal JL (2008) Understanding one-handed use of mobile devices. In: Lumsden J (ed.) Handbook of research on user interface design and evaluation for mobile technology. IGI Global, Hershey, pp 86–101. http://www.irma-international.org/chapter/ understanding-one-handed-use-mobile/21825/

Karlson AK, Iqbal ST, Meyers B, Ramos G, Lee K, Tang JC (2010) Mobile taskflow in context: a screenshot study of smartphone usage. In: Proceedings of the ACM conference on human factors in computing systems (CHI'10). ACM Press, New York, pp 2009–2018. https://doi.org/10.1145/ 1753326.1753631

Kern D, Marshall P, Schmidt A (2010) Gazemarks: gaze-based visual placeholders to ease attention switching. In: Proceedings of the ACM conference on human factors in computing systems (CHI'10). ACM Press, New York, pp 2093–2102. https://doi.org/10.1145/1753326.1753646

Kim L, Albers MJ (2001) Web design issues when searching for information in a small screen display. In: Proceedings of the ACM conference on computer documentation (SIGDOC'01). ACM Press, New York, pp 193–200. https://doi.org/10.1145/501516.501555

Kosch T, Hassib M, Woźniak PW, Buschek D, Alt F (2018) Your eyes tell: leveraging smooth pursuit for assessing cognitive workload. In: Proceedings of the ACM conference on human factors in computing systems (CHI'18). ACM Press, New York. Paper No. 436. https://doi.org/10.1145/ 3173574.3174010

Kristoffersen S, Ljungberg F (1999) Making place to make IT work: empirical explorations of HCI for mobile CSCW. In: Proceedings of the ACM conference on supporting group work (GROUP'99). ACM Press, New York, pp 276–285. https://doi.org/10.1145/320297.320330

Le HV, Mayer S, Bader P, Henze N (2018) Fingers' range and comfortable area for one-handed smartphone interaction beyond the touchscreen. In: Proceedings of the ACM conference on human factors in computing systems (CHI'18). ACM Press, New York. Paper No. 31. https://doi.org/10. 1145/3173574.3173605

Levy DM, Wobbrock JO, Kaszniak AW, Ostergren M (2011) Initial results from a study of the effects of meditation on multitasking performance. In: Extended abstracts of the ACM conference on human factors in computing systems (CHI'11). ACM Press, New York, pp 2011–2016. https:// doi.org/10.1145/1979742.1979862

Levy DM, Wobbrock JO, Kaszniak AW, Ostergren M (2012) The effects of mindfulness meditation training on multitasking in a high-stress information environment. In: Proceedings of graphics interface (GI'12). Canadian Information Processing Society, Toronto, pp 45–52. https://dl.acm. org/citation.cfm?id=2305285

Li KA, Baudisch P, Hinckley K (2008) Blindsight: eyes-free access to mobile phones. In: Proceedings of the ACM conference on human factors in computing systems (CHI'08). ACM Press, New York, pp 1389–1398. https://doi.org/10.1145/1357054.1357273

LiKamWa R, Zhong L (2011) SUAVE: sensor-based user-aware viewing enhancement for mobile device displays. In: Adjunct proceedings of the ACM symposium on user interface software and technology (UIST'11). ACM Press, New York, pp 5–6. https://doi.org/10.1145/2046396.2046400

Lim H, An G, Cho Y, Lee K, Suh B (2016) WhichHand: automatic recognition of a smartphone's position in the hand using a smartwatch. In: Adjunct proceedings of the ACM conference on human-computer interaction with mobile devices and services (MobileHCI'16). ACM Press, New York, pp 675–681. https://doi.org/10.1145/2957265.2961857

Lin M, Price KJ, Goldman R, Sears A, Jacko, JA (2005) Tapping on the move—Fitts' law under mobile conditions. In: Proceedings of the 16th annual information resources management association international conference (IRMA'05). Idea Group, Hershey, pp 132–135. http://www.irma-international.org/proceeding-paper/tapping-move-fitts-law-under/32557/

Lin M, Goldman R, Price KJ, Sears A, Jacko J (2007) How do people tap when walking? An empirical investigation of nomadic data entry. Int J Hum-Comput Stud 65(9):759–769. https:// doi.org/10.1016/j.ijhcs.2007.04.001

Lu J-M, Lo Y-C (2018) Can interventions based on user interface design help reduce the risks associated with smartphone use while walking? In: Proceedings of the 20th congress of the international ergonomics association (IEA'18). Advances in intelligent systems and computing, vol 819. Springer Nature, Switzerland, pp 268–273. https://doi.org/10.1007/978-3-319-96089-0_29

Lumsden J, Brewster S (2003). A paradigm shift: alternative interaction techniques for use with mobile and wearable devices. In: Proceedings of the conference of the IBM centre for advanced studies on collaborative research (CASCON'03). IBM Press, Indianapolis, pp 197–210. https:// dl.acm.org/citation.cfm?id=961322.961355

MacKay B, Dearman D, Inkpen K, Watters C (2005) Walk 'n scroll: a comparison of software-based navigation techniques for different levels of mobility. In: Proceedings of the ACM conference on human-computer interaction with mobile devices and services (MobileHCI'05). ACM Press, New York, pp 183–190. https://doi.org/10.1145/1085777.1085808

MacKenzie IS (1992) Fitts' law as a research and design tool in human-computer interaction. Hum-Comput Interact 7(1):91–139. https://doi.org/10.1207/s15327051hci0701_3

MacKenzie IS, Castellucci SJ (2012) Reducing visual demand for gestural text input on touchscreen devices. In: Extended abstracts of the ACM conference on human factors in computing systems (CHI'12). ACM Press, New York, pp 2585–2590. https://doi.org/10.1145/2212776.2223840

Macpherson K, Tigwell GW, Menzies R, Flatla DR (2018) BrightLights: gamifying data capture for situational visual impairments. In: Proceedings of the ACM SIGACCESS conference on computers and accessibility (ASSETS'18). ACM Press, New York, pp 355–357. https://doi.org/ 10.1145/3234695.3241030

Maehr W (2008) eMotion: estimation of user's emotional state by mouse motions. VDM Verlag, Saarbrücken. https://dl.acm.org/citation.cfm?id=1522361

Manalavan P, Samar A, Schneider M, Kiesler S, Siewiorek D (2002) In-car cell phone use: mitigating risk by signaling remote callers. In: Extended abstracts of the ACM conference on human factors in computing systems (CHI'02). ACM Press, New York, pp 790–791. https://doi.org/10.1145/ 506443.506599

Mankoff J, Hayes GR, Kasnitz D (2010) Disability studies as a source of critical inquiry for the field of assistive technology. In: Proceedings of the ACM SIGACCESS conference on computers and accessibility (ASSETS'10). ACM Press, New York, pp 3–10. https://doi.org/10.1145/1878803. 1878807

Mäntyjärvi J, Seppänen T (2003) Adapting applications in handheld devices using fuzzy context information. Interact Comput 15(4):521–538. https://doi.org/10.1016/S0953-5438(03)00038-9

Marentakis GN, Brewster SA (2006) Effects of feedback, mobility and index of difficulty on deictic spatial audio target acquisition in the horizontal plane. In: Proceedings of the ACM conference on human factors in computing systems (CHI'06). ACM Press, New York, pp 359–368. https://doi.org/10.1145/1124772.1124826

Mariakakis A, Goel M, Aumi MTI, Patel SN, Wobbrock JO (2015) SwitchBack: using focus and saccade tracking to guide users' attention for mobile task resumption. In: Proceedings of the ACM conference on human factors in computing systems (CHI'15). ACM Press, New York, pp 2953–2962. https://doi.org/10.1145/2702123.2702539

Mariakakis A, Parsi S, Patel SN, Wobbrock JO (2018) Drunk user interfaces: determining blood alcohol level through everyday smartphone tasks. In: Proceedings of the ACM conference on human factors in computing systems (CHI'18). ACM Press, New York. Paper No. 234. https://doi.org/10.1145/3173574.3173808

Mark G, Gonzalez VM, Harris J (2005) No task left behind? Examining the nature of fragmented work. In: Proceedings of the ACM conference on human factors in computing systems (CHI'05). ACM Press, New York, pp 321–330. https://doi.org/10.1145/1054972.1055017

Mark G, Gudith D, Klocke U (2008) The cost of interrupted work: more speed and stress. In: Proceedings of the ACM conference on human factors in computing systems (CHI'08). ACM Press, New York, pp 107–110. https://doi.org/10.1145/1357054.1357072

Mayer S, Lischke L, Woźniak PW, Henze N (2018) Evaluating the disruptiveness of mobile interactions: a mixed-method approach. In: Proceedings of the ACM conference on human factors in computing systems (CHI'18). ACM Press, New York. Paper No. 406. https://doi.org/10.1145/3173574.3173980

McFarlane DC (2002) Comparison of four primary methods for coordinating the interruption of people in human-computer interaction. Hum-Comput Interact 17(1):63–139. https://doi.org/10.1207/S15327051HCI1701_2

McKnight AJ, McKnight AS (1993) The effect of cellular phone use upon driver attention. Accid Anal Prev 25(3):259–265. https://doi.org/10.1016/0001-4575(93)90020-W

Miniotas D, Spakov O, Evreinov G (2003) Symbol creator: an alternative eye-based text entry technique with low demand for screen space. In: Proceedings of the IFIP TC13 9th international conference on human-computer interaction (INTERACT'03). IOS Press, Amsterdam, pp 137–143. http://citeseerx.ist.psu.edu/viewdoc/summary?doi=10.1.1.97.1753

Miyaki T, Rekimoto J (2009) GraspZoom: zooming and scrolling control model for single-handed mobile interaction. In: Proceedings of ACM conference on human-computer interaction with mobile devices and services (MobileHCI'09). ACM Press, New York. Article No. 11. https://doi.org/10.1145/1613858.1613872

Mizobuchi S, Chignell M, Newton D (2005) Mobile text entry: relationship between walking speed and text input task difficulty. In: Proceedings of ACM conference on human-computer interaction with mobile devices and services (MobileHCI'05). ACM Press, New York, pp 122–128. https://doi.org/10.1145/1085777.1085798

Moraveji N, Olson B, Nguyen T, Saadat M, Khalighi Y, Pea R, Heer J (2011) Peripheral paced respiration: influencing user physiology during information work. In: Proceedings of the ACM symposium on user interface software and technology (UIST'11). ACM Press, New York, pp 423–428. https://doi.org/10.1145/2047196.2047250

Moraveji N, Adiseshan A, Hagiwara T (2012) BreathTray: augmenting respiration self-regulation without cognitive deficit. In: Extended abstracts of the ACM conference on human factors in computing systems (CHI'12). ACM Press, New York, pp 2405–2410. https://doi.org/10.1145/2212776.2223810

Mott ME, Wobbrock JO (2019) Cluster touch: improving smartphone touch accuracy for people with motor and situational impairments. In: Proceedings of the ACM conference on human factors in computing systems (CHI'19). ACM Press, New York. To appear

Mustonen T, Olkkonen M, Häkkinen J (2004) Examining mobile phone text legibility while walking. In: Extended abstracts of the ACM conference on human factors in computing systems (CHI'04). ACM Press, New York, pp 1243–1246. https://doi.org/10.1145/985921.986034

Naftali M, Findlater L (2014) Accessibility in context: understanding the truly mobile experience of smartphone users with motor impairments. In: Proceedings of the ACM SIGACCESS conference on computers and accessibility (ASSETS'14). ACM Press, New York, pp 209–216. https://doi.org/10.1145/2661334.2661372

Newell AF (1995) Extra-ordinary human-computer interaction. In: Edwards ADN (ed) Extra-ordinary human-computer interaction: interfaces for users with disabilities. Cambridge University Press, Cambridge, pp 3–18

Ng A, Brewster SA, Williamson JH (2014a) Investigating the effects of encumbrance on one- and two- handed interactions with mobile devices. In: Proceedings of the ACM conference on human factors in computing systems (CHI'14). ACM Press, New York, pp 1981–1990. https://doi.org/10.1145/2556288.2557312

Ng A, Williamson JH, Brewster SA (2014b) Comparing evaluation methods for encumbrance and walking on interaction with touchscreen mobile devices. In: Proceedings of the ACM conference on human-computer interaction with mobile devices and services (MobileHCI'14). ACM Press, New York, pp 23–32. https://doi.org/10.1145/2628363.2628382

Ng A, Williamson J, Brewster S (2015) The effects of encumbrance and mobility on touch-based gesture interactions for mobile phones. In: Proceedings of the ACM conference on human-computer interaction with mobile devices and services (MobileHCI'15). ACM Press, New York, pp 536–546. https://doi.org/10.1145/2785830.2785853

Nicolau H, Jorge J (2012) Touch typing using thumbs: understanding the effect of mobility and hand posture. In: Proceedings of the ACM conference on human factors in computing systems (CHI'12). ACM Press, New York, pp 2683–2686. https://doi.org/10.1145/2207676.2208661

Oney S, Harrison C, Ogan A, Wiese J (2013) ZoomBoard: a diminutive QWERTY soft keyboard using iterative zooming for ultra-small devices. In: Proceedings of the ACM conference on human factors in computing systems (CHI'13). ACM Press, New York, pp 2799–2802. https://doi.org/10.1145/2470654.2481387

Oulasvirta A (2005) The fragmentation of attention in mobile interaction, and what to do with it. Interactions 12(6):16–18. https://doi.org/10.1145/1096554.1096555

Oulasvirta A, Tamminen S, Roto V, Kuorelahti J (2005) Interaction in 4-second bursts: the fragmented nature of attentional resources in mobile HCI. In: Proceedings of the ACM conference on human factors in computing systems (CHI'05). ACM Press, New York, pp 919–928. https://doi.org/10.1145/1054972.1055101

Paredes PE, Ordoñez F, Ju W, Landay JA (2018) Fast and furious: detecting stress with a car steering wheel. In: Proceedings of the ACM conference on human factors in computing systems (CHI'18). ACM Press, New York. Paper No. 665. https://doi.org/10.1145/3173574.3174239

Parhi P, Karlson AK, Bederson BB (2006) Target size study for one-handed thumb use on small touchscreen devices. In: Proceedings of the ACM conference on human-computer interaction with mobile devices and services (MobileHCI'06). ACM Press, New York, pp 203–210. https://doi.org/10.1145/1152215.1152260

Parnin C, DeLine R (2010) Evaluating cues for resuming interrupted programming tasks. In: Proceedings of the ACM conference on human factors in computing systems (CHI'10). ACM Press, New York, pp 93–102. https://doi.org/10.1145/1753326.1753342

Pascoe J (1998) Adding generic contextual capabilities to wearable computers. In: Proceedings of the IEEE international symposium on wearable computers (ISWC'98). IEEE Computer Society, Los Alamitos, p 92. https://doi.org/10.1109/ISWC.1998.729534

Pascoe J, Ryan N, Morse D (2000) Using while moving: HCI issues in fieldwork environments. ACM Trans Comput-Hum Interact 7(3):417–437. https://doi.org/10.1145/355324.355329

Perry KB, Hourcade JP (2008) Evaluating one handed thumb tapping on mobile touchscreen devices. In: Proceedings of graphics interface (GI'08). Canadian Information Processing Society, Toronto, pp 57–64. https://dl.acm.org/citation.cfm?id=1375725

Peterson JB, Rothfleisch J, Zelazo PD, Pihl RO (1990) Acute alcohol intoxication and cognitive functioning. J Stud Alcohol 51(2):114–122. https://doi.org/10.15288/jsa.1990.51.114

Pielot M, Kazakova A, Hesselmann T, Heuten W, Boll S (2012) PocketMenu: non-visual menus for touch screen devices. In: Proceedings of the ACM conference on human-computer interaction with mobile devices and services (MobileHCI'12). ACM Press, New York, pp 327–330. https://doi.org/10.1145/2371574.2371624

Price KJ, Lin M, Feng J, Goldman R, Sears A, Jacko JA, Stary C, Stephanidis C (2004) Data entry on the move: an examination of nomadic speech-based text entry. In: Proceedings of the 8th ERCIM workshop on user interfaces for all (UI4All'04). Lecture notes in computer science, vol 3196. Springer, Berlin, pp 460–471. https://doi.org/10.1007/978-3-540-30111-0_40

Qian H, Kuber R, Sears A (2013a) Tactile notifications for ambulatory users. In: Extended abstracts of the ACM conference on human factors in computing systems (CHI'13). ACM Press, New York, pp 1569–1574. https://doi.org/10.1145/2468356.2468637

Qian H, Kuber R, Sears A (2013b). Developing tactile icons to support mobile users with situationally-induced impairments and disabilities. In: Proceedings of the ACM SIGACCESS conference on computers and accessibility (ASSETS'13). ACM Press, New York. Article No. 47. https://doi.org/10.1145/2513383.2513387

Redelmeier DA, Tibshirani RJ (1997) Association between cellular-telephone calls and motor vehicle collisions. N Engl J Med 336(7):453–458. https://doi.org/10.1056/NEJM199702133360701

Reed MP, Green PA (1999) Comparison of driving performance on-road and in a low-cost simulator using a concurrent telephone dialling task. Ergonomics 42(8):1015–1037. https://doi.org/10.1080/001401399185117

Reid-Cunningham AR (2009) Anthropological theories of disability. J Hum Behav Soc Environ 19(1):99–111. https://doi.org/10.1080/10911350802631644

Reis T, Carriço L, Duarte C (2009) Mobile interaction: automatically adapting audio output to users and contexts on communication and media control scenarios. In: Proceedings of the international conference on universal access in human-computer interaction (UAHCI'09). Lecture notes in computer science, vol 5615. Springer, Berlin, pp 384–393. https://doi.org/10.1007/978-3-642-02710-9_42

Richtel M (2010) Forget gum. Walking and using phone is risky. The New York Times, p A1. http://www.nytimes.com/2010/01/17/technology/17distracted.html

Richtel M et al (2009) Driven to distraction. The New York Times. http://topics.nytimes.com/top/news/technology/series/driven_to_distraction/index.html

Roth V, Turner T (2009) Bezel swipe: conflict-free scrolling and multiple selection on mobile touch screen devices. In: Proceedings of the ACM conference on human factors in computing systems (CHI'09). ACM Press, New York, pp 1523–1526. https://doi.org/10.1145/1518701.1518933

Salvucci DD (2010) On reconstruction of task context after interruption. In: Proceedings of the ACM conference on human factors in computing systems (CHI'10). ACM Press, New York, pp 89–92. https://doi.org/10.1145/1753326.1753341

Salvucci DD, Bogunovich P (2010) Multitasking and monotasking: the effects of mental workload on deferred task interruptions. In: Proceedings of the ACM conference on human factors in computing systems (CHI'10). ACM Press, New York, pp 85–88. https://doi.org/10.1145/1753326.1753340

Saponas TS, Harrison C, Benko H (2011) PocketTouch: through-fabric capacitive touch input. In: Proceedings of the ACM symposium on user interface software and technology (UIST'11). ACM Press, New York, pp 303–308. https://doi.org/10.1145/2047196.2047235

Sarsenbayeva Z, Goncalves J, García J, Klakegg S, Rissanen S, Rintamäki H, Hannu J, Kostakos V (2016) Situational impairments to mobile interaction in cold environments. In: Proceedings of the ACM conference on pervasive and ubiquitous computing (UbiComp'16). ACM Press, New York, pp 85–96. https://doi.org/10.1145/2971648.2971734

Sarsenbayeva Z, van Berkel N, Visuri A, Rissanen S, Rintamaki H, Kostakos V, Goncalves J (2017a) Sensing cold-induced situational impairments in mobile interaction using battery temperature. Proc ACM Interact Mob Wearable Ubiquitous Technol 1(3). Article No. 98. https://doi.org/10.1145/3130963

Sarsenbayeva Z, von Berkel N, Luo C, Kostakos V, Goncalves J (2017b) Challenges of situational impairments during interaction with mobile devices. In: Proceedings of the Australian conference on computer-human interaction (OzCHI'17). ACM Press, New York, pp 477–481. https://doi.org/10.1145/3152771.3156161

Sarsenbayeva Z, van Berkel N, Velloso E, Kostakos V, Goncalves J (2018) Effect of distinct ambient noise types on mobile interaction. Proc ACM Interact Mob Wearable Ubiquitous Technol 2(2). Article No. 82. https://doi.org/10.1145/3214285

Saulynas S, Kuber R (2018) Towards supporting mobile device users facing severely constraining situational impairments. In: Extended abstracts of the ACM conference on human factors in computing systems (CHI'18). ACM Press, New York. Paper No. LBW540. https://doi.org/10.1145/3170427.3188642

Saulynas S, Burgee LE, Kuber R (2017) All situational impairments are not created equal: a classification system for situational impairment events and the unique nature of severely constraining situational impairments. In: Proceedings of iConference 2017. http://hdl.handle.net/2142/96688

Sawhney N, Schmandt C (2000) Nomadic radio: speech and audio interaction for contextual messaging in nomadic environments. ACM Trans Comput-Hum Interact 7(3):353–383. https://doi.org/10.1145/355324.355327

Schedlbauer M, Heines J (2007) Selecting while walking: an investigation of aiming performance in a mobile work context. In: Proceedings of the 13th Americas conference on information systems (AMCIS'07). Association for Information Systems, Atlanta. http://citeseerx.ist.psu.edu/viewdoc/summary?doi=10.1.1.102.935

Schedlbauer MJ, Pastel RL, Heines JM (2006) Effect of posture on target acquisition with a trackball and touch screen. In: Proceedings of the IEEE international conference on information technology interfaces (ITI'06). IEEE Computer Society, Los Alamitos, pp 257–262. https://doi.org/10.1109/ITI.2006.1708488

Schildbach B, Rukzio E (2010) Investigating selection and reading performance on a mobile phone while walking. In: Proceedings of the ACM conference on human-computer interaction with mobile devices and services (MobileHCI'10). ACM Press, New York, pp 93–102. https://doi.org/10.1145/1851600.1851619

Schmidt A, Aidoo KA, Takaluoma A, Tuomela U, van Laerhoven K, van de Velde W (1999a) Advanced interaction in context. In: Proceedings of the international symposium on handheld and ubiquitous computing (HUC'99). Lecture notes in computer science, vol 1707. Springer, Berlin, pp 89–101. https://doi.org/10.1007/3-540-48157-5_10

Schmidt A, Beigl M, Gellersen H-W (1999b) There is more to context than location. Comput Graph 23(6):893–901. https://doi.org/10.1016/S0097-8493(99)00120-X

Schneider M, Kiesler S (2005) Calling while driving: effects of providing remote traffic context. In: Proceedings of the ACM conference on human factors in computing systems (CHI'05). ACM Press, New York, pp 561–569. https://doi.org/10.1145/1054972.1055050

Sears A, Young M (2003) Physical disabilities and computing technologies: an analysis of impairments. In: Jacko JA, Sears A (eds) The human-computer interaction handbook, 1st edn. Lawrence Erlbaum, Hillsdale, pp 482–503. http://dl.acm.org/citation.cfm?id=772105

Sears A, Lin M, Jacko J, Xiao Y (2003) When computers fade… Pervasive computing and situationally-induced impairments and disabilities. In: Proceedings of the 10th international conference on human-computer interaction (HCI Int'l'03). Lawrence Erlbaum, Mahwah, pp 1298–1302

Shibata T, Afergan D, Kong D, Yuksel BF, MacKenzie IS, Jacob RJK (2016) DriftBoard: a panning-based text entry technique for ultra-small touchscreens. In: Proceedings of the ACM symposium on user interface software and technology (UIST'16). ACM Press, New York, pp 575–582. https://doi.org/10.1145/2984511.2984591

Simon HA (1971) Designing organizations for an information rich world. In: Greenberger M (ed) Computers, communications and the public interest. Johns Hopkins Press, Baltimore, pp 38–52

Sinclair J (2010) Cultural commentary: being autistic together. Disabil Stud Q 30(1). http://www. dsq-sds.org/article/view/1075/1248

Smith G, Baudisch P, Robertson G, Czerwinski M, Meyers B, Robbins D, Andrews D (2003) GroupBar: the TaskBar evolved. In: Proceedings of the Australian conference on computer-human interaction (OzCHI'03). Ergonomics Society of Australia, Canberra, pp 34–43. http:// citeseerx.ist.psu.edu/viewdoc/summary?doi=10.1.1.3.9622

Soukoreff RW, MacKenzie IS (2004) Towards a standard for pointing device evaluation, perspectives on 27 years of Fitts' law research in HCI. Int J Hum-Comput Stud 61(6):751–789. https://doi. org/10.1016/j.ijhcs.2004.09.001

Strayer DL, Johnston WA (2001) Driven to distraction: dual-task studies of simulated driving and conversing on a cellular telephone. Psychol Sci 12(6):462–466. https://doi.org/10.1111/1467-9280.00386

Su NM, Mark G (2008) Communication chains and multitasking. In: Proceedings of the ACM conference on human factors in computing systems (CHI'08). ACM Press, New York, pp 83–92. https://doi.org/10.1145/1357054.1357069

Sun D, Paredes P, Canny J (2014) MouStress: detecting stress from mouse motion. In: Proceedings of the ACM conference on human factors in computing systems (CHI'14). ACM Press, New York, pp 61–70. https://doi.org/10.1145/2556288.2557243

Tigwell GW, Flatla DR, Menzies R (2018a) It's not just the light: understanding the factors causing situational visual impairments during mobile interaction. In: Proceedings of the Nordic conference on human-computer interaction (NordiCHI'18). ACM Press, New York, pp 338–351. https://doi. org/10.1145/3240167.3240207

Tigwell GW, Menzies R, Flatla DR (2018b) Designing for situational visual impairments: supporting early-career designers of mobile content. In: Proceedings of the ACM conference on designing interactive systems (DIS'18). ACM Press, New York, pp 387–399. https://doi.org/10. 1145/3196709.3196760

Tinwala H, MacKenzie IS (2009) Eyes-free text entry on a touchscreen phone. In: Proceedings of the IEEE Toronto international conference on science and technology for humanity (TIC-STH'09). IEEE Press, Piscataway, pp 83–88. https://doi.org/10.1109/TIC-STH.2009.5444381

Tinwala H, MacKenzie IS (2010) Eyes-free text entry with error correction on touchscreen mobile devices. In: Proceedings of the Nordic conference on human-computer interaction (NordiCHI'10). ACM Press, New York, pp 511–520. https://doi.org/10.1145/1868914.1868972

Tung Y-C, Goel M, Zinda I, Wobbrock JO (2018) RainCheck: overcoming capacitive interference caused by rainwater on smartphones. In: Proceedings of the ACM international conference on multimodal interfaces (ICMI'18). ACM Press, New York, pp 464–471. https://doi.org/10.1145/ 3242969.3243028

Vadas K, Patel N, Lyons K, Starner T, Jacko J (2006) Reading on-the-go: a comparison of audio and hand-held displays. In: Proceedings of the ACM conference on human-computer interaction with mobile devices and services (MobileHCI'06). ACM Press, New York, pp 219–226. https:// doi.org/10.1145/1152215.1152262

van Dantzich M, Robbins D, Horvitz E, Czerwinski M (2002) Scope: providing awareness of multiple notifications at a glance. In: Proceedings of the ACM working conference on advanced visual interfaces (AVI'02). ACM Press, New York, pp 267–281. https://doi.org/10.1145/1556262. 1556306

Vanderheiden GC (1997) Anywhere, anytime (+anyone) access to the next-generation WWW. Comput Netw ISDN Syst 29(8–13):1439–1446. https://doi.org/10.1016/S0169-7552(97)00067-6

Vertanen K, Kristensson PO (2009) Parakeet: a continuous speech recognition system for mobile touch-screen devices. In: Proceedings of the ACM conference on intelligent user interfaces (IUI'09). ACM Press, New York, pp 237–246. https://doi.org/10.1145/1502650.1502685

Vizer LM, Sears A (2017) Efficacy of personalized models in discriminating high cognitive demand conditions using text-based interactions. Int J Hum-Comput Stud 104(C):80–96. https://doi.org/10.1016/j.ijhcs.2017.03.001

Vuchinich RE, Sobell MB (1978) Empirical separation of physiologic and expected effects of alcohol on complex perceptual motor performance. Psychopharmacology 60(1):81–85. https://doi.org/10.1007/BF00429183

Wang Q, Chang H (2010) Multitasking bar: prototype and evaluation of introducing the task concept into a browser. In: Proceedings of the ACM conference on human factors in computing systems (CHI'10). ACM Press, New York, pp 103–112. https://doi.org/10.1145/1753326.1753343

Williamson AM, Feyer A-M (2000) Moderate sleep deprivation produces impairments in cognitive and motor performance equivalent to legally prescribed levels of alcohol intoxication. Occup Environ Med 57(10):649–655. https://doi.org/10.1136/oem.57.10.649

Wobbrock JO (2006) The future of mobile device research in HCI. Workshop on "What is the next generation of human-computer interaction?" In: ACM conference on human factors in computing systems (CHI'06), pp 131–134

Wobbrock JO, Forlizzi J, Hudson SE, Myers BA (2002) WebThumb: interaction techniques for small-screen browsers. In: Proceedings of the ACM symposium on user interface software and technology (UIST'02). ACM Press, New York, pp 205–208. https://doi.org/10.1145/571985.572014

Wobbrock JO, Myers BA, Aung HH (2008) The performance of hand postures in front- and back-of-device interaction for mobile computing. Int J Hum-Comput Stud 66(12):857–875. https://doi.org/10.1016/j.ijhcs.2008.03.004

Wobbrock JO, Kane SK, Gajos KZ, Harada S, Froehlich J (2011) Ability-based design: concept, principles, and examples. ACM Trans Access Comput 3(3). Article No. 9. https://doi.org/10.1145/1952383.1952384

Wobbrock JO, Gajos KZ, Kane SK, Vanderheiden GC (2018) Ability-based design. Commun ACM 61(6):62–71. https://doi.org/10.1145/3148051

Wolf F, Kuber R, Pawluk D, Turnage B (2017) Towards supporting individuals with situational impairments in inhospitable environments. In: Proceedings of the ACM SIGACCESS conference on computers and accessibility (ASSETS'17). ACM Press, New York, pp 349–350. https://doi.org/10.1145/3132525.3134783

World Health Organization (2000) International classification of impairments, disabilities, and handicaps. World Health Organization, Geneva, Switzerland

Yamabe T, Takahashi K (2007) Experiments in mobile user interface adaptation for walking users. In: Proceedings of the international conference on intelligent pervasive computing (IPC'07). IEEE Computer Society, Los Alamitos, pp 280–284. https://doi.org/10.1109/IPC.2007.94

Yang T, Ferati M, Liu Y, Ghahari RR, Bolchini D (2012) Aural browsing on-the-go: listening-based back navigation in large web architectures. In: Proceedings of the ACM conference on human factors in computing systems (CHI'12). ACM Press, New York, pp 277–286. https://doi.org/10.1145/2207676.2207715

Yatani K, Truong KN (2007) An evaluation of stylus-based text entry methods on handheld devices in stationary and mobile settings. In: Proceedings of the ACM conference on human-computer interaction with mobile devices and services (MobileHCI'07). ACM Press, New York, pp 487–494. https://doi.org/10.1145/1377999.1378059

Yatani K, Truong KN (2009) An evaluation of stylus-based text entry methods on handheld devices studied in different user mobility states. Pervasive Mob Compu 5(5):496–508. https://doi.org/10.1016/j.pmcj.2009.04.002

Yesilada Y, Harper S, Chen T, Trewin S (2010) Small-device users situationally impaired by input. Comput Hum Behav 26(3):427–435. https://doi.org/10.1016/j.chb.2009.12.001

Yin Y, Ouyang TY, Partridge K, Zhai S (2013) Making touchscreen keyboards adaptive to keys, hand postures, and individuals: a hierarchical spatial backoff model approach. In: Proceedings of the ACM conference on human factors in computing systems (CHI'13). ACM Press, New York, pp 2775–2784. https://doi.org/10.1145/2470654.2481384

Ylipulli J, Luusua A, Kukka H, Ojala T (2014) Winter is coming: introducing climate sensitive urban computing. In: Proceedings of the ACM conference on designing interactive systems (DIS'14). ACM Press, New York, pp 647–656. https://doi.org/10.1145/2598510.2598571

Zamora W, Calafate CT, Cano J-C, Manzoni P (2017) Smartphone tuning for accurate ambient noise assessment. In: Proceedings of the ACM conference on advances in mobile computing and multimedia (MoMM'17). ACM Press, New York, pp 115–122. https://doi.org/10.1145/3151848.3151854

Zhang Y, Hornof AJ (2014) Understanding multitasking through parallelized strategy exploration and individualized cognitive modeling. In: Proceedings of the ACM conference on human factors in computing systems (CHI'14). ACM Press, New York, pp 3885–3894. https://doi.org/10.1145/2556288.2557351

Zhao S, Dragicevic P, Chignell M, Balakrishnan R, Baudisch P (2007) Earpod: eyes-free menu selection using touch input and reactive audio feedback. In: Proceedings of the ACM conference on human factors in computing systems (CHI'07). ACM Press, New York, pp 1395–1404. https://doi.org/10.1145/1240624.1240836

Zhou Y, Xu T, David B, Chalon R (2016) Interaction on-the-go: a fine-grained exploration on wearable PROCAM interfaces and gestures in mobile situations. Univers Access Inf Soc 15(4):643–657. https://doi.org/10.1007/s10209-015-0448-6

Zucco JE, Thomas BH, Grimmer K (2006) Evaluation of four wearable computer pointing devices for drag and drop tasks when stationary and walking. In: Proceedings of the IEEE international symposium on wearable computers (ISWC'06). IEEE Computer Society, Los Alamitos, pp 29–36. https://doi.org/10.1109/ISWC.2006.286339

Chapter 6
Ageing and Older Adults

Sri Kurniawan, Andrew Arch and Sean-Ryan Smith

Abstract Between 2015 and 2050, the proportion of the world's population over 60 years will nearly double from 12 to 22%. Maintaining a high quality of life for these people has become an important issue throughout the world. The Web has been shown to have a positive experience on the quality of life and well-being of older adults, by assisting them to maintain an independent living. However, many older adults seem to shy away from the Web due to various problems they experience when interacting with the Web. To understand the nature of these problems, this chapter presents the functional impairments and the attitudes that might contribute to older adults' hesitation of utilising the Web. This chapter then discusses the changes that happen with age and their effects on Web interaction. It then moves to the standards surrounding Web accessibility, more specifically WCAG, and how they assist older adults. Finally, it discusses activities that older adults perform on the Web.

6.1 Introduction

According to the WHO (2018a), the pace of population ageing is much faster than in the past. Between 2015 and 2050, the proportion of the world's population over 60 years will nearly double from 12 to 22%. In some countries, it will be much higher than this, e.g. Germany has forecast 30% of its population that will be over 65% by 2050 and Japan has forecast 40% (He et al. 2016). By 2020, the number of people aged 60 years and older will outnumber children younger than 5 years.

As we progress through the natural ageing process, we experience some degenerative effects of ageing, which can include diminished vision, varying degrees of

S. Kurniawan (✉) · S.-R. Smith
University of California Santa Cruz, 1156 High Street, SOE3, UCSC, 95064 Santa Cruz, USA
e-mail: skurnia@ucsc.edu

S.-R. Smith
e-mail: sewsmith@ucsc.edu

A. Arch
Intopia Digital, PO BOX 198, 3442 Woodned, VIC, Australia
e-mail: andrew@intopia.digital

© Springer-Verlag London Ltd., part of Springer Nature 2019
Y. Yesilada and S. Harper (eds.), *Web Accessibility*, Human–Computer Interaction Series, https://doi.org/10.1007/978-1-4471-7440-0_6

hearing loss, psychomotor impairments, as well as reduced attention, memory and learning abilities. This can heavily affect the accessibility of the Web, which has become an increasingly vital tool in our information-rich society; the Web plays an important role in keeping people connected and providing access to services.

Before discussing the effects of ageing on Web interaction, there is a need to define what 'older adults' means. First of all, the term 'older adults' had often been referred to as 'elderly'. The term 'older' has been defined in numerous ways. Bailey cited a variety of research in which the 'old age' categories vary broadly, including studies in which 'older users' were defined as 'over 40' (Study 2), 'over 50' (Study 3) and 'over 58' (Study 1) (Bailey 2002). Orimo et al. (2006) stated that conventionally, those over 65 years are called 'elderly', with those 65–74 years old are called 'early elderly' and those over 75 years old as 'late elderly'. The same article tells a story of the origin of the use of 65 years of age as the retirement age. Apparently, more than a century ago, Prince Bismarck of Germany selected 65 as the age of which the citizens can participate in the national pension plan, believing that most people would have died before reaching that age (Orimo et al. 2006). Indeed, according to World Health Organization, most developed world countries have accepted the chronological age of 65 years as a definition of 'elderly' or older person (WHO 2002).

Ageing research shows that sensory changes that are typically associated with old age are really the result of a gradual sensory decline that typically begins between the ages of 40–55 years old—earlier than the age most people consider themselves 'old' (Straub 2003). One thing that is apparent, however, is that the individual variability of sensory, physical and cognitive functioning increases with age (Myatt et al. 2000) and this functioning declines at largely varying rates in older adults (Gregor et al. 2002).

6.2 Physical Changes

6.2.1 Vision

Vision is the most common physiological change associated with ageing (AgeLight 2001), and the one that affects Web interaction the most. As Jakob Nielsen stated, 'The most serious accessibility problems given the current state of the Web probably relate to blind users and users with other visual disabilities since most Web pages are highly visual' (Nielsen 1996).

One of the most common changes in vision is caused by the yellowing of the lens due to discolouration of the eye's fluid. This gives the impression of looking through a yellow filter (Sekuler et al. 1982). Along with this, any colour blindness in the eye caused by glaucoma or general genetic colour blindness normally worsens with age due to decreased blood supply to the retina (AgeLight 2001). These make it difficult for older adults to tell the difference between colours of a similar hue and low contrast. It is therefore advisable to use highly contrasting colours to improve legibility and to present users with their own colour option for fonts and backgrounds to allow them to customise the site to their own needs. Where colours are specified, they should be highly saturated. Primary colours are believed to be the best for older adults (AgeLight 2001). Maximising differences between hue, lightness and saturation and using high contrasting colours also helps to provide maximum legibility.

The pupil of the eye shrinks with age. The lens becomes thicker and flatter, and the pupil is less able to change diameter, therefore, letting in less light. The retina of an average 60-year old receives just 33% of the light of the retina of the average 20-year old (Armstrong et al. 1991). Ageing eyes are also more sensitive to glare, a condition known as 'night blindness', caused by reduced transparency in the lens. To aid this, it is best to use light-coloured text on a dark background and try to avoid using fluorescent colours or pure white that can appear very bright.

Ageing eyes are also very susceptible to fatigue and tend to be dry due to a decrease in the amount of blinking. Some design choices can provide respite to tired eyes. Using Sans Serif fonts such as Arial of at least 12–14 pt are suggested, as the fonts do not have decorative edges (Ellis and Kurniawan 2000). Allowing bigger gaps between lines and using white space can also produce less eye strain as can minimising the use of long strings of capital letters, e.g. it is much better to put 'This Is A Title' instead of 'THIS IS A TITLE', as in the later, there is little differentiation between capital letters leading to eye strain. A third of people aged over 65 have a disease affecting their vision (Stuart-Hamilton 1999). Some of the most common ones are discussed below.

Age-Related Macular Degeneration (AMD)

AMD, sometimes known as 'senile maculopathy', is a genetic disease and the most common cause of severe visual impairment amongst older adults (Ford 1993). Macular disease refers to the breakdown or thinning of the most sensitive cells of the eye clustered in small area in the centre of the retina known as the macula (Fine et al. 1999).

Macular disease affects central vision only; sufferers still can see adequately at the peripherals of their vision, a term commonly described as 'polo mint vision' due to the hole in the centre of their vision (Ford 1993). While never resulting in total blindness, AMD is often severe enough for the sufferer to be classed as partially sighted or blind. Symptoms of macular disease usually start around the early mid-50s, typically starting in just one eye. In early stages of macular degeneration, it is difficult to read small or faint print, but as the disease worsens and spreads to both eyes, it becomes difficult even to read large print or to determine any specific details such as pictures.

Due to these symptoms, any Web pages should be designed with large fonts (minimum of size 12–14 pt) or the options to increase font size. Any other page elements such as buttons, links and images should be reasonably large. The site should not use bright colours that can cause glare and should avoid using colours in the short-wave spectrum. However, the background of the site should not be too dark as the text will become unreadable due to AMD sufferer's diminished contrast sensitivity. Web pages should also not link from a bright page to a dark page or vice versa.

Cataracts

Cataract refers to the loss of transparency or clouding of the lens of the eye, and it is predominantly an age-related disease (Sekuler et al. 1982). The lens is responsible for focusing light coming into the eye onto the retina to produce clear, sharp images. However, when the lens of the eye becomes clouded, the eye is no longer able to adequately process light coming into the eye.

Cataracts are the most common cause of vision loss in people aged over 55 (St. Lukes 2005). Cataracts are caused by an accumulation of dead cells within the lens. As the lens is within a sealed capsule within the eye, dead cells have no way to get out, and therefore, accumulate over time causing a gradual clouding of the lens.

The clouding of the lens means that less violet light enters and reaches the retina making it harder to see colours like blue, green and violet than reds, oranges and yellows (AgeLight 2001).

Due to this, Web pages should be designed to use colours within the red/orange/yellow spectrum and avoid using colours in the blue/green/violet spectrum. Using colours of similar hues should also be avoided, as it is harder for people with cataracts to determine the difference. Fonts should be a minimum of size 12 pt to allow for the lack of detail in the sufferers' vision. Blinking or flashing icons or animations should be avoided, as they are difficult to see with the user's diminished peripheral vision. The use of advertisements or 'page cluttering' icons or images such as page counters should be omitted from the site as these tend to draw the users attention away from the text, making it harder for them to find the content they are looking for. It has been found that large areas of white space with a small block of text in the middle are easier for the user to read as they can tell where the text is even with diminished ability to see detail due to vision clouding; therefore, maximising white space around the text is a good way to improve readability for users with cataracts (AgeLight 2001).

Presbyopia

Presbyopia is an age-related disorder where the eyes lose the ability to focus on objects or detail at close distances. The onset of presbyopia normally starts in the 40s but is a disorder that happens to all people at some time in their life (Lee and Bailey 2005). Despite its symptoms, presbyopia is not related to nearsightedness, which is due to an abnormality in the shape of the eye. Instead, it is caused by the gradual lack of flexibility in the crystalline lens of the eye due to the natural ageing process (St. Lukes 2005). It is not a disease and cannot be avoided; however, it can easily be treated with reading glasses or eye surgery. People with presbyopia usually have a diminished visual field and tend to compensate for this by moving their head from side to side when reading, instead of sweeping their eyes from left to right.

Glaucoma

Glaucoma is a group of diseases that can damage the optic nerve and cause blindness. While not a direct age-related disorder, it most commonly affects people over 60 or

African Americans over 40 years of age. Symptoms include loss of peripheral vision starting with detail and increasing until the sufferer has a form of tunnel vision where the sufferers gradually lose their peripheral vision. If left untreated, this tunnel vision will continue to move inwards until no vision remains.

While there are various causes of glaucoma, the most common is open-angle glaucoma where fluid builds up in the anterior chamber of the eye causing pressure that damages the optic nerve (National Eye Institute 2004). As with presbyopia, the sufferer has a decreased angle of vision, and so must turn their head to view what a normal person could view in their peripheral vision.

6.2.2 Hearing

Twenty per cent of people between 45 and 54 years have some degree of hearing impairment. The figure rises to 75% for people between 75 and 79 years of age (Kline and Scialfa 1996). Older adults have reduced ability to detect high-pitched sounds (Scheiber 1992). Interfaces that use sound to get attention will need to use lower frequency sounds for older users. It is found that a beep that sweeps across 0.5–1.0 kHz is reasonably effective (Zhao 2001). Recorded voice should also use speakers with low-pitched voices.

Older adults have more problems localising sound than younger persons, which is more apparent in persons with presbycusis (Kline and Scialfa 1996). They have a reduced ability to follow fast speech (more than 140–180 words per minute) and conversation in the noisy surrounding (Hawthorn 2000). Providing audio captions for online news, especially when the journalists reported the news over noisy backgrounds (e.g. an onsite natural disaster report), will help older users.

Even though one might argue that hearing loss does not severely affect Web interaction (as the Web adopts a visual paradigm), unfortunately, hearing loss was reported to be significantly correlated with the severity of cognitive dysfunction in older adults, and therefore carries problems associated with cognitive impairment (Uhlmann et al. 1989). We are also seeing significant increases in video on the Web—YouTube alone had 300 h uploaded every minute in 2018 (Aslan 2018).

6.2.3 Psychomotor

In older adults, response times increase significantly with more complex motor tasks (Spiriduso 1995) or in tasks with a larger number of choices (Hawthorn 2000). Older adults perform poorly when tracking a target using a mouse (Jagacinski et al. 1995), make more sub-movements when using a mouse (Walker et al. 1997) and experience an increase in cursor positioning problems if the target size is small such as the size of letters or spaces in text (Charness and Bosman 1990). Siedler and Stelmach (1996) have also reported that older adults have 'less ability to control and modulate the forces they apply'. Finally, older adults are more cautious in their movement strategies because the likelihood of errors for fast-moving targets increases with age (Hawthorn 2000).

Some older adults suffer from age-related diseases that affect their psychomotor abilities, such as multiple sclerosis, arthritis, osteoporosis, stroke and Parkinson's disease. Multiple sclerosis (MS) is a disorder of the central nervous system marked by weakness, numbness, a loss of muscle coordination and problems with vision, speech and bladder control. Arthritis is inflammation of joints causing pain, swelling and stiffness. Osteoporosis is a loss of normal bone density, mass and strength, leading to increased porousness and vulnerability to fracture. Stroke refers to damage to the brain caused by interruption to its blood supply or leakage of blood outside of vessel walls. Depending upon where the brain is affected and the extent of the decreased blood supply to the brain, paralysis, weakness, a speech defect, aphasia or death may occur. Finally, Parkinson's disease is a progressive disorder of the nervous system marked by muscle tremors, muscle rigidity, decreased mobility, stooped posture, slow voluntary movements and a mask-like facial expression. As the above symptoms indicate, any of these diseases can severely affect older adult's psychomotor abilities.

Older adults also tend to have reduced grip strength and flexibility, and thus a more limited range to move the mouse. Declines in motor control may result in the inability to hold the mouse still and rapidly push the button at the same time, a movement often required when interacting with GUI.

A 1997 study revealed that the most common problem faced by older participants was using the mouse, both for pointing and clicking (21%) and for scrolling (24%). It was noted that because of arthritis or tremors, some older adults were incapable of the fine movements required to manoeuvre a mouse. They had difficulty placing the cursor within a search engine box, placing the mouse in the arrowed boxes, scrolling and coordinating the movement of the mouse and clicking it (IFLANET 1997).

Touch screens and tablets may benefit some older adults with limited psychomotor abilities but target size for touch can still be problematic along with dexterity for swiping.

6.3 Cognitive Changes

6.3.1 Attention

Attention is the ability to focus and remember items in the face of distracting stimuli being presented, which may have to be processed simultaneously mentally (Stuart-Hamilton 2000). Older adults experience more difficulties in trying to focus and maintain attention on activities over long periods of time or require quick and continuous scanning, which is particularly fatiguing (Vercruyssen 1996), and activities that require concentration on a specific task in light of distracting information (Kotary and Hoyer 1995). Selective attention (a type of attention that involves focusing on a specific aspect of an experience while ignoring other aspects) therefore becomes more difficult for older adults. Highlighting important information and using perceptual organisation such as grouping would help older adults focus on the necessary information more effectively (Czaja 1997).

Divided attention is the ability to attend simultaneously and process more than one task at the same time (Hawthorn 2000). The ability to sustain divided attention in the performance of tasks declines with age, particularly in complex tasks (Hartley 1992). The ability to form newly automated responses, which is the ability to respond to stimuli automatically without conscious effort or control, particularly in visual searches becomes more difficult (Hawthorn 2000), and while older adults are able to learn new responses, they continue to remain attention demanding and, hence, contribute to cognitive load (Rogers et al. 1994). Where automated responses have been learned in older adults, these can become disruptive when learning new tasks because it is difficult to unlearn responses where the person is unconscious of the response (Rogers et al. 1994). Visual information processing also slows down with ageing (Cerella et al. 1982).

6.3.2   Memory

There is general agreement in the literature on cognitive ageing that memory performance declines with age and that such age-related decrements in performance are much greater in relation to some tasks than in others (Grady and Craik 2000). Memory is a key performance factor in all cognitive tasks, which includes learning, planning, perception, decision-making, prioritising and creativity (Hoisko 2003). Declines occur in intellectual performance (Zajicek 2001) and the ability to process items from long-term memory into short-term memory, which is distinct from simply being able to recall items (Salthouse 1994) and which explains older adults' problems with text comprehension (Light 1990).

With long-term memory, studies have found there is a decline in episodic memory (memory for specific events) and procedural memory (memory for how we carry out tasks) (Hawthorn 2000). Memory is particularly relevant to learning, in that in order to learn, one must acquire the information and retain it in memory. Research shows that older adults retain skill levels in areas of expertise they have learnt, although it becomes more difficult to learn a new motor skill (Cunningham and Brookbank 1988) and more demanding to learn new complex tasks, particularly where the tasks are not meaningful to the user (Stokes 1992). Older adults also experience a significant decline in capability on performance of memory tasks that require recall of content; however, there is little decline in memory tasks involving recognition (Rybash et al. 1995). Research also suggests that older adults tend not to adopt organising material strategies, unless informed to do so (Ratner et al. 1987), which could also suggest why older adults have poorer learning than younger adults do.

Because of the decline in cognitive ability, older users face many difficulties with using Web pages. As people age, there is a general overall slowing of brain processing speed (Czaja and Sharit 1998). The largest impact seems to be with tasks that require the most cognitive processing, such as with working memory, overall attentional capacity and visual search performance. Age effects are smallest for tasks where knowledge is an important aspect of the task and largest for tasks where successful performance is primarily dependent on speed (Czaja and Sharit 1998).

Various design suggestions to mediate cognitive decline in older adults have been proposed. For example, the use of a certain style in text writing, i.e. the information must be presented in a clear way using simple language and active voice, was suggested (National Institute of Aging and the National Library of Medicine 2002). Older adults may have problems recalling things such as a specific Web page location (i.e. Uniform Resource Locator or URL), previously followed links or the current location in a particular website (Mead et al. 1997). Recall takes more cognitive effort than recognition does; therefore, well-designed visual cues such as text links, buttons and icons could significantly support older users. Graphical cues are useful in providing users with a sense of current location, and therefore, reducing the demand on working memory to remember where they had been and where they are within the Web structure (Ellis and Kurniawan 2000).

It is anticipated that the current work of the W3C Web accessibility cognitive task force (Web Accessibility Initiative 2017) will contribute significantly to addressing cognitive issues overall in future version of the Web accessibility guidelines. This work will also benefit older adults.

6.4   Behavioural Changes

There are some notable behavioural changes associated with advanced ageing. The first notable change is increased cautiousness (hesitancy about making responses that may be incorrect) (Salthouse 1991). One most commonly cited explanation for this change is the decline in speed across a variety of situations (Birren 1970). An older adult has longer reaction times, and it has been suggested that this is caused by inefficient central nervous system (CNS) functioning. Indeed, the CNS is also at the root of sensory and perceptual changes that occur with age. To cope with these changes, older adults modify their behaviour and attempt to compensate, resulting in, among others, increased cautiousness and a lack of confidence. Providing assurance to an older user that the user is in the right (or wrong) path to their information target can alleviate the lack of confidence in older adults.

Older adults have less confidence in their ability to use computer technology, including the Web, which causes computer phobia, anxiety, resistance and negative attitude towards computers (Christopher 1999). This is partly due to the fact that some older adults have never used or been shown how to use computer technology and have never had the opportunity to learn. The same research pointed out that older adults are more receptive to using computers when they perceived the technology as being useful and the tasks that they were able to perform with the technology as being valuable and beneficial. One study found that introducing the technology in a highly interactive and understandable manner was one factor that was likely to influence the receptivity of older adults towards computers and the Web (Edwards and Englehardt 1989).

One piece of good news is that the influence of learned habits on behaviour is unchanged with age (Grady and Craik 2000). This might mean that whilst problems associated with physical and cognitive changes that come with ageing will still affect how older adults use the Web, the next cohort of older adults might not have problems associated with lack of exposure with computers and the Web.

6.5   Web Accessibility Needs of Older Adults

Older adults are increasingly accessing the online world. The Pew Research Centre (2017) estimates that roughly two-thirds of those ages 65 and older in the US go online, however, people aged 65–69 are about twice as likely as those over 80 to go online. The Australian Communications and Media Authority (2016) estimates that 79% of older Australians (over 65) have accessed the Internet at some point in their lives, with 71% going online in the 3 months to June 2015. In the United Kingdom, Age UK (2016) estimate that 80% of 65–74 age adults were recent internet users in 2016 but only 44% of people 75 years and over. These estimates of the numbers of older adults going online increase with every survey and are seen around the world.

However, as explained earlier, ageing brings with it changes in ability. While we tend to think of disability in boxes such as vision, hearing, physical and cognitive, when we age it is likely that all of these abilities will decline to a lesser or greater extent and we will all be impacted in some of the ways described earlier. Many older adults consider themselves just to be 'ageing' rather than having a disability; however, depending on the number and severity of impairments, they will effectively experience disability.

When people lose abilities later in life, they are much less likely than younger people to adopt new compensating technologies if the learning curve is significant. With declining hearing, turning on captions or fitting a hearing aid is an easy adjustment with a very small learning curve. However, learning to use a screen reader if a person's sight deteriorated significantly as described earlier is a much more complicated task with a very large learning curve. This a common finding in studies of older adults use of technology. For example, Gitlow (2014) found that barriers to use included age-related changes such as vision and hearing loss and fine motor difficulties.

The Web Content Accessibility Guidelines (WCAG) 1.0 were released in 1999 (Chisholm et al. 1999) but had a heavy emphasis on technical requirement to get the markup correct so that assistive technologies, especially screen readers, could interpret the markup correctly. WCAG 2.0 (Caldwell et al. 2008) was released in 2008 with more emphasis on usability in addition to technical requirements and WCAG 2.1 (Kirkpatrick et al. 2018) released in 2018 added additional usability factors.

Arch et al. (2009) summarised a large amount of previous literature on the impact of ageing on accessing the Web including

- discussions of the general functional and sensory limitations often experienced as part of the ageing process,
- collections of broad recommendations for making websites more accommodating for older users,
- studies of how particular limitations experienced by older users impact Web use, and
- studies of the impact of specific web design aspects, such as forms, on older users.

They concluded that, for most older adults, it will be usability aspects, rather technical aspects, that will have the largest impact of older adults' ability to use the web.

As discussed in Part 3 (Standards Guidelines and Trends), WCAG comprises four principles—Perceivable, Operable, Understandable and Robust. Older adults browse the Web for information, interaction with commercial organisations and government for purchasing goods and services, and communication with family, friends and others. Arch and Abou-Zahra (2010) compiled a list of WCAG 2.0 success criteria that collectively address many of the needs of older adults with impairments and disability; WCAG 2.1 extended the criteria applicable to older adults. The W3C publishes sufficient techniques, advisory techniques and failure techniques—updated on a regular basis—to assist designers and developers conform with these criteria.

It is expected that future versions of the Web accessibility guidelines will provide even more support for older adults as they consider additional evidence from ongoing research, including addressing additional cognitive and low-vision issues.

The needs of older adults are addressed below under the four WCAG principles and list the relevant success criteria from WCAG 2.1.

6.5.1 Perceivable Information and User Interfaces

Text size, style and layout

Many older adults require large text due to declining vision, including text in form fields and other controls. Text style and its visual presentation impact how hard or easy it is for people to read; this can have a large impact on older adults with declining vision.

- 1.4.4—Resize text (AA),
- 1.4.8—Visual Presentation (AAA),
- 1.4.10—Reflow (AA) and
- 1.4.12—Text Spacing (AA).

Colour and contrast

Most older adults' colour perception changes with the yellowing of the lens, changing colour perception and they lose contrast sensitivity. Eye diseases discussed earlier also often lead to a decrease in contrast sensitivity.

- 1.4.1—Use of Colour (A),
- 1.4.3—Contrast (Minimum) (AA),
- 1.4.6—Contrast (Enhanced) (AAA) and
- 1.4.11—Non-text Contrast (AA).

Multimedia

Because of many older adults' hearing or vision declines, they often need transcripts, captions and clear audio. Some may also benefit from audio description.

- 1.2.1—Audio-only and Video-only (Prerecorded) (A),
- 1.2.2—Captions (Prerecorded) (A),
- 1.2.4—Captions (Live) (AA),
- 1.2.3—Audio Description or Media Alternative (Prerecorded video) (A),
- 1.2.5—Audio Description (Prerecorded video) (AA),
- 1.2.7—Extended Audio Description (Prerecorded video) (AAA),
- 1.2.8—Media Alternative (Prerecorded) (AAA),
- 1.2.9—Audio-only (Live) (AAA) and
- 1.4.7—Low or No Background Audio (Prerecorded) (AAA).

Text-to-speech (speech synthesis)

Some older adults use text-to-speech (speech synthesis) software, which is becoming increasingly available in browsers and operating systems. Others utilise text-to-speech options made available on many sites such as ReadSpeaker (Hoya), Browsealoud (Texthelp) and Recite (Recite Me) to listen to the information rather than reading it.

- 1.1.1—Non-text Content (A) and
- 1.3.1—Info and Relationships (A).

CAPTCHA

CAPTCHA stands for 'Completely Automated Public Turing tests to tell Computers and Humans Apart' and is used on many websites to reduce spam responses and security risks. Older adults with declining eyesight may not be able to discern the characters in an old-fashioned CAPTCHA, especially because CAPTCHAs often have low contrast and extremely busy backgrounds. Newer CAPTCHAs such as reCAPTCHA (Google) can be equally as hard to use if you trigger the 'match the pictures' challenge and your eyesight has declined with age.

- 1.1.1—Non-text Content (A) includes a requirement for alternative CAPTCHAs.

However, audio CAPTCHAs are equally hard to decipher due to the background noise or the distorted speech used and criteria 1.4.7 partly addresses this issue.

Device orientation

Some older adults are unable to hold their 'mobile' devices and have them sitting on a table or on their laps for use. As a result, they may not be able to rotate if required.

- 1.3.4—Orientation (AA).

6.5.2 Operable User Interface and Navigation

Links

Links that are clear to understand and visually identifiable will assist older adults with declining vision and cognition.

- 2.4.4—Link Purpose (In Context) (A),
- 2.4.9—Link Purpose (Link Only) (AAA),
- 2.4.7—Focus Visible (AA) and
- 1.4.11—Non-text Contrast (AA).

Navigation and location

Many older adults need navigation and location indicators to be particularly clear due to declining cognitive abilities. Most older adults are not digital natives and some struggle with website navigation.

- 2.4.5—Multiple Ways (AA),
- 2.4.8—Location (AAA) and
- 2.4.2—Page Titled (A).

Mouse use

It is difficult for some older adults to use a mouse and click small targets due to declining vision or dexterity. They can have similar issues with touch screens.

- 2.4.7—Focus Visible (AA),
- 3.3.2—Labels or Instructions (A),
- 1.4.4—Resize Text (AA),
- 1.4.13—Content on Hover or Focus (AA),
- 2.5.2—Pointer Cancellation (A) and
- 2.5.5—Target Size (AAA).

Keyboard use and tabbing

Some older adults cannot use a mouse well or at all and may instead use a keyboard to navigate; this may even be the case with mobile devices for those with limited dexterity or sense of touch.

- 2.1.1—Keyboard (A),
- 2.1.2—No Keyboard trap (A),
- 2.1.3—Keyboard (No Exception) (AAA),
- 2.4.1—Bypass Blocks (A),
- 2.4.3—Focus Order (A) and
- 2.4.7—Focus Visible (AA).

Distractions

Older adults can be particularly distracted by any movement and sound on Web pages or find concentration difficult in these situations.

- 2.2.2—Pause, Stop, Hide (A),
- 1.4.2—Audio Control (A),
- 2.3.3—Animation from Interactions (AAA) and
- 2.2.4—Interruptions (AAA).

Sufficient time

It takes some older adults longer to read text and complete transactions due to declining vision, dexterity or cognition.

- 2.2.1—Timing Adjustment (A),
- 2.2.3—No Timing (AAA),
- 2.2.6—Timeouts (AAA) and
- 2.2.2—Pause, Stop, Hide (A).

6.5.3 Understandable Information and User Interface

Page organisation

Many older adults are inexperienced Web users without advanced browsing habits, and therefore read the whole page, so good page organisation is important.

- 2.4.6—Headings and Labels (AA),
- 2.4.10—Section Headings (AAA) and
- 1.4.8—Visual Presentation (AAA).

Understandable language

Many older adults find it increasingly difficult to understand complex sentences, unusual words and technical jargon.

- Guideline 3.1 Readable
- 3.1.3—Unusual Words (AAA),
- 3.1.4—Abbreviations (AAA) and
- 3.1.5—Reading Level (AAA).

Consistent navigation and labelling

For people who are new to the Web—many older adults—and older adults with some types of cognitive decline, consistent navigation and presentation are particularly important.

- 3.2.3—Consistent Navigation (AA) and
- 3.2.4—Consistent Identification (AA).

Pop-ups and new windows

Some older adults experiencing cognitive decline can be confused or distracted by pop-ups, new windows or new tabs.

- 3.2.1—On Focus (A) and
- 3.2.5—Change on Request (AAA).

Page refreshes and updates

Some older adults with declining vision or cognition can miss content that automatically updates or refreshes in a page.

- 3.2.1—On Focus (A),
- 3.2.2—On Input (A) and
- 3.2.5—Change on Request (AAA).

Form completion

It is difficult for some older adults to understand the requirements of forms and online transactions and to recover from errors they may make.

- 3.3.2—Labels or Instructions (A),
- 3.3.5—Help (AAA),
- 3.2.4—Consistent Identification (AA),
- 3.3.4—Error Prevention (Legal, Financial, Data) (AA),
- 3.3.6—Error Prevention (All) (AAA),
- 3.3.1—Error Identification (A) and
- 3.3.3—Error Suggestion (AA).

6.5.4 Robust Content and Reliable Interpretation

Older equipment/software

Some older adults will be using older browsers that might not be as capable or fault tolerant as current releases.

- 4.1.1—Parsing (A).

Since the first edition of this book in 2008, there have been an increasing number of popular articles discussing the requirements of older adults on the Web, many from a UX or design perspective. Many issues identified in these articles overlap with the WCAG criteria:

- **Font size**—identified by Adiseshiah (2017), Campbell (2105), Ivil (2016), Moth (2013), Nielsen (2013), Hopping Mad (2013) and Interaction Design (2016);
- **Colour and contrast, including non-text contrast**—identified by Adiseshiah (2017), Campbell (2105), Ivil (2016), Moth (2013), Nielsen (2013), Hopping Mad (2013) and Interaction Design (2016);
- **Readability and plain language**—identified by Adiseshiah (2017), Ivil (2016) and Hopping Mad (2013);
- **Captions and transcripts**—identified by Adiseshiah (2017), Campbell (2105), Ivil (2016) and Interaction Design (2016);
- **Target size**—identified by Adiseshiah (2017), Campbell (2105), Ivil (2016), Moth (2013), Nielsen (2013), Hopping Mad (2013) and Interaction Design (2016);
- **Navigation options**—identified by Adiseshiah (2017), Ivil (2016), Nielsen (2013) and Hopping Mad (2013);
- **Timeouts**—identified by Campbell (2105);
- **Clear links**—identified by Ivil (2016);
- **Consistent identification**—identified by Ivil (2016);
- **Text spacing**—identified by Petrie et al. (2013), Moth (2013) and Nielsen (2013); and
- **Form labels, instruction and error messages**—identified by Moth (2013), Nielsen (2013) and Hopping Mad (2013).

6.6   Web Activities of Older Adults

The pervasiveness of Web technology appears to be growing in line with the ageing of the population. Unfortunately, ageing users face many challenges when trying to get access to the Web due to declines in vision, hearing, mobility and cognitive abilities. Advances in Web tools have allowed for improved accessibility of websites, thereby increasing the level of Web activity amongst older adults. Despite these advances, there is still a lack of proper support for the growing numbers of older adults engaging in online activities. It is, therefore, important to take into account the specific needs of older adults when making design decisions for Web tools to foster online activity as discussed earlier.

6.6.1 Social Networking and Social Media

Social media or social networking websites (SNS) are becoming more popular and prevalent across all age groups. As most of the world becomes connected, the more opportunities there are for individuals to stay connected with one another. SNS afford users with a consistent Web-based communication channel through which social relationships can grow and foster. For older adults, especially those living alone or away from loved ones, this form of communication can mean interacting with friends and family who they might otherwise be unable to see or visit. Additionally, SNS foster the development of new social relationships as well as allow for communal interactions across a diverse range of interests and hobbies. It was reported by Perrin that the percentage of older American adults using SNS has grown from around 2% in 2005 to 35% in 2015 (Perrin 2015). The trend is similar internationally with 43% of older Australians engaging with social media (Australian Communications and Media Authority 2016). This growing trend in older adults using SNS appears to be continuing while usage among younger adults appears to be tapering off. Despite the increase of older adults using SNS, there are still challenges limiting the adoption of SNS by older adults.

In 2013, a study was conducted to understand the obstacles facing older adults when it comes to SNS (Braun 2013). The author designed the study based on the technology acceptance model (TAM) (Davis 1989; Venkatesh and Morris 2003) to investigate predictive features for use of SNS by older adults. They found that perceived usefulness, trust in SNS and Internet use were strong indicators of SNS use (Braun 2013). Factors hypothesised to be of greater significance than in actuality for influencing SNS use were social pressures and perceived ease of use. The author reasons that ease of use was not as significant a factor as thought due to ease of use being measured for websites in general rather than specifically for SNS, in addition to participants already being competent Internet users. They also note that social pressures may be more significant for technology that is mandatory rather than voluntary, a result supported by other studies (Venkatesh and Davis 2000).

Recommendations for encouraging older adults to use SNS include providing assistance during the account setup process for SNS and providing instructions for general use of SNS, outlining the usefulness of SNS by highlighting features most relevant to older adults, and focusing on the security and safety of SNS (Braun 2013). As the results from the study by Braun showed, Internet use and familiarity were strong indicators for SNS use. Therefore, helping older adults getting setup with SNS and guiding them through the process of using SNS provide a baseline level of familiarity for their continued use. Moving forward, highlighting and demonstrating useful features for older adults that are specific to the SNS (e.g. connecting with loved ones) can potentially increase the perceived usefulness of SNS and thus encourage SNS use. Though there are justified concerns over security and safety when using SNS, a possible solution to help build trust for older adults with SNS might be to clearly show the various security options available to them, thereby demonstrating their control over their information on SNS (Braun 2013).

6.6.2 Health and Well-Being Information Searching

As highlighted above, as we age, one's mental, physical and emotional functions are impacted. It is not surprising that a primary area of interest for older adults is health and well-being, not only related to concerns, but also recommendations and guidance. Fortunately, with more and more information becoming readily available through the Internet, people are able to find health-related information that might have otherwise only been obtainable through an in-person doctor or professional visit. It was estimated in 2013 by a Pew Internet Project study that 35% of U.S. adults have searched for health information online specifically to figure out medical conditions for themselves or others (Fox 2013). Not only are Internet users searching for information via health websites, but they are also engaging in health information exchange through SNS. An earlier study reported that 18% of Internet users have used the Web to find other people with similar conditions (Fox 2011). Of these users, 23% of users who had chronic conditions reported using the Internet to interact with others online.

The ability to search and understand health information through digital sources for the purpose of applying said understanding to real-world health problems and decisions is referred to as eHealth literacy (Norman 2006). A telephone study in 2015 was conducted with 493 older adults living in Florida to investigate factors that influence eHealth literacy and use of the Web for health information by older adults (Tennant 2015). The authors found that younger age and higher amounts of device usage were significant positive indicators of eHealth literacy and use of the Web for health information. Furthermore, higher education levels were shown to positively influence eHealth literacy, while being female was a significant positive indicator of use of the Web for health information. It was discovered that, though participants felt confident in their ability to search and find health information online, they found it challenging to discern the quality of online sources. The authors highlight a lack of interventions to increase the confidence and literacy of older adults in eHealth and suggest further investigations into improving older adults' confidence in eHealth literacy via training. Not only can Web training increase the confidence of older adults, it has been shown to potentially improve their overall sense of well-being (Shapira 2007). Moreover, the advances in Web tools and services afforded by social network websites (e.g. groups, events, marketplaces) will continue to create social opportunities for user health information and support.

6.6.3 Web Services

The permeation of Web technology also lends itself towards older adults within the workforce. With technology taking on a bigger role within the workforce, it is important for those older adults in the workforce to be competent and familiar with online tools. Ibarra and colleagues investigated the landscape of Web tools available for online contribution and volunteering opportunities for older adults (Ibarra 2016). They looked into the role technology plays in online contribution, the types of online activities supported by these Web services, and the motivations and rewards for such activities through various studies. It is not surprising that online tools have advanced to allow for more opportunities for individuals to engage socially and be involved with communities across the world. As such, some examples of technology being used in unexpected ways to allow for older adults to contribute online include the use of Skype for tutoring students by retired school teachers (Clark 2011) or the Speaking Exchange project, which uses video conferencing to connect young Brazilians learning English with English-speaking older adults (FCB Brasil 2014). Ibarra et al. also highlight a significant lack of opportunities and tools specifically designed for older adults to enable online contribution, despite the fact that older adults have the capacity to make meaningful contributions (Ibarra 2016; Kobayashi 2015).

6.6.4   Internet-of-Things

Internet-of-Things (IoT) is the concept of digitally connected devices sharing data to provide services and functionality to a user. Current examples of IoT technology include the Nest thermostat or smart speakers such as Amazon Alexa or Google Home. A prominent benefit of IoT devices for older adults includes health monitoring and assistance. Through these connected devices and sensors, health-related services, such as medication tracking through smart pillboxes (Yang 2014), can be specifically tailored for the user. Moreover, guidance and assistance can be delivered directly to users via IoT devices such as smart speakers or activity trackers (e.g. smartwatches) (Angelini 2013). As these technologies continue to blur the lines between the physical and digital worlds, new support opportunities for older adults will continue to emerge. It is imperative to include the ageing population when exploring the design space of IoT devices and applications.

A particular application of IoT devices that are gaining more exposure in the ageing population is ambient-assisted living (AAL). AAL refers to a communication network of sensors and devices specifically aimed to help support and assist a user in their daily life while maintaining user safety and independence (Dohr 2010). These technologies enable health monitoring (Pollack 2005; Dohr 2010), detect possible emergencies and falls (Santos 2016), and offer guidance (Pollack 2005) to aid older adults living independently, or ageing in place. Though IoT and AAL technologies offer various benefits to potentially improve the quality of life of older adults, they do not come without a tradeoff. In order for such technology to carry out the functions required for services, data must be acquired and shared through the communication network. This sharing of potentially sensitive data is not limited to IoT and AAL services, but can apply to general Web-based services and tools. The issue of information privacy is a critical concern for most older adults when deciding to use Web tools and services.

6.6.5 Online Privacy, Trust and Behaviour

One of the biggest concerns for older adults when dealing with the Internet and Web-based technologies is privacy. In 2017, Zeissig et al. reported their findings in a German study of 200 older adults and their perceptions of online privacy (Zeissig 2017). Privacy of data and concerns of information security are among the top barriers for acceptance of online technology by older adults. Though there are similar levels of concerns over privacy between younger and older adults (Zeissig 2017; Hoofnagle et al. 2010), differences in attitude come into play when taking into account the context of Internet usage. Bergström points out, for example, that older adults were more concerned with credit card and online financial security, whereas younger adults expressed concern over online social content (Bergström 2015).

Zeissig et al. (2017) report that privacy self-efficacy, awareness and experience influenced the attitudes of older adults towards privacy as well as the protection behaviour (Zeissig et al. 2017). They found that protection behaviour was higher in older adults than younger adults. This finding, however, is based on the self-reported measure of the user's perception of their protection behaviour and may not fully represent the actuality of their behaviour. They point out various issues that could potentially lead to low protection behaviour in older adults, including possible complexities of online privacy protection tools and users' potential lack of awareness of which specific information is private and protected.

6.7 Authors' Opinion of the Field

This chapter has discussed the changes that occur with ageing, how these changes might affect older adults' interaction with the Web and how WCAG can address those needs. Although it is apparent that most functional abilities decline with ageing, not all is doom and gloom. Some abilities (e.g. those related to semantic memory) do not decline until very late in life. In addition, various studies pointed out that older adults are able to learn new skills as well as their younger counterparts and are able to perform some tasks equally well as younger persons do. The advances in medical science and nutrition are pushing the boundaries of old age and preventing, or minimising, the impacts of some of the declines in ability.

Older adults are arguably the fastest growing segment of potential customers of the Web, and as such it would be economically wise for Web designers to consider the impairment that comes with ageing and how to facilitate effective interaction given these limitations. Many issues can actually be addressed through good Web design, following guidelines such as WCAG, and proper documentation and training. As many ageing studies pointed out (e.g. Knowles and Hanson 2018), the biggest barrier of technology use by older adults is not ageing-related functional impairment, but rather hesitation of exploration due to fear of the unknown and the consequence of incorrect actions.

Nevertheless, one size does not fit all and whilst good practise in Web design can assist older users; some extra consideration and possibly assistive technology might be required in more severe cases of age-related impairments. Simpler assistive technologies with natural language voice interfaces and powered by Artificial Intelligence may make it easier for older adults to get online and remain online in the future. Another possible solution is through personalising Web interface to reflect older adult's developing needs. However, as noted earlier, older users may be less confident when it comes to using the Web, even when they arrive from a generation that has grown up with computers, and they are likely to be more nervous about personalisation if that involves making changes themselves. An easy way out for this is to ensure that configuration is made simple and applied in such a way that users can see the effect of personalisation immediately.

The list of changes that come with ageing and suggestions to accommodate older adults when designing for the Web presented in this chapter is not an exhaustive list. There is always a need to involve the older population when designing for them, and this includes designing for the accessible Web, as only by involving prospective users can we understand and incorporate their requirements and needs. On that note, it is pleasing to see the increasing number of mainstream articles and blog posts that have appeared since the first edition of this book that discusses the needs of older adults from a design and a development perspective.

It is clear that as we continue to live longer and more of the world becomes digitally connected, it is crucial to consider the needs of older adults when designing for the Web. The Web has become a fluid ecosystem capable of fostering unique communication channels between users of all demographics. In order for these communication opportunities to continue to grow, however, it is imperative that they be accessible by all. Current Web trends highlighted in this and other chapters show continued signs of progress towards a more accessible and dynamic Web ecosystem. The ability for older adults to more easily share and exchange knowledge across the Web has opened the door for more emergent Web interactions that may not have otherwise been apparent. This is especially true for Web tools and services being used for social good, e.g. Web tools allowing older adults to share their knowledge (Clark 2011; Ibarra 2016) and offer meaningful contributions online (Kobayashi 2015). It remains, however, that more work still needs to be done to specifically include older adults, especially those with special needs, in the design process of Web technology.

6.8   Future Directions

When we discuss older adults, there are two future directions that we can foresee. In the future, we are talking about a different cohort of 'older adults', the cohort who grows up with the Web. Although undoubtedly this cohort would still experience functional ability declines that come with ageing, we can expect a different set of behaviours in regard to acceptance of Web technology and the requirement to learn about the evolving Web when they are older.

In terms of technology, the sort of evaluations, methodologies and applications that we can expect in the future are covered extensively from Part II onwards. Some of these are relevant to people with disabilities in general, and some are particularly useful for older Web users. A very good example is Voice XML as well as other voice-based systems such as Google Home, Amazon Echo and Apple HomePod. These applications will definitely benefit older Web users due to their potential to supplement visually oriented Web with sounds, which will help older adults with reduced vision (when voice is used as output) or motor ability (when voice is used as input).

We are noticing an increasing discussion and recognition of the requirements of older adults when using the Web. This is due in part to recognition that the 'silver dollar' is increasing as the 'baby boomers' move into older age. It is also due in part to the fact that website owners, designers and developers are starting to think about

- themselves and situational disability,
- their ageing family members getting online, and
- their future selves staying online in older age (Roselli 2017).

Not only is it important to consider the needs of this potentially new cohort of older adults as consumers of Web technology, it is likely to be the case that they themselves will contribute directly to the design and development of such technology. It is important to improve education and training interventions for older adults in Web tools and services. With the advent of IoT and smart environments, the ability to offer just-in-time training and guidance to users might allow for a more dynamically trained and long-lasting workforce. Moreover, such context-aware environments and IoT devices would allow for new paradigms of telehealth and telemedicine for older adults, thereby potentially aiding in the continued increase of the average lifespan of all individuals. It is thus urgent to make sure that all individuals have access to such technologies moving forward.

6.9 Conclusion

As WHO stated, populations around the world are rapidly ageing. Over the past century, the life span for both men and women has increased dramatically. For example, in 1910, the life expectancy of a man was 48 years and a woman was 52 years. In 2010, this has increased to 76 years for men and 81 for women. The hope is that societies can invest in 'Healthy Ageing'. WHO defines 'Healthy Ageing' as the process of developing and maintaining the functional ability that enables well-being in older age (WHO 2018b).

With ageing, there is a dynamic interplay between factors that leads to neurodegeneration and cognitive impairment and factors that lead to neuroplasticity and improved cognitive function. The most important changes are declines in cognitive tasks that require one to quickly process or transform information to make a decision, including measures of speed of processing, working memory and executive cognitive function. Cumulative knowledge and experiential skills are well maintained into advanced age (Murman 2015). Visual and hearing impairments are also common in old age. It has been suggested that at least 50% of individuals aged 75 and older show some degree of measurable hearing loss and that best-corrected visual acuity starts to decline after age 45 (Valentijn et al. 2005).

The United Nations in the Convention for the Rights of People with Disability (2006), which had been signed by 161 countries by the end of 2017, effectively states that access to the Internet for information and services is a human right and that 'access for persons with disabilities' is required. As we have shown in this chapter, disability is a fact of ageing even if many older adults do not recognise their impairments as such.

This chapter has highlighted how the current Web accessibility guidelines can benefit older adults. Incorporating the latest W3C guidelines for Web accessibility as it evolves will help to ensure older adults can continue to access the Web.

It is clear from this chapter that Web services need to consider the specific needs of older adults earlier in the design process to account for this growing population of Web users. Additional resources devoted to training and educating older adults in Web technologies should be put in place to ensure the ageing population has proper access to available Web services and tools and is assisted to adjust to the changes in technology used to access the Web. Web competency is especially imperative for older adults who wish to share their skills and knowledge and contribute to online communities or workforces. However, lack of confidence and self-efficacy brought on by low competency and trust in Web services is still an obstacle to overcome. Increased transparency and simplicity of Web information can help reduce this issue and may bolster older adults' confidence and trust in Web services, thereby improving the Web landscape for all users.

References

Adiseshiah E (2017) UX Design thinking from a senior citizen's perspective. https://usabilitygeek.com/ux-design-thinking-senior-citizen-user/. Accessed 6 Jul 2018

Age UK (2016) The Internet and older adults in the UK. https://www.ageuk.org.uk/globalassets/age-uk/documents/reports-and-publications/reports-and-briefings/active-communities/rb_july16_older_people_and_internet_use_stats.pdf. Accessed 6 Jul 2018

AgeLight LLC (2001) Technology and generational marketing strategies: interface design guidelines for users of all ages. http://www.agelight.com/Webdocs/designguide.pdf. Accessed 6 Jul 2018

Arch A, Abou-Zahra S (2010) Developing websites for older adults: how web content accessibility guidelines (WCAG) 2.0 applies. Accessed at https://www.w3.org/WAI/older-users/developing/. Accessed 6 July 2018

Arch A, Abou-Zahra S, Henry S (2009) Older users online: wai guidelines address older users web experience, Accessed at https://www.w3.org/WAI/posts/2009/older-users-online. Accessed 6 Jul 2018

Armstrong D, Marmor MF, Ordy JM (1991) The effects of aging and environment on vision. Plenum Press, New York

Aslan S (2018) YouTube by the numbers: stats, demographics & fun facts, accessed at https://www.omnicoreagency.com/youtube-statistics/. Accessed 29 Aug 2018

Australian Communications and Media Authority (2016) Digital lives of older Australians, Accessed at https://www.acma.gov.au/theACMA/engage-blogs/engage-blogs/Research-snapshots/Digital-lives-of-older-Australians. Accessed 6 Jul 2018

Bailey B (2002) Age classifications. UI design update newsletter, http://www.humanfactors.com/downloads/jul02.asp. Accessed 6 Jul 2018

Barnes SB (2006) A privacy paradox: social networking in the United States. First Monday, 11(9)

Bergström A (2015) Online privacy concerns: A broad approach to understanding the concerns of different groups for different uses. Comput Hum Behav 53:419–426

Birren (1970) Cited in Eisdorfer C, Lawton P (1973) The psychology of adult development and aging. American Psychological Association, Washington, DC

Brasil FCB (2014) CNA-Speaking exchange [Video file]

Braun MT (2013) Obstacles to social networking website use among older adults. Comput Hum Behav 29(3):673–680

Caldwell B, Cooper M, Guarino Reid L, Vanderheiden G (2008) Web content accessibility guidelines 2.0 https://www.w3.org/TR/WCAG20/. Accessed 6 Jul 2018

Campbell O (2105) Designing for the elderly: ways older adults use digital technology differently. Accessed at https://www.smashingmagazine.com/2015/02/designing-digital-technology-for-the-elderly/. Accessed 6 Jul 2018

Cerella J, Poon LW, Fozard JL (1982) Age and iconic read-out. Journal of Gerontology 37:197–202

Charness N, Bosman E (1990) Human factors in design. In: Birren JE, Schaie KW (eds) Handbook of psychology of aging, 3rd edn. Academic, San Diego, pp 446–463

Chisholm W, Vanderheiden G, Jacobs I (1999) Web content accessibility guidelines 1.0. Accessed athttps://www.w3.org/TR/WCAG10/. Accessed 6 July 2018

Christopher P (1999) Older adults—special considerations for special people. http://www.gsu.edu/mstswh/courses/it7000/papers/newpage31.htm. Accessed 6 Jul 2018

Clark J, Hall I (2011) The Skype Grannies Project. Technical report, Research Centre for Learning and Teaching, Newcastle University

Cunningham WR, Brookbank JW (1988) Gerontology: the psychology. Biology and sociology of ageing, Harper and Row, New York

Czaja S (1997) Using technologies to aid the performance of home tasks. Handbook of human factors and the older adult, chapter 13:311–334

Czaja SJ, Sharit J (1998) Age differences in attitudes toward computers. J Gerontol 53B(5):329–340

Davis FD (1989) Perceived usefulness, perceived ease of use, and user acceptance of information technology. MIS Q 319–340

Dohr A, Modre-Opsrian R, Drobics M, Hayn D, Schreier G (2010) The internet of things for ambient assisted living. In: 2010 seventh international conference on information technology: new generations (ITNG). IEEE, pp 804–809

Edwards R, Englehardt KG (1989) Microprocessor-based innovations and older individuals: AARP survey results and their implications for service robotics. Int J Technol Aging 2:56–76

Ellis RD, Kurniawan SH (2000) Increasing the usability of online information for older users: A case study in participatory design. International Journal of Human-Computer Interaction 2(12):263–276

Fine SL, Berger JW, Maguire MG (1999) Age related macular degeneration. Mosby Inc, Missouri

Ford, M. (1993) Coping again. broadcasting support services, pp. 6–28

Fox, S. (2011) Peer-to-peer healthcare. Pew Internet & American Life Project

Fox S, Duggan M (2013) Health online 2013. Pew Internet & American Life Project, Washington, DC, p 1

Gitlow, L. Technology Use by Older Adults and Barriers to Using Technology, Journal Physical & Occupational Therapy In Geriatrics, Vol 32(3) https://doi.org/10.3109/02703181.2014.946640. Accessed 6 Jul 2018

Google (undated) reCAPTCHA, accessed at https://developers.google.com/recaptcha/. Accessed 6 Jul 2018

Grady CL, Craik FIM (2000) Changes in memory processing with age. Curr Opin Neurobiol 10:224–231

Gregor, P., Newell, A.F. and Zajicek, M (2002) Designing for dynamic diversity – interfaces for older adults. In: Proceedings of the fifth international ACM conference on Assistive technologies. ACM Press, New York, pp. 151–156

Hartley, A.A. (1992) Attention. In: F.I.M. Craik, T.A. and Salthouse (Eds.), The handbook of aging and cognition. Erlbaum, Hillsdale, NJ

He, W., Goodkind, D. and Kowal, P. (2016) An Aging World: 2015, accessed at https://www.census.gov/library/publications/2016/demo/P95-16-1.html. Accessed 28 Aug 2018

Hawthorn, D. (2000) Possible implications of aging for interface designers. Interacting with Computers 12, 507–528.Hoisko, J. (2003) Early Experiences of Visual Memory Prosthesis for Supporting Episodic Memory. International Journal of Human-Computer Interaction, 15(2), 209–230

Hoofnagle, C. J., King, J., Li, S., & Turow, J. (2010) How different are young adults from older adults when it comes to information privacy attitudes and policies?

Hopping Mad Designs (2013) Tips for Designing a Website for Seniors and the Elderly accessed at https://hoppingmad.com.au/blog/tips-for-designing-a-website-for-seniors-and-the-elderly/. Accessed 6 Jul 2018

Hoya Speech Company (undated). ReadSpeaker accessed at https://www.readspeaker.com/. Accessed 6 Jul 2018

Ibarra F, Korovina O, Baez M, Casati F, Marchese M, Cernuzzi L, Barysheva GA (2016) Tools enabling online contributions by older adults. IEEE Internet Comput 20(5):58–65

IFLANET (1997) older adults and the Internet. http://www.ifla.org/IV/ifla63/44pt2.htm. Jagacinski, R.J., Liao, M.J. and Fayyad, E.A. (1995) Generalised slowing in sinusoidal tracking in older adults. Psychology of Aging 9, 103–112

Interaction Design Foundation (2016) Improving the User Experience for the Elderly accessed at https://www.interaction-design.org/literature/article/improving-the-user-experience-for-the-elderly. Accessed 6 Jul 2018

Ivil, L. (2016) Designing A Dementia-Friendly Website Accessed at https://www.smashingmagazine.com/2016/05/designing-a-dementia-friendly-website/. Accessed 6 Jul 2018

Kirkpatrick, A., O'Connor, J., Campbell, A. and Cooper, M. (2018) Web Content Accessibility Guidelines 2.1 accessed at https://www.w3.org/TR/WCAG21/. Accessed 6 Jul 2018

Kline DW, Scialfa CT (1996) Sensory and perceptual functioning: basic research and human factors implications. In: Fisk AD, Rogers WA (eds) Handbook of human factors and the older adult. Academic Press, San Diego

Knowles B, Hanson V (2018) The wisdom of older technology (non)users. Commun ACM 61(3):72–77

Kobayashi, M., Arita, S., Itoko, T., Saito, S., & Takagi, H. (2015, February). Motivating multigenerational crowd workers in social-purpose work. In Proceedings of the 18th ACM Conference on Computer Supported Cooperative Work & Social Computing (pp. 1813–1824). ACM

Kotary L, Hoyer WJ (1995) Age and the ability to inhibit distractor information in visual selective attention. Exp Aging Res 21(2):159–171

Lee, J, and Baily, G. (2005) Presbyopia: All about sight. http://www.allaboutvision.com/ conditions/presbyopia.html. Accessed 6 Jul 2018

Light LL (1990) Memory and language in old age. In: Birren JE, Schaie KW (Eds.), Handbook of the psychology of aging, Third Ed., Academic Press, San Diego, pp. 275–290

Mead, SE., Spaulding, VA., Sit, RA., Meyer, B. and Walker, N. (1997) Effects of age and training on world wide Web navigation strategies. In: Proceedings of the Human Factors and Ergonomics Society 41st annual meeting Human Factors and Ergonomics Society, Santa Monica, pp. 152–156

Moth, D. (2013) Six design tips for making your website senior friendly accessed at https://econsultancy.com/blog/62815-six-design-tips-for-making-your-website-senior-friendly. Accessed 6 July 2018

Murman DL (2015) The Impact of Age on Cognition. Seminars in Hearing 36(3):111–121

Myatt ED, Essa I, Rogers W (2000) Increasing the opportunities for ageing in place. In: Proceedings of the ACM Conference on Universal Usability, ACM Press, New York/ Washington, DC, pp. 39–44

National Eye Institute (2004) What is Glaucoma? http://www.nei.nih.gov/health/glaucoma/ glaucoma_facts.asp#1. Accessed 6 July 2018

National Institute on Aging (2009) Making Your Website Senior Friendly, http://www.lgma. ca/assets/Programs~and~Events/Clerks~Forum/2013~Clerks~Forum/COMMUNICATIONS-Making-Your-Website-Senior-Friendly–Tip-Sheet.pdf. Accessed 6 July 2018

National Institute on Aging and the National Library of Medicine (2002) Making your Website More Senior Friendly: A Checklist, http://www.usability.gov/checklist.pdf. Accessed 6 July 2018

Nielsen, J. (2013) Seniors as Web Users. https://www.nngroup.com/articles/usability-for-senior-citizens/. Accessed 6 July 2018. Accessed 6 Jul 2018

Nielsen J (1996) Accessible Design for Users with Disabilities. http://www.useit.com/alert box/9610.html. Accessed 6 Jul 2018

Norberg PA, Horne DR, Horne DA (2007) The privacy paradox: Personal information disclosure intentions versus behaviors. Journal of Consumer Affairs 41(1):100–126

Norman CD, Skinner HA (2006) eHealth literacy: essential skills for consumer health in a networked world. Journal of medical Internet research, 8(2)

Orimo H, Ito H, Suzuki T, Araki A, Hosoi T, Sawabe M (2006) Reviewing the definition of "elderly". Geriatrics & gerontology international 6(3):149–158

Perrin A (2015) Social media usage. Pew research center, 52-68

Petrie H, Kamollimsakul S, Power C (2013) Web accessibility for older adults: effects of line spacing and text justification on reading Web pages, ASSETS '13 Proceedings of the 15th International ACM SIGACCESS Conference on Computers and Accessibility

Pew Research Centre (2017) Tech Adoption Climbs Among Older Adults accessed at http://www. pewinternet.org/2017/05/17/tech-adoption-climbs-among-older-adults/. Accessed 6 Jul 2018

Piper, A.M., Brewer, R. & Cornejo, R. Technology learning and use among older adults with late-life vision impairments, Univ Access Inf Soc (2017) 16: 699. https://doi.org/10.1007/s10209-016-0500-1. Accessed 6 Jul 2018

Pollack ME (2005) Intelligent technology for an aging population: The use of AI to assist elders with cognitive impairment. AI magazine 26(2):9

Ratner HH, Schell DA, Crimmins A, Mittleman D, Baldinelli L (1987) Changes in adults prose recall: aging or cognitive demands. Dev Psychol 23:521–525

Recite Me (undated) Recite, accessed at http://www.reciteme.com/. Accessed 6 Jul 2018

Rogers WA, Fisk AD, Hertzog C (1994) Do ability related performance relationships differentiate age and practice effects in visual search? J Exp Psychol Learn Mem Cogn 20:710–738

Roselli, A (2017) Selfish Accessibility, https://wordpress.tv/2017/06/21/adrian-roselli-selfish-accessibility-3/ & https://www.slideshare.net/aardrian/selfish-accessibility-wordcamp-europe-2017. Accessed 6 Jul 2018

Rybash JM, Roodin PA, Hoyer WJ (1995) Adult Development and Aging. Brown and Benchmark, Chicago

Salthouse TA (1991) Theoretical perspectives on cognitive aging. Lawrence Erlbaum Associates, Hillsdale

Salthouse, TA. (1994) The aging of working memory. Neuropsychology 8, 535–543 Scheiber, F. (1992) Aging and the senses. In: JE. Birren, RB. Sloane, GD. Cohen (Eds.)

Santos J, Rodrigues JJ, Silva BM, Casal J, Saleem K, Denisov V (2016) An IoT-based mobile gateway for intelligent personal assistants on mobile health environments. Journal of Network and Computer Applications 71:194–204

Shapira, N., Barak, A., & Gal, I. (2007) Promoting older adults' well-being through Internet training and use

Siedler R, Stelmach G (1996) Motor Control. In: Birren JE (ed) Encyclopedia of Gerontology. Academic Press, San Diego, pp 177–185

Spiriduso WW (1995) Aging and motor control. In: Lamb DR, Gisolfi CV, Nadel E (eds) Perspectives in Exercise Science and Sports Medicine: Exercise in Older Adults. Cooper, Carmel, pp 53–114

St. Lukes Eye (2005) Cataracts. http://www.stlukeseye.com/Conditions/Cataracts.asp. Stokes, G. (1992) On Being Old. The Psychology of Later Life. The Falmer Press, London

Stokes G (1992) On being old. The Falmer Press, London, The Psychology of Later Life

Straub, K. (2003) The Gradual Graying of the Internet. http://www.humanfactors.com/downloads/jun03.asp. Accessed 6 Jul 2018

Stuart-Hamilton I (1999) Intellectual changes in late life. In: Woods ERT (ed) Psychological Problems of Ageing. Wiley, New York

Tennant B, Stellefson M, Dodd V, Chaney B, Chaney D, Paige S, Alber J (2015) eHealth literacy and Web 2.0 health information seeking behaviors among baby boomers and older adults. Journal of medical Internet research, 17(3)

Texthelp (undated) Browsealoud, accessed at https://www.texthelp.com/en-gb/products/browsealoud/. Accessed 6 Jul 2018

Uhlmann RF, Larson EB, Rees TS, Koepsell TD, Duckert LG (1989) Relationship of hearing impairment to dementia and cognitive dysfunction in older adults. The Journal of American Medical Association 261(13):1916–1919

United Nations (2006) Convention on the Rights of Persons with Disabilities (CRPD) accessed at https://www.un.org/development/desa/disabilities/convention-on-the-rights-of-persons-with-disabilities.html. Accessed 23 Aug 2018

Valentijn SA, Van Boxtel MP, Van Hooren SA, Bosma H, Beckers HJ, Ponds RW, Jolles J (2005) Change in sensory functioning predicts change in cognitive functioning: Results from a 6-year follow-up in the Maastricht Aging Study. J Am Geriatr Soc 53(3):374–380

Venkatesh V, Davis FD (2000) A theoretical extension of the technology acceptance model: Four longitudinal field studies. Manage Sci 46(2):186–204

Venkatesh, V., Morris, M. G., Davis, G. B., & Davis, F. D. (2003) User acceptance of information technology: Toward a unified view. MIS quarterly, 425–478

Vercruyssen M (1996) Movement control and the speed of behaviour. In: Fisk AD, Rogers WA (eds) Handbook of human factors and the older adult, academic press. San Diego, CA

Walker N, Philbin DA, Fisk AD (1997) Age related differences in movement control: adjusting sub-movement structure to optimize performance. Journal of Gerontology: Psychological Sciences 52B(1):40–52

Web Accessibility Initiative (2017) Cognitive and Learning Disabilities Accessibility Task Force, accessed at https://www.w3.org/WAI/PF/cognitive-a11y-tf/. Accessed 29 Aug 2018

WHO (World Health Organization) (2002) Proposed working definition of an older person in Africa for the MDS Project. http://www.who.int/healthinfo/survey/ageingdefnolder/en/. Accessed 6 Jul 2018

WHO (World Health Organization) (2018a). Ageing and health. http://www.who.int/en/news-room/fact-sheets/detail/ageing-and-health. Accessed 6 Jul 2018

WHO (World Health Organization) (2018b). What is Healthy Ageing? http://www.who.int/ageing/healthy-ageing/en/. Accessed 6 Aug 2018

Yang G, Xie L, Mäntysalo M, Zhou X, Pang Z, Da Xu L, Zheng LR (2014) A health-IoT platform based on the integration of intelligent packaging, unobtrusive bio-sensor, and intelligent medicine box. IEEE Trans Industr Inf 10(4):2180–2191

Zajicek, M. (2001) Special interface requirements for older adults. Workshop on Universal Accessibility of Ubiquitous Computing: Providing for the Elderly. http://virtual.inesc.pt/wuauc01/procs/pdfs/zajicek_final.pdf

Zeissig EM, Lidynia C, Vervier L, Gadeib A, Ziefle M (2017). Online privacy perceptions of older adults. In: International conference on human aspects of IT for the aged population. Springer, Cham, pp. 181–200

Zhao H (2001) Universal usability web design guidelines for the elderly, age 65 and older, April. http://www.otal.umd.edu/uupractice/elderly/. Accessed 6 Jul 2018

Zickuhr K, Smith A (2012) Digital differences

Chapter 7
Speech and Language

Abi Roper, Stephanie Wilson, Timothy Neate and Jane Marshall

Abstract This chapter introduces speech and language from a clinical speech and language therapy perspective. It describes key challenges that can impact speech and language with a focus on the needs of individuals with aphasia, an acquired language disorder. The specific impact that aphasia may have upon Web accessibility is discussed with reference to existing work which illuminates what we currently do and do not know about speech, language and Web accessibility. The authors provide guidance for accommodating the needs of users with aphasia within the design of Web interactions and propose future directions for development and research.

7.1 Introduction

The term 'speech and language' can be used to encompass descriptions of both the way in which we produce verbal communication and the underlying knowledge, organisation and use of words and discourse. Using this definition, speech and language pervade many aspects of our lives. Beginning with our earliest interactions as babies, speech and language enable us to learn from and influence the people and artefacts within our environment. Our capacity to use speech and language varies across the lifespan, between individuals and across different environments. Web interactions typically presuppose a certain level of speech or language capacity and can preclude users with either permanent or situational speech and language needs. Using insights from the field of speech and language therapy/pathology, this chapter

A. Roper (✉)
Centre for Human Computer Interaction Design & Division of Language and Communication Science, City, University of London, Northampton Square, London EC1V 0HB, UK
e-mail: Abi.Roper.1@city.ac.uk

S. Wilson · T. Neate
Centre for Human Computer Interaction Design, City, University of London, Northampton Square, London EC1V 0HB, UK

J. Marshall
Division of Language and Communication Science, City, University of London, Northampton Square, London EC1V 0HB, UK

© Springer-Verlag London Ltd., part of Springer Nature 2019
Y. Yesilada and S. Harper (eds.), *Web Accessibility*, Human–Computer
Interaction Series, https://doi.org/10.1007/978-1-4471-7440-0_7

first introduces the reader to a range of speech and language needs and then provides more detailed discussion of one specific condition (aphasia) before discussing the ways in which such a language need might impact upon Web accessibility.

7.1.1 Demographics on Speech and Language Needs

There are around 40 million people in the United States of America[1] living with communication disabilities and 2.2 million in the United Kingdom (DWP 2013). Estimates suggest that 1–2% of the population have need of speech and language therapy services at any one time and around 20% of people will experience speech and language difficulties within their lifespan (Law et al. 2007). One of these difficulties is aphasia, a disorder of language typically caused by stroke. Estimates suggest there are around 2 million people in the United States of America[2] and 350,000 in the United Kingdom[3] currently living with aphasia.

7.1.2 Specific Speech and Language Needs

When considering the range of individuals affected by speech and language issues, difficulties can be distinguished into those which mainly affect speech, and those which mainly affect language. Within the clinical realm of speech and language therapy/pathology, 'speech' refers to the way we say sounds and words, while 'language' relates to the actual words we use or understand and the ways we use them.[4]

Issues affecting speech production can include physical conditions which affect the face, mouth, tongue or vocal cords (including cleft lip and palate, head and neck cancer, muscle weakness or spasticity) and also conditions which affect speech fluency (such as stammering or apraxia of speech). Challenges with speech perception include hearing and auditory processing issues.

Issues related to language can affect one or more of four key domains—language production through speech or sign, language comprehension through speech or sign, language production through writing and language comprehension through reading. Conditions can be present from birth (for example, developmental language disorder, dyslexia or learning difficulties) or acquired later in life (for example, though brain injury or dementia with resultant aphasia). Individuals with aphasia will form the focus of this perspective on speech and language Web accessibility; however, the wider lessons may be applied to a range of language needs, including people with low levels of literacy, non-native language users, those with developmental dyslexia

---

[1] https://www.asha.org/About/news/Quick-Facts/.

[2] https://www.aphasia.org/aphasia-faqs/.

[3] https://www.stroke.org.uk/what-is-stroke/what-is-aphasia/aphasia-and-its-effects.

[4] https://www.asha.org/public/speech/development/language_speech.htm.

and, with regards to situational disabilities, those with other issues which are placing demands on their cognitive system. It is worth noting that the closest developmental counterpart to aphasia—developmental language disorder—has currently received comparatively little exploration in relation to Web accessibility. Readers are encouraged to consider insights from both this chapter and the chapter 'Cognitive and Learning Disabilities' within this book, to inform their understanding of Web accessibility for individuals with developmental language needs.

7.2 Overview of Aphasia

Any of the factors reported in Sect. 7.1.2 can have an influence on an individual's opportunity to fully engage with Web content and functionality. Here, we focus on the needs of people with language difficulties—specifically those with aphasia following a brain injury such as stroke.

Aphasia can impact upon any or all of the four key language components: reading, writing, spoken or signed language production and spoken or signed language comprehension. Difficulties may vary according to the size and location of the associated brain injury.

7.2.1 Written Language Production

Writing and typing can be affected by a number of factors in aphasia. These can include difficulties in being able to find the desired words from the internal lexicon, difficulties in composing grammatically accurate sentences and difficulties in spelling. One further important factor is the common co-occurrence of hemiplegia (paralysis) or hemiparesis (weakness) of one arm and hand. In aphasia, the right hand is usually affected. This may mean that linguistic challenges are exacerbated by reduced dexterity and a dependence on a person's non-dominant left hand for writing and typing. For example, precise typing or continuous control of computing devices (e.g. mouse, touchpad or graphics tablet) is likely to be particularly challenging.

7.2.2 Written Language Comprehension

Written language comprehension is often impaired in aphasia. This problem may be additional to the production difficulties or may stand alone, i.e. skills in reading and writing can dissociate in aphasia. People with aphasia may find it difficult to extract meaning from individual written words and across sentences and paragraphs—experiencing challenges at a single word level and/or at a grammatical level. Written language comprehension difficulties can also make it hard to self-monitor the accuracy of any written language a person has produced themselves—giving rise to additional challenges in the online proofreading and spell checking non-aphasic readers typically employ to check and correct their written errors. Further, this inability to self-correct may mean that errors created by compensatory features such as autocorrect and spellcheckers may go unidentified, meaning that correctly spelt—but nonetheless incorrectly selected—words may be mistakenly included.

7.2.3 Spoken or Signed Language Production

As for written language, spoken or signed languages can be variably affected from one individual to another. The most common feature of aphasia is anomia—a difficulty in finding the target word or sign to express a thought or to name a person or an object. Whilst a person's ability to understand an object's use and to recognise a known individual is retained, their capacity to find the label for that object or individual from within their lexicon is reduced or diminished. A variety of outcomes may occur in response to these word-finding difficulties, including production of similar sounding or looking words or signs, similar meaning words or signs or the production of neologisms or non-words/non-signs. For speech users, additional challenges in producing the desired speech sounds for a target word can also co-occur when individuals experience accompanying apraxia of speech (a difficulty in eliciting volitional speech movements).

7.2.4 Spoken or Signed Language Comprehension

Comprehension of spoken or signed language is the final feature which can be affected for individuals with aphasia. Again, comprehension might be affected in the extraction of meaning at the level of the individual word or sign, and/or at the phrase or discourse level. Many factors are known to affect comprehension in aphasia. For example, concrete or highly imageable words are typically understood more easily than abstract words (Bird et al. 2003). Similarly, highly familiar words are easier than rare terms. At the level of the sentence, complex structures such as embedded clauses and passives are particularly problematic (Thompson et al. 1997). As noted for written language comprehension, challenges here can make it difficult for a person to monitor the accuracy of their own spoken or signed language production reducing opportunities for error monitoring and self-correction.

7.3 Supporting Access to Written, Spoken or Signed Communication

Within the discipline of speech and language therapy, a number of approaches have been established that can support individuals with aphasia to access the four key components of language use previously identified. Some facilitatory strategies for both face-to-face and Web communication are outlined next.

7.3.1 Written Language Production—What Helps?

Some individuals with aphasia can make use of retained spoken abilities to support their written language production. For example, those with strengths in spoken language may be able to use speech-to-text software to support their written language production (Caute and Woolf 2016). Tools developed for people with dyslexia, which provide features such as word prediction, spellchecking and text-to-speech reading back, can also be facilitative (Marshall et al. 2018). [See 'Technology for Dyslexia' within this book for further, detailed discussion of this topic.] Therapy techniques developed for handwriting have also been adapted for computer delivery and use. An example of a multimedia input method is presented in the W^2ANE tool (Ma et al. 2009), which authors propose may support people with aphasia to construct communicative phrases. Within the context of Web accessibility then, we see support for features such as speech-to-text, word prediction, spellchecking and multimedia input.

7.3.2 Written Language Comprehension—What Helps?

Adaptation of written materials can greatly improve access for individuals with aphasia. For example, while the dense and detailed text of a printed novel may prove impenetrable, increasing the text size and reducing the number of words presented on a page—through the use of an e-reader—can greatly improve access to written language for some readers with aphasia (Caute et al. 2016). Simplified phrase structure, the use of lots of white space and the judicious inclusion of associated, clear images can all further improve an individual's access to written language (Herbert 2012). Technology can also be used to supplement written text with more accessible modalities. For example, Moffat et al. (2004) show that word triplets, which accompany text with graphics and sound, give people with aphasia more opportunity to comprehend written words. The lessons for Web accessibility here are in support of re-sizable text, good use of white space, clear image use and multimodal delivery of content.

7.3.3 Spoken or Signed Language Production—What Helps?

Individuals with spoken language difficulties can be aided by the use of external referents, such as pointing to an image or object, circumlocution (the process of describing the features of a target word/sign or production of a related word/sign) and the use of gesture. Some individuals might also use strengths in written language to support their expression, by writing key words or numbers. Others might be able to utilise drawing to help get their message across. Co-communicators can also assist by giving the individual plenty of time to speak or sign and by presenting alternative options where appropriate. A number of computer tools have been used to support spoken language production in aphasia. An example is sentence shaper (Linebarger et al. 2007) which enables the person to compose, edit and create chunks of spoken discourse. Mainstream video conferencing technologies, such as Skype can also support remote communication, and help to overcome some of the particular challenges of using the telephone—a medium which obscures all but the auditory information being presented by a speaker. Lessons for Web accessibility in this domain include the provision of additional time to produce spoken inputs, the capacity to capture and reuse small segments of speech, the use of non-verbal input methods such as touch selection and the support of video-based chat as an alternative to voice only interaction.

7.3.4 Spoken or Signed Language Comprehension—What Helps?

It is not always obvious whether someone has understood what has been spoken or signed to them. One way to support individuals with aphasia is to check if they have understood at appropriate intervals in conversation. Additionally, simplifying the language that is being used, repeating key points and using gesture, writing and drawing can all serve to aid comprehension. Slowing the rate of speech is also important to aid understanding. When considering Web access, we can look to evidence from Fridriksson et al. (2009), who found that for language therapy, where words were presented in both audio and video formats (i.e. showing the speakers face in addition to hearing their voice), individuals made significant improvements in word learning. A contrasting condition where words were presented in audio-only format did not produce therapeutic improvements. This indicates that the provision of video instruction/presentation in addition to audio presentation can enhance access to digital audio spoken content. When looking to enhance access to video media further, we can consider the preferences of participants in a study by Rose et al. (2010), who expressed a clear desire for the use of subtitling alongside video content. The lessons here speak for inclusion of check-in points to ensure that a user has understood the audio or video content provided, opportunities to slow the rate of speech audio, the provision of a video of a speaker's face alongside any audio narration and the provision of subtitles to accompany video content.

7.3.5   Physical and Perceptual Barriers Caused by Stroke—What Helps?

The physical barriers relating to right-sided weakness can mean that people with aphasia have difficulty engaging with complex, small interfaces due to the fact that they are often using one hand to interact. One viable support feature here is to increase the size of any interactive features in the interface. The use of only one hand is also an essential factor to consider for mobile computing. Ensuring that mobile devices have a stand is often critical. Separate to this, additional stroke-related visual impairments, such as hemianopia, may also affect an individual's ability to visually scan a computer screen. Clear, central placement of any journey-critical navigation can help to address this.

7.4   Other Accessibility Issues

Beyond specific aspects directly related to the language content presented on the Web, research has revealed a number of more subtle ways in which aphasia can impact upon digital interactions. Menger et al. (2016), for example, highlight issues around remembering password and login details. Likewise, Greig et al. (2008) and Moffat et al. (2004) both cite the need for simple navigation methods within interfaces—avoiding the use of complex hierarchical menus. In a review of accessibility for mobile computing, Brandenburg et al. (2013) additionally advocate the use of multimodal content and input (e.g. by supplementing written text with pictures and/or spoken words), aphasia-friendly text (e.g. clear font, short sentences and adequate use of spacing), large 'buttons', a predictable, consistent interface and visually simplistic screens.

7.5   Aphasia-Specific Recommendations

Our group, at City, University of London, has run a series of research projects that have appraised existing technologies (Marshall et al. 2018; Woolf et al. 2016; Caute & Woolf 2016) and developed new tools (Galliers et al. 2017; Roper et al. 2016; Galliers et al. 2011) for people with aphasia. Using inclusive techniques, such as co-design, all our work has involved people with aphasia from the outset (Roper et al. 2018; Grellmann et al. 2018; Wilson et al. 2015). We have drawn on this work to develop a checklist of dos and don'ts for developers and researchers to consider when designing Web and other digital experiences for people with aphasia. Based on a synthesis of the evidence and experience garnered through collaborations between researchers in human–computer interaction and research speech and language therapists in language and communication science, we propose the following[5]:

Dos

- Keep text short and simple;
- Include a text label with every icon;
- Minimise distractions;
- Let users control the pace of the interaction and
- Limit the number of steps.

Don'ts

- Use complex sentences;
- Rely on image or text alone;
- Clutter the screen;
- Use timeouts and
- Use complex user journeys.

The above list is non-exhaustive and evolving. We hope, however, it will provide a starting point for researchers and developers to reference when considering the needs of users with aphasia and other language needs within the process of Web design.

7.6   Discussion

The preceding discourse has sought to illustrate a variety of factors which should be considered when approaching the question of Web accessibility in specific relation to issues of language. We make a case for considering needs along four parameters—written production, written comprehension, spoken or signed production and spoken or signed comprehension. Researchers and developers have a host of tools at their disposal to extend and supplement existing Web design, from word prediction and spellchecking, through to labelled, picture-based input and the multimodal presentation of information. Issues can be further addressed through the adherence to the presented summary list of dos and don'ts. Within the wider context, readers are encouraged to refer to the chapter 'Standards, Guidelines and Trends' within this book for details of the W3C, (World Wide Web Consortium) Web Content Accessibility Guidelines version 2.1. (WCAG 2.1 2018). Here, in addition to the needs of those with cognitive or speech disabilities (whose challenges have been identified in

---

[5] A poster of these dos and don'ts can be downloaded from blogs.city.ac.uk/inca/outputs. The format is based on the gov.uk accessibility poster set available via https://accessibility.blog.gov.uk/2016/09/02/dos-and-donts-on-designing-for-accessibility/.

previous versions of the guidelines), this most recent version specifically acknowledges, for the first time, the need to consider the requirements of users with language disabilities when designing for the Web.

7.7 Future Directions

Looking forward, video and voice present interesting future challenges and opportunities for users with language needs. The increasing ubiquity of video media online offers new opportunities for access to Web content for many people with language disabilities. Existing work on effective methods for supporting access to written language content presentation should now be extended to consider the most effective methods for ensuring access to video content. Additionally, increasingly prevalent speech recognition interfaces such as Amazon Echo and Google Home may offer good opportunities for spoken language practice for users with language needs, but should offer alternative input modes too—to avoid alienating users with unclear or unpredictable speech and language expression.

We now consider the future implementation of accessibility guidance. As is the case for other cognitive or learning difficulties, many of the linguistic barriers to Web access cannot be identified through the use of automated accessibility checkers. For this reason, we argue that—particularly for the group of users with language needs—the practice of user testing is particularly important in order to achieve accessible Web interactions. Important work is yet to be done to establish the most effective methods to accommodate users with speech and language needs within the user-testing context. Alongside the exploration of video and speech accessibility for the Web, operationalising user-testing methods for people with speech and language needs provides a rich seam of future research in the field.

7.8 Author's Opinion of the Field

The increasing recognition of speech and language needs as a discernible accessibility issue marks definite progress in the path towards improving Web access for users affected by speech and/or language disabilities. Further research on this area is necessary in order to determine how needs are currently being met (or not) for members of this population. Within this chapter, we have drawn upon existing evidence from the fields of human–computer interaction, and speech and language therapy/pathology. We believe that pursuing collaborative work across these disciplines will serve to further distil the knowledge so it may be applied most effectively to the topic of Web accessibility. Perhaps most critical to achieving this aim, however, will be the consultation of and advocacy by users with speech and language needs themselves.

7.9 Conclusions

Aphasia is a highly prevalent disability with profound consequences for those affected. Social isolation and reduced quality of life are common. Engagement with technology could ameliorate some of these effects. However, the risks of digital exclusion in aphasia are high. The linguistic impairments of aphasia mean that the language demands of many technologies cannot be met, and additional stroke-related impairments affecting physical and sensory functioning add to the barriers. Good, aphasia-friendly design can mitigate many of these risks and open up the benefits of the digital world to this group. The benefits do not stop there. Design that includes people with aphasia will open technologies to many other disadvantaged groups, such as people with low levels of literacy, second language users and people with cognitive difficulties. By designing for aphasia, we can design for a more inclusive world.

References

Bird H, Howard D, Franklin S (2003) Verbs and nouns: the importance of being imageable. J Neurolinguistics 16(2–3):113–149

Brandenburg C, Worrall L, Rodriguez AD, Copland D (2013) Mobile computing technology and aphasia: an integrated review of accessibility and potential uses. Aphasiology 27(4):444–461

Caute A, Cruice M, Friede A, Galliers J, Dickinson T, Green R, Woolf C (2016) Rekindling the love of books–a pilot project exploring whether e-readers help people to read again after a stroke. Aphasiology 30(2–3):290–319

Caute A, Woolf C (2016) Using Voice Recognition Software to improve communicative writing and social participation in an individual with severe acquired dysgraphia: an experimental single case therapy study. Aphasiology 30(2–3):245–268. https://doi.org/10.1080/02687038.2015.1041095

Department for Work and Pensions (2013) Family resources survey. United Kingdom 2011/2012. Online at https://www.gov.uk/government/statistics/family-resources-survey-201112

Fridriksson J, Baker JM, Whiteside J, Eoute D, Moser D, Vesselinov R, Rorden C (2009) Treating visual speech perception to improve speech production in nonfluent aphasia. Stroke 40(3):853–858

Galliers J, Wilson S, Marshall J, Talbot R, Devane N, Booth T, Woolf C, Greenwood H (2017) Experiencing EVA park, a multi-user virtual world for people with aphasia. ACM Trans Access Comput (TACCESS) 10(4):15

Galliers J, Wilson S, Muscroft S, Marshall J, Roper A, Cocks N, Pring T (2011) Accessibility of 3D game environments for people with aphasia: an exploratory study. In: Proceedings of the 13th international ACM SIGACCESS conference on Computers and accessibility. ACM, pp 139–146

Greig C-A, Harper R, Hirst T, Howe T, Davidson B (2008) Barriers and facilitators to mobile phone use for people with aphasia. Top Stroke Rehabil 15(4):307–324

Grellmann B, Neate T, Roper A, Wilson S, Marshall J (2018) Investigating mobile accessibility guidance for people with aphasia. ASSETS '18, Galway, Ireland, 22–24 October 2018

Herbert R (2012) Accessible information guidelines: making information accessible for people with aphasia. Stroke Association

Law J, Gaag A, Hardcastle WJ, Beckett DJ, MacGregor A, Plunkett C (2007) Communication support needs: a review of the literature. Scottish Executive

Linebarger M, McCall D, Virata T, Berndt RS (2007) Widening the temporal window: processing support in the treatment of aphasic language production. Brain Lang 100(1):53–68

Ma X, Nikolova S, Cook PR (2009) W2ANE: when words are not enough: online multimedia language assistant for people with aphasia. In: Proceedings of the 17th ACM international conference on multimedia. ACM, pp 749–752

Marshall J, Caute A, Chadd K, Cruice M, Monnelly K, Wilson S, Woolf C (2018) Technology-enhanced writing therapy for people with aphasia: results of a quasi-randomized waitlist controlled study. Int J Lang Commun Disord

Menger F, Morris J, Salis C (2016) Aphasia in an internet age: wider perspectives on digital inclusion. Aphasiology 30(2–3):112–132

Moffatt K, McGrenere J, Purves B, Klawe M (2004) The participatory design of a sound and image enhanced daily planner for people with aphasia. In: Proceedings of the SIGCHI conference on human factors in computing systems. ACM, pp 407–414

Roper A, Davey I, Wilson S, Neate T, Marshall J, Grellmann B (2018) Usability testing – an aphasia perspective. ASSETS '18, Galway, Ireland, 22–24 October 2018

Roper A, Marshall J, Wilson S (2016) Benefits and limitations of computer gesture therapy for the rehabilitation of severe aphasia. Front Hum Neurosci 10:595

Rose T, Worrall L, Hickson L, Hoffmann T (2010) Do people with aphasia want written stroke and aphasia information? A verbal survey exploring preferences for when and how to provide stroke and aphasia information. Top Stroke Rehabil 17(2):79–98

Thompson CK, Lange KL, Schneider SL, Shapiro LP (1997) Agrammatic and non-brain-damaged subjects' verb and verb argument structure production. Aphasiology 11(4–5): 473–490

Wilson S, Roper A, Marshall J, Galliers J, Devane N, Booth T, Woolf C (2015) Codesign for people with aphasia through tangible design languages. CoDesign 11(1):21–34

Web Content Accessibility Guidelines 2.1 (2018) W3C World Wide Web consortium recommendation 05 June 2018 (https://www.w3.org/TR/2018/REC-WCAG21-20180605/, Latest version at https://www.w3.org/TR/WCAG21/)

Woolf C, Caute A, Haigh Z, Galliers J, Wilson S, Kessie A, Hirani S, Hegarty B, Marshall J (2016) A comparison of remote therapy, face to face therapy and an attention control intervention for people with aphasia: a quasi-randomised controlled feasibility study. Clin Rehabil 30(4):359–373

Part II
Conducting Research

Chapter 8
Inclusive Writing

**Tom Babinszki, Anna Cavender, Michael Gower, Jeffery Hoehl,
Darcy Lima, Erich Manser and Shari Trewin**

Abstract This chapter introduces inclusive writing and how to incorporate it into research. We give general guidelines on language choice and suggestions on writing for and about specific user groups. However, language is constantly evolving. Preferred language for writing about people with disabilities changes over time, and with context, and can be a source of disagreement even within a user group. The inclusive writing approach proposed here covers three key points: use the included terminology and considerations as a starting point; verify language choices and other assumptions through feedback with participants; and strive for respect in all research interactions. The chapter also explores how careful thinking about language can make an entire research project more accessible and inclusive.

T. Babinszki · M. Gower (✉)
IBM Research, Cleveland, OH, USA
e-mail: gowerm@ca.ibm.com

T. Babinszki
e-mail: tbabins@us.ibm.com

A. Cavender · J. Hoehl · D. Lima
Google, Mountain View, CA, USA
e-mail: annacc@google.com

J. Hoehl
e-mail: hoehl@google.com

D. Lima
e-mail: darcy@google.com

E. Manser
IBM Research, Littleton, MA, USA
e-mail: emanser@us.ibm.com

S. Trewin
IBM Research, Yorktown Heights, NY, USA
e-mail: trewin@us.ibm.com

© Springer-Verlag London Ltd., part of Springer Nature 2019   135
Y. Yesilada and S. Harper (eds.), *Web Accessibility*, Human–Computer
Interaction Series, https://doi.org/10.1007/978-1-4471-7440-0_8

8.1 Introduction

Research confirms that labeling something changes how people perceive it. In one famous study from the 1970s, altering the verb to describe a car crash caused study participants to remember seeing glass when none was present and to significantly alter estimations of vehicle speed (Loftus and Palmer 1974). Language has that ability to change our perceptions or to expose our assumptions.

It is within this context that we can begin to address inclusive writing. When adjectives and other parts of speech used to describe things become nouns for people, they shape how we perceive those people. The associations often take on derogatory common usage in a society—labels like *cripple*, *mental*, and *dumb*.

This chapter addresses how we can transform the language we use in research papers—as well as other facets of the research process—through inclusive thinking. It examines the power and limitations of labels and terminology. We provide some context and general guidelines for writing and language—considerations and techniques that have worked well in other places. We also caution against relying entirely on them.

The ideas presented in this chapter resulted from an attempt at a more inclusive writing process. We sought the involvement of co-authors with disabilities, and then gathered additional input from employees with disabilities in our companies. Quotes from that process appear throughout this chapter. We hope that by working toward a position that offers a multiplicity of opinion, we have illustrated a key aspect of inclusive writing.

This chapter begins by establishing inclusion as the desired outcome of an ongoing process. That process seeks to end the exclusion of persons with disabilities from active participation in all aspects of research, whether as researchers or study participants. The chapter then offers sections with specific guidance on how to achieve inclusion through:

- General language usage (Sect. 8.2.2);
- Usage for specific groups and contexts (Sect. 8.2.3); and
- Making content accessible (Sect. 8.2.5).

We then discuss the question "Can terminology alone achieve inclusion?" We close with sections on future directions for inclusive writing and our opinions of the field.

8.2 Working Toward Inclusive Writing

I think the truly "proper" way to write about disability is simply to engage people with disabilities. Don't make assumptions; we're right here, all around. Ask if something is offensive, or unrealistic, or authentic.

— Erich (co-author)

8.2.1 Inclusion

Interest in Web accessibility often arises from a desire to make the Web more inclusive, although opinions differ on the best definition of Web accessibility (Yesilada et al. 2012). The technology industry is seeing a change in focus from accessibility as an engineering discipline to a broader charge of creating products that include the broadest group of people (more details in Chap. 18). Inclusive writing is an important aspect of inclusion, and it starts with inclusive thinking. The following illustration (Fig. 8.1), based on a famous graphic from the United Nations Committee on the Rights of Persons with Disabilities (Hehir et al. 2016), helps define what we mean by inclusion.

This illustration shows four circles labeled exclusion, separation, integration, and inclusion. Some darker, solid dots (blue) are inside each circle while another set of lighter, bordered dots (orange) are positioned variously inside or outside each circle. For exclusion, the orange, bordered dots are scattered outside the circle. In separation, the orange dots are still outside the circle, but are now contained in their own, smaller circle. With integration, that smaller circle of dots is now inside the larger circle but still holds the orange dots separate from the blue dots. And finally, inclusion shows all dots, blue and orange, intermingled freely within the large circle.

When writing about disability, drawing upon the sentiment captured by the inclusion circle provides useful direction. Demonstrating consideration for a person's disability, if not done with inclusion in mind, can inadvertently feel like separation or integration rather than inclusion.

Early in the process of discussing this article, I was asked about Disability Etiquette. When I hear that term, it feels like the Separation circle—that same sort of "separate-but-equal" connotation, as in "let's develop a specific set of rules for dealing with these people over here".

— Erich (co-author)

Being inclusive means engaging in honest conversations with people with disabilities and using those discussions to inform and transform your language and process.

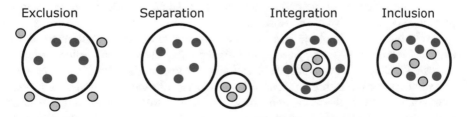

Fig. 8.1 Circle illustration of the terms exclusion, separation, integration, and inclusion

8.2.2   General Language Usage

Is it really about how others see you, or how you see yourself? "Disabled" to me
does not mean "lesser". It just means someone with part of themselves that does not
function as "normal".

— Yvette

This chapter focuses on inclusive language for use in academic papers, a key
form of research communication. Typically, the research being described will include
studies with human participants or involve technology intended for use by a specific
group of people. It is important to not only convey respect for the participants in
research studies but also to accurately and precisely describe these groups to readers.

Although preferences vary between and within groups and contexts, this section
gives general guidance, as identified through articles and existing style guides (e.g.,
National Center on Disability and Journalism 2018), that can serve as a starting point
for rethinking bias and language choices.

To improve readability, terms have been italicized rather than put in quotes in this
and the subsequent section.

8.2.2.1   Use Neutral Wording

People respond to nuances of speech, consciously and subconsciously. The abstract
from the 1970s experiment mentioned in the chapter introduction (Loftus and Palmer
1974) can help illustrate this.

> …subjects viewed films of automobile accidents and then answered questions about events
> occurring in the films. The question, "About how fast were the cars going when they smashed
> into each other?" elicited higher estimates of speed than questions which used the verbs
> *collided, bumped, contacted,* or *hit* in place of *smashed.* On a retest one week later, those
> subjects who received the verb *smashed* were more likely to say "yes" to the question, "Did
> you see any broken glass?", even though broken glass was not present in the film.

Whether using verbs or adjectives, examine the bias inherent in the language you
use. Describing study participants as *stroke sufferers* or *stroke victims* conveys a very
different attitude toward the participants and their situation than the more neutral
phrasing *people who have had a stroke.*

Avoid words that imply judgment, either positive or negative, such as *normal,*
healthy, victim of, suffering from, and *afflicted with.* These terms reflect bias or
projected feelings about an individual's situation. Some people with disabilities feel
that when a word like *normal* or *healthy* is used to describe those without a disability,
its obvious antonym (*abnormal, unhealthy*) is being used to describe them. Therefore,
the more laden with negative connotations the obvious antonym, the more offended
some people may be.

Neutral phrases that you can use as an alternative include *sighted person, hearing*
person, persons without disabilities, neurotypical, and *typically developing* (for a
child).

8.2.2.2   Use Person-Focused Descriptions

The first time I used people first language to describe myself, I started crying. I had no idea how much of a difference it could make to not define who I am by my conditions.

— Matt

As a general guideline, avoid using disabilities as nouns to describe people (e.g., *the blind, a quadriplegic*). These terms remove personhood and define individuals by their disabilities. This can be problematic in many ways, not least of which is that people can have more than one disability. Instead, consider using adjectives or qualifying phrases to describe a user population or when discussing study participants.

Use person-focused descriptions to emphasize the person over their disability or medical diagnosis, for example, *person with dementia*. Other examples of person-focused phrases include *people with disabilities, people experiencing disabilities, a quadriplegic person*, and *person who uses a wheelchair*,

Note that "person-focused" does not always mean "person-first." While many groups generally prefer person-first language (e.g., *person with a visual impairment*), it is common in some communities to prefer identity-first language (e.g., *Deaf person, autistic person*) (Dunn and Andrews 2015). We will discuss this more in Sect. 8.2.3.

One exception is that the names of some advocacy groups include *the Blind* or *the Deaf*; this usage often has historical roots but generally does not make sense for common speech or writing. When talking about actual, specific people, *blind people* or *people who are blind* would be better choices. For example, "We tested this feature with the blind" would be better as "We tested this feature with blind people."

8.2.2.3   Avoid Euphemistic Terms

I intentionally chose the word "condition" over "disease;" but recently, I have started to think that "condition" is such an arbitrary word. Maybe I should just use disease, despite the fact that "disease" connotes some progressively worsening illness.

— Larissa

Euphemisms can arise for any number of reasons, including when people wish to avoid stating something directly, when they are uncomfortable with a topic, or when existing terms have taken on negative associations. While euphemisms may be employed successfully to enhance inclusion, there is also risk associated with their usage, as illustrated in this passage:

> Our data suggest that *special needs* has already become a dysphemism (a euphemism more negative than the word it replaces). *Special needs* will likely become a slur, if it is not already, and it might eventually become a dysphemistic metaphor, akin to *dumb, lame, crippled, ...* (Gernsbacher et al. 2016)

It is best to avoid euphemisms, such as *physically challenged, special, differently abled, handi-capable, angel*. These phrases are generally regarded by the disability community as patronizing and inaccurate.

While these terms might not be inherently offensive, they often appear when people are trying to be careful or do not know the history behind a term. They can also be used in an attempt to avoid using *disabled*, which seems wrong to many people because it sounds nonfunctional (i.e., a disabled car cannot move, a disabled player cannot play), but is the commonly accepted term.

It is best to avoid the word *handicapped*. *Handicapped* as a synonym for "disabled" is outdated. Confusingly, *handicap* can also be used both as a synonym for "barrier" (for example, "The stairs leading to the stage were a handicap to him."), and as a term meaning an enhancement intended to address an unequal situation, as in a golf handicap. Instead of *handicapped parking space*, say *accessible parking* or *accessible parking spot*.

8.2.3 Usage for Specific Groups and Contexts

A key means of achieving *inclusive* writing is by adopting the terminology preferred by the participants in a study.

While opinion varies among individuals and groups, and terminology can change by region and culture (Lazar et al. 2017), the following subsections provide context for specific disabilities, and capture some current preferences within disability types as categorized in the Foundations part of this book. The intention is not to capture all the nuance and detail for each disability community, but to provide some background and context for current language preferences, from which you can build a more inclusive research project. Note that individuals might identify as having more than one disability or none at all.

8.2.3.1 Visual Disabilities

Low vision, visually impaired, blind, and *legally blind* can mean different things in different cultures and regions. The common term *low vision* encompasses a broad range of considerations, and more precise terms or descriptions of symptoms or conditions may be necessary for clarity.

Low vision is often described in terms of a corrected visual acuity. However, many visual impairments do not align with this categorization. Users may be sensitive to light (photophobia), unable to perceive motion (akinetopsia), or have a reduced visual field, for example.

Low vision can also cover a reduced ability to discern colors. While *color blind* is not a particularly accurate term, it is firmly established and more readily understood than *color vision deficiency*, which tends to be used by professionals such as optometrists. Likewise, *red-green color blind* covers the most common forms of color blindness (deuteranomaly and protanomaly).

In general, person-first language is preferred when referring to people who are blind or visually impaired.

Terms to avoid include *the blind*, *sight-deficient*, *people with sight problems*, *unsighted*, and *visually challenged*.

8.2.3.2   Deafness and Hearing Loss

I am not a fan of "hearing impaired"... While it does not bother me extensively, I think someone who uses that term reveals themselves to not have much knowledge and awareness of the deaf and hard of hearing community.

— Erik

Some people are not "deaf" and are truly "hearing impaired". They still have significant use of their hearing, but may have some mild to moderate hearing loss. They tend to not consider themselves deaf. On the other hand, I tend to refer to myself as either deaf or hearing-impaired depending on the situation.

— Yvette

The terms *Deaf* (with a capital D), *deaf*, *hard of hearing*, *hearing loss*, and *hearing impaired* all have different meanings within the D/deaf community.

This area is a notable exception to the person-first guideline: *Deaf person* is generally preferred to *person who is deaf*.

Deaf (capitalized) refers to people who are audiologically deaf to any degree, use sign language as their primary mode of communication, and identify with the Deaf community and Deaf cultural values. Sometimes *deaf* is used to refer to any non-hearing person.

Hard of hearing can refer to people who use assistive listening devices and might or might not be a part of the Deaf community. Hard of hearing people may communicate through sign language, spoken language, lip-reading, and/or may rely on some residual hearing to communicate.

When referring to a general group, use *deaf and hard of hearing*. The *deaf and hard of hearing community* can refer to those who are audiologically and culturally d/Deaf, support sign language usage, and benefit from disability legislation. Sign language usage is often a trait that differentiates between *deaf* and *Deaf*.

Hearing impaired is a term used in medical writing to designate that an individual's hearing threshold differs from the "normal" human audio spectrum (typically measured from 250 Hz to 8 kHz in an audiogram). Because it negatively emphasizes a deficiency, members of the Deaf Community often reject the term. Hearing is not the norm by which most deaf people wish to be measured. However, people who do not identify with the deaf and hard of hearing communities, such as those who have experienced hearing loss later in life, may be comfortable with the term *hearing impaired*.

The *Deaf world* is a term to avoid, since it can seem to reinforce the concept of Separation shown in our graphic on inclusion. Other terms to avoid: *deaf-mute*, *deaf and dumb*, *the deaf*, and *hearing disabled*.

8.2.3.3   Physical Disabilities

As a category, *physical disabilities* typically refer to limitations to a person's dexterity, movement, or stamina. In the context of Web accessibility, this often relates to abilities to use hands and arms to manipulate technology. The term *mobility impairment* refers broadly to movement in general, particularly walking or moving about, while *dexterity impairment* is suitable when the focus of the work is on using a mouse/keyboard, a touch screen, or other manual computer interaction.

Commonly accepted terms include *person with a motor disability*; *person with an ambulatory disability; person with a physical disability*; *person with a mobility impairment*; *person with a dexterity impairment*; *person who uses a wheelchair, walker, or cane*; *wheelchair user*; *wheelchair rider*; *person with restricted or limited mobility, amputee* (OK); *person with an amputation* (better); *residual limb* (when referring to the remaining limb).

Avoid negative terms such as *confined/restricted to a wheelchair, wheelchair-bound, deformed, crippled, physically challenged, lame, gimp*, and *stump* (when referring to the remaining part of an amputated limb).

8.2.3.4   Cognitive and Learning Disabilities

As described in Chap. 5, cognitive function has many dimensions, such as memory, reasoning, attention, executive functioning, understanding verbal, visual, mathematical or textual communication, and using language (Seeman and Cooper 2015). Autism spectrum disorder, dyslexia, dyscalculia, aphasia, Down syndrome, and attention-deficit hyperactivity disorder all fall under this umbrella. Since the term *cognitive disability* is quite broad, it is important to be as specific as possible about what disabilities the research concerns.

Among the autism community, identity-first language is generally preferred (*autistic person*), but some individuals might prefer *person with autism*. It can also be useful to specify *autistic adult* or *autistic child* if that is relevant. Some people may also prefer *autist*. Some people use *neurotypical* and *neurodiverse* (or *neurodivergent*) when discussing autism. It is worth noting that *neurodiverse* can include more than just autism. Conversely, *neurotypical* does not just mean "not autistic."

Society has used many labels over time that are best to avoid. For example, avoid *the developmentally disabled, retarded, demented, deficient, insane, slow* or *slow learner, abnormal* or *normal, mongoloid, idiot, crazy, mental, permanent child, will always be N years old*.

Commonly accepted terms include *person with a cognitive disability, neurodiverse, person with a learning disability, person with an intellectual disability, person with a developmental disability*, and *person with Down syndrome* (or other specific medically diagnosed condition). For children without cognitive or learning impairment use *typically developing*.

8.2.3.5 Psychosocial Disabilities

The UN Convention on the Rights of People with Disabilities (UN General Assembly 2007) uses the phrase *"psychosocial disability"* to describe disabilities arising from mental health conditions, specifically challenges or limits that impact a person's ability to fully participate in life. The term *"psychosocial"* refers to the interaction between a person's psychology and the social world, following the social model of disability. Not everyone living with a mental health condition will experience psychosocial disability.

There can be negative stereotypes and stigma associated with mental health conditions. As with other areas, avoid using terms that define a person in terms of their mental health status, such as *a depressed person* or *a schizophrenic*. Other terms to avoid are *crazy*, *insane*, or other terms used in a derogatory fashion.

8.2.3.6 Ageing and Older Adults

For the first time in history, there are more elderly people than children in many countries. More than one out of five people will be age 60 or older by 2050, according to the UN (United Nations 2015). Studies on ageing and longevity abound, and the vocabulary to describe the global ageing population is likely to evolve rapidly.

There is a statistical likelihood for individuals to experience the onset of disabilities as they age. The 2016 American Community Survey (US Census Bureau 2016) found a marked increase in those aged 75 and over identifying as having hearing (22.4%), vision (9.7%), ambulatory (32.6%), cognitive (13.9%), independent-living (24.8%), and self-care (13.6%) difficulties.

Despite this trend, there is no generally accepted vocabulary for writing about ageing and ageing individuals (or even agreement on whether it is spelled with an *e*), but terms such as *older adults*, *older persons*, *elder* (as an adjective or part of a compound word, such as *eldercare*), or *ageing population* are in current use. The terms *seniors* and *senior citizens* have been popular but are now less often used.

Many older adults are healthy and active, and do not consider themselves to be disabled even though they may have some age-related impairments. Disabilities that onset in older adults are sometimes phrased in terms of "difficulties."

Avoid: *The elderly, the aged, 80 years young*. Be cautious with *seniors, senior citizens*. When referring to an actual study, specify the age category ("people older than 75").

8.2.3.7 Speech and Language

Historically, the keyboard and monitor have been the primary mechanisms for ensuring accessible Web input and output. With the advent of mobile assistants like Siri, voice input and speech output are now poised to become a primary means of interaction (for example, the original versions of Amazon's Alexa and Google Home have no keyboard *or* display screen). Such conversation-based interaction offers real benefits to those who cannot see, read, or easily manipulate devices; however, the potential barriers increase for users who cannot hear or speak.

Language disorders affect how a person expresses his or her thoughts or understands spoken and written language. Speech disorders affect an individual's ability to produce speech. As is noted in the full chapter on speech and language (Chapter 7), the category can also encompass many considerations such as perception of speech (i.e., hearing), which are dealt with separately here and elsewhere in this book.

When referring to people with speech or language disabilities, "disorder" is often preferred, as in *speech disorder, language disorder*, or a specific condition such as *apraxia* or *aphasia* (the focus of the Speech and Language chapter). Considerations may also be phrased as "difficulties", as in *individuals with language difficulties*. Terms to avoid include *mute* or *dumb*.

8.2.4 Describing Research Participants

The previous section provides suggestions for appropriate language to use when referring to disability groups. When writing research findings, it is also important to give the most precise description possible of those who participated. Precise descriptions allow readers to better understand the context of the research, to interpret the findings, and to make comparisons to other studies.

Common approaches to describing participants in research studies include simply stating the broad population sampled (e.g., "people with visual impairment") or providing descriptions based on a medical diagnosis. Both approaches often fail to provide enough information. Instead, some advocate descriptions that include participant abilities, background, experience, and objective assessment information (Sears and Hanson 2011).

For scientific writing, both medical and experiential characteristics can be important. On the cultural side, people with congenital and acquired disabilities may have very different responses to the same technology, due to the differences in their prior experience. For example, people who were born blind and those with acquired vision loss may have different preferences in how graphics are presented to them. Similarly, in sign language research participants' level of fluency and years of experience with sign language are important factors.

When it is necessary to give a description of participants' abilities and disabilities, it is not sufficient to describe participants simply as "visually impaired" or having a "cognitive disability". These are broad terms that cover a range of very different health conditions and impairments. Naming a health condition such as stroke, cerebral palsy, or multiple sclerosis is also not usually sufficient, because the same health condition can have very different impairments that result in different impacts on technology usage. For example, the effect of a stroke on an individual's abilities depends on the location of the brain damage caused by the stroke and can vary enormously. Ideally, a research paper should quantify the relevant abilities of the participants as precisely as possible, using established metrics. For example, "All participants had central visual acuity of 20/200 or less in the better eye, with correction, or a visual field of 20 degrees or less."

While it is always important to give the ages of participants, for research with older adults this does not convey much information about the visual, cognitive, and motor abilities they bring to the study. In many cases, these abilities are a stronger determinant of outcomes than age alone (Smith et al. 1999; Trewin et al. 2012). Reporting measures of visual, physical, and cognitive abilities provide a much better basis for understanding the findings than age alone.

Be cautious in the use of medical terminology. For example, in medical writing, cognitive impairments may be described as *deficits*, a term with strong negative connotations. This and other medical terms may be appropriate in computer science when describing a specific medical condition or group of participants but should not be used as a general term of reference (e.g., *people with deficits*).

8.2.5   Making Content Accessible

Inclusive language is the focus of this chapter, but we would be remiss if we did not mention considerations for the format of content itself. Research papers tend to have very prescriptive formatting requirements, but other content that a researcher produces, such as presentations, articles, and video, offers a broader scope for creating material that is more accessible. Ensuring that research findings and outcomes are accessible is an important way to include all audiences.

8.2.5.1   Sensory Characteristics

Graphs, charts, and illustrations can enhance the understanding for many users, but these elements are not consumable by someone who is blind. Captions and surrounding text should explain the key information that authors intend users to derive from such visual information. Where possible, tabular data on which graphs are based should be provided for users who cannot read or understand the images.

People who are blind or have low vision may not be able to perceive or follow information if it is conveyed by shape and/or location. Describing information in ways other than just by position or shape will allow more people to consume the information conveyed.

Finally, if color alone is used to convey information, users who perceive color differently (i.e., "color blind") or not at all (i.e., "monochromacy") will not be able to access it. Offering additional cues, such as pattern or text, can help make such distinctions accessible to a wider audience.

The inclusion figure from Sect. 8.2.1 can serve as an example of the process of making content accessible. The drawing itself helps readers, especially those with some cognitive disabilities, to understand the concept. As different readers reviewed this drawing, it was transformed to make it more inclusive; the shapes and colors used were altered so different low-vision readers could discern them. The text following the drawing became more descriptive, so that blind readers could better understand the context.

8.2.5.2   Format

Where information is typically provided in a physical format such as a poster, be sure to make an electronic, text-based version available as well. Text can be transformed by assistive technologies into a format that users can adapt to their requirements. Likewise, video and audio materials should not only be captioned (and in the case of videos, described) but be made available as text transcripts.

These considerations should apply not just to content covering the results of research, but to the materials used during all facets of research, such as surveys, consent forms, and instructions, so that people with disabilities can take part as sponsors, participants, or researchers. For research information that appears on the Web, the content should comply with the Web Content Accessibility Guidelines 2.1 (Kirkpatrick et al. 2018), from which much of this information was garnered, as well as Tips for Getting Started Writing for Web Accessibility (White et al. 2016).

8.3   Discussion: Can Terminology Alone Achieve Inclusion?

I am beyond tired of the fuss with words. When we are talking, it's just too easy to forget the correct word of the day. The tone of the conversation is what I'm interested in.
                                                                                — Mary

Much of this article is given over to prescriptive advice on proper terms to use when discussing disabilities and the people who have them. However, following the advice of this or any guide without contemplation or validation can lead to problems. Language is evolving. Over time, commonly accepted terms change, grow, or shrink in popularity or take on negative connotations they may not have had in the past. This phenomenon is discussed in detail in Sect. 8.4.

But even ignoring the longer-term evolution of language, there are two main cautions for prescriptive use of language:

- **Disparate opinion**: Not everyone within a community will agree on terminology.
- **Context matters**: Some terms may be commonly accepted in certain contexts such as in the medical or professional fields, even though their use in social settings would be inappropriate.

8.3.1 Disparate Opinion

When trying to achieve inclusive language, be aware that individuals or groups who self-identify with a disability may have significant differences of opinion about what they wish to be called and what any term means. Also, terminology preferred by a community or individual may not be aligned with professional descriptions. In one example, a UK study (Kenny et al. 2016) found that 3470 responses to a survey revealed significant differences on language used by members of the UK autism community.

> The term 'autistic' was endorsed by a large percentage of autistic adults, family members/friends and parents but by considerably fewer professionals; 'person with autism' was endorsed by almost half of professionals but by fewer autistic adults and parents.... These findings demonstrate that there is no single way of describing autism that is universally accepted and preferred by the UK's autism community and that some disagreements appear deeply entrenched.

Differences in perspective have also been a focus of comedian Zach Anner.

> Other callers were distraught that I had chosen to describe myself as 'a disabled person' rather than their preferred 'differently-abled' or 'a person with a disability.' I fully understand the intention behind person-first language. I agree full-heartedly with the goals of this movement. But here's the thing… It just never rang true for me.

Acknowledging different terms that are in favor before settling on one for the duration of a paper is one approach to ensuring respect while maintaining consistency. Another approach is to use the terms interchangeably. By seeking input and verifying editorial decisions with participants or stakeholders, researchers can help ensure a respectful outcome.

8.3.2 Context Matters

This chapter focuses on writing and working in the field of human–computer interaction (HCI). HCI researchers work in a variety of settings, including clinical medical environments, homes and workplaces, educational venues, and other institutions, in addition to laboratory studies. Each of these settings may have its own norms of vocabulary.

In a hospital or other medical setting, the term *patients* may be an appropriate term for participants, but in a laboratory study at a university, it is not. In HCI, community-preferred language is generally more appropriate than clinical language. An exception is the language used to characterize study participants, for which medical terminology may be the most precise and unambiguous choice. When using clinical terms, consider including medical definitions of the terms, for clarity of meaning. For example, a paper may characterize study participants as having "moderate hearing loss (unable to hear sounds lower than 40–69 dB)."

In cases where you make language choices that differ from user group preferences, it may be helpful to acknowledge the difference and explain the context.

8.3.3 Inclusive Thinking in Research

Beyond considerations for terminology, inclusive thinking can transform research papers, not only making the language more accurate and respectful but also informing the process of creating research.

The difference between the principles of integration and inclusion in a research project can be nuanced. If a research project's purpose is to examine trends between users whose physical or cognitive abilities differ, then integrating users with disabilities into the project will be intentional. But where physical and cognitive abilities are not drivers of the research question, a researcher who acts from a point of inclusion will ensure the project is still constructed in such a way that anyone can participate. By following accessible design practices, regardless of the anticipated participants, people with disabilities can be included. This takes the concept of inclusion beyond considerations for the language used in research papers.

8.4 Future Directions

8.4.1 Evolving Language

You might get the language perfect today and two years from now you would be dead wrong.

— John

The tendency for language and terms to undergo a complete transformation in meaning (from positive to negative) is most noticeable in rapidly maturing and evolving fields of study. In his article "Language and disability" (Foreman 2005), Phil Foreman recounts the evolving language in one Australian publication:

> A perusal of the earliest issues of the Journal from just over 30 years ago reveals the use of words and phrases that have almost totally disappeared from current Australian usage. Examples of these include "mongolism", "mongol patients", "the retarded", "the handicapped", "mentally sub-normal", "mental deficiency", "Down's children", "retardates", "grossly retarded children", and so on. That they seem so terribly out-dated now is a reflection on the rapidity of language change, and not any criticism of the authors or editors. I cringe at my own writing from that period, but am aware that it was current usage at the time.

Similarly, the article Writing About Accessibility (Hanson et al. 2015) was updated just 7 years after initial publication (Cavender et al. 2008) due to changes in terminology, for example, changing the term *mental retardation* to *intellectual disability*. Disability culture advocates have recently challenged the use of person-first

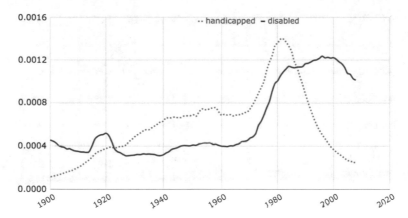

Fig. 8.2 Frequency (in hundredth of percents) of published books (from 1900 to 2008) in which the terms handicapped and disabled appear, according to Google NGram

language, arguing for the positive benefits of identity-first language (e.g., *disabled people*) (Dunn and Andrews 2015). In the face of inevitable change, even the best-intentioned authors will find their language ageing with something less than grace.

Consider, for example, the terms *handicapped* and *disabled*. As Fig. 8.2 illustrates, the term *handicapped* rose rapidly in popularity during the 1970s and 1980s and then swiftly dropped in usage to present day. Concurrently, the term *disabled* dipped a bit during the early part of the twentieth century, picked up in usage during the 1980s, and surpassed *handicapped* during the 1990s. Though *disabled* decreased a bit in usage at the end of the twentieth century, it continues to maintain a pronounced higher usage as compared to *handicapped* at present day.

The terms *the elderly* and *older adults* provide another interesting example, illustrated in Fig. 8.3. It shows a steep rise in the use of the term *the elderly* in the 1960s and 70s, peaking around 1985 then falling, while the term *older adults* grows steadily but slowly in popularity from around 1970 to 2008, though in 2008 was still less popular than *the elderly*.

These examples illustrate the changing and evolving nature of language over time. This chapter outlines the currently accepted language around technology, research, and disability while recognizing that the individual terms used today may very well become terms to avoid tomorrow. Working from a mindsight of inclusion can help us make informed and careful language choices that match the sentiment of the time, and should increase the longevity of our work, even in a field with rapidly evolving language.

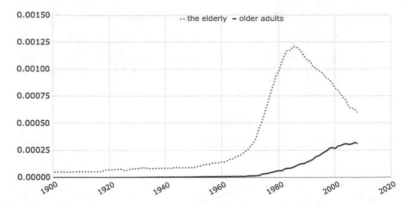

Fig. 8.3 Frequency (in hundredth of percents) of published books (from 1900 to 2008) in which the terms the elderly and older adults appear, according to Google NGram

8.5 Authors' Opinion of the Field

8.5.1 Directives for Inclusive Writing

When it comes to inclusive writing for research papers, there are some high-level guiding considerations which can help inform all aspects of the project.

For general discussion concerning participants:

1. Strive for respect in all interactions with study participants.
2. Choose language that represents the preferences of the participants and their communities.

For discussions on disabilities which are relevant to the research question:

3. Strive for accuracy in describing *relevant* key characteristics of participants.

These directives may seem contradictory at times, but they can help clarify what language best meets the needs of a paper.

8.5.2 Strive for Respect in All Interactions with Study Participants

Publishing a research paper represents the culmination of a project. However, if a project team desires to fully meet the objective of being inclusive, the process needs to begin much earlier in the research process than during the paper writing.

Any written or oral communication should be considered, as should a researcher's assumptions and preconceptions. Areas of the research process where inclusive writing could be demonstrated include the following:

- Initial calls for participants (both the language and the medium used);
- Screening questions; and
- Consent forms, study instructions, questionnaires, and interviews.

By addressing such points, the project team's efforts will help establish an environment that is more conducive to the drafting of a paper that conveys respect to all those involved.

8.5.3 Reflect User Preferences

Incorporating participants' preferences and perspectives can help create an inclusive environment. Ask participants if they self-identify as having any disability, ask them how they wish to describe their disability and themselves, and then incorporate their preferences into all interactions. Where group participation occurs and the topic in discussion includes participant disabilities, be aware of community preferences for language. Acknowledging a difference between community and clinical language can also be useful.

8.5.4 Strive for Accuracy in Describing Relevant Characteristics of Participants

For scientific writing, it is essential to be clear and accurate when describing both participants in studies and intended users of a technology. Consider which characteristics of participants or users are important in the context of the work and be as precise as possible. Instead of broad descriptions like "older adults", consider whether the quality of interest is in fact a specific cognitive ability such as working memory or hand dexterity. Measure and describe that quality in research participants, rather than relying on age as a proxy for these abilities or using broad terms. Use medical terminology when it is necessary to communicate a more accurate description of participants' abilities.

8.6 Conclusions

The best way to make writing more inclusive is to adopt a mindful approach throughout a study, from its conception to the drafting of the paper. Discussing the topic with participants and understanding current professional terminology can help inform the authors' task. It can be humbling understanding that today's inclusive terms will likely over time become viewed as dated or even disparaging, but authors can take comfort knowing that respectful tone in a paper can be detected long after the language of the day has evolved.

References

Cavender A, Trewin S, Hanson VL (2008) General writing guidelines for technology and people with disabilities. SIGACCESS Access Comput 92:17–22. https://doi.org/10.1145/1452562.1452565

Dunn DS, Andrews E (2015) Person-first and identity-first language: developing psychologists' cultural competence using disability language. Am Psychol 70:255–264

Foreman P (2005) Language and disability. J Intellect Dev Disabil 30(1):57–59

Gernsbacher MA et al (2016) Special needs' is an ineffective euphemism. Cogn Res Princ Implic 1:29 (PMC. Web. 22 June 2018)

Hanson VL, Cavender A, Trewin S (2015) Writing about accessibility. Interactions 22(6):62–65

Hehir T, Grindal T, Freeman B, Lamoreau R, Borquaye Y, Burke S (2016) A summary of the evidence on inclusive education. ABT Associates https://alana.org.br/wp-content/uploads/2016/12/A_Summary_of_the_evidence_on_inclusive_education.pdf. Accessed 1 July 2018

Kenny L, Hattersley C, Molins B, Buckley C, Povey C, Pellicano E (2016) Which terms should be used to describe autism? Perspectives from the UK autism community. Autism 20(4):442–462. The National Autistic Society

Kirkpatrick A, O'Connor J, Cooper M (2018) Web content accessibility guidelines (WCAG) 2.1. W3C Recommendation 5 June 2018. https://www.w3.org/TR/WCAG21/. Accessed 1 July 2018

Lazar J, Feng JH, Hochheiser H (2017) Research methods in human-computer interaction, 2nd edn. Morgan Kaufmann, Cambridge

Loftus E, Palmer J (1974) Reconstruction of automobile destruction: an example of the interaction between language and memory. J Verbal Learn Verbal Behav 13:585–589

National Center on Disability and Journalism (2018) Disability language style guide. http://ncdj.org/style-guide/. Accessed 2 July 2018

Seeman L, Cooper M (2015) Cognitive accessibility user research. W3C First Public Working Draft 15 January 2015 https://www.w3.org/TR/coga-userresearch/. Accessed 1 July 2018

Sears A, Hanson VL (2011) Representing users in accessibility research. In: Proceedings of the SIGCHI conference on human factors in computing systems (CHI '11). ACM, New York, NY, USA, pp 2235–2238. https://doi.org/10.1145/1978942.1979268

Smith M, Sharit J, Czaja S (1999) Aging, motor control, and the performance of computer mouse tasks. Hum Factors 41(3):389–396. https://doi.org/10.1518/001872099779611102

Trewin S, Richards JT, Hanson VL, Sloan D, John BE, Swart C, Thomas JC (2012) Understanding the role of age and fluid intelligence in information search. In: Proceedings of the 14th international ACM SIGACCESS conference on computers and accessibility (ASSETS '12). ACM, New York, NY, USA, pp 119–126. https://doi.org/10.1145/2384916.2384923

UN General Assembly (2007) Convention on the rights of persons with disabilities: resolution/adopted by the General Assembly, 24 Jan 2007, A/RES/61/106. Available at http://www.refworld.org/docid/45f973632.html. Accessed 3 July 2018

United Nations, Department of Economic and Social Affairs, Population Division (2015) World population ageing 2015 (ST/ESA/SER.A/390)

US Census Bureau (2016) 2016 American community survey 1-year estimates. https://factfinder.census.gov/bkmk/table/1.0/en/ACS/16_1YR/S181. Accessed 31 Aug 2018

White K, Abou-Zahra S, Henry SL (2016) Tips for getting started writing for web accessibility. Available at https://www.w3.org/WAI/tips/writing/. Accessed 31 Aug 2018

Yesilada Y, Brajnik G, Vigo M, Harper, S (2012) Understanding web accessibility and its drivers. In: Proceedings of the international cross-disciplinary conference on web accessibility (W4A '12). ACM, New York, NY, USA, Article 19, 9 pp. https://doi.org/10.1145/2207016.2207027

Chapter 9
Working With Participants

Christopher Power and Helen Petrie

Abstract Involving users in the design and evaluation of websites is one of the keys to ensuring they are accessible to as wide a range of people as possible. In this chapter, we present the core barriers and solutions that are often encountered by participants in user research activities that are undertaken as part of modern user-centred design processes. We close the chapter with a discussion of future areas of research around measurement of accessible user experiences and a short list of key things to remember when undertaking user research with people with disabilities.

9.1 Introduction

Working with users in a participatory, cooperative and meaningful way is now an important aspect of modern web design. Whether it is to understand the goals of users, co-design of new websites[1] or evaluate the experience users have with them, involving users in all stages of user research is vital. This increased emphasis on user research means we have to make our design processes inclusive and accessible as well.

When user researchers work with users as a regular part of their design work, it is essential to include people with disabilities and older adults. Inclusion at early stages of design shifts the discussion of accessibility away from being something that is done as a special case, as a niche design problem, or as something done after the fact, to being about designing for the diversity of users from the outset (Clarkson and Coleman 2015; Clarkson et al. 2013). From this diversity, there will come a variety of challenging and potentially conflicting requirements (Newell and Gregor

---

[1] In this chapter, we use website broadly to mean both more traditional content-heavy websites and more modern interactive web applications.

C. Power (✉) · H. Petrie
Department of Computer Science, University of York, York YO10 5GH, UK
e-mail: christopher.power@york.ac.uk

H. Petrie
e-mail: helen.petrie@york.ac.uk

© Springer-Verlag London Ltd., part of Springer Nature 2019
Y. Yesilada and S. Harper (eds.), *Web Accessibility*, Human–Computer Interaction Series, https://doi.org/10.1007/978-1-4471-7440-0_9

2000), and creative designs that are sensitive to those different needs are needed to resolve them. This is easier to do throughout a design process rather than as a later adjustment at the end of a design cycle.

When it comes to the evaluation of websites, there is a need for pragmatic yet robust user evaluation with people with disabilities and older adults to ensure that there are no barriers to using it for them Sears and Hanson (2011), Newell et al. (2007). Often this takes the form of checklists to ensure technical accessibility, and then collecting a broad set of problems that users encounter after technical accessibility has been achieved (Power and Petrie 2007; Power et al. 2012). However, it is not sufficient to just ensure that there are no barriers, it is necessary to understand the lived experience of people who use our websites, as to whether or not the planned accessible design choices actually meet their needs and preferences (Hedvall 2009a).

This chapter provides an overview of the common issues that researchers encounter in working with people with disabilities and older adults in user research along with solutions and hints regarding how to make user research activities more inclusive. We discuss activities that employ *generative user research methods*, which are intended to help inform design and *evaluative user research methods* that are used to evaluate technology. In this chapter, we do not aim to give complete details of the different methods, but will instead leave that to other authors within this volume for readers who want to read more about each of them. We aim to provide an overview of these methods such that they could fit in user-centred design processes which is a common framework of design processes used by many web designers. For those who work with other models such as design thinking (Brown 2009), or the double diamond (British Design Council 2007) or more holistic individual approaches (Hedvall 2009a), the framing we provide should be readily adaptable to any of those approaches.

9.2 General Advice

In this section, we discuss a wide range of issues that relate to working with participants no matter the activity you are undertaking or the setting in which researchers are conducting their sessions with people with disabilities. Specifically, we discuss the ethical conduct of working with participants, participant recruitment and engagement, the physical environments in which studies frequently occur, the preparation of alternative format or enhanced materials, the provision and support of individual assistance and issues of language relating to working with people with disabilities.

9.2.1 Ethical Conduct

Before starting any user research with people with disabilities, as with all research with humans or animals, ethical approval should always be should obtained for the activities to be undertaken. For researchers in universities and research institutes, this is standard practice and there are well-developed procedures for such approval. For commercial organisations undertaking user research, there may not be an appropriate authority to give ethical approval. In such cases, creative alternatives are needed. At the very least, the protocol for the research should be checked by someone in the organisation not involved in the research against an ethical research checklist (Rosnow and Rosenthal 2012). A larger organisation may be able to set up its own ethics committee with a combination of people from within the organisation and several 'critical friends' from outside the organisation. In addition, in some countries, some groups of people with disabilities (for example, those with intellectual disabilities) and older people are considered 'vulnerable' groups, so researchers and practitioners need to obtain specific approval for working with these groups. In the United Kingdom, this is a Disclosure and Barring Service Check Disclosure & Barring Service (2018).

9.2.2 Recruitment and Engagement

Recruiting sufficient numbers of participants from particular populations can be one of the most frustrating aspects of conducting user research with people with disabilities and older people. However, with some patience and persistence, this problem can be overcome. For participants with particular disabilities, there are often local or national organisations which can be approached. However, such organisations do not usually have large numbers of people from their particular group ready and waiting to be involved in research. It may be necessary to give a talk about the research at a general members meeting, take part in some of the organisation's activities or write a short article for a newsletter. These activities may seem time-consuming in the short term, but in the long term can build very valuable partnerships with such organisations. Once some participants are recruited and have been involved in research, snowball recruiting can be very valuable in expanding the pool of participants. This involves asking participants to suggest being involved in research to other people from the same group that they know. This is best done after an individual has been involved in some research and has hopefully found it an interesting experience, so can make a positive recommendation.

Recruiting older participants is somewhat easier, as there are many organisations of older people and many activities which attract older people which can help with recruitment. In addition, we have found that retired people are often curious about learning more about new technologies and are more flexible and giving with their free time. We have found that publicising our research through the local community centres, golf clubs and volunteer groups has been very helpful in recruiting older participants.

An important aspect of recruiting participants is to make the research an interesting experience for them. This may include explaining the background of the research, explaining the choice of methods used in the research and providing feedback after the research is complete about how it influenced the development of the system (for example, by providing a short report for participants). In addition, participants' should be offered a pleasant social experience, perhaps meeting a number of members of the organisation, having a tour of the organisation and appropriate refreshment breaks during the research session. Finally, appropriate recompense for the time and effort should be offered to participants. In cases where participants are working on site with us, we offer the equivalent to the salary we pay casual research assistants, as this is a very similar role being fulfilled by the participant. In some situations, such as for tax reasons, it is necessary to offer a gift voucher rather than cash, and many participants find this more appropriate. Some participants ask that their 'fee' get donated to a charity and if a user organisation or charity has helped recruit participants, we recommend researchers make a donation to that organisation as well.

When participants are recruited it is important to provide some information about what will be involved in participating in the research. Participants should be led through a *briefing*. This may involve some elaboration of the research goals but not revealing so much that it risks biasing the participants' reactions. For example, in our work researching at the strategies of people with disabilities on the web (Power et al. 2013), we had to be very careful while explaining to the participants that we wanted to understand how they browse the web, without revealing that we were looking at low-level interactions they were having with the web content. However, a fine balance must be struck where they are given sufficient information so they can give informed consent, and as such they must have a reasonable idea of what is going to happen and how they can withdraw or refrain from doing something they are asked to do. Further, participants should also understand what will happen to the data collected from them in the session, how it will be stored, for how long and who will have access to the data. When the participant is clear about all these aspects, they should be asked to sign an informed consent form to this effect.

At the end of the session, the participant should be *debriefed*. In particular, if there was anything which was not revealed in the briefing session, this should now be fully discussed with the participant and they should be given ample opportunity to ask questions or make comments about the research. This not only helps in creating an interesting experience for the participants, but can often reveal important information that was not gathered during the research session itself.[2]

9.3 Physical Setting

When conducting user research with people with disabilities and older people, it is particularly important to think about the physical setting of the session. Researchers should identify how participants will travel to the venue, whether public transport accessible to the participants, and whether they can they find their way from the

---

[2]*Note* If new information comes to light that researchers want to use as primary data as a result of these after session discussions, researchers should confirm with participants that they can indeed use it.

public transport to the exact location in the venue. Similarly, if participants come by taxi, participants need to be able to make the journey from the taxi into the venue. Taxi drivers have been known to drop blind participants outside a large university building with instructions 'it's over there'.

For participants with mobility disabilities, researchers should ensure that lifts[3] are available and that there are no stairs impeding entrances to rooms. The most embarrassing moment in the research career of one of the authors was when a wheelchair using participant finished an evaluation at about 5:30 pm in a room on an upper floor of a university building. It was discovered only then that the lifts in the building were turned off at 5 pm, something the researcher had never realised. No porters or security staff could be found, so eventually two very strong Ph.D. students carried the participant in his wheelchair down the stairs. So a careful pilot of the physical facilities, at the appropriate times of day is always reassuring. Researchers need to ensure that surfaces are such that they can navigate easily (i.e. no heavy carpet) and that there is sufficient clearance for wheelchair access in both the doors and the interior furniture. Finally, researchers should ensure that there are displays, surfaces and/or materials at a height that is accessible for participants who use wheelchairs so they can participate in the full range of research activities.

9.3.1 Preparation of Materials

When conducting different user research activities, some research participants will require alternative or enhanced formats for different types of media or communication that are used before, during or after the actual sessions.

Participants with print disabilities (e.g. people who are blind, have low vision or have dyslexia) often need different formats or alternatives to print materials. This can include large print, wider line spacing, alternative colour schemes or in some cases Braille transcriptions. It is also important to remember that participants who are pre-lingually Deaf (that is were born Deaf or lost their hearing before they acquired spoken language) may be reading text in a second language (their first language being a sign language), and so they may need simpler written materials than other participants.

However, which specific alternative formats are required are specific to the individual participating, and so it is vital to ask as a matter of course which format individuals would prefer. In general, we have also found it useful, where possible, to provide information ahead of time instead of on the day of the session. This gives participants not only the opportunity to check to ensure the format meets their needs but also gives them the opportunity to review the documents ahead of time for preparation for sessions (Kroll et al. 2007). A common omission made by new researchers is to not provide information sheets, consent forms or recruitment notices in alternative formats as researchers tend to focus on the main protocol materials.

---

[3]Elevators for some of our readers!

If sessions include any audio material, it is necessary to provide at a minimum a transcript of that material for people with hearing disabilities, and if using video it is preferable to provide captioning of video content, and if working with participants who are blind, audio description, which describes what is happening in the visual content of the video, may be necessary to fully explain video content.

9.3.2   Individual Assistance

Participants may wish to bring someone to assist them in research sessions. In some cases, this will be one or more professional personal assistants who are employed by individuals to assist in their day-to-day care. In other cases, participants may bring a family member or close friend acting as a carer, guardian or providing other needed support.

For participants who are Deaf, it is important to establish what their level of competence in the spoken language is and whether they would be more comfortable with a sign language interpreter. An important misconception of newcomers to accessibility research is that people who are Deaf and use sign language will bring their own sign language interpreter with them. However, if working with sign language using people who are Deaf, researchers should arrange for appropriate interpreters to attend activity sessions. It is important to spend some time with the interpreters before the sessions, briefing them on any technical words or concepts which will be used, so they can be confident in interpreting.

In each of these cases, when planning user research activities, researchers should plan for refreshments and meals for those individuals, as well as for the participants, and provide places where they can wait comfortably if they are not going to be present in the planned activity sessions all the time. Some participants may bring a service animal, often a guide dog, with them. In these cases, most service animals will wait patiently with their owner until they are needed. However, providing a water bowl and identifying a place where the animal can have a comfort break would be appreciated by both the participant and the service animal!

9.3.3   Language

Researchers who are new to working with people with disabilities often are concerned about how to discuss a participant's disability or refer to groups of people with disabilities. This section is specifically about the use of language when working with people with disabilities, for purposes of writing inclusively, please refer to the chapter on inclusive writing in this volume.

In general, people should not be referred to by their medical condition (e.g. having glaucoma or cerebral palsy) except in specific medical contexts or if it is directly relevant to the research at hand. Further, the accessibility research field has evolved so that we do not refer to people as having specific functional limitations (e.g. visual impairment). The reason for this is that we are almost always discussing individuals' capabilities in relation to technology and whether the technology meets their needs and preferences. Thus, in this chapter, we adopt the 'people first' language of disability, such as referring to people with visual disabilities or people with learning disabilities. In particular, many people find it offensive to be identified just by their disability or group. So avoid using terms such as 'the blind', 'dyslexics' or 'the elderly'. However, we recommend that when working with individuals and their identity as a person with a disability that researchers ask as to how that person would like to be referred as there can be many cultural and individual differences.

On a related point, when preparing materials for evaluations, researchers need to think carefully about terms used such as information sheets, consent forms and other materials. References to 'clicking' on particular components of a website assumes the use of a mouse, while statements that orient by direction, such as 'using the box below', assume participants can get a visual overview of the two-dimensional nature of the screen. Care should be taken to check materials for such language prior to sessions and in pilot trials of studies.

9.4 Generative User Research

With the above general guidance in mind, we now turn to the methodologies for understanding users and their needs and preferences. There are a wide variety of user research methodologies used across the field of human–computer interaction (HCI) that can be applied in web accessibility studies. However, broadly speaking, there is a common set that reoccurs across both research and practice on web accessibility. While there are more contextual design-based methods or ethnographic methods that could be applied (Holtzblatt and Beyer 2016), in general, there are few examples of these being used in web accessibility research. Therefore, in this section, we focus on three different and distinct methods such as online questionnaires, interviews and focus groups.

9.4.1 Questionnaires

In user research, questionnaires represent one of the most efficient ways to collect data from users. A well-crafted questionnaire distributed on the web could net a user researcher many dozens or hundreds of responses from across a wide range of people with disabilities or older people. However, there are a number of common pitfalls that can be encountered by researchers.

First, the survey platform itself needs to be technically accessible, meaning it complies with necessary web standards so that users of assistive technologies can successfully engage with the questions. Fortunately, many surveys now claim to be compliant with technical accessibility standards; however, the coverage of accessibility standards is varied at the time of writing across products. For example, Qualtrics (2018) and SurveyMonkey (2018) both provide statements that a set of their templates comply to both WCAG 2.0 and Section 508, with WebAIM (2018) providing external validation of this claim at the time of writing. Similarly, QuestionPro (2018) claims to meet Section 508. SnapSurveys (2018) claims compliance to 'web accessibility guidelines' and Section 508, but on further investigation the guidelines compliance is to WCAG 1.0. Google Forms (Google 2018), one of the widely used free survey platforms, offers no statement about accessibility conformance, but does state that their forms can be used with screen readers for both creation of and responses to questionnaires. However, like many systems that allow content creation by non-technical authors Sloan et al. (2006), Power and Petrie (2007), Power et al. (2010), such compliance statements largely only apply if the authors ensure that the content is accessible. Common problems often encountered in surveys by participants with disabilities and older adults that we have noted include the following:

- Logos and other images lacking alternative descriptions, which means they are inaccessible to screen reader users.
- Buttons not being labelled with words like Previous, Next and Done, but which instead have caret characters such as '≫' or '≪' that are misread by screen readers.
- Generic error messages on each question which result in users being disorientated, being unable to link specific error messages to specific questions.
- Questionnaires with an autoscroll feature, usually question by question, which result in a variety of barriers related to users either not having control of what is in their viewport on a screen magnifier, or requiring extra key presses for people using keyboard navigation.
- Poor layout of questions which results in large gaps between question text and interactive elements of the question.
- Exceptionally long or complicated texts which are inaccessible to a variety of users with learning disabilities, cognitive disabilities or those who have lower literacy.
- Questions without numbers, which prevent individuals from being able to orient themselves within the survey.

Even if all the above problems have been avoided, it is valuable to check the questionnaire with a screen reader and using keyboard only navigation to ensure that there are no unexpected problems in a template due to the content that was added to it.

9.4.2 Interviews and Focus Groups

While questionnaires can provide a good means of gathering large amounts of information quickly, during the initial stages of user research, it can be difficult to contextualise the data collected either due to the quantitative nature of much of the data collected, and the tendency for participants to not answer more broad and open answered questions. In these cases, supplementary information will often be gathered through interviews or focus groups. Focus groups in particular are useful for starting a co-design process with target users, ideating around possible design ideas for a particular website.

In terms of the practicalities of focus groups, much of the advice discussed in other sections of this chapter are relevant such as making sure the venue and all materials such as consent forms are accessible to the participants. In addition, there needs to be careful consideration of how the interaction will work. People with visual disabilities may not necessarily pick up non-verbal cues about when it is appropriate to start speaking, so the facilitator may need to be more directive than usual in guiding people when to speak and not letting people speak over each other (which renders a recording of the discussion difficult to transcribe). Focus group facilitators sometimes use visual aids in focus groups, such as a list of topics on a large flip chart or screen, and these need alternatives with participants with visual disabilities. Participants who are Deaf may have an interpreter and the logistics of including an interpreter and the additional time that may add to the focus group need to be considered. Balch and Mertens (1999) provide excellent guidance on conducting focus groups with participants who are Deaf or have hard of hearing. Similarly, Kaehne and O'Connell (2010) provide useful information about conducting focus groups with participants with learning disabilities and Prior et al. (2013) provide useful information about conducting focus groups with participants with profound speech and physical disabilities.

While it may seem economic and interesting to include people with different disabilities in the same focus group, we have found that this can be problematic both practically and in terms of the content elicited. In practical terms, mixing participants with different sensory disabilities can create challenges. For example, a participant who is blind cannot see when an interpreter is signing and may talk over them. Similarly, we have encountered situations where a participant who was blind found it confusing when a participant who was Deaf had a person of a different gender interpreting their sign language to spoken language. More generally, the pace of discussion with participants with different communication needs can be quite variable, and mixing participants who need different paces can cause confusion and frustration within the group.

In terms of content elicited, because different groups of participants may have different issues with websites and use different assistive technologies to access the web, mixed focus groups can become discussions explaining the issues and technologies to each other. In some circumstances, this could be interesting and useful, but in other circumstances, it can take away valuable time in a discussion that could be about a topic the user researcher wishes to understand.

One key question about focus groups is how many participants to include. Recommendations for focus groups in general range widely from 3 to 12 people (Preece et al. 2015; Lazar et al. 2017; Adams and Cox 2008). Number of participants is always a balance between getting views from a range of individuals versus having enough time for each individual to express their views on the various topics of interest. Sani et al. (2016) investigated the effects of small (3–4 participants) versus larger (6–7 participants) focus groups with older participants across several technology-related topics. They found that the number of contributions per participant was much higher in the small focus groups (42.5 contributions/participant) compared to the larger groups (25.3 contributions/participant). However, the number of different contributions in a given amount of time was much higher in the larger focus groups (larger: 20.5 contributions/10 min, small: 14.3 contributions/10 min). This suggests that if user researcher is looking for depth of information, then small focus groups are probably preferable, whereas for breadth of views, larger groups are probably preferable.

Interviews with participants with disabilities or older adults are generally an easier proposition. The usual procedures for interviews should be followed, with additional considerations as discussed on other sections of this chapter in relation to the preparation of materials, venue and language.

9.5 Evaluative User Research

Evaluations of websites are a key activity undertaken for a variety of different purposes. In some cases, researchers are undertaking formative evaluations to collect information from participants in order to refine the design through an iterative design cycle. In other cases, researchers are conducting summative evaluations of a website collecting information about a variety of usability and user experience measures of a nearly finished website. Finally, researchers may also be conducting experiments or other types of studies to try to understand the impact of different design choices on the experiences of different groups of people with disabilities or older adults, which can use techniques from either formative or summative evaluations.

For any of the above, the first step is to make sure that the website has a sufficient level of accessibility that it can be used by the participants involved in the test. This sounds like a bit of a paradox: having to do accessibility testing in order to do accessibility testing! However, if a participant is unable to even get started on a website during an evaluation, then both the participants' time and researchers' time are wasted. For example, consider the example of testing a new editor in a virtual learning environment with screen reader users, or any user who navigates with a keyboard (Power et al. 2010). If it is impossible to reach the component of the web page where someone needs to enter text because it is either not in the tab order or entirely inaccessible by keyboard, then the test cannot succeed in collecting any meaningful data about the editor itself. As such, it is necessary that any website that will be used in evaluations be tested for technical accessibility and, preferably, confirmed to be compatible with key assistive technologies.

If an evaluation is going to be conducted in a user experience laboratory or other settings other than the participant's own home or work or study venue, it is often impossible for participants to bring their own equipment with them for use in an evaluation. It is important to identify during recruitment what different types of technology participants use and ensure that it is installed and thoroughly tested on any systems used in evaluative research studies. For testing websites, this includes both the browser and the participants' preferred assistive technologies. Further, prior to undertaking any tasks specifically related to research questions, participants need to be given the opportunity to configure different pieces of technology such that they are comfortable working with the equipment. Exact replication of their home, work or study systems is unlikely to be possible all the time.

Alternatively, researchers can conduct remote evaluations with participants, which requires less setup, configuration and travel on the part of the participants; however, some control is then given up by the researcher. These types of evaluations can be done either asynchronously, where participants conduct evaluations and then send in results to the researcher or in situations where qualitative or observational data is required, synchronously through online meeting services (Brush et al. 2004; Petrie et al. 2006; Bruun et al. 2009; Power et al. 2011). When conducting remote evaluations or any kind, it is important that participants be given appropriate training material in advance of any testing, along with additional support in installing any extra software or settings on their systems (Petrie et al. 2006).

In formative evaluations, in which participants are documenting user problems on websites, it is common to use a concurrent verbal protocol (CVP) or a retrospective verbal protocol (RVP), where the most recent research with participants who are not disabled indicates CVP is generally superior to RVP (Alhadreti and Mayhew 2018). However, when working with blind users, RVP appears to reveal more user problems relating to users interacting with a website, as opposed to content or information architecture problems (Savva et al. 2016). However, the workload in RVP is substantially higher, even when taking into account the offloading of concurrent problem identification. As such, if tasks are particularly long, RVP may result in fatigue in participants (Savva et al. 2015).

Researchers use summative evaluations to collect a wide variety of different performance and reference information in relation to their websites. This can include task success rates, efficiency, standardised scales or more complex measures such as mental and physical workload in the NASA Task Load Index (Hart 2006).

However, while there can be some challenges related to providing these different measures in an accessible way (e.g. reading off pairwise comparisons in the NASA-TLX which can be time-consuming and potentially fatiguing for participants), the more important challenge of this type of research is in interpreting the data. For example, consider an evaluation of a search system in which data is collected from both screen reader participants and sighted participants using a keyboard and mouse on a variety of website designs. It is likely that screen reader users will be slower to interact with a website, meaning intergroup comparisons may not be valuable in answering research questions except in very specific cases.

A similar problem occurs when researchers use standardised scales about usability such as the SUPR-Q (Sauro 2015) or other user experience measures. Many of these scales have not been validated with people with disabilities, and given the lived experiences of people with disabilities are very different than those of their non-disabled peers, it can be very difficult to predict how these scales will perform, and may be of questionable value if comparing between groups. As a result, these sorts of measures should be used with caution by user researchers when drawing conclusions about the interactions of particular groups of participants (Cairns and Power 2018).

9.6 Discussion

In the above sections, we have discussed how to involve participants with disabilities in both generative and evaluative research. Many of the challenges, such as recruiting participants, preparing rigorous studies and ensuring research is undertaken in a careful and considered way that respects the dignity of the participants, are common across all user research. When working with participants with disabilities, we must consider the point of view of those participants who need adjustments and accommodations in both the physical and digital environments to ensure that the methods we use are accessible as possible.

We will now explore some of the future directions that user research methodologies can take in the next decade of web accessibility and beyond.

9.7 Future Directions

There are a variety of open questions in both generative and evaluative user research methodologies for working with participants with disabilities and older participants that should be explored.

In generative research, there are open questions about how key data collection instruments, be they Likert items or more complex measurement scales, interact with the modalities in which they are presented. For example, when translating a list of items from visual presentation into audio, is there a primacy effect for the first item or a recency effect for the last? How can we detect such effects and are there ways to mitigate them if they do indeed exist?

More urgently, as emphasis for web design continues to push to be more participatory, with co-design being common, we need exemplar research methods that allow different groups of people with disabilities to participate. For example, what are appropriate and acceptable ways to include people with disabilities who have different needs and preferences in activities like affinity diagrams, empathy maps or scenario generation, all of which involve a great deal of collaboration, movement around a space and working with post-its or other types of visual materials? Currently, there are few examples in website design research and practice.

In evaluative research, the big open questions revolve around how we capture the accessible user experiences of people with disabilities on websites (Horton and Quesenbery 2014). It is largely an open question about what are the important measures to capture about the experiences of our users. The measures that are captured currently still largely reflect traditional usability measures, such as task success and speed to completion, with the occasional capture of workload measures. Even with these measures, there is a lack of consensus of what is considered 'good' or 'acceptable' for different groups of users with disabilities and older users, and increasingly it is thought that these experiences are individual to users, and are deeply influenced by the interaction between technical accessibility and the lived experiences of users (Power et al. 2018; Magnusson et al. 2018; Hedvall 2009b). For example, Sayago and Blat (2008) found that older people were not concerned about how fast they could interact with technologies, but were very concerned about not making errors, with quite a different pattern of attitudes compared to younger people. Further, there is a lack of comparison between different domains to nuance that discussion. For example, one would expect that users would want to ensure near 100% completion rates for banking, but the occasional problem when surfing Wikipedia for leisure may be more tolerable, or perhaps not, as the case may be.

Beyond these questions, there is an open question of what are the key experiential measures that should be used on the web with people with disabilities. While there is clearly a link between accessibility of an experience, there is substantial work to be done in identifying which are the experiential indicators that will help drive design for web professionals (Aizpurua et al 2015).

All of these questions are fertile areas for new researchers to improve our user research practices in web accessibility.

9.8 Author's Opinions on the Field

Often in accessibility work, we encounter work that has not involved participants with disabilities in the generative or evaluative research on the web. The reasons for this are many and varied, but a common refrain is that it is either too difficult or too time-consuming to work with people with disabilities as part of a research plan. We believe that it is essential that this attitude change across web accessibility. In order for web accessibility to continue to move forward, we need far more in-depth work with participants with disabilities.

We encourage user researchers reading this chapter who have never worked with people with disabilities or older adults to rise to this challenge and enjoy the opportunity of working with these distinctive groups of participants. Working with participants with disabilities and older adults in the design process often presents some of the most challenging and interesting design opportunities for the web. Similarly, an evaluation of a new website that yields a positive and accessible user experience can be equally one of the most rewarding and satisfying experiences that web designers will have in their career.

9.9 Conclusions

Increasingly, web design employs both generative and evaluative user research to provide rich experiences to their users. Working with users with disabilities and older users throughout the user research activities in the design process is essential to ensuring a truly accessible website. The following is a short list of key things that user researchers should keep in mind when working with people with disabilities and older users as part of their user research activities which include the following:

- Always treat participants with respect and dignity from initial recruitment to the closing of your research activities. This includes ensuring ethical treatment of participants, using user-sensitive language, paying fair remuneration for their time and ensuring that the facilities are supportive of their needs and the needs of their assistants, if appropriate.
- Anticipate the needs and preferences of participants for alternative format materials well before they arrive, seeking preferences from participants regarding how they will interact with materials in your studies.
- Ensure all websites meet at bare minimum technical accessibility standards and preferably testing with a number of different assistive technologies prior to the start of a study.
- Identify what methods and measures will best support gathering the data needed for making your website as accessible as possible, including whether participants need to be locally supported in a lab or if a remote evaluation is possible in an individual's home environment.

Acknowledgements The authors would like to thank the hundreds of participants who have worked with us over the years in making the web a more inclusive place for people with disabilities and older adults.

References

Adams A, Cox A (2008) Questionnaires, in-depth interviews and focus groups. In: Cairns P, Cox A (eds) Research methods for human computer interaction. Cambridge University Press, Cambridge, pp 17–34

Aizpurua A, Arrue M, Vigo M (2015) Prejudices, memories, expectations and confidence influence experienced accessibility on the Web. Comput Hum Behav 51:152–160

Alhadreti O, Mayhew P (2018) Rethinking thinking aloud: a comparison of three think-aloud protocols. In: Proceedings of the 2018 CHI conference on human factors in computing system. ACM, Providence, p 44

Balch GI, Mertens DM (1999) Focus group design and group dynamics: lessons from deaf and hard of hearing participants. Am J Eval 20(2):265–277

British Design Council (2007) Eleven lessons: managing design in eleven global companies-desk research report. British Design Council

Brown T (2009) Change by design. Harper Collins, New York City

Brush A, Ames M, Davis J (2004) A comparison of synchronous remote and local usability studies for an expert interface. In: CHI'04 extended abstracts on human factors in computing systems. ACM, Providence, pp 1179–1182

Bruun A, Gull P, Hofmeister L, Stage J (2009) Let your users do the testing: a comparison of three remote asynchronous usability testing methods. In: Proceedings of the SIGCHI conference on human factors in computing systems. ACM, Providence, pp 1619–1628

Cairns P, Power C (2018) Measuring experiences. New directions in third wave human-computer interaction: volume 2-methodologies. Springer, Berlin, pp 62–80

Clarkson PJ, Coleman R (2015) History of inclusive design in the UK. Appl Ergon 46:235–247

Clarkson PJ, Coleman R, Keates S, Lebbon C (2013) Inclusive design: design for the whole population. Springer Science & Business Media, Berlin

Disclosure & Barring Service (2018) https://www.gov.uk/government/organisations/disclosure-and-barring-service. Accessed 1 Sept 2018

Google (2018) https://www.google.co.uk/forms/. Accessed 1 Sept 2018

Hart SG (2006) NASA-task load index (NASA-TLX); 20 years later. In: Proceedings of the human factors and ergonomics society annual meeting. Sage Publications, Los Angeles, pp 904–908

Hedvall PO (2009a) The activity diamond: modeling an enhanced accessibility. Lund University, Certec-Department of Design Sciences, LTH

Hedvall PO (2009b) Towards the era of mixed reality: accessibility meets three waves of HCI. Symposium of the Austrian HCI and usability engineering group. Springer, Berlin, pp 264–278

Holtzblatt K, Beyer H (2016) Contextual design: design for life. Morgan Kaufmann, Burlington

Horton S, Quesenbery W (2014) A web for everyone: Designing accessible user experiences. Rosenfeld Media

Kaehne A, O'Connell C (2010) Focus groups with people with learning disabilities. J Intellect Disabil 14(2):133–145

Kroll T, Barbour R, Harris J (2007) Using focus groups in disability research. Qual Health Res 17(5):690–698

Lazar J, Feng JH, Hochheiser H (2017) Research methods in human-computer interaction. Morgan Kaufmann, Burlington

Magnusson C, Hedvall PO, Breidegard B (2018) Design for me? In: International conference on computers helping people with special needs. Springer, Berlin, pp 93–99

Newell AF, Gregor P (2000) "User sensitive inclusive design"—in search of a new paradigm. In: Proceedings on the 2000 conference on universal usability. ACM, Providence, pp 39–44

Newell A, Arnott J, Carmichael A, Morgan M (2007) Methodologies for involving older adults in the design process. In: International conference on universal access in human-computer interaction. Springer, Berlin, pp 982–989

Petrie H, Hamilton F, King N, Pavan P (2006) Remote usability evaluations with disabled people. In: Proceedings of the SIGCHI conference on human factors in computing systems - CHI '06, p 1133. https://doi.org/10.1145/1124772.1124942

Power C, Petrie H (2007) Accessibility in non-professional web authoring tools: a missed web 2.0 opportunity? In: Proceedings of the 2007 international cross-disciplinary conference on Web accessibility (W4A). ACM, Providence, pp 116–119

Power C, Petrie H, Sakharov V, Swallow D (2010) Virtual learning environments: another barrier to blended and e-learning. In: International conference on computers for handicapped persons. Springer, Berlin, pp 519–526

Power C, Petrie H, Freire AP, Swallow D (2011) Remote evaluation of wcag 2.0 techniques by web users with visual disabilities. In: International conference on universal access in human-computer interaction. Springer, Berlin, pp 285–294

Power C, Freire A, Petrie H, Swallow D (2012) Guidelines are only half of the story: accessibility problems encountered by blind users on the web. In: Proceedings of the SIGCHI conference on human factors in computing systems. ACM, Providence, pp 433–442

Power C, Petrie H, Swallow D, Murphy E, Gallagher B, Velasco CA (2013) Navigating, discovering and exploring the web: strategies used by people with print disabilities on interactive websites. In: IFIP conference on human-computer interaction, Springer, Berlin, pp 667–684

Power C, Cairns P, Barlet M (2018) Inclusion in the third wave: access to experience. In: New directions in third wave human-computer interaction: volume 1-technologies. Springer, Berlin, pp 163–181

Preece J, Rogers Y, Sharp H (2015) Interaction design: beyond human-computer interaction. Wiley, New York

Prior S, Waller A, Kroll T (2013) Focus groups as a requirements gathering method with adults with severe speech and physical impairments. Behav Inf Technol 32(8):752–760

Qualtrics (2018). http://www.qualtrics.com. Accessed 1 Sept 2018

QuestionPro (2018). http://questionpro.com/. Accessed 1 Sept 2018

Rosnow RL, Rosenthal R (2012) Beginning behavioral research: a conceptual primer, 7th edn. Pearson, London

Sani ZH, Petrie H, Swallow D, Lewis A (2016) Three case studies on methods of working with older people on the design of new technologies. Stud Health Technol Inf 229:153–164

Sauro J (2015) SUPR-Q: a comprehensive measure of the quality of the website user experience. J Usability Stud 10(2):68–86. http://www.upassoc.org

Savva A, Petrie H, Power C (2015) Comparing concurrent and retrospective verbal protocols for blind and sighted users. In: Human-computer interaction. Springer, Berlin, pp 55–71

Savva A, Petrie H, Power C (2016) Types of problems elicited by verbal protocols for blind and sighted participants. In: International conference on computers helping people with special needs. Springer, Berlin, pp 560–567

Sayago S, Blat J (2008) Exploring the role of time and errors in real-life usability for older people and ict. In: International conference on computers for handicapped persons. Springer, Berlin, pp 46–53

Sears A, Hanson V (2011) Representing users in accessibility research. In: Proceedings of the SIGCHI conference on Human factors in computing systems. ACM, Providence, pp 2235–2238

Sloan D, Stratford J, Gregor P (2006) Using multimedia to enhance the accessibility of the learning environment for disabled students: reflections from the skills for access project. ALT-J 14(1):39–54

SnapSurveys (2018). https://www.snapsurveys.com/. Accessed 1 Sept 2018

SurveyMonkey (2018). http://www.surveymonkey.com. Accessed 1 Sept 2018

WebAIM, (2018) Qualtrics survey platform: accessibility certification. https://webaim.org/services/certification/qualtrics. Accessed 1 Sept 2018

Chapter 10
Working with Companies, Charities and Governmental Organisations

Andrew Arch, Lisa Seeman, Sarah Pulis and Glenda Sims

Abstract While discussing how government, charities and companies can work together, this chapter particularly describes how researchers can work with people with disabilities and disability organisations to create more inclusive research. It addresses issues for people working on general research that need to address the needs of real people as well as research focusing on disability. Ultimately, the aim should be to incorporate people with disabilities as participants and stakeholders in all areas of research.

10.1 Introduction

In this chapter, we discuss some of the issues and advantages of conducting research with the private sector and disability organisation as partners as well as discussing public–private partnerships. This chapter particularly focuses on how to conduct research that includes disability organisations and individuals with disabilities. It includes guidance and advice on working with users with disabilities for research studies. This chapter also addresses some of the pitfalls and challenges faced by the research community in inclusive research, and the risks to emerging technologies and society if these are not addressed.

The need to include people with disabilities in research is paramount. If the actual users are not included then their needs and practical requirements will not be ade-

A. Arch (✉) · S. Pulis
Intopia, Parramatta, NSW 2150, Australia
e-mail: andrew@intopia.digital

S. Pulis
e-mail: sarah@intopia.digital

L. Seeman
Athena ICT, Jerusalem, Israel
e-mail: lisa.seeman@zoho.com

G. Sims (✉)
Deque Systems, Inc., Austin, TX, USA
e-mail: glenda.sims@deque.com

© Springer-Verlag London Ltd., part of Springer Nature 2019
Y. Yesilada and S. Harper (eds.), *Web Accessibility*, Human–Computer
Interaction Series, https://doi.org/10.1007/978-1-4471-7440-0_10

quately represented in the outcomes. Arguably, research is a pillar for new ideas, directions and developments in society. Hence, the more that people with disabilities are involved in research the more inclusive our society will become.

Ideas that benefit people with disability and older people with impairments often also benefit the rest of the community and can have commercial benefits. A three-way partnership between academia, the commercial sector and disability organisations enables developing a research question and solutions that meet the needs of people with disability and can contribute to a more inclusive society.

10.2 Building a Public–Private Partnership

Public–private partnerships (PPPs) bring stakeholders from different sectors and disciplines together to solve complex issues and drive innovation. Theoretically, this should be the perfect environment for fostering inclusive research and innovation. It is likely that people with disabilities will have more ideas of what can be done to improve life for all citizens, including during times of stress and ill health. People with disabilities are often early adopters of new technologies and supports, so their participation in these partnerships seems to be a classic example of where diversity can benefit all participants. In practice, however, PPPs do not often include people with disabilities.

Hubs that recruit and encourage citizens' participation are often not inclusive. People with disabilities may be unable to easily participate or feel unwelcome when doing so.

For public–private partnerships to approach their potential, it is essential for people with disabilities and other disadvantaged citizens to participate. Many of the ideas below on inclusive research cultures can help as can the section on building in the user. Making sure social media and outreach initiatives are accessible and easy to use is part of that or people with disabilities will be unaware of the initiatives that exist. When they are aware, offering to provide support for people with disabilities in any public invitations will let them know that they are welcome. Actively encouraging people with disabilities is also important, doing this via disability organisations' social media channels and support groups that focus on needs for people with disabilities is often effective.

All PPPs should consistently check that feedback is being received from people in different disability groups (such as different vision impairments, hearing impairments, cognitive and learning disabilities, mobility impairments, and neurodiversity and mental health). A lack of feedback often stems from inaccessible communications channels or feedback mechanisms that are hard to use by people with disabilities. Important input and feedback are thus not collected and people with disability are left out of the conversation. The result is a failure of the goals of many PPPs.

10.3   Partnering with Corporate

Engaging corporate organisations in inclusive research often requires aligning research aims with corporate goals. For example, a corporation focused on gaining market share or improving their value proposition is unlikely to be energised by arguments that only focus on moral need. A corporate partner will usually require strong evidence-based research hypotheses and statistics that help ground the research.

There is a strong business case for organisations understanding and solving problems for people with disability (see Rush 2018). One example is ageing. Ageing is often accompanied by impairment or disability such as age-related forgetfulness, declining strength and dexterity, and declining vision and hearing. This market is always worth corporate attention with most countries experiencing ageing populations as discussed at length in Chap. 7. The proportion of the world's population over 60 years is expected to nearly double in the next 15 years. Germany has forecast 30% of its population will be over 65 by 2050 and Japan has forecast 40%. Furthermore, 70% of the disposable income in the US is in the hands of the mature market. Making this an essential market and enabling autonomy as we age is clearly an essential human need.

Solving problems for people with disabilities can also be part of a long-term strategy of solving the hard problems; necessity is the mother of invention. Having a real-life problem to solve has always enabled innovation. Finding ways to drive innovation can be a challenge.

The Microsoft Inclusive Design toolkit (Microsoft 2018) focuses on three principles of inclusive design: recognise exclusion, learn from diversity and solve for one, extend to many. Finding solutions for people with disability has led to technology innovations that have become everyday products.

For example, speech and voice commands were originally used for the vision impaired to enable them to use visual interfaces. Pull down kitchen shelving, draws in freezers and large handles on kitchen utensils are design examples that originated from enabling people with disabilities. Rose (2018) spoke about disability as a driver of innovation at UX Australia in 2018.

Once the technology is used by this fast adoption market, it is relatively easy to pivot the innovation to new markets.

10.4   Partnering with Government

Many governments are investing significantly in independent living research as they face ageing populations. As discussed in detail in Chap. 7, ageing often brings many forms of impairment and disability and there are many funded opportunities to undertake significant research in this area as discussed above.

In recognition of the value of PPPs, many government research funds around the world like the Australian Research Council (ARC) now strongly encourage partnerships between researchers and industry, government and community organisations. Including people with disabilities on the research team *and* in the user research can best fulfil this requirement.

10.5 Partnering with Disability Organisations

Accessibility research that includes people with disabilities at all phases can lead to valuable data and deeper insights. All accessibility research activities benefit from inclusion of people with disabilities. Examples of research activities include the following:

- Design of the research study—researchers with disabilities can be an important part of overcoming implicit and unconscious bias in the design of the research study itself. See 'There's gender bias in medical research. Here are 3 keys to fixing it' (Berg 2018) for similar challenges and opportunities in medical research and 'Technically Wrong' (Wachter-Boettcher 2018) for a broader discussion of bias.
- Participate as a test subject in the research study—for valid research, real people with real disabilities must be the active test participants. A person simulating a disability (for example, a sighted person wearing a blindfold) is not credible. A person without a disability claiming to represent a group of people with disability may have personal insights to contribute, but again is not fully credible.
- Analyse the data and write the research study report—a researcher with a disability brings a vast amount of experience and in-depth understanding from their life experiences. Their expertise in living with a disability can help unearth subtle data patterns that a researcher without disabilities may miss. See 'Research to Action: Partnering with people with disabilities for research' (Centre for Applied Disability Research undated) for details including improved data analysis, increased quality and validity.

10.6 Creating an Inclusive Research Culture

An inclusive research culture should consist of including diverse users in your research team *and* conducting research with diverse users to be sure the widest range of possible needs are considered. This approach should also enable you to develop good partnerships with disability organisations that represent the people with disability you are interested in researching with.

10.6.1   Commitment and Common Understanding

Your organisation may already have formal, or informal, inclusion or accessibility policies that you should familiarise yourself with initially. They may also have policies around the employment of people with disability that could also be useful for engagement of people with disability as part of your team. Additionally, many countries have legal requirements around accessibility as discussed in Chap. 15 and captured in 'Web Accessibility Laws and Policies' (Mueller et al. 2018).

Many large organisations, including educational institutions, will have disability champions (e.g. Australian Public Service) and/or disability networks that research teams should also liaise with as part of the organisation's ongoing commitment. Some organisations will also be members of disability forums that can support your organisation (e.g. Australian Network on Disabilities and the UK Business Disability Forum). These internal teams or external organisations might also be able to connect you with users to participate in your research from within your organisation and from the broader community.

As part of your research planning, you also need to have a common understanding of the people you want to include in your research. This may extend beyond people with disability to include other groups in the community that experience similar issues due to the environment, education, culture, etc. For example, reach can be an issue for people of short stature as well for people in wheelchairs; reading may be an issue for refugees as well as those with learning or cognitive disabilities.

From a research standpoint, diversity and inclusion should go beyond disability needs and include a more diverse range of people as given below:

- older people who may have age-related impairments that are not necessarily considered as having a disability,
- people from different countries who may have language difficulties as well as people with learning difficulties,
- people from different cultures who may not understand local cultural nuances as well as autistic people,
- people experiencing injury or illness which could lead to temporary or ongoing disabilities,
- people who have limited access to technology due to affordability and
- people with mental health, emotional issues, and other neurological conditions.

From a digital standpoint, inclusion should go beyond technical conformance with international standards such as the Web Content Access Guidelines to effectiveness, efficiency and satisfactory experience for all. Abou-Zahra and Brewer sum this up nicely in Chap. 14:

> …accessibility is more than the standards and guidelines. In fact, accessibility is the societal inclusion of people with disabilities, rather than merely the technical solutions that are part of inclusion.

10.6.2   Infrastructure

For successful and collaborative partnership or research, all new and existing infrastructure must be inclusive. This includes buildings, facilities and communication and collaboration tools.

The following lists are provided to help the reader provide an accessible environment:

Accessible buildings and facilities include the following:

- ensuring buildings have accessible entrances and interiors and people with disabilities can access all shared spaces such as kitchens or meeting rooms;
- providing access to facilities such as accessible and inclusive toilets, buttons that are easily findable, highly visible, tactile, understandable and within reach for all;
- providing technology aids such as hearing loops.

Accessible communication, collaboration and information include the following:

- ensuring communication, authoring and presentation tools such as email, document creation and software for conferencing and collaboration are accessible;
- training teams in accessible content creation, and working with individuals on the format that best meets their needs and preferences;
- ensuring internal tools such as human resources, finance and organisation information including intranets are accessible;
- acquiring survey and analytical tools that can be used by everyone.

Often the provision of accessible infrastructure becomes a procurement issue and standards or local requirements such as Section 508 (section508.gov) and the European accessibility requirements for ICT products and services adopted by Europe and Australia (EN 301 549 from ETSI) can assist.

10.7   Building the User into Research Projects

For a research project to be successful, focusing on the user and their needs is integral to any research study. There are two distinct methods in which people with disabilities can participate in research: as co-researchers who may be actively involved in guiding, planning and conducting research or as participants in research or usability studies.

10.7.1   Inclusive Research

Inclusive research is research that actively involves people with disabilities in the research process. Partnering with people with disabilities not only fulfils the goal of 'nothing about us without us' but also leads to groundbreaking discovery and innovation.

In a literature review, Smith-Merry (2017) found that most inclusive research projects where conducted mainly in mental health and intellectual disability. Examples can also be found in other areas, such as individuals on the autism spectrum (Autism CRC 2019) and social care (SCIE 2013).

There are many ways people with disability can be actively involved in the research process, including the following:

- giving feedback on research hypotheses and priorities;
- participating in advisory groups;
- advising on recruitment for research activities;
- co-designing research methodologies and co-facilitating research sessions;
- assisting with the dissemination of research findings.

Many innovative companies, like IBM and Apple, have discovered inclusive research to be as a powerful catalyst for success.

IBM has a long history in inclusive accessibility research, including both physical and cognitive disabilities. For example, an artificial intelligence smartphone guide for the blind was developed by Dr. Chieko Asakawa, an IBM Fellow and a blind researcher.

> This project combines artificial intelligence (AI), computer vision, image recognition, location technology, mobile technology and voice navigation to help visually impaired people find places independently. For visually impaired people navigating and getting where they need to go, location technology with four to five meters of precision is not sufficient. Our solution offers high precision location technology with one to two meters of accuracy.
>
> Social interaction can also be a big challenge for the visually impaired. With advanced computer vision, the app can tell users not only who's coming their way but also the person's facial expression. This allows the user to greet the person with confidence.—(Zhou 2018)

The benefits of inclusive research and the need to involve the end users in researching, services and products for them has led to funding bodies making the involvement of people with lived experience part of the research requirements for securing funding.

Consider having partners that have the necessary lived experience in the proposal. This can include joint proposals with non-profits that represent the user. Care should be taken that the end users themselves are involved and not just people paid or volunteering to assist or support them.

Advisory board members that represent user groups can increase the project's reach beyond the number of paid partners that can realistically be included in a proposal. However, for this to be effective, it is our experience that advisory board members should still receive payment as their time and budget are limited.

10.7.2   Participatory Research

Whereas inclusive research involves collaboration with people with disability, participatory research involves them directly in the research as participants. Typically, a research project will include focus groups, contextual observation and usability testing with participants. Chapter 10 discusses methods for generative and evaluative user research. Chapter 12 discusses quantitative and qualitative evaluation methods.

10.7.2.1   Recruiting People with Disabilities

Developing relationships with people with disabilities is a key to inclusive web accessibility research. You can directly engage with this community by attending conferences or connecting with disability networks. The International Association of Accessibility Professionals (IAAP) maintains a list of conference events and meetups around the world (IAAP undated).

As Shawn Lawton Henry explains in 'Just Ask: Integrating Accessibility Throughout Design' (Henry 2007), establishing contacts with international, national or regional disability organisations can help you find the diverse participants you need.

Another valuable connection is universities and colleges that have Services for Students with Disabilities divisions. Reach out directly to your local higher education institution and ask if they can help you recruit researchers and participants with disabilities. Note, that due to privacy requirements, the Services for Students with Disabilities will not be allowed to give you direct access to a list of students or staff with disabilities, but they can email those groups about your research opportunities.

It should be noted that many types of disabilities are not well represented in the university population, often because of the lack of support though their education, physical challenges during their education, and sometimes because of the disability itself. This is especially true in areas of cognitive disability. A student with specific learning disabilities, although bright, may leave education that was a source of frustration for many years. Similarly, age appropriate forgetfulness and slow down in learning will not be represented in the student population. The reader will be aware that people with intellectual disabilities are also less likely to be represented in most university populations. Further, these disabilities are often undeclared and many people with these difficulties are not even aware of their disability, have not contacted the student disability services, and rather blame themselves for their challenges in coping.

A simple post on social media may generate more participants than the university services. Posting without naming the disabilities can also help, as many people are unaware of the disability name. For example, a post stating 'We are designing a train schedule app for people who are bad at numbers' might get more responses than 'We are designing a train schedule app for people with dyscalculia'.

Medical professionals, such as geriatric doctors, educational psychologists or rehabilitation professionals can also offer participation in your research to their patients or clients. Providing them with a clear understandable and accessible information sheet will allow them to inform their patients without breaching confidentiality.

For example, an academic researcher in the United States, recruiting for people with disabilities might have a recruiting plan like this:

Category	Number of test subjects	Test subject parameters	Recruitment source[a]
Visual (Blind)	5	Screen reader user (only using screen reader does not use vision for tasks)	Local blindness association or National Federation of the Blind
Low vision	5	Screen magnifier user (with visual acuity between 20/70 and 20/200) that uses 4× to 6× magnification	Local blindness or low-vision association or National Federation of the Blind
Auditory (Deaf)	5	User who relies on captions/transcripts (not audio)	Local deafness association or National Association of the Deaf
Motor	5	Sighted user who either uses keyboard alone (no mouse) and/or assistive technology that serves the same purpose as a keyboard	Local independent living organisation or National Council on Independent Living
Cognitive/learning (focus, including specific learning disabilities and dementia)	5	User that has/had a documented 504 plan (or doctor's diagnosis) for focus issues	Local support groups, associations for the ageing or medical professionals
Cognitive/learning (dyslexia)	5	User that has/had a documented 504 plan (or doctor's diagnosis) for dyslexia	Local support groups or medical professionals
Cognitive/learning (memory)	5	User that has/had a documented 504 plan (or doctor's diagnosis) for memory issues	Assisted living facilities, National Council on Independent Living, organisations for people with age-related memory issues such as dementia, medical professionals or local support groups
Cognitive/learning (executive function)	5	User that has/had a documented 504 plan (or doctor's diagnosis) for executive function issues	As above or rehabilitation centres
Speech	5	User unable to use their voice to interact with a voice-controlled computer	Local support organisations or medical professionals

[a]University services for students with disabilities might be able to assist with recruitment depending on the demographic being sought. Social media posts can also help find local participants

As you build your network, it may be helpful to search the web for your local, state or country 'disability organization'. Also, consider looking at the International Disability Alliance that lists over a 1000 disability networks led by people with disabilities (International Disability Alliance. undated).

You may choose to outsource your recruiting. Some respected recruiters in this field are US-based Knowbility's Access Works program (Knowbility 2018), EU-based Open Inclusion (Open Inclusion 2017) and Australia-based Intopia Connect (Intopia 2018).

10.8 Making Your Work Available to the Widest Possible Audience

In academia, the phrase 'publish or perish' is often used to describe the need for academic researchers to quickly and regularly publish research papers in academic journals in order to further one's career or profile. It is also important that information and findings are made available to audiences outside the academic sphere. Publishing your results only in academic journals can often create barriers that arise from complex language, inaccessible formats or paywalls.

10.8.1 Language

Use language that is suitable to your audience. Use plain language and consider reading level.

> A communication is in plain language if its wording, structure, and design are so clear that the intended audience can easily find what they need, understand what they find, and use that information.
>
> Source: International Plain Language Federation, What is plain language.

Be aware that you may identify an intended audience, but your actual audience may be much broader. Do not assume that your research with one audience may not have applicability or be of interest to other audiences.

Think about providing an easy-to-read summary of complex content that requires an advanced reading level; see providing a text summary that can be understood by people with lower secondary education level reading ability (W3C 2016) for guidance.

Also consider providing alternative or different ways of presenting the same information. A text article can be accompanied by illustrations or presented as an infographic or in video format (all in accessible formats of course).

10.8.2 Format

For information to be understandable, it must also be published in a way that can be adapted by the user. People may want different font size, colour or style, or use assistive technologies to access your information.

When information is published in an academic journal that is not accessible, approach the publisher about a systemic change to make all their publications accessible. If this is not possible, at a minimum negotiate an accessible version of your report or documents.

Chapter 20 provides more information on creating accessible documents and publications.

10.9 Discussion

While there are tensions and conflicts between academia, government, the private sector and disability organisations, there is a strong need to work together and respect the aims of each.

In this chapter, we have highlighted the benefits of multi-stakeholder research and including disability organisations and individuals with disability in the research planning activities and providing feedback into ongoing development. The best outcomes will come from an inclusive research approach combined with participatory studies.

Having an inclusive culture is paramount to stakeholders coming together in a collaborate way to achieve research outcomes that meet the needs of all involved. While the focus in this book is disability, to be truly inclusive the needs of other minority groups must also be considered. This includes people whose first language is not your own, people who may experience barriers but not identify as having a disability such as older people and those with low literacy and numeracy.

10.10 Future Directions

There is an emerging and critical need to collect ideas from people living with a disability in public–private partnerships and solution research. It is essential that it is easy for ideas to be submitted. People living with physical, cognitive and mental health challenges are precisely the people who understand the problems caused by our increasingly complicated society but their ideas are lost for precisely the same reasons.

As new technologies are being developed, new risks for inclusion emerge. For example, conversational interfaces and voice systems that a user interacts with by listening to spoken prompts from an automated system and responding via speech or sometimes selecting a number on a keypad. This creates new accessibility challenges for people with speech, memory or language impairments; see Cognitive Accessibility Issue Papers—Voice Systems (Seeman and Cooper 2019).

Another issue is in data-driven systems in smart systems and artificial intelligence. When a group is left out of the data collection, their voice and feedback become increasingly hidden and under-represented. Similarly, when research and artificial intelligence agents "learn" on large datasets or behaviours, there may be a bias towards 'the middle of the bell curve'. This results in some minority groups being excluded and the algorithm not being representative of the population.

At the time of writing, the Australian Human Right Commission is undertaking a 3-year project to understand the human rights implications of new and emerging technologies. The project, Human Rights and Technology (AHRC 2018), will look at the following:

- The challenges and opportunities for human rights of emerging technology.
- Innovative ways to ensure human rights are prioritised in the design and governance of emerging technologies.

There have also been calls in Australia (Bajkowski 2019) and other countries for regulation on AI as the pace of development of smart technology leaves the 'old, dumb law' struggling to keep up. These problems become more critical as our fast-changing society becomes more dependent on new technologies, and the time for these technologies to become ubiquitous decreases.

However, it is worth noting that the same technologies have often created unprecedented opportunities to improve the lives of people with disabilities. Artificial intelligence holds the promise of new levels of automated help and support, and new channels of communication may enable people previously excluded.

Ensuring research participants include all different disability types is essential for creating a harmonious and inclusive society for all our citizens.

10.11   Author's Opinion of the Field

In writing this chapter and working with organisations such as G3ICT, it becomes clear that there are important directions that need to be addressed. The practice of recruiting participants in universities results in a strong sample bias against those with educational challenges and those who have long finished their education. In addition, many people are living with hidden disabilities and are afraid to come forward for the support they need because of the discrimination that is likely to follow. It is the authors opinion that disabilities like dyscalculia (a condition that impairs people ability to use numbers and numerical concepts) is underdiagnosed for these reasons. Similarly, many people hide their memory loss as they age because of embarrassment and fear that they will lose their job and standing in the community. More work is needed as to good practice to recruiting diverse populations without omitting these undeclared disabilities.

In 2017, one of the authors of this chapter investigated establishing an industry think tank to identify new issues and opportunities for inclusion as technology changes—sometimes outside what we typically think of as accessibility. For example, as bots become more ubiquitous, speech disabilities will become more of an issue, along with cognitive disabilities and emotional disabilities. As more devices have multi-modal interactive interface, accessible APIs become essential to enable the interface to change to a form that an individual can understand and use whenever and wherever they encounter it. The Global Public Inclusive Infrastructure (GPII undated) project is endeavouring to promote and actively work on this.

The plan for the think tank was to create a 3- or 5-year plan to identify arising issues and gaps, provide a roadmap for the future and identify APIs that could help assistive technology meet user needs in the future. Unfortunately, this initiative did not progress. However, in writing this chapter, the need for this kind of initiative becomes more obvious. In fact, it seems clear that we need to identify the risks and opportunities for inclusion as new technologies emerge, so that all sectors of society are included rather than some being excluded. Accelerating the process of standardisation may be required to enable new accessibility needs to be included into critical services that matches the rate of their adoption. The law also needs to keep up with the pace of technological change and the new challenges it brings.

There is also a need for better supporting materials for researchers, to aid inclusion and diverse participation of people with all disability types. Finally, it is the opinion of the authors that support should be available to enable better communication between researchers, government, corporations and disability organisations or individuals with disability. This is a significant need for both the research and development community and the people impacted by this research.

10.12 Conclusions

While different parties to the research will have different focuses, expectations or drivers, it is essential that research incorporates people with a wide range of disabilities and inclusion needs in all facets of the research process. This includes contributing ideas, actively participating as co-researchers, participating in all forms of research and testing and providing feedback.

Care needs to be taken that all disability groups are represented including people with different learning and cognitive disabilities, as well as people with sensory and physical disabilities. Additionally, people who may encounter similar barriers to people with disabilities must also be included.

The combination of academia, industry, government and disability representation together brings a strength that cannot be achieved apart. The result will be outcomes that will give the broadest benefit to the greatest number of people.

References

AHRC (2018) Human rights and technology. https://tech.humanrights.gov.au/. Accessed 23 Jan 2019

Australian Network on Disabilities. Undated. https://www.and.org.au/. Accessed 5 Jan 2019

Australian Public Service. Undated. APS disability champions network: role of disability champions. https://www.apsc.gov.au/aps-disability-champions-network-role-disability-champions. Accessed 12 Dec 2018

Australian Research Council website. https://www.arc.gov.au/. Accessed 23 Jan 2019

Autism CRC (2019) Inclusive research practice: engaging autistic individuals and their families in research within Autism CRC. https://www.autismcrc.com.au/knowledge-centre/resource/inclusive-research. Accessed 29 Jan 2019

Bajkowski J (2019) David Thodey and friends push hard for AI regulation ahead of election. https://www.itnews.com.au/news/david-thodey-and-friends-push-hard-for-ai-regulation-ahead-of-election-518433. Accessed 29 Jan 2019

Berg S (2018) There's gender bias in medical research. Here are 3 keys to fix it. https://www.ama-assn.org/practice-management/physician-diversity/theres-gender-bias-medical-research-here-are-3-keys-fix-it. Accessed 9 Jan 2019

Business Disability Forum. Undated. https://businessdisabilityforum.org.uk/. Accessed 5 Jan 2019

Centre for Applied Disability Research. Undated. https://www.cadr.org.au/lines-of-inquiry/research-to-action-partnering-with-people-with-disability-for-research. Accessed 8 Jan 2019

ETSI, CEN, CENELEC (2018). Accessibility requirements for ICT products and services. https://www.etsi.org/deliver/etsi_en/301500_301599/301549/02.01.02_60/en_301549v020102p.pdf - accessed 7 January 2019

GPII website. Undated. The Global Public Inclusive Infrastructure. https://gpii.net/. Accessed 29 Jan 2019

Henry SL (2007) Recruiting participants with disabilities. http://uiaccess.com/accessucd/ut_plan.html#recruiting. Accessed 15 Dec 2018

IAAP. Undated. Events. https://www.accessibilityassociation.org/content.asp?contentid=168. Accessed 17 Dec 2018

International Disability Alliance. Undated. IDA members. http://www.internationaldisabilityalliance.org/content/ida-members. Accessed 17 Dec 2018

International Plain Language Federation. Undated. What is plain language? https://plainlanguagenetwork.org/plain-language/what-is-plain-language/. Accessed 22 Dec 2018

Intopia (2018) Intopia connect. https://connect.intopia.digital. Accessed 17 Dec 2018

Knowbility (2018) AccessWorks, Usability and Accessibility Testing. https://access-works.com/. Accessed 17 Dec 2018

Microsoft (2018) Inclusive design. https://www.microsoft.com/design/inclusive/. Accessed 29 Jan 2019

Mueller, Mary Jo, Jolly, Robert and Eggert, Eric (Eds). (2018). Web Accessibility Laws & Policies (W3C). https://www.w3.org/WAI/policies/. Accessed 20 December 2018

Open Inclusion (2017) https://openinclusion.com/. Accessed 17 Dec 2018

Rose Z (2018) Disability as a driver of innovation in UX presentation at UX Australia 2018. http://www.uxaustralia.com.au/conferences/uxaustralia-2018/presentation/disability-as-a-driver-of-innovation-in-ux/. Accessed 29 Jan 2019

Rush S (ed) (2018) The business case for digital accessibility (W3C). https://www.w3.org/WAI/business-case/. Accessed 20 Dec 2018

Section508.gov. Undated. Section 508 of the Rehabilitation Act of 1973. https://www.section508.gov/. Accessed 7 Jan 2019

Seeman L, Cooper M (2019) Cognitive Accessibility Issue Papers W3C Editor's Draft 24 January 2019. https://w3c.github.io/coga/issue-papers/. Accessed 29 Jan 2019

Smith-Merry J (2017) Research to action guide on inclusive research. Centre for Applied Disability Research. www.cadr.org.au. Accessed 29 Jan 2019

Social Care Institute for Excellence (2013) Co-production in social care: What it is and how to do it. Adults' Services: SCIE guide 51. London: Social Care Institute for Excellence

W3C (2016). G86: providing a text summary that can be understood by people with lower secondary education level reading ability. https://www.w3.org/TR/WCAG20-TECHS/G86.html. Accessed 18 Dec 2018

Wachter-Boettcher S (2018) Technically wrong. W. W. Norton and Company, p 240

Zhou R (2018) Accessibility: the intersection of innovation and inclusion. https://www.ibm.com/blogs/think/2018/05/accessibility-research/. Accessed 20 Dec 2018

Chapter 11
End-User Evaluations

Sukru Eraslan and Chris Bailey

Abstract The past few years have seen tremendous development in web technologies. A range of websites and mobile applications have been developed to support a variety of online activities. The ubiquitous nature and increasing complexity of technology mean that ensuring accessibility remains challenging. Accessibility evaluation refers to the process of examining a product and establishing the extent to which it supports accessibility through the identification of potential barriers. While accessibility guidelines can guide the development process and automated evaluation tools can assist in measuring conformance, they do not guarantee that products will be accessible in a live context. The most reliable way to evaluate the accessibility of a product is to conduct a study with representative users interacting with the product. This chapter outlines a range of methods which can be used to ensure that a product is designed to meet the requirements and specific needs of users, from the ideation phase to the design and iterative development. The strengths and weaknesses of each method are described, as well as the primary considerations to ensure that the results of a study are reliable and valid, and also participants are treated ethically. This chapter concludes with a discussion of the field as well as an examination of future trends such as how data from user studies can be used to influence the design of future accessibility guidelines to improve their efficacy.

11.1 Introduction

Websites should be designed in a way so that they are accessible to users in the target population. When users access websites on devices with small screens, they should be able to complete their tasks. Similarly, when visually disabled users access

S. Eraslan (✉)
Middle East Technical University, Northern Cyprus Campus, 99738 Kalkanlı,
Güzelyurt, Mersin 10, Turkey
e-mail: seraslan@metu.edu.tr

C. Bailey
Enabling Insights Ltd., London, UK
e-mail: chris@enablinginsights.co.uk

© Springer-Verlag London Ltd., part of Springer Nature 2019   185
Y. Yesilada and S. Harper (eds.), *Web Accessibility*, Human–Computer
Interaction Series, https://doi.org/10.1007/978-1-4471-7440-0_11

websites with their screen readers, they should not be distracted by unnecessary clutter which can cause a failure of task completion. Accessibility guidelines and automated evaluation tools provide guidance on how to develop usable and accessible websites, but unfortunately they do not guarantee that websites will be accessible to all users in the target population in a live context. Since user evaluations can identify usability and accessibility problems which are not discovered by conformance evaluation, they are crucial for designing usable and accessible websites (Henry 2018). Without end-user evaluations, researchers cannot ensure that all functionality of websites is accessible to all users in the target population.

End-user evaluations can be conducted at different stages of website development. For example, researchers can conduct a user evaluation during website development to identify user requirements for the final version of the website and investigate possible problems that the users can experience. When the website is finalised, another user evaluation can be conducted to ensure that there are no problems in accessing and using the website. If any problem is detected, then the issue should be resolved before releasing the website. Iterative development of a website would allow the detection of accessibility issues in the development stage and minimise problems in the final version of the website.

There are many methods available which can be used for end-user evaluations, including observations, questionnaires, interviews, eye tracking, etc. When researchers conduct an end-user evaluation for a particular website, they usually prepare a set of tasks and they observe how users interact with the website while performing these tasks. An interview, questionnaire or both can then be used to further investigate their overall experience with the website.

A representative sample of the target population is crucial for end-user evaluations. If the sample does not represent the target population, then the results of the evaluation will not be reliable. External factors which can affect the results should also be controlled. However, over control of these factors may cause a problem in representing a real-life situation, and again the results may not be reliable. Data from user evaluations should be analysed carefully as the incorrect interpretation of the data can cause other problems. When researchers conduct a user evaluation, they are also responsible for safeguarding the general welfare of their participants.

The remainder of this chapter first gives the overview of commonly used evaluation methods and explains what should be taken into consideration for designing an effective end-user evaluation. It then discusses the strengths and limitations of end-user evaluations and provides some future directions. Finally, it gives the authors' opinions of the field and provides concluding remarks.

11.2   Overview

There are a range of user-centred design methods that can be conducted when performing a user study. The most important consideration is to select the most appropriate method(s) to support the goal of the research. If background research is conducted to shape the development of a new product, then qualitative methods such as interviews and focus groups could be the most appropriate. If the goal is to elicit feedback or measure performance on an existing or prototype product, then observational studies or user studies following the think aloud protocol may yield the most effective results. Conducting research in accessibility can present significant challenges in recruiting suitable participants. It is important to factor this in the research timeline and consider if remote studies are possible to include participants who may experience difficulties travelling on-site for a laboratory-based study.

An overview of several commonly used research and evaluation methods are provided in Sect. 11.2.1. The key factors of designing an effective study including sampling of participants, internal and external validity, ethical treatment of participants and data analysis are covered in Sect. 11.2.2.

11.2.1 Commonly Used Evaluation Methods

Evaluation methods in user studies generally collect either quantitative or qualitative data. Some methods allow the collection of both quantitative and qualitative data for measuring the user's performance in terms of success, speed and satisfaction (Leavitt and Shneiderman 2006). In all cases, users will perform representative tasks on the interface to achieve a previously defined goal.

Quantitative evaluations are concerned with the collection and analysis of measurable numeric performance data that are obtained from users' interaction with a product. The collection and analysis of numerical data can describe, explain, predict or control variables and phenomena of interest (Gay et al. 2009). As these results are numeric, the results can be analysed using a range of techniques for statistical analysis (Dix et al. 2004). Quantitative evaluations are especially useful for benchmarking, that is, measuring and comparing users' performance on an interface over time. While generally not considered the best practice in the context of market research, there are benefits to recruiting the same participants for accessibility benchmarking studies as the participants' familiarity with the interface reduces the learning curve and can provide more useful results. Previously reported issues can be resolved in subsequent iterations of the design of the product.

Qualitative evaluations are more focused on gaining non-numeric information. These evaluations are conducted to gain an insight into users' existing experiences, their expectations and impressions of an interface, identify elements which cause negative user experience and potentially explore design solutions. Data from such evaluations is subjective as it is influenced by factors such as familiarity with the technology being tested, but the data can subsequently be coded to establish patterns and trends in users' opinions or users' feedback can be used to enhance the overall user experience of the product by removing barriers to the users' interaction.

The rest of this section provides an overview of some of the commonly used quantitative and qualitative evaluation methods, which are summarised in Table 11.1.

Table 11.1 The commonly used evaluation methods

Method	Data gained	Common uses
Performance measures	Quantitative	Collect numerical data to establish how well interface supports users
Logging user actions	Quantitative	Gather longitudinal data about a user's interaction with a product
Questionnaires	Quantitative/Qualitative	Collect information about users and their preferences
Observation	Qualitative	Obtain information on interaction in a live context
Interviews	Qualitative	Collect users' knowledge, thoughts, feelings and attitudes towards a product
Think aloud	Qualitative	Obtain users' thoughts and opinions about a product for identifying positive and negative aspects of their interaction
Eye tracking	Quantitative	Understand users' visual paths on page
Crowdsourcing	Quantitative/Qualitative	Collect numerical and non-numerical data from a large number of users at remote locations

11.2.1.1   Performance Measures

To investigate how well a user can interact with a digital product such as a website, it is necessary to decide which attributes of performance you wish to investigate and then define metrics with which to measure them (Brajnik 2006). If we look at the field of usability, there are five attributes of human–computer interaction that could be investigated in a user study (Nielsen 2003):

- Learnability: How easy is it for users to accomplish basic tasks the first time they encounter the design?
- Efficiency: Once users have learned the design, how quickly can they perform tasks?
- Memorability: When users return to the design after a period of not using it, how easily can they re-establish proficiency?
- Errors: How many errors do users make, how severe are these errors, and how easily can they recover from the errors?
- Satisfaction: How pleasant is it to use the design?

International standards can also provide guidance. ISO-9241-11 defines usability in terms of effectiveness, efficiency and satisfaction in a specified context of use (see the 'Usability, Universal Usability, and Design Patterns' chapter). The intention was to emphasise that usability or accessibility is an outcome of interaction rather than a property of a product and it is now widely accepted (Bevan et al. 2015). If using these standards as a benchmark, then attributes and subsequent metrics can be defined as follows:

- Effectiveness: The accuracy and completeness with which users achieve specified goals. It can be measured as the extent to which participants complete the defined task, expressed as the completion rate.
- Efficiency: The resources expended in relation to the accuracy and completeness with which users achieve specified goals. It can be measured in the time taken to complete the defined task, expressed as the time taken from the start to end time of the task.
- Satisfaction: The comfort and acceptability of use. User satisfaction is measured through standardised satisfaction questionnaires (SUS) which can be administered after each task and/or after the usability test session.

Experiments to measure user performance with an interactive system can be conducted throughout the product development life cycle; from the initial stages by testing paper prototypes and throughout the design process including interactive phases of development. Performance measures need to be tailored to reflect the stage of development being tested. For example, it would be appropriate to measure the satisfaction of a user's interaction with paper prototypes, but not efficiency.

When considering the specific context of accessibility research, examples of performance measures that can be obtained during user evaluations, but are not limited to, are as follows:

- The number of users who complete a task successfully.
- The time taken to complete a task.
- The number of errors a user makes while completing a task (such as selecting an incorrect link).
- The frequency that users can recover from such errors.
- The number of accessibility barriers that the user encounters.
- The number of observations of user frustration.

It should be noted that while some measures can be measured quantitatively, others can be measured qualitatively or by a combination of both. While task completion rate is purely a quantitative measure, the number of observations of user frustration can be measured quantitatively, but additional qualitative data is required to understand the reason behind the frustration. Measures may also be tailored to suit the user group being investigated. For example, visually disabled users who use screen readers generally take significantly longer to complete tasks on a website than sighted users (Borodin et al. 2010). Therefore, when conducting a study with visually disabled users, emphasis may be placed on measures such as effectiveness and satisfaction, over others such as efficiency.

In some domains, such as industry, when testing the accessibility of a product, the emphasis is placed on detecting and investigating solutions to accessibility barriers in a product. The use of research to detect barriers, rather than performance, is emphasised by practitioners (Brajnik 2006; Clegg-Vinell et al. 2014). By using a combination of quantitative and qualitative measures when investigating accessibility barriers encountered by a user, rich and useful data can be gained to remove these barriers and enhance the product.

11.2.1.2 Logging User Actions

Logging user actions is a quantitative research method which allows researchers to capture a continuous stream of data in real time as tasks are performed. Therefore, it is capable of providing valuable insights about users' interactions with websites. By using this method, researchers can capture large amounts of data from multiple users over a long period where log files are typically recorded by web servers and client logs (Nielsen 2004; Burton and Walther 2001). This method can be used to generate inferences about website design, to test prototypes of websites or their modifications over time and to test theoretical hypotheses about the effects of different design variables on web user behaviour (Burton and Walther 2001).

The logging process can occur with users in their natural environments without a researcher being present and therefore less invasive than qualitative evaluation techniques. While users are initially aware that they are being observed, over time the process becomes invisible and users often forget that logging is taking place. However, while users can often behave as though logging is not occurring, the evaluator should always inform users of what actions will be captured and why. Failure to do so raises serious ethical issues, and in some countries covertly capturing user data is illegal. The primary advantage of using logging for evaluations is that analytical data collection is typically built into the server or hosting providers software. This can produce records of server activity that can be analysed to describe user behaviour within the website. A typical application of web server logging is to enhance navigation for the user by establishing common paths through a website. An analysis of the logs can reveal the navigation path users take during their browsing sessions.

Metrics that can be obtained from logging user actions can be grouped into two categories; session-based and user-based metrics. Session-based metrics can be used to measure the average number of page views per session, the average duration of the session and the first (entry) and last (exit) pages of the session. User-based metrics can measure the number and frequency of visits, total time spent on the site, the retention rate (number of users who came back after their first visit) and conversion rate (the proportion of users who completed expected outcomes) (Kuniavsky 2003). These metrics can be correlated to the performance measures described in Sect. 11.2.1.1. Session-based metrics can be used to gain insight into the efficiency of users' interaction and identify pages which may present accessibility issues such as the exit page. User-based metrics can also be used to gain an insight into efficiency, but also give an insight into possible satisfaction with the site (frequent and repeated visits) as well as effectiveness (depending on the conversion rate).

One limitation of this method is that it may not provide sufficient insight into reasons behind users' breakdown in their interactions with a website—for example, failure to complete the checkout process of an e-commerce site. Quantitative data will detail the number of users who did not complete the interaction, but the reasons behind this breakdown would need to be explored with further research. Evaluators can understand what users did when interacting with a website, but cannot necessarily understand why they did it, and if they achieved their goal in a satisfactory manner (Nielsen 2004).

11.2.1.3 Questionnaires

One of the most reliable quantitative research methods to investigate and collect information about users and their opinions is to distribute a questionnaire to the target user group. A questionnaire or survey is a set of questions that when distributed to the target user group creates a structured way to ask a large number of users to describe themselves, their needs and their preferences. When done correctly, they produce a high degree of certainty about the user profile in areas such as demographics which cannot be so easily obtained when using qualitative methods. Special care should be taken over the design of the questionnaire to ensure that the questions are clearly understood and not leading, and also the results are accurate and provide sufficient detail to collect the desired information. These issues can arise due to the lack of direct contact with the participants, and therefore the questionnaire should be trialled beforehand (Kuniavsky 2003).

The questionnaire itself can consist of closed questions, open questions or a combination of the two. Closed questions typically pose a question and provide a predetermined limited set of responses which are accompanied by a numerical scale. Closed questions are heavily influenced by the commonly used System Usability Scale (SUS) used in usability testing. As an example, a question could be posed as 'I was able to complete the form without any difficulties', with the following predetermined responses: (1) Strongly Disagree, (2) Disagree, (3) Neither agree nor disagree, (4) Agree and (5) Strongly Agree. In this case, a score of five would indicate the form is accessible, while a score of one would indicate it is not. While such a question would gain an insight into the overall accessibility of a form, it would not provide detail around any accessibility barriers or features that prevented—or supported—form completion. If this detail was required, it would be necessary to complement it with an open question.

Open questions are phrased to allow the respondent to answer in free text and provide more detail. The data can subsequently be coded to establish any patterns and trends. Again, using a form to provide context, an open question could be phrased as 'Please describe your experience when using the form on the website?'. Such a wording avoids making assumptions about the user being able to complete the form and allows the user to express their opinions. For example, a screen reader user could respond that required form fields were not announced to them and this response provides specific insight into possible accessibility problems.

Questionnaires can be delivered electronically to a large sample of users or can be completed manually on paper in conjunction with observational or think aloud research sessions. The former is useful when starting research into the accessibility of a product as it can provide useful demographic information and influence the design of observational and think aloud research sessions. For example, responses to open-ended questions could provide insight into specific areas or components of the product that require further investigation and testing. If large-scale questionnaires are used, then an incentive for participation should be offered. If used in conjunction with other research methods, they can provide a written record of responses directly from the user and provide information that can be used for benchmarking the accessibility of a product if further research is conducted.

11.2.1.4   Observation

Ethnography and observations are often used as part of a contextual inquiry and are used to gain a better understanding of users in their natural environments. Observational research methods involve observing users in the place where they would normally use the product (e.g. work, home, etc.) to gather data about who that target users are, what tasks and goals they have related to an existing product (or proposed enhancements) and the context in which they work to accomplish their goals. The outputs from this qualitative research can lead to the development of user profiles, personas (archetype users), scenarios and task descriptions on which the design team can base design decisions on empirical evidence throughout the development life cycle (Rubin and Chisnell 2008).

Observation of users while operating an interface provides real-time interaction information and can be performed by curing both the pre-design and post-design stages of a project. Observations conducted during the pre-design phase can be used to identify required enhancements to a newer version of a product or to establish user requirements for a new product. When conducted during the post-design stage, evaluations are used to identify task, performance and environmental factors which could negatively impact their experience. For example, evaluations can be conducted to ensure a product meets users' expectation and to identify required enhancements by gaining data on accessibility and usability barriers.

Observations conducted in a live context can be unstructured and discrete, meaning the researcher will take detailed notes but rarely interfere with the research setting ensuring the authenticity of the work. Alternatively, the researchers can intervene when they observe a breakdown in a user's interaction to determine the cause of the problem, evaluate the impact and provide an insight into a possible solution. Care must be taken to ensure that an inexperienced researcher does not influence the user's interaction and behaviour. Similarly, collecting a video and audio recording of the session can be useful when analysing the session, with the proviso that users who are aware they are being recorded may not behave exactly as they would in a regular context as they may feel uncomfortable. Due to the nature of observational studies being conducted in a live context, the research design should be well planned, the objectives should be clear and the researcher should be suitably trained and experienced. For further details on observational research design, the issues that need to be considered, see (Leedy and Ormerod 2016).

11.2.1.5   Interviews

Interviews are a useful method to investigate users' needs, preferences and desires in a detailed way. They can be used to deepen understanding of users and discover how individuals feel about a product, including why and how they use it. Interviews allow the researcher to gain an understanding about why users hold certain opinions, beliefs and attitudes towards a product. To ensure the interviewer does not influence the results, it is important to conduct non-directed interviewing to make sure the interview process does not lead or bias the answers. It ensures that the participants' true thoughts, feelings and experiences are gained without being filtered through the preconceptions of the interviewer (Kuniavsky 2003).

Interviews can be used to explain general data obtained from large-scale questionnaires or surveys, adding more depth and understanding to previously gained data due to the potential to ask very specific questions. Any uncertainties or ambiguity in a response can be quickly clarified. Due to the one-to-one nature, interviews can be an effective method to explore sensitive topics which people may not feel comfortable discussing in groups and they can allow a greater level of rapport to be built with participants. Interviews offer some flexibility in that they can be structured, semi-structured or ad hoc. Structured interviews are best used if accurate comparisons between users' responses are required. The larger sample size is reached if they are conducted over the telephone or the Internet by several interviewers. Semi-structured interviews allow the interviewers more flexibility to explore topics and themes which emerge during the interview and can offer a more informal approach. Ad hoc interviews are best used when performing guerrilla research or when performing a contextual inquiry and they are the most flexible method. Interview questions must be phrased to be open ended to more easily elicit useful responses from participants. The wording of the questions should not be loaded or worded in a way that could influence the response. Questions with complex answers should not be posted as binary questions, for example, instead of asking 'Is X feature of a screen reader useful to you?', ask 'Can you tell me how you use a screen reader?'. Finally, the interviewers should be wary of asking people to predict their future needs or assume that they will be able to answer every question.

There are also several participant behaviours that can influence the results which the interviewer needs to be aware of. Participants may not always say what they truly believe; this could be as they feel they want to avoid conflict; they may say yes when they mean no. Indicators of this include hesitation when responding or inconsistency with previous answers. More subtle cues may be noted by observing body language, such as someone shaking their head no when answering positively to a question. Participants may also give a different answer to the question asked. This could be because they misheard or did not understand the question, or might have the agenda they wish to discuss. It is important to listen carefully, as the information may still be relevant in the context of the interview script. It may be necessary to repeat the question by using the different wording of phrasing, and persistence may be required to obtain the required data (Kuniavsky 2003).

Group interviews with several participants can be conducted in the form of focus groups. Focus groups are an established user-centred design research method which captures shared experiences in a live situation. They are generally used in the early stages of a research investigation to gain qualitative feedback which can shape the development of a digital product. Focus group interviews involve a group of six to eight people who come from similar social and cultural backgrounds or who have similar experiences or concerns. They gather together to discuss a specific issue with the help of a moderator in a setting where participants feel comfortable enough to engage in a dynamic discussion for 1 or 2 hours. Focus groups do not aim to reach a consensus on the discussed issues. Rather, focus groups 'encourage a range of responses which provide a greater understanding of the attitudes, behaviour, opinions or perceptions of participants on the research issues' (Hennick 2007). Focus groups enable participants to share and discuss their thoughts and attitudes and provide a balanced understanding of their experience and perceptions for analysis. It is also possible to investigate the appropriateness of potential design solutions for new products. Due to their flexibility, multiple topics or themes can be explored in a session and they can be used for formative assessment with the use of visual probes, such as design mock-ups. The facilitator must ensure they manage the discussion to ensure that all participants are involved as one drawback of focus groups is that the discussion can be dominated by one or two individual participants (Breen 2006). While focus groups are an established user-centred design method, their roots in market research have led to a discussion on their suitability for HCI research. Great care should be taken in the research design to reflect the task-based investigation required for focus groups in the field of usability—and by extension—accessibility investigations (Rosenbaum et al. 2002).

Evaluating and analysing the results of interviews have the disadvantage of being time-consuming and being difficult to analyse. However, an experienced researcher can encourage the participant to provide an in-depth discussion that yields rich data to reveal strong conclusions when correctly analysed and coded (Jay et al. 2008).

11.2.1.6 Think Aloud

The think aloud protocol was originally developed to understand users' cognitive process as it encourages them to comment on their actions out loud when performing tasks on a system (Lewis 1982). The think aloud protocol is commonly used during user-testing sessions as it can provide a detailed insight into users' thoughts, feelings and actions during their interactions with a product. Using current or intended users of the product as participants in the think aloud protocol provides a closer view of how users use the product and reveals practical problems related to task performance (Holzinger 2005). It does not only highlight issues with the product that are detected during a live context of use but it can also provide suggestions for possible design solutions (Rubin and Chisnell 2008).

Think aloud testing sessions can be held on a one-to-one basis, with one facilitator working with one participant in a laboratory setting, or there may be an additional observer present. The observer may be in the laboratory with the facilitator and participant or they may be viewing the session in a separate observation room. Testing sessions may also be conducted remotely by using remote screen sharing software. In that case, a video–audio connection is required to view and hear the participant. If a researcher wants to observe the interactions of participants with a particular website remotely, then dedicated software such as Morea[1] can be used to assist with post-session analysis. Morea is a software application that allows researchers to observe and record users' interactions with a product remotely. It uses a timeline metaphor to allow researchers to place markers when observing a session which can then be reviewed and used for more in-depth analysis.

The key aspect of the think aloud protocol is that participants are encouraged to verbalise their thoughts, feelings, opinions, expectations and frustrations around their interactive experience in the form of a 'running commentary'. Participants are asked to explain their actions, such as their justification for following a certain navigation path on a website or what motivated their recent action. Crucially, this allows researchers to see and understand the cognitive processes associated with task completion and identify any barriers (Yen and Bakken 2009).

Asking participants to think aloud during their sessions also reveals important clues about how they are thinking about the product or system they are using and whether the way it works matches up with the way it was designed. In effect, does it match the participants' mental model? Participants may filter their verbalisation, so they may consciously or unconsciously leave things out as they talk. Likewise, it is impossible for a participant to articulate everything that is going through their mind during the session. Thinking aloud can also help participants think through the design problem and form ideas for recovering. One important reason to avoid asking participants to think aloud is when you measure time on tasks. Thinking aloud slows performance significantly (Rubin and Chisnell 2008).

11.2.1.7 Eye Tracking

Eye tracking has widely been used to understand how users interact with web pages for enhancing the design and usability of web pages (Ehmke and Wilson 2007; Yesilada et al. 2013; Eraslan et al. 2013). While users are reading web pages, their eyes become relatively stable at certain points called fixations and the sequences of these fixations show their scanpaths (Poole and Ball 2005). By tracking eye movements of users on web pages, we can discover which elements are used and which paths are followed by users. Table 11.2 shows some popular eye-tracking metrics along with their common interpretations, see more in Ehmke and Wilson (2007). For example, if users are asked to search for a specific item on a particular web page and they make many fixations and follow unnecessarily long paths to complete their tasks, then their searching behaviours tend to be considered as inefficient on that page for the given task.

---

[1] https://www.techsmith.com/morae.html.

Table 11.2 Some popular eye-tracking metrics along with their common interpretations

Metric	Interpretation
Fixation duration	Longer fixation duration, more difficult to extract information or more engaging
Number of fixations overall	Higher number of fixations overall, less efficient searching
Number of fixations on a particular element	Higher number of fixations on an element, more noticeable or important element
Scanpath length	Longer scanpath, less efficient searching
Transitions between areas	More transitions between elements, more uncertainty in searching

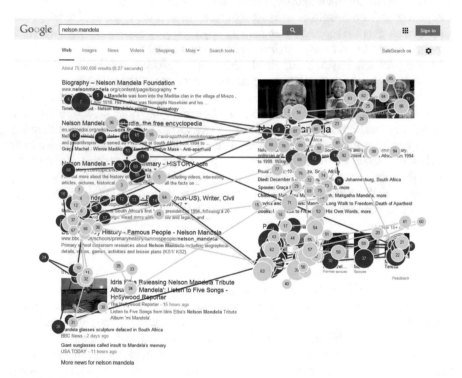

Fig. 11.1 A scanpath visualisation with a gaze plot on the search results page on the Google website (Eraslan et al. 2016a, c, 2017c)

Eye-tracking data can be visualised by using different ways (Blascheck et al. 2017). Figure 11.1 shows an example of a scanpath visualisation with a gaze plot on the search results page on the Google website. The circles illustrate the fixations where the larger circles illustrate the longer fixations. When multiple scanpaths are visualised on the same page with gaze plots, they will overlap and become difficult to analyse. In addition to visualisation techniques, some other techniques have also been

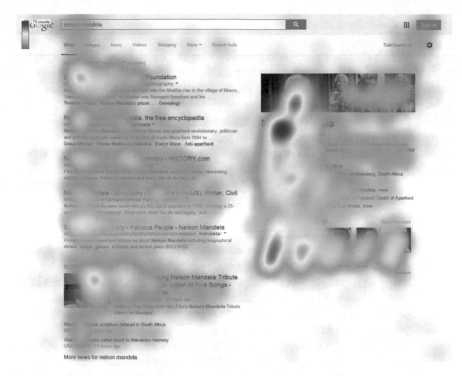

Fig. 11.2 A heat map on the search results page on the Google website (Eraslan et al. 2016a, c, 2017c)

proposed and used in the literature to analyse scanpaths for different purposes, such as computing a similarity score between two scanpaths, determining transition probabilities between elements, detecting patterns in a set of scanpaths and identifying a common scanpath of multiple users (Eraslan et al. 2015).

Fixations can also be aggregated based on certain features, such as duration or count, to generate a heat map. Figure 11.2 shows an example of a heat map on the search results page on the Google website. Heat maps consist of different colours where the red colour usually illustrates the most commonly used elements, whereas the green colour illustrates the rarely used elements. However, these maps do not illustrate sequential information.

Even though eye tracking gives valuable insights about how users interact with web pages, it does not tell why certain elements are fixated by users. Besides this, there can be some involuntary eye movements which are made by users without any specific objective. Furthermore, eye-tracking studies can be costly due to the expensive equipment and can be time-consuming as eye-tracking sessions cannot be conducted in parallel when there is only one eye tracker.

11.2.1.8 Crowdsourcing

Oxford English Dictionary[2] defines crowdsourcing as 'the practice of obtaining information or input into a task or project by enlisting the services of a large number of people, either paid or unpaid, typically via the Internet'. As researchers usually experience difficulties in finding participants for their user studies (Eraslan et al. 2016a, 2017c), they can use this approach to access a wider and diverse set of people from remote locations and ask them to assess a particular software product (Sherief et al. 2014). In particular, they can ask participants to perform certain tasks on a particular website in their environments and fill in a questionnaire in regards to their overall experience (see Sect. 11.2.1.3). The questionnaire can involve a set of questions which aim to identify what kinds of problems can be encountered. The actions of the participants can also be logged to be analysed (see Sect. 11.2.1.2).

Eraslan et al. (2018) recently propose a methodology for creating a corpus of eye-tracking data on web pages by using crowdsourcing. This corpus can allow researchers to access the eye-tracking data collected on different kinds of web pages, thus providing an opportunity to investigate how people interact with different kinds of web pages, such as web pages with various levels of visual complexity. The analysis of eye-tracking data on different kinds of web pages provides valuable insights for possible problems for other similar web pages.

Even though crowdsourcing allows to collect data from a large number of users, the analysis of the collected data is crucial. There can be many factors which can affect users' evaluations, such as expertise, disabilities, experience, etc. The reliability of the collected data should also be checked as this method can reveal unreliable data due to low control. For example, if a questionnaire is conducted to evaluate a website, some participants may fill in the questionnaire randomly. When crowdsourcing is used, researchers should ensure that they obtain sufficient data from users to investigate the reliability of the collected data and analyse the data by considering different factors.

11.2.2 Designing an Effective Study

User studies have their own characteristics, research questions, hypotheses and methodologies, but they should be designed effectively in order to achieve reliable results. These studies should be conducted with a representative sample of the target population and the sample size can vary due to the heterogeneity of the population (Sect. 11.2.2.1). Researchers should also consider how to control external factors which can affect dependent and independent variables (i.e. internal validity) and how to have generalizable results (i.e. external validity) (Sect. 11.2.2.2). When researchers plan their quantitative and/or qualitative data analysis beforehand, they can directly start to analyse the data once the data collection stage is completed (Sect. 11.2.2.3).

---

[2]https://en.oxforddictionaries.com/definition/crowdsourcing.

Since users are included in these studies, ethical issues should be taken into consideration to assure the rights and welfare of the participants (see Sect. 11.2.2.4). All of these issues are briefly explained below.

11.2.2.1   Sampling

When researchers want to carry out an end-user evaluation for a particular product, they need to select their participants from their target population. Specifically, when researchers want to evaluate a website designed for a specific field, their participants should have knowledge in this field. Generally speaking, if a user evaluation is conducted with more participants, then its results will be more generalisable. However, the generalisability of the results does not depend on only the sample size but also depends on the representatives of the target population. In particular, visually disabled users access web pages with their screen readers that follow the source code of the pages (Yesilada et al. 2007). Therefore, these users tend to follow similar strategies when they interact with web pages, even though there can be some differences because of their screen readers. When researchers want to assess the accessibility of a particular website for visually disabled users, they can have a representative sample with a small number of participants. However, if the heterogeneity of the target population is high, then a larger sample size will be needed for a representative sample. Hence, researchers should first investigate and understand how the individuals of the target population are similar or different from each other to determine their sample size.

After a user evaluation study, researchers typically analyse their results by applying some statistical tests. The number of participants required for a specific statistical test to achieve a particular statistical power can be estimated based on statistical approaches. Studies with low statistical power tend to have a Type II error which is a failure to detect a significant difference (Gravetter and Wallnau 2008). G*Power is a software application which is designed to estimate the required sample size based on the study design.[3] For example, when the Mann–Whitney U Test is planned to be used to compare two unrelated groups based on a particular dependent variable, this software application can be used to estimate the required sample size to achieve specific statistical power. To achieve at least 95% statistical power, the required sample size is determined as 92 with this application when the other parameters are set to their default values (Effect size d: 0.5, α err prob: 0.05, Allocation Ratio: N2/N1).

11.2.2.2   Validity

While an end-user evaluation is being performed, there can be some confounding variables which are outside factors possibly affecting both dependent and independent variables (Eysenck 2005). Assume that researchers want to investigate whether

---

[3]http://www.gpower.hhu.de/en.html.

a particular task on a specific web page can be completed within a given duration by two separate user groups which have different levels of computer knowledge. If they conduct their studies with mainly male users, there can a problem for internal validity. Specifically, when two different groups of users will be compared based on a particular dependent variable, all the other variables should be the same to achieve the highest internal validity. Therefore, when researchers set up their studies, they should take confounding variables into consideration. However, it is difficult to achieve very high internal validity because of external factors, such as individual preferences, knowledge, familiarity, etc. For example, there are different kinds of small-screen devices available. If a user evaluation is carried out with a specific small-screen device, the internal validity can be decreased as some of these users can be more familiar with the device in comparison with others. The users can be allowed to use their devices, but in that case the individual settings of the devices could also negatively affect the internal validity.

On the other side, if all the confounding variables are eliminated, then the evaluation design will not represent the real world, and this situation will negatively affect the external validity which is related to the generalisability of the findings. When the sample is not representative of the target population, the external validity will also be negatively affected. Both the real-world conditions and the representatives of the sample are crucial for achieving high external validity. Thus, when researchers design a user evaluation, they should consider both internal validity and external validity based on their objectives.

11.2.2.3   Data Analysis

When researchers design a user evaluation, they also need to make a plan on how they will analyse the data that will be collected in the evaluation. The data should be carefully analysed with appropriate methods and techniques to interpret the data accurately. Incorrect interpretation of data can result in unsuccessful evaluation even though its data collection stage does not have any problem. Data analysis mainly depends on the type of the data collected which can be quantitative or qualitative.

There are many statistical methods that can be used for analysis of quantitative data such as the time required by the user to complete a task, the number of incorrect links choices, etc. For example, when researchers want to investigate whether people with autism can complete a specific task as efficiently as people without autism, they can use the independent T-Test or its non-parametric alternative Mann–Whitney U Test to investigate if these two groups are significantly different from each other based on a particular dependent variable, such as the time required by the user to complete a task (Pallant 2007; Eraslan et al. 2017a). There are some assumptions that should be satisfied to apply the T-Test. For example, the values of the dependent variable for both groups should be normally distributed. If these assumptions are not met, then the Mann–Whitney U Test should be used. When the sample size is small, some sampling methods can also be used to eliminate the effects of the individuals. For example, some subsamples can be randomly created by using the bootstrapping technique where a specific participant is not seen in more than one subsample (Hesterberg 2015).

When a user evaluation provides some qualitative data such as manuscripts from interviews, observations and think aloud studies, researchers can use different techniques to analyse them to discover patterns and relationships between these patterns. Specifically, they can use an iterative approach to first divide larger units into smaller units and then sort and categorise them to draw an overall conclusion.

11.2.2.4 Ethical Issues

Ethical issues should be considered when users are involved in studies. Even though web accessibility evaluation does not threaten physical welfare of participants, researchers are responsible for safeguarding general welfare of their participants. At the beginning of the study, the participants should be informed about the study to understand the main objectives of the study, how it will be conducted, how long it will take and their rights. They will then need to sign a consent form. It is unethical, and also illegal in some countries, to capture data from users without their consent.

Researchers typically experience difficulties in finding participants for their studies (Eraslan et al. 2016a, 2017c). People typically participate in these studies because of their interest, their willingness to help the researchers and/or small gifts which are given after the studies. Therefore, researchers should avoid asking them to complete very complicated questions and keeping them in a laboratory for a long period as they may become tired and stressed, and then decide to withdraw from the study.

Researchers should avoid collecting sentinel information from their participants. Web pages with sensitive information are typically not suitable for user evaluations. For example, a social media account of a particular user is not appropriate as it is likely to include sentinel information and users may not want to share their sentinel information. Similarly, personal email pages should also not be used in a user evaluation. Researchers should take care of sentinel data. In particular, electronic sentinel data collected from the participants should be stored securely on a computer, and written information should be stored in a locked drawer. Researchers should also not pass them to any third party.

When the analysis of the data is reported, the data should be anonymised. It means that participant names and any other information that may identify the participants should not be provided, thus no one can recognise who the data belongs to. To maintain the anonymity, a code can be given to each participant, and the participants can be referred with their codes.

If people with disabilities are invited to a laboratory for a user evaluation study, the laboratory should be accessible for them and well equipped to ensure that they feel comfortable. For example, if participants have some physical disabilities, the laboratory should be set up properly, and therefore they can easily move around.

Many universities have an ethics committee to check whether a particular study is suitable in terms of ethical issues and approve the study to proceed. The committee can also check the study case by case whether it follows the ethical rules.

11.3   Discussion

One of the most important aspects of the research design is to ensure that the hypotheses and research questions are clearly identified and defined. Without this, the goal of the research may be unclear, and the subsequent research design may be flawed. The research design defines what methods will be used, how the study will be conducted, what equipment will be required, what data will be collected, how it will be obtained and then subsequently analysed. Well-defined research questions are required to understand what participants will be recruited, how many will participate, what information is required from them, such as what tasks they will perform. A literature review of existing research in the field can provide guidance on how these should be defined.

The research design should include both independent and dependent variables. An independent variable is a variable which is changed or controlled in a scientific experiment to test the effects on the dependent variable, whereas a dependent variable is a variable which is being tested and measured in the research study. The dependent variable is 'dependent' on the independent variable. As the experimenter changes the independent variable, the effect on the dependent variable is observed and recorded. While purely exploratory studies may not have clear hypotheses and can deliver valid results, there should still be high-level research question(s) that are being investigated.

The tasks that participants are required to complete during the evaluation should be chosen appropriately to answer the research questions or test the hypotheses. If the goal of the research is to progress or reinvestigate existing research, then these can be drawn from a review of existing literature. Conversely, new tasks may need to be defined depending on the context of the investigation. The tasks should be designed to be typical of what target users would complete in a live context. Although it may not be necessary to test all elements of an interface, the tasks should cover the core functionality of the product or interface being evaluated. The preparation of the tasks should be influenced by the overall hypothesis and research questions.

One of the possible limitations of user studies, especially in the domain of accessibility research, is to ensure that the results are generalisable. Participants with disabilities have such a broad spectrum of capabilities and needs which makes difficult to draw definite conclusions. Taking screen reader users as an example, the preferred choice of assistive technology and the varying level of competence and experience can greatly influence the results. Assume that highly competent and experienced screen reader users and novice screen reader users are asked to interact with the same interface and the think aloud protocol is used. Experienced participants are likely to report fewer issues in comparison with novice participants due to their knowledge of how to 'work around' possible problems with the interface or the fact that they do not consider them to be 'issues' as such. Some of these limitations can be addressed by ensuring the number of participants is appropriate to ensure that statistical significance can be achieved. A purely quantitative study will require a higher number of participants. Recruiting large numbers of suitable participants can be challenging, but it depends on the methods used. It is perhaps easier to recruit a large number of participants for a survey than it is for an observational study. A study designed to obtain qualitative data can be conducted with a smaller number of participants. If the study design is appropriate, then the results can have a high level of validity.

Regardless of the goal of the research, a participant screener should be produced to ensure that the participants recruited for the study are appropriate. A screener defines the characteristics of those who will be recruited to participate in the study. Again, if we use the example of screen reader users, certain parameters around the type of assistive used, the frequency of use, competency and previous exposure to the platform being tested may be defined. This way ensures that the most appropriate participants are recruited for the study.

The environment being tested is also an important consideration. For example, a 'live' website could provide the most realistic context of use, but if a longitudinal study is being conducted, the changes in the interface may influence the results as new variables may be introduced. As far as possible, the interface being tested should be consistent throughout the study. Developing a stable testing environment for the research can provide a solution to this potential problem.

Before commencing a live study, a pilot session should be conducted under similar conditions to the live study by using the same protocol and materials. The pilot study could be considered a 'rehearsal' for the real study. Its purpose is to identify any methodological flaws in the study design before engaging with participants in the real study. It allows any issues to be resolved without compromising the results of the study. In particular, a pilot study for an interview would allow checking the phrasing and wording of questions to ensure that they can be clearly understood and are not leading. A pilot study for think aloud user-testing sessions would allow testing the instructions given to participants to ensure that they are feasible and can be completed, and checking that the number of instructions is appropriate for the length of the session.

If the research design—and subsequent investigation—is found to be ineffective, then the rigour of the research could be questioned due to the lack of reliability and validity. Reliability refers to the extent to which the results of the investigation (or a series of investigations) are consistent and can therefore be applied to the larger population. Validity consists of two components which are external validity and internal validity. External validity refers to the extent to which the conditions of the study represent what would happen in a live context. In contrast, internal validity refers to the extent that the study measured or observed the appropriate criteria to meet the aims of the research, as defined by the hypotheses and research questions. As previously discussed, reliability can be addressed by ensuring that a screener is used to recruit appropriate participants and the sample size is sufficient. External validity can be assured by ensuring that the participants conduct tasks which are typical of what they would conduct in a live context (the 'real world') and the variables are controlled. Again, as previously discussed, internal validity can be assured by ensuring that the hypotheses and research questions are clearly defined and the research design is sufficiently implemented to support these. Conducting a pilot study can assist in achieving these goals.

The goal of any user study is that it should be reproducible and can be validated by an external party. It is important to ensure that the research design (such as hypotheses and research questions) is well defined and the materials used during the study (such as a discussion guide) are produced and made available so that the study can be repeated. If we consider the fact that multiple iterations of the design of an interface are to be tested for benchmarking purposes, the conditions of the experiment may need to be replicated to measure either an improvement in user performance or decrease in effectiveness. If the results of the study in an established field contradict with other studies, then other practitioners or the original researchers may wish to examine the datasets or indeed repeat the study to ensure that the reliability and validity of the investigation can be verified.

11.4   Future Directions

People can now use a range of different technologies to interact with websites. In particular, people with motor impairments can use eye-tracking technology to interact with web pages (Menges et al. 2017). However, when the elements of web pages are very close to each other, users can experience some problems in fixating and selecting these elements by using their eyes due to the accuracy rate of eye trackers. All of these kinds of technologies and their limitations should also be taken into consideration during website development. When an end-user evaluation is conducted for a particular website, there should be a set of tasks which can test whether the website is accessible by using different technologies.

There have been some recent studies to predict whether a particular user has autism or dyslexia by using their eye-tracking data (Rello and Ballesteros 2015; Yaneva et al. 2018) After the successful prediction, websites can be automatically adapted or transcoded to be more accessible for these users by meeting their needs. Different approaches are available to transcode web pages such as page rearrangement, simplification and alternative text insertion (Asakawa and Takagi 2008). Therefore, these approaches should first be investigated with a series of user studies to determine the most suitable transcoding approach(es). In these studies, a sufficient number of participants should be recruited from the target population and they should be asked to perform various tasks on the original version and the transcoded versions of web pages for comparison purposes.

Although web accessibility guidelines are beneficial for web designers to develop accessible and usable websites, some of these guidelines, especially the ones for people with autism, have not been validated by using an empirical study with the relevant user groups (Eraslan et al. 2017a; Yaneva et al. 2018). Empirical validation with users would strengthen the reliability of these guidelines.

Different metrics have recently been proposed to analyse how users interact with web pages (Eraslan et al. 2014; Eraslan and Yesilada 2015). Specifically, Eraslan et al. (2016b) have recently proposed an algorithm called Scanpath Trend Analysis (STA) which analyses eye movements of multiple users on a particular web page and discovers the most commonly followed path on the page in terms of its visual elements as the trending path (Eraslan et al. 2016d, 2017b). This path provides a better understanding of how users interact with web pages in general, and it can be used for different purposes. For example, it can be used to transcode web pages to make trending elements more accessible (Yesilada et al. 2013) or it can be used to investigate whether users follow the expected path for a particular goal (Albanesi et al. 2011). If there are two different groups of users in the target population, the STA algorithm can be applied to the samples of these two groups separately and their results can be compared to investigate how these groups are similar to each other. In this case, researchers can recognise whether a particular website is used similarly by different groups of users.

11.5   Authors' Opinion of the Field

End-user evaluations are required to determine the true picture of the accessibility of the interface being tested. They should be considered a required supplement to other evaluation methods, such as conformance review against accessibility guidelines, as research has already shown the limitations of accessibility guidelines. In recognition of the need for formal accessibility guidelines to evolve to be more user centred, following the recent update of version 2.0 to 2.1 of the Web Content Accessibility Guidelines (WCAG), the Accessibility Guidelines Working Group of the W3C is developing another revision to the formal accessibility guidelines which follows a research-focused and user-centred design methodology with the aim of producing more relevant and appropriate guidelines (for more details about the guidelines, see the 'Standards, Guidelines and Trends' chapter). Testing with users will be required to define such guidelines. The aim of any user study could be to identify any—or all—of the following:

- Understand the accessibility requirements of the users and gauge their opinions;
- Identify accessibility issues in the interface for the users being investigated;
- Investigate the severity of the issues and
- Explore potential design solutions to any issues.

   The last few years have seen a shift towards a human approach to accessibility, rather than one which recognises accessibility primarily as a binary technical requirement that a product either 'meets' or does 'not meet'; end-user evaluations will remain a core element of this. Accessibility may not be considered as an intrinsic characteristic of a digital resource, but it is determined by a range of complex political, social and other wider contextual factors (Cooper et al. 2012). The authors believe a true human-centred model of accessibility must consider the full range of their users' technical, operational and psychological requirements. This is one of the key principles of the Web Accessibility Code of Practice, which has been formalised into a British Standard (BS8878) based on a user-centred approach to accessibility, to provide products that are conformant with guidelines, usable and satisfying.

Accessibility should not be considered as a separate quality attribute in isolation. Accessibility, usability and user experience are all interdependent quality attributes of a product. They all need to be at an optimal level to ensure that the product can be used effectively.

We can consider the concept of accessibility as having three separate, but interdependent and overlapping components as given below (Bailey and Gkatzidou 2017):

- Technical accessibility: This component refers to the fundamental requirements for users to be able to access a product, services or physical environment. It includes conformance with accessibility guidelines and compatibility with assistive technologies. Therefore, this component represents the basic user needs.
- Operational accessibility: Once users have access, this component refers to how well they can use and operate the product or navigate the physical environment. It refers to attributes such as efficiency (e.g. can the users accomplish tasks in a reasonable time frame?), error rate and error recovery (e.g. how many errors do the users make? how well do the users recover from them?). This component also represents the extent to which the product or feature set meets the users' expectations.
- Psychological accessibility: Once users can access and use a product, services or premises, this component refers to aspects including but not limited to, how useful the users find its functionality or facilities, how appropriate they are for the users and how satisfying they are for the overall experience of the users. Therefore, this component represents the users' desires.

We consider the psychological element of accessibility to be of great importance. For some audiences, specifically older users, there may be no technical or operational barriers to accessibility when attempting to use a product; the barrier may be psychological and can be due to a general lack of confidence when using digital technology from the user. For example, users may have had a negative experience with an online banking service in the past and they may be unwilling to use, or may assume they cannot use, the service again today, despite the accessibility and usability being significantly enhanced during this time.

When considered together, the defined attributes of accessibility include those described in Yesilada et al. (2012). We emphasise that all components can be evaluated and measured using methods described in this chapter. For example:

- Guideline conformance reviews and testing with end users' assistive technologies can be used to measure technical accessibility.
- Observational or think aloud methods with users can be used to measure operational accessibility.
- Questionnaires and interviews designed to capture both quantitative and qualitative data can be used to measure psychological accessibility.

No single method can comprehensively measure all attributes or all of the aims described earlier. However, when a research study is carefully designed, it can be possible to obtain some insights.

Recent developments have suggested that future research could utilise crowd-sourcing (Sect. 11.2.1.8) as a solution to remedy the issue of recruiting a statistically significant number and a sufficiently diverse range of participants to provide reliable and valid results (Kouroupetroglou and Koumpis 2014; Li et al. 2017; Song et al. 2018). We expect further research in this area to contribute significantly to this field.

11.6 Conclusions

This chapter highlights the need for end-user evaluations to provide accessible web-sites. It gives an overview of the commonly used evaluation methods. There is no unique method which is valid for all end-user evaluations. Some evaluations need to combine multiple methods, whereas some of them can be conducted with a particular method. In addition to the right selection of the methods, the study should be effectively designed, especially by choosing the representative sample from the target population, controlling external and internal factors appropriately, and carefully considering ethical issues.

References

Albanesi MG, Gatti R, Porta M, Ravarelli A (2011) Towards semi-automatic usability analysis through eye tracking. In: Proceedings of the 12th International Conference on Computer Systems and Technologies, ACM, New York, NY, USA, CompSysTech '11, pp 135–141. https://doi.org/10.1145/2023607.2023631

Asakawa C, Takagi H (2008) Transcoding. In: Harper S, Yesilada Y (eds) Web accessibility, Springer, London, a foundation for research, human computer interaction series, pp 231–260

Bailey C, Gkatzidou V (2017) Considerations for implementing a holistic organisational approach to accessibility. In: Proceedings of the 14th Web for All Conference on the Future of Accessible Work, ACM, New York, NY, USA, W4A '17, pp 7:1–7:4. https://doi.org/10.1145/3058555.3058571

Bevan N, Carter J, Harker S (2015) Iso 9241–11 revised: what have we learnt about usability since 1998? In: Kurosu M (ed) Human-computer interaction: design and evaluation. Springer International Publishing, Cham, pp 143–151

Blascheck T, Kurzhals K, Raschke M, Burch M, Weiskopf D, Ertl T (2017) Visualization of eye tracking data: a taxonomy and survey. Comput Graph Forum 36(8):260–284. https://doi.org/10.1111/cgf.13079

Borodin Y, Bigham JP, Dausch G, Ramakrishnan IV (2010) More than meets the eye: a survey of screen-reader browsing strategies. In: Proceedings of the 2010 International Cross Disciplinary Conference on Web Accessibility (W4A), ACM, New York, NY, USA, W4A '10, pp 13:1–13:10. https://doi.org/10.1145/1805986.1806005

Brajnik G (2006) Web accessibility testing: when the method is the culprit. In: Miesenberger K, Klaus J, Zagler WL, Karshmer AI (eds) Computers helping people with special needs. Springer, Berlin, pp 156–163

Breen RL (2006) A practical guide to focus-group research. J Geogr High Educ 30(3):463–475. https://doi.org/10.1080/03098260600927575

Burton MC, Walther JB (2001) The value of web log data in use-based design and testing. J Comput-Mediat Commun 6(3):JCMC635. https://doi.org/10.1111/j.1083-6101.2001.tb00121.x

Clegg-Vinell R, Bailey C, Gkatzidou V (2014) Investigating the appropriateness and relevance of mobile web accessibility guidelines. In: Proceedings of the 11th Web for All Conference, ACM, New York, NY, USA, W4A '14, pp 38:1–38:4. https://doi.org/10.1145/2596695.2596717

Cooper M, Sloan D, Kelly B, Lewthwaite S (2012) A challenge to web accessibility metrics and guidelines: putting people and processes first. In: Proceedings of the International Cross-disciplinary Conference on Web Accessibility, ACM, New York, NY, USA, W4A '12, pp 20:1–20:4. https://doi.org/10.1145/2207016.2207028

Dix A, Finlay J, Abowd G, Beale R (2004) Evaluation techniques. In: Human-computer interaction, 3rd edn. Pearson Prentice Hall, pp 318–363

Ehmke C, Wilson S (2007) Identifying web usability problems from eye-tracking data. In: Proceedings of the 21st British HCI Group Annual Conference on People and Computers: HCI...but not as we know it - volume 1, British Computer Society, Swinton, UK, UK, BCS-HCI '07, pp 119–128

Eraslan S, Yesilada Y (2015) Patterns in eyetracking scanpaths and the affecting factors. J Web Eng 14(5–6):363–385

Eraslan S, Yesilada Y, Harper S (2013) Understanding eye tracking data for re-engineering web pages. In: Sheng QZ, Kjeldskov J (eds) Current trends in web engineering. Springer International Publishing, Cham, pp 345–349

Eraslan S, Yesilada Y, Harper S (2014) Identifying patterns in eyetracking scanpaths in terms of visual elements of web pages. In: Casteleyn S, Rossi G, Winckler M (eds) Web engineering. Springer International Publishing, Cham, pp 163–180

Eraslan S, Yesilada Y, Harper S (2015) Eye tracking scanpath analysis techniques on web pages: a survey, evaluation and comparison. J Eye Mov Res 9(1). https://bop.unibe.ch/JEMR/article/view/2430

Eraslan S, Yesilada Y, Harper S (2016a) Eye tracking scanpath analysis on web pages: how many users? In: Proceedings of the ninth biennial ACM symposium on eye tracking research & applications, ACM, New York, NY, USA, ETRA '16, pp 103–110. https://doi.org/10.1145/2857491.2857519

Eraslan S, Yesilada Y, Harper S (2016b) Scanpath trend analysis on web pages: clustering eye tracking scanpaths. ACM Trans Web 10(4):20:1–20:35. https://doi.org/10.1145/2970818

Eraslan S, Yesilada Y, Harper S (2016c) Trends in eye tracking scanpaths: segmentation effect? In: Proceedings of the 27th ACM Conference on Hypertext and Social Media, ACM, New York, NY, USA, HT '16, pp 15–25. https://doi.org/10.1145/2914586.2914591

Eraslan S, Yesilada Y, Harper S, Davies A (2016d) What is trending in eye tracking scanpaths on web pages? In: Spink A, Riedel G, Zhou L, Teekens L, Albatal R, Gurrin C (eds) Proceedings of the 10th International Conference on Methods and Techniques in Behavioral Research (Measuring Behavior 2016), Dublin City University, MB 2016, pp 341–343

Eraslan S, Yaneva V, Yesilada Y, Harper S (2017a) Do web users with autism experience barriers when searching for information within web pages? In: Proceedings of the 14th Web for All Conference on the Future of Accessible Work, ACM, New York, NY, USA, W4A '17, pp 20:1–20:4. https://doi.org/10.1145/3058555.3058566

Eraslan S, Yesilada Y, Harper S (2017b) Engineering web-based interactive systems: trend analysis in eye tracking scanpaths with a tolerance. In: Proceedings of the ACM SIGCHI symposium on engineering interactive computing systems, ACM, New York, NY, USA, EICS '17, pp 3–8. https://doi.org/10.1145/3102113.3102116

Eraslan S, Yesilada Y, Harper S (2017c) Less users more confidence: how AOis dont affect scanpath trend analysis. J Eye Mov Res 10(4). https://bop.unibe.ch/JEMR/article/view/3882

Eraslan S, Yesilada Y, Harper S (2018) Crowdsourcing a corpus of eye tracking data on web pages: a methodology. In: Grant R, Allen T, Spink A, Sullivan M (eds) Proceedings of the 11th International Conference on Methods and Techniques in Behavioral Research (Measuring Behavior 2018), Manchester Metropolitan University, MB2018, pp 267–273

Eysenck MW (2005) Psychology for AS level, 3rd edn. Psychology Press, Hove, East Sussex
Gay L, Mills G, Airasian P (2009) Educational research: competencies for analysis and applications, 9th edn. Prentice Hall, Upper Saddle River, New Jersey
Gravetter FJ, Wallnau LB (2008) Statistics for behavioral sciences, 8th edn. Wadsworth Publishing
Hennick M (2007) International focus group research: a handbook for the health and social sciences. Cambridge University Press, Cambridge
Henry SL (2018) Involving users in evaluating web accessibility. https://www.w3.org/WAI/test-evaluate/involving-users/. Accessed 15 Aug 2018
Hesterberg TC (2015) What teachers should know about the bootstrap: resampling in the undergraduate statistics curriculum. Am Stat 69(4):371–386. https://doi.org/10.1080/00031305.2015.1089789, pMID:27019512
Holzinger A (2005) Usability engineering methods for software developers. Commun ACM 48(1):71–74. https://doi.org/10.1145/1039539.1039541
Jay C, Lunn D, Michailidou E (2008) End user evaluations. In: Harper S, Yesilada Y (eds) Web accessibility. A foundation for research, human computer interaction series. Springer, London, pp 107–126
Kouroupetroglou C, Koumpis A (2014) Challenges and solutions to crowdsourcing accessibility evaluations. https://www.w3.org/WAI/RD/2014/way-finding/paper5/. Accessed 9 July 2018
Kuniavsky M (2003) Observing the User Experience: A Practitioner's Guide to User Research (Morgan Kaufmann series in interactive technologies). Morgan Kaufmann Publishers Inc., San Francisco
Leavitt M, Shneiderman B (2006) Research-based web design and usability guidelines. Department of Health and Human Services, Washington DC, US
Leedy P, Ormerod J (2016) Practical research: planning and design, 11th edn. Pearson
Lewis C (1982) Using the think aloud method in cognitive interface design. IBM Research Report, RC–9265 (#40713), IBM Thomas J. Watson Research Center, Yorktown Heights, NY
Li L, Wang C, Song S, Yu Z, Zhou F, Bu J (2017) A task assignment strategy for crowdsourcing-based web accessibility evaluation system. In: Proceedings of the 14th Web for All Conference on the Future of Accessible Work, ACM, New York, NY, USA, W4A '17, pp 18:1–18:4. https://doi.org/10.1145/3058555.3058573
Menges R, Kumar C, Müller D, Sengupta K (2017) Gazetheweb: a gaze-controlled web browser. In: Proceedings of the 14th Web for All Conference on the Future of Accessible Work, ACM, New York, NY, USA, W4A '17, pp 25:1–25:2. https://doi.org/10.1145/3058555.3058582
Nielsen J (2003) Usability 101: introduction to usability. http://www.useit.com/alertbox/20030825.html. Accessed: 09 July 2018
Nielsen J (2004) Risks of quantitative studies. https://www.nngroup.com/articles/risks-of-quantitative-studies/. Accessed 01 July 2018
Pallant J (2007) SPSS survival manual: a step by step guide to data analysis using SPSS version 15, 4th edn. Open University Press/McGraw-Hill, Maidenhead
Poole A, Ball LJ (2005) Eye tracking in human-computer interaction and usability research: current status and future. In: Prospects, Chapter in C. Ghaoui (Ed.): encyclopedia of human-computer interaction. Idea Group Inc., Pennsylvania
Rello L, Ballesteros M (2015) Detecting readers with dyslexia using machine learning with eye tracking measures. In: Proceedings of the 12th Web for All Conference, ACM, New York, NY, USA, W4A '15, pp 16:1–16:8. https://doi.org/10.1145/2745555.2746644
Rosenbaum S, Cockton G, Coyne K, Muller M, Rauch T (2002) Focus groups in HCI: wealth of information or waste of resources? In: CHI '02 extended abstracts on human factors in computing systems, ACM, New York, NY, USA, CHI EA '02, pp 702–703. https://doi.org/10.1145/506443.506554
Rubin J, Chisnell D (2008) Handbook of usability testing: how to plan, design and conduct effective tests. Wiley, New York
Sherief N, Jiang N, Hosseini M, Phalp K, Ali R (2014) Crowdsourcing software evaluation. In: Proceedings of the 18th International Conference on Evaluation and Assessment in Software

Engineering, ACM, New York, NY, USA, EASE '14, pp 19:1–19:4. https://doi.org/10.1145/2601248.2601300

Song S, Bu J, Wang Y, Yu Z, Artmeier A, Dai L, Wang C (2018) Web accessibility evaluation in a crowdsourcing-based system with expertise-based decision strategy. In: Proceedings of the internet of accessible things, ACM, New York, NY, USA, W4A '18, pp 23:1–23:4. https://doi.org/10.1145/3192714.3192827

Yaneva V, Ha LA, Eraslan S, Yesilada Y, Mitkov R (2018) Detecting autism based on eye-tracking data from web searching tasks. In: Proceedings of the internet of accessible things, ACM, New York, NY, USA, W4A '18, pp 16:1–16:10. https://doi.org/10.1145/3192714.3192819

Yen PY, Bakken S (2009) A comparison of usability evaluation methods: heuristic evaluation versus end-user think-aloud protocol–an example from a web-based communication tool for nurse scheduling. In: AMIA annual symposium proceedings, American Medical Informatics Association, vol 2009, p 714

Yesilada Y, Stevens R, Harper S, Goble C (2007) Evaluating DANTE: Semantic Transcoding for Visually Disabled Users. ACM Trans Comput-Hum Interact 14(3):14. https://doi.org/10.1145/1279700.1279704

Yesilada Y, Brajnik G, Vigo M, Harper S (2012) Understanding web accessibility and its drivers. In: Proceedings of the International Cross-Disciplinary Conference on Web Accessibility, ACM, New York, NY, USA, W4A '12, pp 19:1–19:9, https://doi.org/10.1145/2207016.2207027

Yesilada Y, Harper S, Eraslan S (2013) Experiential transcoding: An eyetracking approach. In: Proceedings of the 10th International Cross-Disciplinary Conference on Web Accessibility, ACM, New York, NY, USA, W4A '13, pp 30:1–30:4, https://doi.org/10.1145/2461121.2461134

Chapter 12
Reproducible and Sustainable Research Software

Caroline Jay and Robert Haines

Abstract To ensure that you are conducting research to the highest scientific standards, data collection and analysis procedures should be robust, well-described, and open to scrutiny. In principle, this may sound straightforward; in practice, it is very hard to achieve. Here we examine what it means, and what it involves, for Web accessibility researchers to make computational research methods reproducible—such that the data and methods are available to and usable by others—and sustainable—such that they continue to be available and usable over time.

12.1 Introduction

Until recently, the reproducibility of a research study was determined almost entirely by how well it was described in the resulting paper. It was not common practice to publish data, nor to provide anything more than the names of the procedures used to analyse it, not least because, prior to the advent of the Web, providing public access to these things in full was virtually impossible.

Many domains now find themselves in the midst of a reproducibility crisis: results that had formed the foundations of theory for many years appear not to hold when the experiments are rerun (Baker 2016). There are, of course, many complex reasons for this. The current culture within academic publishing encourages the dissemination of striking, novel advances, rather than incremental work, or negative results. The fact that details regarding the precise setting of the study, the sample, and tiny tweaks to the data collection and analysis methods can all have a big impact on the results is often obscured. To address this, we need to capture the research process as accurately as possible, to ensure that the results are understood within the appropriate context. The increasing use of computation in research, from the perspective of both collecting

C. Jay (✉)
School of Computer Science, University of Manchester, Manchester, UK
e-mail: caroline.jay@manchester.ac.uk

R. Haines
Research IT, University of Manchester, Manchester, UK
e-mail: robert.haines@manchester.ac.uk

© Springer-Verlag London Ltd., part of Springer Nature 2019
Y. Yesilada and S. Harper (eds.), *Web Accessibility*, Human–Computer
Interaction Series, https://doi.org/10.1007/978-1-4471-7440-0_12

and analysing data, provides an opportunity to do this, as computational methods and data can, in theory, be provided in full and stored indefinitely.

What does this mean for Web accessibility researchers? Consider a study examining Web usage over time. A software tool can be used to log and analyse information about online activity, and this data can then be stored and analysed computationally, to provide insights into behaviour (Apaolaza et al. 2015). If we make the data and the analysis scripts available, another researcher should be able to repeat the analysis, and obtain the same results. If we make the collection tool available as well, it should be possible to rerun the experiment at a later point in time, and see whether the results still hold, or whether the conclusions resulting from the original study should be updated. Trying to retain as much detail about the research process as possible, and open up this information to scrutiny, underpins the philosophy of *reproducibility* in research. In practice, however, ensuring the *sustainability* of the software that underpins this—such that it continues to be usable—is technically challenging. In the example above, if the tool used to collect Web interaction data is tied to a particular browser, for instance, then it may not work with other browsers, of even future versions of the same browser.

Using reproducible methods enables other researchers both to verify our results, and to make further use of them in the future, but this is only possible if they persist over time. Sustainability is the capacity to endure. It is an intrinsic requirement of reproducibility and repeatability: if the software methods used to undertake a piece of research do not survive, the research cannot be repeated. The Software Sustainability Institute defines 'Software Sustainability' in the following terms: "the software you use today will be available—and continue to be improved and supported—in the future" (About the Software Sustainability Institute 2018). Embedding sustainability in the research software engineering process is key to enabling reproducible research methods, for if the software that underpins research—whether that is a simple script to produce a single figure in a paper, or a complex experimental platform—does not endure, then the research is not reproducible.

In order for computational research to be truly reproducible, every action taken by the computer should be stored and made available (Wilkinson 2016). Pseudocode is not sufficient, as abstracting algorithms, or translating them into words, results in problematic ambiguities and misunderstandings that may not be apparent to either the researcher writing the pseudocode, or the researcher reading it (Thimbleby 2003).

There is currently not a single, optimal way to conduct reproducible research; rather, a collection of good practices are being iteratively developed and adopted by a community of researchers who are trying to advance the way we conduct and publish science. An essential component is making data available in an institutional or public repository (see, for example, Figshare 2018; Mendeley Data 2018; Zenodo 2018; DataHub 2018 and DANS 2018). When publishing in such a repository, materials are assigned a Digital Object Identifier (DOI) which can then be used to cite them (The Digital Object Identifier System 2018). This confers the additional advantage that others can reuse and cite these materials too, allowing researchers to gain credit for careful data collection and curation.

A foundation for developing reproducible and sustainable software methods is provided by adopting basic software engineering best practice, such as version control, documentation and automated testing. Beyond this, technologies such as Jupyter notebooks (Project Jupyter 2018) can help to guide readers through the analysis process, and Docker containers (2018) can make tools available on different platforms. In the next sections, we outline some of the main techniques people are using to help support reproducibility within their research. The precise nature of software that may be used in Web accessibility research varies considerably, and we therefore consider sustainable software practices in general terms, which can be applied to all kinds of software development, from building complex applications, to writing data analysis scripts.

12.2 Good Software Practices

When producing any kind of software for research, whether it is a data analysis script, a tool for logging data, or an application to visualize results, it is of the utmost importance that it does what it is supposed to be doing. A few, experimental lines of R or Python used to conduct a simple analysis procedure may be straightforward to write and verify manually. As software grows in complexity, the likelihood it contains unknown errors increases considerably, and more formal mechanisms for checking and maintaining its functionality are required. Following good software engineering practices provides a solid foundation for supporting the sustainability of research software, and thus the reproducibility of the resulting research.

12.2.1 Version Control

A Version Control System[1] (VCS) tracks changes that are made to a software codebase. As well as providing a way for a developer to rollback any unwanted code changes, should they turn out to be unneeded or incorrect in some way, these systems also enable teams of people to work on the same code simultaneously, without overwriting each others' work. These is useful when several people need to contribute to building an application, or are sharing the development of a tool used within a research project. Typically, all members of a development team would have a copy of the code-base on their own computers, and when they then need to share their changes with the rest of the team, the VCS provides 'merging' functionality to ensure that each person's changes are preserved correctly. Modern examples of version control software include 'git' (Git 2018) and 'mercurial' (Mercurial 2018).

A useful feature of a VCS is that development can be split across multiple 'branches'. In this sense a branch is a new line of parallel development that is separate from the default, or 'master', branch. Branching is typically used to develop and test

---

[1] Also known as a Source Code Management (SCM) System.

new features before merging them into the main line of development. This makes it easy to abandon a feature if it is no longer required or if development goes down a blind alley.

12.2.2 Documentation

It is important to document research methods fully. If software makes up any part of that method, then it too should be documented. There are two aspects of documentation that are particularly useful: user documentation—how to use the software (what it does); and developer documentation—how to modify or extend the software (how it works). This second aspect is often just as important to the original authors of the software as it is to anyone else; if a particular function has been coded in an obscure way—maybe because it has been optimized for speed or memory usage—then an explanation of how it works and the reasons why can greatly reduce confusion in the future.

12.2.3 Software Testing

Testing is the process by which software *functionality* and *quality* is assessed. This is often described as *verification and validation* (V&V). These two terms are often confused, or thought to be the same thing, but the difference can be succinctly expressed (Boehm 1989) as:

- *Validation*: Are we building the right software? Is it fulfilling the users' requirements?
- *Verification*: Are we building the software right? Is it free of defects and failures?

Most testing of the code itself is done by running the software in a controlled environment, and verifying the correctness of the result. Generally, we test small parts of the code—called units—in isolation so that errors can more easily be located as and when they occur. Most programming languages have fully featured testing facilities either built in, or as part of their standard library.

Testing can feel like a lot of extra work, especially if you are working on a project alone, so it pays to think about where testing can have the most useful effects. Tests are code, so they need to be maintained as all the other code does, and tests can contain errors, so care must be taken when writing them. A good rule of thumb is to test code against examples of real world data (or subsets thereof) and any edge-cases that you can think of.

A useful side-effect of maintaining a comprehensive test suite, is that it can be used by other developers as another source of documentation. If there is any doubt about how the software is supposed to operate—for example what parameters a library function expects, or what the output of a function might be—the tests will provide programmatic evidence of the function in use.

12.2.4 Code Review

Version control, documentation and testing can catch the majority of technical problems that might occur within a code-base, but to further aid maintainability and to aid validation of the functionality within it, many teams use 'code review'. This is the practice of a second, possibly more experienced, developer examining code before it is merged into the main repository. Some teams work in pairs, in a practice known as 'pair programming', in which developers take turns to 'drive' (write the code) and 'observe' (analyse the problem, and review code in real time); other teams have code review as a part of the version control process (checked in code is held in a staging area until someone else can check it and approve it). When working alone, code review may not be practical, or indeed desirable, as it requires multiple people to be conversant with the code being written, and most of the benefits of code review are brought to bear in teams.

Code review can pick up maintainability issues, such as badly formatted code—for example, the Python community maintains a style guide to aid developers in producing consistent, readable code (PEP 8—Style Guide for Python Code 2018)—and validation issues, such as a mis-reading of the required user specifications for the software. This helps to guard against a situation where tests all pass, but this is masking the fact that the software is not actually fulfilling its intended purpose.

12.3 Notebooks and Executable Papers

Notebooks and executable papers can both help to document the steps that have been taken while working through a particular programme of research. As a result they provide a detailed 'recipe' for repeating or reproducing research. Notebooks are particularly useful for documenting the steps undertaken during experiments and data analysis, and an executable paper pulls together the whole research pipeline—which may include notebooks—into a single workflow with the published paper as its output. Notebooks and executable papers are both important mechanisms for providing detailed provenance of an experiment.

12.3.1 Notebooks

Notebooks have emerged as an increasingly important tool in the drive towards reproducible research. There are two main types of notebook commonly used in research:

the electronic lab notebook (ELN) and the interactive computing notebook. The former is analogous to an experimental lab notebook, where methods are described and results collected, often during non-computational work, such as 'wet-lab' biological experiments. The latter is an interactive computing environment, typically within a Web browser, where code can be written and executed line-by-line, with results calculated immediately and displayed in-line. Such notebooks can be used to create and share documents that contain live code, equations, visualizations and narrative text. Typical uses for notebooks include data cleaning and transformation, numerical simulation, statistical modeling, data visualization and machine learning (Project Jupyter 2018).

12.3.2 Executable Papers

A paper is said to be executable if it includes the code required to generate its results alongside the text itself (Strijkers 2011). The intention is that this will make verifying and reproducing a paper's findings much easier. If the code is included then it can be inspected to make sure that it does what it should, and that there are no errors. Re-running the code with newly collected data can form part of the replication steps required to demonstrate external validity of the methods detailed in the paper.

There are, at the time of writing, no agreed standards for executable papers, and no end-to-end toolkits for the creation of them. Some journal venues have indicated that they will start publishing papers in an executable form, but at the moment it is more common for the final output of an executable paper—generally a PDF file—to be published, and the executable part of it provided as supporting material.

12.4 Containers and Virtualization

One of the hardest reproducibility problems to solve with research software, especially when working openly and sustainably, is that of packaging and distributing the resultant application. The nature of research software often means that it is at the cutting edge, and therefore that it needs cutting edge, or specially configured, dependencies to run. This might be the latest version of a library, or other tool, that is not yet available within standard installs of the popular operating systems. Installing these dependencies might be possible for the original developers of the software, but may be beyond the skills of much of the intended user base.

A solution to this problem is to distribute the software with all of its dependencies included and configured in a 'Virtual Machine' (VM) or a 'Container'. Both of these provide the means to package an entire software environment in a 'sandbox' which can be distributed and run safely, without impacting anything outside of it. The difference between them is the level at which that sandbox sits; a container encompasses the application and its dependencies only, whereas a virtual machine replicates the whole operating system. A further advantage of encapsulation is that the three most popular operating systems—Windows, Mac OS and Linux—all support VMs and containers, so software written for one is accessible on the others too.

The creation, and subsequent maintenance, of VMs and containers can be automated to further aid reproducibility and sustainability. Both types of encapsulation can be configured with simple text files so that new versions can be built alongside the software they hold in a unified build process. Container systems, such as Docker (2018) and Singularity (2018), provide their own simple configuration languages for this purpose, and containers can be built by extending other containers, so different experiments can be built up using layers of research software if required. Vagrant (2018) is a tool for building and managing virtual machines using simple workflows, again allowing multiple experiments to be built from a common base of software systems.

12.5 Software and Data Citation

In an increasingly open and reproducible world, more and more people are publishing their research software, methods and data. In order to further encourage this happening, and to properly attribute credit to the authors of these outputs, it is important to cite all materials used in our own research correctly. This means that any software and data used should also be cited alongside more traditional research outputs, such as publications.

The FORCE11 Software Citation Working Group has developed a set of Software Citation Principles, to motivate and guide the citing of non-standard research outputs (Smith et al. 2016). The most important step that you can take to help people to cite your work is simply to *tell people how to cite your work*. With a software output, this could be as easy as adding a line to the 'ReadMe' file in your source code, but what should that line say? You could ask people to cite your software directly, or you could ask them to cite a paper that describes what your software does. When citing other people's work, the best approach is to *cite it the way they ask you to*. The rest of this section gives details of ways to make citing your work easier for others, which in turn can be looked for and used when you are citing others' work too.

12.5.1 Software Papers

If a paper exists solely to describe software—that is, it does not describe any experiment or research that has been done with the software, except as an example of its use—then it is known as a 'software paper'. Software papers are a convenient way of describing your software, potentially in a domain-neutral way, and making it easily citable in one step. As a software paper is a paper, then it can be cited as such, and all publication venues understand this type of citation. Example venues for publishing a software paper are the Journal of Open Source Software (JOSS) (2018) and the Journal of Open Research Software (JORS) (2018). As implied by their titles, both of these journals require that software be published under an open source licence to be eligible for publication.

12.5.2   Archiving Software to Be Cited

Software, especially research software, has a life of its own outside of the publication cycle: it can be added to, maintained and fixed. If this happens then the version of a piece of software that two papers use might be different enough that they should be distinguished somehow. Should you write a new software paper for each version that you release? And even if you did, with the many ways that software can be distributed, how could anyone be sure that they had the correct corresponding version?

A neat solution to this problem is to archive significant versions of your software in a repository. For these purposes you should use an 'archival' repository, such as Figshare (2018) or Zenodo (2018). GitHub is a repository, but it is not archival; it lacks defined long-term retention periods and persistent links to content. Using an archival repository assigns a Digital Object Identifier (DOI) to each version of your software (The Digital Object Identifier System 2018). To make this easier, it is possible to use an automated workflow to archive your software every time you tag a version in GitHub (Making Your Code Citable 2018).

Once you have a DOI for your software then a particular version can be easily cited using that DOI in a way that all journals can accept.

12.5.3   Providing Citation Metadata with Your Software

It is useful to provide specific metadata about your software to aid people in citing your work. Most software comes with plenty of metadata associated with it, such as dependency lists and packaging information, but none of this on its own is specific to citation.

One of the simplest ways of adding citation metadata to your software is to add a plain text file to its source code with details on how you would like it to be cited (Encouraging citation of software—introducing CITATION files 2018). Separating this information out from the ReadMe, in a file named 'CITATION', makes it more obvious that it is there, and what its purpose is. The fact that this information now exists and is clearly marked already reduces the main barrier to people citing your code—that of knowing how to cite it. This sort of metadata is not machine readable, however, so cannot be used for any automated collection of citation metadata in the future (Encouraging citation of software—introducing CITATION files 2018).

To address this specific concern an attempt has been made to formalize CITATION files into something that can be read by both humans and machines: 'CITATION.cff' files (2018). This type of CITATION file contains metadata in a minimally structured format, and the standard provides a minimal set of keys that should be included so that the work can be cited.

The CodeMeta Project provides a more comprehensive metadata schema (Jones et al. 2017). It aims to combine the metadata one might need for citation and attribution (authors, title), with that required by replication (version, dependencies) and discovery (keywords, descriptions) into one machine readable format. Adding a 'codemeta.json' file to your source code directory is another way of telling people how to cite your software.

12.6 Privacy and Ethics

A key concern when recording any kind of online information is privacy. IP addresses are now regarded as a form of personal information within Europe (and must therefore be stored in accordance with data protection laws) and keystroke, URL/URI and location data contain a wealth of information which can potentially be used to identify individuals. Whilst it is considered best practice from a scientific perspective to make datasets as open as possible, and to maintain provenance—from the raw data, through any stages of processing, to the final results of the analysis—it is essential that this does not happen at the expense of exposing participant identity, and this is a particular consideration when examining real world behaviour on the Web. Care should be taken at the experimental design stage to collect only the data necessary for the experiment, and to avoid recording identifying information wherever possible. There may be times when it is necessary to collect data that is potentially identifying, and only publish a summary of this (for example, in a thematic analysis of qualitative data). Although this obfuscates the analysis process, such that it is not possible for a reader to determine exactly how the results were reached, maintaining the privacy of the research participants must remain paramount.

12.7 Discussion

That reproducible and sustainable research software is rapidly increasing in importance is not in doubt. It will continue to be more important as time goes on and even more research is performed *in silico*. We have described here a number of tools and techniques that can be employed to ensure that your research software is reproducible and sustainable. Not all of them will be appropriate in all situations. It is important to be pragmatic, and use the right combination of methods to give the right level of reproducibility and sustainability for your desired outcomes. Knowing what to use, and when, requires experience that can only be gained by trying things out and occasionally getting things wrong. We believe that the benefits of making the extra effort to increase the reproducibility and sustainability of your software will be repaid both to yourself and those who build upon your research in the future.

12.8 Future Directions

Publishing research such that all data and associated software—including Web applications, data logging tools and analysis scripts—are available and operable, has the potential to transform science. At present, there remain many technical challenges to achieving this, which are being incrementally addressed, via motivated researchers, and slowly but increasingly, mandates from publishers. The majority of venues still have few guidelines about publishing research software, but over the coming years, this is likely to change. The benefits to making software open, and building it to maximise sustainability, are clear from a scientific perspective. As our understanding of how to build and effectively archive software grows, the more robust and reproducible our science will become.

12.9 Author's Opinion of the Field

At present, the Web accessibility field—like many in computer science—is not as advanced in its expectations of making source and analysis code available as domains such as astrophysics. Open source software is not the norm, nor is it required by publishers within the field. Over time, this is likely to change. Organisations like the ACM are beginning to encourage artifact review and Association for Computing Machinery (2018), which acknowledges and rewards the publication of research software that meets certain repeatability, replicability or reproducibility criteria. Those Web accessibility researchers ahead of this curve, who take care to use good practices when developing software, and make an effort to archive and cite data and software, are likely to reap significant benefits in terms of the perceived trustworthiness and value of their work.

12.10 Conclusions

Conducting truly reproducible research is difficult. A key part of building reproducibility into the research process is ensuring that any software used, be it a tool for collecting data, or a script for analysing it, is sustainable, i.e., it will continue to be available and usable in the future. Following software best practices such as version control, documenting software and ensuring it is properly tested, provide the foundation for sustainability. Software notebooks can help to elucidate the analysis process, such that others can understand and repeat it, and containers reduce software dependencies, helping to make applications available across platforms. Finally, making software openly available, via a public repository, and obtaining a DOI for it, will allow others to use research software, and provide its authors with credit for producing it.

References

About the Software Sustainability Institute. https://software.ac.uk/about. Accessed 28 Jun 2018

Apaolaza A, Harper S, Jay C (2015) Longitudinal analysis of low-level Web interaction through micro behaviours. In: Proceedings of the 26th ACM conference on hypertext and social media, association for computing machinery, p 337. https://doi.org/10.1145/2700171.2804453

Association for computing machinery—artifact review and badging. https://www.acm.org/publications/policies/artifact-review-badging. Accessed 14 Sep 2018

Baker M (2016) 1,500 scientists lift the lid on reproducibility. Nature 533:452–454. https://doi.org/10.1038/533452a

Boehm BW (1989) Software Risk Management. IEEE Computer Society Press

Citation file format specification. https://citation-file-format.github.io/1.0.3/specifications/. Accessed 14 Sep 2018

DANS—data archiving and network services. https://dans.knaw.nl/en. Accessed 29 Aug 2018

DataHub—frictionless data. https://datahub.io/. Accessed 29 Aug 2018

Docker. https://www.docker.com/. Accessed 21 Sep 2018

Encouraging citation of software—introducing CITATION files. https://www.software.ac.uk/blog/2016-10-06-encouraging-citation-software-introducing-citation-files. Accessed 14 Sep 2018

Figshare—credit for all your research. https://figshare.com/. Accessed 29 Aug 2018

Git. https://git-scm.com/. Accessed 29 Aug 2018

It's impossible to conduct research without software, say 7 out of 10 UK researchers. https://www.software.ac.uk/blog/2014-12-04-its-impossible-conduct-research-without-software-say-7-out-10-uk-researchers. Accessed 12 May 2018

Jones MB et al (2017) CodeMeta: an exchange schema for software metadata. version 2.0. KNB data repository. https://doi.org/10.5063/schema/codemeta-2.0

Making your code citable. https://guides.github.com/activities/citable-code/. Accessed 28 Sep 2018

Medeley data. https://data.mendeley.com/. Accessed 29 Aug 2018

Mercurial SCM. https://www.mercurial-scm.org/. Accessed 29 Aug 2018

PEP 8—Style guide for python code. https://www.python.org/dev/peps/pep-0008. Accessed 22 Jun 2018

Project Jupyter. http://jupyter.org/. Accessed 15 Sep 2018

Singularity. https://www.sylabs.io/. Accessed 21 Sep 2018

Smith AM, Katz DS, Niemeyer KE (2016) Software citation principles. FORCE11 Software Citation Working Group. PeerJ Comput Sci 2:e86. https://doi.org/10.7717/peerj-cs.86

Strijkers R et al (2011) Toward executable scientific publications. Procedia Comput Sci 4:707–715. https://doi.org/10.1016/j.procs.2011.04.074

The digital object identifier system. https://www.doi.org. Accessed 22 Jun 2018

The Journal of Open Research Software. https://openresearchsoftware.metajnl.com/. Accessed 22 Sep 2018

The Journal of Open Source Software. http://joss.theoj.org/. Accessed 22 Sep 2018

Thimbleby H (2003) Explaining code for publication. Softw Pract Exp 33:975–1001

Vagrant. https://www.vagrantup.com. Accessed 21 Sep 2018

Wilkinson MD et al (2016) The FAIR Guiding Principles for scientific data management and stewardship. Sci Data 3:160018. https://doi.org/10.1038/sdata.2016.18

Zenodo—research. Shared. https://zenodo.org/. Accessed 29 Aug 2018

Part III
Society and Standards

Chapter 13
Standards, Guidelines, and Trends

Shadi Abou-Zahra and Judy Brewer

Abstract The World Wide Web, the Web, is technically a family of open standards that defines the protocols and formats needed for the Web to function. These technical standards are the backbone of Web accessibility. They define critical accessibility features of Web technologies, as well as interoperability with assistive technologies. At the same time, these technical standards are rapidly evolving as the Web continues to expand in volume and in functionality, as different industry and technology sectors continue to converge onto the Web, and as our expectations for the Web continue to expand. Recent advances in Web technologies include enhanced support for mobile content and applications, real-time communication, immersive environments, multimedia, and automotive systems. Concurrently, Web-based applications are increasingly making use of advances in Artificial Intelligence (AI), Internet of Things (IoT), and Open Data. While such technological advances provide immense opportunities for the inclusion of people with disabilities, they require dedicated efforts to understand the diverse accessibility needs and to develop clear accessibility requirements for designers and developers of digital content, tools, and technologies for desktop and mobile devices. The World Wide Web Consortium (W3C) is the leading standards body for the Web and has a long history of commitment to accessibility. The W3C Web Accessibility Initiative (WAI) utilizes a multi-stakeholder consensus approach to pursue the goal of ensuring accessibility for people with disabilities on the Web. This includes designing and implementing particular accessibility features in core Web standards such as HTML and CSS, as well as developing and maintaining a set of Web accessibility guidelines, which are recognized internationally by business and government. This participatory effort involving representation of people with disabilities, industry, research, public bodies, and other experts promises to address evolving trends on the Web to help ensure accessibility for people with disabilities.

S. Abou-Zahra (✉) · J. Brewer
Web Accessibility Initiative (WAI) of the World Wide Web Consortium (W3C),
Sophia Antipolis, France
e-mail: shadi@w3.org

© Springer-Verlag London Ltd., part of Springer Nature 2019   225
Y. Yesilada and S. Harper (eds.), *Web Accessibility*, Human–Computer
Interaction Series, https://doi.org/10.1007/978-1-4471-7440-0_13

13.1   Introduction

From a user experience perspective, *"Web accessibility means that websites, tools, and technologies are designed and developed so that people with disabilities can use them"* (Lawton Henry 2018). This encompasses people with diverse abilities including auditory, cognitive and learning, neurological, physical, speech, and visual disabilities. It also involves people using a wide range of assistive technologies and adaptive strategies to interact with the Web. For example, one individual with dyslexia may use screen reader software when reading text, while another individual with dyslexia may use standard browser settings to change the appearance of the text to facilitate reading. Web accessibility encompasses this broad range of highly individualized abilities, and combinations of hardware, software, and assistive technologies.

From a technical perspective, Web accessibility means understanding the diverse user needs and translating them into specific technical requirements for designers and developers of websites, tools, and technologies. For example, to address the two scenarios of people with dyslexia described above, underlying technologies need to support reading content aloud and customizing its appearance in order to meet those user needs. HTML defines structures, such as headings, lists, and tables, to support reading content aloud, while Cascading Style Sheets (CSS) provides mechanisms to support customizing its appearance. On a next level, Web browsers need to either provide functionality to read content aloud and to customize its appearance, or to enable open access for assistive technologies that provide such functionality. Lastly, designers and developers of websites need to make correct use of HTML and CSS to provide the accessibility features for these two user scenarios within the content.

"Essential Components of Web Accessibility" (Lawton Henry 2018) defines:

- **Content** is anything provided on the Web, including text, forms, images, videos, sounds, and applications—this includes any markup and coding involved.
- **Technical specifications** include core Web standards, such as HTML, SVG, and CSS that are used by Web designers and developers to create Web content.
- **Accessibility guidelines** are technical standards that define specific accessibility requirements for designers and developers of Web content and software.
- **Developers** are anyone involved in the creation of content, including designers, programmers, quality assurance testers, and nontechnical content authors.
- **Authoring tools** are any tools designed to support the production of Web content, including content management systems (CMS), and code, and text editors.
- **Evaluation tools** are any tools designed to support evaluation of the accessibility of Web content, including automated and manual checkers and testing tools.
- **User agents** are any tools designed to support accessing and interacting with Web content, including browsers, media players, and some mobile applications.
- **Assistive technologies** are any tools designed to support people with disabilities in interacting with Web content, including software- and hardware-based tools.
- **Users** are individuals accessing and interacting with Web content, including people using assistive technologies and adaptive strategies (Fig. 13.1).

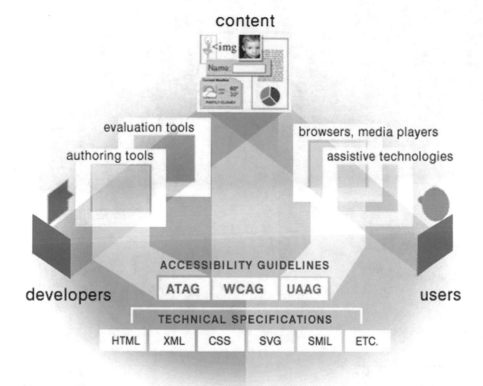

Fig. 13.1 Essential components of web accessibility

From a production perspective, Web accessibility means integrating accessibility requirements into the design, development, and maintenance processes of websites, tools, and technologies to ensure equal access for people with disabilities, while, at the same time, improving usability and promoting inclusion for all users. That is, while accessibility focuses on ensuring equal access for people with disabilities, it benefits many more people. Accessibility is ideally addressed from the onset as part of an inclusive design approach to maximize inclusion of all users (Lawton Henry et al. 2016). For example, addressing the prior two scenarios of people with dyslexia not only results in better accessibility for these two individuals but also results in better usability for anyone who prefers a different appearance of the text and better inclusion for individuals who may not be fluent in the primary content language.

The common denominator among these perspectives is systematic gathering and analysis of diverse user scenarios, deducing technical user needs and accessibility requirements, and documenting these in standards, guidelines, and other supporting resources for designers and developers of websites, tools, and technologies. This requires extensive involvement of a broad range of key stakeholders, including user representatives, research, industry, and other experts, in an open consensus process

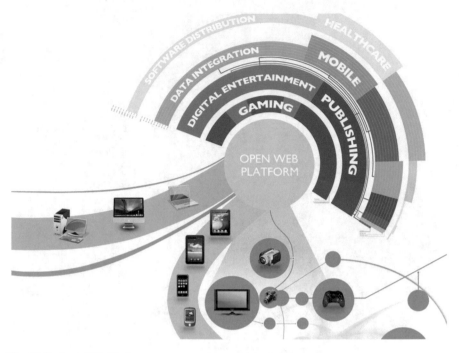

Fig. 13.2 Open Web Platform

that ensures balanced perspectives and rigorous vetting. This process has been successfully pursued at the World Wide Web Consortium (W3C) for over two decades.

13.2 Technical Specifications

Since its inception in 1989, the Web has been continually growing in both size and in functionality, and converging with different media, industries, and technologies. Besides desktop and laptop computers, access to the Web through mobile devices, including smart phones, personal digital assistants, and tablet computers, have been continually growing. In some regions, access through these devices has surpassed access through desktop computers. Also, smart televisions, digital cameras, games consoles, and many other devices are now increasingly web-enabled. This increased variety of interactions over the Web together with increased functionality supported by core Web standards such as HTML5 provides a rich platform for industry sectors to converge onto the Web. For example, digital publishing, online games, digital entertainment, data integration, software distribution, and healthcare are, more than ever, increasingly based on standards forming an *Open Web Platform* (Fig. 13.2).

Today, W3C alone counts over 250 completed standards ("Recommendations") and over 350 technical publications ("Working Group Notes") (All Standards and Drafts 2018), many of which define core functionality of the Web. Further standards, such as HTTP, JavaScript, and PDF are developed by other organizations, including the Internet Engineering Task Force (IETF), the European Computer Manufacturer Association (ECMA), and the International Organization for Standardization (ISO).

A simple example of accessibility support provided by core Web standards is the structural components, such as headings, lists, and tables, defined by HTML. Such structures allow assistive technologies, such as screen readers, to indicate structural information while reading content aloud, for example, to announce headings, lists and list items, and table cells in association with their table headers. This also allows more effective navigation for keyboard users, for example, skipping from section to section and through form controls and widgets. Without structural components in core Web standards, such as in HTML, screen reader users would need considerably more effort to understand the content, and keyboard users would need considerably more effort to navigate through the content, and they would both be disadvantaged.

A more advanced example of accessibility support is communicating changes to the content following user interactions and updates from the server. For example, confirming when users add items to shopping carts and indicating change of prices while purchasing items need to be communicated to users in appropriate modalities. Another example of advanced accessibility support is the capability to define how content is presented and how it adapts to various user settings. For example, settings could include increasing the text size (only) or enlarging the entire display (zoom).

Accessibility support is ideally specified directly within core Web standards and supported by mainstream browsers. Designing and promoting the implementation of accessibility features is a fundamental objective of the W3C Web Accessibility Initiative (WAI), which was established in 1997 to develop "*strategies, standards and resources to help make the Web accessible to people with disabilities*" (Web Accessibility Initiative (WAI) 2018). It is an integrated part of W3C, along with other activities on internationalization, privacy, and security. Together these efforts help achieve universality, which is making the Web "*work for all people, whatever their hardware, software, language, location, or ability*" (Lawton Henry 2018).

One of the priorities of WAI is to review all W3C specifications for accessibility during their development to ensure they address requirements for accessibility. This includes tracking the development of W3C specifications and ensuring coordination on addressing potential accessibility barriers and opportunities. It also includes recruiting expertise on the intersection of accessibility and the particular technology in development, which is not always easy for emerging technologies that do not yet have significant numbers of accessibility experts available. Taken as a whole, Web standards from W3C, such as HTML and CSS, provide robust accessibility support.

In some situations, however, it is necessary to develop technical specifications that exclusively define accessibility support features. For example, W3C Accessible Rich Internet Applications (WAI-ARIA) (Lawton Henry 2018) was developed during a period when HTML4 did not support for accessibility features that are now supported by HTML5, such as certain types of structural components. Yet WAI-ARIA continues to be needed, particularly for situations in which designers and developers do not use native HTML5 elements and instead create custom components. WAI-ARIA is also necessary to provide accessibility support for other technologies, such as W3C Scalable Vector Graphics (SVG), which do not provide the same level of built-in support for accessibility, such as the definition of user interface components.

13.3 Accessibility Guidelines

With the general term *accessibility guidelines*, we refer to standards that define the user requirements for designers and developers, rather than defining protocols and formats. For example, an accessibility requirement is identifying headings within the content. Such a requirement is reflected across the *components of Web accessibility*:

- **Technical specifications**: define the structural components to identify headings
- **User agents**: process headings and communicate them to assistive technologies
- **Designers and developers**: identify headings according to the specification used
- **Authoring tools**: help designers and developers to identify headings effectively
- **Evaluation tools**: check if designers and developers identify headings correctly

The scope of accessibility guidelines is typically the latter four bullets, where the first is discussed in the previous section of this chapter. However, it is important to note the interrelation between these components. For example, continuing with the headings example above, both HTML and WAI-ARIA provide markup to identify headings. This means that designers and developers can use different *techniques* to meet this accessibility requirement. However, in doing so, they need to understand how well different user agents and assistive technologies support these techniques. Also authoring and evaluation tools need to support these different techniques and support the designers and developers in selecting the appropriate ones for each task.

13.3.1 WAI Guidelines

In addition to ensuring accessibility support in core W3C Web standards, the W3C Web Accessibility Initiative (WAI) develops and maintains a set of complementary guidelines for Web accessibility. These are internationally recognized by businesses and governments and are commonly collectively referred to as the *WAI Guidelines*:

- **Web Content Accessibility Guidelines (WCAG)** (Lawton Henry 2018) defines requirements for Web content, including desktop and mobile websites and apps.
- **Authoring Tool Accessibility Guidelines (ATAG)** (Lawton Henry 2015) defines requirements for authoring tools, including content management systems (CMSs).
- **User Agent Accessibility Guidelines (UAAG)** (Lawton Henry 2015) defines requirements for Web browsers, media players, and mobile applications.

These WAI Guidelines are developed using the same open and consensus-based development process as technical specifications from W3C. This ensures rigorous vetting and broad consensus for the resulting work. Part of the obligation of WAI is to ensure a broad participation and representation of all key stakeholders, including people with disabilities and representatives of disability organizations who are often underrepresented in standardization. Such a participatory approach helps ensure the inclusion of all perspectives, to achieve broad consensus (Fig. 13.3).

Particularly, the development of WCAG requires broad review and well-balanced discussion to ensure the adequate definition of the accessibility requirements. The open process of W3C allows the direct participation of key stakeholders from industry, the disability community, government, researchers, and other stakeholder groups. At the same time, it ensures opportunities for review and comments from the public to ensure community responsiveness and public accountability. The process also defines clear conflict escalation and resolution mechanisms to ensure a consensus-based process. This, in turn, requires multi-stakeholder involvement to provide the necessary views and input. This allows for a more balanced discussion and review.

13.3.1.1 Web Content Accessibility Guidelines (WCAG)

The first version of the W3C Web Content Accessibility Guidelines (WCAG) was released in 1999 (Chisholm et al. 1999). The standard is based on requirements originally developed by Trace Center of the University of Wisconsin-Madison. It focused on HTML as the predominant format at the time. WCAG 1.0 was adopted by many governments and businesses as the standard for Web accessibility. However, also derivatives of this standard started to emerge and to gain popularity. This included

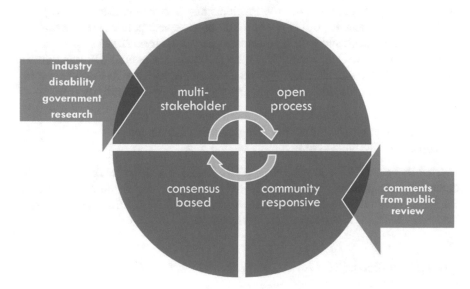

Fig. 13.3 Open collaboration

different variations of the standard used by the US Access Board, by the European Union countries, and other countries.

In 2008, W3C released the second generation WCAG 2.0 (Caldwell et al. 2008). It solves central issues that the WCAG 1.0 derivatives were trying to resolve, which is to be more independent of technologies and to apply to dynamic applications. WCAG 2.0 defines accessibility requirements that are agnostic to the Web technology and techniques that content authors use to meet the user needs, and agnostic to the Web browser and assistive technologies that users utilize to access and interact with Web content. These accessibility requirements are also formulated as testable statements to help content authors better determine when they have met them. An example of this is the requirement from WCAG 1.0 to *"provide sufficient contrast"* between foreground and background color combinations, which did not define specific thresholds for *sufficient*, making it difficult for authors to know when they met the requirement. WCAG 2.0 defines a specific algorithm to calculate *"color luminosity ratio,"* with thresholds of 4.5:1 and 7:1, to help ensure testability.

Meanwhile, civil and disability rights have been strengthening in many regions of the world. In particular, the Convention on the Rights of Persons with Disabilities (CRPD) of the United Nations (UN) (Convention on the Rights of Persons with Disabilities 2006) was adopted by most countries around the world. In many countries, this led to an increased awareness of disability and efforts on accessibility. Additionally, the market for digital accessibility has been maturing over the years, and the fragmentation around WCAG 1.0 was increasingly a barrier. WCAG 2.0 provided the technical basis to support harmonization, which has been increasing since its release. This includes the adoption of WCAG 2.0 as ISO standard 40500 (ISO/IEC 40500 2012), in European standard EN 301 549 (Accessibility Requirements Suitable for Public Procurement of ICT Products and Services in Europe 2014), and in the technical standards of US Section 508 procurement policy (Information and Communication Technology (ICT) Standards and Guidelines 2017).

In June 2018, W3C released WCAG 2.1 (Kirckpatrick et al. 2018) as an update to WCAG 2.0. It does not replace WCAG 2.0 nor change any of its existing requirements. Instead, it adds requirements, primarily to improve accessibility for:

- People with cognitive and learning disabilities
- People with low vision, often not using assistive technologies
- People with disabilities using mobile technology

That is, WCAG 2.1 is a superset of WCAG 2.0 and is therefore fully backwards compatible. Despite its recent release, WCAG 2.1 has been rolled into an update of the European standard EN 301 549, which was released in August 2018 (Accessibility Requirements for ICT Products and Services 2018).

13.3.1.2   Authoring Tool Accessibility Guidelines (ATAG)

As opposed to content authors, the W3C Authoring Tools Accessibility Guidelines (ATAG) addresses the designers and developers of authoring tools. This includes a broad range of software ranging from markup editors and Integrated Development Environments (IDE) to more comprehensive Content Management Systems (CMS), Learning Management Systems (LMS), and social media platforms. All these tools generate content, and thus play an essential role in ensuring the accessibility of the Web. In particular, this includes two important aspects of content authoring:

- Ensure that the content generated by authoring tools supports accessibility
- Ensure that the authoring tools themselves have accessible user interfaces

The first version, ATAG 1.0 (Treviranus et al. 2000), was released in February 2000, soon after the release of WCAG 1.0. At the time, this linkage was a benefit, as WCAG and ATAG were closely aligned with each other. However, as work on WCAG 2.0 advanced, it was clear that also an updated version of ATAG would be needed. In 2015, W3C released ATAG 2.0 (Richards et al. 2015), which provided improvements, including alignment with WCAG 2.0. Yet one challenge with this standard remains, which is its applicability to a wide range of contexts. For example, the types of tools that it addresses are broad, including graphical and text editors that are software or web based. In addition, the industries in which authoring tools are used have considerably different workflows. For example, Learning Management Systems (LMS) used in the educational sector differ from Content Management Systems (CMS) that are more commonly used for website production, and from social media platforms.

13.3.1.3   User Agent Accessibility Guidelines (UAAG)

W3C User Agent Accessibility Guidelines (UAAG) 1.0 (Jacobs et al. 2002) was released in 2003. The term *User Agent* refers to any piece of software used to access, interact with, and render content. Typically, these are Web browsers but can also be media players and some types of assistive technology. Some types of mobile applications are considered user agents because they access and render Web content for users, and allow users to interact with rendered Web content. The rapid uptake of mobile applications to access Web content was one of the main motivations for the development of UAAG 2.0 (Allan et al. 2015). This was released in 2015 as a W3C Working Group Note, which is not as a full Web standard.

User agents have critical roles in Web accessibility because they ultimately define the connection between content authors and users. For example, when Web browsers do not support particular accessibility features of core technical specifications, such as audio description tracks for videos, then Web content authors cannot rely on these particular features as viable techniques to provide accessibility. In WCAG 2.0, this concept is defined as "*accessibility supported ways of using Web technologies.*" This requires content authors to assess support for particular accessibility features before they can be used as a means of providing accessibility. Sometimes such support, in particular, for new features, varies considerably among different browsers and tools.

In fact, while support for accessibility features has improved greatly over the past few years, designers and developers still spend a considerable amount of their time working around inconsistent support in Web browsers and in assistive technologies. In particular, some assistive technologies are developed and maintained by smaller project teams with limited resources to identify and fix bugs. Increasingly, feedback on such bugs is provided by members of the accessibility community. This includes a recent proliferation of accessibility consultancies. One explanation for this trend is that as the market for Web accessibility has continued to grow, and accordingly, the incentives for "getting it right" have also increased for designers and developers.

13.3.2 Other Guidelines

There are several guidelines, beyond the WAI Guidelines, that meet our definition for *accessibility guidelines*. Sometimes, guidelines are formal standards developed by standards development organizations (SDOs), and sometimes, they are informal standards developed by government agencies and other entities. Some guidelines are normative (required in a particular context), while others are informative. Some guidelines focus specifically on accessibility, while others apply more broadly. For example, generic guidelines for designers and developers may include accessibility considerations. Some guidelines focus exclusively on Web, while others apply more broadly to digital accessibility. For example, guidelines could apply to information and communication technologies (ICTs), and relate to the Web as part of that scope.

13.3.2.1   US Section 508 Technical Standard

Section 508 of the United States Rehabilitation Act uses procurement regulations to specify accessibility considerations for federal agencies "*developing, procuring, maintaining, or using electronic and information technology*" (Text of Section 508 of the Rehabilitation Act of 1973, as Amended (29 U.S.C. §794d) 2018). Section 508 is enacted in a technical rule that establishes specific accessibility requirements (Information and Communication Technology (ICT) Standards and Guidelines 2017). These requirements apply to any *Information and Communication Technology (ICT)*, including hardware and software. For example, the US Section 508 Technical Standard applies to printers and ATMs, as well as to websites and mobile applications that are developed, procured, and otherwise acquired by US federal agencies.

The prior version of this technical standard was based on WCAG 1.0 with some significant differences, including modified, removed, or added requirements. It was sometimes difficult to meet both accessibility guidelines because of the differences. The current version of this technical standard has been updated to fully align with WCAG 2.0. In fact, US Section 508 Technical Standard now refers to WCAG 2.0 not only for Web content but also for non-Web electronic documents and software, such as software and documents on the computer rather than published on the Web.

13.3.2.2   CEN/CENELEC/ETSI EN 301 549

Mandated by the European Commission (EC), the three official European standards organizations (ESOs), CEN, CENELEC, and ETSI, released a first version of the European Standard (EN) 301 549 in 2014 (Accessibility Requirements Suitable for Public Procurement of ICT Products and Services in Europe 2014). The intended use of this standard was also procurement by public bodies, only this time in Europe. EN 301 549 was aligned with the updated US Section 508 Technical Standard, and it similarly references WCAG 2.0 for Web content, non-Web electronic documents, and non-Web software. However, this adoption of WCAG 2.0 for non-Web contexts was not initially envisioned by W3C and technical clarification was needed.

Following this need to clarify the application of WCAG 2.0 to non-Web contexts in Europe and in the United States, W3C convened a task force to develop the supporting document "Guidance on Applying WCAG 2.0 to Non-Web Information and Communication Technologies (WCAG2ICT)" (Lawton Henry and Brewer 2018). This nonnormative document provides clarification on the applicability of WCAG 2.0 requirements to documents and software that are not web-based. For example, it clarifies the use of labels and captions for these contexts, which sometimes differ.

In August 2018, the ESOs released an updated version of EN 301 549 (v2.1.1), "Accessibility requirements for ICT products and services" (Accessibility Requirements for ICT Products and Services 2018). This version of the EN was revised to specifically meet the policy requirements of the "European Web Accessibility Directive (WAD)" (Mueller et al. 2018). It references both WCAG 2.0 and WCAG 2.1 for Web content, and it aligns with WCAG 2.1 for non-Web documents and software.

13.3.2.3   National Standards on Web Accessibility

Among the expanding number of laws and policies on accessibility, many countries formally adopted standards on Web accessibility (Mueller et al. 2018). Several countries adopted the WAI Guidelines, in particular, WCAG, while others developed local standards. For example, in Australia, Japan, and Spain, national standardization bodies developed Web accessibility standards (Accessibility Requirements Suitable for Public Procurement of ICT 2016; JIS X 8341-3 2016; UNE 139803 2012). In France, Germany, and India, government agencies developed Web accessibility standards (Référentiel Général d'Accessibilité pour les Administrations (RGAA) Version 3 2017; Verordnung zur Schaffung barrierefreier Informationstechnik nach dem Behindertengleichstellungsgesetz (Barrierefreie-Informationstechnik-Verordnung - BITV 2.0) 2011; Guidelines for Indian Government Websites 2009). Typically, these local standards are based on WCAG 2.0, though they sometimes include few differences that in some cases may reduce the opportunity to share implementation support. Australian standard AS 301 549 is, instead, based on EN 301 549.

13.3.2.4   ISO/IEC TR 29138-1 User Needs Summary

ISO/IEC TR 29138-1:2009 (ISO/IEC TR 29138-1 2009) defines accessibility considerations for people with disabilities, independently of any particular technology, hardware, or software. For example, it states that some people may not be able to perceive auditory information and therefore require alternatives. This level of user requirements is addressed by accessibility guidelines, such as WCAG. However, this level of requirements may be useful in developing novel accessibility functionality for emerging technologies.

13.3.2.5   ISO/IEC FDIS 30071-1 Code of Practice

ISO/IEC FDIS 30071-1 (ISO/IEC FDIS 30071-1 2018) is currently under development. It is based on British Standard BS 8878 (BS 8878 2010) and defines requirements on the development process rather than on the resulting products and services. That is, it complements accessibility guidelines, such as WCAG, by guiding designers and developers throughout the production process. Initially, this standard was focused on websites and applications but it has been broadened to support the production of any ICT product and service.

13.4   Discussion

Web accessibility is backed by a comprehensive set of international standards. They include technical specifications with built-in accessibility features, such as HTML5; technical specifications that provide enhanced accessibility features, such as WAI-ARIA; and accessibility guidelines such as WCAG 2. In addition to these standards, the W3C Web Accessibility Initiative (WAI) maintains a comprehensive collection of educational and training resources to support designers, developers, quality assurance testers, project managers, and others to create accessible content and applications. These resources are openly available under the royalty-free W3C licensing.

This wealth of resources, combined with growing awareness for disability rights in many parts around the world, has continually enlarged and strengthened a global market for Web accessibility. The successes in Web accessibility raise questions of technical, societal, and sometimes philosophical nature. Often the questions are not limited to Web accessibility and relate to broader aspects of disability, accessibility, and inclusion. Some discussions evolve over time, while others recur periodically. Often these discussions are initiated when new technologies are deployed or when laws and policies are strengthened. The following are examples of these discussions.

13.4.1 Scope of the Term Accessibility

The W3C Web Accessibility Initiative (WAI) and many other organizations define the scope of *accessibility* to equivalent use for people with disabilities (Lawton Henry 2018). It comes from the disability rights movement and the call to end discrimination of people due to disability. It is rooted in the principle that disability is part of human diversity, just like age, race, ethnicity, gender, sexual orientation, religion, and such.

Yet accessibility, in particular, Web accessibility, provides benefits to many more societal groups beyond people with disabilities. For example, Web accessibility also improves overall usability and supports inclusion of people with less digital literacy. Some argue that limiting the scope of accessibility to people with disabilities excludes other groups and keeps accessibility as a niche for a smaller group.

A counter-argument is that keeping the focus of accessibility on people with disabilities does not exclude it from being part of *inclusion* for everyone. In fact, the W3C Web Accessibility Initiative (WAI) states that Web accessibility is most efficiently implemented when it is part of a broader process for inclusive design (Lawton Henry et al. 2016). For example, designing content so that it is accessible for people with disabilities and usable for people new to computers is good practice.

Specifically, there are concerns that if the term accessibility is broadened beyond people with disabilities, already underserved disability groups could be further excluded, rather than included. For example, rare types of disabilities and disorders that would seem numerically small in the broader context of inclusion for everyone would potentially receive less focus and attention than they currently frequently do.

13.4.2 Conformance and Compliance

Accessibility guidelines are sometimes enforced by laws and policies (Mueller et al. 2018). Where this is the case, it creates a relationship between *conformance* with the standard and *compliance* with policies, sometimes with legal implications. While this helps drive accessibility, it can also create tension when the relationship is too prescriptive. For example, it can result in designers and developers focusing their efforts on meeting the technical standards rather than focusing on the users.

Part of this comes from the conformance models used by accessibility guidelines. Technically, a failure to meet a given accessibility requirement would mean that the content does not conform to WCAG, regardless of its impact on the user. However, it is not trivial to define robust measurements for accessibility. Already in 2011, the W3C Web Accessibility Initiative (WAI) organized a research symposium on "Web Accessibility Metrics" (Web Accessibility Metrics Symposium 2011) to explore approaches to measuring the extent of conformance. The symposium identified key criteria for qualitative metrics, including *validity*, *reliability*, *sensitivity*, *adequacy*, and *complexity* of the metrics (Vigo et al. 2012). Yet to date, no methodology is known to address these quality criteria to an adequate level.

Another part of this comes from the compliance models used by accessibility laws and policies, which are sometimes perceived as being too rigid. Some include a concept of *undue burden* or similar to address situations when meeting the standard may be too difficult. A few countries, such as The Netherlands, allow public bodies to provide justification and a plan for complying with the policy when they currently do not comply (Mueller et al. 2018). Such approaches provide more flexibility for different situations. However, they are typically also more difficult to maintain.

13.4.3   Underserved Disability Groups

Some accessibility guidelines focus on particular disability groups. The W3C *WAI Guidelines* follow a universal design approach to include all disabilities potentially impacted by accessibility barriers in technologies covered by these standards. That does not mean that all user groups are equally well addressed in these standards. As discussed in earlier sections, in addition to addressing advances in mobile technology, part of the motivation for developing of WCAG 2.1 was to improve coverage of requirements for specific user groups that are less well addressed in WCAG 2.0.

The broad spectrum of people with cognitive and learning disabilities continues to be an especially challenging topic. This is in part because the user needs for some groups are still not adequately understood by researchers and standards developers. It is also in part because some well-understood user needs are not easy to formulate as actionable, testable, and practical criteria for accessibility. For example, defining universally applicable criteria for *easy to read* is difficult to achieve in any one language, let alone for internationally applicable standards. Another factor leading to underserving disability groups is underrepresentation in the standardization process.

13.5   Future Directions

Initially, the Web was a static, document-oriented media. Soon, form elements were introduced that allowed basic client–server interactions. Later, the *Document Object Model (DOM)* and related application programming interfaces (APIs) allowed rich web-based applications on desktop and mobile devices. These are transforming entire industries that are increasingly basing their core infrastructures on cloud computing, software as a service (SaaS), and other web-based technology. In turn, this continues to strengthen the need and case for Web accessibility—without reliable access to the Web, people with disabilities are excluded from parts of modern society that are increasingly web based. This includes but is not limited to education, health care, employment, civic participation, entertainment, and societal interaction.

The Web is also continuing to expand into many different devices beyond the desktop computer. Accessing the Web using laptop computers, mobile phones, and tablet computers has become more common than via desktop computers. This trend extends to televisions, ticketing and information kiosks, home appliances and entertainment systems, gaming consoles, and many more. In fact, today we speak of connected homes, offices, mobility, public spaces, and entire *smart cities* driven by Web-based products and services. This also increases the need and the case for Web accessibility—connected and smart ICTs provide unprecedented opportunities for people with disabilities, yet only if these are designed to be accessible. Otherwise, they have the opposite potential, of excluding people with disabilities from society.

13.5.1 Ubiquitous Web Interfaces

Previously, boundaries of the Web were clearer and more distinct. Using the Web implied using external services, such as purchasing products from an online shop or completing tax forms online. Many other activities, such as creating documents and spreadsheets, exchanging emails, managing notes and calendars, instant messaging, and telephony, required separate software and seemed quite separate from the Web. Today, these kinds of tasks are frequently carried out through Web-based interfaces, and boundaries of the Web have diminished due to several technological advances:

- **Rich applications**: Today, Web-based applications provide rich functionality that is nearly equivalent to native software that is developed for a particular operating system. In fact, native software, in particular, mobile applications, increasingly use Web-based technologies. The so-called *hybrid apps* use native software as a shell to interact with operating systems, and Web-based interfaces to provide content, including user interactions and functionality. In this way, complex applications, such as word processors, calculators, and many more are commonly web-based.
- **Media integration**: Previously, video and audio content on the Web required an external media player for playback. Today, Web technologies such as HTML5 provide native capabilities for video and audio. These are becoming increasingly robust across platforms. Consequently, developers can increasingly rely on the Web for media delivery, for example for broadcasting and streaming services. Continued integration, for example, with immersive environments including augmented and virtual reality, will further open the doors to other digital industries.
- **Increased access**: External applications such as extensions and plugins for Web browsers used to be necessary to give web-based applications access beyond the mere user interface. Today, standards such as W3C Real-time Communication Between Browsers (WebRTC) enable web-based applications for telephony and peer-to-peer interaction such as instant messaging. Other standards allow access to device sensors, such as camera, microphone, and touchscreen. These standards enable web-based applications with functionality comparable to native software.

This growth of the Web is expected to continue in the coming years. As the Internet of Things (IoT) evolves and grows, web-based technologies continue to provide an attractive interface to the Internet. This trend is critical to Web accessibility for two main reasons: first, the Web is built on open, royalty-free standards, which provide open access to assistive technologies and services. Second, most Web standards are developed by W3C, which has a strong commitment to accessibility. However, this commitment is not a given and requires a dedicated effort by the entire community. For example, the accessibility of immersive environments still requires intensive research and development effort. Collaborative efforts in and around W3C groups are necessary to ensure accessibility of the Web as it continues to evolve. In particular, it includes a deep understanding of user needs in diverse digital environments and the development of corresponding accessibility features in Web technologies.

13.5.2 *Artificial Intelligence and Big Data*

Many concepts of data processing and analysis, machine learning, and artificial intelligence date back to the early days of computing in the 1950s. Several cycles of evolution occurred in tandem with advancements in memory, computing power, and computer networks. In recent years AI, in particular, machine learning, reemerged with substantial gains in capabilities. Backed by the enormous amounts of data that exist on the Web today, including text, images, video, and audio content, developers are able to train machine-learning algorithms with greater success than earlier. This ranges from relatively simple applications such as recognizing images, voices, and gestures, to complex applications in healthcare, mobility, robotics, and automation.

Processing large amounts of data to train artificial intelligence applications offers immense potential for Web accessibility. For example, uses of artificial intelligence could increase support for relatively simple tasks such as recognizing accessibility barriers in code segments and user interfaces to support content authors and website owners in ensuring accessibility. Developers of Web accessibility testing tools are experimenting with this technology to provide better products and services (Abou-Zahra et al. 2018), which can be a basis for further development in the field.

AI can be instrumental in solving current challenges in accessibility. Automatic image recognition and audio captioning are already used by researchers and vendors (Abou-Zahra et al. 2018). Increased automation supported by machine learning could enable assistive technologies are less dependent on content authors providing accessibility features. AI could help make emerging digital technologies, such as immersive environments, accessible. Specifically, AI can provide mechanisms to recognize objects and interactions in virtual, augmented, and mixed reality environments to provide more accessible technology experiences.

Beyond these possibilities, more advanced developments in AI, such as affective computing, can be instrumental in better addressing the accessibility needs of neurodiverse users who are currently substantially underserved by accessibility guidance and the technical solutions. For example, recognizing the emotional state of the user and adapting content and functionality accordingly. Likewise, people with diverse types of cognitive, learning, and language disabilities may require individualization and customization of content rather than static accessibility features. They can also benefit from accessibility features that are dynamically generated by AI technology.

13.5.3 Personalization and Adaptation

While also not novel, recently the trend towards personalization and adaptation of Web content has been gaining in popularity. In part, this is driven by advances in artificial intelligence, including improved mechanisms for individualization and customization of Web content. However, there needs to be a common understanding of specific needs for personalization and adaptation. For example, there is a need for a standardized taxonomy of the types of objects that users may want to personalize, and how users may want to personalize them. A type of object could be "button," and one way of personalizing a "button" could be to "change the label" or to "change the appearance on the screen." Such definitions would allow assistive technologies and services, possibly using artificial intelligence techniques, to recognize buttons in the content and adapt them according to the needs and preferences of the specific user.

Recently W3C added two related requirements to the Web Content Accessibility Guidelines (WCAG) 2.1—Success Criteria 1.3.5 "Identify Input Purpose" and 1.3.6 "Identify Purpose" (Kirckpatrick et al. 2018). The first criterion requires content authors to use semantics already provided by HTML to identify input fields, so that these can be recognized by Web browsers and assistive technology. For example, Web browsers increasingly provide functionality to autofill input fields based on previous entries saved in the browser. This reduces the effort for people with reduced dexterity to type and for people with some forms of cognitive and learning disabilities who may otherwise have difficulty remembering required information, such as their email address. The second criterion requires the purpose of all user interface components, icons, and regions to be "programmatically determined." This facilitates personalization and adaptation of Web content by assistive technology. However, this second requirement is currently at Level AAA conformance.

The addition of these two success criteria, however, indicates the importance of personalization and adaptation techniques to facilitate Web accessibility. In addition to these criteria, W3C recently published a complementary set of specifications to support Web content personalization and adaptation for accessibility:

- W3C Personalization Semantics Explainer 1.0
- W3C Personalization Help and Support 1.0
- W3C Personalization Tools 1.0

Currently, these are rather early drafts ("First Public Working Draft") yet indicate an important trend in Web accessibility research, development, and standardization.

13.5.4 Next Generation Accessibility Guidelines

To better reflect the technological trends and developments outlined in the previous sections, a new generation of accessibility guidelines is needed. In particular, it is questionable whether the current limitation around *Web content* in the Web Content

Accessibility Guidelines (WCAG) is adequate for some types of applications, which operate beyond the user interface alone. For example, a web-based teleconferencing system using WebRTC should ensure sufficient quality-of-service (QoS) aspects to ensure accessibility. This could include ensuring sufficient transmission quality for sign language, audio descriptions, and real-time text (RTT). Typically, such aspects were not part of Web content and applications because they were provided through external software, such as Web browser extensions, add-ons, and plugins. Today, it is possible to create such applications directly in the browser using Web technology.

Due to the continual expansion of the Web, more accessibility considerations are needed to address the enlarged scope of the Web. For example, as the Web of Things (WoT) continues to evolve as part of the Internet of Things (IoT), specific questions relating to interoperability, accessibility support, configurability, privacy, security, and safety need to be addressed (Abou-Zahra et al. 2017). The same applies to biometrics, immersive environments, device sensors, and other functionality. In many cases, the user needs are not yet well understood and require further research. For example, making augmented, virtual, and mixed reality environments accessible requires a dedicated research of diverse user needs.

At the same time, continually adding more accessibility requirements to existing accessibility guidelines creates challenges. On the one hand, accessibility guidelines need to be more usable, friendly, and less complex in order to increase acceptance by designers and developers. On the other hand, they need to have stable references to allow policies and implementations to transition from one stable version to another. These and other considerations are flowing into the design and development of the next generation WAI Guidelines, referred to by the project name "Silver" (Silver Task Force Wiki: Main Page 2018). One of the aims is to pursue a more modular approach to address different types of digital applications and content, and a reorganization of requirements to address the enlarged scope of the Web today.

13.6   Authors' Opinion

Web standards, including accessibility guidelines, are the core building blocks for Web accessibility. However, accessibility is more than just standards and guidelines. Accessibility is the foundation for societal inclusion of people with disabilities. In the fields of Web design and development, this means understanding the user needs and involving the users throughout the process. Within that process, standards and guidelines define accessibility requirements that designer and developers need to meet, and supporting materials help guide the implementation process. Involving people with disabilities throughout the standardization process is critical to ensure development of effective standards and guidelines that address real-world situations.

Yet maintaining that focus on users and involving them throughout the design and development processes is difficult to accomplish in practice. Among designers and developers, there is commonly a lack of awareness of the accessibility needs of people with disabilities. In turn, designers and developers often tend to focus solely on technical aspects of accessibility and to neglect the user perspective. Moreover, in standardization, there is commonly a general lack of awareness of accessibility, requiring that it be continuously re-explained. Ideally, people with disabilities are part of the standardization process. Yet this requires standardization processes that are inclusive and ensure that people with disabilities can participate, to voice and explain their needs and to assess whether these have been implemented effectively.

We have come a long way in Web accessibility and successfully addressed many challenges along the way. For example, when the first dynamic Web applications emerged, in the era of Dynamic HTML (DHTML), it posed a challenge for different disability groups, and in particular screen reader users. Yet at the same time, richer and often more intuitive and usable applications provided improved accessibility for other disability groups. To address this gap, WAI-ARIA was developed in order to enable accessible rich Web content and applications. Similarly, there were also gaps when audiovisual formats were converging onto the Web, and when the Web was being increasingly accessed through mobile devices and applications, because these uses were not initially part of the technology nor of the related Web standards.

Ensuring accessibility requires a continued process as new technologies emerge and converge onto the Web. Currently, we seem to be in the middle of a new phase of changing technologies and requirements on the Web. In particular, developments at W3C in WebVR, WebRTC, WoT, and even standards for the automotive industry pose new opportunities and challenges for accessibility. Artificial intelligence is rapidly advancing with exciting new opportunities for accessibility; however, it is currently not yet sufficiently reliable for many of the tasks it could solve in the future, and requires dedicated and coordinated efforts in research and development.

The W3C Web Accessibility Initiative (WAI) has played a crucial role in many of the developments in Web accessibility over the past two decades. It continues to provide a suitable venue for users, industry, researchers, governments, experts, and other stakeholder to come together and address the upcoming challenges in ensuring accessibility of the World Wide Web, as it continues to provide new opportunities.

13.7 Conclusion

The Web continues to be one of the most important technologies for the inclusion of people with disabilities. In many parts of the world, the Web is part of all aspects of everyday life, and this tendency is only increasing. The Web is also continually growing in scope, in the technical capabilities it offers, and in the volume of content and applications that it provides. It evolved rapidly from an initially static and rather document-oriented media to what the World Wide Web Consortium (W3C) meanwhile refers to as the "Open Web Platform." This platform provides unprecedented opportunities for the inclusion of people with disabilities, to be equal part of society.

Web standards play a critical role in realizing these opportunities. Standards are key enablers for assistive technologies and services. They define the core protocols and formats of the Web and allow the design and development of custom solutions to accommodate the accessibility needs of people with disabilities. Web standards from W3C are, in addition, provided under royalty-free licensing and open to anyone wanting to develop web-based products and services. W3C also has a history of strong commitment to accessibility, which ensures that accessibility features are built directly into the core Web standards, as well as the continual evolution of the WAI Guidelines and other technical and educational solutions for Web accessibility.

Yet, the continual rapid growth and evolution of the Web is creating a challenge for accessibility. A substantial of work has already been successfully carried out by the W3C Web Accessibility Initiative (WAI) to address accessibility of rich Web applications and interactive content, multimedia content, and mobile accessibility. This includes continued improvement of accessibility support in core Web standards such as HTML5, continued evolution of WAI-ARIA and related APIs, as well as continued evolution of the WAI Guidelines and their supporting resources. Yet the work ahead requires continued attention and dedicated effort. In particular, ensuring accessibility of the Web of Things (WoT), web-based immersive environments, and other emerging Web technologies requires continued attention and dedicated effort.

At the same time, these continual technological advances also provide immense opportunities for accessibility. For example, the Internet of Things (IoT) promises fundamental accessibility not only online but also of the physical world. It allows more interoperable, affordable, and available smart environments, such homes and workplaces, as well as smart mobility, such as self-driving cars. Also, developments in artificial intelligence, including machine learning, pattern recognition, and affective computing allow new forms of Human–Computer Interaction (HCI), such as voice-based interaction, and new types of assistive technologies and services. This allows inclusion for disability groups that are currently underserved by technology.

A key ingredient to ensuring continued successes in Web accessibility standards and guidelines is multi-stakeholder collaboration in an open and consensus-based process, such as that of the W3C Web Accessibility Initiative (WAI). While such a process involves higher overhead for consensus finding and consensus building, it also ensures more rigor through the involvement of different perspectives. It proved to be successful but it requires continued vigilance of the accessibility community.

References

Abou-Zahra S et al (2017) Web standards to enable an accessible and inclusive internet of things (IoT). Web4All 2017. http://hdl.handle.net/1721.1/107831. Accessed 31 Oct 2018

Abou-Zahra S et al (2018) Artificial intelligence (AI) for web accessibility: is conformance evaluation a way forward? Web4All 2018. http://hdl.handle.net/1721.1/116479. Accessed 31 Oct 2018

Accessibility Requirements for ICT Products and Services (2018) CEN/CENELEC/ETSI. https://www.etsi.org/deliver/etsi_en/301500_301599/301549/02.01.02_60/en_301549v020102p.pdf. Accessed 31 October 2018

Accessibility Requirements Suitable for Public Procurement of ICT (2016) Standards Australia. https://infostore.saiglobal.com/en-gb/Standards/AS-EN-301-549-2016-100620_SAIG_AS_AS_211428/. Accessed 31 Oct 2018

Accessibility Requirements Suitable for Public Procurement of ICT Products and Services in Europe (2014) CEN/CENELEC/ETSI. https://www.etsi.org/deliver/etsi_en/301500_301599/301549/01.01.01_60/en_301549v010101p.pdf. Accessed 31 Oct 2018

All Standards and Drafts (2018) W3C. https://w3.org/TR/. Accessed 31 Oct 2018

Allan J et al (eds) (2015) User agent accessibility guidelines (UAAG) 2.0. W3C. https://w3.org/TR/UAAG20/. Accessed 31 Oct 2018

BS 8878 (2010) Web accessibility. Code of practice. BSI. https://shop.bsigroup.com/ProductDetail/?pid=000000000030180388. Accessed 31 Oct 2018

Caldwell B et al (eds) (2008) Web content accessibility guidelines (WCAG) 2.0. W3C. https://w3.org/TR/WCAG20/. Accessed 31 Oct 2018

Chisholm W et al (eds) (1999) Web content accessibility guidelines (WCAG) 1.0. W3C. https://w3.org/TR/WCAG10/. Accessed 31 Oct 2018

Convention on the Rights of Persons with Disabilities (2006) United Nations (UN). https://www.un.org/development/desa/disabilities/convention-on-the-rights-of-persons-with-disabilities.html. Accessed 31 Oct 2018

Guidelines for Indian Government Websites (2009) Department of administrative reforms and public grievances. https://web.guidelines.gov.in/. Accessed 31 October 2018

Information and Communication Technology (ICT) Standards and Guidelines (2017) US Federal Register. https://www.federalregister.gov/documents/2017/01/18/2017-00395/information-and-communication-technology-ict-standards-and-guidelines. Accessed 31 Oct 2018

ISO/IEC TR 29138-1 (2009) Accessibility considerations for people with disabilities—part 1: user needs summary. ISO. https://www.iso.org/standard/45161.html. Accessed 31 Oct 2018

ISO/IEC 40500 (2012) W3C web content accessibility guidelines (WCAG) 2.0. ISO. https://www.iso.org/standard/58625.html. Accessed 31 Oct 2018

ISO/IEC FDIS 30071-1 (2018) Development of user interface accessibility—part 1: code of practice for creating accessible ICT products and services. ISO. https://www.iso.org/standard/70913.html. Accessed 31 Oct 2018

Jacobs I et al (eds) (2002) User agent accessibility guidelines (UAAG) 1.0. W3C. https://w3.org/TR/UAAG10/. Accessed 31 Oct 2018

JIS X 8341-3 (2016) Guidelines for older persons and persons with disabilities-Information and communications equipment, software and services-part 3: web content. JIS. https://webdesk.jsa.or.jp/books/W11M0090/index/?bunsyo_id=JIS%20X%208341-3:2016. Accessed 31 Oct 2018

Kirckpatrick A et al (eds) (2018) Web content accessibility guidelines (WCAG) 2.1. W3C. https://w3.org/TR/WCAG21/. Accessed 31 Oct 2018

Lawton Henry S (ed) (2015) Authoring tool accessibility guidelines (ATAG) overview. W3C. https://w3.org/WAI/standards-guidelines/atag/. Accessed 31 Oct 2018

Lawton Henry S (ed) (2015) User agent accessibility guidelines (UAAG) overview. W3C. https://w3.org/WAI/standards-guidelines/uaag/. Accessed 31 Oct 2018

Lawton Henry S (ed) (2018) Introduction to web accessibility. W3C. https://w3.org/WAI/fundamentals/accessibility-intro/. Accessed 31 Oct 2018

Lawton Henry S (ed) (2018) Components of web accessibility. W3C. https://w3.org/WAI/fundamentals/components/. Accessed 31 Oct 2018

Lawton Henry S (ed) (2018) Web content accessibility guidelines (WCAG) overview. W3C. https://w3.org/WAI/standards-guidelines/wcag/. Accessed 31 Oct 2018

Lawton Henry S (2018) Accessible rich internet applications (WAI-ARIA) overview. W3C. https://w3.org/WAI/standards-guidelines/aria/. Accessed 31 Oct 2018

Lawton Henry S, Brewer J (eds) (2018) Guidance on applying WCAG 2.0 to non-web information and communication technologies (WCAG2ICT) overview. W3C. https://w3.org/WAI/standards-guidelines/wcag/non-web-ict/. Accessed 31 Oct 2018

Lawton Henry S, Abou-Zahra S, White K (eds) (2016) Accessibility, usability, and inclusion. W3C. https://w3.org/WAI/fundamentals/accessibility-usability-inclusion/. Accessed 31 Oct 2018

Mueller et al (eds) (2018) Web accessibility laws & policies. W3C. https://www.w3.org/WAI/policies/. Accessed 31 Oct 2018

Référentiel Général d'Accessibilité pour les Administrations (RGAA) Version 3 (2017) Secrétariat Général pour la modernisation de l'action publique, Premier ministre, République Française. http://references.modernisation.gouv.fr/referentiel/. Accessed 31 Oct 2018

Richards J et al (eds) (2015) Authoring tool accessibility guidelines (ATAG) 2.0. W3C. https://w3.org/TR/ATAG20/. Accessed 31 Oct 2018

Seeman L et al (eds) (2018a) Personalization semantics explainer 1.0 (working draft). W3C. https://www.w3.org/TR/personalization-semantics-1.0/. Accessed 31 Oct 2018

Seeman L et al (eds) (2018b) Personalization help and support 1.0 (working draft). W3C. https://www.w3.org/TR/personalization-semantics-help-1.0/. Accessed 31 Oct 2018

Seeman L et al (eds) (2018c) Personalization tools 1.0 (working draft). W3C. https://www.w3.org/TR/personalization-semantics-tools-1.0/. Accessed 31 Oct 2018

Silver Task Force Wiki: Main Page (2018) W3C. https://www.w3.org/WAI/GL/task-forces/silver/wiki/Main_Page. Accessed 31 Oct 2018

Text of Section 508 of the Rehabilitation Act of 1973, as Amended (29 U.S.C. §794d) (2018) US Access Board. https://www.access-board.gov/the-board/laws/rehabilitation-act-of-1973#508. Accessed 31 Oct 2018

Treviranus J et al (eds) (2000) Authoring tool accessibility guidelines (ATAG) 1.0. W3C. https://w3.org/TR/ATAG10/. Accessed 31 Oct 2018

UNE 139803 (2012) Requisitos de accesibilidad para contenidos en la Web. UNE. https://www.une.org/encuentra-tu-norma/busca-tu-norma/norma?c=N0049614. Accessed 31 Oct 2018

Verordnung zur Schaffung barrierefreier Informationstechnik nach dem Behindertengleichstellungsgesetz (Barrierefreie-Informationstechnik-Verordnung - BITV 2.0) (2011) Bundesministerium des Innern. https://www.gesetze-im-internet.de/bitv_2_0/BJNR184300011.html. Accessed 31 Oct 2018

Vigo M et al (eds) (2012) Research report on web accessibility metrics (working draft). W3C https://www.w3.org/TR/accessibility-metrics-report/. Accessed 31 Oct 2018

Web Accessibility Initiative (WAI) (2018) W3C. https://w3.org/WAI/. Accessed 31 Oct 2018

Web Accessibility Metrics Symposium (2011) W3C. https://www.w3.org/WAI/RD/2011/metrics/. Accessed 31 Oct 2018

Chapter 14
Web Accessibility Policy and Law

Jonathan Lazar

Abstract This chapter provides an overview of law and policy concepts related to web accessibility. Laws and policies can include a broad range of methods and documents, including national, regional, and provincial statutes, national and more local regulation, case law, policy, enforcement action, as well as treaties and human rights documents. The chapter continues by discussing the coverage of these laws and policies: what types of organizations, what types of disabilities, and what types of content are covered by the laws? Technical standards, user involvement, and transparency are also discussed. The concluding sections discuss future directions in web accessibility law and policy, what is currently needed, and some of the actions that we can individually take as members of the accessibility community.

14.1 Introduction

Designing digital technologies and content so that they can be utilized by the greatest number of possible users is simply good design. However, given tight development timelines and pressures to produce applications and web sites, developers sometimes will just focus on producing a product as quickly as possible, without consideration to the user needs. Often, the users most left out are individuals with disabilities, those who utilize alternate forms of input or output, such as screen readers, alternate keyboards, captioning, voice recognition, and/or no pointing devices. Web accessibility is technically possible, and the guidelines and techniques for ensuring accessible web sites are well known (see the chapter "*Standards, Guidelines and Trends*" by my friend Shadi Abou-Zahra). The reasons for these oversights, for excluding people with disabilities, are potentially many—developers might not be aware of accessibility, it is possible that they didn't learn about web accessibility in their formal technical training, or they might not realize how many potential users of their site have disabilities. There are literally hundreds of possible excuses, most of which are not convincing. For instance, a common excuse given by those who post videos on

J. Lazar (✉)
College of Information Studies, University of Maryland, 20742 College Park, MD, USA
e-mail: jlazar@umd.edu

© Springer-Verlag London Ltd., part of Springer Nature 2019   247
Y. Yesilada and S. Harper (eds.), *Web Accessibility*, Human–Computer
Interaction Series, https://doi.org/10.1007/978-1-4471-7440-0_14

the web is that they didn't realize that they need to caption videos, and they don't know how—they say, "this is a new technique for us!" despite the fact that captioning video for the Deaf and Hard of Hearing is a technique that has been around for more than 40 years.

In many ways, all users, at some time, put up with poorly designed interfaces. The difference is that for users with disabilities, poorly designed web sites aren't just an annoyance, rather the web sites exclude the users with disabilities from access. And when you can't access the most basic commerce e-sites, online education, employment applications, and social networking, you, as an individual with a disability, are excluded from commerce, education, employment, and socialization (Lazar 2013). When web sites are inaccessible, individuals with disabilities are given second-class status. Much as disability rights laws and human rights laws ensure that those with disabilities are included in society in general, these laws also make sure that people with disabilities aren't excluded from society via web sites which are inaccessible. And it does make a difference: when statutes related to web accessibility are present, corporations are more likely to do thorough accessibility testing, and follow accessibility standards (Loiacono and Djamasbi 2013).

The area of law and policy can often be confusing and frustrating for computer scientists and other people with a STEM background, because law has very different approaches to learning, different methods of analysis, different terminology, and even different standards for writing. Terms like "circuit-split" and "address" have completely different meanings in law than they do in STEM-related fields. When computer scientists (or other STEM professionals) say something like, "The law says…" or "there is a law," it is important to immediately stop and specify what the law is, providing details, otherwise, they will not be taken seriously by those in law and policy, and they will instead only increase the amount of confusion. This chapter is designed to provide a summary of law and policy issues, related specifically to web accessibility. It is written for computer scientists, rather than for lawyers, and assumes an understanding of the technical components of web accessibility (available in other chapters of this book, primarily the chapters in PART 4: Technical Foundations).

14.1.1 Types of Laws and Policies

Legal requirements for web accessibility don't just fall under the category of either "law or policy." There are a wide range of legal and policy approaches, under which web accessibility may be a requirement. These types of national, regional, and provincial approaches may include statute, regulation, case law, policy, and enforcement action. Aside from legal approaches within one country, there are also treaties and human rights documents (often based out of the United Nations, and discussed in Sect. 3 of this chapter), and multinational alliances (e.g., the European Union and their Mandate 376 on accessible ICT procurement).

Where statutory laws exist, in some cases, the statutes may be at the national level (e.g., the Equality Act in the UK), or the statutes may be at the provincial/regional level (e.g., Provincial laws in Canada, such as the Accessibility for Ontarians with Disabilities Act, the Accessibility for Manitobans Act, and the Nova Scotia Accessibility Act, see Malhotra and Rusciano 2017 for more information). Furthermore, there can be both national and regional laws co-existing. For instance, in the United States, there is the Americans with Disabilities Act (ADA) at the federal level, but 18 US states have statutes related to technology accessibility (Shaheen and Lazar 2018). For example, the Unruh Act in California provides for financial damages which are not available under the federal-level ADA. And the state of Maryland has a new 2018 law (HB1088—State Procurement—Information Technology—Nonvisual Access) which fines vendors who sell ICT to the Maryland state government, claim it is accessible when in fact it is not accessible, and do not make it accessible.

Statutes may also grant administrative agencies the authority to create, amend, and repeal regulations which provide more detailed technical advice. In general, regulations are seen as technical guidance on implementation, and are easier to modify on a more regular basis, as compared to a statute. Furthermore, in most countries that have regulations, regulatory processes are designed for maximum input from experts, scientists, industry, and all stakeholders including the general public. The same can generally not be said of statutes, which are often created in a process which is primarily political. Put another way, the statute defines the overall policy goal, but the regulation describes the techniques needed to reach that policy goal.

It's important to note the distinction between common law countries and civil law countries. In common law countries, case law can establish precedents, which create legal requirements that can have higher priority than statutes. Common law countries tend to include much of the English-speaking and/or Commonwealth countries (the US, UK, Canada, India, Australia, etc.). In civil law countries, there are comprehensive encoded rules that detail procedures and remedies. Civil law countries tend to include much of the Asian, European, and South American countries. Furthermore, laws can be structured in a way that they encourage a private right of action, so for instance, in the United States, the ADA encourages private enforcement through court cases. There is a similar tradition of private attorney generals in the UK, Australia, and Canada, which encourage citizens to bring cases to enforce disability rights (Lazar et al. 2015), and some of the best-known cases in related to web accessibility include National Federation of the Blind v. Target (in the USA), Maguire v. Sydney Organizing Committee for the Olympic Games (in Australia), and Jodhan v. Attorney General of Canada (Lazar et al. 2015). In addition, some civil law countries, including Spain, have stipulations in the law allowing people with disabilities to take ICT accessibility cases to court (Lazar et al. 2015).

Statutes, regulations, and case law aren't the only forms of law and policy related to web accessibility. Government agencies in charge of legal compliance and enforcement (e.g., ministries of education, offices of civil rights, human rights ombudsmen), can often choose which incidents to investigate, negotiate, and prosecute, and which ones to ignore. These agencies can make web accessibility a priority, or they can make web accessibility a rule that is frequently ignored. Furthermore, government agencies can put out guidance, policies, or other forms of nonregulatory rules, that all covered entities are expected to follow. And, when there are multiple legal investigations and resulting settlements using a similar format and having similar expectations and requirements, these settlements can, in a way, become a sort of informal policy, setting a baseline for what is expected. So, for instance, one can look at the terms of four settlements which were negotiated by either the U.S. Department of Justice Civil Rights Division, or the U.S. Department of Education Office of Civil Rights, which can provide examples of how settlements can become an informal policy. In 2013 and 2014 settlements with Louisiana Tech University and the University of Montana, respectively, the universities were required to provide training about accessibility to all faculty and staff, and file annual reports on their accessibility compliance (Lazar et al. 2015). The settlements involving H&R Block (a tax preparation company) and Peapod (a grocery delivery company) both required compliance with WCAG 2.0 AA, designating an employee as the web accessibility coordinator, performing usability testing involving consumers with disabilities at least once a year, and giving annual training on web accessibility to all employees involved with web development or web content, as well as additional requirements (Lazar et al. 2015). These settlements helped set an informal expectation for what universities and companies were expected to do.

These forms of "soft policy" are often effective in getting covered entities to comply and make their web sites accessible. Policies related to web accessibility can also appear in unexpected locations, such as a state-level Educational Technology Plan (Shaheen and Lazar 2018). Nongovernmental entities may choose to create internal policies related to web accessibility for their organization. Nongovernmental entities may also create policies and resources for public use, which can encourage improved accessibility. Examples of this include the Web Accessibility Toolkit, put out by the Association of Research Libraries (http://accessibility.arl.org/), and the National Association of State Chief Information Officers (NASCIO) Policy-Driven Adoption for Accessibility (http://www.nascio.org).

14.2   Coverage of Laws and Policies

From personal experience, when computer scientists are trying to give presentations about web accessibility or broader digital accessibility, they are often asked questions related to law. These questions are often focused on issues of coverage—"is my organization covered? What types of disabilities are covered? Do I need to make all of my videos accessible?" The next section provides details on issues related to coverage.

14.2.1 What Types of Organizations Are Covered?

The laws and policies need to clearly state what types of individuals and organizations are covered. Government web sites? Private homepages? Universities? Businesses? For any laws related to web accessibility, the coverage, who and what are addressed by the laws, need to be clear. In many national laws, there is a clear distinction between government and public accommodations. So, it may be very clear and obvious that a government (federal, or state/provincial/regional government) web site must be accessible. But what about a web site for a store? For a hotel? If a national law defines a category of "public accommodations" under human rights or civil rights laws, this can be useful in determining coverage. It seems unlikely that a separate law on web accessibility could provide enough detail about what types of websites are and are not covered under the law, so typically, the default is to use existing definitions of coverage, related to disability, civil, and human rights laws.

This issue of coverage is an important one, and defined in ways that computer scientists and engineers may not always expect. The Equality Act in the United Kingdom, is a well-known law that provides broad coverage, including public facilities, education, transportation, and employment. In the US, the Americans with Disabilities Act describes 12 categories of public accommodations. The ADA statute does not yet specifically mention digital content and technology, even though digital content and technology are addressed by the "effective communication requirement" of the ADA. The U.S. Department of Justice first stated publicly in 1996, that the protections of the Americans with Disabilities Act apply to web sites as a part of the effective communication requirement. Regulatory processes that describe specific requirements for websites under Title II (state and local government) and III (public accommodations) of the ADA had been ongoing since 2010, although the regulatory rulemaking process was canceled in 2017. The U.S. Departmental of Justice, as recently as October 2018, reconfirmed in a letter to a congressman, that the ADA applies to web sites of public accommodations (U.S. Department of Justice 2018). However, the ADA regulations do not yet define a technical standard or a specific threshold of coverage, giving broad flexibility to businesses, and this has led to confusion and a multitude of lawsuits (although theoretically, allowing for flexibility and innovation is a good thing).

There is currently a "circuit-split" in the U.S. case law (where different court of appeals circuits have different interpretations), about whether web sites are covered under the Americans with Disabilities Act (ADA), depending on the integration or "nexus" between the physical store and the web site. Some circuit courts (9th, 11th) require a nexus between a physical store (which is covered under Title III as a public accommodation), and a web site (which is a service of the physical store), for the web site to be covered under the ADA. Other circuits (1st, 2nd, and 7th) say that a consumer web site, by itself, counts as a public accommodation. Put into real-world examples, the Target.com web site is covered by the ADA in the 9th circuit only because of the strong integration between the physical store and the web site, but Netflix is covered under the ADA in the 1st circuit, even without any relationship to a physical store. Issues such as the relationship between the web site and the physical store, can matter greatly in a legal context. While the US and UK have broad coverage of organizations, other countries frequently limit their organizational coverage to government agencies or government-funded organizations or projects (e.g., the Stanca Act in Italy).

14.2.2 What Types of Disabilities Are Covered?

Another consideration in terms of coverage is, which disabilities are covered? In theory, whatever disabilities are covered under a national or regional disability rights law, should be covered when it comes to web accessibility. Disability rights laws can cover a broad set of disabilities, including medical issues such as AIDS, anxiety, diabetes, and gluten intolerance, none of which will change the approach for input or output for a given web site. The UN Convention on the Rights of Persons with Disabilities, in Article 1, defines persons with disabilities as "those who have long-term physical, mental, intellectual, or sensory impairments which in interaction with various barriers may hinder their full and effective participation in society on an equal basis with others" (United Nations 2018). The Americans with Disabilities Act defines an individual with a disability as one who has "a physical or mental impairment that substantially limits one of more major life activities [of that person]" (Bagenstos 2013).

It gets trickier when it comes to disabilities that do impact input/output, primarily with cognitive impairments. Unlike medical disabilities such as gluten intolerance, cognitive disabilities do impact the user interaction with a web site. However, unlike perceptual and motor disabilities, the research on web accessibility in the context of cognitive impairment is over a shorter period of time and is more limited (Lazar et al. 2015). There is a strong legal basis for requiring cognitive accessibility (Blanck 2014), however, the understanding of how to technically address the majority of cognitive impairments within interface design, is simply not there yet. A noteworthy effort is the Cognitive and Learning Disabilities Accessibility Task Force from the Web Accessibility Initiative (see https://www.w3.org/WAI/PF/cognitive-a11y-tf/ for more information).

It's also important to note that different laws around the world, often use different terminology to describe similar disabilities. So, for instance, in the United Kingdom, "visually impaired" often means someone with residual vision while "blind" means someone with no residual vision, but the term "blind" is used more broadly in the US to describe anyone with any level of vision loss (Lazar et al. 2015). Across both countries and different disciplines, the terms cognitive impairment, intellectual disability, and learning disability are used sometimes to mean the same thing, and other times to mean completely different things. In addition, different disability communities prefer different types of terminology. So, most disability communities prefer "people-first" language (e.g. a person with Autism, a person with Down syndrome), however, the Blind and the Deaf in many countries prefer to be called "Blind People" or "the Deaf or Hard of Hearing" and in fact, for those who are part of Deaf culture, they do not consider themselves as having any type of disability (Lazar et al. 2015).

14.2.3   What Type of Content Is Covered?

Theoretically, if an organization is covered by a legal requirement for accessible web content, then all types of their web-based content should be covered. However, since web protocols are used to deliver content both inside and outside of an organization, it's not as simple a question as it first appears to be. What about content delivered via a web browser, but only to employees inside a company? What about videos delivered to a small group of employees, none of whom have disabilities? What about course content that is provided to a limited group of students?

Generally, when laws refer to web site accessibility, they refer to publicly available content. So, content that is behind a password wall, and used only for a university course which has no students with disabilities enrolled, might not be required to be accessible. However, once that same content is put on a public MOOC (Massive Open Online Course), that same content may be covered under a disability rights law or perhaps a law guaranteeing access to education) (Ziegler and Sloan 2017). What about online gaming? Must that be legally accessible? What if online gaming is not public, but is used for educational purposes or for evaluating potential employment? What does the law say about that? (Chakraborty 2017). Determining coverage can get trickier when the content is not public, access is limited to a few people, and the content is delivered via a web browser but may not be perceived to be traditional "web content." In extreme examples, organizations may choose to, unfortunately, remove content from public access, rather than comply with accessibility requirements under the law. In 2017, UC-Berkeley removed more than 20,000 educational video and audio files from the web, rather than make those files accessible, as was requested by the U.S. Department of Justice. Instead, the university said that all future content will be accessible, but it decided that it did not want to spend the money on making legacy content accessible (Straumsheim 2017).

14.2.4   What Is the Technical Standard?

A fascinating difference between the worlds of law and computing, is that what is considered a technical standard in computing, is not always given priority in law. When it comes to web accessibility, from a technical point of view, there is only one clear standard—the Web Content Accessibility Guidelines. The Web Content Accessibility Guidelines (WCAG) is a set of technical standards which define best practices for making web content accessible. Originating from technical standards created in the mid-1990s at the Trace Center, WCAG 1.0 was approved by the Web Accessibility Initiative of the World Wide Web Consortium (W3C) in 1999. WCAG

2.0 was finalized in 2008, and WCAG 2.1 was released in June 2018. These standards have been in use for approximately 20 years. W3C has 475 member organizations, including large technical companies such as Microsoft, Google, and Apple, and the standards are developed using an open, public process, with all stakeholders able to provide input, including using existing, published accessibility research. WCAG allows for much flexibility and innovation in how organizations meet the accessibility success factors of WCAG. There are complementary standards for web browsers (user agent accessibility guidelines) and developer tools (the authoring tool accessibility guidelines), both of which are based on WCAG. There are also guidelines for applying WCAG to non-web content (WCAG2ICT). The suite of technical standards from the Web Accessibility Initiative is accepted around the world as the gold standard for making web content (and related technologies) accessible, and has also been adopted by the ISO. Most governments around the world that require accessible web content, use the WCAG as a component of their law.

Given the agreement of WCAG as a technical standard, with no competitors claiming to be a technical standard for accessibility, it is surprising that the world of law and policy may not understand the situation in the same way. For instance, in the original version of Section 508 of the Rehabilitation Act in the United States, the technical standard used was a modified version of WCAG 1.0, not the exact version. In a recent case in Federal district court in the US, the court penalized a plaintiff who had asked that a defendant be required to make their web site compliant with WCAG 2.0, saying that due to the primary jurisdiction doctrine and due process, a plaintiff loses simply for asking for the WCAG 2.0 in a court case (Lazar 2018). That case, *Robles v. Domino's Pizza LLC*, was reversed and remanded by the 9th Circuit Court of Appeals in January 2019, and is awaiting the next actions by the parties involved. Often, organizations misunderstand guidelines such as the WCAG, and instead of viewing them as "well-accepted and no-cost guidance of the highest quality" (which they are) they view them as mandates that provide no flexibility or creativity (which is simply not accurate).

14.2.5   What Level of Involvement in the Process? And How Will Content Be Evaluated?

It's important to involve users throughout a web development process and through the ongoing interface and content updates, and to utilize user-based forms of evaluation (such as usability testing). These are two key concepts of human–computer interaction and user-centered design. Yet these concepts are often missing from policies and laws related to accessibility (Lazar et al. 2015). If WCAG is the "what," then user involvement is the "who" and the "how," yet laws and policies are often silent on how these approaches should be utilized, or sometimes, silent on even the existence of these approaches.

You will likely not create a successful web site that meets the needs of users with disabilities, if the users with disabilities aren't involved with the development or evaluation. Yet frequently, policies are unclear about the role of involvement. With no guidance, different government agencies often use completely different approaches, with varying results (Lazar et al. 2017a). The three most common forms of accessibility evaluation are usability testing, expert reviews (also known as manual inspections), and automated testing (Lazar et al. 2015). Users with disabilities are only involved with one of those—usability testing. It's interesting to note that the term "trusted tester" is used in this context in two completely different ways. The "trusted tester" program at Google is a program to involve users with disabilities in the early-stage evaluation of Google products for accessibility (a usability testing approach to evaluation). The "trusted tester" program run out of the U.S. Department of Homeland Security, is a program to train Federal employees on the basics of standards and testing, and then those employees must score at least 90% on a certification exam to become a "trusted tester" (an expert review approach to evaluation), but which doesn't involve any users with disabilities.

While the results of evaluation methods are designed to inform software engineers, web designers and developers, and web content managers, compliance monitoring is a higher level, policy activity, to monitor how an organization is doing with web accessibility (Lazar et al. 2015). Ongoing compliance monitoring is especially important for web accessibility (more than, say, for a hardware device) because web sites and web content, are constantly changing, and are often managed by a diverse set of individuals, many of whom may not have expertise on web accessibility. Compliance monitoring includes monthly, semi-annual, or annual reports about progress on web accessibility, or triggers for evaluating accessibility, including versioning updates, major content updates, or technology procurement (Lazar et al. 2015).

14.2.6   What Information Must Be Publicly Posted?

One of the greatest challenges with implementing web accessibility is the limited amount of transparency that organizations provide. "Privacy statements" are now considered standard practice on the web. And the number of sites that have web accessibility statements is small but growing. The key problem with most accessibility statements is that they say very little. The statements often say something like, "we aim to be accessible" and "if you have any problems, email or call this person," but the statements do not give any details on whether the site is compliant with WCAG 2.0, whether it has been evaluated with any screen readers or other assistive technology, or whether any usability testing, involving people with disabilities, has taken place. Having information on what parts of a web site are accessible, and what parts are not, would be very useful information for users, even though few sites provide that information. In a 2011 research study, of 100 U.S. Federal government homepages evaluated, 22% listed specific accessibility features available on a web site, but only 3% provided information on how the site became or remained accessible and compliant with Section 508 of the Rehabilitation Act (Olalere and Lazar 2011). Compare that with Sweden, where the automated evaluations of governmental web accessibility, are publicly posted (Gulliksen et al. 2010). When automated evaluations are regularly performed, a more typical approach is that individuals responsible for managing web accessibility and doing web content management can see the reports, but the public cannot access them (Mirri et al. 2011). This is often the case in the U.S. Federal government, where those who are involved with accessibility compliance, reported that they were concerned about the idea of others seeing the evaluation reports of their web accessibility (Lazar et al. 2017a).

14.3   Discussion

When you are an accessibility researcher, practitioner, or teacher, law is a topic that is very important to your work. Even though most of us who work in accessibility don't have legal backgrounds, it is necessary to understand the basics of law, at least in the country in which your work is primarily based. If you teach students about accessibility from a technical or design point of view, you need to include the basics of the legal framework for accessibility present in your country.

Laws and policies not only impact on accessibility practice, but they influence accessibility research. This can occur in a number of different ways. Regulations can change how HCI researchers can involve human participants in their research, removing or creating various approvals (such as institutional review boards or ethics reviews), that are needed before research can begin. See either (Lazar et al. 2016) or (Lazar et al. 2017b) for more information on doing research involving human participants and especially participants with disabilities. Other ways that laws and policies can impact on accessibility research is by prioritizing (for good or bad) some disabilities over others. This can occur if research funding agencies (governments or nongovernmental organizations) provide more funding for accessibility research focusing on one disability more than another, or if governmental jurisdictions have laws that specifically cover some disabilities (for instance, some U.S. states have laws that specifically relate to the Blind and/or the Deaf, in isolation from other disabilities).

I would encourage all accessibility researchers, practitioners, and teachers (and let's face it, most of us play multiple roles), to get involved with law and policymaking. We have much to offer those who create laws and policies, by explaining the reality of accessibility, the technical details, the processes, and how accessibility is often easier to do than people perceive it to be. Make sure to ask questions and to try to ascertain, what are the research questions that could be helpful to those involved in law and policy? When you get involved with law and policy communities, I encourage you to remember three things (Lazar 2014):

1. Know the specifics of the law/policy/regulation. If you can't identify the specifics, you will lose any perceived trust that you might have with lawyers and policy-makers.
2. Know the specific number of people with disabilities (and with specific disabilities) within your political/legal region. Those in law and policy-related positions often want to know how many people are actually affected. Make sure to also include in your discussions and figures, those without disabilities who also benefit from the accessibility features. So, for instance, it's not just the Deaf and Hard of Hearing who use captioning!
3. Understand the importance of doing longitudinal data, and try to collect some longitudinal data. So, for instance, a policy goal might be the improvement in web accessibility over time, but not necessarily perfection. You can have a great impact on the worlds of law and policy, by documenting how a technical accessibility situation is getting better or worse, over a period of time. Those in law and policy-related positions, respond better to longitudinal data than one-point-in-time data.

14.4   Future Directions

There is much work that needs to be done in the law and policy realm, related to web accessibility. Many of the technical solutions for web accessibility already exist. Yet the web seems to be getting less accessible over time. There are a number of potential future directions in law and policy to help improve this situation. One potential solution is for governments, if they are not ready to require more accessibility and do government-based testing, to require more transparency when it comes to web accessibility. So, if public accommodations are required to state whether their facility is physically accessible or not, why shouldn't they also be required to state outright, whether their web site is accessible, and if so, what types of testing and/or evaluation are performed to ensure accessibility? The topic of web accessibility is often "hidden away" and so consumers and society are often not even aware of this major problem. Laws requiring transparency in consumer transactions would also be helpful. For instance, none of the app stores currently provide information on which apps are accessible and which are not, forcing consumers with disabilities to purchase an app without first knowing whether it would work for them.

Better software tools which allow for more accurate automated testing of web site accessibility (even a limited set of features but with high accuracy), would also help in increasing transparency. It is hoped that in the future, the integration of Artificial Intelligence approaches into web accessibility testing tools, will increase the accuracy of these tools, making them more useful for determining legal compliance with web accessibility requirements (which currently, the tools are not accurate at ascertaining).

A common question that I get asked, is do I think that there will be more web accessibility lawsuits in the future, or fewer? I think that there is a good chance, in the short-term, that in the USA, there will be more lawsuits (note: because I am not familiar enough with the legal systems outside of the US, I hesitate to make any guesses about lawsuits in other countries). Because the U.S. Department of Justice suspended the regulatory process related to web accessibility under the Americans with Disabilities Act, the clear and specific guidance that all organizations were hoping for related to web accessibility, will not occur anytime soon. The U.S. Department of Justice has been clear that web accessibility is a requirement for public accommodations already covered under Title III of the ADA, yet the various Courts of Appeals have interpreted the requirements differently, related to the connection between a physical store and a web site. So, while the legal requirement might be "web accessibility," more granular questions of "what type of organization is covered, what type of content is covered, and what type of disability is covered?" are currently unclear in the law. Given the lack of clarity, one can expect that the number of lawsuits in the USA will increase in the short-term. However, a number of major actions (e.g., a regulatory process restarting, a new congressional bill signed into law) could dramatically reduce the number of lawsuits due to increased clarity. Furthermore, draconian actions could also limit lawsuits. For instance, 100 US congresspeople recently wrote a letter to the DOJ asking them to publicly declare that people with disabilities should not have the right to file a lawsuit for web accessibility (U.S. House of Representatives 2018). Thankfully, the DOJ wrote back, as described earlier, reaffirming the right to web accessibility, and noting how the congresspeople completely misunderstood a recent legal ruling in the *Robles v. Dominos Pizza LLC* case (U.S. Department of Justice 2018).

With the law and policy context, three international legal and policy initiatives have the potential to influence web accessibility in the future: (1) the UN Convention on the Rights of Persons with Disabilities, (2) the Marrakesh Treaty to Facilitate Access to Published Works for Persons Who Are Blind, Visually Impaired or Otherwise Print Disabled, and (3) the UN Sustainable Development Goals.

While disability has been mentioned within UN Human Rights documents since 1948, and was the focus of the 1975 Declaration of Rights of Disabled Persons, the UN Convention on the Rights of Persons with Disabilities (CRPD), adopted in 2006, was the first treaty that established the rights of nondiscrimination, accessibility and inclusion (Lazar et al. 2015). Currently, more than 160 countries have signed and ratified the CRPD. Web accessibility is well-established within the text of the CRPD. Article 9 of the CRPD states that countries should "...promote access for persons with disabilities to new information and communications technologies and systems, including the Internet...[and] promote the design, development, production and distribution of accessible information and communications technologies and systems at an early stage, so that these technologies and systems become accessible at minimum cost" (United Nations 2018). Article 21 of the CRPD encourages "Providing information intended for the general public to persons with disabilities in accessible formats and technologies appropriate to different kinds of disabilities in a timely manner and without additional cost....[and] Urging private entities that provide services to the general public, including through the Internet, to provide information and services in accessible and usable formats for persons with disabilities" (United Nations 2018). While Articles 9 and 21 are generally seen as the key articles related to web accessibility, other articles of the CRPD could be easily contextualized within web accessibility (e.g., Articles 22 and 31, relating to privacy of data and information from persons with disabilities, and Article 24 related to education) (Lazar and Stein 2017). For more information about ICT accessibility and the CRPD, the reader is suggested to consult either the Lazar and Stein (2017) book, or the work of the G3ICT, the Global Initiative for Inclusive ICTs (http://www.g3ict.org). Of particular note is the Country-based dashboard at (https://g3ict.org/country-profile), where the reader can find 121 individual country report cards, tracking the progress in implementing digital accessibility for countries that have become parties to the CRPD.

The Marrakesh Treaty to Facilitate Access to Published Worlds for Persons who are Blind, Visually Impaired, or otherwise Print Disabled (simply known as the "Marrakesh Treaty"), was adopted in 2013, and currently has 40 countries which are parties to the treaty. The treaty is technically an intellectual property treaty, focused on copyright, administered by the World Intellectual Property Organization (WIPO), however, it clearly has human rights goals (and the WIPO web site openly states that). There are two key components of the Marrakesh Treaty. One component is that, for countries that are parties to the treaty, they must have exceptions in their domestic copyright law, so that accessible formats can be made of copyrighted materials, by authorized entities, for noncommercial purposes, to be distributed only to people who are Blind, Visually Impaired, or otherwise Print Disabled. The other major component of the Marrakesh Treaty is that it requires for countries that are parties to the treaty, to allow for the import and export of accessible format copies (cross-border flows of digital materials, in accessible formats, which are copyrighted). The United States recently ratified the Marrakesh Treaty, although it has yet to be deposited with WIPO (ARL 2018).

The Sustainable Development Goals (SDG), also coming from the United Nations, are a set of 17 goals that relate to sustainable development with a target date of 2030. Disability and accessibility is a key component of multiple goals within the SDG. Goal 4, related to quality education, specifically states: "ensure equal access to all levels of education and vocational training for the vulnerable, including persons with disabilities" and "Build and upgrade education facilities that are child, disability and gender sensitive." Goal 10, related to reduced inequalities, specifically discusses disability in the context of "empower and promote the social, economic and political inclusion of all, irrespective of age, sex, disability..." The concepts of nondiscrimination, accessibility, and inclusion (from the CRPD) have been integrated throughout the SDG. It is unclear at this point, whether the SDG will have a direct impact on web accessibility in development, although the topic is one that merits further research.

14.5   Author's Opinion of the Field

I might have a very unique view of the field. My education, and my graduate work, is as a human–computer interaction researcher. I have worked on accessibility research for nearly 20 years, and on broader HCI research for over 20 years. Over time, I was asked to get involved in a number of law and policy-related projects; whenever I gave presentations, I was frequently asked many questions related to policy and law. I worked as an expert consultant on legal cases, and as adjunct chair of public policy for SIGCHI from 2010–2015.

All of these activities led to my decision to take a leave of absence for a year from my professorship, and go back to school to earn an LL.M. degree (an advanced masters degree in law). I structured my LL.M degree, from the University of Pennsylvania, around disability rights law and technology law, to better understand the legal issues surrounding digital accessibility. While I am clearly committed to these topics, I am aware that most researchers and practitioners won't be able to commit to working towards a degree in law. However, every accessibility researcher and practitioner can commit to learning more about the laws and policies that relate to digital accessibility in their own country and state/province. HCI and accessibility research is generally international, with research collaborations crossing national borders. Yet laws and policies end at a national or even a regional border. So, we can't all learn the same law and policy together as an HCI/accessibility community, because the laws and policies differ so much from country to country. Yet we still need to encourage everyone to learn about the laws and policies in their own national and local jurisdictions. Even getting more researchers and practitioners to be more specific when referring to legal requirements, stating the statutory source, would be a major leap forward, and that seems like something that is currently within reach.

14.6   Conclusions

While there are a number of different areas of HCI that might interact with law (e.g., privacy, security, intellectual property, and telecommunications), laws and policies seem to have the greatest impact on accessibility. It's time for our community to step up, become more informed on law and policy, and get more comfortable identifying and explaining laws, and interacting with those working in law and policy.

References

Association of Research Libraries (2018) ARL Celebrates President Trump's Signing of the Marrakesh Treaty Implementation Act, Urges Administration to Complete Implementation. Available at: https://www.arl.org/news/arl-news/4646-arl-celebrates-president-trumps-signing-of-the-marrakesh-treaty-implementation-act-urges-administration-to-complete-implementation#. W9cn2ScpCqA. Accessed 29 Oct 2018

Bagenstos S (2013) Disability rights law: cases and materials, 2nd edn. Foundation Press

Blanck P (2014) eQuality. Cambridge University Press, Cambridge, UK

Chakraborty J (2017) How does inaccessible gaming lead to social exclusion?. In: Lazar J, Stein M (eds) Disability, human rights, and information technology. The University of Pennsylvania Press, Philadelphia, pp 212–223

Gulliksen J, von Axelson H, Persson H, Göransson B (2010) Accessibility and public policy in Sweden. Interactions 17(3): 26–29

Lazar J (2013) Locked out: investigating societal discrimination against people with disabilities due to inaccessible websites. Presentation at the Radcliffe Institute for Advanced Study at Harvard University, video available at: https://www.youtube.com/watch?v=XB3EbVpiPeY. Accessed 29 Oct 2018

Lazar J (2014) Engaging in information science research that informs public policy. Libr Q 84(4):451–459

Lazar J (2018) Due process and primary jurisdiction doctrine: a threat to accessibility research and practice? In: Proceedings of the ACM conference on accessible computing (ASSETS), pp 404-406

Lazar J, Stein MA (cds) (2017) Disability, human rights, and information technology. The University of Pennsylvania Press, Philadelphia

Lazar J, Goldstein DF, Taylor A (2015) Ensuring digital accessibility through process and policy. Morgan Kaufmann/Elsevier Publishers, Waltham, MA

Lazar J, Abascal A, Barbosa S, Barksdale J, Friedman B, Grossklags J, Gulliksen J, Johnson J, McEwan T, Martinez-Normand L, Michalk W, Tsai J, VanDerVeer G, vonAxelson H, Walldius A, Whitney G, Winckler M, Wulf V, Churchill E, Cranor L, Davis J, Hedge A, Hochheiser H, Hourcade J-P, Lewis C, Nathan L, Paterno F, Reid B, Quesenbery W, Selker T, Wentz B (2016) Human-computer interaction and international public policymaking: a framework for understanding and taking future actions. Found Trends Hum. Comput Interact 9(2):69–149

Lazar J, Williams V, Gunderson J, Foltz T (2017a) Investigating the potential of a dashboard for monitoring US federal website accessibility. In: Proceedings of the 50th Hawaii international conference on system sciences, pp 2428–2437

Lazar J, Feng J, Hochheiser H (2017b) Research methods in human-computer interaction, 2nd edn. Elsevier/Morgan Kaufmann Publishers, Cambridge, MA

Loiacono ET, Djamasbi S (2013) Corporate website accessibility: does legislation matter? Univers Access Inf Soc 12(1):115–124

Malhotra R, Rusciano M (2017) Using provincial laws to drive a national agenda: connecting human rights and disability rights laws. In: Lazar J, Stein M (eds) Disability, human rights, and information technology. The University of Pennsylvania Press, Philadelphia, pp 94–110

Mirri S, Muratori LA, Salomoni P (2011) Monitoring accessibility: large scale evaluations at a geo political level. In: Proceedings of the 13th international ACM SIGACCESS conference on computers and accessibility, pp 163–170

Olalere A, Lazar J (2011) Accessibility of US federal government home pages: Section 508 compliance and site accessibility statements. Gov Inf Q 28(3):303–309

Shaheen NL, Lazar J (2018) K–12 technology accessibility: the message from state governments. J Spec Educ Technol 33(2):83–97

Straumsheim C (2017) Berkeley will delete online content. Inside Higher Ed. Available at: https://www.insidehighered.com/news/2017/03/06/u-california-berkeley-delete-publicly-available-educational-content. Accessed 29 Oct 2018

United Nations (2018) Convention on the rights of persons with disabilities. Available at: https://www.un.org/development/desa/disabilities/convention-on-the-rights-of-persons-with-disabilities/convention-on-the-rights-of-persons-with-disabilities-2.html. Accessed 29 Oct 2018

U.S. House of Representatives (2018) June 20, 2018 Letter to Attorney General Jeff Sessions from 100 members of congress. https://www.adatitleiii.com/wp-content/uploads/sites/121/2018/06/ADA-Final-003.pdf. Accessed 29 Oct 2018

U.S. Department of Justice (2018) September 25, 2018 Letter to Rep Ted Budd from Assistant Attorney General Stephen Boyd. https://www.adatitleiii.com/wp-content/uploads/sites/121/2018/10/DOJ-letter-to-congress.pdf. Accessed 29 Oct 2018

Ziegler M, Sloan D (2017) Accessibility and online learning. In Lazar J, Stein M (eds) Disability, human rights, and information technology. The University of Pennsylvania Press, Philadelphia, pp 158–181

Chapter 15
Tackling the Inaccessibility of Websites in Postsecondary Education

Jane Seale, Sheryl Burgstahler and Björn Fisseler

Abstract The focus of this chapter is the accessibility of the websites of postsecondary/higher education institutions. We will critique the ability and willingness of these institutions to respond to anti-discrimination and equality legislation by addressing the access needs of the increasing number of disabled students who are enrolling in postsecondary/higher education institutions. This critique will entail a review of the range of approaches that institutions employ to make their websites accessible; a case study of "best" accessibility practice in the field and a consideration of the challenges and opportunities that institutions face in seeking to improve website accessibility.

15.1 Introduction

The focus of this chapter is the accessibility of the websites of higher education institutions (HEIs). For the purposes of this book chapter, higher education (HE) is used very broadly to mean postsecondary (sometimes called post-compulsory) education, which is normally delivered by a university or college. Throughout the accessibility research and practice literature in HE, two main drivers for improvements to the accessibility of websites in higher education have been identified and discussed exhaustively: (1) increasing numbers of disabled students (Asuncion et al. 2010) and (2) anti-discrimination and equality legislation (Guyer and Uzeta 2009). These drivers, combined with the fact that HEIs are perceived to be at the forefront of technological advances, have led to a widespread assumption that HE websites should be exemplary in terms of their compliance with accessibility standards and guidelines. In this chapter, we will examine the reality of this assumption by reviewing the range

J. Seale (✉)
The Open University, Milton Keynes, UK
e-mail: jane.seale@open.ac.uk

S. Burgstahler
The University of Washington, Seattle, WA, USA

B. Fisseler
FernUniversitÄt in Hagen, Hagen, Germany

© Springer-Verlag London Ltd., part of Springer Nature 2019
Y. Yesilada and S. Harper (eds.), *Web Accessibility*, Human–Computer Interaction Series, https://doi.org/10.1007/978-1-4471-7440-0_15

of approaches that HEIs employ to make their websites accessible, providing a case study of "best" accessibility practice in the field and discussing the challenges and opportunities that HEIs face in seeking to improve website accessibility.

15.2   How Accessible Are Websites in Higher Education? A Review of the Research

Accessibility researchers have been evaluating the accessibility of university websites since the turn of the century. Seale (2014) conducted a review of web accessibility studies published between 2000 and 2011. She noted that in HE there had been three main approaches to evaluating web accessibility: First, evaluating the core or main home page of HEIs; second, evaluating library home pages; and third, examining the websites of programs with a disability, special education, or access focus where it was assumed that there was a responsibility to produce the accessibility practitioners of the future. Other approaches include comparing higher education institutional websites to those of non-educational organizations or comparing the accessibility of institutional websites across time (See Table 15.1).

Irrespective of what the focus of the evaluation was or the evaluation methods used, the results of Seale's review suggest that the websites of HEIs were not models of best accessibility practice prior to 2011 and there is little evidence to suggest that accessibility is improving (Seale 2014).

The studies included in Seale's (2014) review focused largely on university websites in countries such as United States (US), Canada, United Kingdom (UK), South East Asia, and Australia. An inspection of web accessibility studies conducted since 2011 reveal a wider geographical focus (Seale 2018). Universities in countries such as Portugal (e.g., Espadinha et al. 2011), Spain (Chacon-Medina et al. 2013), Cyprus (e.g., Iseri et al. 2017), Argentina (e.g., Laitano 2015), and Turkey and Central Asia (Ismailova and Kimsanova 2017; Ismailova and Inal 2018) are now included in the focus of accessibility researchers. Studies also continue in countries such as the US (e.g., Kimmons 2017) and Australia (e.g., Billingham 2014). Across these countries, the studies reveal that a large proportion of University websites are still failing a range of accessibility and usability tests; leading researchers such as Kimmons (2017 p. 448) to conclude

> These types of errors are simple to correct and seem to reflect systemic willingness to ignore basic accessibility requirements.

We would concur with Kimmons (2017) that the lack of accessibility in HE is systemic. Because of this, it is our contention that we need to understand in more detail the factors that influence systemic discrimination and inequalities for disabled students. In the next section, we will begin this examination by exploring the potential factors that influence approaches to making their websites more accessible.

Table 15.1 Comparisons of the accessibility of university websites over time

Authors	What was evaluated	Region	Results
Hackett and Parmento (2005)	Home pages of 45 HEIs, who were members of the Association of American Universities between 1997–2002	US	Found that accessibility decreased over time. In 1997, 64.4% of the pages were considered accessible. In 2002, just 15.6% were considered accessible
Bailey and Burd (2005)	Websites of public organizations, FTSE companies, and universities. Size of sample is not declared	UK	Found a general increase in accessibility for all three groups. Universities for the most time had the lowest percentage of substantially inaccessible websites although most were still moderately inaccessible
Comeaux and Schmetzke (2007)	56 ALA-accredited library school and library websites 49 US 7 Canadian	US and Canada	For library websites, 51% of US sites were considered accessible (Bobby approved) in 2002 compared to 55% in 2006. 43% Canadian sites were approved in 2002 compared to 57% in 2006 For Library School sites, 31% of US sites approved in 2002 compared to 41% in 2006. 14% Canadian sites were approved in 2002 compared to 86% in 2006
Providenti (2004) Providenti and Zai (2007)	Home pages of academic libraries of Bachelor's degree-granting institutions: 31 in 2003 and 32 in 2007	Kentucky, US	In 2003, 3% used valid HTML compared to 6% in 2007 In 2003, 12% were 508 compliant compared to 12% in 2007 In 2003, 3% passed priority one and priory two of Web Content Accessibility Guidelines (WCAG) compared to 3% in 2007
Krach (2007)	Home pages of 51 college websites	US	In 2001, 29.4% met priority one (WCAG), compared to 58.8% in 2007

(continued)

Table 15.1 (continued)

Authors	What was evaluated	Region	Results
Alexander (2004) Alexander and Ripon (2007)	Four pages from 41 university websites: home page, The home page; The main prospective students' page (or an alternative and roughly equivalent page where there was no prospective student's page). An orientation page for incoming students in 2007 (or alternative where necessary); A student accommodation page (or alternative where necessary). Results for 2003 and 2007 were compared	Australia	Overall accessibility slightly worsened over time. 100% of sites and 92% of pages still failed to meet basic standards. The biggest problem was still failure to provide text alternatives
Curl and Bowers (2009)	45 baccalaureate social work websites in 2003 and 2008	US	An overall improvement was demonstrated between 2003 and 2008; however, 75.6% of programs still had one or more priority one accessibility barriers in 2008
Wijayaratne (2008); Wijayaratne and Singh (2010)	Home page and library page of 31 members of Asian Association of Open Universities in 2008 and 30 in 2010	Asia	In 2008, 6 university home pages and four library home pages were free from errors. In 2010, across all the 30 institutions, just four home pages and two library pages were free of accessibility errors
Thompson et al. (2010)	127 homes pages were tested over a five period: once in 2004–2005 and once in 2009	US	Significant positive gains in accessibility were revealed on some measures but declined in others. Improvements were made for issues that were basic and easy to implement. There was a decline in keyboard accessibility

15.3 What Factors Influence the Approaches Higher Education Institutions Take to Making Their Websites More Accessible?

Outside of HE, there is an abundance of advice outlining the steps that organizations should take in order to change their accessibility working practices (See, for example, the Chap. 14 in this book on "Standards, Guidelines and Trends"). This advice is often presented as a series of logical steps or phases. For example, the Web Accessibility Initiative (WAI) developed a generic guide that outlines activities to integrate accessibility into private or organizational websites (WAI 2016). The guide outlines four different areas of action, which are not necessarily carried out in sequence, but should be repeated over time to ensure a certain level of accessibility:

- Initiate: This area of action is about learning the basics of web accessibility, exploring the organization's current state of accessibility, setting objectives of what to achieve until when, and infusing web accessibility into the organizational culture.
- Plan: This is essential to effectively implementing the accessibility effort and includes creating an accessibility policy, assigning responsibilities, reviewing the current environment and websites, determining resources for accessibility activities, and establishing a monitoring framework in order to track progress. Another important aspect of planning is to engage with stakeholders, as the ongoing support of management and stakeholders is needed to achieve the self-imposed goals.
- Implement: When it comes to implement accessibility, the most important aspect is to weave accessibility into the HE core with minimal overhead. The WAI suggest building skills and expertise among key stakeholders, to assign tasks according to the set objectives and identified responsibilities, to evaluate the process early and regularly, and to track and communicate the progress toward accessibility goals.
- Sustain: Accessibility is no one-time goal but has to be maintained for completed projects and be the foundation for new projects. Monitoring the websites for accessibility issues helps to identify when changes in content introduce new errors. Furthermore, the stakeholders and management need permanent attention so that they continually prioritize accessibility.

We will look at each of these four areas of action in turn and discuss what issues arise for HEIs with regard to potential implementation of each area of action.

15.3.1 Initiate: Infusing Web Accessibility into the Organizational Culture

The need to embed accessibility within an organization's culture is frequently mentioned in the literature. For example, Leitner et al. (2016) utilize case studies in three industry sectors to identify factors that influence the implementation of web accessibility and to explain the managerial rationale behind the decision. One of the reasons they identified for why implementations fail was lack of social values anchored in the corporate culture. Hoover (2003) examined factors related to the implementation of accessibility as an innovation and one of the four factors they identified was the values and beliefs of the organization. It is too simplistic, however, to conclude that all that HEIs need to do is embed accessibility into their culture. The social values of underpinning accessibility are linked to democratization, inclusion, and social justice. For many HEIs, however, particularly the high status "Ivy League" and equivalent institutions, the culture is one of the elitism, where excellence is linked to notions of difference, rather than notions of equity (Luna 2009). The increasing marketization and commodification of HE and the positioning of students as consumers of education have led to an increasing business culture. This has the potential to prompt HEIs to consider the strong financial case for accessibility and indeed many advocates have pointed to the high percentage of disabled students in HE (and hence, the high number of customers with an accessibility need) as a driver for accessibility (Seale 2006). Despite such advocacy, accessibility is not yet seeping into the culture and values of the HE sector, largely because there are so many other initiatives that compete for priority. For example, for professors/lecturers, accessibility competes with doing research, obtaining personal qualifications and writing applications for research grants. For managers, accessibility competes with other compliance issues and other marginalized student groups—as accessibility is often seen as a "thing for the disabled only," so to speak. For web developers/learning developers, accessibility might compete with using latest technologies, teaching and learning innovations, and time-to-market issues.

15.3.2 Plan: Developing a Policy, Assigning Responsibilities, and Determining Resources

A core component of planning for accessibility is developing an organizational accessibility policy that responds to national and international accessibility-related policies and laws (Kline 2011; see also Chap. 14). Added to this, many accessibility commentators outside and inside HE points to the need for organizations to identify accessibility-related roles and responsibilities and to allocate resources. Velleman et al. (2017), for example, talk about the assignment of responsibilities, while Linder et al. (2015) identify a need to better articulate who is responsible for online accessibility initiatives and policies and the need for institutional investment in terms of technology, staffing, and other resources. Hoover (2003) argues that organizations need to allocate sufficient resources and appoint a change agent.

The way HEIs are organized can make the development of an agreed accessibility policy, identification of roles and responsibilities and appropriate change agents difficult. They are frequently organized into semi-autonomous Faculties or Schools, with their own unique organizational structures and line management systems. Many operate as mini-businesses within the larger HEI business. Such structures can work against the creation of an accessibility policy as it can be difficult to develop a shared understanding of what accessibility means, a shared set of goals, and shared set of responsibilities. In addition, any successful change agent within an institution will need to be able to successfully negotiate the organizational complexities that we have outlined. The challenge of this should not be underestimated, and therefore we would suggest that appointing a change agent is no guarantee of success. Furthermore, in the light of this, we are not surprised that Linder et al. (2015) noted a sense of institutions within the HE sector being overwhelmed with regard to responding to accessibility drivers. Implementing accessibility plans in HE is complex. The reasons for implementing accessibility can be articulated quite simply—but operationalizing accessibility is not simple.

15.3.3   Implement: Building Skills and Expertise

It is universally argued that successful accessibility implementation will depend on an organization's capacity to implement the required changes and that this in turn will depend on the education, knowledge, and experience of the various stakeholders (Hoover 2003; Velleman et al. 2017). Building skills and expertise among many stakeholders can be the key to success for HEIs, as some departments consider themselves as having sole responsibility for the websites and have issues in sharing responsibilities. So getting more stakeholders onboard can help to improve overall accessibility as well as integrate the goals into policies throughout the organization. However, there are issues that need to be addressed when attempting to build skills and expertise. Issues are such as (1) looking for evidence-based approaches to capacity building and asking the question: "What approaches are proved to be work (we will address this issue in more detail in the final section of this chapter) and (2) are training and skills development programs the right medium for attempting to change organizational cultures and values associated with accessibility?

15.3.4   Sustain: Monitoring Progress

Sustaining accessibility might be the hardest part for an institution, as accessibility is no "quick win," but the result of an ongoing effort. Sustaining an accessibility initiative will depend in part on monitoring progress in order to ensure that the momentum keeps going forward. HE as a sector is no stranger to monitoring. In an era of accountability and austerity, HEIs are audited on all kinds of things. In fact, HEIs are good at audits! They can tick boxes to say things have been done and even provide evidence to that effect [as can indeed any organization] but that does not mean that they are meaningfully "done". This means we have to identify the drivers that will encourage an HEI to engage meaningfully and genuinely in the sustainability of accessibility initiatives. One driver could be the use of student feedback for continuous improvement. The critical audiences are the prospective students, as these are the ones who go on the HEI's websites and look for news and information. If the websites are not accessible for them, these prospective students could be lost for the individual institution. But of course, depending on the culture and values of an organization, they may or may not care about the loss of a disabled student whose access needs were not met.

In this section, we have offered our insight into why implementing approaches to accessibility within HEIs can be challenging and complex. This does not mean that there are no beacons of good practice within HE. We would point the reader to the California State University (2009) Accessible Technology Initiative (ATI) and the Penn State University (n.d.) ATI, for examples. In addition, we will now offer you a detailed case study of what is widely acknowledged to be a successful accessibility initiative within an HEI, drawn from the experience and practice of one of the co-authors, Sheryl Burgstahler.

15.4   The University of Washington: A Case Study in Addressing Web Accessibility

As has been well documented in the literature, it is not easy to create a campus environment that systematically moves a postsecondary institution toward a more inclusive online environment. The University of Washington (UW) has been working toward Information Technology (IT) accessibility since 1984. Back then, its efforts mostly related to the selection, procurement, and use of assistive technology. Over time, however, a more comprehensive approach has emerged in which UW tackles the problem of inaccessible websites from multiple angles—from bottom-up and top-down, from reactive to proactive steps, from policy to practice. With a seemingly constant arrival of new technology, staff, and websites, the UW has found that diverse and relentless efforts are required to make progress toward the elusive goal of campus-wide web accessibility. This section of the chapter shares the UW's journey.

15.4.1   The Foundation for the UW Approach

The UW approach to the promotion of accessible web design is underpinned by four pillars: (1) UW values, (2) compliance awareness, (3) a civil rights, social justice approach with respect to access issues for individuals with disabilities, and (4) a Universal Design (UD) framework.

15.4.2   UW Values

According to its website "The UW educates a diverse student body to become responsible global citizens and future leaders through a challenging learning environment informed by cutting-edge scholarship." It lists its values to be integrity, diversity, excellence, collaboration, innovation, and respect. This vision and these values promote a campus culture that is accessible, inclusive, and equitable. Accessible web design efforts reflect this institutional image.

15.4.3   Compliance Awareness

The legal basis for UW web accessibility efforts is primarily section 504 of the Rehabilitation Act of 1973 (US Department of Labor 1973), the Americans with Disabilities Act of 1990 and its 2008 Amendments (US Department of Labor 1990), and Washington State Policy#188 on IT Accessibility (State of Washington Office of the Chief Information Officer 2016), which

> ...establishes the expectation for state agencies that people with disabilities have access to & use of information & data & be provided access to the same services & content that is available to persons without disabilities...

The definition of "accessible" with respect to IT, including websites, comes from the federal government:

> ...a person with a disability is afforded the opportunity to acquire the same information, engage in the same interactions, & enjoy the same services as a person without a disability in an equally effective & equally integrated manner, with substantially equivalent ease of use. The person with a disability must be able to obtain the information as fully, equally & independently as a person without a disability. (South Carolina Technical College System 2013)

15.4.4   Civil Rights and Social Justice

Much of the work in providing access to individuals with disabilities at the UW, like most postsecondary institutions in the United States, involves the self-disclosure of a disability and appropriate documentation to a disabilities services office followed by the approval of accommodations by that office which is shared with faculty and staff who must do their part in implementing them. Typical accommodations include sign language interpreters; extra time and alternative locations for exams; and remediation of inaccessible websites, documents, videos, and other IT. Much of this work is based on the medical model of disability which focuses on individual functional limitations and how an inaccessible product or environment can be altered to make it more accessible to someone with these limitations. The UW has made gradual steps toward a civil rights, social justice model of IT accessibility where more focus is on the product (e.g., a website) or environment (e.g., a location where computers are placed for student use), and how it can be proactively designed to be accessible to a broad audience, thus minimizing the need for accommodations for specific individuals with disabilities. For example, when a course website is accessibly designed, there is no need for an accommodation for a student who is blind to access its content.

15.4.5 A Universal Design Framework

Universal design (UD) is the framework used to guide IT accessibility efforts because of its consistency with the other three foundational pillars. UD, with its earliest applications in the design of physical spaces and commercial products, is defined as "the design of products and environments to be usable by all people, to the greatest extent possible, without the need for adaptation or specialized design" (North Carolina State University 1997). UD is an attitude, goal, and process that values diversity, equity, and inclusion; promotes best practices and does not lower standards; is proactive and can be implemented incrementally; and benefits everyone and minimizes the need for accommodations (See also Chap. 24 written by David Sloan and Sarah Horton).

15.4.6 The UW Approach to the Accessibility of IT

Influenced by these four key pillars, UW accessibility-related activities focus on leadership, policies, guidelines, resources, and practices.

15.4.7 Leadership

UW leadership includes (1) an IT Accessibility Coordinator, (2) an IT Accessibility Task Force, (3) an IT Accessibility Team, and (4) IT Accessibility Liaisons. The Coordinator is the UW Director of the UW's Accessible Technology Services (ATS). The Task Force, co-led by the IT Accessibility Coordinator, represents stakeholders campus-wide; meets monthly to draft policies, procedures, and resources; implements practices within the spheres of influence of the membership; and reports progress and makes recommendations to the upper administration in an annual report. The IT Accessibility Team includes twelve members of ATS who engage in accessible IT efforts, most working part-time on this effort and each with special areas on which they focus, including a member who works to help webmasters make their current websites accessible and learn to make future web pages more accessible. IT Accessibility Liaisons are individuals from campus units who have some basic knowledge about IT accessibility and agree to continue to increase their knowledge, attend three Liaison meetings each year, and promote accessibility in their respective units.

15.4.8   Policy, Guidelines, and Resources

With much input from the Task Force, the UW developed an IT accessibility policy, guidelines (pointing to WCAG 2.0 AA as the standard); a checklist for following the guidelines; step-by-step strategies for making websites and other IT accessible; and resources. In addition, whenever possible, web accessibility policies and practices are integrated into existing policies and practices regarding the procurement, development, and use of IT and regarding accessibility and diversity efforts in other application areas. The approach is also synchronized with campus-wide IT security efforts, thus learning from these experiences and identifying efficiencies that can be achieved when IT security and accessibility teams work together (e.g., in the IT procurement process).

15.4.9   Practices

The UW approach includes multiple ways to increase awareness, expertise, and practices with respect to web accessibility. A website provides a single location to find current policies and recommended practices (University of Washington, n.d.). Accessibility training is integrated within more general courses on the use of specific IT; stand-alone trainings on accessible website design are also offered. ATS supports a web accessibility special interest group and hosts meetings where webmasters can receive specific consultation on how to improve the accessibility of their websites. Although individual units are responsible for the accessible design of their websites, ATS secured financial resources to fund limited captioning of videos and remediation of documents that are considered high impact. ATS engages with vendors to increase the accessibility of existing products the UW uses and to promote the procurement of accessible products in the future. ATS staff members also help IT staff campus-wide integrate accessibility into their workflows. ATS has also invested in multiple products to improve accessibility including the negotiation of contracts and relationship building with caption and document remediation vendors, website accessibility checkers, and an accessibility add-on feature to its campus learning management system that checks for and help remediate IT with respect to accessibility. Annually, ATS gathers data summarizing services offered and data regarding the accessibility of IT and plans future activities based on these results.

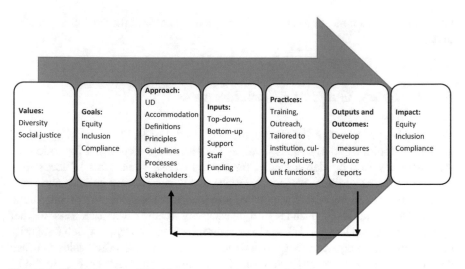

Fig. 15.1 The University of Washington approach to accessibility

15.4.10 Lessons Learned

Experiences at the UW suggest that the following strategies be considered by others implementing a campus-wide initiative to improve the accessibility of websites:

- Engage all key stakeholder groups, encourage each to build web accessibility into their workflows, and offer multiple ways for them to gain knowledge and otherwise engage in web accessibility efforts.
- Build the program on current policies and procedures and address web accessibility from a broad perspective with respect to more general as well as IT accessibility efforts.
- Undertake efforts that are both reactive and proactive, both top-down and bottom-up.

And, perhaps most importantly, promote accessibility within the unique context of the institution with respect to values, goals, approaches, inputs, practices, outputs and outcomes, and impact. The following image provides a visual representation of how this approach is implemented at the UW (See Fig. 15.1).

15.5 Discussion

At the beginning of this chapter, we noted that there was a common perception that there are two main drivers for improvements to the accessibility of websites in HE have been identified and discussed exhaustively: (1) increasing numbers of disabled students in HE and (2) anti-discrimination and equality legislation. We then presented evidence from both literature and an institutional case study to suggest that many more factors drive or influence an institution's approach to accessibility including contextual factors such as institutional values and stakeholders. Inaccessibility therefore is not as "simple to correct" as Kimmons (2017) would suggest. In this section, we will seek to develop this argument further by discussing what we see as two imperatives for future research in the field: The imperative to stop seeking overly simplistic solutions and the imperative to acknowledge the influence of powerful and newly emerging cultures within HE.

15.5.1 The Imperative to Stop Seeking Overly Simplistic Solutions

One of the consequences to having an overly simplistic view of the drivers and factors that influence accessibility is that it can lead to a tendency to seek overly simplistic solutions. Seale (2014) gives a range of examples of this phenomenon including looking to guidelines and standards; promoting Universal Design as a universal solution and calling for the training of all university staff. Seale (2014) gives a detailed critique of each of these and argues that the calls for such solutions often fail to point to any evidence that the proposed solutions will actually work.

If we take the call for more accessibility training as an example to illuminate our argument, Seale's review of the accessibility training literature reveals that there is a lack of consensus about what the content of the training should be, with some arguing for a focus on technical issues, some for disability awareness and others for design approaches. There is also a lack of detailed debate about the best ways to deliver accessibility training with many simply opting for obvious technological delivery mechanisms such as online courses, virtual environments, and disability simulations. Furthermore, there is very little discussion about whether and how theories about the best way to learn can and should underpin the design of accessibility-related training learning and development. The closest the discourse comes to touching on pedagogy is to call for the embedding of "accessibility" within other courses. Finally, there is no debate about what evidence there is that training works, what evidence is required to show that training is effective, and the factors that might influence effectiveness studies. There has been a tendency instead to offer anecdotal evidence for the effectiveness of training. Seale concluded her critique of the accessibility literature by arguing that accessibility training should show staff how they can link knowledge to action and adapt that knowledge to meet different needs and contexts and recognize that training and professional development is not just about changing individual practice, but it is about changing institutional culture. Accessibility training, therefore, might offer one part of the solution to the inaccessibility of university websites, but it is not a simple fix. It is our contention that this is true for many other accessibility "solutions" that have been offered to the field.

15.5.2　The Imperative to Acknowledge the Influence of Powerful and Newly Emerging Cultures Within Higher Education

The management of HEIs has changed in the past decades and moved toward what has been called "New Public Management" (Deem and Brehony 2005; Broucker and Wit 2015). It is argued that HEIs are more and more "governed by objectives," driven by quality standards and control, and have to make more efficient and effective use of increasingly scarce or stagnating resources. Accessibility as a concept, initiative, and practice must therefore fit into these changed framework conditions and currently it is not entirely clear whether this is possible. For example, accessibility has to compete for resources with other initiatives such as diversity management and gender equality and at the moment we do not know how HEIs negotiate or manage such competitions for resources.

One way that HEIs might manage such competition is by investing in accessibility just enough to avoid being sued, but no further. So accessibility could be described as a question of compliance with legal requirements and internal guidelines (Roberts et al. 2011). HEIs may therefore make sure that the Internet and intranet sites are accessible and take care of learning material, videos, and other digital assets. Being inclusive, however, requires more than mere compliance, as the case study of the University of Washington testified to. The HEI as a whole has to be far more proactive, open, and welcoming to a diverse student body. But there is a perception in large parts of HE that it is not cost-effective to attract marginalized groups, because they claim specific support (resources) and yet might not graduate. Such costs and uncertain results could conflict with the goals of New Public Management, like producing more successful students. The extent to which new management cultures across the HE sector are sympathetic or antagonistic to the principles of inclusion and accessibility would seem worthy of further research.

15.6　Future Directions

We began this chapter by presenting a review of current accessibility research in the field of HE which has focused on evaluating the accessibility of university websites. If future research is to make a genuine and meaningful contribution to improving the accessibility of websites for disabled students in HE, then it is our contention that we must stop doing the easy technical stuff—auditing existing websites—and engage instead with the difficult stuff—developing and evaluating solutions to the socio-cultural and political barriers to accessibility both within the sector as a whole and within individual institutions. This requires interdisciplinary research teams capable of embracing complexity. Computer Scientists and Human–Computer Interaction specialists cannot solve the problem of inaccessible websites in HE on their own.

15.7 Authors' Opinion of the Field

It is our view that future research in the field of accessibility and HE must understand and seek to develop accessibility within the unique context of the institution with respect to values, goals, approaches, inputs, practices, outputs and outcomes, and impact; address the roles, perceptions and needs of all the relevant stakeholders within an institution including managers and those who have to respond to the pressures of increasing student success while reducing costs and provide robust evidence that proposed solutions predicated on developing new accessibility practices actually work.

As authors of this chapter, our own personal response to these challenges is to form a network (called ED-ICT) which consists of researchers in the US, Canada, UK, Israel, and Germany. The aims of the network are to synthesize and compare the research evidence that is available across the five countries regarding the relationship between students with disabilities, Information and Communication Technologies (ICT), and post-compulsory education; construct theoretical explanations for why ICTs have not yet brought about the reductions in discrimination, disadvantage, and exclusion that were predicted when equality and discrimination-related laws were published across the five countries and provide new perspectives about potential future solutions regarding how post-compulsory education institutions can better use ICTs to remove the ongoing problems of disadvantage and exclusion of students with disabilities.

15.8 Conclusion

In conclusion then, we have presented evidence to show that websites in HE are not models of best accessibility practice and why implementing approaches to accessibility within HEIs can be challenging and complex. We have argued that for research and practice to develop in the future it is important that we stop seeking overly simplistic solutions and acknowledge the influence of powerful and newly emerging cultures within HE. Finally, we suggested that in order to be successful, future accessibility initiatives will require interdisciplinary research teams capable of embracing complexity in order to take into account institutional contexts, many different stakeholders involved, and the need for evidence that is robust enough to move institutions and stakeholders to change.

Acknowledgements This chapter is based in part on work supported by the National Science Foundation (Grant number CNS-1539179) and The Leverhulme Trust (Grant Number IN-2016-018). Any opinions, findings, and conclusions or recommendations are those of the authors and do not necessarily reflect the policy or views of the funders, and you should not assume their endorsement.

References

Alexander D (2004) WebWatch: how accessible are Australian university web sites? Ariadne (38). http://www.ariadne.ac.uk/issue38/alexander/

Alexander D, Rippon S (2007) University website accessibility revisited. In: Proceedings of AusWeb07. http://ausweb.scu.edu.au/aw07/papers/refereed/alexander/pa/per.html. Accessed 16 Feb 2010

Asuncion JV, Fichten CS, Cwojka C, Barile M, Nguyen MN, Wolforth J (2010) Multiple perspectives on the accessibility of e-Learning in Canadian colleges and universities. Assist Technol Off J RESNA 22:187–199

Bailey J, Burd E (2005) Web accessibility evolution in the United Kingdom. Paper presented at the seventh IEEE international symposium of web site evolution, 26 Sept 2005

Billingham L (2014) Improving academic library website accessibility for people with disabilities. Libr Manag 35:565–581. https://doi.org/10.1108/LM-11-2013-0107

Broucker B, Wit KD (2015) New public management in higher education. In: The Palgrave international handbook of higher education policy and governance. Palgrave Macmillan, London, pp 57–75

Chacón-Medina A, Chacón-López H, López-Justicia MD, Fernández-Jiménez C (2013) Dificultades en la Accesibilidad Web de las Universidades Españolas de acuerdo a la Norma WCAG 2.0. Rev Esp Doc Científica 36:e025

California State University (2009) Accessible technology initiative. http://teachingcommons.cdl.edu/access/. Accessed 1 Sept 2018

Comeaux D, Schmetzke A (2007) Web accessibility trends in university libraries and library schools. Libr Hi Tech 25:457–477. https://doi.org/10.1108/07378830710840437

Curl AL, Bowers DD (2009) A longitudinal study of website accessibility: have social work education websites become more accessible? J Technol Hum Serv 27:93–105. https://doi.org/10.1080/15228830902749229

Deem R, Brehony KJ (2005) Management as ideology: the case of 'new managerialism' in higher education. Oxf Rev Educ 31:217–235. https://doi.org/10.1080/03054980500117827

Espadinha C, Pereira LM, da Silva FM, Lopes JB (2011) Accessibility of Portuguese public universities' sites. Disabil Rehabil 33:475–485. https://doi.org/10.3109/09638288.2010.498554

Guyer C, Uzeta M (2009) Assistive technology obligations for postsecondary education institutions. J Access Serv 6:12–35. https://doi.org/10.1080/15367960802286120

Hackett S, Parmanto B (2005) A longitudinal evaluation of accessibility: higher education web sites. Internet Res 15:281–294

Hoover SJ (2003) IT professionals' response to adoption and implementation of innovations in the workplace: incorporating accessibility features into information technology for end users with disabilities. Doctor of Philosophy thesis, University of Minnesota

Iseri EI, Uyar K, Ilhan U (2017) The accessibility of Cyprus Islands' higher education institutions websites. Procedia Comput Sci 120:967–974. https://doi.org/10.1016/j.procs.2017.11.333

Ismailova R, Inal Y (2018) Accessibility evaluation of top university websites: a comparative study of Kyrgyzstan, Azerbaijan, Kazakhstan and Turkey. Univers Access Inf Soc 17: 437–445. https://doi-org.libezproxy.open.ac.uk/10.1007/s10209-017-0541-0

Ismailova R, Kimsanova G (2017) Universities of the Krgyz Republic on the web: accessibility and usability. Univ Access Infor Soc 16:1017–1025. https://doi.org/10.1007/s10209-016-0481-0

Kimmons R (2017) Open to all? Nationwide evaluation of high-priority web accessibility considerations among higher education web-sites. J Comput High Educ 29:434–450. https://doi.org/10.1007/s12528-017-9151-3

Kline J (2011) Strategic accessibility: enabling the organisation. Live Oak Book Company

Krach SK (2007) Snapshot-ten years after the law: a survey of the current status of university web accessibility. J Spec Educ Technol 22:30–40. https://doi.org/10.1177/016264340702200403

Laitano MI (2015) Accesibilidad web en el espacio universitario público argentino. Rev Esp Doc Científica 38:e079. https://doi.org/10.3989/redc.2015.1.1136

Leitner M-L, Strauss C, Stummer C (2016) Web accessibility implementation in private sector organizations: motivations and business impact. Univers Access Inf Soc 15:249–260. https://doi.org/10.1007/s10209-014-0380-1

Linder KE, Fontaine-Rainen DL, Behling K (2015) Whose job is it? Key challenges and future directions for online accessibility in US Institutions of Higher Education. Open Learn J Open Distance E-Learn 30:21–34. https://doi.org/10.1080/02680513.2015.1007859

Luna L (2009) But how can those students make it here? Examining the institutional discourse about what it means to be 'LD' at an Ivy League university. Int J Incl Educ 13:157–178. https://doi.org/10.1080/13603110701322852

North Carolina State University (1997) The principles of universal design. https://projects.ncsu.edu/design/cud/about_ud/udprinciplestext.htm. Accessed 15 June 1998

Penn State University (n.d.) Accessible Technology & Information Committee. http://accessibility.psu.edu/ati/. Accessed 1 September 2018

Providenti M, Zai R (2007) Web accessibility at Kentucky's academic libraries. Library Hi Tech 25:478–493. https://doi.org/10.1108/07378830710840446

Providenti M (2004) Library web accessibility at Kentucky's 4-year degree granting colleges and universities. D-Lib Magazine, 10, 9. http://www.dlib.org/dlib/september04/providenti/09providenti.html

Roberts JB, Crittenden LA, Crittenden JC (2011) Students with disabilities and online learning: a cross-institutional study of perceived satisfaction with accessibility compliance and services. Internet High Educ 14:242–250. https://doi.org/10.1016/j.iheduc.2011.05.004

Seale J (2006) E-learning and disability in higher education: accessibility theory and practice, 1st edn. Routledge, Oxford

Seale J (2014) E-learning and disability in higher education: accessibility theory and practice, 2nd edn. Routledge, New York

Seale J (2018) Disability, ICT, post-compulsory education & employment: in search of new designs for technology. http://ed-ict.com/workshops/tel-aviv/. Accessed 20 March 2018

South Carolina Technical College System (2013) Resolution agreement, OCR compliance review No. 11-11-6002. https://www2.ed.gov/about/offices/list/ocr/docs/investigations/11116002-b.pdf. Accessed 15 June 2018

State of Washington Office of the Chief Information Officer (2016) Policy #188—Accessibility. https://ocio.wa.gov/policy/accessibility. Accessed 15 June 2018

Thompson T, Burgstahler S, Moore E (2010) Web accessibility: a longitudinal study of college and university home pages in the northwestern United States. Disabil Rehabil Assist Technol 5:108–114. https://doi.org/10.3109/17483100903387424

US Department of Labor (1990) Information and technical assistance with the Americans with disabilities act. https://www.ada.gov/ada_intro.htm. Accessed 15 June 2018

US Department of Labor (1973) Section 504, Rehabilitation Act of 1973. https://www.dol.gov/oasam/regs/statutes/sec504.htm. Accessed 15 June 2018

University of Washington (n.d.) Accessible technology at the UW. http://www.washington.edu/accessibility/. Accessed 15 June 2018

Velleman EM, Nahuis I, van der Geest T (2017) Factors explaining adoption and implementation processes for web accessibility standards within eGovernment systems and organizations. Univ Access Inf Soc 16:173–190. https://doi.org/10.1007/s10209-015-0449-5

Web Accessibility Initiative (2016) Planning and managing web accessibility. In: Planning and managing web accessibility. https://www.w3.org/WAI/planning-and-managing/. Accessed 21 May 2018

Wijayaratne A, Singh D (2010) Is there space in cyberspace for distance learners with special needs in Asia? A review of the level of web accessibility of institutional and library home pages of AAOU members. Int Inf Libr Rev 42:40–49 https://doi.org/10.1016/j.iilr.2010.01.002

Wijayaratne A (2008) Web accessibility: does it have a role in delivering distance education? Paper presented at the fifth PAN Commonwealth forum on open learning, July 2008, London

Chapter 16
Policy and Standards on Web Accessibility for Cognitive and Learning Disabilities

Clayton Lewis and Lisa Seeman

Abstract Access to the Web for people with cognitive, language, and learning differences and limitations is widely recognized as important and becoming more important as Web content and Apps become ubiquitous. Yet progress has been slow, as indicated by limited support for cognitive accessibility within the Web Content Accessibility Guidelines process. How can this progress be accelerated, and how can research contribute to the increase in cognitive accessibility that is needed?

16.1 Introduction

As explained in other chapters of this book, access to the Web is increasingly important for people to be able to control their own life, access to critical services as well as social participation of all kind, including education, employment, and education. Accessibility to the digital world is widely acknowledged as by the United Nations and individual governments to be a right for people with disabilities. This is as true for people with cognitive, language, and learning differences and limitations as it is for anyone else.

The framework for support for accessibility for people with cognitive and learning disabilities in policy is included international law or treaties, such as the UN Convention on the Rights of Persons with Disabilities (the CRPD).[1] However, despite the understanding of the need and the obligation via international treaties, specific guidelines or precedent in law is lacking to the extent of lack of accessible access to basic, critical, online services.

---

[1] Convention on the Rights of Persons with Disabilities http://www.un.org/disabilities/documents/convention/convoptprot-e.pdf.

C. Lewis (✉)
Department of Computer Science, University of Colorado Boulder, Boulder, USA
e-mail: clayton.lewis@colorado.edu

L. Seeman
Athena ICT, Beit Shemesh, Israel
e-mail: Lisa.seeman@zoho.com
URL: http://accessibility.athena-ict.com/

© Springer-Verlag London Ltd., part of Springer Nature 2019
Y. Yesilada and S. Harper (eds.), *Web Accessibility*, Human–Computer
Interaction Series, https://doi.org/10.1007/978-1-4471-7440-0_16

This clearly impacts the rights of people with cognitive disabilities to control their own lives and participate in society. There has been evidence to suggest that this lower level of accessibility support for people with cognitive disabilities can be a contributory factor to their lower life expectancy. Addressing this issue should be considered urgent.

The focus of this chapter is to review and discuss the state of accessibility support in standards and policy for the inclusion of people with cognitive, learning, and intellectual disabilities. It will also discuss how policy and research could be advanced in the future. We'll use the shorthand COGA to stand for "cognitive accessibility".

16.1.1 People with Cognitive and Learning Disabilities and the Web

As discussed in Chap. 4, there are many diverse cognitive and learning disabilities. Most groups struggle with using the Web and are often unable to use Web content because of the design choices of the content provider. In some cases, different groups will have similar user needs. For example, most COGA user groups will struggle with filling out forms or entering data. In these cases, single solutions can aid all the different user groups, such as allowing the user to select from a choice of valid options.

In other cases, user needs may be different for diverse COGA user groups. For example, people with severe language impairments may benefit from sites with less text and may be helped on graphics and familiar symbols. On the other hand, persons living with early-stage dementia will still have reading skills and may understand the words well, but will not be able to learn symbols used in modern interfaces. People with dyscalculia may not be able to use numerical references such as percentages signs. A textual explanation of quantities may be easier for these users to understand, but harder for others.

In many cases, however, there are techniques that help particular COGA user groups, but also increase the usability of the content for most users. Examples include:

- People with language-related disabilities may have a limited vocabulary and may need common words, short chunks of text, and simple language. Other users will also appreciate this clarity and simplicity.
- People with an impaired executive function may struggle to learn new interface paradigms, but will be able to use familiar, well-known symbols and standard interface patterns. Users who can learn new paradigms may be glad not to have to.
- People with impaired memory may be unable to remember new symbols, jargon or interface paradigms. They may be unable to login and forget passwords and access codes. Login mechanism such as conforming to the Web Authentication specification can enable them to use their preferred login method.
- People with impaired attention may be unable to complete a task if there are distractions and interruptions. If they also have an impaired short-term memory,

then they will not remember what they were doing before they were distracted and therefore be unable to continue the task from a midpoint after being distracted. Reducing distractions and having a clear heading that reminds them of what they are doing can help these users in particular, but make the system easier to use for everyone.

16.2 Policy and COGA

As discussed in Chap. 4, attitudes to People with cognitive disabilities are slowly improving. However, even with these improvements, digital inclusion for COGA is far behind the inclusion for other groups of disabilities. Part of this has been attributed to these disabilities being undeclared. People with cognitive disabilities may be less likely to request accommodations, fearing discrimination. They may also not be aware of their disability or the accommodations that they are entitled to.[2]

Another issue is the lack of guidance given in widely adopted standards. Standards available are often fragmented by disability group and available guidance is often vague and is not testable.

However, possibly the core barrier is still attitudes and misinformation. For example, developers, standards organizations and businesses that may feel people with cognitive disabilities cannot use computers. Misconceptions about what COGA use groups can do and the prevalence in people with learning and cognitive disabilities in skilled and intellectual and analytical vocations is discussed in chap. 4.

While accommodations for COGA groups are lacking, demographic trends are increasing the numbers of people worldwide with cognitive, language, and learning differences and limitations. One factor is the aging population in many countries, leading to greater numbers of people with cognitive decline and dementia (see the background in Ren et al. 2018). Another factor is the increased life expectancy for people with developmental disabilities (Lim et al. 2018). The lack of accommodation and inclusion for this growing demographic adds increasing stress and expense on caregivers, as people who could control their own life, are unable to do so without external support. Hence improving accommodations for COGA groups is not only a human rights issue but is also becoming essential from an economic perspective as the cost of care providers for COGA user groups rises.

16.2.1 Overview of Support in Policy and Standards

Arguably the most important definition of rights for people with disabilities is the UN Convention on the Rights of Persons with Disabilities Convention on the Rights of

---

[2]https://www.w3.org/TR/coga-gap-analysis/#introduction.

Persons with Disabilities[3] or CRPD. The CRPD has 177 ratifications and the optional protocol was had 92 accessions.[4]

This convention defines persons with disabilities to include those who have long-term physical, mental, intellectual or sensory impairments, clearly covering COGA use groups.

The principles of the Convention include nondiscrimination; full and effective participation and inclusion in society; equality of opportunity; and accessibility.

General obligations of the signatories (Article 4) include: adopt all appropriate legislative, administrative, and other measures for the implementation of these rights, and to take all appropriate measures, including legislation, to modify or abolish existing laws, regulations, customs, and practices that constitute discrimination against persons with disabilities.

The rights are further detailed in the remainder of the document. Article 9 defines the right to accessibility as *"To enable persons with disabilities to live independently and participate fully in all aspects of life, States Parties shall take appropriate measures to ensure to persons with disabilities access, on an equal basis with others, ... including information and communications technologies and systems..."* and to promote access for persons with disabilities to new information and communications technologies and systems, including the Internet.

It is also worth noting that the convention requires other rights which can be infringed on when access to information application and forms are not equal. Arguably, this could include access to justice and even the right to life, in cases where medical support, appointments and critical information are inaccessible.

Similarly, in the European Union Charter of Fundamental Rights, support for inclusion and accessibility for people with cognitive disabilities can be easily inferred from Article 26, "Integration of persons with disabilities". Here the Union recognizes and respects the right of persons with disabilities to benefit from measures designed to ensure their independence, social and occupational integration and participation in the life of the community. Similarly, in Article 25, the rights of the COGA groups with age-related forgetfulness and people living with dementia can be included as part of the rights of the elderly to lead a life of dignity and independence and to participate in social and cultural life.[5]

Other directives also imply accommodation for people with cognitive disabilities, such as The Employment Equality Directive (2000/78/EC). The Directive implemented the principle of equal treatment in employment and training. The European Council Employment Guidelines also define next steps as policies aimed at combating discrimination against groups such as persons with disability.[6]

---

[3]Convention on the Rights of Persons with Disabilities http://www.un.org/disabilities/documents/convention/convoptprot-e.pdf.

[4]https://www.un.org/development/desa/disabilities/convention-on-the-rights-of-persons-with-disabilities.html.

[5]http://www.europarl.europa.eu/charter/pdf/text_en.pdf

[6] Employment Eq http://eur-lex.europa.eu/LexUriServ/LexUriServ.do?uri=CELEX:32000L0078:en:HTMLuality Directive (2000/78/EC)

While these are a comprehensive declaration of rights and obligations of the states, they are also abstract. As policies are added to implement these principles, unfortunately, they too often provide less support for COGA user groups.

16.2.2 The Web Content Accessibility Guidelines (WCAG)

The most important specification in the world of digital accessibility is the Web Content Accessibility Guidelines (WCAG) process of the Web Accessibility Initiative of the W3C. These guidelines are referred to by legislation across the globe as the benchmark for digital and Web accessibility. Unfortunately, this does not present a very bright picture for COGA, despite a great deal of work and discussion. In the first major revision of WCAG, producing WCAG 2.0 in 2008, many COGA advocates were concerned that key COGA features, for example, mandating the use of clear and simple language, or logins that do not rely on password or memory, were deemphasized in the transition from WCAG 1.0 to WCAG 2.0.

A major concern about WCAG as a whole was the generally low level of compliance (despite the fact that WCAG guidelines, which are in themselves purely informational, are given regulatory force in many jurisdictions) and the extra author burden these provisions may cause. Some people felt that lack of clear operational criteria, that is, simple ways for organizations to know whether or not they are in compliance with the provisions of WCAG, inhibited compliance. WCAG 2.0, therefore, emphasized framing guidelines that could be given very clear operational criteria. Using clear and simple language, it was felt, cannot be defined in a sufficiently clear way; although efforts were made using RDF (Resource Description Framework) techniques to reduce ambiguity that would enable simplification (Judson et al. 2005), they were not accepted. (The World-Wide Augmentative and Alternative Communication project (Poulson and Nicolle 2004) also had concept coding proposals that were tested along similar lines.)

Dissatisfaction about the situation following WCAG 2.0 led to a concerted response, a task force https://www.w3.org/WAI/PF/cognitive-a11y-tf/ within the WAI to focus specifically on improving the COGA situation in further revisions of the guidelines. When the guidelines were next revised, to produce WCAG 2.1 with a target date in 2018, many ideas from the COGA task force were proposed. As it happened, however, only a very small proportion of these suggestions were adopted (3 downgraded out of a proposed 38 new criteria), leaving COGA advocates feeling that cognitive access is still not being adequately promoted in the content guidelines.

As a result, the WCAG COGA task force is creating as part of their gap analysis[7] a separate note on how to make content useable for COGA use groups. Although this note does not have strong testability criteria included, it will have guidance on what aspects are considered testable. It also has guidance for usability testing, persona

---

[7]https://www.w3.org/TR/coga-gap-analysis/.

design, and other support for inclusive content and applications. Testable criteria may be added at a later date.[8]

16.2.3 Other Standards and Policies

There is some COGA support in other standards. For example, TC/SC/standard for Information technology, includes some user accessibility needs for COGA groups, such as to the user need to understand the information presented. The reader may note that these requirements, although good, leave the content provider without clear guidance of what to do. They are also not requirements.

ETSI, The European Telecommunications Standards Institute, is another important standards organization on a European level. The key ETSI standard for accessibility EN 301 549 is targeted at referencing WCAG 2.1 and in doing so may be the first piece of legislation to point to WCAG 2.1. However, as the COGA requirements were largely rejected by WCAG, it is unlikely that the revision of EN 301 549 will provide significant COGA support. The ETSI team on accessibility of mobile ICT for persons with cognitive disabilities has published ETSI Guide (EG) 203 350, which is harmonized with the work of the W3C COGA taskforce proposals. This may positively impact EN 301 549.

Some disabilities organizations have created guidelines or policies of COGA. Some examples are the EU easy to read standard[9] and the British dyslexia style guide.[10]

Another area of policy that reflects some COGA needs is the use of plain language. Plain language is typically a requirement of government communication. For example, in the US the Plain Writing Act of 2010 was signed on October 13, 2010. While the Act does not cover regulations, two separate Executive Orders emphasize the need for plain language.[11]

It is also worth mentioning that Spain launched an experimental standard on easy reading in 2018 (UNE 153101EX) and this may suggest a start of legislation that supports COGA independent of WCAG requirements.[12]

---

[8]To be published at https://www.w3.org/tr/coga-useable/ (was https://www.w3.org/TR/coga-gap-analysis/index.html#appendix-making-content-usable-for-people-with-cognitive-and-learning-disabilities).

[9]http://easy-to-read.eu/.

[10]https://www.bdadyslexia.org.uk/common/ckeditor/filemanager/userfiles/About_Us/policies/Dyslexia_Style_Guide.pdf.

[11]https://plainlanguage.gov/law/.

[12]Lectura Fácil   http://www.aenor.es/aenor/normas/normas/fichanorma.asp?tipo=N&codigo=N0060036&PDF=Si#.WyIcOy2RhE7 .

16.2.4   Reflections

Stepping back, what are the causes of this state of affairs, where the needs of people with cognitive disabilities are excluded from policies even though their right to accessibility is acknowledged? One likely cause is poor COGA in the WCAG process itself. The online tools used for deliberation in the guidelines development process are quite difficult to use for anyone, but especially for people with cognitive limitations and differences. For example, issues are referred to using numeric tags; if one has trouble remembering what these tags refer to, as many people with cognitive differences do, it is difficult to follow and contribute to the discussion. This is consequential in what is in many ways a political process, where a sense of balance of opinion among participants is often important. Not all groups find it equally easy to represent their opinions in the process.

A related issue is that many COGA users do not like to declare or discuss their cognitive impairments. This may have a larger effect as industry play a significant role in standards committees such as WCAG. Inside these companies, people with physical disabilities often participate in the companies' contributions to creating the standard and advocate for it inside the organization. However as discussed above, people with cognitive disabilities may be less vocal and less likely to declare these cognitive issues, especially in the workplace. This may result in less internal advocacy inside many of the organizations that participate in standards groups.

The search for easy to measure metrics is another issue. Many stakeholders have a strong need for metrics that enable them to measure conformance automatically. This can create a bias in the guidelines toward requirements that support automated testing and metrics. The requirement for COGA, on the other hand, tends to be harder to test via an automated and mechanism while adequately addressing the core user need.

An example of this is readability metrics. Some readers may be aware of the existence of a number of readability formulae, that can be used to measure the comprehensibility of texts, and may wonder why effective guidelines could not be framed around these measures. The difficulty, clearly articulated by Redish (2000), is that these formulae work by measuring certain correlates of comprehensibility, and not comprehensibility itself. For example, texts with longer sentences tend to be less comprehensible than texts with shorter sentences. But short sentences are not, in themselves, easier to understand. Therefore, taking a text that has a poor readability score, and shortening its sentences, will not necessarily increase its actual readability, even though its readability score will improve. In fact, often, shortening sentences leads to less comprehensibility, because the semantic connections among ideas in the text may be lost. Hence guidelines that support an easy to measure readability criteria may not consistently address the user need of understandability.

Another way to understand what is happening is to observe that readability formulae are based on correlations observed only in *naturally occurring* text. For example, among a large collection of naturally occurring texts, it will be found that those with shorter sentences are easier to understand, on the average. But deliberately shortening the sentences in a text creates an *artificial* text, not a naturally occurring text, and the correlation does *not* hold among these artificial texts.

A further cause is that participants in the WCAG process sometimes cite lack of evidence of effectiveness in declining to support this proposal or that. For example, the discussion of efforts to require plain and simple language included a call for "usability research" to confirm the value of meeting proposed guidelines. So, would providing the requested research make a difference?

Many have suggested this, including the current first author, in the previous edition of this book (2008). But considering the slow progress we have seen, over several years, one must ask if this diagnosis is too simple.

In fact, the COGA task force of the W3C and WCAG assembled a great deal of research in support of its recommendations. For example, one part of the suggested COGA language guidance called for alternatives to figurative language, such as the use of expressions like "kick the bucket" in English for "die". There is a substantial literature showing that many people have difficulty understanding expressions like these, and the COGA task force reviewed this research. But the research isn't specifically "usability research", conducted in the context of the use of the Web. Rather, the studies are conducted as lab research by psychologists. In the complex WCAG consensus process, such a distinction can be all that's needed to defer a recommendation.

So, can we make progress just by doing this "usability research" on the Web? Could we settle these questions by comparing user performance on a batch of Web pages, with two versions, one revised to follow a proposed set of guidelines, and one unrevised?

Problems are immediately apparent. What kind of user performance would one measure, and how could one be confident that the revisions would impact this performance? Putting that another way, what if the original Web site, even if not as good as the revised one in some ways, is adequate? The original site may use figurative language, for example, but not in a way that affects user performance. Further, some users may find the content of the site easy to understand, based on prior knowledge, and hence be relatively insensitive to the changes, while others may find neither version intelligible. And of course, people are always variable. For many reasons, one may fail to get a crisp result favoring a sound guideline.

Do these difficulties mean that the whole idea of making Web pages more cognitively accessible is doomed? No. There is a crucial difference between *user testing*, used to improve a particular site, and *user research* intended to establish the value of a design guideline. In the former case, one examines the results of user testing to identify barriers of whatever kind, not just those associated with some particular guideline, and, in an iterative process, seeks to remove them. Problems are identified in the context of use, not on the basis of abstract descriptions of site features. So the prospects for user testing are better than for user research. But, so far, at any rate, the WCAG process seeks user research, rather than user testing.

Nevertheless, in our view, many improvements in COGA can and should be mandated in the WCAG process, despite these difficulties. After all, few if any existing WCAG guidelines have been adopted because of user research, a point to which we return below. But we also feel that the difficulties, and in particular the key role of context of use, do call for some revision in how we promote accessibility.

To develop this idea, let's return to Redish's work on the comprehensibility of text. The work goes beyond the problem of correlations in readability measures that we discussed earlier. She points out that the comprehensibility of a text depends not only on the characteristics of the text but also on what people know. That is, comprehensibility cannot be determined out of context.

Redish has described (personal communication, 2018) the experience of revising the model lease that was in use in a particular community. The purpose of a model lease is to lay out provisions that tenants and landlords can generally agree on. When a landlord accepts a model lease, tenants need not fear that they are signing a document with some hidden trap that advantages the landlord over them. It's clearly helpful if the model lease is easy for people to understand, and Redish and collaborators were retained to improve the language.

One of the important terms in a lease is "security deposit", a sum of money paid in advance by the tenant and returned at the end of the lease, with deductions if the tenant has damaged the premises. This phrase contains two words, totaling seven syllables. Further, both words have Latin roots, rather than Germanic roots, and often such words are less familiar, in English vocabulary. Good practice suggested replacing this phrase with one that used shorter, more familiar words. Redish and her collaborators chose "promise money".

The team made other revisions in the lease, and tested the comprehensibility of two versions, one with "security deposit" and one with "promise money". Testing with economically poor, often low literacy renters, they watched as many stumbled over the words "security deposit", in that version of the lease. Those who saw the other version had no trouble reading "promise money". However, renters who saw "security deposit" had no trouble understanding what it meant, once they had decoded it, while those who read "promise money" asked "What's that?" or said, "I've never seen that before." People found "promise money" easier to read, but *harder to understand*. In Redish's words, "Moral of the story: Plain language is dependent on audience and context."

Related concerns arise with other aspects of COGA. Lewis (2007) argues that "simplicity", as it might be used to indicate that a Web site will or will not be easy to use or understand, is similarly a relational property. That is, a site that is "simple" for one user may be "complex" for another. In particular, some users may benefit from interactions organized so that they are asked to choose among only a few alternatives at a time. In order to select among a given number of alternatives, overall, this means they must make a number of choices, each of which has only a few alternatives. Other users may find it easier to choose among more alternatives, if they don't have to make as many different decisions. This could be true if they find it difficult to keep a goal in mind through a long sequence of steps (Hoehl 2016, found that young adults with cognitive limitations often preferred "wide" sites that presented many choices.) Here again, it emerges that guidelines that mandate particular structure for sites or interactions cannot deliver "simplicity" for all users.

This reasoning points to an aspect of Web accessibility that is assuming increased prominence: personalization. Rather than mandating that sites should use this or that presentation, the mandate would be that users can choose a presentation that meets their individual needs. This is consistent with emergent wisdom in other areas of accessibility, such as the need to allow users to adapt such aspects of presentation as font, font size, and color contrast so as to meet their individual needs.

Some COGA opportunities are being pursued in the context of a personalization task force within the Web Accessibility Initiative https://www.w3.org/WAI/ARIA/task-forces/personalization/work-statement. For example, proposals are well advanced that would permit users to substitute symbols from a familiar symbol set for idiosyncratic symbols that a site designer might use for common functions like "search", "compose", or "back". Proposals for providing literal forms to replace figurative language and forms to replace language that uses numbers (for example, replacing "9 out of 10" by "almost all", for users who have difficulty comprehending numerical information) are under consideration. As these proposals mature they may be accepted in the WCAG process.

Promising and important though we think this work is, we note that it is limited in scope. It does not address the comprehensibility of text on a Web site in general. There are other aspects of the work of the Personalization Task Force that have a wider scope, such as provisions for marking controls or pieces of content as more or less commonly needed, so that a simplified presentation could omit them. But an observer of the WCAG process may well question whether these features will pass muster in WCAG, given the subjectivity involved in judging how commonly needed control is, or how important it might be, even if not used very often. Here too the importance of the context of use emerges as crucial. What is needed is a mix of guidance from the standards and intent of the author to make the content easier to use and understand. Simply conforming to a binary measurement will not guarantee the result in most cases.

Considering all this, how might generally good COGA be achieved? How can the context of use, as well as the characteristics of sites, be reflected in a system for promoting accessibility? A process of user testing, in which people with a variety of cognitive limitations try to use a site to accomplish tasks that are representative of those the site aims to support, would be appropriate. This parallels the accepted best practice in user experience design, a field of design that substantially overlaps COGA proposals for WCAG (see, e.g., Jakob Nielsen, https://www.nngroup.com/articles/usability-101-introduction-to-usability/).

Today, this kind of process is taken to be outside the scope of the current WCAG process. Whatever people think of the practical value of user tests, they believe that a requirement to carry out actual user testing to assess accessibility would be seen as too burdensome, and would be widely flouted, undermining the effectiveness of the WCAG overall (see Note 1).

In response to this situation, the COGA task force has moved away beyond the WCAG requirements to emphasize user needs and guidance for meeting them, as opposed to testable criteria. Although the provisions of this guidance are human testable, they may not serve the industry needs for automated measurement (see Note 2).

16.3 Discussion

The COGA Task Force is on track to publish their recommendations as a supplement or a note. This has freed the task force from the legislative burden associated with WCAG, and can also enable them to change their scope to include user testing and process. The current working draft of the guidance contains user needs, process discussion, and design requirements. Although the design requirements are often human testable, the advice focuses on being understandable by content creators rather than measurable by automated testing.[13]

In the wake of the WCAG 2.1 effort, participants have recognized the failure of the process to yield substantial enhancement of COGA (though some modest gains were achieved). This concern joins with other concerns in a broad effort to rethink the accessibility guidelines for the Web, called Silver https://www.w3.org/WAI/GL/task-forces/silver/.

Without taking away from the need to continue to press for COGA within the current WCAG process, we suggest that Silver may offer an opportunity to add significant elements to the overall Web accessibility enterprise, with the potential to address some of the opportunities that the current process has failed to address. It is beyond the scope of this chapter to develop these ideas in detail, but some aspects of a possible extended process do have implications for the research enterprise. We consider those here.

The most important feature of an extended process would be adding evaluation of the development *process* to the current evaluation of a development *product*. That is, while compliance with current WCAG is established by checking various aspects of a Web site, compliance with the extended guidelines would require checking various aspects of how a Web site is designed and maintained. In particular, the extended guidelines would require that developers carry out user testing with diverse users as part of the development process, and that they have a means of responding to issues that are identified in this testing process. Similarly, site owners would be asked to show that they have a means of obtaining and responding to feedback from users about accessibility problems, once the site is deployed. This kind of *process* certification, while quite different from the current WCAG framework, is being considered for Silver. It has precedents in other fields, for example, the ISO 9001 certification (https://www.iso.org/iso-9001-quality-management.html). We briefly discuss other aspects of this idea, and its relationship to current WCAG, in Note 3. Similar sugges-

---

[13]To be published at https://www.w3.org/tr/coga-useable/ (was https://www.w3.org/TR/coga-gap-analysis/index.html#appendix-making-content-usable-for-people-with-cognitive-and-learning-disabilities).

tions are included in the note on COGA being prepared to accompany the WCAG 2.1 guidelines, mentioned earlier.

Another direction for advancing COGA in policy may be litigation. In many countries, once the rights have been established in the law, the practical ramifications are set via president. For example, the Americans with Disabilities Act clearly defines the rights of people with disabilities to equal access to public services. However, it took landmark court cases brought by the nonvisual community to establish that the ADA applied to services offered over the internet, and not just to brick and mortar business establishments. A similar legal case could establish that this law includes COGA. It is hoped that the guidance in the note by the COGA task force may help to support such legal action. The fact that the guidance will be of the form of a note and not a standard may make this route more difficult.

16.3.1 The Role of Research

We've expressed reservations, above, about the ability of user research to support cognitive accessibility. But other kinds of research are needed. One clear need is for research on accessibility evaluation that can cope with the diversity of user needs seen in the COGA space. Evaluations based on large group comparisons, sometimes called A-B testing (Kohavi et al. 2009), will likely not be effective, because the variability of users and contexts makes generalization difficult (this argument is developed in the case of programming language design in Lewis 2017a). Rather, methods that can interpret results from a diversity of small scale assessments are needed.

This situation is parallel to that prevailing in educational research, where many scholars argue that randomized controlled trials, considered the gold standard by some influential groups, are unable to cope with the diversity of learners and contexts. Margaret Eisenhart (2009) calls for "theoretical generalization", which produces generalizable findings not by statistical reasoning but by framing and testing theories of what is happening in particular settings. Statistical methods work by ignoring variability among people, by averaging, and thus can only find things that are true of most people, or work for most people, within some identified population. Theoretical generalization can respond to anyone, even one person, to whom the theory is applicable.

Within human–computer interaction, the widely used Cognitive Dimensions Analysis framework (see resources at http://www.cl.cam.ac.uk/~afb21/ CognitiveDimensions/) is based on theoretical generalization. The framework identifies structures in situations that, if found, strongly suggest likely positive or negative effects. For example, "hidden dependencies" are relationships within a system that tie different aspects of the system together, without the connection being apparent to a user. Thus when changing one thing, the user finds they have unintentionally changed something else. One can see that hidden dependencies suggest potential problems, wherever they occur, without making any statistical determination of how often or where they occur.

A great deal of existing accessibility work is already based, though only implicitly, on theoretical generalization. The requirement that headings need to be marked in documents, to support screen reader users, is not based on or supported by A-B testing or other statistical reasoning (as we remarked earlier). Rather, the way in which the lack of headings interferes with access for screen reader users is clear within a common sense analysis of the situation.

To support the development of a framework for COGA, parallel to Cognitive Dimensions Analysis, researchers should seek to develop logical analyses of the innovations they explore, that is, statements of the circumstances in which they can be expected to deliver benefits. Thus, instead of focusing on establishing that a feature delivers benefit to some group of people, using statistical methods (which often fail anyway, because of the difficulty of amassing large enough samples), researchers should articulate what it is about a situation, and a person, that indicates that the feature will be useful. For example, the psychological research identified by the COGA task force shows that some people have difficulty interpreting figurative language, so one can anticipate that this will create an accessibility barrier in a context in which interpreting such language is important for a task.

Research results framed in this way can feed usefully into the development processes that would be mandated under an extended accessibility regime. In the extended regime, in addition to seeing whether is feature is mandated by a guideline, developers will be seeking solutions to observed accessibility problems, either ones they observe during their own user testing or that are revealed in responses from users in the field. So even if WCAG does not adopt a guideline on figurative language, dealing with this problem would be promoted in the extended regime, where it arises in the context of use.

16.4   Future Directions

There are other classes of research that would gain impact within an extended accessibility regime. First, there is a need for research on software architectures that can support quite radical restructuring of Web sites. We lack software structures that can do this, smoothly trading off the breadth and depth of choice trees, for example, as suggested in the analysis in Lewis (2007), discussed earlier. The Fluid Project (www.fluidproject.org) can be cited as an effort that is aimed in this direction, strategically, with its effort to support flexibility in how information is represented and how users interact with it. But even this effort does not yet support the restructuring of choice trees.

We also need research on how to revise text so as to meet the needs of individual users. Advances in machine learning are providing new ways to rewrite the text, so as to reduce vocabulary, or decrease length by providing summaries that may be more easily understood in some situations. But we lack ways to tie such revisions to the reader's personal vocabularies and background knowledge.

Further, another way in which revision of text has to be variable is the context of use. Consider a description of a support service for people with disabilities, such as were provided by the Medicaid Reference Desk Web site (Lewis and Ward 2011). One user may want to understand what a service is, while another may want to understand whether they are eligible. A good summary for the first user may not be good for the second, and vice versa. This happens because the two summaries would retain and discard different information. Here again one cannot say that one summary is easier to understand than the other, independent of context. So COGA requires flexibility in presentation, rather than presentation in some mandated form. Research is needed on how to make this flexibility widely available to Web content creators (and consumers).

Another target for research in Natural Language Processing is support for the personalization features mentioned earlier, substituting for figurative language, and language that relies on numbers. Support for these features is likely to be spotty and brittle as long as it relies on human inspection and editing.

All of these natural language processing tools could be used either by site creators, as part of their editing workflow, or by end users. The latter use has the advantage that it could make even noncompliant sites more accessible. It is worth mentioning that many corporations are implementing or even adding to the research topics addressed by COGA. Honorable mentions include Microsoft (see https://www.microsoft.com/en-us/accessibility/features?activetab=pivot_1:primaryr4) and IBM's Content Clarifier (see https://www-03.ibm.com/able/content-clarifier.html).

The WAI Personalization Taskforce, mentioned earlier, is keeping a wiki (https://github.com/w3c/personalization-semantics/wiki/Implementations-of-Semantics) that includes implementations of desirable features, and also research projects. Some notable projects are the Unicef sponsored work on enabling conversion of symbols to symbols that are understood by the individual user. The European Commission is sponsoring work in the topic as well such as the SMART4MD application for people with mild dementia and their carers (http://www.smart4md.eu/). The EasyReading project (http://www.easyreading.eu/) will improve the accessibility of web pages by developing a software framework that helps people with cognitive disabilities to understand and navigate Web content which is created with paper researchers with cognitive disabilities as a framework for integrating different engines and support.

Providing a tool that can render inaccessible content, in an accessible way, is part of Vanderheiden's InfoBot program for future accessibility https://raisingthefloor.org/get-involved/challenges/infobot-grand-challenge/. A related, but contrasting, vision that researchers can explore is that of a means of representing content in a way that is independent of any particular presentation, and from which any needed presentation can be developed. As applied to COGA, this would mean that a single description of a service could be created, from which a description that communicated only the nature of the service, or a description that communicated only eligibility, could be created, to use the example mentioned earlier. Similarly, presentations using different vocabulary or assuming different background knowledge could be developed from the underlying content representation. This very demanding, but very attractive idea derives from the thinking of T V Raman and Jason White (see Raman 1996; Raman and Gries 1997; Lewis 2017b).

The COGA task force has identified two more areas of research in their gap analysis (https://www.w3.org/TR/coga-gap-analysis/). These fall outside the scope of Web accessibility, narrowly considered, but are strategically important. First, the spread of smart systems that rely on digital user data and behaviors to adapt and change the system poses challenges. For example, mature smart cities may use digital data-driven smart systems to regulate city services. If any group of users is not represented in these data, the system will not work well for them. For example, older people and people with learning disabilities may be less likely to use the city's bill paying system or parking app. As a result, their parking needs and struggles may be excluded from the digital data that drives these services. COGA researchers need to combat these biases.

Second, conversational interfaces, such as Apple's Siri, Amazon's Alexa, Google's Assistant, IBM's Watson API, and Microsoft's Cortana are increasingly popular and are supporting a wider array of services. While not Web-based, in themselves, these are becoming integrated with the Web; for example, a Web site can use specific markup to automatically create conversational access to some of its content via Google Assistant. What issues and opportunities do these interfaces present for people with cognitive disabilities? For example, Autistic people may have days when they are nonvocal. Stress can exacerbate people's ability to cope in times of additional anxiety, or "bad days". Can a conversational system be developed, integrated with the Web that would allow people to control their home automation (for example) via either a visual or a conversational interface, as they choose? It should be noted that as these systems become more ubiquitous and integrated into everyday task, the accessibility for people with cognitive disabilities of the visual interface becomes more and more essential.

One more kind of research is especially needed in the research ecosystem that would be promoted by the changed perspective on certification that we are suggesting. Where will ideas for new and useful COGA features come from, to feed the kind of research on features we've described above? We need more observational studies of users with cognitive differences, to understand the barriers to access they encounter, and to learn how they cope with these. A key advantage of the extended accessibility regime is that the wide-scale participation of people with cognitive differences in user testing will produce a great deal of new knowledge within development organizations. The research community, as well, can contribute in this way.

16.5 Authors' Opinion of the Field

Despite halting progress to date, cognitive accessibility will make progress in the coming years. Driven by demographic trends, enabled by new technological supports, many based on machine learning, and by increased participation of people with cognitive disabilities, and supported by enhancements in institutional support for accessibility, this progress will deliver more Web sites offering superior cognitive access. Research will play a key role in developing the tools and features that will enable this progress. However, activism by people with cognitive disabilities maybe required to help this progress affect policy.

16.6   Notes

Note 1: The dynamics of ideas about "testing" within the WCAG consensus process are complex. It appears necessary to distinguish at least three kinds of "testing": mechanical checking of a requirement, checking of a requirement by human experts, and gathering data from actual user tests. The first two are widely accepted, with the caveat that checking by experts has to be expected to lead to wide agreement among experts, that is, not to rely on variable, subjective judgements. Starting from a broad "common sense" requirement, such as the requirement for "plain and simple language" in the WCAG 1.0 guidelines, advocates have to make the requirement narrower, and more specific, to meet objections that a guideline has to be checkable by an objective process. Narrowing the requirement means backing off from a requirement on a site as a whole, to just some limited part, like headings. Making it more specific means designating particular lists of permitted vocabulary, and a mechanism for extending the lists when particular terminology is clearly needed, as in the Redish "security deposit" example. But even this kind of proposal does not get consensus support, perhaps because (on the one hand) people are concerned about how it would be determined that a given extension to the vocabulary is needed (would experts agree on this? How would they learn enough about the situation to have an opinion?) On the other hand, some COGA advocates might feel that the coverage of the narrowed requirement is clearly inadequate.

The tensions over these matters in the WCAG process are significant. Even when proposed COGA guidelines are limited in scope, with well-defined core vocabularies, such as are used extensively for teaching people with significant language impairments, and with exceptions provided for unclear cases, the burden may be considered too great to be accepted.

Note 2: While these testability concerns are relevant for many of the proposed COGA requirements they were not decisive for other important proposals from the COGA task force. For example, many people with memory impairments cannot manage applications with long secure passwords and user IDs. A proposal to require an alternate login mechanism that does not require memory or copying skills was rejected, even though there are ways to meet the requirement that are easily checkable. Enabling alternative login mechanisms such as conformance to the Web authentication specification or login via Facebook or Google would be easy to check. But other concerns, such as wide support, wide applicability, lack of support in existing user agents, and author burden, were all considerations that caused these proposals to be rejected by the larger WCAG group.

Note 3: Effective assessment of an organization's development and maintenance processes would be expensive. Further, many small organizations might not wish to commit themselves to the necessary investment. These issues could be dealt with by making the proposed process certification even more clearly voluntary than the current WCAG guidelines. (In themselves, the current guidelines are purely advisory, as we've mentioned earlier, but they have been given regulatory force in many contexts around the world.) Only organizations wishing to demonstrate their commitment would participate.

Parallels in other domains demonstrate that it is possible to motivate organizations to devote substantial resources to establish measures of quality, even without a legal or regulatory requirement. The LEED certification process for green buildings has been very effective, even though the investments required to earn certification, and the cost of the certification itself, are considerable. The same is true of the ISO 9001 certification for quality management mentioned above. In the case of LEED, organizations evidently feel that the public recognition of their efforts on behalf of environmental sustainability, as attested by a trusted third party, is of great value. Given a similar framework, it seems quite likely that many organizations would seek similar recognition for their efforts to make their Web sites accessible.

A more fully voluntary, aspirational system might avoid some of the resistance that sometimes crops up in the WCAG process today. Organizations sometimes express a willingness to do things that they strongly resist being *required* to do.

As applied to accessibility, including COGA, organizations would qualify for certification by establishing such points as the following:

that they consistently test their Web products with a diverse audience, including people with disabilities, during development;

that they demonstrate that their processes respond effectively to accessibility problems identified in testing;

that their process for developing new content includes attention to accessibility early in design;

that their maintenance processes ensure that new content is added, or existing content is updated, without loss of accessibility;

that they have and use a means to gather and respond to accessibility problems identified by their users; and

that their development process monitors developments within the WAI and aligns with these as they mature.

Organizations once certified would provide documentation at intervals demonstrating continued adherence to these requirements (ISO 9001 has such a recertification requirement.).

While our focus here is on COGA, there is a good reason to think that this proposed regime would have benefit for other forms of access as well, including those forms that are perhaps reasonably well supported by WCAG as it is today. People often emphasize the gap between apparent compliance with WCAG, as it is operationalized, and actual accessibility, where such matters as complexity of screen reader navigation, or the actual content of image descriptions, or link labels, are concerned. Under the proposed certification regime, these things would be subject to improvement in response to actual user testing (and user experience with the deployed site.).

At this writing, some of these ideas are being considered in the Silver discussions. Organizations could earn points for adopting appropriate development processes, moving beyond the current compliance framework.

In this extended regime, would the WCAG guidelines still be necessary? Very much so. If individual development organizations seek to remove access barriers in uncoordinated ways, users would face the burden of learning to use incompatible tools, and assistive technology vendors would face a fragmented market. So WCAG should continue to manage, and mandate, agreed common practices.

References

Eisenhart M (2009) Generalization from qualitative inquiry. Generalizing from educational research: Beyond qualitative and quantitative polarization, 51–66. Ercikan K, Roth WM (eds) (2009) Generalizing from educational research: Beyond qualitative and quantitative polarization. Routledge

Hoehl JA (2016) Exploring web simplification for people with cognitive disabilities (Doctoral dissertation, University of Colorado at Boulder). https://search-proquest-com.colorado.idm.oclc.org/docview/1794655985?pq-origsite=gscholar

Judson A, Hine N, Lundälv M, Farre B (2005) Empowering disabled users through the semantic web: the concept coding framework an application of the semantic web. In: Proceedings of WEBIST 2005: 1st international conference on web information systems and technologies, pp 162–167

Kohavi R, Longbotham R, Sommerfield D, Henne RM (2009) Controlled experiments on the web: survey and practical guide. Data Min Knowl Disc 18(1):140–181

Lewis C (2007) Simplicity in cognitive assistive technology: a framework and agenda for research. Univ Access Inf Soc 5(4):351–361

Lewis C (2017a) Methods in user oriented design of programming languages. In Proc. Psychology of programming interest group. http://www.ppig.org/sites/ppig.org/files/2017-PPIG-28th-lewis.pdf

Lewis C (2017b) Representation, inclusion, and innovation: multidisciplinary explorations. Synth Lect Hum-Cent Inf 10(4):i-93

Lewis C, Ward N (2011) Opportunities in cloud computing for people with cognitive disabilities: designer and user perspective. International conference on universal access in human-computer interaction. Springer, Berlin, Heidelberg, pp 326–331

Lim JC, Bessey LJ, Joshi P, Boyle LL (2018) Intellectual Disability in the Elderly. In: Psychiatric disorders late in life. Springer, pp 253–262

Poulson David, Nicolle Colette (2004) Making the Internet accessible for people with cognitive and communication Impairments. Univ Access Inf Soc 3:48–56

Raman TV (1996) Emacspeak–A speech interface. In: Tauber MJ (ed), Proceedings of the SIGCHI conference on human factors in computing systems (CHI '96). ACM, New York, NY, USA, pp 66–71

Raman TV, Gries D (1997) Documents mean more than just paper! Math Comput Model 26(1):45–53

Redish J (2000) Readability formulas have even more limitations than Klare discusses. ACM J Comput Doc (JCD) 24(3):132–137

Ren L, Zheng Y, Wu L, Gu Y, He Y, Jiang B, Zhang J, Zhang L, Li, J (2018) Investigation of the prevalence of cognitive impairment and its risk factors within the elderly population in Shanghai, China. Sci Rep 8(1):3575

Chapter 17
Inclusion

Cynthia C. Shelly

Abstract While the field of accessibility of websites, software, and apps has primarily dealt with the technical aspects of the products themselves, inclusion deals with the experience of people using these technology products as part of their lives. Inclusion means that the widest range of users are able to have an experience with the product that helps them to be part of society and commerce. This chapter discusses the inclusion of people from a variety of marginalized groups, on the internet and web, in employment, and in the development of commercial web and app products. It covers some of the history of disability inclusion, and how changes in user and employee expectations, and changes in technology, will impact inclusion for people with disabilities going forward.

17.1 Introduction

Noun: **inclusion**

1. The action or state of including or of being included within a group or structure.

   federal legislation now mandates the inclusion of students who are English language learners
   — Google definition (Google 2018)

Inclusion is broader than accessibility. Where accessibility is focused on disability, inclusion considers all forms of social stratification, such as class, race, gender, income, geography, language, sexual orientation, and disability. Where accessibility is focused on making it possible for a person with a disability to access a resource, inclusion is about making that access straightforward, enjoyable and fair.

Inclusion is more than connectivity. The Inclusive Internet Index breaks internet inclusion into four categories: Availability, affordability, readiness, and relevance. Readiness and relevance deal with the relationship between the population to be served and the content being provided by connectivity. Are the users literate? Do

---

C. C. Shelly (✉)
Starbucks Coffee Company, Seattle, WA, USA
e-mail: cshelly@starbucks.com

© Springer-Verlag London Ltd., part of Springer Nature 2019
Y. Yesilada and S. Harper (eds.), *Web Accessibility*, Human–Computer
Interaction Series, https://doi.org/10.1007/978-1-4471-7440-0_17

they trust the system? Is the content in their language, and covering topics that matter to them? "An inclusive internet is not just accessible and affordable to all. It is also relevant to all, allowing usage that enables positive social and economic outcomes at individual and group level." (Economist Intelligence Unit 2017). Inclusion is more than usability. Where usability deals with whether a particular website, application or product is straightforward and enjoyable, inclusion goes beyond the product itself to the social aspects around the use of that product by people from marginalized groups. The related field of Inclusive Design is about expanding the group of users served by a product (May 2018). The Inclusive Design Research Center defines it as "[D]esign that considers the full range of human diversity with respect to ability, language, culture, gender, age and other forms of human difference."

Inclusion is deeper than diversity. Where diversity is about allowing people from marginalized groups to join mainstream educational and professional organizations, inclusion is about making the experience of the marginalized people living and working in those environments straightforward, enjoyable and fair. "Diversity is about quantity. Inclusion is about quality…We used to think that diversity was a goal in itself until we discovered that unless the environment, the friendship, the neighborhood, and the workplace are inviting, fair, and respectful, diversity is not going to thrive." (Myers 2012).

17.2   Overview

17.2.1   Accessibility, Usability, and Inclusion for the Internet and the Web

Discussion of Internet inclusion usually centers on connectivity and the Digital Divide. It asks questions about whether people can connect to the Internet in developing countries, whether Internet service is available and affordable to low-income people and communities around the world, whether people with low literacy can find useful content, whether content is available in a variety of languages, and whether women, young people, and LGBTQIA people can find content that is relevant to them. Discussion of web inclusion is centered on accessibility for people with disabilities, and the technical implementation issues surrounding it. In the field of web development, the terms inclusion, usability, compliance, and accessibility are often confused or used interchangeably. However, it is important to understand the separate, related threads of these ideas.

Accessibility is an engineering concern. It asks questions like: Does the website or app correctly implement Application Programming Interfaces (APIs) to make it possible for an assistive technology to interoperate with it? Does it work with settings for colors and fonts and sounds on the device? Does it pass the tests in a particular automated tool? Can a user with a disability and a high level of technology skill find a way, no matter how difficult, to access the content?

It as a design concern. Usability deals with whether users of a website or app can complete tasks it is designed to enable, and whether they can complete those tasks in a reasonable amount of time. Some usability testing measures how satisfied a user is with a site or app. When the users with disabilities take part in usability studies, and their satisfaction is measured, it can uncover the user experience of users with disabilities.

Compliance is a management concern. It asks questions about what standards have been applied and what percentage of tested features meet the standard. It is concerned with large datasets and changes over time. Depending on the standard used, a product might be compliant, and still not be accessible or usable.

Inclusion is more than accessibility, usability or compliance. It is about the social environment in which the website or app exists. It's about how a product interacts with people and the environment, and what kind of experience it provides. Inclusion goes beyond usability, into the social aspects around the development and use of a website or app. It is about whether people with disabilities were involved in the design and construction of the product, and whether their needs were considered with equal weight to those of other users. Did the market research include people with disabilities? Did the designers understand how someone with color blindness or hearing loss would use the product? What the experience might be for users with a variety of disabilities? What differences and similarities their experience would have with anyone else's? Were there members of the product, design and engineering teams with disabilities?

Designing for inclusion encompasses both making a product usable by the widest range of people and making products that minimize or counteract stigma. Designers have a tendency, when designing for people with disabilities, to prioritize utilitarianism over beauty. This can contribute to the stigma associated with disability products. "Glasses or spectacles are frequently held up as an exemplar of design for disability. The very fact that mild visual impairment is not commonly considered to be a disability, is taken as a sign of the success of eyeglasses" which moved from an unstyled medical appliance in the 1930s to a fashion accessory in the 1990s. This change has made customers and fun, where there used to be patients and stigma. User experience is an important part of inclusion, but it is not all that is needed. (Usability.gov)

While this book is about accessibility and disability inclusion on the web, disability is but one aspect of the broader effort to include marginalized populations in society, and the web is just one part of society. It is important to recognize the intersectional nature of inclusion when designing and marketing products. Accessibility is a necessary component of inclusion, both of individuals with disabilities and in the broader sense, but it is not sufficient.

17.2.2 *Nothing About Us Without Us*

The movement toward disability inclusion begins with the Disability Rights Movement of the 1960s and 1970s. Groups of veterans and people with different disabilities began working together in an environment where civil rights were top of mind. Activists argued that disability is "a social construct of discrimination and unmerited stigma" and not a medical condition.

Before that time, people with disabilities were typically either institutionalized or cared for at home, with little opportunity for education or employment. Ed Roberts, who sued to gain admission to the University of California, is often credited with starting the Disability Rights Movement. Roberts was admitted to Berkeley, but was not allowed to attend after the University learned of his disability. He successfully sued, gaining admission in 1969. More students with disabilities followed, and together with advocates, they began the Independent Living Movement, eventually founding Independent Living Centers across the US (Nielsen 2013).

Disability activism continued in a civil rights model through the 1970s and 1980s. In the US, the 1970s saw legislation to expand access to workplaces and education. These rules were eventually consolidated into the Americans with Disabilities Act in 1990. During this period, the idea of inclusion in decision-making become more prevalent. The drive to fully participate in society, what we would call inclusion today, underpinned these efforts. In his 1986 article "Independent Living and the Medical Model of Disability," Simon Brisenden discusses the importance of viewing disability as a social construct, a product of the environment.

> The most important factor is not the amount of physical tasks a person can perform, but the amount of control they have over their everyday routine. The degree of disability does not determine the amount of independence achieved. We believe that the choice of independent living is not a privilege conferred on us by a generous society, but is the right of all individuals, regardless of disability, to live in the community. We see it as a right that has to be restored to us rather than a freely given gift. (Brisenden 1986)

Understanding disability as a product of the social environment, rather than a medical problem or deficit, was a necessary first step to including people with disabilities fully in society. It is possible to change the social environment, and not necessary to change the people.

17.2.3 Full and Equal Enjoyment

> The purpose of the present Convention is to promote, protect and ensure the full and equal enjoyment of all human rights and fundamental freedoms by all persons with disabilities, and to promote respect for their inherent dignity.
>
> Persons with disabilities include those who have long-term physical, mental, intellectual or sensory impairments which in interaction with various barriers may hinder their full and effective participation in society on an equal basis with others.
>
> — Article 1 United Nations Convention on the Rights of Persons with Disabilities

The United Nations Convention on the Rights of Persons with Disabilities (UNCRPD), adopted in 2006, incorporates inclusion at its core. Article 1, above, spells out clearly how the treatment of people with disabilities in society had evolved. As a comparison, the 1990 Americans with Disabilities Act defines its goal in the negative. It aims to eliminate discrimination. The UNCRPD uses positive language that aligns with the idea of inclusion. It aims "promote, protect and ensure full and equal enjoyment" of human rights and dignity.

In the 12 years since the UNCRPD, this idea has become mainstream. Publications targeted at engineers and designers regularly talk about how to achieve accessibility for people with disabilities. For example, Designing for Accessibility and Inclusion, in the April 2018 issue of Smashing Magazine, states: "To design for accessibility means to be inclusive to the needs of your users. This includes your target users, users outside of your target demographic, users with disabilities, and even users from different cultures and countries." (Lambert 2018).

Similarly, publications for managers and human resources professionals have started to discuss inclusion rather than diversity. Project Include, founded by Silicon Valley activist Ellen Pao, is an example of a high-profile organization pushing for inclusion as part of corporate culture (Project Include 2018). The 2017 book The Future-Proof Workplace includes an entire chapter on workplace inclusion and how managers can confront their own unconscious biases. Searching Amazon for "inclusion" results in a large selection of mainstream management books.

Part of this shift in attitude toward inclusion appears to be generational. A 2018 Deloitte study of the attitudes of workers in the Millennial generation showed that Millennials view inclusion as necessary for business success, where Baby Boomers and Generation X viewed it as something to do for moral reasons. When asked about diversity, more Millennials in that study mentioned "A variety/mix/multiple facets/spectrum," "Differences," and "Tolerance, inclusiveness and openness" than mentioned demographics. 31% thought that disability was an important area of diversity for businesses to address. It fell between gender and ethnicity, and was fourth most common area mentioned (Deloitte 2018). That is quite a change in the 50 years since Ed Roberts was denied admission to UC Berkeley.

17.2.3.1 Enjoyment and Customers with Disabilities

Enjoyment is a high standard. To realize the goals of the UN, people with disabilities must be included not only in civic life, but in commercial life as well. That requires expanding the idea of people with disabilities beyond simply "users" to fully realized people: Customers with disabilities, employees with disabilities, vendors with disabilities, etc. As inclusion efforts expand beyond required activities like work, school, and paying taxes, users can simply choose to opt out of an experience if it isn't enjoyable. A product has to be enjoyable for people with disabilities to use, or it won't win these customers. When designing for enjoyment, designers must take into account more than functionality. They must design for relatability and fun. That requires convincing stakeholders that the business benefit of inclusion outweighs the costs in time and money to incorporate high-quality design features for different types of users. It requires business decision makers to understand that people with disabilities constitute a sufficiently large market. "Inclusion marketing" is the idea that by "including customers with disabilities in your target customer base, you make a meaningful difference by showing this underserved population that they are wanted, valued and significant." (Ruh 2018).

While accessibility, usability, and compliance are fairly well-understood practices, enjoyability is tricky to measure, and to achieve. This is something that comes up often in my work at Starbucks, to make our mobile app inclusive and accessible. Fun is a crucial element of our product, and we want that to be true for every customer who tries our app or comes to our stores. No one is required to buy coffee with our app, and the experience is intended to be a treat. We don't want it to be a trial for anyone. Customers with disabilities have told is in interviews how empowering and important it is for them to be able to buy their own coffee, on their own, without having to rely on an assistant or on the barista. While users might be willing to put up with software that's not enjoyable to use when it's required as part of their jobs, commercial apps are discretionary. Customers want their experience to be more than accessible; they want it to be fun.

To have the maximum impact on the "degree of user experience your product will aim to provide for its users, including those with disabilities," a development team should look at the core goals of its product, and make the experience great for all users who are trying to accomplish that goal. Less important goals and use cases can be prioritized lower (Hassell 2014). The most important parts of your website or product are the ones that users are most likely to encounter. Having a great experience there will have the biggest impact on how included they feel.

Inclusion is an attitude and an approach to people and work. But, to be effective, it has to be implemented. For a website or app, that means that it has to be designed, engineered, tested, deployed, updated and marketed. At each of these steps, the people doing the work need to keep inclusion in mind. Succeeding in this endeavor usually requires cultural changes in an organization. One way to start to create a culture of inclusion is for the team to be put in direct contact with real people who are struggling to use their product. For products covered by the twenty-first-century Communications and Video Accessibility Act (CVAA) in the United States, this type of testing is required by law, but any product team can do it whether or not it's required (FCC 2010). To be effective, team members should be coached in inclusive listening practices. As they gain skills around listening to concerns with an open mind, avoiding defensiveness, and asking probing questions to uncover users' needs, they will start to be able to use their existing problem-solving skills to address the needs of customers with disabilities. Teams that are themselves inclusive, with representation from a wide range of people, will have a head start on this process.

17.2.3.2 Inclusion and Employees with Disabilities

[P]eople should be judged in the workplace, based upon their ability to do the job, and not based upon the fears, myths and stereotypes that one may have due to their race, or gender, or disability, or age, religion or national origin.

— Paul Miller, Commissioner of the United States Equal Opportunity Commission Speaking on the occasion of the 35th anniversary of the Commission, 2000

The reality … is that there is no 'us' and 'them.' People with disabilities are the largest minority group, and any one of us can become a member at any time – either through injury or illness or age. (Chisholm and May 2008)

Everyone wants to be treated fairly, and to have the opportunity to live their best life. That is the moral basis for inclusion, and for the related ideas of diversity and equal opportunity. While many of the intersectional facets on which discrimination is based are immutable, disability is not. Anyone can become disabled at any time. The inclusion of people with disabilities in civic life, in the workplace, in education, and in product development is part of creating a just and fair society. Over the last 20 years, arguments for diversity have focused more on the business case, but the move toward inclusion incorporates some of the earlier thinking on morality and fairness.

That is not to say that the business case is unimportant, or that it incorporates wishful thinking about the positives of inclusion. Studies of the impacts of school desegregation in the United States show clear evidence of improvements in outcomes in inclusive environments (Riley 2016). "Educational gains related to integration largely flow from contact with better prepared students and teachers, and the variety of cultures, experiences and worldviews present in diverse classrooms. Different perspectives contribute to enhanced classroom discussion, flexible and creative thinking, and the ability to solve complex problems." (Orfield et al. 2014). Similarly, in a 2018 survey of Millennial workers worldwide, there was "a very strong correlation between perceptions of workforce diversity and loyalty, and how well respondents say their companies perform financially." (Deloitte 2018). This idea is expressed in mainstream management literature as well: "Creating a culture that fully embraces, and includes, all participants is essential for a future-proof organization. Inclusion is the new paradigm that replaces the old paradigm of diversity. And the first step is honesty." (Sharkely and Morag 2017).

There is also widespread agreement that diverse teams make better products. Globalization and migration have created markets that are more diverse. When teams include people from a variety of backgrounds, individual team members are more likely to be aware of the needs and requirements of potential customers who share their background. An example of the market risk of a non-inclusive team is the "Shirley Cards" used to calibrate early color photographic film. The models were all white women, and the film was calibrated to show their features in an attractive and detailed way. Color calibration was not done with models who had other skin tones. Photos of darker skinned people taken with the film did not show their facial features well. The film was not designed in an inclusive way and did not serve a diverse market well (Roth 2009).

Leveraging the skills and experiences of diverse workers for business reasons is a business strategy. It is not charity. Consumers have positive attitudes toward companies that hire people with disabilities, and will sometimes make buying decisions based on that (Ruh 2018). Research done by The Center for Talent Innovation in 2017 showed that 30% of white-collar employees in the United States had disabilities, while only 3.2% had disclosed those disabilities to their employers. More than a third of those employees said they had experienced discrimination because of their disabilities. However, in organizations with inclusive management, defined as "leaders who cherish difference, embrace disruption, and foster a speak-up culture," (Hewlett et al. 2013) employees with disabilities were less likely to have "their ideas ignored, face discrimination, or feel stalled in their careers". (Sherbin et al. 2017). Matt May, Director of Inclusive Design at Adobe, suggests managers can increase inclusion in their organizations by asking one inclusion-related question in every meeting (May 2018). "Inclusive leader behaviors effectively "unlock" the innovative potential of an inherently diverse workforce, enabling companies to increase their share of existing markets and lever open brand new ones." (Hewlett et al. 2013).

17.3 Discussion

Inclusion is the right thing to do, but it is also the smart thing to do. Customers are diverse, and so our products must be diverse to include them, serve them, and sell to them. This creates a positive feedback loop. As people with disabilities are increasingly able to access technology for work and commerce, their spending power increases, and businesses have more incentive to develop products that meet their needs. To understand what those needs are, businesses have more incentives to hire people with disabilities.

17.3.1 Inclusion as a Driver of Innovation

Design depends largely on constraints

Iconic furniture designer Charles Eames, quoted in Design Meets Disability (Pullin 2011)

Many of the technology products we rely on today were first invented to help include people with disabilities in society.[1] The microphone and telephone were inspired by Alexander Graham Bell's interest in deaf education. The typewriter was invented to allow a blind woman to write letters. Email was a way for Vince Cerf, who has hearing impairment, to communicate with his wife, who is deaf. The speech recognition technology used by personal assistants like Siri and Alexa was first developed to allow input for people who couldn't use a keyboard. Optical Character Recognition (OCR) was first used to make books available to people who were blind. The Segway scooter was based on a design for a two-wheeled wheelchair. Eye gaze tracking, first used to help people with locked-in syndrome communicate, is now used in usability research, digital cameras, and automobile safety systems (Steenhout 2018). The constraints of these use cases pushed inventors in to think in new directions.

This is true for design esthetics as well as functionality. The Eames chair, which inspired so much of the mid-century design, started from a project to build a

---

[1] https://www-s.acm.illinois.edu/conference/1997/chron2.html.

lightweight prosthetic leg for WWII veterans. As Pullin describes in Design Meets Disability:

> it was the peculiar constraints of the US Navy brief that led the Eameses to develop their own technology for forming plywood in complex curvature in the first place, in order to make a lightweight yet stiff structure that accommodated the form and variation of the human body. But this technique had a far-reaching influence on the future work of the design partnership and design in general. Organic plywood forms underpinned the iconic mainstream furniture manufactured by Herman Miller in the 1940s and 1950s.
>
> — Design Meets Disability

Some of the most beautiful and useful things we use in the modern world were first made to include someone with a disability.

17.4 Future Directions

Inclusion has become a mainstream idea, with multiple large companies employing executives charged with making their organizations more inclusive for employees and customers. A great deal of writing, some cited earlier, is occurring regarding how to include people in an intersectional way across the civic, professional, educational, commercial, and social realms. The work is happening in academic, management, and mainstream venues, and in multiple countries, and appears to be growing in scope and popularity. The idea of inclusion is popular among younger people. As the idea of inclusion becomes even more mainstream, and is applied to more areas of society, it is important to ensure that disability remains a part of the discussion. The number of mainstream management publications referencing disability inclusion is encouraging.

Members of the Millennial generation view inclusion differently than older workers. They see it as an open environment that allows them to express their differences in the workplace, and that contributes to business goals. It will be interesting to see how this interacts with diversity and inclusion efforts for people with disabilities and other marginalized groups. How will these new inclusive teams tackle challenges that will inspire the next level of innovations?

In the technology industry specifically, tools for supporting inclusive product development for the web and mobile apps are improving quickly. It is becoming more possible for organizations in retail, banking, government and other sectors to build accessible technology in a cost-effective way. Accessibility and inclusion are more culturally typical, and are taught more in university computer science, design and human factors classes. Inclusive education in universities, as well as primary and secondary schools, is increasing the chances that young people will have personal experience with people with disabilities, engendering more empathy and a deeper understating of use cases. Technology workers are more likely than in the past to have some familiarity with accessibility at both a conceptual and implementation level, and to expect that supporting accessibility and inclusion is a normal part of product development. As these employees move into management roles, we can expect to see a greater level of support and innovation in the field of disability inclusion.

One promising example of inclusive technology is the new avatars for Microsoft Xbox, which can be configured to use a variety of virtual prosthetics and assistive technology, to be visibly pregnant, or to have nonbinary gender, along with existing support for different skin tones, hair types, and facial features. Another is modern digital photography tools that can be calibrated to optimize for a variety of skin tones, solving the "Shirley Card" problem discussed earlier. Finally, many mainstream companies make an effort to make their websites comply with accessibility standards and test their usability with people with disabilities, making basic functionality available to more people. This trend shows no sign of slowing.

New technologies, such as wearable devices, drones, personal assistants, and smart home devices provide new challenges and opportunities as well. Many of these can be used to support independent living by people with disabilities, but only if they are designed and built with inclusion in mind. How will existing accessibility guidelines and tools apply to these technologies? Some initial research has begun into creating accessibility guidelines for wearable devices, recommending multimodal interaction and feedback mechanisms (Wentzel et al. 2018). Similarly, the Worldwide Web Consortium (W3C) has started researching accessibility concerns and opportunities related to the Internet of Things (Abou-Zahra et al. 2017). These technologies are still in the early stages of development and standardization, and it is encouraging to see accessibility being considered as part of the early thinking.

17.5   Author's Opinion of the Field

The change of focus from accessibility as an engineering discipline to the inclusion of the broadest group of people is exciting. It allows for more people, including people with business and design skills, to get involved in making the web and apps work for more people. Some engineers are changing their focus from directly implementing accessible websites, or doing manual consulting work, to building tools and reusable components that simplify the process of developing accessible websites and applications. This will allow more organizations to implement accessibility in a cost-effective way. The combination of better tools, more people insisting on inclusive development practices, and more focus on designing the whole experience of our products for a broad range of users gives me a great deal of hope that websites and apps will continue to become more inclusive of more people over time.

I also see an alignment with a general social trend of intentional inclusion of marginalized populations in employment and society. As product teams become more diverse and inclusive, their products do as well. At the moment, disability inclusion is not always part of the general trend toward inclusion, and this is something those of us in the field will need to continue to champion. Smaller companies, even those with inclusion as part of their missions, sometimes don't have a disability as part of their strategy of inclusion. I would like to see more outreach to smaller companies and their funders to begin counting disability as part of their intersectional inclusion efforts. That said, the large tech companies are doing a good job, with Apple, Google, Adobe, and Microsoft all listing inclusion as a goal, and making inclusive hiring a part of their work. Companies that serve retail customers are also making efforts to be more inclusive, in both their physical locations and their applications. Companies have started to think of inclusion efforts as part of doing business.

17.6   Conclusions

It is important to think about the humans who will use technology, and not only the technology itself. For the web and mobile apps to be truly inclusive of all people, and especially people with disabilities, they must be designed with those users in mind. People with disabilities are customers, employees, students, and government officials. When products are designed to be inclusive, people with disabilities can complete their task like anyone else, in an efficient, effective, and enjoyable way.

References

Abou-Zahra S, Brewer J, Cooper M (2017) Web standards to enable an accessible and inclusive internet of things (IoT). http://hdl.handle.net/1721.1/107831. Accessed 1 Sept 2018

Americans with Disabilities Act of 1990, As Amended (1990) https://www.ada.gov/pubs/ada.htm. Accessed 28 Aug 2018

Brisenden S (1986) Independent living and the medical model of disability. Disabil Handicap Soc (known as Disability and Society since 1993) 1(2):173–178. http://www.cilt.ca/Documents%20of%20the%20CILT%20Website/Ind_Living_Medical_Model.pdf. Accessed 29 Aug 2018

Charlton JI (2000) Nothing about us without us, disability oppression and empowerment. University of California Press. ISBN: 0520224817

Chisholm W, May M (2008) Universal design for web applications: web applications that reach everyone. O'Reilly Media. ISBN: 0596518730

Commissioner Paul Miller (2000) Importance of equal employment opportunity. Transcript of speech at US EEOC 35th Anniversary. https://www.eeoc.gov/eeoc/history/35th/videos/paulmiller-text.html. Accessed 1 Sept 2018

Deloitte (2018) 2018 deloitte millennial survey. https://www2.deloitte.com/global/en/pages/about-deloitte/articles/millennialsurvey.html. Accessed 29 Aug 2018

Federal Communications Commission (2010) 21st century communications and video accessibility act (CVAA) consumer guide. https://www.fcc.gov/consumers/guides/21st-century-communications-and-video-accessibility-act-cvaaAccessed 1 Sept 2018

Google (2018) Define inclusion. https://www.google.com/search?q=define+inclusion. Accessed 28 Aug 2018

Hassell J (2014) Including your missing 20% by embedding web and mobile accessibility. BSI British Standards Institution. ISBN: 0580812049

Hewlett SA, Marshall M, Sherbin L, Gonslaves T (2013) Innovation, diversity, and market growth. Center for Talent Innovation. http://www.talentinnovation.org/_private/assets/IDMG-ExecSummFINAL-CTI.pdf. Accessed 1 Sept 2018

Lambert S (2018) Designing for accessibility and inclusion in smashing Magazine. Accessed 28 Aug 2018

Leon J (2018) Ed Roberts in ENCYCLOPÆDIA BRITANNICA. https://www.britannica.com/biography/Ed-Roberts. Accessed 29 Aug 2018

May M (2018) The same, but different: breaking down accessibility, universality, and inclusion in design. https://theblog.adobe.com/different-breaking-accessibility-universality-inclusion-design/. Accessed 28 Aug 2018

Myers V (2012) Moving diversity forward: how to go from well-meaning to well-doing. American Bar Association. ISBN: 1614380066

Nicolas S (2018) The evolution of assistive technology into everyday products. https://incl.ca/the-evolution-of-assistive-technology-into-everyday-products/. Accessed 1 Sept 2018

Nielsen KE (2013) A disability history of the United States (ReVisioning American History). Beacon Press. ISBN: 0807022047

Orfield G, Siegel-Hawley G, Kucsera J (2014) Sorting out deepening confusion on segregation trends. The Civil Rights Project. https://www.civilrightsproject.ucla.edu/research/k-12-education/integration-and-diversity/sorting-out-deepening-confusion-on-segregation-trends/Segregation-Trends-Dispute-CRP-Researchers.pdf. Accessed 1 Sept 2018

Project Include (2018) https://medium.com/projectinclude. Accessed 29 Aug 2018

Pullin G (2011) Design meets disability. MIT Press. ISBN: 0262516748

Riley S (2016) How Seattle gave up on busing and allowed its public schools to become alarmingly resegregated. In: The stranger, 13 Apr 2016. https://www.thestranger.com/features/2016/04/13/23945368/how-seattle-gave-up-on-busing-and-allowed-its-public-schools-to-become-alarmingly-resegregated. Accessed 1 Sept 2018

Roth L (2009) Looking at Shirley, the Ultimate Norm: colour balance, image technologies, and cognitive equity. Can J Commun 34(2009):111–136. https://www.cjc-online.ca/index.php/journal/article/view/2196/3069. Accessed 1 Sept 2018

Ruh D (2018) Inclusion branding. Ruh Global, LLC. ISBN: 1732043205

Sharkey L, Barrett M (2017) The future-proof workplace Wiley, New York. ISBN: 11928757X

Sherbin L, Kennedy JT, Jain-Link P, Ihezie K (2017) Disability and inclusion, US Findings. Center for Talent Innovation. http://www.talentinnovation.org/_private/assets/DisabilitiesInclusion_KeyFindings-CTI.pdf. Accessed 1 Sept 2018

The Economist Intelligence Unit (2017) The inclusive internet index: bridging digital divides. https://theinclusiveinternet.eiu.com/assets/external/downloads/3i-bridging-digital-divides.pdf. Accessed 28 Aug 2018

United Nations Convention on the Rights of People with Disabilities (2006) https://www.un.org/development/desa/disabilities/convention-on-the-rights-of-persons-with-disabilities.html. Accessed 28 Aug 2018

University of Illinois (2018) Many technologies originally developed to help people with disabilities led to the development of many of today's information products. https://www-s.acm.illinois.edu/conference/1997/chron2.html. Accessed 1 Sept 2018

Usability.gov (2017) Usability testing. https://www.usability.gov/how-to-and-tools/methods/usability-testing.html. Accessed 29 Aug 2018

Wentzel J, Velleman E, van der Geest T (2018) Wearables for all: development of guidelines to stimulate accessible wearable technology design. https://ris.utwente.nl/ws/portalfiles/portal/5423202/wearables.pdf. Accessed 1 Sept 2018

Wireless RERC (2017) Accessibility, usability, and the design of wearables and wirelessly connected devices.   http://www.wirelessrerc.gatech.edu/sites/default/files/publications/research_brief_ accessibility_usability_and_the_design_of_wearables_and_wirelessly_connected_devices_0. pdf. Accessed 1 Sept 2018

Part IV
Technical Foundations

Chapter 18
Assistive Technologies

Hugo Nicolau and Kyle Montague

Abstract Over the last three decades, the Web has become an increasingly important platform that affects every part of our lives: from requesting simple navigation
instructions to active participating in political activities; from playing video games to
remotely coordinate teams of professionals; from paying monthly bills to engaging is
micro-funding activities. Missing on these opportunities is a strong vehicle of info-,
economic-, and social-exclusion. For people with disabilities, accessing the Web is
sometimes a challenging task. Assistive technologies are used to lower barriers and
enable people to fully leverage all the opportunities available in (and through) the
Web. This chapter introduces a brief overview of how both assistive technologies
and the Web evolved over the years. It also considers some of the most commonly
used assistive technologies as well as recent research efforts in the field of accessible
computing. Finally, it provides a discussion of future directions for an inclusive Web.

18.1 Introduction

The Web is now ubiquitous in almost every facet of our lives. No longer is the
Web merely our source of information, it has become the place we do business,
communicate, socialise, shop, entertain ourselves, and even receive health and social.
Many of us are never disconnected from the Web, thanks largely to the reduction
in cost of portable and wireless mobile technologies, we live our lives both in the
physical world around us and the virtual world that sits on top of it. The modern web
has been integrated into the rich sensing capabilities of our ubiquitous computing

H. Nicolau (✉)
Department of Computer Science and Engineering, Instituto Superior Técnico, INESC-ID,
Av. Prof. Cavaco Silva, 2744-016 Porto Salvo, Portugal
e-mail: hman@inesc-id.pt

K. Montague
Open Lab, School of Computing, Newcastle University, Urban Sciences Building,
1 Science Square, Newcastle upon Tyne NE4 5TG, England
e-mail: kyle.montague@ncl.ac.uk

© Springer-Verlag London Ltd., part of Springer Nature 2019
Y. Yesilada and S. Harper (eds.), *Web Accessibility*, Human–Computer
Interaction Series, https://doi.org/10.1007/978-1-4471-7440-0_18

devices, enabling novel interaction opportunities for content creators, and potential new challenges for people with disabilities.

The first generation of the web was predominantly static pages that offered read-only experiences of published content from few savvy outlets and positioned the rest of us as information consumers. The Web we know today allows anyone to become a content creator, with purpose-built web tools and dedicated sites to support publishing of rich media and interactive content to the masses. These tools and sites have quickly transformed the landscape of the Web and further solidified its position in society as the place where we communicate and share our ideas. Where previously the Web took a backseat to the accessing a physical instance or service, now we see many examples where the Web is the only way to access something including jobs, products and financial support. To that end, it is now more vital than ever before that people have access to the Web, exclusion online will undoubtedly lead to exclusion in society. Therefore, we need to ensure that everyone has equal opportunity to access the Web regardless of any physical or cognitive abilities.

18.2   History of Assistive Technologies

Since the dawn of the human–computer interaction research field, several approaches to create accessible computing systems have been proposed. Unavoidably, many of them share the same overall goal: provide access to the widest range of users. This section describes some of the most relevant perspectives on accessible computing and how they evolved over time.

Assistive Technology is a term that includes all software and hardware solutions for people with disabilities (Cook and Hussey 2001). Its main goal is to enable users to perform tasks they were once unable to accomplish, thus increasing their independence. These technologies are seen as being useful only to a minority by means of assistive components that bridge the gap between users and systems. Since these components are not part of the original solutions, they often require additional adaptation costs. Systems are seen as immutable entities and the burden of change lies with users. While this approach may be useful in some cases, such as for white canes, wheelchairs or hearing aids, it becomes obsolete when considering interactive computer systems. Approaches to Engineering Human Performance, focus on building models to provide effective system adaptations by matching the products' demands with users' capabilities (Kondraske 1995; Persad et al. 2007). However, similarly to Assistive Technology, this approach assumes that the product is immutable.

From the mismatch between immutable systems and the diversity of users' capabilities, two schools of thought emerged: designing for all and designing for the individual. Although they share the same goal of creating accessible computing systems, they have unique perspectives on how to tackle the overarching problem.

Stephanidis (1995) proposed the concept of User Interfaces for All (UI4All), promoting the use of unified interfaces to support user-independent interface development. In a unified user interface, only the core functionality is developed, while abstract user interface representations map to one concrete interface template, either at configuration- or run-time. Later, Universal Design (Vanderheiden 1998), Design for All (Stephanidis et al. 1998), and Universal Usability proposed similar concepts and introduced the visionary goal of an information society for all. These approaches focus on applying a set of guidelines, methods, and tools to develop technological products and services that are accessible and usable by the widest range of users, therefore avoiding the need for adaptations. They follow an 'one size fits all' approach to provide universal access.

The second school of taught was pioneered by Newel (1995) where he proposed the concept of Extraordinary Human–Computer Interaction by depicting the parallel between 'ordinary' people operating in 'extraordinary' environments (e.g. adverse noise and lightning conditions) and 'extraordinary' (disabled) users operating in ordinary environments. For the first time, the author relates individual human abilities to context. Later, Newel and Gregor (2000) proposed User-Sensitive Inclusive Design where they acknowledge that Design for All is a difficult, if not impossible, task:

> Providing access to people with certain types of disability can make the product significantly more difficult to use by people without disabilities, and often impossible to use by people with a different type of disability.

The use of the term Inclusive rather than Universal reflects the view that Inclusivity is a more achievable, and in many situations, appropriate goal than Universal Design or Design for All.

More recently, Wobbrock et al. (2011) proposed ability-based design, which focuses on users' abilities throughout the design process in an effort to create systems that leverage the full range of individual potential. This concept provides a unified view of able-bodied and disabled users, as well as health- and context-related impairments (Sears et al. 2003). The authors focus on how systems can be made to fit the abilities of whoever uses them, either through automatic adaptation or customization. Unlike universal design approaches that design for what everyone can do, ability-based design focus on what the user can do.

Over the last two decades, the field of accessible computing has been evolving, and consequently the term Assistive Technologies has also been shifting. It is nowadays an 'umbrella' term that includes a wide range of technologies from hardware and software to adaptive and customizable solutions. Throughout this chapter, we will use this wide definition when reporting on the several technologies that strive for inclusion of people with disabilities in the Web.

18.3   Modern Web Technology: HTML5

Tim Berners-Lee set out to create a network-accessible, organised store of information, built from documents that could be interconnected by their associations, providing effective means of navigation by its users. In the early years of the World-WideWeb aka the Web, the documents and information were predominantly text documents described in HTML (HyperText Markup Language) that allowed for basic structure and formatting—such as headings and the essential hypertext links. The Web was intended for archival and publishing purposes, offering read-only interactions to its users.

Fast forward a decade and the notion of a Web 2.0, a read–write web that would enable bidirectional interaction. Where users were not simply content consumers of the Web, but its creators and curators. Everyone could participate and contribute to the vast, growing web of knowledge through personal blog and wikis; or curate and publish their own aggregations of web content using the popular RSS (Rich Site Summary) format—making it possible for anyone to create associations between stored pieces of information and share them with the world. As the Web matured, so too did the infrastructure it was built upon—and so began the rise of the RIA (Rich Internet Application) leveraging the interactive affordances of the JavaScript, Flash and Flex languages.

The latest paradigm shift is known as the Semantic Web. Where previously information was structured and curated purely for humns, the Semantic Web aims to make a machine-readable web of data. Using the RDF (Resource Description Framework) specification, metadata can be associated with individual pieces of data allowing their discovery, description and reuse across applications and enterprises. In 2014 the W3C published the latest version of the HTML standard, HTML5, which boasted new features to better support mobile devices, natively handle multimedia content and new elements to enrich the semantic description of page content. DOM (Document Object Model) has also been included as part of the HTML5 specification, providing a tree structure representation of the page that can be programmatically read and manipulated. DOM integration is key to the success of many Assistive Technologies discussed within this chapter.

Fig. 18.1 illustrates the aforementioned newly added HTML5 semantic elements. Not only do these tags describe and structure the content to be displayed, they carry inherent meaning that can be leveraged by machines, browsers and assistive technologies. The <nav> tag is used here to define a set of navigation links, while <main> identifies the primary content of the document. Documents can consist of one or more <article> containers, which are used to describe self-contained pieces of content. Articles can define their own <header> to introduce the content, and <footer> to name the author and copyright details for the individual article (Fig 18.2).

While the HTML5 page contains semantic elements, the visual representation of the content is no different from traditional HTML using <div> containers to structure the content. However, these simple changes to the ways we build the web will enable new innovations in intelligent agents and assistive technologies to the benefit of everyone.

In addition to the new semantic tags, HTML5 includes features to natively handle multimedia and graphical content and better support mobile devices with API (application programme interface) integration to leverage their rich sensing and interaction capabilities. HTML5 allows developers to directly work with a user's geolocation, camera, microphone, local storage, Bluetooth and soon NFC (Near Field Communication) sensing to create cross-platform context- and location-aware experiences

```
1  <!DOCTYPE html>
2  <html>
3      <head>
4          <meta charset="UTF-8">
5          <title>Document title</title>
6      </head>
7      <body>
8          <header>
9              <nav>
10                 <a href="/">Home</a></li>
11                 <a href="/about/">About</a></li>
12                 <a href="/contact/">Contact</a></li>
13             </nav>
14             <h1>Top-level heading</h1>
15         </header>
16         <main>
17             <article>
18                 <header>
19                     <h2>Sub-heading</h2>
20                     <p>articles should be used to describe independent, self-contented content.</p>
21                 </header>
22                 <p>the body content of the article.</p>
23                 <figure>
24                     <img src="daschund.jpg" alt="two daschunds sleeping">
25                     <figcaption>Fig1. - Mac and Crunchie, Newcastle, UK.</figcaption>
26                 </figure>
27             </article>
28         </main>
29         <footer>
30             <p>Posted by: Hugo Nicolau and Kyle Montague</p>
31         </footer>
32     </body>
33  </html>
```

Fig. 18.1 A sample Webpage which is marked up with HTML5 tags

that rival native mobile apps (Anthes 2012). As more developers embrace HTML5 to create rich experiences for mobile devices; we can expect to see positive side effects for web accessibility. These websites were found to be inherently more accessible largely thanks to their design being intended to adapt to device specific characteristics (Richards et al. 2012), which in turn is advantageous for assistive technologies that augment the presentation and interaction experiences.

18.4   Visual Abilities

A screen reader is a technology that assists people with little or no functional vision in interacting with computing devices. It resorts to text-to-speech software to translate visual information of computer interfaces. Over the years, several screen readers have been developed to support various operating systems such as Microsoft Windows (e.g. JAWS, NVDA), Linux (e.g. ORCA), OSX/iOS (e.g. VoiceOver), and Android (e.g. Talkback). Web-based screen readers (Bigham et al. 2008) have also been developed and require no additional software to be installed on the client machine (e.g. WebAnywhere, ChromeVox). These assistive technologies capture the displayed information on the screen and provide a set of navigational commands to aid users in interacting with applications. Commands are usually keyboard shortcuts or touchscreen gestures. For instance, when using the built-in screen reader of Android, i.e. Talkback, users move their fingers on the screen and the interface ele-

Home About Contact

Top-level heading

Sub-heading

articles should be used to describe independent, self-contented content.

the body content of the article.

Fig1. - Mac and Crunchie, Newcastle, UK.

Posted by: Hugo Nicolau and Kyle Montague

Fig. 18.2 How the HTML5 in Fig 18.1 would be rendered by a browser

ments being touched are read aloud. A double tap is used to select the last element. Horizontal swipes can also be used to scroll through all elements on display.

Most screen readers have some type of specialised web mode that enables quick navigation through the DOM structure. One could argue that screen readers no longer read the screen as they use the underlying structure of the page rather than the visual layout. Screen readers convert a two-dimensional page to a one-dimensional text string (i.e. linearization). Thus, browsing the Web can become a difficult and frustrating process (Borodin et al. 2010). To deal with these issues, researchers have been investigating novel ways of adapting web pages and their content (i.e. transcoding) to the needs of blind people (Lai 2011; Ackermann et al. 2012; Yesilada et al. 2013; Valencia et al. 2013; Fernandes et al. 2015). Common approaches include using heuristics, users' preferences, annotations, and semantic information. Moreover, as the Web evolves, increasingly types of content are being used and generated by its users: from scientific formulas (Sorge et al. 2014) and diagrams (Sorge et al. 2015) to videos (Encelle et al. 2013) and other dynamic content (Brown et al. 2009). Current research efforts aim at providing blind users with the means to access and manipulate such content.

Screen readers are generally able of providing both speech and Braille output. The latter needs an external device, such as a Braille pin-display, and can be used as a complement or replacement of speech output. Braille pin-displays generally include a Braille keyboard and interactive tactile cells that enable novel shortcuts, text-entry, or even drawing (Bornschein et al. 2018). Recently, several research efforts aimed at leveraging Braille as an input method for touchscreen devices (Southern et al. 2012; Azenkot et al. 2012; Trindade et al. 2018) as well as an output strategy (Nicolau et al. 2013, 2015).

While screen readers and Braille-related devices were mainly developed for blind users, people that experience low-vision generally use a multitude of assistive technologies to access screen content, such as screen magnifiers, increased text size, inverted colours, text-to-speech, modified contrast, and zooming tools. Knowing what tools are available and how to use them efficiently can be challenging (Szpiro et al. 2016).

Speech input and conversational agents are another form of assistive technology that are being increasingly integrated on mobile platforms. Google Assistant and Siri enable users to perform numerous actions such as search the Internet or create calendar events solely using speech input. Commercial dictation systems such as Dragon Naturally Speaking are also used for text input. Additionally, users can speak commands such as 'move left' and 'undo' to edit text. Speech input has also been used to aid users in web browsing actions. Ashok et al. (2015) proposed a speech-enabled screen reader that leverages a custom dialog model, designed exclusively for non-visual web access (Ashok et al. 2014). Although speech is a natural and efficient interaction modality it is often highly dependent on recognition accuracy. These solutions are sometimes used in combination with keyboards as correcting input errors is a cumbersome and time-consuming process (Azenkot and Lee 2013).

In recent years, we witnessed a novel trend of using the Web as a platform to improve accessibility, namely through human computation. Human workers, volunteers, and friends can help blind people in multiple tasks (e.g. labelling, object recognition, navigation) with higher accuracy than automatic solutions (Takagi et al. 2008; Gardiner et al. 2015; Rodrigues et al. 2017). The Social Accessibility project was one of the first to connect blind users to volunteers who can help them solve web accessibility problems (Takagi et al. 2008). VizWiz (Bigham et al. 2010) recruits web-based workers to answer visual (real-world) questions in nearly real-time. Blind people take a picture, speak a question to be answered from the photo, and then receive answers in about 30 seconds. Commercial systems, such as BeMyEyes, have leverage this approach and extended it to live video calls.

18.5 Physical Abilities

Being able to physically interact with the browser is essential to engage with online content. The Web we know today boasts interfaces that are rich in interactive media; framed by complex screen layouts requiring a significant degree of control to navigate and move through them. Where previously websites consisted of large volumes of text and hyperlinks, requiring the user to perform a single click to select, modern websites now take advantage of expressive gestural inputs and create custom interface elements to produce completely bespoke and immersive experiences for their visitors. If not done right these rich interactive spaces can become physically demanding and challenging to explore, particularly for individuals that require assistive technologies to engage with them. There are positive measures that developers can take to support users with physical access needs, such as providing keyboard shortcuts and alternative modes of interaction. However, for a large population these provisions are not enough, and more is needed. Over the years there have been many technologies created to improve the physical accessibility of the Web, both hardware and software solutions.

A common software augmentation used by individuals with reduced motor control is Switch Access Scanning (SAS), whereby a selection focus indicator moves through the website highlighting (visually or otherwise) each item on the screen for a period of time. When the desired target is highlighted the user performs the selection interaction i.e. presses the switch. This method can be very slow depending on the scanning pattern (e.g. linear scanning from top left to bottom right, grouped scanning by rows then columns within the selected row) and the dwell time for selection. SAS bares some resemblances to non-visual screen exploration via a Screen Reader. SAS can also support text-entry with the addition of an on-screen soft keyboard; this approach is also used by many AAC (Assistive Augmented Communication) interfaces as the input and outputs of SAS can be individually tailored with custom hardware or mixed-modalities for outputs, making it a strong candidate for universal access.

Gaze tracking technologies such as Tobii Dynavox[1] are used by individuals that find traditional mouse pointer control challenging or impossible. Commodity gaze trackers consist of IR cameras that are able to track the pupil movements and fixations of the eye and map these to the on-screen pointer. Targets are typically selected based on a dwell or fixation over the intended element. Speech input and conversational agents, as used to support visual abilities, are also popular methods of interaction for individuals with reduced motor control where their speech is otherwise unimpacted.

For individuals whom experience intermittent reduced motor control (e.g. people with Parkinson's Disease) or those with a higher degree of motor control, SAS are an excessive adaptation; solutions such as screen magnification to increase target sizes or personalisation of keyboard and mouse configurations to reduce unintentional inputs are more appropriate.

Other approaches to support target acquisition include predictive models for mouse endpoints (Ruiz et al. 2008; Dixon et al. 2012; Pasqual and Wobbrock 2014) and adaptive gesture models for touchscreen interactions (Montague et al. 2014; Mott

---

[1] https://www.tobiidynavox.com/.

et al. 2016). However, the lack of mainstream support for these technologies means they are not widely adopted. Solutions that are better integrated into the browser or operating system hold greater potential for individuals with reduced motor control. IBM Research have proposed several examples such as, Trewin's Dynamic Keyboard, a desktop assistive technology, which would simultaneously monitor and adjust keyboard configurations to correct for common input errors (Trewin 2004).

Physical adaptation of computers and input devices to improve their accessibility is a well-documented strategy for many individuals with motor impairments, as evidenced by the wealth of Youtubers sharing their creations (Anthony et al. 2013). Given that an individual's needs are often in their nature unique to that individual, the Do-it-Yourself approach to assistive technology has become popular in recent years thanks to the rise in maker culture and the advancements in consumer electronics and 3D printers (Hurst and Tobias 2011).

Through platforms like Thingiverse, [2] designers and makers have started to create a plethora of open source 3D models for everyday assistive technologies. Anyone can download these designs and customise and remix them to meet their individual preferences and needs—using freely available open source software. These are truly exciting innovations for the assistive technology domain.

18.6 Hearing Abilities

The Web is becoming increasingly media-rich; from text and audio to video and immersive content. People who experience hearing loss and deafness usually need visual access to aural information. Common accessibility services include captioning and subtitles. These can be either open or closed. While closed captions/subtitles can be turned off, open captions/subtitles are part of the video itself. The Web has enabled these services to be provided via remotely-located captioning services for live events, such as classroom lectures, work meetings, personal conversations, public events, and so forth. For instance, Skype, a commercial video conference software, already provides real-time automatic subtitling (translation) services.

Although captioning solutions can be used in many domains, they have been particularly successful in educational and classroom settings (e.g. Federico and Furini 2012; Lasecki et al. 2014a; Kushalnagar et al. 2017). While Automatic Speech Recognition has been proposed as a cost-effective solution (Federico and Furini 2012; Berke et al. 2018), alternative approaches have leveraged non-experts crowd workers to provide real-time and accurate captions (Lasecki et al. 2012). Indeed, human computation has been promised as a technology for affordable, accurate, and real-time captioning in real-world conditions (Lasecki et al. 2014a; Gaur et al. 2016). This is in contrast with professional captioning services that can cost dozens of dollars per hour.

---

[2]https://www.thingiverse.com/.

Other common approach to access aural information is via sign language translation. For many individuals, captioning can be difficult to follow when the speed of verbatim captioning exceeds their reading abilities (Jensema et al. 1996). While many use a sign language over a written language to communicate, sign language translation is less common in web content. Kushalnagar et al. (2017) proposed a closed ASL interpreting, which similarly to closed captioning can be toggled on/off. Additionally, the closed interpreter's size, position, and transparency can be customizable. Similar work was proposed by Hughes et al. (2015) for mobile captions.

Recent developments in web technologies have enabled the creation of cross-platform accessibility services. Web services such as X3D are being leveraged in the creation of virtual signing characters in translation systems (Boulares and Jemni 2012). Research into virtual characters has reach a level of refinement that is now possible to build a model of human form that is articulate and responsive to perform sign languages (Kipp et al. 2011). Nevertheless, producing linguistically accurate, easily understandable, and user acceptable virtual signers is an open challenge (Kacorri et al. 2017). Similarly, automatically recognise and understand sign language is an open research problem that can benefit Deaf signers (Huenerfauth and Hanson 2009).

Finally, the Web has also been used as an authoring and sharing platform of educational resources that were hard to create just a few years ago. For instance, the ASL-STEM Forum[3] is a grassroots online community that brings together educators, interpreters, captioners, and students to build and disseminate American Sign Language technical vocabulary.

18.7   Cognitive and Learning Abilities

Our cognitive function and learning abilities impact a wide range of interaction capabilities; spanning from the ways in which we do things, to the feelings we experience. When designing for cognitive and learning abilities it is vital to recognise the complexity of human cognition and the breadth of the individual functions. Given the challenges of this domain and the additional considerations needed to work with people within this context, it is no surprise that it has received less attention that other more easily understood areas of accessible computing.

In reality it is impossible to distil a single checklist to create websites that are fully accessible by individuals with low cognitive and learning abilities. However, technologies that seek to reduce the complexity to consume and engage with the content or provide intelligent support, make the Web more inclusive to these individuals.

Text simplification, is a technique used to reduce the complexity of text by simplifying the structure and grammar while maintaining the underlying meaning and information. Both automatic (Watanabe et al. 2009) and human-computation solutions to summarise or re-narrate text on the web (Dinesh and Choppella 2012) have demonstrated the relatively simple workflows needed as well as the wider benefit to

---

[3]https://aslstem.cs.washington.edu/.

other web users (e.g. visually impaired people). With the current push to create a semantic web of machine-readable data, works exploring machine learning and text translation models could yield exciting new opportunities for more accessible text content on the web.

Beyond the complexity of the text itself, web accessibility researchers have also demonstrated the importance of text layout and presentation to create readable web content (de Santana et al. 2012; de Santana et al. 2013; Rello et al. 2012) including the selection of appropriate colours, fonts, visual presentation and supporting media types.

One of the most powerful things the web has enabled is communication—specifically the ability to be directly connected to a friend, family member or carer anywhere in the world via text, audio or video at the push of a button. The web holds tremendous potential to support individuals with cognitive impairments (and their caregivers) to maintain meaningful relationships and live independently, whilst receiving the support they need from family and loved ones (Martins et al. 2014).

18.8 Ageing

Older adults starting to use the web face difficulties distinct from younger users. Problems include navigating web pages (back and history functions), longer times to complete tasks, select targets, and links, finding new information and revisiting sites. They usually require more practice than younger people (Sayago and Blat 2007; Tullis 2007; Fairweather 2008), and present lower levels of confidence when using technology (Marquié et al. 2002).

It is worth highlighting that it is not age per se that affects older users' web experience but a combination of factors (Crabb and Hanson 2016), including the type of and level of impairment. Some may not need any assistive technologies, other may need multiple technologies to access the Web. As age-related declines are often in more than one ability (and with various levels of impairment), their combination can make accessibility more challenging than for people with a single disability (Gregor et al. 2002).

Current browsers (and Operating Systems) already include several accessibility features, such as font enlargement, colour modification, screen magnification, and text declutter. Further adaptations that extended the browsers' functionality through scripting are available via add-ons. Examples include screen readers, voice input, display customization, and navigational enhancements. Although many options are already available, they required awareness of their existence and relevance to individual needs. Moreover, they require users to be able to activate and customise them, which may require excessive cognitive demands.

Even when accessibility features are available, they are usually grouped under the banner of 'disability', which might not match users' views of themselves. Indeed, older people do not identify themselves as having impairments; rather, just as novice users with low computer literacy skills. Automated or semi-automated adaptations have been proposed as a solution to all these problems (Sloan et al. 2010); however, accurately detecting users' accessibility needs and selecting appropriate adaptations is an open research challenge.

Other approaches to assistive technologies include simplified browsers targeted at older, novice users (Muta et al. 2005; Milne et al. 2005). However, these solutions tend not to be used by the larger population since (1) it may be difficult to get help from people that are unfamiliar with the simplified browser, (2) they hide functionality and (3) they mark the user as 'different'. Specialised browsers with voice augmentation have also been investigated (Sato et al. 2011), showing that they can increase confidence levels of older adults when accessing the web.

An interesting alternative to browsers consists of bypassing all learning challenges by resorting to familiar devices to access web content. SOMFA (Social Media For All) is a platform that finds, retrieves, transforms and displays social media content over TV Sets (Borrino et al. 2009). Other example includes the CaringFamily service[4] that enables older adults to use email via fax.

Over the years, solutions to web access have been increasingly considering older adults as individuals rather than disabled versions of younger users. They view web pages differently (Tullis 2007), have unique browsing behaviours (Fairweather 2008), and make conscious decisions about what technologies (not) to use (Knowles and Hanson 2018).

18.9 Discussion

Beyond having access to the information contained within, the web serves a greater purpose within today's society—it is a communication infrastructure like no other before. Governments are using the web to engage and interact with their citizens on local democracy; Educational institutions have prioritised eLearning environments to students; Health and social care are shifting to data-driven and technology-enabled consultations and interactions with patients. It is vital that everyone has equal access to the web and the services that exist within it.

Assistive Technologies work to support individuals overcoming those barriers to access by augmenting the ways in which the content is presented, navigated and manipulated. However, assistive technologies are not always mainstream or can be mass produced, often resulting in added complexities to maintain support and can incur significant costs to the end user.

HTML5 specifications and the push to support a diverse set of personalised mobile experiences are helping to create a more malleable and accessible web. As the underlying structure of the web improves, new integrations and interaction adaptations are made possible, helping to create a more inclusive web.

While there is no doubt that a number of assistive technologies have been designed to support specific abilities, such as braille displays for vision or gaze tracking

---

[4]www.caringfamily.com.

for motor control—many accommodate a broad range of needs and abilities (e.g. screen magnification and closed captioning), with some obtaining mainstream status; designed for ease and convenience, not 'disabilities' (e.g. speech control and conversational agents).

As new technologies emerge, there will always be the need for niche and bespoke adaptations to support individuals with differing abilities. However, the current vision for the Web is leading towards rich semantic document descriptions, supporting ubiquitous interactions through with flexible modes presentation and engagement tailored to the specific context, device and user.

18.10 Future Directions

Developments in assistive technologies have opened up the Web to user groups that experience some form of impairment. It is now possible to access a wide range of online applications and services that promote greater independence and quality of life. Still, much work remains to be done to build an inclusive Web.

We are increasingly witnessing the appearance of intelligent and personalised assistive technologies that adapt to people's abilities. Such technologies are powered by advances in machine learning techniques and/or human-computation approaches. Having systems that continuously assess, model and adapt themselves to individuals and situations is the holy grail of accessible computing. It is also noteworthy that personalization is not restricted to software. The recent emergence of Makers movement (e.g. project e-NABLE[5]) and the renewed culture of gadget-oriented products, opened new and exciting opportunities for hardware customization. No longer must assistive technologies be produced in small volumes at significant cost to the manufacturer and end user, nor need they just be for utilitarian purposes. It is possible to design for fun, play, and games. This year Microsoft announced the launch of the Xbox Adaptive Controller,[6] a gamepad designed to be augmented and customised via simple plug-and-play connections to meet the individual needs of the gamer; Nintendo also announced Labo,[7] a DIY kit for creating custom gamepads with cardboard—a trend that will hopefully continue in the future.

18.11 Authors' Opinion of the Field

Until recently, most Assistive Technologies focused on providing access to products or services via software or hardware solutions. However, in recent years, we have witnessed technologies that go beyond just 'bridging the gap' between users and

---

[5]http://enablingthefuture.org/.
[6]https://www.xbox.com/en-US/xbox-one/accessibility.
[7]https://labo.nintendo.com/.

systems but use the Web as a platform for real-world inclusion. Examples include commercial tools such as Google Maps or BeMyEyes,[8] or research projects such as VizWiz (Bigham et al. 2010), Legion Scribe (Lasecki et al. 2014a) or Tohme (Hara et al. 2014). These solutions open new opportunities for people with disabilities allowing them to perform tasks that were once arduous or impossible to accomplish in the real-world.

Despite all its potential, technology can equally impose new barriers to widen the 'digital divide'. Examples include people that make conscious decisions about not using certain technologies, which can result in different forms of social exclusion (Knowles and Hanson 2018).

These are exciting times to create novel inclusive technologies that can have a broad impact on people's lives: from software solutions to Internet-enabled devices that sense and act on the built environment.

It is therefore crucial that accessibility studies aim to understand the broader impact of web technologies, beyond traditional performance measures and focus on its social impact; going beyond utility and access towards assessing empowerment and agency.

18.12 Conclusions

Gone are the days when websites were designed to target the young, able-bodied, technology savvy users that would access the content from their keyboard and mouse desktop environments. Technology in one form or another has permeated into every facet of human lives spanning the broad range of demographics and severing a broader range of functions. Portable networked-devices have allowed us to form a symbiotic relationship with the Web, simultaneously drawing from and contributing to the vast knowledge base of interconnected documents and datasets. To deny access to such a resource seems criminal, yet for many individuals the much of the web remains inaccessible and unexplored.

Beyond having access to the information contained within, the web serves a greater purpose within today's society—it is a communication infrastructure like no other before. Governments are using the web to engage and interact with their citizens on local democracy; Educational institutions have prioritised eLearning environments to students; Health and social care are shifting to data-driven and technology-enabled consultations and interactions with patients. It is vital that everyone has equal access to the web and the services that exist within it.

As the underlying technologies and conceptual vision of the web evolve to towards a semantic web of machine-readable data designed to be discovered, manipulated and presented in new forms, assistive technologies are well positioned to benefit from those efforts regardless of the developer's web accessibility knowledge.

---

[8]https://www.bemyeyes.com/.

New trends in human-computation and machine learning technologies are bringing about a new era of assistive technologies designed to leverage the web to support interactions in the real-world. In particular, these innovations hold promise for individuals with reduced cognitive and learning abilities leading independent lives.

References

Ackermann P, Velasco CA, Power C (2012) Developing a Semantic User and Device Modeling Framework That Supports UI Adaptability of Web 2.0 Applications for People with Special Needs. In: Proceedings of the International Cross-Disciplinary Conference on Web Accessibility. ACM, New York, NY, USA, p 12:1–12:4

Anthes G (2012) HTML5 leads a web revolution. Commun ACM 55:16–17. https://doi.org/10.1145/2209249.2209256

Anthony L, Kim Y, Findlater L (2013) Analyzing user-generated youtube videos to understand touchscreen use by people with motor impairments. In: Proceedings of the SIGCHI conference on human factors in computing systems. ACM, New York, NY, USA, pp 1223–1232

Arch A (2009) Web accessibility for older users: successes and opportunities (keynote). In: Proceedings of the 2009 international cross-disciplinary conference on web accessibility (W4A). ACM, New York, NY, USA, pp 1–6

Ashok V, Borodin Y, Stoyanchev S et al (2014) Wizard-of-Oz evaluation of speech-driven web browsing interface for people with vision impairments. In: Proceedings of the 11th web for all conference. ACM, New York, NY, USA, pp 12:1–12:9

Ashok V, Borodin Y, Puzis Y, Ramakrishnan IV (2015) Capti-speak: a speech-enabled web screen reader. In: Proceedings of the 12th web for all conference. ACM, New York, NY, USA, p 22:1–22:10

Azenkot S, Lee NB (2013) Exploring the use of speech input by blind people on mobile devices. In: Proceedings of the 15th international ACM SIGACCESS conference on computers and accessibility - ASSETS '13, pp 1–8

Azenkot S, Wobbrock JO, Prasain S, Ladner RE (2012) Input finger detection for nonvisual touch screen text entry in Perkinput. In: Proceedings of graphics interface. Canadian information processing society, Toronto, Ont., Canada, Canada, pp 121–129

Berke L, Kafle S, Huenerfauth M (2018) Methods for evaluation of imperfect captioning tools by deaf or hard-of-hearing users at different reading literacy levels. In: Proceedings of the 2018 CHI conference on human factors in computing systems. ACM, New York, NY, USA, pp 91:1–91:12

Bigham JP, Prince CM, Ladner RE (2008) WebAnywhere: a screen reader on-the-go. In: Proceedings of the 2008 international cross-disciplinary conference on web accessibility (W4A). ACM, New York, NY, USA, pp 73–82

Bigham JP, Jayant C, Ji H et al (2010) VizWiz: nearly real-time answers to visual questions. In: Proceedings of the 2010 international cross disciplinary conference on web accessibility (W4A). ACM, New York, NY, USA, pp 24:1–24:2

Bigham JP, Williams K, Banerjee N, Zimmerman J (2017) Scopist: building a skill ladder into crowd transcription. In: Proceedings of the 14th web for all conference on the future of accessible work. ACM, New York, NY, USA, pp 2:1–2:10

Bonavero Y, Huchard M, Meynard M (2015) Reconciling user and designer preferences in adapting web pages for people with low vision. In: Proceedings of the 12th web for all conference. ACM, New York, NY, USA, pp 10:1–10:10

Bornschein J, Bornschein D, Weber G (2018) Comparing computer-based drawing methods for blind people with real-time tactile feedback. In: Proceedings of the 2018 CHI conference on human factors in computing systems. ACM, New York, NY, USA, pp 115:1–115:13

Borodin Y, Bigham JP, Dausch G, Ramakrishnan IV (2010) More than meets the eye: a survey of screen-reader browsing strategies. In: Proceedings of the 2010 international cross disciplinary conference on web accessibility (W4A). ACM, New York, NY, USA, pp 13:1–13:10

Borrino R, Furini M, Roccetti M (2009) Augmenting social media accessibility. In: Proceedings of the 2009 international cross-disciplinary conference on web accessibility (W4A). ACM, New York, NY, USA, pp 54–57

Boulares M, Jemni M (2012) Mobile sign language translation system for deaf community. In: Proceedings of the international cross-disciplinary conference on web accessibility. ACM, New York, NY, USA, pp 37:1–37:4

Brown A, Jay C, Harper S (2009) Audio presentation of auto-suggest lists. In: Proceedings of the 2009 international cross-disciplinary conference on web accessibility (W4A). ACM, New York, NY, USA, pp 58–61

Cook AM, Hussey S (2001) Assistive technologies: principles and practice, 2nd edn. St. Louis, Mosby

Crabb M, Hanson VL (2016) An analysis of age, technology usage, and cognitive characteristics within information retrieval tasks. ACM Trans Access Comput 8:10:1–10:26. https://doi.org/10.1145/2856046

de Santana VF, de Oliveira R, Almeida LDA, Baranauskas MCC (2012) Web accessibility and people with dyslexia: a survey on techniques and guidelines. In: Proceedings of the international cross-disciplinary conference on web accessibility. ACM, New York, NY, USA, pp 35:1—35:9

de Santana VF, de Oliveira R, Almeida LDA, Ito M (2013) Firefixia: an accessibility web browser customization toolbar for people with dyslexia. In: Proceedings of the 10th international cross-disciplinary conference on web accessibility. ACM, New York, NY, USA, p 16:1—16:4

Dinesh TB, Choppella V (2012) Alipi: tools for a re-narration web. In: Proceedings of the international cross-disciplinary conference on web accessibility. ACM, New York, NY, USA, pp 29:1—29:2

Dixon M, Fogarty J, Wobbrock J (2012) A general-purpose target-aware pointing enhancement using pixel-level analysis of graphical interfaces. In: Proceedings of the SIGCHI conference on human factors in computing systems. ACM, New York, NY, USA, pp 3167–3176

Encelle B, Beldame MO, Prié Y (2013) Towards the usage of pauses in audio-described videos. In: Proceedings of the 10th international cross-disciplinary conference on web accessibility. ACM, New York, NY, USA, p 31:1–31:4

Fairweather PG (2008) How older and younger adults differ in their approach to problem solving on a complex website. In: Proceedings of the 10th international ACM SIGACCESS conference on computers and accessibility. ACM, New York, NY, USA, pp 67–72

Federico M, Furini M (2012) Enhancing learning accessibility through fully automatic captioning. In: Proceedings of the international cross-disciplinary conference on web accessibility. ACM, New York, NY, USA, p 40:1–40:4

Fernandes N, Guerreiro T, Marques D, Carriço L (2015) Optimus web: selective delivery of desktop or mobile web pages. In: Proceedings of the 12th web for all conference. ACM, New York, NY, USA, pp 20:1–20:4

Gardiner S, Tomasic A, Zimmerman J (2015) SmartWrap: seeing datasets with the crowd's eyes. In: Proceedings of the 12th web for all conference. ACM, New York, NY, USA, pp 3:1–3:10

Gaur Y, Lasecki WS, Metze F, Bigham JP (2016) The effects of automatic speech recognition quality on human transcription latency. In: Proceedings of the 13th web for all conference. ACM, New York, NY, USA, pp 23:1–23:8

Gregor P, Newell AF, Zajicek M (2002) Designing for dynamic diversity: interfaces for older people. In: Assets '02: proceedings of the fifth international ACM conference on assistive technologies. ACM, New York, NY, USA, pp 151–156

Hanson VL (2009) Age and web access: the next generation. In: Proceedings of the 2009 international cross-disciplinary conference on web accessibility (W4A). ACM, New York, NY, USA, pp 7–15

Hara K, Sun J, Moore R et al (2014) Tohme: detecting curb ramps in google street view using crowdsourcing, computer vision, and machine learning. In: Proceedings of the 27th annual ACM symposium on user interface software and technology. ACM, New York, NY, USA, pp 189–204

Huenerfauth M, Hanson V (2009) Sign language in the interface: access for deaf signers. Univers Access Handbook NJ Erlbaum, p 38

Hughes CJ, Armstrong M, Jones R, Crabb M (2015) Responsive design for personalised subtitles. In: Proceedings of the 12th web for all conference. ACM, New York, NY, USA, pp 8:1–8:4

Hurst A, Tobias J (2011) Empowering individuals with do-it-yourself assistive technology. In: The Proceedings of the 13th international ACM SIGACCESS conference on computers and accessibility. ACM, New York, NY, USA, pp 11–18

Jaballah K (2012) Accessible 3D signing avatars: the tunisian experience. In: Proceedings of the international cross-disciplinary conference on web accessibility. ACM, New York, NY, USA, pp 24:1–24:2

Jensema C, McCann R, Ramsey S (1996) Closed-captioned television presentation speed and vocabulary. Am Ann Deaf 284–292

Kacorri H, Huenerfauth M, Ebling S et al (2017) Regression analysis of demographic and technology-experience factors influencing acceptance of sign language animation. ACM Trans Access Comput 10:3:1–3:33. https://doi.org/10.1145/3046787

Kipp M, Nguyen Q, Heloir A, Matthes S (2011) Assessing the deaf user perspective on sign language avatars. In: The proceedings of the 13th international ACM SIGACCESS conference on computers and accessibility. ACM, New York, NY, USA, pp 107–114

Knowles B, Hanson VL (2018) The Wisdom of Older Technology (Non)Users. Commun ACM 61:72–77. https://doi.org/10.1145/3179995

Kondraske GV (1995) A working model for human system-task interfaces. Biomed Eng Handb 2:147

Kushalnagar R, Seita M, Glasser A (2017) Closed ASL interpreting for online videos. In: Proceedings of the 14th web for all conference on the future of accessible work. ACM, New York, NY, USA, p 32:1–32:4

Lai PPY (2011) Application of content adaptation in web accessibility for the blind. In: Proceedings of the international cross-disciplinary conference on web accessibility. ACM, New York, NY, USA, pp 6:1–6:4

Lasecki W, Miller C, Sadilek A et al (2012) Real-time captioning by groups of non-experts. In: Proceedings of the 25th annual ACM symposium on user interface software and technology. ACM, New York, NY, USA, pp 23–34

Lasecki WS, Kushalnagar R, Bigham JP (2014) Helping students keep up with real-time captions by pausing and highlighting

Lasecki WS, Kushalnagar R, Bigham JP (2014) Legion scribe: real-time captioning by non-experts. In: Proceedings of the 16th international ACM SIGACCESS conference on computers & accessibility. ACM, New York, NY, USA, pp 303–304

Marquié JC, Jourdan-Boddaert L, Huet N (2002) Do older adults underestimate their actual computer knowledge? Behav Inf Technol 21:273–280. https://doi.org/10.1080/0144929021000020998

Martins J, Carilho J, Schnell O et al (2014) Friendsourcing the unmet needs of people with dementia. In: Proceedings of the 11th web for all conference. ACM, New York, NY, USA, pp 35:1–35:4

Milne S, Dickinson A, Gregor P et al (2005) Not browsing, but drowning: designing a web browser for novice older users. In: Proceedings of HCI international, pp 22–27

Montague K, Nicolau H, Hanson V (2014) Motor-impaired touchscreen interactions in the wild. In: 16th international ACM SIGACCESS conference on computers and accessibility (ASSETS)

Mott ME, Vatavu R-D, Kane SK, Wobbrock JO (2016) Smart touch: improving touch accuracy for people with motor impairments with template matching. In: Proceedings of the 2016 CHI conference on human factors in computing systems. ACM, New York, NY, USA, pp 1934–1946

Muta H, Ohko T, Yoshinaga H (2005) An activeX-based accessibility solution for senior citizens. In: Proceedings of the center on disabilities technology and persons with disabilities conference 2005

Newell AF (1995) Extra-ordinary human-computer interaction. Cambridge University Press, New York, NY, USA, pp 3–18

Newell AF, Gregor P (2000) User sensitive inclusive design: in search of a new paradigm. CUU '00: proceedings on the 2000 conference on universal usability. ACM, New York, NY, USA, pp 39–44

Nicolau H, Guerreiro J, Guerreiro T, Carriço L (2013) UbiBraille: designing and evaluating a vibrotactile Braille-reading device. In: Proceedings of the 15th international ACM SIGACCESS conference on computers and accessibility. ACM, New York, NY, USA, pp 23:1–23:8

Nicolau H, Montague K, Guerreiro T, et al (2014) B#: chord-based correction for multitouch braille input. In: Proceedings of the SIGCHI conference on human factors in computing systems. ACM, New York, NY, USA, pp 1705–1708

Nicolau H, Montague K, Guerreiro T et al (2015) Holibraille: multipoint vibrotactile feedback on mobile devices. In: Proceedings of the 12th web for all conference. ACM, New York, NY, USA, pp 30:1–30:4

Pasqual PT, Wobbrock JO (2014) Mouse pointing endpoint prediction using kinematic template matching. In: Proceedings of the 32nd annual ACM conference on human factors in computing systems. pp 743–752

Persad U, Langdon P, Clarkson J (2007) Characterising user capabilities to support inclusive design evaluation. Univers Access Inf Soc 6:119–135

Rello L, Kanvinde G, Baeza-Yates R (2012) Layout guidelines for web text and a web service to improve accessibility for dyslexics. In: Proceedings of the international cross-disciplinary conference on web accessibility. ACM, New York, NY, USA, pp 36:1–36:9

Richards JT, Montague K, Hanson VL (2012) Web accessibility as a side effect. In: Proceedings of the 14th international ACM SIGACCESS conference on computers and accessibility. ACM, New York, NY, USA, pp 79–86

Rodrigues A, Montague K, Nicolau H et al (2017) In-context Q&A to support blind people using smartphones. In: Proceedings of the 19th international ACM SIGACCESS conference on computers and accessibility. ACM, New York, NY, USA, pp 32–36

Ruiz J, Tausky D, Bunt A et al (2008) Analyzing the kinematics of bivariate pointing. In: Proceedings of graphics interface 2008. Canadian information processing society, Toronto, Ont., Canada, Canada, pp 251–258

Sato D, Kobayashi M, Takagi H et al (2011) How voice augmentation supports elderly web users. In: The Proceedings of the 13th international ACM SIGACCESS conference on computers and accessibility. ACM, New York, NY, USA, pp 155–162

Sayago S, Blat J (2007) A preliminary usability evaluation of strategies for seeking online information with elderly people. In: Proceedings of the 2007 international cross-disciplinary conference on web accessibility (W4A). ACM, New York, NY, USA, pp 54–57

Sears A, Lin M, Jacko J, Xiao Y (2003) When computers fade: pervasive computing and situationally-induced impairments and disabilities. In: Proceedings of HCI international, pp 1298–1302

Sloan D, Atkinson MT, Machin C, Li Y (2010) The potential of adaptive interfaces as an accessibility aid for older web users. In: Proceedings of the 2010 international cross disciplinary conference on web accessibility (W4A). ACM, New York, NY, USA, pp 35:1–35:10

Sorge V, Chen C, Raman T V, Tseng D (2014) Towards making mathematics a first class citizen in general screen readers. In: Proceedings of the 11th web for all conference. ACM, New York, NY, USA, pp 40:1–40:10

Sorge V, Lee M, Wilkinson S (2015) End-to-end solution for accessible chemical diagrams. In: Proceedings of the 12th web for all conference. ACM, New York, NY, USA, pp 6:1–6:10

Southern C, Clawson J, Frey B et al (2012) An evaluation of BrailleTouch: mobile touchscreen text entry for the visually impaired. In: Proceedings of the 14th international conference on human-computer interaction with mobile devices and services. ACM, New York, NY, USA, pp 317–326

Stephanidis C (1995) Towards user interfaces for all: some critical issues. In: Yuichiro Anzai KO, Mori H (eds) Symbiosis of human and artifact future computing and design for human-computer interaction proceedings of the sixth international conference on human-computer interaction (HCI International '95). Elsevier, pp 137–142

Stephanidis C, Salvendy G, Akoumianakis D et al (1998) Toward an information society for all: an international R&D agenda. Int J Hum Comput Interact 10:107–134

Szpiro SFA, Hashash S, Zhao Y, Azenkot S (2016) How people with low vision access computing devices: understanding challenges and opportunities. In: Proceedings of the 18th international ACM SIGACCESS conference on computers and accessibility. ACM, New York, NY, USA, pp 171–180

Takagi H, Kawanaka S, Kobayashi M et al (2008) Social accessibility: achieving accessibility through collaborative metadata authoring. In: Proceedings of the 10th international ACM SIGAC-CESS conference on computers and accessibility. ACM, New York, NY, USA, pp 193–200

Trewin S (2004) Automating accessibility: the dynamic keyboard. In: Proceedings of the 6th international ACM SIGACCESS conference on computers and accessibility. ACM, New York, NY, USA, pp 71–78

Trindade D, Rodrigues A, Guerreiro T, Nicolau H (2018) Hybrid-Brailler: combining physical and gestural interaction for mobile braille input and editing. In: Proceedings of the 2018 CHI conference on human factors in computing systems. ACM, New York, NY, USA, pp 27:1–27:12

Tullis TS (2007) Older adults and the web: lessons learned from eye-tracking. In: Stephanidis C (ed) Universal acess in human computer interaction. Coping with diversity. Springer, Berlin, pp 1030–1039

Valencia X, Arrue M, Pérez JE, Abascal J (2013) User individuality management in websites based on WAI-ARIA annotations and ontologies. In: Proceedings of the 10th international cross-disciplinary conference on web accessibility. ACM, New York, NY, USA, pp 29:1–29:10

Vanderheiden GC (1998) Universal design and assistive technology in communication and information technologies: alternatives or complements? Assist Technol Off J RESNA 10:29

Watanabe WM, Junior AC, Uzêda VR et al (2009) Facilita: reading assistance for low-literacy readers. In: Proceedings of the 27th ACM international conference on design of communication. ACM, New York, NY, USA, pp 29–36

Wobbrock JO, Kane SK, Gajos KZ et al (2011) Ability-based design. ACM Trans Access Comput 3:1–27. https://doi.org/10.1145/1952383.1952384

Yesilada Y, Harper S, Eraslan S (2013) Experiential transcoding: an eyetracking approach. In: Proceedings of the 10th international cross-disciplinary conference on web accessibility. ACM, New York, NY, USA, pp 30:1–30:4

Chapter 19
Documents and Publications

Vivienne Conway and Amanda Mace

Abstract The purpose of this chapter is to describe some of the issues related to creating accessible documents and publications. Publications include both formal publications such as those created by publishing houses and those created informally such as a corporate organization's annual report. Until the last few years, most organizations relied heavily on the Portable Document Format (PDF) and this is gradually being replaced by the ePUB format as the accepted international standard. However, issues still exist in the best method to create these documents, how accessibility is assessed, and how to ensure accessibility is maximized for users. This chapter also looks at some of the new technology in document creation, remediation and assessment.

19.1 Introduction

In this chapter, we deal with issues that occur in the creation of accessible documents, both formally published documents such as journals and books, and informal documents such as annual reports, company documents and newsletters. We examine issues regarding the format choice of the document, and accessibility issues that arise in the various format choices.

We often think of a document as a physical piece of paper, a magazine, a legal set of papers etc., with a digital document being one of these that you download from a website, or that someone sends you as an email attachment.

Rothberg (2017) describes a digital document as an onion. The centre of the onion is the content—the text, images, embedded media and user interaction. Surrounding the content is the structure of the document headings, chapters, page breaks. The next layer is the delivery format, and the final layer is the cataloguing information to enable the document to be located within a system. According to Rothberg, we use standards such as HTML5, WAI-ARIA, and ePUB to make these documents accessible. The inner layer (words, images, etc.) use HTML and ARIA, which are then arranged with

V. Conway (✉) · A. Mace
Web Key IT Pty Ltd, 10 Tonrita Pace, Wanneroo, WA 6065, Australia
e-mail: v.conway@webkeyit.com

© Springer-Verlag London Ltd., part of Springer Nature 2019
Y. Yesilada and S. Harper (eds.), *Web Accessibility*, Human–Computer
Interaction Series, https://doi.org/10.1007/978-1-4471-7440-0_19

semantic structure and wrapped in a delivery format using the ePUB accessibility standard. Lastly, the accessibility features are available to the metadata in ePUB or on the web page or in the metadata through the publisher workflow. According to Rothberg, ePUB is the core standard for creating a document that is accessible by users, particularly those using assistive technology (Rothberg 2017).

We find a great emphasis on multiple formats for documents, rather than relying on one medium. Kasdorf (2017b) states that publications are not specifically Web publications, but delivered via the web, '...the publication as a whole is not a single "thing" on the Web. Those publications are typically on a platform that uses the Web for delivery, but those platforms are not the Web' (Kasdorf 2017b).

Not only are we living in a time of change within the digital environment, including how we publish, and what tools we use to publish, but also what tools users are employing to enjoy the content. While this chapter deals mainly with publishing formats such as PDF, ePUB etc., we also include Braille publishing. The use of formats other than Braille for visually impaired students greatly increases their opportunities for success in schools, and enables them to blend more easily into the classroom (Cicerchia 2015). Fewer children are learning Braille in schools, with more users relying on in-built accessibility in documents. This may be partially due to the lack of appropriately skilled Braille teachers. Vision Australia, in their submission to the Australian Government enquiry into access for students with disabilities, discussed the inconsistency of funding distribution for resources between regions/schools, stating:

> This inconsistency in the allocation of supports has resulted in some students remaining virtually and functionally illiterate because funding is not available to provide them with teaching support to learn braille (Vision Australia 2015).

19.2   History—Documents in Digital Form, Trends

When WCAG 2.0 was released by W3C in 2008, there were no guidelines for documents that are downloaded from the Web. We now have the Guidance on Applying WCAG 2.0 to Non-Web Information and Communications Technologies, and guidance on maximizing ePUB for accessibility, given it is based on HTML5 (W3C 2013).

A PDF document is designed to ensure all information on the page remains in the same format when printed—page numbers do not change, images remain the same, etc. When a low-vision reader zooms in for magnification on a PDF document, the PDF cannot rescale, meaning depending on the magnification of the PDF, the user may need to scroll horizontally to see the content. In contrast, with an ePUB document which is magnified, the user can manipulate the text on the page, making the actual text larger, viewing shorter pages with larger text size. The term for this feature is 'reflow'. For a user with a visual impairment, the difference between ePUB and PDF becomes obvious.

Different formats serve different purposes. A PDF document works well in printed form and sometimes for desktops, laptops and tablets. ePUB is better suited for mobile devices and assistive technology (but is not easy to create as we will discuss later), and HTML is as accessible as ePUB, but misses some of ePUB's special capabilities. Hence, we are left with creating multiple versions of a document (Kasdorf 2017b).

Adobe's PDF has changed from its original intent in the early 1990s as a secure means of sharing and printing documents into a format incorporating multimedia and forms. With the incorporation of Optical Character Recognition (OCR), scanned PDF documents are editable —a huge breakthrough allowing people using assistive technology to read historical documents such as old newspapers. Much of the early work in OCR was conducted by Kurzweil who is credited with developing the first OCR programme to recognize any style of print (Kurzweil 2018).

19.2.1 OCR and Readability

OCR is a technology which enables scanned documents and images to be transformed into searchable and editable document formats. OCR can be a powerful tool with large-scale possibilities, but it is entirely dependent on the quality of the image being scanned. The power of text recognition in the mobile context, working with smartphones, smart glasses etc., is exciting and many companies, such as Microsoft, are using this technology for applications such as Seeing AI. However, OCR technology is not reliable requiring human intervention to ensure it reads accurately for the users of assistive technology.

One of the issues with reliance on OCR to make a PDF accessible is the quality of the print. OCR works well when high resolution and print quality are evident. For example, it may misread the letter 'S' for the number '5' or number '0' and letter 'O'. Results with OCR may differ based on the fonts, layout of the scanned image, language used, etc. It relies on the print being in good condition. Tears, low colour contrast, fading and distortion, such as water damage, impact the effectiveness of the OCR technology. Degradation of print, as well as the quality of the actual programme being used, also play a part in the quality of the outcome. The better the quality of the print, the better the output.

The other major issue with OCR is that while it recognizes text, the text itself requires appropriate 'tagging' to be correctly read by assistive technology and understood by its users. The term 'tagging' refers to programmatically defining structure such as headings, tables, etc. in PDF for them to be available and contextual to the user of assistive technology. For example, tagging headings allows those tagged elements to become bookmarks and/or navigational aids in a converted document.

19.2.2 Mobile Responsive Requirements

Scalability is no longer an 'optional' feature. With society's heavy reliance on mobile devices, the design of websites has changed. So too, digital documents need to change. 'Mobile responsive' refers to the design approach intended to provide an optimal viewing experience across a wide range of devices, including tablets and mobile phones. It also ensures ease of reading and navigation with minimal resizing and scrolling. Currently, PDF and other word processing documents do not provide a responsive design solution.

19.2.3 Documents as Forms

Creating accessible forms requires additional effort from the author to ensure accessibility. All input fields and elements need to be clearly identified using the correct structure. This information also needs to be available to assistive technology, such as screen readers.

The order in which keyboard focus is received is imperative. Each interactive element should be available using the keyboard alone and move in a logical manner. If the tabbing sequence is not logical it adds to confusion and frustration for the user. In current popular programmes, the ability to use every interactive element with only a keyboard is fraught with inconsistencies and access limitations.

It seems practical to provide clear instructions; however, this is often overlooked. Consider, for example a date format. If the author does not inform the user they would like the date in the format of; day, month and year, and the user inputs the date using a month, day, year format, it can create unintentional and avoidable errors. There are different methods for dealing with user errors, but the most effective method is prevention wherever possible with clear instructions to the user.

Often, authors inform users an input field is required by the presence of an asterisk in pure red colour next to the required element. There are two accessibility issues with this use of the asterisk. First, some screen readers do not read out punctuation. Users would, therefore, miss out on the information conveying a required field. Second, the pure red regular-sized text fails colour contrast requirements at the WCAG 2.1 AA level. This also applies to using pure red text to highlight important notes or instructions.

It is important to note that while in 'focus mode', a screen reader will skip over content that is not an interactive element. Placing important information or instructions at the beginning of the form, or as part of the label applied to the element ensures the user has all the necessary information.

19.3   Companies Leading the Way in Accessible Software

Several companies are making a concerted effort to implement built-in features to help people with varying capabilities read and author documents. For example, both Microsoft and Adobe Acrobat offer automated tools to audit accessibility issues.

Microsoft continues to add features which make the experience for reading documents and presentations made in the Office Suite more accessible. The ability to identify low colour contrast with the Accessibility Checker tool, available for Microsoft Office Suite 2010 and onwards, takes another step towards helping authors make informed choices. The checker finds issues and categorizes them as Error, Warning or Tip. Microsoft has not stopped at flagging errors and warnings, it also provides feedback for the author with advice: 'Why fix this?' and 'How to fix this.' This tool is useful, and results display in a pane on the right side of the checked document. As fixes occur, errors and warnings disappear from the tools' pane (Microsoft 2018).

Microsoft provides users the ability to select an auto-generated description using Microsoft's cloud-powered intelligent services, creating a description based on AI. They also provide pre-written alternative text for their icons feature and have added the ability for authors to select when the image is purely for decoration and is unnecessary for the assistive technology user.

Digital Access at Vision Australia created the Document Accessibility Toolbar for the ribbon menu in Microsoft Word. The toolbar collates accessibility features into one area to more easily produce and check Word documents for accessibility. It is compatible with Microsoft Office 2010–2016 on a PC (Microsoft 2018).

Acrobat Reader provides several preferences that make the reading of PDF documents more accessible for users with vision or motion impairments. These preferences control how PDF documents appear on the screen and how they are read by a screen reader (Adobe 2018a).

Adobe Acrobat have also provided accessibility features, including the Accessibility Setup Assistant where many of the accessibility preferences and settings are located. For document creators, Adobe Acrobat Pro also features an accessibility tool. This tool is only found in the Pro version of Adobe Acrobat and offers options such as 'auto-tagging a PDF', adjusting the reading order and generating an accessibility report. Running a 'Full Check' from the Accessibility tool produces a list of accessibility issues in the left-hand side column. Right- clicking on an error provides the author options to fix, skip, explain, etc. accessibility issues.

Adobe Acrobat Reader and Pro DC both have 'Read Out Loud' a built-in Text-to-Speech tool. It reads a PDF text aloud, including the alternate text for images and descriptive tooltips for input fields. The PDF, however, must be tagged and made accessible, otherwise, it may read incorrectly, not be read, or it may be read in the wrong order.

CommonLook PDF GlobalAccess software along with Adobe Acrobat are the only software programmes recognized by W3C for PDF remediation. It is a plug-in for Adobe Acrobat with one interface to navigate for accessibility testing and remediating documents. Like Adobe Acrobat Pro, the accessibility checker automatically detects common accessibility issues against several accessibility standards using a checkpoint-by-checkpoint report (CommonLook 2018).

It would be remiss not to mention Open Access Technologies (OAT), who developed an automated PDF remediation platform. OAT employ web-crawling technology to identify the number of PDFs on a website and discern whether they are tagged PDF files. Untagged documents require tagging before using the automated checker. However, previously tagged documents are scanned with the accessibility checker and the user is advised if a PDF requires remediation. Remediation combines automated added tags, bookmarks, etc. and manually required information such as descriptive alternative text attached to images. Content from both the manual and the automated remediation are merged and the remediated documents are returned to the website (Open Access Technologies Inc. 2018).

Automated accessibility checkers do not replace the need for manual checking, as they are unable to effectively audit to the standard of the accessibility guidelines (Gilakjani 2012). It is important to remember that the 'checking' in all automated tools is incomplete. For example, a tool may verify alternative text is present, but it cannot verify the actual text; where human intervention and auditing is required.

19.4 Issues of Accessibility for Documents

19.4.1 The Case for HTML Forms

Using form documents is common practice. Forms are often created in a word processing programme and converted to a PDF. Once a PDF is created, either the creator inserts interactive form elements or automatically detects form fields in the PDF using a programme such as Adobe Acrobat Pro or simply leaves it as is. If the latter is chosen, the document user must print the form, complete it manually, electronically scan and return it to the author, or provide the completed form in person or by mail. If either of the two former options are chosen, the author must correctly, tag, label and prepare the form. Because of the variables which play a part in ensuring a PDF form is accessible, it is considered best practice to provide an alternative. According to Konicek et al., there are fewer complications to creating accessible HTML than in attempting to create accessible PDF documents (Konicek et al. 2003). The solution to using documents for forms is to utilize HTML instead. Using HTML means the form will become accessible to search engines, browsers and mobile devices. HTML was specifically designed for screen viewing, which gives it a more user-friendly on-screen appearance than the more printer-focused PDF documents. HTML also means content is more interactive, using all the semantic options available in the code. It is easy to share by hyperlink (even with large file sizes) and is less CPU-intensive on the server. There is no need to save or delete files with HTML. Design-wise, by using HTML branding and formatting consistently, the design, look and feel is controlled with CSS (Cascading Style Sheets). Consistency is aided with CMS controlling rules for structure, business rules and code. However, PDF documents are currently the widely accepted standard. They currently have the advantage of easily being saved by the client and being available offline.

Aside from PDF forms, the other common format is DOCX in Microsoft Word. These require the creator to insert interactive form elements or retain as a print-only version. There are inconsistencies and keyboard access issues arising with the programmers' interactive form elements, which requires thorough manual testing. Microsoft Word allows the author to restrict editing to form elements only, but this feature is not always used, thus leaving the document exposed to the risk of editing.

19.4.2 Embedding Rich Media

Embedding rich media such as video gives the author an opportunity to capture the user's attention. Rich media including, Flash (SWF), audio (MP3) and video (MP4) can be incorporated into document files. Embedding such content requires the author to provide an alternative equivalent, giving the user the option of reading the information in an accessible format. In most cases, this involves ensuring a transcript is available which presents the information in the MP3 or MP4 format. Requirements for MP4 content also state captions must be available to users. Adding Audio Description offers the person with a visual impairment an understanding of the video content in an MP4, and is best practice. One could argue the same way a wheelchair ramp assists a parent with a pram or stroller. Audio Description can be beneficial for a much broader audience. Auditory learning assists with language development and learning outcomes (Gilakjani 2012). People on the autism spectrum experience difficulty recognizing emotional cues. Audio Descriptions provide this context to those users.

19.4.3 InDesign—For Print

Graphic designers often rely on programmes such as InDesign and Photoshop. Although InDesign offers the ability to export to HTML and PDF, it can also generate a downloadable file on the website. InDesign wasn't developed for creating web browsing materials. The result is almost always inaccessible content. Manual remediation is required for PDF or in the HTML code depending on the exported choice (Adobe 2018b).

19.4.4 Digitization and Preservation

It is nearly 30 years since the first digitizing of historical material began. Libraries, governments of all levels, cultural and religious groups, and social clubs will continue to take advantage of the Internet to share their resources worldwide. This is one of the benefits of PDF and highlights the importance of OCR. It enables people without access to libraries, museums, and archives access to use the knowledge of the past. Digitization is an amazing tool. Digital copies of documents reduces the handling of fragile originals and allows better preservation. It is necessary to digitize legacy materials such as historical newspapers and secondly to understand the manual process for correcting and tagging to enable users access to documents.

19.4.5 Graphs, Maps and Complex Illustrations

Alternative text (alt text) for informative images describes the image or the purpose of the image coded during document creation. The alternative text provides equivalent information about the image for those who are unable to see it. For complex illustrations, infographics, maps and graphs, alt text may not be sufficient. The key to text alternative is the word 'alternative'. A data table may provide an alternative for charts and graphs. A paragraph giving clear directions about the inaccessible map is an alternative. The curse and beauty of the accessibility guidelines is they often do not provide the right way to fix an issue, because there are numerous options available. The result is 'free reign' for creativity and innovation. In general, there are numerous way to provide an alternative.

19.5 How to Check Documents for Accessibility

Checking documents for accessibility is most effective with a combination of manual and automated approaches. While an automated tool cannot be used on its own to ensure a document is accessible, it can be helpful when used with a manual audit. A manual audit consists of assessing a document against each of the guidelines. Manual assessment includes testing all interactive elements with a keyboard to ensure keyboard access, logical focus order and visibility of focus indicator. The tester or auditor will also check reading order of the content, reviewing alternative text to ensure its appropriateness, etc. Often testers will use assistive technology such as screen readers and voice activation software to test the document and better understand the experience for someone using assistive technology. Testers navigate a document without a mouse, using keyboard-only techniques to ensure that people with print disabilities can navigate easily.

In a normal workflow, each organization will need to decide who checks documents for accessibility. This can include Marketing, Communications, one of the Content Editors, or an Accessibility expert. Thus, someone who understands accessibility needs to take on this responsibility.

On two occasions, the authors were requested to remediate a complaint form a user had identified as inaccessible. The irony is obviously not lost—a user is unable to use a complaint form to complain about the lack of accessibility of material, because they were unable to complete the inaccessible form.

List of Typical Issues Found When Checking Documents

1. Untagged documents.
2. Illogical reading order.
3. Irregular tables.
4. Data tables with incorrect table headers.
5. Incorrectly nested headings.
6. Headings which appear to be headings, but are not tagged as such.
7. Document title not set.
8. Language not defined in properties or is set to the wrong language.
9. Image without alt text.
10. Colour contrast issues.
11. Form elements without tooltips for those using assistive technology.
12. Illogical focus order for form elements.
13. Author listed as an individual and not the organization/company.

19.6   Issues in Academic Publishing and the Shift to EPUB

When thinking about 'publishing' we tend to think only of formal publishing, for example an academic publishing house for books and journals. Publishing houses are now equipped to produce documents in the ePUB format. In Australia, government agencies are required to produce an Annual Report, and this is a publication, albeit a more informal form with a small distribution. Governments have typically produced this document in PDF, printed and submitted to the government for approval, and then posted online as a PDF. If they decide to publish this as an ePUB document, a simple method is needed for an organization to produce this form of the document.

There are advantages for electronic publishing in contrast to the traditional physical monograph in terms of ease of distribution. This is especially true when it concerns the distribution of material for people with disabilities. Many people with disabilities have been disadvantaged in education, recreation, and employment because of print access (Konicek et al. 2003). There has been some disagreement between authors, conference committees, and publishing houses regarding formats required for academic publishing. This is particularly obvious with conferences or journals, involved in the field of digital accessibility. Publishers often insist upon a format and provide a template, causing issues for the user of the publication, with the result of an inaccessible publication. According to House, Orme and Bide, the publishers have been accused of deliberately locking the print disabled out of content. Publishers did not understand accessibility at the time, and how to implement best accessibility practice, a situation that is changing. Writers of conference papers and journals often do not understand digital accessibility as it relates to documents, even when their own discipline relates to overall accessibility issues (House et al. 2018, p. 31). As conference chairs, authors, programme chairs, peer reviewers and document remediators, we have observed these issues first-hand, with frustration.

Conference organizers issue statements to authors that they need to ensure submitted copy is accessible, and often provide a list of requirements and templates, stipulating font, size, justification requirement, alternative text for images/tables/graphs, MathML for equations, use of simple versus complex tables, proper structure such as headings etc. Most authors tend to ignore this information in their desire to submit a paper to a reputable journal or conference. Conference organizers are often under time constraints and often return the paper for accessibility revision by the author. The author may not know how or has been given an inaccessible template to use. The conference organizers may attempt to fix the document themselves, but not have the subject matter experts (SME's) available to properly describe the graphic content.

Everyone in the publication chain needs to ensure they do not rely solely on the advances in technology to solve the problems of digital accessibility in the publishing industry. As House et al. state, 'making all publications accessible to people with print impairments at the same time and at the same price as for readers without impairment—is made massively simpler by technology' (House et al. 2018).

Kasdorf discusses a number of issues that make it problematic to produce accessible academic publications and states '...publishers have typically been reluctant to invest in the effort to make their publications fully accessible' (Kasdorf 2018, p. 11). He states several reasons for this including some of the difficulties involving MathML and the fact that many browser systems do not render math correctly. Despite the publishing constraints like cost, workflow, author vs publisher responsibility etc., Kasdorf states many of the issues can be handled through the move to the ePUB3 format.

19.7   Publishing Formats

Kasdorf discusses the issues of PDF for academic publishing with various professionals including George Kerscher, Chief Innovation Officer of the DAISY Consortium (Kercher in Kasdorf 2018, p. 12), who stated, 'The inherent accessibility of an EPUB far surpasses that of PDF in many ways'. This view is substantiated by Madeleine Rothberg of the National Center for Accessible Media who stated in Kasdorf's paper 'ePUB is better on structural grounds and far easier to author for accessibility than PDF is' (Rothberg in Kasdorf 2018, p. 12).

Surprisingly, one of the basic issues for digital accessibility in publications, from website to document is that of image description. For many in the accessibility discipline, this is 'Accessibility 101', describing images to enable the user with assistive technology to understand the meaning (W3C 2008). This means not just giving a literal description of what is in the image, but what information the image provides. The situation becomes difficult and costly for the publisher. They often employ SME's to describe the image or rely on the author's ability to do it properly and provide the information. Obviously, the author is the one most likely to have the information, but they often do not understand how or why to provide the description. This becomes problematic for complex graphs, mathematical equations, etc. Stating something is a graph containing the results of the work is not the equivalent information the visual user receives. Providing a graphic relying on the use of colour to differentiate information, does not provide the colour blind user with meaningful information. Complex legends are elements the person with cognitive limitations would struggle to comprehend. Unless the publisher has the SME's in-house, the author will need information on the requirements to provide this information correctly at the time of writing. It is much easier to create something accessible by design, than to retrofit.

We tend to view new publications in the 'born digital' concept, but as Kasdorf states, this does not mean 'born accessible'. Although HTML5 and ePUB3 possess the 'ability' to be accessible, this does not mean they 'ensure' accessibility. Knowledge is required to use them properly.

One issue still proving problematic is the use of mathematical equations, necessary for statistical proof and result demonstration in academic publications. Publishers are now using MathML when producing equations. However, according to Kerscher, MathML 'almost never makes it downstream to the user of assistive technology' (Kasdorf 2018, p. 17). Browsers have not yet fully incorporated the ability to render MathML. Browser software is relied upon by ePUB reading systems, which do not effectively render math. One of the solutions discussed in Kersher's work is MathJax, which uses JavaScript (Cervone et al. 2016a, b):

> One can use MathJax (and its accessibility extension) in ePUB if there is a JavaScript engine available. Alternatively they can use MathJax to pre-render Maths (e.g. as SVG (and automatically generate alternative text/descriptions for the elements (Sorge 2018).

MathJax, as a result of research in accessibility, is used extensively in the production of books and journals containing mathematical equations. DAISY, Benetech and others are also working on methods to ensure publishers can create accessible math including the textual description for interpretation by assistive technology (Cervone et al. 2016a, b; Kasdorf 2018).

Access to 'remediated' published material has also been a contentious issue. In the USA, once a published item has been remediated for a single user's needs (such as a journal article or textbook for a student), the material can only be provided for the individual student and cannot be shared with other students with similar needs (Kasdorf 2018, p. 14). This places a financial burden on the university, requiring the work to be repeated if required. In the UK, the Equalities Act 2010 grants an exception with specific limitations to allow access to the material once remediated

(House et al. 2018, p. 32). The goal of the Marrakesh Treaty to Facilitate Access to Published Works for Persons Who Are Blind, Visually Impaired or Otherwise Print Disabled is to establish exceptions allowing sharing of documents between participating countries. This enables people who are visually impaired and print disabled to access accessible documents, while discouraging unauthorized copying of documents (World Intellectual Property Association (WIPO) 2013).

Some publishers are now seeking accessibility certification of publications to ensure they meet international accessibility requirements and to secure competitive advantage. Firms such as Benetech, a Silicon Valley not-for-profit organization have developed similar schemes.

> "Global Certified Accessible is part of Benetech's Born Accessible initiative, which encourages the education community to request accessible digital content and engages the publishing community to produce content that is accessible from the moment it is created. As a result of the recently released ePUB Accessibility Specification 1.0 and the growing demand for accessible materials, leading publishers and educational institutions are increasing their support for accessibility as a business and a classroom imperative" (Benetech 2018).

As mentioned above, the internationally accepted standard for publishing is now ePUB. To assist with the work required, Google has funded a resource for publishers, educators, developers and consumers, through a DAISY Consortium initiative (Inclusive Publishing 2018b). The following website acts as a hub with four main areas of resources:

19.7.1   EPUB Accessibility Specifications

EPUB Accessibility 1.0 sets the guidelines in which to authors and evaluators can evaluate content against. This provides a means of certifying accessible ePUB documents. To meet conformance formal requirements, need to be met. It's important to recognize that these guidelines stand on their own without repeating the requirements of WCAG. While the requirements are not the same, WCAG remains relevant and important in creating accessible ePUB documents. EPUB Accessibility 1.0 adds requirements that are not a part of WCAG, meaning an ePUB Publication can conform to WCAG without conforming to EPUB Accessibility 1.0 (www.idpf.org/epub/a11y/) (International Digital Publishing Forum 2017).

19.7.2   Ace by DAISY

The DAISY Consortium created Ace by DAISY, a free and open source accessibility checking tool. This tool helps to evaluate ePUB documents based on the EPUB Accessibility 1.0 requirements helping authors and publisher assess for conformance. As an automated checker it can replace the manual audit process, however, it does assist in the reviewing (https://inclusivepublishing.org/toolbox/accessibility-checker/) (Inclusive Publishing 2018a).

19.7.3   EPUB 3 Support Grid

The Grid is a resource complying and sharing information regarding ePUB3 support, including what support is available on reading systems, apps and devices for accessibility features. The Book Industry Study Group's Content Structure Committee heads up the work to provide results of tests conducted by publishers, service providers, and vendors (http://epubtest.org/) (Book Industry Support Group 2018).

19.7.4   Inclusive Publishing

Inclusive Publishing is a DAISY Consortium Initiative. This information hub provides relevant news and events. It also has a host of resources and advice for creating content accessible for all (https://inclusivepublishing.org) (Inclusive Publishing 2018c).

Kasdorf and others such as the IDPF and W3C share the sentiment that ePUB is the way of the future, "There is worldwide interest in EPUB 3—this fully accessible digital publishing standard will change the world forever" (Kasdorf 2018, p. 12).

19.8   W3C and Publishing

The World Wide Web Consortium (W3C) has been involved in developing standards since it began. Since publishing has been extensively web based for years, it is only natural W3C moved towards developing adequate publishing standards for web-based publications. In this effort, it launched a Publishing Working Group (PWG) in June 2017 with the Charter active until 2020:

> The mission of the Publishing Working Group is to enable all publications—with all their specificities and traditions—to become first-class entities on the Web. The group will provide the necessary technologies on the Open Web Platform to make the combination of traditional publishing and the Web complete in terms of accessibility, usability, portability, distribution, archiving, offline access, and reliable cross referencing

Part of the charter for the PWG is to produce ePUB 4 and in the charter, it states:

> "EPUB has become one of the fundamental technologies for the global publishing ecosystem … It is the preferred format for a broad range of types of publications, not only for distribution but increasingly also for authoring and production workflows. As part of the work on Web Publications, described in this charter, it is essential that a next generation of EPUB,

currently referred to as EPUB 4, retain the specificity, portability, predictability, accessibility, and internationalization required by the publishing ecosystem while benefitting from the improved features and functionalities offered by Packaged Web Publications. EPUB 4 should not be in conflict with Web Publications; it should be a type of Web Publication that provides the predictability and interoperability that this ecosystem has come to rely on" (W3C 2018).

Discussing the importance of the development of ePUB4, Kasdorf states that as publishing has moved from print dominance to web dominance, it has motivated the merger of the International Digital Publishing Forum (IDPF) with W3C (W3C 2017). This means 'future publications will be able to make use of all the features available on the Web, and produce publications that can be displayed, without any specific actions, in any Web browser' (Kasdorf 2017a). Discussing the importance of this merger, Kerscher states 'By combining our organizations, we not only align our technology roadmaps, but also accelerate the adoption of content that is natively accessible and device-friendly for all types of publishing, whether you are reading on the Web or offline' (W3C 2017).

19.9   The Document Journey

Most PDF documents on the web are not created in the format in which they are shared. Typically, a PDF document (mostly text, linear format) begin life as an MS Word document. A PDF brochure (graphics, creative layout) often starts life as an InDesign document. Documents are converted to their published formats, usually via 'Save as' or 'Export' although some are converted using third-party products, e.g. PDFCreator. Features existing in the original document do not always transfer to the final PDF version. Issues exist relating to consistency and reliability with multiple methods.

19.10   Changing Standards

19.10.1   Traditional Publishing Standards and Practices

Until recently, standard practice was to produce a document using InDesign or Microsoft Word and save it in PDF or at best PDF/UA, believing it would be accessible. The 'UA' stands for 'Universal Accessibility', and is designed to allow for greater accessibility and reliability in PDF (May (2013). Kerscher discusses the limitations of PDF, even when optimized by the PDF/UA specification, stating that it is not considered capable of competing with the new web and ePUB-based specifications. 'We are testing the accessibility of EPUB with a full range of reading systems on all platforms, and the use by persons who are blind, those who have low vision and need to increase the font size, or persons with dyslexia and learning disabilities who benefit by a change in font, increase spacing between lines, etc. The nature of PDF prevents these types of presentational changes' (Kerscher in Kasdorf 2018, p. 12).

19.10.2 EPub Challenges

For the informal publisher, the process of converting digital documents into accessible ePUB documents can be complicated. There are many software tools offering to convert source documents into ePUB format, but they are inconsistent, and assistive technology, such as a screen reader is often unable read the final product. The support of HTML in ePUB is a catalyst for accessibility professionals to recommend it. It is unfortunate many open source conversion tools do not maintain accessibility features such as, headings, alternative text, bookmarks, etc. to the ePUB file. PDF, although popular amongst organizations for documents, loses much of the structure needed to create an accessible ePUB when converted from other programmes such as Adobe Acrobat's InDesign or Microsoft Word. Without a basis for accessibility in a PDF document, the option is creating an accessible document in the authoring tool to convert its features to an ePUB format. If an author or organization considers the intention of the document, for example that the document will be available digitally, the author can ensure the source document is available for ePUB conversion.

Publishing houses and other publishing professionals typically have their own software tools. Sometimes, they develop software personalized for their own use. By creating both the platform and interface, they have an opportunity to ensure quality of the final product.

Tools and software, are continuing to improve, and new tools are developed, offering easier, and more efficient methods for authors to create accessible ePUB documents. Microsoft are considering a 'save as ePUB' that would work in a manager similar to the 'save as PDF' for the future, however, a date for release has not yet been announced.

19.11 Discussion

There are a number of 'best practice' guidelines for creating accessible documents that are highlighted below. Using these guidelines does not guarantee perfect accessibility for everyone, however, incorporating best practice procedures will assist with the production of a more easily navigated and understood document.

Heading Structure

Accessible documents contain appropriate heading structure. This structure is based on 'Headings' "styling elements or tags. Headings provide a hierarchy of information, which is then portrayed through assistive technology. For this reason, an author should change the style of a heading level to be suitable to the document design rather than not use headings or use incorrectly nested headings because of preset heading styles. As a rule, there should only be one heading Level 1 (H1) per page. H1 identifies the highest level of information in the document structure. An H1 is used for chapter titles—main section headings representing the top level of information. Headings should be consistent and each level nested in a hierarchical order. To nest headings correctly a heading level 1 (H1) would describe the main purpose of the document, following but a heading level 2 (H2), followed by a H2 or heading level 3 (H3), an H3 would be followed by a H3 or a heading level 4 and so forth.

Text Alternatives

Images, infographics and graphs require text alternatives. For informative images, descriptive alternative text is applied. Assistive technology reads aloud the alternative text, ensuring the reader does not miss information. Purely decorative images which convey no information, may be tagged as artefact, background or decorative, enabling assistive technology to omit announcing the images and not present them to the reader. The alternative options for infographics, charts and graphs can include a descriptive paragraph, a data table or alt text. These ensure the reader of the document understands the information being conveyed.

Data Tables

Data tables should have table headers applied. Assistive technology reads tables row by row across the columns, which may not make sense to someone using a screen reader or Braille display. Tagging table headers enables these technologies to give context for each data cell to the reader. For example, a screen reader will read the table header cell first prior to each data cell. Tables are sometimes used for layout purpose but can sound cluttered and confusing for screen reader users. Document creators also have the option of using the table summary element. When done correctly, the screen reader user will hear that there is a table present with 'x' rows and 'x' columns.

Reading Order

Assistive technology relies on the reading order of a document to be logical and flow in a manner that does not confuse or change the context of the content. By checking and correcting the reading order, the author provides the reader using assistive technology an opportunity to understand the content in the way it was intended.

Colour Contrast

According to The Colour Blindness Awareness Organisation, colour blindness affects approximately 1 in 12 men and 1 in 200 women worldwide (Colour Blind Awareness 2017). This statistic highlights the need to examine colour contrast in documents. People who are colour blind, have reduced vision or other vision impairments require contrast between text and background to read it. Consider the way that colour is used. Colour alone should not be the only way to portray information. Readers who cannot see colour are unable to access the information.

19.12 Future Directions

By now you may be wondering about the future for published documents. Some are wondering if we will have printed documents in the future, and if we will continue to produce physical documents. There will always be historical records in the physical form. For many who love the texture of a physical book in our hands, we hope they will not disappear.

When examining digital publishing, change is inevitable. How many of us will print out online documents in the future? Many of us are looking forward to the time when we will not need to print, sign and scan/email documents because an organization requires an original signature. Perhaps we will see a biometric method for signing documents become the norm.

Perhaps the most significant change will be universal reading software to allow a user to read a document in any form. Allowing the reader, particularly those with disabilities the choice of how to read or complete a document will be a major advance for the publishing world.

Kasdorf's final comment sums up the desire of everyone associated with document accessibility:

> We are not far from the day when the version of a book or a journal article that is suitable for a user who needs assistive technology is not a special version at all: it is just the same EPUB that everybody else gets. And it is available for the same price, and at the same time, as the copy that everyone else gets (Kasdorf 2018, p. 18).

19.13 Author's Opinion of the Field

When we think about digital accessibility, we are usually thinking 'website accessibility'. The reality is that everything we access with an Internet connection, is considered 'digital' and comes under the International Standards, usually the Web Content Accessibility Guidelines (WCAG 2.1 currently, and its subsequent iterations). For many users the inaccessibility of documents is far more than a nuisance. They are unable to read the document, sign when necessary and generally interact with material from legal forms to online books, putting them at a distinct disadvantage. While the International standard is moving to ePUB, the authors are of the opinion this will not be complete until it is universal and not only for the formal publishing houses. It does not necessarily follow that an ePUB built upon HTML will automatically be more accessible. We still need to face the accessibility challenges described in this chapter, including complex issues of mathematical equations, technical drawings and graphs. We believe the merger of the standards under W3C, will provide the impetus for a more accessible publishing future.

There is considerable optimism in the adoption of international publishing standards, we need to understand that issues of digital accessibility apply equally to documents and websites.

19.14 Conclusions

In this chapter, the authors have examined a number of issues regarding informal and formal publishing, including history, format, accessibility issues in publishing, and changing standards. We have examined some of the current problems encountered when publishing documents in different formats and we conclude there is not a 'one size fits all' publishing option. We do, however, see movement towards that goal.

References

Adobe (2018a) Accessibility features Adobe Acrobat Reader. https://helpx.adobe.com/in/reader/using/accessibility-features.html

Adobe (2018b) InDesign: the next page in layout design. https://www.adobe.com/au/products/indesign.html

Benetech (2018). Benetech establishes global certified accessible program to ensure content serves all students equally. https://benetech.org/benetech-establishes-global-certified-accessible-program-to-ensure-content-serves-all-students-equally/

Book Industry Support Group (2018) EPUB3 support grid. http://epubtest.org/

Cervone D, Krautzberger P, Sorge V (2016a) New accessibility features in MathJax. J Technol Pers Disabil 4:167–175

Cervone D, Krautzberger P, Sorge V (2016b) Towards universal rendering in MathJax

Cicerchia M (2015) Visual impairment in the classroom. https://www.readandspell.com/visual-impairment-in-the-classroom

Colour Blind Awareness (2017) Colour blind awareness. http://www.colourblindawareness.org/

CommonLook (2018) CommonLook PDF global access—product overview. https://commonlook.com/accessibility-software/commonlook-pdf-globalaccess/commonlook-pdf/

Gilakjani AP (2012) Visual, auditory, kinaesthetic learning styles and their impacts on English language teaching. J Stud Educ 2(1):104–113. https://doi.org/10.5296/jse.v2i1.1007

House E, Orme R, Bide M (2018) Towards universal accessibility: the UK policy landscape and supporting technology. Learn Publ 31(1):31–34. https://doi.org/10.1002/leap.1144

Inclusive Publishing. (2018a) ACE by Daisy, accessibility checking tool. https://inclusivepublishing.org/toolbox/accessibility-checker/

Inclusive Publishing (2018b) Your information hub for creating digital publications for all. https://inclusivepublishing.org/. Accessed 2 May 2018

Inclusive Publishing (2018c) Your information hug for creating digital publications for all. https://inclusivepublishing.org/

International Digital Publishing Forum (2017) EPUB accessibility 1.0: conformance and discovery requirements for EPUB publications. http://www.idpf.org/epub/a11y/

Kasdorf B (2017a) The importance and the need for ePUB 4. https://w3c.github.io/publ-bg/docs/EPUB4_business_case.html

Kasdorf B (2017b) Publishing@W3C: the convergence is well underway. http://apexcovantage.com/blog/publishingw3c/

Kasdorf B (2018) Why accessibility is hard and how to make it easier: lessons from publishers. Learn Publ 31(1):11–18. https://doi.org/10.1002/leap.1146

Konicek K, Hyzny J, Allegra R (2003) Electronic reserves: the promise and challenge to increase accessibility. Libr Hi Tech 21(1):102–108. https://doi.org/10.1108/07378830310467445

Kurzweil R (2018) Kurzweil computer products: excerpt from the age of spiritual machines. http://www.kurzweiltech.com/kcp.html

May M (2013) Adobe accessibility: what is PDf/UA all about anyway? http://blogs.adobe.com/accessibility/2013/06/pdf-ua-2.html

Microsoft (2018) An inclusive office 365. https://www.microsoft.com/en-us/accessibility/office?activetab=pivot_1%3aprimaryr2

Open Access Technologies Inc (2018) Open access technologies. http://www.openaccesstech.com/about/

Rothberg M (2017) Industry update (wileyonlinelibrary.com) Received: 1 Oct 2017|Accepted: 21 Nov 2017. Publishing with accessibility standards from the inside out. Learn Publ 2018(31):45–47. https://doi.org/10.1002/leap.1149

Sorge V (2018) Accessibility and MathJax. Accessed 20 June 2018

Vision Australia Submission to the Inquiry into current levels of access and attainment for students with disability in the school system, and the impact on students and families associated with inadequate levels of support (2015)

W3C (2008) Understanding WCAG 2.0: non-text content, understanding SC 1.1.1. http://www.w3.org/TR/UNDERSTANDING-WCAG20/text-equiv-all.html

W3C (2013) Guidance on applying WCAG 2.0 to non-web information and communications technologies (WCAG2ICT). http://www.w3.org/TR/wcag2ict/

W3C (2017) New roadmap for future of publishing is underway as W3C and IDPF officially combine (Press release). https://www.w3.org/2017/01/pressrelease-idpf-w3c-combination.html.en

W3C (2018) Publishing working group charter. https://www.w3.org/2017/04/publ-wg-charter/

World Intellectual Property Association (WIPO) (2013) Summary of the Marrakesh treaty to facilitate access to published works for persons who are blind, visually impaired, or otherwise print disabled (MVT). http://www.wipo.int/treaties/en/ip/marrakesh/summary_marrakesh.html

Chapter 20
Inclusively Designed Authoring Tools

Jutta Treviranus, Jan Richards and Colin Clark

Abstract Authoring tools play two very critical roles in Web accessibility. They offer a powerful mechanism for promoting the creation of accessible Web content. They are also the key to ensuring that people with disabilities are not just consumers, but also producers of Web content, an essential criterion for full participation in our Web-mediated society. This chapter discusses the important role that inclusively design authoring tools play in achieving equitable participation in the complex adaptive system that is the Web.

20.1 Introduction

It would be no exaggeration to say that the Web has become a fundamental element of our society and daily life. Almost all critical functions are mediated in some way through the Web, from education, to employment, entertainment, civic engagement, commerce, and socialization. Equitable participation in our society requires access to the Web. To date the primary focus of Web accessibility advocacy has been on Web content accessibility. Implicit in this prioritization is the assumption that people with disabilities are primarily consumers, not producers of Web content. Another assumption is that it is realistic to expect all Web authors to understand and consistently apply Web Content Accessibility Guidelines. There are problems with both these assumptions. Authoring tools provide a means to circumvent these problematic assumptions.

Most Web content is created using some type of authoring tool with relatively few authors continuing to code Web pages by hand using raw HTML. These authoring

J. Treviranus (✉) · C. Clark
Inclusive Design Research Centre, OCAD University, Toronto, ON, USA
e-mail: jtreviranus@ocadu.ca

C. Clark
e-mail: cclark@ocadu.ca

J. Richards
Inclusive Design Research Centre, Metrolinx, Toronto, ON, USA
e-mail: jan.richards2@gmail.com

© Springer-Verlag London Ltd., part of Springer Nature 2019   357
Y. Yesilada and S. Harper (eds.), *Web Accessibility*, Human–Computer
Interaction Series, https://doi.org/10.1007/978-1-4471-7440-0_20

tools greatly influence the Web content created: some markup is automatically generated for the author by the tool, the tool presents authors with choices and advice, authors are offered pre-authored content and templates, and authors are assisted in checking and revising their content. Each of these tool functions presents an opportunity to promote the creation of accessible Web content or, conversely, a risk of introducing accessibility barriers, often without author awareness.

Similarly, the ability for people with disabilities to participate in producing content, media, interactions, or applications is dependent on the accessibility of the authoring tool interface. From a systems-thinking perspective, the larger Web ecosystem will only become more equitable once persons with disabilities can participate fully in constructing and advancing the ecosystem. This requires accessible authoring and development tools.

This chapter will discuss the role authoring tools can play in promoting broader, proactive compliance to Web accessibility guidelines and the importance of authoring tools in the equal participation of people with disabilities in our Web-mediated society.

20.2   Overview of the Field

A cursory review of publishing and discourse on the topic of Web accessibility shows a preponderance of information, legislation, and discussion regarding Web content accessibility and Web content accessibility guidelines with less focus on authoring by people with disabilities or the use of authoring tools to promote accessibility. The Web Accessibility Initiative of the World Wide Web Consortium (W3C-WAI) was established in April 1997 with three major guideline initiatives: Web content, authoring tools, and user agents. Since then at least 40 jurisdictions around the world have adopted legislation regarding Web content accessibility, the majority based upon the W3C Web Content Accessibility Guidelines (WCAG).

The Authoring Tools Accessibility Guidelines 1.0 (ATAG) first became a W3C recommendation with version 1.0 in February 2000. ATAG version 2.0 followed in September 2015. These guidelines describe how to create a Web authoring tool that both assists all authors to create accessible Web content (that conforms to WCAG) and that can be used by people with disabilities. The guidelines are primarily intended for developers of authoring tools. Authoring tools are very broadly defined to encompass any Web-based or non-Web-based application(s) that can be used by authors (alone or collaboratively) to create or modify Web content for use by other people (other authors or end users) (Richards et al. 2015). The "for other people" requirement rules out the many Web applications that allow people to modify Web content that only they themselves experience (e.g., Web-based email display settings) or that only provide input to automated processes (e.g., library catalog search page).

Authoring tools include the following:

- Web page authoring tools (e.g., WYSIWYG HTML editors);
- software for directly editing source code;
- software for converting to Web content technologies (e.g., "Save as HTML" features in office document applications);
- integrated development environments (e.g. for Web application development);
- software that generates Web content on the basis of templates, scripts, command-line input, or "wizard"-type processes;
- software for rapidly updating portions of Web pages (e.g., blogging, wikis, online forums);
- software for generating/managing entire Websites (e.g., content management systems, courseware tools, content aggregators);
- email clients that send messages using Web content technologies;
- multimedia authoring tools;
- software for creating mobile Web applications.

In the almost 20 years since ATAG 1.0 became a recommendation there has been increasing interest in accessibility by authoring tool developers, but there is still a long way to go before authors will be able to rely on their tools to create accessible content in the way that they can already rely on them to produce browser-interoperable or consistently formatted content. This is partly due to the unstable or volatile authoring tool market. Over the two decades, several applications have approached ATAG compliance only to be merged and absorbed. Research projects demonstrate the viability of ATAG compliance in promising prototypes but fail to transfer to mainstream markets. Aspects of ATAG guidelines have been adopted by document authoring tools; however, the accessible content produced may not survive conversion.

The lack of readily available ATAG functionality has resulted in the proliferation of inaccessible content and the need for costly remediation. A new industry has emerged whose primary function is to repair and remediate inaccessible content. Governments and other public institutions have resorted to removing access to content that does not comply when the cost and effort of repairing the content become too burdensome. One recent example is the removal of over twenty thousand free video lectures by the University of California, Berkeley following a Department of Justice complaint (Ernst 2017). The tragedy of this incidence is that students with disabilities are both blamed for the removal and among the students most in need of affordable access to content.

Other chapters in this book cover the fundamental importance of Web accessibility to the lives of people with disability but also to society as a whole. The economic, educational and social impact of lack of equal access to the Web is grave and far-reaching. Policy, advocacy, and legislation encouraging Web accessibility have focused on the Web Content Accessibility Guidelines. Despite legislation in many jurisdictions (some with very serious consequences associated with noncompliance) episodic snapshots of the state of Web accessibility globally, beginning with the United Nations Nomensa study in 2006 show that the majority of Web sites, including government Web sites, are still not WCAG compliant. It would appear that current strategies to encourage Web accessibility have not been as successful as hoped and efforts should be focused on new or additional strategies. Web accessibility advocacy based solely on WCAG assume that all Web authors can acquire the specialized knowledge required to meet the guidelines. However, authoring tools have become so ubiquitous and automated that at this point Web authors comprise a wide cross-section of the population, including professional Web editors, employees whose occasional task it is to author Web content, grandparents, young children, and hobbyists. To fully understand and adhere to the accessibility guidelines requires strong motivation and commitment on the part of the authors. The authors must also constantly update their knowledge as technologies change.

Another support for accessible Web content is the use of checking or evaluation tools (Abou-Zahra 2007). These tools process a Web page or site to detect and report any accessibility issues. The checking tools detect as many problems as possible automatically but leave a number of issues to human judgment that cannot be automatically detected (e.g., that alt-text is appropriate). Some tools guide the author through a series of questions to determine whether the content is accessible. The difficulty with a checker-only approach is that the checking occurs once the Web content has already been created. Addressing Web accessibility problems at this stage requires retrofitting existing content and occasionally completely recreating a site. Many authors rely solely on the automatic checking component of these tools, ignoring the time-consuming manual checking steps that are required to assess conformance with some aspects of WCAG.

Authoring tools that are compliant to ATAG address these barriers to creating accessible content. Theoretically, using an ATAG compliant authoring tool to produce accessible content does not require knowledge of the WCAG guidelines or even motivation or commitment to create accessible content on the part of the content author. An authoring tool can encourage accessible practices and accessible authoring choices from the very beginning, thereby precluding costly and onerous retrofitting or reworking of sites. However, before this strategy can be effective, ATAG compliant authoring tools must be developed and broadly deployed. The advocacy effort to achieve this should not be as difficult as achieving WCAG compliance as the number of developers of authoring tools is far smaller than the number of authors of Web content. What is needed is a concerted effort by policymakers, advocates and companies developing authoring tools.

It appears, however, that there is a nascent recognition of the strategic role of authoring tools in the Web accessibility ecosystem with many fragmented efforts to support accessible authoring.

At the time of publication, examples of good practices include the following:

- accessibility wizards and checkers in Microsoft Office suite and Adobe Acrobat;
- accessible authoring support in Google Doc and Drive;
- ATAG 2.0 support in the open source content management system Drupal (Drupal Groups 2011);
- ATAG 2.0 support in the textbox.io editor (Textbox.io 2016), and

- ATAG 2.0 support in the XHTML WYSIWYG editor XStandard (XStandard 2018);
- Browser extensions such as Web Developer, which add developer tools to a browser, including accessibility supports (Pederick 2018);
- Community efforts to support accessible authoring of educational content such as the REBUS project for accessible open textbooks online (Rebus Community 2017);
- Media accessibility tools such as CADET: Caption and Description Editing Tool by the National Center for Accessible Media (National Centre for Accessible Media 2017).

There are hopeful signs that the trend toward integration of accessibility in the authoring process will become expected functionality in Web authoring tools. This can be boosted by focusing on equivalent advocacy toward authoring as has been focused on Web content accessibility guidelines.

20.3 Encouraging the Creation of Accessible Content

Authoring tools influence the design of the Web content created in a large number of explicit ways but also in some that are subtle and even hidden. The styles of influence differ according to the type of tool used whether it is a WYSIWYG tool, a tool that supports direct manipulation of the markup or a tool that automatically converts content to a Web format. Web accessibility is largely based upon the choice of formats or technologies used (e.g., W3C open standards), the appropriate choice and use of markup (e.g., use of headers rather than fixed text styling), the creation of equivalent content in accessible formats (e.g., alt-text, captions, descriptions), appropriate structuring and description of content (e.g., for forms, tables, document structure) and avoidance of certain content or authoring techniques (e.g., blinking, color-coding). Authoring tools can generate accessible content, influence the choices made, guide and support good authoring practices, educate in explicit or subtle ways and encourage the adoption of accessible authoring habits and conventions.

Little research has been conducted to determine the most effective means of encouraging accessible authoring practices. General user interface design research can be applied, but even here much of the research is anecdotal. Determining the criteria for successful support of accessible authoring within an authoring tool is a rich and worthwhile research agenda that can be informed by user interface design research and research into change management and learning. This section outlines some of the techniques gleaned from informal heuristic evaluations, anecdotal observations, and experiences contributed by tool designers in developing ATAG versions 1.0 (Treviranus et al. 2000) and 2.0 (Richards et al. 2015).

Many authoring tools or authoring tool functions make choices for authors by automatically generating markup, structure or file formats. This includes the choice of markup in WYSIWYG tools and conversion-to-HTML functions in Word Processors.

These automatic processes can deploy accessible technologies or markup by default. This is a highly reliable and predictable method of creating accessible content.

When the author has a choice, given that there are accessible choices and inaccessible choices (or more and less accessible choices), there are many strategies that can be employed to ensure or encourage an accessible choice. These choices may be presented in menus, toolbars, dialog boxes, palettes, or other user interface mechanisms. At the most basic level, the choices available should include accessible choices. This is not always the case. For novice or less experienced authors the order of choices influences the choice made, the first choices are the most likely to be selected. The prominence of the choice may also influence the decision. For example, if the accessible alternative is nested within several layers of menus it is less likely to be chosen than if it is at the top level and obviously displayed. However, for most authors, it is important that the accessible choice not be seen as an add-on or nonintegrated alternative.

Some accessible practices require more than a set of accessible choices and cannot be performed automatically. This includes the creation of alt-text or other equivalent content such as captions for audio content, labels for form or table elements and other authoring practices. In these cases, authoring tools can use various mechanisms to guide and support authors such as dialog boxes, wizards or intelligent agents. Authoring tools can also provide supportive tools such as alt-text libraries to make the task easier.

Wizards, assistants, or intelligent agents have had a mixed reception in user interface design. Wizards are more likely to be received positively when the user wishes to accomplish a goal that has several steps, when the steps need to be completed in a set sequence or when users lack necessary domain knowledge. Wizards that attempt to anticipate a user's choice or intention are frequently dismissed as are wizards that are inflexible or wizards that accomplish tasks that can be accomplished by other means.

While the goal is to encourage accessible authoring, an authoring tool cannot be dictatorial or inflexible, authors will usually respond by making perfunctory steps to comply, finding workarounds that are less than satisfactory from an accessibility perspective, or rejecting the tool. An example of this might be a dialog box that will not let the author proceed unless alt-text is filled into a text field when an image is inserted. The author who wishes to insert the images in a batch will likely fill in any text to proceed rather than taking the time to create an appropriate label. The author should be given sufficient flexibility and leeway regarding the timing, order of steps and choice of authoring options to avoid feeling constrained and at odds with the authoring tool. It may also be the case in multi-person workflows that the person inserting certain content (e.g., images) will be different than the person making that content accessible (e.g., alt-text copy editor).

Similarly, intrusive prompts, pop-up windows, or warnings, although they are powerful mechanisms to address accessibility issues, interrupt the workflow and can be seen as annoying by the author. These are more likely to be well received if the author has chosen to activate them and can turn them off.

An assistive function that has become expected and has gained user trust is the spell-checking function. In standard spell checkers, errors are highlighted in an unobtrusive manner and can be dealt with immediately or in a batch. Similarly, Web authors have come to trust and implement other checking tools for issues such as HTML validity, broken links, and spelling/grammar. Accessibility checking and repair functions integrated into an authoring tool can mimic these more familiar tools to encourage greater acceptance. Checking and repair integrated into an authoring tool has the advantage of enabling checking and repair at the time of authoring when the cost of revision is minor rather than after the fact when a number of dependent steps may need to be reversed to address accessibility problems.

Most authors leave preference settings in the default or "factory preset" state, unless prompted to create a preference profile upon setup. To support the goal of accessible authoring, most accessibility supports, such as accessibility checking and repair, should therefore be 'on' by default.

Many authors implement templates, style sheets, and pre-authored content such as clip art or scripts and applets. This has become even more prevalent with the increased use of dynamic, database-driven Web sites delivered through content management systems. If these templates and pre-authored content elements are WCAG compliant there is a high likelihood that the sites they form the basis of will also be WCAG compliant. However, there are instances when the author should be encouraged to modify the content, for example, when images are to be repurposed, stock alt-text may no longer be appropriate for the new purpose and authors should be instructed to modify the alt-text in line with the new meaning to be communicated by the image.

Pre-authored applets, scripts or online user interface elements that are part of many content management systems including learning management systems should be accessible. With the prevalence of open-source content management projects exemplary accessible components can be shared and freely adapted across systems making it easier to include accessible versions of functionality. Examples of such sets of reusable components are the Fluid Infusion framework and component library (Inclusive Design Research Centre 2016) and the CAST Figuration framework (CAST 2018).

Ideally, accessible authoring should become a natural, integrated part of the authoring workflow. Accessible authoring practices should become habitual and assumed. Standard conventions for existing content types and for emerging content types should include accessible practices. An authoring tool can encourage this by integrating accessibility features and accessible authoring steps into any multistep process, as well as including accessible examples in any examples given in help, tutorials, documentation, or intelligent assistants. All tutorials, help, documentation, or intelligent assistants should integrate accessible authoring practices in the standard authoring practices demonstrated or described.

It's also important to recognize that the lifecycle of Web content is often intertwined with that of office documents. For example, office document reports or presentations may be converted into Web content formats (e.g., HTML, PDF) for wider dissemination. Unfortunately, if the office documents include numerous accessibility issues, it can be onerous to fix these during conversion and potentially a waste of authoring effort if there are subsequent changes to the original office document. Therefore, it would be advisable for the office tools earlier in the lifecycle to support accessible authoring in the same way as tools at the end. Several of the more popular document authoring tools are integrating basic accessibility supports such as checkers.

20.3.1 Authoring Tools that Are Accessible to People with Disabilities

It is just as important that people with disabilities be able to use authoring tools to produce Web content as it is that content be accessible to people with disabilities. This requires that the authoring tool user interface follow standard user interface accessibility guidelines. Standard accessible user interface techniques are ably covered in a number of resources and will not be addressed in this chapter (Treviranus et al. 2000). In addition to standard accessible user interface principles, there are a number of unique accessibility challenges that are presented by the task of authoring that should also be addressed.

One unique accessibility challenge associated with authoring is that the default presentation or rendering of the content that the author is creating may not be accessible to the author. The author should, therefore, be able to configure the tool interface and rendering of the content independent of the final default rendering, while authoring. For example, an author with low vision may require text to be presented in a 46-point size with a dark background and light foreground text. This may not be the desired rendering of the Web site the author is creating. This can be addressed by allowing the author to adjust the presentation of the user interface and content without affecting the styling of the authored content.

Standard authoring tasks include cutting, copying, moving and pasting content. Typically, this involves mouse-based, visually dependent highlighting, dragging, and dropping. When the application is designed accessibly this can be achieved using keyboard equivalents, however, moving to and selecting the desired chunk of content can be a considerable challenge when relying on the keyboard. Enabling navigation using the structure (e.g., from one H1 to the next, through all H2s nested within an H1 and then to the first paragraph) and selection of structural chunks (e.g., header, body, paragraph, etc.) makes this important task much more efficient and accessible.

Authoring is frequently a collaborative task. When authoring a largely text-based document, change tracking commonly relies on color-coding and other purely visual cues. Modally independent alternatives must be developed for these cues (e.g., text-based alternatives or markup that can be interpreted as a change in voice if read by a screen reader). When the collaborative environment or application is used to create or to communicate through graphic information, such as a whiteboard application, more creative solutions are needed to make the information and the collaboration accessible. One approach is a whiteboard that offers a palette of vector graphic shapes in place of free-hand drawing. These shapes can be combined or grouped and new combinations can be added to the palette. For example, a triangle on top of a rectangle with smaller rectangles can be combined to be a rudimentary house that can then be added to the palette. If each of these shapes and grouping of shapes has an associated text label, an individual who is blind can decipher the visual model being collaboratively constructed. The facility for a collaborative peer to also add a text description of the graphically presented information will add to the accessibility of the collaboration.

Real-Time Authoring

The most challenging online authoring environments from an accessibility per-spective are communication environments in which the information is created syn-chronously or in real time and must be responded to in real time. These include text chats, voice over IP, and video over IP. These present a particularly difficult challenge because there is little opportunity to create equivalent content for audio or visual information. Surprisingly even text-chat environments continue to present barriers even though the communication medium is text. The primary accessibility barrier in text chat environments is that screen readers and refreshable Braille dis-plays are unable to logically handle focus. Thus, a screen reader will intersperse speaking a message being constructed by the screen reader user with messages com-ing in from other participants. When real-time communication occurs using speech or video, providing equivalent content such as captions or descriptions is much more challenging. Two options include relying on ad hoc peer captioning or description or using a video or audio relay service (i.e., access to professional transcribers or sign interpreters through a remote link). The communication environment or application should provide input supports to enable this peer or relay translation.

20.4   Discussion and Future Directions

20.4.1   Individual Optimization or "One Size Fits One"

Many Web sites currently offer the opportunity to log in and create a personalized profile that persists on the site, or to express personal preferences regarding the inter-face or content on the site. This provides the opportunity to optimize the site for each individual user. This can be an effective mechanism for delivering individually optimized accessibility as well. Standards and specifications, collectively referred to as "AccessForAll", specify a common language for expressing accessibility pref-erences and needs and a matching set of common terms to describe resources and functions, in very functional terms, that apply to users with and without disabilities (Jackl et al. 2004; Norton and Treviranus 2003; Treviranus et al. 2007). If these are commonly implemented, a user with a disability or any user can have a portable preference profile that they can take from application to application. These profiles can also be context specific to accommodate varying needs caused by the device used, the environment or other circumstances that may cause a shift in needs or preferences. For the site author, this means that all accessibility guidelines do not need to be addressed in a single instance of the site, the content and interface can be dynamically transformed or replaced depending on the user.

This functionality has been implemented in tools such as FLUID UI options or FLOE Learner Options, an extensible component-based open source tool that can be embedded in a Website to enable personalization (Fluid Project 2018). This functionality is being replicated in a browser plug-in called UIO+ (Inclusive Design Research Centre 2018a).

Automated personalization and a portable personal preference manager as cloud services have been the deliverables of a number of projects led by a consortium associated with Raising the Floor and the Global Public Inclusive Infrastructure project (GPII 2018, Raising the Floor 2018).

20.4.2   Automatic and Crowdsourced Accessibility

With the maturation of artificial intelligence and the associated audio and visual pattern recognition, a number of efforts to automate modal translation are emerging. Examples include automated captioning, automated alt-text generation and automated video description. Examples include automatic alt-text on Facebook (Facebook 2018) and automated captioning on YouTube. These have generated a great deal of controversy as early efforts are plagued by errors and sometimes embarrassing or unhelpful mistranslations. There is disagreement whether automatic captions speed and assist manual captioning, and whether automatic alt-text and descriptions promote or work against the responsible human effort to accurately describe visual material (Kafle and Huenerfauth 2017). It is difficult to predict when the threshold of machine translation accuracy will equal or surpass human accuracy. This is likely to be inconsistent across languages, fields, and subject matter. Until that time, human verification will remain good practice.

Crowdsourcing efforts such as Amara offer another alternative. These enlist volunteers as well as professional help to translate and caption video content (Amara 2018). The workflow may include reviewing for accuracy thereby circumventing the drawbacks of purely automated translations.

20.4.3   Learning to Code and Coding to Learn

With the increasing emphasis on digital literacy and the importance of understanding and using code in primary education, code authoring tools are another aspect of authoring that must be addressed to enable full participation by individuals with disabilities. Learning to code is increasingly part of the required curriculum for primary-level students in many countries today. In Canada, coding education is now mandatory in three provinces, and is an encouraged part of the curriculum in most other provinces. Much attention has been paid to the role that learning to code can play in preparing students for employment within the new digital economy. The role of programming in teaching life skills, developing social connections, supporting reflective learning, and cultivating creative thinking, however, has been under-recognized and under-researched. These capacities are increasingly essential for success in the flexible, collaborative, and changing environment of the digital economy.

Students with disabilities, especially those who have language, learning, physical, or cognitive difficulties, are often unable to participate in today's classroom coding activities or are relegated to passive roles while their peers actively engage in solving problems together computationally. Most of the educational programming tools and curricular resources currently in use in classrooms were not designed to be accessible to students with disabilities. Teachers need greater assistance in modifying learning resources to suit their students' needs, and students lack the ability to personalize their learning experience with these tools. Yet students with disabilities often also have the most to gain from the opportunities afforded by learning to code, especially when taught in collaborative and creative settings. Shared programming activities can help contribute to the development of expressive communication, literacy, sequencing, and metacognition—skills that are essential for learning as well as daily life and work.

Today's educational programming systems often do not have sufficient flexibility to accommodate the needs of students who may have difficulty reading or who need additional guidance, time, or help focusing or remembering. Most popular visual programming environments are incompatible or untested with commonly used assistive technologies. Often, programming environments are insufficiently flexible to accommodate system-wide changes to magnification, spacing, or text size, and do not provide simplified modes that help make it easier for students to read or focus on the salient parts of the system. Most current programming environments limit coding representations to either text- or visual-centric forms of presentation and interaction, which limits collaboration between students with disabilities and their peers.

When unable to participate in the activities and technologies required to learn programming, students with disabilities are at a significantly greater risk of being left behind as the new knowledge economy continues to increasingly demand computational literacy as well as the critical and creative thinking necessary to adapt to rapid change and innovation.

While coding is seen primarily as a means for developing skills that will support future employment and career opportunities in technology, coding education is equally important as a way to develop social, daily living, metacognition, and creative skills—coding to learn. Students who are supported in developing self-reflection or metacognition skills regarding their own learning needs are more likely to succeed in the learning process, and to ultimately be better prepared for navigating the constant change and lifelong learning required for participation in the knowledge economy. For all students, especially those with cognitive and learning disabilities, participation in coding lessons can help teach crucial collaborative and communication skills, strategies for problem solving, task sequencing, spatial awareness, and metacognitive skills such as those involved in giving instructions to others. Participation by students with disabilities in shared coding activities also helps support a sense of belonging and equality with their peers in the school community and provides valuable collaborative problem-solving experience for all students. Most importantly, coding provides students with new ways to discover and create personal outlets for communication and creative expression. Learning to code can empower students to be active producers of their digital environments, rather than just consumers of prefabricated apps and games. This empowerment is particularly valuable for those who depend on assistive technologies or personalized user interface adaptations; programming literacy can provide them with new means to reconfigure, script, or develop their own personally tailored access tools and features.

Some strategies for establishing inclusive coding to learn environments are the following:

- Supporting multiple simultaneous representation of a program's structure, composition, and state. Students should be able to create programs using visual, textual, auditory (such as text to speech) or haptic (e.g., robot or game-based) interfaces, and share these programs with students who use a different representation.
- Providing the ability for instructors or students to define customized goals, rewards, and learning scaffolds, to help support fine-grained, incremental skill development.
- Enabling users to personalize the coding environment's user interface, including simplification modes that support incremental learning; display flexibility; support for alternative modes of control, including eye gaze and switch access.
- Designing collaborative, creative programming activities in which each student may use their own personalized interface while also being able to work on shared projects and learning activities together with peers.

Some work has already been done to apply these and other techniques for making coding more accessible. For example, the Noodle (Lewis 2014) and Blocks4all (Milne 2017) environments provide text-to-speech based interfaces that aim to make node-based and block-based programming paradigms more accessible to programmers with visual impairments. The AccessCS4all project provides an accessible curriculum and a new programming language, Quorum, which is designed to support students with disabilities (Ladner and Stefik 2017). Robot-based programming, in combination with explicit instruction pedagogy, has been used successfully to teach students with intellectual disabilities how to program using the Blockly environment (Taylor 2017).

Given commitments to equitable education, this is a critical area for further future research and development.

20.5 Author's Opinion of the Field

Despite extensive accessibility advocacy, policy and legislation; relatively few Web authors are aware of accessibility guidelines or knowledgeable in accessible authoring practices or see accessibility as a priority. Moreover, the growth of the Web and the simplification of authoring interfaces has meant that almost everyone is now a Web author in some way. Most authors of Web content, however, use some form of authoring tool to create Web content. Education, advocacy, or compliance evaluation programs will not effectively address the prevalence of inaccessible Web content and sites. These approaches demand skills and conventions that do not match the reality of Web authoring, not all authors need to know the technical minutiae of accessible authoring practices, as all authors do not need to know about HTML to author Web content. Evaluation and repair programs or conformance testing occurs after a Web site is created (often after it is publicly available) causing the author or evaluator to retrofit or rewrite content.

The best and most efficient strategy for insuring that content is accessible is to broadly implement the use of authoring tools that create accessible content. This strategy would ensure that even authors who are not knowledgeable about or moti- vated to create accessible content do so, almost unconsciously. In this way, accessible authoring would also be an integrated part of the process rather than an afterthought, reducing the time required to repair accessibility problems. This approach can be accomplished by promoting—through legislative or policy mechanisms such as pro- curement regulations—the use of authoring tools that are compliant with ATAG.

The Web Accessibility Initiative was founded in an era when there was a clear distinction between content, authoring tools, and browsers or user agents. Today these distinctions are blurring. Many Web environments have become collaborative authoring environments where the distinction between content, authoring, and view- ing becomes an academic rather than practical distinction. Forums, Blogs, Wikis, sites such as Flickr, YouTube, and Facebook, can be seen as content, authoring, and special-purpose user agents. The Web Accessibility Initiative is embarking on a new conception of accessibility guidelines to address this convergence (W3C Web Accessibility Initiative 2018). This new conception could be based on more practical classifications of functionality such as professional and amateur authoring, dynam- ically generated and manually authored content, software development kits, and component libraries. This new conception could also take into account accessibility through personal optimization rather than through a single universally accessible resource.

One of the key challenges the accessibility field has faced is the reputation of accessibility among Web developers. Accessibility has been characterized as anti- innovation, anti-creativity. Developers have been cautioned or prevented from using new technology due to accessibility concerns. Accessibility evaluation is frequently seen as a policing, or punitive function. The sad irony is that the accessibility chal- lenge is more in need of innovation and creativity than many other areas. Fortunately, it can be shown that inclusive design spurs creativity and innovation and benefits everyone. To achieve an inclusive Web, accessibility advocates must work to ally accessibility with innovation and creativity. This can be achieved in large part by focusing on integrated accessible authoring rather than compliance testing and by the promotion of more flexible accessibility strategies such as personal optimization which support the use of a variety of strategies and allows experimentation with new technologies that are yet to be accessibility vetted for all users.

With the dominance of social media, it has become even more critical that people with disabilities have equal access to communication over the Web - to both receiving and expressing information. This is true from the perspective of the individual and the community. New technology-enabled social practices intensify the effect of nonparticipation. All things popular and current rise to the top and gain additional significance. With practices such as "likes" the values of popularity and newness gain prominence. This reinforces the popular view and any perspective in the minority will never win the popularity contest. Perspectives that cannot participate are rendered invisible. If people with disabilities do not have accessible means of contributing, their perspective and needs will disappear. Equal participation may also bring about the promotion of more inclusive alternatives to popularity as influential values in these online communities (Treviranus and Hockema 2009). This participation is complicated by concerns regarding data abuses and misuses and data privacy. Addressing the needs of people with disabilities who are among the most vulnerable to data abuse and misuse, but also have the most compelling uses of smart systems, is a highly promising means of addressing the current data ethics dilemmas.

Inclusive design promotes adding considerations of process and systems thinking to considerations of the outcome criteria for accessibility (Inclusive Design Research Centre 2018b). To realize an accessible Web ecosystem and sustain equitable participation by persons with disabilities in our Web-mediated society, we must go beyond mandating a checklist of accessibility criteria. The three dimensions of inclusive design include: (1) recognizing individual differences, enabling self-awareness of unique personal needs and supporting that difference in an integrated system; (2) ensuring that the process of design and development is accessible and inclusive and inviting individuals who cannot use or have difficulty using current designs to participate in the process; and (3) considering the complex adaptive system that any design is embedded in and designing in such a way that initiates virtuous cycles that ultimately benefit the system as a whole. Web pages that respond to the individual needs of each visitor help to address the first dimension. Inclusively designed authoring tools address both the second and third dimension: enabling inclusive participation and proactively integrating accessibility into the overall Web ecosystem so that it is a natural part of the workflow and development process.

20.6   Conclusions

Authoring Tools are a critical piece of the Web accessibility puzzle, they offer a powerful and effective mechanism for supporting the creation of accessible Web content and they are the key to equal participation on the Web. As more and more critical functions occur on the Web and as the Web becomes our source for socialization and community this equal participation becomes even more critical. A principle that has been underemphasized in Web accessibility efforts is that people with disabilities must be producers as well as consumers on the Web. This has become even more important with the dominance of social media. If participation is inaccessible to people with disabilities, the contributions, creativity, as well as the needs of a large segment of society will become invisible. The research agenda to address accessible authoring is of great magnitude but also of great significance.

Acknowledgments The authors wish to acknowledge the input and feedback of Susie Blackstien-Adler in discussing coding to learn, and the contributions of the Inclusive Design Research Centre team in all sections of the chapter.

References

Abou-Zahra S (March 2007) Evaluation and Report Language (EARL) overview. https://www.w3.org/WAI/standards-guidelines/earl/. Accessed 21 Oct 2018

Amara (2018) Caption, subtitle and translate video. https://amara.org/en/. Accessed 21 Oct 2018

CAST (2018) CAST figuration. http://figuration.org/. Accessed 21 Oct 2018

Drupal Groups (2011) Drupal compliance overview of ATAG 2.0. https://groups.drupal.org/node/164389. Accessed 21 Oct 2018

Ernst D (2017) Berkeley removing 20 K free videos after DOJ ruling, closed-captioning compliant. The Washington Times. https://www.washingtontimes.com/news/2017/mar/7/berkeley-removing-20k-free-educational-videos-afte/. Accessed 21 Oct 2018

Facebook (2018) How does automatic alt text work. https://www.facebook.com/help/216219865403298?helpref=faq_content. Accessed 21 Oct 2018

Fluid Project (2018) An Infusion framework demo. https://build.fluidproject.org/infusion/demos/prefsFramework. Accessed 21 Oct 2018

GPII (2018) The Global public inclusive infrastructure. https://gpii.net. Accessed 21 Oct 2018

https://about.rebus.community/2017/01/the-rebus-approach-to-accessibility-inclusivity/. Accessed 21 Oct 2018

Inclusive Design Research Centre (2016) Fluid infusion framework and components. https://fluidproject.org/infusion.html. Accessed 21 Oct 2018

Inclusive Design Research Centre (2018) Introducing UI options plus (UIO+). https://floeproject.org/news/2018-01-31-uioPlus.html. Accessed 21 Oct 2018

Inclusive Design Research Centre (2018) The inclusive design guide. https://guide.inclusivedesign.ca Accessed 21 Oct 2018

Israel M, et al (2015) Empowering K–12 students with disabilities to learn computational thinking and computer programming. Teaching Except Child 48.1: 45–53. http://www.academia.edu/download/41724995/TEC_Computing_August_2015.pdf

Jackl A, Treviranus J, Roberts A (2004) IMS access for all meta-data overview. Accessed 1 May 2007 from http://www.imsglobal.org/accessibility/accmdv1p0/imsaccmd_oviewv1p0.html

Kafle S, Huenerfauth M (2017, October). Evaluating the usability of automatically generated captions for people who are deaf or hard of hearing. In: Proceedings of the 19th international ACM SIGACCESS conference on computers and accessibility. ACM, pp 165–174

Kazakoff Elizabeth R, Sullivan Amanda, Bers Marina U (2013) The effect of a classroom-based intensive robotics and programming workshop on sequencing ability in early childhood. Early Childhood Educ J 41(4):245–255

Ladner Richard E, Stefik Andreas (2017) AccessCSforall: making computer science accessible to K-12 students in the United States. ACM SIGACCESS Access Comput 118:3–8

Lewis C (2014) Work in progress report: nonvisual visual programming. Psychol Programm Interest Group. http://users.sussex.ac.uk/~bend/ppig2014/14ppig2014_submission_5.pdf

Milne Lauren R (2017) Blocks4All: making block programming languages accessible for blind children. ACM SIGACCESS Access Comput 117:26–29

National Centre for Accessible Media (2017) CADET: caption and description editing tool. http://ncamftp.wgbh.org/cadet/. Accessed 21 Oct 2018

Nomensa (2006) United Nations global audit of web accessibility. Available from Nomensa at http://www.nomensa.com/resources/research/united-nations-global-audit-of-accessibility.html

Norton M, Treviranus J (2003) IMS learner information package accessibility for LIP best practice and implementation guide. Accessed 1 Mar 2007 from http://www.imsglobal.org/accessibility/acclipv1p0/imsacclip_infov1p0.html

Pederick C (2018) Web developer. https://chrispederick.com/work/web-developer/. Accessed 21 Oct 2018

Raising the Floor (2018) Our approach – AccessForAll. https://raisingthefloor.org/who-we-are/our-approach/. Accessed 21 Oct 2018

REBUS Community (2017) The rebus approach to accessibility and inclusivity

Richards J, Spellman J, Treviranus J (2015) Authoring tool accessibility guidelines 2.0. Accessed 10 June 2018 from https://www.w3.org/TR/2015/REC-ATAG20-20150924/

Taylor M (2017) Computer programming with early elementary students with and without intellectual disabilities. Electron Theses Dissertations. 5564. http://stars.library.ucf.edu/etd/5564

Textbox.io (2016) Textbox.io 2.0 ATAG 2.0 Conformance claim. http://textbox.io/wp-content/uploads/2016/07/Textbox.io2_.0ATAG2.0ConformanceClaim.pdf. Accessed 21 Oct 2018

Treviranus J, Hockema S (2009, September) The value of the unpopular: counteracting the popularity echo-chamber on the Web. In: 2009 IEEE Toronto international conference on science and technology for humanity (TIC-STH). IEEE, pp 603–608

Treviranus J, McCathieNevile C, Jacobs I, Richards J (2000) Authoring tool accessibility guidelines 1.0. Accessed 1 May 2007 from http://www.w3.org/TR/2000/REC-ATAG10-20000203

Treviranus J, Nevile L, Heath A (2007) Individualized adaptability and accessibility in elearning, education and training. ISO/IEC JTC1/SC36 International Standard 24751, parts 1, 2 and 3

W3C Web Accessibility Initiative (2018) Essential components of web accessibility. https://www.w3.org/WAI/fundamentals/components/. Accessed 21 Oct 2018

W3C Working Draft 23 March 2007, Accessed August 1 2007 from http://www.w3.org/TR/EARL10-Schema/

XStandard (2018) The XHTML WYSIWYG editor for desktop and web applications. http://xstandard.com/en/documentation/xstandard-dev-guide/features/. Accessed 21 Oct 2018

Chapter 21
Dynamic Web Content

Renata Pontin de Mattos Fortes, Humberto Lidio Antonelli and Willian Massami Watanabe

Abstract Web applications have provided a good deal of information that is dynamically rendered to users in accordance with their needs. The continuous evolution of web technologies has enhanced the flexibility of interactions with increasingly varied and resourceful web interfaces (i.e. rich interfaces) that support dynamic web content. However, the increase in web interactivity has created accessibility barriers, because users of Assistive Technology (AT) tools may not be aware of the web's dynamic behaviour and its available controls. The goal of this chapter was to clarify technical factors, as well as to address the main concerns and their outcomes that developers have to deal with, and provide a brief account of current trends in research on this subject. For this reason, this chapter describes the main mechanisms used in web applications that are responsible for providing the dynamic content. In addition, there is a discussion of questions regarding the accessibility of the web resources that form the dynamic content.

R. P. de Mattos Fortes (✉) · H. L. Antonelli
University of São Paulo, São Carlos, SP, Brazil
e-mail: renata@icmc.usp.br

H. L. Antonelli
Federal Institute of Education, Science and Technology of São Paulo, São Carlos,
SP, Brazil
e-mail: humbertoantonelli@usp.br

W. M. Watanabe
Federal University of Technology – Paraná, Cornélio Procópio, PR, Brazil
e-mail: wwatanabe@utfpr.edu.br

© Springer-Verlag London Ltd., part of Springer Nature 2019
Y. Yesilada and S. Harper (eds.), *Web Accessibility*, Human–Computer
Interaction Series, https://doi.org/10.1007/978-1-4471-7440-0_21

21.1 Introduction

The World Wide Web was originally conceived to provide a technological infrastructure that could make content available in a simple and powerful standard format, by displaying information in hypertext (Berners-Lee and Fischetti 2000). Initially, information was made available statically and user interactions were limited to providing navigation links and data entry forms. Although this interaction model was simple and universal, the scope of web applications was modest and quite limited. The reason for this was that users did not have the same degree of interactivity as that provided by the desktop applications. However, the Web has evolved since its creation in 1989, and a good deal of progress has been made in the related technologies over the years. Moreover, since the beginning of Web 2.0, the nature of interactive web content has changed dramatically (Hall et al. 2009). In this new scenario, the complexity and the number of functionalities available to users have greatly increased. Modern solutions have led to more sophisticated user interaction and client-side processing, as well as asynchronous communications, multimedia and other benefits.

The concept of Web 2.0 was officially introduced in 2004, by Dale Dougherty, and formally defined by Tim O'Reilly, when the term became popular (O'Reilly 2005). This concept was not a revolutionary step or technological upgrade, although it led to a direct change in how people could participate in the Web by ensuring they could obtain dynamic content just by using their browsers. In other words, the Web offers new perspectives to users, such as a development and working platform (O'Reilly 2005). By allowing greater interactivity, with the possibility of providing users with reading and writing content, the Web became bidirectional, which is one of the main features of Web 2.0. The fact that it was possible to collaborate in the production of information from different standpoints was regarded by this new generation as an important milestone (Murugesan 2007).

Currently, the Web is mainly recognised as a means of providing universal access to information. A large number of services, news and advertisements can be accessed by any device connected to the Internet from anywhere in the world. In particular, the continuous evolution of the Web has brought about greater dynamism and flexibility by allowing an increasing interaction in 'rich' interfaces. However, this increase in web interactivity has been accompanied by accessibility barriers, since users of Assistive Technology (AT) tools may not be aware of how the dynamic content operates and how to interact with it (see 'Assistive Technologies' chapter).

This chapter provides an overview of the relationship between dynamic web content and accessibility. Our aim is to clarify technical factors, as well as the main concerns the developers have to deal with, and briefly examine current research in this area.

21.2 Overview

Web content, whether dynamic or static, refers both to what is rendered by the browser and contained in the available web pages. The two possible ways of providing the type of content that dynamically changes while a user navigates on the web page are: (a) requesting content to the server, using AJAX so that parts of the content in the *Document Object Model* (DOM) remain unchanged, or (b) interacting in the page that causes changes in the DOM of the page, using JavaScript language to manipulate the DOM. Both types of dynamic content changes cause the users to feel that they have exclusive access with the web page during the interaction, and their demands for contents are quickly met.

As web applications have increased their interactivity by enabling users to influence how content is delivered (Cooper 2007), the user interfaces have also become richer and more interactive (Gibson 2007). The effect of these new interfaces is due to the use of technologies that go beyond the markup language, such as CSS, JavaScript, DOM and AJAX, among others, and result in what is called *Rich Internet Applications* (RIA). Although this is a widespread concept in the web community, the term RIA still lacks a formalised definition that is widely accepted. RIAs can be characterised as web applications that seek to provide the features and functionalities available, in the same way as the traditional desktop applications (Casteleyn et al. 2014).

RIA usually refers to a set of heterogeneous solutions which are aimed at adding new capabilities to the conventional Web (Fraternali et al. 2010). The purpose of RIAs is to improve multimedia interactivity and communication by combining user interface functionalities of desktop applications with the wide reach of the Web (Casteleyn et al. 2014). User-centric web applications have increasingly adopted the use of RIA technologies, which require more advanced presentational and interactive features, thus resulting in an application that offers a more intuitive, agile and effective user experience.

A significant number of websites have implemented RIAs or widget components. Collaborative publishers, social networks and live content (in real time) are popular examples of RIAs (Hooshmand et al. 2016). The popularity of RIAs stems from their ability to provide a more effective and better-quality presentation and interaction than traditional web applications, which consist of several pages that have to be updated at each user interaction. The adoption of RIAs is a means of achieving improved responsiveness, interaction and a better user interface, with the goal of enhancing the user's experience (Pansanato et al. 2015). These applications usually depend on client-side technologies, combined with asynchronous communication. Accordingly, as soon as JavaScript/AJAX codes run, they can modify various features (including page content, layout, etc.) that are represented in the DOM structure.

DOM represents the semantic structure of a web page in a data structure of a 'tree' type (Connor 2012). This data structure maps the HTML features and the contents of a web page, which are stored in *Random Access Memory* (RAM) on the client

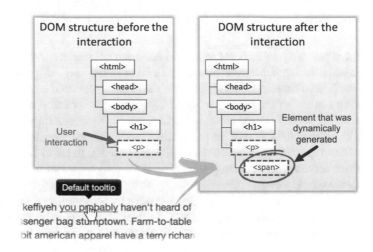

Fig. 21.1 Example of the DOM structure with the elements of a web page, over an interaction

machine while rendering the page in the browser. Figure 21.1 displays a set of HTML elements of a web page to compose the sheets in the DOM structure.

RIAs are able to (a) modify the layout, (b) alter the cross-sectional content, and (c) send and retrieve information (among other features) asynchronously, by only using the technologies on the client-side. *Asynchronous JavaScript and XML* (AJAX) is one of the leading technologies that is implemented in RIAs, and that enhances user interaction. Web interfaces that use AJAX are usually formed of individual components, which can be deleted, added or updated with new content at runtime. However, when these elements are handled with AJAX, the application behaviour becomes unpredictable and sets up barriers that prevent disabled users from accessing the available content (Brown and Harper 2011).

As Fig. 21.1 shows, the 'nodes' of the DOM structure represent the various structural parts of the document that the browser or AT will have access to. When this structure is changed by means of JavaScript/AJAX, the rendering of the web page also changes, so that new content can appear in an arbitrary way. On the other hand, AT ensures that the information on a web page contains a content structure that can be accessed in a linear fashion.

Users with disabilities may face difficulties in recognising the dynamic component within the interface and determining its functionalities, especially when there is no feedback from the changes in the interface states that resulted from the interactions. An example of these difficulties is that the web page regions may be updated as a result of an external event when the user's attention (focus) may be elsewhere. In these live regions, the content is not always updated as a result of a user's interaction and this practice has become common with the increasing use of AJAX. Hence, ATs are unaware of the changes that occurred in the web page or can not process them for the user because these areas have been updated asynchronously outside the user's attention area. In addition, these changes may correspond to a complex graph of states (Mesbah et al. 2012), which if not created correctly can lead to several problems with regard to accessibility, especially for disabled people (Connor 2012; Fogli et al. 2014).

Disabled people have difficulties or handicaps when carrying out everyday tasks, depending on the type of disability they suffered from Maciel (2000). Studies have shown that of all the groups of users with some type of disability, those who were blind had the greatest difficulty in navigating on the Web (Petrie et al. 2004; Power et al. 2012). Several problems faced by blind users have been addressed in the literature (Geraldo and Fortes 2013). Among them, two are directly related to RIA: (a) dynamic content modification and (b) the implementation of RIAs without regard for accessibility requirements. These problems can be considered to be serious, because they can cause disorientation to users of AT tools (a screen reader in the case of the blind) and, in many cases, deny access to the available information (see 'Non-visual Browsers' chapter).

The development of websites that follow accessibility guidelines is of crucial importance, since the interaction of visually impaired users is only possible by using an AT tool (screen readers). While disabled users are interacting, these tools act as an interface that facilitates access to the available information (see 'Assistive Technologies' chapter). However, the content must be made available in a minimally accessible format before the AT tools can operate properly and in a way expected by users (W3C 2014).

Most of the AT tools interact with user agents (browsers, for example) by calling an accessibility API, which defines the interface for accessing all the important objects on the user's screen. Thus, accessibility can be achieved in two key ways: by interacting with the accessibility APIs or by direct access with the content of the DOM (W3C 2014). However, the reduction of accessibility barriers should always be regarded as a continuous goal that must be pursued, since it is clear that individual differences require a wide range of solutions, which do not remove any or all of the accessibility barriers. Figure 21.2 illustrates the operation of obtaining access to an RIA.

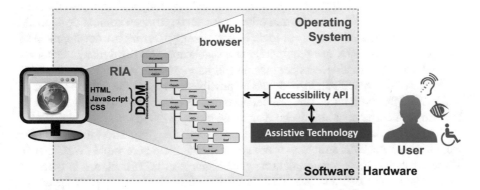

Fig. 21.2 Outline of an RIA interaction by users with disabilities

Accessibility involves the principle that everybody has the right to access information, regardless of disability, geographical location, language or other factors (Thatcher et al. 2002, 2006). In addition, it should be noted that after the founding of the Web (in 1989), its British inventor, Tim Berners-Lee[1] pointed out that *the power of the Web is in its universality. Access by everyone, regardless of disability, is an essential aspect*. Thus, before Web 2.0 can be made accessible to every user, web applications must incorporate more semantic information and predictable behaviour so that users of AT tools can interact properly with the available content. To achieve this end, W3C has been working on a number of specifications that can assist in providing accessible web applications. Next, we summarise the Web Standards related to the W3C specifications, regarding dynamic web content.

The following subsections describe the technical aspects of the web which provide a means for users to be supplied with dynamic content, especially those related to the accessibility guarantees that must be honoured. First, there is a description of the widgets that are usually implemented as a means of dynamically changing the content of a web page; after that, we examine AJAX, which is often adopted as an architectural framework for allowing parts of a web page to be kept the same while other parts have been brought from the server side asynchronously. Further emphasis is laid on the questions of accessibility with regard to dynamic web content. In addition, there are some reflections on Focus Management, since this is a particular requirement that must be taken into account when there are 'silent' changes during a web page rendering. The aim of the following subsection is to outline the main procedures that developers should be aware of when evaluating dynamic web content.

21.2.1 Standards

The *Accessible Rich Internet Applications* (WAI-ARIA) standard introduces a framework to improve the accessibility and interoperability of web applications for the users of AT tools (W3C 2017). It is a technical specification that has been recommended by an official W3C since March 2014, and is mainly aimed at the (i) developers of browsers, AT resources and other user agents; (ii) web content developers; and (iii) developers of assessment tools of accessibility. During the development of web pages, WAI-ARIA has provided appropriate semantics for dynamic elements (widgets) to make them accessible, usable and interoperable with the use of an AT. By means of this specification, it should be possible to identify the different types of widgets and their structures, and provide an ontology of the corresponding functions that can be incorporated into the content (Valencia et al. 2013).

WAI-ARIA defines a set of attributes (roles, states and properties) that should be included in the HTML structure of widgets to make them accessible (W3C 2017). These attributes add semantic data to general-purpose HTML elements (such as <div> and <span>) and provide information about the behaviour of these ele-

---

[1] World Wide Web Inventor and W3C Director.

ments for AT resources and user agents. The WAI-ARIA attribute set comprises the following attributes, which should be incorporated into the technologies used in RIAs (W3C 2017):

- *Roles*: these allow developers to include semantic information about the behaviour of a particular element or set of HTML elements. AT resources and user agents (browsers) can use this information to provide accessible interaction for people with disabilities. According to the WAI-ARIA specification, the roles can be categorised as follows:

  - *Abstract Roles*—to define abstract concepts of taxonomy and serve as the basis for the construction of all other roles. This means that developers need not make use of these roles, since they are extended by the others.
  - *Widget Roles*—to define standalone user interface components, such as progress bar, menu items, tips box and others; or composite user interface components, such as combo boxes, menus, tab lists boxes and others.
  - *Document Structure Roles*—to define structures that arrange the content of a web page. Examples include content that generally contains a graphical document, heading and a collection of function buttons or controls.
  - *Landmark Roles*—are regions in a web page with a cluster of key points, which a user may want to access quickly. Examples of these roles include the main area of the page (`main`), navigation blocks (`navigation`), and search regions (`search`).
  - *Live Region Roles*—some of the roles can be classified as live content regions, where an automatic content update occurs as a result of an external event, that is, updates that do not depend on user interaction. Examples of these regions include chat widgets, weather forecasts or a sports score section that is periodically updated to reflect game statistics.
  - *Window Roles*—to define structures that act as windows within the browser or application, such as Dialogs.

- *States* and *Properties*: to declare attributes in HTML elements in order to tell the AT resources and operating systems how to interact with them, even when they are changed asynchronously, sometimes without user interaction. The attributes used to represent states and properties refer to similar functionalities, since both provide specific information about an object and form a part of a role. According to the WAI-ARIA specification, states and properties are treated as attributes prefixed with '`aria-`'. However, the two concepts (states and properties) are kept separate because property values are less likely to be dynamically changed than state values, which are often changed as a result of user interaction.

The WAI-ARIA specification clearly defines the requirements for implementation that can ensure user interaction by informing the users what features of the web page are interactive and how to interact with them (W3C 2017). By implementing WAI-ARIA appropriately, a web component can increase literally its features, as well as include more semantics. In this way, it can be customised to maximise its accessibility for user of AT. On the other hand, when WAI-ARIA is implemented inappropriately, the accessibility of widgets can be compromised, making them virtually unusable by users of AT. Therefore, extreme caution should always be applied when deploying RIA. In addition, developers are responsible for finding alternatives to the exclusive use of the mouse to interact with the widgets. Finally, dynamic features should be included in the structure of the web page, in particular the region where the interaction took place (W3C 2017).

21.2.2   Widgets

RIAs provide better interaction capabilities for users. The content of these dynamic web applications relies on interactive features (widgets), which combine client-side technologies with asynchronous communication to create and control them (Caste-leyn et al. 2014). A widget can be defined as a unit of content within a web page; examples of widgets include user interface components available in JavaScript toolkits such as Dialogs, Tooltips, Drop-down menus, Date pickers, Drag-and-drop controls, Window widgets and Suggestion boxes. Figure 21.3 shows three of these widgets.

Widgets are self-contained client-side applications which are based on web standards and packaged for distribution (W3C 2012). Chen et al. (2013) define a widget as a coherent unit of content contained within a web page that users can interact with. They also include interface components which supply information and update data using web standards to communicate with the server such as weather forecasting, news items, social media publications, among other services.

The user interface of a widget is based on (i) HTML so that its content can be structured, (ii) CSS to define the way it is displayed, and (iii) JavaScript to implement its behaviour when an event (e.g. clicks, mouse over or key presses) is triggered. For instance, when building a Drop-down menu widget, developers might use the following:

- *HTML*: to structure the Drop-down menu elements in an unordered list (using `<ul>` and `<li>` elements);
- *CSS*: to declare the position of the widget and the layout details, such as border, colour and other information;

Fig. 21.3 Examples of widgets: *Date picker*, *Drop-down menu* and *Colour picker*, respectively

- *JavaScript*: to implement a mouseover listener function which shows further options of the menu, by changing the DOM structure of the web page.

The following example (Listing 1) only refers to the HTML implementation of the *Drop-down menu* widget, as displayed in Fig. 21.3. Most of the widget's implementations available on the Web have tended to follow this example, which does not comply with WAI-ARIA specification.

Listing 1 Example of HTML implementation of *Drop-down menu* widget

```
1  <ul id="menu">
2      <li id="ui-1" class="disabled">Toys (n/a)</li>
3      <li id="ui-2">Books</li>
4      <li id="ui-3">Clothing</li>
5      <li id="ui-4">Electronics
6          <ul>
7              <li id="ui-5" class="disabled">Home Entertainment</li>
8              <li id="ui-6">Car Hifi</li>
9              <li id="ui-7">Utilities</li>
10         </ul>
11     </li>
12     <li id="ui-8">Movies</li>
13     <li id="ui-9"> Music
14         <ul>
15             <li id="ui-10">Rock
16                 <ul>
17                     <li id="ui-11">Alternative</li>
18                     <li id="ui-12">Classic</li>
19                 </ul>
20             </li>
21             <li id="ui-13">Jazz
22                 <ul>
23                     <li id="ui-14">Freejazz</li>
24                     <li id="ui-15">Big Band</li>
25                     <li id="ui-16">Modern</li>
26                 </ul>
27             </li>
28             <li id="ui-17">Pop</li>
29         </ul>
30     </li>
31     <li id="ui-18" class="disabled">Specials (n/a)</li>
32 </ul>
```

In the previous example, users of AT tools may face serious barriers when interacting with this widget due to the lack of accessibility requirements defined by WAI-ARIA. One of these barriers refers to updates in the web interface, which are not realised by AT tools and, consequently, the users are not informed about the updates. The following example (Listing 2) refers to the HTML implementation of the same previous *Drop-down menu widget*. However, in this example, we have included the WAI-ARIA specification attributes.

Listing 2 Example of HTML implementation of *Drop-down menu* widget with WAI-ARIA attributes

```
1  <ul id="menu" role="menu" tabindex="0" aria-activedescendant="ui-17">
2      <li aria-disabled="true" id="ui-1" tabindex="-1" role="menuitem">Toys (n/a)</li>
3      <li id="ui-2" tabindex="-1" role="menuitem">Books</li>
4      <li id="ui-3" tabindex="-1" role="menuitem">Clothing</li>
5      <li aria-haspopup="true" id="ui-4" tabindex="-1" role="menuitem">Electronics
6          <ul role="menu" aria-expanded="false" aria-hidden="true">
7              <li aria-disabled="true" id="ui-5" tabindex="-1" role="menuitem">Home
               Entertainment</li>
```

```
8              <li id="ui-6" tabindex="-1" role="menuitem">Car Hifi</li>
9              <li id="ui-7" tabindex="-1" role="menuitem">Utilities</li>
10          </ul>
11     </li>
12     <li id="ui-8" tabindex="-1" role="menuitem">Movies</li>
13     <li aria-haspopup="true" id="ui-9" tabindex="-1" role="menuitem"> Music
14        <ul role="menu" aria-expanded="true">
15             <li aria-haspopup="true" id="ui-10" tabindex="-1" role="menuitem">Rock
16                <ul role="menu" aria-expanded="false" aria-hidden="true">
17                     <li id="ui-11" tabindex="-1" role="menuitem">Alternative</li>
18                     <li id="ui-12" tabindex="-1" role="menuitem">Classic</li>
19                </ul>
20             </li>
21             <li aria-haspopup="true" id="ui-13" tabindex="-1" role="menuitem">Jazz
22                <ul role="menu" aria-expanded="false" aria-hidden="true">
23                     <li id="ui-14" tabindex="-1" role="menuitem">Freejazz</li>
24                     <li id="ui-15" tabindex="-1" role="menuitem">Big Band</li>
25                     <li id="ui-16" tabindex="-1" role="menuitem">Modern</li>
26                </ul>
27             </li>
28             <li id="ui-17" tabindex="-1" role="menuitem">Pop</li>
29          </ul>
30       </li>
31       <li aria-disabled="true" id="ui-18" tabindex="-1" role="menuitem">Specials (n/a)
            </li>
32   </ul>
```

The differentials of this implementation conform to the WAI-ARIA specification and include the following six attributes: `role`, `aria-disabled`, `aria-haspopup`, `aria-expanded`, `aria-hidden` and `aria-activedescendant`. It is worth noting that the visual display will remain the same if the WAI-ARIA attributes are not defined. However, the use of these attributes improves the interaction for users of AT tools by providing further information, which would be inaccessible without the WAI-ARIA.

However, just specifying the attributes in the HTML code is not enough to design an accessible web application. Developers must also implement dynamic interaction controls in a scripting language (W3C 2017). All the dynamic elements must have a well-defined keyboard navigation scheme (through focus management in the web application), that takes into account the possible use of AT resources.

21.2.3   AJAX

The acronym AJAX stands for 'Asynchronous JavaScript and XML', a term coined by Jesse James Garrett in Adaptive Path in February 2005.[2] AJAX encompasses the use of several other technologies apart from JavaScript and XML, such as DOM, HTML, JSON or any other markup or programming language that can be retrieved from a server. Mahemoff (2007) defines AJAX as an architectural style that allows content to be loaded in a web page asynchronously through the use of JavaScript, without the need for a complete update of the Web page.

The AJAX differential is related to how web technologies can work together to deliver a more interesting and productive application for the user, by making

---

[2]http://adaptivepath.org/ideas/ajax-new-approach-web-applications.

rich interactions possible through logical constructions designed for the document adaptation of documents based on script languages (Schmidt et al. 2008). In an AJAX application, JavaScript acts as a connecting interface between the various components, by defining the user workflow and the business logic of the application. A user interface upgrade takes place through DOM manipulation, which enables the content to be modified, incorporated or removed, through user interaction. CSS also makes it possible to modify the interactive mode interface in AJAX applications through the DOM by means of JavaScript. Finally, the XMLHttpRequest object is used to talk to the server asynchronously, which involves responding to user requests and fetching updated data, while the user is in the application.

AJAX is one of the leading technologies that is implemented in RIAs, which provide enhanced user interaction. RIAs that use AJAX usually consist of individual components, which can be deleted, added or updated with new content at runtime. However, when these elements with AJAX are manipulated, it makes the behaviour of the application unpredictable, since it sets up barriers that prevent disabled users from accessing the available content (Brown and Harper 2011).

Users with disabilities may face difficulties in recognising the dynamic component within the interface and determining its functionalities, especially when there is no feedback from the changes in the interface state as a result of the interactions. An example of these kinds of difficulties is updating web page regions that are caused by an external event when the user's attention may be elsewhere. In these live regions, content is not always updated as a result of a user interaction and this practice has become common with the increasing use of AJAX. Hence, ATs might be unaware of changes that occurred in the web page or unable to process them for the user because these areas have been updated asynchronously without user being aware of it. In addition, these kinds of changes may correspond to a complex graph of states (Mesbah et al. 2012), which if not created correctly can lead to several accessibility problems, especially for disabled people (Connor 2012; Fogli et al. 2014).

In light of this, web applications that implement AJAX mechanisms for updating content must be based on the concept of 'live regions' (W3C 2017). Many web applications also update timeline posts, sent an instant message between users and auto-update scoreboards. These widgets often depend on AJAX for updating content and providing it to users. The feedback in the interface is usually displayed by means of visual effects in the parts of the web page which were updated, together with new information. Live regions are areas of the DOM tree which can be used to tell users about these updates brought by AJAX. There are different types of live region roles which can be included in the web page, such as `alert`, `log`, `marquee`, `status` and `timer`. These roles differ in accordance with the type of message which will be sent to the users. For instance: `alert` live regions will present the updates associated to warning or error messages for validating a form input; `log` live regions can be used to show a chronological sequence of updated messages (used in chats or scoreboards); among other usages. Changes in the DOM structure of these elements will be informed to users, even if the user is navigating in other parts of the web application.

In Live regions, developers can configure other properties to determine how users should be notified about changes and which changes should be communicated. Updates in the Live region can be conducted in an assertive way, by interrupting the task a user is carrying out in the web application (`aria-live='assertive'`); or in a polite manner (`aria-live='polite'`), which avoids interrupting the users. Furthermore, developers can also configure which type of DOM changes should be communicated to users by means of the aria-relevant attribute. For instance, Live regions can only be used to notify additions or removals of DOM elements from the Live region.

21.2.4 Focus Management

The WAI-ARIA specification describes an accessibility framework for RIA (W3C 2017) and one mandatory requirement is Focus Management. Many users are not capable of interacting with web applications through pointer devices, such as the mouse. Hence, web applications must create alternative keyboard interaction scenarios for accessing every kind of functionality, as laid down by guideline 2.1 of WCAG 2.0 (W3C 2008). Since many RIAs include interactive controls which trigger dynamic updates in the DOM structure, developers must make them accessible by implementing a mechanism for navigating with the aid of these controls and interacting with them by using the keyboard. These mechanisms are mainly implemented in web applications by means of the Focus event and programmatically determining the sequence of elements which require attention.

Guideline 2.1 of WCAG 2.0 specifies a technologically neutral design solution for handling keyboard navigation (Reid and Snow-Weaver 2008). The web standard based solution for implementing guideline 2.1 is explained in the WAI-ARIA specification (W3C 2013), which stipulates that all the functionalities available in an RIA component must be completely operable by the keyboard. HTML features such as `links`, `anchors` and `forms` behave in a predictable way and have native keyboard interactive mechanisms in the browser. However, in RIA, the interactive scenarios of widgets are not always predictable and often take place with generic markup which does not always include native keyboard interaction. In view of this, the developers themselves must implement these keyboard interaction scenarios in their applications.

Widgets rely on programmatic resources for creating complex interaction scenarios in HTML elements. The features which handle mouse interaction, for instance, must be embedded in the tab order of the browser, so that they can handle keyboard events by using the HTML attribute `tabindex` with a non-negative value (W3C 2013). The tab order of the browser consists of a list of elements that can be found in the DOM structure which are highlighted (focused on) in the interface and respond to keyboard events. This list also defines the order of elements which will be highlighted, such as when the user moves the cursor in the web application, generally by using the TAB key to move forward or the SHIFT+TAB keys to move backward. This navigation strategy is also referred to as Focus navigation.

Every HTML element in the DOM structure of a web application contains a tabindex attribute with an integer numerical value. If an HTML element has a negative value for the tabindex attribute, this element is not embedded in the tab order and, hence, is not capable of handling keyboard events. On the other hand, if an HTML element has a non-negative tabindex attribute, this element is included in the tab order of the browser and can listen to/handle keyboard events.

HTML standard interactive elements such as links, inputs and buttons natively have a non-negative tabindex attribute. However, other HTML elements such as div and span, which are often used to implement widgets in RIA, natively have a negative tabindex attribute value (−1). Hence, the web developer is responsible for changing this behaviour in HTML elements to incorporate widget controls in the tab order and enable keyboard navigation.

Furthermore, implementing an effective navigation through the functionalities of widgets is of critical importance to ensure the RIA is usable. Using Focus navigation strategies for navigating through a large number of widgets controls can be tedious and leads to behaviour that is inconsistent when compared with the navigation mechanisms of desktop applications (W3C 2013). The WAI-ARIA states that Focus navigation (setting non-negative tabindex attributes for elements and navigating using the TAB or SHIFT+TAB keys) should be implemented for navigating between widgets, while the navigation inside a widget should be implemented by means of other keyboard shortcuts.

21.2.5 Evaluation

The process of developing RIAs and their components is highly specialised and enables a wide range of resources to be explored, by characterising the different forms of interaction that come with Web 2.0. Although the WAI-ARIA specification provides the general guidelines for an accessible application, it does not ensure compliance with its technical specifications. However, making an evaluation is essential for any development process to produce an interactive system with high quality of use (Dix et al. 2003; Shneiderman et al. 2009).

The purpose of the web accessibility evaluation is to determine how easy it is for disabled people to access the applications and at what level, while pointing out the existing barriers so that they can be analysed and properly corrected (Abou-Zahra 2008). When conducting accessibility evaluations, developers can reflect on what users need and what barriers they might face. This means that they can correct problems arising from the use of a system before it becomes a part of the users' daily life. In view of this, an interactive system should be assessed from different perspectives, but particularly from the standpoint of those who conceive, build and use it. Accessibility evaluation techniques can be divided into three basic types

(Abou-Zahra 2008). These can be combined in an evaluative process (depending on the purpose and context of the project).

Manual Evaluation This is an analytical method that plays an essential role in evaluating websites (Brajnik 2008). It is based on the opinions of the evaluators, which include faults (from the perspective of the accessibility requirement that have been violated) and possible solutions (Brajnik et al. 2011). In carrying out the assessment, the evaluators use a set of accessibility recommendations to check whether a web application complies with these recommendations (Abou-Zahra 2008; Brajnik et al. 2011). Brajnik (2008) emphasises that the choice of the set of recommendations can affect the quality of the evaluation. The ability of the evaluators to use and understand them is another essential factor, since the level of knowledge of the evaluators has a significant effect on the results (Brajnik 2008; Brajnik et al. 2010; Yesilada et al. 2009). Finally, the evaluation that is conducted manually is a means of checking the points that the automatic tools are not able to analyse completely. In addition, a manual evaluation can check whether there are any false positives or false negatives.

Evaluating RIAs through manual inspections can be frustrating for evaluators, since the attributes of the WAI-ARIA specification do not show signs of visual changes. In this case, the evaluators may use one or more AT resources, which support the WAI-ARIA markup, to check whether or not the web application is accessible. Operating systems currently offer a native screen reader, but there are other free alternatives, such as NVDA.[3] In addition, there are several commercial screen reader solutions that offer limited but free techniques for testing, such as JAWS.[4]

Using screen readers to conduct a manual evaluation, however, can be difficult at first and become tiring over a period of time. Screen readers often have a feature to assist the output of texts that are synthesised from 'voice'. This alternative allows evaluators to analyse the content without having to listen to the reading several times. Another strategy is to use software for the screen reader emulator, such as Fangs.[5] However, before determining whether AT resources are displaying their content correctly, it is highly recommended that evaluators confirm whether the source code complies with markup language standards, and is suitable for the style sheets, and scripts. The WAI-ARIA specification provides general recommendations that assist in the design of accessible RIAs, but it lacks the means to ensure compliance with its technological implementation specifications (Watanabe et al. 2017).

To briefly summarise, manual inspection methods support the identification of possible accessibility problems of a more technical nature, since they are largely based on criteria defined by the general guidelines. Although these methods are a good starting point for reducing potential accessibility barriers in web applications, tests should also be conducted with disabled users (see 'Working with Participants' chapter).

---

[3]http://www.nvaccess.org.
[4]http://www.freedomscientific.com/Products/Blindness/JAWS.
[5]http://www.standards-schmandards.com/projects/fangs/.

Tests with users This focuses on end users, and investigates how well technical solutions address the needs of these individuals in a specific context of use (Abou-Zahra 2008). This evaluation method should involve a representative sample of disabled users, who are individually invited to carry out the tasks defined for the test, while the evaluators observe their behaviour (Brajnik 2008). At the end of the test, a list of the problems faced by the users is compiled on the basis of the audio and video recordings, as well as the notes made by the evaluators; as a result, levels of seriousness can be assigned to each problem that was identified (Brajnik et al. 2011).

The evaluators usually use the 'Think Aloud protocol' during the testing session. In this technique, the assessor asks the user to verbalise everything he/she thinks while interacting with the system (Lewis 1982; Nielsen 1993; Rubin and Chisnell 2008). In addition, the tests should be carefully worded to ensure the evaluation is effective and prevent the evaluator from having an influence on the problems are detected or classified (Abou-Zahra 2008; Brajnik 2008). Tests with users are regarded as an essential evaluation method to provide evidence about the degree of accessibility of a web application, when used by the target audience for which it was designed (Petrie and Bevan 2009). However, the task of evaluating all the web pages that comprise a particular website, with different user profiles is not trivial. When disabled users are taken into account, the complexity of using this type of test is further increased, given the difficulty of recruiting users with specific types of disability (Freire 2012).

Automatic Tests It is one of the simplest ways of evaluating the accessibility of a web application, since they involve automatic evaluation tools. Automatic tests are conducted without any human involvement in the evaluation process (Abou-Zahra 2008), since automatic tools are employed to check to what extent a web page complies with a given set of accessibility recommendations (Brajnik et al. 2011). Thus, these tests should be carried out periodically on large numbers of web pages, without greatly increasing the expenditure on development.

Although automatic testing is an important assessment technique in an evaluator's portfolio, this type of evaluation may not be able to overcome all the accessibility barriers, since the tools only take into account of the features that are encoded on the web page (Kelly et al. 2005). Thus, additional methods are required, such as manual inspection, since automatic tools are not able to check certain visual factors, such as whether the textual alternatives provide information that is equivalent to that represented by the image (Abou-Zahra 2008; Brajnik 2008). Currently, there are several automatic accessibility evaluation tools as listed by the W3C,[6] which are employed to determine whether websites are in compliance with the main accessibility guidelines adopted internationally. It should be noted that all of the tools are available online, and accessible from browsers. Moreover, web page evaluations can be carried out on the basis of the URL and from the source code provided directly in a data entry form. Although most current automated tools can assist in the evaluation of accessibility of a website, they only check the static content of the web page. Automatically testing the accessibility of RIAs is not an easy task owing to the formation of a dynamic

---

[6]https://www.w3.org/WAI/ER/tools/.

structure at runtime. Thus, only WCAG 2.0 is not capable of automatically checking all the accessibility requirements of these applications (Ballis et al. 2011).

The use of the WAI-ARIA specification has been the subject of many studies (Doush et al. 2013; Ohara et al. 2016; Schiavone and Paternò 2015; Tateishi et al. 2007; Watanabe et al. 2017). However, one of the main limitations of evaluative approaches is how to discover the dynamic elements (widgets) automatically, since there is no standard source code model that can be compared directly. Although Doush et al. (2013) adopted an approach to automatically identify and classify these features, the strategy is only conceptual and just serves as a possible reference point for designing automatic evaluation tools. In addition, any automatic tool that seeks to evaluate the accessibility of RIAs must be able to generate and execute different event sequences so that all possible dynamic states of the web application can be analysed. In short, the automatic evaluation of accessibility in RIAs is still an open question that needs to be further investigated.

21.3 Discussion

The Web faces challenges in terms of barriers to accessibility, which include a wide range of features related to users as human beings, such as their skills, culture, language, special needs and other factors. Despite this, strenuous efforts have been made to overcome the effects of accessibility barriers on the Web (Naftali et al. 2010). In light of this, accessibility on the Web has been included as a research area with the aim of offering everybody the means to perceive, understand, navigate and interact with the Web. People who are barrier-free (or are only affected by minor barriers), and also supported by AT resources, can also contribute to the web content (Thatcher et al. 2006).

According to W3C (2005), web accessibility encompasses the entire range of disabilities that affect web access, whether visual, auditory, cognitive, speech-based, physical or neurological. The ideas and concepts related to the subject also extend to the inclusion of elderly people, who, even though they are not classified as people with disabilities, generally have handicaps caused by the ageing process, which hampers their interaction with the Web. In addition, web accessibility benefits people without disabilities (Connor 2012), since the creation of accessible websites increases usability in general, by allowing everyone, without exception, to make use of available material in accordance with their own preferences, such as the use of any browser, access platform (desktop or mobile), among other devices. Thus, from the different perspectives addressed in the literature on web accessibility, Petrie et al. (2015) proposed an all-inclusive definition aiming at every kind of person and situation:

> 'all people, particularly disabled and older people, can use websites in a range of contexts of use, including mainstream and assistive technologies; to achieve this, websites need to be designed and developed to support usability across these contexts'.

In ensuring that websites can be really accessible to any user, it is also important for user agents to be accessible, such as web browsers, multimedia players, AT resources and so on. Hence, Web Accessibility Initiative has drawn up the *User Agent Accessibility Guidelines* (UAAG), which aims to define standards and make recommendations for the development and operation of the software through which the Web and its resources can be accessed, as well as other forms of AT (W3C 2015b). Ultimately, the *Web Content Accessibility Guidelines* (WCAG) are geared towards creating web content, as they give recommendations on how to make content available on websites more accessible to people with disabilities. The first version of the WCAG was used to improve the accessibility of websites (Reid and Snow-Weaver 2008).

However, since its release in 1999, web applications have ceased to be static and simple, there are now more complex and rich interactions caused by the extensive development of RIAs (Watanabe et al. 2012). As a result, AT tools are not always able to recognise the dynamic changes and updates generated by the use of JavaScript/A-JAX because the web page is no longer a part of a static and linear structure, and can be modified during the user interaction (Watanabe et al. 2012). In light of this, W3C has developed the 'WAI-ARIA' as a part of the HTML5 specification, to address the increasing complexity of web interfaces with RIAs, and to enable AT users to interact with these applications (W3C 2017). Unlike WCAG, which aims at making web content accessible without taking into account of the technological factors involved in its development, WAI-ARIA is a technical specification for devising several dynamic components of the web interface in an accessible way. Thus, it should be emphasised that WAI-ARIA complies with the recommendations of WCAG 2.0 so that, in fact, the RIAs are accessible.

It can be seen that the relationship between the web browser and AT resources takes place through an accessibility API. This relationship allows information to be shared (roles, states, events, notifications, information-based relationships and descriptions) of RIA application data that need to be processed when the user requires a special means of access. While the user is interacting with RIA, the web browser is responsible for transmitting the relevant information to the accessibility API. As a result, AT tools are able to inform users about which events and modifications in the interface are significant and need to be displayed, so that the content can be conveyed to the user in an accessible way.

Even though the WAI-ARIA specification provides the design solutions for implementing accessibility requirements in RIA, the research community presents reports that web applications still lack the implementation of these requirements, despite the increasing popularity of RIA and HTML (Watanabe et al. 2015a, b). These kinds of reports have brought light on the development of frameworks and tools for assisting web developers while implementing accessible RIA.

21.4   Future Directions

Many development efforts have been dedicated to supporting more and more technological resources to increase user engagement to contribute to dynamic web content
and facilitate their interaction on web pages. Web mediating collective partnerships
is an irreversible global tendency. In this context, new challenges for developers of
web tools and services constantly arise. Developers increasingly need the support of
tools that assist them in the development and evaluation of RIAs.

   One future trend in this study field is related to the accessibility verification tools
for RIAs, which are currently not yet enabled to identify and classify widgets and their
subcomponents in order to facilitate an automated conformance analysis of WAI-
ARIA. Many efforts on this subject need to be made by Computer scientists. Thereon
this area, researches have focused on the elaboration of frameworks for evaluating
accessibility in RIA (Doush et al. 2013), identification of widgets (Antonelli et al.
2018; Chen et al. 2013; Melnyk et al. 2014), evaluation of accessibility in RIA
widgets (Watanabe et al. 2017) and dynamic injection of WAI-ARIA (Brown and
Harper 2013).

   A recent demand is regarding the adoption of *Model–View–Presenter* (MVP)
design pattern by web developers, in which the presenter layer provides a single,
well-defined place for the code that can implements, for example, a 'user story'.
Thus, it is the presenter, not the view, that responds to user interface events (Mezzalira 2018). In fact, this user interface architectural pattern aims to improve the
separation of concerns in presentation logic. Many frameworks have implemented
MVP pattern, and *Google Web Toolkit* (GWT)[7] is a notable example that propels
developers. Other front-end web frameworks explore different RIA models regarding the use of declarative programming components, such as React.js, Angular and
Vue. These frameworks support developers in the implementation of customised
interaction scenarios, facilitating the construct of *Single-Page Application* (SPA).
Future works in the area also have to support these types of changes in the technological architecture of web applications. The general contributions should work
towards assisting web developers in their coding activities and possibly reducing the
cost of deploying accessible RIAs.

   In fact, there is an irreversible trend of web development supported by these
frameworks, therefore, resources should also be provided for developers to ensure
the 'rich' web pages are accordingly obeying accessibility requirements.

21.5   Author's Opinion of the Field

The evolution of web technologies has boosted the amount of dynamic content in
an irreversible way. Users are becoming even more demanding with regard to user
experience, especially if RIAs are able to provide rapid feedback, and requested

---

[7]http://www.gwtproject.org/.

data delivery, while at the same time giving the impression that they are exclusively catering for their individuals requirements. In fact, currently society is information-oriented, and this is resulting in demands for changeable data on a huge scale. The dynamics of web content reflects this reality.

The considerable improvements in interaction provided by RIAs make web dynamic content available in a suitable way and provide an appropriate means of customising interfaces that are in tune with the needs of each individual user when interacting with the web page components. It is worth noting that users are being given a kind of freedom of choices during their navigation. The technological resources (languages, frameworks, architectural styles, design patterns, etc.) in the web context have shown a fast-paced evolution, and W3C has always made efforts to aggregate the demands of the public with the specialist community to maintain universal access to all the content in the web.

Thus the principle of universality, with regard to usability and accessibility in web pages, which can include any kind of innovative technology, should always be ensured. We strongly support this cause and think that an educational approach must be given priority. For example, correct adoption of features with their suitable (i.e. semantically relevant) attributes, means that the dynamic content should be made accessible the browsers. Another suggestion is to provide a simpler and cheaper means of evaluating the accessibility of RIAs. For example, this might entail a scenario where a regular developer would be able to conduct automatic tests and rapidly be aware of the difficulties that disabled people face during their web navigation and interaction.

21.6 Conclusions

The Web is undergoing a constant evolutionary process, which means it can now provide greater interactivity to the users through web applications with more sophisticated and dynamic interfaces. However, these kinds of applications need to address accessibility requirements (BRASIL 2016; U.S. Government 2014; W3C 2008, 2015a, b, 2017), so that any user can properly interact with the available content.

With the evolution of technologies on the Web, advances have been made to allow greater user participation. Web applications that are increasingly interactive have enhanced its potential to provide dynamic content. However, dynamic content on web pages requires making structural changes, which are not always properly mapped so that they can be controlled and address the needs of users who require AT.

Developers, in general, do not have enough knowledge of AT to be aware of the accessibility requirements involved in web page structures or the extent to which they can enable a high level of interactivity and allow changes in content material during the browser rendering. It should be noted that the RIAs applications have become popular too and had a great effect on matters related to accessibility. The WAI-ARIA that provides general guidance on the requirements for the development of affordable RIAs should also be widespread. However, unlike WCAG, WAI-ARIA does not address ways to ensure that the recommendations described are properly checked and put into practice. We suspect that the systems for assessing compliance with these requirements in RIAs need to be made easier for developers.

For this reason, the attempts by the scientific community to adopt effective approaches for assessing accessibility in RIA are having a positive effect, since there has been a continuous evolution in this area of research with timely and promising contributions (Doush et al. 2013; Fernandes et al. 2011, 2013; Ohara et al. 2016; Schiavone and Paternò 2015; Tateishi et al. 2007; Watanabe et al. 2012, 2017). However, a lack of knowledge of accessibility is one of the main obstacles to the development of web applications with accessible dynamic content.

Acknowledgements We would like to thank CAPES/CNPq–Brazil and the FAPESP (process: 2015/24525-0) for their financial support.

References

Abou-Zahra S (2008) Web accessibility evaluation. In: Yeliz Yesilada SH (ed) Web accessibility: a foundation for research. Springer, London, pp 79–106. https://doi.org/10.1007/978-1-84800-050-6_7

Antonelli HL, Igawa RA, Fortes RPdM, Rizo EH, Watanabe WM (2018) Drop-down menu widget identification using HTML structure changes classification. ACM Trans Access Comput 11(2):10:1–10:23. https://doi.org/10.1145/3178854

Ballis D, Kutsia T, Linaje M, Lozano-Tello A, Perez-Toledano MA, Preciado JC, Rodriguez-Echeverria R, Sanchez-Figueroa F (2011) Automated specification and verification of web systems providing RIA user interfaces with accessibility properties. J Symb Comput 46(2):207–217. http://www.sciencedirect.com/science/article/pii/S0747717110001380

Berners-Lee T, Fischetti M (2000) Weaving the web: the original design and ultimate destiny of the World Wide Web by its inventor, 1st edn. HarperBusiness, New York

Brajnik G (2008) Beyond conformance: the role of accessibility evaluation methods. Springer, Berlin, Heidelberg, pp 63–80. https://doi.org/10.1007/978-3-540-85200-1_9

Brajnik G, Yesilada Y, Harper S (2010) Testability and validity of WCAG 2.0: the expertise effect. In: Proceedings of the 12th international ACM SIGACCESS conference on computers and accessibility, ASSETS '10. ACM, New York, pp 43–50. https://doi.org/10.1145/1878803.1878813

Brajnik G, Yesilada Y, Harper S (2011) The expertise effect on web accessibility evaluation methods. Hum Comput Interact 26(3):246–283, https://doi.org/10.1080/07370024.2011.601670

BRASIL (2016) e-MAG: Modelo de Acessibilidade em Governo Eletrônico. Ministério do Planejamento, Orçamento e Gestão. Secretaria de Logística e Tecnologia da Informação, Brasília - DF. https://www.governodigital.gov.br/cidadania/acessibilidade/emag-modelo-de-acessibilidade-em-governo-eletronico

Brown A, Harper S (2011) Ajax time machine. In: Proceedings of the international cross-disciplinary conference on web accessibility, W4A '11. ACM, New York, pp 28:1–28:4. https://doi.org/10.1145/1969289.1969325

Brown A, Harper S (2013) Dynamic injection of WAI-ARIA into web content. In: Proceedings of the 10th international cross-disciplinary conference on web accessibility, W4A '13. ACM, New York, pp 14:1–14:4. https://doi.org/10.1145/2461121.2461141

Casteleyn S, Garrigós I, Mazón JN (2014) Ten Years of rich internet applications: a systematic mapping study, and beyond. ACM Trans Web 8(3):18:1–18:46. https://doi.org/10.1145/2626369

Chen A, Harper S, Lunn D, Brown A (2013) Widget identification: a high-level approach to accessibility. World Wide Web 16(1):73–89. https://doi.org/10.1007/s11280-012-0156-6

Connor JO (2012) Pro HTML5 accessibility, 1st edn. Apress, New York

Cooper M (2007) Accessibility of emerging rich web technologies: web 2.0 and the semantic web. In: Proceedings of the 2007 international cross-disciplinary conference on web accessibility (W4A), W4A '07. ACM, New York, pp 93–98. https://doi.org/10.1145/1243441.1243463

Dix A, Finlay JE, Abowd GD, Beale R (2003) Human-computer interaction, 3rd edn. Prentice-Hall Inc, Upper Saddle River

Doush IA, Alkhateeb F, Maghayreh EA, Al-Betar MA (2013) The design of RIA accessibility evaluation tool. Adv Eng Softw 57:1–7. http://www.sciencedirect.com/science/article/pii/S0965997812001512

Fernandes N, Lopes R, Carriço L (2011) On web accessibility evaluation environments. In: Proceedings of the international cross-disciplinary conference on web accessibility, W4A '11. ACM, New York, pp 4:1–4:10. https://doi.org/10.1145/1969289.1969295

Fernandes N, Batista AS, Costa D, Duarte C, Carriço L (2013) Three web accessibility evaluation perspectives for RIA. In: Proceedings of the 10th international cross-disciplinary conference on web accessibility, W4A '13. ACM, New York, pp 12:1–12:9. https://doi.org/10.1145/2461121.2461122

Fogli D, Parasiliti Provenza L, Bernareggi C (2014) A universal design resource for rich internet applications based on design patterns. Univers Access Inf Soc 13(2):205–226. https://doi.org/10.1007/s10209-013-0291-6

Fraternali P, Rossi G, Sánchez-Figueroa F (2010) Rich internet applications. IEEE Internet Comput 14(3):9–12

Freire AP (2012) Disabled people and the web: user-based measurement of accessibility. Ph.D. thesis, University of York, Inglaterra. http://etheses.whiterose.ac.uk/3873/

Geraldo RJ, Fortes RP (2013) Dificuldades de usuários cegos na interação com a web: uma análise sobre as pesquisas. Revista de Sistemas e Computação (RSC) 3(2):146–160

Gibson B (2007) Enabling an accessible web 2.0. In: Proceedings of the 2007 international cross-disciplinary conference on web accessibility (W4A), W4A '07, vol 1. ACM, New York, pp 1–6. https://doi.org/10.1145/1243441.1243442

Hall W, Roure Dd, Shadbolt N (2009) The evolution of the web and implications for eResearch. Philos Trans: Math Phys Eng Sci 367:991–1001. https://doi.org/10.2307/40485755

Hooshmand S, Mahmud A, Bochmann GV, Faheem M, Jourdan GV, Couturier R, Onut IV (2016) D-ForenRIA: distributed reconstruction of user-interactions for rich internet applications. In: Proceedings of the 25th international conference companion on World Wide Web, international World Wide Web conferences steering committee, Republic and Canton of Geneva, Switzerland, WWW '16 Companion, pp 211–214. https://doi.org/10.1145/2872518.2890547

Kelly B, Sloan D, Phipps L, Petrie H, Hamilton F (2005) Forcing standardization or accommodating diversity?: a framework for applying the WCAG in the real world. In: Proceedings of the 2005 international cross-disciplinary workshop on web accessibility (W4A), W4A '05. ACM, New York, pp 46–54. https://doi.org/10.1145/1061811.1061820

Lewis C (1982) Using the thinking-aloud method in cognitive interface design. IBM TJ Watson Research Center, Yorktown Heights

Maciel MRC (2000) Portadores de deficiência. São Paulo em Perspectiva 14(2):51–56

Mahemoff M (2007) Padrões de Projetos Ajax. Alta Books, Rio de Janeiro, RJ

Melnyk V, Ashok V, Puzis Y, Soviak A, Borodin Y, Ramakrishnan IV (2014) Widget classification with applications to web accessibility. Springer International Publishing, Cham, pp 341–358. https://doi.org/10.1007/978-3-319-08245-5_20

Mesbah A, van Deursen A, Roest D (2012) Invariant-based automatic testing of modern web applications. IEEE Trans Softw Eng 38(1):35–53

Mezzalira L (2018) Front-end reactive architectures: explore the future of the front-end using reactive JavaScript frameworks and libraries, 1st edn. Apress, London. https://doi.org/10.1007/978-1-4842-3180-7

Murugesan S (2007) Understanding Web 2.0. IT Prof 9(4):34–41

Naftali M, Watanabe W, Sloan D (2010) W4A 2010: a web accessibility conference report from the Google W4A student award winners. SIGWEB Newsl 1:1–1:5. https://doi.org/10.1145/1836291. 1836292

Nielsen J (1993) Usability engineering. Morgan Kaufmann Publishers Inc, San Francisco

Ohara T, Iwata H, Shirogane J, Fukazawa Y (2016) Support to apply accessibility guidelines to web applications. Int J Comput Commun Eng 5(2):99–109

O'Reilly T (2005) What is web 2.0. http://oreilly.com/web2/archive/what-is-web-20.html

Pansanato L, Rivolli A, Pereira D (2015) An evaluation with web developers of capturing user interaction with rich internet applications for usability evaluation. Int J Comput Sci Appl 4(2):10. http://dpi-journals.com/index.php/IJCSA/article/view/1569/1384

Petrie H, Bevan N (2009) The evaluation of accessibility, usability, and user experience. In: The universal access handbook. Human factors and ergonomics. CRC Press, pp 1–16. http://www.crcnetbase.com/doi/abs/10.1201/9781420064995-c20

Petrie H, Hamilton F, King N (2004) Tension, what tension?: website accessibility and visual design. In: Proceedings of the 2004 international cross-disciplinary workshop on web accessibility (W4A), W4A '04. ACM, New York, pp 13–18. https://doi.org/10.1145/990657.990660

Petrie H, Savva A, Power C (2015) Towards a unified definition of web accessibility. In: Proceedings of the 12th web for all conference, W4A '15. ACM, New York, pp 35:1–35:13. http://dl.acm.org/citation.cfm?id=2746653

Power C, Freire A, Petrie H, Swallow D (2012) Guidelines are only half of the story: accessibility problems encountered by blind users on the web. In: Proceedings of the SIGCHI conference on human factors in computing systems, CHI '12. ACM, New York, pp 433–442. https://doi.org/10.1145/2207676.2207736

Reid LG, Snow-Weaver A (2008) WCAG 2.0: a web accessibility standard for the evolving web. In: Proceedings of the 2008 international cross-disciplinary conference on web accessibility (W4A), W4A '08. ACM, New York, pp 109–115. https://doi.org/10.1145/1368044.1368069

Rubin J, Chisnell D (2008) Handbook of usability testing, 2nd edn. Wiley, Indianapolis

Schiavone AG, Paternò F (2015) An extensible environment for guideline-based accessibility evaluation of dynamic web applications. Univers Access Inf Soc 14(1):111–132. https://doi.org/10.1007/s10209-014-0399-3

Schmidt KU, Dörflinger J, Rahmani T, Sahbi M, Stojanovic L, Thomas SM (2008) An user interface adaptation architecture for rich internet applications. In: ESWC'08: proceedings of the 5th European semantic web conference on the semantic web. Springer-Verlag, Berlin, Heidelberg, pp 736–750

Shneiderman B, Plaisant C, Cohen M, Jacobs S (2009) Designing the user interface: strategies for effective human-computer interaction, 5th edn. Addison-Wesley Publishing Company, Reading

Tateishi T, Miyashita H, Naoshi T, Saito S, Ono K (2007) DHTML accessibility checking based on static JavaScript analysis. Springer, Berlin, Heidelberg, pp 167–176. https://doi.org/10.1007/978-3-540-73283-9_20

Thatcher J, Bohman P, Burks M, Henry LS, Regan B, Swierenga S, Urban DM, Waddell DC (2002) Constructing accessible web sites, vol 34. Glasshaus Birmingham, Birmingham

Thatcher J, Kirkpatrick A, Urban M, Lawson B, Henry SL, Burks MR, Waddell C, Heilmann C, Rutter R, Regan B, Lauke PH (2006) Web accessibility: web standards and regulatory compliance, 1st edn. Apress, Berkeley

US Government (2014) Section 508. https://www.section508.gov/

Valencia X, Arrue M, Pérez JE, Abascal J (2013) User individuality management in websites based on WAI-ARIA annotations and ontologies. In: Proceedings of the 10th international cross-disciplinary conference on web accessibility, W4A '13. ACM, New York, pp 29:1–29:10. http://dl.acm.org/citation.cfm?id=2461128

W3C (2005) Introduction to web accessibility. http://www.w3.org/WAI/intro/accessibility

W3C (2008) Web content accessibility guidelines (wcag) 2.0. http://www.w3.org/TR/WCAG20/

W3C (2012) Packaged web apps (widgets) – packaging and XML configuration (second edition). W3C recommendation. http://www.w3.org/TR/widgets/

W3C (2013) WAI-ARIA 1.0 authoring practices - an author's guide to understanding and implementing accessible rich internet applications. W3C working draft. http://www.w3.org/TR/wai-aria-practices/

W3C (2014) WAI-ARIA 1.0 user agent implementation guide. https://www.w3.org/TR/wai-aria-implementation/

W3C (2015a) Authoring tool accessibility guidelines 2.0. https://www.w3.org/TR/ATAG20/

W3C (2015b) User agent accessibility guidelines 2.0. https://www.w3.org/TR/UAAG20/

W3C (2017) Accessible rich internet applications (WAI-ARIA) 1.1. https://www.w3.org/TR/wai-aria-1.1/

Watanabe WM, Fortes RPM, Dias AL (2012) Using acceptance tests to validate accessibility requirements in RIA. In: Proceedings of the international cross-disciplinary conference on web accessibility, W4A '12. ACM, New York, pp 15:1–15:10. https://doi.org/10.1145/2207016.2207022

Watanabe WM, Dias AL, Fortes RPdM (2015a) Fona: quantitative metric to measure focus navigation on rich internet applications. ACM Trans Web 9(4):20:1–20:28. https://doi.org/10.1145/2812812

Watanabe WM, Geraldo RJ, Fortes RPM (2015b) Keyboard navigation mechanisms in widgets: an investigation on ARIA's implementations. J Web Eng 14(1–2):41–62. http://dl.acm.org/citation.cfm?id=2871254.2871258

Watanabe WM, Fortes RPM, Dias AL (2017) Acceptance tests for validating ARIA requirements in widgets. Univers Access Inf Soc 16(1):3–27. https://doi.org/10.1007/s10209-015-0437-9

Yesilada Y, Brajnik G, Harper S (2009) How much does expertise matter?: a barrier walkthrough study with experts and non-experts. In: Proceedings of the 11th international ACM SIGACCESS conference on computers and accessibility, Assets '09. ACM, New York, pp 203–210. http://dl.acm.org/citation.cfm?id=1639678

Chapter 22
Scientific Documents

Volker Sorge, Dragan Ahmetovic, Cristian Bernareggi and John Gardner

Abstract Scientific documents are a very specialised type of literature not only in terms of their topics and intended audience, but also in terms of their content and how it is presented. They generally use highly topical vernacular, mathematical formulas, diagrams, data visualisations, etc. While any single one of these features on its own poses a considerable accessibility problem, their combination makes the accessibility of scientific literature particularly challenging. However, with nearly all aspects of learning, teaching, and research moving to the web, there is a need to specifically address this problem for science on the web. In this chapter, we present an overview of the main challenges that arise when making scientific texts accessible. We will particularly concentrate on the accessibility problem for scientific diagrams and discuss the more common techniques for making them accessible via screen-reading, sonification and audio-tactile presentation. This chapter gives an overview of the current state of the art, sketches some of the technical details on how to create accessible diagrams and closes with some open research questions.

22.1 Introduction

Since the beginning of this millennium, we have seen massive changes in our habits to learn, teach and study the sciences. There has been a trend in online learning and massive open online courses (MOOC). And even where traditional teaching methods

V. Sorge (✉)
University of Birmingham, Birmingham, UK
e-mail: v.sorge@cs.bham.ac.uk

D. Ahmetovic
Università degli Studi di Torino, Turin, Italy
e-mail: ahmetovic.dragan@gmail.com

C. Bernareggi
Università degli Studi di, Turin, Italy
e-mail: cristian.bernareggi@unimi.it

J. Gardner
ViewPlus Inc., Corvallis, OR, USA
e-mail: john.gardner@viewplus.com

are still employed, teaching material moved more and more to online resources and learning management systems. We no longer research a subject by going to the library and finding a book or reading a paper, but we search the internet for information and read a relevant online article. Even in advanced academia, research is now rarely communicated in traditional paper form, or their electronic equivalent such as PDF documents, but via digital libraries and web documents. While in many countries legislation mandates the accessibility of teaching material, online or otherwise, in primary and secondary education, for advanced scientific material, as used in further and higher education, this is rarely the case. The situation is even worse in advanced academia, where publications are often only aimed at a small number of experts worldwide and accessibility considerations are generally ignored.

Documents in the traditional STEM fields[1] are often a combination of text, tables, formulas, and diagrams, each have to be made accessible with different techniques, often with different systems or in separate workflows. Access to scientific material, therefore, presents a major challenge for readers with visual impairments—and to some degree for readers with learning disabilities like dyslexia or dyscalculia—that goes far beyond the problem encountered in the ordinary document or web accessibility.

Traditionally, scientific literature was made accessible in a manual process, generally on a by-need basis and often restricted to monographs important for teaching a particular subject. Texts could be translated into Braille, with formulas being set in specialist formats and experts preparing tactile versions of diagrams. Alternatively, subject matter experts would make audio recordings of literature, pronouncing formulas unambiguously, giving detailed explanations of diagrams and illustrations.

In the age of the web, these traditional workflows often fail, mainly for two reasons: first, teaching material can now be assembled and customised quickly and easily by everyone. Thus teachers, lecturers and professors prefer to use their own notes for teaching, multiplying the number of material that needs to be made accessible on a daily basis for teaching alone. However, even if the material has been made accessible sufficiently, providing alternative text for images and formulas etc., the second main problem is that web documents are often ephemeral. That is, they can change easily overnight; a formula is updated or a diagram is changed making even the best alternative text description obsolete. Consequently, new ways of making STEM content have to be developed in the age of the web.

22.2   Scientific Documents and the Web

Scientific documents have a number of particularities that raise the barrier for their accessibility. We briefly give an overview of the particularly challenging components they exhibit, before focusing on diagrams for the remainder of the chapter.

---

[1]STEM is an acronym for Science, Technology, Engineering, Mathematics.

Highly specialised vernacular—Most scientific subjects come with their own particular language, use highly specialised terms that can not be found in ordinary dictionaries or that are taken from other languages, such as Latin. Consequently, using ordinary assistive technologies like screen readers can often lead to mispronunciations or incorrectness (e.g. notations like Greek letters are omitted) that are intolerable for scientific subjects, where precision of expression is often the key.

Setting screen readers to read specific words more slowly or letter by letter can help to work around these problems. However, the obvious drawback is that readers have to spend considerably more time on the text as well as loose the reading flow, which is far from ideal.

Tables—Many sciences rely on presenting data, to convey information or backup experimental results, often in a tabular form. But unlike ordinary tables, where standard row by row or column by column reading is sufficient to comprehend their content, scientific tables often need to be viewed comparatively or holistically. For example, the distribution of zeros in a table can convey more meaning than the actual numerical values of all the other entries.

While for readers with learning impairments, techniques such as highlighting can be helpful, for readers with visual impairments that rely on extreme magnification or on screen readers, it is nearly impossible to get a picture of a table as a whole and linear exploration will generally not reveal the information as intended by the author. One solution is to employ advanced screen reading techniques such as cursor virtualisation, which can help a reader to jump between different cells of a table. In addition, tables can be authored with appropriate ARIA annotations (Diggs et al. 2017) to guide screen reader users to a non-linear navigation.

Formulas—Mathematical, statistical or chemical formulas can be found across the majority of scientific texts. As maths accessibility is a long standing issue, there exists assistive technology specialising on mathematics (Soiffer 2005; Cervone et al. 2016; Sorge 2018) as well as some support for mathematics in general screen reading technology (Scientific 2019; Apple 2019; Sorge et al. 2014; Texthelp 2019). However, the reading of complex formulae and the pronunciation of mathematical expressions can vary considerably over different subject areas or STEM disciplines. As a very simple example consider the imaginary number: it is normally represented by i, but in many engineering disciplines j is used, as i denotes current. Simply put, the further advanced or specialised a scientific text, the less likely it is for current screen reading technology to be sufficient to handle formulas correctly.

As formulas play an exceptional role in education and maths accessibility is a research area in its own right, they are treated separately in the next chapter.

Diagrams—Graphical illustrations are an important means of conveying information in STEM subjects and they are ubiquitous in teaching material. While good visualisations are commonly used to great effect for the sighted world, they are practically useless to a visually impaired and particularly a blind audience. Indeed, often diagrams not only complement the exposition in the text, but are used in lieu of an exposition, with the consequence that if one cannot read the diagram, one cannot understand the document.

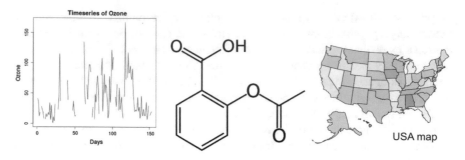

Fig. 22.1 Some common examples of scientific diagrams: A timeseries plot for the distribution of Ozone; a chemical molecule diagram for Aspirin; and a political map of the USA

There exist a number of taxonomies to classify diagrams. For the purpose of our discussion, we will adopt the following rough division:

Data Visualisations plot a relationship between two or more variables. They include histograms, function graphs, scatter plots, and time series, for which an example is presented on the left in Fig. 22.1. They are commonly used for the visualisation of statistical data and in other areas of mathematics either over discrete or continuous ranges of values.

Relationship Diagrams illustrate collections of items and relationships between them. Common examples are network diagrams, organisational charts, phylogenetic trees, molecule diagrams. An example of the latter is given in the middle of Fig. 22.1. They are generally of a graph-like nature and aim for clarity using ordered and clean layout.

Schematics are the abstract, often simplified graphical depiction of complex systems and relationships. Examples are drawings of machinery or electric circuits in engineering, but also drawings of organisms in the life sciences or maps, such as the example in the Fig. 22.1. In addition to interspersed descriptive text, they often use colour to distinguish and emphasise objects and relationships.

In addition to these types of diagrams, it is not uncommon to find more artistic illustrations in the scientific literature, such as botanical drawings of plants. However, as these are becoming less common in advanced scientific material and in particular more modern work, they are of less practical importance.

22.3 Well-Structured and Information-Rich SVG

Traditionally diagrams on the web were embedded as bitmap images such as Jpeg, PNG, or GIF. While bitmaps can be made accessible to some degree by providing an alternative text description using the HTML `alt` attribute for image tags, this can at best be viewed as a stopgap solution. First, although alt attributes are voiced by screen readers, some impose a limit on the number of words they will speak. In addition, unlike for regular text, users can generally not interact with alternative texts, such as going back or stepping through it word-by-word. Second, and more importantly, complex diagrams are difficult to describe in one-liners or even more extended text. Consider the example of the Aspirin diagram from Fig. 22.1: simply announcing 'Aspirin' would certainly defeat the aim of the diagram to convey the molecules structural layout visually. Providing a description of that structure in terms of lines and characters and how they are connected would not only be very long but also make it nearly impossible for a reader to form the correct mental image of the displayed structure.

Thus, to benefit from a diagram like their sighted peers, blind readers must have a means to interact with the diagram, to explore it step-by-step and at their own speed, and possibly to experience the diagram's structure in alternative formats. To this end, we need to embed semantic information on the diagram into its drawing. The HTML5 web standard (Berjon et al. 2013) offers its own dedicated image format with Scalable Vector Graphics (SVG) (Dahlström et al. 2011) that offers these possibilities. As a vector graphics format, it allows to specify components in terms of shapes and properties with coordinates where to place them instead of black and white or coloured pixels as in bitmap graphics. SVG images are drawn by the browser rather than simply displayed, which has not only the advantage that they scale lossless visually but also that they and their components are elements of the browsers DOM and can, therefore, be made accessible similar to any other part of the document.

One important prerequisite, however, is that the SVG is well constructed: consider the Aspirin molecule from Fig. 22.1 again. One can construct the SVG simply as a collection of 18 lines and 5 characters with the appropriate coordinates. While this would draw the diagram correctly, it would not capture any of the relations between the components that are so obvious to the sighted reader. But SVG does not only offer elements for painting, but also elements that are not rendered and can help to structure and annotate a drawing. In particular, it offers the *container element* g that allows to group related elements together and that can be arbitrarily nested, giving us an easy means to express semantic relations between components. We observe how this can be done with our Aspirin example as depicted in Fig. 22.2.

Grouping base elements and ordering—A natural initial step for introducing groups is by combining drawn elements that form a single semantic entity. For example, while double bonds consist of two lines, they should be grouped together into a single entity. Elements can then be arranged in an order that roughly corresponds to their structural layout in the diagram.

Creating abstract containers—We can hierarchically combine elements into groups representing semantically interesting components. For example, a chemical molecule is generally composed of one or more sub-components like rings, carbon chains or functional groups. Aspirin consists of three such components: A benzene ring and two functional groups, ester and carboxylic acid. Consequently, we can model these using three containers grouping the single bonds and atoms they comprise together.

Fig. 22.2 Structural overview of the Aspirin molecule consisting of one benzene ring with two attached functional groups: ester and carboxylic acid. Note that single and parallel lines represent single and double bonds, respectively. O and H denote Oxygen and Hydrogen atoms, while carbon atoms together with attached hydrogen atoms are understood to be at junctions of bonds, giving Aspirin 9 carbon atoms altogether

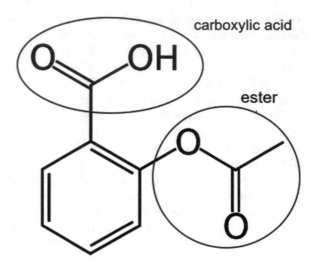

As a result, we get a highly structured SVG consisting of 5 individual elements: the three components and the two bonds connecting each functional group to the ring.

Embedding alternative structures—Often, hierarchically structuring an SVG is not enough to embed all the semantic relations we would like. For example, chemical molecules are in most cases complex graph structures. However, an SVG is a tree and therefore does not have the same expressive power. It is already impossible to indicate that the benzene container is a ring using a simple structuring approach. Once we have structures where two or more abstract containers need to share one or more components, e.g. two functional groups share atoms and bonds, we need to use an auxiliary structure to hold this information.

In this case, one can represent the graph structure as a separate XML element that is either embedded into the SVG in a different namespace or as an invisible structure in the DOM of the web page. The elements in the XML graph are related to the SVG components via their unique element ids. This technique was first introduced in Sorge et al. (2015) in the context of chemical diagrams. Smith et al. (2018) use a similar approach to introduce an auxiliary XML structure to represent information on animated physics simulations.

Inserting textual information—In addition to expressing semantics via grouping, SVG offers ways to embed textual information with the `title` and `desc` elements. The former can provides short information on an element that browsers can display as tooltip on mouse hovering. The latter is used to provide a more detailed description for an element. As each container or graphics element in an SVG can have associated `title` and `desc` elements, we can annotate drawings very detailed.

As an example consider the map of the USA in Fig. 22.1. We would annotate each state with a `title` element containing its name, while the `desc` element could hold additional information, such as the state's capital or its population.

22.4   Audio-Tactile Access

Converting content into tactile formats (e.g. braille notation) is a traditional way to provide access for the visually impaired to documents and graphics. Although it is generally assumed that blind people all read braille and understand graphics by feeling tactile replicas, this is not necessarily the case. Reliable statistics are not available, but estimates are that 10–15% of blind people read braille and only 2–3% are comfortable with tactile graphics. This number decreases for people who develop a visual impairment later in life. In STEM, the percentage is almost certainly larger, but it is still small. This is compounded by the fact that it is often difficult to convey tactilely all the information that is readily available visually: tactile resolution is considerably smaller than image resolution, making it difficult to clearly separate features in crowded diagrams; colours can only be modelled to a limited extent by different textures before they become indistinguishable; text in graphics cannot always be fitted as Braille and needs to be abbreviated or supplied in an extra key. All this make pure tactile graphics often difficult and cumbersome to read.

22.4.1   Overview on Audio-Tactile STEM Graphics

Audio-tactile diagrams try to solve this problem by complementing the tactile experience with audio feedback that can give information to components or explain elements that are difficult to represent tactilely. The concept was first introduced by Parkes in 1988 as audio/touch technique (Parkes 1988, 1991) as a way that even non-braille readers and people with other print disabilities can access graphical information. The user obtains the two dimensional overview of a tactile graphic and hears information spoken when they indicate a text label or some graphical object.

The potential of using audio-tactiles in teaching was realised quite early (Lötzsch 1994; Loetzsch and Roedig 1996) and a particular emphasis was given to their use in teaching and examining mathematics and sciences in primary and early secondary education (Gardner 2005; Landau et al. 2003). Another major application is the creation of audio-tactile maps (Miele et al. 2006). Technically, the talking graphic uses an interface (e.g. a touchscreen or finger-detecting camera) that sends spatial information to a phone, tablet, computer, or other devices that then can provide spoken or non-speech audio information about whatever is at the indicated position on the graphic. Diagrams have to be represented either in proprietary file formats (Landau et al. 2003) or standard SVG format appropriately enriched with metadata (Gardner 2016) as described in the previous section. This latter make it particularly useful for adaptation to the Web and we will concentrate on those in the remainder of this section.

Audio-tactile diagrams are also closely related to audio-haptic approaches, where sound and haptic feedback are combined (Iglesias 2004). For example (Gorlewicz et al. 2014) is an approach to teach mathematics using tablets that provide normal audio feedback together with vibration when graphical components are touched.

22.4.2   Creating Audio-Tactile SVG

When Creating good enough audio-tactile replicas of more complicated STEM graphics, care has to be taken to create both good tactile diagrams and speech data. In the US, the Braille Authority of North America (BANA) has established guidelines (North America 2010) for tactile graphics. Only trained transcribers can make diagrams that meet these standards, so officially sanctioned tactile graphics are very expensive. Good enough tactile graphics can be made by normal sighted human beings using common drawing software and printed using a graphics-capable embosser. For example, embosser from the ViewPlus line (ViewPlus 2018a) by default, emboss images as a tactile greyscale. Dark regions are embossed with tall dots and lighter regions with progressively lower dots. Simple line drawings, block images, and some colour images with good colour contrast can directly produce acceptable tactile images.

To add audio, we need diagrams as SVG files with appropriate metadata. They need a meaningful title and a description explaining what the image is supposed to convey. In addition, we need to add `title` elements to all the semantically meaningful components. If the title is not sufficiently descriptive, or if the author wants to convey related information, it should be given in the object description (i.e. the `desc` element). SVG also permits graphical features or text to be fitted to invisible overlay objects with titles and descriptions. This feature allows us to make even more abstract information tactile diagram. Consider again our Aspirin diagram from Fig. 22.1 semantically enriched with abstract containers and descriptions for functional groups as discussed in Sect. 22.3. In that form, a reader can only get audio feedback for the drawn elements, i.e. bonds, double bonds, oxygen, etc. To allow users to find the omitted carbon atoms we add invisible rectangles to the SVG at the junctions of the bonds with a title of 'Carbon'. Similarly, we add invisible bounding polygons around the containers representing the functional groups. This has the effect that, if the reader touches, for instance, inside the ring structure 'Benzene ring' will be spoken, while touching one of the ring's boundary lines, the corresponding bond will be announced. Note that the resulting audio-tactile image still retains the original visual properties, making a graphic accessible to both sighted and non-sighted readers at the same time.

22.5   Screen Reading

While audio-tactile graphics present an ideal means for readers to engage with diagrams, they have two major drawbacks: first, reading them requires to run additional, often proprietary software outside a web browser, that might not be available on all platforms. Second, they are relatively costly, both due to the price of embossers as well as the time it takes to emboss a tactile graphic, which is a consideration if one only wants to glance briefly at a diagram when reading an article.

Consequently, there are attempts to enable screen reading and interaction with graphics directly in browsers similar to working with ordinary text and to some extent mathematics. We have already commented on the disadvantages bitmap graphics have, due to the limitations of alternative text. However, although SVG effectively offers all the technical specification that can enable effective presentation of graphical material to visually impaired readers, support for working with SVG in mainstream screen readers is still relatively poor. One reason is the rather late adoption of SVG as an official HTML5 standard and in particular its implementation in all major browsers; in Internet Explorer some SVG support exists only since version 9. Moreover, screen readers often have problems with highly nested structures that require non-linear progression through DOM elements. Nevertheless, there are some successful approaches to making complex STEM diagrams web accessible with general screen readers, either by using ARIA constructs to guide screen readers or by turning SVG images effectively into rich web applications using JavaScript functionality.

22.5.1 Accessible SVG Using ARIA

Since SVG elements implement the same interface as regular DOM elements, they are amenable to WAI-ARIA technology (Diggs et al. 2017) for creating Accessible Rich Internet Applications. One such approach is implemented in the Highcharts library (Moseng et al. 2019) for generating data visualisations and maps. It allows authors to put a simple accessibility layer over visualisations. Technically, this is done by giving components of a diagram an entry in the tabbing structure of the web site via the `tabindex` attribute. Speech content that we would otherwise embed as `title` or `desc` elements, can instead be added via the `aria-label` attribute. For example, when considering the US states map in Fig. 22.1, each SVG element representing a state gets a `tabindex="-1"` and an `aria-label` with state name and any other information we want to convey. This allows the reader to browse through the different states once the map is focused, using left and right arrow keys. The screen reader will read the information embedded in the `aria-label`. Further visual effects like highlighting can be added by the change of CSS styling on focus events.

The advantage of this approach is that it can be employed without the need for any special application or hardware, using any screen reader on any platform. If JavaScript is available in the display engine, events can be exploited for visual style changes. However, care has to be taken on the order in which elements of the SVG are arranged as the tab order determines the order in which they can be presented to the user. This highlights the major drawback of this approach: the limitations it imposes on the freedom for the user to explore the diagram. For example, the states on the map can only be explored in a fixed order, not giving the reader the choice of seeing what neighbouring states lie north, south, east or west. Similarly, it is difficult to present information in a hierarchical manner by giving users the option to dive deeper into particular components, such as exploring cities or provinces of a state. Since the SVG elements can only be presented linearly; it is either all or nothing.

22.5.2 SVG as Rich Web Application

This problem can be solved by using bespoke navigation structures as introduced in Sect. 22.3. Examples of this approach are navigatable molecule diagrams (Sorge et al. 2015) and data visualisations (Fitzpatrick et al. 2017) as well as animated physics simulations (Smith et al. 2018).

The basic idea is to combine the SVG with a corresponding graph data structure and use JavaScript code to drive the navigation as soon as the user inspects the diagram. The SVG itself is turned into a rich web application, by annotating it with the ARIA `role="application"` attribute. This allows a user to switch from normal reading mode into diagram exploration mode (often with keystroke `Enter`). These hands control from the screen reader to the JavaScript application until explicitly left (usually with the `Escape` key). Further communication with the screen reader is achieved by using an ARIA live region; this is a DOM element that screen readers monitor and, whenever it is updated, its new content is voiced.

We observe how this works in practice using the Aspirin molecule as an example. Below is the graph data structure that implements navigation on the molecule in three layers: the entire molecule ($m1$), its three main components ($as1$, $as2$, $as3$), and for each of these, the layer of atoms and bonds:

When a reader enters the molecule, they can use the arrow keys to navigate the graph: initially, the entire molecule will be announced; that is, 'Aspirin' would be pushed to the live region and voiced by the screen reader. Keystroke `Down Arrow` will enter the next lower level and the benzene ring $as1$ will be spoken. Keystrokes `Right Arrow` and `Left Arrow` navigate to the functional groups ester ($as2$) and carboxylic acid ($as3$), respectively, while `Down Arrow` keystroke will allow the reader to walk around the single atoms of the ring (Fig. 22.3).

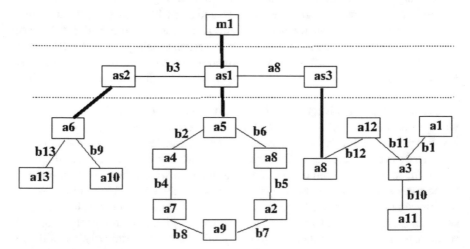

Fig. 22.3 Abstract Navigation graph for Aspirin: The labels a_i and b_i on vertices and edges correspond to ids of the drawn elements for atoms and bonds in the SVG. $as1$, $as2$, $as3$ represent the benzene ring, ester, and carboxylic acid components, respectively, and $m1$ the entire molecule

Note that the navigation structure is connected to the SVG via ids of the drawn elements, which allows effects like synchronised navigation highlighting, zooming and magnification. Having full control via a JavaScript application also makes it easy to offer other options to the reader, like toggling expert and novice explanations of the chemistry, changing navigation styles, or switching languages. But the reliance on JavaScript leads also to a disadvantage: in environments where JavaScript is not available, for instance in some ePub readers, this approach is not suitable.

22.6 Sonification

Up to here, our techniques to make STEM diagrams accessible relied on verbal explanations of their content. An alternative for non-visual exploration and editing of graphical representations is *sonification*, the transformation of any data relation into non-speech sound (Hermann 2008; Sarkar et al. 2012). Data sonification can be achieved thanks to the ability of the human auditory system to identify even slight changes in a sound pattern so that, the amount of information conveyed through an auditory representation can be, in some cases, very close to the visual equivalent (Balik et al. 2014; Harada et al. 2011). Based on this perceptual capability, many different solutions have been developed, in particular: sonification systems to explore any kind of visual scenarios (including images in STEM subjects) and sonification techniques to explore exclusively images in STEM subjects.

22.6.1 Background

Sonification techniques can be classified into two main categories, according to the exploration method adopted (Yeo and Berger 2005): *scanning* methods, in which image data is sonified in a predefined sequence, and *probing* methods, where the user can dynamically and interactively choose the portion of the image to be sonified.

Examples of systems for exploring any kind of visual scenario, based on the scanning method, are 'The vOICe' (Meijer 1992), where frames captured through a camera are sonified by mapping the vertical position of each pixel to frequency, the horizontal one to time and brightness to loudness (Dallas and Erickson 1983), and 'EyeMusic' (Abboud et al. 2014), that represents colour images through pleasant sounds. The position is mapped to a note in a pentatonic scale, the luminance to the attenuation of the note and the colour to distinct musical instruments. The evaluations of both blind subjects show that they can be used to explore basic geometric shapes. However, it is not clear whether they are adequate for exploring more complex representations.

Probing technique try to leverage both sonification and proprioception[2] to facilitate the selection of the portion of the image to be sonified. Generally, the image is presented on a touchscreen and exploration is achieved by sliding the finger over the touchscreen. The portion of the image pointed by the finger is sonified. For example, 'EdgeSonic' (Yoshida et al. 2011), uses two sonification modalities: local area and distance to edge. In the former, the user slides the finger over the touchscreen and once a line is touched, a sound is played. In the latter, a pulse train signal is used to represent the finger's distance to the closest line. The game 'Invisible Puzzle' (Gerino et al. 2015a, b; Mascetti et al. 2017) requires the player to recognise many different shapes (e.g. geometric shapes, daily life objects) through both probing and scanning methods, using 6 novel image sonification techniques. Evaluation of both systems have demonstrated that users are able to recognise geometric shapes after few minutes of training.

In addition, there has been considerable research specific for application of sonification in STEM. It is worth noting that research has investigated solutions both for all scientists and for blind people: Many different sonification techniques have been investigated to assist scientists in data analysis. For example, to mine databases of time series through musical melodies (Last and Gorelik 2008), monitor network traffic (Emsley et al. 2017) or to monitor real-time data streams (Hermann 2011). While all of these models can be adapted for integration into assistive technologies (Walker and Mauney 2010), there has also been work specifically targeting support for blind people to sonify data visualisations—especially function graphs—and relationship diagrams, in particular graphs (in the graph theoretical sense).

Particularly, the work on data visualisations has found its way into commercial products. For example, *Audio Graphing Calculator* (Gardner 2002) sonifies function diagrams by mapping coordinates to sound frequency. *SAS Graphics Accelerator* (SAS 2019) enables blind people to interactively explore bar charts, time series plots, heat maps, line charts, scatter plots and histograms and *Desmos* (Desmos 2019) leverages proprioception and sonification to explore function diagrams on touchscreen devices.

The evaluation with blind people gives evidence of the effectiveness of this sonification especially for understanding the trend of the function as well as maximum or minimum points. However, it also suggests that sonification on its own is not enough. Consequently, approaches that complement sonification with verbal explanations have been developed. For example, *Audio Functions* (Taibbi et al. 2014) combines scanning, probing and speech. A user can explore a function graph on a tablet by listening to the sonified diagram as a whole or by sliding the finger over the touchscreen following the sonified curve or along the x-axis and listen to the sonified function value. Further information about the function diagram (e.g. concavity and point coordinates) are optionally provided by speech. Analogously, *graCALC* (Goncu et al. 2015) is a graphing calculator that adds an overview containing a sonification

---

[2]Proprioception, in this context, refers to the awareness of the reader of their relative position in the graphic that is explored.

of the diagram and an automatically generated description in order to help the blind person in the initial navigation.

For relationship diagrams, exploration of directed and undirected graphs through sonification was notably analysed in the PLUMB system (Cohen et al. 2005) (later extended also to support other data structures Calder et al. 2007). It presents a graph on a tablet and a continuous sound varying in pitch and loudness guides the fingertip along edges to discover nodes. Names of edges and nodes are communicated by speech. Some events relevant for exploration, such as (e.g. entering/exiting a node) are signalled through auditory icons. A similar approach, but also including editing of structures, is followed in the Graph Sketching tool (GSK) (Balik et al. 2014).

22.6.2 Sonification on the Web

As opposed to sonification in general, sonification for the web has been explored only relatively recently, mainly because the technical prerequisites were not available: a dedicated `audio` tag has been introduced in HTML 5 only since 2014. The Web Audio API (Adenot and Toy 2018) that allows developers to add audio effects to web pages, has only been formalised since 2011 and implementation in major browsers are not all yet fully compatible. And even then, practical obstacles remain, such as sounds often being played with delays in a browser, which makes real-time sonification difficult.

Nevertheless, there is already some work exploiting these features initially for function graphs as well as other STEM graphics. Both the Desmos graphics calculator (Desmos 2019) and the Highcharts (Moseng et al. 2019) library support the sonification of x-y plots on the web using the Web Audio API. While the latter uses SVG representations as discussed in the previous sections, the former draws programmatically inside `canvas` elements (Cabanier et al. 2015). Wörtwein and Schauerte (2015) goes beyond simple plots by also sonifying charts and maps, in particular floor maps. When tracing graphics on a touch device the distance to the nearest wall are modelled with increasing and decreasing sounds. Cherston et al. (2016) introduces the auditory representations of real-time particle collision data from high energy physics. While this application is not aimed at a blind audience only, it illustrates the potential for sonification for complex data visualisation and simulations.

Finally, as a practical example, we consider sonification of a timeseries plot like the one presented in Fig. 22.1 can be created using the SVG and the Web Audio API. First, we note that the data in the plot is created with one or more SVG `path` elements, which is effectively a set of (x, y)-coordinate pairs $\{(x_0, y_0), (x_1, y_1), \ldots (x_n, y_n)\}$, each representing the endpoint of a line. We use a simple *oscillators* to create sound. An oscillator represents an audio source that generates a periodic waveform (e.g. a sine wave) for a given frequency. We then turn the coordinates of the path into frequency over time as follows: decide on a base frequency f_0; for simplicity we take $f_0 = \sigma(y_0)$, where σ is a suitable scaling function. Then map all remaining y

coordinates to frequencies $f_i = \sigma(y_i)$. Similarly, create time n intervals $[t_{i-1}, t_i]$, $i = 1, \ldots, n$ by setting $t_i = \tau(x_i)$, where τ is a suitable scaling function. We then create n oscillators $o_i, i = 1, \ldots, n$ with frequency f_i. A sonification is then created by running oscillator o_i in interval $[t_{i-1}, t_i]$. Note that, the created sound will be rather crude. More pleasing results can be achieved by applying smoothing methods or modulating externally loaded sounds instead of using oscillators.

While this approach gives us a scanning method for sonification, we can easily see how one could create a probing method by combining this technique with the interactive diagram exploration from the previous section, if we allow the reader to step through recursively decreasing parts of the data plot and add a sonification to each sub-interval separately.

22.7 Discussion

The techniques discussed in this chapter demonstrate that there are already ways to give full access to scientific web documents to all readers, regardless of their disabilities. The evolution and availability of current web technologies (HTML 5, SVG, ARIA, Web Audio, etc.) can ultimately ensure seamless non-visual exploration of graphical content dynamically generated on the web, without the need for specialist software tools or browser extensions. However, an important prerequisite for all of the presented techniques to allow meaningful non-visual presentation of the content is that the SVG diagrams are sufficiently semantically rich, which leaves the question of how the relevant information can be obtained and embedded. There are effectively three ways to do this:

Authoring—The straight forward method is to annotate components during authoring. SVG drawing tools like Inkscape (2019) allow to add title and descriptions to each object's properties. Similarly, the Highcharts library (Moseng et al. 2019) for generating data visualisations, maps, etc. offers methods to allow authors to annotate SVG drawings programmatically.

Automatic Generation—Of course, authors often care more about visuals than accessibility, so it is always preferred if annotations can be generated automatically. Since the majority of SVG images are not drawn individually by hand but generated programmatically as output of some scientific calculation programme, diagrams could be generated accessibly at point of production.

Fitzpatrick et al. (2017) and Godfrey et al. (2018) presents a way to produce data visualisations like the time series shown in Fig. 22.1 from the statistic software package R (R Core Team 2017) that generates fully accessible diagrams directly from the statistical model. Speech rules are triggered during SVG output that add `title` and `desc` elements to each of the drawn components such as the ticks on the axes, as well as to grouped elements like the x- and y-axes and most importantly to the actually presented data elements.

Retrofitting—Since many diagrams are created 'naively', either by authors or software, and there is a need to make legacy content accessible, the final alternative is to retroactively add the semantic information. Specialised software like IVEO Transformer (ViewPlus 2018b) can assist in transforming bit map images to good tactile copies. It can OCR (optical character recognition) text, replace colour by automatically generated tactile patterns and add Braille for 'stand alone' tactile images. Users can elect to put lines at edges of coloured objects and to reduce or eliminate colour fill. A pencil allows objects to be added or removed. Finally, the transformer provides a way to improve the tactile image without changing its visual.

Much more challenging is to automatically generate semantic information for an already existing diagram, by means of image analysis and pattern recognition. For example, (Sorge et al. 2015) presents an approach that analyses bitmap images of molecule drawings like our Aspirin example, automatically recognises the chemical structure and semantically interprets it to the extent that it can not only correctly describe all atoms and bonds, but also recognises the intermediate components, i.e. the ring and the two functional groups, and names and describes correctly. This results in an SVG together with an external annotation structure as mentioned in the previous section, which can be used to make the molecule diagram accessible either by screen readers or as audio-tactile graphics. While this method has the advantage that even poorly authored images and legacy documents can be made accessible, its drawback is that, in case of recognition errors, incorrect descriptions might be generated.

22.8   Author Opinion

It is our opinion that the future for fully accessible scientific documents lies in the web and its technologies. Its ubiquity and transferable standards will help to eliminate the need for creating bespoke, often platform specific specialist software tools for accessing material in different subjects. This will not only enable more robust and future-proof documents but in particular will relieve readers from the need to buy, use and learn new software tools for every subject matter. There might be some need to extend the ARIA standard to allow for more flexible exploration techniques to avoid the need for screen reading software to become expert systems on each scientific subject. However, we should not fall into the trap of designing subject specific representation standards for the web. The example of the web standard for mathematics MathML, which has existed for many years and is yet to be implemented in most browsers, demonstrates that these efforts can easily become cul-de-sacs. Instead we should acknowledge that the representation standards are already there, and we only have to fill them meaningfully. In other words the most important task is to close the semantic gap between representation and accessibility, by retrieving, generating and fitting the necessary information into visual content ideally without manual intervention.

Unfortunately, it would be too much to hope for authors to change their ways of preparing scientific documents to be accessible out of the box. However, many components like diagrams, formulas, tables are generated with scientific software in which this information is readily available but often ignored when the visual output is generated. There is therefore a need to both educate system developers about accessibility needs and to provide bespoke accessibility extensions. Scientifically there is plenty of demand for developing techniques in image analysis, pattern recognition and semantic analysis as well as exploiting advances in machine learning and AI to recognise, understand, classify and semantically enrich existing visual components to make documents fully accessible.

22.9 Future Directions

Immediate future work should consist of porting existing accessibility techniques to the web. For example, audio-tactile enabled SVGs can be embedded into websites, but to take full advantage of their capabilities they still need to be opened in a special software application. It is ongoing work to enable the audio feedback directly from within browsers. And this is by no means purely derivative work: Creating general methods that work on all software platforms and devices—desktops, tablets, phones—simultaneously are of higher scientific value, than building a bespoke system for one particular operating system, only.

Although many accessibility techniques have been investigated and evaluated with blind and visually impaired students, large-scale longitudinal studies aimed at measuring the effectiveness and the acceptance of the presented techniques in the context of STEM education have not yet been conducted (Davison 2012). These studies, however, would be of great value to lead visually impaired students in the choice of the suitable tools in their scientific curriculum.

It is clear that well designed, semantically rich diagrams are an important prerequisite for making scientific content accessible. To that extent effective and reliable methods for the automatic, or automated, conversion and semantic enrichment of existing diagrams are needed, combining areas of image analysis and document understanding. Likewise better support for editing information-rich diagrams are needed, ideally on the web. While, for example techniques for editing graphical representations assisted by sonification exist, they are still very limited. Touchscreen and wearable devices able to localise the position of many body parts (e.g. fingers, arms, head) even in a three-dimensional space are getting more and more widespread also among visually impaired people. These devices prove to be a suitable platform to investigate the editing of graphical representations driven by sonification.

Finally, the new medium of the web enables us to go beyond what is possible on static media like paper, leading to more reader engaging approaches to present science, by providing animated graphics as well as interactive simulations. For an example of interactive statistics see Stark and Sticigui (2018) and for physics simulations see Smith et al. (2018). Both projects serve as a research base for advanced accessibility techniques in interactive graphics.

22.10 Conclusions

Accessibility to scientific material, and in particular diagrams, is one of the most challenging tasks in accessibility research. It is not merely a niche concern, as access to education is a human right, and restricting disabled students from learning scientific subjects due to lack of accessible material is a clear discrimination. In fact, the societal importance of this work cannot be overestimated as the need to participate in the information society where, for instance, data visualisation commonly occur in news, sports and even in the social media, requires that complex, data-intensive content can be accessed by all, everywhere and on any device.

References

Abboud S, Hanassy S, Levy-Tzedek S, Maidenbaum S, Amedi A (2014) Eyemusic: introducing a "visual" colorful experience for the blind using auditory sensory substitution. Restor Neurol Neurosci 32(2):247–257

Adenot P, Toy R (2018) Web audio api. W3c working draft, world wide web consortium. http://www.w3.org/TR/webaudio

Apple: voiceover (2019). www.apple.com/accessibility/osx/voiceover

Balik S, Mealin SP, Stallmann M, Rodman R, Glatz ML, Sigler VJ (2014) Including blind people in computing through access to graphs. In: ASSETS14 - proceedings of the 16th international ACM SIGACCESS conference on computers and accessibility, pp 91–98

Berjon R, Faulkner S, Leithead T, Navara ED, O'Connor E, Pfeiffer S, Hickson I (2013) Hypertext markup language (html) version 5.0. W3c candidate recommendation, world wide web consortium. http://www.w3.org/TR/html5

Cabanier R, Mann J, Munro J, Wiltzius T, Hickson I (2015) Html canvas 2d context. W3c recommendation, world wide web consortium. http://www.w3.org/TR/2dcontext

Calder M, Cohen RF, Lanzoni J, Landry N, Skaff J (2007) Teaching data structures to students who are blind. In: Proceedings of the 12th annual SIGCSE conference on innovation and technology in computer science education, ITiCSE '07. ACM, New York, pp 87–90. https://doi.org/10.1145/1268784.1268811

Cervone D, Krautzberger P, Sorge V (2016) Towards universal rendering in mathjax. In: Proceedings of the 13th web for all conference. ACM, p 4

Cherston J, Hill E, Goldfarb S, Paradiso JA (2016) Sonification platform for interaction with real-time particle collision data from the atlas detector. In: Proceedings of the 2016 CHI conference extended abstracts on human factors in computing systems, CHI EA '16. ACM, pp 1647–1653. https://doi.org/10.1145/2851581.2892295

Cohen RF, Yu R, Meacham A, Skaff J (2005) Plumb: displaying graphs to the blind using an active auditory interface. In: Proceedings of the 7th international ACM SIGACCESS conference on computers and accessibility, Assets '05. ACM, New York, pp 182–183. https://doi.org/10.1145/1090785.1090820

Dahlström E et al (2011) Scalable vector graphics (svg) 1.1. W3c recommendation, world wide web consortium. www.w3.org/TR/SVG

Dallas Jr SA, Erickson AJ (1983) Sound pattern generator. US Patent 4,378,569

Davison BK (2012) Evaluating auditory graphs with blind students in a classroom. SIGACCESS Access Comput 102:4–7. https://doi.org/10.1145/2140446.2140447

Desmos: graphing calculator (2019). www.desmos.com/calculator

Diggs J, McCarron S, Cooper M, Schwerdtfeger R, Craig J (2017) Accessible rich internet applications (wai-aria) 1.1. W3c recommendation, international digital publishing forum. www.w3.org/TR/wai-aria

Emsley I, De Roure D, Chamberlain A (2017) A network of noise: designing with a decade of data to sonify janet. In: Proceedings of the 12th international audio mostly conference on augmented and participatory sound and music experiences, AM '17. ACM, New York, pp 36:1–36:5. https://doi.org/10.1145/3123514.3123567

Fitzpatrick D, Godfrey AJR, Sorge V (2017) Producing accessible statistics diagrams in R. In: Proceedings of the 14th web for all conference. ACM, p 4

Gardner J (2005) New technologies for accessible tactile math and accessible graphics. In: Proceedings of the national federation of the blind goals for achieving math accessibility summit

Gardner JA (2002) Access by blind students and professionals to mainstream math and science. In: Proceeding of the 8th international conference on computers helping people with special needs. Springer

Gardner JA (2016) Universally accessible figures. In: International conference on computers helping people with special needs. Springer, pp 417–420

Gerino A, Picinali L, Bernareggi C, Alabastro N, Mascetti S (2015a) Towards large scale evaluation of novel sonification techniques for non visual shape exploration. In: Proceedings of the 17th international ACM SIGACCESS conference on computers and accessibility, ASSETS '15. ACM, New York, pp 13–21. https://doi.org/10.1145/2700648.2809848

Gerino A, Picinali L, Bernareggi C, Mascetti S (2015b) Eyes-free exploration of shapes with invisible puzzle. In: Proceedings of the 17th international ACM SIGACCESS conference on computers and accessibility, ASSETS '15. ACM, New York, pp 425–426. https://doi.org/10.1145/2700648.2811335

Godfrey AJR, Murray P, Sorge V (2018) An accessible interaction model for data visualisation in statistics. In: International conference on computers helping people with special needs. Springer

Goncu C, Marriott K (2015) Gracalc: an accessible graphing calculator. In: Proceedings of the 17th international ACM SIGACCESS conference on computers and accessibility, ASSETS '15. ACM, New York, pp 311–312. https://doi.org/10.1145/2700648.2811353

Gorlewicz JL, Burgner J, Withrow TJ, Webster RJ III (2014) Initial experiences using vibratory touchscreens to display graphical math concepts to students with visual impairments. J Spec Educ Technol 29(2):17–25

Harada S, Takagi H, Asakawa C (2011) On the audio representation of radial direction. In: Proceedings of the SIGCHI conference on human factors in computing systems, CHI '11. ACM, New York, pp 2779–2788. https://doi.org/10.1145/1978942.1979354

Hermann T (2008) Taxonomy and definitions for sonification and auditory display. In: Susini P, Warusfel O (eds) Proceedings of the 14th international conference on auditory display (ICAD 2008). IRCAM

Hermann T, Hunt A, Neuhoff JG (2011) The sonification handbook. Logos Publishing House

Iglesias R, Casado S, Gutierrez T, Barbero J, Avizzano C, Marcheschi S, Bergamasco M (2004) Computer graphics access for blind people through a haptic and audio virtual environment. In: Proceedings of the 3rd IEEE International workshop on haptic, audio and visual environments and their applications, HAVE 2004. IEEE, pp 13–18

Inkscape 0.92—draw freely (2019). http://inkscape.org

Landau S, Russell M, Gourgey K, Erin JN, Cowan J (2003) Use of the talking tactile tablet in mathematics testing. J Vis Impair Blind 97(2):85–96

Last M, Gorelik A (2008) Using sonification for mining time series data. In: Proceedings of the 9th international workshop on multimedia data mining: held in conjunction with the ACM SIGKDD 2008, MDM '08. ACM, New York, pp 63–72. https://doi.org/10.1145/1509212.1509220

Loetzsch J, Roedig G (1996) Interactive tactile media in training visually handicapped people. Institut National de la Sante et de la Recherche Medicale: colloques et seminaires, pp 155–160

Lötzsch J (1994) Computer-aided access to tactile graphics for the blind. In: International conference on computers for handicapped persons. Springer, pp 575–581

Mascetti S, Gerino A, Bernareggi C, Picinali L (2017) On the evaluation of novel sonification techniques for non-visual shape exploration. ACM Trans Access Comput 9(4):13:1–13:28. https://doi.org/10.1145/3046789

Meijer PB (1992) An experimental system for auditory image representations. IEEE Trans Biomed Eng 39(2)

Miele JA, Landau S, Gilden D (2006) Talking TMAP: automated generation of audio-tactile maps using Smith-kettlewell's TMAP software. Br J Vis Impair 24(2):93–100

Moseng Ø et al. (2019) Highcharts—make your data come alive. https://www.highcharts.com

Braille Authority of North America (2010) Guidelines and standards for tactile graphics. http://www.brailleauthority.org/tg

Parkes D (1988) Nomad, an audio-tactile tool for the aquisition, use and management of spatially distributed information by visually impaired people. In: Proceeding of the second international symposium on maps and graphics for visually handicapped people

Parkes D (1991) Nomad: enabling access to graphics and text based information for blind, visually impaired and other disability groups. Technol People Disabil 5:690–714

R Core Team: R: A language and environment for statistical computing. R Foundation for Statistical Computing, Vienna, Austria (2017). www.R-project.org

Sarkar R, Bakshi S, Sa PK (2012) Review on image sonification: a non-visual scene representation. In: 2012 1st International conference on recent advances in information technology (RAIT). IEEE, pp 86–90

SAS: SAS graphics accelerator (2017). https://support.sas.com/software/products/graphics-accelerator

Scientific F (2019) Jaws. https://freedomscientific.com/Products/Blindness/JAWS

Smith T, Greenberg J, Reid S, Moore E (2018) Architecture for accessible interactive simulations. In: Proceedings of the 15th web for all conference. ACM

Soiffer N (2005) Mathplayer: web-based math accessibility. In: Proceedings of the 7th international ACM SIGACCESS conference on computers and accessibility. ACM, pp 204–205

Sorge V (2018) Speech rule engine version 2.2.2. http://github.com/zorkow/speech-rule-engine

Sorge V, Chen C, Raman T, Tseng D (2014) Towards making mathematics a first class citizen in general screen readers. In: 11th Web for all conference. ACM, Seoul, Korea

Sorge V, Lee M, Wilkinson S (2015) End-to-end solution for accessible chemical diagrams. In: Proceedings of the 12th web for all conference. ACM

Stark PB (2018) Sticigui. www.stat.berkeley.edu/~stark/SticiGui

Taibbi M, Bernareggi C, Gerino A, Ahmetovic D, Mascetti S (2014) Audiofunctions: eyes-free exploration of mathematical functions on tablets. In: Computers helping people with special needs. Springer

Texthelp: Equatio (2019). www.texthelp.com/en-gb/products/equatio

ViewPlus (2018a) http://viewplus.com/viewplus-embossers-at-a-glance

ViewPlus (2018b) http://viewplus.com/product/tiger-software-suite

Walker BN, Mauney LM (2010) Universal design of auditory graphs: a comparison of sonification mappings for visually impaired and sighted listeners. ACM Trans Access Comput 2(3):12:1–12:16. https://doi.org/10.1145/1714458.1714459

Wörtwein T, Schauerte B, Müller KE, Stiefelhagen R (2015) Interactive web-based image sonification for the blind. In: Proceedings of the 2015 ACM on international conference on multimodal interaction, ICMI '15. ACM, pp 375–376. https://doi.org/10.1145/2818346.2823298

Yeo WS, Berger J (2005) A framework for designing image sonification methods. In: Proceedings of international conference on auditory display

Yoshida T, Kitani KM, Koike H, Belongie S, Schlei K (2011) Edgesonic: image feature sonification for the visually impaired. In: Proceeding of the 2nd augmented human international conference. ACM

Chapter 23
Mathematics and Statistics

Neil Soiffer and Steve Noble

Abstract Math accessibility work dates back to the 1990s, but these efforts have accelerated rapidly in the last 5 years. It has moved from research into widely used systems that include JAWS, NVDA, VoiceOver, and TextHELP. The current systems convert MathML into speech and braille, and allow the users to navigate expressions for better comprehension. Further work on better semantic speech that uses page content or other clues to determine the meaning of the notation and how it should be spoken is ongoing. Work on accessible typed input, braille input, speech input, and accessible ways of doing math (not just reading it) is also underway. Beyond equations, the research on audio and tactile methods of presenting plots and charts has also been performed, and is being incorporated into commonly used software.

23.1 Introduction

Work on making math accessible dates back to the early 1990s with pioneering work by T. V. Raman for his Ph.D. thesis (Raman 1994) and Stevens and Edwards (1994). For more references to early work, see Karshmer et al. (2007).

In the last 5–10 years, much of the work has focused on reading (both speech and braille) and navigating math. The results of that work are embedded in several popular tools including JAWS, NVDA + MathPlayer (Soiffer 2015), ChromeVox (2013), Safari + VoiceOver, TextHELP, and MathJax (Cervone et al. 2016). With the exception of NVDA + MathPlayer, these systems are limited to working in browsers; MathPlayer + NVDA also works in Word documents and PowerPoint with math created by MathType.

N. Soiffer (✉)
Talking Cat Software, 9215 NW Lovejoy St, Portland, OR 97229, USA
e-mail: soiffer@alum.mit.edu

S. Noble (✉)
University of Louisville, 5401 Amalfi Ave, Louisville, KY 40219, USA
e-mail: steve.noble@louisville.edu

© Springer-Verlag London Ltd., part of Springer Nature 2019   417
Y. Yesilada and S. Harper (eds.), *Web Accessibility*, Human–Computer Interaction Series, https://doi.org/10.1007/978-1-4471-7440-0_23

In this chapter, we cover key topics in math accessibility. Although most of our focus is on making mathematical expressions accessible, there is much more to math than simply their algebraic representation. In early grades, manipulatives are quite common to introduce the notion of numeracy, fractions, and shapes. Visual representations continue to be important as students learn more math. Even though functions are usually written in an algebraic notation, they are often plotted to give the student a better understanding of the function. Similarly, as students begin to learn statistics, the data they collect or are given is often displayed in formats ranging from scatter plots to pie charts. We discuss efforts to make these graphs accessible and what the future might hold as technology progresses. Beyond visual representations of data, diagrams are often used to illustrate problems and their solutions. Making these diagrams accessible is briefly covered in this chapter; it is discussed more fully in Chap. 22, *Scientific Documents and Diagrams*.

23.2 Math Accessibility

Math accessibility involving algebraic expressions encompasses input techniques, output techniques, and ways of interacting with the mathematical content. These techniques span different modalities such as keyboards, speech, and braille. Research into these techniques and modalities is discussed below.

23.2.1 Algebraic Expressions

Algebraic expressions are notations used in the beginning in pre-algebra and continue on through advanced math. These include fractions, powers, and roots. The solution to the quadratic equation illustrates many of these notations along with a few of the special symbols used in math:

$$x = \frac{-b \pm \sqrt{b^2 - 4ac}}{2a}$$

Notations used in early grades such as 2D addition and long division are somewhat different. They tend to be more tabular and are arranged so that each digit has its own column. In addition, they often represent a process for solving the problem in that there are borrows/carries, or intermediate stages shown. For example:

$$
\begin{array}{r}
\overset{1}{3}8 \\
+53 \\
\hline
91
\end{array}
\qquad
\begin{array}{r}
42 \\
17\overline{)714} \\
68 \\
\hline
34 \\
34 \\
\hline
0
\end{array}
$$

Although elementary notations are widely used in textbooks in grades 1–6, support for them in math editors is not widespread; they were added to MathML 3.0 in 2010. For accessibility, only MathPlayer added support for speech and navigation of elementary math, but this support has never been part of a study to determine how useful it is. There is little support for them in MathML to braille conversion tools.

23.2.1.1   Converting Math to Speech

There are many different ways to speak an expression. Common forms of human speech tend to be ambiguous, relying on the listener either being familiar with the equation or being able to see it. Several methods have been tried to make speech unambiguous. The most common technique and most universal given limitations of various speech engines is to use lexical cues/bracketing words such as "fraction … over … end fraction" to signal when a two-dimensional notation begins and ends.

An alternative to lexical cues is to use sounds or spearcons to reduce the time to read an expression (Murphy et al. 2010). Some sounds such as a rising tone to signal an opening parenthesis and a falling tone for a closing parenthesis have been proposed and tested in limited settings. Spearcons are a modification of that idea. They are words that are sped up so that they are no longer intelligible, but the listener may subconsciously understand them.

A supplement or replacement for some lexical cues is to use prosody changes: pauses, rate, volume, and pitch to distinguish various parts of an expression. This was first done in the pioneering work by Raman in his AsTeR system for reading math paper (Raman 1994). The changes need to be carefully crafted because mathematical notation can be nested. For example,

$$
2^{2^{2^{2^n}}}
$$

If a higher pitch is used for superscripts/exponents, the changes need to be both easily distinguishable and avoid becoming distorted when highly nested.

Another technique used to disambiguate expressions but still minimize the disruptive effects of lexical cues is to use conventions for how some expressions are spoken. For example, MathPlayer's Simple Speech style uses the convention that simple fractions such as $\frac{x}{y}$ speak without bracketing words, but more complex ones will be bracketed with "fraction…over…end fraction". Because simple expressions are relatively common, this can significantly reduce the number of words used to speak math expressions.

Prosody pauses are particularly important to group subexpressions and produce natural speech in much the same way that a pause is used when commas are encountered when reading the text. Although many of these ideas have been around for over 20 years, the user studies have been limited. The ClearSpeak project performed one of the few user studies investigating student preferences for prosody changes (speed and pitch) versus lexical cues (Frankel and Brownstein 2016). It found subjects (who were blind or visually impaired) preferred spoken lexical cues over pitch and rate changes.

Lexical cues help resolve ambiguity when you can't see the expression, but are "verbal noise" to those who can see. The extra words may hinder understanding for people with a learning disability (Lewis et al. 2013). MathPlayer allows the users to specify their disability and will avoid bracketing words for people with a learning disability.

A user's level of expertise is another reason that speech might need to change. As a beginner, a longer form of speech might be used such as "the square root of 2" but as one becomes more accustomed to the subject, a shortened form such as "root 2" might be used. In calculus, "the derivative of sin of x with respect to x" might shorten to "d sin x d x".

Another reason speech might differ is a semantic reading versus a syntactic one. When expressions are spoken in the classroom, the speech typically includes semantics. For example, most teachers would say "x squared" as opposed a syntactic way of speaking it such as "x with a superscript of 2". Although teachers have expressed preferences that computers should read the math similarly to how they speak it, no studies have been done to evaluate preferences for syntactic or semantic verbal renderings, nor have studies been done comparing the rate of comprehension for them.

It is important to note that there are differences in how teachers and others speak the same expression. For example, $\sin^{-1} x$ is commonly spoken as "sine inverse of x", "the inverse sine of x" and "arc sine of x" (the "of" is often elided in more terse forms of speech). Even at a basic level of how a parenthesized expression is spoken, there are many differences such as "left parenthesis ... right parenthesis", "left paren ... right paren", "open paren ... close paren", "open ... close", and "quantity ... end quantity",

One of the difficulties in speaking math semantically is inferring semantics from the notation—the same notation is reused in math repeatedly. For example, a bar over an expression can be a line segment, complex conjugate, or mean. Knowledgeable sighted readers typically don't have a problem deciding the meaning and hence how it should be spoken. Knowing the subject area usually resolves how it should be spoken, but divining the subject area typically requires more information than is found in a single expression. MathPlayer can make use of meta information embedded in the page; MathJax's speech rule engine looks at the surrounding context to try to deduce the subject area. Looking at multiple equations in a section can also lead to clues to the subject. Automatically deducing the subject area remains an area of research.

Although there is a strong trend to produce correct semantic speech, the Math-Speak (Isaacson et al. 2009) style of speech is mostly syntactic because it tries to map directly onto the Nemeth braille code which is a syntactic code. For example, the Nemeth code for x^2 has characters that correspond to the words "x superscript 2 baseline." Some semantic interpretation was added to the MathSpeak specification as an option for users because this form of speech can be very verbose and unfamiliar for people who are not used to it. Because the verbose form maps one to one to the Nemeth code from which it was developed, it is useful as a means to describing math when someone wants to braille what is spoken or read what is brailled.

23.2.1.2 Braille Output

There are many braille math codes used around the world, although most have only a relatively small number of users. Currently, the two most common codes used for math in braille documents intended for English speakers are the Nemeth Braille Code (1972) and the Unified English Braille (UEB) (International Council on English Braille 2014). UEB is a unified code for literary, mathematics, and computer science text elements. Nemeth code is a math-only code and has been used for many years; its use spread well beyond the US where it was developed. UEB is an attempt to unify the braille codes used in English-speaking countries and is now used by all large English-speaking countries. UEB includes a math braille code that differs from Nemeth code in many ways. Most prominently, it requires a number indicator to indicate that the code for a letter such as "a" really means "1". Because of this, it is much more verbose than Nemeth code. This can be a problem when reading math, especially on a braille display that might be limited to 40 or 80 characters. In the US, the Braille Authority of North American allows the use of either UEB or Nemeth for math in braille documents. Using UEB for all contents including math is a contentious topic in the US educational system (Miller 2016).

JAWS, NVDA + MathPlayer, and VoiceOver + Safari display braille math codes on a refreshable braille display. All of them display the entire math expression on the display. For textual content, dots 7 and 8 on a display indicate the current focus. For math, none of these systems use dots 7 and 8. A small user study conducted by Pearson in October 2015 (Pearson 2015) noted that participants were confused when dots 7 and 8 were not used to communicate the user's input position. The Pearson Accessible Equation Editor (AEE) was updated to indicate the current input position using dots 7 and 8, as well as the current editor selection with dot 8 on the braille display to provide tactile feedback similar to what users expect for textual content. The Pearson editor is currently the only math editor to do this.

23.2.1.3 Display

It used to be common to use raster images for math in web pages. Their use has decreased significantly in recent years in web pages. In its place, MathML and TeX (often rendered by a polyfill such as MathJax or KaTeX), along with SVG is used. These technologies allow the math to scale with the font size, so that the math can be enlarged without degrading the quality. The ISO 32000-2 PDF specification also recommends using MathML in what is called the tag tree for accessibility; as a vector format, math has always scaled well in PDF. Native math in a Google doc and math in Microsoft Word or Apple Pages also scale well.

In print, larger math expressions are broken over lines. AsTeR supported verbally eliding subexpressions and MathJax has experimented with this technique also. In AsTeR, a substitution was made and the large expression with the substituted variable was spoken. For example,

$$\int_1^0 \frac{x^2 - 1}{(x^2 + 8x + 15)} dx$$

is spoken as "integral with respect to x from 0 to 1 of f of x dx, where f is fraction x squared minus 1 divided by x squared plus 8 × plus 15". In contrast, MathJax + SRE just collapses the large part and says (using MathSpeak) "integral subscript 0 superscript 1 baseline collapsed fraction d x". MathPlayer's overview mode reads this as "integral from 0 to 1 of fraction"; users can navigate to hear details about the fraction.

For people with learning disabilities, synchronized highlighting of speech and text has been shown to be helpful (Hecker et al. 2002; Petrie et al. 2005). No studies have been done to evaluate the effectiveness of math comprehension when synchronized highlighting of math elements is available with math speech in contrast to speech output alone, However, the MeTRC study (Lewis et al. 2013) found that students with learning disabilities made twice as many errors reading math as they did reading text. Thus, it seems very likely that synchronized highlighting is important for math also. This conclusion is further suggested by the earlier SMART study, in which 100% of teachers reported that "the way the words and symbols light up and read out loud at the same time helped students read their math;" while 79% of the students said the same thing (Lewis et al. 2010). TextHELP—the maker of the Read & Write software used in both the MeTRC and SMART studies—originally used synchronized highlighting with MathPlayer and IE; it now makes use of MathJax to do that.

People who are severely dyslexic may benefit from specific fonts and/or coloring. Although special fonts for dyslexic readers have been devised, several studies have cast doubt on their usefulness (Rello and Baeza-Yates 2013; Wery and Diliberto 2017). These studies do show that italic fonts tend to be a bad idea; italic fonts are typically used for variables in math. There do not appear to be any studies related to math, fonts, and dyslexia. Colors can be useful to distinguish between commonly confused symbols (Pinna and Deiana 2018) such as 3 and 8 and 2 and 5. A school for severely dyslexic students has devised a coloring scheme for math that includes those ideas along with using background colors to distinguish similar operators such as "+" and "÷" (J. Larson, personal communication, June 10, 2018). Boldface is also used to make characters with thin lines such as "−" more prominent. An example is shown below.

$$8(-6+2) \div 3 =$$

To date, no software does this coloring.

23.2.1.4 Navigation

Navigation of math is now supported by most accessible math software. In a Clear-Speak study (Frankel et al. 2017), it was the highest rated feature studied. Three forms of navigation were tested: character level, notational (2D structures such as division act like a character when arrowing left/right), and structural (left/right arrow keys move from operand to operator to operand). For the latter two modes of navigation, up/down arrows are used to move into and out of 2D notational structures. Participants liked all three and found the different navigation modes useful in different circumstances. Most systems only support notational navigation; MathPlayer supports all three. An additional difference between MathPlayer and other systems is that in MathPlayer, the left and right arrow keys move out of 2D structures such as fractions; in most other systems, users must utilize the up arrow to get to the correct level (e.g., the fraction), and then move left/right. MathPlayer's ease of use features can be a problem for advanced screen reader users who typically repeatedly "bang" on the arrow keys to move through expressions to get to a place of interest. The beginning/ending of 2D notations are useful "walls" for such users. MathPlayer added an option so that advanced screen reader users stay in the notation, unless, they also hold down the shift key or they use the up-arrow key to move to the appropriate level. Although not studied, the ability to navigate up and down a column, such as in a matrix, a system of equations, or in an elementary math problem is likely very important.

When moving around, it is sometimes useful to be able to remember a location. MathPlayer's navigation supports user-defined placeholders. Although ClearSpeak study participants liked that feature, it was not widely used and was rated lower than most other features.

Summaries/Outlines/Overviews of larger expression have been tried a number of times in software. Gillan et al. (2004) did a study that showed providing an outline slowed solution time. Nonetheless, they added outlines to their MathGenie solution because they felt it would be useful. As part of a ClearSpeak navigation study, a summary mode was added to MathPlayer; user feedback from studies was that it was not that useful. The study authors feel part of this is because the implementation was crude relative to other features.

As noted earlier, only the Pearson AEE changes a braille display to indicate the location of the navigation. Because math expressions, particularly those that require navigation, can use far more characters than fit on a braille display, it might be a good idea to make sure that as much as possible of the current focus of navigation fits on the braille display.

23.2.1.5   Input/Editors

Entering and editing math employs all of the above techniques and raises additional issues. TeX and ASCIIMath are two input notations for specifying both characters and layout. Because they are linear and use a standard keyboard, they are inherently accessible to someone using speech or braille output. However, they only support character-by-character navigation and speech. Also, it is easy to make a mistake when using them. They must be converted to MathML (which screen readers can speak) and/or converted to braille to verify they were entered correctly. Furthermore, for someone with a mobility disability who wants to use speech-to-text input, or who needs to use some form of adapted mouse, touch screen or screen scanning and switch technology, the process to enter math expressions using only character input becomes a lengthy and physically taxing experience. Until recently, these were the only accessible math editor options.

While some direct edit/WYSWYG math editors have been found to be adaptable and very useful for individuals with mobility-related disabilities, most are not accessible to someone who is blind (Choi and Chan 2015). Two exceptions to this are ChattyInfty (Yamaguchi and Suzuki 2012) and AEE. Math editors typically use palettes and keyboard shortcuts for all the special characters and notations. Keyboard shortcuts are especially useful for speech-input users, as they can be programmed as unique spoken phrase commands. Palettes can also very useful for screen scanning and switch access users, but must be focusable and keyboard accessible—with appropriate labels—in order to be accessible to blind individuals using screen readers or braille displays.

One recent extension of WYSWYG math editors is to allow natural language input, where one speaks or types in common mathematical phrases such as "not equal to" or "x squared" and the editor converts the phrase to math notation. TextHELP's EquatIO implements this idea by integrating typing into its math speech recognition system: as speech is recognized, the words are put into an editable area. To speed typing, ranked input suggestions appear as one types. While no studies have evaluated the effectiveness of this approach, it may present some benefits for people with certain types of learning disabilities or memory deficits who find palette and keyboard shortcut approaches difficult to use. Speech input is discussed more fully below.

One problem that is specific to math is that math uses many more characters and notations than there are keys on a keyboard. For example, Greek letters are frequently used in math as are symbols such as $\leq$ and ∞. Linear formats use character strings for these special symbols. For example, TeX uses "\leq" and "\infty" for $\leq$ and ∞, respectively; ASCIIMath uses "<=" and "oo". Most WYSIWYG editors use hierarchical palettes of symbols. Many of the systems support hundreds of symbols in their palettes. For example, MathType's standard palette contains about 210 symbols (notations such as square roots are not part of that count); WIRIS's standard palette has about 370 symbols. Organizing this information to make it easy to find and access is a challenge. A study by Dave Schleppenbach (personal communication 2014) revealed that just 10 operators accounted for 95% of all operators found in a US algebra textbook he examined. A follow-up study by Soiffer (2018a) verified that the claim is true across several algebra textbooks. As subject area advanced, so did the number of symbols used in the books, but even for calculus, only 40 symbols not on a keyboard accounted for 99.95% of the characters used in math expressions. Additionally, the context of what has been entered can be used to show likely characters and notations for further input. Making common choices easy to access is very helpful to those who are limited to mainly sequential access, such as screen reader users and switch users.

As math is entered and edited, changes to the insertion cursor, selection, and expression need to be communicated to screen readers. Best practices in regard to the amount of information communicated when inserting, selecting, or deleting have yet to be established (e.g., "fraction deleted" vs. saying the contents of a deleted fraction vs. saying nothing). Even best practices for something as common as typing a "backspace" after a fraction have yet to be established. The behavior of where a backspace ends up differs between common editors: AEE, Mathematica, and Desmos's editor move to the end of the denominator; MathType, WIRIS, and Word select the fraction; and ChattyInfty deletes the fraction.

23.2.1.6 Braille Input

The most commonly used approach to braille math input is to capture braille cells one by one and translate input from braille to other formats, either on user request, or on word or equation boundaries. This approach leads to a user experience where the math markup is not kept up to date with user input, which impedes communication with non-braille users.

Pearson's AEE uses a transformational approach where each braille input cell directly modifies the underlying content MathML markup (Dooley and Park 2016). Since this same method is used to process keyboard input, the resulting input behavior remains similar for braille and keyboard users, and supports immediate interactive feedback between input and output formats. Desmos' calculator (Desmos 2018) supports braille input and output and acts in a similar manner, but uses LaTeX as the underlying representation (J. Merill, personal communication, August 7, 2018).

Being able to enter math expressions in running text (i.e., in-line expressions), while relatively simple for sighted users with applications like MathType, presents special challenges for a blind person wishing to use their braille display to input math on a computer. Having students explain steps while working out mathematical solutions is a very common teaching tactic, and is commonly required when students take math tests in school. Further, research with sighted students have demonstrated that students who embed mathematical representation into their descriptions of science concepts performed better on test questions than students who just wrote in text, or those who used text and embedded graphs (Hand et al. 2009). Blind students have traditionally been able to do this with the mechanical Perkins Brailler, but this capability has thus far been impossible for someone wanting to input both math and text in the same input field from a braille display on a computer. The AEE, however, has recently integrated this capacity in its "text plus math" mode, which translates

Nemeth braille strings into Content MathML, while literary braille is translated into simplified HTML as the student enters braille on the display.

In braille, knowing where certain math structures begin and end is vital to disambiguation. Constructs like superscripts, roots, and fractions are some common examples. In all these cases, special braille characters mark the start and end of the notation. This poses a problem for editors though that want to display converted braille during editing. For example, typing a backspace after a fraction raises the question of what should happen with the braille "end fraction" character. In a small Pearson user study conducted in July 2016 (Pearson 2016) users preferred having backspace move inside the fraction, although some confusion was noted because the close fraction symbol in braille did not go away (because the fraction still remained). Since the ability to edit math on a computer with a braille display is relatively new, more research will be needed to establish best practices.

23.2.1.7 Speech Input

MathTalk (McClellan 2005) was an early attempt at speech input using Dragon Dictate (now using Dragon Naturally Speaking), but has had limited success, perhaps because it requires the use of the phonetic alphabet ('a' is spoken as "alpha", "b" as "bravo", etc.) and requires slow, clear speech due to the quality of speech recognition when it came out in 1997. Mathifier (Batlouni et al. 2011) was another older system. The authors noted that math has a relatively limited lexicon and grammar. They tried to improve the speed and accuracy of recognition by limiting recognition to that smaller language. Mathifier was based on CMU's Sphinx 4 speech recognizer (Lamere 2001) which relies on Hidden Markov Models to recognize words. They achieved 80–85% accuracy with six testers; this is likely too low to be useful.

With the advent of machine learning via recurrent neural networks, speaker-independent speech input on phones, home assistants, and other devices has become popular. These systems work well when given large amounts of data (speech) for training. However, math-related speech has not been part of the training and so they are less successful in interpreting math. AEE uses the latest version of Dragon Naturally Speaking, which is based on deep learning. It makes use of grammar rules with a limited lexicon to help improve accuracy with math, but still requires the use of the phonetic alphabet for letters and requires users to learn the grammar. EquatIO, successor to g(Math), uses Google Speech recognition with special filters to correct for common mistakes that Google speech makes with mathematical speech; it does not use the phonetic alphabet. No studies have been run to determine error rates on these two systems.

23.2.1.8 Handwritten Input

A number of applications such as Windows' Math Input Panel, WIRIS, and MyScript allow handwritten math. The accessibility of such systems has not been studied.

Handwriting poses challenges for the physically disabled as well as people who are blind, although those who lost their sight after learning math are often able to write math legibly. Most of the handwriting systems support conversion to MathML, so the recognized result can be spoken or brailled. This means the result can be checked, but correcting a mistake may be difficult for those who are blind. Similarly, because they don't have spoken feedback, once a user with no sight has moved their hand any changes are not possible to the handwriting. However, because the handwritten math can be converted to MathML or another form, it can be brought into an accessible editor.

23.2.2 Plots, Charts, and Diagrams

As students are introduced to the notation of algebraic notation and functions, they are also introduced to plotting as a way to visualize the meaning of the functions. Similarly, as students are introduced to statistics, the data and tables they collect or are given is often more easily understood via plotting, bar charts, etc. Beyond visual representations of data, diagrams are often used to illustrate problems and their solutions. This is particularly true for geometry.

23.2.2.1 Sonification

The use of audio tone generation to map an aural analog to line graphs has been commonly used in recent years. Such a practice is understood as an extension of "sonification:" the use of nonspeech audio to convey information. Sonication, at its broadest level, can be viewed as the transformation of data relations into perceived relations in an acoustic signal for the purposes of facilitating communication or interpretation (Kramer et al. 1999). While sonification as a broad term includes such practices as audio icons, earcons, and even audio output from Geiger counter and SONAR devices, a growing body of research has focused on extensions to mathematics (Banf 2013).

Early research applying sonification to mathematical graphing of lines on a Cartesian plane primarily looked at line graphs containing a single data series (Mansur 1975), but later researchers have also found success with sonifying graphs containing two data series (Brown et al. 2002). Common practice for sonification of graphs is to rely upon the length of the audio tone to depict travel along the x-axis while the y-axis is aurally depicted by pitch, where a descending audio frequency is used to represent lower y values and an ascending frequency represents higher y values. While such analogs are highly relative and inherently inexact, one study with sighted subjects found an average of 80% accuracy when users were asked to draw an approximation of the sonified graph they had just heard (Brown and Brewster 2003).

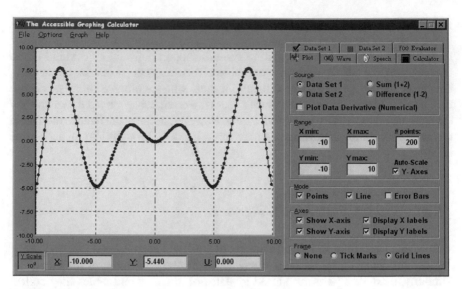

Fig. 23.1 Screenshot of AGC showing a function plot

In addition to the basic aspects of audio signal duration and pitch, later applications have attempted to use stereo effects of left–right audio panning, varieties of tone timbres, as well as amplitude and frequency modulation (Song 2011). Over time, common practices have emerged such as using changes in the stereo field to reflect the value of the x-axis, the use of concurrent static or white noise to indicate when the y-axis value is below zero, and various types of chirps, pops or other audio cues to denote when a line has crossed the x-axis, the y-axis, or an intersection point with another drawn line. Simultaneous audio graphs of two or more lines is commonly accomplished through changes in audio timbre, such as using a composite audio signal mimicking the sound of a violin for one line and the sound of a flute for a second line.

One of the earliest publicly released implementations of graph sonification for blind users was pioneered by John Gardner as part of Oregon State University's Science Access Project. Initially developed in 1996 as a DOS application, TRI-ANGLE included one of the first commonly available Audio Graphing Calculators (AGC) designed for use by someone who is blind (Gardner et al. 1998). The AGC permits the user to compute a function y of x or import a data file of x, y values, and then generate a tone plot audio display. According to Gardner, tests with sighted undergraduate students who had an only brief exposure to the AGC interface were able to "…extract information from audio graphs almost as accurately as from visual graphs" (Gardner et al. 2002). Due to the difficulty in visualizing two graphs from simultaneous tone plots, the AGC instead provided a comparison of two graphs displaying tone plots of the difference (or sum) of two graphs. After the closure of Oregon State's Science Access Project, the Audio Graphing Calculator was eventually released as a commercial product by ViewPlus Technologies (Fig. 23.1).

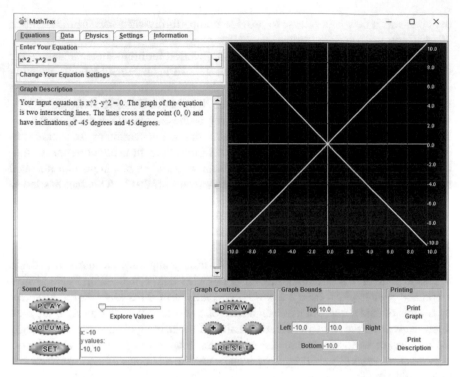

Fig. 23.2 Screenshot of MathTrax showing an equation plot

Robert Shelton of the NASA Learning Technologies team developed MathTrax. It became a popular implementation of graph sonification not long after its release in 2004 (Nguyen 2011). MathTrax was designed as a software-based graphing calculator which draws graphs visually, generates descriptions of graphs using text, and creates a sonified audio output using rising and falling frequencies. MathTrax was built on top of the underlying Java-based Math Description Engine (MDE), also developed by NASA and released as open-source code. The MDE is a library of interactive software modules that combines mathematical analysis, graphing and sonification. The MDE modules use rule and computation-based AI to synthesize text descriptions for graphs of mathematical equations, tables of data, and simulations. The sonification engine then renders the resulting graph as a mixture of stereo tones (Fig. 23.2).

Although MathTrax remains available on the NASA Website, it has not been updated since 2008. Continuing development of the open-source MDE code was briefly picked up by Benetech, but the GitHub repository has been dormant since 2014 (Benetech 2014). Another Java-based sonification implementation, the Sonification Sandbox, was created by the Sonification Lab at the Georgia Institute of Technology. The Sonification Sandbox allows the user to map data to multiple auditory parameters and add context using a graphical interface. First released in 2002, the last update to the code was a new beta release to provide compatibility with Java 7 in December, 2014 (Georgia Tech Sonification Lab 2014).

More recent implementations of graph sonification for blind students include the Desmos Graphing Calculator and the Orion TI-84 Plus handheld talking graphing calculator. Both of these products continue using common practice graph sonification methods originally developed in applications like the AGC and MathTrax.

Moving beyond the sonification of line graphs, the use of audio tones to map more complex statistical data has been incorporated in the SAS Graphics Accelerator. In contrast to the ability to understand data sets through sight using common visualization methods, human hearing is much more capable of picking up on nuanced changes in patterns over time in audio signals (Neuhoff 2011). This fact has led to many novel applications of sonifying large data sets which have been found promising in such diverse uses as studying migration patterns of Pacific salmon (Hegg et al. 2018), climate data (George et al. 2017), and stock market information (Chabot and Braasch 2017).

In the SAS Graphics Accelerator, sonification techniques are used to provide access to chart-like information involving complex data visualizations such as heat maps and scatter plots. Heat maps are especially useful for large data sets where thousands of data points often pile up on top of each other in certain areas of the plot. Such maps are often difficult to read visually and creators typically use increasingly darker hues of various colors to distinguish dense areas of the plot, making them a significant accessibility challenge. Such maps are almost impossible to use effectively as a tactile graphic.

The SAS Graphics Accelerator solves this problem by manipulating the pitch of the melodic sound representing the number of data points in the corresponding cell in the heat map (commonly referred to as the z-axis). A low pitch represents a small number of data points and a high pitch represents a large number of data points in a given cell. Empty cells are represented by a non-melodic audio cue. A second melodic sound (utilizing a different instrument timbre) represents the height of the data point on the y-axis, and the position of any sound between the left and right speakers represents the position of the cell on the x-axis. When the two melodic sounds are played at the same time, each column sounds as a chord and provides an overall sense of the relationship between the two variables. The users can also explore each row as a melody, and further explore by cell and query for the numeric value to quickly find important data points such as densest cell in the heat map (Holton 2018).

Exploration of data is the focus of work to make creation and viewing of histograms, box plots, scatter plots, and time series accessible in R (Godfrey et al. 2018). The output is generated as SVG with XML annotations. The result is opened automatically in a browser and users can hear textual overviews or navigate via arrow keys to subcomponents to hear more details. At the lowest level, data values can be heard.

23.2.2.2 Tactile Visualizations

For students who are blind, tactile diagrams can be generated on braille embossers that can print raised dots at several different heights. This gives students a way to feel a diagram and get a good sense of what a diagram is if it is simple enough. However, converting an image to a tactile graphic requires selecting the important features from a high-resolution image and incorporating them into a low-resolution tactile printout. A particularly hard problem is converting the text to braille and placing it on the image. Braille must be printed at a fixed size and it must be horizontal. This may take up a considerable amount of space and may interfere with the tactile graphic itself because the braille is also tactile. The Tactile Graphics Assistant automates much of this process, with particular attention paid to extracting the text, removing it from the image, and then placing it back into the tactile graphic (Jayant et al. 2007). However, recognition and OCRing of math in diagrams were problematic. Human intervention is still required in some cases, but the amount of time needed to produce a tactile image ranged from 6.3 min per figure for a precalculus book to 25 min per figure for a computer architecture book that had very complex figures; these numbers represent significant reductions in time to produce the tactile graphics by hand.

Baker explored using QR codes in place of braille or touch and using a smartphone to read the QR code (Baker et al. 2016). Based on a sample of 82 images from a precalculus book, QR codes required 47% less space than braille (a scan distance of six inches was used as a basis for the QR code size). Additionally, the diagrams with QR codes are accessible by those with poor or no braille skills. Since less than 10% of blind people in the United States are braille readers (National Federation of the Blind 2009), the developers wanted to support this larger audience of blind readers. Three techniques were tested for aiming the camera: silent, verbal, and finger pointing. There was no statistical preference for either of these methods among the 10 participants. When compared with braille, braille readers preferred braille due to its immediacy, but testers who were not proficient with braille preferred the QR codes. Participants found it difficult to read the tactile graphic with one hand and aim the camera with the other. Baker also reports on preliminary work using Google Glass as the camera. The wide-angle lens used by Google Glass made it difficult to read small QR codes. Instead, they put a larger QR code on the back which embedded coordinate info of the labels in it; small tactile markers were used on the front side at the location of each label. After scanning the QR code on the back, the user would turn tactile graphics over and the system would track the user's finger position and use that to know which label to read when the user spoke "Read Label". No user tests were reported with this system. Due to the expense of using Google Glass, the authors propose using this alternative idea with a phone in a stand pointed at the tactile graphic.

Parks pioneered a method to link audio to tactile graphics in his Nomad system (Parkes 1998). This was further developed in IVEO (Gardner and Bulatov 2006). IVEO runs on a standard computer and makes use of a touch sensitive screen/tablet. An SVG image is converted to an embossed image and placed on the tablet screen. The text is associated with specific regions in the SVG and when these are touched on the tablet, the text is spoken with a synthesized voice; later versions allowed recording human voices. Testing focused on whether tactile images and audio descriptions could be produced by nonexpert users (they could); it did not examine the usefulness of the images and audio by users. A separate study by Brock compared raised line maps and raised line maps with audio feedback (Brock et al. 2014). This study found that with interactive audio maps, learning was shorter (textual information that didn't fit on the maps was referenced on a second embossed sheet of paper for the noninteractive map) and satisfaction higher; comprehension was similar (all test participants were braille readers). Tactile images and audio feedback can be used for various types of plots and provides an alternative to the audio-based sonification methods discussed above. However, it does require preparation of both the tactile graphic along with associating text with locations in the tactile image.

In the last few years, 3D printing has moved into the mainstream as 3D printers have become much cheaper and much easier to use. 3D printers can be used to make geometric shapes useful for all students. 3D shapes can be especially useful for students who are blind because studies have found that those students have trouble recognizing a 3D object in a 2D tactile drawings (Picard and Lebaz 2012). Klatzky found students who are blind are better in recognizing 3D models (Klatzky and Lederman 2007). 3D printers can also be used to make raised line drawings for plots, etc. Perhaps one of the main advantages of 3D printers over braille embossers is the ability to create different heights and different textures, something that is backed up by comments made by some users in a small study by Brown and Hurst (2012). They also experimented with using alphanumeric characters instead of braille due to low braille literacy rates; only one of their six study participants had fluency in braille. The small size of characters used (space constraints prevented larger letters) made them harder to read than braille characters. It is possible to combine 3D printing and touch feedback by using a printer with two printheads and using a conductive material in the second printhead so touch is transmitted to the underlying touch display (Götzelmann 2018).

23.2.2.3   Haptics

Although some researchers use the term haptics to include tactile feedback of 2D images and 3D models, we reserve the use of the term to refer to force feedback and vibratory feedback for virtual objects and diagrams. Most research into haptics takes one of three approaches: using an apparatus that provides force feedback in three dimensions; using gloves with vibration or feedback for the fingers; using vibration motors in mobile phones or added to touchscreens to provide feedback. Audio feedback is often used in conjunction with haptic feedback to provide additional information.

Early research with force feedback often used the Phantom, a device that can be maneuvered in space that allows users to explore virtual 3D objects. Later research used the Novint Falcon, a much lower cost device with less degrees of freedom of movement than the phantom. Both devices can be thought of as a stylus that allows touching the virtual object at a single point (i.e., touching the object with just your finger). Yu used a Phantom to see whether users could accurately recognize plots with two lines on them; the lines were distinguished from each other by having different friction (Yu et al. 2001). They compared having a background grid versus not having a grid. While the grid helps locate features of the plot, it interferes with finding the plot lines, does not provide precise information about the location of points on the lines, and counting grid lines takes mental effort. Blind testers were divided about their usefulness. The authors felt providing verbal feedback for location when a button is pressed is a better solution. One point they noted was they used raised lines which are easy to slip off; they thought recessed lines would work better. A follow-up study by Brewster (2002) verified this. Additionally, the lines were identified uniquely via force feedback "clicks" and line end points also were identified via vibration to distinguish them from sharp bends. With these changes, the users had high success rates identifying the number of lines (97%), the number of bends (89%), and the number of intersections (92%).

Gloves or vibration motors attached to each finger provide feedback to each finger rather than having just a single point of contact. The "gloves" with motors are typically very cheap to make: $6 for the Vision Glove system (Manshad and Manshad 2008). However, most systems require a high-quality touch sensitive screens so that the system knows where the fingers are. The screen is the major component of the cost. The Vision Glove was tested with 13 people who had visually impairments. The test compared using the gloves to using a stylus on the touch screen; both used audio feedback when trying to find a line, circle, or parabola. With the glove, a vibration in different fingers indicated the direction to move. It took less time to find the graphs when wearing the gloves, but at the cost of more interactions. The GraVVITAS system (Goncu and Marriott 2011) used a touchscreen capable of tracking four fingers, although initial testing found the training to distinguish between vibrations on all four fingers was longer than participants could spend, so only the index finger on each hand was used. Their initial studies involved lines, triangles, rectangles, and circles with filled interiors. The perimeters produced one vibration pattern when touched and the interiors produced a different pattern. They investigated using sound instead when a shape was touched but found there was a slight preference for vibration; additionally, they wanted to use sound for providing details about the shapes/locations. They investigated using 3D sound to indicate object positions near the finger locations and compared that to using 3D sound to indicate the object's position between the two fingers. Users manually would turn on/off each mode. They found testers liked both and that they were complementary: the two finger positioning sounds provided an overview as the user slid their hand down the screen and the other method was used to find particular objects. They tested various different objects including a line graph with two lines/sets of data. Users were able to recognize the individual lines and answer qualitative and quantitative questions about the data. Because of resolution issues with the size of fingers, the authors felt that adding a zoom and pan feature is important.

The FeelX glove (Soviak et al. 2016) improves on this design by using a 2×4 pin grid for each finger. Unlike with the previous two systems, a touchscreen is not used.

Instead, the gloves have LEDs on the fingertips that is read by an infrared camera mounted on a stand. This reduces the overall system costs and allows for multi-touch to be accurately tracked over a large area. The FeelX glove was tested in one and four finger modes. The test involved identifying horizontal and vertical lines, rectangles, triangles, and circles. Results were significantly better in the four-finger mode in terms of accurate image recognition, speed of recognition, and user opinion. One issue that surfaced in their studies was that users wanted the ability to click on the screen while wearing the glove. They also complained about the ergonomics/fit of the prototype glove. Both of these studies were aimed at objects on a screen. Dhaher developed a low cost 10 finger prototype for exploring both 2D and 3D virtual objects (Dhaher and Clements 2017). Early testing revealed two needs:

- The hands needed to be constrained to the tracking space and also placed at some initial position relative to the virtual object being explored. To do this, a box was built with an acrylic glass sheet on which to rest the hand.
- Using all ten fingers was not practical with their setup, so they reduced the number of fingers tracked from five on each hand to two on each hand. They also claimed using only the index and middle fingers on each hand simulates how most people read braille.

They did not report any test results involving object recognition, etc.

Like other forms of haptics mentioned, vibration feedback on phones and tablets is still in its infancy. Researchers are interested in taking advantage of it because it could leverage mainstream technology that students commonly have. Most studies so far focus on point or shape detection. Bateman looked at strategies testers used to find a point on the screen: systematic sweeping (back and forth from top to bottom), failed sweeping (gaps left in the sweep), rapid unstructured exploration, and no discernible strategy (Bateman et al. 2018). Not surprisingly, systematic sweeping did well with 92% accuracy in finding the dot. Surprisingly, rapid unstructured sweeping did best and found the dot 100% of the time. The other two methods succeeded 74% of the time. The authors attribute the success of the rapid unstructured exploration on finding the corners quickly (hence, the boundaries) and that the rapid motion covers much of the screen in a short period of time. In another study (Toennies et al. 2011), the authors compared audio and haptic feedback for point location and shape detection. The results were relatively good for both methods and there was no statistical difference between auditory feedback and haptic feedback. Gorlewicz worked with commercially available tablets set to vibrate at different frequencies when lines were crossed while being traced by one's fingers. It also generated various audio tones when the student's fingertip touched a specific point along the line, curve, or shape displayed on the screen (Gorlewicz et al. 2014). In this way, the students found it easier to distinguish between the gridlines and the points on the grid. Pilot studies on user comprehension of grids and points were conducted with students with visual impairments, and explored the perception of objects through haptic feedback alone, auditory feedback alone, and combinations of the two. The results showed that when both methods were combined, each student could successfully find and locate 100% of displayed points on a grid.

An alternative to vibration feedback is variable friction. This is exemplified in the TeslaTouch (Xu et al. 2011) and the TPad (Mullenbach et al. 2013). Both provide feedback to a moving finger that makes the glass surface feel like a raised or textured surface. Xu et al. (2011) report on attempts to emulate braille that failed, but filled shapes had about an 80% recognition rate. Chu et al. (2017) is a more recent exploration of distinguishable patterns using a TPad phone.

23.3 Discussion

23.3.1 Mathematical Expressions

Although text-to-math speech has made great progress in the last five years and is now part of the major screen readers, the easy part is done. The harder part is getting the correct semantics and producing more natural/higher quality speech. As mentioned earlier, knowing the context of the math, in particular, knowing the subject area allows conversion to subject-specific speech and more importantly, avoids speaking the notation incorrectly. Some work has been performed using textual context and looking at more than one expression on a page to figure this out. More work needs to be done in this direction. The development of a standard that allows an author to embed the information in metadata in a page or as part of the math itself would simplify the work and help avoid errors at least for pages that contain that metadata.

Another difficult area involves cleaning up the markup being read. There are often many ways in which a notation can be displayed. For example, the combinatorial notation $\binom{n}{m}$ can be encoded as a 2×1 table with parentheses around it or as a fraction whose fraction line has zero width. Similarly, there are many look-alike characters in Unicode. For example, a minus sign $(-)$ could properly be either U+002D or U+2212; some authors mistakenly use the look-alike character U+2013 (en-dash). Multiplication dot ($\cdot$U+00B7) is another example that has several look-alikes: $\cdot$ (U+22C5 dot operator), • (U+2022 bullet), and ● (U+2219 bullet operator). The multitude of ways that an equation can be represented in MathML (and other formats) has led some authors to advocate using a canonical MathML representation (Archambault and Moço 2006; Formánek et al. 2012). Using a canonical representation helps the generation of speech, etc., along with aiding in mathematical searches. Both MathPlayer and SRE canonicalize MathML for speech generation.

Taken together, the complications involved in understanding the semantics of the expression and the need to use canonical MathML means that good speech generation is a significant programming effort. Further effort is required to produce good speech in the presence of encoding errors in the math. These complications will likely push AT vendors in the future toward using third-party software that specializes in math rather than implementing their own solutions. Note that although a third-party tool *could* be used on the server to clean the math up, unless such a tool is universally used

Fig. 23.3 Quadratic equation and the equivalent DotsPlus representation

$$x = \frac{-b \pm \sqrt{b^2 - 4ac}}{2a}$$

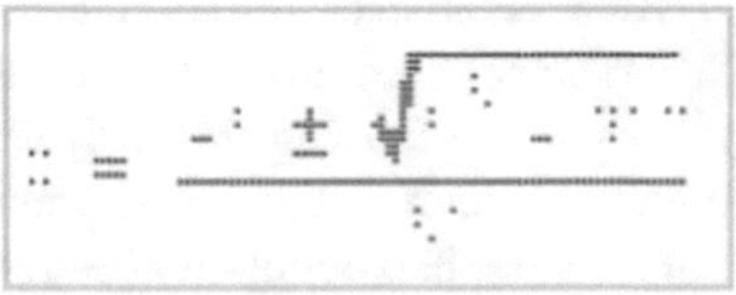

which seems unlikely, a client-side solution will be needed to ensure high-quality speech.

Although speech is very important, many teachers for the blind feel math braille literacy is essential for understanding math (Kapperman and Sticken 2003). However, as mentioned earlier, the percentage of the blind community that know braille, let alone a braille math code is quite low. Gardner developed DotsPlus (Gardner 1995) as an alternative to learning a braille math code, especially for those who lost their sight after learning some math. DotsPlus uses braille for letters, digits, and punctuation, but embosses roots, fractions lines, and symbols like $+$, $=$, and $\sum$ using a tactile representation of their printed shape (Fig. 23.3).

While some people liked DotsPlus, it suffers from three drawbacks: embossing loses the immediacy of a refreshable braille display; braille readers were forced to move up and down for fractions, superscripts, etc., which is unnatural; and DotsPlus can't be used for input. Standard braille math codes continue to be the best method for representing math in braille.

23.3.2 Plots, Charts, and Diagrams

Data sonification and auditory display methods are likely to mature as mainstream analytical tools for examining multivariate data and time series data in particular. As the theory and best practices for creating effective sonifications continues to advance, research-based sonification models for such purposes will become accepted. Just as with many other aspects of accessibility engineering, once such auditory displays become commonly available in the mainstream, people with disabilities will be able to reap the benefits of this newly available technology.

To date, commercially available refreshable braille displays have been limited to one line of 8-dot braille. This is about to change with the Graphiti tablet (APH 2018), a 40 × 60 grid of pins that occupies 8.5 × 11.5 inches. It plugs into a USB slot and supports both input and output along with haptic feedback. The pins are too widely spaced to support braille, but charts, graphs, and geometric figures along with dynamic content (about one-second refresh rate) are supported. Because of the low resolution, various filters are available to bring out important features in an image, but no one filter will work for every image. Demonstrations do not currently include audio feedback, but that seems a likely candidate for future development. It is also likely that if the Graphiti tablet is commercially successful, larger and denser displays will follow.

23.4 Future Directions

An area that has not received much attention to date is doing math on a computer versus just entering math. Theorist (now LiveMath) (Avitzur 1998) was a very early application that allowed users to drag a subexpression from one side of an equation to the other side and it would do simple things such as change the sign if the term was added/subtracted or change multiplication into division. Each change would be recorded as a new step. Other supported operations include switching terms (commutative law) and distributing multiplication over addition. DUDAMATH (Dudamath.com 2018) and Graspable math (Weitnauer et al. 2016) are more recent web-based applications with nice animations as part of the drag-and-drop process. None of these applications are accessible to screen reader users although there is nothing to prevent developers from making drag-and-drop accessible or providing some alternative means such as selection followed by invoking a command ("move to right hand side" or "distribute"). MathShare (Soiffer 2018b) is specifically designed to be an inclusive application for doing math. It supports crossing things out, cleaning them up, and providing reasons for each step. Accessible semantic drag and drop as discussed above is planned for future versions together with the ability to specify what automatic features can be used for each problem. It is likely that accessible applications focused on doing math will be a direction of research.

One important factor in this direction is finding ways to help students with limited working memory. This includes students who are blind and access math via speech along with students with various types of learning disabilities. For this group of students, expression outlines/summaries help students find and focus on parts of problems. Process Driven Math (Perez et al. 2017; Noble et al. 2018) is a technique developed at Auburn University Montgomery that appears to be useful for these groups of students. The ability to pick out subproblems, work on them, and bring them back into the main line of editing is another area that will likely be pursued.

Haptics is an area of active research, but so far, results have been modest. Hanson et al. (2016) compared force feedback (Falcon), vibrotactile feedback (Android tablet), and tactile graphics (embossed paper with no feedback) for a science assessment task about water molecules and evaporation. The basic setup involved a cylinder and round water molecules inside of it. The evaluation consisted of counting the number of water molecules. The tactile graphic performed best, although the authors noted they couldn't factor out the students' familiarity with tactile graphics. Because the Falcon presented a 3D scenario, finding the molecules was more difficult than the 2D versions used on the tablet and paper. Force feedback and haptics allow for dynamic motion of the water molecules, but that capability wasn't tested to see if it increased the students' understanding. This study provides a cautionary tale that at least with the current state of the art, sometimes old technologies have better outcomes. However, perhaps with multi-touch displays and better vibrotactile feedback, haptics may someday become a complimentary or even preferred technology for understanding plots, charts, or mathematical diagrams.

23.5 Author's Opinion of the Field

Every day, in every classroom, children in kindergarten through high school take a math class. Hence, it should not be a surprise that educators, students, and parents consider math accessibility to be an important problem to solve. The interest in math accessibility extends to browser manufacturers, AT vendors, and other software developers such as those making EPUB readers. The sad fact is that although companies and software developers agree that math accessibility is important, most vendors don't prioritize math accessibility—it seems to always be a planned future improvement. The development of open-source software libraries such as liblouis and SRE offer some hope that vendors will make use of the libraries in their code because the libraries reduce the burden of implementing accessible math. However, adoption still requires effort to understand how to use the code and to convert internal formats to the library's formats. Even then, vendors still worry about bug fixes and feature enhancements because open-source code, while changeable, is not theirs and no one in their company understands it or "owns" it. User pressure on developers can make a big difference as it did to get JAWS to incorporate support for MathML, but that took many years before the company prioritized the work.

Beyond getting companies to add math accessibility to their products, getting the word out about accessible math products to general education teachers and teachers for the visually impaired is a big task. General education math teachers rarely see students with significant impairments such as blindness and so do not choose the software they use (if they use software at all) based on its accessibility. Teachers of the visually impaired are rarely well versed in math, and so they are rarely skilled in knowing how to teach math and knowing what tools are useful for students to learn and do math. Although user disability conferences such as CSUN can be a starting point for passing on information about user math accessibility tools, hands-on learning likely will only happen when math specialists at schools for the blind learn the tools and pass that knowledge on to teacher trainees and other teachers who update their skills as part of a continuing education program.

STEM is widely regarded as a rewarding and well-rewarded career to enter. Many initiatives have been pushed to increase the number of students pursuing STEM. Sadly, partly due to lack of access, students with significant visual impairments pursue STEM careers at a much lower rate than students without those impairments (Gottfried et al. 2014). Although technology has vastly increased the ability of STEM professionals to solve challenging problems, math education in the schools has not changed much. Calculators have mostly eliminated the teaching of approximation techniques for square roots and trig functions. However, advanced algebra and calculus courses still spend a lot of time teaching students the mechanics of simplifying a rational function, taking a derivative, and solving system of equations. This happens despite software such as Mathematica, Maple, and MATLAB that eliminate the need for mechanical manipulation having been around for over 20 years. The mechanical steps taught in school are particularly hard for many students with a range of disabilities, yet they are no more important to solving a math problem than learning the proper spelling of words is to creating a good story. Professionals mainly rely on software to work toward a solution to a problem. Mathematical problem solving takes place in the mind: seeing how to translate a problem to a diagram and/or a set of equations, simplifying or solving those perhaps with tools, and then interpreting the results, whether it be an equation, an approximation, or data sets. Perhaps the biggest change in math accessibility will not come from the creation and adoption of better accessible math tools, but changes to the way math is taught so that students are free to imagine and explore potential solutions to problems without getting bogged down in the mechanics of solving the problem.

23.6 Conclusions

There has been a great deal of progress in getting math to speak in screen readers, although high-quality semantic speech is still an area of research. It is equally important to be able to navigate math because moderate to complicated expressions are hard to comprehend unless heard in smaller chunks. The ability to navigate expressions has also seen a lot of progress and is enabled in most common screen readers. Similarly, braille output to a refreshable braille display is common, although only a few braille math codes are currently supported. The large number of braille math codes and the relatively small number of users of most of them make support for these other braille math codes less likely. Accessible math editors for users who are blind remain rare, as is braille math input. Even when braille input is possible, typically only Nemeth or UEB are supported.

Most work on accessibility has focused on the visually impaired. Very little work has been done for people with physical handicaps although speech input is starting to get attention because the underlying speech recognition engines used for normal text have improved greatly in the last few years. However, much work needs to be done to correct mistakes and understand how to edit expressions with speech only. Some work has been done for people with reading disorders such as dyslexia. In particular, synchronized highlighting of speech and text is part of some systems. However, other techniques for severely dyslexic students such as font and color changes are not yet part of systems. Similarly, work still needs to be done for students with learning disabilities including those with limited short-term memories.

Plots, charts, and diagrams are important to math. There are several tools that sonify plots and charts. Software that allows for automatically navigating them is now starting to appear. Prior work required preparing tactile output and attaching textual descriptions. The newer approaches remove some of the requirements for sighted assistance in preparing materials. Refreshable grids with a large number of pins along with 3D printing of shapes will further enhance the accessibility and immediacy of diagrams and pictures commonly used in textbooks.

References

APH (n.d) Introducing graphiti—a revolution in accessing digital tactile graphics and more! (WWW Document). https://www.aph.org/graphiti/. Accessed 31 July 2018

Archambault D, Moço V (2006) Canonical MathML to simplify conversion of MathML to Braille mathematical notations. In: Lecture notes in computer science computers helping people with special needs, pp 1191–1198. https://doi.org/10.1007/11788713_172

Avitzur R (1998) Direct manipulation in a mathematics user interface. In: Texts and monographs in symbolic computation computer–human interaction in symbolic computation, pp 43–60. https://doi.org/10.1007/978-3-7091-6461-7_4

Baker CM, Milne LR, Drapeau R, Scofield J, Bennett CL, Ladner RE (2016) Tactile graphics with a voice. ACM Trans Access Comput 8:1–22. https://doi.org/10.1145/2854005

Banf M (2013) Auditory image understanding for the visually impaired based on a modular computer vision sonification model

Bateman A, Zhao OK, Bajcsy AV, Jennings MC, Toth BN, Cohen AJ, Horton EL, Khattar A, Kuo RS, Lee FA, Lim MK, Migasiuk LW, Renganathan R, Zhang A, Oliveira MA (2018) A user centered design and analysis of an electrostatic haptic touchscreen system for students with visual impairments. Int J Hum-Comput Stud 109:102–111. https://doi.org/10.1016/j.ijhcs.2017.09.004

Batlouni S, Karaki H, Zaraket F, Karameh F (2011) Mathifier—speech recognition of math equations. In: 2011 18th IEEE international conference on electronics, circuits, and systems. https://doi.org/10.1109/icecs.2011.6122273

Benetech MDE (2014) GitHub repository. https://github.com/benetech/mde. Accessed 24 July 2018

Brewster S (2002) Visualization tools for blind people using multiple modalities. Disabil Rehabil 24:613–621. https://doi.org/10.1080/09638280110111388

Brock AM, Truillet P, Oriola B, Picard D, Jouffrais C (2014) Interactivity improves usability of geographic maps for visually impaired people. Hum Comput Interact 30:156–194. https://doi.org/10.1080/07370024.2014.924412

Brown C, Hurst A (2012) VizTouch: automatically generated tactile visualizations of coordinate spaces. In: Proceedings of the sixth international conference on tangible, embedded and embodied interaction—TEI 12. https://doi.org/10.1145/2148131.2148160

Brown L, Brewster S, Ramloll R, Riedel B, Yu W (2002) Browsing modes for exploring sonified line graphs. In: Vol. II Proceedings of HCI 2002, pp 6–9

Brown LM, Brewster SA (2003) Drawing by ear: interpreting sonified line graphs. Georgia Institute of Technology

Cervone D, Krautzberger P, Sorge V (2016) New accessibility features in MathJax. J Technol Pers Disabil, 167–175. scholarworks.csun.edu/handle/10211.3/180124

Chabot Samuel, Braasch Jonas (2017) High-density data sonification of stock market information in an immersive virtual environment. J Acoust Soc Am 141(5):3512

Choi Kup-Sze, Chan Tak-Yin (2015) Facilitating mathematics learning for students with upper extremity disabilities using touch-input system. Disabil Rehabil Assist Technol 10(2):170–180

ChromeVox Version 1.27 Release Notes (2013) ChromeVox 1.27 release notes. www.chromevox.com/27/release_notes.html. Accessed 30 Nov 2017

Chu S, Zhang F, Ji N, Zhang F, Pan R (2017) Experimental evaluation of tactile patterns over frictional surface on mobile phones. In: Proceedings of the fifth international symposium of Chinese CHI on—Chinese CHI 2017. https://doi.org/10.1145/3080631.3080639

Desmoslaccessibility [WWW Document] n.d. [WWW Document] Desmos graphing calculator. https://www.desmos.com/accessibility. Accessed 29 July 2018

Dhaher Y, Clements R (2017) A virtual haptic platform to assist seeing impaired learning: proof of concept. J Blind Innov Res 7. https://doi.org/10.5241/7-123

Dooley SS, Park SH (2016) Generating Nemeth Braille output sequences from content MathML markup. J Technol Pers Disabil, pp 156–160. http://scholarworks.csun.edu/handle/10211.3/180122

Dudamath.com. (2018). Dudamath—math in the making. [online] Available at: http://www. dudamath.com/. Accessed 30 July 2018

Formánek D, Líška M, Růžička M, Sojka P (2012) 24th OpenMath workshop, 7th workshop on mathematical user interfaces (MathUI), and intelligent computer mathematics work in progress. In: Proceedings of CEUR workshop. Neuveden, Aachen, pp 91–103

Frankel L, Brownstein B (2016) An evaluation of the usefulness of prosodic and lexical cues for understanding synthesized speech of mathematics. ETS research report series 2016(2):1–19. https://doi.org/10.1002/ets2.12119

Frankel L, Brownstein B, Soiffer N. (2017) Expanding audio access to mathematics expressions by students with visual impairments via MathML. In: ETS research report series

Gardner JA (1995) ACM SIGCAPH computers and the physically handicapped, pp 4–5

Gardner JA, Bulatov V (2006). Scientific diagrams made easy with IVEO™. In: Lecture notes in computer science computers helping people with special needs, pp 1243–1250. https://doi.org/10.1007/11788713_179

Gardner JA, Lundquist R, Sahyun S (1998) TRIANGLE: a tri-modal access program for reading, writing and doing math. In: Proceedings of the CSUN international conference on technology and persons with disabilities, vol. 123. Converging Technologies for Improving Human Performance, Los Angeles

Gardner JA, et al (2002) Tiger, AGC, and win-triangle, removing the barrier to sem education. In: Proceedings of the 2002 CSUN international conference on technology and persons with disabilities

George, S St, et al (2017) Making climate data sing: using music-like sonifications to convey a key climate record. Bull Am Meteorol Soc 98(1):23–27

Georgia Tech Sonification Lab, Sonification Sandbox (2014) Sonification sandbox downloads. http://sonify.psych.gatech.edu/research/sonification_sandbox/download.html. Accessed 31 July 2018

Gillan DJ, Barraza P, Karshmer A, Pazuchanics S (2004) Cognitive analysis of equation reading: application to the development of the math genie. In: Computers Helping People with Special Needs, pp 628–628

Godfrey AJR, Murrell P, Sorge V (2018) An accessible interaction model for data visualization in statistics. In: Lecture notes in computer science computers helping people with special needs, pp.590–597. https://doi.org/10.1007/978-3-319-94277-3_92

Goncu C, Marriott K (2011) GraVVITAS: generic multi-touch presentation of accessible graphics. In: Human-computer interaction—INTERACT 2011. Lecture notes in computer science, pp 30–48. https://doi.org/10.1007/978-3-642-23774-4_5

Gorlewicz JL, et al (2014) Initial experiences using vibratory touchscreens to display graphical math concepts to students with visual impairments. J Spec Educ Technol 29(2):17–25

Gottfried MA, Bozick R, Rose E, Moore R (2014) Does career and technical education strengthen the STEM pipeline? Comparing students with and without disabilities. J Disabil Policy Stud 26:232–244. https://doi.org/10.1177/1044207314544369

Götzelmann T (2018) Visually augmented audio-tactile graphics for visually impaired people. ACM Trans Access Comput 11:1–31. https://doi.org/10.1145/3186894

Hand B, Gunel M, Ulu C (2009) Sequencing embedded multimodal representations in a writing to learn approach to teaching electricity. J Res Sci Teach 46:225–247. https://doi.org/10.1002/tea.20282

Hansen EG, Liu L, Rogat A, Hakkinen MT, Darrah M (2016). Designing innovative science assessments that are accessible for students who are blind. J Blind Innov Res 6. https://doi.org/10.5241/6-91

Hegg JC, et al (2018) The sound of migration: exploring data sonification as a means of interpreting multivariate salmon movement datasets. Heliyon 4(2):e00532

Hecker L, Burns L, Katz L, Elkind J, Elkind K (2002) Benefits of assistive reading software for students with attention disorders. Ann Dyslexia 52:243–272. https://doi.org/10.1007/s11881-002-0015-8

Holton B (2018) Reviewing charts and graphs with SAS accessibility. AFB AccessWorld 19(7) July 2018

International Council on English Braille (2014) Unified English Braille guidelines for technical material, 2008 version updated August 2014. http://www.iceb.org/guidelines_for_technical_material_2014.pdf. Accessed 27 July 2018

Isaacson MD, Schleppenbach D, Lloyd L (2009) Increasing STEM accessibility in students with print disabilities through MathSpeak. J Sci Educ Stud Disabil 14(1):25–32. https://doi.org/10.14448/jsesd.03.0002

Jayant C, Renzelmann M, Wen D, Krisnandi S, Ladner R, Comden D (2007) Automated tactile graphics translation. In: Proceedings of the 9th international ACM SIGACCESS conference on computers and accessibility—Assets 07. https://doi.org/10.1145/1296843.1296858

Kapperman G, Sticken J (2003) A case for increased training in the Nemeth code of braille mathematics for teachers of students who are visually impaired. J Vis Impair Blind 97:110–112

Karshmer A, Gupta G, Pontelli E (2007) Mathematics and accessibility: a survey. In: Proceedings 9th international conference on computers helping people with special needs, vol. 3118

Klatzky RL, Lederman SL (2007) Object recognition by touch. In: Blindness and brain plasticity in navigation and object perception. Lawrence Erlbaum Associates, New York

Kramer G, et al (1999) The sonification report: status of the field and research agenda. Report prepared for the national science foundation by members of the international community for auditory display. In: International community for auditory display (ICAD), Santa Fe, NM

Lamere P et al (2001) The Cmu Sphinx-4 speech recognition system

Lewis P, Noble S, Soiffer N (2010) Using accessible math textbooks with students who have learning disabilities. In: Proceedings of the 12th international ACM SIGACCESS conference on computers and accessibility. ACM

Lewis P, Lee L, Noble S, Garrett B (2013) KY Math Etext Project- a case study: math curriculum digital conversion and implementation. Inform Technol Disabil E-J 13(1)

Manshad MS, Manshad AS (2008) Multimodal vision glove for touchscreens. In: Proceedings of the 10th international ACM SIGACCESS conference on computers and accessibility—Assets 08. https://doi.org/10.1145/1414471.1414523

Mansur DL (1975) Graphs in sound: a numerical data analysis method for the blind. M.Sc. thesis, Department of Computing Science, University of California

McClellan N (2005) Voice math with MathTalk using either dragon naturally speaking or microsoft Speech engine. In: CSUN conference proceedings

Miller C (2016) UEB and Math: where are we headed? Paths to literacy. www.pathstoliteracy.org/blog/ueb-and-math-where-are-we-headed, 30 Mar

Murphy E, Bates E, Fitzpatrick D (2010) Designing auditory cues to enhance spoken mathematics for visually impaired users. In: Proceedings of the 12th international ACM SIGACCESS conference on computers and accessibility. ACM

Mullenbach J, Shultz C, Piper AM, Peshkin M, Colgate JE (2013) Surface haptic interactions with a TPad tablet. In: Proceedings of the adjunct publication of the 26th annual ACM symposium on user interface software and technology—UIST 13 adjunct. https://doi.org/10.1145/2508468.2514929

National Federation of the Blind (2009). The braille literacy crisis in America (rep.). The Braille Literacy Crisis in America. National Federation of the Blind, Baltimore, MA

Neuhoff JG (2011) Perception, cognition and action in auditory displays. In: The sonification handbook, pp 63–85

Noble S, Soiffer N, Dooley S, Lozano E, Brown, D (2018, March). Accessible math: best practices after 25 years of research and development. J Technol & Pers Disabil 6:284–296. Retrieved from http://hdl.handle.net/10211.3/203002

Nguyen DM (2011) The use of MathTrax in algebra teaching. Electron J Math Technol 5(2)

Parkes D (1998) Tactile audio tools for graphicacy and mobility "A circle is either a circle or it is not a circle". Br J Vis Impair 16:99–104. https://doi.org/10.1177/026461969801600304

Pearson School Assessments (2015) Usability test results. In: Internal report

Pearson School Assessments (2016) Usability test results. In: Internal report

Perez L, Gulley A, Prickett L (2017) Improving access to higher education with UDL and switch access technology: a case study. In: Empowering learners with mobile open-access learning initiatives. IGI Global, pp 13–30

Petrie HL, Weber G, Fisher W (2005) Personalization, interaction, and navigation in rich multimedia documents for print-disabled users. IBM Syst J 44:629–635. https://doi.org/10.1147/sj.443.0629

Picard D, Lebaz S (2012) Identifying raised-line drawings by touch: a hard but not impossible task. J Vis Impair Blind 106(7):427–431

Pinna B, Deiana K (2018) On the role of color in reading and comprehension tasks in Dyslexic children and adults. I-Perception 9(3):204166951877909. https://doi.org/10.1177/2041669518779098

Raman TV (1994) Audio system for technical readings. Cornell University

Rello L, Baeza-Yates R (2013) Good fonts for dyslexia. In: Proceedings of the 15th international ACM SIGACCESS conference on computers and accessibility—ASSETS 13. https://doi.org/10.1145/2513383.2513447

Soiffer N (2015) Browser-independent accessible math. In: Proceedings of the 12th web for all conference on—W4A 15. https://doi.org/10.1145/2745555.2746678

Soiffer N (2018a) Improving usability of math editors. In: Proceedings of the internet of accessible things on—W4A 18. https://doi.org/10.1145/3192714.3192835

Soiffer N (2018b) The Benetech math editor: an inclusive multistep math editor for solving problems. In: Lecture notes in computer science computers helping people with special needs, pp 565–572. https://doi.org/10.1007/978-3-319-94277-3_88

Song H (2011) Evaluation of the effects of spatial separation and timbral differences on the identifiability of features of concurrent auditory streams. http://hdl.handle.net/2123/7213

Soviak A, Borodin A, Ashok V, Borodin Y, Puzis Y, Ramakrishnan I (2016) Tactile accessibility. In: Proceedings of the 18th international ACM SIGACCESS conference on computers and accessibility—ASSETS 16. https://doi.org/10.1145/2982142.2982175

Stevens R, Edwards A (1994) MathTalk: the design of an interface for reading algebra using speech. Computers for Handicapped Persons, pp 313–320

The Nemeth Braille Code for Mathematics and Science Notation (1972) Revision (1979) American Printing House for the Blind, Louisville, Kentucky

Toennies JL, Burgner J, Withrow TJ, Webster RJ (2011) Toward haptic/aural touchscreen display of graphical mathematics for the education of blind students. In: 2011 IEEE world haptics conference. https://doi.org/10.1109/whc.2011.5945515

Weitnauer E, Landy D, Ottmar E (2016) Graspable math: towards dynamic algebra notations that support learners better than paper. In: 2016 future technologies conference (FTC). https://doi.org/10.1109/ftc.2016.7821641

Wery JJ, Diliberto JA (2017) The effect of a specialized Dyslexia font, OpenDyslexic, on reading rate and accuracy. Ann Dyslexia 67(2):114–127. PMC. Web. 30 July 2018

Xu C, Israr A, Poupyrev I, Bau O, Harrison C (2011) Tactile display for the visually impaired using TeslaTouch. In: Proceedings of the 2011 annual conference extended abstracts on human factors in computing systems—CHI EA 11. https://doi.org/10.1145/1979742.1979705

Yamaguchi K, Suzuki M (2012) Accessible authoring tool for DAISY ranging from mathematics to others. In: Lecture notes in computer science computers helping people with special needs, pp 130–137. https://doi.org/10.1007/978-3-642-31522-0_19

Yu W, Ramloll R, Brewster S (2001) Haptic graphs for blind computer users. In: Lecture notes in computer science, haptic human–computer interaction, pp 41–51. https://doi.org/10.1007/3-540-44589-7_5

Chapter 24
Usability, Universal Usability, and Design Patterns

David Sloan and Sarah Horton

Abstract The concept of universal usability brings practical purpose to web accessibility efforts by focusing on enabling diverse populations to successfully and independently use the web for meaningful goals. Design patterns have emerged as a means
to capture and standardize research-derived knowledge in the accessible interface and
interaction design through presenting definitions and examples of how commonly
used interface components can be designed with accessibility in mind. A design
system and code library with patterns that incorporate accessibility features is a
powerful tool for ensuring people with disabilities benefit from new technologies.
Additionally, patterns benefit general usability by improving the learnability and
memorability of interaction patterns. Guidelines that encourage or enforce standard
interaction patterns, like Apple's Human Interface Guidelines (Apple in Human
interface guidelines, 2018), improve user experience and in turn, increase loyalty
behaviors such as repurchase and referrals (Hoisington and Naumann in Qual Prog
36(2):33–41, 2003). In this chapter, we reaffirm the relationship between accessibility and universal usability, reflecting on developments since the Universal Usability
chapter in the first edition of this book (Horton and Leventhal in Universal usability.
Springer, 2008). With today's more mature technology platform and profession, we
explore the use of accessible design guidelines and patterns to provide interactions
that are usable by everyone.

24.1 Introduction

Universal usability is defined by Ben Shneiderman in his 2000 *Communications
of the ACM* article of that title as "…having more than 90% of all households as
successful users of information and communications services at least once a week"

D. Sloan (✉) · S. Horton
The Paciello Group, 17757 US 19 North, Clearwater, FL 33764, USA
e-mail: dsloan@paciellogroup.com

S. Horton
e-mail: shorton@paciellogroup.com

© Springer-Verlag London Ltd., part of Springer Nature 2019   445
Y. Yesilada and S. Harper (eds.), *Web Accessibility*, Human–Computer
Interaction Series, https://doi.org/10.1007/978-1-4471-7440-0_24

(Shneiderman 2000, p. 85). To work toward inclusiveness through universal usability, technologists must focus on three challenges:

1. Support a wide range of technologies.
2. Accommodate diverse users.
3. Help users bridge the gap between what they know and what they need to know (Shneiderman 2003, p. 15).

The Universal Usability chapter in the first edition of this book explored methods and considerations to address these challenges, including:

- Universal access, covering the level of availability of technology to people,
- Usability, covering the degree to which digital products support successful task completion, and
- Universal design, covering the degree to which digital products can be used regardless of disability (Horton and Leventhal 2008).

In this edition, we provide an update on progress in these areas, and extend the exploration of universal usability to cover design patterns and design standards as a means of improving universal design, and learnability of technology.

24.2 Accessibility Supports Diversity

An analysis of technology trends over the last ten years will show that there is an increasing range of devices through which people, including people with disabilities, access, and interact with digital products. With the growing importance of technology in everyday life, there has been an increased focus on the rights of people with disabilities not to encounter discrimination online. Organizations within and beyond the technology industry have embraced the perspective of accessibility as not just a risk management exercise, but also an opportunity to design better solutions for more people. These factors shape a positive response to the first two of Shneiderman's challenges, "support a wide range of technologies" and "accommodate diverse users."

24.2.1 Access to the Internet Is Not yet Universal

According to the International Telecommunications Union (2017), global trends between 2015 and 2017 show a gradual increase in the use of the internet, and a more significant increase in mobile cellular telephone subscriptions. During the same time period, the proportion of households with access to the internet has grown from around 20% in 2005 to 50% in 2017. This change hides a significant difference across the world.

Estimated figures for 2017 indicate that:

- In the Developed World, over 80% of households have access to the internet.
- In the Developing World, less than 40% of households have access to the internet.

While access to information and communication services has clearly increased, Shneiderman's figure of 90% has not yet been reached, and progress toward it varies globally.

24.2.2   Technology Has Advanced Accessibility Support

Looking more specially at the challenge of supporting a wide range of technologies, we must reflect on changes in consumer technology used to access and interact online. Since the publication of the first edition of this book, technological development has continued apace, with a clear significance for people with disabilities.

The emergence of smartphones and tablet devices as popular alternatives to the more traditional desktop or laptop computer is illustrated by usage statistics from the ITU, where global mobile cellular subscriptions have increased from just over 2 billion in 2005 to an estimated figure of over 7 billion in 2017.

With increased connectivity and reduced cost of devices and network access, mobile access is possible to a greater number of people. The motivation for access is fueled by the increased use of social media, media streaming, and online retail. Smart consumer products are displaying and communicating data through very different interfaces to the traditional website displayed on a browser and desktop computer.

The growth in usage of mobile devices is mirrored when looking at people with disabilities. Data collected by WebAIM's Screen Reader User Surveys show that the percentage of respondents who use a mobile screen reader had increased from 12.2% (135 respondents) in January 2009 to 88% (1557 respondents) in November 2017 (WebAIM 2017). While WebAIM notes some limitations to conclusions that can be drawn from the data due to the distribution method for the survey and potential for skew, including the inclusion of non-disabled screen reader users, the figures nevertheless give some indication that mobile device usage amongst screen reader users has grown substantially over the last 10 years.

For people with disabilities, the emergence of tablet and smartphone devices, in particular, has presented significant opportunities. The portability of mobile devices combined with the opportunities provided by location-aware interactions can help people with disabilities achieve increased independence (Kane et al 2009).

Another advantage mobile devices offer people with disabilities is the availability and integration of a range of accessibility features and assistive technologies in the device's operating system. Embedded assistive technologies are standard on mobile operating systems, such as VoiceOver on Apple's iOS devices and TalkBack on Android devices. The accessibility options are available that are helpful for people with disabilities and also other users, such as the pinch-to-zoom feature widely available on touchscreen devices. These features help make the consumer products more usable to a wider audience, out of the box, without the need for locating, installing, and using third-party assistive technology, or relying on custom "accessible" versions that might create stigmatization.

As demands for technology accessibility have grown, there is greater commercial value in investing in and communicating accessibility features of web sites and applications, and products used to generate online content. In the US, Section 508 of the Rehabilitation Act places responsibilities on federal agencies to procure and provide technology that meets accessibility standards, including WCAG, for web resources. This, in turn, places demands on vendors to invest in accessibility, and to publicize accessibility information, for example using the Voluntary Product Accessibility Template®. While these efforts are driven by a desire to serve the US federal market, a public declaration of accessibility and an underlying commitment to enhancing accessibility helps purchasers regardless of sector or location.

24.2.3   Inclusive Design Is Becoming Valued in Mainstream Technology

While Shneiderman introduced the concept of universal usability, the term "inclusive design" is emerging as a dominant descriptor of an approach to digital product creation that recognizes and attempts to accommodate human diversity, including disability. Writing in the Adobe Blog, May (2018) explains how inclusive design was selected as a term that most effectively encapsulated Adobe's efforts to introduce diversity and inclusion into product design:

> Inclusive design is a term that leads people to think about an expanding audience, with expanding wants and needs, which, in turn, gives them more to think about as they design products. (May 2018)

There is plenty of evidence that inclusive design is becoming more valued in the design of digital products and services. An organization's level of motivation for inclusive design may traditionally be seen as a function of the point where they balance the benefits (access to a larger audience, altruism, or risk reduction) and limitations (perceived effort or constraints on what can be produced).

From a benefits perspective, there is an obvious argument that inclusive designs enable more people to successfully use products by reducing barriers to access and interaction. Related to this is a strong moral argument for ensuring that as technological innovations become prominent across education, government, healthcare, retail, finance, and other sectors, they do not unjustifiably create new barriers for groups already vulnerable to exclusion.

From a limitation perspective, there is a business argument around return on investment. To maximize profit, efforts may begin with an initial focus on a majority of a population with similar needs. Only later should attention turn to smaller populations with more distinct needs, who may need features that might be perceived to detract from a desirable solution. This argument clearly presents problems for accessibility if people with disabilities are perceived as a small population that requires specialized features.

The moral argument for and business argument against suddenly align when considering accessibility as a civil rights issue. We have already mentioned Section 508 of the Rehabilitation Act in the US as a driver for increased publicity of accessibility features of digital products. Legislation that protects the rights of people with disabilities from unjustified discrimination, such as the 1990 Americans with Disabilities Act (ADA) or the UK's Equality Act of 2010, also becomes a motivator for organizations who want to manage risk. Some risk management focuses on compliance with technical accessibility standards, or even choosing to do nothing and accept the potential consequences of legal action. When risk management prioritizes people with disabilities and successful task completion, the result is greater attention to universal usability.

Beyond these arguments, accessibility advocates have joined with others in the design industry to argue the benefits of accessibility in design strategy. Instead of seeing diverse populations on the margins of a homogeneous population, and as a group that can be deprioritized, focusing on diverse populations *first* and understanding and meeting those needs helps create more innovative and effective solutions. In Change by Design, Tim Brown encourages designers to seek rewards:

> By concentrating solely on the bulge at the center of the bell curve we are more likely to confirm what we already know than learn something new and surprising. (Brown 2009)

Focusing on people with disabilities as part of a user-centered design approach helps design and development teams recognize spectrums of capabilities across many dimensions—vision, hearing, dexterity, concentration, memory, and literacy, amongst others. These capabilities have long been recognized as also being constrained by the device a user may use, or the environment in which a digital product is used, and therefore, a disability-sensitive approach to design helps anticipate and accommodate diverse designs and usage environments (Newell and Gregor 2000).

This observation is reflected in a number of resources intended to support inclusive design. Version 2.1 of the Web Content Accessibility Guidelines (WCAG) was published in June 2018, driven by the need to provide better coverage for accessibility of mobile and touchscreen interactions. Building on WCAG, designers have access to principles of accessible user experience and inclusive design (Horton and Quesenbery 2014; Swan et al. n.d.). Microsoft launched an Inclusive Design resource that promotes the value of designing for diversity, and provides a toolkit for design and development teams to think more inclusively in their projects (Microsoft 2018).

Microsoft's Inclusive Design initiative is an example of how major players in the technology industry have become more visible in talking about accessibility and support for people with disabilities, in their design activities and in advertising of products. An advertisement from Apple for their FaceTime video conferencing product included sign language users communicating through FaceTime.

The Teach Access initiative (Teach Access 2018) is another example of how the technology industry is placing increased value on accessibility and inclusive design as a valued professional skill. A number of technology companies have partnered with disability advocacy organizations and higher education institutions in the United States in a range of activities intended to grow the pool of future employees with requisite knowledge and skills in the accessibility. Amongst these activities is providing support to faculty who would like to develop teaching methods and topics to cover accessibility more extensively. The immediate beneficiaries of this initiative are students, who have greater exposure to accessibility as a topic and thus the opportunity to develop a professional skill that is valued in the industry. The long-term beneficiaries are people who benefit from inclusively designed digital products.

There is also evidence of a growing focus on organizational strategy for accessibility and inclusion, as a way to ensure that human diversity is recognized and managed systemically and in a sustainable way (Klein 2011).

24.3 Patterns Help Bridge the Gap

The value of design is debated and attention to user interface design is often deprioritized. In a technology-driven industry, designers and usability professionals must make a case for investing time and resources in good design and universal usability (Marcus 2002; Nielsen Norman Group n.d.; Shneiderman 2003). Additionally, consistency is not always valued in product development. Instead, the design is seen as a differentiator, and digital products are designed to have distinctive user interfaces. These factors make Shneiderman's third challenge for universal usability, "Help users bridge the gap between what they know and what they need to know," more difficult to achieve.

24.3.1 Design Patterns Improve Usability

Nielsen's five quality components of usability are the following:

Learnability: How easy is it for users to accomplish basic tasks the first time they encounter the design?
Efficiency: Once users have learned the design, how quickly can they perform tasks?
Memorability: When users return to the design after a period of not using it, how easily can they reestablish proficiency?
Errors: How many errors do users make, how severe are these errors, and how easily can they recover from the errors?
Satisfaction: How pleasant is it to use the design? (Nielsen 2012).

Of these, learnability and memorability are influenced by familiarity. Interfaces are easier to learn and remember when they use familiar components and interactions, or design patterns.

Design patterns arise from proven approaches to interaction design—for example, buttons to perform an action and links to navigate to a new page or screen. A design approach becomes a pattern when it is widely adopted and becomes a convention. Users benefit from design patterns because they can take advantage of what they know and apply it to diverse digital products and devices. Without design patterns, or with conflicting design patterns, users must continuously relearn how to operate digital products.

Consistency is a design principle that maintains that people can learn more quickly when elements that have the same or similar purpose are presented in a consistent way visually and functionally. Internal consistency is one factor, where a digital product presents similar content and features in a consistent way. With external consistency, content and features are designed to be consistent with established design standards. Another design principle that is supported by design patterns is Recognition Over Recall, which maintains that it's easier to work with familiar content and features than it is to recall commands or remember steps in a process. When design patterns are used for content and functionality, people can recognize the pattern and know how it works (Lidwell et al. 2010). Adopting a common set of design patterns is one way to utilize consistency and recognition over recall to improve usability.

Considered in the context of Nielsen's five quality components of usability, design patterns are a way to improve learnability and memorability of user interfaces and establishing a common set of design patterns could be a "major breakthrough in usability."

> Standardize and you simplify lives: everyone learns the system only once. (Norman 2013)

However, Norman cautions about timing for standardization:

> But don't standardize too soon; you may be locked into a primitive technology, or you may have introduced roles that turn out to be grossly inefficient, even error-inducing. Standardize too late, and there may already be so many ways of doing things that no international standard can be agreed upon. (Norman 2013)

Technology is maturing and with it, design insights and methods. With the current support for accessibility and attention to quality user experiences, it is time to standardize on design patterns and improve universal usability. Otherwise, the current free-for-all approach to digital product design will yield so many variants that it will become increasingly more difficult to define and adopt a standard approach.

24.3.2   Accessible Design Patterns Support Universal Usability

Design patterns have long been seen as a valuable tool in supporting user-centered, usable interaction design, and have emerged as a tool to support accessible design. Borchers defined a design pattern as:

> A structured textual and graphical description of a proven solution to a recurrent design problem. (Borchers 2001, p. 7)

This definition emphasizes the nature of a pattern as a way to capture research-derived knowledge of how to tackle a frequently occurring issue, in a language that is understandable by multi-disciplinary teams. Design patterns have thus been identified as a means to convey knowledge about the accessible interface and interaction design in a way that is reusable by designers and developers.

Many efforts exist to provide design patterns within different contexts:

- Operating systems. For example, Apple (2018) offers guidance and specifications for how to design and provide specific components, like navigation bars and sliders, on mobile devices.
- Platforms and frameworks. For example, jQuery provides a library of reusable components, such as dialogs and datepickers (jQuery Foundation 2018).
- Company design standards. For example, IBM's Design Language (IBM n.d.) and MailChimp's pattern library (MailChimp n.d.) are both aimed at enhancing the user experience by standardizing on visual and interaction design.

These efforts are local in scope, providing guidance and resources to improve usability through familiarity within the context of a specific technology or company. Design systems have the added benefit of improving processes and reducing technical debt within an organization. MailChimp's pattern library summarizes these benefits:

- We can **build consistently**, focusing our energy on workflows and logic, not web forms and list items.
- We can **reuse code** instead of reinventing the wheel or roping in an engineer.
- We can **see all of our patterns in one place**, quickly revealing maintenance issues (MailChimp n.d.).

On the other hand, accessibility has provided a push toward establishing universal design standards to support accessibility. WCAG is a global standard that provides specifications for designing and building accessible components. The design patterns that are part of the WAI toolkit provide the same detailed guidance as the design systems referenced above and have the benefit of incorporating accessibility features.

In 2014, the W3C published version 1 of the WAI-ARIA specification, an extension to the HTML, CSS, and JavaScript core web technologies to address accessibility shortcomings of rich internet application development approaches. Version 1.1 of WAI-ARIA followed in 2017.

To support adoption of this specification, the W3C has also published WAI-ARIA Authoring Practices (W3C 2018), a definition of how a range of user interface components, from simple buttons to complex interactions like interactive data tables and tab panels, can be implemented using the WAI-ARIA specification. For each user interface component, the Authoring Practices document describes:

- the intended purpose of the component, indicating appropriate usage context;
- the appropriate use of WAI-ARIA code to define name, role, and current state or value of the component and subcomponents, indicating where these values would need to be updated by scripting in response to significant events like a user keypress or mouse click;

- recommended keyboard support.

Each component's pattern also includes links to approved working examples of the implementation, which helps meet the graphical requirement of Borchers' definition of a design pattern.

The value of the WAI-ARIA Authoring Practices is in its definition of how web technologies can be implemented following WCAG to implement patterns in diverse environments and with diverse tools. These patterns, in turn, can be inherited by other style guides and patterns at a more local level.

Activity in the web industry has also seen a number of efforts from industry, academia, and grassroots efforts from developers to provide working validated examples of interface component design that exhibit best practice in accessibility. These examples are typically based on the WAI-ARIA specification, and include amongst others:

- Fluid Infusion Framework and Components, from the Inclusive Design Research Centre at OCAD University (Inclusive Design Research Centre n.d.).
- Inclusive Components, by Heydon Pickering (n.d.).
- Open Accessibility Framework (OAF), a set of accessible components for different development environments, an output of the AEGIS project (AEGIS n.d.).

Work toward a standard approach to accessible design patterns is more mature and global than general design pattern efforts. We can use accessibility to focus attention on the value of standardizing design and incorporating accessibility features and help "bridge the gap" for all users by providing accessible design patterns.

24.4   Discussion

In the fast-paced world of the technology industry, new pattern libraries are regularly emerging, demonstrating novel approaches to interface design, and solving other challenges, such as performance. One shortcoming will be if "accessible design patterns" continue to exist as a separate entity to design patterns more generally. The existence of design patterns branded as accessible suggests shortcomings of other patterns. The most desirable goal must be to integrate accessibility best practices into mainstream design patterns.

What will it take to blend local efforts to establish a design language and global efforts to ensure people with disabilities can use technology? And how can we build on global efforts to support accessibility and improve universal usability through standardization of design patterns?

24.4.1 Accessibility and Ease of Use Are Essential to Adoption

The tech industry is driven by a culture of invention and innovation. New technology products jostle to "hook" potential consumers and thereby reap the benefits of a captive audience. One of the factors described in Eyal's book, Hooked: How to Build Habit-Forming Products, is "variable reward," which draws our attention to novelty.

> Novelty sparks our interest, makes us pay attention, and—like a baby encountering a friendly dog for the first time—we seem to love it. (Eyal 2014, p. 98)

It is no wonder that standardization in user interface design is not widely embraced by digital product developers. In an industry that looks to novelty as a way of profiting, the use of tried-and-true components and patterns to increase familiarity and improve usability may be seen as a potential risk to revenue. Additionally, pattern libraries reduce the necessity for creative designs and custom code and may reduce or change the role of members of the product team, including designers, developers, researchers, and testers. If a digital product makes use of proven patterns, how do these roles remain relevant?

Creativity and invention should focus on the experiences afforded by digital products. Consumers value what technology allows us to do, over the novel ways in which it works. Innovation activities should focus on providing a novel and valued content and functionality, and digital products should use design patterns to make those features easy to learn and use. As Lynch and Horton explain in Web Style Guide, "The interface is the frame, not the painting."

> In general, people find the familiar easier to use and remember, and if your site follows these familiar patterns, users will quickly adapt and begin to focus on your unique content, features, or products. (Lynch and Horton 2016, p. 226)

People do want novelty, but not solely in design. Part of what makes the "hook" cycle work is the action phase, where success depends on usability and ease of use. "The more effort…required to perform the desired action, the less likely it is to occur" (Eyal 2014, pp. 8, 61). For end users, design patterns minimize the required effort to interact with a digital product, and between products. This benefits usability when user knowledge of prior experiences can be reapplied, and supports Nielsen's usability heuristic of recognition rather than recall (Budiu 2014); consistency in appearance and behavior supports people with cognitive impairments that may affect memory and learning. When patterns incorporate best practice in accessibility, beneficiaries include people with disabilities.

Design and development teams also benefit from using patterns with known high levels of accessibility, by saving time through the reduced need to test and evaluate interfaces for accessibility. The granular nature of patterns for specific user interface components may also provide an obvious opportunity for benchmarking performance, helping design and development teams further optimize their efforts. With design patterns, design and development teams can capitalize on prior research into accessibility and deliver interface solutions that provide users with disabilities with a familiar and consistent user experience.

24.5 Future Directions

Research and design of accessible design patterns is a rich area for exploration, with potentially another positive outcome of a universal design approach to usability and accessibility. Like curb cuts and access ramps, applying design approaches to accessibility will lead to innovative approaches that will improve interface design generally. Prioritizing people with disabilities will force attention to the implications of technology on individuals and society, and evolve technology culture from "move fast and break things" to "above all, do no harm."

24.5.1 Universal Usability is an Opportunity to Innovate

A recurring challenge to universal usability is resistance due to the perceived stifling of innovation and creativity. This is despite the many real-world examples of product innovation with roots in attempts to solve a disability-related challenge, from typewriters and cassette recorders to predictive text input and speech recognition. Pullin (2009) describes how there has also been a shift in design approaches to assistive technology—from a medical challenge that prioritizes managing a condition to a design challenge that values esthetics and social inclusion.

Design patterns can help systemize the existing knowledge in inclusive interaction, while still affording the possibility for patterns to be evaluated, refined, and improved over time. But they can also provide a platform for innovation, in the same way, that automotive design operates within certain constraints established by safety and efficiency concerns, adheres to certain conventions of control placement, form, and operation, yet still provides substantial scope for manufacturers to innovate and compete on different levels.

A clear opportunity exists for greater involvement of people with disabilities in user research and design activities, and with an aging population where accessibility needs increase, there is a logical economic argument for doing so. This can include involvement in exploratory user research activities to understand a design problem space, and in participatory design, activities to collaboratively identify and evaluate potential solutions, for example, as described by Politis et al. (2017). The result is a richer understanding of a problem space and solutions that might not have been considered had people with disabilities not been involved.

24.5.2 Universal Usability Helps Make Technology Humane

The dominant technology companies of the late 2010s adopted a business model driven by gathering and selling user data; by encouraging social interaction that is not always healthy. Concerns have been raised over directions of the technology industry and in particular on ethical values, from workplace sexism to misuse of data (Monteiro 2017). Can a focus on diversity help to reset how we use technology for good?

When technology design processes and business goals do not prioritize identifying and managing sensitive or stressful situations, harmful consequences can result (Meyer and Wachter-Boettcher 2016). This includes making assumptions about users and their characteristics, and a lack of recognition of diversity.

Given the commercial priorities of an organization selling digital products or services, influencing behaviors to accommodate diversity may require a complex mix of pressures. We have already explored how a greater focus on people with disabilities could help design and development teams better understand a problem space and identify more effective solutions. There are opportunities to realize the additional benefit of a focus on disability as increased sensitivity to the potential negative consequences of design decisions, and thus greater awareness of the range and nature of the impact of design decisions.

24.6 Authors' Opinion of the Field

We have made great strides in recent times to move from a perspective of accessibility as a compliance exercise toward one that focuses on supporting task completion and goal achievement by people with disabilities. We have also seen increases in access to and accessibility of devices and platforms, which supports greater use of the web by diverse populations. But when we look back at Shneiderman's definition of universal usability, we can see there is more to be done.

As we rely more on technology-based solutions for activities that are essential to independence, we must make accessibility a requirement, and incorporate accessibility into accessible interaction design patterns that are tested and refined through careful and ongoing research. An accessible pattern library, widely adopted, could be the basis of a global design system to support universal usability. From there, we must prepare technology professionals to use such solutions as standard tools in their toolkit.

24.6.1   *Universal Usability Is Essential to an Inclusive Society*

Technology's potential to improve the quality of life is proven, and most people use some form of technology to make tasks easier, more efficient, and more effective. Technology can reduce the disabling aspect of an impairment that otherwise gets in the way of accomplishing tasks. As a screen reader-using participant, in a usability study conducted by the authors put it:

> I mean big picture, I think that we could mitigate blindness as a disability in 20 years vis-a-vis technology.

Our reliance on technology-based solutions is increasing exponentially. It is difficult to imagine accomplishing instrumental activities of daily living—activities that allow people to live independently—without using technology (Wikipedia 2018). Managing money, shopping, communicating, transportation, etc., are made easier through technology. In many cases, these activities are *only* achieved using technology.

Technology is both an opportunity and a risk to people with disabilities. As reliance on technology increases, we must make universal usability a requirement, and thereby foster a healthy, inclusive society rather than cause increased exclusion by erecting technology barriers.

24.6.2   *Design Research Must Define Universally Usable Patterns*

Creating and validating the effectiveness and universal usability of design patterns is an ongoing endeavor and needs an accompanying research agenda. Historically, accessibility-related activity has focused on technology standards and solutions, e.g., defining code attributes to make smarter interfaces that work better with assistive technology, building software solutions to enlarge text and invert colors. Less attention goes to approaching the human factors side of accessibility, exploring design's role in providing technology that is optimally usable for with people with disabilities. If we are to advance standard design patterns as a means to "bridge the gap" to intuitive interaction for everyone, we must be prepared to present solid patterns that have been refined through research methods, and that will continue to be tested and refined to account for advancements in technology and diverse contexts of use.

24.6.3   *Education Must Prepare Responsible Technologists*

The people side of technology is generally underrepresented in research and scholarship. There is still work to do to increase the prominence of usability and user-centered design in design, engineering, and computer science programs; and while evidence from the U.S. indicates accessibility is now taught across a large proportion of educational institutions, lack of recognition as a core topic presents a challenge in increasing coverage of accessibility in the curriculum (Shinohara et al 2018).

PEAT (Partnership on Employment and Accessible Technology) conducted an industry survey in 2018 on employer perspectives on accessibility skills in recruitment and found that "60% said it was difficult or very difficult for their organization to find job candidates with accessibility skills. 0% said it was easy or very easy."

> All our developers should know or at least be familiar with accessibility. Most of the time when asked about accessibility they don't even know what it is. (PEAT 2018)

The Teach Access project described earlier in this chapter is one effort toward addressing shortcomings in how we prepare future designers and engineers to build accessible technologies. The challenge is to extend efforts beyond computing science education to all educational pathways followed by digital designers, developers, and content authors of the future. Everyone involved in creating digital technologies needs to learn what it means to build responsibly. "It's time we recognize that the digital things we're making are the places where many of our most important social interactions are happening, and start designing them accordingly" (Arango 2018).

24.7 Conclusions

Universal usability remains a viable target for digital accessibility efforts. Accessibility standards and laws provide a strong foundation for increasing attention to human factors in general, with the goal of designing technologies that are humane and inclusive. The scholarly community should support industry efforts by establishing a research agenda focused on developing and maintaining accessible design patterns and promoting their use as a proven means to improve universal usability, and educating future technologists to aim for universal usability.

References

AEGIS (n.d.) Open accessibility framework. http://www.aegis-project.eu/index.php?option=com_content&view=article&id=191&Itemid=80. Accessed 14 Oct 2018

Apple (2018) Human interface guidelines. https://developer.apple.com/design/human-interface-guidelines/. Accessed 14 Oct 2018

Arango J (2018) Living in information: responsible design for digital places. Two Waves Books/Rosenfeld Media, Brooklyn, NY

Borchers J (2001) A pattern approach to interaction design. Wiley, Chichester

Brown T (2009) Change by design. HarperBusiness, New York

Budiu R (2014) Memory recognition and recall in user interfaces. https://www.nngroup.com/articles/recognition-and-recall/. Accessed 14 Oct 2018

Eyal N (2014) Hooked: how to build habit-forming products. Portfolio/Penguin, New York

Google (n.d.) Material design. https://material.io Accessed 14 Oct 2018

Hoisington S, Neumann E (2003) The loyalty elephant. Qual Prog 36(2):33–41. American Society
    for Quality
Horton S, Leventhal L (2008) Universal usability. In: Harper S, Yesilada Y (eds) Web accessibility:
    a foundation for research. Springer
Horton S, Quesenbery W (2014) A web for everyone. Rosenfeld Media, New York
IBM (n.d.) IBM design language. https://www.ibm.com/design/language/. Accessed 14 Oct 2018
Inclusive Design Research Centre (n.d.) Fluid infusion framework and components. https://
    fluidproject.org/infusion.html. Accessed 14 Oct 2018
International Telecommunications Union (2017) Measuring the information society report 2017,
    vol 1. https://www.itu.int/en/ITU-D/Statistics/Documents/publications/misr2017/MISR2017_
    Volume1.pdf. Accessed 14 Oct 2018
jQuery Foundation (2018) jQuery UI.n https://jqueryui.com. Accessed 14 Oct 2018
Kane S, Jayant C, Wobbrock J, Ladner R (2009) Freedom to roam: a study of mobile device adoption
    and accessibility for people with visual and motor disabilities. In: Proceedings of ASSETS'09.
    ACM Press, New York, pp 115–122
Kline J (2011) Strategic accessibility: enabling the organization. Live Oaks
Lidwell W, Holden K, Butler J (2010) Universal principles of design. Rockport Publishers, Glouces-
    ter, MA
Lynch P, Horton S (2016) Web style guide: foundations of user experience design. Yale University
    Press, New Haven
MailChimp (n.d.) MailChimp pattern library. https://ux.mailchimp.com/patterns. Accessed 14 Oct
    2018
Marcus A (2002) Return on investment for usable UI design. User Exp 1(3):25–31
May M (2018) The same, but different: breaking down accessibility, universality, and
    inclusion in design. https://theblog.adobe.com/different-breaking-accessibility-universality-
    inclusion-design/. Accessed 14 Oct 2018
Meyer E, Wachter-Boettcher S (2016) Design for real life. A Book Apart
Microsoft (2018) Inclusive design. https://www.microsoft.com/design/inclusive. Accessed 14 Oct
    2018
Monteiro M (2017) A designer's code of ethics. https://muledesign.com/2017/07/a-designers-code-
    of-ethics. Accessed 14 Oct 2018
Newell A, Gregor P (2000) User-sensitive inclusive design—in search of a new paradigm. In:
    Proceedings of ACM conference on universal usability (CUU). ACM, New York, pp 39–44
Nielsen J (2012) Usability 101: introduction to usability. https://www.nngroup.com/articles/
    usability-101-introduction-to-usability/. Accessed 14 Oct 2018
Nielsen Norman Group (n.d.). Return on investment (ROI) for usability, 4th edn
Norman D (2013) The design of everyday things. Basic Books
PEAT (n.d.) The accessible technology skills gap. http://www.peatworks.org/skillsgap. Accessed
    14 Oct 2018
Pickering H (n.d.). Inclusive Components. https://inclusive-components.design. Accessed 14 Oct
    2018
Politis Y, Robb N, Yakkundi A, Dillenburger K, Herbertson N, Charlesworth B, Goodman L (2017)
    People with disabilities leading the design of serious games and virtual worlds. Int J Serious
    Games 4(2)
Pullin G (2009) Design meets disability. MIT Press, Cambridge, MA
Shinohara K, Kawas S, Ko A, Ladner R (2018) Who teaches accessibility? A survey of U.S.
    computing faculty. In: Proceedings of the 49th ACM technical symposium on computer science
    education (SIGCSE '18). ACM, New York, pp 197–202
Shneiderman B (2000) Universal usability. Commun ACM 43(5):84–91. ACM, New York
Shneiderman B (2003) Leonardo's laptop: human needs and the new computing technologies. MIT
    Press, Cambridge, MA
Swan H, Pouncey I, Pickering H and Watson L (n.d.) Inclusive design principles. https://
    inclusivedesignprinciples.org. Accessed 14 Oct 2018

Teach Access (2018) http://teachaccess.org/. Accessed 14 Oct 2018

W3C (2018) WAI-ARIA authoring practices 1.1. https://www.w3.org/TR/wai-aria-practices-1.1/. Accessed 15 Oct 2018

WebAIM (2017) Screen reader user survey #7 results. https://webaim.org/projects/screenreadersurvey7/. Accessed 14 Oct 2018

Wikipedia (2018) Activities of daily living. https://en.wikipedia.org/wiki/Activities_of_daily_living. Accessed 14 Oct 2018

Chapter 25
Multimedia Accessibility

Carlos Duarte and Manuel J. Fonseca

Abstract Multimedia content is growing at an increasing pace. Making this content accessible to people with impairments is not only paramount but also a growing challenge in itself. Access services for people with visual or hearing impairments have been studied and refined over the last years, resulting in standards and laws to ensure that minimum amounts of accessible content are produced. Professional content producers have the knowledge and skills required to do so. However, individuals creating multimedia content to publish on the Internet usually lack both. In this chapter, we review existing access services, comprised of subtitles, sign language and audio descriptions. We complement this with a summary of research efforts that could assist both in the production and consumption of access services. Finally, we discuss how emerging technologies and techniques, like machine learning or crowdsourcing, can help us tackle the sheer amount of access services that need to be created to ensure all have equal access to produced content.

25.1 Introduction

Multimedia content has become available to large numbers of the world population since the mass commercialisation of television (TV) begun. To ensure this content is also accessible to people with disabilities a variety of access services have been made available over the years. These include subtitling and sign language interpretation for people with hearing impairments and audio description for people with visual impairments. The provision of these access services is the responsibility of the TV broadcasters or content providers and regulated by the laws of individual countries.

Multimedia availability increased even further with the emergence of the Web. Not only some of the content broadcasted on TV found a new medium for dissemination,

C. Duarte (✉) · M. J. Fonseca
LASIGE, Departamento de Informática, Faculdade de Ciências,
Universidade de Lisboa, Lisbon, Portugal
e-mail: caduarte@fc.ul.pt

M. J. Fonseca
e-mail: mjfonseca@fc.ul.pt

© Springer-Verlag London Ltd., part of Springer Nature 2019   461
Y. Yesilada and S. Harper (eds.), *Web Accessibility*, Human–Computer
Interaction Series, https://doi.org/10.1007/978-1-4471-7440-0_25

but now every individual could become a producer of audio or visual content that she or he could make publicly available on the Web. This evolution raised a new set of challenges for producing and disseminating accessible multimedia. Some of the existing access services for TV could not be readily reutilised for the Web. Many multimedia players are not accessible. Individual producers are not aware of how to produce accessible content.

Furthermore, content producers, professional or otherwise, are not able to know in advance who will consume their content and under what circumstances. Thus, it is a good practice to always make content accessible to everyone. They should not consider only people with impairments (e.g. visual impairments, hearing impairments) but also other people consuming the content in conditions or contexts that limit their options.[1] For instance, users with a low bandwidth connection, in a noisy environment (e.g. a crowded pub or bar), or in a place where they can not disturb others (e.g. a library). People that are not able to hear a video will scroll past it if it is not captioned, irrespectively of the reason they cannot hear it.

In this chapter, we start by covering existing access services and some of the regulations they are subjected to. We follow with a discussion of existing multimedia accessibility problems on the Web and present existing research that aims to tackle those. Before concluding we present an overarching discussion of this topic, some future avenues and our opinion of the field.

25.2 Access Services

Access to multimedia, or to any other type of content, should consider the ability to perceive the content, to understand the content and to operate the mechanisms that allow the content to be reproduced. Multimedia access services focus on offering the possibility to perceive the content and target two main user groups. People with hearing impairments that can watch the content but not hear it benefit from subtitling and sign language interpretation. People with visual impairments that can hear the content but not see it benefit from audio descriptions.

Another user group that can also benefit from access services are people with cognitive impairments. Although access services target content perception, perceiving the same content from multiple channels can improve the ability of users with some cognitive impairments to understand the content (Sloan et al. 2006; Khan 2010). The impact of multimedia on people with dyslexia is also under investigation although conclusive results have not been achieved yet (Wang et al. 2018; Knoop-van Campen et al. 2018).

Finally, in order for users to benefit from existing access services, the media player itself must be accessible. In what concerns media player accessibility, a further group of users must also be considered: those with physical impairments. For access

---

[1] Discussed in the 'Situationally-Induced Impairments and Disabilities' chapter in the first part of this book.

services that are provided for broadcast content, this usually means that the TV set, including the remote control, must be accessible. For access services provided for Web-based content, the media player must take into account the needs of different groups of users so that the interface is perceivable, understandable and operable. In Sect. 25.3, we will further discuss the issues of media players' accessibility. In the following paragraphs, we elaborate on the characteristics of access services.

25.2.1   Subtitles

Subtitles are text provided and synchronised with multimedia to provide the speech in the media content.[2] Another commonly used term for subtitles is captions. However, in some countries, captions refer to more than the dialogue transcription, including also sound effects and possibly the speaker's identification. Depending on the platform and service, subtitles can be visible continuously (open subtitles) or the user can select to display them in the picture as desired (closed subtitles). When considering the TV platform, one common use for subtitles in countries that broadcast foreign language programmes is to subtitle those programmes when they are not dubbed in the national language. In these situations, the subtitles make the media content accessible not only for those with hearing impairments but for the general population.

Even though subtitles are the access service with higher availability, they are still far from being universal. Figure 25.1, published in the European Commission's 'Study on Assessing and Promoting e-Accessibility' (Kubitschke et al. 2013), shows that about half of the broadcasted programmes in the EU around 2013 had subtitles (with public broadcasters having a higher availability of subtitles than commercial ones). Although the study focuses on the EU countries, it also includes data from four non-EU countries for comparison: Australia, Canada, Norway and the USA. In all of these countries, at least 85% of the programmes have subtitles, which is a number aligned to the rate in some of the EU countries (like France, Holland, Slovenia and the UK), but much better than the average of the EU. Unfortunately, we are not aware of a more recent analysis as encompassing as this one is for TV-based media or a similar one for Web-based media.

Producing subtitles for media content equates to creating a file with time codes indicating the start and stop times for presenting the subtitle together with the subtitle's text. There are several tools available to help in subtitling efforts.[3] More recently, efforts have been made to create auto-captioning services. We will discuss some of these in Sect. 25.3.

---

[2] As defined in the Web Content Accessibility Guidelines 2.0 (https://www.w3.org/TR/2006/WD-WCAG20-20060427/appendixA.html).

[3] For example, the National Association for the Deaf publishes a list of captioning tools (https://dcmp.org/learn/213).

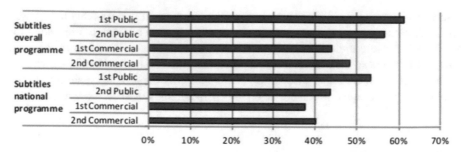

Fig. 25.1 Average share of programmes with subtitles in the overall programme across all countries included in the study (Adapted from Kubitschke et al. 2013)

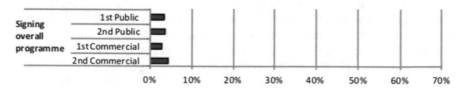

Fig. 25.2 Average share of programmes with sign language in the overall programme across all countries included in the study (Adapted from Kubitschke et al. 2013)

25.2.2 Sign Language

Sign language interpretation consists in the translation of spoken words into a language that conveys meaning through combinations of hand shapes, facial expressions and movements of the hands, arms and body.[4] Unlike subtitles, signing is traditionally provided in an open implementation, i.e. it is overlaid on the media content and users are not able to decide whether to enable its presentation or not. However, recent research efforts are addressing this issue and enabling closed sign language, as we will show later in the chapter.

Sign language provision is the least available of all access services. Figure 25.2, adapted from the study on e-Accessibility mentioned above, shows that only around 5% of all programmes have sign language interpretation, without significant variations between public and commercial broadcasters. This low percentage of programmes with sign language is common across EU (Portugal being an exception with an average of 12%) and non-EU countries.

The difficulties and costs associated with producing sign language access services are certainly not foreign to its low availability. Sign language interpretation requires capturing video of a human sign language interpreter and then overlay that video over the media content that is to be published or broadcast. Dissimilar to subtitles, which can be created without any significant infrastructure on a voluntary basis, the production of sign language interpretation is a professional task. Due to the required

---

[4]As defined in the Web Content Accessibility Guidelines 2.0 (https://www.w3.org/TR/2006/WD-WCAG20-20060427/appendixA.html).

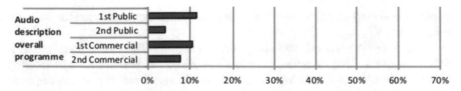

Fig. 25.3 Average share of programmes with audio description in the overall programme across all countries included in the study (Adapted from Kubitschke et al. 2013)

expressive richness in facial expressions and the movements of the hand, arms and body (Smith and Nolan 2016), solutions based on computer graphics, making use of avatars, have been unsuccessful so far (Wolfe et al. 2016), albeit having the promise of reducing the production costs for signing (Kacorri et al. 2015). Section 25.3 provides more details on this topic.

25.2.3 Audio Description

Audio description is a narration added to the soundtrack of media content to describe important visual details that cannot be understood from the main soundtrack alone.[5] This narration takes place between pauses in the dialogue and usually describes characters, their actions, scene changes or on-screen text.

The availability of audio description in EU based countries is barely better than that of sign language. Figure 25.3, adapted from the same study, shows that only between 4 and 11% of the broadcast programmes have an audio description available. Remarkably, the North American countries represented in this study have higher levels of audio description available, with Canada channels varying between 17 and 29% and the USA's first public channel having 85%.

The production process of audio descriptions is similar to that of subtitles. The outcome is also a file with time codes and text which means the same production tools can be used. However, while subtitles are visually displayed together with the video, audio descriptions are read aloud by a screen reader or the media player (as long as it supports audio description).

25.2.4 Standards and Regulation

Media content is available across multiple platforms (TV, Web) and devices (TVs, desktops and laptops, tablets and smartphones). Often the content produced for one

---

[5]As defined in the Web Content Accessibility Guidelines 2.0 (https://www.w3.org/TR/2006/WD-WCAG20-20060427/appendixA.html).

platform is also available in the other. This situation is especially true for contents created for TV.

National or international laws and directives regulate TV content producers and TV broadcasters. One example is the EU's Audiovisual Media Service Directive (https://ec.europa.eu/digital-single-market/en/audiovisual-media-services-directive -avmsd). This directive coordinates, at the EU level, the multiple national legislation on audiovisual media, both for TV broadcasts and on-demand services. Existing regulations ensure that, at least, part of the broadcast content meets accessibility guidelines. However, content created by individuals to be published on the Web is not subject to regulations. Individual creators also do not have access to the same grade of tools that professional content producers have. This lack of resources makes it fundamental to provide easy ways to produce accessible media so that the ever-increasing amount of media made available is also accessible to as much as possible of the population.

Guidance on how to make accessible media is available to content creators. The Web Content Accessibility Guidelines (https://www.w3.org/TR/WCAG21/) (WCAG) provide orientation on how to make Web content accessible. They include guidelines applicable to media content, like *Guideline 1.2 Time-based Media* that specifies properties for captions, audio description and sign language, for example. To provide access to this content, media players also need to possess specific characteristics. A set of guidelines exists that can be applied to create accessible media players. The User Agent Accessibility Guidelines (https://www.w3.org/TR/ UAAG20/) (UAAG) focus on the principles that should orient content reproducing tools, including media players. Similarly to WCAG, the UAAG include guidelines applicable to media playback, such as *Guideline 2.10 Provide control of time-based media*.

25.3 Multimedia Accessibility Research

Most of the multimedia content published on the Web, in particular videos, are created by individuals who are not subject to regulations and do not have access to the tools needed to make the content accessible. In this section, we present some research works that could help individuals make their content more accessible to hearing and visually impaired people.

25.3.1 Overcoming the Absence of Sound

25.3.1.1 Subtitles

Automatic Speech Recognition (ASR) software can convert speech into text, thus overcoming the absence of sound. It has evolved over the years, promising accuracies very close to 99% when correctly trained, used for dictating purposes and while using good quality microphones in a controlled acoustic environment. However, for conversations, video lessons, broadcast news, phone calls or other scenarios where we are dealing with spontaneous speech that occurs in an acoustically, linguistically and structurally different environment, their accuracy worsens (Maybury 2007). However, and despite speech recognition being far from entirely satisfactory, it has been improving over the years, making it the most affordable alternative to manually creating captions for video material.

In 2009, YouTube introduced the automatic captions system, which uses Google's ASR technology[6] to perform speech transcription. This was a significant step to make videos accessible, considering YouTube is the biggest repository of videos on the Internet and the most visited by all types of users. Combined with auto-caption, Google added their translation mechanism to offer captions in different languages. In 2017, they added a new functionality to the automatic captioning system allowing it to describe sound effects.[7] More recently, in 2018, Google introduced their Live Automatic Speech Recognition (LASR) technology,[8] which can automatically generate English captions for live videos, with error rates and latency approaching industry standards.

However, subtitling a video stream is not just about applying ASR. Federico and Furini (2012) presented an architecture that automatically creates captions for video lessons, by combining an off-the-shelf ASR software with a novel caption alignment mechanism to produce a time-coded transcript. Their approach overcomes the absence of timing information in the textual transcript produced by the off-the-shelf ASR by smartly introducing unique audio markups into the audio stream before giving it to the ASR software.

Shiver and Wolfe (2015) performed two studies focused on multimedia accessibility for Internet users who were born deaf or became deaf at an early age. In the first study, they identified priorities for improving accessibility for deaf people. The most identified topic was the lack of accessibility to online news. Users also mentioned that they prefer captions over transcripts because the former is synced with the video. In the second study, the authors asked participants to evaluate different types of caption styles, including those generated using ASR. Results confirmed that users prefer to have videos with captions, even when they are automatically generated and consequently with some errors, than without captions.

Toledo et al. (2005) proposed a sensorial substitution system to help deaf people understand the location of sources of sound information. Their system presents visual elements in see-through glasses and captures the environment's acoustic information around the user. The sound sources are represented as Gaussian curves, where their orientation conveys the angle of the sound source, their size the power of the sound, and colour bands dividing the Gaussian depict the different frequency components of the sound. Although this solution was devised to transmit acoustic information in

[6]https://googleblog.blogspot.com/2009/11/automatic-captions-in-youtube.html.

[7]https://ai.googleblog.com/2017/03/adding-sound-effect-information-to.html.

[8]https://youtube-creators.googleblog.com/2018/02/updates-to-youtube-live-streaming.html.

real time about the surrounding environment, the visual representation of the sound sources can be adapted to become another type of information that can be used to make videos more accessible.

Multimedia solutions can also be used to improve the accessibility of interactions between people with different characteristics. Peng at al. recently proposed Speech-Bubbles (Peng et al. 2018), a real-time speech recognition interface prototype on an augmented reality head-mounted display, to help deaf people comprehend speech from hearing users in face-to-face group conversations. Experimental results demonstrated that SpeechBubbles was suitable for group conversations between deaf and not deaf people.

25.3.1.2 Sign Language

Kim et al. (2004) proposed a solution for communication among deaf people in real time, which uses an intelligent avatar communication system. It supports Korean, Chinese and Japanese sign languages to overcome the linguistic barrier between different languages. Sign language translation between the languages is incorporated, as well as CG animation techniques and emotional expression methods to produce more realistic gesture images. Experimental results show that the methods could be used for sign language communications between Korean, Japanese and Chinese deaf people on the Internet.

In de Araújo et al. (2014), the authors presented a solution for automatic generation and insertion of sign language video tracks into captioned digital multimedia content. Their approach can convert subtitles into sign language, in real time, embedding it in the multimedia content as an extra layer of accessible content. A 3D avatar reproduces the sign language.

Even if a video or movie has a supporting video with an interpreter performing sign language, some information is still lost due to the inability to look at both the video and the interpreter simultaneously. To alleviate this issue, Kushalnagar et al. (2017) proposed a tool called closed interpreter, which can be toggled on and off by the user. Additionally, the interpreter size and its transparency and location can also be adjusted by the user. A study with deaf and hard of hearing users to find what they like about videos that come with interpreters and to identify the benefits of the offered adjustability showed that users preferred customisable interpreters over the static because they could adjust the location and transparency of the interpreter and see both the video and the interpreter.

These results are supported by a more recent study by Terrill Thompson (2018), who conducted interviews and focus groups to develop a better understanding of how persons with impairments interact with video players. The author found that for a synchronised sign language window to be effective, users should be able to control its size, position and opacity so they can place it in the perfect position relative to the video.

25.3.2 Overcoming the Absence of Image

Rich and multimedia content brings severe problems to screen reader users because when the audio starts playing they have to deal with two audio streams at the same time: one delivering the original audio from the video, and the other delivering the audio from the screen reader. Moreover, there is only one physical volume control, and it is not possible to control each sound separately. A possible solution is to use two concurrent speech channels placed in a 3D space simultaneously, along the lines of Guerreiro's work (Guerreiro and Gonçalves 2016), which takes advantage of the *Cocktail Party Effect* to present several contents at the same time. For our context, one channel could be used for the main audio of the video and the other for the screen reader audio.

Flash applications (videos or interactive games) are still available on the Internet. When we think of them, accessibility is not one of the characteristics that we associate with them. In Krüger (2008), the author demonstrated that it is possible to create accessible Flash applications for both blind and sighted users. The author adapted an existing e-learning application to make it accessible, without the need of changing its user interface. According to the author, no separated versions of the original applications were needed. Consequently, already existing Flash applications could be made accessible to blind users, without rebuilding the overall application.

Another multimedia content that poses challenges concerning accessibility is video games. In Allman et al. (2009), the authors presented a modified version of the *Rock Band®* computer game, to allow people with no or limited vision to enjoy the game. Their solution represents visual information through haptic and audio feedback. In particular, they convey the original drumming activity of *Rock Band®* through vibrations on the upper and lower arm (for drumhead clues) and the ankle (for kick drum clue). Auditory information is used to provide feedback about the correctness of the hit. Evaluation with subjects with various levels of visual impairment revealed that they were able to master the system almost immediately. This shows that it is possible to convey visual information to users through other modalities, making multimedia content more accessible.

25.3.3 Multimedia Players

When choosing how to deliver multimedia content, it is important to consider options that are fully accessible. Thus, a player should at least: (i) support closed captions; (ii) support audio description and enable users to toggle the narration on and off; (iii) have buttons and controls that can be operated without a mouse; (iv) have buttons and controls labelled adequately so they can be operated using a screen reader; (v) be fully functional across platforms and in all major browsers.

This list is complemented by a set of requirements presented by González et al. (2011) that should be included in a media player to make it accessible. In particular, a media player should: (i) provide different alternatives together with the video, such as captions, audio description, sign language, transcription or extended audio description; (ii) provide access to all its features via mouse, keyboard or assistive technologies (e.g. screen readers); (iii) provide help and access to documentation to inform about its accessible features and how to use them.

In the last years, several media players have been developed to satisfy these requirements (or at least most of them). Among those, we have Mediasite,[9] Video.js,[10] iTunesU,[11] YouTube[12], and Able Player.[13]

Able Player is a free open-source HTML5 media player, and one of the most accessible media players available. It is WCAG 2.0 Level AAA compliant and accommodates Sign Language tracks. Able Player has fully accessible player controls and, where necessary, uses ARIA[14] to expose interface elements to screen readers. It is the only media player that fully supports the HTML5 <track> element, including all five kinds of text tracks (Thompson 2015).

25.4 Discussion

The overall coverage of media that is made accessible is still too low as could be seen in Sect. 25.2. This is true for TV broadcast, where legislation seems to be the primary driver for ensuring that broadcast media is accessible, and for the media made available online on the Web. Unfortunately, enforcing legislation on the Internet is harder. With the know-how for creating accessible media available, the initial challenge facing the accessibility community is to find ways to support the creation of accessible media in a way that requires a low amount of resources (human and material) and effort. Only with this kind of support, the **quantity of access services** will increase and approximate the needs of the population.

The following challenge facing the accessibility community is to ensure the **quality of access services**. While it is paramount that we have means to produce accessible content, the quality of this content must be enough to make it useful. The efforts mentioned above of Google's YouTube to provide auto-captions are a perfect illustration of the tension that arises between quantity and quality. While YouTube's auto-caption service is excellent from the perspective of quantity (delivering an access service for all videos in the supported languages) it still does not deliver a quality access service when the audio track in the video does not possess the needed characteristics. Consequently, it is important that the accessibility community in collaboration with each

---

[9]http://delta.ncsu.edu/learning-technology/classroom-content-capture/.

[10]http://www.videojs.com/.

[11]http://itunes.ncsu.edu/.

[12]http://www.youtube.com/.

[13]https://github.com/terrill/ableplayer.

[14]Accessible Rich Internet Applications (WAI-ARIA) (https://www.w3.org/TR/2014/REC-wai-aria-20140320/).

country's regulatory agencies be able to provide measures of the quantity of access services provided (this is what has been done so far) but also of the quality of those access services.

A further challenge that impacts the accessible media production process is the source of the media. With the advance and democratisation of technology, ever more people are media content producers. The initial impact of this situation is that there are more media to make accessible by more people that do not have the expertise to do it. Further analysing this issue reveals that the amount of live media being broadcast or distributed on the Internet is also increasing. Ensuring the accessibility of live media is much more challenging than recorded media. For sign language interpretation and audio description current solutions are based on human intervention, with sign language interpreters ensuring translation of live events and trained audio describers verbally depicting events as they unfold. Automated procedures that can increase the amount of subtitles can also be used to provide subtitles for live content and thus are the more promising avenue for production of accessible live media.

In addition to the challenges faced for creating access services, a different set of challenges needs to be addressed for multimedia players, i.e. for using the created access services to ensure an accessible playback of the content. As presented in Sect. 25.3.3, a variety of media players is already available capable of implementing access services. The challenges often lie in making sure that the media players themselves are accessible in addition to the content they playback. Kushalnagar et al. (2017) present one example of how that can be achieved. With their solution, a media player could use eye tracking to automatically pause a sign language interpreter when viewers are not looking at it, and resume it when they gaze again on the interpreter and speed up the replay speed of the interpreter to catch up to the current point in the video.

25.5 Future Directions

Machine learning based solutions are becoming pervasive across a range of domains. Multimedia accessibility is not an exception. We have presented above current research efforts and globally available services that already make use of it. The first inroads happened for subtitle generation that took advantage of evolving speech recognition systems to automate the generation workflow. These solutions are evolving to automate also the creation of audio descriptions by recognising other sounds in addition to speech (Ichiki et al. 2018). The challenges for automated sign language generation are very different. Current limitations of avatar-based signing result from the difficulty in conveying all the richness that sign language requires to transmit information. Nevertheless, some advances are underway, beginning with signing in specific domains like weather news presentation (Azuma et al. 2018; Oh et al. 2014).

Another future direction in the field of multimedia accessibility that can benefit from the increasing reach of the Web is the crowdsourcing of access services.

Crowdsourcing can also be used in combination with machine learning approaches. This is already being explored for subtitle generation (Huang et al. 2017).

Emotions that people convey while talking are valuable to produce a more engaging conversation. This is also true for dialogues that take place in multimedia content. While people usually express themselves with different tones to convey their moods, deaf individuals are not able to capture it. They rely on visuals cues which may not be enough for them to infer the emotions conveyed. Individuals with cognitive impairments also have difficulties in interpreting emotions (McCade et al. 2011). Therefore, future research on how to identify the emotions being conveyed and how to represent them in an effective way for deaf individuals or cognitively impaired individuals is an additional avenue for exploration.

25.6   Author's Opinion of the Field

As we already mentioned, the amount of multimedia content on the Web is increasing exponentially. Multimedia consumption is increasing, with about one-third of online activity being spent watching video.[15] Correspondingly, multimedia content production is also increasing, with the latest estimates indicating that 72 h of video are uploaded to YouTube every 60 s (see footnote 15), for instance.

We, obviously, believe that ensuring accessibility to multimedia content is a very relevant topic. Primarily, we all have a social responsibility in ensuring that everyone has access to publicly available content, including multimedia content. Furthermore, the World Health Organization (WHO 2011) estimates that the disability prevalence in the world population is around 15% (representing approximately 1 billion individuals). This means that from a business perspective there is a huge market for accessible services, including everything that can be promoted through or take advantage of multimedia delivery.

With access services becoming standardised, our opinion is that the greatest challenge for the near future is in devising ways to assist in the generation of access services for the content that individuals are now able to create and share online. Ideally, access services would be generated automatically, but that is still out of our reach. However, if we are able to provide content producers or communities of content consumers with tools that reduce the effort required for the production of access services, we should be able to see an increase in the accessibility of available multimedia content.

Another trend that must not be overlooked is the platform of choice for consumption of the content. Mobile devices are already responsible for half of the video content watched (see footnote 15). Therefore, it is essential that mobile applications that offer multimedia content are made accessible, following trends in Web media players.

---

[15] 37 Staggering Video Marketing Statistics for 2018 | Wordstream (https://www.wordstream.com/blog/ws/2017/03/08/video-marketing-statistics).

25.7 Conclusions

The amount of available multimedia content keeps increasing at a great pace. To make this multimedia accessible to all population is a massive trial that must be addressed at all points in the production to the consumption chain. First, access services must be created to ensure that people with visual or hearing impairments can access the content. Then, playback mechanisms, which themselves must also be accessible, need to be compatible with these access services so that consumers can, in fact, access the content.

In this chapter we tried to provide an overview of the status of multimedia accessibility, describing what access services exist, their purpose and presenting a panorama of their usage, with a greater focus on broadcast multimedia. We complemented this with a summary of existing research efforts that have the potential to lessen the required resources for the production of access services or to improve the accessibility of playback tools. Finally, we discussed how machine learning, possibly supported by crowdsourcing, has the potential to improve the quantity and quality of access services.

Acknowledgements This work was supported by national funds through Fundação para a Ciência e Tecnologia, under LASIGE Strategic Project—PEst-OE/EEI/UI0408/2014.

References

Allman T, Dhillon RK, Landau MA, Kurniawan SH (2009) Rock vibe: rock band®computer games for people with no or limited vision. In: Proceedings of the 11th international ACM SIGACCESS conference on computers and accessibility, Assets '09, ACM, New York, USA, pp 51–58

Azuma M, Hiruma N, Sumiyoshi H, Uchida T, Miyazaki T, Umeda S, Kato N, Yamanouchi Y (2018) Development and evaluation of system for automatically generating sign-language CG animation using meteorological information. In: Miesenberger K, Kouroupetroglou G (eds) Computers helping people with special needs. Springer International Publishing, Cham, pp 233–238

de Araújo TMU, Ferreira FL, Silva DA, Oliveira LD, Falcão EL, Domingues LA, Martins VF, Portela IA, Nóbrega YS, Lima HR, Filho GLS, Tavares TA, Duarte AN (2014) An approach to generate and embed sign language video tracks into multimedia contents. Inf Sci 281:762–780. Multimedia modeling

Federico M, Furini M (2012) Enhancing learning accessibility through fully automatic captioning. In: Proceedings of the international cross-disciplinary conference on web accessibility - W4A '12, ACM Press, New York, USA, p 1

González M, Moreno L, Martínez P, Iglesias A (2011) Web accessibility requirements for media players. In: Campos P, Graham N, Jorge J, Nunes N, Palanque P, Winckler M (eds) Human-computer interaction - INTERACT 2011. Springer, Berlin, pp 669–674

Guerreiro JA, Gonçalves D (2016) Scanning for digital content: how blind and sighted people perceive concurrent speech. ACM Trans Access Comput 8(1):2:1–2:28

Huang Y, Huang Y, Xue N, Bigham JP (2017) Leveraging complementary contributions of different workers for efficient crowdsourcing of video captions. In: Proceedings of the 2017 CHI conference on human factors in computing systems, CHI '17, ACM, New York, USA, pp 4617–4626

Ichiki M, Shimizu T, Imai A, Takagi T, Iwabuchi M, Kurihara K, Miyazaki T, Kumano T, Kaneko H, Sato S, Seiyama N, Yamanouchi Y, Sumiyoshi H (2018) Study on automated audio descriptions overlapping live television commentary. In: Miesenberger K, Kouroupetroglou G (eds) Computers helping people with special needs. Springer International Publishing, Cham, pp 220–224

Kacorri H, Huenerfauth M, Ebling S, Patel K, Willard M (2015) Demographic and experiential factors influencing acceptance of sign language animation by deaf users. In: Proceedings of the 17th international ACM SIGACCESS conference on computers and accessibility, ASSETS '15, ACM, New York, USA, pp 147–154

Khan TM (2010) The effects of multimedia learning on children with different special education needs. Procedia - Soc Behav Sci 2(2):4341–4345. Innovation and creativity in education. http://www.sciencedirect.com/science/article/pii/S1877042810007305

Kim S-W, Li Z-X, Aoki Y (2004) On intelligent avatar communication using Korean, Chinese and Japanese sign-languages: an overview. In: Proceedings of the 8th control, automation, robotics and vision conference (ICARCV'04), vol 1, pp 747–752

Knoop-van Campen CAN, Segers E, Verhoeven L (2018) The modality and redundancy effects in multimedia learning in children with dyslexia. Dyslexia 24(2):140–155. https://onlinelibrary.wiley.com/doi/abs/10.1002/dys.1585

Krüger M (2008) Accessible flash is no oxymoron: a case study in E-learning for blind and sighted users. In: Miesenberger K, Klaus J, Zagler W, Karshmer A (eds) Computers helping people with special needs. ICCHP 2008. Springer, Berlin, pp 362–369

Kubitschke L, Cullen K, Dolphin C, Laurin S, Cederbom A (2013) Study on assessing and promoting E-accessibility, Technical report, European Commission DG Communications Networks, Content and technology

Kushalnagar R, Seita M, Glasser A (2017) Closed ASL interpreting for online videos. In: Proceedings of the 14th web for all conference on the future of accessible work - W4A '17, ACM Press, New York, USA, pp 1–4

Maybury M (2007) Searching conversational speech. In: Proceedings of the SIGIR workshop on searching spontaneous conversational speech (SSCS'07)

McCade D, Savage G, Naismith SL (2011) Review of emotion recognition in mild cognitive impairment. Dement Geriatr Cogn Disord 32(4):257–266. https://www.karger.com/DOI/10.1159/000335009

Oh J, Jeon S, Kim M, Kwon H, Kim I (2014) An avatar-based weather forecast sign language system for the hearing-impaired. In: Iliadis L, Maglogiannis I, Papadopoulos H (eds) Artificial intelligence applications and innovations. Springer, Berlin, pp 519–527

Peng YH, Hsi M-W, Taele P, Lin T-Y, Lai P-E, Hsu L, Chen TC, Wu, T-Y, Chen Y-A, Tang H-H, Chen MY (2018) Speechbubbles: enhancing captioning experiences for deaf and hard-of-hearing people in group conversations. In: Proceedings of the conference on human factors in computing systems (CHI '18), ACM, New York, USA, pp 293:1–293:10

Shiver BN, Wolfe RJ (2015) Evaluating alternatives for better deaf accessibility to selected web-based multimedia. In: Proceedings of the 17th international ACM SIGACCESS conference on computers accessibility - ASSETS '15, ACM Press, New York, USA, pp 231–238

Sloan D, Stratford J, Gregor P (2006) Using multimedia to enhance the accessibility of the learning environment for disabled students: reflections from the skills for access project. ALT-J 14(1):39–54. https://doi.org/10.1080/09687760500479936

Smith RG, Nolan B (2016) Emotional facial expressions in synthesised sign language avatars: a manual evaluation. Univers Access Inf Soc 15(4):567–576

Thompson T (2015) Video for all: accessibility of video content and universal design of a media player, 2nd edn. Harvard Education Press, Boston, pp 259–273

Thompson, T (2018) Media player accessibility: summary of insights from interviews and focus groups. J Technol Pers Disabil 6:325–335

Toledo J, Torres J, Alonso S, Toledo P, González EJ (2005) SLOAS: hearing with the eyes. In: Proceedings of the 4th WSEAS international conference on electronic, signal processing and control, pp 27:1–27:5

Wang J, Dawson K, Saunders K, Ritzhaupt AD, Antonenko PP, Lombardino L, Keil A, Agacli-Dogan N, Luo W, Cheng L, Davis RO (2018) Investigating the effects of modality and multimedia on the learning performance of college students with dyslexia. J Spec Educ Technol 33(3):182–193. https://doi.org/10.1177/0162643418754530

WHO (2011) World report on disability, World Health Organization

Wolfe R, Efthimiou E, Glauert J, Hanke T, McDonald J, Schnepp J (2016) Special issue: recent advances in sign language translation and avatar technology. Univers Access Inf Soc 15(4):485–486

Part V
Techniques and Tools

Chapter 26
Tools for Web Accessibility Evaluation

Julio Abascal, Myriam Arrue and Xabier Valencia

Abstract The objective of Web accessibility evaluation is to verify that all users are able to use the Web, this means that they can perceive, understand, navigate, and interact with it (Henry 2018a). Since the manual verification of the fulfilment of guidelines that specify accessibility requirements can often turn out to be difficult and cumbersome, it is crucial to have appropriate computer tools available to assist this activity. There exist numerous applications that perform diverse types of automatic accessibility evaluations. On the other hand, on-site and remote evaluations with users can also be supported by specific tools. Even manual evaluations may be supported by crowdsourcing-based tools. All these innovations may have crucial importance in the advancement of Web accessibility. This chapter studies the need for tools in this field, reviews the main characteristics of the tools used for Web accessibility evaluation, and reflects upon their future.

26.1 Introduction

The Web was designed to be universally accessible, which means that it can be accessed by everyone, whatever their hardware, software, language, culture, location, or physical or mental ability (Henry and McGee 2018). Nevertheless, in practice this does not always happen, mainly because websites are often designed without considering human diversity, leading to poorly designed websites containing accessibility barriers.

Research on Web accessibility ranges from web content evaluation and the design and development of tools (to support both web developers when creating accessible content and users navigating the Web), to increase the understanding of the behaviour of users on the Web. These activities include the definition of accessibility guidelines; the design of evaluation methods and assessment metrics; the development of author-

J. Abascal (✉) · M. Arrue · X. Valencia
Egokituz Laboratory of Human-Computer Interaction for Special Needs, Informatics School, University of the Basque Country/Euskal Herriko Unibertsitatea, Donostia, Spain
e-mail: julio.abascal@ehu.eus

© Springer-Verlag London Ltd., part of Springer Nature 2019
Y. Yesilada and S. Harper (eds.), *Web Accessibility*, Human–Computer Interaction Series, https://doi.org/10.1007/978-1-4471-7440-0_26

ing and evaluation tools; the development of appropriate assistive technologies; and the study of the needs and behaviour of users when they navigate the Web.

The World Wide Web Consortium (W3C) through the Web Accessibility Initiative (WAI) is one of the main organisations promoting Web accessibility. The WAI promotes the creation of international standards that describe guidelines for the different components involved in accessible web development. One of the most widely known set of guidelines is the Web Content Accessibility Guidelines (WCAG) (Chisholm et al. 1999; Caldwell et al. 2008; Kirkpatrick et al. 2018). However, other organisations and companies have also issued accessibility guidelines: the US Government Section 508 (2018), IBM Web Accessibility Checklist (IBM 2017) or the BBC (2018) have developed their own, inspired in many cases by the W3C guidelines [Read Part 3 'Standards, Guidelines and Trends' for further details].

In order to check whether accessibility guidelines have been properly implemented into websites, it is of utmost importance to conduct accessibility evaluations not only after the website has been made available online, but also during the development process.

The availability of tools for the automatic evaluation of websites appears to be key to the advancement of web accessibility. Three types of software tools are relevant to this chapter:

- Automatic evaluation tools are applications that analyse web page code to verify the compliance of specific sets of guidelines. Even if they are limited to the evaluation of criteria that can be matched in the code, they provide the main starting point to accessible design.
- Crowdsourcing-based social accessibility contributes to methods and tools (which add accessibility metadata) to enable adequate rendering of the content. It is also a way of recruiting people for manual Web accessibility evaluation.
- Tools to support remote user evaluations achieve trustworthy accessibility evaluations by managing data from real users accessing the Web in real work environments.

26.2   Web Content Accessibility Evaluation Methods

Web accessibility evaluation can be defined as the assessment of how well a website can be used by users with disabilities (Harper and Yesilada 2008) and it is an essential process in order to check that the adopted accessibility standards have been met. Web accessibility evaluation encompasses a wide range of disciplines and skills (Abou-Zahra 2008). It can require knowledge not only about technical aspects related to web technologies, guidelines, standards and evaluation tools, but also non-technical aspects such as the involvement of end users in the evaluation process. For this reason, diverse methods are used to assess the accessibility of websites, which are usually clustered in three main categories: automated testing, manual inspection and user testing. Figure 26.1 shows a detailed taxonomy of Accessibility

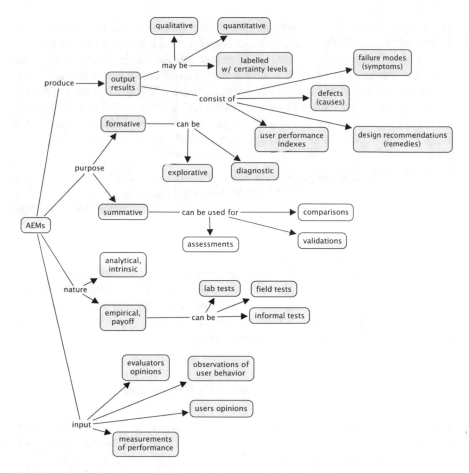

Fig. 26.1 Taxonomy of accessibility evaluation methods (Brajnik 2008b)

Evaluation Methods (AEMs), classified by purpose, type of results and type of input information used (Brajnik 2008b).

Automated Testing This kind of evaluation is performed by applications running locally or online. They analyse the page code to verify the compliance of specific accessibility guidelines. In fact, only guidelines that can be translated to code pieces can be verified by these tools. For this reason, automated testing is normally used as a first accessibility test that allows basic accessibility barriers to be detected (and sometimes fixed). In this way, they save time and resources and provide basic support to developers building and maintaining accessible websites.

Manual Inspection Accessibility inspections are conducted by expert human evaluators (Brajnik 2008a). Generally, they entail checking if a page satisfies a list of accessibility criteria. Most frequently a conformance or guidelines review is performed. This consists of checking if a website meets a set of accessibility guidelines.

For example, Barrier Walkthrough (Brajnik 2009) is a manual inspection method to evaluate Web accessibility in which the inspector identifies the frequency and severity of a list of accessibility barriers present in a website. Brajnik defines a barrier as any condition that makes it difficult for people to achieve a goal when using the website through specified assistive technology (Brajnik 2008a). The manual inspection also includes screening techniques that involve using a website in such a way that certain sensory, motor or cognitive capabilities are artificially reduced (Henry 2007). It is convenient to use manual inspection techniques throughout the design process as they can early identify potential design problems.

User Testing This kind of evaluation is usually based on informal empirical usability tests, where participants with disabilities are asked to individually perform a number of tasks. Depending on the design of the test, participants provide their feedback in various ways (e.g. concurrent or retrospective think-aloud protocols, questionnaires or interviews), and the behaviour and interactions of participants are recorded and observed by evaluators, who can then synthesise their findings. The assessment obtained from the actual experience of the users is the most reliable accessibility evaluation method [Refer to Part 2 'End User Evaluations' for more information]. Nevertheless, user testing is not easy to perform, and frequently it turns out to be slow and expensive. Support software for user testing is being produced in order to make these evaluations easier and to speed them up.

26.2.1 Methodologies for Accessibility Evaluation

Diverse methodologies for accessibility evaluation have been proposed. They vary in objective, scope, thoroughness, breadth, etc. For instance, the Website Accessibility Conformance Evaluation Methodology (WCAG-EM) 1.0 (Velleman and Abou-Zahra 2014), the TECED Accessibility Evaluation Methodology (TECED 2017) or the Accessibility Compliance and Remediation Methodology (ACRM) by AccessIT (AccessIT 2017). Many of these include an initial automatic evaluation using various (typically three) automated tools. The reason being that automatic tools can produce different evaluation results for the same page because they use different code specifications for the guidelines, and their searching/matching methods also differ. Most methodologies include manual evaluations by one or more experts. Finally, the evaluation by actual users performing real tasks is required. Nevertheless, it has not yet been fully established how these methods should be combined and organised in order to evaluate Web accessibility in a comprehensive manner (Yesilada et al. 2012).

The WAI's website contains a list of accessibility evaluation resources (Henry 2018b) and indicates different approaches for evaluating websites for accessibility. While it does not provide details on testing techniques, it contains information about general procedures and tips for accessibility evaluation in different situations, such as preliminary checks, Conformance Evaluation Methodology (WCAG-EM) (Velleman and Abou-Zahra 2014), involving users in the evaluation or the selection of automated tools, etc.

26.3   Automated Web Accessibility Evaluation Tools

The automation of the accessibility evaluation process is of particular interest in the field of accessibility evaluation research. Even if automated tools cannot replace human evaluation, they play an important role in accessibility evaluation despite their limitations. When used appropriately, they can provide developers and evaluators with support and significantly reduce the time and effort required to conduct an evaluation. Ivory and Hearst (2001) highlighted some of the advantages of using automated tools:

- The evaluation process becomes less time consuming with the consequent reduction in costs.
- The errors detected are more consistent.
- It is possible to foresee the effort needed in the evaluation process, in terms of time and financial cost.
- The evaluation scope is broadened, as it is possible to analyse diverse aspects of the interface in a shorter period of time.
- It becomes easier for inexperienced evaluators to perform usability and accessibility evaluations.
- Comparison of the suitability of different user interface design alternatives is made easier.
- It is easier to incorporate evaluation tasks during the development process.

Although useful, these tools have also some weaknesses that we must be aware of before using them. As a number of accessibility guidelines require human judgement to assess whether or not they are being met, automated evaluation tools are not able to deal with those guidelines. The diverse implementations of the search/match algorithm and the different codification of the guidelines can result in the production of false negatives (accessibility barriers that are not detected) or false positives (reported false issues). In addition, the effectiveness of the automated tools may vary depending on the number of tests implemented and how they are applied. In fact, the completeness, correctness and specificity of the results produced by a tool are used in order to measure its effectiveness (Brajnik 2004).

According to Vanderdonckt (1999), the development process of high-quality accessibility evaluation tools consists of diverse milestones. In this process, the accessibility guidelines are the essential component as they are required to:

- Collect, gather, merge and compile guidelines from available resources.
- Sort and organise the guidelines within a framework.
- Give a computational representation to the guidelines for manipulation by computer-based tools.

The effectiveness of a tool depends on the computational representation given to the guidelines. The definition of guidelines is made in natural language and may vary in its content and level of specification. The guidelines may have a different format and may be defined to a different level of detail (Abascal and Nicolle 2001; Mariage et al. 2005). The correctness of an automated tool depends on the ability of the development team to give correct computational representations to the guidelines. While several accessibility guidelines can be completely verified by computer-based tools, a number of guidelines cannot be accurately represented in a computational way because they require human judgement. For the latter, the tool can only produce recommendations for manual verification.

Therefore, most evaluation tools produce two types of results:

- Errors: when accessibility barriers have been detected in the code.
- Warnings: when specific characteristics found in the code may contain barriers, the presence of which, however, can only be verified by a human inspector.

Some tools also include general recommendations about the guidelines that cannot be searched in the code by the tool and must always be checked by human experts. Successive versions of WCAG produced by the WAI endeavoured to reduce the risk of giving incorrect computational representation to guidelines. To this end, versions 2.0 and 2.1 of WCAG contain success criteria that are testable statements, reducing the ambiguity and interpretability of guidelines in previous versions.

Specific technologies are used to define and programme automated accessibility tests. A practical option is to use XPath and XQuery expressions that can be directly applied to the evaluation of the HTML code of the web pages (Arrue et al. 2008; Luque et al. 2005). For example, the technique H36 'Using alt attributes on images used as submit buttons' of the WCAG 2.0 states that image type input elements require alternative texts to provide a functional label. Using XQuery, a test for verifying this technique can be defined as follows:

let $var: = doc("web_page.xml")//INPUT[@TYPE="img" and not(@ALT)

This query detects those image type input elements, which do not have alternative text (defined by the *alt* attribute).

26.3.1 Metrics and Personalised Accessibility Evaluation

Automatic accessibility evaluation tools report their results using metrics. A metric produces a score calculated from predefined parameters that have been counted, measured or calculated from the failures or successes detected in the selected guidelines.

26.3.1.1 Qualitative Metrics

Accessibility evaluation methods have to provide clear and useful results to inform the user whether or not a web page can be effectively used by people with diverse disabilities. The WACAG 2.0 guidelines provide three levels of conformance depending on the Web page satisfying all the Success Criteria for each level (or the provision of a conforming alternate version): A, AA and AAA. In addition to this score, most automatic evaluation tools give pointers to the code segments that fail specific checkpoints [Read Part 5 'Automatic Web Accessibility Metrics' for further information].

26.3.1.2 User-Tailored Evaluation

The qualitative score of WCAG is useful to verify whether a website legally fulfils accessibility requirements or not, but it may not be informative enough for the requirements of individuals. Systems able to provide more detailed data about the fulfilment of the WCAG 2 four principles present more detailed information about the type of barriers in a specific website which people with specific disabilities may come across. For example, the score on the *perceivable* principle can mostly be associated with sensory disabilities, while the score on *operable* principally affects (though not exclusively) people with motor disabilities. The *understandable* principle is mainly related to cognitive accessibility and the *robust* principle takes into account the technology (equipment and applications) used to access the Web, including Assistive Technology (Aizpurua 2017).

More detailed personalization of the accessibility evaluation is possible when the criteria to be evaluated can be fine-tuned. In this case, only the guidelines affecting a specific person (also taking into consideration their particular impact on the specific user) are evaluated. In this way, some tools can be tailored to particular features of specific types of users (Vigo et al. 2007b). For instance, Mauve (HIIS Lab/ISTI-CNR 2018) offers the possibility of evaluating web content using end-user-specific guidelines (such as usability criteria identified to improve web navigation for vision-impaired people). Other tools include options to select and configure the checkpoints to be verified (Arrue et al. 2008). For example, TAW includes a standalone application (CTIC 2018b) which allows the selection of checkpoints to be checked as well as the creation of new custom rules.

26.3.1.3 Quantitative Metrics

A web page that fails a specific checkpoint one in ten times is nearer to being accessible than a page that fails the same checkpoint ten out of ten times, nevertheless, both are scored equally by qualitative metrics. In order to take into account how far a web page is from being accessible, quantitative metrics have been proposed (Vigo and Brajnik 2011). These metrics take into account the relative frequency and the impact of each failure, providing a more discriminative accessibility score. Their results are useful to monitor the evolution of the accessibility of a website, for instance. Vigo et al. (2007a) used this system to create a web service called EvalBot that was able to rank by personal accessibility (using their own quantitative metrics) the first 20 websites proposed by a web search engine when answering a query.

26.3.2 Available Automated Evaluation Tools

A number of automated accessibility evaluation tools have been implemented. A comprehensive list of available web accessibility evaluation tools can be found on the W3C-Web Accessibility Initiative (WAI) website (Egger and Abou-Zahra 2016). Its advanced search functionality enables evaluation tools to be looked for according to various criteria: sets of guidelines, language, type of tool, technology, provided assistance, scope and license type.

Accessibility evaluation tools can be classified following diverse criteria:

- Free versus commercial: while a few of them are commercial tools, the majority of them are freely available.
- Platform: depending on where they run they can be classified in local or standalone applications, online services or browser extensions.
- Evaluation scope: distinguishes the evaluation of single pages, sets of pages, and complete websites.
- Evaluation only versus evaluation and repair: while most tools only provide the option to evaluate, some tools are also able to provide guidance on the repair process.
- Ways for reporting accessibility issues: the evaluation reports generated may contain step-by-step evaluation guidance, or may display information about barriers within web pages, or even modified presentations of web pages.
- Guidelines used: the standards or guideline sets they employ for evaluating accessibility.

Numerous automated accessibility evaluation tools, such as AChecker (AChecker 2011; Gay and Li 2010), or Mauve (HIIS Lab/ISTI-CNR 2018; Schiavone and Paternò 2015; Paternò and Schiavone 2015) are freely available. While other tools, such as WAVE (WebAIM 2018), TAW (CTIC 2018a), or Tenon (2018), in addition to a free version have a commercial version.

Several tools can perform accessibility checks during the development process, by installing plugins within the development tool. This is the case, for instance of aDesigner (Eclipse 2018), Continuous Accessibility Testing for Eclipse (WEBaccessibility 2018), or Accessibility checker for CKEditor 4 (CKEditor 2018). Besides the accessibility evaluation, these tools can also provide other functionalities such as simulation of disabilities (aDesigner) or assistance to repair the accessibility barriers discovered (Accessibility checker).

There are tools which can be installed as add-ons in a web browser to evaluate the accessibility of the created web pages, such as aXe (2018), which enables accessi-

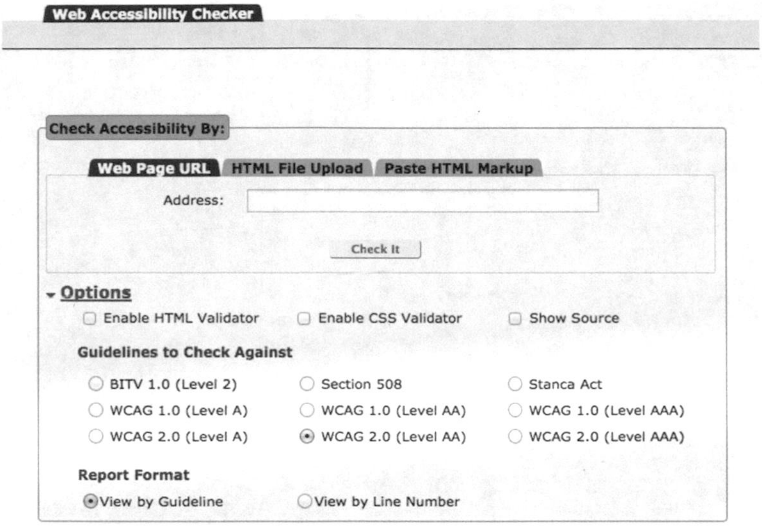

Fig. 26.2 A screenshot of AChecker evaluation tool main web page

bility evaluations to be run without sending the page code to external servers. Other tools, such as Audits (Basques 2018), are already integrated into the web browser. For example, audits can measure the accessibility of the page, its adequacy for best practices, and it can also simulate how the web page would be displayed in some mobile devices.

26.3.3 AChecker: An Example of Use of an Automated Evaluation Tool

Applying automated tools for accessibility evaluation is a simple and fast way to obtain a report containing accessibility errors and warnings. Most of the tools provide a form in which the evaluator may insert the URL of the web page to evaluate. Some tools also provide a feature to evaluate directly inserted HTML code or the code of an uploaded file. All these features are included in AChecker and can be seen in Fig. 26.2. In addition, this tool includes diverse features for configuring the evaluation process: selecting the technologies to be verified (HTML/CSS), the guidelines to be tested (BITV 1.0, Section 508, WCAG 1.0, WCAG 2.0, etc.), and the format of the report (by guideline, by line number).

The report obtained by the evaluation tools contains the necessary information to assist evaluators in understanding the detected errors/warnings as well as to repair them. Figure 26.3 shows a report obtained by AChecker. It contains links to get more

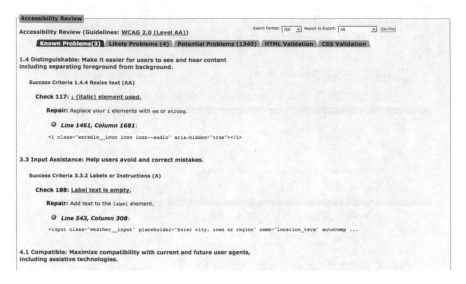

Fig. 26.3 A report from AChecker

information about the checks and the line and column number where the error was found.

26.3.4 Limitations of Automated Accessibility Evaluation

Although automated evaluation tools can assist evaluators in the evaluation process, they should not be the only method used for the accessibility evaluation of websites. As stated by the WAI (Abou-Zahra et al. 2017) 'We cannot check all accessibility aspects automatically. Human judgment is required. Sometimes evaluation tools can produce false or misleading results. Web accessibility evaluation tools cannot determine accessibility, they can only assist in doing so'.

In fact, a number of studies have been carried out in order to detect the limitations of automated evaluation. Thatcher et al. (2006) used 40 different benchmark tests to test 6 evaluation tools obtaining a failure rate between 5 and 42%. In another study carried out by Brajnik (2004) comparing the results obtained by two different automated evaluation tools, 33% of false positives and up to 35% of false negatives were detected. Vigo et al. (2013) analysed the coverage of six automated evaluation tools based on WCAG 2.0 guidelines conformance and found that, at most, 50% of the success criteria were covered.

Therefore, evaluators are often obliged to apply more than one automated tool and then to compare and aggregate the results in order to obtain better evaluation results. To aggregate and summarise the results from diverse tools can be difficult. For this reason, the WAI defined Evaluation and Report Language (EARL) (Abou-Zahra and

Henry 2011), a machine-readable format, for expressing test results. Its objective is to facilitate the processing of test results obtained from different testing tools. The EARL 1.0 version is available on the WAI/W3C website. Unfortunately, it would appear that little, if any, progress has been made since 2011.

26.4 Crowdsourcing-Based Tools for Web Accessibility

Website owners have the responsibility to make their content accessible. However, since accessibility evaluation and barrier removal are complex tasks, the rate of non-accessible content produced is constantly increasing. There are various reasons behind this: development haste, ignorance, lack of adequate tools, etc.

On the other hand, users with disabilities are aware of the barriers they find when accessing a specific website. Usually, they can report them to the owner via feedback forms or email, but even if their criticisms are taken into account, issuing a fixed version of the website usually takes time. Some authors think that involving a larger community of volunteers collaborating to fix accessibility bugs may help to increase the rate of accessible websites.

Crowdsourcing-based tools aim to reduce the burden on owners of accessibility evaluation and fixing and to shorten the time required to provide an accessibility barrier-free version by recruiting volunteers throughout the world to cooperate in barrier detection and elimination.

The underlying idea is that the inclusion within the page code of adequate metadata is a key issue to ensure web accessibility. Metadata provide structural information required by adapted browsers and screen readers to understand text structure and hierarchy (tables, headings, lists, etc.) in order to render it adequately. In addition, metadata complement information presented in inaccessible modes with alternative information in accessible modes (e.g. a text to describe a picture) (Takagi et al. 2008).[1] The availability of sufficient accessibility metadata rapidly alters the situation: the user is notified when new metadata has been added to overcome a reported barrier. When the user re-visits the page the available metadata is used to adequately render its content (Brady and Bigham 2015).

Adding semantic value to the different elements of the web is very laborious. This means correctly identifying elements of the web page and establishing what its purpose is (for example, whether it is an element of a navigation menu, or part of the main content or a decorative element, etc.) Even though there are methods that facilitate the annotation process of the elements, such as those proposed by Takagi et al. (2002) or Harper and Bechhofer (2007), the annotation process is still very expensive. However, with adequate tools, crowdsourcing can greatly help alleviate these problems since work can be divided into small tasks to be carried out by remote workers.

---

[1]Transcoding methods also depend on the availability of metadata [See Part 4: "User Interface Adaptation for Accessibility" for more information on transcoding].

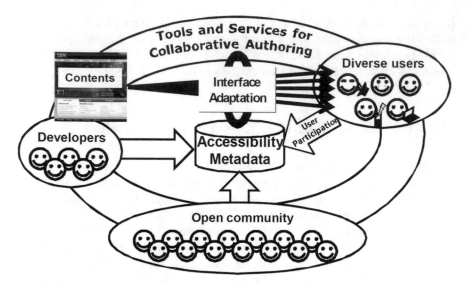

Fig. 26.4 Concept of social accessibility approach [Taken from (Takagi et al. 2008)]

Since the quantity and quality of accessibility metadata embedded in the content by web designers and developers is not sufficient, Takagi et al. (2008) propose the application of crowdsourcing methods to revert the situation. Appointing a large community of supporters would enable the following scenario: when a user finds an accessibility barrier the problem is reported to the volunteer community. The volunteers create and publish the required accessibility metadata (after a discussion if necessary). The user is prompted and then can access the page without problems.

26.4.1 Tools for Crowdsourcing-Based Social Accessibility

Following the Social Accessibility approach, Takagi et al. (2008) created a pilot system for collaborative metadata authoring aimed at achieving web accessibility.

The community was composed of three types of stakeholders: **users** with diverse accessibility needs, who reported their accessibility evaluations; **volunteers** were members of the open community, who received users' reports and collaborated to propose adequate metadata to render the reported accessibility barrier accessible; finally, **website owners and developers**, who received these metadata with a view to future accessibility improvements (Fig. 26.4).

In this way, users and volunteers were able to improve the accessibility of any content on the Internet by collaboratively authoring the accessibility metadata. In order to enable the collaboration process, Takagi et al. (2008) proposed new types of authoring tools and collaboration services following these principles:

- The authoring tools should be usable enough to allow non-technical and accessibility novice volunteers to join in.
- The collaboration services should help participants to work together in the right direction and achieve appropriate sets of metadata.
- The service should effectively motivate volunteers to contribute to the activity, and should reduce their stress load by giving them opportunities to ask questions and to get instructions.

To this end the following tools were designed:

- Some client-side code, installed in the user browser, supplied scripts to handle both problem reports and transcoding (which used the added metadata to render the web page more accessible). Since the pilot system was aimed at blind users provided with screen readers, the end user component was mainly written using screen reader scripts transparent to the users' regular Web access.
- A browser plug-in, installed in the supporter browser. This plug-in offered an extension sidebar with various functions: a popup appearing whenever a request was issued by a user; an authoring view, which had a simulation area of the reading text with a screen reader; a pushbutton to submit the created metadata to the server; and a 'page map' function to give a visual overview of the accessibility status of the page.
- Each participant was provided with a portal function that contained basic information, activity ratings, rankings among participants, pending requests, and hot sites where problems were reported or where metadata was actively being created.

Tools for collaboration were created to enable collective creation of metadata. Real-time collaboration was performed by means of a group chat. For complex requests, supporters had access to a Web form to send an email query to ask the requester (end user) for clarification. Asynchronous collaboration was carried out by means of a discussion thread associated with each request and metadata item, linked to the toolbar or the portal page. Finally, to accumulate the acquired knowledge supporters were able to describe and publish guidelines for other supporters by creating new Wiki pages in a Wiki integrated into the system.

26.4.2 Crowdsourcing-Based Web Accessibility Evaluation

Since automatic Web accessibility evaluation can only cover part of the checkpoints, manual evaluation by human experts is required for the remaining ones. To recruit enough experts to evaluate large numbers of web pages is not easy. To solve this problem, crowdsourcing-based Web evaluation has been proposed. The basic idea is to divide the accessibility evaluation into small 'minitasks' and to submit these to several evaluators working in parallel. Each mini-task is carried out by a number of evaluators. The result for each mini-task can be 'accessible', 'inaccessible' or none. The accessibility score result is obtained by the majority of the answers received.

Since expertise among evaluators can be very diverse, more complex metrics have been tried, in order to reduce the weight of non-expert opinions and to boost the importance of expert scores. For instance, Song et al. (2018), distribute a number of 'golden tasks' which have been previously rated by experts. They use the answers from the evaluators to rate their expertise and subsequently assign a weight to their scores. Additionally, these authors consider the time required to answer 'accessible' (allegedly requiring more time) or 'non-accessible' (supposedly requiring less time) to identify possible inaccurate or random answers. In this way, they achieve reasonably accurate evaluations investing half the time of similar crowdsourcing Web evaluation systems.

26.5 Support Tools for Web Accessibility Evaluations with End Users

User testing for web accessibility evaluation has some drawbacks in comparison to other evaluation methods. For example, higher cost, longer development times, difficulty of finding an appropriate sample of users representative of the target audience, etc. Moreover, setting up a user testing session requires taking into consideration many potentially challenging aspects: it is necessary to install the appropriate assistive technology type and version required by each user, to ensure certain room facilities, etc. Nevertheless, user testing is an essential part of the accessibility evaluation process if the barriers usually experienced by real users are to be accurately detected and identified. Therefore, tools to support user testing are highly desired.

26.5.1 Types of User Tests

Similarly to other experimental studies, Web accessibility evaluations with users can be carried out with supervision (moderated evaluations) or unsupervised (unmoderated evaluations).

For moderated evaluations one or more supervisors are in charge of preparing the set-up, explaining the procedures and observing or recording the participants while they are trying to perform the given tasks. Direct observation of participants enables evaluators to obtain valuable information about the barriers they face, the strategies used to overcome them as well as how they use their assistive technology. Moderated evaluations are usually carried out in a laboratory, enabling valuable information to be gathered about the participants. However, it is not always easy to recruit the appropriate number of participants with the required characteristics. Moreover, they may have difficulties to travel to the experiment location. In order to adequately carry out the accessibility evaluation, assistive technologies should be properly configured for each participant. Otherwise, they might experience barriers due to the inadequate configuration of the assistive technology, altering the results of the accessibility evaluation (Petrie et al. 2006).

Alternatively, remotely carried out evaluations mitigate some of the aforementioned issues. Participants are not required to travel to the laboratory, they have their environment already adapted to their needs and the interaction with the Web is carried out in a more naturalistic manner. Remote evaluations can also be moderated, when an evaluator supervises the tasks using communication software such as, for example, a videoconference system, screen-sharing software, etc. (Hammontree et al. 1994). However, the moderated remote evaluation also has drawbacks such as the lack of control over participant environment (noise, interruptions, etc.) or the difficulty to install and configure special software if required.

These problems are alleviated by carrying out unmoderated evaluations in which participants carry out the tasks whenever and wherever they want without any supervision. In such evaluations, multiple tests are carried out simultaneously. Data are analysed once the evaluations have been finished. In this case, the required tasks should be carefully described in order to make sure that participants have understood the test correctly. Tasks should be short enough to maintain the participant's attention, taking into consideration that, in online studies, participants' attention tends to fade after 20 or 30 min (Albert et al. 2010).

Unmoderated remote evaluations enable a wider population to be reached and are carried out in a more realistic environment. In this case, participants use their own computer as they would usually do. However, there are also several risks: the total lack of control over the evaluation environment and participant. They might suffer distractions such as, for example a telephone call, other people in the room, etc. In addition, even if the participant is focused on carrying out the tasks, it is often the case that fewer accessibility barriers or usability issues are reported (Andreasen et al. 2007).

Evidently, the large amount of valuable information about the interaction of the user with web pages, obtained through logging web usage can be used to analyse several types of accessibility barriers. However, these data have also limitations that make it difficult to detect exactly were the accessibility barriers are. For example, no information can be obtained about why a user performs specific actions or how users utilise assistive technology (Petrie et al. 2006).

26.5.2   Architecture of Tools for Remote Web User Evaluations

Depending on the required purpose and functionality, user testing tools can be installed on the computer, in a proxy (configuring the browser to redirect web requests through the tool) or inserting new code into the target page. Let us describe the most commonly used architectures, the types of data collected, and some applications.

Tools that are used to carry out remote or in situ user evaluations are usually located in one of three locations: a server, a proxy between the server and the participant device or the client (device). In the following paragraphs, the strengths and weaknesses of each approach are discussed and summarised.

26.5.2.1 Located on the Server Side

When the user evaluation tool is located on a server (Scholtz et al. 1998; Etgen and Cantor 1999; Paganelli and Paternò 2002; de Santana and Baranauskas 2015; Google 2018), participants can carry out the experimentation transparently and comfortably. Some code is added to the web pages to gather the required events. Therefore, no installation or configuration is required by participants. The only requirement is to access the test web page and to perform the pertinent tasks.

This system has a major drawback: only pages located in the same server can be analysed, hence no third party web pages can be considered. Another inconvenience is the lack of control over the evaluation. For example, if the participant navigates to a page that is out of the server, closes the navigator tab, opens a new one, etc., large quantities of data are lost affecting the quality of the evaluation.

26.5.2.2 Located on the Proxy Side

Proxy tools are located between the participants' device and the website server (Hong et al. 2001; Atterer et al. 2006; Loop[11] 2018). In order to perform the tasks relating to the evaluation, each participant has to use a web browser configured to access the Internet through the proxy. Alternatively, researchers can provide a link to the proxy from which participants start the test and the following web page requests are made through the proxy. All the requests made by the web browser (texts, images, videos, etc.) are first caught by the proxy, which adds the necessary code to gather user interface events before reaching the participants' device.

As opposed to tools located on servers, proxy tools make it possible to analyse any existing web page. In this way, researchers can analyse how the users navigate in different types of web pages, observe their interests, measure accessibility, etc. Nevertheless, proxy systems also have some drawbacks. When the test is made through a proxy without browser configuration, the data is lost when participants close tabs or when they type URLs manually. Adequately configuring the web browser avoids these problems but it makes the process more obstructive than when accessing from a URL. In addition, proxy systems usually have restrictions with secure web pages and dynamic content.

26.5.2.3   Located on the Client Side

These tools are located on the participants' device, usually as a browser add-on, but web browsers especially designed for user evaluations can be also found (Claypool et al. 2001; Arrue et al. 2018; TechSmith 2018). With this approach, all the web pages can be analysed. The number of events that can be gathered is larger since browser selections such as back, history, or the context menu produced by the right click can be gathered. These events are appropriate to learn the interest that a participant has for a web page, for instance if it has been saved, printed or added to the bookmarks.

As opposed to proxy or server systems with client tools there is no problem closing tabs or inserting the desired URL manually. Clients can handle dynamic content and secure connections without problems. Nevertheless, data from secure connections have to be carefully handled, no keyboard events or information about web pages elements can be gathered, as this information can be used to get personal data such as passwords, bank accounts, etc. The need to perform a previous software installation before starting the experimental session is a major drawback, proving to be rather obstructive for the participant. In all three cases, when user interface events are gathered, a transmission mechanism is needed to send the data from the browser to the server.

26.5.3   Collected Data

Various types of data that are useful to enhance web accessibility can be obtained from tools that locally or remotely carry out user evaluations.

Early tools were only able to gather log data generated by servers (Hallam-Baker and Behlendor 2018) or the path followed by the participant (Scholtz et al. 1998). These logs are generated by the server to get information about its performance or the problems that may occur. It records the request (texts, images, etc.) made by the web browser in a known format (*host, ident, authuser, date, request, status, bytes*). However, with adequate data processing methods, data useful for finding problems related to navigation within the web pages in a site can be obtained. However, data obtained from server logs is limited and no information about the user interaction in a web page can be obtained.

On the other hand, with the use of technologies, such as JavaScript or Java Applets, events generated by the cursor or keyboard can be gathered (Kacmarcik and Leithead 2018). These events provide richer information about the participant compared to server logs (Atterer et al. 2006).

The most relevant events for obtaining information about the participant are those related to the mouse (*mouseup, mousedown, mousemove*), touch (*touchstart, touchend, touchmove, touchleave*), keyboard (*keyup, keydown*) or with the web browser (back-forward buttons, contextual-menu, zoom, etc.). These events usually provide information about the position (x, y) where the event was triggered, information about elements related to the event, which button or keys were pressed to trigger the event, etc. This information can be used to calculate measurements (cursor speed, time on page, trajectory linearity, etc.) to determine when the user is having problems, to detect accessibility issues or to classify the input device used.

For example, Mackenzie et al. (2001) defined seven accuracy measures (Target Re-entry, Task Axis Crossing, Movement Direction Change, Orthogonal Direction Change, Movement Variability, Movement Error and Movement Offset) to evaluate differences between the pointing devices. Later, Kates et al. (2002) added six new characteristics (Distance Travelled Relative to Cursor Displacement, Distribution of Distance Travelled for a Range of Cursor Speeds, Sub-movements, Cursor Distance Travelled Away from the Target, Distribution of Distance Travelled for a Range of Curvatures, Distribution of Distance Travelled for a Range of Radii from the Target). With these, it is possible to detect accessibility difficulties during target selection on the web page of people with reduced mobility.

Another alternative for detecting accessibility issues is to find the common events streams (event sequence) of a page. Studying the events streams with a post hoc analysis, several accessibility issues can be revealed such as, the lack of contrast, the confusion of text with links or unexpected usage patterns (de Santana and Baranauskas 2015). Vigo and Harper (2017) on the other hand, identified four strategies that might indicate navigation problems (*quick preview, asking for help, retracing* and *quick revisitation*) and created algorithms to detect those problems during navigation. This strategy enables the provision of interventions as the problems occur, making web navigation easier.

It is also possible to obtain information about the characteristics of the participants with data obtained from events (Hurst et al. 2008; Valencia et al. 2015) or to analyse the input performance from natural interactions (Gajos et al. 2012). Gajos et al. (2012) used an algorithm to extract the deliberated point and click movements to obtain laboratory like measurements. Hurst et al. (2008), distinguished between young, young adults, older adults and people with Parkinson's disease using their input events obtained in laboratory settings. Valencia et al. (2015) instead, obtained different measures from natural web navigation that can be used to detect accessibility issues or to identify the assistive technology used by the users. Another possible use of the information obtained from events is to extract the interest of the person on a page. For instance, the time spent on the page and the amount of scrolling were found as good interest indicators by Claypool et al. (2001).

26.5.4 Remotest: A Tool to Assist Evaluations with Users

Remotest is an application that assists researchers to define experiments, manage experimental remote/in situ sessions and analyse the gathered interaction data (Arrue et al. 2018). The main objective of the evaluations is to measure the accessibility and usability of a website during use. The platform admits a wide range of experiments. Various examples are, to study the user behaviour when performing a task in different websites, to analyse and compare navigational strategies of different types of participants when interacting with the same website, to evaluate the accessibility-in-use of several websites, to gather significant information through surveys, to measure user satisfaction when using a certain web service, to analyse user performance improvement when interacting with adapted versions of original web pages, etc.

The platform is split into four modules:

- The **Experimenter Module**: helps to specify the type of experiment, tasks, stimuli, the procedure of the experimental session, data to gather and sample.
- The **Coordinator Module**: stores and manages the experiments, creates stimuli to be presented during the experimental sessions (questionnaires, task description web page, task completion alert, etc.) and stores interaction data.
- The **Participant Module**: conducts the experimental sessions following the specification established by the Experimenter and Coordinator Modules. It presents login procedures, questionnaires, task descriptions pages, etc. It also tracks the participant throughout the experimental session and collects interaction data.
- The **Results Viewer Module**: deals with the presentation of the interaction data gathered in experimental sessions. For this purpose, it implements functions for collecting the data from the Coordinator Module, structuring it in understandable blocks of events and presenting them to the experimenter through a web application. In addition several statistical values, grouped by pages, tasks or users, can be visualised.

Remotest has been used to detect accessibility barriers related to motor and vision restrictions (Valencia et al. 2015). In addition, the results provided by remotest have been used to create adaptation techniques for transcoding and to evaluate the efficacy of the transcoded pages (Valencia 2017).

26.6 Discussion

Automatic tools can help make pages more accessible but it is essential that developers must receive training which enables them to gain a better understanding of the guidelines, their application and of the users themselves. Knowing the users would also foster a greater awareness of the need for web accessibility something which is otherwise often seen as being of secondary importance.

The disparity of results from web accessibility evaluations is also a problem. Not only do the various automatic evaluation tools provide different results, the evaluations carried out by different experts rarely reach the same conclusions. Therefore, it is necessary to study what the causes for this divergence are, and what can be done to achieve more coherent results.

A simpler wording for the guidelines might facilitate their applications and unambiguous machine-readable specifications would presumably help to produce more uniform results.

Another problem is the time required to perform web page accessibility evaluations. When the evaluation is made during the development process the extra time required is minimal. But analysing existing websites can be quite laborious when a site has numerous pages. Therefore, it is necessary to explore new ways to facilitate the evaluation process. For example, automatic evaluation tools could incorporate machine-learning modules to elucidate compliance and even the arrangement of some rules that cannot currently be evaluated. For example, automatic tools could be used to find out the suitability of alternative text and even to propose a substitute text, to check the complexity of the texts, suitability of the structure, etc. It could also be complemented with crowdsourcing techniques, to evaluate the adequacy of the results obtained by machine-learning techniques.

It cannot be overlooked that in order to entirely guarantee web page accessibility, it is necessary that the pages be tested by people with disabilities. Remote evaluation tools, are a cheap option that can reach larger samples of users. Despite the advantages of remote testing, 'in situ' user tests continue to be vital for developers to be able to see how users navigate, what difficulties they come across and what strategies they use to overcome those difficulties.

26.7   Future Directions

Advances in the definition of more specific accessibility guidelines which can be matched with the page code will contribute to more effective automatic accessibility evaluation. Unambiguous guidelines would also help to decrease the discrepancy between the accessibility reports generated by the various automatic evaluators, as well as between different human experts.

The integration of automatic accessibility evaluation tools into common use for professional web design and development frameworks will facilitate the creation of accessible pages and will combat the resistance of some designers to tackling accessibility issues.

Adaptability to the specific user of the accessibility evaluation would allow a more practical approach to help each individual to find pages that do not have accessibility barriers for her or him.

Methodologies, with their supporting tools, that include the complete series of evaluation, (automatic, by experts and by users, preferably in real scenarios) would ensure higher levels of accessibility.

26.8   Author's Opinion of the Field

Web accessibility is perceived by numerous designers as requiring extra effort and producing no extra benefits. Frequently, accessibility is only considered when legal or marketing requirements impose its fulfilment. This is due to the fact that designers often lack training in accessible design, and do not have the development tools that could help them in this field.

To reverse this tendency, it is essential that designers accept accessibility as a factor of quality, and they perceive it as a step towards their quality objective. To this end, accessibility must be integrated in the same way as any other requirement within the methodologies and tools that developers use every day.

Therefore, the advancement of web accessibility is closely tied to the availability of advanced, easy to use, tools that are well integrated into the professional design and development frameworks. These tools must be effective in helping the designer to develop websites that fulfil standard web accessibility guidelines and to test them efficiently. The scope of the required tools is broad: not only for automatic accessibility verification, but also, for support to expert inspections and different types of user testing.

26.9   Conclusions

Progress in web accessibility is closely associated with the availability of tools for design, evaluation and reparation. Automatic web accessibility evaluation has proved to be an essential starting point towards obtaining accessible websites, but it is important to underline its limitations: it can only detect failure to fulfil accessibility guidelines that can be expressed in machine-readable mode. More general guidelines must be checked by human experts. Moreover, the absence of detected compliance failures does not guarantee full accessibility. An evaluation by an ample and diverse sample of real users can detect barriers which are invisible to automatic evaluators and experts.

Most accessibility guidelines focus on 'general accessibility', which could be too restrictive for particular users with specific accessibility problems. Tailoring the evaluation to the concrete needs of specific users can help them to find sites which are useful for them, even if they may not be generally accessible. This kind of personalised evaluation may also help in page transcoding for specific users.

User tests are usually conducted with a small number of users working in artificial environments. A key issue to enhance web accessibility is to be able to evaluate the existence of barriers while people are using the Web with their own equipment (frequently including well-adapted assistive technology). To this end, tools to gather usage data from remote users and to efficiently process these data are indispensable.

Acknowledgements The authors are members of the EGOKITUZ/ADIAN research team, supported by the Basque Government, Department of Education, Universities and Research under grant (IT980-16).

References

Abascal J, Nicolle C (2001) Why inclusive design guidelines? In: Nicolle C, Abascal J (eds) Inclusive design guidelines for HCI, Taylor & Francis, London, pp 3–13

Abou-Zahra S, Henry SL (eds) (2011) WAI/W3C evaluation and report language (EARL) overview. https://www.w3.org/WAI/standards-guidelines/earl/. Accessed 1 Aug 2018

Abou-Zahra S, Steenhout N, Keen L (eds) (2017) Selecting web accessibility evaluation tools. https://www.w3.org/WAI/test-evaluate/tools/selecting/. Accessed 1 Aug 2018

Abou-Zahra S (2008) Web accessibility evaluation. In: Harper S, Yesilada Y (eds) Web accessibility: a foundation for research. Springer, London, pp 79–106

AccessIT (2017) Accessibility compliance and remediation methodology (ACRM) http://www.dor. ca.gov/Access-IT/documents/ACRM%2005102017.docx. Accessed 1 Aug 2018

AChecker (2011) Web accessibility checker. https://achecker.ca/checker/. Accessed 1 Aug 2018

Aizpurua A (2017) Contributions to web accessibility: device-tailored evaluation, user-tailored interface generation and the interplay with user experience. PhD Dissertation, University of the Basque Country/Euskal Herriko Unibertsitatea

Albert W, Tullis T, Tedesco D (2010) Beyond the usability lab: conducting large-scale online user experience studies. Morgan Kaufmann, San Francisco

Andreasen MS, Nielsen HV, Schrøder SO, Stage J (2007) What happened to remote usability testing?: An empirical study of three methods. In: Proceedings of the SIGCHI conference on human factors in computing systems (CHI '07). ACM, New York, pp 1405–1414. https://doi.org/ 10.1145/1240624.1240838

Arrue M, Valencia X, Pérez JE, Moreno L, Abascal J (2018) Inclusive web empirical studies in remote and in-situ settings: a user evaluation of the RemoTest platform. Int J Hum–Comput Interact. https://doi.org/10.1080/10447318.2018.1473941

Arrue M, Vigo M, Abascal J (2008) Including heterogeneous web accessibility guidelines in the development process. In: Gulliksen J, Harning MB, Palanque P, van der Veer GC, Wesson J (eds) Engineering Interactive Systems EHCI 2007. Lecture notes in computer science, vol 4940. Springer, Berlin, Heidelberg, pp 620–637

Atterer R, Wnuk M, Schmidt A (2006) Knowing the user's every move: user activity tracking for website usability evaluation and implicit interaction. In Proceedings of the 15th international conference on world wide web. ACM, New York, pp 203–212. https://doi.org/10.1145/1135777. 1135811

aXe (2018) Easy accessibility testing with aXe. https://www.axe-coreorg/. Accessed 1 Aug 2018

Basques K (2018) What's new in DevTools (Chrome 60). https://developers.google.com/web/ updates/2017/05/devtools-release-notes#lighthouse. Accessed 1 Aug 2018

BBC (2018) BBC digital guidelines accessibility standards and guidelines. http://www.bbc.co.uk/ guidelines/futuremedia/accessibility/. Accessed 1 Aug 2018

Brady E, Bigham J (2015) Crowdsourcing accessibility: human-powered access technologies. Found Trends Hum-Comput Interact 8(4):273–372. https://doi.org/10.1561/1100000050

Brajnik G (2004) Comparing accessibility evaluation tools: a method for tool effectiveness. Univ Access Inf Soc 3(3):252–263. https://doi.org/10.1007/s10209-004-0105-y

Brajnik G (2008a) A comparative test of web accessibility evaluation methods. In: Proceedings of the 10th international ACM SIGACCESS conference on computers and accessibility. ACM, New York, pp 113–120. https://doi.org/10.1145/1414471.1414494

Brajnik G (2008b) Beyond conformance: the role of accessibility evaluation methods. In: Hartmann S, et al (eds) Web information systems engineering WISE 2008. Lecture notes in computer science, vol 5176. Springer, Berlin, Heidelberg, pp 63–80

Brajnik G (2009) Barrier walkthrough. https://users.dimi.uniud.it/~giorgiobrajnik/projects/bw/ bwhtml. Accessed 1 Aug 2018

Caldwell B, Cooper M, Reid LG, Vanderheiden G (2008) WAI/W3C web content accessibility guidelines (WCAG) 20. http://www.w3.org/TR/WCAG20/. Accessed 1 Aug 2018

Chisholm W, Vanderheiden G, Jacobs I (eds) (1999) WAI/W3C web content accessibility guidelines 10 http://www.w3.org/TR/WAI-WEBCONTENT/. Accessed 1 Aug 2018

CKEditor (2018) Accessibility checker. https://ckeditor.com/cke4/addon/a11ychecker. Accessed 1 Aug 2018

Claypool M, Le P, Wased M, Brown D (2001) Implicit interest indicators. In Proceedings of the 6th international conference on intelligent user interfaces. ACM, New York, pp 33–40. https://doi.org/10.1145/359784.359836

CTIC (2018a) TAW web accessibility test. https://www.tawdisnet/?lang=en#. Accessed 1 Aug 2018

CTIC (2018b) TAW monitor. https://www.tawdisnet/proj#c2. Accessed 1 Aug 2018

de Santana VF, Baranauskas MCC (2015) WELFIT: A remote evaluation tool for identifying web usage patterns through client-side logging. Int J Hum-Comput Stud 76:40–49. https://doi.org/10.1016/j.ijhcs.2014.12.005

Eclipse (2018) ACTF aDesigner. http://www.eclipseorg/actf/downloads/tools/aDesigner/. Accessed 1 Aug 2018

Egger E, Abou-Zahra S (2016) WAI/W3C web accessibility evaluation tools list. https://www.w3.org/WAI/ER/tools/. Accessed 1 Aug 2018

Etgen M, Cantor J (1999) What does getting WET (web event-logging tool) mean for web usability. In Proceedings of 5th human factors and the web conference, NIST, Gaithersburg, 3 June 1999

Gajos KZ, Reinecke K, Herrmann C (2012) Accurate measurements of pointing performance from in situ observations. In: Proceedings of the SIGCHI conference on human factors in computing systems. ACM, New York, pp 3157–3166. https://doi.org/10.1145/2207676.2208733

Gay GR, Li CA (2010) Open, interactive, customizable, web accessibility checking. In: Proceedings of the 7th international cross disciplinary conference on web accessibility. ACM, New York, p 2. https://doi.org/10.1145/1805986.1806019

Google (2018) Google analytics. http://www.google.com/analytics/. Accessed 1 Aug 2018

Hallam-Baker PM, Behlendor B (2018) W3C extended log file format. https://www.w3.org/TR/WD-logfile. Accessed 1 Aug 2018

Hammontree M, Weiler P, Nayak N (1994) Remote usability testing. Interactions 1(3):21–25. https://doi.org/10.1145/182966.182969

Harper S, Bechhofer S (2007) SADIe: Structural semantics for accessibility and device independence. ACM Trans Comput-Hum Interact (TOCHI) 14(2):10. https://doi.org/10.1145/1275511.1275516

Harper S, Yesilada Y (eds) (2008) Web accessibility: a foundation for research. Springer, London

Henry SL (2007) Just ask: integrating accessibility throughout design. http://uiaccess.com/accessucd/. Accessed 1 Aug 2018

Henry SL (ed) (2018a) WAI/W3C introduction to web accessibility web accessibility initiative WAI (W3C). https://www.w3.org/WAI/fundamentals/accessibility-intro/#what. Accessed 1 Aug 2018

Henry SL (ed) (2018b) WAI/W3C evaluating web accessibility overview. https://www.w3.org/WAI/eval/Overview. Accessed 1 Aug 2018

Henry SL, McGee L (eds) (2018) Accessibility. https://www.w3.org/standards/webdesign/accessibility. Accessed 1 Aug 2018

HIIS Lab/ISTI-CNR (2018) MAUVE multiguideline accessibility and usability validation environment. http://mauve.isti.cnr.it/. Accessed 1 Aug 2018

Hong JI, Heer J, Waterson S, Landay JA (2001) WebQuilt: a proxy-based approach to remote web usability testing. ACM Trans Inf Syst 19(3):263–285. https://doi.org/10.1145/502115.502118

Hurst A, Hudson S E, Mankoff J, Trewin S (2008) Automatically detecting pointing performance. In: Proceedings of the 13th international conference on intelligent user interfaces. ACM, New York, pp 11–19. https://doi.org/10.1145/1378773.1378776

IBM (2017) IBM accessibility checklist. https://www.ibm.com/able/guidelines/ci162/accessibility_checklist.html. Accessed 1 Aug 2018

Ivory MY, Hearst MA (2001) The state of the art in automating usability evaluation of user interfaces. ACM Comput Surv (CSUR) 33(4):470–516. https://doi.org/10.1145/503112.503114

Kacmarcik G, Leithead T (eds) (2018) W3C UI events. https://www.w3.org/TR/uievents/. Accessed 1 Aug 2018

Keates S, Hwang F, Langdon P, Clarkson P J, Robinson P (2002) Cursor measures for motion-impaired computer users. In Proceedings of the 5th international ACM conference on assistive technologies. ACM, New York, pp 135–142. https://doi.org/10.1145/638249.638274

Kirkpatrick A, O'Connor J, Campbell A, Cooper M (2018) WAI/W3C web content accessibility guidelines (WCAG) 21. https://www.w3.org/TR/WCAG21/. Accessed 1 Aug 2018

Loop[11] (2018) Loop[11]. http://www.loop11.com/. Accessed 1 Aug 2018

Luque V, Delgado C, Gaedke M, Nussbaumer M (2005) Web composition with WCAG in mind. In: Proceedings of the 2005 international cross-disciplinary workshop on web accessibility (W4A). ACM, New York, pp 38–45. https://doi.org/10.1145/1061811.1061819

MacKenzie I S, Kauppinen T, Silfverberg M (2001) Accuracy measures for evaluating computer pointing devices. In: Proceedings of the SIGCHI conference on human factors in computing systems. ACM, New York, pp 9–16. https://doi.org/10.1145/365024.365028

Mariage C, Vanderdonckt J, Pribeanu C (2005) State of the art of web usability guidelines. In: Proctor R, Vu K (eds) The handbook of human factors in web design. Erlbaum, Lawrence, pp 688–700

Paganelli L, Paternò F (2002) Intelligent analysis of user interactions with web applications. In: Proceedings of the 7th international conference on intelligent user interfaces. ACM, New York, pp 111–118. https://doi.org/10.1145/502716.502735

Paternò F, Schiavone AG (2015) The role of tool support in public policies and accessibility. Interactions 22(3):60–63. https://doi.org/10.1145/2745395

Petrie H, Hamilton F, King N, Pavan P (2006) Remote usability evaluations with disabled people. In: Proceedings of the SIGCHI conference on human factors in computing systems. ACM, New York, pp 1133–1141. https://doi.org/10.1145/1124772.1124942

Schiavone AG, Paternò F (2015) An extensible environment for guideline-based accessibility evaluation of dynamic Web applications. Univ Access Inf Soc 14(1):111–132. https://doi.org/10.1007/s10209-014-0399-3

Scholtz J, Laskowski S, Downey L (1998) Developing usability tools and techniques for designing and testing websites. In: Proceedings of the 4th conference on human factors and the web, Basking Ridge, New Jersey, 5 June 1998

Section 508 (2018) Website policies. https://www.section508.gov/content/accessibility. Accessed 1 Aug 2018

Song S, Bu J, Wang Y, Yu Z, Artmeier A, Dai L, Wang C (2018) Web accessibility evaluation in a crowdsourcing-based system with expertise-based decision strategy. In: Pearson E, Sorge V (eds) W4A, ACM, pp 23:1–23:4. ISBN: 978-1-4503-5651-0

Takagi H, Asakawa C, Fukuda K, Maeda J (2002) Site-wide annotation: reconstructing existing pages to be accessible. In: Proceedings of the fifth international ACM conference on assistive technologies. ACM, New York, pp 81–88. https://doi.org/10.1145/638249.638265

Takagi H, Itoh T, Kawanaka S, Kobayashi M, Asakawa C. (2008) Social accessibility: achieving accessibility through collaborative metadata authoring. In: Proceedings of the 10th international ACM SIGACCESS conference on computers and accessibility. ACM, New York, pp 193–200. https://doi.org/10.1145/1414471.1414507

TECED (2017) Accessibility evaluation methodology. http://teced.com/services/web-accessibility/accessibility-evaluation-methodology/. Accessed 1 Aug 2018

TechSmith (2018) Morae. http://www.techsmith.com/moraehtml. Accessed 1 Aug 2018

Tenon (2018) LLC simplify your accessibility. https://tenon.io/. Accessed 1 Aug 2018

Thatcher J, Burks MR, Heilmann C, Henry SL, Kirkpatrick A, Lauke PH, Lawson B, Regan B, Rutter R, Urban M, Waddell CD (2006) Web accessibility: web standards regulatory compliance. Apress, New York

Valencia X (2017) A web transcoding framework based on user behaviour evaluation. Dissertation, University of the Basque Country

Valencia X, Pérez JE, Muñoz U, Arrue M, Abascal J (2015) Assisted interaction data analysis of web-based user studies. In: Abascal J, Barbosa S, Fetter M, Gross T, Palanque P, Winckler M (eds) Human-computer interaction—INTERACT 2015. Lecture notes in computer science, vol 9296. Springer, Cham, pp 1–19

Vanderdonckt J (1999) Development milestones towards a tool for working with guidelines. Interact Comput. Elsevier 12(2):81–118. https://doi.org/10.1016/S0953-5438(99)00019-3

Velleman E, Abou-Zahra S (eds) (2014) W3C/WAI Eval TF WAI/W3C website accessibility conformance evaluation methodology (WCAG-EM) 10. https://www.w3.org/TR/WCAG-EM/. Accessed 1 Aug 2018

Vigo M, Brown J, Conway V (2013) Benchmarking web accessibility evaluation tools: measuring the harm of sole reliance on automated tests. In: Proceedings of the 10th international cross-disciplinary conference on web accessibility. ACM, New York, pp 1–10. https://doi.org/10.1145/2461121.2461124

Vigo M, Arrue M, Brajnik G, Lomuscio R, Abascal J (2007a) Quantitative metrics for measuring web accessibility. In: Proceedings of the 2007 international cross disciplinary conference on web accessibility. ACM, New York, pp 99–107. https://doi.org/10.1145/1243441.1243465

Vigo M, Brajnik G (2011) Automatic web accessibility metrics: where we are and where we can go. Interact Comput 23(2):137–155. https://doi.org/10.1016/j.intcom.2011.01.001

Vigo M, Harper S (2017) Real-time detection of navigation problems on the World 'Wild' Web. Int J Hum-Comput Stud 101:1–9. https://doi.org/10.1016/j.ijhcs.2016.12.002

Vigo M, Kobsa, A, Arrue M, Abascal J (2007b) User-tailored web accessibility evaluations. In: Proceedings of the 18th conference on hypertext and hypermedia (HT '07). ACM, New York, pp 95–104. https://doi.org/10.1145/1286240.1286267

WEBaccessibility (2018) Continuous accessibility testing. https://webaccessibility.com/. Accessed 1 Aug 2018

WebAIM (2018) WAVE web accessibility evaluation tool. http://wave.webaim.org/. Accessed 1 Aug 2018

Yesilada Y, Brajnik G, Vigo M, Harper S (2012) Understanding web accessibility and its drivers. In: Proceedings of the international of the 2012 cross-disciplinary conference on web accessibility. ACM, New York, pp 1–9. https://doi.org/10.1145/2207016.2207027

Chapter 27
Automatic Web Accessibility Metrics

Where We Were and Where We Went

Giorgio Brajnik and Markel Vigo

Abstract This chapter starts by depicting how the topic of web accessibility metrics was in 2011, analyses what has happened since, and discusses the challenges that accessibility metrics face today. More specifically, we review a variety of metrics and a quality framework for metrics based on validity, reliability, sensitivity, adequacy and complexity. We then describe what new metrics were defined and how metrics have been used in the last 7 years, which range from assessments of accessibility awareness, of accessibility progress, to in-depth analyses within the banking sector, in country-based and continent-based assessments. We illustrate metrics that use new kinds of data, like human judgements or questionnaires, that in some case are used to deal with validity and reliability of metrics. The chapter ends with a discussion of the challenges ahead.

27.1 Introduction

In the Conclusions of a previous paper of ours, we wrote (Vigo and Brajnik 2011):

> Accessibility metrics are going to be more and more important in the years to come due to their applicability in scenarios that benefit both developers and end users.

The goal of this chapter is to see to what extent that has occurred in the last decade and to review some of the most relevant projects that have been pursued and suggest possible future roadmaps.

We expect this analysis will benefit different kinds of readers. Those who need to monitor web accessibility awareness and accessibility implementation can benefit from this new state of the art because they can understand if existing metrics and approaches are suitable to them. Those who are tasked with deciding to develop new

G. Brajnik (✉)
Department of Mathematics, Informatics and Physics, University of Udine, Udine, Italy
e-mail: giorgio.brajnik@uniud.it

M. Vigo
School of Computer Science, University of Manchester, Manchester, UK
e-mail: markel.vigo@manchester.ac.uk

© Springer-Verlag London Ltd., part of Springer Nature 2019
Y. Yesilada and S. Harper (eds.), *Web Accessibility*, Human–Computer
Interaction Series, https://doi.org/10.1007/978-1-4471-7440-0_27

accessibility metrics could find interesting suggestions on which metric could be more appropriate. And finally, researchers should be able to find new research areas. In 2011, we reviewed several metrics:

- The 'failure-rate' between actual and potential points of failure of a subset of 8 checkpoints from the WCAG 1.0 set (Sullivan and Matson 2000).
- The 'Kit for the Accessibility to the Internet', a set of applications to enhance the accessibility of web pages for visually impaired users (González et al. 2003). Besides metrics leading to percentages, in the kit, there are also other ones yielding absolute number of items, such as the number of colours used as background, as mentioned by WCAG 1.0 checkpoint 2.2. In addition, a normalised overall accessibility value is calculated using the Web Quality Evaluation Method, Web-QEM (Olsina and Rossi 2002).
- Navigability and listenability metrics for blind users (Fukuda et al. 2005). The former takes into account broken links, correct usage of headings and fast navigation mechanisms such as 'skip-links', adequate labelling of controls in forms and whether tables are not used for layout purposes. Listenability considers the existence and appropriateness of alt attributes, redundant text and how Japanese characters are arranged so that pages can be adequately be read by screen readers.
- Tree-maps to display/visualise the accessibility level of a website (Bailey and Burd 2005). The authors claim that this information visualisation technique is more interactive and easier to comprehend for website accessibility maintenance. Each node within the tree represents a web page, and it is visualised as a rectangle, whose area and colour correspond to the inverse of the value of the Overall Accessibility Metric (OAM), which depends on the number of violations of WCAG 1.0 checkpoints multiplied by a coefficient that accounts for different levels of confidence.
- Page Measure (PM) to analyse the correlations between the accessibility of websites and the policies adopted by software companies regarding usage of Content Management Systems or maintenance strategies (Bailey and Burd 2007). Page Measure is defined similarly to OAM, but weights correspond to checkpoint priorities.
- The Web Accessibility Barrier (WAB) metric aiming at quantitatively measuring the accessibility of a website based on 25 WCAG 1.0 checkpoints (Hackett et al. 2004).
- The Web Accessibility Quantitative Metric (WAQM) (Vigo et al. 2007) overcomes some limitations of the above metrics (i.e. lack of score normalisation and consideration of manual tests) by automatically providing normalised results that consider the weights of the WCAG 1.0 priorities, and by exploiting the information in the reports produced by the evaluation tool EvalAccess.
- T1 normalises WAB and is applied to different user groups by selecting the subsets of WCAG 1.0 checkpoints that impact on the blind and the deaf (Sirithumgul et al. 2009).
- In the context of the Unified Web Evaluation Methodology (UWEM) a few metrics have been proposed during its development process. In version UWEM 1.2

(Velleman et al. 2007) the accessibility score of a page is the mean of the failure-rates produced by all checkpoints.

- A3 was suggested in Bühler et al. (2006), as an extension of the UWEM 0.5 metric.
- The Web Interaction Environments (WIE) metric yields the proportion of WCAG 1.0 checkpoints that are violated on a page Lopes and Carriço (2008).

We then experimentally analysed Failure-Rate, Page Measure, WAB, A3, UWEM 1.2, WAQM and WIE, comparing them against a quality framework (Vigo and Brajnik 2011), which we recap below. We also review what has happened since, and discuss future challenges in light of these findings.

27.2 Where We Were

Around the years 2009–2011, we observed an increase in papers reporting numeric outputs to convey the result of accessibility evaluations. A common characteristic of these studies was that all metrics were different and the rationale for defining the metrics was often not included. This had several drawbacks in that not only were not the results of the accessibility evaluation studies comparable, but neither were the metrics. These limitations motivated us to propose a framework for automatic accessibility metrics (Vigo and Brajnik 2011) that would allow:

- comparing existing metrics;
- helping researchers to use those metrics that were more appropriate for their research objectives;
- highlighting the weaknesses of existing approaches, which would have informed a research agenda for those interested in measuring accessibility.

27.2.1 A Quality Framework of Accessibility Metrics

The framework specifies five quality properties:

- **Validity**, which is how a metric reflects the accessibility of the website to which it is applied. It can be defined at least in two ways: *validity with respect to accessibility-in-use* reflects how well scores produced by a metric predict the effects that real accessibility problems will have on the quality of interaction as experienced by real users when interacting with real pages for achieving real goals. The second definition characterises validity in terms of how well scores mirror all and only the true violations of checkpoints/requirements of a given standard (e.g. WCAG 2.0), namely, *validity with respect to conformance*.
- **Reliability** relates to the reproducibility of scores: i.e. the extent to which scores are consistent when evaluations of the same websites are carried out in different contexts (different tools, people, goals or time). There are two kinds of reliability

that are related with the tools used to run evaluations: intra-tool reliability is related to how results change depending on the settings of a given tool, which affect which pages are crawled and how guidelines are applied. Inter-tool reliability has to do with how reports produced by different tools differ when similar settings and the same guidelines are used.

- **Sensitivity** is about the extent that changes in the output of the metric are quantitatively related to changes in the accessibility of the site being analysed. With a sensitive metric, small changes in accessibility of pages produce large changes of the scores. An ideal metric shows low sensitivity, in order to behave in a robust way against small changes in the input, which can be caused by many unexpected and uncontrollable factors. Too sensitive metrics lead to results that are dependent on small variations in the accessibility of pages, making comparisons very difficult because differences may be influenced by confounding factors.
- **Adequacy** encompasses several properties of accessibility metrics: the type of data used to represent scores, including ordinal WCAG conformance levels {nonconformant, A, AA, AAA} where distance between accessibility levels is not represented, ratio scales that include 0 and 1 and are based on the usual integer, or rational numbers and interval scales (like the ones used for Celsius/Fahrenheit degrees). Another property is the resolution of the scale (e.g. values in [0,1] or in {0,1,..., 10}); it is particularly useful if it can be easily transformed to [0,1] (i.e. normalisation) and actual distribution of scores (i.e. the span covered by actual values of the metric). A metric that uses just a few ordinal values (such as WCAG conformance levels) is not very useful for monitoring purposes because small changes in accessibility are not detected.
- **Complexity** can be defined in two ways: internal complexity which measures the number of variables that are needed to compute the metric and the algorithmic complexity (time and memory requirements) of the algorithm computing it, whereas external complexity indicates the availability of tools that compute the metrics.

27.2.2 Application Scenarios of Automatic Accessibility Metrics

The relevance of these qualities is determined by the purpose of the metrics, which depends on the scenarios where metrics are used:

- **Quality assurance**. Web accessibility is explicitly considered in several web quality models (Mich et al. 2003; Olsina et al. 2008; BS and ISO 2011). When considering web accessibility from a quality control perspective, there is a need for finer grades than just conformance ordinal levels, so that developers or test engineers can keep track of accessibility in agile iterative development. With proper metrics, they could also assess the relative accessibility levels of different sections of a website, and prioritise accordingly the necessary effort. Since content is frequently updated/added by other users it is even harder to monitor the overall quality of the website, including accessibility. For these reasons, high-quality automatic accessibility metrics could play crucial roles in quality management processes.

- **Benchmarking**. Policies have been passed worldwide in order to promote/enforce a barrier-free web. In order to ensure that regulations are met, national and international accessibility observatories are being developed, like the European Internet Accessibility Observatory. These projects keep track of the accessibility level of pages and to do so they need accurate measurement methods and tools.

- **Search engines**. Search engines can make use of the accessibility level as a criterion to rank their results. Sorting search results according to accessibility or usability criteria improves the search experience of users with visual disabilities (Ivory et al. 2004). Since it is questionable whether trading-off content relevance against accessibility is really worthwhile, results could be sorted by content relevance and each item can be annotated with its accessibility score.

- **User-adapted interaction**. Adaptation techniques are believed to be effective ways to provide an accessible web environment for people with disabilities and the elderly. For instance, adaptive navigation could increase user orientation by providing guidance using techniques such as link recommendation, non-relevant link hiding or link annotations. In this scenario, accessibility scores can be used as a criterion for an end user to decide to follow a link or not.

27.2.2.1 Mapping the Framework to Application Scenarios

We mapped the framework of accessibility metrics into the application scenarios we identified in Table 27.1. Three levels of demand define how the degree of fulfilment of these qualities is relevant for each scenario: properties that must be fulfilled for the correct application of a metric to a scenario are marked as Required; when Desirable properties are fulfilled this leads to benefits in the application scenario, although failure to fulfil does not prevent the metric from being used in the scenario; finally, those properties that do not make a considerable difference are labelled as Optional.

27.3 What Happened Since

Since 2011 the web accessibility scene has changed. Several studies have shown differences in awareness of accessibility, in how accessibility features were implemented (for a comprehensive overview, see Part 3 of this book, 'Society and Standards' and Part 4, 'Technical Foundation'), in how accessibility can be evaluated (for an updated overview of automated tools (see Abascal et al. 2018) and for evaluation techniques (see Eraslan and Bailey 2018; Power and Petrie 2018)), and of course in accessibility techniques. Some of these studies relied on old and new web accessibility metrics.

Table 27.1 Mapping of the quality framework onto the application scenarios using levels of fulfilment: Required, Desirable and Optional

	Quality assurance	Benchmarking	Search engines	Adaptive interaction
Sufficient validity	Accessibility-as-conformance	Accessibility-as-conformance	Accessibility-as-conformance	Accessibility-in-use
Key reliability	Inter-tool (R)	Inter-tool (R)	Intra-tool (D)	Intra-tool (R)
Low sensitivity	O	R	R (rankings) O (annotations)	R
Adequacy				
Type of data	Ratio	Ratio or ordinal	Ordinal (rankings) Ratio (annotations)	Ratio
Normalisation	O	D	O (rankings) R (annotations)	O
Precision	R	R	D (rankings) R (annotations)	D
Distribution	R	D	O (rankings) R (annotations)	D
Low internal complexity	O	O	R	R

27.3.1 Drivers for Web Accessibility Metrics

One thing that has changed is that more attention is being paid to web accessibility metrics. We notice there are several drivers that push researchers to look at web accessibility metrics as ways to support decision-making. Some of the drivers are different and new compared to what we described back in 2011 (Vigo and Brajnik 2011).

Accessibility metrics have been used to determine the evolution of web accessibility in the public and private sector. A longitudinal study was conducted to evaluate the accessibility of 20 governmental websites in the UK and in the US and 60 among the topmost Alexa websites (Hanson and Richards 2013), over a period of 12 years starting in 1999, when WCAG 1.0 was published. The overall goal of the study was to determine if over such a time period there was progress in web accessibility and if the pace of the progress differed between governmental and top websites. Results showed that both types of websites show low conformance levels with WCAG. Over the time period, though, evidence of improvement can be seen, with government sites showing more improvement than top websites. Awareness of accessibility was also measured, showing that it kept increasing and that it reached 65% for governmental sites and 20% for top websites. To perform such a study, authors implemented 'ad hoc' metrics: some metrics were defined to measure the level of awareness of accessibility in terms of the number of pages that have a link or text with the word 'accessibility'. Other metrics were based on the percentage of violations of specific success criteria in relation to the total number of possible violations. Success criteria that were covered were lack of descriptive text for content images, decorative images, buttons; presence of 'skip navigation' links; titles used in frames, iframes and pages; number of page headings; usage of attribute 'lang'; and parsing errors in HTML.

Another study characterised web accessibility within the banking sector, in Spain (Lorca et al. 2016). The overall goal of this study is to see how web accessibility differed between two different types of Spanish banks, saving ones (non-profit and owned by the government) and commercial ones (owned by shareholders). Several experimental hypotheses were formulated whose validity was determined by using WAB*, a variant of the WAB accessibility metric (Zeng 2004), applied to 43 saving banks and 30 commercial ones. Some of the hypotheses were:

- saving banks are more likely to achieve a higher accessibility: this hypothesis was not supported by the data;
- prior economic performance influences accessibility: not supported by data;
- size of the bank is negatively related to accessibility: supported by the data.

To perform such a study, researchers needed quantitative metrics that are suitable for complex statistical analyses. Web accessibility metrics are thus seen as enabling mechanisms for such studies. We find it interesting that results obtained by using web accessibility metrics are used to understand what relationship holds between accessibility and different factors characterising the domain, namely, ownership of a bank institution, its performance and its size. Researchers also used results of metrics for suggesting that a category of banks (i.e. saving banks) should do more in terms of accessibility in order to be more successful.

Similarly, motivated by the business opportunities that may be missed if banking services are not accessible for people with disabilities, an analysis of the accessibility of 100 US bank and finance sites was conducted (Wentz et al. 2018). The authors report the most frequently violated WCAG 2.0 success criteria including '1.4.3 Poor contrast ratio', '1.4.4 Ability to resize text without assistive technology' and '4.1.1 Valid HTML markup'. Metrics are reported as aggregates of success criteria violations: for instance, the average violation per Federal Reserve district, being the banks located in the Boston area the ones with the highest number of violations.

Another driver for web accessibility metrics comes from worldwide analyses of accessibility and inclusion. A report shows how different countries (204) have policies that are related to accessibility covering diverse sectors such as education, emergency response services, health services, workplace, teleworking, smart cities (G3ict 2016). Such a study was performed through questionnaires sent to more than 100 respondents in those countries.

The results show that, among others, only 41% of the countries have commitments to accessibility in legislation and official policies; that only 13% of the countries ensure at least a partial level of accessibility for governmental communications to the public; that only 9% define procurement rules with some sort of accessibility requirements; that no more than 36% of the countries have policies for assistive technology for the different types of disabilities. Regarding the level of accessibility implementation, 66% of the countries have emergency response services that are not accessible; 51% have inaccessible primary and secondary education; 65% have inaccessible health services; and 58% have inaccessible workplaces. Besides this data, a major finding of the report was the widespread and systematic lack of data that is needed to support tracking the progress. To this end, the report recommends creating a country-level monitoring framework. This framework could benefit from well designed and understood web accessibility metrics that encompass subjective data like those collected through questionnaires, but enrich them with data collected also from standard accessibility criteria violations.

There are numerous examples of country-level surveys including Mexico (Ochoa and Crovi 2018), Kyrgyzstan (Ismailova 2017), Saudi Arabia (Al-Khalifa et al. 2017), Italy (Gambino et al. 2016) and Finland (Nurmela et al. 2013) which focus mostly on government sites.[1] Despite the methodological problems of relying on automated tools alone (Vigo et al. 2013), full reliance on automated tools is common to these kinds of studies—sometimes minimal human checks are reported. The computed metrics are along the lines of:

- The absolute number of violations as reported by automated tools (Ismailova 2017).
- The average of violations by category (Al-Khalifa et al. 2017).
- Normalisation (using linear transformations), weights allocation (through analytic hierarchy processes) and aggregation of the number of violations (Ochoa and Crovi 2018).

Monitoring services are scarce and their coverage is typically at a continent level: examples along these lines are the Iberoamerican Observatory (OIA) (Benavidez et al. 2014) and the European Internet Inclusion Initiative (EIII) (Mucha et al. 2016). The former uses the metric implemented by the tool implemented by the OIA (i.e. eXaminator Fernandes and Benavidez 2011), where violations are assigned a weight depending on their severity and frequency of the tests executed. The EIII metric generates a page score that computes the number of instances where tests failed over the number of all instances were applied (Nietzio et al. 2011).

The accessibility directive issued in 2016 by the European Parliament (European Parliament 2016) gives quite a substantial emphasis on periodical monitoring of accessibility conformance levels of public bodies' websites within the member states. It stresses that quantitative information should be regularly collected and that the procedure should be transparent, reproducible and leading to comparable results.

The same driver for accessibility metrics applies also to the Chinese government, which annually monitors the level of accessibility of websites deemed essential for the daily life of people with disabilities (Song et al. 2017, 2018a, b). In order to monitor a relatively large set of websites (98 websites with a total of more than 300,000 pages), a new metric called WAEM is used, Web Accessibility Experience Metric. WAEM is based on the fraction of pages of a website that contain automatically determined violations of WCAG 2.0 criteria (used to compute the *pass rate of*

---

[1]Note that this list is not exhaustive.

the success criterion), which is combined with weights that are computed through a machine learning algorithm that optimises an objective function. This function considers agreement of the pass rate of checkpoints for a website with a set of pairwise preference judgements provided by human judges. In an experiment with 30 judges who explored for 20 min the homepages of 45 websites, WAEM gave promising results.

In a subsequent study, the authors factored the reliability of human judgements in their metrics (Song et al. 2018a). Results applied to 46 websites with more than 300,000 pages, combined with judgements provided by 94 judges, show that the new metric, Reliability-Aware-WAEM, outperforms several other metrics, including UWEM, WAB, WAQM and WAEM. RA-WAEM reaches 87% of accuracy, which in this case is defined as the fraction of human judgements that agree with the ordering of websites derived by the metrics.

Finally, they propose a system that uses a multistaged approach to evaluate accessibility and to measure it (Song et al. 2018b). First, an automated tool is used for evaluating certain success criteria; second, a crowdsourcing approach is used to obtain binary judgements on whether remaining success criteria are satisfied or not by a web page; third, the WAEM metric is used to obtain an overall accessibility score. To compensate for the fact that crowdsourcing workers might show different levels of expertise in accessibility, a set of 'golden tasks' are used: their outcomes was known beforehand, and they were submitted to each worker (who were not aware) to gauge the level of attention that was paid in executing the task and also their expertise. The time needed to declare a page as being accessible is monitored as a second indicator of the accuracy of a worker. If this value falls below a dynamic threshold, then the result of the task is rejected. An experimental evaluation of the system showed that 24,000 tasks were completed in 31 hours, leading to quite a valid and reliable evaluation of web accessibility even when employing workers that were not expert in accessibility.

27.4   Discussion

Back in 2011, informed by the outcomes of our analysis, we proposed research avenues to explore validation, reliability, sensitivity, adequacy and tailorability aspects of metrics. We now revisit these and reflect about whether the research projects discussed earlier in Sect. 27.3 have made any progress along the lines of our proposal, and highlight the most important challenges for accessibility metrics.

27.4.1   Type of Information

Based on the above review of the current state of the art, and compared to the previous decade, in many cases, the same kinds of data were used as a basis for the metrics.

However, an interesting finding is that new kinds of data are also being considered by some metrics. Many works we analyse in this chapter employ very basic metrics that are derived from automatically computed violations of success criteria, as in the case of Hanson and Richards (2013), Wentz et al. (2018). Some include the total number of violations (Ismailova 2017) and simple aggregates such as the arithmetic mean (Al-Khalifa et al. 2017). In these cases, web accessibility is treated as a multidimensional property, making it impossible to use it for ranking websites because a partial order will in general ensue.

In some cases, metrics include also the maximum number of possible violations of a success criterion. When also weights are being used to combine violations of different success criteria, metrics can be normalised, making it possible the comparison between different websites.

We observe that there are metrics defined on the basis of existing ones, or minor variations of them. For instance, the metric used in EIII could be understood as a variation of the WAB metric (Zeng 2004); so does the work of Lorca et al. (2016); the OIA metric is basically an aggregation of the failure-rate metric (Sullivan and Matson 2000). Some adopt a pragmatic approach by employing metrics that are by-products of tools (Fernandes and Benavidez 2011).

Interestingly, new metrics use other data, such as pairwise human judgements, like in Song et al. (2017), Song et al. (2018a), Ochoa and Crovi (2018). These judgements can be quickly provided by human judges and are reliable, if automated quality checks are used. While the idea of integrating automatically generated data with human judgements was explored in Brajnik and Lomuscio (2007), the novelty relies on considering binary judgements. As a further advancement, hybrid evaluations relying on crowdsourcing define novel mechanisms for combining data computed automatically and data produced by humans (Song et al. 2018b).

Finally, metrics for measuring accessibility awareness were also defined (Hanson and Richards 2013) as well as metrics based on questionnaires (G3ict 2016).

27.4.2 Validity

One research avenue that we identified was 'validation of metrics'. There are two main challenges in metric validation: first, there is no 'gold standard' with respect to which to compare the output produced by a metric. Second, the reliance on tools and their limited coverage, completeness and correctness (Brajnik 2004; Vigo et al. 2013) introduces uncertainty if not errors. While both challenges affect the two types of validity we introduced in Sect. 27.2, validity with respect to conformance is more sensitive to the reliance on tools, as the main purpose of automated tools is to evaluate the conformance of websites against accessibility criteria. Validity in use is sensitive to the lack of ground truth and the lack of tools capable of reporting accessibility problems as they occur on a given website. Approaches to evaluate accessibility-in-use have also been proposed (Vigo and Harper 2013), where a system detected accessibility barriers by monitoring browsing behaviours that are known to be indicators of problematic interactions.

We observe different levels of attention being paid by researchers on how validity is handled: some works are fully reliant on tools and do not even acknowledge the methodological considerations of such an approach, while some others use more than one tool (which, at least, would maximise coverage). In some cases, researchers decided to use simplified metrics, like those based on counting violations of individual success criteria that were carefully chosen to yield valid results. Notice that the problem with these metrics based on only a subset of criteria is related with the poor coverage, and therefore the potentially large number of false positives, i.e. missed problems, that affect the values computed by the metric. The usage of these metrics to quantify accessibility as a whole, as opposed to just tallying the different kinds of violations, is subject to underestimation of the measured accessibility.

Other researchers, though, think that user involvement is central to the metric being used. For example, hybrid approaches implicitly address the validity of metrics; human judgements are added in order to change the weights that are associated to violations of success criteria and in this way weights mitigate the impact of false positives or negatives yielded by the evaluation tool. We suggested that human judgements concerning the validity of the results of an evaluation tool are used to modulate the values of the metric (Brajnik and Lomuscio 2007). Some of the approaches that we reviewed in this chapter, such as Song et al. (2017), Song et al. (2018a), Ochoa and Crovi (2018), are based on using human judgements concerned with the accessibility of websites. This choice helps overcoming an important limitation of the former approach, namely, the fact that asking human judges to assess the validity of the results of tools cannot cope with the problem of false negatives. However, also this road faces potential flaws in that some users are not aware of the accessibility problems they encounter (Takagi et al. 2009), which suggests that particular attention needs to be paid to validate the input collected from users. Furthermore, these approaches mix the two types of validity, in-use versus conformance-based: data produced by evaluation tools refer to accessibility-as-conformance whereas data collected by users refer to accessibility-in-use. It is likely that this difference plays an important role on validity of a hybrid metric.

We observe the use of crowdsourcing to increase validity of the violations that are reported, in this case by delegating to human judgement the success criteria that cannot reliably be evaluated automatically. We are glad to see this latter case being an approach that includes an implementation of a suggestion we made in Vigo and Brajnik (2011) of seeding pages with known accessibility problems and using them to estimate the validity of judgements, and therefore the metrics.

None of the most recent papers performed a detailed sensitivity analysis of validity along the lines we then suggested, namely: how validity changes when guidelines are changed, how validity changes when a subset of guidelines is used, how validity is affected when testing Rich Internet Applications, how validity changes when the tool is replaced, can validity be estimated. Therefore we believe these questions are still important ones to be answered.

No approach has tackled the problem of applying metrics to Rich Internet Applications (like single-page applications), and use also violations of ARIA techniques as an input for metrics. This is also an area that needs to be covered.

27.4.3 Reliability

Ideally, metrics should be independent of tools and the particular context in which an evaluation is performed. Reliability of metrics is considered by some approach: for example, in Song et al. (2018a) reliability of human judgements is automatically assessed, and it affects the final scores. Other studies, to be on the safe side, considered three metrics together, WAB, UWEM and WAB* (Lorca et al. 2016).

Reliability was also discussed in Hanson and Richards (2013), when the authors found their results were significantly different from previous studies. One possible reason was that the tool used had a more accurate way of identifying violations of success criteria involving images.

One of the causes of low reliability that we identified in 2011 is the sampling method adopted to select the pages to be evaluated. The work done by Zhang et al. (2015) addresses this aspect and shows how a particularly chosen sampling approach improves results when using WAQM. The same sampling approach was used also in subsequent studies (Song et al. 2018b).

It would be interesting to assess the reliability of the two major components that contribute to measures of accessibility, the tool used to identify violations of accessibility criteria and the data and formulae used to compute the final score. If the adopted tool would produce results in a standard representation, such as EARL, and computation of metrics would rely on the same representation, then these analyses could be more easily performed, for example by switching evaluation tools.

As mentioned above, the EU directive (European Parliament 2016) stresses that metrics should be transparent and lead to reproducible and comparable results. Transparency refers to the fact that details regarding how data are collected and values are computed should be made explicit. Comparability is motivated by the fact that values produced by different member states need to be homogeneous in order to produce European level dashboards and reports. It is unfortunate that no mention is made to the validity aspect of adopted metrics.

27.4.4 Sensitivity and Adequacy

While sensitivity deals with the magnitude of variation in a metric score caused by a change in the accessibility of a given web page, adequacy is about how meaningful and suitable are the scores generated by metrics. These two qualities are closely related in that a metric with a too-low or too-high sensitivity maybe not very useful. Works analysed in this chapter do not conduct research around these two qualities but some of them are exemplar of the problems caused by inadequate sensitivity. For instance, the work by Ochoa and Crovi (2018) reports the top 199 sites of their analysis, with scores ranging from 99.961 to 99.016. Without discussing the validity of this metric, the high resolution of the results leads to the question of whether such small differences are meaningful.

We noticed that recently new drivers have been considered; for example, to measure the level of accessibility awareness. Another important driver comes from accessibility policies within individual organisations. In Brajnik and Graca (2018) the authors present a survey and analysis of different accessibility policies defined by higher educational institutions. In many cases, these policies include a description of the methods to be used to assess the accessibility level of the website and implicitly refer to accessibility metrics. We believe that deciding which metric to use for measuring accessibility would greatly improve the overall effectiveness of such policies. Determining the most adequate metric to be used for this kind of assessments is not trivial because of the large variety of web content that is normally present in such websites.

27.4.5   User-Tailored Metrics

This research path in 2011 proposed designing metrics that would convey the fact that accessibility barriers affect different users in a different manner, even those who use the same assistive technology. We were not able to find examples of research focused on *adaptive* metrics but there are instances where weights are allocated based on expert judgement (Ochoa and Crovi 2018; Song et al. 2018a). These methods could potentially be used to collect weights to define metrics that correspond to certain stereotypes of users. While we acknowledge that all users have different needs, accessibility barriers affect users of assistive technologies in a different manner. For instance, the lack of an `alt` attribute is more problematic for a screen reader user than for a deaf user.

This kind of tailoring could be used to assess the accessibility level with respect to specific users, and to monitor how it changes. Similar approaches could be used to compute metrics that refer to certain user platforms, such as touch versus keyboard interaction.

27.5   Future Directions

Several open issues remain, which are challenges that we expect should be tackled in the future.

The validity of metrics is often neglected, or taken for granted. We argue that if an accessibility metric has to be used, some sort of validity claim needs to be made and corresponding evidence should be explicit. Hybrid approaches are a promising direction, but human judgements need to be filtered in order to consider different levels of expertise of judges (see Brajnik et al. 2011) and possible contextual aspects, such as disability type or user platforms.

Using only a subset of known criteria for assessing levels of accessibility, based on automatically determined violations, can be viewed as a quick way to estimate the overall accessibility level. However, the correlation between such an overall accessibility level and numbers of detected violations needs to be studied. Ideally, if such a correlation is found and it turns out to be marked and statistically significant, then such a quick estimate could be safely used as a proxy for the overall accessibility level. Appropriate simplified sampling approaches could also be studied. The gain is efficiency, as no human judgements are needed and a simplified automatic evaluation of websites would suffice.

The sensitivity of validity of a metric should be studied with respect to various factors that can play a role, such as different accessibility guidelines, sub-setting accessibility criteria, different genres of websites or different evaluation tools. These studies could shed light on how general validity claims could be and if there are hidden factors that can affect them.

Reliability of accessibility metrics is also an important topic for future studies. We still need to better understand how large should be the changes in accessibility scores when using different tools, or when using different metrics, or when using different sampling methods, or when integrating different data. Once that is known, it would let practitioners have expectations regarding variability of scores, and would help them make appropriate claims and decisions based on such scores.

Determining the most appropriate metrics to be used for specific kinds of purposes and websites (such as metrics to assess levels of adoption of accessibility policies for higher educational institutions) is also an interesting research goal to pursue.

Finally, determining how to tailor metrics to different kinds of users is also required to establish a mapping between characteristics of metrics and the scenarios in which they are used.

27.6 Authors' Opinion of the Field

We believe that the field of web accessibility metrics has made some progress in the last decade. Yet, it is still immature.

As mentioned in the previous section, there are a few important challenges that still need to be tackled, the most pressing ones being validity and reliability of accessibility metrics. Once standard methodologies for assessing these quality attributes of metrics are defined and established, and consensus within the community has been achieved, then the quality of metrics will increase and consequently will do their usefulness. We expect this to match an increasing demand that new drivers for metrics will place.

27.7 Conclusion

In this chapter, we started from the conclusions that we wrote in Vigo and Brajnik (2011), analysed what has happened since in terms of accessibility metrics, and discussed challenges that accessibility metrics face.

In particular, the quality framework for accessibility metrics was reviewed. By and large, among the five quality aspects included in the framework, the most important quality aspects affecting metrics were validity and reliability. This is true now as well.

Since 2011 several things have happened. More and more attention has been paid to accessibility metrics, which have been used to monitor progress in accessibility adoption, in general or within specific sectors (like banking); they have been used to assess the existence of and compliance with accessibility policies in different countries; they are referred to in EU directives, and have been used in several country-level assessments of accessibility.

New metrics have been proposed, and in some cases, the issues of reliability and validity have been addressed, especially by integrating data that are automatically collected with data derived from human judgements.

We hope that in the years to come, by addressing the challenges that we discussed above, web accessibility metrics become the centre of a vibrant scientific research activity, so that future studies can shed more light on the quality of web accessibility metrics. Existing gaps constitute research opportunities to be pursued.

References

Abascal J, Arrue M, Valencia X (2018) Tools for web accessibility evaluation. In: Yesilada Y, Harper S (eds) Web accessibility. Springer. This volume

Al-Khalifa HS, Baazeem I, Alamer R (2017) Revisiting the accessibility of Saudi Arabia government websites. Univers Access Inf Soc 16(4):1027–1039 Nov

Bailey J, Burd E (2005) Tree-map visualization for web accessibility. In: COMPSAC '05: proceedings of the 29th annual international computer software and applications conference (COMPSAC'05) vol 1. IEEE Computer Society, Washington, pp 275–280

Bailey J, Burd E (2007) Towards more mature web maintenance practices for accessibility. In: IEEE workshop on web site evolution, WSE07. IEEE Press, pp 81–87

Benavidez C, Cardoso C, Fernandes J, Gutiérrez y Restrepo E, Gutiérrez H, Martínez-Normand L (2014) Iberoamerican observatory of web accessibility. In: Miesenberger K, Fels D, Archambault D, Peñáz P, Zagler W (eds) Computers helping people with special needs. Springer International Publishing, pp 101–108

Brajnik G (2004) Comparing accessibility evaluation tools: a method for tool effectiveness. Univers Access Inf Soc 3(3):252–263

Brajnik G, Graca S (2018) On accessibility policies for higher education institutions. In: Proceedings of the 15th web for all conference, ACM. https://doi.org/10.1145/3192714.3192833

Brajnik G, Lomuscio R (2007) SAMBA: a semi-automatic method for measuring barriers of accessibility. In: Trewin S, Pontelli E (eds) 9th international ACM SIGACCESS conference on computers and accessibility, ASSETS, Tempe, AZ, ACM Press

Brajnik G, Yesilada Y, Harper S (2011) The expertise effect on web accessibility evaluation methods. Hum Comput Interact 26(3):246–283

BS and ISO (2011) Systems and software engineering systems and software quality requirements and evaluation (square) system and software quality models - BS ISO/IEC 25010:2011

Bühler C, Heck H, Perlick O, Nietzio A, Ullveit-Moe, N (2006) Interpreting results from large scale automatic evaluation of web accessibility. In: Computers helping people with special needs, ICCHP06, LNCS 4061. Springer, pp 184–191

Eraslan S, Bailey C (2018) End user evaluations. In: Yesilada Y, Harper S (eds) Web accessibility. Springer. This volume

European Parliament (2016) Directive (eu) 2016/2102 of the European parliament and of the council of 26 October 2016 on the accessibility of the websites and mobile applications of public sector bodies. https://eur-lex.europa.eu/legal-content/EN/TXT/?uri=uriserv:OJ.L_.2016.327.01.0001. 01.ENG

Fernandes J, Benavidez C (2011) A zero in echecker equals a 10 in examinator: a comparison between two metrics by their scores. In: Connor JO, Vigo M, Brajnik G (eds) W3C symposium on website accessibility metrics, page article 8

Fukuda K, Saito S, Takagi H, Asakawa C (2005) Proposing new metrics to evaluate web usability for the blind. In: Extended abstracts of proceedings of the SIGCHI conference on human factors in computing systems, CHI'05. ACM Press, pp 1387–1390

G3ict (2016) Convention on the rights of persons with disabilties - 2016 ICT accessibility progress report. Technical report, G3ict. www.g3ict.org

Gambino O, Pirrone R, Di Giorgio F (2016) Accessibility of the italian institutional web pages: a survey on the compliance of the italian public administration web pages to the stanca act and its 22 technical requirements for web accessibility. Univers Access Inf Soc 15(2):305–312 Jun

González J, Macías M, Rodríguez R, Sànchez F (2003) Accessibility metrics of web pages for blind end–users. In: Cueva Lovelle JM et al (ed) Web engineering, number 2722 in Lecture notes in computer science. Springer, pp 661–707

Hackett S, Parmanto B, Zeng X (2004) Accessibility of internet web sites through time. In: Proceedings of ACM SIGACCESS conference on computers and accessibility. ACM Press, pp 32–39

Hanson VL, Richards JT (2013) Progress on website accessibility? ACM Trans Web 7(1). https://doi.org/10.1145/2435215.2435217

Ismailova R (2017) Web site accessibility, usability and security: a survey of government web sites in Kyrgyz Republic. Univers Access Inf Soc 16(1):257–264

Ivory MY, Yu S, Gronemyer K (2004) Search result exploration: a preliminary study of blind and sighted users' decision making and performance. In: CHI '04 extended abstracts on human factors in computing systems, CHI EA '04. ACM, New York, pp 1453–1456

Lopes R, Carriço L (2008) The impact of accessibility assessment in macro scale universal usability studies of the web. In: International cross-disciplinary conference on web accessibility, W4A08. ACM Press, pp 5–14

Lorca P, de Andrés J, Belén Martínez A (2016) Does web accessibility differ among banks? World Wide Web 19:351–373. https://doi.org/10.1007/s11280-014-0314-0

Mich L, Franch M, Gaio L (2003) Evaluating and designing web site quality. IEEE MultiMed 10(1):34–43

Mucha J, Snaprud M, Nietzio A (2016) Web page clustering for more efficient website accessibility evaluations. In: Miesenberger K, Bühler C, Penaz P (eds) Computers helping people with special needs. Springer International Publishing, Cham, pp 259–266

Nietzio A, Eibegger M, Goodwin M, Snaprud M (2011) Towards a score function for wcag 2.0 benchmarking. In: Connor JO, Vigo M, Brajnik G (eds) W3C symposium on website accessibility metrics, page article 11

Nurmela K, Pirhonen A, Salminen A (2013) Accessibility of public web services: a distant dream? In: INTERACT 2013. IFIP international federation for information processing

Ochoa RL, Crovi DM (2018) Evaluation of accessibility in mexican cybermedia. Univers Access Inf Soc

Olsina L, Rossi G (2002) Measuring web application quality with WebQEM. IEEE Multimed 9(4):20–29

Olsina L, Papa F, Molina H (2008) How to measure and evaluate web applications in a consistent way. Springer, London, pp 385–420

Power C, Petrie H (2018) Working with participants. In: Yesilada Y, Harper S (eds) Web accessibility. Springer. This volume

Sirithumgul P, Suchato A, Punyabukkana P (2009) Quantitative evaluation for web accessibility with respect to disabled groups. In: International cross-disciplinary conference on web accessibility, W4A09. ACM Press, pp 136–141

Song S, Wang C, Li L, Yu Z, Lin X, Bu J (2017) WAEM: a web accessibility evaluation metric based on partial user experience order. In: Proceedings of the 14th web for all conference. ACM, 21 p

Song S, Bu J, Shen C, Artmeier A, Yu Z, Zhou Q (2018a) Reliability aware web accessibility experience metric. In: Proceedings of the 15th web for all conference, ACM. https://doi.org/10.1145/3192714.3192836

Song S, Bu J, Wang Y, Yu Z, Artmeier A, Dai L, Wang C (2018b) Web accessibility evaluation in a crowdsourcing-based system with expertise-based decision strategy. In: Proceedings of the 15th web for all conference, ACM. https://doi.org/10.1145/3192714.3192827

Sullivan T, Matson R (2000) Barriers to use: usability and content accessibility on the web's most popular sites. In: Proceedings of the 2000 conference on universal usability, CUU '00. ACM, New York, pp 139–144

Takagi H, Kawanaka S, Kobayashi M, Sato D, Asakawa C (2009) Collaborative web accessibility improvement: challenges and possibilities. In: Proceedings of the 11th international ACM SIGACCESS conference on Computers and accessibility, Assets '09. ACM, New York, pp 195–202

Velleman E, Strobbe C, Koch J, Velasco CA, Snaprud M, Nietzio A (2007) D-WAB4: unified web evaluation methodology (UWEM)1.2. Technical report, WAB Cluster

Vigo M, Brajnik G (2011) Automatic web accessibility metrics: where we are and where we can go. Interact Comput 23(2):137–155

Vigo M, Harper S (2013) Evaluating accessibility-in-use. In: Proceedings of the 10th international cross-disciplinary conference on web accessibility, W4A '13. ACM, New York, pp 7:1–7:4

Vigo M, Arrue M, Brajnik G, Lomuscio R, Abascal J (2007) Quantitative metrics for measuring web accessibility. In: W4A '07: proceedings of the 2007 international cross-disciplinary workshop on web accessibility (W4A). ACM Press, New York, pp 99–107

Vigo M, Brown J, Conway V (2013) Benchmarking web accessibility evaluation tools: measuring the harm of sole reliance on automated tests. In: Proceedings of the 10th international cross-disciplinary conference on web accessibility, W4A '13. ACM, New York, pp 1:1–1:10

Wentz B, Pham D, Feaser E, Smith D, Smith J, Wilson A (2018) Documenting the accessibility of 100 US bank and finance websites. Univers Access Inf Soc

Zeng X (2004) Evaluation and enhancement of web content accessibility for persons with disabilities. Ph.D. thesis, University of Pittsburgh

Zhang M, Wang C, Bu J, Yu Z, Lu Y, Zhang R, Chen C (2015) An optimal sampling method for web accessibility quantitative metric. In: Proceedings of the 12th web for all conference, ACM. https://doi.org/10.1145/2745555.2746663

Chapter 28
Tools and Applications for Cognitive Accessibility

K. Miesenberger, C. Edler, P. Heumader and A. Petz

Abstract Cognitive Accessibility is an important aspect of Web accessibility addressing a considerably large number of users and showing a high impact on general usability. Cognitive accessibility has been on the agenda in Web accessibility since its beginning but the body of R&D is much smaller and also guidelines, standards, techniques, and tools are vaguer as well as addressed at a lower priority. The recent focus on cognitive accessibility in W3C/WAI changes the situation. This chapter discusses the state of the art and the different domains, where R&D is needed for guidelines and standards, inclusion and participation of end users, take-up of the digital potential in service provision and new tool development based on user tracking/understanding and Artificial Intelligence (AI). We conclude by proposing a new concept of user involvement and a framework for R&D supporting the integration of profiling, annotating, adapting and translating content for personalized Cognitive Accessibility and using/adapting proven and stable HCI concepts.

28.1 Introduction and Challenge

Assistive Technology (AT) and accessibility of digital systems and services and in particular the Web, which becomes the common access point to all systems and services, is key for easier and better communication and participation in the digital society for People with Disabilities (PwD). As the W3C Web Accessibility Initiative (WAI) states: "The Web is increasingly an essential resource for many aspects of

K. Miesenberger (✉) · P. Heumader · A. Petz
Johannes Kepler University Linz, Linz, Austria
e-mail: klaus.miesenberger@jku.at

P. Heumader
e-mail: peter.heumader@jku.at

A. Petz
e-mail: andrea.petz@jku.at

C. Edler
Technical University Dortmund, Dortmund, Germany
e-mail: cordula.edler@icloud.com

© Springer-Verlag London Ltd., part of Springer Nature 2019   523
Y. Yesilada and S. Harper (eds.), *Web Accessibility*, Human–Computer
Interaction Series, https://doi.org/10.1007/978-1-4471-7440-0_28

life: education, employment, government, commerce, health care, recreation, social interaction, and more. The Web is used not only for receiving information, but also for providing information and interacting with society. Therefore, it is essential that the Web be accessible in order to provide equal access and equal opportunity to people with disabilities" (W3C/WAI 2018). People who cannot use the common Web interfaces will have an increased feeling of being alienated.

Progress can be seen in making the Web accessible for people with sensory and motor disabilities. The principles of perceiving and operating with content in alternative and accessible ways are well understood. Guidelines, techniques, and tools are at hand for evaluating accessibility and supporting developing more accessible systems and services. This allows efficient use of assistive functionalities already integrated into mainstream end user tools as well as connecting personal Assistive Technologies (ATs). Despite seeing the fast-growing potential of ICT and the Web for people with disabilities, it is evident, that this potential is widely unused due to lacking AT and accessibility implementation, what leads to an increased digital divide. But the field can make use of globally accepted strategies, standards, and resources developed by and in cooperation with W3C/WAI to make the Web accessible to people with disabilities, what includes also pushing social, economic, and legal actions.

The situation is considerably different for cognitive accessibility. Cognitive access goes beyond getting hold of the content in terms of sensory perception and physical interaction, what might not be the issue for people with cognitive disabilities or might be only a part of the challenge. Cognition demands for decoding, processing, understanding of content perceived, and making it part of a mental structure to allow becoming active and participating (Rumelhardt 2017). Of course, as we will outline, methods, technique and digital tools/ATs have been developed for cognitive support. But in many aspects and in contrary to other groups of people with disabilities, these services are much less general and most often go beyond what can be expected from mainstream web design, development and content authoring (WebAIM 2016).

This is also reflected in the fact, that cognitive accessibility is not accordingly defined in measurable criteria in the valid Web Content Accessibility Guidelines WCAG2.0 (W3C/WAI/WCAG2.0 2018). Only recently efforts for WCAG2.1 (W3C/WAI/WCAG2.1 2018), in particular by the Cognitive Accessibility Group (W3C/WAI/COGA 2017), focus on cognitive accessibility by providing more measurable success criteria and in particular semantic enrichment for personalization of content to support cognitive accessibility. Also, here it becomes evident and challenging that cognitive accessibility in many aspects is part of individual service provision by closely related people and specialist developing and adapting content for very personal skills, communication cultures, and knowledge spaces. Making digital content accessible as well as using ATs has to respect this personal sphere and integrate into established service frameworks to exploit its potential. Requirements, concepts, and techniques to support understanding and processing content are much less uniform and might differ inside the target group, from organization to organization, person to person, and situation to situation (Matausch et al. 2010).

Individual skills and know-how based on a personal learning and support history, which is embedded in often difficult socio-psychological settings, tend to a much more diverse and difficult set of requirements which are much harder to capture for general mainstream design, development, and content authoring requirements. A user and situation centered approach to cognitive accessibility and support for better understanding, navigating, using, and interacting with digital content, therefore, has to take at least three aspects or better levels into account, which have to work together:

a. The level of general mainstream.
   This level comprises general mainstream design, development, and content authoring guidelines, methods, techniques, and tools for translations into concepts as, e.g., Plain Language (e.g., PLAIN 2011) or Easy to Read (e.g., Inclusion Europe 2016; IFLA 2010) including aspects of annotation or translation with symbols and pictures to improve general legibility, readability, and usability.
   WCAG 2.1 and general Web Usability trends let us expect a new level of requirements in terms of legibility, readability, and understandability as well as semantic enrichment to make content machine understandable for new ATs (supported/automated services) for personalized accessibility and usability.
b. The level and process of personalized services and support in changing contexts.
   This level is of importance because "general cognitive accessibility" is still perceived as "one size fits it all" and neither specific enough nor sufficient for the majority of users with cognitive disabilities (Edler and Weber 2010; Matausch and Peböck 2010; Miesenberger 2014).
c. The level of ATs to (re)present and tools for support or automation of the generation, enrichment, or translation of the above aspects/levels.
   New AI-based technologies and approaches to track, monitor, and translate individual requirements into machine-understandable profiles for content adaptation will allow supporting and automating cognitive accessibility at all levels (Miesenberger 2014a).

To address these levels in R&D we start with an overview on the considerable diversity and size of the target group (2) followed by the presentation and discussion of the state of the art in service provision (3) as well as in digitization and AT for better cognitive accessibility (4).

Additionally, we will look into the ongoing work on guidelines, standards, techniques, and tools (WCAG 2.0, WCAG 2.1) for Cognitive Accessibility and related content personalization (5). In (6), we will give a specific focus on user involvement and participatory approaches (IPAR-UCD) for eliciting personal requirements in individual service contexts. This all together forms the base for (7), the discussion of a possible innovative R&D framework for supporting and automating Cognitive Accessibility called "EasyReading", which integrates ICT tools for tracking the cognitive status of the user, profiling for more personalized ATs for translation into Plain Language, Easy to Read or Symbol Languages or content annotation/enrichment (for e.g., symbols, images, videos).

This R&D framework allows users to work independently with original content. We propose IPAR-UCD and EasyReading as best practice examples for the way forward in R&D for improving Cognitive Accessibility.

A critical reflection and conclusions on the subject area and the presented research and development activities (8) finishes this part.

28.2 Cognitive Accessibility: Who Is It?

For a definition of the target group, we can build on and refer to the International Classification of Functioning, Disability and Health of the World Health Organization (WHODAS 2001) and the definition of intellectual disabilities of the American Association of Intellectual and Developmental Disabilities (AAIDD 2010). This includes people with disorders or functional problems related to memory, problem-solving, attention/awareness, reading, writing, and graphical comprehension with the consequence of decreased participation (W3C/WAI 2012a). This broad variety of reasons leading to reduced reading, understanding, and working skills on the Web includes (WebAim 2013)[1]:

People with cognitive disabilities related to functionality such as

- Intellectual disabilities including memory/problem-solving (conceptualizing, planning, sequencing, reasoning and judging thoughts and actions).
- Attention (Attention Deficit/Hyperactivity Disorder—ADHD), awareness.
- Reading, linguistic, verbal comprehension (e.g., Dyslexia dyscalculia).
- Developmental disorder.
- Autism Spectrum Disorders (ASD), High Functioning Autism (HFA, e.g., Asperger's Syndrome).
- Mental health disorders.
- People with low language skills and not fluent in a language.
- People with auditory disabilities affecting reading/using written content.

Statistics (WHO 2001) let us estimate that the group of people with cognitive disabilities is as big as 1–3% of the population. Formal and informal services providers, relatives and friends, doctors/clinicians, cognitive psychologists, therapists, and educators also have to be considered as users benefiting from R&D, techniques and tools for making content cognitive accessible for their daily tasks.

And the number of end users which can benefit from better cognitive accessibility is much bigger as studies outline for selected regions and countries: 25% of adults do not reach the level of literacy and reading skills expected after 9 years of formal education; in some countries, this figure is as high as 40–50%. In particular, the aging of society underlines the need for cognitive accessibility (W3C/WAI/COGA 2017). These user groups include people with migration background and those with considerable disadvantages in education. We should consider including also situational and contextual use of content in globalized settings demanding for information that is usable and readable cross-borders and cultures as well as understood by the biggest

---

[1]Chapter 5 discusses definition approaches of cognitive disabilities and in particular the social situation of people with cognitive disabilities.

possible user group with many nonnative users. Finally, the aging population, as aging is closely related to disabilities, and users with low digital literacy are major groups benefiting from better readability and understandablity. This lets us underline that the target group of cognitive accessibility and the return of investment is most often underestimated.

Therefore, Cognitive Accessibility significantly contributes to a more general improvement of usability in terms of "the extent to which a product can be used by specified users to achieve their goals with effectiveness, efficiency, and satisfaction in a specified context of use" by supporting learnability, memorability, error prevention and handling, trust, and satisfaction (ISO 2010). The more ICT and the Web become a part of everyday lives the bigger the impact of usability and Cognitive Accessibility will be.

The striking advantage of this (W3C) definition and approach is the fact that—if understood, followed, and implemented correctly—the above classification(s) become obsolete and superfluous by changing the focus from (different levels of) disability to a generally enhanced usability by personalization—independent from a disability. This would also affect and in best case change the widespread need for "objectivatisation by measurement and quantification" to be seen in today's research and development frameworks. By its non-reflected use, this classification provides an "easy way" to discuss *about* people with disabilities and on how to support them—a passive process for the intended target group—and last but not least keeps people and society far away from recognizing the fact that everybody—independently from a potential (cognitive) disability benefits from information, documents, and websites that are consistently structured, follow an idiomatic "golden thread", are easily perceived and written in a way that eases understanding without being bored nor feeling offended by the used language level, e.g., supported by technology that is only to be seen in case needed, adapts to different competence and learning levels and provides individualized access to information.

This interpretation—together with adequate technology and framework—has the potential to serve and equally empower the biggest possible user group independent understanding, learning, discussing, and working with the same materials instead of keeping some of them by definition/categorization at a standardized (lower) level and in extreme cases completely away from the digital original.

The majority of users acts as a consumer and at the same time provider/author of information, independently from a possible (cognitive) disability. This makes it necessary that the rules and guidelines to be followed are presented and implemented in a way that can be understood and used by everyone, including people with an above categorized "cognitive disability".

This leads by itself either to a deadlock with discrimination and exclusion, puts (via legal regulations deriving from pure rules and guidelines) additional workload and needed efforts to developers and content providers which ultimately results in costs for experts/institutions working afterward on implementing the asked level of accessibility—OR—to a combination of ICT and automated technological tools that keep developers and content providers from dealing with language levels and reading skills by understanding basic levels and presenting information at an individualized level with individualized support (enrichment, annotation, translation) for everyone, a decoupling of "syntax from semantics"—what we already were able to observe in parts with the implementation of CSS.

The formal translation and adaptation of information into Easy To Read (E2R) as well as individualized personal assistance with surfing the web and using information will be needed nevertheless, but the threshold to self dependently be part of the "same community" will be significantly lower and the output in information significantly higher in quality and quantity.

28.3 Cognitive Accessibility: Practice and Service Provision

W3C/WAI underlines that people with cognitive disabilities need adapted and personalized content that suits specific needs, rather than just content with a very general reduced reading complexity (Miesenberger 2014a). But what is to be used for whom in what situation varies a lot—and is even more scattered when it comes to the roles the players in this field have and the question who should be responsible for (what part of) "cognitive accessibility".

Accordingly broad is the actual practice. The state of the art in service provision for cognitive accessibility, both at the level of mainstream design, development, and content authoring as well as specialized service provision by experts for cognitive disabilities, refers to the concepts as Plain Language and Easy to Read. Both origin from very practical demands before becoming subject of the R&D field of Cognitive Accessibility. Both are techniques to improve legibility, readability, and usability of content and are not own languages with own grammatical structures. The guidelines and techniques address the way of using the respective language (IFLA 2018a).

Plain Language (PLAIN 2011) is a professional reaction, in particular by the public sector, to the outlined low literacy level in society—or better to the level and excessive use of needed (?) legal jargon in the communication between public administration and citizens. To improve the quality of services for citizens but also to support efficiency and effectiveness of public services provision a general focus on understandability became indispensable. The guidelines address demands and known issues in design, development, and content authoring.

Easy to Read (Inclusion Europe 2016; IFLA 2010) also started as a practical approach to support cognitive accessibility and provides sets of guidelines and techniques on how to design, develop, and in particular rework content to provide access for very specific target groups (Bock and Lange 2015; Netzwerk Leichte Sprache 2014). The main driving force has been more the support of service provision for personalized access for users with cognitive disabilities connecting with and participating in the translation process to guarantee that requirements are met.

Both concepts first of all not only address wording and language use but also encourage to use other media to support understandability—and read sometimes as if the result of following those concepts would be diametrically opposed to effective W3C guidelines for accessible web design (see Chaps. 14 and 17):

- **Language use**:
Easy Read formats are aimed at adults and should not be childish/cartoon-like in applying guidelines:

  - Explain the concept and define purpose.
  - Include only important and directly relevant information.
  - Write using clear text—"plain language".
  - Use a minimum of 16 points for body text.
  - Use active, not passive form: Make it personal.
  - Keep sentences short—20 words maximum.
  - Break up text with bullet points.
  - Use fact boxes to explain complex terms.
  - List the boxed words at the back of the document.
  - Do not use abstract terms.
  - Use humor but only if appropriate.
  - Do not use acronyms—spell words out in full.
  - Do not use jargon.
  - Annotate and include pictures, graphics, and symbols.

- **Images**:
Used the right way, pictures, and/or symbols can be very powerful in supporting the text and by making content easier to understand.

  - Use images to support words.
  - Use the correct image in the correct place.
  - Images should be easy to understand—keep as clear and simple as possible.
  - Only show one idea at a time.
  - Use pictures to illustrate the most important points—not all text will need an image next to it.
  - Do not use abstract images.
  - Think about combining photographs and images.
  - Use images that represent your audience and that they can relate to.
  - Drawings are better than photographs at showing a single concept or a key message.
  - Keep the image on a clear background so it is easy to see.

- **Audio and Video**:
Audio and Video are a helpful support/alternative for those having problems in understanding written text with or without supplementing symbols/pictures. The materials should also be short, clear and to the point.
- **Design and Process**:

  - Include end users in design, development, and testing.
  - Use appropriate e2r design methods.

Even if the core principles of Easy to Read and Plain Language are similar, there is a difference in the target group where Easy to Read also aims at higher levels of cognitive constraints demanding for alternative methods, techniques and tools (e.g., Symbol Languages, using cards or personal pictures, techniques known from Augmentative and Alternative Communication—AAC). Easy to Read is, therefore, no general solution but a solution for specified, individual groups. Providing specific or even personalized alternatives is seen as a key factor also for motivation and personal learning and development for such groups (Matausch-Mahr 2017).

Both approaches focus on the process and workflow of content creation or reworking. They integrate the definition of the intended target group and their involvement to allow elicitation of personal requirements (and not estimations about them), use guidelines and tools (e.g., WCAG, ATAG, UAAG, Plain Language, Easy to Read) and user testing as part of the process of sequential or parallel design, development, and content authoring. They discuss aspects of education, training and the involvement of external experts in design, development, and content authoring (e.g., Matausch et al. 2012).

More recent developments propose to respect different levels of language use when defining and implementing Easy to Read. E.g., the Capito-Method (CFS—Consulting, Franchise and Sales 2018; Gross 2015; Fröhlich 2015), developed by a group of service organizations with a practical background and an extensive experience in writing and formatting information for people with cognitive disabilities. The Capito-Method defines about 170 criteria grouped into three literacy levels oriented at the CEFR, the "Common European Framework of Reference" for Languages (Council of Europe 2001). Based on this, it provides a quality standard to orient toward and to be used. Besides text, it includes aspects of general media accessibility known from WCAG.

Critical reflections of the state of the art (e.g., W3C/WAI 2012a; Maaß 2015; Jekat et al. 2015; Seitz 2014) led to renewed practices as the above. Reflections and evident deficits to be considered as key research questions are

- Lack in the theoretical foundation of practices and approaches.
- Stigmatizing effects of special annotation, adaptation, and translation.
- A stabilization of institutionalized settings due to (re)establishing dependencies due to the use of a language specific to contexts and organizations.
- The fixation on the "written only" use of language.
- The lack in respecting the users' individual knowledge and development/training/raised skills.
- The separation of users from the (digital) original content leading to limited possibilities of mastering content independently and of individual learning—practice tends to develop own language spaces with segregating and already mentioned institutionalizing effects.

The mentioned orientation towards more measureable guidelines, process orientation and user involvement and this critical reflection outline that R&D for advancement is therefore needed in

(a)   Assessing the actual goals, skills, and requirements ("profiling") for,
(b)   Selecting the most appropriate cognitive support and training, and
(c)   Making (personal, responsive) tools available to changing contexts for a more efficient design, development, and content authoring practice both at mainstream and specialized service level.

This also underlines that users with cognitive disabilities and their services have a strong need for personalization of presentation and interaction and benefit most from an individual selection and combination of features, tools, and services and adaptation/recombination of services in changing contexts—as everybody else in mainstream uses a changing mixture of books/www/Wikipedia, YouTube or, for e.g., asking a friend for finding out how to solve an issue.

28.4   Digitization and Assistive Technology in Cognitive Accessibility

Over decades a comprehensive apparatus of concepts, methods, techniques, and tools to support people with cognitive disabilities has been developed, mostly in settings for (medical) diagnosis, therapy, education, training, and daily living support services. They all provide important and useful features and potential for improving cognitive accessibility and for supporting services as mentioned above. We list some here and refer to more in-depth analysis and discussions:

- **Plain Language and Easy to Read Tools**: Linguistics, language technology, and Natural Language Processing (NLP) research grammar and style-checking for what is sometimes called Controlled Language) (McCarthy 2011; Fuchs 2010), translation (Chiang 2012), annotation and enhancement (Nikolova et al. 2011) and summarizing (Hovey 2005; Nenkova and McKeown 2012). First solutions merit attention for integration into Cognitive Accessibility frameworks.
- **Technical Writing**: Markel (2012) focuses on strict language rules for usability and applicability, often enforced by legal requirements, and due to globalization on text production that is suitable for (semi-)automated translations (e.g., to avoid figurative language and ambiguities). These approaches are of particular interest for R&D as according to market studies (e.g., Liesem 2011) everyday content of product descriptions, press handouts, and emails from computer and software companies were difficult to understand by most people.
- **Annotating Content with Alternative Expressions, Images and Multimedia** (e.g., explorative text, symbols, pictures, graphs, animations, videos), in particular, used and based on R&D for speech disabilities and Augmentative and Alternative Communication (AAC) (e.g. ISAAC 2018; Fager 2012) are a valuable source for supporting cognitive accessibility. This also includes research related to Natural Language Processing for automatic annotations.
- **Text to Speech/Speech to Text:** Switching from written format to audio or vice versa or using both formats in parallel is beneficial for many users with cognitive

disabilities (e.g., Raskind 1998). R&D of such tools, e.g., speech synthesis and speech recognition, progressed over the last years and became common on computers and mobile devices. Tools or specific functionalities like a screen reader, speech output, screen enlargement, and systems for multimedia access to digital content as the Digital Accessible Information SYstem (DAISY 2018) are to be analyzed for cognitive accessibility.

- **Captioning**: Captioning is used for people not speaking the language in use, for hearing impaired and deaf people or for blind and visually impaired people ("audio description"). Techniques, services, and know-how in designing captions for different target audiences are of particular interest for cognitive accessibility (e.g., Media Access Group 2014).
- **Adaptability of Structure and Layout**: This issue has been high on the agenda since long (e.g., in WCAG) and many aspects entered mainstream due to the demand for responsive design (Jiang 2014)—in particular, related to device independence and usability (e.g., Mohorovici 2013).

Other supportive functionalities and tools of interest to be analyzed include

- **Memory support** (recorder, collections such as dictionaries, wikis, and marker),
- **Conceptualizing and problem-solving** (forms, mind maps, templates, concept tools, summarizing tools, tables of content, lists)
- **Tools for workflow support** and **mind mapping** (for e.g., daily living, job)
- **Focused attention and motivation tools**
- **Tools for text and information production**: recording, editing, speech/handwriting recognition, spelling/grammar checkers, word/concept prediction, predictive typing
- **Alternative input devices**: adaptive/onscreen keyboards, touch devices, switch interaction, scanning interfaces.

This description and analysis clearly show that many tools and ATs are available but usage is not sufficiently/efficiently integrated into workflows and service infrastructures. It furthermore underlines the lack and need to focus on personalization of presentation and interaction with close contact to the (digital) original. Users with cognitive disabilities benefit most from an individualized selection and mix of features, tools, and services—not only in changing contexts.

To come back to the discussion on roles and responsibilities from the beginning of this part, most individuals do (per se) not need all information in Easy to Read what is a sine qua non for a known and specific target group using specific services and elements of personal assistance.

Consequently, the responsibility for providing materials in fully blown Easy to Read is not well allocated with "All content providers"—and not even in the case of Plain Language the general audience is able to comply to all rules.

But every content provider should and must be asked to deliver information in a way and supported by tools that take care for structuring, wording, and a common language level adapted to be understood also by machines and automated tools providing enrichment, annotation and translation. Therefore not only users, but also designers, developers, content authors, and service providers benefit most from tools supporting personalized approaches at all parts of the "value chain".

28.5 Guidelines, Standards, and Techniques for Cognitive Accessibility

As outlined, for a long time the primary focus in accessibility has been on *perceiving* (alternatives for vision and auditory disabilities) and *handling* (motor/mobility disabilities) digital content and interaction. Cognitive accessibility has played only a minor role in these developments. According to the WebAIM (2016), cognitive disability has been for long the least studied, understood, and discussed type of disability among Web developers. As also outlined it makes the situation even more complex, that many cognitive disabilities are difficult to diagnose and characterize because of the diversity in categorizing the characteristics of people with even similar forms of cognitive disabilities.

Although accessibility issues arising from cognitive constraints are a topic in recommendations, guidelines, standards, and even legislation, the actual implementation of Cognitive Accessibility is still lagging (e.g., Miesenberger 2014, Chaps. 14 and 17). This is partly a result of social and educational traditions and practices which exclude or do not focus on accessibility and AT; some developers are also hesitant or even reluctant to implement independent and user-driven participation (e.g., W3C/WAI 2012a, b; Schluchter 2010; Müller 2013; Edler 2015). Another aspect keeping Cognitive Accessibility from the mainstream is due to the outlined fact, that it goes way beyond perceptive and operational accessibility which is easier to measure and support by ICT/AT. Cognitive Accessibility requires more personal support for presentation, decomposition of complexity, amendment, and explanation of content (e.g., Borg 2015; Blanck 2014).

As a consequence, guidelines, standards, techniques, and tools on cognitive accessibility or understandability are still vague what impacts on practice as designers and developers might be confronted with unrealistic expectations as, for e.g., providing personalized content in Easy to Read or even with symbol annotations, what is much more a task for professional educators and service providers. It is still rather unclear what is to be done by (a) mainstream designers, developer, and content providers, by (b) ATs and tools, and (c) by service providers or care givers (Miesenberger 2014).

The World Wide Web Consortium (W3C) Web Accessibility Initiative (WAI) develops and maintains guidelines that are internationally recognized as the standard for Web accessibility: The Web Content Accessibility Guidelines (WCAG 2.0), also available as ISO/IEC 40500: 2012, are the most valuable starting point for better Web accessibility outlining 12 guidelines, which are organized around 4 principles of Web accessibility: perceptibility, operability, understandability, and robustness. Each guideline has a set of constituent success criteria, each given a priority level (A, AA, AAA).

Understandability is a principle with success criteria focusing on readability/understandability, predictable design and behavior and avoiding/recovering from errors. This establishes a close relation to concepts as Plain Language and Easy to Read. Also other criteria such as under the principle of operability the guideline "control of time limits" (2.2, becoming more specified within WCAG 2.1 as Guideline 2.2.6 on "Timeouts" (level AAA)) and "supporting orientation/navigation by structure" (2.4) contribute to cognitive accessibility. But in terms of measurable success criteria for readability and understandability, they stay rather vague. In relation to the three levels of Cognitive Accessibility outlined, it is unclear where to allocate tasks and responsibilities between designers, developers, content authors and AT and service providers. There is no support in recommending or defining responsibilities in the process of personalized access to content. More guidance would be needed for the different stakeholder groups. And most importantly all of the elements addressing cognitive disabilities in WCAG2.0 were assigned with lower priority making them broadly ignored in practice (e.g., Grotlüschen 2011). This outlines an extended R&D agenda for better integrating Cognitive Accessibility into Web Accessibility.

In other W3C/WAI guidelines, which reach much less attention in the accessibility discourse, as the User Agent Accessibility Guidelines (W3C/WAI/UAAG), the Authoring Tool Accessibility Guidelines (W3C/WAI/ATAG), and the Accessible Rich Internet Applications (W3C/WAI/ARIA) we can find a very similar situation when it comes to cognitive accessibility.

WCAG2.0 was updated by W3C/WAI to version 2.1 with a clear focus on improving the standard for people with cognitive and learning disabilities amongst other goals as more clear guidelines for low vision and updating for mobile accessibility. "Easy to Read on the Web" (Miesenberger and Petz 2014a) and the Cognitive and Learning Accessibility Task Force (COGA) founded in 2013 propose a roadmap for better accessibility and usability of Web content for users with cognitive disabilities (W3C/WAI/COGA 2017, 2018a, b, c) and propose changes to existing and new success criteria. This includes

- Including semantics, symbols, and personalization for presenting information in different ways (1.3).
- Providing enough time and (few exceptions) (2.2).
- Using measures to avoid misuse of personal data and making sure that data are used only in case of informed consent.
- Hinder harmful and unsafe mechanisms such as selling products (2.3).
- Using a clear (easy to read oriented) writing style for instructions, labels, navigation, and important information (3.1).
- A new guideline in WCAG 2.1 under 3.4 to

  - use an easy to read oriented layout (color, size, spacing, positioning, symbol support).
  - using manageable small, stepwise chunks of information for text and other media.

- Emphasizing a clear and understandable layout and a consistent style for the same information and controls and that the purpose of a page and section which is obvious for all users and extraneous information is separated. This will impact on different language skills, memory, attention, focus, and executive functions (3.2.4).
- Emphasizing caution when requiring additional skills as for managing captchas and avoid or help to restore when getting lost (3.2.4).
- Indicate success or failure for all actions, avoid mistakes, and help to restore from mistakes based on easy to read feedback and finding mistakes.
- Proposing higher levels for success criteria (A, AA, AAA) for issues related to cognitive accessibility to increase impact, awareness, and enforcement at legal level.
- The work is accompanied by studies and experimenting how AI could help improving accessibility in relation to automation of support features for accessibility based on user tracking and understanding in changing contexts (e.g., Abou-Zahra et al. 2018).

This identifies a strong need for ongoing and enforced support of the work on Cognitive Accessibility in the W3C/WAI context. Even if still vague and hard to measure in many aspects, there is a strong need for R&D and we expect considerable steps forward both in design, development, and authoring of content as well as ATs for automation/support of making content cognitive accessible.

28.6   Discussion of the State of the Art

With the focus on Cognitive Accessibility in WCAG 2.1 a very positive global shift of efforts to close the gap in supporting users with cognitive disabilities can be identified. The discussions underline the complexity of Cognitive Accessibility by going beyond sensory presentation and motoric interaction. This raises the awareness that Cognitive Accessibility can't be expected as an issue which could be "solved" by design/development/content authoring as it is done for perceiving and operating content. User and situational requirements are much more diverse that a "one size fits it all" approach could work. Seeing the actual problems in the implementation of accessibility at very basic sensory and operational level let us expect that Cognitive Accessibility, implemented in the way as it is in WCAG 2.0, would overload design/development/content authoring and would neglect the key aspect of cognitive disabilities which in many aspects demand for human and personal services to access and participate in content, interaction, and communication.

Thinking, researching, planning, supporting, and implementing Cognitive Accessibility at least at the three levels mentioned in the introduction is, therefore, indispensable: (a) Design/development/authoring has to provide semantic-rich content, which is machine readable and automatable for personalization and content adaptation/annotation/translation. As this is a key asset for improving usability in general, we expect Cognitive Accessibility to be part of and based on a next level of personal Web usability. (b) Service practice has to take up the potential of digital technology in service and care provision with the goal of independent access to as much as possible original content. Making digital tools and content/tool personalization part of therapy, training, and education is indispensable for improved Cognitive Accessibility and exploiting the digital potential. (c) New AI-based ATs for content adaptation/annotation/translation for Cognitive Accessibility are needed which use tracking and profile building for content adaptation/annotation/translation to integrate the actual and changing status of the user and his service infrastructure. This includes R&D in automated (tracking) but in particular, also IT supported human-supported and -reflected profile building and continuous adaptation for transfer in diverse life context under control of users.

Cognitive Accessibility has to be understood as an ecosystem which includes, professionally develops and seamlessly integrates stakeholder roles at these three levels. This avoids unrealistic expectations from web design/development/authoring. And in particular, it makes uses of the considerably large and powerful field of service provision pushing it to a new level of addressing the ultimate goal of improved independence and self-determined participation when using digital technology. Finally, it also provides an R&D agenda for the AT and service sector aiming at interfaces under control of users, supported by care providers for personal Cognitive Accessibility and based on standardized semantic-rich content. So far there is a lack of definition, guidance and shared responsibilities between these roles.

In addition, core technical challenges lay within the questions of tracking, profile building, and managing, which include aspects of automation and including support of carers. The profile must not only reflect the actual status but must orient towards and support learning and more independence and also cross-organizational transitions from institution to institution, education level to education level, job to job, private activity to private activity.

A key challenge can also be found in the interface design and adaptation. Stable and manageable interaction concepts are needed which allow managing more and more complex content. In the same way, as the success of digital technology in the mainstream is based on stable, ubiquitous and easy to use interaction concepts, the benchmark for R&D is seen if the HCI concepts allow users with cognitive disabilities to more independently and efficiently manage original content to stay with and contribute to mainstream discourses. Traditional content adaptation services as Easy to Read are seen critical as they do not support coping with original content and they develop an own language and interaction style and culture what tends to separate from mainstream discourses. This makes users even more dependent on often not affordable services. Content adaptation/annotation/translation needs to address the challenge of allowing the user to stay in the mainstream discourse. Only when needed, based on observation, tracking, or experiences stored in the profile, content adaptation/annotation/translation should be provided as temporal overlay or alternative. HCI and digital technology do have the power of providing interaction concepts supporting both the needed personalization without losing contact and learning to deal with the original content and staying in mainstream discourses.

This also draws the line for AI-based AT development for Cognitive Accessibility in terms of automated but also supported human-controlled content adaptation/annotation/translation at the original. There is clear evidence about the limits of automated services. But when integrated into the mentioned ecosystem, AT development can rely on extensive corrective factors, both in terms of sensor and AI-based tracking as well as user/service driven adaptation.

Out of the many directions and domains for future R&D, which come up in discussing the state of the art, we select and conclude with two challenges, which are seen as critical to support the work on Cognitive Accessibility in terms of WCAG2.1, new AI-based ATs and accessibility features and service practice: First we address the need for new and better approaches to user involvement at the three levels of roles outlined. What has been a key success factor for accessibility, AT and the inclusion of other groups of people with disabilities is still missing or at very early stages for people with cognitive disabilities. Second, we present a framework for Cognitive Accessibility R&D which allows better mastering the outlined complexity by integrating smaller scaled or bigger work and projects into proven concepts and tools, in particular, based on adaptable HCI concepts.

28.7 Future Direction I: Participatory Approaches to Services, Engineering, and Research for Cognitive Accessibility

Cognitive accessibility demands for personalization to address the changing and diverse personal requirements. The state of the art in service provision, Web Engineering, and content authoring (e.g., Edler 2010; W3C/WAI/Coga 2018a, b, c, Chaps. 10 and 12) underline that a higher level of understandability and usability can be only reached if based on individual user-centered, personal services, and personalization. There is a strong need for methods and tools to better involve users with cognitive disabilities.

User involvement in general, for e.g., in usability or user-centered design and involving users with disabilities, in particular, is a success story and has become an indispensable aspect of accessibility, AT and digital inclusion (e.g., Sharma 2008; Edler 2010; Kwiatowska 2012). Working with intrinsically motivated end users and starting from real user needs instead of assumptions about them has been pushing projects to a much higher level of quality. Cognitive accessibility again is lagging behind due to communication barriers, lack of methods, techniques, and tools for user involvement (Bohman 2016). It is underlined that here R&D works mostly based on expert opinions and a mediated understanding of the user (e.g., Janz 2009). The core demand for participation in all domains related to the users is much less reached for this group (Keates 2003). Recent innovative approaches, pushed by the UN-Convention on the Rights of People with Disabilities (UNCRPD) (United Nations

2006), show potential to help to close this gap. This includes two domains, which are compatible but not yet linked (Bergold 2013; Walmsley 2003):

- Approaches such as Participatory Action Research are used in the practice of social and educational research and do not differ fundamentally from other current social science approaches (e.g., Kemmis 2011). In particular, the same scientific criteria for qualitative research and analytical methods shall be used to evaluate the process and research results. Another quality criterion of integrative research is the complete and high-quality participation of users with cognitive disabilities. The IPAR method is a variant of Participatory Action Research (PAR), which combines the approaches of inclusive and participatory action research. IPAR directly involves people with disabilities (Ollerton 2012) in all steps of action research.
- User-Centered Design (UCD) is a design methodology that puts users in the center of the process. In particular, when it comes to systems and tools for mass-consumer markets the involvement of users at all stages of the process has proven to be essential for better usability and improved product/output quality. Studies underline that reasonable investment in UCD leads to a substantial return in terms of higher efficiency, less maintenance, less complaints, and higher usage/client rates. Also in AT research and Accessibility user involvement at all stages of the engineering process is one of the major guiding principles and a key success factor. Walozek (2004) recommends: "With the ever growing spread of computers into our daily lives, software application design is more and more focusing on untrained and casual users. These users have very different requirements from professional users who for a long time dominated the business scene. Developers need to take this new breed of users seriously and design applications that do not frustrate them."

Such inclusive approaches of course demand for making an extended set of educational, cognitive, psychological, and linguistic know-how available. The even bigger challenge is how to integrate such approaches into the design, development, and content authoring process and establishing the needed communicative and cooperative infrastructure including adapted engineering usability methods. Three levels of user involvement with cognitive disabilities should be considered:

- Of course, it would be ideal that users participated in all phases of the process taking over ownership of the idea and the product under discussion. This seems to be only in reach for the content of core demand and it is to be underlined that up to date also here, in contrary to the other accessibility groups, user involvement is most often not even considered.
- Another participative approach would be contacting/consulting end users at certain points of the process, in particular when requirements, designs, wording, interaction concepts, levels of personalization/adaptation are under discussion or are to be tested in development cycles from low to hi-fi. Also, this will be restricted to domains with a strong interest and support by the group and of course restricts participation considerably.
- For general accessibility involving users with cognitive problems in most cases, besides big and public systems, will be out of reach. But at least methods, tech-

niques, and tools as Personas, Users Stories, or User Simulators might help in raising awareness and guiding the process toward respecting guidelines as WCAG 2.0/2.1. Better, more attractive, easy to access, and well-connected tools and techniques are needed to promote and strengthen the usage at this minimum level of user involvement for better cognitive accessibility. This forms a challenging research agenda, which should use an inclusive setting in itself.

For all participatory approaches, a set of prerequisites has to be put in place to establish a user-centered/oriented design, development, and content authoring context starting from accessible communication and participation infrastructures, for e.g.,:

- Is an appropriate understanding in place how users work with systems and tools, what ATs they might use, what requirements are to be respected in terms of, for e.g., timing and usage of media, ATs or personal assistance?
- Has an appropriate infrastructure for communication been established allowing expressing, discussing, noting, controlling been established?
- Is the topic/system understood as relevant and important for participation; do end users have the possibility to influence topic, goal, and parameters defining the project/activity?
- Do users understand their role and the expected contribution?
- Do users have the feeling that their opinion and know-how is respected and requested at an equal level?

In general, Software/Web/Usability/User Experience Engineering focuses on a UCD process to take the requirements of users in varying contexts into account. This has become a key aspect in engineering and methods/tools are used and researched to efficiently integrate it such as Cognitive Walk-Through, Card Sorting, Personas, User Stories, focus groups, observation, interviews, keyboard/mouse logging, eye tracking (e.g., Kaur 2016). The process of integrating and applying these steps has changed from a more sequential ("waterfall") over incremental ("iterative, spiral") toward dynamic and adaptive ("agile") process models, in particular, to support better addressing usability and UCD. All methods, techniques, and tools have to be reworked and adapted for usage in such inclusive settings (Nind 2013; Strnadova and Cumming 2013; Ollerton 2012).

It is, therefore, recommended that R&D and work on guidelines and practice focus on making these techniques, tools and the engineering process more open for participation of people with cognitive disabilities to make it a guiding principle and common practice in the mainstream, AT development and use as well as service practice (Newell 2000). This should support addressing the challenges of WCAG2.1 in terms of more measurable success criteria, personalization and semantics/AI-based automatization/support of cognitive accessibility. This integrates traditional approaches and expertise as Easy to Read, Plain Language, and symbol systems into an inclusive, personal, and participatory R&D setting in line with the UNCRPD.

Finally, it is to be mentioned that new technologies of user tracking and understanding, also based on AI, should allow new approaches to personalization of content. The base for such solutions is the understanding of the user, his knowledge space and preferences what again asks for user participation. Therefore, the outlined innovative approaches for involving users with cognitive disabilities are fundamental for such new innovative solutions for supported and/or automated personalization based on tracking and understanding the user, what leads us to the final chapter.

28.8   Future Direction II: A Framework for Content Personalisation for Cognitive Accessibility

According to W3C/WAI/COGA (2018a), people with cognitive disabilities need adapted content that suits their specific needs, rather than just content with a very general reduced reading complexity. But what is to be used for whom in what situation varies a lot. A conversion of content into Easy to Read or the use of symbols, for example, might be useful for several users with a cognitive disability but might be rejected by another person. Of course, there are techniques that are helpful for the majority of people with cognitive disabilities like exchanging a difficult to read font for a more readable font. However, as cognitive skills and preferences are very personal a general approach for cognitive accessible webpages and content for the majority of the people is not feasible. Therefore, there is a demand for personalized content and user interfaces that are tailored for the individual user.

As outlined, Cognitive Accessibility demands personal adaptation of content that in many cases goes beyond what can be expected from the mainstream. Cognitive Accessibility, therefore, demands for integrating the stakeholder groups at the levels of designers, developers, and content authors, service provision and AT-tool support. Therefore, a framework or platform for R&D and practice seems to be essential, which allows integrating and cooperation in these diverse and changing contexts.

In this chapter, we bring such an approach into the discussion which is based on work in the EU-funded project EasyReading (2018). EasyReading proposes an integrated research agenda starting from user involvement (see Chap. 7) for design and adaptation of HCI concepts working, user tracking, and profiling (influenced and managed by users and caregivers) over upcoming AI-based content adaptation, annotation, and translation toward personalized access with the ultimate goal to allow users to work more independent with and at the original web content.

Personalization is based on personal data, which are traditionally in the hands of supporting staff or educators. Transferring, modeling, and storing them in a profile is a first R&D challenged to support digital Cognitive Accessibility. An evolving user profile that stores the abilities and preferences (e.g., HCI and interaction concepts or presentation of data and content) of the user as well as the actual status of the user is therefore needed.

User agents and ATs can utilize this profile to adapt Web content to personalize content, structure, and the way the user interacts with content. This adaption and personalization should only be triggered on demand by the actual user. This might trigger a learning effect as the user interacts with the original webpage and not

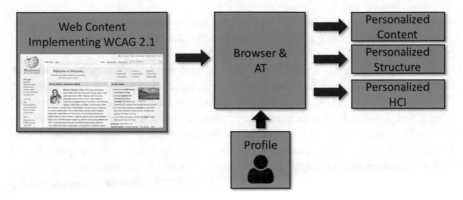

Fig. 28.1 Personalization workflow

with an alternative version of the webpage that is tailored for people with cognitive disabilities.

Figure 28.1 shows the workflow of personalization based on personal profiles, content adaptation/annotation/translation using (upcoming AI based) automated ATs or ICT/AT supported services that can be classified in the following domains:

- Personalized Structure: Structure and layout of Web content can be adjusted for the individual so that it is easier to read and to navigate.
- Personalized Content: Content of webpages can be optimized for the individual user, e.g., by using the appropriate language level, symbol annotation or Text-ToSpeech.
- Personalized HCI: Personalized HCI concepts describe all mechanisms that allow users to operate a computer. This is usually a combination of input through input devices like a mouse and widgets like buttons that can be triggered by the user to interact with the user interface. With personalized HCI complex widgets can be substituted by other widgets that suit the needs and preferences of the individual user.

Current tools and ATs supporting such personalization and simplification did not receive much support from WCAG. This changed now with WCAG 2.1 which focused also more on cognitive accessibility of Web content. Among other improvements two very interesting guidelines that would enable producers of assistive technologies to build better solutions for personalization were developed:

- 1.3.5 Identify Input Purpose Level AA
- 1.3.6 Identify Purpose Level AAA.

These guidelines oblige Web designers/developers/content authors to enrich HTML elements with metadata so that input elements, user interface components, icons, and regions can be programmatically determined. When the intent and meaning of components is known, adaption, personalization, and simplification of content are facilitated. Preferred layouts, stylings but also symbols can be applied to webpages that support these guidelines allowing consistent navigation and look and feel while exploring the Web (W3C/WAI/COGA 2018b).

The EasyReading framework for intelligent, adaptive, and personalized interfaces that allows to combine different sorts of content, structure, and layout simplification for the individual user. Only when adapted and used in practice the actual personalized interaction is put in place, which might need more adaptation at the beginning, but gets reduced over time based on user tracking or by careful intervention as users learn to better cope with the original content. The EasyReading framework integrates tested and proven interface concepts, respects the user's level of understanding, needs, abilities, behaviors, and patterns of emotions in diverse situations based tracking, sensor fusion and reasoning and integrates into real-life environments, allowing the framework to react in a way which really makes a difference.

Thereby EasyReading invites to research and expands in the different domains (interface concepts, tracking, profile building and management, adaptation/annotation/translation of content. Smaller scaled R&D can focus on very specific aspects of Cognitive Accessibility without losing the holistic context for testing, experimenting, and implementing. In particular, the work on guidelines, standards, and techniques gains an operational setting to discuss where to allocate requirements and how to make them operational.

And EasyReading is seen as an important step to better include service practice into the Cognitive Accessibility move. They can start from own specific contexts and use the framework to support and expand services towards the ultimate goal of more independent and inclusive participation. It respects and values individual needs and contexts and provides support for personal care (tools for better service practice in particular with profile and backend for carers). With a strong focus on AT and tool support based on AI for automated content adaptation, annotation and translation it motivates to exploit the potential of digitization.

28.9   Critical Reflection and Conclusions

With no doubt Cognitive Accessibility is most important to overcome still discriminating practice. Additionally, it is obvious that Cognitive Accessibility has the biggest potential in accessibility domain for impacting on better usability in general. As R&D is too fragmented and in many aspects separated from practice, a promising way forward is a more holistic approach, where small-scaled R&D can be based on and integrated into a proven state of the art. Complementing to this, day-to-day practice can use a step-by-step approach toward0. innovation respecting personal and situational requirements.

The discussion on including Cognitive Accessibility into WCAG 2.1 in a better measurable manner needs careful considerations on allocating the requirements to different stakeholders/roles to avoid overload, in particular for the mainstream. We expect extensive support when Cognitive Accessibility is in line with improving general usability through semantics and AI-based functionalities. The considerably big care sector has to play a much more visible role in Cognitive Accessibility both in R&D and practice when including AI-based tools for automated and supported tracking, profiling, and content personalization. And, to close the circle, this must start from semantically rich original contents and by supporting personalization. Therefore, better measurable Cognitive Accessibility can be expected as in line with responsive design that is ready for personalization in general. From here AI-based AT-tool R&D and service practice will reach out to better inclusion, leading to a manageable and beneficial standard in Cognitive Accessibility—way more comprehensive and for sure beyond the "typical" user group(s) one thinks about first.

Progress and success in Cognitive Accessibility are expected, therefore, as a mix of better general usability based on semantic rich personalized content aiming at accessibility and supporting better AI-based user tracking, profiling, and ICT/AT tools. Finally and in particular, we need the involvement and efficient change management in service provision taking over digitization as *their* asset to reach inclusion.

References

AAIDD American Association of Intellectual and Developmental Disabilities (2010) Intellectual disability: definition, classification, and systems of supports, 11th edn. http://aaidd.org/intellectual-disability/definition. Accessed 15 Aug 2018

Abou-Zahra S, Brewer J, Cooper M (2018) Artificial Intelligence (AI) for web accessibility: is conformance evaluation a way forward? Web4All 2018, 23–25 April, Lyon, France, ACM

Bergold J (2013) Partizipative Forschung und Forschungsstrategien, eNewsletter Wegweiser Bürgergesellschaft 08/2013. https://www.buergergesellschaft.de/fileadmin/pdf/gastbeitrag_bergold_130510.pdf. Accessed 15 Aug 2018

Blanck P (2018) The struggle for web eQuality by persons with cognitive disabilities. Behav Sci Law. http://bbi.syr.edu/news_events/news/2014/02/BlanckWebAccessibility2014BSLOnline.pdf. Accessed 15 Aug 2018

Bock B, Lange D (2015) Was ist eigentlich, Leichte Sprache? In: Candussi K, Fröhlich W (Hrsg): Leicht Lesen, Der Schlüssel zur Welt; Böhlau Verlag Wien Köln Weimar, S. 65–79

Bohmann P (2016) Cognitive impairments part 1 – we still know too little, and we do even less. http://webaim.org/articles/cognitive/cognitive_too_little/. Accessed 15 Aug 2018

Borg J, Lantz A, Gulliksen G (2015) Accessibility to electronic communication for people with cognitive disabilities: a systematic search and review of empirical evidence. J Univ Access Informat Soc 14:547. https://doi.org/10.1007/s10209-014-0351-6. Springer, Heidelberg

CFS – Consulting, Franchise & Sales (2018) Capito-network. http://www.capito.eu/. Accessed 15 Aug 2018

Chiang D (2012) Grammars for language and genes. Springer's series in Theory and Applications of Natural Language Processing, Springer, New York, Heidelberg

Council of Europe (2001) Common European framework of reference for languages: learning, teaching, assessment. Appl Linguist. Cambridge University Press (2001). https://books.google.at/books?id=PygQ8Gk4k4YC. Accessed 15 Aug 2018

DAISY Consortium (2018) Digital accessible information system. http://www.daisy.org. Accessed 15 Aug 2018

Easy Reading (2018) Keeping the user at the digital origina. http://www.easyreading.eu/. Accessed 15 Aug 2018

Edler C (2015) E-Inklusion und Cognitive Accessibility, Menschen mit kognitiven Behinderungen nutzen Tablets im Alltag. Merz Medien und Erziehung 2015(04):74–81

Edler C, Weber H (2010) Supporting the web experience of young people with learning disabilities. In: Miesenberger K et al 12th International conference on computers helping people with special needs (ICCHP 2010), pp 649–656. Springer, Heidelberg

Fager S et al (2012) Access to augmentative and alternative communication: new technologies and clinical decision-making. J Pediatr Rehabil Med 5(1). IOS Press, Amsterdam

Fröhlich W, Candussi K (2015) Informationsbarrieren und Wege zu ihrer Überwindung. In: Candussi K, Fröhlich W (Hrsg): Leicht Lesen, Der Schlüssel zur Welt; S. 9–38, Böhlau Verlag (Wien 2015)

Fuchs NE (ed.) (2010) Controlled natural language, international workshop on controlled language applications. Lecture Notes in Computer Science, Springer, New York, Heidelberg

Gross S (2015) Regeln und Standards für leicht verständliche Sprache. In: Candussi, K., Fröhlich, W.: Leicht Lesen: Der Schlüssel zur Welt, Böhlau Verlag Wien, pp 88–105. https://doi.org/10.7767/9783205203292-005

Grotlüschen A, Riekemann W (2011) Leo – Level one study, Literacy of adults at the lower rungs of the ladder. Press broschure. http://blogs.epb.uni-hamburg.de/leo/files/2011/12/leo-Press-brochure15-12-2011.pdf. Accessed 15 Aug 2018

Hovy E (2005) Automated text summarization. The Oxford Handbook of Computational Linguistics, pp 583–598

IFLA International Federation of Library Association and Institutions (2018) Guidelines for easy-to-read materials. https://www.ifla.org/files/assets/hq/publications/professional-report/120.pdf. Accessed 15 Aug 2018

ISAAC (2018) International society for augmentative and alternative communication. https://www.isaac-online.org. Accessed 15 Aug 2018

ISO International Standard Organisation (2010) ISO 9241-210:2010 Ergonomics of human-system interaction—part 210: human-centred design for interactive systems. https://www.iso.org/standard/52075.html. Accessed 15 Aug 2018

Inclusion Europe (2016) Information for all – European standards for making information easy to read and understand. http://easy-to-read.eu/wp-content/uploads/2014/12/EN_Information_for_all.pdf. Accessed 15 Aug 2018

Janz F, Terfloth K (eds) (2009) Empirische Forschung im Kontext geistiger Behinderung. Universitätsverlag Winter GmbH, Heidelberg

Jekat S, Jüngst H, Schubert K, Villiger C (eds) (2015) Sprache barrierefrei gestalten. Frank & Timme, Berlin

Jiang W et al (2014) Responsive web design mode and application. Advanc Res Technol Indust Appl (WARTIA). IEEE

Kaur S et al (2016) Analysis of website usability evaluation methods. In: 3rd international conference on computing for sustainable global development (INDIACom). IEEE

Keates S, Clarkson P (2003) Countering design exclusion: bridging the gap between usability and accessibility. Universal Access in the Information Society, vol 2, no 3, pp 215–225. Springer, Heidelberg

Kemmis S (2011) A self-reflective practitioner and a new definition of critical participatory action research. In: Mockler N, Sachs J Rethinking educational practice through reflexive inquiry. Springer, New York, pp 11–29

Kwiatkowska G, Tröbinger T, Bäck K, Williams P (2012) Multimedia advocacy – a new way of self expression and communication for people with intellectual disabilities. In: Miesenberger K et al (eds.) ICCHP 2012, Part II, Springer, Heidelberg. pp 361–368

Liesem K, Kränicke J (2011) Professionelles Texten für die PR-Arbeit. VS Verlag für Sozialwissenschaften, Springer Fachmedien Wiesbaden GmbH, Wiesbaden

Maaß C (2015) Leichte Sprache, das Regelbuch. Lit-Verlag, Berlin

Markel MH (2012) Technical communication: situations and strategies, 10th edn. St. Martin's Press

Matausch-Mahr K, Pudelko A, Gubler E, Danner J, Mühlbachler K, Pfeiffer C, Weber S, Herlitz B (2017) Leicht verständliche Sprache: ein Motivator für Kommunikation. In: Blechschmidt

A, Schräpler U (Hrsg.): Unterstützt erzählen – Erzählen unterstützen. ISBN 978-7965-3628-1; Schwabe AG, Basel, pp S. 131–142

Matausch K, Peböck B (2010) EasyWeb – a study how people with specific learning difficulties can be supported on using the internet. In: Miesenberger K et al 12th international conference on computers helping people with special needs (ICCHP 2010), Springer, Heidelberg

Matausch K, Peböck B, Pühretmair F (2012) Accessible content generation an integral part of accessible web design. In: DSAI'2012 international conference on software development for enhancing accessibility and fighting info-exclusion. Elsevier, Amsterdam

McCarthy PM, Boonthum CH. (eds.): Applied natural language processing and content analysis: advances in identification, investigation and resolution. Informat Sci Ref

Media Access Group (2014) Captioning and video description for the web. http://main.wgbh.org/wgbh/pages/mag/pdfs/marketing_web.captioning.pdf. Accessed 15 Aug 2018

Miesenberger K, Petz A (2014) Easy-to-read on the web: state of the art and further research directions. In: Miesenberger K et al 14th international conference on computers helping people with special needs. ICCHP 2014, proceedings. Springer Heidelberg, pp 318–326

Miesenberger K, Petz A, Matausch K (2014a) Research report on easy to read on the web. W3C WAI Research and Development Working Group (RDWG) Notes (Editors' draft). http://www.w3.org/WAI/RD/2012/easy-to-read/. Accessed 15 Aug 2018

Mohorovičić S (2013) Implementing responsive web design for enhanced web presence. In: Information & communication technology electronics & microelectronics (MIPRO). IEEE

Müller S, Fleischer S (2013) Medienkompetenz und geistige Behinderung-Einsatz von Medien im Schulalltag von geistig behinderten Heranwachsenden. spektrum – Jugend und Information in der mediatisierten Gesellschaft, 2013/03, pp 55–59

Nenkova A, McKeown K (2012) A survey of text summarization techniques. In: Aggarwal CC, Zhai CH Mining text data. Springer, NewYork, Heidelberg

Netzwerk Leichte Sprache, Ratgeber für Leichte Sprache (2014) https://www.bmas.de/DE/Service/Medien/Publikationen/a752-leichte-sprache-ratgeber.html. Accessed 15 Aug 2018

Newell AF, Gregor P (2000) User sensitive inclusive design – in search of a new paradigm. In: Proceedings conference on universal usability. ACM (2000)

Nikolova S, Boyd-Graber J, Fellbaum Ch (2011) Collecting semantic similarity ratings to connect concepts in assistive communication tools. In: Mehler A et al (ed.) Modeling, learning, and processing of text technological data structures

Nind M (2013) Understanding quality in inclusive research: a process of dialogue. In: Nordic network on disability research conference, Turku, Finland. https://eprints.soton.ac.uk/352715/1/_soton.ac.uk_ude_PersonalFiles_Users_man_mydocuments_conference%2520papers_NNDR_NNDR%25202013_Nind_Understanding%2520quality.pdf

Ollerton JM (2012) IPAR, an inclusive disability research methodology with accessible analytical tools, Original practice development and research. Int Pract Development J 2(2), Article 3. http://www.fons.org/library/journal/volume2-issue2/article3

PLAIN (2011) Plain language action and information network: federal plain language guidelines. https://www.plainlanguage.gov/media/FederalPLGuidelines.pdf. Accessed 15 Aug 2018

Raskind M, Higgins E (1998) Assistive technology for postsecondary students with learning disabilities. J Learn Disabil 31(1)

Rumelhart DE (2017) Schemata: the building blocks of cognition. In: Theoretical issues in reading comprehension. Routledge, pp 33–58

Schluchter J (2010) Medienbildung mit Menschen mit Behinderung. Kopaed, München, p 172

Seitz S (2014) Leichte Sprache? Keine einfache Sache, Politik und Zeitgeschichte 64(9–11):3–6

Sharma V, Simpson R, LoPresti E, Mostowy C, Olson J, Puhlman J, Hayashi S, Cooper R, Konarski E, Kerley B (2008) Participatory design in the development of the wheelchair convoy system. J NeuroEng Rehabil 5(1):1

Strnadova I, Cumming T (2013) People with intellectual disabilities conducting, research: new directions for inclusive research. https://www.researchgate.net/publication/258856612_

People_with_Intellectual_Disabilities_Conducting_Research_New_Directions_for_Inclusive_
Research. Accessed 15 Aug 2018

United Nations (2006) Convention on the rights of persons with disability. http://www.un.org/
disabilities/convention/conventionfull.shtml (2006). Accessed 15 Aug 2018

W3C/WAI/ARIA (2017) Accessible rich internet applications (WAI-ARIA) 1.1. https://www.w3.
org/TR/wai-aria/. Accessed 15 Aug 2018

W3C/WAI/ATAG (2015) Authoring tool accessibility guidelines (ATAG) 2.0. https://www.w3.org/
TR/ATAG20/. Accessed 15 Aug 2018

W3C/WAI/COGA:(2018a) Cognitive Accessibility User Research: http://w3c.github.io/coga/user-
research/. Accessed 15 Aug 2018

W3C/WAI/COGA (2017) Cognitive and learning disabilities accessibility task force (cognitive
A11Y TF). https://www.w3.org/WAI/PF/cognitive-a11y-tf/. Accessed 15 Aug 2018

W3C/WAI/COGA (2018) Cognitive accessibility roadmap and gap analysis. https://rawgit.com/
w3c/coga/master/gap-analysis. Accessed 15 Aug 2018

W3C/WAI/COGA (2018b) Coga.Personalization. https://github.com/ayelet-seeman/coga.
personalisation. Accessed 15 Aug 2018

W3C/WAI/UAAG: (2015) User Agent Accessibility Guidelines (UAAG) 2.0. https://www.w3.org/
TR/UAAG20/. Accessed 15 Aug 2018

W3C/WAI/WCAG2.0: (2018) Web Content Accessibility Guidelines (WCAG) 2.0. https://www.
w3.org/TR/WCAG20/. Accessed 15 Aug 2018

W3C/WAI/WCAG2.1: (2018) Web Content Accessibility Guidelines (WCAG) 2.1. https://www.
w3.org/TR/WCAG21/. Accessed 15 Aug 2018

W3C/WAI (2018) Developing a web accessibility business case for your organization. https://www.
w3.org/WAI/bcase/Overview.html Accessed 15 Aug 2018

W3C/WAI (2012) Text customizatioin for readability online symposium. http://www.w3.org/WAI/
RD/2012/text-customization/. Accessed 15 Aug 2018

W3C/WAI (2012a) Diversity of the web. Diversity of abilities: cognitive and neurological. https://
www.w3.org/WAI/intro/people-use-web/diversity#cognitive. Accessed 15 Aug 2018

WHO World Health Organization (2001) The World Health Report 2001 – Mental Health: New
Understanding, New Hope. p. 178 Geneva:

WHODAS World Health Organisation Disability Assessment Schedule (2001) International classification of functioning, disability and health (ICF). http://www.who.int/classifications/icf/en/.
Accessed 15 Aug 2018

Walmsley J, Johnson K (2003) Inclusive research with people with learning disabilities. Jessica
Kingsley, London

Waloszek G (2004) SAP Design Guide. http://www.sapdesignguild.org/resources/simplification/
index.htm. Accessed 15 Aug 2018

WebAim: (2016) Cognitive Disabilities Part 1- We Still Know Too Little, and We Do Even Less.
http://webaim.org/articles/cognitive/cognitive_too_little. Accessed 15 Aug 2018

WebAim: (2013) Evaluating Cognitive Web Accessibility, available at: http://webaim.org/articles/
evaluatingcognitive. Accessed 15 Aug 2018

Chapter 29
User Interface Adaptation
for Accessibility

Sergio Firmenich, Alejandra Garrido, Fabio Paternò and Gustavo Rossi

Abstract In this chapter, we discuss methods and tools for adapting user interfaces to make them more accessible. We introduce the problem of user interface adaptation and characterize different techniques to be adapted to the user interface. We show that there is a broad range of methods and tools to transform existing interfaces to make them accessible. We describe such approaches by grouping them in two types of solutions: those that provide built-in adaptation mechanisms for the application and those which are external to the application.

29.1 Introduction

Adapting a user interface (UI), for example, to make it accessible, implies changing, or adjusting its structure, contents, and/or available actions according to the users' current goals and abilities (including the context of use). This adaptation may be initiated and controlled by the user, or built-in in the application itself or performed by a third party (not the user, not the original application).

The need for UI adaptation has been recognized by Edmonds since the early 80s (Edmonds 1982). The traditional idea that one system fits all is antagonistic toward the special needs or preferences of different users. Even the same user may change her ability regarding the task she performs with the system, and the interface should evolve (adapt) accordingly. Edmonds also introduced the concept of dynamic

S. Firmenich · A. Garrido · G. Rossi (✉)
LIFIA, Facultad de Informática, Universidad Nacional de La Plata and CONICET,
50 y 120 s/n, La Plata, Argentina
e-mail: gustavo@lifia.info.unlp.edu.ar

S. Firmenich
e-mail: sfirmenich@lifia.info.unlp.edu.ar

A. Garrido
e-mail: garrido@lifia.info.unlp.edu.ar

F. Paternò
CNR-ISTI, HIIS Laboratory, Via G. Moruzzi 1, 56124 Pisa, Italy
e-mail: fabio.paterno@isti.cnr.it

© Springer-Verlag London Ltd., part of Springer Nature 2019
Y. Yesilada and S. Harper (eds.), *Web Accessibility*, Human–Computer
Interaction Series, https://doi.org/10.1007/978-1-4471-7440-0_29

adaptation or self-adaptive interfaces, i.e., those which do not need the intervention of the developer or the user to perform the adaptation.

We are accustomed to different degrees of adaptation in the interfaces we regularly use. A simple example is the Windows start menu, which changes its contents dynamically according to the most (recently) used applications. Amazon adapts the contents presented to each user in relation to their browsing and shopping story, adjusting the recommended products in their home page and in every sub-store. It also adapts forms (e.g., to perform the check-out process) according to the information it has about the user (e.g., frequently used address, check-out preferences, etc). Email applications (Google, Yahoo, etc) let end-users change the structure, look and feel, and available operations of their site.

When dealing specifically with accessibility, different factors might impact on the need to adapt the UI. In the past, research work has focused on user-related factors such as perceptual skills, motor or sensing abilities, preferences, emotional state, cultural and education issues, in addition to the ability of the application to support users in their task, and afford to adapt regarding the user acquired experience. However, the emergence of mobile computing and the possibility of using application software in different contexts brought other factors into consideration such as those related with technology (screen resolution, connectivity, battery life, etc.) or the environment (location, noise, etc) (Paternò 2013). In any case, just considering the myriad of different requirements for accessibility related to specific motor or sense abilities let us conclude that adaptation is a must.

There are many considerations to take when building adaptation in interfaces for accessibility, and many dimensions to classify them. We next summarize some of the most important topics related to the general problem of adaptation, and the rest of the chapter will discuss some of the peculiarities of each approach.

- Who configures the adaptation: There may be coarse-grained interface variants, for example, for a particular disability, which is configured during design time. Alternatively, the interface may be self-adaptive, i.e., it learns about the user's needs dynamically, or the user may configure the adaptation herself.
- What is adapted: According to Brusilovsky (2001), a Web interface may be adapted regarding its structure, contents, and/or links. We may refine this coarse-grained classification considering, for example, what is adapted regarding the contents' presentation: it may be its media transforming text into audio (as in screen readers) or other properties such as size and colour (of text or images), volume (audio), etc.
- How we represent the user model: A critical issue is the representation of the systems knowledge about the user and her context, including preferences, abilities, device, environmental context, social context, etc. This representation must be expressive enough to capture all the information needed to perform the adaptation, and it must be dynamic in terms of both the information and its structure. Additionally, the user model may be deduced from the users actions or built by the user by configuring some options.
- When adaptation occurs: Assuming that the interface changes automatically in response to its experience with users, we must decide the rhythm of change. This

decision is not minor since, for example, changing too often might affect stability of the interface and therefore comprehension and usability.

- Where adaptation occurs: The adaptation may occur inside the system or may be external and performed by a third party or application built explicitly to fulfill this purpose.

Each one of these issues requires more than a book chapter, but for the sake of clarity and conciseness, we will address only some of them and provide pointers to others. The next section introduces a classification of User Interface Adaptation types, which includes a brief revision of existing literature.

29.2   Classifying Adaptive Interfaces

There are many different classifications in the literature for UI adaptation. One of them distinguishes between adaptable versus adaptive systems (Stephanidis and Savidis 2001). In the case of adaptable systems, end users have the capability to adapt the UI to their needs, i.e., users are in control of the adaptation, whereas adaptive systems have internal mechanisms to directly perform the adaptation, with little or no control from users. Other classifications exist that categorize the involvement of the user versus system at different stages of the adaptation, like Dieterich's taxonomy (Dieterich et al. 1993) and the recent PDA-LPA taxonomy (Bouzit et al. 2017), which provides a fine-grained characterization of end-user involvement versus system self management with respect to Perception, Decision, Action, Learning, Prediction, and Adaptation.

While the above are relevant classifications, they tend to leave out coarse-grained architectural differences that have appeared with recent technological innovations. A similar argument can be made about McKinley's taxonomy (McKinley et al. 2004), which considers three dimensions: How to adapt, Where to adapt, and When to adapt, but does not provide insight into the design and implementation of different adaptation techniques (Bouzit et al. 2017).

Another classification divides adaptive systems from the point of view of the development approach, in window managers and widget toolkits on the one hand, and model-driven engineering on the other hand (Akiki et al. 2014). Thus, this classification misses adaptive frameworks. Furthermore, although several approaches exist to create adaptive Web applications for accessibility, other approaches have emerged to allow users to adapt their preferred Web applications even beyond what these applications support.

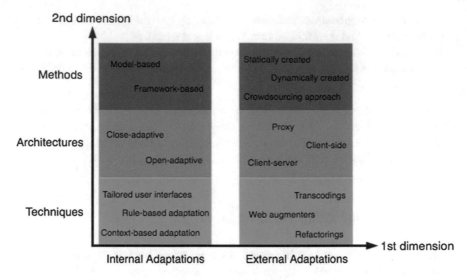

Fig. 29.1 Classification of user interface adaptation for accessibility

Based on the above discussion, we propose a classification structured into two dimensions (see Fig. 29.1). First, a coarse-grained partition between two broad types of adaptations:

- Those which are built in the original system, together with those that may be added because the original system provides some infrastructure to allow for new adaptations. In general, we may say that these are adaptation-aware systems, because the system was constructed to be able to perform some adaptations. Instances of this category are model-driven adaptive systems. We call them **Internal Adaptations**.
- Those which are external to the system, i.e., the original developers did not create a system with adaptation capabilities but the system is adapted from the outside by third-party software artifacts, or with techniques that intervene at a later stage, from which the Web application is unaware. Instances of these techniques are transcoding (Asakawa and Takagi 2008), augmentation (Bigham 2007), and refactoring (Garrido et al. 2013). We call them **External Adaptations**.

The second dimension in our classification aims at characterizing the different approaches in each partition with a finer grained definition with regard to:

- the **technique** by which the adaptation mechanism is activated;
- the **architecture** that establishes adaptation mechanism constraints;
- the **method** for developing the adaptation.

The next two sections analyze, correspondingly, internal and external UI adaptation approaches for improving or supporting Web applications accessibility.

29.3 Internal Approaches for UI Adaptation

There has been a number of interesting contributions in the area of methods and tools for accessible UIs adapted to people with various disabilities. This is an important area since there are many people with disabilities that can only access their applications through assistive technology, and they need adapted versions of their applications in order to accomplish their tasks with them.

29.3.1 Techniques

There are two main types of techniques to activate internal adaptations: tailored application versions and rule-based adaptive solutions. The former is mainly used at design time or at the beginning of a user session so that users (in some cases with the support of developers) can directly select one of the versions available or configure the desired version. The latter is more often used to obtain adaptive solutions where the applications modify some parts depending on dynamic contextual events, whose occurrence trigger specific rules that can change UI aspects. We can add a further technique: context-aware (Run-time adaptivity, system-initiated), which is related to run-time adaptivity, i.e., the context and all user activities are captured as the user interacts with the system, and the system acts accordingly.

29.3.1.1 Tailored User Interfaces

One of the first contributions in this area has been the result of the AVANTI project (Stephanidis et al. 1998), which aims to adapt Web applications in terms of content, navigation, and presentation for people with disabilities. It classifies users to different stereotypes, and, accordingly, it presents optional content and chooses appropriate information from alternatives.

In model-based approaches (Paternò 2005), the basic idea is to start with logical descriptions and then derive implementations for the target platforms and users. In the human–computer interaction area, the CAMELEON reference framework (Calvary et al. 2002) was introduced to distinguish the various possible abstraction levels in describing UIs: task and domain models, abstract UIs (the interaction is described independently from the possible modality used), concrete UI (the interaction is described dependent of some specific modalities but independent of specific implementation languages). The Supple system (Gajos et al. 2006) is an example of model-based system. It has focused on automatically generating UIs at design time for people with disabilities from logical descriptions taking into account device, tasks, preferences, and abilities. The UI generation is organized as a discrete optimization problem solved by using a branch-and-bound algorithm. The Supple authors focused on how to exploit Supple in order to support disabled users, for example, by automatically generating UIs for a user with impaired dexterity based on a model of her actual motor abilities. The authors have carried out laboratory experiments that indicate positive results in terms of speed, accuracy, and satisfaction of users with motor impairments.

A different approach has been adopted in The Global Public Inclusive Infrastructure (GPII), proposed by Vanderheiden and Treviranus (2014), which is an infrastructure aimed at automatically providing disabled users with solutions able to enhance their interaction with different public services. For instance, someone needing to access an inaccessible service, in a specific moment and in a concrete place, can obtain an accessible interface from GPII. To accomplish this process, users store their preferences in a local device or in the cloud. Subsequently, they carry out the login process wherever they are and GPII provides them with a tailored UI and the required assistive technologies. This seems useful but limited support since it can just provide access to a few predefined versions or configurations of the application, while the wide variety of possible user characteristics and preferences as well as contexts of use call for more flexible adaptations, which should be able to provide changes in the UI at various granularities.

29.3.1.2   Rule-Based Adaptation

In rule-based approaches, the rules generally indicate some events or conditions that should trigger the consequent adaptation. Miñón et al. (2016) have investigated how to exploit such rules in the model-based generation of accessible UIs. The adaptations can be applied in any of the CAMELEON abstraction levels at design time. For instance, adaptation rules related to task sequencing should be considered at the task and domain level, whereas adaptation rules related to some specific UI modalities have to be considered at the concrete UI level. At run-time, the solution proposed involves obtaining the necessary level of abstraction by means of an abstraction process in order to apply adaptation rules when a change in the context occurs, and then generate again the final UI. Ghiani et al. (2014) have put forward a proposal for obtaining run-time adaptation able to support dynamic reverse engineering of Web pages in order to obtain their model-based description, and then generate an implementation using different modalities more suitable for the new context of use. Yang and Shao (2007) have introduced the use of an expert system, JESS (Java Expert System Shell), in managing the adaptation rules. It uses a special algorithm called Rete to match the rules to the facts, which should be faster than a simple set of cascading "if. . .then" statements in a loop. A JESS rule is defined in such a way to trigger actions after matching knowledge base patterns. The adaptation knowledge base consists of a fact base, i.e., context profiles, and a rule base, i.e., adaptation rules. W3Touch (Nebeling et al. 2013) has not used model-based languages for supporting Web pages adaptation. For this purpose, it considers user interaction, in particular, the occurrence of missed links or frequent zooming as indicators of layout issues, however the adaptation rules supported do not consider the use of multimodality. In this case, the adaptation rules can be defined based on the logged events and may only be restricted to specific devices and viewing conditions. The possibility of using rules to specify the desired adaptations has raised interest in environments able to support the specification of such rules even by people who are not professional developers. An example of tool addressing this topic is TARE (Ghiani et al. 2017) that aims to provide an easy to understand way to specify contextual events and conditions as well as the corresponding actions, which can modify the application or even the state of surrounding appliances (e.g., lights, radio). This tool has been used in projects aiming to support elderly, thus giving them or their caregivers the possibility to personalize their applications according to specific situations.

29.3.1.3   Context-Based Adaptation

The increasing availability of various types of sensors, both personal and environmental sensors, has made it possible to detect useful information concerning the context of use in which users are interacting with the application, and then adapt the UI accordingly. The possible contextual aspects can involve the user (the tasks to perform, the emotional state, the current disabilities, etc.), the environment (e.g., light, noise, position), and the technologies (the available devices, appliances, and objects). Such technological evolution has also stimulated the development of solutions exploiting multimodal UIs, in which the adaptation can involve different communication channels between the user and the system. An example of accessible solution in this area is provided by Ghiani et al. (2009), who support the blind by exploiting the haptic channel as a complement to the audio/vocal one. It includes vibrotactile feedback enhancement for orientation and obstacle avoidance obtained through the use of unobtrusive actuators applied to two of the user's fingers combined with an electronic compass and obstacle detector sensors connected wirelessly to the mobile device. The user localization is obtained with the support of RFID tags associated with objects of interest. Later, Ahmetovic et al. (2016) proposed a smartphone-based system that provides turn-by-turn navigation assistance based on accurate real-time localization over large spaces. In addition to basic navigation capabilities, the NavCog system also informs the user about nearby points-of-interest (POI) and accessibility issues (e.g., stairs ahead). For this purpose, the system makes use of a network of Bluetooth low energy (BLE) beacons to localize the user with an approach based on the K-nearest neighbor (KNN) algorithm.

   In this perspective, Hussain et al. (2018) support rule-based adaptivity by collecting real-time data from multimodal data sources, e.g., smartwatch, mobile phone, camera, Kinect. It aims to generate the UI at runtime, without redeploying the system, and with the help of authoring tools, new rules are added without affecting the running system. Additionally, the adaptation on UI is made when the context is changed, which is observed by implicit and explicit (user feedback) ways. It also aims to receive user feedback: the implicit feedback is acquired from the user behavioral responses, which are collected automatically when users interact with the system, while the explicit feedback is acquired through questionnaires. However, currently the rule authoring is able to manage only basic-level adaptation rules.

29.3.2 Architectures

The support for adaptation can be obtained through different architectures. According to Sottet et al. (2007), a system is close-adaptive when adaptation is self-contained. It supports the innate adjustments planned at the design stage as well as new adjustments produced by its own internal learning mechanisms. The system is open-adaptive if new adaptation plans can be introduced during run-time. Thus, in close-adaptive systems rules are prefixed. Adaptation rules are designed at development time. Whenever a new rule is to be added, the system needs to be redeployed. This is the case for MyUI (Peissner et al. 2012) in which relevant interaction patterns are identified for the target users and devices, but if the targets change then the UI parametrization and preparation needs to be performed again before deployment. In order to obtain more open solutions, Miñón et al. (2016) propose an architecture in which there is an autonomous Adaptation Integration System, which applies adaptation rules to model-based descriptions of the interactive application. The rules consider user disability (cognitive impairment, motor impairment, deafness, etc.) and various granularity levels (single element, group element, presentation, application). Lastly, the adapted UI is generated. The resulting adaptation process tends to be slow and not very flexible. An efficient and flexible architecture for open-adaptive solution is presented by Ghiani et al. (2017). It is based on rules repositories and a middleware able to detect dynamic events in the context of use. Adaptation rules associated with a given application can be added and executed at any time. They are provided to an architectural component called adaptation engine in a trigger-action format. The adaptation engine subscribes to the underlying middleware (Context Manager) in order to be notified when relevant events occur. In this case, the corresponding actions are transmitted to the application for actually performing the desired adaptation to its UI or the state of some connected appliances. This type of architecture has then also been adopted in Hussain et al. (2018), which also considers the use of models for context, user, and device. In this approach, in the offline phase of adaptive UI design, all the relevant models are built and the adaptation rules are generated using a rule authoring tool. The created rules subscribe to the relevant events in a context evaluator. Then, the monitoring module is responsible for data collection while user is interacting with the system through different sensors and trackers (e.g., facial, vocal, eye, and analytics). The evaluator component evaluates the acquired information and decides whether adaptation is required on the UI or not.

29.3.3 Methods

In this section, we discuss the methods proposed for development of adaptable UIs for accessibility. A first distinction can be made between approaches using some model-based descriptions of the UI and framework working directly on the Web implementation.

29.3.3.1   Model-Based Methods

In model-based methods, we can distinguish two types of approaches: static and dynamic. In static model-based approaches, there is the possibility to provide some relevant model-based description and then generate the implementation version for the target users. In the dynamic approaches, the use of models can be updated according to some contextual dynamic change in order to obtain updated implementation without having to deploy again the application. Examples of the static approaches are MARIAE (Paternò et al. 2011) and Supple (Gajos et al. 2006). Supple automatically generates UIs, taking as inputs device-specific constraints, such as screen size and a list of available interactors, a typical usage trace, a functional specification of the interface, which describes the types of information that need to be communicated between the application and the user, and a cost function. The goal is to automatically generate, ability-based UIs that should significantly improve speed, accuracy, and satisfaction of users with motor impairments compared to manufacturers' default interfaces. Miñón et al. (2016) propose to make the model-based development more open to dynamic environments. The basic idea is that when some dynamic contextual change occurs, a model-based description is provided to an adaptation integration system, which is able to access a repository of adaptation rules, apply them to the model-based description, which is then passed again to the tool for model-based implementation generation. A solution aiming to obtain adaptation in terms of interaction modalities with the support of model-based descriptions is proposed by Ghiani et al. (2014). The goal is to overcome some limitations of responsive design (Marcotte 2011), which is able to consider only changes in device resolution and orientation and supports only graphical UIs. An approach aiming to obtain dynamic adaptation with the support of models is in Hussain et al. (2018). It considers context, user, and device models. It needs an offline phase during which all the relevant models are built and the adaptation rules are generated using a rule authoring tool. The rules are then applied during actual use of the application.

29.3.3.2   Framework-Based Methods

Current frameworks (for example, Bootstrap) mainly provide support for adaptation according to the responsive design approach, which support adapting to various device features through fluid layout and stylesheets. They also provide the possibility of associating various visual attributes with groups of devices identified by some features detected through media queries. However, such adaptations are too limited for supporting accessibility because they do not consider the many types of contextual events that can influence user interaction and the various possible user disabilities. The context toolkit (Salber et al. 1999) was among the earliest supports for developing context-enabled applications by providing a library to facilitate integration with sensors. It initially considered a limited set of events and led to meld the context awareness code with the application. Later, the Context Toolkit has been augmented with support to facilitate development and debugging of context-dependent applications (Dey and Newberger 2009). However, such approaches mainly refer to providing changes in the appliances states as a consequence of the detected events, and pay little attention to UI adaptations. W3Touch is an interface instrumentation toolkit for web designers to collect user performance data for different device characteristics in order to help them identify potential design problems for touch interaction. Web designers can visualize the data aggregated by W3Touch and use simple metrics to automate the adaptation process for many different viewing and interaction contexts.Thus, it provides a more flexible support but still without considering accessibility issues with particular attention. To facilitate the development of frameworks able to address such issues the W3C has developed the WAI-ARIA standard (WAI-ARIA (W3C) 2019), which helps with dynamic content and advanced UI controls developed with Ajax, HTML, JavaScript, and related technologies. Further aspects about dynamic content concerning accessibility may be found in chapter "Dynamic Web Content" in this book.

29.4 External Approaches for UI Adaptation

This category, as explained earlier, belongs to approaches for adapting a system from the outside, i.e., the target system is unaware of the adaptations. The benefits of these approaches are mainly that they may be applied to any Web system, i.e., the system does not need to be constructed in any particular way or depending on any infrastructure (which simplifies development) and often provide the final users with the possibility to control the adaptation and personalize it. In the context of accessibility, however, users controllability may not always be an advantage, since depending on the disability, it may require the assistance of third persons, like family members or caregivers. Adapting third- party Web contents is an old idea that has been applied in very distinct ways, and may involve end-users alone or contemplate a volunteer role.

29.4.1 Techniques

In this section, we will talk about two mainstream techniques for manipulating existing and third-party Web content: traditional transcoding and client-side adaptation.

Both client-side adaptation and transcodings are very powerful and have been applied with very similar goals in some approaches, while very different in others. Even the terms are used indistinctly sometimes and also combined, such as client-side transcoding, or browser-side transcoding (Díaz and Arellano 2015). Originally, transcodings systems were defined as those that transcode a resource before it is delivered to their target client (Asakawa and Takagi 2008). Once the resource (mainly an HTML page together with CSS and JavaScript) is delivered to the client, it behaves as usual, meaning that even if the Web content was adapted (transcoded) by an intermediary server, once it is loaded and rendered on the Web Browser, it is still a normal Web site, and the adaptation mechanisms are restricted to this situation. Client-side adaptation approaches, on the other hand, manipulate the content after it is loaded and rendered in the client, because these techniques manipulate the actual DOM that Web browsers create for the loaded HTML pages. Client-side approaches bring new opportunities in comparison with intermediary servers. This architectural difference (architectural aspects for external adaptation approaches are discussed on Sect. 29.4.2), directly impacts on how the adaptation mechanisms are defined and triggered, and subsequently on how easy it is to apply some adaptation technique/method. With this in mind, we separate this subsection into transcoding systems and pure client-side adaptation. For each of these techniques for manipulating existing Web content, we discuss their main uses and scope.

29.4.1.1 Transcodings

The problem of improving accessibility by adapting third-party Web content was first tackled by approaches inspired in transcoding systems. Transcoding was defined as a system that transforms content or a program on the fly at an intermediary server, resulting in other formats; this served, for instance, to change the content encoding on the fly using a proxy (Asakawa and Takagi 2008). The same idea of using an intermediate server to manipulate existing content was applied to improve accessibility of third-party websites. According to Asakawa and Takagi (2008), transcodings methods (text magnification, content reorder, page simplification, etc.) are applicable on an intermediary server (proxy) and also directly at client-side by using client-side adaptation scripts. In the same article, Asakawa established two main techniques for transcodings, which are the use of annotations and simplification based on differential analysis.

Basically, these accessibility transcodings act like transformation functions that, once a target UI element is specified, apply a transformation method. Content annotation was and still is a widely used technique for deciding which transformation method to apply over which UI elements for a given Web page. Approaches around this idea were very well described in a previous chapter focused specifically on transcodings (Asakawa and Takagi 2008). Since that time, there have been new works on transcoding tackling different problems. For instance, some works have explored other ways to do annotations via CSS. Other works have taken advantage of the collaborative nature of annotation-based systems, which allows a whole community of end-users to create and share annotations (Takagi et al. 2008, 2009). In some cases, these kinds of approaches may involve a volunteer role, coined to create the annotations when these require some technical skill.

Web applications became more complex at client-side, for instance, by incorporating asynchronous content load and later RIA concerns. In the context of Accessible-Rich Internet Applications (ARIA), some approaches proposed to incorporate RIA functionalities as a new application for transcoding (Lunn et al. 2009; Brown and Harper 2013).

Several aspects related to this technique are discussed in the chapter "Document Engineering" from this book.

29.4.1.2 Client-Side Adaptation

With the evolution of client-side Web technologies, another approach that has emerged to adapt existing third-party Web contents (perhaps the most popular in terms of actual users) is the one based on Web browser extensibility, that enables third-party client-side adaptation based on Web content manipulation once it is loaded in the Web browser, without previous intervention of any proxy server. This idea of extending the Web browser for adapting Web pages was stated as Web augmentation several years ago (Bouvin 1999), and newer literature reinforce this idea and define accessibility as a dimension to improve existing Web sites through the use of Web augmentation software (Díaz and Arellano 2015).

Despite that transcodings can be performed at client-side, other contributions for external adaptation for improving accessibility, in particular those based on client-side, are not easily classifiable into the categories Asakawa defined in the context of traditional transcodings for accessibility (Asakawa and Takagi 2008). New and often used techniques such as user interaction analysis, eye tracking, etc., are tied to client-side adaptation, because these mechanisms need to work when the Web site is already in use (i.e., once it is loaded, parsed, and rendered on the Web browser), and not before it is delivered to the client, as it occurs in proxy servers.

For instance, Hanson and Crayne (2005) discussed how older end-users may personalize their web browsing activities by applying client-side adaptations. Another similar approach, called Farfalla (Mangiatordi and Sareen 2011), similarly proposes to augment Web pages with a toolbar that let end-users customize some aspects of content presentation such as magnify text, change font size, etc. Also this kind of adaptations could be applied automatically if the client-side component may read a user profile from which it takes the information to make adaptation decisions (Peinado and Ortega-Moral 2014). Renarration UI (Prasad et al. 2017) is another similar client-side approach, that also offers a fixed set of transformations the user may perform over the Web sites s/he is visiting.

Other approaches propose an architecture that serves to install artifacts created by the community, instead of offering a fixed set of available transformations. For instance, Accessmonkey (Bigham 2007) proposes a weaving engine together with an authoring tool that, correspondingly, let end-users install and create scripts that are run in the Web browser.

The case of Accessmonkey is a specialization of a general-purpose engine called Greasemonkey, which executes JavaScript scripts when a specific (or a set of) URL is loaded (Pilgrim and Mark 2005). In both cases, however, the reason for the creation of a new adaptation artifact is a non-satisfied users need or preference.

Another approach, called Client-Side Web Refactoring (CSWR) (Garrido et al. 2013), is similar in terms of how the adaptation is performed (through DOM manipulation), but it is different in terms of its motive. In the case of CSWR, the transformations of UI elements are driven with the philosophy of well-known code refactoring (Fowler and Beck 1999). This means that these transformations are motivated by accessibility "bad smells" and the result must guarantee that the original application functionality is still available.

Finally, client-side approaches that work inside Web browsers bring new possibilities. For instance, Puzis et al. (2013) propose an automation assistant for people with vision impairments. This work is interesting because the automation assistant is an agent that adapts the interaction with Web applications, which is very important today, given the complex business processes behind Web applications. The approach proposes a model that uses the navigational history and the current Web site to predict browsing actions (such as filling a text input, or click a button).

29.4.2   Architectures

The techniques described above are mainly deployed using at least one of the following architectures:

- Intermediate Proxy Server: In this architecture, the transformation machinery is hosted in a proxy server that transforms the content delivered by the application server before this content reaches the client, i.e., the user's Web browser. Necessarily, Web browsers must be configured to work with the desired proxy. Extensibility in this approach is achieved, mainly, by annotation. Examples of approaches using this architecture, which are mainly transcoding systems, are SADIe (Lunn et al. 2008), Social4All (Crespo et al. 2016; Takagi et al. 2009; Asakawa and Takagi 2000).
- Client-Side: The client is any software able to communicate with a Web server and rendering the HTML responses. According to this definition, specialized Web browsers are considered a client-side mechanism, even if they apply static transformations, such as the emblematic IBM Home Page Reader (Lunn et al. 2008). This is a good example of a transcodings system without using an intermediate server. However, most of the latest works on client-side external adaptation rely on well-known standards Web browsers, because they have high user adoption, and allow very powerful extensibility mechanisms through which Web content transformation is very easy to achieve. A Web browser extension is aware of every event happening during the navigation session. In this way, when a Web page is loaded, the extension recognizes this event, and it is able to manipulate the loaded DOM to change it. By altering the DOM at client-side, users perceive the Web page adaptation. Examples of approaches using this architecture are Farfalla (Mangiatordi and Sareen 2011), Accessmonkey (Bigham 2007), CSWR (Garrido et al. 2013), Social Accessibility (Takagi et al. 2008).
- Client–Server: there are several approaches, such as Social Accessibility, that propose collaboration among users and volunteers. Also, it is common to require a user profile to make it available from every user's devices (Hanson and Richards 2005). In this way, although stand-alone client-side components are enough to perform the adaptation, it is not enough to contemplate every concern behind the problem of making the Web more accessible, such as collaboration, crowdsourcing, profiling, etc., which are important concerns to be considered. This is the reason

for the existence of client–server architectures, in which the client part performs the adaptation but consumes services provided by the server counterpart to achieve its goals.

A priori, it seems that the power of HTML transformation (or its run-time version: DOM manipulation) of intermediary proxies and client-side adaptation is equivalent, and, in some way, it is true. Thus, although technically almost any UI transformation could be made in any of these architectures, what is not equal is when and under what stimulus or events the alteration is made. This is crucial nowadays, because Web 2.0 and RIA applications make it difficult to transform the whole UI without contemplating user's behavior, just because the content delivered to the client-side not necessarily contains all the UI, but contain a basic layout that will be populated at client-side asynchronously. This problem was reported before (Hanson and Richards 2005), where the authors describe that obtaining a trustable version of the UI (which is the input for the transcoding process) in a proxy server is very complicated given the dynamism with which the UI is composed. Besides this aspect, in other cases the authors say it is directly impossible because of the use of SSL connections.

While dealing with dynamic Web sites (those fully interactive Web sites using CSS, HTML, and JavaScript) is difficult through an intermediate server, this is straightforward in the case of client-side architectures, because these approaches are mostly based on DOM manipulation. When the adaptation is performed at client-side, any aspect of the user interaction may be easily used as part of the adaptation system. This aspect is mandatory for some approaches like refactoring, in which the "bad smells" may be detected automatically by analyzing user interaction at the client-side (Grigera et al. 2017). Another interesting aspect is composition. In client-side approaches, several end-user tools may be integrated, for instance CSWRs may be used for structural and behavioral adaptations but combined with Farfalla (Mangiatordi and Sareen 2011) to adapt other aspects of content presentation, such as color schemes. In the case of intermediate servers, the configuration in cascade of several servers is hard to achieve.

Finally, these architectures may be analyzed also from the point of view of openness. Often they are a natural environment for installing (by plug and play) new kind of adaptation artifacts and for authoring processes. The use of visual tools for content annotation or UI transformation is based on the interaction between users or volunteers with Web content, in some cases, applying changes on the fly (Garrido et al. 2013); then running the end-user created artifacts at client-side is very convenient.

29.4.3   Methods

In this dimension, we discuss the methods in which the adaptations are created or built into the adaptation system. That is, on the one side there are adaptations statically created into the system and later provided by way of a fixed menu of options, and on the other side of the spectrum there are no adaptations provided statically but all of them are created dynamically by volunteers or end-users. In the middle, we may find a range of hybrid methods which provide some adaptations but leave the door open to receive new ones. Thus, we could also say that this dimension is about the openness of the adaptation system.

Among augmentation systems which are closed to new adaptations we may cite the work of Chung et al. (2013) for deaf people, the work of Hanson and Crayne for older adults (Hanson and Crayne 2005), and the more recent Farfalla project (Mangiatordi and Sareen 2011). In the first case, Chung et al. propose an algorithm to simplify the grammatical structure of complex sentences in news articles to make them easier to understand by deaf people, in addition to showing a graphical representation of the relationships among sentences (Chung et al. 2013). In the case of the Farfalla system, which is an active project similar to the older work of Handon and Crayne, there are a fixed number of adaptations provided in a sidebar menu for the user to control: font size, contrast and color combination, mouse pointer size, capitalized text for easier reading and on-screen keyboard (Mangiatordi and Sareen 2011). Nevertheless, Farfalla is an open-source project that invites for participation, so volunteers could actually add more adaptations by coding them in the Farfalla source code.

There are many examples of open augmentation systems, for instance, Access-monkey (Bigham 2007). With respect to the transcoding technique, it is specially suited for an open adaptation method, that is, a mechanism to add semantic annotations into the transcoding system. The reason is that semantic annotations are very tight to the particular web application being adapted, so the cost of creating an scalable transcoding system is not affordable by a single group of people. Although there are some proposals to add annotations automatically from CSS classes (Lunn et al. 2008), or automatic transcoding of images into text (Bigham et al. 2006), they did not prosper since automatic methods have accuracy limitations (Takagi et al. 2008). Instead, from their early works, the research group of Chieko Asakawa created authoring tools for volunteers to add annotations to their transcoding system (Asakawa and Takagi 2000). The annotations thus created are added into an annotation database organized by target URL. Other transcoding systems that rely on external annotations are Dante Yesilada et al. (2004) and WebAdapt2Me (2019).

It is worth to note that when an adaptation system has to rely on users to grow, it must necessarily provide a simple and possibly visual interactive tool to make the task very easy and promote adoption among volunteers. Takagi et al. discuss the advantages of open transcoding systems, and present the "Social Accessibility Approach" (Takagi et al. 2008). These authors take a step further by adopting a crowdsourcing approach, i.e., calling the entire community of users to create annotations by providing them with a collaborative authoring platform. Another tool that proposes the use of a crowdsourcing platform if Social4All (Crespo et al. 2016). Using the Social4All platform, volunteers create adaptation profiles for any website, each profile containing a set of adaptations to solve WCAG issues. Last but not least, crowdsourcing has also been proposed in the context of refactoring systems (Garrido et al. 2017). In this case, a crowdsourcing platform is proposed not only for creating new adaptations (applying CSWRs), but also for users to report bad smells manually or collect them automatically, and for the crowd to evaluate the effectiveness of solutions.

29.5   Discussion

Though not stated explicitly in the previous sections, external and internal approaches to UI adaptation also have a difference in the role of end-users in the process of building the adaptable/adaptive interface. In internal approaches, the burden of designing and implementing the adaptation machinery (be it in the form of rules or other different approach) often lies on developers, even if recently some work to enable non professional developers to specify their personalization rules has been put forward. Meanwhile, in some external approaches for adaptation, end-users (not directly involved in the design of the target application) might help in the process through crowdsourcing. In internal approaches, as explained in Sect. 29.3, designers are profiting from long software engineering and user modeling experience in the construction of flexible systems, which can be either seamlessly modified at design time, or can adapt dynamically when the context changes. User interfaces are certainly one part of the system and flexibility in UIs, e.g., for improving accessibility, is a good example of the impact of modularity in system design. In order to limit the effort in designing adaptation in internal approaches, there have been recent proposals aiming to allow even people without programming experience to provide the desired adaptation rules.

External approaches, meanwhile, are relatively new. Specially, the growth of client-side adaptations could not be predicted 10 years ago when the future seemed to bring the growth of proxy-based solutions (Asakawa and Takagi 2008). While transcoding-based approaches have some years now, the increasing and overwhelming growth of social networks have made end-users much more aware of their own (for example, accessibility) problems; these problems are not only shared between them but they are also involving themselves in finding solutions, e.g., via crowdsourcing. This involvement, which is also pushed by the popularity of end-user approaches, puts also some pressure on the improvement of internal approaches and on designers themselves, since it shows that those features not originally provided by designers can be eventually added by the end-users.

Something that the literature is still missing, to the best of our knowledge, is a thorough experimentation on very important aspects like user adoption, real coverage of user needs, and also a comparison of the effectiveness of the different approaches discussed in this article. We consider this a crucial task in the near future.

29.6   Future Directions

Even though UI adaptation is a consolidated topic in the literature, there are still areas in which research is needed. Some of them are mentioned here.

- Regarding model-based approaches for internal adaptation, one problem that has hindered part of their popularity is the relative low penetration of model-based and model-driven development in industry. This topic has been extensively discussed elsewhere (Whittle et al. 2014). Better and more stable tool support might help these approaches to gain penetration. Better training and education is needed (as in other fields related more directly with accessibility).

- In Framework-based approaches for adaptation, there is also a growing interest to include accessibility issues. For example, the accessibility plugin for the Bootstrap framework (BootstrapAccessibilityPlugin 2019). Yet, covering the broad possibilities of adaptation for accessibility is a missing issue in Web development frameworks (not only considering adaptation as a target issue).
- Regarding external approaches, most of them share a complex weakness, which is the evolution of the source Websites. All external approaches maintain some kind of reference to the targets UI elements that will be adapted. When the Website changes, these references may become old, and the adaptation mechanism may not work. Since authoring tools are becoming a common place for scripts or annotation creation, it is important also to support the maintenance of artifacts, and not just their building. We believe that automatic or semi-automatic testing and end-user driven maintenance must be faced both at methodological and at technical level.
- Though not explicitly discussed in this chapter, new interaction techniques (like those based on gestures or eyes gaze) are beginning to gain momentum for improving accessibility (Kumar et al. 2017). However, little work has been done on adapting the interaction technique to the needs of the end-user (see, for example, Yoda 2018). Moreover, there is a bunch of work in gesture recognition within the field of robotics and rehabilitation (see, for example, Lin et al. 2017). The combination of adaptive interaction techniques with other technologies such as the Internet of Things (see Chapter "Internet of Things" in Part 6 of this book) will leverage existing techniques.
- Finally, the extensive application of Artificial Intelligence (AI) techniques (such as machine learning) will have an impact in UI adaptation. In fact, rule-based approaches like those discussed in Sect. 29.3.1.2 have their roots in the work on expert systems in the early 90s. Abou-Zahra et al. (2018) discuss different aspects in which AI will improve Web accessibility and particularly, interface adaptation. For example, natural language processing may be used to allow text adaptation (e.g., simplifying text) for people with cognitive disabilities. Besides, AI might help to better learn the preferences and needs of people with changing conditions and therefore help in content adaptation. Related with this last trend, Galindo et al. (2017) present an approach to provide UI adaptation driven by emotions. They also use a rule-based adaptation engine which interacts with an inference engine to detect the actual user emotion.

29.7   The Author's Opinion of the Field

A disability is an impairment that may be cognitive, developmental, intellectual, mental, physical, sensory, or some combination of these. Such impairments may impact the way how people can interact with Web applications in different ways. Thus, it becomes crucial to provide user interfaces that can change presentation, navigation, and content according to the user abilities and preferences. Over time, developers and designers have started to become aware of such important issues, and we can find several applications that provide some level of adaptation. Unfortunately, often they are not sufficient to meet users needs, and more flexible and usable solutions are necessary.

The technological fast evolution makes this issue more challenging because people are more and more used to access their applications through a variety of devices ranging from wearables to large screens, also exploiting different interaction modalities, and there are various emerging JavaScript frameworks that are changing the way how people develop their applications. Flexible solutions should allow developers and designers to control the adaptation of their user interfaces at various granularity levels (single elements, groups, pages, etc.) and for various types of attributes. The adaptation should consider the various contextual aspects in order to be more effective, also considering emotional and environmental parameters. This area can benefit from the use of intelligent techniques that, based on the analysis of previous interactions, can predict the most suitable adaptations. However, more importantly, the users should be in control of the adaptation; they should know when the adaptation is triggered, where, how, and why it is applied. In this way, new tools may be developed to empower even nonprofessional developers to directly personalize their applications according to their actual and dynamic needs.

29.8 Conclusions

In this chapter, we have discussed several issues related to UI adaptation for accessibility. Adapting the UI to the special needs of different kinds of users is a must and the problem has been discussed in the literature for more than 30 years. While each particular user or user profile might pose a different challenge, there are already techniques that allow fine-grained personalization of the interface to improve its accessibility and usability.

We have presented a discussion of the proposed solutions in which we separate those approaches in which the interface adaptation is somewhat "built-in" in the system design and those in which adaptation occurs "outside" of the original application.

In both types of approaches, there are a wide range of different techniques that so far have shown to be powerful enough to face existing challenges to achieve adaptation. While in "internal" approaches much of the burden for foreseeing adaptation is often dealt with by designers, even if some end-user development approach is emerging, in "external" ones, there is a tendency to involve end-users either by building their own adaptations or solving others' problems via crowdsourcing.

However, there is yet much work to do as mentioned in Sects. 29.5 and 29.6. New implementation frameworks (such as Angular, Node.js) pose new technical issues in applying the adaptation solutions. More generally, further longitudinal studies are needed with final users representing the various target communities in order to validate the various technical solutions and their actual effectiveness.

Acknowledgements The authors acknowledge the support from the Argentinian National Agency for Scientific and Technical Promotion (ANPCyT), grant numbers PICT-2015-3000 and PICT-2015-2050.

References

Abou-Zahra S, Brewer J, Cooper M (2018) Artificial intelligence (AI) for web accessibility. In: Proceedings of the internet of accessible things on - W4A 2018. ACM Press, New York, pp 1–4. https://doi.org/10.1145/3192714.3192834. ISBN 9781450356510

Ahmetovic D, Gleason C, Ruan C, Kitani K, Takagi H, Asakawa C (2016) NavCog. In: Proceedings of the 18th international conference on human-computer interaction with mobile devices and services - MobileHCI 2016. ACM Press, New York, pp 90–99. https://doi.org/10.1145/2935334.2935361. ISBN 9781450344081

Akiki PA, Bandara AK, Yu Y (2014) Adaptive model-driven user interface development systems. ACM Comput Surv 47:1–33. https://doi.org/10.1145/2597999. ISSN 03600300

Asakawa C, Takagi H (2000) Annotation-based transcoding for nonvisual web access. In: Proceedings of the fourth international ACM conference on Assistive technologies - Assets 2000, pp 172–179. https://doi.org/10.1145/354324.354588

Asakawa C, Takagi H (2008) Transcoding. In: Web Accessibility. Springer, London, pp 231–260. https://doi.org/10.1007/978-1-84800-050-6_14

Bigham JP, Kaminsky RS, Ladner RE, Danielsson OM, Hempton GL (2006) WebInSight: In: Proceedings of the 8th international ACM SIGACCESS conference on computers and accessibility - Assets 2006. ACM Press, New York, p 181. https://doi.org/10.1145/1168987.1169018. ISBN 1595932909

Bigham JP (2007) AccessMonkey: enabling and sharing end user accessibility improvements. ACM SIGACCESS Access Comput 89:3–6. https://doi.org/10.1145/1328567.1328568

BootstrapAccessibilityPlugin,   https://www.paypal-engineering.com/2014/01/28/bootstrap-accessibility-plugin-making-the-popular-web-development-framework-better/

Bouvin NO (1999, February) Unifying strategies for Web augmentation. In: Proceedings of the tenth ACM conference on hypertext and hypermedia: returning to our diverse roots. ACM, pp 91–100. https://doi.org/10.1145/294469.294493

Bouzit S, Calvary G, Coutaz J, Chene D, Petit E, Vanderdonckt J (2017) The PDA-LPA design space for user interface adaptation. In: 2017 11th international conference on research challenges in information science (RCIS). IEEE, pp 353–364. https://doi.org/10.1109/RCIS.2017.7956559. ISBN 978-1-5090-5476-3

Brown A, Harper S (2013) Dynamic injection of WAI-ARIA into web content. In: Proceedings of the 10th international cross-disciplinary conference on Web Accessibility - W4A 2013. ACM Press, New York, p 1. https://doi.org/10.1145/2461121.2461141. ISBN 9781450318440

Brusilovsky P (2001) User modeling and user-adapted interaction 11:87. https://doi.org/10.1023/A:1011143116306

Calvary G, Coutaz J, Bouillon L, Florins M, Limbourg Q, Marucci L, Paternò F, Santoro C, Souchon N, Thevenin D, Vanderdonckt J (2002) Cameleon reference framework in cameleon reference framework

Chung J-W, Min H-J, Kim J, Park JC (2013)Enhancing readability of web documents by text augmentation for deaf people. In: Proceedings of the 3rd international conference on web intelligence, mining and semantics - WIMS 2013. ACM Press, New York, p 1. https://doi.org/10.1145/2479787.2479808. ISBN 9781450318501

Crespo RG, Espada JP, Burgos D (2016) Social4all: definition of specific adaptations in web applications to improve accessibility. Comput Stand Interfaces 48:1–9. https://doi.org/10.1016/J.CSI.2016.04.001. ISSN 0920-5489

Dey AK, Newberger A (2009)Support for context-aware intelligibility and control. In: Proceedings of the 27th international conference on Human factors in computing systems - CHI 09. ACM Press, New York, p 859. https://doi.org/10.1145/1518701.1518832. ISBN 9781605582467

Díaz O, Arellano C (2015) The augmented web. ACM Trans Web 9:1–30. https://doi.org/10.1145/2735633. ISSN 15591131

Dieterich H, Malinowski U, Kuhme T, Schneider-Hufschmidt M (1993) State of the art in adaptive user interfaces. Adapt User Interfaces: Princ Pract 10:13

Edmonds E (1982) The mancomputer interface: a note on concepts and design. Int J Man-Mach Stud 16:231–236. https://doi.org/10.1016/S0020-7373(82)80060-6 ISSN 00207373

Fowler M, Beck K (1999) Refactoring: improving the design of existing code. Addison-Wesley, Boston. ISBN 0201485672

Gajos KZ, Long JJ, Weld DS (2006) Automatically generating custom user interfaces for users with physical disabilities. In: Proceedings of the 8th international ACM SIGACCESS conference on computers and accessibility - Assets 2006. ACM Press, New York, p 243. https://doi.org/10.1145/1168987.1169036. ISBN 1595932909

Galindo JA, Dupuy-Chessa S, Céret E (2017, August) Toward a generic architecture for UI adaptation to emotions. In: Proceedings of the 29th conference on l'Interaction Homme-Machine. ACM, pp 263–272. https://doi.org/10.1145/3132129.3132156

Garrido A, Firmenich S, Grigera J, Rossi G (2017) Data-driven usability refactoring: tools and challenges. In: 2017 6th International workshop on software mining (SoftwareMining). IEEE, pp 52–55. https://doi.org/10.1109/SOFTWAREMINING.2017.8100854. ISBN 978-1-5386-1389-4

Garrido A, Firmenich S, Rossi G, Grigera J, Medina-Medina N, Harari I (2013) Personalized web accessibility using client-side refactoring. IEEE Internet Comput 17:58–66. https://doi.org/10.1109/MIC.2012.143. ISSN 1089-7801

Ghiani G, Leporini B, Paternò F (2009) Vibrotactile feedback to aid blind users of mobile guides. J Vis Lang Comput 20:305–317. https://doi.org/10.1016/j.jvlc.2009.07.004. ISSN 1045926X

Ghiani G, Manca M, Paternò F, Porta C (2014) Beyond responsive design: context-dependent multimodal augmentation of web applications. Springer, Cham, pp 71–85. https://doi.org/10.1007/978-3-319-10359-4_6

Ghiani G, Manca M, Paternò F, Santoro C (2017) Personalization of context-dependent applications through trigger-action rules. ACM Trans Comput-Hum Interact 24:1–33. https://doi.org/10.1145/3057861. ISSN 10730516

Grigera J, Garrido A, Rivero JM, Rossi G (2017) Automatic detection of usability smells in web applications. Int J Hum-Comput Stud 97:129–148. https://doi.org/10.1016/j.ijhcs.2016.09.009

Hanson VL, Crayne S (2005) Personalization of web browsing: adaptations to meet the needs of older adults. Univers Access Inf Soc 4:46–58. https://doi.org/10.1007/s10209-005-0110-9. ISSN 1615-5289

Hanson V, Richards J (2005) Achieving a more usable World Wide Web. Behav Inf Technol 24:231–246. https://doi.org/10.1080/01449290412331327465. ISSN 0144-929X

Hussain J, Ul Hassan A, Muhammad Bilal HS, Ali R, Afzal M, Hussain S, Bang J, Banos O, Lee S (2018) Model-based adaptive user interface based on context and user experience evaluation. J Multimodal User Interface 12:1–16. https://doi.org/10.1007/s12193-018-0258-2. ISSN 1783-7677

Kumar C, Menges R, Müller D, Staab S (2017) Chromium based framework to include gaze interaction in web browser. In: Proceedings of the 26th international conference on World Wide Web companion - WWW 2017 companion. ACM Press, New York, pp 219–223. https://doi.org/10. 1145/3041021.3054730. ISBN 9781450349147

Lin Y, Breugelmans J, Iversen M, Schmidt D (2017) An adaptive interface design (AID) for enhanced computer accessibility and rehabilitation. Int J Hum-Comput Stud 98:14–23. https://doi.org/10. 1016/J.IJHCS.2016.09.012. ISSN 1071-5819

Lunn D, Bechhofer S, Harper S (2008) The SADIe transcoding platform. In: Proceedings of the 2008 international cross-disciplinary workshop on Web accessibility (W4A) - W4A 2008. ACM Press, New York, p 128. https://doi.org/10.1145/1368044.1368073. ISBN 9781605581538

Lunn D, Harper S, Bechhofer S (2009) Combining SADIe and AxsJAX to improve the accessibility of web content. In: Proceedings of the 2009 international cross-disciplinary conference on web accessibililty (W4A) - W4A 2009. ACM Press, New York, p 75. https://doi.org/10.1145/1535654. 1535672. ISBN 9781605585611

Mangiatordi A, Sareen HS (2011) Farfalla project: browser-based accessibility solutions. In: Proceedings of the international cross-disciplinary conference on web accessibility - W4A 2011. ACM Press, New York, p 1. https://doi.org/10.1145/1969289.1969317. ISBN 9781450304764

Marcotte E, Impr. EMD (2011) Responsive web design, Eyrolles, ISBN 2212133316

McKinley PK, Sadjadi SM, Kasten EP, Cheng BH (2004) A taxonomy of compositional adaptation. Rapport Technique numéro MSU-CSE-04-17

Miñón R, Paternò F, Arrue M, Abascal J (2016) Integrating adaptation rules for people with special needs in model-based UI development process. Univers Access Inf Soc 15:153–168. https://doi. org/10.1007/s10209-015-0406-3. ISSN 1615-5289

Nebeling M, Speicher M, Norrie M (2013) W3touch. In: Proceedings of the SIGCHI conference on human factors in computing systems - CHI 2013. ACM Press, New York, p. 2311. https://doi. org/10.1145/2470654.2481319. ISBN 9781450318990

Paternò F (2005) Model-based tools for pervasive usability. Interact Comput. https://doi.org/10. 1016/j.intcom.2004.06.017. ISSN 09535438

Paternò F (2013) User interface design adaptation in the encyclopedia of human-computer interaction. In: The encyclopedia of human-computer interaction, 2nd edn

Paternò F, Santoro C, Spano LD (2011) Engineering the authoring of usable service front ends. J Syst Softw. https://doi.org/10.1016/j.jss.2011.05.025. ISSN 01641212

Peinado I, Ortega-Moral M (2014) Making web pages and applications accessible automatically using browser extensions and apps. Springer, Cham, pp 58–69. https://doi.org/10.1007/978-3-319-07509-9_6

Peissner M, Häbe D, Janssen D, Sellner T (2012) MyUI. In: Proceedings of the 4th ACM SIGCHI symposium on engineering interactive computing systems - EICS 2012. ACM Press, New York, p 81. https://doi.org/10.1145/2305484.2305500. ISBN 9781450311687

Pilgrim M, Mark (2005) Greasemonkey hacks. O'Reilly, Sebastopol. ISBN 0596101651

Prasad GVRJS, Soumya MS, Choppella V (2017) Renarrating web pages for improving information accessibility. In: 2017 12th international conference on intelligent systems and knowledge engineering (ISKE), IEEE, pp 1–8. https://doi.org/10.1109/ISKE.2017.8258772. ISBN 978-1-5386-1829-5

Puzis Y, Borodin Y, Puzis R, Ramakrishnan I (2013) Predictive web automation assistant for people with vision impairments. In: Proceedings of the 22nd international conference on World Wide Web - WWW 2013. ACM Press, New York, pp 1031–1040. https://doi.org/10.1145/2488388. 2488478. ISBN 9781450320351

Salber D, Dey AK, Abowd GD (1999) The context toolkit. In: Proceedings of the SIGCHI conference on human factors in computing systems the CHI is the limit - CHI 1999. ACM Press, New York, pp 434–441. https://doi.org/10.1145/302979.303126. ISBN 0201485591

Sottet J-S, Ganneau V, Calvary G, Coutaz J, Demeure A, Favre J-M, Demumieux R (2007) Model-driven adaptation for plastic user interfaces. Springer, Heidelberg, pp 397–410. https://doi.org/ 10.1007/978-3-540-74796-3_38

Stephanidis C, Paramythis A, Sfyrakis M, Stergiou A, Maou N, Leventis A, Paparoulis G, Karagiannidis C (1998) Adaptable and adaptive user interfaces for disabled users in the AVANTI project. Springer, Heidelberg, pp 153–166. https://doi.org/10.1007/BFb0056962

Stephanidis C, Savidis A (2001) Universal access in the information society: methods, tools, and interaction technologies. Univers Access Inf Soc 1(1):40–55. https://doi.org/10.1007/s102090100008. ISSN 1615-5289

Takagi H, Kawanaka S, Kobayashi M, Itoh T, Asakawa C (2008) Social accessibility. In: Proceedings of the 10th international ACM SIGACCESS conference on computers and accessibility - Assets 2008. ACM Press, New York, p 193. https://doi.org/10.1145/1414471.1414507. ISBN 9781595939760

Takagi H, Kawanaka S, Kobayashi M, Sato D, Asakawa C (2009) Collaborative web accessibility improvement. In: Proceeding of the eleventh international ACM SIGACCESS conference on computers and accessibility - Assets 2009. ACM Press, New York, p 195. https://doi.org/10.1145/1639642.1639677. ISBN 9781605585581

Vanderheiden GC, Treviranus J, Ortega-Moral M, Peissner M, de Lera E (2014) Creating a global public inclusive infrastructure (GPII). Springer, Cham, pp 506–515. https://doi.org/10.1007/978-3-319-07509-9_48

WAI-ARIA (W3C), Web accessibility initiative (WAI) – W3C. https://www.w3.org/WAI/standards-guidelines/aria/

WebAdapt2Me. https://www-03.ibm.com/press/us/en/pressrelease/19515.wss

Whittle J, Hutchinson J, Rouncefield M (2014) The state of practice in model-driven engineering. IEEE Softw 31:79–85. https://doi.org/10.1109/MS.2013.65. ISSN 0740-7459

Yang SJ, Shao NW (2007) Enhancing pervasive web accessibility with rule-based adaptation strategy. Expert Syst Appl 32(4):1154–1167. https://doi.org/10.1016/j.eswa.2006.02.008

Yesilada Y, Harper S, Goble C, Stevens R (2004) DANTE. In: Proceedings of the 13th international World Wide Web conference on alternate track papers and posters - WWW Alt. 2004. ACM Press, New York, p 490. https://doi.org/10.1145/1013367.1013540. ISBN 1581139128

Yoda I (2018) A study of the adaptive gesture interface for the severely physically handicapped. Impact 2018:41–43

Chapter 30
Transcoding

Chieko Asakawa, Hironobu Takagi and Kentarou Fukuda

Abstract "Transcoding for Web accessibility" is a category of technologies to transform inaccessible web content into accessible content on the fly. It was invented to help people with disabilities access inaccessible web pages without asking the content authors to modify their pages. It does this by converting the content on the fly in an intermediary server between the web server and the web browser. The technology has matured along with voice browsing technology from circa 1992 and was actively used in the 2000s. In this chapter, we will first cover the history of the transcoding technologies, and then introduce technical details of these transcoding systems. Finally, we discuss future directions and technical problems.

30.1   Introduction

Table 30.1 is a list of major transcoding systems. This list is not comprehensive, but covers the major types of historical and current transcoding systems. In this section, we will briefly look back at the history of transcoding for web accessibility by introducing these systems.

In order to look back at the history, we need to follow two technology streams in the 1990s, one for web accessibility technologies and transcoding technologies. These two types of technologies yielded a new category of technologies by 2000. We will briefly introduce these two streams.

The web was invented in 1992, and it quickly spread all over the world. Over the next decade, web accessibility technologies appeared and matured. From the beginning of web accessibility efforts, the content transformation was a central topic to make general Web content accessible especially for blind users.

Lynx, a text-based web browser developed in 1992, was one of the earliest knownonvisual web access systems [Lynx]. It has a function to convert pages writ-

C. Asakawa
IBM Thomas J. Watson Research Center, New York, USA

H. Takagi · K. Fukuda (✉)
IBM Research, Tokyo, Japan
e-mail: kentarou@jp.ibm.com

© Springer-Verlag London Ltd., part of Springer Nature 2019
Y. Yesilada and S. Harper (eds.), *Web Accessibility*, Human–Computer
Interaction Series, https://doi.org/10.1007/978-1-4471-7440-0_30

Table 30.1 Transcoding systems

Year	Name	Developer/organization	Final status	Where transformation	Input format	Output format	Main target user	Main methods	Metadata	References
1992	Web-BBS gateway	Asahinet	Commercial	Intermediary (BBS server)	HTML	Terminal	General user	Serialization and link numbering		Asakawa (2005)
1997	IBM home page reader	IBM	Commercial	Client-side (Application)	HTML	HTML	Blind	Table header inference, alt text inference, etc.		Asakawa and Lewis (1998), Asakawa and Itoh (1998, 1999) and Laws and Asakawa (1999)
1998	HTML-VoiceXML	Siemens		Intermediary (VoiceXML server)	HTML	VoiceXML	General user	Segmentation		Goose et al. (1998)
1998	BETSIE	BBC	Public (open source)	Server-side	HTML	HTML	Blind and low vision	Content reordering	Specialized for BBC	BETSIE
1998	Access gateway		Public (open source)	Intermediary (Web server)	HTML	HTML	Blind and low vision	Serialization, etc.		Brown and Robinson (2001)
2000	Aurora	IBM Research—Almaden		Intermediary (Proxy server)	HTML	HTML	Blind and general user	Simplification	External annotation	Huang (2000a, b)

(continued)

Table 30.1 (continued)

Year	Name	Developer/organization	Final status	Where transformation	Input format	Output format	Main target user	Main methods	Metadata	References
2000	Accessibility transcoding	IBM Research—Tokyo		Intermediary (Proxy server)	HTML	HTML	Blind and low vision	Simplification, reordering, etc.	External annotation	Asakawa and Takagi (2000) and Takagi and Asakawa (2000)
2001	ITry/LYCOS transcoder	IBM Japan and LYCOS Japan	Public	Intermediary (Web server)	HTML	HTML	Blind, low vision and seniors	Reordering, magnification, color change, etc.	External annotation	Maeda et al. (2004)
2003	LIFT text transcoder	Usable Net	Commercial	Intermediary (Web server)	HTML	HTML	Blind (compliance)	Text only	External annotation (XSLT)	LiFT
2004	Hearsay	State Univ. of New York at Stony Brook	Public (open source)	Intermediary	HTML	HTML	Blind	Automatic segmentation		Ramakrishnan et al. (2004), Borodin (2006) and Borodin et al. (2007)

(continued)

Table 30.1 (continued)

Year	Name	Developer/organization	Final status	Where transformation	Input format	Output format	Main target user	Main methods	Metadata	References
2004	Web Adapt2Me	IBM T. J. Watson Research Center	Commercial	Client-side (Browser plug-in)	HTML	HTML	Low vision and seniors	Magnification, device adaptation		Hanson (2001), Hanson and Richards (2004), Richards and Hanson (2004) and WA2M
2004	Dante	University of Manchester		Intermediary	HTML	HTML	Blind and low vision	Table of contents, simplification, etc.	External annotation	Plessers et al. (2005) and Yesilada et al. (2007)
2006	Web in Sight	University of Washington	Public	Intermediary	HTML	H TM L	Blind and low vision	Insertion of alternative texts	External annotation and automatic analysis	Bigham et al. (2006) and Bigham (2007)

(continued)

Table 30.1 (continued)

Year	Name	Developer/organization	Final status	Where transformation	Input format	Output format	Main target user	Main methods	Metadata	References
2006	SADle	University of Manchester		Intermediary (Proxy server) and Client-side	HTML	HTML	Blind and low vision	Simplification, reordering, etc.	CSS (class and id) and external annotation	Harper and Patel (2005a), Harper et al. (2006a) and Bechhofer et al. (2006)
2007	A browser for multimedia	IBM research—Tokyo	Public (open source)	Client-side	DHTML and flash	HTML	Blind	Insertion of alternative texts, multimedia control, audio description, etc.	External annotation	Miyashita et al. (2007) and Sato et al. (2007)
2008	Web anywhere	Univ. of Washington	Public (open source)	Intermediary (Proxy server) and Client-side	HTML	HTM L + Speech	Blind	Self-voicing web browser inside a web browser		Bigham et al. (2008)

(continued)

Table 30.1 (continued)

Year	Name	Developer/organization	Final status	Where transformation	Input format	Output format	Main target user	Main methods	Metadata	References
2008	Social accessibility	IBM research -Tokyo	Public	Client-side (JAWS Script and JavaScript)	HTML	HTML	Blind	Insert of alternative texts and headings, reordering, etc.	External annotation	Takagi et al. (2008)
2009	Automatic captions	YouTube	Commercial	Server-side	Video	Video with captions	Hearing impaired and general user	Automatic caption generation and automatic translation		Harrenstien (2009)
2013	Client-side Web refactoring (CSWR)	Univ. Nacionalde La Plata	Public	Client-side	HTML	HTML	Blind	Split page, contextualize menu, distribute menu, postpone selection, etc.	External annotation	Garrido et al. (2013)
2013	Experiential transcoding	Millde east technical Univ.	Public (open source)	Client-side	HTML	HTML	Small screen device user	Reorder or select visual elements based on scanpath	External annotation ("scanpath" based on eye-tracking data)	Akpınar and Yeşilada (2015)

(continued)

Table 30.1 (continued)

Year	Name	Developer/organization	Final status	Where transformation	Input format	Output format	Main target user	Main methods	Metadata	References
2014	Personalized rendering on mobile browsers	Samsung R&D Institute		Client-side	Rendered (HTML, etc.)	Converted	Small screen device user	Rendering adjustments (Zoom—level, color profile, brightness/contrast)		Sunkara et al. (2014)
2015	Smart wrap	Carnegie Melbn Univ.	Public	Client-side (Browser plug-in)	HTML	HTML	Blind and low vision	Convert data sets (tables, lists, etc.) into accessible table	External annotation	Gardiner et al. (2015)
2016	Automatic alternative text	Facebook	Commercial	Server-side	HTML	HTML	Blind and low vision	Automatic alternative text insertion		Wu et al. (2017)

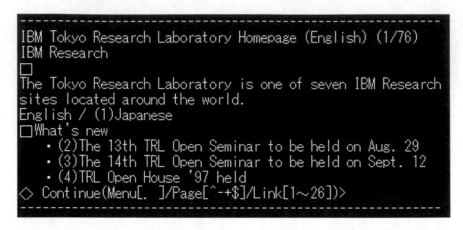

```
--------------------------------------------------------------
IBM Tokyo Research Laboratory Homepage (English) (1/76)
IBM Research
□
The Tokyo Research Laboratory is one of seven IBM Research
sites located around the world.
English / (1)Japanese
□What's new
    • (2)The 13th TRL Open Seminar to be held on Aug. 29
    • (3)The 14th TRL Open Seminar to be held on Sept. 12
    • (4)TRL Open House '97 held
◇ Continue(Menu[. ]/Page[^-+$]/Link[1~26])>
--------------------------------------------------------------
```

Fig. 30.1 Simulated screenshot of BBS-based web access system (authors' recreation)

ten in the Hypertext Markup Language (HTML) into text-only presentations on the client-side, and allows the users to navigate in the content by pressing the cursor keys. For example, the users could move to the next or previous link texts with the arrow keys. This allowed blind users to access the web with a DOS screen reader, using telnet to a UNIX server. For some years, such as "serialization of content" and "text-only conversion" were the basic functions for transcoding systems.

In the same year (1992), a Japanese text-based Bulletin Board System (BBS) provider started a text-based web browsing service through their BBS service (Asakawa 2005). This system was similar to Lynx, but the transformation was done on the server's side, acting as an intermediary in their BBS server. Whenever a user accessed a page, the BBS server obtained the target page from the web server, and transformed it into the text format, assigning sequential numbers to each link. The users were required to remember a target's link number, and input it into the command line of the BBS system to follow that link. Blind users could use the BBS system by using a DOS screen reader, and it meant they could access the web nonvisually. This system can be regarded as one of the earliest server-side transcoding systems, providing practical nonvisual access (Fig. 30.1).

In the mid-1990s, the focus of web access systems shifted from transformation to screen reading. In those days, the functionality of web browsers was evolving rapidly because of fierce competition among browsers. This was later called the "Browser War." Tracking these improvements, screen readers were also updated frequently to read text on various web browsers.

Screen reading is an approach that reads information on the screen "as it is." This approach is important to give blind users equal access to the information on the screen, but meanwhile, the web content is becoming much more visual, with two-dimensional layouts and embedded rich media. In addition, e-business appeared using HTML forms, and these forms were scarcely supported by screen readers at that time.

In the late 1990s, standalone voice browsers were developed to make the nonvisual web browsing much easier by integrating content transformation and optimized key operations (Asakawa and Lewis1998; Asakawa and Itoh 1998, 1999; DeWitt et al. 1998). IBM Home Page Reader (HPR) was developed and became an official product in 1997 (Laws and Asakawa 1999; Asakawa 2005). It was a standalone browser with its own HTML parser, transformation engine, and custom key combinations. It included various transformation functions. For example, if an image link did not have a corresponding alternative text, HPR picked some part of the destination Uniform Resource Identifier (URI) to give an idea of the destination. HPR also analyzed complicated tables and automatically inferred which cells were the table headers (Asakawa and Itoh 1999), and then allowed users to dynamically jump to these headers with table navigation keyboard commands. These transformation functions worked well to improve the usability of web access in combination with advanced nonvisual rendering functions, such as using a female voice for clickable elements, and sound icons and slower reading for headings. These early web accessibility technologies can be regarded as transcoding systems both on the client-side (HPR) or on using a server-side intermediary (the BBS).

Meanwhile, transcoding technologies continued to evolve. Transcoding is a general concept of transforming content or a program on the fly in an intermediary server, resulting in other formats. The initial targets in the 1980s were programs and encoded media content. In those cases, the original "transcoding" stood for "transformation of machine code" or "transformation of media-encodings."

Along with the rapid spread of the web, the concept and the term "transcoding" were soon applied in a broader sense to the transformation of web content written in HTML. This was at the same time as the web accessibility technologies were developing (in the 1990s). Initially, the main target was mobile devices (Bickmore and Schilit 1997; Hori et al. 2000; Buyukkokten et al. 2000). The approach was applied to make web content "adaptive" for mobile devices by adapting various methods, such as simplification, fish-eye rendering, optimized navigation, and so on. This was the beginning of transcoding for adaptation, but for diverse devices rather than for diverse users (see "User Interface Adaptation for Accessibility" in PART 5 and "Mobile Web" in PART 6 for more details about UI adaptation and mobile web accessibility, respectively).

In the late 1990s, the "adaptation of devices" shifted to the concept of "adaptation to users." In 1997, (Barrett et al. 1997) developed a web personalization system by using an intermediary transcoding approach. Their Web Intermediaries (WBI) was a framework to develop transcoding systems, and they developed personalization functions, such as a personal history, shortcut links, page watching, and web traffic lights, on top of the framework (Maglio et al. 2000, WebSphere Transcoding Publisher). The key innovation of this system was the profile repository ("user model" in the paper). The repository supported content adaptation for each user. This idea directly inspired the idea of personalization (adaptation) for people with disabilities.

From that time (circa 1998), web pages were becoming increasingly visual. Web designers and content owners tend to lay out various kinds of information in one page with various types of visual effects. This trend made web access more difficult for users of screen readers or voice browsers. The effectiveness of nonvisual web access was declining, and many blind users became discouraged with web browsing even though the numbers of sighted Web users were increasing explosively. The web accessibility transcoding systems were invented to reverse this trend by transforming the inaccessible content on the fly to make it more accessible.

BETSIE [Betsie] and the Access Gateway (Brown and Robinson 2001) were among the earliest practical transcoding systems for web accessibility. BETSIE was a transcoding system used by the BBC site to automatically create a text-only version of its web site, developed by the BBC in 1998. Surprisingly, the system had been supported until (2010), more than 10 years after its introduction. It can create pages optimized for visually impaired users by moving the main content to the top of the page, and changes colors for high contrast color sets. The system is exploiting specific characteristics of the template of the BBC web site, and therefore it can only handle pages from that site.

The Access Gateway, developed in 1998, is a transcoding server for general web pages. A user can get a personalized web page by entering the URI of the target page, and then pressing the "Get page" button. It has a preference page for setting detailed options, such as font sizes, image replacement, color scheme changes, and various user-specific controllable options. This system was the first transcoding server available to the public and capable of handling any page on the Internet.

Based on this research and these developments, Asakawa and Takagi developed an accessibility transcoding proxy in 2000 (Asakawa and Takagi 2000; Takagi and Asakawa 2000). The system had two major features, a user profile repository and a combination of automatic transcoding and annotation-based transcoding. The user profile repository allowed storing each user's profile on the server-side, and used it to provide comprehensive adaptations for each user.

There is a need to automatically transform content in order to handle arbitrary pages on the Internet. To tackle this issue, Facebook automatically generates alternative texts for photos posted to SNS by using object recognition technology, (Simonite 2017; Wu et al. 2017). It enables screen reader users to understand what kind of things might be contained in the photos. However, the automatic transformation has clear limitations. For example, it is difficult to compensate for the missing information such as missing labels for form elements, etc., appropriately. Complicated transformation, such as reordering of content, is also difficult to achieve automatically. We developed some heuristics to tackle these issues, but the heuristics were flawed, both quantitatively and qualitatively.

Annotation-based transcoding is a method to address some of these problems. It is a method to transform contents by referring to manually created external metadata, which adds missing semantic information for appropriate transformations of a target page. In order to make transcoding effective, especially for blind users, it is necessary to transform content drastically but accurately. The external annotation approach supports this level of transcoding. The most important drawback of this approach is the workload of creating annotations for pages. We will discuss this topic in Sect. 30.3.1.

At the same time, two other accessibility transcoding systems were developed within IBM, one in the Watson Research Laboratory and one in the Almaden Research Laboratory. Watson's system focused on adaptations for senior citizens, and was first developed as a server-side proxy (Hanson 2001), before moving to client-side transcoding (Hanson and Richards 2004; Richards and Hanson 2004). The system was productized and has been deployed at various sites [WA2M]. The system from Almaden Research (Huang and Sundaresan 2000a, b) focused on the simplification of e-business applications, such as auctions and search engines. This used precise annotation and first transformed the web pages into semantically structured XML documents, and then the pages for users were generated from the XML documents.

Such research established the area of accessibility transcoding as a part of web accessibility research, and various types of research started based on these results. Dante (Yesilada et al. 2003; Plessers et al. 2005) is an annotation-based transcoding system, which is characterized by a metaphor for nonvisual navigation, called the travel metaphor (Goble et al. 2000). They created a taxonomy for nonvisual navigation based on their metaphor, such as directions, navigation points, travel assistance, decision points, and reference points. Since it takes time to navigate among the component items on a page by using nonvisual key navigation, the travel metaphor is a powerful metaphor to establish a well-designed taxonomy.

The SADIe (Harper and Patel 2005; Harper and Bechhofer 2005; Bechhofer et al. 2006; Harper et al. 2006a, b) has both automatic (rule-based) and (annotation-based) semantic transcoding function, and it is characterized by its use of "inlined" metadata as a form of Cascading Style Sheet (CSS) information. CSS is the standard mechanism to format and to layout web pages by adding styling/layout attributes to HTML elements by referring identification information, such as "id" and "class" attributes. SADIe is utilizing this identification information as "inlined metadata" for distinguishing semantics of partial contents in a page. The effective utilization of internal metadata will be an important research topic to make the transcoding more feasible in a real environment (see Sect. 30.3.1).

HearSay (Ramakrishnan et al. 2004; Borodin 2006; Borodin et al. 2007) is an automatic transcoding system from existing web pages to VoiceXML [W3CVoice]. The system is characterized by its automatic segmentation algorithm, which can avoid the use of annotation. It has functions to analyze the visual structure of a page based on the Document Object Model (DOM [DOM]) tree structure (using the HTML tags) of the page. (Goose et al. 1998, 2000) is one of the earliest studies in this category, and (Shao et al. 2003) tried to apply annotation-based transcoding for HTML to VoiceXML transformation.

Transcoding technology was also adopted by web accessibility service businesses, which become active after the U.S. Section 508 [Section 508] took effect. In 2003, UsableNet, Inc. started a transcoding service, "LIFT Text Transcoder" [LiFT]. This is a service to generate "text only pages" without modifying the original content based on transcoding techniques. Their approach is a standard approach to the transcoding system, with basic transformations that can automatically create a text-only and serialized page. In order to compensate for the automatic transformation, an XSLT-based annotation can be used. This covers various functions, such as reordering of content, adding alternative text to images, and adding heading tags to plain texts. They are selling services to create annotations and to transform customers' content into accessible text-only pages.

As the years pass, transcoding technologies are becoming more ubiquitous in web systems, both on the client-side and server-side (Bigham et al. 2008; Takagi et al. 2008; Garrido et al. 2013; Sunkara et al. 2014; Akpınar and Yeşilada 2015; Gardiner et al. 2015). On the server-side, many web sites, and content management systems provide functions to personalize features such as the colors, layouts, and font sizes of pages by using a settings panel (e.g., Rainville-pitt and D'Amour 2007).

Some browser plug-ins have been developed to enable client-side transcoding. Greasemonkey [Greasemonkey] is a popular plug-in for the Firefox browser to allow people to create transcoding functions on the client-side. We can easily integrate transcoding functions by creating simple JavaScript programs. This plug-in is not used only for accessibility, but various scripts to improve accessibility have developed on the framework. The Accessmonkey (Bigham and Ladner 2007) is a similar Firefox plug-in, but is focusing on accessibility purposes.

Some client-side assistive technologies are available on the market for senior citizens, such as WebAdapt2Me and the EasyWeb Browsers, both from IBM. They have some transcoding functions to change color schemas and font magnification functions, and also have text-to-speech services related to mouse operations. Transcoding functions are also added to assistive technologies for visually impaired people. Jaws [Jaws], the most popular screen reader, has a function to serialize the current web page. This function serializes layout tables and makes nonvisual navigation simpler for screen reader functions.

In the late 2000s, the challenge in the web accessibility field was moved to the accessibility of dynamic web content, such as DHTML (simulated graphical user interfaces on a web page using JavaScript) and Flash (a widely used animation format developed by Adobe Systems). At that moment, no general methodology had been widely accepted to make such content accessible, and so accessibility is rarely taken into account for this content. An example is that buttons were rarely operable with a keyboard, and cases where the reading order of elements was not logical to support understanding the meaning of the content.

Sato's Flash transcoding system (Sato et al. 2007) is an example of an attempt to transcode dynamic content for accessibility. The system has functions to associate the most probable text object as an alternative text for a button, and to make inaccessible buttons accessible since some visible button are not presented as buttons for screen readers. Miyashita et al. (2007) developed an annotation-based client-side transcoding system for dynamic content and multimedia content, such as DHTML, Flash, and movies. In this system, metadata can be regarded as a transformation language for transforming a dynamic XML object model structure to a simple tree structure for nonvisual access. This process is done completely on the client-side. In addition, the system can also provide audio description for movies based on the annotation. Another example that tackled to multimedia content is automatic captions in YouTube (Harrenstien 2009; Simonite 2017). It provides captions for movies by leveraging a combination of automatic speech recognition and machine translation technologies.

To improve the accessibility of dynamic web content, Accessible-Rich Internet Applications (WAI-ARIA) 1.0 [WAI-ARIA] was published from W3C in 2014. WAI-ARIA enables web developers to properly convey user interface behaviors and structural information to assistive technologies in document-level markup by using its ontology of roles, states, and properties. This concept was incorporated into HTML 5 [HTML5] that is a new standard for the web. Simultaneously with WAI-ARIA, accessibility support was considered in major JavaScript libraries such as in jQuery UI [jQuery UI].

30.2 Overview

Throughout the history of transcoding technologies, various types of transformation functions were developed. In this section, we will give an overview of these transformation methods.

30.2.1 Text Magnification

Text Magnification is the most common adaptation method for web pages for sighted users. This function has become ubiquitous in modern browsers. This method can be applied for a wide variety of users, such as senior citizens with mild vision problems, senior citizens with cataracts, or people with poor eyesight. Even for people with good eyesight, it helps when their screen resolution is too fine for web pages (of course, magnification does not provide any benefit for blind users).

Currently, this method is popular both for server-side systems and for client-side systems. Many content management systems provide personalization functions for font sizes, and many major web sites have the personalization function to give users preferable impression to their sites.

Web browsers have been improved to include this function. Thus, users can magnify pages whenever they want, even if a site does not provide a personalization function. We could say that this function graduated from being limited to transcoding and has become a mandatory function in web systems.

30.2.2 Color Scheme Changes

Color scheme changes are beneficial for people with some types of eye conditions, such as cataracts, glaucoma, or color vision deficiency (see "Visual Disabilities" in PART 1 for more details). Since our society has many people with these conditions, this method was one of the major methods for transcoding systems. For HTML content, this method can be implemented by simply changing the Cascading Style Sheet (CSS) for the page (Iaccarino et al. 2006a, etc.). CSS properties can be overwritten by external style sheets, so it is easy to change colors from a default to some other color schema. As in the case of text magnification, currently, this method is popular both for server-side systems and for client-side systems.

Another type of technique is the image processing-based adaptation (Nam et al. 2005; Iaccarino et al. 2006b; Sunkara et al. 2014, etc.). By using image processing techniques, it is possible to optimize the visual presentation for each disability, such as cataracts or color vision deficiencies, by using specific color schemes with the bitmap images. For example, (Iaccarino et al. 2006b) is a method to shift a color range to the ideal range for people with color vision deficiency. It shifts sets of confusing colors to other colors that can be discriminated between, such as red and green colors, by using image processing techniques on the fly. This type of precise color scheme adaptation provides great benefits to the users, especially for images and multimedia content that cannot be managed by CSS. However, many issues have to be addressed to make it practical, especially for performance and scalability.

30.2.3 Serialization

Serialization is a method to remove HTML tags that are used only for layout purposes, such as layout tables, and to generate serialized content (e.g., Brown and Robinson 2001). Serialized content is beneficial both for blind and for low-vision users. Each voice browser has table navigation functions that allow users to navigate in two-dimensional tables by using the directional cursor keys [HPR]. Blind users can understand the structure of a data table by using this navigation function. In contrast, some tables are used merely for layout purposes, such as aligning contents horizontally in table cells with an invisible border. These "layout tables" are generally regarded as a misuse of tables, since the layout should properly be controlled by style sheets, but they are very common. These layout tables interfere with table navigation. For example, if a data table is contained within a layout table, the voice browsers cannot distinguish between the data tables and layout tables, and they try to verbalize the current complicated location (including the cell numbers) for the layout tables. The serialization transcoding can address this issue by eliminating the layout tables.

For low-vision users, serialization is beneficial by eliminating troublesome horizontal scrolling when a page is magnified. If the page was designed using CSS functions, the page can easily be serialized by simply disabling the style sheets. However, if layout tables are used in the page, it is necessary to scroll both vertically and horizontally to see the full content. Vertical scrolling can be done with the usual page up/down operations, but a need for horizontal scrolling clearly lowers the usability.

In the 2010s, Responsive Web Design and Adaptive Web Design (Marcotte 2010; Gustafson 2011) that aim to automatically adapt (resize, hide, shrink, etc.) web page to make it looks good on each user's environment (screen size, device, etc.) became popular. Simultaneously with it, the use of a layout table decreased significantly. However, to show dataset, such as a list of products in web shop, there still exist layout tables and serialization approach is required to enable visually impaired users to access these datasets (Gardiner et al. 2015).

30.2.4 Alternative Text Insertion

"Alternative text" is a concept of adding short descriptions to non-text objects in a page. This is critical to allow blind users to access web content, since images without alternative text are fundamentally unrecognizable for voice access users. The use of alternative text is one of the most important concepts to make web content accessible.

It is technically hard to automatically detect appropriate alternative text for arbitrary images, even when using Optical Character Recognition (OCR) techniques. Even when an image has text, it is usually highly decorated, which is why an image was used for that text. For other images, such as an icon, there is no text and it is difficult to automatically analyze a description from the image.

Every screen reader has a function to read a part of a URI if no other alternative text is assigned to an image with a link. The early versions of HPR read the last two "words" in the URI (and ignoring the file extension). For example, if the URI linked to an image is "http://www.example.com/news/articles/images/new.gif" then it is read as "images new." This is a primitive but general heuristic method to cope with the problem of missing an alternative text.

The annotation-based method was invented to augment pages by providing accurate but manually created alternative text [Dardailler]. Annotation is a type of metadata used for transcoding (see Sect. 30.3.1). The transcoder has a repository of alternative text. Alternative text is indexed to URIs and image file names in the repository, and the transcoding system automatically retrieves an appropriate text by using the URLs and filenames as keys and then assigns a proper text to each image. The essential drawback of this method is that a human annotation author should describe the annotations manually. The workload of annotation authoring has prevented this approach from being widely used in practical environments.

WebInSight (Bigham et al. 2006; Bigham 2007) is a transcoding system, which is focused on inserting alternative texts. The system is characterized by combining three different methods, context labeling, OCR image labeling, and human labeling. Context labeling is a method to get appropriate texts from linked pages for image links without alternative texts. There is an empirical rule that the linked page's title or headings (especially texts in <h1>) are often appropriate for the alternative text. The system applies this rule for the transcoding. OCR image labeling is a method to analyze alternative texts by using OCR techniques. They optimized an OCR engine for detecting alternative texts, and achieved 65% accuracy. Recently, by using object recognition technology, Facebook automatically generates alternative texts for photos posted to SNS (Simonite 2017; Wu et al. 2017). It enables screen reader users to understand what kind of things might be contained in the photos. Even there remain several limitations in these Machine Learning and AI-based approaches, automatically generated accessibility information is a great help to blind users.

At the same time, it is desirable to provide more accurate/appropriate texts while considering the context of web content, and therefore the system also provides a method for human labeling. This is an annotation-based transcoding method. Because of the importance of alternative texts, these transcoding methods will continue to be improved.

30.2.5   Page Rearrangement

Page rearrangement is a method to change the layout of a page to be suitable for screen readers or for magnification (e.g., Takagi et al. 2002; Harper 2006a, b). In the 2000s, the trends of web authoring were shifted to present various types of information in one page. For this purpose, various types of visual effects, such as background colors, layout tables, spacing, or horizontal lines are used to visually separate the components of the content. Each component has a "role" in the page, such as header or footer of the page, index list, advertisement, main content, shopping list, and so on. These components and their roles are easily recognized visually at a glance. For example, if a page has a header at the top of the page and an index at the left, then the main content area is usually at the center of the page, logically after the header and the index. This means that most users want to skip that unnecessary information by using navigation keys in order to reach the main content area, while sighted users can skip those components by merely moving their eyes to the main content at once.

Page rearrangement is a method to solve this issue, by making the visual components nonvisually distinguishable for screen reader users, or by providing semantically organized serialization for magnifier users. BETSIE [Betsie] is the first system, which can rearrange the order of components to be suitable for screen readers. It moves the main content to the top of the page, before the header or index, and thus screen reader users and magnifier users can immediately access the main content. BETSIE is an automatic transcoder, but specialized for the BBC site. Therefore, it recognizes the main content area specific hints, such as the size of a table. These hints and rules can be regarded as metadata.

Social accessibility project enabled full-page rearrangement based on manually created annotation information (Takagi et al. 2008). Figure 30.2 shows an example of the transformation. First, the system retrieves corresponding annotation data from the annotation database (see Sect. 30.3.1). Then it rearranges the page by referring to the roles and the importance values assigned to each component. The order of arrangement is determined based on the importance values, so that the main content will be moved to the top and nonessential information (e.g., advertisements) will be moved to the bottom. In addition, it inserts some delimiter text to show the borders of the components based on the title information included in the annotation, and it also inserts a page index at the top of each page to jump directly to each component.

This type of annotation-based rearrangement can provide highly accessible web content. It can also be applied to generate pages for telephone access. However, the workload of annotation authoring is a problem. That is why many page segmentation algorithms have been proposed. We will discuss the issue of the workload for annotation authoring in Sect. 30.3.

Various segmentation methods have been invented to realize automatic reordering and segmentation-based navigation supports (Goose et al. 1998; Buyukkokten et al. 2001; Fukuda et al. 2003; Ramakrishnan et al. 2004, etc.). The technique is a challenging research topic since it is necessary to semantically "accurately" partition pages into sub-contents in order to realize meaningful support for nonvisual access. If a detected boundary shifts an element, the result will be impacted severely. CSurf (Mahmud et al. 2007a, b) is a tool to support nonvisual navigation by using the automatic context detection, but not fully reordering pages. This approach will not be severely impacted by fine-grained accuracy of an automatic detection algorithm. This system shows that it is important not to apply the reordering method directly to the automatic segmentation method, instead, to invent new types of navigation supports based on automatic segmentation algorithms.

Recent standards such as WAI-ARIA [WAI-ARIA] and HTML 5 [HTML5] also tackled to this segmentation problem. By using Landmark Roles of WAI-ARIA and new elements of HTML 5, such as header, footer, main, nav, article, section, and aside, web authors can easily specify the segments and its roles in their web content. If there exist this structural and semantic information, screen reader users can easily access their desired content within a page. In addition, the concept of page rearrangement is now part of major web design trends (Marcotte 2010; Gustafson 2011).

30.2.6   Simplification

Page simplification is a method that presents users with only the important parts of a page by eliminating the nonessential parts. As mentioned in the rearrangement section, each page has various types of components. While rearrangement retains all of the content, simplification removes unnecessary components from the target page and allows users to access only the important or interesting parts. This method is also called page clipping. It is popular for transcoding systems for mobile devices since these devices only have small screens and this method is especially suitable for small displays.

The most popular method for simplification is the annotation-based transformation. For rearrangement, annotation authors must describe all of the components in the page for the annotation of that page. In contrast, for simplification, the annotations only need to describe the components that are to be preserved or removed. This characteristic lowers the cost of annotation authoring, and make this method more cost effective compared with page rearrangement methods.

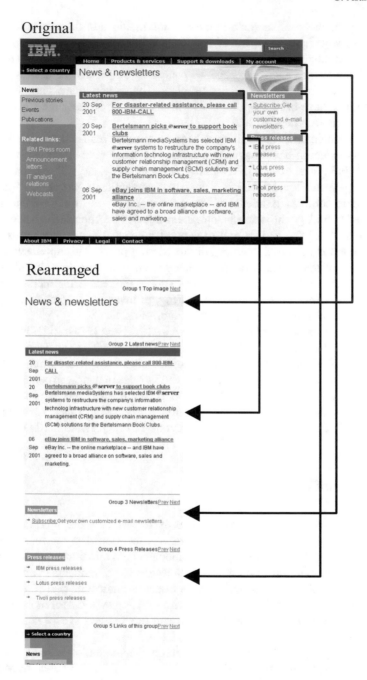

Fig. 30.2 Example of page rearrangement (excerpt from Takagi et al. 2002)

Not only annotation-based transcoding, but also various types of automatic transcoding methods have been developed. The page segmentation algorithms can be applied to simplify a page, if they have a function to detect an important component in a page. Differential analysis method (Takagi and Asakawa 2000) is one of the methods (see Sect. 30.3). This method analyses the difference between two HTML documents based on DOM structure. The basic assumption is that the most important component is the most unique component, which is not included in any other pages. Therefore, if all of the duplicated components are removed, the remaining components should be the unique and important component in the page. For example, header, footer, and index are included in other neighbor pages, so they can be eliminated.

One of the drawbacks of this method is concern about losing important content. Ideally, the same information available to sighted users should be presented non-visually, even after the transformations. Especially for compliance to accessibility regulations, it is necessary to preserve all of the content in each page. Also, the lost material will interfere with the business models of many sites by removing their advertisements. As described in the previous subsection, the recent web standards enable the authors to easily include structural and semantic information into their web page. With the expansion of these techniques, the role of simplification can be considered as finished.

30.3 Discussion

Transcoding is a method to transform content on the fly. That is why the architectures can be classified by the location of the transformation engines, from server-side transformations to client-side transformations. In Table 30.1, the column "where transformation occurs" shows these locations. We classified this column into mainly three categories, server-side, intermediary (proxy server), and client-side. The server-side implies the transcoding system is integrated into a web server and only used for a specific site. Usually, transcoders in this category are not visible to end users since they are just a part of the web site. These transcoders are usually integrated as a part of the web server and include any support systems such as reverse proxies used for security or load-balancing. BETSIE is an exception among server-side transcoders. This system is actually a kind of web server-style intermediary transcoder (see below) but is only capable of supporting the BBC sites.

The "intermediary" is an approach to transform content between the browser at the end user's side and the web server. This approach is the archetypical architecture for transcoding systems since originally transcoding referred only to this approach. Figure 30.3 shows the basic architecture of this intermediary approach. There are two types of implementation, one that uses a proxy setting and one that explicitly uses a web server.

Proxy transcoders work as an HTTP proxy and transform the content on the fly. Each user must set the address of the transcoding server in their browser, but the

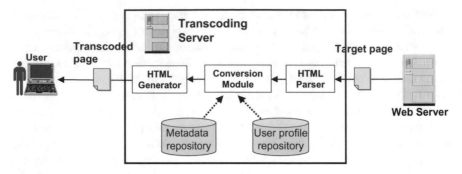

Fig. 30.3 Typical architecture for intermediary setting

transcoding process is then transparent. They simply use their browser as usual, and the transcoder transforms each page on the fly. This is an ideal environment that was the original conception when accessibility transcoding was invented.

Web server transcoders are slightly different from proxy transcoders since the user does not need to change any proxy setting in the browser. The user accesses an initial entry page for the transcoder and accesses the target page, and all links in that page are modified so that the following accesses will also be processed by the transcoding server. For example, when using Access Gateway, a user first needs to access a starting page, and submit the target page's URI to the system. Then it transforms the target page, and sends the modified page to the user. If the user submitted URI "www.ibm.com," then the URI of the modified target page will become "http://access.accu.org/cgi-bin/access?Aesu=1&Au=www.ibm.com." This means that the server-side script "/cgi-bin/access" has processed the target page and sent it to the browser.

Both of these methods have drawbacks and advantages (see Table 30.2). Using a web server does not require any changes on the client-side, while the systems with proxy settings require users to change the proxy configuration of their browsers. The coverage of available pages for the proxy setting approach is wider than with a web server setting since the web server setting approach requires the transcoder to rewrite all of the URIs in the links in a page so that following the hyperlink will also go through the transcoding system. This requirement often breaks JavaScript associated with links, and the URIs in JavaScript code are usually not modified during the transcoding since it is technically difficult to analyze JavaScript sufficiently.

It is not so technically difficult to migrate the proxy setting approach to the web server setting approach. Therefore, some systems are capable of both approaches. In fact, the Asakawa and Takagi transcoder was originally developed using the proxy setting approach (as Accessibility Transcoder in 2000), but was later migrated to the web server approach for a public service demonstration with a Japanese web portal provider (as the ITry/Lycos transcoder in 2001 (Maeda et al. 2004)). The system is classified into "server-side," since the system worked only for the target portal site, and ran within their server environment. However, the system was just the same as the

Table 30.2 Comparison of location of transcoding engines

		Advantage	Drawbacks
Server-side		– Can be maintained along with web servers	– Only for a specific site
Intermediary	Web server	– Does not require users to change their browser settings	– Coverage is limited, since all links in a target page should be rewritten by the transcoder, and this causes various problems – Impossible to transcode pages with DHTML or AJAX
	Proxy	– Transcoding process is transparent from users	– Require users to change their browser setting – Impossible to transcode pages with DHTML/AJAX. (Better than Web server setting, but worse than client-side transcoding)
Client-side		– More stable than intermediary setting – Possible to provide additional assistive functions (e.g., TTS) – Possible to transcode DHTML pages (with limitations)	– Require users to install client-side components

"intermediary," and simply added some HTML generation code and link rewriting code to implement the web server setting approach.

The client-side transcoding is a method to transform the content, usually inside a browser, not an intermediary server. Figure 30.4 shows a general architecture for this approach. There is no intermediary between the web server and the browser. The pages are loaded by the browser as usual. Once a page is loaded, the component for transformation detects it, usually by receiving the page loading completion event (the "onload" event), and then starts the transformations. Modern browsers expose the internal HTML tag structure as a DOM tree structure, and it is possible for browser plug-in components to access the in-memory DOM structure through the DOM API, the most popular API not only for transcoding systems but also for JavaScript and other XML processing.

The trend of transcoding architecture is changing along with the changes in general web architectures. Currently, the processing engine is moving from the server to the client based on client-side scripts, usually written in JavaScript. AJAX and mash-up provide developers with new paradigms to build new web applications by combining existing services written in JavaScript. This general trend directly affects the architecture of transcoding systems. It is technically too difficult and impractical

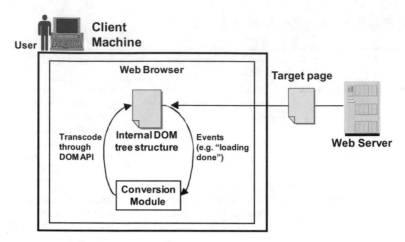

Fig. 30.4 Typical architecture for the client-side transcoding

to transcode JavaScript code on the fly by adapting the intermediary approach. That is why transcoding systems are shifting to client-side approaches (see Table 30.1).

In the Sect. 30.2, various types of transcoding methods were introduced. In this section, we will discuss the techniques underlying these methods, and also discuss problems with these methods.

30.3.1 Annotation-Based Transcoding

Annotation-based transcoding is a method to transform content by referring to external (or inlined) annotation information, which is metadata for making transformations more accurate and usable for end users compared to automatic transcoding. We introduced many annotation-based transcoding methods in Sect. 30.2, such as the insertion of alternative texts, rearrangement, and simplification. This method can generate highly usable and accurate pages, but the workload for annotation authoring is the most significant and essential drawback.

Annotation-based transcoding was originally developed for mobile devices (Hori et al. 2000; Nagao 2000). One of the basic methods for transcoding for small screen devices is page fragmentation, which divides pages into fragments, displays the fragments one by one, and allows users to navigate among these smaller pages. This process was called "re-authoring" of content. In order to implement this function, Hori, et al. applied an annotation-based approach. They defined an annotation language based on RDF [RDF], which could describe alternative content for parts of the target page, give hints for fragmentation, and supply criteria to select appropriate alternative content.

Asakawa and Takagi (Asakawa 2000; Takagi 2000) developed an annotation-based transcoding system for web accessibility in 2000, based on previous work including Hori's system and Nagao's system. At that time, they soon noticed differences between transcoding systems for mobile devices and for accessibility, because the required coverage of the annotation systems was different. For mobile access, site owners usually did not want to make their whole site visible, but just the most important parts of their site, or some specific web applications, such as the pages for a specific event or a web form for registration. They also wanted visually "precise" transcoding, and that the resulting pages should be "well designed". Therefore, the annotations did not need to cover as many pages but were intended to be as fine-grained as possible to precisely control the transcoding (see "Mobile Web" in PART 6 for more details about Mobile Web accessibility).

In contrast, the site owners wanted to make their "whole site" accessible by using transcoding systems, since the users normally want access to an entire site. It was natural that blind users want to access the same information as sighted users, but with a usable interface. The users were always frustrated when they found pages without annotations. Another reason was compliance. It is normally necessary to make all of a site compliant to satisfy web accessibility regulations. Therefore, the site owners were attracted to the possibilities of cost reduction for making their entire sites accessible by using transcoding technology.

In order to achieve "whole-site" transcoding, there are three major technical challenges. In the paper in 2002 (Takagi et al. 2002), we introduced the first and second challenges, but the third challenge emerged with the development and adoption of DHTML technologies.

1. Reduction of the workloads for annotation authoring. One obvious answer is by adapting generalized annotations for similar web pages.
2. Adaptation of annotations for changing pages. Web pages are not static, but are continuously changing their content and layout, and new pages are created each day.

"Annotation matching" and "component pointing" are the key technologies to cope with these problems. Each annotation file should have descriptions for component definitions or alternative tests, and each description should have the location of the target object in the page. This pointing technology can be called "component pointing." This pointing mechanism is essential for transcoding systems. Several methods have been proposed (Huang and Sundaresan 2000a, b), but XPath [XPath] is the de facto standard method for transcoding systems. XPath is a pointing language for addressing a part of an XML document, based on the XML DOM structure. In the following discussion, we will use XPath notation as the method for component pointing.

Figure 30.5 shows an example of the annotation description and reordering based on the description. Figure 30.5 (A) is a part of the original web page. The annotation description (B) includes two "groups (sub-contents)" and their XPath descriptions. One group has an "advertisement" role and another has "proper content" role. That is why the order is switched in the result page (C). In the (C), boundary messages,

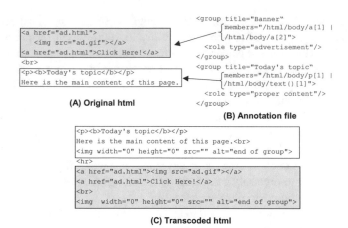

(A) Original html

(B) Annotation file

(C) Transcoded html

Fig. 30.5 Example of XPath-based annotation description (excerpt from Takagi and Asakawa 2000)

"end of group" are inserted between groups to clearly indicate semantic boundary nonvisually.

Each annotation-based transcoding system should have a repository of annotations (Fig. 30.3). An annotation database selects a corresponding annotation file by calculating the fit between a target page and an annotation file based on some matching algorithm. We call this an annotation matching algorithm. Any annotation-based system has such an algorithm. If an algorithm can appropriately apply an annotation to all of the applicable pages on the site, the workload will be drastically reduced (Challenge 1). If an algorithm can apply appropriate annotations to dynamically created pages and DHTML pages, whole-site transcoding will be feasible.

The simplest method is page by page matching (Hori et al. 2000). Each annotation has a list of corresponding URIs, and the database simply replies with the annotation for the listed URI. This method is completely rigid and deterministic, so it can handle neither newly created pages nor dynamically changing pages. In addition, it is difficult to apply one annotation to many similar pages, since the developer needs to list all of the corresponding pages.

A more advanced and widely used method involves regular expressions (Asakawa and Takagi 2000) for the URI patterns. In this case, the transcoder only sends the target page's URI to retrieve a corresponding annotation file. The database looks for a regular expression matching the target URI, and the annotation file associated with the matched regular expression will be returned to the transcoder as a result of the query. The basic assumption is that pages with similar layouts tend to have similar URIs. As an example, in the New York Times web site (www.nytimes.com), URIs involve a date, category, and part of the title: http://www.nytimes.com/2007/03/10/washington/10gun.html.

Therefore, we can expect URIs in this site may follow a specific rule: http://www.nytimes.com/[year]/[month]/[date]/[category]/[word/from/title].html.

This rule can be converted into a regular expression format, such as http://www\.nytimes\.com/20[0-2][0-9]/[0-1][0-9]/[0-3][0-9]/(international|politics|business|national|washington|world)/.+¥.html.

If all article pages in this site have sufficiently similar structures, then one annotation using this regular expression will cover all of the article pages throughout the site.

There are still problems with regular expression-based matching using XPath pointing. For example, on one specific day, a table announcing a "Special Sale," could appear in a page whose URI matches the regular expression. In the DOM tree, a new table has been inserted between the second table and the third table, so the third table of the annotation has become the fourth table. The XPath for an annotation that referred to the old third table should be changed to "table[4]", but this system would expect the special sale announcement will disappear in the near future. This means an annotation author would need to check and rewrite the XPath statements repeatedly, adapting to changing page layouts. At other times, it might be necessary to modify the regular expression in order to adapt to (distinguish between) pages with similar URIs but different layouts. This rewriting and generalization process is extremely tedious and time consuming.

To solve the issue of "changes in pages" and reduce the workload of annotation authoring, (Takagi et al. 2002) developed an annotation matching algorithm, called the dynamic annotation matching algorithm. The fundamental idea of this algorithm is to regard the annotation description itself as a pattern for the layout. Each annotation is associated with one layout pattern. Layout patterns are essentially lists of XPath statements involved in each annotation file. Each XPath statement must start with a body tag, and therefore each layout pattern takes the form of a subtree with one root node and several paths extending from the root to specific nodes. Patterns typically have ten to thirty branches from a root node (a body tag). When an annotation author submits a file, the database automatically generates a layout pattern by listing the XPath statements involved in each annotation file. At processing time, the transcoder sends a target's DOM Tree structure to the database, and the database evaluates each layout pattern with the target's DOM.

This method releases the annotation authors from the loop of checking and fixing XPath statements and regular expressions since the database can automatically retrieve corresponding annotations. The workload for maintenance can also be lightened. If an unmatched page is found, an annotation author can simply create an annotation file for the page and submit it, without worrying about the XPath statements and regular expressions. Therefore, the workload of the annotation authors can be drastically reduced by this algorithm. In addition, an annotation authoring tool and annotation management tools were developed to reduce the workload of authoring and management.

Asakawa and Takagi confirmed the workload reduction by creating a set of annotations for an existing major site with around 8000 pages. In this trial, about 250 annotation files could cover the whole site, and it took 30 h and 20 min to create the annotation documents. This workload was less than one normal workweek. They also opened a public transcoding site for an Internet portal service provider. The target site had more than 20,000 pages. They created annotations without dynamic annotation matching, which took about 200 h. This was reduced to about 20 h with the newer algorithm.

The next trend is the use of inline metadata. In the mid-2000s, web pages became to be designed by using CSS or dynamically controlled by JavaScript. For these purposes, programmers usually assign identifiers ("id" attributes) and properties ("class" attributes) to important elements in a page. These inline properties can be regarded as a kind of "annotation" since the components are usually marked to control their visual appearance by applying style sheets or marked to dynamically update information in some part of the screen. This means that no workload is required to implement transcoding if this new metadata is sufficient for the purposes. This is a strong advantage based on full use of the latest web authoring trends. SADIe is a system to transform content based on these inline annotations. The system is fully utilizing the inline metadata for CSS to point at target elements in pages. The annotations are described as ontological data corresponding to the CSS files, which define the types of transcoding that takes place, such as simplification, reordering (rearrangement), and other transformations.

We think this approach has huge potential, and especially if a vocabulary can be standardized for accessibility transcoding. Microformat is an approach to use "class" attributes to insert metadata into XHTML pages. The associated community has already defined some vocabulary items, such as contact information, review text, and so on [Microformats]. The landmark roles of WAI-ARIA [WAI-ARIA] and new elements of HTML 5 [HTML5], such as header, footer, main, nav, article, section, and aside, allows web authors to specify the segments and its roles by using usual HTML element and attribute. If these authors use this vocabulary for their pages, then those pages can be automatically personalized according to the user profiles.

30.3.2 Simplification Based on Differential Analysis

Page simplification is one of the major methods for generating accessible web content. Various methods have been proposed to support usable but simplified pages. This section introduces an automatic transcoding method based on differential analysis, which Asakawa and Takagi developed in 2000.

Differential analysis is a technique to compare two pages and obtain only the differing parts of their content (Douglis et al. 1998, HTML Diff). Various methods have been proposed for this purpose, but they used Dynamic Programming (DP) matching for their system, since the algorithms can be easily customized for the transcoding purposes, and the performance is good. Basically, DP matching finds the longest common string that is included in two strings. For example, the longest common string for "abcdef" and "abdgf" is "abdf." They applied this method to calculate the differences between two HTML object models.

The calculation process is as follows:

1. Parse two HTML files and convert them into DOM) trees
2. Traverse and serialize the DOM trees
   This process converts the DOM tree for each HTML file into a string structure of nodes. The nodes that should be included in the string structure, such as BR and TABLE tags, are selected using HTML TAG information.
3. Calculate the Longest Common "Node" String (LCNS) using DP matching.
   This string consists of the content that is the same in the two HTML files, so those nodes should be removed.
4. Remove the nodes in the LCNS from an original DOM tree.
   Finally, the nodes in the LCNS are actually removed from the DOM tree for the target HTML page.

As already mentioned in Sect. 30.2, transcoding systems need to determine a set of pages, which may have a similar layout or content as the target page, in order to apply differential analysis for the transcoding. Their system (Takagi and Asakawa 2000) had functions to list some categories of pages to be compared, and then select the smallest page as the result of simplification.

1. List URIs in the target page
   After a target HTML file is loaded, the system parses it and lists all URIs described in the HREF attributes of anchor tags. From the list, the system selects files, which exist in the same directory with the target file, and then adds them to a candidate list.
   Example target: http://www.asahi.com/0423/news/national23008.html
   Selected candidate file: http://www.asahi.com/0423/news/national23010.html
2. Select files having the same parent directory as the target file
   The following two index.html files exist in different directories, "cuba.boy.07" and "spokane.slayings.ap," but their parent directory is the same as "2000/US/04/22/".
   http://www.cnn.com/2000/US/04/22/cuba.boy.08/index.html
   http://www.cnn.com/2000/US/04/22/spokane.slayings.ap/index.html
3. List each index file for each directory
   A site often provides an index file (often named "index.html" or "default.asp") not only for the site's top page, but also for each directory. It is often useful for the system to compare such an index file with a target file to get the difference, because they tend to use a common template for all of the files in the same directory. For example, for http://www.cnn.com/2000/US/04/22/cuba.boy.07/index. html, the following directories which might contain index pages can be extracted from this URI:
   http://www.cnn.com/2000/US/04/22/
   http://www.cnn.com/2000/US/04/
   http://www.cnn.com/2000/US/
   http://www.cnn.com/2000/
   http://www.cnn.com/
4. Search previous pages from cache database

The system uses not only the neighboring pages, but also cached files. The module searches the files in the cache database, and selects any old files for the same target URI. These files are added to the candidate list.

30.4   Future Directions

Web technology is continuously in a revolutionary era. Previously, web pages were "documents," and basically expressed only structured text content. However, the technical advancement around scripting technologies is shifting the web from document-oriented content model to a more dynamic visual application model. This shift gives us huge challenges to achieve accessible web environment for future contents. We believe accessibility improvement methodologies that used in transcoding technologies can be applied to help make these dynamic visual applications accessible for low or nonvisual users.

We tried to classify these challenges into several categories of "access models." The "access model" is a basic concept for making a category of contents accessible, which we defined for this classification.

"Documents and Hypertexts" access model
Contents should be essentially text-based, which is consisted of heading, paragraphs, tables and hypertext links. Nonvisual users can navigate through contents by using heading navigation, table navigations, and hypertext link jumps. Recently, more precise navigation methods, such as jump to the main content, landmark navigation, etc., can be achieved by using structural and semantic information based on WAI-ARIA and HTML 5. This access model is the most matured and well established through the web accessibility activities, and various guidelines are instituted, various authoring tools support this model, various accessibility checking tools exists, and screen readers and voice browsers support this model.

"GUI" access model
Contents can be regarded as a graphical user interface. It covers HTML forms, simple Flash contends, Java applets, and form-oriented DHTML applications. Nonvisual users can access all these contents by using basic GUI operation functions, such as a tab for moving among GUI widgets and enter for selection. Each GUI widget has its own (but common) operations, such as press down cursor for changing the selection in a pull-down menu. This access model is also well established through the development of screen readers for GUIs. Flash accessibility supports this access model, the Java accessibility API supports this, and DHTML accessibility (WAI-ARIA) also supports this access model.

"Documents and Hypertexts" and "GUI" access models are well established, but followings are not established yet, and increasing in the new dynamic visual content era. We believe transcoding technologies can help these contents accessible by transforming contents in a dynamic way. We will briefly describe the possible contribution to improve accessibility for the following access models.

"Vector graphics" access model
Recently, accessibility support in each graphics format based on Machine Learning and AI technologies are widely spread and expand its coverage. However, an access model for vector graphics is not established well yet. This access model is critical since modern browsers support vector graphics, such as Canvas and SVG, natively. In addition, we are using diagrams massively in our business process and education process. Transcoding technology can improve this situation by analyzing graphics on the fly and creates a more accessible format for screen readers or pictorial Braille. Some of the image processing technologies and pattern matching technologies can be used, as well as, XML and metadata-based transformation techniques.

"Multimedia" access model
This access model is becoming mainstream of web contents as multimedia contents. In order to make these contents accessible, we need to apply "GUI access model" to GUI components and also need to provide movie control functions for streaming movies. In HTML 5, external text resources, such as captions, audio descriptions, etc., can be associated with multimedia contents by using track element. If these metadata and controls can be applied on the fly intermediary, it will contribute to improve multimedia contents accessible.

"Interactive animation" access model
Interactive animation means dynamic vector graphics, which moves according to users' mouse operations. This is not an "access model," since there is no method for accessing this type of contents. At this movement, we need to make each content accessible in an ad hoc way. By applying a transcoding approach, there is a possibility to transform interactive animations into other access models, such as "GUI" or "Movie + GUI." It is obvious that rich metadata is required to realize this conversion.

The point for transcoding approaches for these access models are the concept of adaptive user interfaces. We defined the adaptive user interface as a simplified and optimized the alternative interface for content, which is hardly accessed by using assistive technologies. The traditional approach is the screen reading, which reads a screen "as it is seen by vision." However, introduced a new type of contents are highly visual and dynamic, so it is difficult to provide a usable interface for nonvisual users by applying the screen reader approach. So, we believe that the transcoding approach for adaptive user interfaces have the possibility to provide new types of usable interface for nonvisual users (see "User Interface Adaptation for Accessibility" in PART 5 for more details about UI adaptation).

30.5 Author's Opinion of the Field

Originally, transcoding meant intermediary approach between a web server and a browser. With the power of recent Machine Learning and AI technologies, this approach is really beneficial and effective to provide accessibility information for multimedia content (Harrenstien 2009; Simonite 2017; Wu et al. 2017). However, the emergence of client-side scripting based on JavaScript makes the intermediary approach difficult. In order to intermediary transform dynamic web contents written procedural scripts, static analysis technology is required. Contents written in declarative XML-based languages can be transformed by applying various transcoding methods, however, procedural scripts cannot be transformed intermediary since static analysis is not matured technology for practical transformation. It is essentially difficult to infer the result by execution of a part of script codes without executing them. Some static analysis methods have been developed for accessibility, but it is only applicable for validation of metadata, such as for WAI-ARIA. Therefore, client-side transcoding is becoming mainstream of transcoding technologies. As already mentioned in Sect. 30.3, transcoding systems are shifting to client-side approaches. The trend will continue for some years as long as the script-based dynamic contest era continues.

30.6   Conclusions

This chapter overviewed transcoding technologies for improving the web's accessibility. First, history was introduced with the list of transcoding systems. These systems were invented from the transcoding systems for mobile devices and voice browsing technologies. Various transcoding methods were proposed throughout history, and these methods were also overviewed in Sect. 30.2. The architecture is one of the characteristic points for transcoding systems since it defines the coverage of each system. Two basic technologies were introduced in the Sect. 30.3 to give examples of technical details for transcoding systems. Finally, we discussed the future direction of transcoding systems. The possibility of the transformation of rich and dynamic contents and the concept of adaptive interfaces are discussed in Sect. 30.4.

The web is progressing to be more dynamic to realize real-time web-based collaboration and to provide a more visual and interactive user experience for sighted users. Researchers and developers of accessibility technologies should not avert from these contents. Accessibility technologies should be drastically improved to cope with these trends. We hope the transcoding approach introduced in this chapter will help consider the possibility to realize fully accessible and dynamic next-generation web environment.

References

About jQuery UI; see https://jqueryui.com/about/, Accessed 1st Aug 2018
Akpınar E, Yeşilada Y (2015) "Old habits die hard!": eyetracking based experiential transcoding: a study with mobile users. In: Proceedings of the 12th Web for all conference (W4A '15). ACM, New York, NY, USA, Article 12

Asakawa C, Lewis C (1998) Home page reader: IBM's talking Web browser. In: Closing the gap conference proceedings

Asakawa C, Itoh T (1998) User interface of a home page reader. In: Proceedings of the Third international ACM conference on assistive technologies (Marina del Rey, California, United States, 15–17 Apr 1998). Assets '98. ACM Press, New York, NY, pp 149–156

Asakawa C, Itoh T (1999) User interface of a nonvisual table navigation method. In: CHI '99 extended abstracts on human factors in computing systems (Pittsburgh, Pennsylvania, 15–20 May 1999). CHI '99. ACM Press, New York, NY, pp 214–215

Asakawa C, Takagi H (2000) Annotation-based transcoding for nonvisual Web access. In: Proceedings of the fourth international ACM conference on assistive technologies (Arlington, Virginia, United States, 13–15 Nov 2000). Assets '00. ACM Press, New York, NY, pp 172–179

Asakawa C (2005) What's the Web like if you can't see it?. In: Proceedings of the 2005 international cross-disciplinary workshop on Web accessibility (W4a) (Chiba, Japan, 10–10 May 2005). W4A '05, vol 88. ACM Press, New York, NY, pp 1–8

Bickmore TW, Schilit BN (1997) Digestor: device-independent access to the World-Wide Web. In Proceedings of the 6th international World-Wide Web conference

Barrett R, Maglio PP, Kellem DC (1997) How to personalize the Web. In: Proceedings of the SIGCHI conference on human factors in computing systems (Atlanta, Georgia, United States, 22–27, Mar 1997). S. Pemberton, Ed. CHI '97. ACM Press, New York, NY, pp 75–82

Bechhofer S, Harper S, Lunn D (2006) SADIe: semantic annotation for accessibility. In: 5th international semantic web conference (ISWC'06), Athens, GA, USA, pp 101–115

Bigham JP, Kaminsky RS, Ladner RE, Danielsson OM, Hempton GL (2006) WebInSight: making Web images accessible. In: Proceedings of the 8th international ACM SIGACCESS conference on computers and accessibility (Portland, Oregon, USA, 23–25 Oct 2006). Assets '06. ACM Press, New York, NY, pp 181–188

Bigham JP (2007) Increasing Web accessibility by automatically judging alternative text quality. In: Proceedings of the 12th international conference on intelligent user interfaces (Honolulu, Hawaii, USA, 28–31 Jan 2007). IUI '07. ACM Press, New York, NY, pp 349–352

Bigham JP, Ladner RE (2007) Accessmonkey: a collaborative scripting framework for Web users and developers. In: Proceedings of the 2007 international cross-disciplinary conference on Web accessibility (W4a) (Banff, Canada, 07–08 May 2007). W4A '07, vol 225. ACM Press, New York, NY, pp 25–34

Bigham JP, Prince CM, Ladner RE (2008) WebAnywhere: a screen reader on-the-go. In: Proceedings of the 2008 international cross-disciplinary conference on Web accessibility (W4A) (W4A '08). ACM, New York, NY, USA, pp 73–82

Borodin Y (2006) A flexible vxml interpreter for non-visual Web access. In: ACM conference on assistive technologies (ASSETS)

Borodin Y, Mahmud J, Ramakrishnan IV, Stent A (2007) The hearsay non-visual Web browser. In: Proceedings of the 2007 international cross-disciplinary conference on Web accessibility (W4a) (Banff, Canada, 07–08 May 2007). W4A '07, vol 225. ACM Press, New York, NY, pp 128–129

Brown SS, Robinson P (2001) A World Wide Web mediator for users with low visions, presented at CHI2001 Workshop 14, Seattle, Washington, US, 31 Mar–5 Apr 2001

Buyukkokten O, Garcia-Molina H, Paepcke A, Winograd T (2000) Power browser: efficient Web browsing for PDAs. In: Proceedings of the SIGCHI conference on human factors in computing systems (The Hague, The Netherlands, 01–06 Apr 2000). CHI '00. ACM Press, New York, NY, pp 430–437

Buyukkokten O, Garcia-Molina H, Paepcke A (2001) Accordion summarization for end-game browsing on PDAs and cellular phones. In: Proceedings of the SIGCHI conference on human factors in computing systems (Seattle, Washington, United States). CHI '01. ACM Press, New York, NY, pp 213–220

Dardailler D. The ALT-server ("An eye for an alt"). http://www.w3.org/WAI/altserv.htm

De Witt JC, Hakkinen MT (1998) Surfing the Web with pwWebSpeak (tm), In: Proceedings of the technology & persons with disabilities conference (CSUN 98)

Document Object Model (DOM), World Wide Web Consortium, http://www.w3.org/DOM/

Douglis F, Ball T, Chen Y-F, Koutsofios E (1998) The AT&T internet difference engine: tracking and viewing changes on the web. World Wide Web 1:27–44

Fukuda K, Takagi H, Maeda J, Asakawa C (2003) An assist method for realizing a Web page structure for blind people. In: Proceedings of HCI international 2003 (Universal Access in HCI), June 2003, pp 960–964

Gardiner S, Tomasic A, Zimmerman J (2015) SmartWrap: seeing datasets with the crowd's eyes. In: Proceedings of the 12th Web for all conference (W4A '15). ACM, New York, NY, USA, Article 3

Garrido A, Firmenich S, Rossi G, Grigera J, Medina-Medina N, Harari I (2013) Personalized Web accessibility using client-side refactoring. IEEE Internet Comput 17(4):58–66

Goble C, Harper S, Stevens R (2000) The travails of visually impaired Web travellers. In: Proceedings of the eleventh ACM on hypertext and hypermedia (San Antonio, Texas, United States, May 30–June 03, 2000). HYPERTEXT '00. ACM Press, New York, NY, pp 1–10

Goose S, Wynblatt M, Mollenhauer H (1998) 1–800-hypertext: browsing hypertext with a telephone. In: Proceedings of the ninth ACM conference on hypertext and hypermedia: links, objects, time and space—structure in hypermedia systems: links, objects, time and space—structure in hypermedia systems (Pittsburgh, Pennsylvania, United States, 20–24 June 1998). HYPERTEXT '98. ACM Press, New York, NY, pp 287–288

Goose S, Newman M, Schmidt C, Hue L (2000) Enhancing Web accessibility via the vox portal and a Web hosted dynamic HTML <->VoxML converter,?? 2000-voxML

Greasemonkey; see https://addons.mozilla.org/ja/firefox/addon/748

Gustafson A, Adaptive Web design: crafting rich experiences with progressive enhancement, 1st edn, Easy Readers, LLC (30 May 2011)

HTML 5, World Wide Web Consortium. https://www.w3.org/TR/html5/

HTML Diff: C3 Project, Stanford University. http://www-db.stanford.edu/c3/c3.html

Hanson VL (2001) Web access for elderly citizens. In: Proceedings of the 2001 EC/NSF workshop on universal accessibility of ubiquitous computing: providing for the Elderly (Alcácer do Sal, Portugal, 22–25 May 2001). WUAUC'01. ACM Press, New York, NY, pp 14–18

Hanson VL, Richards JT (2004) A Web accessibility service: update and findings. In: Proceedings of the 6th international ACM SIGACCESS conference on computers and accessibility (Atlanta, GA, USA, 18–20 Oct 2004). Assets '04. ACM Press, New York, NY, pp 169–176

Harper S, Patel N (2005) Gist summaries for visually impaired surfers. In: Proceedings of the 7th international ACM SIGACCESS conference on computers and accessibility (Baltimore, MD, USA, 09–12 Oct 2005). Assets '05. ACM Press, New York, NY, pp 90–97

Harper S, Bechhofer S (2005) Semantic triage for increased Web accessibility. IBM Syst J 44(3):637–648

Harper S, Bechhofer S, Lunn D (2006a) Taming the inaccessible Web. In: Proceedings of the 24th annual conference on design of communication (Myrtle Beach, SC, USA, 18–20 Oct 2006). SIGDOC '06. ACM Press, New York, NY, pp 64–69

Harper S, Bechhofer S, Lunn D (2006b) SADIe: transcoding based on CSS. In: Proceedings of the 8th international ACM SIGACCESS conference on computers and accessibility (Portland, Oregon, USA, 23–25 Oct 2006). Assets '06. ACM Press, New York, NY, pp 259–260

Harrenstien K (2009) Automatic captions in YouTube https://googleblog.blogspot.com/2009/11/automatic-captions-in-youtube.html

Hori M, Kondoh G, Ono S, Hirose S, Singhal S (2000) Annotation-based Web content transcoding. In: Proceedings of the ninth international World Wide Web conference (WWW9) (May 2000)

Huang AW, Sundaresan N (2000a) Aurora: a conceptual model for Web-content adaptation to support the universal usability of Web-based services. In: Proceedings on the 2000 conference on universal usability (Arlington, Virginia, United States, 16–17 Nov 2000). CUU '00. ACM Press, New York, NY, pp 124–131

Huang AW, Sundaresan N (2000b) A semantic transcoding system to adapt Web services for users with disabilities. In: Proceedings of the fourth international ACM conference on assistive technologies (Arlington, Virginia, United States, 13–5 Nov 2000). Assets '00. ACM Press, New York, NY, pp 156–163

Iaccarino G, Malandrino D, Scarano V (2006a) Personalizable edge services for Web accessibility. In: Proceedings of the 2006 international cross-disciplinary workshop on Web accessibility (W4a): building the mobile Web: rediscovering accessibility? (Edinburgh, U.K. 22–22 May 2006). W4A, vol 134. ACM Press, New York, NY, pp 23–32

Iaccarino G, Malandrino D, Del Percio M, Scarano V (2006b) Efficient edge-services for colorblind users. In: Proceedings of the 15th international conference on World Wide Web (Edinburgh, Scotland, 23–26 May 2006). WWW '06. ACM Press, New York, NY, pp 919–920

JAWS, Freedom Scientific Inc.; see http://www.freedomscientific.com/

Laws C, Asakawa C (1999) IBM home page reader: the voice of the World Wide Web. In: Proceedings of technology and persons with disabilities conference (CSUN 1999)

LiFT; see http://www.usablenet.com/products_services/text_transcoder/text_transcoder.html, Accessed in 2005. (demo site: https://transcoder.usablenet.com/tt/)

Lynx; see http://lynx.browser.org/

Maeda J, Fukuda K, Takagi H, Asakawa C (2004) Web accessibility technology at TRL. IBM Res Dev J 48(5/6)

Maglio P, Barrett R (2000) Intermediaries personalize information streams. Commun ACM 43(8):96–101

Mahmud J, Borodin Y, Das D, Ramakrishnan IV (2007a) Combating information overload in non-visual Web access using context. In: Proceedings of the 12th international conference on intelligent user interfaces (Honolulu, Hawaii, USA, 28–31 Jan 2007). IUI '07. ACM Press, New York, NY, pp 341–344

Mahmud JU, Borodin Y, Ramakrishnan IV (2007b) Csurf: a context-driven non-visual web-browser. In: Proceedings of the 16th international conference on World Wide Web (Banff, Alberta, Canada, 08–12 May 2007). WWW '07. ACM Press, New York, NY, pp 31–40

Marcotte E, Responsive Web Design, a list apart. https://alistapart.com/article/responsive-web-design, 25 May 2010

Miyashita H, Sato D, Takagi H, Asakawa C (2007) Aibrowser for multimedia—introducing multi-media content accessibility for visually impaired users. In: Proceedings of the ninth international ACM SIGACCESS conference on computers and accessibility (ASSETS 2007)

Microformats; see http://microformats.org/

Nagao K (2000) Semantic transcoding: making the World Wide Web more understandable and usable with external annotations. In: Proceedings of international conference on advanced in infrastructure for electronic business, science, and education on the internet

Nam J, Ro Yong Man, Huh Y, Kim M (2005) Visual content adaptation according to user perception characteristics. IEEE Trans Multimed 7(3):435–445

Plessers P, Casteleyn S, Yesilada Y, De Troyer O, Stevens R, Harper S, Goble C (2005) Accessibility: a Web engineering approach. In: Proceedings of the 14th international conference on World Wide Web (Chiba, Japan, 10–14 May 2005). WWW '05. ACM Press, New York, NY, pp 353–362

Rainville-pitt S, D'Amour J (2007) Using a CMS to create fully accessible websites. In: Proceedings of the 2007 international cross-disciplinary conference on Web accessibility (W4a) (Banff, Canada, 07–08 May 2007). W4A '07, vol 225. ACM Press, New York, NY, pp 130–131

Ramakrishnan IV, Stent A, Yang G (2004) Hearsay: enabling audio browsing on hypertext content. In: Proceedings of the 13th international conference on World Wide Web (New York, NY, USA, 17–20 May 2004). WWW '04. ACM Press, New York, NY, pp 80–89

Resource Description Framework (RDF); see http://www.w3.org/RDF/

Richards JT, Hanson VL (2004) Web accessibility: a broader view. In: Proceedings of the 13th international conference on World Wide Web (New York, NY, USA, 17–20 May 2004). WWW '04. ACM Press, New York, NY, pp 72–79

Sato D, Miyashita H, Takagi H, Asakawa C (2007) Automatic accessibility transcoding for flash content. In: Proceedings of the ninth international ACM SIGACCESS conference on computers and accessibility (ASSETS 2007)??

Section 508 of the Rehabilitation Act; see http://www.section508.gov/

Shao Z, Capra RG, III, Pérez-Quiñones MA (2003) Transcoding HTML to VoiceXML using annotation. In: Proceedings of the 15th IEEE international conference on tools with artificial intelligence, pp 249, Nov 03–05

Simonite T (2017) Machine learning opens up new ways to help people with disabilities. In: MIT technology review. https://www.technologyreview.com/s/603899/machine-learning-opens-up-new-ways-to-help-disabled-people/

Sunkara S, Tetali R, Bose J (2014) Responsive, adaptive and user personalized rendering on mobile browsers. In: 2014 international conference on advances in computing, communications and informatics (ICACCI), New Delhi, pp 259–265

Supporting Accessibility: Betsie, Text Only, and the Semantic Web; see http://www.bbc.co.uk/blogs/bbcinternet/2012/02/accessibility_betsie_text.html

Takagi H, Asakawa C (2000) Transcoding proxy for nonvisual Web access. In: Proceedings of the fourth international ACM conference on assistive technologies (Arlington, Virginia, United States, 13–15 Nov 2000). Assets '00. ACM Press, New York, NY, pp 164–171

Takagi H, Asakawa C, Fukuda K, Maeda J (2002) Site-wide annotation: reconstructing existing pages to be accessible. In: Proceedings of the Fifth international ACM conference on assistive technologies (Edinburgh, Scotland, 08–10 July 2002). Assets '02. ACM Press, New York, NY, pp 81–88

Takagi H, Kawanaka S, Kobayashi M, Itoh T, Asakawa C (2008) Social accessibility: achieving accessibility through collaborative metadata authoring. In: Proceedings of the 10th international ACM SIGACCESS conference on computers and accessibility (Assets '08). ACM, New York, NY, USA, pp 193–200

[WAI-ARIA] World Wide Web Consortium, Voice Browser Working Group. http://www.w3.org/Voice/ Accessible Rich Internet Applications (ARIA), World Wide Web Consortium. https://www.w3.org/TR/wai-aria/

WebAdapt2Me, IBM Corporation; see https://www-03.ibm.com/press/us/en/pressrelease/19515.wss

WebSphere Transcoding Publisher, IBM Corporation; see ftp://public.dhe.ibm.com/software/webserver/transcoding/brochures/G325-3987.pdf, Accessed 1st Aug 2018)

Wu S, Wieland J, Farivar O, Schiller J (2017) Automatic alt-text: computer-generated image descriptions for blind users on a social network service. In: Proceedings of the 2017 ACM conference on computer supported cooperative work and social computing (CSCW '17). ACM, New York, NY, pp 1180–1192

XML Path Language (XPath): World Wide Web Consortium (W3C). http://www.w3.org/TR/xpath

Yesilada Y, Stevens R, Goble C (2003) A foundation for tool based mobility support for visually impaired web users. In: Proceedings of the 12th international conference on World Wide Web (Budapest, Hungary, 20–24 May 2003). WWW '03. ACM Press, New York, NY, pp 422–430

Yesilada Y, Stevens R, Harper S, Goble C (2007) Evaluating DANTE: semantic transcoding for visually disabled users. ACM Trans Comput-Hum Interact 14(3):14

Chapter 31
Technologies for Dyslexia

Maria Rauschenberger, Ricardo Baeza–Yates and Luz Rello

Abstract Nowadays, being excluded from the web is a huge disadvantage. People with dyslexia have, despite their general intelligence, difficulties for reading and writing through their whole life. Therefore, web technologies can help people with dyslexia to improve their reading and writing experience on the web. This chapter introduces the main technologies and many examples of tools that support a person with dyslexia in processing information on the web, either in assistive applications for reading and writing as well as using web applications/games for dyslexia screening and intervention.

31.1 Introduction

The *American Psychiatric Organization* defines dyslexia as a *specific learning disorder* which affects around 5–15% of the world population (American Psychiatric Association 2013) (more information can be found in this book in the chapter *Cognitive and Learning Disabilities*). A person with dyslexia has difficulties to read and write independently of intelligence, the mother tongue, social status, or education level. Hence, people with dyslexia understand the meaning of the words but do not always know how to spell or pronounce the word correctly. This means that children with dyslexia do not show any obvious difficulties in other areas. This is the reason why *dyslexia* is also called a *hidden* disorder. Often, this results in bad grades in school and frustration for the children (40–60% of children with dyslexia show symptoms of psychological disorders (Schulte-Körne 2010) like negative thoughts,

M. Rauschenberger (✉) · R. Baeza–Yates
Universitat Pompeu Fabra, Carrer de Roc Boronat, 138, 08018 Barcelon, Spain
e-mail: Maria.Rauschenberger@upf.edu

R. Baeza–Yates
e-mail: ricardo.baeza@upf.edu

L. Rello
IE Business School, IE University, Calle de María de Molina, 11-13-15, 28006 Madrid, Spain
e-mail: luzrello@acm.org

© Springer-Verlag London Ltd., part of Springer Nature 2019
Y. Yesilada and S. Harper (eds.), *Web Accessibility*, Human–Computer Interaction Series, https://doi.org/10.1007/978-1-4471-7440-0_31

sadness sorrow, or anxiety) and the parents over many years. Moreover, these are common indicators for detecting a person with dyslexia.

As a matter of fact, children with dyslexia can learn the spelling of words or decode words for reading but they need more time to practice. For example, for German, Schulte-Korne et al. state that children need two years instead of one for learning how to spell phonetically accurate words (Schulte-Körne 2010). Hence, to give children with dyslexia more time to practice, avoid frustration and the possibility to succeed, early detection is needed. Although a person with dyslexia is able to gain reading comprehension and spelling accuracy, a certain degree of difficulty will most probably remain and assistive applications for reading and writing are helpful.

Even though language acquisition depends on the syllabic complexity and orthographic depth of a language (Seymour 2003), results show that similarities between readers with dyslexia in English and German are far bigger than their differences (Ziegler et al. 2003). Also, similar types of errors were found in texts written by people with dyslexia for English, Spanish (Rello 2014) and German (Rauschenberger et al. 2016). Multiple factors have been investigated to find the causes of dyslexia and measuring it, as well as the skills that need to be trained to improve reading and writing (Catts et al. 2017).

It has been argued that dyslexia might be mainly phonological and perception differences could be explained with electric oscillations (Goswami 2011). Furthermore, previous research has related speech perception difficulties to auditory processing, phonological awareness and literacy skills (Rolka and Silverman 2015; Tallal 2004). Phonological deficits of dyslexia have also been linked to basic auditory processing (Hämäläinen et al. 2013). The auditory perception of children with dyslexia has been proven to be related to the sound structure (Huss et al. 2011), as well as to the auditory working memory (Männel et al. 2016). Nondigital approaches, e.g., Jansen et al. (2002) try to predict the literacy skills of children with the phonological perception, phonological working memory processing, long-term memory, and visual attention (quoted after Steinbrink and Lachmann 2014).

Another line of research suggests that reading impairments are due to the visual-spatial attention and poor coding instead of phonological difficulties (Vidyasagar and Pammer 2010). In fact, non-similar sounds might be used as a compensation strategy to cope with dyslexia, which breaks down when we have phonetic ambiguity, that is, we see a symptom of the problem but not the real cause.

Apart from this, visual discrimination and search efficiency are being used as predictors for future reading acquisitions (Franceschini et al. 2012). Even more, recently, the missing visual asymmetry is proposed as one of many reasons which might cause dyslexia (Le Floch and Ropars 2017).

Lately, it has been shown that computer games are a convenient medium to provide an engaging way to significantly improve the reading (Gaggi et al. 2017; Kyle et al. 2013) and the spelling (Gaggi et al. 2017; Rello et al. 2014) performance of children with dyslexia. Additionally, it was shown that children with dyslexia could be detected easily and cost-efficient with a web tool that, among other things, analyses word errors from people with dyslexia (Rello et al. 2016).

A person with dyslexia has difficulties to learn how to read and write through their whole life depending on the assistive tools used as well as the detection date or/and intervention method duration (more information can be found in this book in the chapter *Assistive Technologies*). Since there are already various software tools, we present the main similarities through tables and point out key differences in the text.

The next section give an overview of applications to support people with dyslexia to make the web accessible when reading or writing as well as the relatively new field of online tools for screening and intervening with web technologies to cope with dyslexia. We argue that web accessibility for dyslexia is more than only tools which help to read and write (Rello 2015). We end with a discussion, future directions and conclusions.

31.2   Assisted Reading for Dyslexia

Assisted reading can be accomplished with the existing readers or new applications, especially designed for people with dyslexia. In both cases, what is important are the available features and how they can be customized. The British Dyslexia Association updated their *Style Guide* in 2018 on the presentation of content, writing style, and text to speech (TTS), which we take into account for the comparison of applications (British Dyslexia Association 2018).

In the next subsection, we give an overview of different approaches to design text customization, test simplification, and text to speech to improve the reading performance and/or comprehension for people with dyslexia.

31.2.1   Text Customization

How a text is presented and how a person with dyslexia likes to perceive it, is very personal (Gregor and Newell 2000). Therefore, different parameters can help to improve the readability for individuals depending on the customization.

But not every parameter improves the reading performance or comprehension. Various studies explore the different parameters for readability, comprehension, and reading performance. For example, studies provide evidence that the font type has an impact on the readability, i.e., *italics* and *serif* should be avoided (Rello and Baeza-Yates 2016, 2017; British Dyslexia Association 2018). Fonts like *Arial, Courier, Helvetica* and font families like *roman, sans serif* and *mono-spaced* are suggested to increase readability. On the other hand, fonts specifically created for people with dyslexia (Wery and Diliberto 2017) have not be proven better than conventional fonts (Rello and Baeza-Yates 2016). Also, there is evidence that the font size has an significant impact on the readability while line spacing does not Rello et al. (2013).

The background color is also important since people without dyslexia chose black over white as the most readable option compared to people without dyslexia (93.88%

Table 31.1 Parameters that can be customized in assistive reading tools

Parameter		Font	Size	Spacing
Tools				
AccessibleNews	Rello et al. (2012)		✓	✓
Amazon Kindle	Amazon (2018), Wikipedia (2018a)	✓	✓	✓
Apple Books	Apple (2018), Wikipedia (2018b)	✓	✓	
ClaroRead	Claro Software Ltd. (2015)	✓	✓	✓
DysWebxia	Rello (2014), Rello and Baeza-Yates (2014)	✓	✓	✓
Firefixia	de Santana et al. (2013)	✓	✓	✓
Google Play Books	Google (2018), Wikipedia (2018c)	✓	✓	✓
IDEAL	Kanvinde (2012)	✓	✓	✓
MultiReader	Petrie et al. (2005)		✓	
Text4All	Topac (2012)	✓	✓	✓
WebHelpDyslexia	de Avelar et al. (2015)	✓	✓	✓

compared to 60% Rello and Baeza-Yates 2017). A medium-scale study ($n = 241$) contributed that (1) background colors have an impact on the readability for people with and without dyslexia, (2) warm background colors are beneficial for the reading performance, and (3) cool background colors decrease the readability (Rello et al. 2017). Also, the background color is reported to be correlated with the size of the text (Rello and Baeza-Yates 2017). Another example is line spacing which has not been proven to have a significant effect on readability and personal preferences (Rello and Baeza-Yates 2017).

Already various guidelines British Dyslexia Association (2018), de Santana et al. (2012), Miniukovich (2017), WAI (2018) have been proposed, mainly with recommendations for readability on the web and digital devices. In Table 31.1, we compare the most important parameters to improve the readability of reading applications or/and recommended by guidelines.

The three most popular reading applications are: the *Amazon Kindle* (Amazon 2018; Wikipedia 2018a), *Apple Books* (Apple 2018; Wikipedia 2018b) (previously know as iBooks), and *Google Play Books* (Google 2018; Wikipedia 2018c). Nearly, all applications include the three parameters that should have an effect on readability. However, *MultiReader* can only change one parameter (Size) and two applications can change only two parameters, i.e., *Apple Books* (Font and Size) and *Accessible-News* (Size and Spacing). Apart from readers for e-books or other types of digital documents, the tools are mainly designed for a certain context like reading the news (*AccessibleNews*) or adapting existing web pages (*Text4all*). The *reading ruler* from WebHelpDyslexia is the only feature to address the confusion while reading and changing rows.

Table 31.2 Available text simplification features

Feature		Synonyms	Simplification	Definition
Tools				
AccessibleNews	Rello et al. (2012)			
Amazon Kindle	Amazon (2018), Wikipedia (2018a)	✓		✓
Apple Books	Apple (2018), Wikipedia (2018b)			✓
ClaroRead	Claro Software Ltd. (2015)			
DysWebxia	Rello (2014), Rello and Baeza-Yates (2014)	✓		
Firefixia	de Santana et al. (2013)			
Google Play Books	Google (2018), Wikipedia (2018c)		✓	✓
IDEAL	Kanvinde (2012)			
MultiReader	Petrie et al. (2005)		✓	
Text4All	Topac (2012)	✓		
WebHelpDyslexia	de Avelar et al. (2015)	✓		

31.2.2   Text Simplification

After a text is accurately displayed, the person needs to comprehend the text. One possible help to make understanding a text easier, is simplifying the content. Either a complex word will be replaced with the most simple synonym or various synonyms are presented at the user's request (Rello et al. 2013). Also, a dictionary function is useful to look up foreign words but also non-foreign words with a similar spelling like *quiet* and *quit* to precise their meaning in a given context.

In Table 31.2, we compare the available features for reading applications. The challenges for simplifying with synonyms are polysemic words (Rello and Baeza-Yates 2014). Especially, if synonyms need to be found in a sentence or short phrase as, e.g., in a *Twitter* tweet or a *Reddit* post. Additionally, simplifying depends a lot on the person's ability itself. Since dyslexia is a learning disorder and not a cognitive disability, the simplification depends more on the typographical errors and not on the complexity of the content. Research shows that people with dyslexia encounter specific difficulties with phonetically or orthographically similar words or letters (Wyke 1984; Rello et al. 2016; Rauschenberger et al. 2016). To raise awareness for these kinds of words, *ClaroRead* colors words with a similar pronunciation. Colors are also used to differentiate similar looking letters as in *SeeWord*. In Rello et al. (2013) it is also shown that people with dyslexia prefer to see synonyms of complex words rather than direct text simplification.

Table 31.3 Example tools with and without native text to speech

YES		NO	
Amazon Kindle	Amazon (2018), Wikipedia (2018a)	AccessibleNews	Rello et al. (2012)
ClaroRead	Claro Software Ltd. (2015)	Apple Books	Apple (2018), Wikipedia (2018b)
Google Play Books	Google (2018), Wikipedia (2018c)	DysWebxia	Rello (2014), Rello and Baeza-Yates (2014)
IDEAL	Kanvinde (2012)	Firefixia	de Santana et al. (2013)
MultiReader	Petrie et al. (2005)	Text4All	Topac (2012)
		WebHelpDyslexia	de Avelar et al. (2015)

31.2.3 Text to Speech

Text to speech (TTS) can be used to hear the text without the need to read it. This means that the written text is read to the user by an engine and not recorded before by a person as it is the case for audio books. These tools could be useful for a person with dyslexia as well as for a person with visual impairments among other disabilities. A TTS engine might support different languages and some are already included in popular operating systems. TTS APIs are available in the most used mobile operating systems such as Android or iOS and can be used by any application, although some people report difficulties while using them, for example in iBooks (Pipusbcn 2017).

In Table 31.3, we compare the availability of proprietary text to speech (TTS) in reading applications. This functionality can be used to follow the reading of a text or to confirm what a person has read as training. Useful features support this training with the control of speed, read word by word or read letter by letter line in the *IDEAL eBook Reader*. These features empower a person with dyslexia to learn and read (new, similar, or complicated) words.

31.3 Assisted Writing for Dyslexia

For a person with dyslexia, reading and writing remains a challenge through their life. A study of dyslexia on social media (interview with 11 participants with dyslexia; questionnaire with 492 participants with and without dyslexia Reynolds and Wu 2018) reports that writing is a bigger challenge than reading for a person with dyslexia. The study also reveals that people with dyslexia experience more often negative feedback on the writing which can trigger or increase their stress and anxiety. Therefore, spelling corrections, text suggestions, or dictation are useful features in the daily routine for a person with dyslexia.

In the next subsections, we present tools for spelling correction, text suggestions, and dictation.

31.3.1 Spelling Correction

The analysis of spelling mistakes from children with dyslexia in German and Spanish (Rello et al. 2016; Rauschenberger et al. 2016) shows real word errors as a very common error category, produced by phonetically or orthographically similarity of words or letters (Pedler 2005, 2007) (see also previous section).

Real word errors refer to words which are wrong in the context and are very similar to another word from that language like for German *Schal ("scarf")* and *Schall ("sound")*, for Spanish *pala ("shovel")* and *palabra ("word")* and for English *from* and *form*. These spelling mistakes are for a spellchecker very difficult to find due to the need to understand the semantic context of the sentence or phrase (similarly to text simplification). Spelling correction is useful also for a person without dyslexia since, for example, the frequency on the Spanish web of correct words is 4.63 times more frequent than for words with errors, apart from real word errors (Rello et al. 2016).

To target real word errors, spellcheckers base their approach on language models or on natural language processing. Next, we present some example applications:

- **Babel** (Spooner 1998) was the first to use an user model with human errors and rules addressing the permutation of letters to support the writing of a person with dyslexia. The approach was evaluated with errors from real people by measuring the frequency of suggestion of the correct answer, and the position of the correct answer on the suggestion list when suggested. *Babel* performance as a spellchecker was significantly better in finding real word errors for some key populations using new rules addressing the permutation of letters or user modeling with human errors.
- **PoliSpell** (Quattrini et al. 2013) uses an user model for boundary errors or real word errors and offers a simple user interface for a person with dyslexia to better distinguish suggested words. An evaluation of PoliSpell could not be found.
- **Real Check** (Rello et al. 2015) uses a probabilistic language model, a statistical dependency parser and Google n-grams to detect real-world errors. The evaluation was done with a corpus of real-world errors, comparison of other spellcheckers and an experiment to test the efficiency of the detection. The results from 2015 with a user study with 36 people show that people with dyslexia corrected sentences more accurately and in less time with RealCheck than with other spellcheckers.

31.3.2 Text Suggestions

The use of text suggestions is relevant for different digital contexts such as search interfaces (Morris 2018), text editors, or spellcheckers (Quattrini et al. 2013). As mentioned in the previous section, *PoliSpell* (Quattrini et al. 2013) provides a simple user interface for a person with dyslexia to show predicted correct words. Since a person with dyslexia has difficulties to distinguish phonologically or orthographically similar words (as described before), the visual layout of word predictions or suggestions is also relevant when writing. In addition, we already mentioned that in Rello et al. (2013), people with dyslexia preferred synonym suggestions instead of a direct simplification.

31.3.3 Dictation

Dictation, *speech to text* (STT) (Wagner 2005) or speech recognition (Juang and Rabiner 2004) is the reverse of text to speech from the previous section and means broadly that the spoken words or sentences are recognized and visualized as text. Historically was developed to integrate people with hearing impairments in oral communication. Although these tools are not specifically developed for people with dyslexia, it makes a real-time communication easier and probably with less spelling mistakes if the STT is well designed. A typical use case today are in mobile search interfaces (Morris 2018). Apart from that, speech recognition can be helpful for a person with *dysgraphia* (Mayes 2018) and is already used in professional areas like medicine, business correspondence, or legal briefs (Spehr 2010). With speech recognition included already in every smartphone, it is available for a broad audience and challenges are in accuracy, foreign accents, specific terminology, or language changes. SST is also researched and recommended as an alternative way of learning how to write (Haug and Klein 2018).

31.4 Dyslexia Screening

The previous sections focused on assistive tools for reading and writing when having dyslexia. This section introduces a relatively newer research area, which is the screening of dyslexia through web-based applications or games.

Detection and especially an early detection of dyslexia is important because an early intervention avoids negative effects of dyslexia such as school failure and low self-esteem.

Most current approaches to detect dyslexia require linguistic skills (i.e., phonological awareness, or letter recognition to apply e.g., a German spelling test Grund 2004), expensive personnel (i.e., psychologists), or special hardware (i.e., eye trackers or MRI machines).

The rate of spelling mistakes and reading errors are the most common way to detect a person of dyslexia. Since people with dyslexia exhibit higher reading and spelling error rates than people without dyslexia (Coleman et al. 2008), there are diagnoses of dyslexia based on the errors score (Schulte-Körne et al. 1996). Very often children and their families already experienced lots of failures and frustration due to the, back then, inexplicable problems of learning how to read and write. Hence, spelling tests are forcing children with dyslexia to fail again under observation and puts additional stress and frustration on each child.

Hence, in recent years, computer games are being used to provide support for children with dyslexia in an engaging, convenient, and cost-efficient way (Rello et al. 2014; Kyle et al. 2013). Next, we give an overview of different approaches for screening readers and pre-readers using web applications/games.

31.4.1 Screening for Readers

Screening with applications for readers is mainly based on the perception of linguistic skills (Nessy 2011; Lexercise 2016; Rello et al. 2016) (e.g., phonological awareness, letter recognition) but also on visual or auditory short-term memory (Rello et al. 2016) or phonological processing (Rolka and Silverman 2015). Mainly, these web applications have been designed as a low-cost approach for nonprofessionals as a quick screening tool to identify people that may have dyslexia and should go to see a professional. An overview of the cognitive skills tested in some tools is given in Table 31.4. Next, we detail those tools for detecting children with dyslexia.

- **Dytective** (Rello et al. 2018, 2016) is a web-based game with different stages to detect dyslexia with machine learning prediction models. The stages exist in German, English, and Spanish. Each stage has a new task, e.g., search for a letter by its name in a letter grid (see Fig. 31.1, left) or search for a letter by its sound in a letter grid (see Fig. 31.1, right). *Dytective* in Spanish has an accuracy of almost 85% (Rello et al. 2016) while in English has 83% (Rello et al. 2018) for detecting a person with dyslexia. The most informative features on the individual level are how many correct and incorrect answers a participant has and they plan to include other languages in the future.
- **GraphoGame** (Lyytinen et al. 2015) is a game to teach and to evaluate early literacy skills. From their pre-analysis of children at risk in Finnish, they focus on the delayed letter knowledge. Measurements are, for example, the phonological manipulation, naming speed, or verbal short-term memory. It provides exercises for children aged two to six.
- **Lexercise Screener** (Lexercise 2016) is an English screening tool for detecting dyslexia. Children read familiar words and the parent records the child's response.

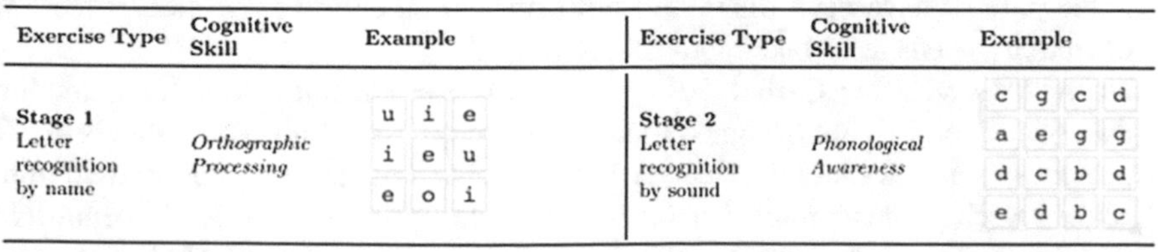

Exercise Type	Cognitive Skill	Example			Exercise Type	Cognitive Skill	Example			
							c	g	c	d
Stage 1 Letter recognition by name	Orthographic Processing	u	i	e	Stage 2 Letter recognition by sound	Phonological Awareness	a	e	g	g
		i	e	u			d	c	b	d
		e	o	i			e	d	b	c

Fig. 31.1 Example exercises of stage 1 (left) and stage 2 (right) from the dyslexia screener *Dytective* (Rello et al. 2016)

Table 31.4 Cognitive skills tested in different dyslexia screening tools for readers

Tools	Dytective 2016, 2018 (Rello et al. 2016, 2018)	GraphoGame 2015 (Lyytinen et al. 2015)	Lexercise 2016 (Lexercise 2016)	Nessy 2014 (Carbol 2014)
Languages	Spanish English	Finnish	English	English
Duration	10–15 min.	n/a	n/a	~20 min.
Skill				
Memory general	✓	✓		✓
Working memory	✓	✓		✓
Visual word memory	✓	✓		✓
Visual sequential memory	✓			✓
Visual alphabetical memory	✓	✓		
Auditory sequential memory	✓			✓
Auditory phonological memory	✓	✓		
Processing speed		✓		✓
Language skills General	✓	✓	✓	
Alphabetic awareness	✓	✓		
Lexical awareness	✓	✓		
Morphological awareness	✓	✓		
Phonological awareness	✓	✓		✓
Semantic awareness	✓			
Syllabic awareness	✓	✓		
Syntactic awareness	✓		✓	
Executive functions General	✓			
Activation and attention	✓			
Sustained attention	✓			
Simultaneous attention	✓			

This requires phonological awareness from the parents, which might be difficult if the parents have been diagnosed with dyslexia themselves. Hence, a lack of objectivity needs to be taken into account.

- **Nessy** (Nessy 2011; Carbol 2014) is an English screening tool for detecting dyslexia. Exercises are designed to test many cognitive skills (see Table 31.4). It provides exercises for children aged 5–16 years and the test takes around 20 min. The research summary published on their website reports the results of the multiple regression analysis between the game and the *comprehensive test of phonological processing* (Bruno 2000) with a strong correlation of almost 0.8.

All of the web applications mentioned before are mainly designed for desktop or laptop computers as well as for tablets.

To sum up, all these screening applications are language dependent. This means on one hand that the content of the application needs to be adapted for every new language which is time and resource consuming. On the other hand, only people who already have language acquisition can be tested (i.e., children need a minimum knowledge of phonological awareness, grammar, and vocabulary of the child to detect or predict dyslexia). In practice, these tools can only screen children after the first year of school and not earlier. Therefore, new ways of detecting the risk of having dyslexia are needed for pre-readers.

31.4.2 Screening for Pre-readers

As we already pointed out, the difficulty in detecting dyslexia before children go to school is the missing phonological awareness. To detect dyslexia in a child before, they gain phonological awareness, new indicators of dyslexia need to be discovered beside the ones mentioned in the previous subsection.

Expensive approaches predict future language acquisition of pre-readers e.g., with brain recordings for newborns (Guttorm 2003), with *rapid auditory cues* for infants (Benasich and Tallal 2002), and with the perception of *visual-spatial attention* for kindergarten children (Franceschini et al. 2012).

As we have seen in the Introduction, other auditory and visual indicators do not require reading ability, and may be useful in detecting dyslexia with a web application. Hence, now we present different examples of approaches that aim to predict dyslexia in pre-readers. All of them base their approach on indicators mainly related to linguistic skills. This rationale is supported by the following assumptions: (1) dyslexia does not develop when children come to school, but is already there before, (2) linguistic related indicators can represent the difficulties a person with dyslexia has with writing and reading, and (3) dyslexia can be measured through the interaction behavior of a person. An overview of the cognitive skills tested in each application is given in Table 31.5.

– **AGTB 5–12** is a computer-based test for children from age five to twelve years old (Hasselhorn 2012). In Germany, one of the first applications that was addressing the visual and phonological working memory (quoted after Irblich et al. 2013), besides the linguistic skills and the working memory. On the product website, it is stated that the Cronbach's Alpha is between 0.58 and 0.98 for children from the age of five till eight (Hasselhorn and Zoelch 2012). *AGTB 5–12* is criticized for the lack of objectivity for some tasks because the supervisor has to decide the grading depending on the subjective knowledge (Irblich et al. 2013). Additionally, the duration of over an hour and the detailed instructions are not suitable for younger children. Although *AGTB 5–12* aims to screen pre-readers is not specifically designed for smaller children.

Table 31.5 Cognitive skills tested in dyslexia screeners for pre-readers

Tools	AGTB 5–12 2012 (Irblich et al. 2013; Hasselhorn and Zoelch 2012)	DYSL–X 2013 (Van den Audenaeren 2013; Geurts et al. 2015)	GC 2017 (Gaggi et al. 2017)	Lexa 2018 (Poole 2018)	MusVis* 2018 (Rauschenberger et al. 2018a)
Languages	German	Italian	Italian	English	German Spanish English
Duration	~87 min.	n/a	Endless	n/a	10–15 min.
Skills					
Memory General	✓			✓	✓
Working M.					✓
Short-term M.	✓				✓
Auditory sequential M.					✓
Auditory phonological M.	✓			✓	✓
Processing speed				✓	✓
Language skills General	✓	✓			
Alphabetic awareness		✓	✓		
Phonological awareness			✓		

DGames has the same functionality as MusVis

- **DYSL-X** (also called DIESEL-X) aims to predict the possibility of a child having dyslexia at the age of five (Van den Audenaeren 2013; Geurts et al. 2015). The three mini games are designed to measure dyslexia using for example indicators like letter knowledge, frequency modulation detection, and end-phoneme recognition (Geurts et al. 2015). The games (for example, see Fig. 31.2d) take one hour to complete. The indicators are, for example, finding a letter that the child has been told.
- **Game–Collection** (CG) has six games each with a different challenge and gameplay (Gaggi et al. 2017). The games use visual and auditory elements and an evaluation was found only on the game interaction. The games explore the visual cues and the temporal time perception for predicting dyslexia at the age of five or six (Gaggi et al. 2012, 2017), although children of age three or four tested the games as well. In the game, called *Paths*, a shape with similarities to the letter *C* is used as an indicator (see Fig. 31.2a). The game, called *Fence Letters*, tries to distract a child while they close the lines to create a letter (see Fig. 31.2c). The usability test reported that children without dyslexia ($n = 17$) got a higher game score, winning a and using less time than children with dyslexia risk ($n = 6$).
- **Lexa** (Poole 2018) is a prototype to detect dyslexia by the auditory processing using oddity and rise time. The simple decision tree analysis of the lab study data (Data was collected by Goswami et al. Goswami 2011) was used to find

the most relevant features. A higher accuracy (89.2 vs. 53.8%) was found if no preprocessing of the feature related to phonological processing was applied. The researchers state that the biggest challenge in creating different rise times sounds and if a child is guessing the answer.

- **MusVis** (Rauschenberger 2016; Rauschenberger et al. 2018a) and **DGames** (Rauschenberger et al. 2018) address the visual and auditory perception with two different games. MusVis was developed based on the experience of a pilot implementation called *DysMusic* (Rauschenberger et al. 2017). The statistical analysis of the game measurements from 178 participants showed 8 significant indicators (e.g., total clicks, time to the first click, hits, and efficiency) for Spanish. Overall languages, four indicators are still significant (e.g., total clicks, time to the first click, hits, and efficiency). **DGames** (Rauschenberger et al. 2018) is a major update from *MusVis* with the learnings of its online study (see Fig. 31.2d). The evaluation of *MusVis* and *Dytective* showed that people with dyslexia do not make more mistakes, in spite that children with dyslexia are historically detected by the spelling mistakes they make. Consequently, non-related linguistic visual and musical content are included in *DGames*.

The web games presented focus mainly on a high-score gameplay, easy instructions, and colorful representation as well as story-based design. Besides AGTB 5–12 (Hasselhorn 2012; Steinbrink and Lachmann 2014), which is the only one that predicts the risk of dyslexia, all games are prototypes and have not been brought to the market until now. However, so far, no evaluation for the prediction accuracy of any of these games has been made public. Also, the focus for the prediction is mainly on having letter knowledge and phonological awareness.

31.5 Dyslexia Intervention

Nowadays, reading and writing is still one of the great abilities to be successful in our society. That is why after an (early) screening with the methods described in the previous section, it is crucial to start also with an (early) intervention. Indeed, an early intervention will give children with dyslexia the possibility to, (a) keep up with their peers in learning how to read and write, (b) avoid frustration, and (c) be not only defined by dyslexia. The success of the intervention depends on the time of diagnosis, mother tongue and the degree of difficulties a person has.

The idea to use computers for education exist quite a while as a historical overview from 1987 shows Kurland and Kurland (1987) and a few years later computer games were already used for learning a language, e.g., Tim 7 on Windows 95 (Soft 2000). But a person with dyslexia has specific difficulties, for example, in associating letter representations and the corresponding phoneme especially to organize the sequence, i.e., phonological awareness and information processing/sequence. That is why different approaches are necessary as well as many repetitions. A game has the potential of longer engagement and a better training effect. The advantages of web application

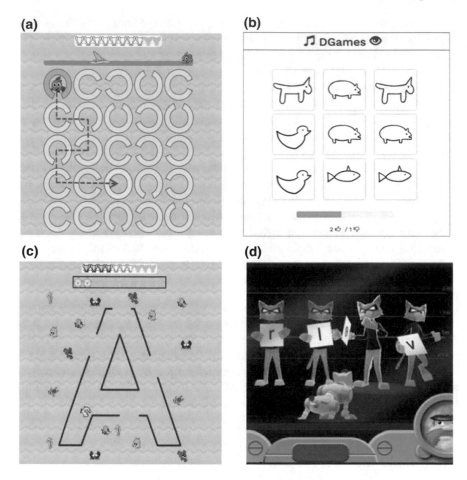

Fig. 31.2 Screen examples: **a** *Paths* game (Gaggi et al. 2012); **b** *DGames* (Rauschenberger et al. 2018); **c** Fence *letters game* (Gaggi et al. 2012); and **d** *DYSL-X* (Van den Audenaeren 2013)

games are: (1) automatically shaping an individual's learning curve, (2) engage in a fun way of learning, (3) potential of long-term commitment to repeat exercises, and (4) easily accessible through different devices, regions, and cultures. In the last decade, the intervention of people with dyslexia has increased with tools such as the examples that we present next. An overview of features for each application is given in Table 31.6.

– **Dyseggxia** is an iOS game made from the knowledge of the analysis from mistakes children with dyslexia made (Rello et al. 2016; Rauschenberger et al. 2015, 2016). The same learning approach is available in three different languages (Spanish, English Rello et al. 2014, and German Rauschenberger et al. 2015). The evaluation was done with 48 Spanish participants and showed that participants significantly improved their spelling compared to the control game (Rello et al. 2014). The

Table 31.6 Cognitive skills trained by applications for dyslexia intervention

Tools	Dysegg. 2014 (Rello et al. 2014)	Dytec. 2016 (Rello et al. 2017; Rello 2018)	Gale. 2016 (Serrano 2016; Dev 2019)	GC. 2012 (Gaggi et al. 2012)	Lern. 2007 (Flug 2016)	Nessy 2014 (Nessy Learning Ltd. 2019)	Proso. 2017 (Holz et al. 2017)
Languages	English German Spanish	Spanish	English Spanish	Italian	German	English	German
Type	Product	Product	Product	Prototype	Product	Product	Prototype
Skills							
Language Skills General	✓	✓	✓		✓	✓	✓
Alphabetic Awareness			✓	✓		✓	
Lexical A.			✓			✓	
Phonemic A.	✓	✓				✓	
Phonological A.	✓	✓	✓	✓			
Syllabic A.		✓	✓				
Syntactic A.					✓		
Orthographic Spelling		✓	✓				✓
Morphological A.		✓	✓				
Analysis of Error Words	✓	✓					
Working Memory		✓					
Executive Functions		✓					
Cognitive Abilities		✓		✓			
Auditory Perception		✓					
Rapid Auditory Skills							✓
Visual-spatial attention		✓		✓			

reading skills were not improved with this training but the experience gained from building this application was used for DytectiveU.

- **DytectiveU** is a computer game that provides a holistic learning approach (Rello et al. 2017; Rello 2018). The 25 cognitive abilities related to dyslexia are trained with 40,000 exercises to also empower the strengths of children with dyslexia. Exercises are designed with the knowledge from the analysis of spelling mistakes from children with dyslexia and natural language processing techniques. A workshop was used to get a first feedback from families and professionals about the functionality, i.e., gamification strategy or use of reports. In a longitudinal evaluation, the participants either had only their professional treatment or additionally played DytectiveU. All participants, independent if having or not a learning disorder (dyslexia or ADHD), significantly improved compared to the control group after playing DytectiveU.

- **Galexia** (Serrano 2016) is an intervention app to train reading fluency and comprehension in a playful environment. The app uses two approaches: Repeating reading and a recent one on accelerated reading, which may *promote rapid and automatic word recognition*. The approaches are combined with a sequential training at syllable, word, and text reading level. The game has been developed to engage participants with the gameplay to play longer without thinking about the intervention purpose. The game is available for children in the second till the sixth grade. The evaluation was done with an intensive training over 6 weeks with 46 participants native Spanish speakers (either diagnosed with dyslexia or poor readers). The results show significant differences for all grades for all fluency reading measures and comprehension measures. However, it can be argued that any child would have improved with such an intensive training since a control group is missing. Galexia is in the Google Play Store in Spanish (Dev 2019) and English (Dev 2019).

- **Game–Collection** (Gaggi et al. 2012, 2017) has different games which aim to screen and treat children at an early age. The screening part of *GC* is described in Sect. 31.4.2. The suggestion is that a daily treatment with these exercises will improve the reading abilities of pre-readers. The additional assumption is that a game can engage and motivate participants to do this daily treatment. Therefore, the first evaluation was done with a high focus on playing the game for pre-readers. The results show that the game is enjoyable and easy to play (67% of the children). The game called *Wizards*, challenges the child with the question "Which sound came first?" as the pre-readers were not able to discriminate the phoneme "A" from "E". They plan to evaluate their prediction approach in the future.

- **Lernserver** (Schönweiss and Schönweis 2014) is a tool to treat dyslexia in German, defining the level of support the child needs from the standard spelling test i.e., *Mnsteraner Rechtschreibanalyse (MRA)* (Mannhaupt 2006), and providing support exercises. Since the screening is done with a conventional printed spelling test *MRA*, we do not include this screening tool in the previous section. The exercises are based on the analysis of 500,000 error words from children classified in 230 error categories (Schönweiss and Schönweis 2014). The learning exercises are selected with an algorithm and a therapist depending on the errors a child makes in an initial test phase of 30–40 min. An evaluation with the *Landesinstitut für Schule* found out that 78.2% of the students ($n = 3798$) improved their writing using this tool (Flug 2016; BVL 2010) without a control group. Therefore, it is unknown if the students improved because of the intervention of the program *Lernserver* or the individual development of the children. In addition, children who did not attend sessions or showed a lack of interest in the program were excluded. This condition then increased the success rate of the study. Participants reported after the training session that they felt more comfortable writing (84%) and noticing their own mistakes (82%). Although *Lernserver* is not a game, participants reported they liked the application but did not like to reduce their free time.

- **Nessy Reading and Spelling** (Nessy Learning Ltd. 2019) is a web application to treat children between the age of 5 and 14 in English and defining individual support after using the *Nessy Screener* (see Sect. 31.4.1. The evaluation published on their website reports that students playing twice a week for 45 min improved on average their reading and writing skills after 18 weeks. Additionally, 84% of the participants reported having fun with this game. More details such as the evaluation measures used and the number of participants are not given.

- **Prosodiya** is a serious mobile game that targets the intervention by learning the syllable stress of the German orthography and embodied training (Holz et al. 2017) for children from ages of 6–12. The six parts and various subparts provide each time different linguistic or orthographic tasks and the whole game aims to use a *rule-based orthographic spelling training* (Holz et al. 2017). The individual training is designed with difficulty levels for each subpart and an integrated learner model. The preliminary study is mainly on the user experience and usability. Children reported that they liked the game which was confirmed by their parents. Additionally, the literacy process of participant was measured with the two standard tests for German: *Diagnistischer Rechtschreibtest* (DRT) (Müller 2003) and *Salzburger Lese-/ und Rechtschreibtest* (SLRT II) (Moll and Landerl 2010). The spelling improvement is reported for six children with the DRT and the reading improvement is reported for three children with the SLRT II. They plan to evaluate the intervention approach in a long-term study with more children.

In many cases, there are no more details probably because some applications are already products and other approaches are not open knowledge or are still under development. Similar approaches for intervention are *GraphoGame* (Lyytinen et al. 2015), *Lautarium* (Prölß 2016), mobile Intervention (Madeira et al. 2015), *LegaKids* (LegaKids Stiftung 2019), or *EasyLexia* (Skiada et al. 2014).

Applications, mentioned above, train mainly for only one language with the exception of *GraphoGame, Dyseggxia, DytectiveU* and *Galexia*.

Nevertheless, similarities have been found in the error categories of children with dyslexia having distinct native languages, e.g., German (Rauschenberger et al. 2016), English, or Spanish (Rello et al. 2016). The obvious reason these intervention approaches target only one language is that languages are different (e.g., in grammatical or orthographic rules). Also, adapting a technique to another language is very time consuming or the approach itself must be changed.

31.6 Discussion

Assistive technologies to improve reading and writing have been developed for years but many challenges remain. Not only people with dyslexia benefits from these developments but every person as well. Some of them are also beneficial for other disorders or disabilities such as text to speech for a person with visual impairments, text simplification for a person with cognitive disabilities or certain layout and presentation characteristics are also better for people without dyslexia, to mention just some cases.

Research is targeting dyslexia to avoid reading and spelling mistakes or to learn from the mistakes people with dyslexia make, which depend on the language. New approaches to screening (Rauschenberger et al. 2018a) or intervene dyslexia (Rello et al. 2014) are based in machine learning. In particular, how to create exercises for intervention depend on the language structure and are difficult to design, even though *DytectiveU* is already working on this. Also challenging is the degree of personalization on individual learning as well as the engagement to keep on practicing. The assumption is that an early detection for pre-readers is more helpful than traditional detection tests. An early detection means also early intervention and probably a faster and lasting knowledge of reading and writing.

Evaluating of a tool improved the reading and writing of a person with dyslexia can be easily examined by measuring the number of errors. But evaluating the longitudinal effect of learning considering external factors is much harder to study. The analysis of data collected through online experiments with a larger number of participants will improve future detection and intervention tools, surely involving machine learning and other data science methods. Indeed, since we are dealing with a social problem, we should make sure we detect everyone with dyslexia and interview many more people over the years instead of not detecting people with dyslexia that may fail at school. This applies for any prediction process related to health issues.

Another interesting recent result is that people with dyslexia do not see misspellings and then their comprehension is not affected by them. This is not the case for people without dyslexia, so adding misspellings in reading comprehension tests levels the field (Baeza-Yates and Rello 2017).

31.7 Future Directions

On one hand, the possibilities to explore dyslexia on the web, with the web, or for the web has increased successfully in the past years. On the other hand, little is known about the social effects: What kind of feedback is a person receiving when writing on the web with spelling mistakes? How is the, apparently, negative feedback affecting a person's writing or personality? Is the time and effort a person with dyslexia has to spend on writing correctly a daily bias because they can not spend time on other things to succeed?

So far, the focus is mainly on writing and reading itself and future research could take advantage of the strength that a person with dyslexia uses to compensate the challenges of reading and writing. As a person with visual impairments trains other perception competences, i.e., hearing or touch sense, a person with dyslexia must train other areas to compensate for the difficulties with texts. These compensation strategies might lead to a better understanding of dyslexia and improve the guidelines for presenting (digital) text or support (digital) writing. Apart from that, the bias a person with dyslexia faces in their daily routine on the web in social media or through conversations has an impact on each individual and on the content of the web. When exploring user created content or predicting diseases a multi-modal approach is needed (i.e., including different computer science fields such as HCI, IR, and ML; as well as other disciplines like psychology) to also capture comorbidity. Assistance when writing on a computer is helpful, but in mobile input techniques such as *swiftkey* or *t9*, an additional challenge is when the spelling of the word is not obvious. At this point, an insuperable issue is writing in different languages with the mobile input methods while having dyslexia. There is no tool to support a person with dyslexia when for example writing in English on Twitter and a moment later in German on Facebook or WhatsApp. Similar words in these languages are frequent (e.g., German *vor* (*"before/in front of"*) and English *for*) and not detected or prevented.

Using web technologies not only to provide assistive but to set up online experiments or large-scale studies is another possible future direction of web accessibility. As well, in the future, the daily routine of the user with the Internet-of-Things for a person of dyslexia might give more information of the origin of dyslexia and how to design better assistive technology.

Recently, the behavior of searchers with dyslexia analyzing web search results have been explored to investigate the relation of lexical and esthetic features on their impact toward text judgment and readability (Morris 2018; Fourney et al. 2018). The formulation of a query, deciding the link to click, and the examination within the document negatively impacts a searcher with dyslexia. The study with 174 adults with dyslexia and 172 without dyslexia suspects that certain parameters improve the web search results readability for both populations, i.e., line length, image size, and sentence text ratio. The authors explored the choice of text relevance and found a central tendency bias, i.e., participants with dyslexia rated on average lower and in a smaller region on the ratings scale. The authors explain this with the assumption that a person with dyslexia has difficulties to differentiate between relevant and nonrelevant documents. More research needs to be done in this problem and other problems where the task is composed of several steps.

31.8 Authors' Opinion of the Field

The use of text customization, simplification, and text to speech are already very well studied with several assistive applications designed. It seems that these research areas has nearly reached their limit. Still updates need to be done for each new device or technology (e.g., tablet, smartphone, and reader), innovation approach (e.g., machine learning algorithm), design evaluation for Usability and User Experience (e.g., with the User Experience Questionnaire Rauschenberger et al. 2013) and especially for each new contribution of the understand dyslexia (e.g., a person with dyslexia is lacking a visual asymmetry Le Floch and Ropars 2017). However, only after we fully understand the difficulties of a person with dyslexia while reading a text, we might reach the end of our research.

The field has evolved and took new directions into the detection and intervention through web-based applications. It is not only about assistive tools to understand what has been written or how to write correctly. Rather, the web is now a place to explore and study dyslexia with web methods.

Communication, training, and support to limit spelling mistakes in the text are the obvious solutions to improve the writing of a person with dyslexia. Early detection is the key for supporting a person with dyslexia to succeed. They can succeed without it but then it is much harder. Therefore, we should not wait for a person to fail before helping.

31.9   Conclusions

The technology presented in this chapter gives an overview of different approaches on how to assist people with dyslexia. The main focus was to show different research areas and their use with relation to the web. The first two sections refer to technology for supporting reading and writing, in the line of traditional assistive web technology. The relative new research field of detection and intervention is creating applications accessible through the web to screen for a person with dyslexia or to treat a person with dyslexia, with newer ones using the power of machine learning. Additionally, this research area opens up the opportunity to use the web for medium-scale online experiments to prove a hypothesis related to underrepresented target groups. Web technologies are now daily used and people with dyslexia should be empowered to use the web through them, as well as use web games to engage for repeatedly and challenging tasks.

References

Amazon (2018) Amazon.com: online shopping for electronics, apparel, computers, books, DVDs & more

American Psychiatric Association (2013) Diagnostic and statistical manual of mental disorders. American Psychiatric Association

Apple (2018) iBooks - Apple (DE)

Baeza-Yates R, Rello L (2017) The impact of misspellings on reading comprehension for people with dyslexia. In: International dyslexia association annual conference

Benasich AA, Tallal P (2002) Infant discrimination of rapid auditory cues predicts later language impairment. Behav Brain Res 136(1):31–49

British Dyslexia Association (2018) Dyslexia Style Guide 2018

Bruno RM (2000) Comprehensive test of phonological processing (CTOPP). Diagnostique 24(1)

BVL LdUM (2010) (Bundesverband Legasthenie Dyskalkulie e.V.). Evaluation Modellprojekt LISA (Evaluation project on LISA). LeDy– Mitgliederzeitschrift Bundesverband für Legasthenie und Dyskalkulie e.V. 1:8–32

Carbol B (2014) Research brief: use of the dyslexia quest app as a screening tool. Schmidt & Carbol Consulting Group, Technical report

Catts HW, McIlraith A, Bridges MS, Nielsen DC (2017) Viewing a phonological deficit within a multifactorial model of dyslexia. Read Writ 30(3):613–629

Claro Software Ltd (2015) Claro software

Coleman C, Gregg N, McLain L, Bellair LW (2008) A comparison of spelling performance across young adults with and without dyslexia. Assess Eff Interv 34(2):94–105

de Avelar LO, Rezende GC, Freire AP (2015) WebHelpDyslexia: a browser extension to adapt web content for people with dyslexia. Proc Comput Sci 67(Dsai):150–159

de Santana VF, de Oliveira R, Almeida LDA, Baranauskas MCC (2012) Web accessibility and people with dyslexia. In: Proceedings of the international cross-disciplinary conference on web accessibility - W4A'12. ACM Press, New York, p 1

de Santana VF, de Oliveira R, Almeida LDA, Ito M (2013) Firefixia. In: Proceedings of the 10th international cross-disciplinary conference on web accessibility - W4A'13. ACM Press, New York, p 1

Dev P, Galexia Educational Games–Apps on Google Play

Dev P, GALEXIA Mejora Fluidez Lectora–Apps bei Google Play

Flug L (2007) Projekt-Evaluation Bremen: Erprobungsphase des Lernservers an Bremischen Schulen (Evaluation project in Bremen: Pilot study with Lernserver at schools in Bremen). http://bit.ly/2bVRdfD. [Accessed 06 Sept 2016]

Fourney A, Ringel Morris M, Ali A, Vonessen L (2018) Assessing the readability of web search results for searchers with dyslexia. In: The 41st international ACM SIGIR conference on research and development in information retrieval - SIGIR'18. ACM Press, New York, pp 1069–1072

Franceschini S, Gori S, Ruffino M, Pedrolli K, Facoetti A (2012) A causal link between visual spatial attention and reading acquisition. Curr Biol 22(9):814–819

Gaggi O, Galiazzo G, Palazzi C, Facoetti A, Franceschini S (2012) A serious game for predicting the risk of developmental dyslexia in pre-readers children. In: 2012 21st international conference on computer communications and networks, ICCCN 2012 - proceedings

Gaggi O, Palazzi CE, Ciman M, Galiazzo G, Franceschini S, Ruffino M, Gori S, Facoetti A, Gaggi O, Palazzi CE, Galiazzo G, Franceschini S, Gori S, Facoetti A (2017) Serious games for early identification of developmental dyslexia. Comput Entertain Comput Entertain 15(4)

Geurts L, Vanden Abeele V, Celis V, Husson J, Van den Audenaeren L, Loyez L, Goeleven A, Wouters J, Ghesquière P (2015) DIESEL-X: a game-based tool for early risk detection of dyslexia in preschoolers. In: Describing and studying domain-specific serious games. Springer International Publishing, Switzerland, pp 93–114

Google (2018) Google Books

Goswami U (2011) A temporal sampling framework for developmental dyslexia. Trends Cogn Sci 15(1):3–10

Gregor P, Newell AF (2000) An empirical investigation of ways in which some of the problems encountered by some dyslexics may be alleviated using computer techniques. In: Proceedings ASSETS'00, ASSETS 2000. ACM Press, New York, pp 85–91

Grund M, Naumann CL, Haug G (2004) Diagnostischer Rechtschreibtest für 5. Klassen: DRT 5 (Diagnostic spelling and reading test for the class 5). Deutsche Schultests. Beltz Test, Göttingen, 2., aktual edition

Guttorm TK, Leppänen PHT, Tolvanen A, Lyytinen H (2003) Event-related potentials in newborns with and without familial risk for dyslexia: principal component analysis reveals differences between the groups. J Neural Trans 110(9):1059–1074

Hämäläinen JA, Salminen HK, Leppänen PHT (2013) Basic auditory processing deficits in dyslexia. J Learn Disabil 46(5):413–427

Hasselhorn M, Schumann-Hengsteler R, Gronauer J, Grube D, Mähler C, Schmid I, Seitz-Stein K, Zoelch C (2012) AGTB 5-12— Arbeitsgedächtnistestbatterie für Kinder von 5 bis 12 Jahren (AGTB 5-12— Working memory tasks to test children at the age of 5 till 12)

Hasselhorn M, Zoelch C (2012) Funktionsdiagnostik des Arbeitsgedächtnisses (Functional diagnostics of the working memory). Hogrefe Verlag, Göttingen

Haug KN, Klein PD (2018) The effect of speech-to-text technology on learning a writing strategy. Read Writ Q 34(1):47–62

Holz H, Brandelik K, Brandelik J, Beuttler B, Kirsch A, Heller J, Meurers D (2017) Prosodiya – a mobile game for German dyslexic children. Springer International Publishing, Cham, pp 73–82

Huss M, Verney JP, Fosker T, Mead N, Goswami U (2011) Music, rhythm, rise time perception and developmental dyslexia: perception of musical meter predicts reading and phonology. Cortex 47(6):674–689

Irblich D, Diakonie SK, Renner G (2013) AGTB 5–12 –Arbeitsgedächtnistestbatterie für Kinder von 5 bis 12 Jahren (AGTB 5–12 - working memory tasks to test children at the age of 5 till 12). Praxis der Kinderpsychologie und Kinderpsychiatrie 62(5):1–389

Jansen H, Mannhaupt G, Marx H, Skowronek H (2002) BISC - Bielefelder Screening zur Früherkennung von Lese-Rechtschreibschwierigkeiten (Early detection with the Bielefelder screening of reading and spelling difficulties). Hogrefe, Verlag für Psychologie, Göttingen

Juang B-H, Rabiner LR (2004) Automatic speech recognition–a brief history of the technology development. Georgia Institute of Technology. Atlanta Rutgers University and the University of California. Santa Barbara 1(1):1–67

Kanvinde G, Rello L, Baeza-Yates R (2012) IDEAL. In: Proceedings of the 14th international ACM SIGACCESS conference on computers and accessibility - ASSETS'12, p 205

Kurland DM, Kurland LC (1987) Computer applications in education: a historical overview. Annu Rev Comput Sci 2(1):317–358

Kyle F, Kujala J, Richardson U, Lyytinen H, Goswami U (2013) Assessing the effectiveness of two theoretically motivated computer-assisted reading interventions in the United Kingdom: GG Rime and GG Phoneme. Read Res Q 48(1):61–76

Le Floch A, Ropars G (2017) Left-right asymmetry of the Maxwell spot centroids in adults without and with dyslexia. Proc R Soc B: Biol Sci 284(1865):20171380

LegaKids Stiftung. Legasthenie und LRS–LegaKids informiert und hilft (Dyslexia–Information and help with LegaKids

Lexercise (2016) Dyslexia test - online from Lexercise. http://www.lexercise.com/tests/dyslexia-test. [Accessed 18 Sept 2017]

Lyytinen H, Erskine J, Hämäläinen J, Torppa M, Ronimus M (2015) Dyslexia - early identification and prevention: highlights from the Jyväskylä longitudinal study of dyslexia. Curr Dev Disord Rep 2(4):330–338

Madeira J, Silva C, Marcelino L, Ferreira P (2015) Assistive mobile applications for dyslexia. Procedia Comput Sci 64:417–424

Männel C, Schaadt G, Illner FK, van der Meer E, Friederici AD (2016) Phonological abilities in literacy-impaired children: Brain potentials reveal deficient phoneme discrimination, but intact prosodic processing. Dev Cogn Neurosci 23:14–25

Mannhaupt G (2006) Münsteraner Screening zur Früherkennung von Lese-Rechtschreibschwierigkeiten (Münsteraner Early Screening for reading and writing difficulties.). Cornelsen, Berlin

Mayes SD, Frye SS, Breaux RP, Calhoun SL (2018) Diagnostic, demographic, and neurocognitive correlates of dysgraphia in students with ADHD, autism, learning disabilities, and neurotypical development. J Dev Phys Disabil

Miniukovich A, De Angeli A, Sulpizio S, Venuti P (2017) Design guidelines for web readability. In: Proceedings of the 2017 conference on designing interactive systems - DIS'17. ACM Press, New York, pp 285–296

Moll K, Landerl K (2010) SLRT II - Lese- und Rechtschreibtest (Reading and spelling test). Verlag Hans Huber, Bern

Morris MR, Fourney A, Ali A, Vonessen L (2018) Understanding the needs of searchers with dyslexia. In: Proceedings of the SIGCHI conference on human factors in computing systems - CHI'18, pp 1–12

Müller R (2003) Diagnostischer Rechtschreibtest für 2. Klassen (DRT 2). (Detection spelling test for class 2.). Beltz, Göttingen

Nessy. Dyslexia screening - Nessy UK. https://www.nessy.com/uk/product/dyslexia-screening/. [Accessed 18 Sept 2017]

Nessy Learning Ltd. Research Evidence - Nessy Reading and Spelling

Pedler J (2005) Using semantic associations for the detection of real-word spelling errors. Proc Corpus Linguist Conf Ser 1(1):N.N

Pedler J (2007) Computer correction of real-word spelling errors in dyslexic text. PhD thesis, Birkbeck College, London University

Petrie HL, Weber G, Fisher W (2005) Personalization, interaction, and navigation in rich multimedia documents for print-disabled users. IBM Syst J 44(3):629–635

Pipusbcn (2017) Use of text to speech in iBooks - Apple Community

Poole A, Zulkernine F, Aylward C (2017) Lexa: a tool for detecting dyslexia through auditory processing. In: 2017 IEEE symposium series on computational intelligence, SSCI 2017 - proceedings, pp 1–5

Prölß A (2016) Evaluation des computergestützten phonologischen Trainingsprogramms Lautarium zur Förderung des Schriftspracherwerbs (Evaluating the computer-based phonologischen spelling approach Lauarium). Doktor der philosophie, Technischen Universität Kaiserslautern

Quattrini Li A, Sbattella L, Tedesco R (2013) PoliSpell: an adaptive spellchecker and predictor for people with dyslexia. In Carberry S, Weibelzahl S, Micarelli A, Semeraro G (eds) User modeling, adaptation, and personalization. Springer, Berlin, pp 302–309

Rauschenberger M (2016) DysMusic: detecting dyslexia by web-based games with music elements. In: The web for all conference addressing information barriers – W4A'16. ACM Press, Montreal

Rauschenberger M, Füchsel S, Rello L, Bayarri C, Thomaschewski J, Silke F, Rello L (2015) Exercises for german-speaking children with dyslexia. Hum-Comput Interact-INTERACT 9296:445–452

Rauschenberger M, Fuechsel S, Rello L, Bayarri C, Gòrriz A (2015) A game to target the spelling of German children with dyslexia. In: Proceedings of the 17th international ACM SIGACCESS conference on computers and accessibility - ASSETS'15. Lisbon, pp 445–446

Rauschenberger M, Rello L, Baeza-Yates R (2018a) A tablet game to target dyslexia screening in pre-readers. In: MobileHCI'18. ACM Press, Barcelona

Rauschenberger M, Rello L, Baeza-Yates R, Bigham JP (2018b) Towards language independent detection of dyslexia with a web-based game. In: W4A'18: the internet of accessible things. ACM, Lyon, France, pp N.N

Rauschenberger M, Rello L, Baeza-Yates R, Gomez E, Bigham JP (2017) Towards the prediction of dyslexia by a web-based game with musical elements. In: Proceedings of the 14th web for all conference on the future of accessible work - W4A'17. ACM Press, Perth, pp 1–4

Rauschenberger M, Rello L, Füchsel S, Thomaschewski J (2016) A language resource of German errors written by children with dyslexia. In: Proceedings of the tenth international conference on language resources and evaluation (LREC 2016). European Language Resources Association, Paris

Rauschenberger M, Schrepp M, Cota MP, Olschner S, Thomaschewski J (2013) Efficient measurement of the user experience of interactive products. How to use the user experience questionnaire (UEQ). Example: Spanish language. Int J Artif Intell Interact Multimed (IJIMAI) 2(1):39–45

Rello L (2014) DysWebxia a text accessibility model for people with dyslexia. PhD thesis, Universitat Pompeu Fabra

Rello L (2015) Dyslexia and web accessibility. In: Proceedings of the 12th web for all conference on - W4A'15. ACM Press, New York, pp 1–4

Rello L (2018) Superar la dislexia. Una experiencia personal a través de la investigación. (Overcome dyslexia. A personal experience through research.). Paidos Educacion

Rello L, Baeza-Yates R (2014) Evaluation of DysWebxia: a reading app designed for people with dyslexia. In: Proceedings of the 11th web for all conference, W4A'14. ACM, New York, pp 10:1–10:10

Rello L, Baeza-Yates R (2016) The effect of font type on screen readability by people with dyslexia. ACM Trans Access Comput 8(4):1–33

Rello L, Baeza-Yates R (2017) How to present more readable text for people with dyslexia. Univers Access Inf Soc 16(1):29–49

Rello L, Baeza-Yates R, Bott S, Saggion H (2013) Simplify or help?: text simplification strategies for people with dyslexia. In: Proceedings of the 10th international cross-disciplinary conference on web accessibility, W4A'13. ACM, New York, pp 15:1—15:10

Rello L, Baeza-Yates R, Llisterri J (2016) A resource of errors written in Spanish by people with dyslexia and its linguistic, phonetic and visual analysis. Lang Resour Eval 51(2):1–30

Rello L, Ballesteros M, Abdullah A, Serra M, Sánchez DA, Bigham JP (2016) Dytective: diagnosing risk of dyslexia with a game. In:Pervasive health 2016. ACM Press, Cancun

Rello L, Ballesteros M, Bigham JP (2015) A spellchecker for dyslexia. In: ASSETS 2015: the 17th international ACM SIGACCESS conference of computers and accessibility, pp 39–47

Rello L, Bayarri C, Otal Y, Pielot M (2014) A computer-based method to improve the spelling of children with dyslexia. In: Proceedings of the 16th international ACM SIGACCESS conference on Computers and accessibility - ASSETS'14. ACM Press, New York, pp 153–160

Rello L, Bigham JP (2017) Good background colors for readers. In: Proceedings of the 19th international ACM SIGACCESS conference on computers and accessibility - ASSETS'17, pp 72–80

Rello L, Kanvinde G, Baeza-Yates R (2012) Layout guidelines for web text and a web service to improve accessibility for dyslexics. In: Proceedings of the international cross-disciplinary conference on web accessibility. ACM, p 36

Rello L, Macias A, Herrera M, de Ros C, Romero E, Bigham JP (2017) DytectiveU. In: Proceedings of the 19th international ACM SIGACCESS conference on computers and accessibility - ASSETS'17. ACM Press, New York, pp 319–320

Rello L, Pielot M, Marcos M-C, Carlini R (2013) Size matters (spacing not): 18 points for a dyslexic-friendly Wikipedia. In: Proceedings of the 10th international cross-disciplinary conference on web accessibility, W4A'13. ACM, New York, pp 17:1–17:4

Rello L, Romero E, Rauschenberger M, Ali A, Williams K, Bigham JP, White NC (2018) Screening dyslexia for English using HCI measures and machine learning. In: Proceedings of the 2018 international conference on digital health - DH'18. ACM Press, New York, pp 80–84

Reynolds L, Wu S (2018) "I'm Never Happy with What I Write": challenges and strategies of people with dyslexia on social media. In: Proceedings of the 12th international conference on web and social media. The AAAI Press, Palo Alto, p 280

Rolka EJ, Silverman MJ (2015) A systematic review of music and dyslexia. Arts Psychother 46:24–32

Schönweiss F, Schönweis P (2014) Lernserver - Individuelle Förderung (Lernserver - individual intervention)

Schulte-Körne G (2010) Diagnostik und Therapie der Lese-Rechtscheib-Störung (The prevention, diagnosis, and treatment of dyslexia). Deutsches Ärzteblatt international 107(41)

Schulte-Körne G, Deimel W, Müller K, Gutenbrunner C, Remschmidt H (1996) Familial aggregation of spelling disability. J Child Psychol Psychiatry 37(7):817–822

Serrano F, Bravo SJF, Gómez-Olmedo M (2016) Galexia: evidence-based software for intervention in reading fluency and comprehension. In: INTED2016, pp 2001–2007

Seymour PHK, Aro M, Erskine JM (2003) Foundation literacy acquisition in European orthographies. Br J Psychol (Lond, Engl: 1953) 94(Pt 2):143–74

Skiada R, Soroniati E, Gardeli A, Zissis D (2014) EasyLexia: a mobile application for children with learning difficulties. Procedia Comput Sci 27:218–228

Soft U (2000) Tim 7, Deutsch, 5. Klasse

Spehr M (2010) Diktieren ist viel schneller als Tippen (Dictating is faster than typing)

Spooner RIW (1998) A spelling aid for dyslexic writers. PhD thesis, University of York

Steinbrink C, Lachmann T (2014) Lese-Rechtschreibstörung (Dyslexia). Springer, Berlin

Tallal P (2004) Improving language and literacy is a matter of time. Nat Rev Neurosci 5(9):721–728

Topac V (2012) The development of a text customization tool for existing web sites. In: The development of a text customization tool for existing web sites. Web accessibility initiative W3C

Van den Audenaeren L, Celis V, Vanden Abeele V, Geurts L, Husson J, Ghesquière P, Wouters J, Loyez L, Goeleven A (2013) DYSL-X: design of a tablet game for early risk detection of dyslexia in preschoolers. In Games for health. Springer Fachmedien Wiesbaden, Wiesbaden, pp 257–266

Vidyasagar TR, Pammer K (2010) Dyslexia: a deficit in visuo-spatial attention, not in phonological processing. Trends Cogn Sci 14(2):57–63

Wagner S (2005) Intralingual speech-to-text conversion in real-time: challenges and opportunities. In: Challenges of multidimensional translation conference proceedings. MuTra, Saarbrücken

Web Accessibility Initiative (WAI) (2018) World Wide Web Consortium (W3C)

Wery JJ, Diliberto JA (2017) The effect of a specialized dyslexia font, OpenDyslexic, on reading rate and accuracy. Ann Dyslexia 67(2):114–127

Wikipedia (2018a) Amazon Kindle

Wikipedia (2018b) Apple Books

Wikipedia (2018c) Google Play Books

Wyke MA (1984) Reading, writing and dyslexia: a cognitive analysis A.W. Ellis, London: Lawrence Earlbaum, 1984, p. 147. Behav Psychother 14(01):95

Ziegler JC, Perry C, Ma-Wyatt A, Ladner D, Schulte-Körne G (2003) Developmental dyslexia in different languages: language-specific or universal? J Exp Child Psychol 86(3):169–93

Chapter 32
Alternative Nonvisual Web Browsing Techniques

I. V. Ramakrishnan, Vikas Ashok and Syed Masum Billah

Abstract People with vision impairments typically use screen readers to browse the Web. To facilitate nonvisual browsing, web sites must be made accessible to screen readers, i.e., all the visible elements in the web site must be readable by the screen reader. But even if web sites are accessible screen reader users may not find them easy to use and/or easy to navigate. For example, locating the desired information may require a tedious linear search of the webpage that involves listening to a lot of irrelevant content. These issues go beyond web accessibility and directly impact web usability. Several techniques have been reported in the accessibility literature for making Web usable for screen reading. This chapter is a review of these techniques.

32.1 Introduction

The Web has permeated all aspects of our daily lives. We use the Web to obtain and exchange information, shop, pay bills, make travel arrangements, apply for college or employment, connect with others, participate in civic activities, etc. It has in effect become the indispensable ubiquitous "go-to utility" for participating in society. A 2016 report by Internet World Stats shows that Internet usage has skyrocketed by more than 1000% since 2000, to include almost half of the global population in 2016 (over 3.6 billion people) (MiniwattsMarketingGroup 2016), making it one of the most widely used technologies.

About 15% of the world's population are living with some form of physical/sensory/cognitive disability (WHO-disability-data 2011). The Web has the potential to provide an even greater benefit to such individuals who once required human

I. V. Ramakrishnan (✉) · V. Ashok · S. M. Billah
Department of Computer Science, Stony Brook University, New York, NY, USA
e-mail: ram@cs.stonybrook.edu

V. Ashok
e-mail: vganjiguntea@cs.stonybrook.edu

S. M. Billah
e-mail: sbillah@cs.stonybrook.edu

© Springer-Verlag London Ltd., part of Springer Nature 2019
Y. Yesilada and S. Harper (eds.), *Web Accessibility*, Human–Computer
Interaction Series, https://doi.org/10.1007/978-1-4471-7440-0_32

assistance with many of the activities mentioned earlier. The Web opens up opportunities to do them without assistance and thereby foster independent living.

People with disabilities rely on special-purpose assistive software applications for interacting with the Web. It is left to web developers to ensure that their web sites are accessible, i.e., the web sites work with such assistive software. To aid web developers in this process, the W3C Web Accessibility initiative (WAI 1997) has formulated the Web Content Accessibility Guidelines (WCAG 2009) on how to make web pages accessible. These guidelines are essentially recommendations to web developers. As an example, one recommendation states that web developers should provide text equivalents for images and semantically meaningful labels to links in web pages.

People with vision impairments browse the Web nonvisually. They form a sizeable fraction of people with disabilities. Specifically, there are nearly 285 million people with vision impairments worldwide—39 million blind and 246 million with low vision (WHO 2014). In the U.S. alone, there are over 23 million Americans suffering from vision loss and over 1.5 million of them use the Internet (AFB 2017).

Ever since the advent of the PC, visually impaired people have used Screen Readers (SRs), a special-purpose software application, to interact with digital content. SRs serially narrate the content of the screen using text-to-speech engines and let users navigate the content using touch or keyboard shortcuts.

Over the years, there has been much progress on screen reading and more broadly on assistive technologies for a broad range of disabilities. It has been driven by several factors: (1) federal mandates such as the ADA (INTRODUCTION TO THE ADA) and the 21st Century Communications and Video Accessibility Act (21st Century Communications and Video Accessibility Act (CVAA)); (2) companies specializing in the development of assistive technologies (Dolphin; Micro; NVAccess; Scientific); large IT companies like Google, Apple and Microsoft incorporating support for accessibility in their products and services (e.g., Microsoft's MSAA & UI Automation (Microsoft; Microsoft), Apple's NSAccessibility (Apple), and GNOME's ATK & AT-SPI (Manning et al. 2008)); (3) business and educational institutions adopting assistive technologies to enhance employment and educational opportunities for people with disabilities. Because of all this progress, these days visually impaired people have several high quality SRs to choose from, e.g., JAWS (JAWS 2013), Window-Eyes (Window-Eyes 2010), SuperNova (SuperNova 2013), NVDA (NVDA 2013) and VoiceOver (VoiceOver 2015).

For visually impaired people, SRs remain the dominant technology for nonvisual web browsing. Web sites that are designed based on WCAG guidelines are accessible to SRs. But making web pages accessible in and of itself does not make them usable—a problem that is primarily concerned with the "how to's" of providing a rich user experience in terms of ease of use, effectiveness in getting tasks done, etc. In this regard, SRs are not very usable or efficient for web browsing (Borodin et al. 2010) and have several notable drawbacks (Lazar et al. 2007).

First, to be efficient, SR users have to remember an assortment of shortcuts and learn a number of browsing strategies; however, most users rely only on a small basic set of sequential navigation shortcuts, which leads to excessive interaction with computers even while performing simple browsing tasks (Borodin et al. 2010).

Second, because one cannot judge the importance of content before listening to it; blind users typically go through reams of irrelevant content before they find what they need, thereby suffering from information overload.

Third, SRs are typically oblivious of the fact that web content is organized into semantic entities (e.g., menus, date pickers, search results, etc.), where each entity is composed of many basic HTML elements; the user may not know what entities are present on the page, whether s/he is navigating inside or outside an entity, where the entity's boundaries are, etc.

These problems become particularly acute when performing tasks in content-rich web sites; for example, while sighted users can purchase something online or make a reservation in just a few minutes, screen reader users often take 10 min or more (Borodin et al. 2010; Puzis et al. 2013). Yet another serious problem of not knowing the entity boundaries is that the SR's sequential readout intersperses content from different semantic entities, which can confuse and disorient the user. Lastly, in addition to not being able to get a quick overview of the entire web page and having to read through content one element at a time, blind users also have to endure the fact that SRs navigate web pages at the syntactic level instead of the semantic one. Consequently, while sighted people see the semantic structure of the web page, blind people have access only to its syntactic structure, and most often have to navigate and listen to individual HTML elements.

The root cause of the usability problems stems from the SR's limited knowledge of the semantics of web content. Research efforts in accessibility have sought to rectify this situation by incorporating *semantic awareness* in nonvisual browsing. At their core, the techniques for semantic awareness infer the semantics by analysis of the content using syntactic and structural cues in web pages, optionally supplemented by explicit knowledge-based encoding the semantics of domain-specific web sites such as travel web sites, shopping web sites, etc. Semantic awareness goes beyond web accessibility. It embodies the state of the art in making web browsing usable for SR users. We will review how semantic awareness is incorporated in nonvisual browsing with SRs next.

32.2 Semantic Awareness in Nonvisual Web Browsing

A web page can be viewed as a collection of semantic entities. Informally, we define a semantic entity to be a meaningful grouping of related HTML elements. As an illustration, Fig. 32.1 is a web page fragment with six semantic entities, numbered 1–6. The number associated with an entity is shown in red at the corner of that entity. For example, entity numbered 4 corresponds to the search-result entity showing the results for an available flight. Notice that it is a grouping of related links, button, images, and text. Similarly, an article entity in a news web page is a collection of

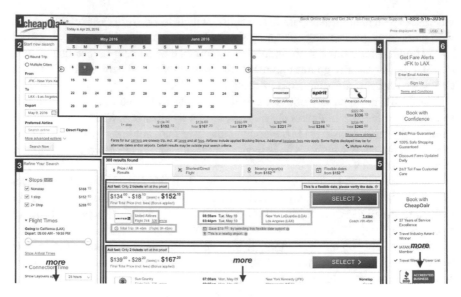

Fig. 32.1 An illustration of web page fragment with six semantic entities, numbered 1–6. The number associated with an entity is shown in red at the corner of that entity

paragraphs and possibly links; a list of items entity can be a simple HTML list or a tabulated list of products with their prices and short descriptions.

Observe how the semantic entities in Fig. 32.1 have clear visual boundaries. Sighted people can easily identify and interact with these entities because of these boundaries and moreover are easy to distinguish from each other. In contrast, blind people have to use the screen reader to figure out and guess where the entity starts and ends and how it is organized.

Early on there has been a lot of research effort on identifying the boundaries of semantic entities. The basis of these efforts is segmentation, described next.

32.2.1 Segmentation

A (logical) segment of a web page corresponds to a contiguous fragment of web elements in the page that are "semantically" related (e.g., semantic entities such as the news headline and article summary, a menu of categories, search results, etc.). As an illustration, the fragments enclosed within the rectangles in Fig. 32.1 are examples of segments.

Organizing a web page into a hierarchy of segments or semantic entities lets users navigate between "meaningful" pieces of information, and results in much better comprehension of the content. This is especially useful for small screen devices where the display area is at a premium, making it all the more important to focus on coherent and relevant chunks of content.

Several techniques for segmenting web pages have appeared in the research literature (e.g., see Álvarez et al. 2010; Cai et al. 2004; Guo et al. 2007; Yi and Liu 2003; Yin and Lee 2004; Yu et al. 2003; Zhai and Liu 2005; Zhu et al. 2006) that utilize a range of features in the pages from visual cues, to spatial locality information, to presentational similarity, to patterns in the content, etc. The web segmentation techniques can be categorized into the following four groups (Eldirdiery and Ahmed 2015):

1. **DOM-Based Approach** These segmentation techniques (Ahmadi and Kong 2008; Bar-Yossef and Rajagopalan 2002; Chakrabarti et al. 2008; Debnath et al. 2005; Kang et al. 2010; Kołcz and Yih 2007; Rajkumar and Kalaivani 2012; Sadet and Conrad 2011; Vineel 2010; Wang et al. 2008; Xiao et al. 2008; Yi and Liu 2003) analyze the DOM to determine the various semantic entities. A few techniques (Ashok et al. 2017; Billah et al. 2017a) even use handcrafted ontologies containing information about typical semantic entities (e.g., filters, forms, menus, product items, etc.) to reinforce DOM analysis for segmentation.

2. **Vision-Based Approach** These segmentation techniques (Cai et al. 2004; Kovacevic et al. 2002; Song et al. 2004; Xiao et al. 2005; Yan and Miao 2009; Zhang et al. 2010) process the webpage rendering information to determine the segments. They partition the page by analyzing the visual cues such as background color, styling, layout, font size, and type, separators such as lines and whitespace, etc.

3. **Text-Based Approach** These segmentation techniques (Hearst 1994; Kohlschütter and Nejdl 2008) look only at the textual content of the web pages. Specifically, they analyze text features such as text density and link density. The primary assumption by these techniques is that text portions with linguistically similar features are likely (statistically) to be part of one segment.

4. **Hybrid Approach** These techniques (Sanoja and Gançarski 2014; Safi et al. 2015; Wang and Liu 2009) combine ideas from the above three approaches in order to overcome their individual shortcomings.

Segmentation has been used in a variety of applications such as adapting content on small screen devices (e.g., Yin and Lee 2004), data cleaning and search (e.g., Yi and Liu 2003; Yu et al. 2003) and web data extraction (e.g., Álvarez et al. 2010; Zhu et al. 2006). Recognizing the importance of segmentation, Apple's VoiceOver also segments web pages with its "auto web spot" feature. More importantly, segmentation is an important component in many techniques that have been developed to enhance web usability for people with visual impairments. We review these techniques next.

32.2.2   Segmentation-Based Techniques for Enhancing Browsing Experience

32.2.2.1   Clutter-Free Browsing

As SR users browse the Web, they have to filter through a lot of irrelevant data, i.e., clutter. For example, most web pages contain banners, ads, navigation bars, and other kinds of distracting data irrelevant to the actual information desired by the users. Navigating to the relevant information quickly is critical for making nonvisual web browsing usable. For finding information quickly, SRs allow keyword searching. This assumes that users already know what they are looking for, which is not necessarily true in all cases, especially in ad hoc browsing.

The relevance of different entities on any page is subjective. However, as soon as the user follows a link it is often possible to use the context of the link to determine the relevant information on the next page and present it to the user first. A technique described in Harper et al. (2004) uses the context of a link, defined as the text surrounding it, to get a preview of the next web page so that users could choose whether or not they should follow the link. The idea of using the words on the link as well as those surrounding it is used in Mahmud et al. (2007) to more accurately identify the beginning of main content relevant to the link, on the following page. For example, clicking on a news link, it will directly place the reading position to the beginning of the news article on the next page. The user can now listen to the article clutter-free.

This focus on removing "clutter" in a web page for readability purposes motivated the Readability (Readability) tool and the "Reader" button in the Safari browser. Both employ heuristics driven by visual and structural cues (such as link density in a node, text length, node position in the tree, representative font size, tags like headers and div) for extracting the main content in a web page. More precise clutter removal is done in Islam et al. (2011) by tightly coupling visual, structural, and linguistic features.

32.2.2.2   Online Transactions

Web transactions broadly refer to activities such as shopping, registrations, banking, and bill payments online. Such transactions involve several steps that typically span several web pages. This can significantly exacerbate information overload on SR users and affect their productivity. In this regard, as was mentioned earlier, while sighted users can purchase something online or make a reservation in just a few minutes, SR users often take 10 min or more (Borodin et al. 2010; Puzis et al. 2013).

Usually one needs to browse only a small fragment of a web page to perform a transaction. This observation is the basis of the method in Sun et al. (2007) for doing web transactions more efficiently and with less information overload. Specifically, a web transaction is modeled as a process automaton (see Fig. 32.2). In that automaton,

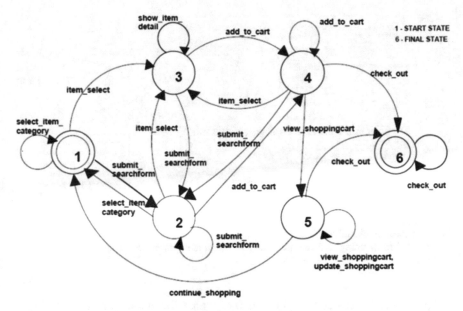

Fig. 32.2 Automaton fragment for online shopping

each node/state represents transaction-specific semantic entities (e.g., search results or product description) it expects to find in the web page that is given as the state's input and the edges/arrows are possible user actions corresponding to the entity represented by the state (e.g., clicking a button). Segmentation is used to identify transaction-specific semantic entities in that page.

Stepping through a transaction corresponds to making transitions in the automaton; at each step, only the entity relevant to that step in the transaction is presented thereby skipping all the other content in the page. The process automaton is learned from labeled training sequences gathered from click streams of user actions. In (JAWS), the construction process of the automata was completely automated.

32.2.2.3   Logical Hierarchy Browsing

Instead of navigating the content element-by-element at the syntactic HTML level, a recent work, Speed Dial (Billah et al. 2017a), offers a novel interaction paradigm that supports hierarchical navigation at the semantic entity level. Speed Dial uses Microsoft's physical off-the-shelf Surface Dial as an input interface device. The Dial accepts a small set of simple input gestures such as press, rotate left, and rotate right. Pressing and holding the Dial activates a radial dashboard menu containing various configuration options that can be accessed by rotating the Dial left or right. The Dial also provides haptic feedback through vibration.

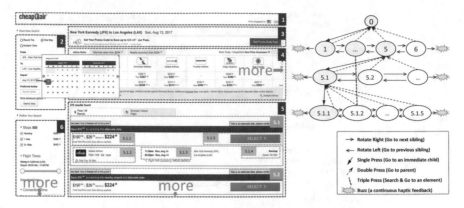

Fig. 32.3 An illustration of Speed-Dial. On the left is a flight-reservation web site, which is divided into six logical blocks or semantic entities. Entity 5 is further divided into (sub)-entities. On the right is the corresponding semantic tree, and a list of valid gestures offered by the Dial to navigate on the tree

Speed Dial interfaces this physical Dial with a Semantic Model consisting of abstract representations of the semantic entities of a web page (e.g., forms, search results, filters, etc., see Fig. 32.3) organized in the form of a hierarchy. As opposed to current screen readers, which navigate through syntactic DOM elements in idiosyncratic patterns, Fig. 32.3 illustrates how Speed Dial navigates at the semantic level. Users can traverse the segments with rotate left and rotate right gestures. Users may move into or out of (sub)segments with press/double press gestures respectively. Haptic feedback, denoted by a "buzz," indicates that one has reached either the first or last element in a segment. When a node is visited, Speed Dial reads out descriptive information of the segment, such as the price of a result item in the example of Fig. 32.3. The illustration above reveals some of the distinctive features of Speed Dial. Unlike the numerous shortcuts in screen readers, there are only a few simple gestures in Speed Dial. Additionally, these gestures are easy-to-remember, easy-to-perform, and uniform across websites—an attribute that is highly desired by blind screen reader users (Billah et al. 2017b).

32.3 Skimming and Summarization

Skimming and summarization are complementary techniques that help the users obtain the gist of a text document. Summarization is a snippet of text, explicitly constructed from the document's text, which conveys the essence of the information contained in the document. Skimming, on the other hand, conveys it by identifying a few informative words in the document. These two topics have attracted the attention of the Information Retrieval and Natural Language Processing research community (Manning et al. 2008; Radev et al. 2002). Summarization and skimming are naturally applicable to web pages, especially for nonvisual browsing as they give the users a "peek" into the content without having to make them listen to it in its entirety.

Using the notion of the context of a web page as a collection of words gathered around the links on other pages pointing to that web page, (Delort et al. 2003) uses this context to obtain a summary of the page. Summarization using context is also explored by the InCommonSense system (Amitay and Paris 2000), where search engine results are summarized to generate text snippets. In BrookesTalk (Zajicek et al. 1999) the web page is summarized as a collection of "significant" sentences drawn from the page. These are sentences containing key trigrams (phrases containing three words) that are identified using simple statistics. The AcceSS system (Parmanto et al. 2005) makes web pages accessible through a transcoding process comprised of summarization and simplification steps. The former uses the idea of the context of a link from Harper et al. (2004) to get a preview of the page and the latter identifies "important" sections to be retained. The Summate system picks a maximum of four sentences from a web page as its gist summary (Harper and Patel 2005).

A method for nonvisual skimming is described in Ahmed et al. (2012). It works as follows: First, every sentence is parsed to extract grammatical relations amongst its words. Second, a lexical tree based on these relations is constructed, where each node of the tree represents a word in the sentence. Third, for every word in this tree, it is grammatical (i.e., POS tags) as well as structural features (related to in-degree/out-degree, etc.) are extracted. These features are given to a trained classifier to determine whether or not to include the word in the skimming summary. Finally, a subtree consisting of the selected words is constructed. This subtree represents the skimming summary that users interact with via an interface.

32.4   Speech-Based Browsing

Speech input has long been recognized as a powerful interaction modality for nonvisual browsing because of its potential to alleviate the shortcomings of an SR's keyboard-based press-and-listen mode of interaction. An exposition of these short-comings and how speech modality can address them appears in Ashok et al. (2015). Several systems support browsing with spoken commands.

Voice browsers like PublicVoiceXML (Public Voice Lab 2002) and JVoiceXML (Schnelle 2013) have an interactive voice interface for browsing web content. Browsing the Web with these voice browsers requires the conversion of web pages to JVoiceXML (VoiceXML 2009), a document format that operates within a controlled domain. In some cases, voice navigation is used for improving one particular aspect of browsing, e.g., Han et al. (2014) focuses on making the menus and submenus appearing on a webpage voice-accessible; Windows Speech Recognition (WSR) (Microsoft 2014) makes it possible to follow a link by speaking its ordinal number and enables a few other basic commands. Alas, neither is accessible to blind users.

An Android accessibility service, JustSpeak (Zhong et al. 2014), can be used with any Android app or accessibility service and is able to process chains of commands in a single utterance. It is limited to a few basic browsing-related commands, specifically: activate, scroll, toggle switch, long press, toggle checkbox. Dragon NaturallySpeaking Rich Internet Application feature (Nuance 2014) enables the user to control certain websites by voice. It provides limited support to select parts of only four (4) websites in specific browsers and lists many additional caveats and limitations, both general and browser specific. But usage of visual cues and a graphical user interface for listing possible utterances/commands significantly reduces Dragon's accessibility for blind people.

Capti-Speak is speech-augmented Screen Reader (Ashok et al. 2015). Capti-Speak translate spoken utterances into browsing actions and generate appropriate TTS responses to these utterances. Each spoken utterance is part of an ongoing dialog. It employs a custom dialog act model (Ashok et al. 2014) that was developed exclusively for "speech-enabled non-visual web access" to interpret every spoken utterance in the context of the most recent state of the dialog, where the state, in some sense, encodes the history of previous user utterances and system responses.

A recent work exploring the applicability of dialog assistants in web screen reading suggests that it has the potential to significantly enhance web usability for SR users (Ashok et al. 2017). In this work, the web screen reading assistant, SRAA, is rooted in two complimentary ideas: First, it elevates the interaction to a higher level of abstraction—from operating over (syntactic) HTML elements to operating over semantic web entities. Doing so brings blind users closer to how sighted people perceive and operate over web entities. Second, the SRAA provides a dialog interface using which users can interact with the semantic entities with spoken commands. The SRAA interprets and executes these commands.

SRAA is driven by a Web Entity Model (WEM), which is a collection of the semantic entities in the underlying webpage. The WEM is dynamically constructed for any page using an extensive generic library of custom-designed descriptions of commonly occurring semantic entities across websites. The WEM imposes an abstract semantic layer over the web page. Users interact with the WEM via natural-language spoken commands (They can also use keyboard shortcuts). By elevating interaction with the web page to the more natural and intuitive level of web entities, SRAA relieves users from having to press numerous shortcuts to operate on low-level HTML elements—the principal source of tedium and frustration. Figure 32.4 below depicts a scenario snippet of how a user interacts with SRAA to review the search results for making a flight-reservation, depicted in Figs. 32.1 and 32.3.

User actions (with keystrokes) and SRAA's internal operations corresponding to user commands appear in the left and right columns respectively. Arrows pointing right and left in the middle column correspond to user's spoken commands and SRAA's synthesized-speech responses. The scenario sequence flows from left-to-right and top-to-bottom. As seen in Fig. 32.4, users no longer need to spend time and effort locating and getting the information, they need; instead, they simply use speech commands to delegate this task to the SRAA, which also resolves any ambiguity in the process (e.g., "sort by price"). Observe the simplicity and ease of interaction with SRAA compared to using only a vanilla screen reader. While sighted users' interaction with the Web is implicitly driven by the semantics of web entities, SRAA

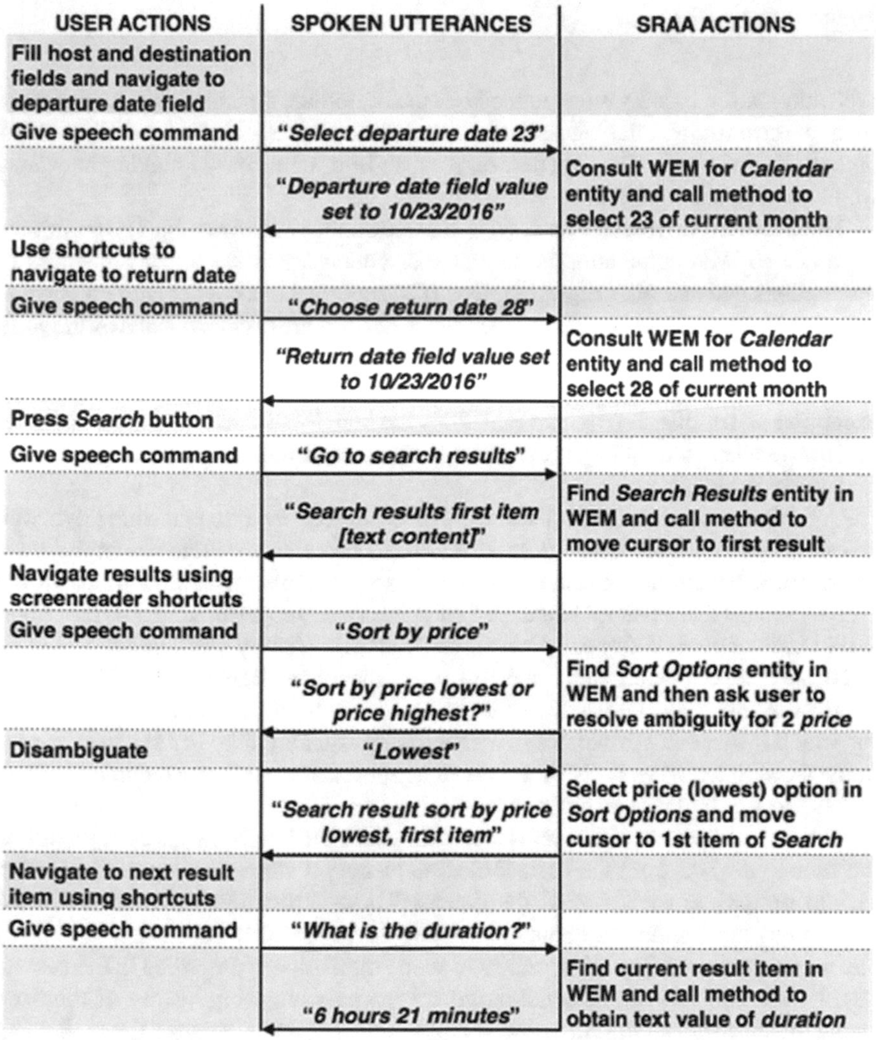

USER ACTIONS	SPOKEN UTTERANCES	SRAA ACTIONS
Fill host and destination fields and navigate to departure date field		
Give speech command	*"Select departure date 23"*	
	"Departure date field value set to 10/23/2016"	Consult WEM for *Calendar* entity and call method to select 23 of current month
Use shortcuts to navigate to return date		
Give speech command	*"Choose return date 28"*	
	"Return date field value set to 10/23/2016"	Consult WEM for *Calendar* entity and call method to select 28 of current month
Press *Search* button		
Give speech command	*"Go to search results"*	
	"Search results first item [text content]"	Find *Search Results* entity in WEM and call method to move cursor to first result
Navigate results using screenreader shortcuts		
Give speech command	*"Sort by price"*	
	"Sort by price lowest or price highest?"	Find *Sort Options* entity in WEM and then ask user to resolve ambiguity for 2 *price*
Disambiguate	*"Lowest"*	
	"Search result sort by price lowest, first item"	Select price (lowest) option in *Sort Options* and move cursor to 1st item of *Search*
Navigate to next result item using shortcuts		
Give speech command	*"What is the duration?"*	
	"6 hours 21 minutes"	Find current result item in WEM and call method to obtain text value of *duration*

Fig. 32.4 Example user interaction scenario with Web Screen Reading Automation Assistance (SRAA)

makes it explicit to the blind users. It brings blind users closer to how sighted people perceive and interact with the Web—which is the highest degree of web usability any technology can expect to achieve.

32.5   Web Automation

Web automation broadly refers to methods that automate typical web browsing steps such as form filling, clicking links and more generally any kind of repetitive steps, on behalf of the user. They,, therefore, play an important role in making nonvisual web browsing more usable.

There are several research prototypes that automate web browsing. The traditional approach to Web automation is via macros, which are prerecorded sequences of instructions that automate browsing steps. The recorded macros are later replayed to automate the same sequence of recorded steps. Macros are usually created by the well-known process of programming by demonstration, where the developer demonstrates to the macro recorder what steps need to be done and in what sequence. With the exception of Trailblazer (Bigham et al. 2009), which is built on top of the CoScripter system (Leshed et al. 2008), most of the macro-based web automation systems are meant for sighted users.

CoScripter system is a tool for recording macros to automate repetitive web tasks and replay them. CoCo (Lau et al. 2010) takes user commands in the form of (restricted) natural language strings in order to perform various tasks on the Web and maps these natural language commands to macros stored in the CoScripter Wiki (Leshed et al. 2008) and CoScripter Reusable History (ActionShot (Li et al. 2010)). While both CoScripter and CoCo are meant for sighted users, TrailBlazer (Bigham et al. 2009) allows SR users to provide a brief description of their tasks for which it dynamically cerates new macros by stitching together existing macros in the CoScripter Wiki. It also attempts to adapt macros explicitly recorded for one website to similar tasks on other sites.

The main drawback with macros is that they lack the flexibility necessary to allow the user to deviate from the prerecorded sequence of steps, or to choose between several options in each step of the macro. Those difficulties make macro-based approaches too limiting to be useful for people with vision impairments. A flexible, macro-less model-based approach to web automation is described in Puzis et al. (2013). The model is constructed based on the past browsing history of the user. Using this history and the current web page as the browsing context, the model can predict the most probable browsing actions that can be performed by the user. The model construction is fully automated. Additionally, the model is continuously and incrementally updated as history evolves, thereby, ensuring the predictions are not "outdated".

32.6   Alternative Browsing Techniques for People with Other Disabilities

There has also been significant research on identifying web accessibility and usability issues and providing alternative interaction techniques for people with other disabilities. We will briefly discuss some of these works, especially regarding dyslexia (de

Avelar et al. 2015; de Santana et al. 2012, 2013; Rello et al. 2012), low-vision (Billah et al. 2018; Christen and Abegg 2017; Hallett et al. 2017; Szpiro et al. 2016; Theofanos and Redish 2005), hearing impairments (Chung et al. 2011; Debevc et al. 2009, 2011; Fajardo et al. 2009), and cognitive impairments (Friedman and Bryen 2007; Rocha et al. 2009).

Dyslexia For people with dyslexia, depending on the severity of their condition, the issues include a wide range of issues such as (a) problems with spelling, reading comprehension, and black text on white background (Freire et al. 2011); and (b) confusing page layout, poor color selections, small font text, and complicated language (The Web: Access and inclusion for disabled people; a formal investigation 2004).

To address these issues, researchers have proposed both guidelines (de Santana et al. 2012; Rello et al. 2012) and browser extensions/toolbars (de Avelar et al. 2015; de Santana et al. 2013). For example, Rello et al. (2012) conducted a study with 22 dyslexic users, and based on their observations, propose several recommendations for selecting font, size, colors, background, paragraph spacing, column width, etc. Similarly, de Santana et al. (2012) propose a set of 41 guidelines for web developers to help make websites more user-friendly for people with dyslexia. These guidelines cover a wide range of aspects such as navigation, colors, text presentation, writing, layout, images and charts, end user customization, markup, videos, and audios. As for browser extensions and toolbars, the examples include Firefixia (de Santana et al. 2013), AccessibleNews DysWebxia (Rello et al. 2012), and WebHelpDyslexia (de Avelar et al. 2015). Firefixia was specially designed to support people with dyslexia to adapt the presentation of Web content according to their preferences. Similarly, WebHelpDyslexia browser extension offers customization features of web pages, based on requirements from problems encountered by users with dyslexia in related studies in the literature.

Low-Vision Low-vision users struggle to browse the web with screen magnifiers. First, magnifiers occlude significant portions of the webpage, thereby making it cumbersome to get the webpage overview and quickly locate the desired content (Szpiro et al. 2016; Theofanos and Redish 2005). Further, magnification causes loss of spatial locality and visual cues that commonly define semantic relationships in the page; reconstructing semantic relationships exclusively from narrow views dramatically increases the cognitive burden on the users. Second, low-vision users have widely varying needs requiring a range of interface customizations for different page sections; dynamic customization in extant magnifiers is disruptive to users' browsing. Third, the effect of magnification and contrast negatively impacted the reading performance and the comprehension (Christen and Abegg 2017; Hallett et al. 2017) of web content, because there's no "one-size-fits-all" accessibility solution for the spectrum of eye conditions that low-vision impairment entails, and the lack of support for word wrapping in screen magnifier.

To overcome many of the above problems, Billah et al. (2018) present SteeringWheel, a semantics-driven magnification interface that preserves local context. In combination with a physical dial, supporting simple rotate and press gestures, users can quickly navigate different webpage sections, easily locate desired content,

Fig. 32.5 Magnification in ZoomText versus SteeringWheel in a travel booking site, where each box is a (logical) segment. Odd numbered arrows show the magnification of the corresponding segment in ZoomText, where even-numbered arrows show the same in SteeringWheel

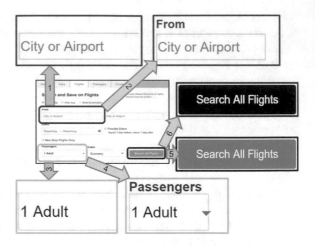

get a quick overview, and seamlessly customize the interface. Locality-preserving magnification addresses the problem of magnification-induced occlusion of the local context. The preservation of local contexts is rooted in these key ideas: First, the focus of magnification is limited at any time to a single segment of "semantically" related page elements (e.g., search results, search forms, news articles, etc.), and the cursor movement is confined (i.e., clipped) to the boundaries of this segment. Elements in such a segment inherently exhibit spatial locality. Second, the magnification factor is differentially applied across the entire segment. In particular, the white space is magnified only to the extent of preserving the spatially encoded semantic relationships of the other nonwhite space elements in the group. Third, certain content elements within a segment are selectively rescaled post magnification, if necessary, so as to retain them in the user's viewport. In Fig. 32.5, the even-numbered arrows point to pieces magnified by SteeringWheel under identical magnification conditions that were used by ZoomText for the same pieces. Notice how all the related contextual elements in the top right and bottom right pieces are all kept together in the magnification viewport.

Hearing Impairment For people with hearing impairment, the primary accessibility concerns are complex texts and multimedia content without text alternative (Pascual et al. 2015). Deaf users might find it difficult to navigate through websites with textual content which, for many of them, constitutes the written representation of a nonnative oral language (Fajardo et al. 2009). Also, for certain web pages, deaf users require the translation of existing written information into their first language, which can be one of many sign languages (Debevc et al. 2011).

Solutions to address the above problems include sign language translators (Chung et al. 2011; Debevc et al. 2009, 2011). For example, Sign Language Interpreter module (SLIM) (Debevc et al. 2009) translates web content and displays the corresponding sign language video on a transparent overlay. In a slightly modified version of SLIM (Debevc et al. 2011), the sign language video is shown only on explicit request. Specifically, special interactive elements are injected into the page content at appropriate locations, using which the users can "trigger" the sign language translation and display of corresponding video.

Cognitive Disabilities Studies (Friedman and Bryen 2007; Rocha et al. 2009) have shown that people with cognitive disabilities mainly face problems with reading text and recognizing hyperlinks. Therefore, the recommendations for addressing these issues include providing audio help (menus using audio) (Rocha et al. 2009), using more pictures, graphics, icons and symbols along with text, using clear and simple text, using consistent navigation and design on every page, and using headings, titles, and prompts (Friedman and Bryen 2007).

32.7 Discussion

The design for usability of interaction with computing devices for people with disabilities is a very broad topic. Usability, unlike accessibility, entails getting tasks done efficiently. This chapter has only touched upon usability in the context of nonvisual desktop web browsing; in particular, it addressed the important problem of making nonvisual desktop web browsing usable by people with vision impairments. The chapter surveyed a slew of techniques in the literature aimed at making web browsing usable. The essential idea underlying these techniques is centered on semantic models of web content, exemplified by semantic web segments for nonvisual web browsing.

We mention a few topics to illustrate the breadth and depth of the problems in the broad area of making interaction with computing devices usable by people with disabilities: Making applications such as Word, Spreadsheets, etc., usable seems to be a relatively unexplored problem. Addressing them will improve the productivity and employability of people with disabilities. Smartphones have become inextricably tied to their daily lives just like the general population. Designing apps on smartphones that are usable is an open research area. People interact with apps using gestures. Typically, smartphones support only a limited number of gestures. For example, blind users have to use swipe gestures in conjunction with smartphone screen readers to locate apps on their smartphones and interact with them, which can quickly get tiring and cumbersome. The challenge here is to make apps usable for people with disabilities despite having only a limited number of gestures at one's disposal.

32.8 Future Directions

Although progress is being made on making the Web more usable by blind computer users, it still remains at a nascent stage. We highlight a few key research topics that will push the frontier of web usability further. First, this chapter demonstrated the importance of semantic model of the Web for web usability. Research needs to be done on how to incorporate semantic model directly into screen readers, thereby elevating the level of interaction from syntactic web elements to semantic elements. Second, voice-based assistants are in vogue these days, such as Apple's Siri and Amazon's Alexa. But they are not yet suited for general purpose web browsing. In the future web semantics can perhaps be directly incorporated into such commercial Assistants. Third, web automation methods are either macro based, which are inflexible, or are restricted to operations on a single page. A flexible method for goal-oriented web browsing will generalize both these methods and would greatly improve usability. Lastly, at their core most of the web accessibility and usability techniques navigate the web content sequentially. Devices with haptic feedback have the potential to overcome some of the above limitations. Haptics engages the sense of *touch*, providing multiple simultaneous channels of information. For example, if touch screens could render any webpage, an inherently 2D structure, in tactile form, the user would be able to explore the 2D structure: feel webpage sections, or the lines of text, or individual controls such as links and buttons. Understanding and remembering webpage layout would be easier if the user could feel section borders. The user could explore the webpage faster than with audio alone, and then decide what content is worth listening to. In Soviak et al. (2016), a haptic glove was proposed to gather tactile feedback requirements for Web browsing. A fully functional tactile system that facilitates exploration of the 2D web page structure randomly, akin to pointing and clicking at any screen element with a mouse is an interesting and important avenue for future research.

32.9 Authors' Opinion

Ever since the advent of the Web, there has been a concerted push to make it accessible to people with disabilities. Most notable in this regard is the W3C Web Accessibility Initiative (WAI 1997) whose efforts contributed to guidelines for making web pages accessible. But making web pages accessible in and of itself does not make them usable—a problem that is primarily concerned with the "how to's" of providing a rich user experience in terms of ease of use, effectiveness in getting tasks done, etc. At the core of all the techniques described in this chapter is a logical model of the screen content, namely the logical segment. Such a model of the screen content is crucial for developing techniques such as those described in this chapter, for making web browsing usable by people with vision impairments. More generally semantic understanding of the content is essential for making browsing usable by people with other kinds of disabilities as well.

32.10 Conclusion

This chapter reviewed techniques, reported in the accessibility research literature, for making web sites easy-to-use with screen readers. The chapter included clutter-removal techniques, support for online transactions, skimming and summarization, interacting using speech, web automation and Assistants. The overall aim of these techniques is to make the Web easy to use, easy to navigate, and avoid information overload. The common thread underlying these techniques was their use of the semantic knowledge of the web content to improve the web-browsing experience for visually impaired screen reader users. The techniques reviewed mostly focused on desktop computing as this is still the primary way people with visual impairments use computers at home, in education and employment.

Acknowledgments   We thank Hae-Na Lee for reviewing the manuscript and the research literature. The preparation of this chapter has been supported by NIH Award: R01EY026621, NIDILRR award: 90IF0117-01-00 and NSF awards: 1805076.

References

21st Century Communications and Video Accessibility Act (CVAA)

AFB (2017) Facts and figures on American adults with vision loss. http://www.afb.org/Section.asp? SectionID=15&TopicID=413&DocumentID=4900. 2015

Ahmadi H, Kong J (2008) Efficient web browsing on small screens. https://doi.org/10.1145/ 1385569.1385576

Ahmed F, Borodin Y, Soviak A, Islam M, Ramakrishnan IV, Hedgpeth T (2012) Accessible skimming: faster screen reading of web pages. In: Paper presented at the proceedings of the 25th annual ACM symposium on user interface software and technology, Cambridge, Massachusetts, USA

Álvarez M, Pan A, Raposo J, Bellas F, Cacheda F (2010) Finding and extracting data records from web pages. J Signal Process Syst 59:123–137

Amitay E, Paris C (2000) Automatically summarising web sites: is there a way around it? In: Paper presented at the CIKM '00: proceedings of the ninth international conference on Information and knowledge management

Apple NSAccessibility. https://developer.apple.com/library/mac/documentation/Cocoa/Reference/ ApplicationKit/Protocols/NSAccessibility_Protocol/index.html-//apple_ref/doc/constant_ group/Focus_change_notifications

Ashok V, Borodin Y, Stoyanchev S, Ramakrishnan IV (2014) Dialogue act modeling for non-visual web access. In: Paper presented at the in the 15th annual SIGdial meeting on discourse and dialogue, SIGDIAL, Philadelphia, PA, USA

Ashok V, Borodin Y, Puzis Y, Ramakrishnan IV (2015) Capti-speak: a speech-enabled web screen reader. In: Paper presented at the proceedings of the 12th web for all conference, Florence, Italy

Ashok V, Puzis Y, Yevgen B, Ramakrishnan IV (2017) Web screen reading automation assistance using semantic abstraction. In: Paper presented at the 22nd ACM international conference on intelligent user interfaces

Bar-Yossef Z, Rajagopalan S (2002) Template detection via data mining and its applications. https:// doi.org/10.1145/511446.511522

Bigham JP, Lau T, Nichols J (2009) Trailblazer: enabling blind users to blaze trails through the web. In: Paper presented at the proceedings of the 13th international conference on intelligent user interfaces, Sanibel Island, Florida, USA

Billah SM, Ashok V, Porter DE, Ramakrishnan IV (2017a) Speed-Dial: a surrogate mouse for non-visual web browsing. In: Paper presented at the proceedings of the 19th international ACM SIGACCESS conference on computers and accessibility, Baltimore, Maryland, USA

Billah SM, Ashok V, Porter DE, Ramakrishnan IV (2017b) Ubiquitous accessibility for people with visual impairments: are we there yet? In: Paper presented at the proceedings of the 2017 CHI conference on human factors in computing systems, Denver, Colorado, USA

Billah SM, Ashok V, Porter DE, Ramakrishnan I (2018) SteeringWheel: a locality-preserving magnification interface for low vision web browsing. In: Proceedings of the 2018 CHI conference on human factors in computing systems, 2018. ACM, p 20

Borodin Y, Bigham JP, Dausch G, Ramakrishnan IV (2010) More than meets the eye: a survey of screen-reader browsing strategies. In: Paper presented at the proceedings of the 2010 international cross disciplinary conference on web accessibility (W4A), Raleigh, North Carolina

Cai D, Yu S, Wen J-R, Ma W-Y (2004) VIPS: a vision based page segmentation algorithm. Microsoft technical report

Chakrabarti D, Kumar R, Punera K (2008) A graph-theoretic approach to webpage segmentation. In: Paper presented at the WWW, Beijing, China

Christen M, Abegg M (2017) The effect of magnification and contrast on reading performance in different types of simulated low vision. J Eye Mov Res JEMR 10

Chung J-W, Lee H-J, Park JC (2011) Improving accessibility to web documents for the aurally challenged with sign language animation. In: Proceedings of the international conference on web intelligence, mining and semantics. ACM, p 33

de Avelar LO, Rezende GC, Freire AP (2015) WebHelpDyslexia: a browser extension to adapt web content for people with dyslexia. Procedia Comput Sci 67:150–159

de Santana VF, de Oliveira R, Almeida LDA, Baranauskas MCC (2012) Web accessibility and people with dyslexia: a survey on techniques and guidelines. In: Proceedings of the international cross-disciplinary conference on web accessibility. ACM, p 35

de Santana VF, de Oliveira R, Almeida LDA, Ito M (2013) Firefixia: an accessibility web browser customization toolbar for people with dyslexia. In: Proceedings of the 10th international cross-disciplinary conference on web accessibility. ACM, p 16

Debevc M, Kosec P, Rotovnik M, Holzinger A (2009) Accessible multimodal web pages with sign language translations for deaf and hard of hearing users. In: 20th international workshop on database and expert systems application. DEXA'09. IEEE, pp 279–283

Debevc M, Kosec P, Holzinger A (2011) Improving multimodal web accessibility for deaf people: sign language interpreter module. Multimed Tools Appl 54:181–199

Debnath S, Mitra P, Lee Giles C (2005) Automatic extraction of informative blocks from webpages. https://doi.org/10.1145/1066677.1067065

Delort JY, Bouchon-Meunier B, Rifqi M (2003) Enhanced web document summarization using hyperlinks. In: Paper presented at the proceedings of the 14th ACM conference on hypertext and hypermedia, Nottingham, UK

Dolphin SuperNova Screen Reader. http://www.yourdolphin.com/productdetail.asp?id=1

Eldirdiery HF, Ahmed AH (2015) Web document segmentation for better extraction of information: a review, vol 110. https://doi.org/10.5120/19297-0734

Fajardo I, Cañas JJ, Salmerón L, Abascal J (2009) Information structure and practice as facilitators of deaf users' navigation in textual websites. Behav Inf Technol 28:87–97

Freire AP, Petrie H (2011) Power CD empirical results from an evaluation of the accessibility of websites by dyslexic users. In: Proceedings of the workshop on accessible design in the digital world. York, pp 41–53

Friedman MG, Bryen DN (2007) Web accessibility design recommendations for people with cognitive disabilities. Technol Disabil 19:205–212

Guo H, Mahmud J, Borodin Y, Stent A, Ramakrishnan I (2007) A general approach for partitioning web page content based on geometric and style information. In: Paper presented at the in proceedings of the international conference on document analysis and recognition

Hallett EC, Dick W, Jewett T, Vu K-PL (2017) How screen magnification with and without word-wrapping affects the user experience of adults with low vision. In: International conference on applied human factors and ergonomics. Springer, pp 665–674

Han S, Jung G, Ryu M, Choi B-U, Cha J (2014) A voice-controlled web browser to navigate hierarchical hidden menus of web pages in a smart-tv environment. In: Proceedings of the companion publication of the 23rd international conference on World Wide Web companion. International World Wide Web Conferences Steering Committee, pp 587–590

Harper S, Patel N (2005) Gist summaries for visually impaired surfers. In: Paper presented at the proceedings of the 7th international ACM SIGACCESS conference on computers and accessibility, Baltimore, MD, USA

Harper S, Goble C, Stevens R, Yesilada Y (2004) Middleware to expand context and preview in hypertext. In: Paper presented at the proceedings of the 6th international ACM SIGACCESS conference on computers and accessibility, Atlanta, GA, USA

Hearst MA (1994) Multi-paragraph segmentation of expository text

INTRODUCTION TO THE ADA

Islam MA, Ahmed F, Borodin Y, Ramakrishnan IV (2011) Tightly coupling visual and linguistic features for enriching audio-based web browsing experience. In: Paper presented at the proceedings of the 20th ACM international conference on information and knowledge management, Glasgow, Scotland, UK

JAWS (2013) Screen reader from Freedom Scientific. http://www.freedomscientific.com/products/fs/jaws-product-page.asp. 2015

Kang J, Yang J, Choi J (2010) Repetition-based web page segmentation by detecting tag patterns for small-screen devices, vol 56. https://doi.org/10.1109/tce.2010.5506029

Kohlschütter C, Nejdl W (2008) A densitometric approach to web page segmentation. https://doi.org/10.1145/1458082.1458237

Kołcz A, Yih W-t (2007) Site-independent template-block detection. https://doi.org/10.1007/978-3-540-74976-9_17

Kovacevic M, Diligenti M, Gori M, Milutinovic V (2002) Recognition of common areas in a web page using visual information: a possible application in a page classification. In: 2002 IEEE international conference on data mining, 2002. ICDM 2003. Proceedings. IEEE, pp 250–257

Lau T, Cerruti J, Manzato G, Bengualid M, Bigham JP, Nichols J (2010) A conversational interface to web automation. In: Paper presented at the proceedings of the 23nd annual ACM symposium on user interface software and technology, New York, New York, USA

Lazar J, Allen A, Kleinman J, Malarkey C (2007) What frustrates screen reader users on the web: a study of 100 blind users. Int J Hum-Comput Interact 22:247–269

Leshed G, Haber EM, Matthews T, Lau T (2008) CoScripter: automating & sharing how-to knowledge in the enterprise. In: Paper presented at the proceeding of the 26th annual SIGCHI conference on human factors in computing systems, Florence, Italy

Li I, Nichols J, Lau T, Drews C, Cypher A (2010) Here's what I did: sharing and reusing web activity with ActionShot. In: Proceedings of the SIGCHI conference on human factors in computing systems. ACM, pp 723–732

Mahmud JU, Borodin Y, Ramakrishnan IV (2007) CSurf: a context-driven non-visual web-browser. In: Paper presented at the proceedings of the 16th international conference on World Wide Web, Banff, Alberta, Canada

Manning CD, Raghavan P, Schütze H (2008) Introduction to information retrieval. Cambridge University Press

Microsoft (2014) Common commands in speech recognition. http://windows.microsoft.com/en-us/windows/common-speech-recognition-commands-1TC=windows-7. 2015

Micro G Window-Eyes. http://www.gwmicro.com/Window-Eyes/

Microsoft microsoft active accessibility: architecture. https://msdn.microsoft.com/en-us/library/windows/desktop/dd373592(v=vs.85).aspx

Microsoft UI automation overview. http://msdn.microsoft.com/en-us/library/ms747327.aspx

MiniwattsMarketingGroup (2016) Internet usage statistics: the Internet Big Picture world Internet users and population stats. http://www.internetworldstats.com/stats.htm

Nuance (2014) Dragon naturally speaking rich Internet application. http://nuance.custhelp.com/app/answers/detail/a_id/6940/~/information-on-rich-internet-application-support. 2014

NVAccess NV access: home of the free NVDA screen reader. http://www.nvaccess.org/
NVDA (2013) nonvisual desktop access. http://www.nvda-project.org/. 2015
Parmanto B, Ferrydiansyah R, Saptono A, Song L, Sugiantara IW, Hackett S (2005) AcceSS: accessibility through simplification & summarization. In: Paper presented at the proceedings of the 2005 international cross-disciplinary workshop on web accessibility (W4A), Chiba, Japan
Pascual A, Ribera M, Granollers T (2015) Impact of web accessibility barriers on users with a hearing impairment. Dyna 82:233–240
Public Voice Lab S (2002) PublicVoiceXML
Puzis Y, Borodin Y, Puzis R, Ramakrishnan IV (2013) Predictive web automation assistant for people with vision impairments. In: Paper presented at the proceedings of the 22th international conference on world wide web, Rio de Janeiro, Brazil
Radev DR, Hovy E, McKeown K (2002) Introduction to the special issue on summarization. Comput Linguist 28:399–408. https://doi.org/10.1162/089120102762671927
Rajkumar K, Kalaivani V (2012) Dynamic web page segmentation based on detecting reappearance and layout of tag patterns for small screen devices. https://doi.org/10.1109/icrtit.2012.6206790
Readability. https://www.readability.com/
Rello L, Kanvinde G, Baeza-Yates R (2012) Layout guidelines for web text and a web service to improve accessibility for dyslexics. In: Proceedings of the international cross-disciplinary conference on web accessibility. ACM, p 36
Rocha T, Gonçalves M, Godinho F, Magalhães L, Bessa M (2009) Accessibility and usability in the Internet for people with intellectual disabilities. In: Proceedings of 2nd international conference on software development for enhancing accessibility and fighting info-exclusion-DSAI, pp 25–29
Sadet A, Conrad S (2011) Page segmentation by web content clustering. https://doi.org/10.1145/1988688.1988717
Safi W, Maurel F, Routoure J-M, Beust P, Dias G (2015) A hybrid segmentation of web pages for vibro-tactile access on touch-screen devices. https://doi.org/10.3115/v1/w14-5414
Sanoja A, Gançarski S (2014) Block-o-Matic: a web page segmentation framework. In: 2014 international conference on multimedia computing and systems (ICMCS), 14–16 April 2014, pp 595–600. https://doi.org/10.1109/icmcs.2014.6911249
Schnelle (2013) JVoiceXML. http://webdesign.about.com/gi/o.htm?zi=1/XJ&zTi=1&sdn=webdesi gn&cdn=compute&tm=171&f=00&tt=14&bt=3&bts=31&zu=http%3A//jvoicexml.sourceforge. net/. 2015
Scientific F JAWS screen reader. http://sales.freedomscientific.com/Category/11_1/JAWS%C2% AE_Screen_Reader.aspx
Song R, Liu H, Wen J-R, Ma W-Y (2004) Learning block importance models for web pages. In: Paper presented at the proceedings of the 13th international conference on World Wide Web, New York, NY, USA
Soviak A, Borodin A, Ashok V, Borodin Y, Puzis Y, Ramakrishnan I (2016) Tactile accessibility: does anyone need a haptic glove? In: Paper presented at the proceedings of the 18th international ACM SIGACCESS conference on computers and accessibility
Sun Z, Mahmud J, Ramakrishnan IV, Mukherjee S (2007) Model-directed Web transactions under constrained modalities. ACM Trans Web (TWEB) 1:12. http://doi.acm.org/10.1145/1281480.1281482
SuperNova (2013) Screen reader from Dolphin. http://www.yourdolphin.com/productdetail.asp?id=1. 2015
Szpiro SFA, Hashash S, Zhao Y, Azenkot S (2016) How people with low vision access computing devices: understanding challenges and opportunities. In: Proceedings of the 18th international ACM SIGACCESS conference on computers and accessibility. ACM, pp 171–180
The Web: Access and inclusion for disabled people; a formal investigation (2004). The Stationery Office
Theofanos MF, Redish JG (2005) Helping low-vision and other users with web sites that meet their needs: is one site for all feasible? Tech Commun 52:9–20

Vineel G (2010) Web page DOM node characterization and its application to page segmentation. https://doi.org/10.1109/imsaa.2009.5439444

VoiceOver (2015) Screen reader from Apple, vol 2011

VoiceXML (2009) W3C—voice extensible markup language. http://www.w3.org/TR/voicexml20. 2015

WAI (1997) W3C web accessibility initiative. http://www.w3.org/WAI/. 2010

Wang J, Liu Z (2009) A novel method for the web page segmentation and identification, vol 1. https://doi.org/10.1109/iccet.2009.149

Wang Y, Fang B, Cheng X, Guo L, Xu H (2008) Incremental web page template detection. https://doi.org/10.1145/1367497.1367749

WCAG (2009) W3C web content accessibility guidelines. http://www.w3.org/TR/WCAG10/. 2010

WHO (2014) Visual impairment and blindness. http://www.who.int/mediacentre/factsheets/fs282/en/. 2015

WHO-disability-data (2011). http://www.who.int/disabilities/world_report/2011/report/en/

Window-Eyes (2010) Screen reader GW Micro, vol 2010

Xiao X, Luo Q, Hong D, Fu H (2005) Slicing*-tree based web page transformation for small displays. https://doi.org/10.1145/1099554.1099638

Xiao Y, Tao Y, Li Q (2008) Web page adaptation for mobile device. https://doi.org/10.1109/wicom. 2008.1182

Yan H, Miao M (2009) Research and implementation on multi-cues based page segmentation algorithm. https://doi.org/10.1109/cise.2009.5363822

Yi L, Liu B (2003) Eliminating noisy information in web pages for data mining. In: Paper presented at the in proceedings of the ACM conference on knowledge discovery and data mining

Yin X, Lee WS (2004) Using link analysis to improve layout on mobile devices. In: Paper presented at the in proceedings of the international World Wide Web conference (WWW)

Yu S, Cai D, Wen J-R, Ma W-Y (2003) Improving pseudo-relevance feedback in web information retrieval using web page segmentation. In: Paper presented at the in proceedings of the international World Wide Web conference (WWW)

Zajicek M, Powell C, Reeves C (1999) Web search and orientation with BrookesTalk. In: Paper presented at the technology and persons with disabilities conference (CSUN)

Zhai Y, Liu B (2005) Web data extraction based on partial tree alignment. In: Proceedings of the 14th international conference on World Wide Web. ACM, pp 76–85

Zhang A, Jing J, Kang L, Zhang L (2010) Precise web page segmentation based on semantic block headers detection

Zhong Y, Raman TV, Burkhardt C, Biadsy F, Bigham JP (2014) JustSpeak: enabling universal voice control on Android. In: Paper presented at the proceedings of the 11th web for all conference, Seoul, Korea

Zhu J, Nie Z, Wen J-R, Zhang B, Ma W-Y (2006) Simultaneous record detection and attribute labeling in web data extraction. In: Proceedings of the 12th ACM SIGKDD international conference on knowledge discovery and data mining. ACM, pp 494–503

Chapter 33
Education and STEM on the Web

Barbara Leporini and Marina Buzzi

Abstract Difficulty accessing digital educational material in the fields of science, technology, engineering, and mathematics (STEM) hinders many students from receiving an education according to his/her preferences and fully enjoying the opportunities offered by our technology-enhanced society. Web resources enhance the delivery of STEM content by offering interactive and visual models, dynamic content, videos, quizzes, games and more. STEM content can be delivered in several ways including visually, vocally, or through a 3-D printed Braille bar or other assistive technology. In this chapter, we focus on the accessibility of STEM Web content for students with disabilities who are prevented from fully accessing digital visual resources, precluding a fully inclusive education. This chapter offers an overview of the state of the art of accessibility of STEM content on the Web, focusing especially on the experience of blind students. Existing issues and the authors' opinions in the field are aimed at motivating future research and development.

33.1 Introduction

Technology now shapes our life in every field, including education. Accessibility is crucial for any student, including those with disabilities. The challenge is delivering the full content in different formats and rhythms, to effectively reach individual perceptive channels and offer an environment in which to interact easily, enabling learning.

The design of digital frameworks for science, technology, engineering, and mathematics (STEM) education should address the needs of students who experience "learning difficulties", utilizing a multidisciplinary approach from different perspectives, integrating several components and carefully considering recent findings in

B. Leporini (✉)
ISTI-CNR, Via Moruzzi 1, Pisa, Italy
e-mail: barbara.leporini@isti.cnr.it

M. Buzzi
IIT-CNR, Via Moruzzi 1, Pisa, Italy
e-mail: marina.buzzi@iit.cnr.it

© Springer-Verlag London Ltd., part of Springer Nature 2019
Y. Yesilada and S. Harper (eds.), *Web Accessibility*, Human–Computer
Interaction Series, https://doi.org/10.1007/978-1-4471-7440-0_33

cognitive psychology and neuroscience (Robotti and Baccaglini-Frank 2017). Studies in cognitive science shed light on the complexity of the brain and perception processes in problem-solving and mathematical skills, by showing a correlation between mathematics outcome, working memory and verbal skills (Devine et al. 2013). It is remarkable that the integration of sensorial, perceptive, tactile, and kinesthetic experiences contributes to the creation of mathematical thinking and the development of abstract concepts (Arzarello 2006). Lack of visual perception, especially from birth, may impact on the acquisition of spatial skills, which are related to mathematics outcome (Rourke and Conway 1997).

In the Digital Age, an accessible education implies delivering the same educational digital content to students with different abilities via diverse perception channels and assistive tools (Basham and Basham 2013). Accessible teaching is crucial for enabling learning in the digital environment; this involves perception, understanding, experience, and the ability to interact with active and dynamic interface elements. However, in spite of a number of studies on accessibility, applications, and assistive tools, various barriers still undermine access to STEM education, hinder careers, and influence the overall quality of life of persons with disability (Israel et al. 2013).

Difficulty accessing mathematics and STEM content, in general, are often experienced by individuals with visual, cognitive, and learning disability. The introduction of digital learning environments can further increase the difficulties experienced. Sightless people have the most evident form of impairment in accessing digital graphic materials, but other students such as people with intellectual and developmental disabilities or dyslexia may also experience important difficulties. For instance, the abstract nature of symbols and math formulae, the representation of equations, and the visual structure of tables and diagrams are all challenges for blind students. Data need to be sequentialized, to be perceived by the aural or tactile channel, and embossed paper can help a student perceive borders and the main features (e.g., geography/geometry charts). Educational materials and environments developed to support students in the learning process should be designed in an accessible and effective manner. While technology and innovation are evolving, including in the accessibility field, STEM education still presents many barriers for users with a disability. Here we intend to analyze the current status and potential prospects to offer a contribution to the field.

In the following, we mainly focus on the needs of totally blind people, who are severely penalized by poor usability of STEM web content and digital environments. They experience great difficulties since the interaction via keyboard, screen reader and voice synthesizer requires more time (serialization) and cognitive effort (the structure is mixed with the content) compared to other disabilities.

First, we introduce an overview of STEM education for people with disability, and then discuss accessibility in education with special attention to STEM via Web. Next, some applications for facilitating access to and manipulation of math content for blind students are illustrated. Last, a discussion on open issues, future research directions, and the authors' opinions regarding this field end the chapter.

33.2 STEM Education for People with Disability

Students with sensory or motor disabilities are often discouraged from pursuing STEM careers since they frequently have poor skills for accessing university STEM studies due to inadequate preparation and limited post-secondary accommodations (Rule and Stefanich 2012). This limitation penalizes people with disability, denying equal participation in the right to follow a full education program.

College enrollment and STEM participation of individuals with ASD (Autism Spectrum Disorder) vs other categories of disability have been investigated by Wei et al. (2013). Despite showing one of the lowest overall enrollment rates, college students with ASD are most likely to pursue STEM majors. This result confirms that students with ASD who have the ability to study are more likely than the general population and other disability groups to study STEM (Wei et al. 2013).

Different disabilities can affect individuals in different ways, and since disability is a complex issue, this means that even people who share the same disability might not experience the same problems. This might also account for the difficulties encountered when designing for various disabilities. Nevertheless, some common challenges are shared by various disabilities (Jenson et al. 2011).

This chapter focuses on students who have difficulty reading printed text, such as those with blindness, low vision, and learning disabilities, and who often rely on speech for information input. It is very important to understand how different abilities can affect an individual, including which assistive technologies may benefit them and which formats of learning materials are compatible with their disability.

Visually impaired students who wish to attend university courses and/or perform a job requiring involving scientific texts, encounter enormous difficulties, and even when they have a high IQ score are often forced to choose other activities. Villanueva and Stefano Di (2017) report a narrative survey concerning 60 blind students in STEM education.

The common core of STEM is mathematics: "From physics to economy, through chemistry, biology, computer science, mathematical expressions are at the heart of modelling and understanding science" (Archambault 2009).

Mathematical language contains two components: meaning and notation (Pierce 2012). The algebraic expressions converted to spoken language by popular screen readers could be misinterpreted if the semantics of the notation typical of mathematics (such as parentheses, scope of operators, fraction, power, root, functions) are not communicated. Ambiguities create an obstacle for the acquisition of basic mathematics, science, and technological topics for people with visual disability. The first problem is due to the poor rendering of math content on the web, due to old browsers or assistive technologies. Fortunately, in recent years the interpretation of math formulae has been gradually incorporated by popular screen readers.

In order to understand the studies and the opportunities available for people with disabilities who access STEM, it is crucial to comprehend the main problems encountered. We hereby intend consider the main lacunae in the education of people with disabilities, with special attention to Web tools and content. Different disabilities imply different adaptation of the material to suit the assistive technology or the individual's learning needs. Material and content available in learning systems or virtual environments require specific personalization, especially when more than one disability is present (Nganji and Brayshaw 2015).

33.2.1 Visual Impairment

A whole range of disabilities affects vision, including partial sight, low vision, color blindness, and total and legal blindness. Since e learning involves significant use of the sense of sight, people with visual impairment risk being excluded if the learning environment is not designed to be accessible, providing an appropriate assistive technology to compensate for vision loss and/or personalizing learning for students with this disability. Various assistive technologies help visually impaired persons access online information—screen magnifiers enlarge content on the screen, screen readers read content to the user, and Refreshable Braille Display Devices provide information by stimulating the sense of touch. For more information, please refer to the chapter "Assistive Technologies" (Nicolau et al.).

An important consideration when designing for individuals with disabilities in Web-based learning environments is to ensure that accessibility requirements are followed closely. Simple requirements such as alternative texts for images are very important, but for more complex content this might not be enough to assure suitable support for learning purposes.

Particular attention and care are required when designing accessibility for STEM topics since it is quite complex to make scientific content usable via assistive technology. For people with severe visual impairment or who are totally blind, appropriate formats of learning materials include Braille, tactile representations, audio, and digital text. Audio allows the use of the sense of hearing to assimilate the information while screen readers can be used to read out the text. Braille is more suitable for those who have been blind from birth and tactile formats may be very important for understanding certain elements and concepts that are more easily perceived via touch. Color-blind individuals instead can exploit any format and enjoy images and videos.

Suitable support is needed to provide totally blind people with equivalent and effective STEM materials. Since some low vision users rely on a screen reader to interact with the user interface, in the following we refer to screen reader users.

Digital content and applications are becoming increasingly useful for visually impaired people, provided they are very confident with the devices, applications as well as assistive technology, and accessibility is guaranteed by the developers and designers. In this perspective, visually impaired students need to acquire a range of technology skills. The use and maintenance of assistive technology is then part of the curriculum for students with visual impairment.

Science, technology, and mathematics are widely based on graphical and visual content. Making this content completely and truly accessible via screen reader is a challenge; sometimes audio descriptions or alternative text for certain graphical content might not be inadequate to fully explain a concept.

Moreover, handling formulae and graphical functions can be very difficult for a blind person. This occurs especially when practicing and performing exercises (Karshmer et al. 1999). Unfortunately, the screen reader is unable by its nature to make fully accessible formulae, graphics, and any other scientific content.

Mathematics is visual in nature and thus can present many challenges for visually impaired students. Specific teaching modalities and adaptations are needed for those students who have impaired vision, for numerous activities and topics (Cooper et al. 2008; in't Veld and Sorge 2018; Karshmer et al. 1999; Wedler et al. 2012) such as numbers and counting, algebra, patterns and functions, geometry and spatial sense, measurement, probability and analysis of scientific data collection, and chemistry, to mention only a few examples.

The main accessibility difficulties for a screen reader user when learning STEM topics can be summarized as follows:

Reading, writing and transcribing formulae. Formulae by their nature are complex and structured, so scientific images are usually used to deliver information. For this reason, it is necessary to fully understand their meaning and their educational value when interacting with such content. An alternative description might not be enough for satisfactory understanding, especially when the student is performing exercises. The student should be able to explore, interact, and use formulae in an effective way. Various applications have been created to compensate for poor Assistive Technology Readiness. However, the copy and paste editors are still difficult to use for very blind users, so different assistive tools for writing and solving formulas, equations, etc., are needed.

Understanding complex tables, graphs, and diagrams. When learning and doing exercises, a STEM student must access graphical content and tables. As mentioned for formulae and equations, a short description would not be suitable for educational purposes. Furthermore, tables can be very complex and structured so they are not easy to explore in a sequential way. Assistive technology is not yet suffiently mature to support such exploration. In addition, when practicing, students should use editors and virtual environments to interact with graphical content and structured data. Unfortunately, those environments can be poorly accessible for screen reader users.

Interacting with virtual and simulation tools. Nowadays several tools offer students the opportunity to manipulate complex objects as well as observing simulations and reproduction of scientific phenomena. Those environments are valuable support for any learners, except for screen reader users. Although many of those tools are available on the Web, current accessibility guidelines are not adequate to ensure their use via assistive technology. Thus, visually-impaired students may be excluded from these activities.

Several tools to make digital textual content accessible are available on the market. However, in the scientific context (formulae, graphs, and tables) the problem is still far from being resolved. As a consequence, even PDF scientific documents offer accessibility issues (Armano et al. 2018). On one hand, the speech synthesizer engines are unable to process images and formulae; on the other hand, the Braille display (the component translating the digital content appearing on the screen) is only able to reproduce formulae written with specialized software. Moreover, the OCR (Optical Character Recognition) scanning of text containing formulae is still difficult and graphs, diagrams, and images are often of low quality and difficult to access. The Infty project (http://www.inftyproject.org) is developing an integrated mathematical document reader system "InftyReader" using an OCR approach.

33.2.2 Hearing Loss

Hearing loss refers to unilateral o bilateral reduced acuity or total loss of hearing. Fortunately, some assistive technologies can now help compensate for some hearing loss. These include assistive listening devices such as hearing loops, which work by amplifying sound and are effective in managing hearing loss. There are also augmentative and alternative communication devices such as touch screens with symbols and specific apps, which can improve an individual's ability to communicate and participate in interactions. People with such impairments would benefit from content that makes use of the sense of vision such as text-based materials and videos with captions. More information is available for the reader in the chapter "Hearing Loss and Deafness" (Kushalnagar).

Math skills of students with hearing impairment are delayed respect to their hearing peers, mainly due to difficulty understanding math language (Ray 2001; Swanwick et al. 2005). Hearing children learn the language from birth and understand everyday language. This favors the understanding and use of mathematical language (Flexer 1999). They learn every day, while a child with hearing impairment has to learn many skills in a structured way. The implication for teachers is that they need to be aware of, and focus on, those areas of learning or language skills that deaf/hearing-impaired children find particularly challenging because it is more difficult for them to simply pick up those skills from their environment.

33.2.3 Learning Difficulties

Learning difficulties can involve students with different needs, including dyslexia, the most common disability amongst higher education students (Mortimore and Crozier 2006). Dyslexia is a neurological disturbance that can affect several areas, resulting in poor spelling, reading, writing and decoding skills, spatial/temporal abilities (e.g., difficulties orienting), motor abilities, and memory.

A previous study suggested that most students with learning difficulties, especially individuals with dyslexia, experience the most difficulty exploiting the visual-verbal channel (Stella and Grandi 2011). Träff and Passolunghi (2015) offer a very interesting overview of developmental dyslexia. The theoretical triple-code model

(Dehaene 1992) and next, the developmental model of numerical cognition suggests that language and phonological abilities underlie the development of early mathematical skills (Von Aster and Shalev 2007). Recent research evidence confirms that reading and phonological difficulties have a negative impact on the ability to acquire age-adequate skills in some areas of mathematics. Specifically, tasks such as word problem solving and multi-digit calculation are challenging for students with dyslexia Träff and Passolunghi (2015). Specific difficulties are experienced by students with Developmental Dyscalculia (DD), a learning difficulty specific to mathematics involving 3–6% of the population (Szucs et al. 2013).

There are various assistive technologies available for students with dyslexia to improve reading and writing on the web (readable type font, an app for conversion/personalization of font/background, line spacing, online cognitive maps, and so on), visual and diagramming tools to help with organization and memorization. They would also benefit greatly from audio and video. The ability to pause, stop, replay, and forward audio and video clips and to use them alongside their notes would be very helpful to them. More information is available in the chapter "Technologies for Dyslexia" (Rauschenberger et al.).

Complex mathematical expressions can be particularly challenging for students with dyslexia. Reducing the amount of complexity of equations/formulae/expressions dynamically collapsing/expanding sub-parts facilitates interaction and solution building. Responsive equations enable a new approach to assisting users with learning disabilities. Specifically, MathJax facilitates the reading of math expressions by

1. Offering collapsing/expanding features to simplify the structure of formulae, and facilitates reading and comprehension. The default state of collapse of an equation depends on context parameters such as screen size, page size, zoom factor.
2. Enabling the interactive exploration of sub-expressions via mouse click, keyboard, or touch events
3. Offering synchronized and customizable highlighting for sub-expressions (Cervone et al. 2016).

33.3   STEM Education on the Web

Nowadays technology offers many opportunities for learners and students. Applications and learning resources are available on the Internet to support education. From the more common sources, such as electronic documents, eBooks, etc., to advanced tools like Virtual Learning Environments (VLE), Learning Management Systems (LMS), apps, and so on, several educational sources are available on the Internet. Unfortunately, due to their nature, digital materials and environments may be not suitable for interaction via assistive technologies, especially screen readers. This occurs for any type of content, including even simple text, depending on how it has been designed. The situation becomes even more complicated when dealing with more complex content such as formulas, graphics, graphic simulation and so on. In this section, we analyze the main resources available on the Web to support education and learning, especially in STEM. More specifically, we refer to them in terms of their accessibility rather than their content.

33.3.1 Math Framework on the WEB

Math content, such as books, formulae, equations, and exercises, can be published on the Web using MathML (Mathematics Markup Language), a specialized markup language defined by the W3C (World Wide Web Consortium) for representing mathematical content in the HTML5 source code.

It enables the inclusion of formulae in documents and the exchange of data between mathematical software (W3C 2015). Unfortunately, only new versions of the popular browser are fully MathML compliant. Old browsers are lacking in native implementation of MathML, thus rendering solutions such as SVG or HTML converters are unable to exploit web accessibility standards such as ARIA (Cervone et al. 2016).

To solve this compatibility problem, a decade ago, the MathJax Consortium started the development of a JavaScript rendering engine for displaying mathematics content in all browsers, for efficient and effective publishing of Mathematics on the Web (Cervone et al. 2016). Visual editors enable the copy and paste function between MathJax and other math editors including Office, LaTeX, and wiki environments (http://www.mathjax.org).

Recently the MathJax team has introduced the semantic interpretation and enrichment of MathML presentation, in order to enhance accessibility features:

- efficient reflow of content in small screens and magnification
- selective and synchronized highlighting and interactive exploration of sub-formulae, very useful for dyslexic readers
- dynamic speech text generation for offering a seamless reading experience to blind users, independent of the adopted platform or assistive technology Cervone et al. (2016).

Another emerging extensible standard for defining the semantics of mathematical objects is standard for OpenMath, coordinated by the OMS (OpenMath Society). It is very important to understand the differences between OpenMath and MathML:

- "OpenMath provides a mechanism for describing the semantics of mathematical symbols, while MathML does not.
- MathML provides a presentation format for mathematical objects, while OpenMath does not" (http://www.openmath.org).

It is important to remark that these technologies are complementary; OpenMath facilitates the automatic processing of math content and can be exploited to build interactive documents and apps.

MathPlayer is a math reader that enables math to be accessed via assistive technology, through both speech and Braille. MathPlayer is based on MathML technology and supports both visual rendering and screen reader interaction in compatible browsers (Soiffer 2007). This offers a powerful environment for accessing Math content. More details are available for the reader in the chapter "Mathematics and Statistics" (Soiffer).

33.3.2 Electronic Documents and Ebooks

On the network, more and more digital documents and eBooks are available for various purposes. For visually impaired people these materials are very interesting because they offer new opportunities to access content and information, provided they have been designed in an accessible manner. Several formats are used to deliver digital documents and eBooks. EPub (Electronic Publishing) and PDF (Portable Digital Format) are two formats widely used on the Web for delivering content.

EPub is the distribution and interchange format standard for digital publications and documents based on Web Standards. EPUB defines a means of representing, packaging and encoding structured and semantically enhanced Web content—including XHTML, CSS, SVG, images, and other resources—for distribution in a single-file format. EPUB enables publishers to produce and send a single digital publication file through distribution and offers consumers interoperability between software/hardware for unencrypted reflowable digital books and other publications (http://idpf.org/epub). Since ePub 3 is based on the open Web platform and HTML5, accessibility may benefit from the work done by the Web Accessibility Initiative (WAI), and many of the features of EPUB 3 will be useful for persons with a disability without additional work from the publisher. However, there are specific accessibility aspects to be considered outside of traditional publisher workflows.

When considering scientific content, e.g., math and formulas, graphics, tables and so on, things are a little more complicated. Images, rich content and other complex features of an eBook by their very nature may be inaccessible to visually impaired individuals. Some images or graphics contain even richer information than the text and therefore, people who cannot see the image can lose out on extra information. This can be a significant issue when considering educational contents and concepts.

Although ePub is an HTML-based format, MathML is not yet supported by e-readers and assistive technology such as screen readers. Similar issues also occur for PDF documents; formulas are still inaccessible even when the source document is in LaTeX format. Studies such as those by Armano (2018) are investigating how to solve the accessibility of PDF documents including formulas.

More details about accessible publishing are available for the reader in the chapter "Alternative Documents and Publications" (Conway and Mace).

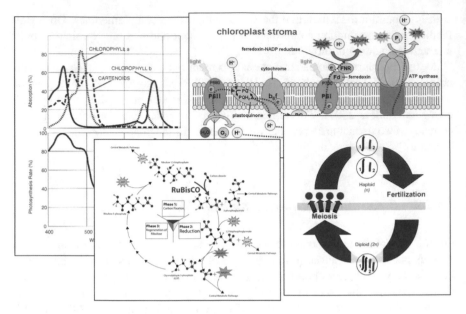

Fig. 33.1 Example of a complex image (*source* CK-12 Foundation)

33.3.2.1 Alternative Descriptions

Text and audio description are the most widely used ways to provide access to images and greatly increase the accessibility of an image for a visually impaired reader. Writing image descriptions is a skill and there are a number of resources available to help everyone in the supply chain prepare these descriptions, which can vary greatly depending on the requirement of the given context.

Images can be very challenging. Figure 33.1 shows a set of four complex images from the textbook CK-12 Biology 1, published in 2010 by the CK-12 Foundation. This image is quite complicated to describe. Its alternative description is "Composite picture illustrating the range of different image types from graphs to flow diagrams and pictures." This is enough to give an idea of the content, but at the same time does not provide enough semantic and useful information about its effective content.

Image description and alternative texts are best created at the authoring stage since the author knows what the image is trying to convey. Images can help sighted people understand textual explanations and are, in fact, accessibility aids themselves in many instances. An accessible image provides a different approach to the visual content, helping both sighted and blind readers access all key points and interpret what the image is supposed to convey.

Creating successful image descriptions is truly a skill, especially concerning educational topics. For this reason, there are several indications, suggestions, and guidelines available on the Web on accessible images and how to create them (Landry 2018; W3C 2015). The Publishing Forum (IDPF) has established Accessibility Standards that call for a detailed description of images but do not offer guidance in their preparation. Publishing guidelines have arisen to fill this gap, but lack a focus specifically on science, technology, engineering, and math content. The Image Description Guidelines (Diagram center 2018a) and Effective Practices for Description of Science Content within Digital Talking Books (National Center for Accessible Media) both offer best practices and sample descriptions for accessible STEM content in educational publications (Gould et al. 2008).

By their nature, some image types are much more complex to describe than others. Typically, these include art, music, maps, and mathematics and science. In scientific books, mathematical symbols and formulae are often produced as images, making them inaccessible to blind readers. If the symbols were produced in MathML or LaTeX, they can be accessed by a screen reader.

Image descriptions can be included in digital publications (e-books, PDFs, ePubs, HTML) through a variety of methods and markup including alt, longdesc, prodnote, describedby, visible text, hidden text. However, not all description delivery methods work on all devices. In addition, the choice of the authoring tool (whether Word, InDesign, Dolphin Publisher, or the like) can affect how the markup is applied. Therefore, the publisher has a number of choices to make depending on the content, workflow, and formats. Tools such as Poet Image Description Tool (http://diagramcenter.org/poet.html) have been proposed as an open Web resource to facilitate the creation of image descriptions within the DAISY format and so within EPUB 3, the mainstream format of choice for accessible content.

33.3.2.2   Audio Descriptions

Audio descriptions are an additional audio track of narration that deliver information about important visual features, such as body language, changes in scenery or context, charts and diagrams. Audio description tracks can prerecorded by persons or via text-to-speech (TTS) engine.

There are two kinds of audio descriptions (W3C 2018):

- *Open audio descriptions* are embedded in the program audio track, cannot be turned off and thus are announced to everyone
- *Closed audio descriptions* can be turned on/off by users.

Frequently, graphs are used in scientific material since they simplify complex information and make it possible to see trends. If for sighted users, they are particularly explicative; for people who cannot see, this type of information may be a serious matter if the alternative content is not well provided. In this case, it is crucial to offer narrative audio descriptions to give the blind user more complex and complete alternative information. Suggestions on how to prepare descriptions for audio books have been proposed in Gould et al. (2008).

33.3.3 Distance Learning

Interactive and dynamic learning materials spread quickly in the field of education. GeoGebra is a very popular web application that has become part of the math curriculum for secondary school students in several countries. It allows teachers to create and share and students to learn and practice online exercises, supporting math achievement. The accessibility of the GeoGebra website was tested against the success criteria A and AA of WCAG 2.0 applying heuristic evaluation of a set of selected webpages in two different platforms by two evaluators. Results showed that most of the success criteria levels were not met, by indicating that GeoGebra is still poorly accessible for people with disabilities (Shrestha 2017).

Learning Managements Systems (LMSs) still present accessibility issues for traditional tasks, such as loading educational content. Three popular open source LMSs—i.e., Moodle, ATutor, and Sakai—have been evaluated in terms of accessibility according to WCAG recommendations (Iglesias et al. 2014). The study revealed accessibility problems for common activities by teachers and learners. Thus, no specific functionality for supporting STEM topics and materials is considered.

The main accessibility issues affecting visually impaired interaction are related to graphical tools, toolbars and formatting palettes, lack of support to upload and add STEM content, and collaborative and cooperative interaction.

Laabidi et al. (2014) have enhanced the popular e-learning platform Moodle, creating its accessible version "MoodleAcc+" defining generic models that may be instantiated on specific needs of the student, and offering a set of tools for authoring and evaluating accessible educational content (for Learner and Author Assistance, Accessible Course Generation, Platform Accessibility Evaluation).

Fortunately, Moodle's accessibility is steadily increasing over time. Armano et al. (2016) evaluated the accessibility of Moodle v. 2.7 for visually impaired people, focusing on mathematics. Four visually impaired individuals with different degrees of impairment carried out various tasks performing different roles, by using different assistive technologies (NVDA and VoiceOver screen readers, Braille displays and magnifiers), operating systems (Win 7, Win 8, Mac OS X) and browsers (Internet Explorer 11, Firefox 41, Safari 8). Participants were able to complete the required tasks, suggesting that Moodle can be considered accessible for the visually impaired.

With regard to distance learning in a synchronous modality, virtual environments are not yet sufficiently mature to be really accessible, especially via a screen reader. Virtual Learning Environments (VLE) or Virtual Classes include tools and simulation environments able to offer rich multimodal Web-based functionalities to the students.

Progress in technology has encouraged the development of virtual reality and simulation environments that allow learners to perform exercises and experiments to practice on specific topics, such as those of science, engineering, and mathematics. Evolution in graphical processing, multimedia, and multimodal interaction opens up new and interesting scenarios for students who, individually or collaboratively and constructively, can apply, experiment, and test thanks to the increase in augmented reality, artificial intelligence, and advanced tools for computational processing and graphics.

While this offers students important new opportunities, it creates new barriers and obstacles for those with serious disabilities, such as students with visual impairment. First, graphical virtual environments are currently far from being accessible to blind users as their content is mostly visual (Maidenbaum et al. 2016). Second, these environments offer functionalities and commands with important accessibility limitations and issues. A VLE includes more components, such as a Virtual Class and a Virtual Laboratory, and offers students a collaborative environment.

Accessibility problems and limitations encountered when interacting via screen readers and magnifying software affect both relatively simple functionalities such as screen sharing, and more complex procedures such as simulation in three-dimensional environments.

The main functionalities to consider in accessibility support for VLE on the web are:

Screen sharing. This modality is increasingly used to show participants the slides and documents prepared for presentation and lessons. As a consequence, not all the topics presented are described, leading to obvious difficulty for non-sighted users who are automatically excluded from this activity. These limitations especially affect scientific and mathematics topics, which are more difficult to understand only through vocal descriptions by the presenter/teacher. Literary content is easier to comprehend even when what is shown on the screen cannot be seen. It is different for more complex content such as mathematics and science.

Collaborative environments. Several actions and activities are required to be carried out in a collaborative way in real time from two or more learners. Nevertheless, the Web pages have been designed keeping accessibility in mind, the functionalities specifically designed to support a collaborative approach still present several accessibility issues. Google Docs and other tools are examples. When editing cooperatively simultaneously with other participants, several issues arise for screen reader users. This occurs even with simple text; we can then imagine what happens with content such as science, engineering, and math. At this time, research in this field to support full accessibility via screen reader is still limited.

Communication and interaction. Several tools for distance learning and virtual environments offer the opportunity for participants to state their presence in the class, to ask a question, and so on. These functionalities are usually made available by installing a plug-in for online conferences, like that of Adobe Connect or other Web conferencing tools offering communication tools, especially for instant messages. Writing more complex content such as expressions, functions or any other science and math content can be a challenge due to the limitations of the tools available for editing such content.

33.3.4   Tutorials and Videos

Numerous sources online are made available through audio and video content in order to make the learning process easier and more immediate. Complete tutorials or online lectures are arranged through multimedia materials (e.g., Web pages embedding clips and videos to explain more specific concepts).

Video tutorials are increasingly used on the Web for various purposes. Science and math content is presented through tutorials and videocasts. Those materials are often inaccessible since the visual content is not described to the user. Usually, a disabled learner can obtain information from the audio description but what is explained via graphical content is lost. As with graphical and more complex content, audio description may not be enough to permit the student to understand and learn specific concepts. Therefore, when providing STEM content via tutorials in video formats, specific audio descriptions should be provided to offer additional information aimed at improving content comprehension by people with a disability, such as blind users. Audio descriptions are largely used for visually impaired people, especially for films (Pettitt et al. 1996). Audio Description allows persons with visual impairment to hear what cannot be seen on film and video, in museum exhibitions, or at theater performances, in a wide range of human endeavors (Snyder 2005). Applying audio description to STEM content would be very useful for improving educational support via tutorials and video content available on the Web.

33.3.5   Interactive Environments

Several online tools support training activities to help students learn and practice numerous activities and consolidate technical concepts. Usually, those tools are designed to be visually oriented in order to facilitate interaction. Many of them offer the opportunity to learn while following Web learning programming or simulation environments. For example, tools such as Scratch (https://scratch.mit.edu/), Blockly (https://developers.google.com/blockly/) and Code Monster (http://www.crunchzilla.com/code-monster) are designed for enabling visually oriented coding, in order to simplify interaction and avoid syntax errors. They are based on an intuitive click-and-drag modality, through which it is possible to easily compose fragments of code by using graphical and colored elements and blocks. Fortunately, an accessible version of this visual programming environment is offered by Google Accessible Blockly, a web application that exploits hierarchical menus, to facilitate interaction when navigating via screen readers. However, Milne and Ladner state the importance of providing accessible tools for all, by making existing block-based environments universally accessible instead of creating a different accessible version. By addressing the main accessibility, problems detected in visual programming environments these authors created Blocks4All, an accessible visual programming environment optimized for touchscreen devices (Milne and Ladner 2018).

Using an interactive environment such as an Integrated Development Environment (IDE) can be a challenge for a disabled person. For example, interacting via screen reader with an IDE can be difficult or impossible for a blind person. Potential difficulties or inaccessible tasks include: (a) getting an overview of the main parts and classes available in the code; (b) localizing the errors in the debugging phase; (c) recognizing indented code, especially when a specific syntax is not used for blocks; (d) delivering the software to test it in a simulation framework; (e) operating with blocks and objects via drag-and-drop; and so on. This is crucial when learning the coding or developing software. To break down these barriers other studies and projects focus on accessible teaching and specifically accessible coding, as discussed in detail in (Diagram Center 2018b). In particular, Quorum (https://quorumlanguage.com/), a programming language offering a fully accessible Integrated Developer Environment (IDE), is a very interesting approach in this field. Quorum enables one to write a program exploiting the accessible SODBeans (Sonified Debugger) IDE. SODBean allows for a self-voicing, fully integrated development environment for Netbeans, a popular Java IDE. Quorum allows the programmer to specify that the output should be spoken aloud in addition to text and graphic format. This is extremely helpful to a blind user to catch bugs in the code but also very useful to quickly include speech output in a program (Diagram Center 2018b).

A similar approach can be adapted to many other contexts. For practice in chemical concepts and experiments, several tools and virtual labs are available on the Web (http://www.acs.org/).

The engineering field also offers numerous tools to support learning. For example, EasyEDA (https://easyeda.com/) and PartSim (http://www.partsim.com/) are Web tools that support the student learning circuit design. Unfortunately, in this case, as well, the approach is totally graphic and interaction via mouse creates obvious problems for people who are blind.

Many specific tools reproduce virtual labs or simulations, as previously mentioned. In the last decade a number of fully software-based virtual laboratories in different fields have been developed. In most cases, they are specific for a certain educational context and do not offer the possibility of generalizing to a platform applicable to a broader class of engineering disciplines. These laboratories offer different levels of technical complexity. Some examples are available at https://phet. colorado.edu/. Potkonjak et al. (2016) offer a review in this field.

33.4 Tools Enabling Math Access for the Blind

Exploiting MathML standards, some applications have been proposed to help blind student's access math via screen reader, in order to enhance interaction in the desktop environment.

STEM is one of the main drivers in a growing economy. For this reason, governments have taken action to encourage STEM education for the entire population. Europe is also promoting math accessibility through projects and actions. Benefits of

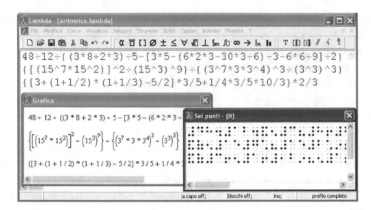

Fig. 33.2 Lambda environment (*source* www.lambdaproject.org/)

ICT for delivering mathematics are still limited for visually impaired people. The EU LAMBDA project created a system based on the functional integration of a linear mathematical engine and an editor for text visualization, writing, and processing. The Lambda Mathematical Code derives from MathML and was designed for interacting via Braille devices and speech synthesizer. It is automatically convertible, in real time, into an equivalent MathML version and then into popular math formats (LaTeX, MathType, and Mathematica). The editor enables one to write and manipulate math expressions in a linear way and provides some compensatory functions. LAMBDA targets high school and university students (Armano et al. 2018). Unfortunately, this assistive tool is not a web application; it needs to be installed in the PC and requires a fee (Fig. 33.2).

Karshmer et al. (2004) propose the UMA system to support math accessibility for blind people. The UMA system includes translators that freely interconvert mathematical documents transcribed in formats used by unsighted persons (the Braille code for scientific expressions, Nemeth and Marburg) to those used by sighted people (LaTeX, Math-ML, OpenMath) and vice versa. The UMA system also includes notation-independent tools for aural navigation of mathematics.

Similarly, Isaacson et al. (2010) created MathSpeak, a tool for supporting students who have difficulty in reading print MathSpeak applies a set of rules for conveying mathematical expressions in a nonambiguous manner. It includes an engine that can easily translate STEM materials into a nonambiguous form, which can be announced via a high-quality synthesizer. It vocally announces mathematics content by adding semantics to interpret its visual syntax (such as parentheses) and to remove ambiguity from spoken expressions. Also, this technology has the potential to increase accessibility to STEM materials. A test with 28 users has shown its efficacy. However, as observed by these authors, access is only the first step in the long process of making STEM accessible to all.

Word integrates an editor (LeanMath) enabling the writing of formulas for visually impaired people, via keyboard shortcuts. LeanMath aims at reinforcing and refreshing lean thinking. Its main application is as an editor for MathType equations in MS Word, a very popular authoring system. Another application providing accessible math input and output for the blind is WAVES (Web Accessible Virtual Electronic Scratchpad) which enables the rapid selection of mathematical symbols, voice output for expressions, and MathML conversion (http://diagramcenter.org/).

33.5 Discussion

Based on the main barriers encountered by people with disability, research and industry have been proposing techniques and tools to overcome some of the issues experienced by disabled learners in STEM education. Unfortunately, many of those solutions are not based on the Web because the tools proposed are dated and the technology at that time was not yet mature for these purposes. Two topics deserve more research and technological effort to enable easy interaction of the blind with math, and STEM content in general: operating with (1) math and formulae, and (2) graphical elements and structured objects.

Operating with Formulae and Web Math via Screen Reader

Bernareggi and Archambault (2007) introduce the interaction issues encountered by a screen reader user when reading and writing formulae and expressions. Speech and Braille understanding of mathematical expressions are somewhat different from visual comprehension. Mathematical notation usually uses two-dimensional structures (fractions, matrices, etc.). A two-dimensional layout can be understood quickly with a rapid overall glance, providing information about the structural elements making up the expression, then by examining details, horizontally or vertically. The sighted reader can immediately and accurately access any specific part of the expression. On the other hand, reading and understanding a mathematical expression through speech output or Braille are impeded by the lack of a solid representation of the structure to explore. These modalities necessarily linearize contents, which makes it difficult to achieve overall understanding and to quickly and easily access specific sub-expressions. Reading a Braille representation of a mathematical expression is mainly a sequential process.

   Math expressions can be understood effectively and efficiently through tactile and auditory perception only when the reader can rapidly and effortlessly access specific parts of the expression and extract the overall structure. Various mathematical and/or scientific Braille notations have been developed in different countries (UNESCO 1990).

   MathML has offered new possibilities for generating speech and Braille representations and giving readers the functions required for optimal understanding. When math formulae are expressed through MathML, software agents can parse the structure to generate speech or Braille alternative descriptions and can allow exploration via the keyboard. Moreover, MathML content can be accessed to output high-quality speech (using prosody, for example).

Recently Da Paixão et al. (2017) have evaluated the effort required by blind users when exploring mathematical formulae, by applying two task models with GOMS (Goals, Operators, Methods, and Selection rules) and KLM (Keystroke-Level Model) to a set of mathematical problems and resources, by selecting optimal paths to simulate the behavior of experienced blind users. Between the three selected screen readers, JAWS, ChromeVox and NVDA (NonVisual Desktop Access), JAWS performed better than ChromeVox and NVDA, although the within-formulae navigation still is poor, making mathematical learning and problem solving on the Web a very complex task for blind users.

Tools have been accordingly proposed to support formula exploration via screen reader (Ferreira and Freitas 2004; Schweikhardt et al. 2006).

The screen reader NonVisual Desktop Access (NVDA) powered by MathPlayer offers an accessible interaction with Word and PowerPoint via speech and Braille. MathPlayer can be integrated into the MS Office environment, extending the Word & PowerPoint button ribbon for self-voicing, which is useful not only for blind students but also for users with other disabilities such as dyslexia.

However, although some solutions have been investigated to support access to math and formulae on the Web, they still do not allow writing and manipulating expressions for exercises and practice. Web pages and applications, as well as the assistive technology, should (1) natively support the reading and exploration of formulas, and (2) allow any user regardless of their abilities to edit and manipulate expressions. OpenMath promises to fill this gap, making documents incorporating math content truly operable. An inclusive effort of different research teams would be valuable for harmonizing and exploiting the full potential of emerging technology for accessibility.

Graphics, Diagrams, and Tables

Accessing graphics, diagrams and any other non-textual representation for STEM content is still an open issue; nevertheless, there are various suggestions proposed for preparing alternative image descriptions. For complex images, the textual or narrative description might not be enough for a full understanding of a certain concept. In addition, alternative descriptions must be prepared for any graphical element. This implies that a blind student cannot perceive any STEM concept available on the Web unless an alternative description has been provided by the developer. For example, a blind student cannot perceive the function originating from any formulae. Alternative descriptions are related only to static graphical objects, and not to dynamically generated ones. A similar issue is related for tables, especially when they are rich in content, very structured and not easy to understand even when sequentialized.

This represents an ongoing interaction issue that is very important for the Web, especially in the education field. Studies such as Taibbi et al. (2014) propose new modalities to support blind students explore functions using audio feedback. Audio-Functions is an iPad app that adopts three sonification techniques to convey information about the function graph. Indeed, early research studies have been carried out, implementing Web tool prototypes to allow blind users to comprehend simple drawings, as well as to create graphics (Roth et al. 2000; Yu et al. 2003).

Exploring and navigating complex and very structured tables can be a challenge. The screen reader announces the content, including the data tables, serializing the structured content as speech. A benefit of the table structure is that users can use table screen reading commands to move their cursor along the rows and columns of the table. Using table navigation mode, the element comparison becomes a simple matter of moving the cursor up and down the column. Table navigation mode allows a screen reader user to move within the logical structure of the table. The screen reader is able to facilitate this exploration since the information is presented as a logical sequence of the cells according to the table structure. Thus, appropriate table structure is very important to truly guarantee accessibility via screen reader. However, tables with many columns and rows for navigation and especially comparison of the elements require great effort via screen reader. Exploring very complex tables, a blind person might encounter crucial difficulties in data navigation. As a consequence, several studies have investigated possible strategies for improving such activity (Gardiner et al. 2016; Kildal and Brewster 2006). Nevertheless, satisfactory data table exploration is still an unresolved issue.

In summary, although various studies have been carried out in the field, people who are blind are still far from finding effective and satisfactory solutions to use in their education, especially in online and collaborative environments.

33.6   Future Directions

Research and development in this field will exploit technology and innovation to improve STEM education on the Web via a multimodal approach.

First, browsers and assistive technologies should appropriately support fluent reading of math formulae via screen reader and Braille display. MathML is a valuable tool for including formulae and expressions along with the Web page code. However, its support needs further investigation and implementation. Browsers, assistive technology, and app developers must work on suitable interaction with the MathML standard. A small step is required for reading: appropriate detection of the included MathML by both browsers and assistive technologies. Further effort would enable the editing of expressions as well as formulae. This is particularly useful for helping students with disability practice and perform exercises, in the evaluation and testing processes as well as when participating in courses on the Web. In this context, integration with the semantic aware OpenMath standard could aid in exploiting the full potential of the Web in delivering accessible math and STEM in general.

Another important direction for research concerns the support of function and graphic perception. Assistive technologies, as well as computer environments, need to be redesigned in order to enhance accessibility support for reading complex tables, or graphics and diagrams. The (vision-impaired) learner should be easily able to read and comprehend fluently a complex object and, importantly, to be able to write and reproduce the concepts learned. Editors and environments should be redesigned in order to offer new multimodal interaction to help all users obtain semantic information and build objects and graphical elements as well.

In some cases, the most appropriate alternative to an image is a tactile version. Tactile perception can provide some additional details, which may not be easily transmitted via alternative or audio descriptions. For instance, a math function may be clearer if perceived by touch rather than via audio description. Apart from children's books, tactile images are not a part of mainstream publishing for books or the Web, but this is an exciting area where technologies as diverse as 3D printing and haptics could create opportunities for accessibility in STEM education. Several studies (Papazafiropulos et al. 2016; McDonald et al. 2014) offer examples of how 3D printing can support learning for people who are blind. The procedure for preparing digital models to be 3D printed includes simplifying the digital content in order to obtain a version that produces an easily perceived tactile image. In this perspective, an online repository with a collection of simplified reproductions as well as a Web-based tool able to guide simplification of a graph or math function could aid STEM education. Furthermore, a plug-in for the browser designed to quickly 3D-print a function, diagram or any other graphical object is a potential direction for visually impaired students.

For instance, a suitable algorithm and procedure implemented via a plug-in could allow the student to easily print a math function or graphic as it is detected when learning on the Web. In addition, a science object such as an atom or a detail of a more complex graphical element could be easily reproduced for touch via a 3D printer.

33.7   Author's Opinion of the Field

More integrated action is needed to enable careers in STEM by people with disability. From a technical perspective, more assistive tools are necessary to deliver accessible STEM content to people with disability, especially via assistive technology. In the author's opinion, co-design together with people with disability is crucial for creating accessible and usable tools. Most accessibility problems result from the evolution in graphic user interfaces, especially with regard to virtual environments. In addition, even simpler tools are increasingly oriented toward a complex or visual approach. Assistive technologies are not yet fully mature for interacting with tools for virtual and simulation environments. The tools should be designed to be accessible to everyone, but at the same time a step forward in assistive technology is needed to effectively include people with disability.

Most web applications are mainly devoted to the notation part of math language, enabling the correct perception of math content, while the accessibility of tools for helping students with disability decode the meaning of math and simplify logical processes in solving exercises is still in progress.

In the authors' opinion, more technology should enhance learning: mobile and web apps, robotics, the IoT with the ability to merge physical, tangible devices and virtual resources should shape the future of STEM teaching. Games such as logic games, chess, circuitry and so on are natural motivators, and by offering enjoyable challenges for children can improve problem-solving and train their logic skills, thus preparing them for STEM. The Web is an essential learning tool, and LMSs would integrate simple accessible tools for practices and problem solving. All this is possible if accessibility support is truly effective.

33.8 Conclusion

This chapter has analyzed the current status of accessibility support for STEM education on the Web. After an introduction to the field, the main issues related to people with disability when accessing the STEM content have been considered in order to understand the effective needs of these students. We have mainly focused on visually impaired people, although other disabilities are discussed. More specifically, the focus was on key problems encountered by visually impaired students because STEM materials and technology aiming to enhance education present great problems when using a screen reader. Accessing scientific material can be a great challenge for screen reading learners.

In conclusion, despite the evolution of technology and progress in research, STEM education on the Web still presents numerous obstacles for people with disability. It is urgent to create additional assistive tools in a multidisciplinary and multisensorial approach, from different perspectives involving psychology and neuroscience, to enable accessible teaching and encourage STEM learning and careers for people with disabilities.

References

Archambault D (2009) Non visual access to mathematical contents: state of the art and prospective. In: Proceedings of the WEIMS conference, vol 2009, pp 43–52

Armano T, Borsero M, Capietto A, Murru N, Panzare A, Ruighi A (2016) On the accessibility of Moodle 2 by visually impaired users, with a focus on mathematical content. Universal Access in the Information Society, pp 1–10

Armano T, Capietto A, Coriasco S, Murru N, Ruighi A, Taranto E (2018) An automatized method based on LaTeX for the realization of accessible PDF documents containing formulae. In: Miesenberger K, Kouroupetroglou G (eds) Computers Helping people with special needs. ICCHP 2018. Lecture notes in computer science, vol 10896. Springer, Cham, pp 583–589

Arzarello F (2006) Semiosis as a multimodal process. Revista Latinoamericana de Investigación en Matemática Educativa RELIME, 9 (Extraordinario 1), pp 267–299

Basham JD, Marino MT (2013) Understanding STEM education and supporting students through universal design for learning. Teach Except Child 45(4):8–15

Bernareggi C, Archambault D (2007) Mathematics on the web: emerging opportunities for visually impaired people. In Proceedings of the 2007 international cross-disciplinary conference on Web accessibility (W4A). ACM, pp 108–111

Cervone D, Krautzberger P, Sorge V (2016) New accessibility features in MathJax

Cooper M, Lowe T, Taylor M (2008, July) Access to mathematics in web resources for people with a visual impairment. In International Conference on Computers for Handicapped Persons. Springer, Berlin, Heidelberg, pp 926–933

Da Paixão Silva LF, de Faria Oliveira O, Freire ERCG, Mendes RM, Freire AP (2017) How much effort is necessary for blind users to read web-based mathematical formulae?: A comparison using task models with different screen readers. In Proceedings of the XVI Brazilian symposium on human factors in computing systems. ACM, p 29

Dehaene S (1992) Varieties of numerical abilities. Cognition 44(1–2):1–42

Devine A, Soltész F, Nobes A, Goswami U, Szűcs D (2013) Gender differences in developmental dyscalculia depend on diagnostic criteria. Learn Instr 27:31–39

Diagram Center (2018a) Image Description guidelines. http://diagramcenter.org/table-of-contents-2.html. Accessed on July 2018

Diagram Center (2018b) Accessible Coding in Education. http://diagramcenter.org/diagram-reports/2017-report/coding.html. Accessed on July 2018

EPUB 3 Accessibility Guidelines (2018) http://kb.daisy.org/publishing/. Accessed on July 2018

Ferreira H, Freitas D (2004, July) Enhancing the accessibility of mathematics for blind people: the AudioMath project. In International conference on computers for handicapped persons. Springer, Berlin, Heidelberg, pp 678–685

Flexer CA (1999) Facilitating hearing and listening in young children. Singular

Gardiner S, Tomasic A, Zimmerman J (2016, Jan) The utility of tables for screen reader users. In: 2016 13th IEEE annual consumer communications & networking conference (CCNC). IEEE, pp 1135–1140

Gould B, O'Connell T, Freed G (2008) Effective practices for description of science content within digital talking books, Dec 2008. http://ncam.wgbh.org/experience_learn/educational_media/stemdx

Iglesias A, Moreno L, Martínez P, Calvo R (2014) Evaluating the accessibility of three open source learning content management systems: A comparative study. Comput Appl Eng Educ 22(2):320–328

In't Veld D, Sorge V (2018) The Dutch best practice for teaching chemistry diagrams to the visually impaired. In: Miesenberger K, Kouroupetroglou G (eds) Computers helping people with special needs. ICCHP 2018. Lecture notes in computer science, vol 10896. Springer, Cham, pp 644–649

Isaacson MD, Schleppenbach D, Lloyd L (2010) Increasing STEM accessibility in students with print disabilities through MathSpeak. J Sci Educ Stud Disabil 14(1):3

Israel M, Maynard K, Williamson P (2013) Promoting literacy-embedded, authentic STEM instruction for students with disabilities and other struggling learners. Teach Except Child 45(4):18–25

Jenson RJ, Petri AN, Day AD, Truman KZ, Duffy K (2011) Perceptions of self-efficacy among STEM students with disabilities. J Postsecon Educ Disabil 24(4):269–283

Karshmer AI, Gupta G, Geiger S, Weaver C (1999) Reading and writing mathematics: The MAVIS1 Project. Behav Inf Technol 18(1):2–10

Karshmer AI, Gupta G, Pontelli E, Miesenberger K, Ammalai N, Gopal D, Batusic M, Stöger B, Palmer B, Guo H-F (2004) UMA: a system for universal mathematics accessibility. In: Proceedings of the ACM SIGACCESS conference on computers and accessibility. ACM Press, Atlanta, GA, USA, pp 55–62

Kildal J, Brewster SA (2006) Exploratory strategies and procedures to obtain non-visual overviews using TableVis. Int J Disabil Hum Dev 5(3):285–294

Laabidi M, Jemni M, Ayed LJB, Brahim HB, Jemaa AB (2014) Learning technologies for people with disabilities. J King Saud Univ-Comput Inf Sci 26(1):29–45

Landry D (2018) Writing image descriptions for course content. https://www.ryerson.ca/content/dam/lt/resources/handouts/WritingEffectiveImageDescriptions.pdf. Accessed Julay 2018

Maidenbaum S, Buchs G, Abboud S, Lavi-Rotbain O, Amedi A (2016) Perception of graphical virtual environments by blind users via sensory substitution. PLoS One 11(2):e0147501

McDonald S, Dutterer J, Abdolrahmani A, Kane SK, Hurst A (2014, Oct) Tactile aids for visually impaired graphical design education. In Proceedings of the 16th international ACM SIGACCESS conference on computers & accessibility. ACM, pp 275–276

Milne LR, Ladner RE (2018, Apr). Blocks4All: overcoming accessibility barriers to blocks programming for children with visual impairments. In Proceedings of the 2018 CHI conference on human factors in computing systems. ACM. p 69

Mortimore T, Crozier WR (2006) Dyslexia and difficulties with study skills in higher education. Stud High Educ 31(2):235–251

National Center for Accessible Media (NCAM) (2018) Guidelines for Describing STEM Images. http://ncam.wgbh.org/experience_learn/educational_media/stemdx/guidelines. Accessed on Julay 2018

Nganji JT, Brayshaw M (2015, July) Personalizing learning materials for students with multiple disabilities in virtual learning environments. In Science and information conference (SAI). IEEE, pp 69–76

Papazafiropulos N, Fanucci L, Leporini B, Pelagatti S, Roncella R (2016, July). Haptic models of arrays through 3D printing for computer science education. In: International Conference on Computers Helping People with Special Needs. Springer, Cham, pp 491–498

Pettitt B, Sharpe K, Cooper S (1996) AUDETEL: enhancing television for visually impaired people. Br J Vis Impair 14(2):48–52

Pierce JR (2012) An introduction to information theory: symbols, signals and noise. Cour Corp

Potkonjak V, Gardner M, Callaghan V, Mattila P, Guetl C, Petrović VM, Jovanović K (2016) Virtual laboratories for education in science, technology, and engineering: a review. Comput Educ 95:309–327

Ray E (2001) Discovering mathematics: the challenges that deaf/hearing-impaired children encounter

Robotti E, Baccaglini-Frank A (2017) Using digital environments to address students' mathematical learning difficulties. In Innovation and technology enhancing mathematics education. Springer, Cham, pp 77–106

Roth P, Petrucci LS, Assimacopoulos A, Pun T (2000) Audio-haptic internet browser and associated tools for blind users and visually impaired computer users

Rourke BP, Conway JA (1997) Disabilities of arithmetic and mathematical reasoning: perspectives from neurology and neuropsychology. J Learn Disabil 30(1):34–46

Rule AC, Stefanich GP (2012) Using a thinking skills system to guide discussions during a working conference on students with disabilities pursuing STEM fields. J STEM Educ 13(1):43

Schweikhardt W, Bernareggi C, Jessel N, Encelle B, Gut M (2006, July). LAMBDA: a European system to access mathematics with Braille and audio synthesis. In: International conference on computers for handicapped persons. Springer, Berlin, Heidelberg

Shrestha P (2017) Evaluation of interactive learning materials for universal design: case of geogebra in norwegian high schools (Master's thesis, Oslo and Akershus Univeristy College of Applied Sciences)

Snyder J (2005, Sept) Audio description: the visual made verbal. In: International congress series, vol 1282. Elsevier, pp 935–939

Soiffer N (2007, Oct). MathPlayer v2.1: web-based math accessibility. In Proceedings of the 9th international ACM SIGACCESS conference on computers and accessibility (pp 257–258). ACM

Stella G, Grandi L (2011) Conoscere la dislessia ei DSA. Giunti Editore

Swanwick R, Oddy A, Roper T (2005) Mathematics and deaf children: an exploration of barriers to success. Deaf Educ Int 7(1):1–21

Szucs D, Devine A, Soltesz F, Nobes A, Gabriel F (2013) Developmental dyscalculia is related to visuo-spatial memory and inhibition impairment. cortex 49(10):2674–2688

Taibbi M, Bernareggi C, Gerino A, Ahmetovic D, Mascetti S (2014, July). Audiofunctions: eyes-free exploration of mathematical functions on tablets. In: International conference on computers for handicapped persons. Springer, Cham, pp 537–544

Träff U, Passolunghi MC (2015) Mathematical skills in children with dyslexia. Learn Individ Differ 40:108–114

UNESCO (1990). World Braille usage, Paris 1990, ISBN 92–3-102323-3/US Library of Congress, Washington D.C. 1990, ISBN 0-8444-0676-7.)

Villanueva I, Di Stefano M (2017) Narrative inquiry on the teaching of STEM to blind high school students. Educ Sci 7(4):89

Von Aster MG, Shalev RS (2007) Number development and developmental dyscalculia. Dev Med Child Neurol 49(11):868–873

W3C (2015) HTML5 image description extension (longdesc), W3C. http://www.w3.org/TR/html-longdesc/. Recommendation 26 Feb 2015

W3C (2018) Production options for audio descriptions, web accessibility tutorials. Guidance on how to create websites that meet WCAG. https://w3c.github.io/wai-media-intro/accessible-media/production-audio-description/

W3C WAI-ARIA Graphics Module (2018) W3C Candidate. Recommendation 29 Mar 2018

Wedler HB, Cohen SR, Davis RL, Harrison JG, Siebert MR, Willenbring D, Hamann CS, Shaw JT, Tantillo DJ (2012) Applied computational chemistry for the blind and visually impaired. J Chem Educ 89(11):1400–1404

Wei X, Jennifer WY, Shattuck P, McCracken M, Blackorby J (2013) Science, technology, engineering, and mathematics (STEM) participation among college students with an autism spectrum disorder. J Autism Dev Disord 43(7):1539–1546

Yu W, Kangas K, Brewster S (2003, Mar) Web-bassed haptic applications for blind people to create virtual graphs. In: Proceedings 11th symposium on haptic interfaces for virtual environment and teleoperator systems, 2003. HAPTICS 2003. IEEE, pp 318–325

Part VI
Ubiquitous Web Accessibility

Chapter 34
Wayfinding

Daisuke Sato, Hironobu Takagi and Chieko Asakawa

Abstract Wayfinding is a fundamental ability for daily living of people with disability. People with visual impairments have difficulty to find and follow an appropriate route, and wheelchair users need to find an accessible route without gaps or stairs. Wayfinding systems allow them to navigate indoor and outdoor environment seamlessly, and assist their daily mobility to schools, offices and any other places they are interested in. This chapter will focus on introducing technologies to enable such wayfinding systems to assist people with disabilities.

34.1 Introduction

The web is widely used as a platform for geographical information. Many web contents are associated with geographical locations and allow people to search and visit places such as shops, hospitals, parks, stations, and any other point of interests (PoIs) they want to visit. Wayfinding system is a category of technologies to connect two basic actions—search a PoI on the Web and visit there—by navigating the user. There are two major groups of users. A wayfinding system allows People with Mobility Impairment (e.g., wheelchair and clutches) to fully utilize their capability by showing the best route for each person and also allows blind and people with visual impairments to walk unknown places by themselves. In other words, wayfinding systems bridge the gap between the web and real experience.

People with mobility impairment need to be aware of accessible routes to their destinations avoiding inaccessible waypoints such as steps, bumpy roads, and narrow corridors. Besides, people with visual impairment face a series of difficulties based on

D. Sato (✉) · H. Takagi
IBM Research, Tokyo, Japan
e-mail: dsato@jp.ibm.com

H. Takagi
e-mail: takagih@jp.ibm.com

C. Asakawa
IBM T. J. Watson Research Center, Pittsburgh, USA
e-mail: chiekoa@us.ibm.com

© Springer-Verlag London Ltd., part of Springer Nature 2019
Y. Yesilada and S. Harper (eds.), *Web Accessibility*, Human–Computer
Interaction Series, https://doi.org/10.1007/978-1-4471-7440-0_34

their degree of disability. Although visually impaired people often had been trained for their mobility and orientation skill to be able to walk by themselves with mobility aid such as white cane and guide dog, unfamiliar places are difficult to navigate without sighted assistance or dedicated assistive technologies for navigation.

"Navigation" task is involving multiple problem-solving. Petrie et al. categorized navigation into micro and macro-navigation (Petrie et al. 1996). Micro-navigation indicates tasks completed with information in the shorter range such as obstacle avoidance. Macro-navigation indicates more distant tasks toward the destination like accessible route finding. "Wayfinding" involves the broader concept of mobility. Sighted people can navigate by themselves toward their destinations by using maps, visual landmarks, signage, and also navigational assistance like GPS. They may also explore the environment without having any destination. Then tend to walk, look around shops and browse. Concerning this aspect, micro-navigation may also involve awareness of surrounding to enable users to get visual information around them and macro-navigation may also involve exploration rather that navigation toward a destination. To this end, an ideal wayfinding system needs to introduce a variety of technologies including the state-of-the-art research topics and still in the middle of a long journey.

Figure 34.1 shows the underlying architecture of a model wayfinding system. (a) Mapping is a category of technologies to generate (b) topological route map and (d) Point of Interest (PoI) data. In practical use cases, most of the process have done manually, but there are various activities to reduce mapping cost (Hara et al. 2013; Mobasheri et al. 2017). A (b) topological route map database is used to calculate a route from a starting point to a destination point. The coverage of the routes in the database should be comprehensive across target areas, consistent and up to date with a real physical environment. An alternative to the topological route map is the walkable area map. In the case, each route is dynamically generated as a path on a two-dimensional space. A (c) route planning engine is responsible for calculating an appropriate route for a user by considering not only distance but also gaps, width, and accessible facilities such as elevators, ramps, and tactile pavement. (d) Point of Interest (PoI) is a broad concept to denote any geographical features which allow the user to be aware of surroundings such as shops and restrooms, to confirm their location by using nonvisual sense such as floor material change and doorways, and to find objects such as elevator buttons and static obstacles. The definition varies in each wayfinding system, and there are various types of PoIs are defined in each system based on the purpose of a system.

A localization engine (e) has a role in calculating reasonably accurate geographical location based on environmental information (e.g., radio wave strength) or internal sensor information (e.g., accelerometer for pedestrian dead reckoning). An (f) obstacle detection engine (f) is responsible for detecting obstacles on a route to avoid collisions dynamically. This component requires real-time sensing and recognition of obstacles and any other surrounding information to help wayfinding. Finally, (g) wayfinding user interface integrates all the information and navigate a user to the destination. The primary interaction modality is similar to in-car navigation systems,

Fig. 34.1 The model
architecture of a wayfinding
system

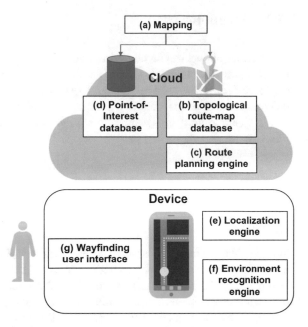

voice navigation commands, and a visual map. Other modalities have been actively
proposed (Dakopoulos and Bourbakis 2010; Giudice and Legge 2008).

Here is a model process of navigation with a wayfinding system. We tried to
design this model as general as possible to cover many navigation systems. So, it
may not exactly match to an existing wayfinding system.

1. A user indicates a destination typically by using conversational interaction with
   the system. ((d) Point of Interest database and (g) Wayfinding user interface)
2. The system localizes the user's location and shows the location on a map or
   announce via voice. ((e) Localization engine)
3. The (c) Route planning engine calculates and searches to find a fastest but accessible route to the destination based on (b) Topological route map database
4. The user inspects and agrees with the proposed route, and the system starts
   navigation. ((g) Wayfinding user interface)
5. The system continuously obtains the current location of the user and provide
   instruction along with the route. ((e) Localization engine)
6. The system automatically senses obstacles around the users to avoid them. ((f)
   Environment recognition engine)
7. The system also provides surrounding information such as shops and restaurants
   the user is passing by and detects the user is arriving at the destination. ((d) Point
   of Interest database).

34.2 Technologies

As described above, wayfinding is involving a variety of technologies. Here we summarize a part of technologies based on the model architecture (Fig. 34.1); (1) static topological route map (b) and POIs (d) to get accessible routes to destinations (c), (2) navigation interface (g) including both macro- and micro-navigation, and (3) localization technologies (e), (4) environment recognition (f) and mapping technologies (a).

34.2.1 Topological Route Map, Point of Interest, and Route Planning

Topological route map database and Point-of-Interest (POI) database are fundamental information sources to enable wayfinding. To navigate a user from a starting point to a destination point, these two points should be connected to a concatenated continuous route without any break. Such a route can be calculated from a topological network of paths across a target area (a floor, a building, an area, or a city). We call such topological network as "Topological route-map" for wayfinding systems (Fig. 34.2).

A topological route map should have information to enable accessible route planning by considering each person's ability. If one segment of a route has a gap or width smaller than the minimum for wheelchairs, the segment should not be a part of a route for users of wheelchairs. Such accessibility information is embedded in a route map or stored as tags on the database which will be used for searching accessible routes.

There are various discussions to standardize topological route map and point of interest, and we analyzed available open proposals at that time to understand com-

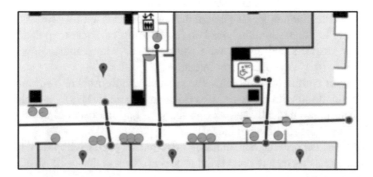

Fig. 34.2 Topological route map with Point of Interest Information for Accessibility (citation from Pérez et al. 2017). Lines indicate topological routes on the map, red balloons indicate shops, green circles indicate accessibility information such as obstacles and special instruction regarding safety

monality and differences to foresee future "one" global standard. Open Street Map provides a guideline for tagging accessibility related information for people with mobility impairments (https://wiki.openstreetmap.org/wiki/Disabilities). A ministry of Japan issued a specification for spatial network model for pedestrians (JMLITT 2018) which allows map provider or local government to share accessibility information for people with mobility impairments. Wayfindr (2018) proposed their open standard of navigation application for visually impaired users which includes taxonomies of accessibility information especially in public transportation, and knowledge of navigational application and environment.

We classified the types of information into eight categories; pathways, doorways, elevators, escalators, stairs, public toilets, facilities, and rooms (Pérez et al. 2017) (Table 34.1). A pathway is one segment of a topological route map. For people with visual impairments, the tactile paving is the necessary information to allow people to choose a route with tactile paving. For people with mobility impairments, access restriction (existence of gap), the width of corridors, and slope (yes/no, gradient) are necessary information to choose the best way. These features should naturally be assigned to a "segment" of a route instead of a "point." On the other hand, "public toilets" are naturally regarded as POIs. They can be destinations of a wayfinding system. The "elevators" are in the middle. They can be regarded as both routes or a point. OpenStreetMap and Wayfindr define them as points, and JMLITT defines them as segments. Such difference may affect the design of route planning algorithms, so standard bodies should carefully determine the best way to encode such features.

Once sufficient information is registered to a topological route map and POI database, it is not difficult to develop a route planning engine. The basic algorithm is almost the same as an algorithm for in-car navigation systems, but accessibility for each user should be considered. For example, a part of visually impaired people prefer to use escalators over elevators, but others prefer the opposite. The necessary width varies in width among wheelchair types (e.g., manual, motorized, and with human assistance), so the challenge of a route planning engine is the adaptation. Also, Bradley and Dunlop (2005) reported a set of instructions is highly accepted by people with visual impairments, but not by sighted people, which indicates the necessity of personalization. How a system can capture the requirements appropriately and reflect them to calculate the best route and instructions.

Despite the fact that visually impaired users tend to rely more on nonvisual information in the real-world environment for navigation such as sound, floor features, and structure, most of the maps do not contain enough nonvisual information as mapping objects. Usually, in orientation and mobility (O&M) training, a trainer describes the environment and the trainee (visually impaired user) confirms the description by their remaining cognitive sensors such as hearing and touch. The trainer will describe sensable landmarks in the environment which the users can feel via their canes or touch, and also surrounding sound or noise for self-localization.

Table 34.1 Comparison of POI, environmental elements, and features considered by three real-world specifications (shared entries bolded)

	OpenStreetMap	Wayfindr	JMLITT
Pathways	• **Type of pathway** • **Width** • **Access restrictions** • **Tactile paving availability** • **Slope (wheelchair access)**	• **Type of pathway** • **Length** • **Tactile paving availability** • Junctions, significant curve, type of tactile paving	• **Type of pathway** • **Width, length** • **Access restrictions** • **Tactile paving availability** • **Slope (gradient, wheelchair access)** • Surface condition, direction of travel, open hours, name
Doorways	• **Type of doorway** • **Width** • **Wheelchair accessible** • **Steps counts** • **Entrance name** • Handle type, opening direction, ramp, handrail, access restrictions, level	• **Type of doorway** • **Venues connected** • Opening button (door side and height)	• **Type of doorway** • **Width** • **Step height** (only one) • **Entrance name**
Elevators	• **Tactile/braille support** • **Levels connected** • **Wheelchair accessible** • Access restrictions, opening hours	• **Audible announcements** • **Tactile/braille support** • **Levels connected** • Call buttons location (side and height) • Side doors open (if more than 1 door)	- *Defined as* <u>*type of pathway*</u> • **Audible announcements** • **Braille support** • **Wheelchair accessible**
Escalators	• **Direction of travel** • **Tactile paving availability** • Width, incline, lanes, access restrictions	• **Direction of travel** (may change—peak hours) • **Tactile paving availability** • Handrail location, side to stand during travel	- *Defined as* <u>*type of pathway*</u> • **Direction of travel** (pathway feature) • **Tactile paving availability**
Stairs	• **Number of steps** • **Handrail location** • **Levels connected** • **Tactile paving availability** • Width, incline, ramp (for wheelchair), name	• **Number of steps** • **Handrail location** • **Levels connected** • **Tactile paving availability** • Type of stairs, landing/flight of stairs	- *Defined as* <u>*type of pathway*</u> • **Number of steps** • **Handrail location** • **Tactile paving availability** • Assistive mechanism available

(continued)

Table 34.1 (continued)

	OpenStreetMap	Wayfindr	JMLITT
Public toilets	• **Wheelchair accessible** • **Gender** • **Opening hours** • Access restrictions, diaper changing table, drinking water, hand washing, paper supply	Not included	• **Accessibility level** (wheelchair accessible and colostomy support) • **Gender** • **Opening hours** • Crib
Buildings/facilities	• **Name** • **Address** • Purpose, levels, entrance, access restrictions	Not included	• **Name** • **Address** • Phone number, opening hours, toilets accessibility level
Rooms/venues	• **Name** • **Purpose** • Level	• **Name** • **Purpose**	Not included

34.2.2   User Interface

This chapter describes user interaction techniques regarding micro-navigation and macro-navigation tasks. Micro-navigation is the term to describe navigation in immediate environments around the users such as obstacle detection and avoidance, finding nearby objects, and navigation after arriving a POI (i.e., shops, restaurants, and restroom), which mainly uses dynamic map information. On the other hand, macro-navigation processes static map information to provide a broad view for navigation including the optimal route finding from a location to another, accessibility features of the routes, turn-by-turn navigation with the shape of the routes. The navigation interfaces have challenges of "real-time, non-visual, and bandwidth." A user interface needs to indicate necessary information in "real-time" in a "non-visual" way not only for people with visual impairments. The narrow "bandwidth" of nonvisual modalities such as speech, sound, and vibration has been a long-term research challenge for wayfinding systems.

34.2.2.1   Interface for Micro-Navigation

With visual cues, people can process micro-navigation subconsciously. It is, however, impossible without vision to do micro-navigation as people can see. Visually impaired people rely on tactile and hearing senses to navigate through the environment. The most basic mobility assistance for micro-navigation is white cane. Visually impaired people need to train their mobility and orientation skill with the mobility assistance how to deal with the real environment without vision. Although people can sense objects in front of them with the white cane, they need to touch the object physically, and the object should be in the range of cane. Besides, echolocation is an ability of hearing sense to locate distant obstacles with the reflection of click sounds like bats (Kolarik et al. 2014). People usually use mouth clicks or finger snapping to generate click sounds. Ifukube et al. (1991) converted ultrasound clicks into hearable sound, which enables people to recognize small objects.

During navigation, a system needs to provide information in real-time. A user's attention is always changing given the flow of surrounding environmental information, but a wayfinding system needs to provide necessary information without any delay through accessible mediums for each user. Especially, for the people with visual impairments, the challenge is nonvisual and real-time navigation interface.

The idea of "digital white cane" attracted many researchers in history, and also several technologies have been productized. The basic concept is to embed additional sensors into a cane and provide them in an accessible interaction medium. These methods are aiming to avoid obstacles and avoid falling for their safety which usually uses ultrasonic sensors to detect something in a range (Borenstein and Ulrich 1997; Wang and Kuchenbecker 2012), or laser sensors to measure distances to find gaps (Yuan and Manduchi 2005). Recently, depth cameras are utilized to detect both obstacles and gaps (Filipe et al. 2012; Takizawa et al. 2012). Most of them convert such visual information into a sound or tactile sensation.

On the other hand, guide dog can support people with visual impairments to walk and find objects as people can see, and the use of a robot to resemble a guide dog has a long history since the 1970s (Tachi and Komoriya 1984). It is not difficult to imagine the value to replace guide dogs with robots. They are tireless, no need to feed, no toilet required, and no training required. However, even with the advancement of robotics technologies, it is not easy to develop a robot which has comparable mobility ability to dogs such as for gaps and stairs. Robot guide dogs provide "walk-ahead" model to a user. The user can intuitively feel the fine-grained movement of a robot, and decide walking speed, direction, sudden stop, and change of direction only by holding the handle without any voice commands. The user interface is seamless to existing guide-dog experience. Moreover, also it can provide the feeling of safety by walking one step ahead of a user. It means that robots always hit the wall or obstacles first and fall first.

The weakness of the robot approach is gaps and stairs. The mobility ability of practical robots is significantly lower than human ability. The recent advancement of the bipedal and quad-pedal robots may solve the challenge soon (Murphy et al. 2011).

Also, robotics technologies have enhanced wheelchairs and allows users with mobility impairments to drive a wheelchair with less control such as by using a brain–machine interface or gaze (Carlson and Millan 2013). The system can estimate a user's intention and make a smooth route toward estimated direction without collision with surrounding obstacles, which is called "shared control" or "shared autonomy" (Philips et al. 2007; Hirzinger et al. 1993).

The micro-navigation has a challenge of more fine-grained and more time-sensitive information presentation to avoid walking people in a collision course and temporal objects in a corridor. Currently, wayfinding systems for the blind depend on traditional methods for micro-navigation. Smartphone-based navigation system depends on manual white cane for obstacle avoidance and other micro-navigation needs. Another approach is the combination with guide dogs. Other systems e.g., iMove provides nonvisual information even when a blind user is following somebody, on a taxi or public transportation. In other words, there is enormous whitespace for innovating the interaction technologies for micro-navigation for the blind.

34.2.2.2 Interface for Macro-Navigation

The primary modality of a macro-navigational interface has not been changed since the accessible wayfinding system research started in the 1980s. The primary medium is a graphical map display with current position and route information. Such display is commonly used by in-car navigation systems and augmented reality navigation is also developed (Narzt et al. 2006). However, the display does not work for people with visual impairments and also the danger to use smartphones while walking is becoming one of the significant challenges of pedestrian safety in urban areas (Richtel 2010). The speed of manual wheelchairs can be competitive or higher than general pedestrians, so visual attention on the surrounding environment instead of looking down screens is essential to improve safety during navigation. The use of augmented reality for wheelchair users may reduce the risk of smartphones while moving. The use of a wearable glass device with displays may help reduce such risks, but more evidence is required.

Therefore, the importance of nonvisual interaction medium is increasing not only for people with visual impairments. The voice commands are also commonly used by in-car navigation systems, but the one of significant difference is the variety of user requirements. NavCog is one of the macro-navigation systems for the indoor environment (Sato et al. 2017), which introduces three types of navigation modes, general pedestrian, wheelchair and visually impaired (see Case study: NavCog). In this way, adaptation is one of the major topics to provide better usability for each type of the users. For example, visually impaired users want to know when they reach turning points, while sighted users feel such navigation as "delayed" because they can see the corners and wanted to know before reaching the turning points.

Loomis et al. (1998) reported a comparison of three auditory display modes; "virtual" where a system indicates the direction of the target location by using stereo sound, "left/right" where a system indicates to turn "left or right" only, and "bearing" where the system indicates the detailed angle like "(turn) left fifty (degree)." Participants completed tasks faster with and preferred "virtual" mode in their experiments. Marston et al. (2007) tested binary indicator with sound or vibration for on-course and off-course. The on-course display gives users signal when they are heading within 20 degrees error, and the off-course is opposite. However, they also reported continuous display for direction is not preferred because users need to pay attention to the system all the time. Marston et al. (2006) and Sato et al. (2017) combines voice commands and vibration for indicating turning direction. Both studies conducted experiments, not in a laboratory but a real field, and carefully designed not to interfere with the environmental sound.

As for the input from the user to the system, the advancement and increasing popularity of conversational user interface will dramatically change the way of wayfinding system navigate in voice. The idea to use conversational interface is not new and has a long history. Strothotte et al. (1996) developed a dialogue system to help wayfinding for blind users. This research may be the first significant attempt in the direction. After years, given the advancement of voice recognition technologies (Saon et al. 2017) conversational interfaces are becoming usable in a practical environment. Sato et al. (2017) utilized a conversational interface for searching a destination with a restaurant recommendation engine. The recent end-to-end neural network approaches are promising to change the technology basis of conversational navigation systems.

Harm de Vries (2018) enabled a virtual agent to determine (human) user's localization through a series of conversation and then navigate him/her to a destination via voice. The system is designed for sighted users, but such an approach can be applied to wayfinding system for accessibility.

34.2.3 Localization Technologies

Localization is a fundamental technology for modern wayfinding systems, and it can drastically improve mobility especially for people with visual impairments. Location of the user in the real world is a kind of the cursor position of screen reader on a computer. The system knows where the user is in the world and what it should read at that position.

There are two big difference between the screen and the real world; information availability and localization error. In the screen, the system can easily get most of the information except semantics of graphics. While, in the real world, almost all of the information is visual and challenging to obtain by the system. In addition, localization has an error, and it causes problems for reading. Imagine, if the cursor on the screen has location error, how the screen reader should manage screen information and user's intention. Wayfinding application needs to handle or ignore such ambiguity and lack of information in the real world. Although localization must improve the quality of the wayfinding application, it is also a challenging research topic. Here, we summarize localization technologies and discuss the future of the localization.

Localization technologies have been evolving in recent decades both for outdoor and indoor. Table 34.2 shows a comparison of major localization technologies.

Recent smartphones have a GPS sensor and archives about 5 m errors in the average [5], which is a promising method to localize users' position outdoor. Some commercial wayfinding applications are using GPS such as [BlindSquare] and [Seeing Eye GPS]. On the other hand, indoor localization has been extensively studied. Among various indoor localization techniques, localization based on Radio wave Sig-

Table 34.2 Comparison of localization technologies (created by the authors by referring papers including (Mautz 2012) and (Murata et al. 2018))

Carrier	Method	Outdoor/indoor	Absolute/relative	Typical accuracy [m]	Available on smartphone
Radio wave	GPS	Outdoor	Absolute	1–10	Yes
	Wi-Fi	Indoor	Absolute	1–10	Yes
	Bluetooth	Indoor	Absolute	1–10	Yes
	RFID	Both	Absolute	0.5–10	No
	UWB	Indoor	Absolute	0.1–1	No
Sound	Ultrasound	Indoor	Absolute	~0.1	Yes
Light	Camera	Both	Both	0.1~	Yes
Magnetic	Magnetic	Indoor	Absolute	1–10	Yes
N/A	PDR	Both	Relative	1%~	Yes

nal Strength (RSS) of Wi-Fi (Bahl and Padmanabhan 2000; Hähnel and Fox 2006; Hilsenbeck et al. 2014) or Bluetooth (Subhan et al. 2011; Faragher and Harle 2015; Murata et al. 2018) is one of the most popular due to its use of off-the-shelf devices and low infrastructure cost. Magnetic field anomaly-based method is also available on magnetometer on smartphone (Haverinen and Kemppainen 2009), which usually needs to rely on RSS-based localization to reduce the possible area for magnetic pattern matching.

Aside from RSS-based methods, various localization techniques have been developed based on RFID (Wang and Katabi 2013), UWB radios (Gezici et al. 2005), ultrasound (Lazik et al. 2015). Most of these approaches require specialized hardware for either the infrastructure or the user, and sometimes both. Image-based localization methods (e.g., Xu et al. (2015)) are promising, but they are not robust enough in scenes having few visual features and appearance changes.

Recent innovation with Wi-Fi localization is the Round-Trip Time (RTT) method which calculates the distance between the device and the Wi-Fi access point not by RSS but RTT. RSS could be noisy due to the interference of the environment, but RTT is more robust and brings better distance estimation (Ciurana et al. 2009). The method requires specified chips for both for mobile device and from access points, but it has been recently available in the market (Google 2018b).

In addition to the above localization method, pedestrian dead reckoning estimates a user's relative movement based on motion analysis (Li et al. 2012; Hilsenbeck et al. 2014). However, the motion estimation can become unreliable when the user's motion profile changes, e.g., a user moves with lower acceleration changes. A recent study (Flores and Manduchi 2018) found significantly larger step counting error for blind walkers than for sighted walkers through analysis of a data set collected from the two groups.

Many studies have been trying to apply one of these localization methods to realize navigation systems for visually impaired people with GPS (Wilson et al. 2007), RFID

(Kulyukin et al. 2005), Camera (Manduchi et al. 2010), Bluetooth (Ahmetovic 2016; Sato et al. 2017), PDR + Human perception (Fallah et al. 2012), and more.

34.2.4 Environment Recognition

Understanding of the dynamically changing surrounding environment is the essential ability to perform better wayfinding. While sighted people can recognize the environment at a glance such as obstacles, walking people, and signages, people with visual impairments needs to rely on his/her nonvisual sense, someone's assist, or technologies. Such environment recognition is one of the fast-growing technology areas thanks to the deep learning revolution in computer vision (Gurari et al. 2018). The recent computer vision evolution is aiming to complete mobility tasks such as autonomous vehicles and autonomous delivery drones. In the coming decades, computers will understand the world, and help persons with disabilities users based on such knowledge.

Obstacle detection techniques and visual sonification are some of the examples of traditional technology field (Dakopoulos and Bourbakis 2010). These technologies transform visual information such as distances or camera pixels into sound or tactile sensation to let visually impaired user grasp the surrounding environment. In other words, it will enhance visually impaired person's nonvisual senses to understand the real world.

Furthermore, the emerging computer vision technologies are not only for mobility but also for recognition and description of the environment. On the Web, the system fully integrates face recognition (Schroff et al. 2015; Taigman et al. 2014) and object recognition (Russakovsky et al. 2015) technologies into the user experience. It adds a tag on your friend's face when you upload a photo to an SNS or describe an object when you post a picture of your couch to a free market site. Microsoft's [Seeing AI] is an app, integrating such vision technologies to allow people with visual impairments to know characters, faces, barcodes, and currencies in the real. By selecting recognition mode and aiming the camera toward the target, the user can get the recognition results instantly.

With the state-of-the-art research, computer vision demonstrates to describe a scene in a picture by a model trained with tons of image data set and a deep neural network technique (Vinyals et al. 2015). Furthermore, the visual question answering method (Antol et al. 2015) allows users to ask the system questions about images, and social scene understanding technique can understand the social behavior of human beings (Bagautdinov et al. 2017; Park 2014).

Although it may take a long time that such technologies become accurate enough for practical usage, it would completely change the daily life of visually impaired users, and it would allow them to go out and enjoy window shopping independently.

34.2.5 Mapping

The mapping, creation of topological route maps and POIs, is a time-consuming task, and it is required to keep reducing the cost, and ultimately automate the process. The most promising way to manage such mapping cost is the combination of manual and automated methods including collaborative editing or crowdsourcing. Palazzi et al. proposed a method to automatically extract accessible routes by analyzing smartphone location history of local wheelchair users for wheelchair tourists to the area (Palazzi et al. 2010). Wheelmap is a crowdsourcing platform where volunteers contribute information about wheelchair-accessible places and have collected over 800 thousands of accessible information all over the world (Mobasheri et al. 2017). Wheelmap uses a limited set of expression ("yes," "limited," or "no") to describe whether the venue is accessible for wheelchair users. The coverage is small given such a manual process (Bakillah et al. 2014). Hara et al. combine computer vision technologies and crowdsourcing to describe accessibility features on sidewalks such as bus stops, benches, and curve cuts via images from Google's Streetview and archive reasonably higher accuracy of tagging with less effort than tagging in the real world (Hara et al. 2013).

34.2.6 Other Technologies

34.2.6.1 Spatial Knowledge Acquisition

Spatial knowledge acquisition of routes and environment is useful for wayfinding, especially for people with visual impairments. They often get spatial knowledge from verbal descriptions and inspection of the route with O&M trainer. Tactile Braille maps and 3D models also enable blind people to explore a map/model with their fingers and are known to provide accurate spatial representations of an environment (Wiener et al. 2010). However, geographic maps are inherently visual and inaccessible for people with visual impairments, thus interaction techniques that allow them to obtain spatial knowledge have been actively studied.

Static maps need to have Braille for text information on the maps, and thus many studies utilize touch-sensitive surfaces for interactive maps which are able to speak text information at where the users are touching. Interactive maps can be categorized into two; digital interactive maps and hybrid interactive maps (Ducasse et al. 2018). Digital interactive maps provide audio, haptic, or force feedback to enable a user to explore digital maps by using a 2D pointing device such as a joystick (Lahav and Mioduser 2000) and touchscreen (Su et al. 2010; Kane et al. 2011). Hybrid interactive maps combine digital interactive maps and physical, tactile surface, which enables users to touch the map with their fingers and easily understand spatial relationships on the maps (Wang et al. 2009; Paladugu et al. 2010).

Another approach is to utilize digital environments where users can freely explore with/without actual move or walking to obtain spatial knowledge virtually. Virtual exploration can also be categorized into two; free exploration and instructional exploration. Free exploration methods often employee virtual white cane (Lécuyer et al. 2003) to enable users to examine the virtual world freely, and some of the methods simulate the real-world acoustic environment (Picinali et al. 2014). Instructional exploration is more focusing on navigations toward destinations, which highlights places where people with visual impairments need to pay attention to their safety and lost-less wayfinding (Yatani et al. 2012; Guerreiro et al. 2017).

34.3 Case Study: NavCog

34.3.1 Overview

As an example of a complete wayfinding system, let us introduce our NavCog system (Sato et al. 2017). NavCog is a smartphone-based wayfinding assistant system characterized by its localization accuracy and features to navigate blind users. We have deployed the system first at a shopping mall in central Tokyo area (Sato et al. 2017; Murata et al. 2018; Takagi 2017), and then an airport, a university campus, a museum, a hotel [NavCog PCB] and other places.

Let us focus on the shopping mall deployment. The system provided three modes, general pedestrian, wheelchair users, and people with visual impairments. Let me take a blind user as an example. The user can first initiate a voice chat to find and decide a destination in the environment like "I want to eat Italian food with my young son," and then the system may reply like "You searched for an Italian restaurant. There are 3 candidates ..." (see Fig. 34.3 left). Once the user decides a destination, NavCog obtains an accessible route to the destination from the map service and information of POIs along with the route (Fig. 34.4). The navigation screen (Fig. 34.2 Right) shows an example of a view of the map in a shopping mall environment. NavCog can provide nonvisual turn-by-turn navigation based on the precise localization and accessible route information. The basic announcement is like "Proceed 10 meters and turn left" at the beginning of a segment of the route, then the user is approaching to the turning point, the system announces "approaching" and "turn left." It also provides information about POIs such as shops and restaurants when the user is passing by. POIs are including not only shops but also essential features of the environment improving accessibility for people with visual impairments such as locations of elevator buttons, doors, and floor material changes. It may help users to locate objects which is difficult to find without visual supports and make them confident by increasing their self-localization capability. NavCog also notifies the user of surrounding POIs such as shops, restaurants, and restrooms when the user is passing by such facilities of the environment. Such POIs could be a nonvisual landmark for them even if they cannot see the actual environment and also be fun

CASE STUDY: NAVCOG

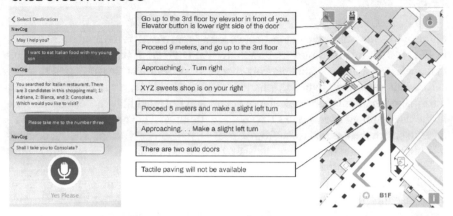

Fig. 34.3 Examples screens of NavCog Application (Left: voice chat to search a destination, Right: route visualization during navigation)

Fig. 34.4 The architecture of NavCog system

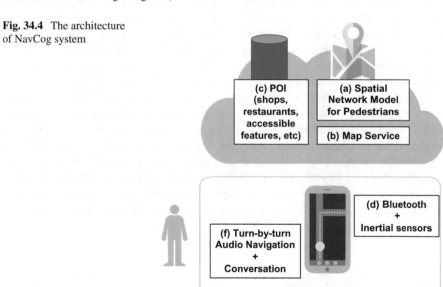

for people with visual impairments during the travel. Usually, it is difficult to know the surroundings while navigating by themselves.

34.3.2 Design

Figure 34.4 shows the architecture of NavCog system based on the model architecture in Fig. 34.1. It provides turn-by-turn nonvisual navigation based on the accessible map, an extension of a spatial network model for pedestrians (JMLITT 2018) which can contain accessible route information. The cloud-side server manages static map information including topological route maps and PoIs including accessible features in the environment (See JMLITT column in Table 34.1). The server also provides APIs to obtain the optimal route from a location to another with specified accessibility options such as avoiding steps and using tactile paving and also to get surrounding PoIs. Most of the components are published as open source under the Human Scale Localization Project [HULOP]. The current system provides navigation based on static map information, but does not provide functions to recognize a dynamic environment.

Localization engine supports multiple platforms such as iOS and Android. NavCog uses a hybrid localization method based on Radio wave Signal Strength (RSS) of Bluetooth Low Energy (BLE) beacons and smartphone sensors such as accelerometers, gyroscopes, altimeters, and magnetometers. Specifically, the engine fuses RSS fingerprinting method and a pedestrian dead reckoning method on the mobile devices. It successfully achieved about 1.5 m average error in a complex environment with multi-stories and multi-buildings (Murata et al. 2018).

In addition to a graphical display of the route on indoor maps, the blind people can get necessary information through voice announcement and haptic feedback based on the route, POIs, and the user's location. When a user reached to the point to turn, it notifies both through voice and vibration. When the user starts turning, it automatically assess the real-time degree based on a gyroscope, and then notify the appropriate angle with voice and vibration again. Also, the system allows the user to talk to the system to find a destination in the environment by using speech to text functionality and conversation scripts. We enabled the voice chat feature both in English and Japanese (see Overview).

34.3.3 Implementation

There are multiple steps to prepare the navigation field. The first step is planning. We needed to obtain the accurate floor maps of the target areas and created a beacon deployment plan, topological route map, and POIs. We had to negotiate with building owners and other stakeholders to obtain the first set of maps. The creation of POIs was a time-consuming task. We had to check detailed accessibility information on-site such as the location of elevator buttons (right or left, chest level or waist-level), appropriate store entrance, the existence of obstacles (chairs, tables, and signboards), usual cue location, nonvisual landmarks (car noise, sound sings), and so on. These POIs are registered to the POI database.

Another hurdle was permission to set up beacons. We deployed BLE beacons (mainly battery powered) all over the environment to cover walkable areas every 7–10 m. In our deployment in Japan especially for areas owned by the central government, we had to acquire special permission to place small beacons. It took months to get approval. The physical beacon setup itself only took several hours. Most of the beacons were placed in hidden places such as a maintenance door on a ceiling, inside indirect lighting appliances, and we found other ways to hide beacons in the well-designed shopping mall environment. Such seamless deployment was one of the requirements of building owners. Another long-term challenge is the battery life. A battery of each beacon only lasts about one year to a few years, so battery replacement is required every year.

After the deployment of the beacons, RSS distribution in the environment needs to be measured by the system. The process is called as RSS fingerprinting. For better localization accuracy, RSS fingerprinting should be done precisely and carefully which will be modeled and trained for the localization. To reduce workload and improve accuracy, we developed a unique indoor vehicle with LiDAR sensor. The location calculated from a LiDAR can be the ground truth to create a localization model, and the indoor vehicle (motorized wheelchair) provide constant speech to fingerprinting. Thanks to such technologies, we have done the fingerprinting within ten hours.

To implement the voice chat interface, a set of corpora for potential queries should be built before the deployment. We had to imagine the questions from users before deployment. We interviewed some experts who usually work at a service desk at the mall and collected real-world questions. We also needed to collect textual explanation of restaurants to create a flexible search engine for restaurants both in Japanese and English. We collected information on the Web and registered to POI database and also the restaurant search engine, such as brief introduction, smoking or not, accessible for wheelchairs (or not), and so on. We also converted menu information usually published as PDF into a textual format. We implemented the voice chat feature by using Watson Assistant [Watson] and our restaurant search engine.

34.3.4 User Evaluation

We conducted multiple evaluation sessions at the venue. One of the evaluation sessions focused on visually impaired people. Ten legally blind users joined an evaluation session in February 2017. The users had 5–10 min of training about the system and asked to visit two fixed destinations and come back to the starting point. The route was about 400 meters in total with three elevator rides. We investigated the navigation performance and localization performance and recorded 360° videos of the travels (Sato et al. 2017).

Of the 260 turns in total, 221 turns were successful on the first attempt. Of the 39 missed turns, 22 were successful on the second attempt. Regarding the turn success rate, the average rate per participant across all routes was 85.0% (SD = 10.6%)

without any correction, and 93.5% (SD = 5.8%) either with the help of the system's failure safe guidance (N = 18) or by participants themselves (N = 4). The overall localization accuracy of the system during the evaluation was measured regarding the Euclidian distance between a user's actual location and estimated location. We extracted 7641 actual location points across the three routes from the participants' results. The average error rate was 1.65 m (SD = 1.13).

All participants considered POIs information to be useful. We noticed that some participants considered POIs would increase the enjoyment of walking places (N = 4). One participant stated that without the system she would have never walked into an interesting shop to buy something unless somehow encouraged to do so and that it was a pleasure to enjoy shopping from the information received. P7 also wished to use POI information to enhance his spatial awareness. While POIs may increase the joy of walking around and improve spatial awareness, two participants specified that they would like to receive POI information only upon request or have two modes of navigation such as exploration mode where a user can receive detailed information about nearby POIs and direction-only mode, which does not provide POI information at all.

34.4   Discussion

Wayfinding is one of the biggest challenges for people with visual impairments because it involves real-world interactions and understandings without vision, hence it is a multidisciplinary field including computer vision, sensory augmentation, spatial awareness, spatial learning, mobile, crowdsourcing, and lots of Web services for spatial knowledge.

Like the Web accessibility, wayfinding may need standards to build up blocks accumulating worldwide efforts. Although some standards for accessible wayfinding have been discussed recently (Wayfindr 2018; JMLITT 2018), they cover limited situations. Meanwhile, unlike the Web accessibility, wayfinding has a long history of practices and researches in many fields and it seems not easy to systematize those enormous efforts. Also, the required technology level varies with expected conditions such as daily familiar environments to occasional unfamiliar environments. Standardization for mobility is likely to be affected more by regional and cultural differences, conditions of visual impairments, and physical mobility capability. If public space is essentially inaccessible, it is not possible to make the environment fully accessible. Even if a station is designed to be accessible, users often need to take a long detour to get the desired destination. In Tokyo, there are some colossal subway transit stations with multiple lines and tens of exits. It is not so easy even for sighted people, but accessibility is far larger challenges. Currently, people with mobility impairments need to plan accessible transportation routes "before" their actual travel by checking accessibility information for train and bus stations to avoid inaccessible transitions [London, Accessible Japan, Google 2018]. We also learned the challenges of real-world deployment such as permission from building owners and governments, esthetic beacon placement, authoring of detailed POI information for accessibility, and data collection for flexible search engines.

34.5   Future Direction

Now, let us foresee the future direction. Accelerating standardization may be one of the key points. In order to promote standardization, we may need to increase the number of users and expand the area where they can try it to gain more feedback. The most critical challenge is the necessity of infrastructure. In the case of NavCog, we used BLE Beacons as the necessary infrastructure. Through our study, the setup workload is manageable even in a real environment, and it can reach sufficient accuracy to provide navigation for people with visual impairments. Other infrastructure-less methods have been developed as explained in Localization technology section. Another approach to reducing the cost of infrastructure is by using a new Wi-Fi standard [IEEE 802.11]. It is one of the candidates to make our public spaces "virtually" infrastructure less if the standard widespread across public spaces. We can expect other technologies will emerge from other areas such as Channel State Information (CSI) of Wi-Fi signals (Wu et al. 2013).

Another technical innovation will exist in computer vision. There is a long history to apply computer vision technologies to help blind pedestrian, but only a few computer vision technologies are used for accessibility in daily life. The emerging "AI glasses" (glass devices with a camera connected to a computer/smartphone) and other new wearable devices will open up a new way to deploy computer vision technologies to help people with visual impairments and other people with disabilities.

34.6   Author's Opinion of the Field

Wayfinding is easy and difficult depending on situations. Even if people cannot see and without mobility aids, they can get their destination by their remaining senses with spatial knowledge in familiar environments. However, it is too difficult to get a destination if it is unfamiliar environments without vision. The ultimate goal of wayfinding technology for people with disabilities is to provide less effort and more comfortable ways to get their destinations.

Toward this goal, we have to overcome issues one by one and allow them to use it anywhere anytime. We expect computer vision technologies will be used to help wayfinding and explain the surrounding environment in real-time in the near future. Ultimate computer vision would complement the lost ability of visually impaired people and would help to build spatial knowledge of real-world environment through its understanding autonomously.

In the foreseeable future, we will see wayfinding systems in public places all over the world. We hope this article will contribute to the penetration of the Wayfinding systems.

34.7 Conclusions

With wayfinding technologies, people with disabilities can expand their opportunity and obtain more comfort and safer mobility. In this section, we tried to overview the current state of wayfinding technologies. We classified components of a model wayfinding system into seven categories, mapping, topological route map database, route planning engine, Point of Interest (POI) database, localization engine, and environment recognition engine.

We then introduced our navigation system as an example of real-world deployment. The system was deployed at many venues including a shopping mall which we explained in detail as an example. Through the deployments and evaluation sessions, we could confirm the effectiveness of indoor localization systems. The feedback from users is mostly positive with high expectations for a future possibility.

Wayfinding is not a topic only for people with disabilities. Parents with baby strollers, older people with walkers, patients in a hospital, travelers with suitcases, foreigners who are not familiar with the area, and any other people who want to move and enjoy urban environment will benefit from a wayfinding system

References

Accessible Japan, Accessible transportation. https://www.accessible-japan.com/transportation/
Ahmetovic D, Gleason C, Ruan C, Kitani K, Takagi H, Asakawa C (2016) NavCog: a navigational cognitive assistant for the blind. In: Proceedings of the 18th international conference on human-computer interaction with mobile devices and services. ACM, pp 90–99
Antol S, Agrawal A, Lu J, Mitchell M, Batra D, Lawrence Zitnick C, Parikh D (2015) Vqa: Visual question answering. In: Proceedings of the IEEE international conference on computer vision, pp 2425–2433
Bagautdinov TM, Alahi A, Fleuret F, Fua P, Savarese S (2017) Social scene understanding: end-to-end multi-person action localization and collective activity recognition. In: CVPR, pp 3425–3434
Bahl P, Padmanabhan VN (2000) RADAR: an in-building RF-based user location and tracking system. In: Proceedings of IEEE INFOCOM 2000, nineteenth annual joint conference of the IEEE computer and communications societies, vol 2, pp 775–784
Bakillah M, Mobasheri A, Rousell A, Hahmann S, Jokar J, Liang SH (2014) Toward a collective tagging android application for gathering accessibility-related geospatial data in European cities. Parameters 10:21
BlindSquare. http://www.blindsquare.com/
Borenstein J, Ulrich I (1997) The guidecane-a computerized travel aid for the active guidance of blind pedestrians. ICRA

Bradley NA, Dunlop MD (2005) An experimental investigation into wayfinding directions for visually impaired people. Personal Ubiquitous Comput. 9(6):395–403. http://dx.doi.org/10.1007/s00779-005-0350-y

Carlson T, Millan JR (2013) Brain-controlled wheelchairs: a robotic architecture. IEEE Robot Autom Mag 20(1): 65–73

Ciurana M, López D, Barceló-Arroyo F (2009) SofTOA: Software ranging for TOA-based positioning of WLAN terminals. In: International symposium on location-and context-awareness. Springer, Berlin, pp 207–221

Dakopoulos D, Bourbakis NG (2010) Wearable obstacle avoidance electronic travel aids for blind: a survey. IEEE Trans Syst Man Cybern Part C (Appl Rev) 40(1):25–35

Ding C, Wald M, Wills G (2014) A survey of open accessibility data. In: Proceedings of the 11th web for all conference. ACM, p. 37

Ducasse J, Brock AM, Jouffrais C (2018) Accessible interactive maps for visually impaired Users. In: Pissaloux E, Velazquez R (eds) Mobility of visually impaired people. Springer, Cham

Fallah N, Apostolopoulos I, Bekris K, Folmer E (2012) The user as a sensor: navigating users with visual impairments in indoor spaces using tactile landmarks. In: Proceedings of the SIGCHI conference on human factors in computing systems. ACM, pp 425–432

Faragher R, Harle R (2015) Location fingerprinting with bluetooth low energy beacons. IEEE J Sel Areas Commun 33(11):2418–2428

Filipe V et al (2012) Blind navigation support system based on Microsoft Kinect. Procedia Comput Sci 14: 94–101

Flores GH, Manduchi R (2018) WeAllWalk: an annotated dataset of inertial sensor time series from blind walkers. ACM Trans Access Comput (TACCESS) 11(1):4

Gezici S, Tian Z, Giannakis GB, Kobayashi H, Molisch AF, Poor HV, Sahinoglu Z (2005) Localization via ultra-wideband radios: a look at positioning aspects for future sensor networks. IEEE Signal Process Mag 22(4):70–84

Giudice NA, Legge GE (2008) Blind navigation and the role of technology. The engineering handbook of smart technology for aging, disability, and independence, pp 479–500

Google (2018a) Introducing "wheelchair accessible" routes in transit navigation https://www.blog.google/products/maps/introducing-wheelchair-accessible-routes-transit-navigation/. Accessed July 2018

Google (2018b) Introducing android 9 pie. https://android-developers.googleblog.com/2018/08/introducing-android-9-pie.html

Guerreiro J, Ahmetovic D, Kitani KM, Asakawa C (2017) Virtual navigation for blind people: building sequential representations of the real-world. In: Proceedings of the 19th international ACM SIGACCESS conference on computers and accessibility (ASSETS '17). ACM, New York, NY, USA, pp 280–289. https://doi.org/10.1145/3132525.3132545

Gurari D et al (2018) VizWiz grand challenge: answering visual questions from blind people. arXiv: 1802.08218

Hähnel BFD, Fox D (2006) Gaussian processes for signal strength-based location estimation. In: Proceeding of robotics: science and systems

Hara K, Le V, Froehlich J (2013) Combining crowdsourcing and google street view to identify street-level accessibility problems. In: Proceedings of the SIGCHI conference on human factors in computing systems. ACM, pp 631–640

Harle R (2013) A survey of indoor inertial positioning systems for pedestrians. IEEE Commun Surv Tutor 15(3):1281–1293

Harm de Vries (2018) "Talk the Walk: Navigating New York City through Grounded Dialogue." https://arxiv.org/abs/1807.03367

Haverinen J, Kemppainen A (2009) Global indoor self-localization based on the ambient magnetic field. Robot Auton Syst 57(10):1028–1035

He S, Chan SHG (2016) Wi-Fi fingerprint-based indoor positioning: recent advances and comparisons. IEEE Commun Surv Tutor 18(1):466–490

Hilsenbeck S, Bobkov D, Schroth G, Huitl R, Steinbach E (2014) Graph-based data fusion of pedometer and WiFi measurements for mobile indoor positioning. In: Proceedings of the 2014 ACM international joint conference on pervasive and ubiquitous computing. ACM, pp 147–158

Hirzinger G et al. (1993) Sensor-based space robotics-ROTEX and its telerobotic features. IEEE Trans Robot Autom 9(5): 649–663

HULOP, Human-scale Localization Platform. https://hulop.mybluemix.net/

IEEE 802.11, Liaison from 3GPP RAN4 on RTT measurement accuracy. (2016) https://mentor.ieee.org/802.11/dcn/16/11-16-1338-00-0000-liaison-from-3gpp-ran4-on-rtt-measurement-accuracy.doc

Ifukube Tohru, Sasaki Tadayuki, Peng Chen (1991) A blind mobility aid modeled after echolocation of bats. IEEE Trans Biomed Eng 38(5):461–465

Kane SK, Morris MR, Perkins AZ, Wigdor D, Ladner RE, Wobbrock JO (2011). Access overlays: improving non-visual access to large touch screens for blind users. In: Proceedings of the 24th annual ACM symposium on user interface software and technology (UIST '11). ACM, New York, NY, USA, pp 273–282. https://doi.org/10.1145/2047196.2047232

Kolarik AJ et al (2014) A summary of research investigating echolocation abilities of blind and sighted humans. Hear Res 310: 60–68

Kulyukin V, Gharpure C, Nicholson J (2005) Robocart: toward robot-assisted navigation of grocery stores by the visually impaired. In: 2005 IEEE/RSJ international conference on intelligent robots and systems, 2005 (IROS 2005). IEEE, pp 2845–2850

Lahav O, Mioduser D (2000) Multisensory virtual environment for supporting blind persons' acquisition of spatial cognitive mapping, orientation, and mobility skills. In: Proceedings of the third international conference on disability, virtual reality and associated technologies, ICDVRAT 2000.

Lazik P, Rajagopal N, Shih O, Sinopoli B, Rowe A (2015) ALPS: a bluetooth and ultrasound platform for mapping and localization. In: Proceedings of the 13th ACM conference on embedded networked sensor system. ACM, pp 73–84

Lécuyer A et al (2003) HOMERE: a multimodal system for visually impaired people to explore virtual environments. IEEE virtual reality, 2003. Proceedings, IEEE

Liu H, Darabi H, Banerjee P, Liu J (2007) Survey of wireless indoor positioning techniques and systems. IEEE Trans Syst Man Cybern Part C (Appl Rev) 37(6):1067–1080

Li F, Zhao C, Ding G, Gong J, Liu C, Zhao F (2012) A reliable and accurate indoor localization method using phone inertial sensors. In: Proceedings of the 2012 ACM conference on ubiquitous computing. ACM, pp 421–430

Loomis JM, Klatzky RL, Golledge RG, Cicinelli JG, Pellegrino JW, Fry PA (1993) Nonvisual navigation by blind and sighted: assessment of path integration ability. J Exp Psychol Gen 122(1):73

Loomis JM, Golledge RG, Klatzky RL (1998) Navigation system for the blind: auditory display modes and guidance. Presence 7(2):193–203

Manduchi R, Kurniawan S, Bagherinia H (2010) Blind guidance using mobile computer vision: a usability study. In: Proceedings of the 12th international ACM SIGACCESS conference on Computers and accessibility. ACM, pp 241–242

Marston JR, Loomis JM, Klatzky RL, Golledge RG, Smith EL (2006) Evaluation of spatial displays for navigation without sight. ACM Trans Appl Perception (TAP) 3(2):110–124

Marston JR, Loomis JM, Klatzky RL, Golledge RG (2007) Nonvisual route following with guidance from a simple haptic or auditory display. J Vis Impair Blind 101(4):203–211

Mautz, Rainer. Indoor positioning technologies (2012)

Ministry of Land, Infrastructure, Transport and Tourism, Japan (2018) Development specification for spatial network model for pedestrians. http://www.mlit.go.jp/common/001244373.pdf. Accessed July 2018

Mobasheri A, Deister J, Dieterich H (2017) Wheelmap: The wheelchair accessibility crowdsourcing platform. Open Geospatial Data, Softw Stand 2(1):27

Murata M, Sato D, Ahmetovic D, Takagi H, Kitani MK, Asakawa C (2018) Smartphone-based indoor localization for blind navigation across building Complexes. International conference on pervasive computing and communications (PerCom)

Murphy, Michael P et al (2011) The littledog robot. Int J Robot Res 30(2):145–149

Narzt W, Pomberger G, Ferscha A, Kolb D, Müller R, Wieghardt J, Lindinger C (2006). Augmented reality navigation systems. Univers Access Inf Soc 4(3):177–187

Paladugu DA, Wang Z, Li B (2010) On presenting audio-tactile maps to visually impaired users for getting directions. In: CHI'10 extended abstracts on human factors in computing systems (CHI EA '10). ACM, New York, NY, USA, pp 3955–3960. https://doi.org/10.1145/1753846.1754085

Palazzi CE, Teodori L, Roccetti M (2010). Path 2.0: A participatory system for the generation of accessible routes. In 2010 IEEE international conference on multimedia and expo (ICME), IEEE, pp 1707–1711

Park HS (2014). Social scene understanding from social cameras (Doctoral dissertation, Carnegie Mellon University)

Pérez JE, Arrue M, Kobayashi M, Takagi H, Asakawa C (2017). Assessment of semantic taxonomies for blind indoor navigation based on a shopping center use case. In Proceedings of the 14th Web for All conference on the future of accessible work. ACM, p 19

Petrie H, Johnson V, Strothotte T, Raab A, Fritz S, Michel R (1996) MoBIC: Designing a travel aid for blind and elderly people. J Navig 49(1):45–52

Petrie H, Johnson V, Strothotte T, Raab A, Michel R, Reichert L, Schalt A (1997) MoBIC: An aid to increase the independent mobility of blind travellers. Br J Vis Impair 15(2):63–66

Philips, Johan et al (2007) Adaptive shared control of a brain-actuated simulated wheelchair. In: IEEE 10th international conference on rehabilitation robotics ICORR 2007. IEEE

Picinali L et al (2014) Exploration of architectural spaces by blind people using auditory virtual reality for the construction of spatial knowledge. Int J Hum Comput Stud 72(4):393–407

Richtel M (2010) Forget gum. Walking and using phone is risky, The New York Times, p 17

Russakovsky O, Deng J, Su H, Krause J, Satheesh S, Ma S, Berg AC (2015). Imagenet large scale visual recognition challenge. Int J Comput Vis 115(3):211–252

Saon G, Kurata G, Sercu T, Audhkhasi K, Thomas S, Dimitriadis D, Roomi B (2017). English conversational telephone speech recognition by humans and machines. arXiv:1703.02136

Sato D, Oh U, Naito K, Takagi H, Kitani K, Asakawa C (2017). Navcog3: An evaluation of a smartphone-based blind indoor navigation assistant with semantic features in a large-scale environment. In: Proceedings of the 19th international ACM SIGACCESS conference on computers and accessibility. ACM, pp 270–279

Schroff F, Kalenichenko D, Philbin J (2015). Facenet: A unified embedding for face recognition and clustering. In: Proceedings of the IEEE conference on computer vision and pattern recognition, pp 815–823

Seeing AI, Microsoft. https://www.microsoft.com/en-us/seeing-ai

Seeng Eye GPS, Sendero Group. http://www.senderogroup.com/products/seeingeyegps/index.html

Strothotte T, Fritz S, Michel R, Raab A, Petrie H, Johnson V, Schalt A (1996). Development of dialogue systems for a mobility aid for blind people: initial design and usability testing. In: Proceedings of the second annual ACM conference on Assistive technologies. ACM, pp 139–144

Su J, Rosenzweig A, Goel A, de Lara E, Truong KN (2010). Timbremap: enabling the visuallyimpaired to use maps on touch-enabled devices. In: Proceedings of the 12th international conference on Human computer interaction with mobile devices and services (MobileHCI '10). ACM, New York, NY, USA, pp 17–26. https://doi.org/10.1145/1851600.1851606

Subhan F, Hasbullah H, Rozyyev A, Bakhsh ST (2011). Indoor positioning in bluetooth networks using fingerprinting and lateration approach. In: 2011 international conference on information science and applications (ICISA 2011). IEEE, pp 1–9

Tachi, Susumu, Kiyoshi Komoriya. (1984) Guide dog robot.In: Autonomous mobile robots: control, planning, and architecture, pp 360–367

Taigman Y, Yang M, Ranzato MA, Wolf L (2014). Deepface: Closing the gap to human-level performance in face verification. In: Proceedings of the IEEE conference on computer vision and pattern recognition, pp 1701–1708

Takagi H. Realizing a barrier-free society. https://www.ibm.com/blogs/research/2017/02/realizing-a-barrier-free-society/

Takizawa, Hotaka et al (2012) Kinect cane: An assistive system for the visually impaired based on three-dimensional object recognition.In: 2012 IEEE/SICE international symposium on system integration (SII), IEEE

Transport for London, Transport accessibility. https://tfl.gov.uk/transport-accessibility/

van Diggelen F, Enge P (2015) The worlds first GPS MOOC and worldwide laboratory using smartphones. In: Proceedings of the 28th international technical meeting of the satellite division of the institute of navigation (ION GNSS+ 2015), pp 361–369

Vinyals O, Toshev A, Bengio S, Erhan D (2015). Show and tell: A neural image caption generator. In: Proceedings of the IEEE conference on computer vision and pattern recognition, pp 3156–3164

Wang J, Katabi D (2013). Dude, where's my card?: RFID positioning that works with multipath and non-line of sight. ACM SIGCOMM Comput Commun Rev 43(4):51–62. ACM

Wang Z, Li B, Hedgpeth T, Haven T (2009) Instant tactile-audio map: enabling access to digital maps for people with visual impairment. In: Proceedings of the 11th international ACM SIGACCESS conference on Computers and accessibility (Assets '09). ACM, New York, NY, USA, pp 43–50. https://doi.org/10.1145/1639642.1639652

Wang, Yunqing, Katherine J, Kuchenbecker. (2012) HALO: Haptic alerts for low-hanging obstacles in white cane navigation. In: 2012 IEEE Haptics Symposium (HAPTICS). IEEE

Watson Assistant, IBM. https://www.ibm.com/watson/ai-assistant/

Wayfindr (2018) Open Standard for audio-based wayfinding. Working Draft ver. 2.0. https://www.wayfindr.net/open-standard. Accessed July 2018

Wiener WR, Welsh RL, Blasch BB (2010). Foundations of orientation and mobility, vol 1. American Foundation for the Blind

Wilson J, Walker BN, Lindsay J, Cambias C, Dellaert F (2007). Swan: System for wearable audio navigation. In: 11th IEEE international symposium on wearable computers, 2007. IEEE, pp 91–98

Wu, Kaishun, et al (2013) CSI-based indoor localization. IEEE Trans Parallel Distrib Syst 24(7):1300–1309

Xu H, Yang Z, Zhou Z, Shangguan L, Yi K, Liu Y (2015). Enhancing wifi-based localization with visual clues. In: Proceedings of the 2015 ACM international joint conference on pervasive and ubiquitous computing. ACM, pp 963–974

Yang Z, Wu C, Zhou Z, Zhang X, Wang X, Liu Y (2015) Mobility increases localizability: A survey on wireless indoor localization using inertial sensors. ACM Comput Surv (Csur) 47(3):54

Yatani K, Banovic N, Truong K (2012). SpaceSense: representing geographical information to visually impaired people using spatial tactile feedback. In: Proceedings of the SIGCHI conference on human factors in computing systems (CHI '12). ACM, New York, NY, USA, pp 415–424. https://doi.org/10.1145/2207676.2207734

NavCog PCB, NavCog at Annual PCB conference on Youtube. https://www.youtube.com/watch?v=KkRigGqTsuc&t=2s

Yuan, Dan, and Roberto Manduchi. (2005) Dynamic environment exploration using a virtual white cane.In: IEEE computer society conference on computer vision and pattern recognition, CVPR 2005. vol 1. IEEE

Chapter 35
Wearables

Shaun K. Kane

Abstract Computing devices have evolved from machines that fill a room, to portable and mobile devices, and now to devices that are worn on our own bodies. Wearable computing devices provide new opportunities for supporting individuals with disabilities via environmental context sensing and ubiquitous input and output. However, designing wearable computing devices to support people with disabilities requires careful design of features, the wearable device itself, and the input and output methods used. This chapter offers an overview of contemporary trends in wearable computing devices for people with disabilities.

35.1 Introduction

While wearable computing devices may be considered a new and emerging technology, body-worn technology devices have an extremely long history among users with disabilities. In fact, among the earliest known devices that may be considered assistive technology are a wooden prosthetic toe from ancient Egypt (c. 950 BCE) and a bronze prosthetic leg from the Roman Empire (c. 300 BCE) (Park 2015). Although fabrication techniques have advanced since then (see chapter on Fabrication, 3D Printing, and Making), the challenges of designing worn assistive technologies exist to this day.

However, the accessibility challenges presented when using wearable technology, and the opportunities presented by wearable technology to enhance the lives of people with disabilities, change from year to year. Today it is not uncommon for an individual in a developed country to be wearing one or more wearable computing devices, such as a smartwatch or fitness tracker, that can sense and record the user's movement; present information via a color display, haptic feedback, or text-to-speech generated on the device itself; and communicate wirelessly with nearby devices or cellular networks. As these devices gain new input, output, and sensing capabilities, it is important to ensure that these devices remain accessible to people with disabilities,

S. K. Kane (✉)
Department of Computer Science, University of Colorado Boulder, Boulder, CO 80309, USA
e-mail: shaun.kane@colorado.edu

© Springer-Verlag London Ltd., part of Springer Nature 2019
Y. Yesilada and S. Harper (eds.), *Web Accessibility*, Human–Computer
Interaction Series, https://doi.org/10.1007/978-1-4471-7440-0_35

and to identify how these devices may be used to support individuals in becoming more independent. As wearable computing devices become more socially accepted and perhaps even expected, we must also ensure that these devices are designed in an inclusive and supportive way, and that they do not exclude or draw unwanted attention to users with disabilities.

In this chapter, we present an overview of the design of wearable computing devices, identify emerging trends in the research and design of accessible wearable computing devices, and offer suggestions for ensuring that wearable computing devices are accessible to all people.

35.2   Characteristics of Wearable Device Interaction

It may be tempting to consider wearable devices as simply an alternative form of common mobile devices such as smartphones and tablets. Indeed, modern wearable devices such as smartwatches and head-mounted displays are often based on the same technology as that used in other mobile devices. However, research has shown that the usage patterns for wearable devices are often quite different than those of other devices, and it is important that designers account for how these devices will be used if they wish to effectively design wearable device interactions.

For example, while early versions of smartwatch operating systems often focused on running applications on the watch itself, research has shown that interactions with apps comprise only about 2% of users' interactions with smartwatches, with considerably more time spent checking the time, reading notifications, and tracking physical activity (Pizza et al. 2016).

While the exact usage patterns of wearable device use will depend on the device, the user, and the context of use, research has shown some systematic differences in how wearable device use differs from the use of mobile devices:

Temporality. In many cases, interactions with wearable computing devices may involve interactions with quite different task durations and interaction frequency. For example, a recent study of smartwatch interaction patterns showed that the average interaction was completed within 6.7 s, while smartphone interactions average 38 s (Pizza et al. 2016). This difference may be due to differences in tasks being performed using a wearable device (e.g., checking the time or step count), as well as differences in the design of the hardware (e.g., displays that are only activated for a few seconds at a time).

Interaction modes. Perhaps due in part to the lack of traditional input methods such as keyboards, mice, and large touch screens, many wearable devices offer alternative interaction modes such as speech and gesture input, as well as haptic and text-to-speech output. It is good design practice to allow system actions to be performed using any of the available input modes. For example, an Apple Watch user can send a message to a friend by dictating the message, by writing out a message by drawing on the device's touch screen, or by choosing from a list of predefined messages. This multimodal interaction also supports accessibility, as some individuals may be unable to use a certain input mode due to their disability, but able to use one of the alternative input modes.

Contextual availability and reachability. As wearable devices are used in a variety of contexts, some features or interaction modes may be unavailable to the user in certain contexts. For example, a user of smart glasses may be unable to input voice commands while on a loud factory floor, or while seated during a theater performance. Similarly, at times the user of a wearable fitness device may be unable to view the device's display, such as if the device is worn underneath clothes, or if it is worn on the wrist while the user is carrying a heavy object.

Whether a device can be accessed also depends upon the user's physical capability to reach that device, and their preferred modes of interaction. For example, a user with a mobility impairment may have difficulty reaching nearby devices (Carrington et al. 2014b), and individuals who favor speech input may reduce device usage when in public spaces (Azenkot and Lee 2013).

Social acceptability. Use of specific computers, mobile devices, and assistive technologies can affect one's sense of self (see e.g., Kane et al. 2009), and it seems that this effect may be magnified for wearable computing devices. Using a wearable computing device in public can affect bystanders' opinion about the wearable device user (Profita et al. 2016a). Characteristics of the wearable device, such as its placement on the body and the mode of interacting with the device, can affect perceptions of the device and its wearer (Profita et al. 2013). Concerns about the social impacts of using devices in public may cause some users to reduce their use of that device in public, or to abandon the use of that device entirely (Kane et al. 2009; Shinohara and Wobbrock 2011).

35.3   A Taxonomy of Wearable Computing Devices

When designing a wearable computing device or application, one must consider a diverse set of factors, including the design of the hardware device itself, the features of the software application, and the modes of interaction between the user and the device. Furthermore, these decisions frequently interact with each other, such that making one choice can reduce choices along with other dimensions. For example, designing a wearable device that is positioned near the user's chest so as to accurately record heart rate, may prevent the device from being easily viewed by the wearer or interacted with using touch.

In this section, we introduce a taxonomy of design dimensions relevant to the design of wearable computing devices and applications (summarized in Table 35.1), and provide examples of how researchers and designers have successfully navigated these dimensions to create accessible wearable devices and applications. Later in this chapter, we will describe emerging trends and upcoming form factors for wearable devices.

Table 35.1 Design dimensions for contemporary wearable computing devices and applications. Devices may support one or more of the elements from each category

Location	Design	Function	Input	Output	Temporality
Head	Anthropomorphic	Computing	Touch	Haptic	Permanent
Torso	Subtle	Fitness	Voice	Speech	Every day
Arms	Stylish	Prosthetic	Motion	Audio	As needed
Legs	Hard materials	Sensory substitution	Activity		Occasional
Accessory	Soft materials	Rehabilitation			
		Guidance			
		Communication			

35.3.1 Location

Among the most significant design decisions related to wearable computing devices is its location on the body. The device's worn location can affect its available modes of interaction, sensing capabilities, size and weight requirements, overall functionality, social impact, and other factors. For example, the placement of a wearable device screen can affect the time needed to notice a visual alert (Harrison et al. 2009), while the location of a wearable touchpad affects whether bystanders see the device as being "normal" or "awkward" (Profita et al. 2013).

These decisions are often closely intertwined. For example, consider the Toyota BLAID, a collar-shaped wearable device to support independent navigation by blind and visually impaired people (Vanian 2016). BLAID's form factor carefully balances its design priorities. First, as the device uses cameras to track objects in the wearer's environment, it must be worn near the user's head so that it has a good view of the environment, and must be worn over any clothes so that the cameras are not occluded. Second, to provide audio and haptic feedback, the device must be placed at an easily reachable point on the body. In balancing these constraints, the designers of BLAID ultimately chose a form factor that wraps around the user's neck in a collar-like shape, providing the system with a clear view of the environment, and supporting touch input and audio and haptic output.

Common body locations for wearable computing devices are: the face, including smart glasses and head-mounted displays; the ears, including hearing aids, headphones, and "hearables" (Johansen et al. 2017); around the neck, such the Toyota BLAID (Vanian 2016); on the torso, such as some heart rate monitors; on the wrists, such as smart watches; on the hands, such as smart gloves (e.g., Huang et al. 2010); and on the legs, such as knee and leg braces (e.g., Ananthanarayan et al. 2013). Most wearable computing devices are designed to be worn on a single body location. Some devices, such as fitness trackers from Misfit Inc. (2018), consist of a modular "core" that can be placed inside different enclosures, such as a wristband, necklace, or simply placed in a pocket. Currently, this approach is optimal for fitness tracking devices, as these devices primarily track overall movement and have little need for displaying information to the user.

Recently, some researchers and designers have begun to consider accessory objects that are frequently used by some people with disabilities as wearable devices, even if they do not match traditional clothing items. Recently, Carrington et al. (2014b) coined the term *chairable technology* to refer to devices placed on or around a power wheelchair. These items, such as smart canes and wheelchair add-ons, share many of the same properties as wearable devices, including issues surrounding device reachability, the need for versatile interaction modes, and an impact on one's social perceptions.

35.3.2 Design and Materials

As all wearable computing systems involve some hardware component, choosing the overall design of the hardware may have significant impacts on adoption and use of the device.

In considering the design of wearable device hardware, especially for assistive devices for people with disabilities, the overall design esthetic for the device must be considered. Should an assistive wearable device attempt to blend in? Should it disguise itself as a mainstream device? Should the device draw attention, reflecting the user's pride in their identity? Wearable device designers have several options for the overall design esthetic of their device:

Anthropomorphic. The design of the assistive device mirrors that of the unaltered human body. This design approach may be most common for prosthetics, for which the design of the device might reflect the user's natural skin tone and body shape. Other wearable devices, such as hearing aids, may adopt the user's skin tone in order to be less conspicuous.

Subtle. The design of the device is intended to avoid attention and blend in with the wearer's clothing. The device may be made from transparent materials or dark colors, or may be hidden on the body. For example, some recent hearing aids take advantage of miniaturization to hide almost entirely behind the ear, showing only a small wire.

Stylish. The design of the device is intended to stand out and draw attention. The device may be larger in size than is necessary, and may be decorated with bright colors or patterns. Prior research that has examined how wearers of hearing aids and cochlear implants share images of their devices online illustrates strategies for decorating one's own assistive devices, including creating visual patterns, adding elements from jewelry, and adding characters or logos to share favorite media characters and sports teams (Profita et al. 2016b). The use of stylish and highly visible devices may serve several purposes, including communicating to others that the individual has a disability (perhaps causing them to adjust their expectations or communication strategy), showing off one's creativity, and demonstrating pride in one's disability.

In addition to the overall design theme of a wearable device, the materials used to create that device may also have a significant impact on the usability and perception of that device. Traditionally, wearable computing devices have followed design trends similar to other electronics in terms of materials (i.e., hard plastic and metal casing) and styles (i.e., black, white, or silver coloring). In recent years, some wearable computing devices have been designed using textiles and other soft materials (Profita et al. 2017). While these textile-based wearables present some trade-offs relative to traditional electronics, such as durability and the need to be washed, they may offer additional comfort, customization, and esthetic appeal that may lead to increased adoption of these devices.

35.3.3 Function

As wearable devices increasingly approach the capabilities and features of standalone computers, they are able to perform a wide variety of functions. However, wearable devices and applications that support people with disabilities often fall into a set of particular functional categories. Here we describe some of the more common functions for assistive wearable devices and applications:

Computing replacement. The wearable device replaces or augments an existing computing device, such as a personal computer or mobile device. This category of the device may feature functions such as mobile notifications or running simplified applications. Many mainstream wearable devices, such as smart watches, offer this functionality.

Fitness. The wearable device tracks exercise and other physical activities. These devices often provide an array of sensors, such as step counters and heart rate monitors. In the past, these devices have often been designed to track activities from typically abled users only, and were unable to track activities from other users such as wheelchair athletes (Carrington et al. 2015). However, mainstream fitness tracking devices have begun to integrate wheelchair activity tracking and more customizable tools for tracking physical activity.

Prosthetic. These devices, which include prosthetic replacements for limbs and other body parts, typically serve as functional or cosmetic replacements for missing limbs. While much research has focused on replacing the sensation, dexterity, and control of biological limbs, relatively little research has explored integrating wearable computing functionality into prosthetics. However, interest in developing prosthetics has recently been energized somewhat by the maker movement, as amateur creators have worked to design, fabricate, and distribute 3D-printed prosthetic limbs (Parry-Hill et al. 2017).

Sensory substitution and augmentation. Wearable devices can provide a sensory substitution for the users with sensory disabilities, relaying information about the environment in another medium. For example, visual information from a wearable device camera can be presented to a blind person as sonified audio (Ward and Meijer 2010) or by tactile patterns delivered to the tongue (Sampaio et al. 2001).

Wearable devices can also be used to augment the senses of users with disabilities. For example, head-mounted smart glasses have been used to represent colors as visual patterns for people with color blindness (Tanuwidjaja et al. 2014), to highlight objects of interest for people with low vision (Zhao et al. 2016), and to display the visual location of environmental sounds for deaf and hard of hearing people (Jain et al. 2015).

Rehabilitation. Wearable devices can also be used to guide individuals through rehabilitation activities, often to restore function that has been lost through some injury. For example, Pt Viz is a textile-based knee brace that uses embedded sensors to track and provide feedback on at-home knee rehabilitation exercises (Ananthanarayan et al. 2013).

Guidance. In addition to substituting one sense for another, wearable devices can assist people with disabilities by detecting information in the environment and providing the user with some instructions or guidance. For example, BLAID is a neck-worn device that uses cameras to recognize objects in the environment such as sidewalks, signs, and other landmarks (Vanian 2016). The user of BLAID can request directions to a specific location, and receives feedback in the form of audio instructions and haptic vibrations.

Communication. Wearable devices can also support individuals who experience difficulties communicating by acting as an augmentative and alternative communication (AAC) device. Benefits of wearable AAC technology include the ability to conform to different activities, including vigorous physical activity, as in some textile-based AAC devices (Profita 2012), and the ability to present communication prompts via a head-mounted private display (Williams et al. 2015).

35.3.4 Input Methods

As stated above, current wearable devices support a diverse set of input methods, including physical buttons, touch screens and surfaces, and voice commands. A user's choice of input method may depend on their physical capabilities (e.g., ability to reach and actuate a user interface), activity (e.g., whether they are carrying something or otherwise encumbered), and social context (e.g., whether they are in a public or private place). When possible, wearable devices should support multiple input methods for performing specific tasks.

In addition to these traditional forms of input, human–computer interaction researchers have explored other modes of wearable device input that may be useful in cases in which the user is physically or situationally constrained. These methods include "no-handed" techniques for controlling a device by moving other parts of the body, such as the feet (Heo et al. 2017), or through alternative input methods such as eye gaze (Esteves et al. 2015). Due to their proximity to the body, wearable devices are also a natural fit for tangible user interfaces (see Tangible Interfaces chapter).

35.3.5   Output Methods

As with input methods, many wearable devices provide a variety of output methods, including text-to-speech, nonspeech audio, and various forms of haptic feedback. Audio feedback may be delivered by traditional speakers, bone conduction speakers, or headphones. Haptic feedback is often delivered via vibration motors, although some recent devices, such as the Apple Watch, have incorporated linear actuators that provide more fine-grained control over haptic feedback. Other wearable device makers continue to explore new output methods, such as the Dot smartwatch (Dot 2018), which uses a small refreshable Braille display to provide Braille output.

When designing output methods for wearable devices and applications, several factors should be considered. First, of course, is the intelligibility of the feedback. Some forms of wearable device output, such as haptic feedback, can be difficult to identify or even to detect when a signal is present (Lee and Starner 2010). Conversely, in some cases, it may be important that feedback from a wearable device is subtle enough that it is not easily detected by anyone other than the wearable device user, as the user may not want others to know that they are receiving assistance from their device. A third consideration is situational awareness: as a wearable device may provide feedback at unexpected times, some users may be concerned that this feedback could reduce their awareness of the surrounding environment. For example, some blind people who use mobile GPS applications have reported wearing bone conduction headphones specifically because they do not occlude the wearer's ears (Kane et al. 2009).

35.3.6   Temporality

A final consideration in designing wearable devices and applications for people with disabilities is considering the frequency of use. How often is a given device used? Some devices may be used every day, such as a wheelchair, and thus may have stronger ties to the wearer's sense of self. Other devices may only be worn during certain activities, such as an artistically designed prosthetic leg, or a prosthetic hand adapter designed for an activity such as playing a musical instrument (Hofmann et al. 2016). Although there are no clear-cut rules for designing a wearable device for specific usage patterns, we might expect that everyday devices should be more versatile and customizable, while single-use devices may be more conspicuous.

A related consideration is the cost and ease of purchasing of a wearable device. For example, as fashionable eyeglasses have become affordable, some individuals now purchase multiple pairs of eyeglasses in different styles, enabling them to match their eyeglasses to their current mood or outfit (Said et al. 2014). Conversely, as hearing aids are often prohibitively expensive, many hearing aid wearers own only one pair of hearing aids, but may instead customize their appearance through colored device cases, stickers, or other temporary decorations (Profita et al. 2016a, b).

35.4   Future Directions

In this section, we describe several emerging trends related to the development of wearable computing devices, and the increasing intersection of mainstream wearable computing devices and assistive technologies for people with disabilities.

35.4.1   New Input and Output Techniques

Along with improvements to processing power, wireless connectivity, and battery life, new models of mobile and wearable technologies are often enhanced through the addition of new sensors and actuators that can support more robust input and output methods. Recent smartphones and smartwatches have incorporated technologies such as pressure-sensing touch screens and 3D camera-based facial recognition. These new interaction methods may enhance the user experience for typical users, but may have even more significant benefits for people with disabilities. For example, pressure-based touch input, similar to that found in recent touch screens, has been shown to be useful in increasing accessibility for people with motor impairments (Carrington et al. 2014a). One opportunity for the designers of wearable devices and applications is to identify new input and output modalities that can be marketable to the general population, while also supporting new forms of accessible interaction for people with disabilities.

35.4.2   Device Personalization

Research has shown that customizing one's assistive technologies can have an impact on how the user sees the technology, how others see the user, and how the user sees themselves (Hofmann et al. 2016; Profita et al. 2016a, b). These studies have shown that off-the-shelf technologies do not always meet users' needs, and that users see some value in personalizing and customizing their devices.

Currently, there exists relatively little support for personalizing and customizing devices, and users of wearable assistive technology sometimes resort to do-it-yourself techniques to customize their devices (Profita et al. 2016a, b). Recognizing that wearable devices are quickly becoming a fashion item, many smartwatch and fitness tracker manufacturers have begun to offer a range of colorful bands and other accessories for their devices. This form of device customization has been further extended by several companies. For example, the Misfit fitness tracker (Misfit Inc. 2018) can be customized at purchase time with several different device shapes and materials, including colorful plastic devices, metallic devices, and even bejeweled devices, each of which can be paired with wristbands or necklaces in a variety of colors and materials. Similarly, UNYQ (Unyq Inc. 2018) enables wearers of leg prostheses to create customized prosthetic covers using a variety of materials, colors, and patterns. Developing new approaches to customizing and personalizing wearable devices could increase the adoption and use of these devices.

35.4.3   Prototyping Toolkits

Designing wearable technology requires considering many issues: hardware form factor, materials, esthetic appearance, computing capabilities, sensors, interaction techniques, application software, and others, resulting in a design process that is extremely complex. Furthermore, as modern wearable technologies rely heavily upon miniaturized components and assembly processes, it is difficult to create realistic prototypes that match both the form factor and functionality of a finished product. Prior research has explored the use of modular electronics kits for quickly prototyping wearable devices (Williams et al. 2015); however, prototypes created using these toolkits differ in several ways from a completed product. As participation from people with disabilities is important throughout the design process, there is great value in exploring techniques for prototyping and testing wearable devices.

35.4.4   Social Acceptability and Policy

The proliferation of wearable computing devices has raised some alarm from various communities and organizations, especially regarding the risks to privacy that may be caused by the presence of ubiquitous recording devices. As an example, the Google Glass head-mounted computer was banned in numerous locations even before it had been widely launched (Gray 2013). Tension over the use of wearable computing devices in public may be harmful to people with disabilities who might otherwise benefit from the use of these devices.

Prior research into the perceptions surrounding mobile device use has shown that, while bystanders may generally have negative attitudes about the use of wearable devices in public spaces, they may have a more positive attitude if they learn that the wearable device user is using the device for accessibility reasons (Profita et al. 2016a, b). The tensions between negative attitudes about wearable computing use, the acceptability of wearable computers for accessibility, and the privacy of any individual wearable device user, is still somewhat unclear, and further research is needed to understand how these tensions might be addressed.

In addition to the potential social repercussions of using wearable computing devices in public, changes in policy that are meant to exclude "recreational" use of wearable devices may cause harm to people with disabilities who benefit from these devices. Addressing this tension between individual privacy and reasonable accommodation for people with disabilities will likely require a new policy that takes into account the benefits and harms of wearable device use in public spaces (Kirkham 2015).

35.5 Design Guidelines

Based on prior research described earlier in this chapter, following these design guidelines may help to ensure that future wearable devices are accessible to end users with disabilities:

Leverage mainstream device platforms when possible. Prior research has shown that people with disabilities often prefer mainstream technologies to specialized assistive technology, even when the assistive technology is optimized for their own abilities. People with disabilities have identified several reasons for preferring mainstream technologies, including lower cast, better availability, higher reliability, and the ability to blend in with others (Kane et al. 2009).

Design hardware and software in collaboration with end users. It is well established that including end users in the design process can lead to more usable and inclusive designs. Because wearable computing involves designing both hardware and software, it is important to involve users in all aspects of system design. There exists an opportunity to explore new prototyping techniques to help guide the development of wearable hardware form factors throughout the development process.

Support robust device placement and interaction methods. By design, many wearable devices are already designed to support users with different physical characteristics, from left- and right-handedness to different sizes of body parts. Ensure that wearable devices and applications support diverse input methods and placement locations. People with disabilities may further subvert expectations about how to use a specific wearable device, such as by wearing them on a different part of the body or even by attaching them to a wheelchair or other assistive device.

Support modular designs and decoration. The appearance of a wearable assistive device can significantly impact the wearer's feelings about the device, and may even impact how the wearer sees themselves (Kane et al. 2009; Shinohara and Wobbrock 2011). Furthermore, the ability to choose the appearance of one's own device can instill further positive feelings in the wearer (Profita et al. 2016a, b). When possible, wearable devices should offer multiple possible designs, or should support end user customization or decoration.

35.6 Author's Opinion of the Field

Wearables are an active and exciting area for innovating in assistive technology. Today's wearable computing platforms enable us to create small computing devices that accept various types of user input and that can connect to the Web and other data sources, making them an ideal platform for assistive devices. As advances in computing technology enable the creation of higher performing and longer lasting devices, assistive technology designers will have even more opportunities to create new and better devices.

However, despite these improvements in technology, the role of wearables in our everyday lives is still in flux. Commercial wearable devices are still limited to a small number of form factors, while other wearable devices primarily exist as DIY prototypes (see chapter on Fabrication, 3D Printing, and Making). Social norms around the use of wearables are still developing, and in some cases, such as in the introduction of Google Glass, the use of wearable devices in public has caused a backlash. As these devices become more common, it seems likely that social norms will develop to include them, and it is possible that broader acceptance of wearable computing devices will also result in broader acceptance of assistive technologies.

35.7   Conclusion

As wearable computing devices become more popular within mainstream technology culture, they offer new opportunities to support the independence of people with disabilities. Conducting an inclusive design process that involves end users in the design of wearable device hardware and software, supporting modular form factors, and considering the social aspects of wearable device use will help to ensure that wearable computing devices will be accessible to individuals of all abilities.

References

Ananthanarayan S, Sheh M, Chien A, Profita H, Siek K (2013) Pt viz: towards a wearable device for visualizing knee rehabilitation exercises. In: Proceedings of the SIGCHI conference on human factors in computing systems. ACM, New York, NY, USA, pp 1247–1250. https://doi.org/10.1145/2470654.2466161

Azenkot S, Lee NB (2013) Exploring the use of speech input by blind people on mobile devices. In: Proceedings of the 15th international ACM SIGACCESS conference on computers and accessibility. ACM, Article 11, 8 p. https://dx.doi.org/10.1145/2513383.2513440

Carrington P, Hurst A, Kane SK (2014a) The gest-rest: a pressure-sensitive chairable input pad for power wheelchair armrests. In: Proceedings of the 16th international ACM SIGACCESS conference on computers & accessibility. ACM, New York, NY, USA, pp 201–208. https://doi.org/10.1145/2661334.2661374

Carrington P, Hurst A, Kane SK (2014b) Wearables and chairables: inclusive design of mobile input and output techniques for power wheelchair users. In: Proceedings of the SIGCHI conference on human factors in computing systems. ACM, New York, NY, USA, pp 3103–3112. https://doi.org/10.1145/2556288.2557237

Carrington P, Chang K, Mentis H, Hurst A (2015) "But, I don't take steps": examining the inaccessibility of fitness trackers for wheelchair athletes. In: Proceedings of the 17th international ACM SIGACCESS conference on computers & accessibility. ACM, New York, NY, USA, pp 193–201. https://doi.org/10.1145/2700648.2809845

Dot (2018) Dot watch. https://dotincorp.com/. Accessed 2 July 2018

Esteves A, Velloso E, Bulling A, Gellersen H (2015) Orbits: gaze interaction for smart watches using smooth pursuit eye movements. In: Proceedings of the 28th annual ACM symposium on user interface software & technology. ACM, pp 457–466

Gray R (2013) The places where Google Glass is banned. https://www.telegraph.co.uk/technology/google/10494231/The-places-where-Google-Glass-is-banned.html

Harrison C, Lim BY, Shick A, Hudson SE (2009) Where to locate wearable displays?: reaction time performance of visual alerts from tip to toe. In: Proceedings of the SIGCHI conference on human factors in computing systems. ACM, New York, NY, USA, pp 941–944. https://doi.org/10.1145/1518701.1518845

Heo S, Annett M, Lafreniere B, Grossman T, Fitzmaurice G (2017) No need to stop what you're doing: exploring no-handed smartwatch interaction. In: Proceedings of the 43rd graphics interface conference. Canadian Human-Computer Communications Society, School of Computer Science, University of Waterloo, Waterloo, Ontario, Canada, pp 107–114. https://doi.org/10.20380/GI2017.14

Hofmann M, Harris J, Hudson SE, Mankoff J (2016) Helping hands: requirements for a prototyping methodology for upper-limb prosthetics users. In: Proceedings of the 2016 CHI conference on human factors in computing systems. ACM, New York, NY, USA, pp 1769–1780. https://doi.org/10.1145/2858036.2858340

Huang K, Starner T, Do E, Weinberg G, Kohlsdorf D, Ahlrichs C, Leibrandt R (2010) Mobile music touch: mobile tactile stimulation for passive learning. In: Proceedings of the SIGCHI conference on human factors in computing systems. ACM, pp 791–800

Jain D, Findlater L, Gilkeson J, Holland B, Duraiswami R, Zotkin D, Vogler C, Froehlich JE (2015) Head-mounted display visualizations to support sound awareness for the deaf and hard of hearing. In: Proceedings of the 33rd annual ACM conference on human factors in computing systems. ACM, New York, NY, USA, pp 241–250. https://doi.org/10.1145/2702123.2702393

Johansen B, Flet-Berliac YPR, Korzepa MJ, Sandholm P, Pontoppidan NH, Petersen MK, Larsen JE (2017) Hearables in hearing care: discovering usage patterns through IoT devices. In: Universal access in human–computer interaction. Human and technological environments. Springer, Cham, pp 39–49. https://doi.org/10.1007/978-3-319-58700-4_4

Kane SK, Jayant C, Wobbrock JO, Ladner RE (2009) Freedom to roam: a study of mobile device adoption and accessibility for people with visual and motor disabilities. In: Proceedings of the 11th international ACM SIGACCESS conference on computers and accessibility. ACM, New York, NY, USA, pp 115–122. https://doi.org/10.1145/1639642.1639663

Kirkham R (2015) Can disability discrimination law expand the availability of wearable computers? Computer 48(6):25–33. https://doi.org/10.1109/MC.2015.167

Lee SC, Starner T (2010) BuzzWear: alert perception in wearable tactile displays on the wrist. In: Proceedings of the SIGCHI conference on human factors in computing systems. ACM, New York, NY, USA, pp 433–442. https://doi.org/10.1145/1753326.1753392

Misfit Inc. (2018) Smartwatches, fitness trackers & wearable technology—Misfit. https://misfit.com/. Accessed 2 July 2018

Park W (2015) The geniuses who invented prosthetic limbs. http://www.bbc.com/future/story/20151030-the-geniuses-who-invented-prosthetic-limbs. Accessed 2 July 2018

Parry-Hill J, Shih PC, Mankoff J, Ashbrook D (2017) Understanding volunteer AT fabricators: opportunities and challenges in DIY-AT for others in e-NABLE. In: Proceedings of the 2017 CHI conference on human factors in computing systems. ACM, New York, NY, USA, pp 6184–6194. https://doi.org/10.1145/3025453.3026045

Pizza S, Brown B, McMillan D, Lampinen A (2016) Smartwatch in vivo. In: Proceedings of the 2016 CHI conference on human factors in computing systems. ACM, New York, NY, USA, pp 5456–5469. https://doi.org/10.1145/2858036.2858522

Profita HP (2012) An electronic-textile wearable communication board for individuals with autism engaged in horse therapy. In: Proceedings of the 14th international ACM SIGACCESS conference on computers and accessibility. ACM, New York, NY, USA, pp 231–232. https://doi.org/10.1145/2384916.2384968

Profita HP, Clawson J, Gilliland S, Zeagler C, Starner T, Budd J, Do EY-L (2013) Don't mind me touching my wrist: a case study of interacting with on-body technology in public. In: Proceedings of the 2013 international symposium on wearable computers. ACM, New York, NY, USA, pp. 89–96. https://doi.org/10.1145/2493988.2494331

Profita HP, Albaghli R, Findlater L, Jaeger P, Kane SK (2016a) The AT effect: how disability affects the perceived social acceptability of head-mounted display use. In: Proceedings of the 2016 CHI conference on human factors in computing systems. ACM, New York, NY, USA, pp 4884–4895. https://doi.org/10.1145/2858036.2858130

Profita HP, Stangl A, Matuszewska L, Sky S, Kane SK (2016b) Nothing to hide: aesthetic customization of hearing aids and cochlear implants in an online community. In: Proceedings of the 18th international ACM SIGACCESS conference on computers and accessibility. ACM, New York, NY, USA, pp 219–227. https://doi.org/10.1145/2982142.2982159

Profita HP, Lightner M, Correll N, Kane SK (2017) Textile-based wearables. http://scholarworks.calstate.edu/handle/10211.3/190201

Said K, Burton MA, Hurst A, Kane SK (2014) Framing the conversation: the role of Facebook conversations in shopping for eyeglasses. In: Proceedings of the 17th ACM conference on computer supported cooperative work & social computing. ACM, New York, NY, USA, pp 652–661. https://doi.org/10.1145/2531602.2531683

Sampaio E, Maris S, Bach-y-Rita P (2001) Brain plasticity:'visual'acuity of blind persons via the tongue. Brain Res 908(2):204–207

Shinohara K, Wobbrock JO (2011) In the shadow of misperception: assistive technology use and social interactions. In: Proceedings of the SIGCHI conference on human factors in computing systems. ACM, New York, NY, USA, pp 705–714. https://doi.org/10.1145/1978942.1979044

Tanuwidjaja E, Huynh D, Koa K, Nguyen C, Shao C, Torbett P, Emmenegger C, Weibel N (2014) Chroma: a wearable augmented-reality solution for color blindness. In: Proceedings of the 2014 ACM international joint conference on pervasive and ubiquitous computing. ACM, New York, NY, USA, pp 799–810. https://doi.org/10.1145/2632048.2632091

Unyq Inc. (2018) Unyq. http://unyq.com/us/. Accessed 2 July 2018

Vanian J (2016) Toyota is building a wearable device for the blind. http://fortune.com/2016/03/07/toyota-wearable-device-blind/. Accessed 2 July 2018

Ward J, Meijer P (2010) Visual experiences in the blind induced by an auditory sensory substitution device. Conscious Cogn 19(1):492–500. https://doi.org/10.1016/j.concog.2009.10.006

Williams K, Moffatt K, McCall D, Findlater L (2015) Designing conversation cues on a head-worn display to support persons with aphasia. In: Proceedings of the 33rd annual ACM conference on human factors in computing systems. ACM, New York, NY, USA, pp 231–240. https://doi.org/10.1145/2702123.2702484

Williams MA, Buehler E, Hurst A, Kane SK (2015) What not to wearable: using participatory workshops to explore wearable device form factors for blind users. In: Proceedings of the 12th web for all conference. ACM, Article 31, 4 p. https://doi.org/10.1145/2745555.2746664

Zhao Y, Szpiro S, Knighten J, Azenkot S (2016) CueSee: exploring visual cues for people with low vision to facilitate a visual search task. In: Proceedings of the 2016 ACM international joint conference on pervasive and ubiquitous computing. ACM, New York, NY, USA, pp 73–84. https://doi.org/10.1145/2971648.2971730

Chapter 36
Tangible Interfaces

Mark S. Baldwin, Rushil Khurana, Duncan McIsaac, Yuqian Sun,
Tracy Tran, Xiaoyi Zhang, James Fogarty, Gillian R. Hayes
and Jennifer Mankoff

Abstract Tangible interfaces are a method of computer interaction that supports communication through the human kinesthetic system, a network of sensory inputs and outputs that allow the body to perceive the physical world. By leveraging the physical properties of objects identified by the kinesthetic system, a tangible interface makes it possible to interact with computational information more naturally than the traditional computer mouse and keyboard. Tangible interaction enables individuals with a range of abilities to use technologies in the same way. In this chapter, we explore the role of tangibility as an assistive technology. We summarize three projects completed by the authors that demonstrate novel ways of deploying tangible interfaces.

M. S. Baldwin (✉) · G. R. Hayes
University of California, Irvine, CA, USA
e-mail: baldwinm@uci.edu

G. R. Hayes
e-mail: gillianrh@ics.uci.edu

R. Khurana · D. McIsaac
Carnegie Mellon University, Pittsburgh, PA, USA
e-mail: rushil@cmu.edu

D. McIsaac
e-mail: dbmcisaac1@gmail.com

Y. Sun · T. Tran · X. Zhang · J. Fogarty · J. Mankoff
University of Washington, Seattle, WA, USA
e-mail: ys47@cs.washington.edu

T. Tran
e-mail: tracyt28@cs.washington.edu

X. Zhang
e-mail: xiaoyiz@cs.washington.edu

J. Fogarty
e-mail: jfogarty@cs.washington.edu

J. Mankoff
e-mail: jmankoff@cs.washington.edu

© Springer-Verlag London Ltd., part of Springer Nature 2019
Y. Yesilada and S. Harper (eds.), *Web Accessibility*, Human–Computer
Interaction Series, https://doi.org/10.1007/978-1-4471-7440-0_36

36.1   Introduction

Making computers accessible poses a significant challenge for researchers and creators of technological systems. When one or more sensory modalities (e.g., vision, audition, and kinesthetic) are impaired, the assumptions of mainstream computational interfaces may be violated, making interaction problematic. Assistive technologies compensate by supporting interaction through a secondary modality. For example, a blind user can interact with a computing system through text-to-speech, a deaf person can interact with auditory information through speech-to-text, and a person with mobility impairment can interact through facial expression. Unfortunately, computational systems are not designed to be operated through a secondary modality, requiring complex workarounds to ensure access. One way to compensate for the absence of primary modality is to augment interaction through multiple secondary modalities.

Tangible interfaces hold promise as tools capable of expanding the ways in which people interact with technology. While computer interfaces designed for the visual and auditory channels remain siloed by modality, a tangible interface is capable of intersecting multiple modalities, allowing its operation to be functionally identical for a range of abilities. In this chapter, we explore the role of tangible interfaces in accessible computing. We start with a brief overview of the history of tangible interfaces followed by a review of the literature. We then report on three exemplary works completed by the authors that explore ways in which tangible interfaces can be used to improve accessible computing. In the first example (Sect. 36.5), we report on the Tangible Desktop, a set of physical devices designed to address some of the challenges faced by blind and low-vision computer users (Baldwin et al. 2017). In the second example (Sect. 36.6), we report on the design and evaluation of SPRITEs, a two-dimensional navigation method that integrates with a keyboard surface (Khurana et al. 2018). In the third example (Sect. 36.7), we report on Interactiles, an unpowered system that enhances tactile interaction on Android touchscreen phones (Zhang et al. 2018). This chapter summarizes these three systems and their previously published evaluation results, discussing an analysis of these three approaches as they relate to and differ from one another.

36.2   What Is a Tangible Interface

Tangibility broadly refers to the ability to manipulate an object through touch. The touch modality is commonly associated with cutaneous and kinesthetic receptors that provide the body with awareness of the size, shape, location, and temperature of physical objects (Klatzky and Lederman 2003). Collectively, these attributes can be used as points of interaction with computational systems to change the state of the system or notify the user of changes to system state. By this definition, the traditional keyboard and mouse can be thought of as tangible interfaces. However, the notion of a tangible interface has evolved to include some level of interaction beyond what occurs through these standard mechanisms for input and output.

Perhaps the most recognized example of a tangible interface that incorporates these principles is the Marble Answering Machine (Bishop 1992). Durell Bishop designed a device for the capture and playback of auditory messages that was controlled through the physical manipulation of glass marbles. When a message was left with the device, it would release a marble into a tray. When the receiver of the message was ready to listen to it, they would remove the marble from the tray and place it back in the machine, triggering message playback. The incorporation of physicality (moving the marble) and information display (the tray of marbles) embody the core properties of a tangible interface—the physical manipulation of the system is directly paired with its system state.

Acknowledging the value of tangible manipulation in systems like the Marble Answering Machine, Ishii and Ullmer formally bridged the digital and physical worlds through a concept they titled "Tangible Bits" (Ishii and Ullmer 1997). Through three interactive prototype systems, they demonstrated how the multisensory experience could enhance human–computer interactions by merging everyday objects and their properties with digital information. The introduction of Tangible Bits ushered forth an era of research focused on bridging the digital world with the physical world. Until recently, technological constraints (e.g., processing power, connectivity, and size) have been one of the largest barriers to widespread adoption of tangible interfaces. Ishii and Ullmer's tangible prototypes were room-sized, intricately connected systems built using bulky, expensive tools. Today, many of the features that Tangible Bits promised can be achieved through palm-sized devices like tablets and smartphones, giving rise to promising commercially available tangible systems.[1]

36.3 Benefits of Tangible Interaction

The human sensory perception system is a powerful tool for interacting with and manipulating objects within the physical world. Humankind's sociocultural heritage is built upon the development and enrichment of physical artifacts through which the modern world has been created. Tool use plays a critical role in how humans learn, build, and interact with the world (Kaptelinin and Nardi 2006).

As tools have moved from physical to digital artifacts, the use of metaphor has played a critical role in guiding the transition. Familiar objects from the physical world have been used as visual cues to explain how digital artifacts should be acted upon and expected to behave (e.g., visual ridges to infer draggability). The success of the graphical user interface demonstrates the power that metaphor has on

---

[1] https://palettegear.com, https://www.microsoft.com/en-us/surface/accessories/surface-dial.

human comprehension, yet the graphical interface alone is incapable of harnessing the expressiveness of tangible objects. In his taxonomy for tangible interfaces, Fishkin argues that physical tangibility broadens the range of metaphorical interaction, eliciting how "a designer can use the shape, the size, the color, the weight, the smell, and the texture of the object to invoke any number of metaphorical links (Fishkin 2004)."

The physical properties that define a tangible interaction promote a natural system of constraints. Shaer et al., identify the constraints of a physical object as guide to understanding its behavior (Shaer et al. 2004). For example, a glass ball is constrained by the physical hardness of its surface, removing compression as a method of interaction. Whereas a rubber ball is malleable, affording compression as a possible method of interaction. Working with both ball materials in a tangible interface, a user can intuit different roles for each by understanding their constraints.

36.4 Tangible Interfaces for Assistive Technology

Tangibility plays an important role within the field of assistive technology, providing an alternative mode of interaction to augment the reduced capacity of one or more human sensory modalities. For example, the output of the marble answering machine discussed earlier, a tray of marbles, is simultaneously capable of communicating its status visually and tactilely. Tangible interaction enables people with a range of disabilities to engage with technological systems that would otherwise be difficult or impossible to use (Chang et al. 2002).

Perhaps the most common example of tangible assistive technology is Braille, an alphabet consisting of raised dots that can be read with the fingers. A commonly used, computational Braille device is the BrailleNote.[2] The BrailleNote combines a braille keyboard (a specialized arrangement of keys used for generating braille characters), refreshable braille display, and file storage capabilities into a single, portable device. The familiarity of braille has led others to explore its role beyond text description. Prescher et al., use a large braille pin display to map the entities found in a graphical display for tactile input and output (Prescher et al. 2010). The same display was later used to drive an interactive drawing environment as a way to teach graphical concepts to blind students (Bornschein et al. 2018). Although both studies discovered interesting ways to communicate visual concepts to blind users, the device they relied on, called the BrailleDis9000, is prohibitively expensive. High costs and device abandonment have likely contributed to the absence of diversity in tangible interfaces for assistive technologies (Hurst and Kane 2013).

More recently, innovations in do-it-yourself (DIY) technologies like 3D printing and low-cost microelectronics have led to a rich atmosphere for creating assistive technologies (Hurst and Tobias 2011). The field of assistive technology faces a variety of challenges, leading researchers to design tangible interfaces for a variety of

---

[2]http://www.humanware.com/en-usa/products/blindness/braillenotes.

domains. Tangible interfaces have been used to support navigation (Ducasse et al. 2016), learning (Stangl et al. 2015; Shi et al. 2017), and adaptation of non-assistive technologies (Guo et al. 2016). In a multiphase study, Tanaka and Parkinson worked closely with blind audio engineers to create a dynamically operated tangible interface for interpreting audio waveforms (Tanaka and Parkinson 2016). They found that by designing for the direct manipulation of sound, rather than mapping to an existing graphical interface, participants found their system intuitive to learn and use.

Although the space for tangible interfaces in assistive technology is diverse, very little work has explored the role of tangibility for the web. In the following three sections, we will present our contributions to this area through a summary of our work on web-based tangible interaction.

36.5 The Tangible Desktop: A Tangible Interface for Desktop Computing

Tactile interaction makes it possible to replace the ephemeral nature of the audio stream with a permanence similar to that of a graphical display. We set out to explore this space by creating peripheral devices that target two common desktop computer activities required for almost all computer use: switching and locating. Our "Tangible Desktop" system is comprised of physical implementations of the computer taskbar and application window scrollbar that were built with inexpensive rapid prototyping tools. In this section, we describe the potential design space for tangible interactions as well as our prototype system developed to test out that design space.

36.5.1 Field Study

To better understand challenges in nonvisual computing, we conducted a field study at Empowertech, a Los Angeles-based nonprofit organization that offers computer training and education for people with disabilities. Over a 4-month period, the first author participated in a blind and low-vision computer skills training class, observing student activity as well as providing general teaching assistance when required. In addition to learning how to use assistive tools like a screen reader and screen magnifier, students were taught basic computer productivity skills. A significant portion of the course material was focused on Internet browsing and basic web browser use. Analysis of the data collected from the field study revealed numerous challenges that blind and low-vision users face when learning to use computers.

Importance of productive web use: Blind and low-vision individuals need computer skills to support their independence as the services that they rely on become increasingly web dependent. The students we observed were enrolled in the class for a variety of reasons. For some, attendance was part of state-funded process to help people with disability secure work. For others, the class was an opportunity to stay active with technology as they transitioned from visual to nonvisual computer use. While all students acknowledged computer skills would add independence to their daily lives, the diversity of motivation increased the friction between user and assistive tool as they attempted to accomplish basic computer tasks. Although all students struggled to navigate through the challenges surrounding screen reader use, those who saw a clear path for their lives beyond the class were better prepared to manage the friction. Others struggled to see the value in learning how to complete the web-based tasks taught in the class. These tensions highlight the importance of productive web use for the blind and low-vision community.

Demands of memorization: Operating a screen reader requires an excessive amount of command memorization. In lieu of the point and click interaction on which sighted computer users rely, nonvisual screen reader use is dependent on keyboard input commands. Encapsulating all of the actions required to perform visually oriented computing tasks for an audio-only interface increases the commands required to perform similar actions through direct manipulation. To accommodate the demands of memorization, students were given audio recorders to record and playback the command shortcuts provided by the instructor. The dependence on this type of secondary assistive device points to the complexities of learning audio-only interfaces. Not only do users have to memorize the commands for the screen reader, but they also have to navigate a complex suite of software applications to complete their tasks. For example, the class instructor routinely emphasized the importance of learning how to use multiple web browsers as some are better at certain tasks than others. From the perspective of an audio-based computer interface, particularly one that is designed to interact with content and applications built for sighted users, memorization is unavoidable.

Better two-way communication: Navigating the complex structures of graphical systems through ephemeral auditory cues impose frequent challenges on users. Even with a reasonable amount of keyboard commands memorized, locating information on screen remained challenging for the students we observed. A common tactic employed by the students was to use the basic navigation controls like the tab and arrow keys to move between elements sequentially. Although effective when content is well structured and limited in size, this approach quickly breaks down as the complexity of content increases. We observed students who assumed they had exhaustively scanned a page when in actuality the information that they desired was unreachable by the commands they were using. Even when information could be located, subsequent visits to the same content required the scanning procedure to be repeated again. Thus, it became clear to us during this fieldwork that two-way communication with the computer, would be required, rather than the parallel but unidirectional flow of keyboard-only input and auditory-only output.

Through our field study, we recognized the difficulties that memorization and auditory information processing present for novice blind and low-vision users. While a nonvisual system will always have to rely on audio in some capacity, we wanted to

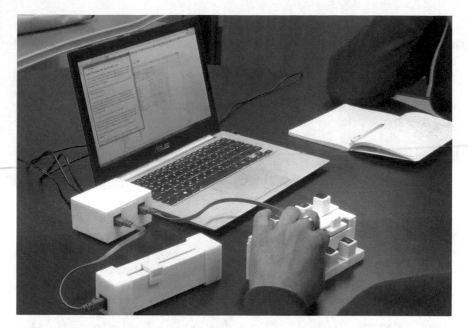

Fig. 36.1 Here the Tangible Desktop is connected to a laptop in a typical configuration. The subject is moving a physical icon to the taskbar to open its associated application. To the right is the Tangible Scrollbar. Both devices are connected to the laptop through a central hub that supplies power and communications over USB

explore alternative input and output strategies that might reduce the amount of command memorization and auditory information required to interact with a computer.

36.5.2   Development of the Tangible Desktop

The Tangible Desktop is designed to probe how tangible interaction might improve computer interfaces for nonvisual access. It is comprised of a set of two physical devices designed to work in coordination to support opening, closing, switching, and scrolling within a windowing desktop environment (see Fig. 36.1). Preliminary conceptual models of the Tangible Desktop were focused on the reappropriation of the visual metaphors that contributed to the success of the graphical user interface (GUI). Just as graphics and iconography within the GUI were designed to mimic physical objects in the real world (e.g., desk blotter, waste bin, and printer), we based our tangible devices on physical representations of graphical objects.

The Tangible Desktop is comprised of three individual tangible components: physical icons, a taskbar, and a scrollbar. The physical icons represent a single computational entity such as a web page, file, folder or application. The taskbar manages the state of each icon enabling a user to tangibly open, close, and switch to the entity associated with an icon. The scrollbar provides support for content traversal through a fixed linear motion. In addition to the tangible interaction offered by the physical format, the taskbar and scrollbar also produce vibrotactile effects to communicate some semantic information haptically to the user. Coordination between the components of the Tangible Desktop is managed by software running on the host computer. The software is responsible for communicating with the hardware and the host operating system.

36.5.3 Using the Tangible Desktop

The following vignette demonstrates a typical usage scenario for the Tangible Desktop:

> Sarah sits down at her desk to continue working on a paper for class. She locates the icon that she had previously associated with her paper and places it in an open slot on the taskbar. She then moves the slide thumb on the taskbar to the position of the new icon. The taskbar recognizes the icon and opens the paper. Sarah needs to finish section four of her paper, so using the scrollbar she moves the slide thumb quickly from left to right counting each vibration along the way. After the fourth vibration she stops moving the slide thumb, switching to her keyboard and screen reader to navigate the rest of the way.

In this scenario, most of the preliminary steps required to begin working on a computer, typically managed through keyboard input and audio output, have been replaced with direct tangible interaction. For example, using a traditional screen reader, opening an existing file requires several keyboard-driven tasks. An individual must first open a file browser or the existing file menu from the desired application, navigate to the file, and select it. Each step requires existing knowledge of which keys to press as well as auditory processing of the screen reader's response to each step. Certainly, through practice, each of these steps can and will become routine, at least for frequently used files. However, by placing the task in the physical world, each step can be combined into a single tangible interaction.

As we developed the Tangible Desktop, we recognized the potential ability of tangible interactions to reduce the amount of audio that screen reader-based environment must output to communicate system state. For our formative evaluation of the Tangible Desktop, we developed a custom web browser with text-to-speech capabilities to support a reduction in audio. By interacting directly with a web browser, we leveraged the openness of web-based documents to capture, parse, and modify document contents as they are rendered. A traditional screen reader communicates web page structure (*i.e., menus, links, headers, and lists*) inline with content. The structural information guides users through the page, providing knowledge about how to interpret and act upon content. Rather than auditorily communicate structural information, our custom browser sends structural information to the Tangible

Desktop to be rendered as tactile information. By separating page content from its structure, the system is able to communicate across two input channels, tactile and auditory, rather than one.

36.5.4 Validation of the Tangible Desktop

For our evaluation study, we mapped our physical icons to individual web pages created for the study, the taskbar was used to switch between each web page, and the scrollbar was used to navigate the selected web page. The results of our study indicated that the introduction of tangible interaction to screen reader use can provide a significant increase in productivity. On average, screen reader participants completed their tasks in 10.05 min with the experimental system as compared to 16.49 min using their own systems, an improvement of 39.0% ($(16.49 - 10.05)/16.49 = .390$), $t(5) = 4.94$, $p < 0.01$ (see Fig. 36.2).

In post-study interviews, participants commented on how much easier they thought using the Tangible Desktop was compared to just the keyboard. Their responses align closely with the established benefits of tangible interfaces like increased reasoning through representation and motor memory (Klemmer et al. 2006). In particular, participants described their sense of touch as a critical tool

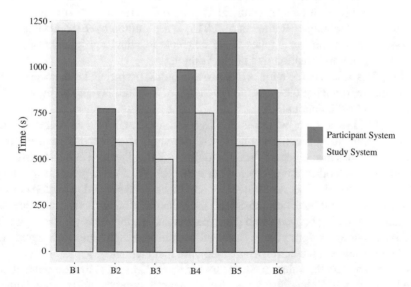

Fig. 36.2 Task completion time comparison between the participant system and experimental system for each participant. Completion times are total elapsed time, so we have not included error bars

for understanding the world. The one-to-one mapping of physical to computational space (e.g., physical icon to web page) gave participants an object to actively manipulate to comprehend their environment.

36.6   SPRITEs: Tangibility at the Keyboard Surface

While the Tangible Desktop provided strong evidence for the importance of tangibility, its form factor lacks portability, and its production is not necessarily easy to scale. In this subsection, we explore a different, more deployable approach by leveraging a device that blind users use every day—the keyboard. The keyboard is not normally thought of as a pointer or mapped directly onto interactive elements on the screen. However, it can be used for spatial interaction. There are typically 90 tangibly distinct keys on most keyboards, laid out (approximately) in a two-dimensional (2D) grid. In addition, unlike other tangible interfaces, a keyboard is essentially free (since every desktop and laptop already has one).

We call our approach SPRITEs (spatially region interaction techniques), and here we summarize (Khurana et al. 2018). SPRITEs build on past work exploring spatial interaction techniques such as gesturing, using keyboards, for sighted users (e.g., Taylor et al. 2014; Zhang and Li 2014). For example, GestKeyboard uses the keyboard surface to enable touchscreen like gestures on an ordinary keyboard (Zhang and Li 2014) while Taylor et al.'s mechanical keyboard (Taylor et al. 2014) and Ramos et al.'s fingers technique (Ramos et al. 2016) sense motion over the keys using IR sensors. However, neither applies these concepts to nonvisual interaction, nor to providing spatial information in a tactile fashion.

SPRITE is a suite of techniques that provide quick, usable, and rich access to web GUIs, thus reproducing the perceptual benefits of a spatial layout for sighted users for a non-sighted individual.

The SPRITEs system, which is deployable on commodity hardware, provides holistic support for a specific domain web browsing. Thus, we designed the interaction techniques available in SPRITEs to function together as a cohesive whole, in concert with each other and a screen reader. The SPRITEs backend service is accessible via a keyboard mode. A simple key combination can be used to switch between the default keyboard behavior and SPRITEs. When SPRITE is active, it creates and maintains a mapping between web page element and keyboard keys. Pressing a key once reads out any information associated with its corresponding web element. A double press invokes the action associated with that element.

We demonstrate the value of SPRITEs for nonvisual access to web content conveyed implicitly to sighted users via spatial layout. Examples of interface elements with this property include menus, tables, and maps. Our validation shows that access to SPRITEs in addition to a screen reader more than triples task completion rates for spatial tasks.

Fig. 36.3 A mockup of AirBnB (https://airbnb.com/s/places) being used with SPRITEs. (left) The initial selection chosen by SPRITEs highlighted when the user presses the topmost key in the rightmost keyboard key. (middle) When the user presses the "\" key, SPRITEs reads out the menu and double pressing "\" activates the menu on the numeric row. (right) Pressing the "1" key reads out the first element in the menu

36.6.1 Using SPRITEs

In the following vignette, we walk through an example of SPRITEs as it might function in a Wiki-like page modeled after AirBnB[3] (See Fig. 36.3).

> Jane is interested in traveling over the holidays, so she opens a web browser and loads the AirBnB 'Places' page, and presses 'ctrl w' on her keyboard to enable SPRITEs mode. The SPRITEs server, running in the background, automatically analyzes the page and extracts hierarchical information about structure, which is mapped onto the column of keys at the rightmost side of the keyboard. All similar web elements are mapped to the same location on the keyboard for consistency (e.g., lists or any grouped items on a page always mapped to numeric row of keyboard) and to help the user build a mental model of the interface.
>
> Jane positions her right hand at right edge of her laptop to find the rightmost column and presses the topmost key (see Fig. 36.3 (left)). SPRITEs outputs "Header" auditorily. When she presses the key again, it outputs "Los Angeles" auditorily. She presses the next key ('\'), and hears "menu". When she presses '\' again, SPRITEs outputs "menu activated on number row" auditorily, informing her that the contents of the menu are now associated with the keys of the number row of her keyboard. Jane now moves her left hand to the top left corner of the laptop keyboard and presses '1' to hear the first menu item. SPRITEs responds "Guide: Downtown photo ops, By Grant Legan, Fashion Photographer". Jane decides she is not interested, she uses her right hand to press the next key in the column, "return", and hears "Header: Havana". She changes her mind and returns to the menu still associated with the number keys.

36.6.2 Evaluation of SPRITEs

We conducted a study comparing the performance of SPRITEs to either a screen reader or screen magnifier depending on each participant's preference. A secondary goal was to explore how SPRITEs impacted participants understanding of webpage organization and spatial layout. Our study used a counterbalanced, within-subjects design to compare SPRITEs to participants' own technology. Ten participants com-

---

[3]https://www.airbnb.com.

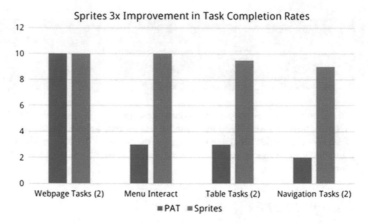

Fig. 36.4 Graph showing task completion rates for different kinds of tasks in our user study

pleted eight tasks in each condition. Tasks were chosen to require linear and hierarchical exploration of web pages, web navigation, and tables.

Our results demonstrated that SPRITEs is valuable for tasks that have traditionally been difficult to support. We found that SPRITEs was particularly useful for interaction with web page elements that have a natural 2D structure, such as menus, tables, and maps. Task completion rates highlighted in Fig. 36.4 show this effect most strongly. For difficult spatial or hierarchical tasks, SPRITEs is three times better than the screen reader on the task completion metric. Overall, rates are equal or better on every task we studied, and the difference in task completion rates is highly significance, despite a small sample.

Because only two or three participants out of ten completed many tasks, the task times of others were not included in our analysis of task completion times. For expert screen reader/magnification participants, their preferred tool was faster than SPRITEs in straightforward linear tasks. In spatial tasks, SPRITEs was faster in four out of five conducted, despite the fact that it was only being compared to the most capable users in each of task (those who completed the task in the PAT condition), two of whom preferred to use screen magnification.

Our observations of SPRITEs use, as well as participant performance, indicate that participants were successfully developing a mental model of the correspondence between keyboard keys and spatial or hierarchical structure of the document. This is a promising sign that SPRITEs may be able to help improve a user's mental model of the interface. Additionally, participants had much less opportunity to learn SPRITEs than they had spent learning to use their preferred technology.

The innate spatial orientation of the keyboard makes it suitable for exploring a range of useful tangible interactions. By integrating the SPRITEs system with the standard computer keyboard, we not only leverage a mainstream tool familiar to all computer users but also enrich nonvisual modalities for increased control of the computing environment.

36.7 Interactiles: Making Tangible Interaction Mobile

Increasing tactile feedback and tangible interaction on touchscreens can improve their accessibility. However, prior solutions have either required hardware customization or provided limited functionality with static overlays. Prior investigation of tactile solutions for large touchscreens also may not address the challenges on mobile devices. We therefore present Interactiles, a low-cost, portable, and unpowered system that enhances tactile interaction on Android touchscreen phones (Zhang et al. 2018). Interactiles consists of 3D-printed hardware interfaces and software that maps interaction with that hardware to manipulation of a mobile app (Fig. 36.5). The system is compatible with the built-in screen reader without requiring modification of existing mobile apps. We describe the design and implementation of Interactiles, and we evaluate its improvement in task performance and the user experience it enables in people who are blind or have low vision.

Interactiles is an inexpensive, unpowered, general-purpose system that increases tactile interaction on touchscreen phones. Its hardware allows users to interact and receive tactile feedback. Its software receives touch input on hardware and invokes the corresponding action on the current running app. The system is designed to work with built-in screen readers and mobile apps without modification to them. The unpowered and portable Interactiles hardware provides tactile feedback to users. Inspired by prior research on capacitive touch hardware components (Chang et al. 2012), our hardware leverages conductive material to connect a users finger to an on-screen contact point, thus registering a touch event.

The Interactiles software is an accessibility service that runs in an app-independent fashion. To increase deployability and generalizability, our software is implemented

Fig. 36.5 Interactiles allows people with visual impairments to interact with mobile touchscreen phones using physical attachments, including a number pad (left) and a multipurpose physical scrollbar (right)

with standard Android accessibility APIs. Our implementation approach was inspired by Interaction Proxies (Zhang et al. 2017), a strategy to modify user input and output on the phone that can be used for accessibility repairs such as adding alternative text or modifying navigation order.

36.7.1 Using Interactiles

The Interactiles system is designed to work with mobile screen readers while providing tactile feedback. Its hardware base is a 3D-printed plastic shell that snaps on a phone, and the shell contains three hardware components: a number pad, a scrollbar, and a control button at the bottom of the scrollbar. Users may flip in and out hardware components for different tasks. When all hardware components are flipped out and the software is off, users have full access to the touchscreen as normal. These hardware components work with our software to achieve five main functions: element navigation, bookmarking, page scrolling, app switching, and number entry. These features are described in the following vignette:

> Steve is interested in purchasing a new backpack. He picks up his Android smartphone and uses Android accessibility to launch Interactiles software and the Amazon mobile app. After searching for backpacks, he flips the scrollbar attached to the phone case over the screen. He moves the scroll thumb vertically to hear information for each product. When he reaches the bottom of the scrollbar, Steve long presses the scroll thumb to move to the next page. As he continues to scroll, when he finds a backpack that he likes he uses the control button to bookmark it. After hearing the details for a few more backpacks, Steve decides to purchase the one that had bookmarked earlier. He presses the control button once to activate the page scrolling mode. He slides the scroll thumb up to scroll back through previous items until he feels the phone vibrate, indicating that he has returned to the bookmark he created.
>
> While Steve is shopping, his phone receives a message notification. He presses the control button to activate app switching mode and hears "Mode: App". He moves the scroll thumb to navigate through the open apps until he hears "Messages". He double-taps the scroll thumb to open the Messages app. Steve presses the control button again to switch back to element navigation mode. Moving the scroll thumb, he hears the subject line for the new message "Hey Steve, on my way to your new place, what's the address again?". After hearing the message, Steve moves the scroll thumb until he reaches the text input field. When he double-taps the scroll thumb, his phone's native soft keyboard pops up and the Interactiles software opens a floating window at the top of the screen. Steve flips the physical number pad attached the phone case on to the screen and uses it to enter the numerical portion of his address. He then proceeds to use the soft keyboard to enter his street address.

36.7.2 Evaluation of Interactiles

To complement the feedback that informed our design of Interactiles, we conducted a study comparing Interactiles with TalkBack (the built-in Android screen reader). This study collected qualitative reactions to Interactiles and compared task completion times and user preferences.

We recruited participants (N = 5) through word of mouth, university services, and mailing lists of organizations of blind people. Three participants were blind while two had some level of impaired vision. In the comparative study, all participants use mobile screen readers, primarily iOS VoiceOver. We employed a within-subjects design to examine the completion time, accuracy, and user preference between two interaction methods: A Nexus 6P phone with TalkBack (the control condition), and the same phone with TalkBack and Interactiles (the experimental condition). Participants had the option to set up the phone with their preferred TalkBack volume and speed settings. Participants were asked to complete four tasks that isolated specific functionality, followed by a more open-ended task to explore the system as a whole.

The specific tasks in the usability study were designed to test each Interactiles feature. Tasks were chosen by considering the difficulties faced in using common apps and how Interactiles might be used in such situations. These tasks covered target acquisition (locate), browsing speed (locate, relocate, app switch), data entry (mixed text/number entry), and spatial memory (relocate).

In terms of speed, Interactiles improved performance times for the app switching and number entry tasks. Participants were uniformly positive about the number pad but were mixed on the usefulness of the scrollbar and control button even though the scrollbar resulted in better task completion time for the previously mentioned task. Average Likert scale ratings for each condition and task can be seen in Fig. 36.6.

Our results demonstrate that Interactiles is particularly useful for app switching and number entry, which are tasks that currently require a mode switch, but may not be as useful for tasks that are already quick even without tangibility such as locate and relocate. Our analysis also explores interactions that may be more helpful to

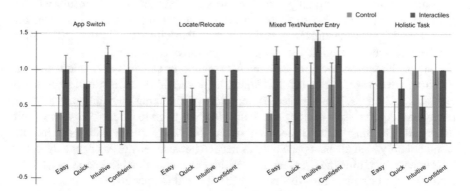

Fig. 36.6 The average Likert scale rating (strongly disagree $= -2$, strongly agree $= 2$) with standard deviation from participants for tasks. Participants were asked how easy, quick, intuitive, and how confident they felt completing each task with the control condition (only TalkBack) and Interactiles. Locate/relocate was rated as one task. P5 did not complete or rate the holistic task

map to a scrollbar and provides design recommendations for future work in tangible mobile touchscreen accessibility.

Interactiles did not provide a major speed advantage for all tasks. However, it did improve task completion time for app switching and number entry. Because participants were beginners with both Interactiles and TalkBack, this suggests that Interactiles may be of value for novice users. Given more time to learn, participants might also be more comfortable with Interactiles and find greater value in its functionality.

Interactiles was least helpful for locating and relocating. It failed to serve as a memory aid and was not reliable enough to be trusted by participants. A secure clip for holding the scrollbar to the screen to maintain screen contact would help to reduce the uncertainty that resulted from inconsistent touch events. The scrollbar may be more useful for known mappings (e.g., a menu) than unknowns (e.g., infinite scroll). In the case of relocation, although Interactiles improved task performance for three out of five participants, participants wanted an additional feature to automatically arrive at bookmarks. Given the speed benefit of bookmarking, this could be of great value. A future implementation might include a short strip of buttons that could be used as bookmarks, similar to saved radio station buttons on cars.

Interactiles was slower for element navigation than TalkBack (i.e., swipe navigation or explore-by-touch). Because of the space limitations in the mobile platform, many apps use linear layouts to deliver content. Even though swipe navigation and explore-by-touch do not have tactility, they work fast enough to help the user form a coherent understanding of the app, especially when content is linear. One reason may be the common use of one-dimensional layout in many small screen mobile apps. Even though swiping and explore-by-touch do not have tactility or much of a physical mapping, they work fast enough to help the user form a coherent understanding of the app, especially if the content is linear. We believe this is the reason the scrollbar did not rate highly with participants, even though it did result in faster completion times for all participants in the app switching task and was faster for three out of five participants in the relocate task. Participants still provided positive feedback on having tangible feedback on the physical scrollbar.

One of the most difficult challenges for tangible or screen reader interaction on mobile platforms is infinite scroll. Ideally, there should be no distinction between elements and pages. The Interactiles approach of chunking elements into discrete pages that requires users to stop processing elements to go to the next page may limit users understanding of the content. However, software implementations of infinite scroll not only load the next page only as needed but also may even change the order of elements each time the user begins scrolling, an action that has been shown to be confusing for blind and low-vision users (Brown and Harper 2013).

Interactiles was most valuable both in task completion times and participant ratings for app switching and number entry. This suggests the interactions to target on mobile might be those that currently already require a mode switch, particularly a difficult one such as opening the symbol keyboard to enter symbols and numbers.

36.8   Discussion

In this chapter, we have presented three systems that introduce tangibility to desktop and mobile systems to improve accessibility. The first system, the Tangible Desktop, placed common graphical interactors into the physical world to reappropriate visual interactions for nonvisual use. The second system, SPRITEs, introduced a spatial navigation mode to the traditional keyboard to increase its utility as a tangible interface. The third system brought tangible interactors to mobile computing using an integrated smartphone case. Although each system set out to solve a different set of accessibility challenges, collectively each project draws attention to the benefits and challenges of building accessible tangible interfaces.

Most promising are the positive results we observed across all three studies, a strong indication that introducing nonvisual and nonauditory modalities to the interaction space is an effective strategy for designing assistive technology systems. In addition to the physical aspects of these projects, each system also took advantage of the human body's proprioceptive abilities to communicate information (e.g., physical icons on the desk (Tangible Desktop), 2D spatial menus (SPRITEs), and scroll thumb location (Interactiles)).

Despite positive results, we must acknowledge the limitations of our evaluation. In particular, the most promising results of the Tangible Desktop and Interactiles studies were with novice participants. In the case of the Tangible Desktop, the most significant improvements were reported on participants who were still actively learning nonvisual computing. Similarly, participants for the Interactiles study were beginners with Android's TalkBack screen reader.[4] The results for novice users uncover two compelling tensions around research-oriented assistive technology development. First, mainstream approaches to accessible computing, be it the desktop or smartphone, are difficult to learn and challenging to master for blind and low-vision users. With SPRITEs and the Tangible Desktop, we observed less improvement with expert users, indicating that given enough time users can efficiently utilize traditional accessibility tools. However, what is less understood are the time commitment requirements to reach efficient use, particularly in comparison to similar tasks for non-accessibility users. Second, all three studies identified length of use as a constraint on uncovering additional benefits (or hindrances) of the intervention. Although lab studies are quite effective at understanding preliminary needs, requirements, and performance, accessible tangible interface research can benefit from longitudinal study. Deeper investigations with tangible interfaces will help answer questions around adoption and learnability.

---

[4]https://developer.android.com/training/accessibility/testing.

36.9   Future Directions

One of the challenges in bringing innovative assistive technologies to market is the costs associated with research, development, and production. The disability community as a whole is simply unable to benefit from the same economies of scale that keep mainstream technology costs low. Economic issues are further compounded by functional needs that can vary between disabilities at a near personal level. One way to address these challenges is by enabling reproduction and adoption of beneficial research-oriented work. As we mentioned in Sect. 36.4, modern DIY techniques have enabled new possibilities for bridging the gap between research and personal use. The projects we have described were developed using design and fabrication technologies that are available to anyone. The Tangible Desktop and Interactiles projects were produced with a commodity 3D printer, the Tangible Desktop used over-the-counter electronics and microcontroller, and SPRITEs relied on standard computing peripherals (e.g., keyboard). By building these projects with tools and technologies available to everyone, we make real-world adoption far more achievable for the communities that we serve. It is our hope that by designing accessible tangible interfaces with a focus on reproduction, we can open new ways of participation with the disability community.

36.10   Authors Opinion of the Field

The research community has established a substantive body of literature that contributes to our understanding of how the kinesthetic system can be used to support computer interaction. While there has been some limited interest commercially, we have yet to see the level of adoption required to make tangible interfaces as ubiquitous as the mobile phone, keyboard, and desktop computer.

As the examples we have provided in this chapter demonstrate, tangible interfaces can support interaction with computational systems in nontraditional and unexpected ways. Rather than negotiate complex relationships between mainstream and assistive technologies, tangible interfaces will make it possible for a much larger cross section of abilities to interact with information in the same way. However, reaching the level of support necessary for day to day utility still requires significant modifications to the traditional computing environment. Fortunately, we are currently experiencing a period of technological advancement that has brought with it compelling new computational devices. Smartwatches, voice assistants, augmented and virtual reality, and the Internet of things (IoT) have reduced our dependence on desktop computing to perform computational tasks and raised new questions about the methods we use to control the digital world.

Tangible interfaces have the potential to unify interaction, but they must be designed with accessibility in mind. For example, a tangible interface that depends on color change to communicate information would exclude people with visual impairments from using it. However, if color change was paired with sound, shape, or temperature, it would be useful for a much broader range of abilities. To ensure that tangible interfaces are accessible, they must be designed to accommodate multiple sensory modalities.

Over the past decade, significant efforts have been made within the industry to ensure that core products meet accessibility guidelines. Most mobile and desktop operating environments now ship with voice assistants, text-to-speech engines, and an accessibility layer to support third-party tools. Ultimately, we view this adoption of accessible thinking as a strong step toward reducing technological barriers for people with disability.

36.11 Conclusion

Tangible interfaces hold promise as way to merge the computational and physical worlds. By combining the unique attributes of real-world objects with digital artifacts, tangible interfaces make it possible to manipulate computational information through the human kinesthetic system. When combined with the visual and auditory forms of computer interaction, it is possible to design interfaces that are useful to all, regardless of ability. In this chapter, we discussed the role that tangible interfaces play in making computing accessible. We presented three projects that demonstrate how tangible interfaces can be used to improve the computing experiences for the visually impaired community. In the first project, the Tangible Desktop, tangible interfaces reappropriated visual metaphors from desktop computing to physical form. The second project, SPRITEs, converted the computer keyboard into a two-dimensional tangible interface for navigating hierarchical structures. Finally, the third project, Interactiles, introduced tangible interaction to touchscreen smartphones. Together, these projects demonstrate novel ways in which tangible interfaces can solve challenges in accessible computing.

References

Baldwin MS, Hayes GR, Haimson OL, Mankoff J, Hudson SE (2017) The tangible desktop: a multimodal approach to nonvisual computing. ACM Trans Access Comput (TACCESS) 10(3):9

Bishop D (1992) Marble answering machine. Royal College of Art, Interaction Design

Bornschein J, Bornschein D, Weber G (2018) Comparing computer-based drawing methods for blind people with real-time tactile feedback. In: Proceedings of the 2018 CHI conference on human factors in computing systems, CHI 18. ACM, p 115:1115:13. https://doi.org/10.1145/3173574.3173689

Brown A, Harper S (2013) Dynamic injection of wai-aria into web content. In: Proceedings of the 10th international cross-disciplinary conference on web accessibility. ACM, p 14

Chang A, O'Modhrain S, Jacob R, Gunther E, Ishii H (2002) Comtouch: design of a vibrotactile communication device. In: Proceedings of the 4th conference on designing interactive systems: processes, practices, methods, and techniques. ACM, pp 312–320

Chang T, Yu NH, Tsai SS, Chen MY, Hung YP (2012) Clip-on gadgets: expandable tactile controls for multi-touch devices. In: Proceedings of the 14th international conference on Human-computer interaction with mobile devices and services companion. ACM, pp 163–166

Ducasse J, Mac MJM, Serrano M, Jouffrais C (2016) Tangible reels: construction and exploration of tangible maps by visually impaired users. In: Proceedings of the 2016 CHI conference on human factors in computing systems, CHI 16. ACM, pp 2186–2197. https://doi.org/10.1145/2858036.2858058

Fishkin KP (2004) A taxonomy for and analysis of tangible interfaces. Pers Ubiquitous Comput 8(5):347–358. https://doi.org/10.1007/s00779-004-0297-4

Guo A, Kim J, Chen XA, Yeh T, Hudson SE, Mankoff J, Bigham JP (2016) Facade: auto-generating tactile interfaces to appliances. In: Proceedings of the 18th international ACM SIGACCESS conference on computers and accessibility, ASSETS 16. ACM, pp 315–316. https://doi.org/10.1145/2982142.2982187

Hurst A, Kane S (2013) Making making accessible. In: Proceedings of the 12th international conference on interaction design and children. ACM, pp 635–638

Hurst A, Tobias J (2011) Empowering individuals with do-it-yourself assistive technology. In: The proceedings of the 13th international ACM SIGACCESS conference on computers and accessibility. ACM, pp 11–18

Ishii H, Ullmer B (1997) Tangible bits: towards seamless interfaces between people, bits and atoms. In: Proceedings of the ACM SIGCHI conference on human factors in computing systems. ACM, pp 234–241

Kaptelinin V, Nardi BA (2006) Acting with technology: activity theory and interaction design. MIT press

Khurana R, McIsaac D, Lockerman E, Mankoff J (2018) Nonvisual interaction techniques at the keyboard surface. In: Proceedings of the 2018 CHI conference on human factors in computing systems. ACM, p 11

Klatzky RL, Lederman SJ (2003) Touch. Handbook of psychology pp 147–176

Klemmer SR, Hartmann B, Takayama L (2006) How bodies matter: five themes for interaction design. In: Proceedings of the 6th conference on designing interactive systems. ACM, pp 140–149

Prescher D, Weber G, Spindler M (2010) A tactile windowing system for blind users. Assets10 (August 2015), 9198. https://doi.org/10.1145/1878803.1878821

Ramos J, Li Z, Rosas J, Banovic N, Mankoff J, Dey A (2016) Keyboard surface interaction: making the keyboard into a pointing device. arXiv:1601.04029

Shaer O, Leland N, Calvillo-Gamez EH, Jacob RJK (2004) The tac paradigm: specifying tangible user interfaces. Pers Ubiquitous Comput 8(5):359–369. https://doi.org/10.1007/s00779-004-0298-3

Shi L, Zhao Y, Azenkot S (2017) Designing interactions for 3D printed models with blind people. In: Proceedings of the 19th international ACM SIGACCESS conference on computers and accessibility, ASSETS 17. ACM, pp 200–209. https://doi.org/10.1145/3132525.3132549

Stangl A, Hsu CL, Yeh T (2015) Transcribing across the senses: community efforts to create 3D printable accessible tactile pictures for young children with visual impairments. In: Proceedings of the 17th international ACM SIGACCESS conference on computers & accessibility, ASSETS 15. ACM, pp 127–137. https://doi.org/10.1145/2700648.2809854

Tanaka A, Parkinson A (2016) Haptic wave: a cross-modal interface for visually impaired audio producers. In: Proceedings of the 2016 CHI conference on human factors in computing systems, CHI 16. ACM, pp 2150–2161. https://doi.org/10.1145/2858036.2858304

Taylor S, Keskin C, Hilliges O, Izadi S, Helmes J (2014) Type-hover-swipe in 96 bytes: a motion sensing mechanical keyboard. In: Proceedings of the 32nd annual ACM conference on Human factors in computing systems. ACM, pp 1695–1704

Zhang H, Li Y (2014) Gestkeyboard: enabling gesture-based interaction on ordinary physical keyboard. In: Proceedings of the SIGCHI conference on human factors in computing systems. ACM, pp 1675–1684

Zhang X, Ross AS, Caspi A, Fogarty J, Wobbrock JO (2017) Interaction proxies for runtime repair
    and enhancement of mobile application accessibility. In: Proceedings of the 2017 CHI conference
    on human factors in computing systems. ACM, pp 6024–6037
Zhang X, Tran T, Sun Y, Culhane I, Jain S, Fogarty J, Mankoff J (2018) Interactiles: 3D printed
    tactile interfaces to enhance mobile touchscreen accessibility

Chapter 37
Mobile Web

Tiago Guerreiro, Luís Carriço and André Rodrigues

Abstract Mobile devices are the tools of the trade to access services and contents on the Internet, already surpassing their desktop counterparts. These gadgets are always available and provide access to social networks, messaging, games, productivity tools, among many others. Accessing the Web with mobile devices, either through a browser or a native application, has become more than a perk; it is a need. Such relevance has increased the need for provide accessible mobile webpages and (Web and native) applications; failing to do so would exclude people with different abilities from a world of opportunities. In this chapter, we focus our attention on the specific challenges of mobile devices for accessibility, and how those have been addressed in the development and evaluation of mobile interfaces and contents. We finish with a discussion on future directions in the field, that outlines the need to learn from the fast emergence of a mobile world, and be prepared for the impact of other upcoming technologies.

37.1 Introduction

Mobile devices paved their way into our daily lives becoming crucial tools in a variety of contexts. These powerful handheld devices have gone long past their initial purpose—one-on-one communication— and are now full-fledged computers. Not so long ago, people would use their desktop computers to play a game, review and edit documents, or check their e-mails; they now also, and likely more often, do it on a mobile phone (Johnson and Seeling 2014). The portability and communication capabilities alongside the bundle of sensors enabled the creation of novel interaction methods and applications. What was once not common or existent for personal

T. Guerreiro (✉) · L. Carriço · A. Rodrigues
LASIGE, Faculdade de Ciências da Universidade de Lisboa, Lisboa, Portugal
e-mail: tjvg@di.fc.ul.pt

L. Carriço
e-mail: lmcarrico@fc.ul.pt

A. Rodrigues
e-mail: afrodrigues@fc.ul.pt

© Springer-Verlag London Ltd., part of Springer Nature 2019   737
Y. Yesilada and S. Harper (eds.), *Web Accessibility*, Human–Computer
Interaction Series, https://doi.org/10.1007/978-1-4471-7440-0_37

computers has become a feature leveraged daily by many (e.g., geolocated or motion-based games and applications, camera-based social interactions). Mobile devices constant availability, portability, connectivity, interactivity, and individuality have enabled us to improve how we work and learn, e.g., mobile learning, beyond what other ICT could do (Terras and Ramsay 2012).

The opportunities created for ubiquitous and enriched access to an ever-increasing world of applications comes along with a variety of challenges. Mobile devices are smaller which makes them challenging in a multitude of ways (Nicolau et al. 2014a; Rodrigues et al. 2015). The sheer amount of applications and tasks (Fig. 37.1), adding up to the small size of the display, makes them cognitively challenging (Page 2014). Mobile devices are also often used under challenging conditions, the so-called situationally induced impairments and disabilities (Sears et al. 2003; Yesilada et al. 2010, 2011), and even more so if you already face a health-induced disability (Nicolau 2012); let us call those situationally augmented impairments and disabilities. Consequently, mobile accessibility affordances need to be carefully understood to maximize the inclusion of all. When we do so successfully, we might even be enabling people who were previously excluded from common usages and tasks to access the Web (Naftali and Findlater 2014).

Mobile devices and their applications have been evolving at an extremely fast pace pushed by major companies like Microsoft, Nokia, and more recently, Apple and

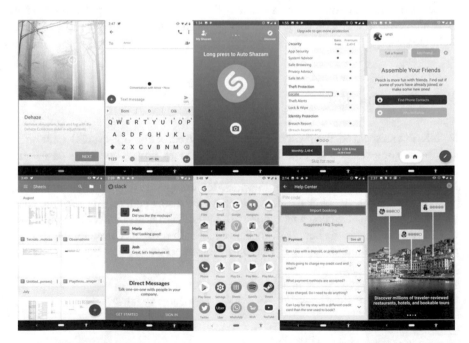

Fig. 37.1 Variety of smartphone applications interfaces that users have to interact with 10 application screens all with very different interfaces. Interfaces with grids, lists, keyboard, no interactive items, logins, tutorials, and tables

Google. This industry-driven evolution is also characterized by a lack of convergence and standardization which has an impact on how accessibility has been taken into account. There have been sparse efforts to provide guidelines and recommendations for the specific case of mobile accessibility at a local level, e.g., BBC, Android, iOS Mobile Accessibility Guidelines. At a more global level, only recently the most accepted sources of accessibility guidelines in the Web have started to pay special attention to mobile accessibility, e.g., Web Content Accessibility Guidelines 2.1 (WCAG 2.1) discussed in Standards, Guidelines, and Trends chapter.

Accessing services and contents on the Web with a mobile device can be done through a browser or a native application. The aforementioned challenges are mostly associated with the device characteristics and applicable to both those types of access. The development of webpages has evolved, with mobile devices as propellers, with a variety of approaches, e.g., mobile-dedicated versions, where a different version is served when the user agent is a mobile device; non-dedicated versions, i.e., responsive design, where the output is differently served depending on the device characteristics. Native applications, on the other hand, are developed with a set of platform versions in mind. In the case of the former, accessibility benefits from the maturity already attained on Web development. In the case of the latter, accessibility benefits from a deeper integration with the operating system and its native accessibility services. A third breed is a hybrid: an application that is natively packaged but which inner contents are a Web view and thus structured in a way that can follow accepted standards and guidelines. Still, in all cases, access to the Web in a mobile device is still limited.

In this chapter, we focus our attention on the challenges that make mobile accessibility a unique endeavor, as well as the state of the art in developing, evaluating, and overall researching toward an accessible mobile world. Mobile accessibility is not a given today. Yet, what we have learned from the disruption caused by the overwhelming growth of mobile devices and applications, should prepare us for future technological revolutions. We discuss the mobile accessibility panorama and point future directions for research in this space.

37.2 Specific Challenges of Mobile Accessibility

For several years, access to the Web was achieved through a desktop/laptop computer with reasonably standard input and output affordances. The keyboard and the mouse, rich in tactile cues, complemented each other but also were enablers of access on their own when coupled with a suitable output interface. Access to the Web on mobile devices started with an attempt to mimic such access, although with less input bandwidth, i.e., using the available keypad and eventually joypad (Trewin 2006). Quickly, the affordances on mobile devices mutated and, with the overwhelming emergence of touchscreens, direct manipulation over a flat screen became the norm.

This brought up challenges for accessible interaction, to add to the ones of size, already a problem in the early mobile phones. We focus our attention in three main challenges that influence the current panorama on mobile accessibility: size and I/O, contexts of use, and lack of convergence.

37.2.1 Device Size and I/O

One of the important differences between mobile devices and personal computers is their size. It has been changing throughout the years, from larger to smaller and back to larger, but still way smaller than their desktop counterparts (Fig. 37.2). This fact impacts content delivery in several forms.

The contents that can fit a mobile device screen, in a way that they are still perceivable, are limited. The approaches to deal with this challenge varied. Early approaches argued for liquid design, where the screen contents would adapt to the device dimensions and resolution. For the majority of websites, this would mean that

Fig. 37.2 Device size evolution, from 2002 to 2014 (retrieved from Wikimedia Commons)

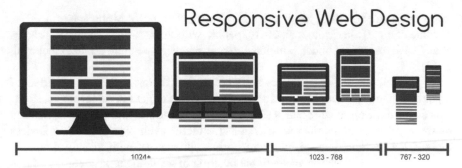

Fig. 37.3 Responsive Web Design. Layout on different devices (retrieved from Wikimedia Commons)

the first render of a webpage would be unreadable (due to its small size), upon which a zoom to a readable level would be required, which can be cumbersome and highly inaccessible. The option to just render a webpage at a readable level leads to the need for continuous scrolling, vertically and horizontally, which can also be damaging for accessibility (e.g., physically and cognitively).

More recently, responsive design, an approach that makes interfaces render differently depending on the device characteristics, had increasing success and adoption (Fig. 37.3). Although not a synonym for accessibility, responsiveness of the design contributed to the overall improvement of the usability of webpages delivered on mobile devices, to everyone. A parallel approach, that also gives adequate relevance to mobile Web, is the creation of mobile-dedicated webpage versions, most often simpler and with more focused content (Fernandes et al. 2015), which has been previously associated with higher accessibility (Lopes et al. 2010).

The approach generally followed in the development of native mobile applications merges the two aforementioned approaches applying responsive design to a selection of contents and widgets normally made available through webpages.

A positive consequence of these most recent approaches to mobile design is that decisions are made regarding which contents are a priority and need to be quickly accessed. Conversely, it is still a challenge to place all the important information available to the users in such a small screen. This creates issues of clogging the screen, applying new metaphors that can be unclear to users (e.g., navigation drawers with cryptic or inexistent affordances), or creating the need to endless scrolls, sometimes bi-dimensionally (Díaz-Bossini and Moreno 2014; Zhou et al. 2012).

A second consequence of reduced device size relates to user input. Mobile devices include a screen occupying their entire front face and have fully adopted direct manipulation. To interact with the device, users are required to tap, double tap, or long press interactive elements, as well as performing a set of gestures. Deriving from this limitation, a first challenge is in defining or adapting target sizes in a way that they can be directly selected by their users. Several researchers have leaned over this problematic, some with particular attention to older people and people with motor impairments (Kobayashi et al. 2011; Zhong et al. 2015; Montague et al. 2014; Nicolau et al. 2014a; Mott et al. 2016), people with visual impairments (Rodrigues et al. 2016), or people under situational impairments (Kane et al. 2008b; Goel et al. 2012).

In parallel, the lack of an always-available keyboard drastically reduces the set of input commands that could allow for more effective navigation. For example, shortcuts on the desktop screen readers allow for more usable and fine-grained navigation between page elements than what is conceivable or even possible with a keyless mobile device. This is even more drastic in applications, with visually impaired users being left to either be aware of the position of an element onscreen (or search for it), or to navigate element by element until they find it (Rodrigues et al. 2015).

Of particular relevance in the mobile context, is the set of gestures used to navigate a webpage or application. As aforementioned, the dimensionality of such set is limited to the users ability to memorize and perform them. An additional problem comes with the possibility for each developer to define gesture recognizers for their webpages and applications, which can be hard to identify and execute. Although there are slight differences in the basic gesture set of iOS and Android applications, for example, we have been witnessing a convergence. This accepted set is a result of past research that has explored which gestures would be more natural to perform (Ruiz et al. 2011). Other researchers have focused on how to adapt the gesture-based interaction to cooperate with a screen reader, and thus enabling nonvisual access to touchscreens (Kane et al. 2008a; Gonçalves et al. 2008). SlideRule (Kane et al. 2008a) was the stepping stone for the non-visual interaction of today's mobile screen readers. Operation of a touchscreen by older adults has also been a matter of study, with recognition to its inherent complexity (Stöß and Blessing 2010). What is clear is that these stereotypical difficulties faced by different populations should be known by developers so that webpages and applications are designed to be at least, stereotypically accessible.

37.2.2   Contexts of Use

Mobile devices are used in a variety of contexts (Dey 2001). These can be extremely challenging and limit how devices and interfaces can be operated. The awareness of the impact of context on mobile interaction brought up the discussions around situationally induced impairments and disabilities (Sears et al. 2003), their similarities with physical and sensorial impairments (Nicolau et al. 2014b; Yesilada et al. 2010; Nicolau 2012), and solutions to overcome these temporary limitations inability (Goel et al. 2012; Kane et al. 2008b). Common examples of situational impairments include the usage of mobile devices outside under high brightness, while walking or taking a public transportation, or even with interacting with gloves.

To design for mobile accessibility, context needs to be fully considered as a sum of the users' abilities, the device, interface, application being used, and the environment where the interaction is taking place. Situationally augmented impairments and disabilities have had limited attention. Concrete examples are of a blind person commuting and using the phone, seeking to input her password privately but without wearing headphones, or of a user with limited motor abilities seeking to input text via eye tracking while paying attention to his surrounding environment (Abdolrahmani et al. 2016).

37.2.3 Lack of Convergence

Mobile devices are not only different from desktop computers, they are also vastly different from each other. With the popularization of smartphones, the variety of devices and platforms rose and segmented the user base. Currently, there are two major mobile operating systems market leaders, Android and iOS (Mobile Operating System Market Share Worldwide StatCounter 2018d), that are very different from each other.

iOS is a closed-source operating system that only allows access through its APIs, apps are only published via their online store and devices are only produced by a single entity (i.e., Apple). Android is open sourced with manufacturers able to adapt its operating system and commercialize devices with a wide range of specifications. Android developers are able to create other stores and have more control over the device; consumers are able to choose from a broader set of devices and applications. However, while the iOS ecosystem remains stable, and Apple ensures continuity between devices, the Android market is heavily segmented. In September 2018, 64% of users are on the latest version of the OS with the rest of the versions having at most 7% (Mobile & Tablet iOS Version Market Share Worldwide StatCounter 2018c), while on Android, the latest version only accounts for 12% with 5 different versions having above 10% market penetration and the highest with just 22% (Mobile & Tablet Android Version Market Share Worldwide StatCounter 2018b).

The consequences of the differences in versions and features for accessibility are that developers and researchers often have to deal with a variety of requirements simultaneously to ensure the Web content created is accessible to users of all versions and devices (Rogers et al. 2016). At times, this can prevent developers from taking advantage of the device's latest features or requires them to provide different experiences depending on capabilities, similar to what had previously happened with different browsers having support for different features. In addition, these updates to features and devices are constant and often in the mobile ecosystem.

37.3 Developing for Mobile Accessibility

Previously, developers only had to take into account a limited set of browsers to ensure their content was accessible on desktop/laptop computers. However, the panorama shifted, with the introduction of a variety of mobile devices and technologies; the problem became vastly more complex (Nielsen 2012). The need to target devices with different affordances spawned a variety of approaches (e.g., dedicated mobile sites, responsive Web design, native applications), each with their own benefits (Charland and LeRoux 2011). In 2011, (Mikkonen and Taivalsaari 2011) anticipated a "battle" between two opposing approaches, native development versus open Web. However, we have yet to witness one approach becoming the one solution.

As predicted by Charland and LeRoux (2011), in the recent years, we have instead seen the rise of hybrid solutions where Web-based content is packaged in native applications. There is no perfect approach as each has its own set of challenges. Native approaches often struggle with fragmentation of platforms, versions, and devices; Web solutions struggle with the ability to take advantage of devices features (i.e., compatibility); and hybrid, to a lesser extend, struggles with compatibility (Ahmad et al. 2018).

There have been efforts to provide a standardized set of guidelines (WCAG) that ensures Web content is accessible by all and easily leveraged by assistive technologies on desktop computers. In the advent of mobile devices, in an effort to unify best practices, in 2008, W3C released the recommendation for Mobile Web Best Practices 1.0 (MWBP Rabin and McCathieNevile 2008). A year later, to consolidate WCAG 2.0 with their MWBP W3C released "Relationship between Mobile Web Best Practices (MWBP) and Web Content Accessibility Guidelines (WCAG)" (Chuter and Yesilada 2009) a report describing their similarities and differences. These were only the first steps, as W3C continued to work toward a single recommendation that would encapsulate all platforms.

In July 2018, W3C released a new recommendation, WCAG 2.1 (Kirkpatrick et al. 2018) that now takes into account a variety of devices, modalities, and features that are used by contemporary mobile devices (e.g., Guideline 1.3.4 Orientation about screen orientation). The core technologies of the Web, such as HTML5 and CSS, are developed at W3C, the same organization responsible for the Web Content Accessibility Guidelines. However, the access points to Web content are no longer just the traditional Web browser, with native and hybrid applications taking a significant role. The lines have blurred to whom is responsible for what, with applications having to take on roles previously held by user agents and vice-versa. For example, the Guideline 2.4—Provide text search from UAAG 2.0 (Allan et al. 2015) which previously user-agents were responsible for, on hybrid and native applications, is up for content developers to implement.

Many of the accessibility efforts for mobile have also been industry led, particularly for native applications. Google, with the vested interest in their mobile operating system (Android), has provided developers with a set of guidelines (Google 2018b) that, when followed, ensured their native assistive technologies are compatible and fully accessible. Apple goes beyond guidelines and provides developers with many predefined controls (e.g., add a contact, detailed info) and views that harmonize the experience throughout different applications (Apple 2018a). Other private companies have made clear guides in an effort to ensure their content is accessible in all device types—BBC guidelines for developers (BBC 2018). Overall, when developing for mobile, one should also take into consideration the native guidelines to maximize compatibility with the native assistive technologies provided in each.

As with traditional Web development, integrated development environments can have an impact in the usability and accessibility of content (Gibson 2007). As reported by Ross et al. (2017), when we use an epidemiology lens to look for the accessibility problems that plague the mobile ecosystems, we become acutely aware of the impact the current main development environments and common use libraries have (e.g., iOS with Xcode Apple 2018b and Android with Android StudioGoogle 2018a). Similarly, the work by Richards et al. (2012) revealed that improvements to Web accessibility came has a side effect of changes in coding practices or trends. Duarte et al. (2016), more recently, explored the impact of development technologies on the accessibility of applications. Moreover, in an era where content is created by users as much, if not more, than by developers, we need new ways to ensure new content remains accessible to all. There is an opportunity to further explore how we can shift development and content authoring practices to have accessibility embedded into its core.

Developers should also be aware of the different modalities and services available for users to consume and create content. Mobile devices are highly integrated platforms with different applications leveraging features from each other (e.g., "Share on Facebook", "Sign in with Google"). In recent years, speech has also become a common modality of interaction; mobile devices are equipped with voice assistants that are able to access content and request services (e.g., Google Assistant on Android and Siri on iOS). These technologies can be leveraged to provide access to many people. If a Web app or a native application with Web content limits its interaction to just the inside of the app or browser, and does not look forward to opportunities to mesh and collaborate with other services, it can negatively impact its accessibility. For example, in the specific case of a voice assistant, when speech is the only modality available to someone, enabling access through it might be the only way to effectively reach the user.

A different approach toward mobile accessibility is to create accessibility services that change the way users interact with content. Some are looking into adapting how content is rendered (Zhang et al. 2017; Zhou et al. 2014) or navigated (Zhong et al. 2014; Rodrigues et al. 2017b), compensating for the accessibility issues introduced by careless developers; others are providing additional Q&A capabilities on top of existing content (Rodrigues et al. 2017a). These services are akin to Web plugins.

One thing is for sure, mobile applications are every day more intertwined. With one piece of content leading to another in a different app and interface; floating windows appearing with extra content from a different service or app. While traditionally on the Web one would not have to consider the interactions between services, other then embedded content, one must always do so on mobile. Nowadays, more than ever, when developing any Web content, accessibility should not be an afterthought.

37.4   Evaluating Mobile Accessibility

Webpages developed for desktop devices quickly became unusable on mobile devices. This fact, and the overwhelming prevalence of mobile device access to the

Web, increased the need for webpages that adapt to the device size, and that focus and reorganize contents for maximum benefit both for the user and the provider. In parallel to the creation of mobile representations of webpages or other types of high responsiveness to device characteristics, the development of native mobile applications accounts by design with the device size restrictions.

Despite the awareness of the relevance of adapting the Web to the mobile reality, the seek for empirical evidence of the different approaches has been limited. There is a large body of work focusing on touchscreen accessibility, text-entry, and other parallel tasks, and less on the impact of design alterations to maximize accessibility. This may be related to the bias of Web accessibility guidelines toward a more traditional setting, i.e. desktop, and the only recent effort to provide guidelines applicable to mobile settings, both webpages and native applications.

There are notable exceptions. Johnson and Seeling (2014) performed one of the first studies comparing desktop and mobile representations of webpages, with the goal of comparing them over time. Most of the differences found related to network demands, particularly, to a lower number of objects (and with smaller size) requested in mobile settings; this study had no particular focus on accessibility. Fernandes et al. (2012) compared the accessibility of mobile and desktop representations of webpages, using an automated evaluator (Fernandes et al. 2014), analyzing the success in complying with standard accessibility guidelines (i.e., WCAG 2.0). This study found that, even without using mobile-specific guidelines, mobile- dedicated representations were less accessible than mobile non-dedicated representations. The latter tend to be simpler, a common consequence of responsive design, but reuse the accessibility knowledge, practices, and code of desktop representations. These results illustrate that the effort to design from scratch for a mobile reality has brought back past challenges for accessibility; the same reality has been patent in the emergence of mobile native applications, that show a multitude of errors that were also common on webpages (Ross et al. 2017).

Automatic evaluations, as those mentioned above, are performed similarly to mobile webpages and desktop representations, most of the times resorting to the same evaluators (Fernandes et al. 2015). However, past work has recognized the differences of the mobile web, particularly by developing evaluators that would take device characteristics in consideration (Vigo et al. 2008). While for mobile webpages are accessible (i.e. its structure and contents can be accessed and processed), to common evaluators, native applications were used for years without the existence of suitable automatic evaluation tools. Nowadays, there are alternatives to assess the accessibility of the applications for the major operating systems, iOS, and Android, but still limited when comparing to webpage evaluators, in their verification of the accepted guidelines (Feiner et al. 2018; Ross et al. 2017).

Several authors have argued for the importance of more in-depth usage analysis, with users, in mobile contexts when evaluating the accessibility of a webpage or application. The reasons for that relate to the suggested inadequacy or incompleteness of accepted guidelines for a mobile context (Clegg-Vinell et al. 2014) and the need to evaluate within context. One example of such studies is the work by Akpinar and Yeşilada (2015) where 50 users participated in a study where they had to interact with original and transcoded versions of webpages, to assess the benefits of an eye-tracking based transcoding approach.

The multitude of contexts where mobile interaction takes place has only recently started to be taken into account in mobile accessibility evaluation. Particularly, this has been achieved by capturing how people with disabilities interact with mobile devices and their applications in real life settings (Kane et al. 2009; Rodrigues et al. 2015; Naftali and Findlater 2014). This allowed researchers to delve into challenges that were not considered nor evaluated in laboratorial or automatic evaluation contexts.

The need to assess the accessibility in context has been brought up before in desktop settings (Hurst et al. 2008, 2013; Vigo and Harper 2013) but has further implications in mobile contexts given their imprevisibility and variety. The consideration of mobile interaction contexts as determinant to understand mobile accessibility is only patent in recent work, and particularly in the way research is conducted (Naftali and Findlater 2014; Rodrigues et al. 2015; Montague et al. 2014, 2015; Nicolau et al. 2017). These works are characterized by using multiple methods that seek to capture a deeper perspective of the impact of the solutions they are assessing. They include observations, interviews, questionnaires; performed through time; sometimes in parallel with objective data collection.

37.5 Discussion

The rise of mobile devices brought not only new challenges to the way Web content is accessed and developed, but also lowered the entry barrier to access Web content. Mobile devices can be cheaper and easier to obtain than desktop computers. In August 2018, worldwide, mobile (smartphone + tablet) already account for 57% of the market share (StatCounter 2018e), and in some countries, mobile users already represent over three-quarters of the total users (Desktop vs Mobile vs Tablet Market Share India StatCounter 2018a). The trend has been for mobile devices to become the primary access point to Web content. The variety of devices, platforms, and applications that have permeated into our daily lives can no longer be an afterthought when developing for the Web.

The standardization and evaluation of the accessibility of Web content have paved the way for changes on how Web content was previously developed on desktop computers and its stereotypical input methods. However, even the less complex context in which interactions take place on desktop computers, guidelines compliance does not translate into an accessible experience. In Power et al. (2012), guidelines only accounted for 50% of the problems 32 blind people encountered when interacting with a variety of websites. We have to continue the efforts towards accessibility but taking into account the complexities that come with mobile technology.

The efforts in research and development since the introduction of smartphones have been mostly targeting the size variance (Kobayashi et al. 2011; Zhong et al. 2015; Montague et al. 2014; Rodrigues et al. 2016) and the novel input modalities

(Kane et al. 2008a; Gonçalves et al. 2008). However, work that explores the issues with mobile devices in a real-world context (Kane et al. 2009; Rodrigues et al. 2015; Naftali and Findlater 2014) has been scarce. One of the possible causes is the complexity of conducting such studies, with concerns to privacy (e.g., collecting user daily text-entry), safety (e.g., texting while driving), and ability to collect data in situ at the right moment. The lack of convergence of the mobile platforms will only increase with the introduction of new devices. While some work has proposed to assess the impact of different development practices and tools (Ross et al. 2017; Richards et al. 2012), there seems to be a gap in knowledge to what are the consequences of the fragmentation of user basis across platforms, versions, and apps.

Multiple methods research may be leveraged as part of a quest for a deeper understanding of the accessibility issues people are facing in the real world. Part of the solution may come from further development of new evaluation metrics for accessibility; automatic evaluators capable of assessing native and hybrid content; and real-world data collection services. Evaluations will need to change in order to keep up with the fast pace at which applications, features, operating system, and devices are being released and updated. The time of static evaluations conducted on a secular version of the system will no longer be relevant. Nowadays, it is time we look beyond traditional contexts where interaction used to take place. Interactions are happening everywhere at any time, and if we neglect working toward accessible models that encapsulate them, we will be excluding a vast number of people.

37.6 Future Directions

With the understanding of the impact of past decisions on the impact of the accessibility, comes a responsibility and an opportunity. It is clear today that the accessibility of a mobile webpage or application is not a localized issue; it is the result of standardization, education and training, development environments, platform accessibility services, awareness to contextual factors, among several others. It is the sum of a set of premises. The first steps to improve the accessibility of current platforms and their contents is to work on these premises, leaving no excuses left for failing. The rise of new technologies, mobile or not, should be informed by the accidented path toward mobile accessibility, and do better (e.g., integrated development environments designed from scratch to enable accessibility).

As reiterated throughout this chapter, mobile devices are embedded in our daily lives. In the foreseeable future, the variety of devices and features will keep on rising, with the introduction of new wearable (e.g., skin wearables), augmented (AR), and virtual reality (VR) devices. The contexts in which mobile interactions take place are complex enough that we have yet to standardize accessibility requirements, or develop tools to evaluate accessibility in situ accurately. With new sensors, interactions methods, and the debut of AR and VR, the contexts in which interactions take place will become a complex intertwining of real and virtual that will present us we a new set of challenges. With new challenges come great opportunities to innovate and think about the possibilities for work, leisure, communication, and assistive technologies.

In the age where everyone has a powerful computer in their pocket, we have not yet seen a true realization of solutions that cater to the individual. With the advances in data science and artificial intelligence in general, it is odd that everyone is still given a predefined solution that works for most but not all. Accessibility of Web content to all does not mean equal interaction or layout. We are all a sum of our experiences, with different abilities and preferences. It is time technology catches up to the real-world understanding in situ, catering to our individual needs and abilities (Wobbrock et al. 2011; Oliveira et al. 2011).

37.7   The authors' Opinion of the Field

Accessing the Web with a mobile device has become too common and relevant to be seen as a secondary concern. In the past, with a focus on content alone, accessibility to the mobile Web was not considered as being that different from accessing the Web on any other device. The contexts where mobile devices are used, the complexity and interwinding of applications, the I/O capabilities of these devices, proved otherwise. To add to it, the lack of specific guidelines and standardization lead to a disparity of approaches, from platforms to devices and even between application versions, that only increase the problem of providing accessibility to the mobile context. Only now, circa 2018, we are witnessing clear efforts to standardize having mobile devices, and their idiosyncrasies, in consideration.

It is timely and relevant to learn from the past experiences and be on the lookout for novel contexts, technologies, and usages, that can render accepted guidelines and procedures as inadequate. With novel technologies emerging (e.g., virtual, augmented, and mixed reality), it is important to consider them, their authoring environments, guidelines for development, and evaluation tools, with a challenging eye to what is known and accepted today.

The matters of context, highly focused in this chapter, are only one example of the importance of a broader view when designing and evaluating with accessibility in mind, on mobile contexts (or other novel contexts we may imagine). The steps given in uncovering associations between emergence of new authoring tools, development technologies, or more broadly diverse aspects that can influence the accessibility of a product, as in the case of an epidemic, call out for wiser discussions around the impact of what is made available.

One particular concern for both practice and research is how mobile accessibility is being evaluated. Beyond the aged discussions on the differences between manual (expert) and automatic evaluations, in challenging contexts, it becomes paramount to assess in-context. In the age of data science, there is an opportunity to continuously assess products, their usages and failures, with a variety of methods, able to uncover accessibility barriers that would be unfindable even by experts using them in their cozy offices.

37.8 Conclusions

The emergence of mobile devices took us all by surprise. From one device to the other, there was rarely time to consolidate and work toward the accessibility of these devices and the contents therein, as it was not a priority. However, these devices have become so relevant in today's society that it is irresponsible to continue this path.

Recent work has presented several ways to improve the accessibility to mobile devices and its contents, and evidence on how these advances can benefit everyone. It is exciting to witness increasing awareness of mobile accessibility; it is with careful excitement that we expect the emergence of new technologies and work toward a less accidented path, with accessibility at the forefront.

References

Abdolrahmani A, Kuber R, Hurst A (2016) An empirical investigation of the situationally-induced impairments experienced by blind mobile device users. In: Proceedings of the 13th web for all conference, ACM, New York, NY, USA, W4A '16, pp 21:1–21:8. https://doi.org/10.1145/2899475.2899482

Ahmad A, Li K, Feng C, Asim SM, Yousif A, Ge S (2018) An empirical study of investigating mobile applications development challenges. IEEE Access 6:17,711–17,728. https://doi.org/10.1109/ACCESS.2018.2818724

Akpinar E, Yeşilada Y (2015) Old habits die hard!: eyetracking based experiential transcoding: a study with mobile users. In: Proceedings of the 12th web for all conference, ACM, New York, NY, USA, W4A '15, pp 12:1–12:5. https://doi.org/10.1145/2745555.2746646

Allan J, Lowney G, Patch K, Jeanne S (2015) User agent accessibility guidelines (UAAG) 2.0 W3C working group note 15. https://www.w3.org/TR/UAAG20/. Accessed 14 Sept 2018

Apple (2018a) Human interface guidelines - accessibility. https://developer.apple.com/design/human-interface-guidelines/ios/app-architecture/accessibility/. Accessed 14 Sept 2018

Apple (2018b) Xcode - apple developer. https://developer.apple.com/xcode/. Accessed 14 Sept 2018

BBC (2018) BBC mobile accessibility. http://www.bbc.co.uk/guidelines/futuremedia/accessibility/mobile. Accessed 14 Sept 2018

Charland A, LeRoux B (2011) Mobile application development: web vs. native. Queue 9(4):20:20–20:28. https://doi.org/10.1145/1966989.1968203

Chuter A, Yesilada Y (2009) Relationship between mobile web best practices (MWBP) and web content accessibility guidelines (WCAG). https://www.w3.org/TR/mwbp-wcag/ Accessed 14 Sept 2018

Clegg-Vinell R, Bailey C, Gkatzidou V (2014) Investigating the appropriateness and relevance of mobile web accessibility guidelines. In: Proceedings of the 11th web for all conference, ACM, New York, NY, USA, W4A '14, pp 38:1–38:4. https://doi.org/10.1145/2596695.2596717

Dey AK (2001) Understanding and using context. Pers Ubiquitous Comput 5(1):4–7. https://doi.org/10.1007/s007790170019

Duarte C, Matos I, Vicente Ja, Salvado A, Duarte CM, Carriço L (2016) Development technologies impact in web accessibility. In: Proceedings of the 13th web for all conference, ACM, New York, NY, USA, W4A '16, pp 6:1–6:4. https://doi.org/10.1145/2899475.2899498

Díaz-Bossini JM, Moreno L (2014) Accessibility to mobile interfaces for older people. Proc Comput Sci 27:57–66. https://doi.org/10.1016/j.procs.2014.02.008, http://www.sciencedirect.com/science/article/pii/S1877050914000106; 5th International conference on software development and technologies for enhancingaccessibility and fighting info-exclusion, DSAI 2013

Feiner J, Krainz E, Andrews K (2018) A new approach to visualise accessibility problems of mobile apps in source code. In: Proceedings of the 20th international conference on enterprise information systems - volume 2: ICEIS, INSTICC, SciTePress, pp 519–526. https://doi.org/10.5220/0006704405190526

Fernandes N, Costa D, Neves S, Duarte C, Carriço L (2012) Evaluating the accessibility of rich internet applications. In: Proceedings of the international cross-disciplinary conference on web accessibility, ACM, New York, NY, USA, W4A '12, pp 13:1–13:4

Fernandes N, Rodrigues A, Duarte C, Hijón-Neira R, Carriço L (2014) Web accessibility of mobile and desktop representations. In: Proceedings of the 28th international BCS human computer interaction conference on HCI 2014-Sand, Sea and Sky-Holiday HCI, BCS, pp 195–200

Fernandes N, Guerreiro T, Marques D, Carriço L (2015) Optimus web: selective delivery of desktop or mobile web pages. In: Proceedings of the 12th web for all conference, ACM, New York, NY, USA, W4A '15, pp 20:1–20:4

Gibson B (2007) Enabling an accessible web 2.0. In: Proceedings of the 2007 international cross-disciplinary conference on web accessibility (W4A), ACM, New York, NY, USA, W4A '07, pp 1–6

Goel M, Findlater L, Wobbrock J (2012) WalkType: using accelerometer data to accomodate situational impairments in mobile touch screen text entry. In: Proceedings of the SIGCHI conference on human factors in computing systems, ACM, New York, NY, USA, CHI '12, pp 2687–2696

Gonçalves D, Jorge JA, Nicolau H, Guerreiro T, Lagoá P (2008) From tapping to touching: making touch screens accessible to blind users. IEEE MultiMedia 15:48–50. https://doi.org/10.1109/MMUL.2008.88

Google (2018a) Android studio - android developers. https://developer.android.com/studio/. Accessed 14 Sept 2018

Google (2018b) Material design - accessibility. https://material.io/design/usability/accessibility.html. Accessed 14 Sept 2018

Hurst A, Mankoff J, Hudson SE (2008) Understanding pointing problems in real world computing environments. In: Proceedings of the 10th international ACM SIGACCESS conference on computers and accessibility, ACM, New York, NY, USA, Assets '08, pp 43–50. https://doi.org/10.1145/1414471.1414481

Hurst A, Hudson SE, Mankoff J, Trewin S (2013) Distinguishing users by pointing performance in laboratory and real-world tasks. ACM Trans Access Comput 5(2):5:1–5:27. https://doi.org/10.1145/2517039

Johnson T, Seeling P (2014) Desktop and mobile web page comparison: characteristics, trends, and implications. IEEE Commun Mag 52(9):144–151. https://doi.org/10.1109/MCOM.2014.6894465

Kane SK, Bigham JP, Wobbrock JO (2008a) Slide rule: making mobile touch screens accessible to blind people using multi-touch interaction techniques. In: Proceedings of the 10th international ACM SIGACCESS conference on computers and accessibility, ACM, New York, NY, USA, Assets '08, pp 73–80

Kane SK, Wobbrock JO, Smith IE (2008b) Getting off the treadmill: evaluating walking user interfaces for mobile devices in public spaces. In: Proceedings of the 10th international conference on human computer interaction with mobile devices and services, ACM, New York, NY, USA, MobileHCI '08, pp 109–118

Kane SK, Jayant C, Wobbrock JO, Ladner RE (2009) Freedom to roam: a study of mobile device adoption and accessibility for people with visual and motor disabilities. In: Proceedings of the 11th international ACM SIGACCESS conference on computers and accessibility, ACM, New York, NY, USA, Assets '09, pp 115–122

Kirkpatrick A, Connor J, Campbell A, Cooper M (2018) Web content accessibility guidelines (WCAG) 2.1 W3C recommendation. https://www.w3.org/TR/WCAG21/. Accessed 14 Sept 2018

Kobayashi M, Hiyama A, Miura T, Asakawa C, Hirose M, Ifukube T (2011) Elderly user evaluation of mobile touchscreen interactions. Human-computer interaction - INTERACT 2011. Springer, Berlin, pp 83–99

Lopes R, Gomes D, Carriço L (2010) Web not for all: a large scale study of web accessibility. In: Proceedings of the 2010 international cross disciplinary conference on web accessibility (W4A), ACM, New York, NY, USA, W4A '10, pp 10:1–10:4

Mikkonen T, Taivalsaari A (2011) Apps vs. open web: the battle of the decade

Montague K, Nicolau H, Hanson VL (2014) Motor-impaired touchscreen interactions in the wild. In: Proceedings of the 16th international ACM SIGACCESS conference on computers & accessibility, ACM, New York, NY, USA, ASSETS '14, pp 123–130

Montague K, Rodrigues A, Nicolau H, Guerreiro T (2015) TinyBlackBox: supporting mobile in-the-wild studies. In: Proceedings of the 17th international ACM SIGACCESS conference on computers & accessibility, ACM, New York, NY, USA, ASSETS '15, pp 379–380

Mott ME, Vatavu RD, Kane SK, Wobbrock JO (2016) Smart touch: improving touch accuracy for people with motor impairments with template matching. In: Proceedings of the 2016 CHI conference on human factors in computing systems, ACM, New York, NY, USA, CHI '16, pp 1934–1946

Naftali M, Findlater L (2014) Accessibility in context: understanding the truly mobile experience of smartphone users with motor impairments. In: Proceedings of the 16th international ACM SIGACCESS conference on computers & accessibility, ACM, New York, NY, USA, ASSETS '14, pp 209–216

Nicolau H (2012) Disabled 'r' all: bridging the gap between health and situational induced impairments and disabilities. SIGACCESS Access Comput 102:21–24. https://doi.org/10.1145/2140446.2140451

Nicolau H, Guerreiro T, Jorge J, Gonçalves D (2014a) Mobile touchscreen user interfaces: bridging the gap between motor-impaired and able-bodied users. Univers Access Inf Soc 13(3):303–313. https://doi.org/10.1007/s10209-013-0320-5

Nicolau H, Guerreiro T, Lucas D, Jorge J (2014b) Mobile text-entry and visual demands: reusing and optimizing current solutions. Univers Access Inf Soc 13(3):291–301

Nicolau H, Montague K, Guerreiro T, Rodrigues A, Hanson VL (2017) Investigating laboratory and everyday typing performance of blind users. ACM Trans Access Comput 10(1):4:1–4:26. https://doi.org/10.1145/3046785

Nielsen J (2012) Mobile site vs. full site. Rimerman S And Walker AM Mobile Usability Berkeley, New Riders, pp 24–25

Oliveira Ja, Guerreiro T, Nicolau H, Jorge J, Gonçalves D (2011) Blind people and mobile touch-based text-entry: acknowledging the need for different flavors. In: The Proceedings of the 13th international ACM SIGACCESS conference on computers and accessibility, ACM, New York, NY, USA, ASSETS '11, pp 179–186. https://doi.org/10.1145/2049536.2049569

Page T (2014) Touchscreen mobile devices and older adults: a usability study. Int J Hum Factors Ergon 3(1):65–85

Power C, Freire A, Petrie H, Swallow D (2012) Guidelines are only half of the story: accessibility problems encountered by blind users on the web. In: Proceedings of the SIGCHI conference on human factors in computing systems, ACM, New York, NY, USA, CHI '12, pp 433–442. https://doi.org/10.1145/2207676.2207736

Rabin J, McCathieNevile C (2008) Mobile web best practices 1.0 basic guidelines W3C recommendation. https://www.w3.org/TR/mobile-bp. Accessed 14 Sept 2018

Richards JT, Montague K, Hanson VL (2012) Web accessibility as a side effect. In: Proceedings of the 14th international ACM SIGACCESS conference on computers and accessibility, ACM, New York, NY, USA, ASSETS '12, pp 79–86

Rodrigues A, Montague K, Nicolau H, Guerreiro T (2015) Getting smartphones to talkback: understanding the smartphone adoption process of blind users. In: Proceedings of the 17th international ACM SIGACCESS conference on computers & accessibility, ACM, New York, NY, USA, ASSETS '15, pp 23–32

Rodrigues A, Nicolau H, Montague K, Carriço L, Guerreiro T (2016) Effect of target size on non-visual text-entry. In: Proceedings of the 18th international conference on human-computer interaction with mobile devices and services, ACM, New York, NY, USA, MobileHCI '16, pp 47–52. https://doi.org/10.1145/2935334.2935376

Rodrigues A, Montague K, Nicolau H, Guerreiro J, Guerreiro T (2017a) In-context Q&A to support blind people using smartphones. In: Proceedings of the 19th international ACM SIGACCESS conference on computers and accessibility, ACM, New York, NY, USA, ASSETS '17, pp 32–36

Rodrigues A, Santos A, Montague K, Guerreiro T (2017b) Improving smartphone accessibility with personalizable static overlays. In: Proceedings of the 19th international ACM SIGACCESS conference on computers and accessibility, ACM, New York, NY, USA, ASSETS '17, pp 37–41. https://doi.org/10.1145/3132525.3132558

Rogers N, Wald PM, Draffan EA (2016) Evaluating the mobile web accessibility of electronic text for print impaired people in higher education. In: Proceedings of the 13th web for all conference, ACM, New York, NY, USA, W4A '16, pp 26:1–26:2

Ross AS, Zhang X, Fogarty J, Wobbrock JO (2017) Epidemiology as a framework for large-scale mobile application accessibility assessment. In: Proceedings of the 19th international ACM SIGACCESS conference on computers and accessibility, ACM, New York, NY, USA, ASSETS '17, pp 2–11

Ruiz J, Li Y, Lank E (2011) User-defined motion gestures for mobile interaction. In: Proceedings of the SIGCHI conference on human factors in computing systems, ACM, New York, NY, USA, CHI '11, pp 197–206

Sears A, Lin M, Jacko J, Xiao Y (2003) When computers fade: pervasive computing and situationally-induced impairments and disabilities. HCI Int 2:1298–1302

StatCounter (2018a) Desktop vs mobile vs tablet market share India. http://gs.statcounter.com/platform-market-share/desktop-mobile-tablet/india. Accessed 14 Sept 2018

StatCounter (2018b) Mobile & tablet android version market share worldwide. http://gs.statcounter.com/os-version-market-share/android/mobile-tablet/worldwide. Accessed 14 Sept 2018

StatCounter (2018c) Mobile & tablet iOS version market share worldwide. http://gs.statcounter.com/os-version-market-share/ios/mobile-tablet/worldwide. Accessed 14 Sept 2018

StatCounter (2018d) Mobile operating system market share worldwide. http://gs.statcounter.com/os-market-share/mobile/worldwide. Accessed 14 Sept 2018

StatCounter (2018e) Desktop vs mobile vs tablet market share worldwide. http://gs.statcounter.com/platform-market-share/desktop-mobile-tablet. Accessed 14 Sept 2018

Stöß C, Blessing L (2010) Mobile device interaction gestures for older users. In: Proceedings of the 6th nordic conference on human-computer interaction: extending boundaries, ACM, New York, NY, USA, NordiCHI '10, pp 793–796

Terras MM, Ramsay J (2012) The five central psychological challenges facing effective mobile learning: a psychological perspective on mobile learning. Br J Educ Technol 43(5):820–832

Trewin S (2006) Physical usability and the mobile web. In: Proceedings of the 2006 international cross-disciplinary workshop on web accessibility (W4A): building the mobile web: rediscovering accessibility?, ACM, New York, NY, USA, W4A '06, pp 109–112

Vigo M, Harper S (2013) Evaluating accessibility-in-use. In: Proceedings of the 10th international cross-disciplinary conference on web accessibility, ACM, p 7

Vigo M, Aizpurua A, Arrue M, Abascal J (2008) Evaluating web accessibility for specific mobile devices. In: Proceedings of the 2008 international cross-disciplinary conference on web accessibility (W4A), ACM, New York, NY, USA, W4A '08, pp 65–72

Wobbrock JO, Kane SK, Gajos KZ, Harada S, Froehlich J (2011) Ability-Based design: concept, principles and examples. ACM Trans Access Comput 3(3):9:1–9:27

Yesilada Y, Harper S, Chen T, Trewin S (2010) Small-device users situationally impaired by input. Comput Human Behav 26(3):427–435

Yesilada Y, Brajnik G, Harper S (2011) Barriers common to mobile and disabled web users. Interact Comput 23(5):525–542. https://doi.org/10.1016/j.intcom.2011.05.005, /oup/backfile/contentpublic/journal/iwc/23/5/10.1016/j.intcom.2011.05.005/2/iwc23-0525.pdf

Zhang X, Ross AS, Caspi A, Fogarty J, Wobbrock JO (2017) Interaction proxies for runtime repair and enhancement of mobile application accessibility. In: Proceedings of the 2017 CHI conference on human factors in computing systems, ACM, New York, NY, USA, CHI '17, pp 6024–6037

Zhong Y, Raman TV, Burkhardt C, Biadsy F, Bigham JP (2014) JustSpeak: enabling universal voice control on android. In: Proceedings of the 11th web for all conference, ACM, New York, NY, USA, W4A '14, pp 36:1–36:4

Zhong Y, Weber A, Burkhardt C, Weaver P, Bigham JP (2015) Enhancing android accessibility for users with hand tremor by reducing fine pointing and steady tapping. In: Proceedings of the 12th web for all conference, ACM, New York, NY, USA, W4A '15, pp 29:1–29:10

Zhou J, Rau PLP, Salvendy G (2012) Use and design of handheld computers for older adults: a review and appraisal. Int J Hum-Comput Interact 28(12):799–826

Zhou L, Bensal V, Zhang D (2014) Color adaptation for improving mobile web accessibility. In: 2014 IEEE/ACIS 13th international conference on computer and information science (ICIS), pp 291–296. https://doi.org/10.1109/ICIS.2014.6912149

Chapter 38
Fabrication, 3D Printing, and Making

Amy Hurst

Abstract This chapter presents an introduction to digital fabrication and the exciting opportunities it offers in the accessibility and assistive technology domain. Digital fabrication tools are more efficient and accessible than manual fabrication tools, allowing for efficient and affordable creation or modification of existing assistive technologies, or novel solutions. This chapter provides an overview of relevant digital fabrication tools (with an emphasis on 3D printing technology) and current online communities to share ideas and designs, and discusses exciting research and practitioner contributions that leverage 3D printing. The chapter concludes with the author's recommendations for how to successfully apply this technology in accessibility projects and areas for future inquiry.

38.1 Introduction to Making, Digital Fabrication, and Accessibility

38.1.1 Maker Culture as Consumerism Alternative

Making things (instead of buying them) is attractive to many people to save money, customize goods to fit needs, and feel less dependent on corporations (Lupton 2006) This practice spans a wide range of activities from gourmet cooking, fashion, home improvement, and electronics. This *"maker"* culture highlights a set of values where sharing, learning, and creativity are valued over profit and social capital (Kuznetsov and Paulos 2010). A culture where people are interested in modifying or creating is not new, and has appeared throughout history notably through amateur radio enthusiasts in the late 1920s, and model railroad enthusiasts in the 1950s (Obrist 2008). According to Von Hippel, 10–40% of users engage in developing or modifying products (Von Hippel 2005).

A. Hurst (✉)
New York University (NYU), New York City, USA
e-mail: amyhurst@nyu.edu

© Springer-Verlag London Ltd., part of Springer Nature 2019
Y. Yesilada and S. Harper (eds.), *Web Accessibility*, Human–Computer
Interaction Series, https://doi.org/10.1007/978-1-4471-7440-0_38

Users that innovate can develop exactly what they want, rather than relying on manufacturers to act as their (often imperfect) agents. Moreover, individual users do not have to develop everything they need on their own: they can benefit from innovations develop and freely shared by others (Von Hippel 2005).

Digital fabrication tools have created a new chapter of people making physical objects, and freely sharing their knowledge, experience, and designs. This phenomenon, and expertise is particularly exciting in the accessibility community where there is a great need for innovation and customization.

38.1.2 Digital Fabrication Overview

Digital Fabrication tools are part of the larger family of *Computer Numeric Controlled* (CNC) automated manufacturing tools that are controlled by a computer and able to follow computer instructions. CNC tools include a wide range of manufacturing and fabrication tools, but the most relevant ones for accessibility are 3D printers that can build solid objects out of plastic, laser cutters that can precisely cut (or etch) flat materials (such as cardboard, acrylic, wood, and metal), vinyl cutters that can cut paper and sticky vinyl, and multi-axis milling machines that can transform metal or wood into almost any 3D shape.

Since the early 2000s, the term CNC tools has expanded to include a new generation of *rapid prototyping tools* that have the potential to make *personal-scale manufacturing* possible. "Personal-scale manufacturing tools enable people that have no special training in woodworking, metalsmithing, or embroidery to manufacture their own complex, one-of-a-kind artisan-style objects" (Lipson 2010). Rapid prototyping tools manufacture objects quickly so they can be used in the iterative design process, with varying quality and durability of output.

Most digital fabrication tools create objects through additive or subtractive techniques. In *additive manufacturing*, a machine builds an object by layering (and bonding) thin pieces of material together. These layers are most commonly bonded together through a glue or melted the material. In *subtractive manufacturing*, a custom object is revealed after precisely removing material from a larger object. There are many tools and techniques used in subtractive manufacturing, but material is commonly with a hard or sharp tool head (most commonly made from metal), or something hot (such as plasma or a laser) to remote material (Table 38.1).

Table 38.1 Overview of common digital fabrication tools

Digital fabrication tool	Type	Common materials
3D printer (FDM)	Additive	Plastic (many types), ceramic, metal
3D printer (SLA)	Additive	Resin, polymers
Laser cutter	Subtractive	Plastic (Acrylic), cardboard, wood, metal
Mill	Subtractive	Foam, wood, metal

38.2 Digital Fabrication Tools, 3D Printers, and Online Communities

This section provides a brief overview of digital fabrication tools, provides a detailed explanation to 3D printing, and describes relevant online communities.

38.2.1 Overview of Digital Fabrication Tools and Software

38.2.1.1 Finding Digital Fabrication Tools

As discussed in Sect. 38.1, there are several additive and subtractive digital fabrication tools that can build custom objects. This section describes current trends and standards in finding these tools, design software, and 3D scanners.

Buying and Sharing Tools: Since the mid-2000s, digital fabrication tools have become more affordable and ubiquitous. Previously, access to these machines was predominantly limited to large manufacturing companies and research labs because the machines were prohibitively expensive. However, there are now many digital fabrication machines that are affordable enough for people to have in their own homes or their local community (Khanapour et al. 2017). Additionally, shared and public workshops and Hackerspaces (hackerspaces.org) are becoming more common, and give individuals the option to rent time on shared machines.

Service Bureaus: Those who do not have access to nearby CNC machines can manufacture almost any part using online services such as Ponoko (Ponoko), and Shapeways (Shapeways), 3D Systems (3D), and eMachine Shop (eMachineShop). These companies tend to offer high-quality manufacturing for a variety of services including 2D and 3D manufacturing of metal, wood, glass, and plastic. They offer reasonable turnarounds, competitive pricing, and support small order volumes.

Assembling, Modifying and Designing Tools: As the increased demand for digital fabrication grows, there remains a steady stream of enthusiasts who engage in assembling, modifying, repairing, and designing custom 3D printers (Replicating). These communities have explored many alternatives in printer designs and contributed to (or inspired) many commercially available 3D printers. This phenomenon is relevant to accessibility as these are the communities that push the status quo on this technology and can support individuals or researchers whose digital fabrication needs cannot be met through current products.

38.2.1.2 Design Software

To build a physical object, digital fabrication machines require instructions about the object to be created. Designs are described using CAD (Computer-Aided Design) tools and files. The specific tools (and subsequent output needed for fabrication) vary according to the digital fabrication technology and the manufacture, however, these are often divided into formats that describe 3D files (.OBJ .STL) or 2D Files (.SVG).

As manufacturing becomes more accessible, it is possible for almost anyone to become a machine operator, but an important question is how novices will create designs. Following in the footsteps of software designed to help nonprogrammers build and customize software (Kelleher et al. 2007), there has been an influx of software projects to help non-engineers design objects for these platforms.

38.2.1.3   Control Software

After an object has been designed, information from the CAD/CAM file must be converted into a machine instruction that will build the object. One important part of this process is for the operator to specify physical aspects of the build. These exact aspects vary by digital fabrication tool, but include details such as the final size, resolution, and density of the object. While there are standard formats for machine instructions (GCODE is very common), the software that the operator uses to specify the build can vary significantly by manufacturer.

38.2.2   Introduction to 3D Printing Technology

This section provides a brief overview of 3D printing technology, and describes fundamental concepts regarding the printers themselves, 3D design software, and 3D scanner technology. While there is much to learn about other digital fabrication tools, 3D printing technology was selected due to its broad popularity and the unique opportunities it has already created in accessibility (see Sect. 38.4.1).

38.2.2.1   Fused Deposition Modeling 3D Printers

Fused Deposition Modeling (FDM) is a very popular, affordable, and easy-to-use consumer 3D printing technique. FDM printer costs range from hundreds to thousands of dollars, and these tools can create plastic models by layering small strands of heated material, which harden and bond together, solidifying into a 3D object. Of the other printer types currently on the market, these printers well suited for prototyping in schools, community centers, and medical settings because the machines are clean, do not use harsh chemicals, and can be found in affordable and small form factors. We describe below important factors to consider when comparing 3D printers. For those interested in a more in-depth comparison of 3D printers, there are multiple organizations that conduct annual reviews and evaluations of 3D printers on the market (Make: 3D Printer, PCMag:).

Build Area. The maximum dimensions of an object that can be produced by a 3D printer is limited by that 3D printer's build area. If an end user wants to create an object that is larger than the maximum build area of a given printer, they may choose to redesign the object so it can be printed in multiple pieces that are later assembled.

Extruder. FDM 3D printers *extrude* precisely heated thermoplastic *filament* (thin strands of material) and a small motor pushes (or extrudes) the melted plastic through a small nozzle. Extruders can vary according to the temperature range they can reliably maintain, layer resolution (measured in microns), and the diameter of the nozzle. 3D printers can vary according to the number of extruders on a machine, and their capabilities. Lower cost FDM printers have one extruder, optimized for lower temperature (210 °C), and more expensive printers will have multiple extruders that can reach higher temperature. While printers with multiple extruders offer more opportunities for customization (color, or combining soft and hard materials), they add to the total cost of the machine, and can add to the complexity of successfully designing and operating the machine.

Filament. FDM 3D printers build objects using a filament that is commonly packaged into spools. Working with filament is much simpler (and cleaner) than the 3D printing materials used by other methods that require pouring and mixing of liquids or powders. FDM 3D printers support a wide range of thermoplastic filaments that have different properties regarding their melting temperature (usually starting at 195 °C), flexibility, recyclability, color, and strength. When working with an FDM printer, the operator must understand specific characteristics of the filament since its the type or formulation can impact 3D printer temperature, extruder speed, resolution, and the potential for the print to fail.

38.2.3   Overview of 3D Design Tools

To create an object that can be printed, users must either have access to an existing 3D model or use Computer-Aided Drafting (CAD) tools to build such a model and then process this file for printing on their specific brand of printer. The section below describes four different 3D modeling tool paradigms common at the time of publication.

Manipulation-Based Design Software. Most 3D models are designed using manipulation-based design software. These tools use 2D representations of 3D objects that can be manipulated using a pointing device. Users can manipulate these 3D objects and the camera angle they are viewed from in real time to create a direct manipulation WYSIWYG (What You See Is What You Get) interfaces that output a standard format. These tools support multiple modes for creating models including combining primitive shapes (such as cubes, triangles, and spheres), or sculpting (which is similar to how a sculptor manipulates clay). These tools range from the simple Tinkercad (Tinkercad) as shown in Fig. 38.1 left, to the complex Blender (Blender) as shown in Fig. 38.1 middle and there are open-source, cloud-based, browser-based, and expensive proprietary versions.

Dialog-Based Design Software. When a user does not have the time or training to design a 3D model using manipulation-based software for a simple design, a dialog-

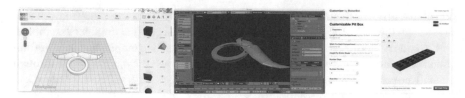

Fig. 38.1 Screenshots of the existing manipulation-based 3D modeling tools. Tinkercad (left), is designed for novices, while Blender (middle), is more advanced. Dialog-based customizer on Thingiverse.com (right)

based system is a welcome alternative. These systems let users design 3D models using familiar GUI iterators such as text boxes, checkboxes, and radio buttons. Thingiverse's Customizer (Customizer), (Fig. 38.1 right) is a popular tool, and Tinkercad recently added a similar functionality to its modeler. While these tools can dramatically simplify the modeling process and make customizing a preexisting design effortless, they limit the designer's freedom based on what they are preprogrammed for.

Tangible Design Platforms. Within the research community, there has been an influx of alternative design tools that enable users to tangibly design 3D models by manipulating physical objects (see Part 4 Chapter 6). A 3D model is then created by 3D scanning these objects (see next section), or the objects have embedded electronics that can specify their configuration to the computer (Follmer et al. 2010; Leduc-Mills and Eisenberg 2010). While users can quickly create low-resolution primitives with these tangible systems, their complexity is usually limited.

Text-Based 3D modelers. There are also several text-based modelers that let users programmatically define 3D shapes such as OpenSCAD (OpenSCAD), and some professional-level manipulation-based modelers support scripting (Scripting). However, these text-based methods are advanced, and have a steep learning curve.

38.2.4   *Capturing Physical Objects with 3D Scanners*

For some projects, it may be more efficient to capture the shape of a physical object using a 3D scanner than design a 3D model. Current 3D scanners use lasers, cameras, or both technologies to measure and capture the shape of a physical object using photogrammetry (Turk and Levoy 1994) or taking measurements of physical objects without touching them, using a camera or laser. Four categories of 3D scanners are described below, and important considerations to consider before selecting a scanning technique.

38.2.4.1   Common Scanner Types

Desktop 3D Scanners: These scanners are small machines (often smaller than 2′ cubed) that are ideal for capturing the shape of an object. Most of these tools rotate the object around its sensor (camera and/or laser) manually or on an automated turntable to maximize its view of the object.

Handheld 3D Scanners: These scanners use similar technology as desktop 3D scanners, but instead, the device is held by the operator and moved around the physical object to control the sensor's field of view.

Environment and Large-Scale 3D Scanners: These scanners are designed to capture details of large objects or environments. These scanners may be portable to scan an environment, such as those used to capture archeological sites, crime scene investigations, or surveying land (Remondino 2011; Sansoni et al. 2009). They may also be installed in a physical environment (Levoy et al. 2000, 3D Photogrammetry) to capture a large object.

Clever 3D Scanning Techniques: There have been several clever DIY projects to build low-cost 3D scanners that leverage off-the-shelf electronics. The two most popular were 3D scanning using a Microsoft Kinect (Izadi et al. 2011, 3D Scanning, Scanect) or stitching together photos taken from a smartphone (Ondruvska et al. 2015, itSeez3D, Scandy). At the time of this publication, these tools have been used to produce reasonable results to capture simple objects (usually between the size of a grapefruit or loaf of bread), or the outline of a figure. Depending on the application, the scans from these tools may be appropriate, or a higher resolution scanner is needed to more accurately capture surface features and precise measurements.

38.2.4.2   Important Considerations

Technical Considerations. When choosing a 3D scanner for a given application, the most important factors to consider are the resolution of the scanner, the time required to scan at a given resolution, the field of view of the scanner (and the size object it is calibrated for), and the form factor of the scanner.

Accessibility Considerations. Just as it is important to match the scanning technology to the application and final object to be captured, one should match the form factor of the tool to the scanning environment and the operator's ability. For example, while handheld scanners are ideal for mobile scanning or objects that cannot be set on a table, these scanners require the operator to carefully hold the scanner and potentially to hold their arm still. Desktop and environmental scanners may be more accessible for the operator, as they require minimal interaction from the operator as the object either stays still during the capture, or the scanner automatically moves the object.

38.2.5 Online Communities

Online communities enable end users, designers, and builders to share experiences, designs, modifications, and inspiration. They have been grouped into two categories below that capture much of the work happening in accessibility and digital fabrication: communities that share stories and inspiration, and online repositories that share instructions and digital files. While some of these communities are professionally curated and tied to companies that sell digital fabrication tools or training materials (Make: Ultimaker, Adafruit, MakerBot Thingiverse), there are also many run by nonprofits or individuals passionate about this accessibility (ATMakers.org, enabling, Adaptive, SMA). The following section further describes current trends in sharing communities and highlights existing communities that are popular for either sharing ideas, stories, and knowledge or being an online repository.

38.2.5.1 Sharing Ideas, Stories, and Knowledge

Many online communities have been created to share ideas, stories, and knowledge around the potential for digital fabrication tools to impact accessibility. This has been happening in both general digital fabrication and making communities, and ones that are exclusively focused on accessibility.

General and Editorially Curated Resources: There are many websites focused on fabrication trends that occasionally post accessibility articles highlighting interesting research innovations, homemade solutions, and interviews with designers or end users. While not committed exclusively to accessibility, these organization help accessibility work get wide attention and appeal, and can serve as a satisfying venue for novice designers to publish their work. Since these communities are professionally curated, the quality of the content is exceptionally high, and their staff engages with members through answering question and moderating discussion. One of the most popular examples is the Makezine Blog (Make:) which is part of Maker Media (publisher of Make: Magazine, and puts on Maker Faires across the world). This blog posts interesting projects and news from professionals and amateurs in the DIY community and engages novices through in-post discussions and active forums. Adafruit, an open-source hardware company that sells custom electronic kits and digital fabrication tools (Adafruit), has built an active online community through blog posts and video. Accessibility projects (and their designers) are often featured on their blog and participate in a weekly live streaming Show and Tell (Using Bluefruit) where designers show their designs and are interviewed by the company's famous co-founders.

Accessibility-Focused Communities: Smaller organizations or individuals actively working to innovate and solve specific accessibility problems. These include parent groups of children with a specific diagnosis (such as the SMA Adaptability Facebook group) sharing resources, experiences, and designs (SMA). AT Makers works to match volunteer engineers to assistive technology users and post tutorials on their website and answers questions via Facebook and Twitter (ATMakers.org). E-nable has become famous for printing 3D prosthetic hands and mobilizing volunteers to print and assemble these devices. Their website features stories of the impact of their work and provides instructions and resources for volunteers to get started (enabling). Finally, the Adaptive Design Association provides classes and workshops and posts instructional videos and educational materials on their website (Adaptive Design).

38.2.5.2   Online Repositories for Sharing on Instructions and Files

The origins of open-source software, or freely sharing source code, can be traced back to the 1950s when researchers started sharing software in user forums. Since then, open-source software has become a popular alternative to mass-marketed software, at a fraction of the cost (or no cost). Open-source hardware is a recent parallel to the open-source software movement: the same values and ideas are present where designs, materials, discussions, and source code are all publicly available. Within the open-source hardware movement online communities have been created to share designs and instructions to build objects. While the online communities described below are not focused exclusively on accessibility, they do feature accessibility projects.

Online Repositories of Designs: Thingiverse was one of the first online communities for sharing completed designs and works-in-progress (MakerBot Thingiverse). In addition to requiring designers to upload all digital files required to build an object, it encourages members to share experiences building these objects, and post modifications or derivatives of designs (through using its customizer tool (Customizer) or uploading new designs). Since their launch in 2008, many other repositories of 3D models have emerged, with varying emphasis on discussion and collaboration (Finger Splints on STL Finder, Ultimaker).

Sharing Instructions: Depending on the project, sharing a file for 3D printing might not be enough information to complete a project, and more instructions are needed. One of the first major online communities to fit this need is Instructables (Autodesk Instructables) which allows users to share instructions on how to make anything. This site supports sharing by allowing photo and video uploads and posting step-by-step instructions in the text. The Adafruit Learning System (Adafruit) is an excellent example of carefully curated instructions that include detailed instructions complete with downloadable files, video tutorials, and links to components that frequently feature accessibility adaptations (Using Bluefruit).

38.3   Accessibility Applications for Digital Fabrication

Digital Fabrication tools have been used across assistive technology and accessibility domains. These tools have been used to create many objects, but popular accessibility applications include custom cases and containers, tactile graphics, personalized objects, and grips. This section describes some of the active domains 3D printing has made strides in related to accessibility.

38.3.1   Tactile Graphics

Tactile graphics are tangible representations of visual content and can be used to make graphs, photos, and diagrams accessible for individuals with vision impairments. It is also popular to use tactile graphics in education to or make abstract information accessible to tactile learners. Prior to the proliferation of digital fabrication tools, tactile graphics were typically made by hand (using a raised paint or embossing tool), swell paper (material that raises a material when heated), or a digital embosser (noisy and expensive machines that "print" embossed designs on paper or a thin plastic) (NFB), or building 3D shapes with clay or found materials. However, 3D printing tactile graphics has proven to be a more scalable solution and offers the opportunity to quickly produce and customize these tactile graphics. Past work has shown demonstrated benefits creating 3D printed tactile graphics for math equations (Brown and Hurst 2012; Hu 2015), story books (Stangl et al. 2014, 2015) and scientific diagrams (Shi et al. 2016a; Horowitz and Schultz 2014).

Tactile Overlays: The other area of tactile graphics that has seen significant advancement with digital fabrication is *tactile overlays*. These are made of thin pieces of plastic (usually 3D printed, but sometimes cut with a laser cutter) that are placed on a flat interactive surface to present informational tactilely. Digital fabrication tools provide the opportunity to create overlays that convey more information about the underlying interface than traditional tactile dots could (such as labeling the buttons on a microwave (Guo et al. 2017). Additionally, there is exciting work looking at automating the process to design custom overlays (Guo et al. 2017; He et al. 2017). Another avenue tactile overlays have made headway is in making LCD touchscreens on smartphones or tables more accessible. These overlays are designed to be raised enough to convey visual information, yet thin enough not to block the touchscreen's sensor. One of the popular areas for this research is in tactile maps (Taylor et al. 2016; Gotzelmann 2016).

38.3.2   Therapeutic and Medical Devices

Perhaps the most visible application of 3D printing and accessibility has been in 3D printing assistive or medical devices such as prosthetics, splints, and grips. These applications offer many opportunities as end users may currently have no solution, or an off-the-shelf solution from a medical professional that is unideal.

Custom Hand Grips: Perhaps the simplest example of a 3D printed assistive technology is creating a custom hand grip for an individual who is either unable to use an existing solution, or using the device is uncomfortable. Depending on the application, custom grips can be made by designing an object that will fit many people, or creating a unique object by taking a mold with an end user's hand and 3D scanning it (Buehler et al. 2016).

Splints: An excellent application of 3D printers is creating splints that can be worn over a joint to minimize movement instead of a cast (Blaya et al. 2017). 3D printing is ideal for this application since custom splints can be created to match an individual's unique body, can be easily removed, offer many customization options (color or design), and an exact replica can be replicated if necessary. 3D printing splints has become so popular and so economical that FDA certified companies began offering this service (Active Armor) for temporary splints due to injury. There have also been other projects to create splints for older adults to minimize arthritis pain (Paterson et al. 2014), and there are many finger splint designs (Finger Splints on STL Finder, Finger Splints on Thingiverse).

Prosthetics: 3D printing prosthetic limbs has become an exciting and popular application of 3D printing and the E-nable community has lead the revolution to mobilize volunteers to print and assemble 3D printed hands (Parry-Hill et al. 2017; Schull 2015). There are currently multiple designs of prosthetic hands (Phillips et al. 2015, enable), and many exciting implications to be used in the developing world (Schmidt et al. 2015; Phillips et al. 2015).

Reviving Historic Designs: The examples above described the role 3D printing can play in creating new assistive technologies. However, it can also play an important role in reproducing past designs. One early example was posted to Open Prosthetics Project (Open Prosthetics) to revive the Trautman Hook (Trautman Hook). The original Trautman hook is from the 1920s and was no longer commercially produced at the time. This group analyzed the original patents of this device to understand the dimensions and functionality, and created 3D models that they 3D printed using inexpensive plastic filament and later 3D printed in metal once they had perfected the design.

38.3.3 Cases and Containers for High-Tech Assistive Technologies

In addition to creating standalone objects, digital fabrication tools offer the possibility to enclose or attach other high-tech assistive technologies. Specifically, 3D printing is an ideal tool to produce custom cases or adaptations for wearables, controllers, or Internet of Thing devices.

Adapting Existing Technology: Sometimes an end user does not need a custom electronic solution. Instead, their accessibility needs can be met through redesigning the form factor of an existing technology, or adjustments it to be more accessible for an end user. One of the most prolific areas is adapting video game controllers for individuals who are not able to access the consumer versions. One early example is

Benjamin Heckendorn's (known for adapting video game consoles and controllers (Heckendorn 2005)) conversion of two-handed game controllers to work with either the left or right hand (Single Handed) using custom 3D printed parts. There are now several groups and stories of people adapting gaming consoles with 3D printers when the commercial version is not accessible to them (Controller Project, 3D Printed Adaptor).

38.3.4   Novel Interactions with 3D Printed Objects

Given the ability to create unique objects, accessibility researchers have developed novel interactive systems that leverage custom 3D printed objects that either have electronics embedded in them, or track interaction through an external source. While not all of these projects were not developed as accessibility devices, they could be used to extend tangible and tactile interactions in assistive technologies such as tactile graphics, communication devices, or interactive surfaces.

Embedding Materials in a 3D Print: Within the HCI literature, there have been several successful efforts to digitally fabricate 3D printed objects with embedded electronics that support interaction. A few examples include an embedded accelerometer in 3D printed objects (Hook et al. 2014), printing objects with conductive surfaces (Gunther et al. 2017), embedding small optical elements (or light pipes) into a 3D print (Willis et al. 2012), or fabricating objects with embedded wire coils that can act as electromagnetic fields (Peng et al. 2016).

Interactive Plastic: There have been interesting innovations in detecting how an end user is interacting with a 3D printed plastic object. Some of these solutions have included using computer vision methods to track what parts of a 3D print are touched by an end user (Shen et al. 2013; Shi et al. 2016b), listening to the sound the object makes when tapped by a specific tool to let the user specify a region of interest (Shi et al. 2016a), or track the deformation of a flexible 3D print that is tracked by a capacitive touchscreen (Schmitz et al. 2017). While the interaction capabilities for this approach may be more limited than embedding electronics, this approach has the advantage of being lower cost, simpler to implement, and working with standard 3D printers.

38.4   Discussion

38.4.1   Opportunities for Digital Fabrication and Accessibility

Digital Fabrication tools offer new and exciting opportunities for accessibility researchers, practitioners, and assistive technology end users to build physical objects. As discussed in Sect. 38.3, these tools have been used to build and customize physical objects such as educational materials, therapy aids, prosthetics, and communication technology. This section briefly outlines some of the key opportunities this technology offers to those interested in accessibility.

Increased Fabrication Safety. Traditional manufacturing tools (band saws, lathes, and drill presses) can be dangerous and there are many operator requirements for safe operation. These frequently include the ability to stand, precise manual dexterity, and accurate vision, all of which limit who can operate these machines. Furthermore, operating these machines requires special training and knowledge, and can be extremely dangerous when misused. Digital fabrication tools remove many of these barriers since they are computer controlled, and the main task of the user moves from operating the machine accessing a computer to control and supervise fabrication.

Accessible Digital Design. Since these machines build objects from digital design files, anyone who can access a computer can become a designer. To create an object for a digital fabrication tool, a user only needs to be able to access a computer and create (or download) a file in the correct format. As discussed in Sect. 38.2, there are many design tools and online communities for individuals to create, share, or download digital design files.

Customization and "Design for 1". Digital fabrication tools are ideal for creating unique physical objects that can be tailored to the specific needs of an individual or application. Since digital fabrication tools use additive or subtractive techniques to build individual objects, it does not cost more time or money to make a set of unique designs compared to identical copies of the same design. This is in stark contrast to traditional manufacturing methods which are optimized for large-scale production of a single design and cannot accommodate modifications.

Fast Turnaround from Idea to Physical Object. The true power of rapid prototyping happens when the duration from idea to physical object is shortened. This frequently occurs when design and fabrication tools are co-located and a designer can easily create a digital design, quickly build a low-fidelity physical model of that object, test the object, and iteratively design it. Once the designer has finalized the design they can make a high-fidelity object in the ideal size, material, and resolution.

Cost Savings. There are many potential financial incentives to use digital fabrication tools in accessibility research and practice. However, perhaps the most significant cost savings is in the ability to avoid the significant markup associated with accessibility items due to medical insurance. While the financial aspects are appealing, there can be risks associated with liability for end users who chose to circumvent existing accessibility delivery systems.

"Making" can be Empowering. Independently solving problems can create a unique sense of satisfaction that is often missing for assistive technology end users. By empowering individuals with the means and knowledge to create their own accessibility solutions (and iterate on these designs as their needs change), they will have full control over most of the factors that are problematic in adoption (described below).

38.4.2   Potential for Digital Fabrication and Assistive
Technology Adoption Rates

While there is a large market for both medical and nonmedical devices that are used as assistive technology, many studies have shown that the overall abandonment rate of assistive technology is high: 29.3% overall (Phillips and Zhao 1993). High abandonment rates leave many individuals without the solutions they need and waste time, money, and energy developing and purchasing technology that is not used.

In a survey of 227 adults with disabilities who use assistive technology, Phillips found that almost one-third of all devices were completely abandoned (Phillips and Zhao 1993). They identify four factors related to abandonment:

(1) **User involvement in device selection**. They found that user opinions matter, and quotes one participant saying, "Listen to me! I know what works for me."
(2) **Ease of procuring the device**. Surprisingly, devices that are easy to obtain (purchased at drugstores, mail-order catalogs, etc.) were not always the most appropriate device for the user's needs.
(3) **Device performance**: Participants cared about reliability, comfort, ease of use, safety, and durability.
(4) **Change in ability** (both improvement and decline) and preferences. User needs, lifestyles, and priorities change over time, resulting in previously used assistive technology devices becoming irrelevant to one's current needs.

Phillips concluded that one of the best ways to fight abandonment is to develop policies and services that emphasize consumer involvement and consider long-term needs (Phillips and Zhao 1993). Digital fabrication tools allow individuals to create and modify their own assistive technology rather than being forced to rely on "off-the-shelf" products. Access to these tools and being involved in the design process may yield technologies with higher adoption rates and avoid these common abandonment issues.

38.5   Author's Opinion of the Field

38.5.1   Recommendations and Best Practices

I have studied the adoption of digital fabrication in multiple accessibility-focused communities including special education, physical and occupational therapy, and popular making. Through this work, my colleagues and I have observed the following challenges regarding the adoption of 3D printing in the accessibility domain.

38.5.1.1 Budget More Time than You Expect

Time is easily the most expensive resource in digital fabrication. Given the afford-ability of many digital fabrication tools, financial cost is rarely the most significant obstacle to adoption and use for creating accessibility solutions. Instead, it is more common for people to underestimate the amount of time required to learn how to use CAD tools, 3D printer operation software, and 3D scanners.

Slow Build Times: Unfortunately, current 3D printers are not fast, and it can take several hours to build a part that is smaller than 4 in.^{2}. Print times vary according to the 3D printers, filament used, and desired resolution and density. However, the traits of objects that are most frequently requested for accessibility applications (durable, soft to the touch, flexible), require settings and filaments that are slow to print with.

Printer Failure: Successfully printing a 3D model is not trivial. In addition to learning the technical skills to operate a 3D printer, an operator must troubleshoot the machine and monitor it to successfully print. Most operators have experienced the frustrating experience of running a 3D printer for several hours only to return to a nest of the wasted filament and a failed part (Fig. 38.2).

Working with Limited Schedules: Unfortunately, most individuals with the accessibility domain knowledge to build custom assistive technologies have busy schedules that do not allow the luxury of devoting significant time to learning and operating digital fabrication tools. For example, in my past research working with Occupational Therapists at in a school setting, it took us weeks to find time in a stu-dent's weekly 45-min OT session to iteratively design a custom hand grip because the therapists had higher priority tasks they needed to work on (Buehler et al. 2016). I believe the only way to address this challenge is to advocate (and budget) for staff time for any new digital fabrication tools an organization is looking to adopt.

38.5.1.2 Select the Right Tools

Given the diversity of fabrication tools, it is important to ensure appropriate tools are selected for the population and the environment. Some general considerations to

Fig. 38.2 Common printer failure where the model came loose from the print bed resulting in wasted filament and time (left). Delicate and full-color 3D print made at a school for the blind (middle). Design exploration (in clay) with therapists in a school setting to create a custom stylus grip for a student (right). All photos were taken by Erin Buehler

consider when making a purchasing decision is to consider the size of the object the machine can produce the materials of the final object.

Matching Output to Application. One troublesome example we observed in (Buehler et al. 2016) was when a school for the blind had a full-color resin composite 3D printer. This machine can create high-quality prints by sealing layers of a resin powder together and inject color into the powder to create full-color prints (see white snowman next to green tree as shown in Fig. 38.2). However, the final product from this kind of machine is fragile and can crumble with frequent handling, or shatter if dropped. The brittleness of the final product is problematic for any tactile graphics that were designed for this setting.

Housing Fabrication Technology. Physical access to the fabrication tools is important to ensure adoption. In my past work, I encountered a school that kept an expensive 3D printer in a locked closet to ensure it was safe. However, since this technology ended up being rarely used because instructors and students had extremely limited access to the technology, and were too worried about breaking it to spend the time exploring its features and learning how to use it.

38.5.1.3   Involve End Users and Clinicians

Working closely with end users is a core principle of user-centered design, and it is important to acknowledge its relevance when designing custom assistive technologies. In addition to increasing the likelihood of building a successful solution that will be used, being involved in the design process can feel empowering.

38.5.2   Future Directions

38.5.2.1   Understanding and Minimizing Liability

We are still understanding the complicated liability questions for using digital fabrication tools to build accessibility and health devices, and the implications of the end users circumventing existing supply chains and insurance when they make their own devices. In my work, I have begun to explore this issue by interviewing Physical Therapists who expressed concern about these implications:

> If a product fails, the manufacturer is liable. If I were to print a piece of equipment for my patient to use, I am now the designer and the manufacturer. I had n't thought about this before, but it makes sense that this would be a concern with 3D printing. – Physical Therapist (McDonald et al. 2016).

Quality Control and Risk Assessment: While the concept of circumventing medical professionals is appealing to reduce cost and decrease device delivery time, there are some serious concerns regarding assessing the safety of the device in terms of durability and impact of long-term use. It is important to acknowledge that not all custom assistive technologies have the same liability concerns, and many popular designs have minimal risk (such as tactile graphics, modified input controllers, or custom phone cases). However, objects that are designed to carry weight, be in close contact with the body for a long time, or fit over body parts may expose the end user to higher risk. For example, when 3D printing splints or prosthetics, it is important to ensure the weight and fit are appropriate, as the end user could encounter injury if it is too heavy, rubs on their bare skin, or is too tight.

Modifying Assistive Technology Under Warranty: As described above, there are many opportunities to modify off-the-shelf technology using custom parts created with digital fabrication tools. However, the liability concerns regarding modifications become murky when discussing assistive technologies acquired through traditional channels and are under warranty. One of the most striking examples is power wheelchairs, which can easily cost $30,000–50,000 (US) before insurance. In past interviews with power wheelchair users, they were eager to make minor modifications to their wheelchair (adding lights or a clock), but generally hesitant to make changes that would void a warranty. However, several people I worked with admitted that their attitude toward breaking the warranty would change depending on the circumstances. One individual said he would be open break the warranty if he were involved in the design process and knew exactly every change that was made to his wheelchair. Another said it would depend on the urgency of the repair or benefit of the modification. He recounted a powerful time when his wheelchair was broken for 6 months and had to stay home, and said:

> When it breaks I stay in bed. – Power wheelchair user (Hurst and Tobias 2011).

38.5.2.2 Lower the Barriers for End Users and Clinicians to Become Designers

The best way to minimize these liability concerns is to involve end users and accessibility experts in the design, fabrication, and evaluation of these devices. In order for this to be feasible, we must ensure these tools are accessible and understandable by these individuals without engineering backgrounds. Despite the significant amount of currently available resources and the benefits of solving accessibility solutions with digital fabrication tools, my research team has observed a lack of participation from end users and individuals with accessibility training in design (Buehler et al. 2015).

Create Accessible Tools. For significant and meaningful participation from assistive technology end users and experts, we need to ensure that all digital fabrication software, tools, and communities are accessible. This includes all design, operation, and scanning tools, as well as online repositories of designs, and online communities that share ideas and feedback. In addition to following the well-established practices described in this book for software accessibility, it is also important to ensure that these tools are accessible to novices with little digital fabrication or engineering experience.

Provide Accessible Training Materials. To ensure end users, clinicians, and other stakeholders stay involved in digital fabrication for accessibility it is important to ensure that the tools and training materials are designed for non-engineers. While those with professional training will likely always be interested (and have access) to these tools, we must strive to ensure these tools are used by a diverse population.

38.5.2.3 Promote Sustainability Through Encouraging Documentation

Finally, it is important to consider the long-term sustainability of any custom accessibility solution. Unlike assistive technologies prescribed by a physician and acquired through insurance, custom-built assistive technology solutions rarely come with a warranty or service plan. This is especially important for devices where someone kindly volunteers to build the device, but the end user does not have the tools or knowledge to move forward if the device breaks or their needs change. These sustainability concerns could potentially be overcome through careful documentation (and publication) of all knowledge and resources necessary to recreate the object, ideally through online communities and repositories that will be around in the long term. However, motivating and training end users to document work is nontrivial and all documentation should be reviewed for completeness, readability, and accuracy. Moving forward, there may be lessons from the open-source software and hardware movements that can be applied to this domain.

38.6 Conclusion

This chapter has described the potential for digital fabrication and accessibility and provided an overview of relevant tools and significant applications. It provides recommendations for accessibility end users, volunteers, or clinicians to consider before starting an accessibility project or buying equipment. It is the author's hope that this resource will be valuable to individuals interested in using digital fabrication tools for accessibility projects.

Acknowledgements The author thanks her past collaborators and students who have participated in the research that informed her views about the potential for digital fabrication and accessibility, and the research that was featured in this chapter. These collaborators and students include Lisa Anthony, Stacy Branham, Erin Buehler, Patrick Carrington, William Easley, Matthew Griffin, Foad Hamidi, Scott Hudson, Shaun Kane, Samantha McDonald, and Jennifer Mankoff.

References

3D Photogrammetry Scanning. https://photogrammetry.irc.umbc.edu/

3D Scanning with Windows 10. https://developer.microsoft.com/en-us/windows/hardware/3d-print/scanning-with-kinect

3D Systems On-demand Manufacturing. https://www.3dsystems.com/on-demand-manufacturing

ActiveArmor 3D Printed Splints. https://activarmor.com/

Adafruit. https://www.adafruit.com/

Adaptive Design Association Inc. http://www.adaptivedesign.org/

ATMakers.org Helping Makers Help Others. http://atmakers.org/

Autodesk Instructables. https://www.instructables.com/

Blaya F, Pedro PS, Lopez-Silva J, D'Amato R, Juanes JA, Lagandara JG (2017) Study, design and prototyping of arm splint with additive manufacturing process. In: Proceedings of the 5th international conference on technological ecosystems for enhancing multiculturality. ACM, pp 57:1–57:7

Blender: the Free and Open Source 3D Creation Suite. https://www.blender.org/

Brown C, Hurst A (2012) VizTouch: automatically generated tactile visualizations of coordinate spaces. In: Proceedings of the sixth international conference on tangible, embedded and embodied interaction. ACM, pp 131–138

Buehler E, Branham S, Ali A, Chang JJ, Hofmann MK, Hurst A, Kane SK (2015) Sharing is caring: assistive technology designs on Thingiverse. In: Proceedings of the 33rd annual ACM conference on human factors in computing systems. ACM, pp 525–534

Buehler E, Comrie N, Hofmann M, McDonald S, Hurst A (2016) Investigating the implications of 3D printing in special education. ACM Trans Access Comput 8(3):11:1–11:28

Customizer on Thingiverse. https://www.thingiverse.com/customizer

eMachineShop. http://www.emachineshop.com

Enabling the Future. http://enablingthefuture.org/

Finger Splints on STL Finder. https://www.stlfinder.com/3dmodels/finger-splint

Finger Splints on Thingiverse. https://www.thingiverse.com/search?q=splint&dwh=85b3643f48f931

Follmer S, Carr D, Lovell E, Ishii H (2010) CopyCAD: remixing physical objects with copy and paste from the real world. In: Adjunct proceedings of the 23rd annual ACM symposium on user interface software and technology, pp 381–382

Gotzelmann T (2016) LucentMaps: 3D printed audiovisual tactile maps for blind and visually impaired people. In: Proceedings of the 18th international ACM SIGACCESS conference on computers and accessibility. ACM, pp 81–90

Gunther S, Schmitz M, Muller F, Riemann J, Muhlhauser M (2017) BYO*: utilizing 3D printed tangible tools for interaction on interactive surfaces. In: Proceedings of the 2017 ACM workshop on interacting with smart objects. ACM, pp 21–26

Guo A, Kim J, Chen XA, Yeh T, Hudson SE, Mankoff J, Bigham JP (2017) Facade: auto-generating tactile interfaces to appliances. In: Proceedings of the 2017 CHI conference on human factors in computing systems. ACM, pp 5826–5838

Hackerspaces.org Wiki. https://wiki.hackerspaces.org/

He L, Wan Z, Findlater L, Froehlich JE (2017) TacTILE: a preliminary toolchain for creating accessible graphics with 3D-printed overlays and auditory annotations. In: Proceedings of the 19th international ACM SIGACCESS conference on computers and accessibility. ACM, pp 397–398

Heckendorn B (2005) Hacking video game consoles: turn your old video game systems into awesome new portables (ExtremeTech). Wiley

Hook J, Nappey T, Hodges S, Wright P, Olivier P (2014) Making 3D printed objects interactive using wireless accelerometers. In: CHI '14 extended abstracts on human factors in computing systems. ACM, pp 1435–1440

Horowitz SS, Schultz PH (2014) Printing space: using 3D printing of digital terrain models in geosciences education and research. J Geosci Educ 62(1):138–145

Hu M (2015) Exploring new paradigms for accessible 3D printed graphs. In: Proceedings of the 17th international ACM SIGACCESS conference on computers and accessibility. ACM, pp 365–366

Hurst A, Tobias J (2011) Empowering individuals with do-it-yourself assistive technology. In: The proceedings of the 13th international ACM SIGACCESS conference on computers and accessibility. ACM, pp 11–18

itSeez3D Mobile Scanning App. https://itseez3d.com/

Izadi S, Kim D, Hilliges O, Molyneaux D, Newcombe R, Kohli P, Shotton J, Hodges S, Freeman D, Davison A et al (2011) KinectFusion: real-time 3D reconstruction and interaction using a moving depth camera. In: Proceedings of the 24th annual ACM symposium on User interface software and technology, pp 559–568

Kelleher C, Pausch R, Kiesler S (2007) Storytelling Alice motivates middle school girls to learn computer programming. In: Proceedings of the SIGCHI conference on human factors in computing systems. ACM, pp 1455–1464

Khanapour PR, DesPortes K, Cochran Z, DiSalvo B (2017) Framing makerspace communities. In: Proceedings of the 7th annual conference on creativity and fabrication in education. ACM, pp 15:1–15:4

Kuznetsov S, Paulos E (2010) Rise of the expert amateur: DIY projects, communities, and cultures. In: Proceedings of the 6th Nordic conference on human-computer interaction: extending boundaries, pp 295–304

Leduc-Mills B, Eisenberg M (2010) The UCube: a child-friendly device for introductory three-dimensional design. In: Proceedings of the 10th international conference on interaction design and children, pp 72–80

Levoy M, Pulli K, Curless B, Rusinkiewicz S, Koller D, Pereira L, Ginzton M, Anderson S, Davis J, Ginsberg J, Shade J, Fulk D (2000) The digital michelangelo project: 3D scanning of large statues. In: Proceedings of the 27th annual conference on computer graphics and interactive techniques. ACM Press/Addison-Wesley Publishing Co., pp 131–144

Lipson H, Kurman M (2010) Factory@ home: the emerging economy of personal fabrication. A report commissioned by the US Office of Science and Technology Policy

Lupton E (2006) DIY: design it yourself: a design handbook. Princeton Architectural Press

Make: 3D Printer Buyer's Guide. https://makezine.com/comparison/3dprinters/

Make: We Are All Makers. https://makezine.com/

MakerBot Thingiverse. https://www.thingiverse.com/

Maloney JH, Peppler K, Kafai Y, Resnick M, Rusk N (2008) Programming by choice: urban youth learning programming with scratch. SIGCSE Bull 40(1):367–371

McDonald S, Comrie N, Buehler E, Carter N, Dubin B, Gordes K, McCombe-Waller S, Hurst A (2016) Uncovering challenges and opportunities for 3D printing assistive technology with physical therapists. In: Proceedings of the 18th international ACM SIGACCESS conference on computers and accessibility. ACM, pp 131–139

NFB Introduction to Tactile Graphics. https://nfb.org/images/nfb/publications/jbir/jbir11/jbir010205.html

Obrist M (2008) DIY HCI. VDM Verlag

Ondrúska P, Kohli P, Izadi S (2015) Mobilefusion: real-time volumetric surface reconstruction and dense tracking on mobile phones. IEEE Trans Vis Comput Graph 21(11):1251–1258

OpenSCAD: The Programmer's Solid 3D CAD Modeller. http://www.openscad.org/

Parry-Hill J, Shih PC, Mankoff J, Ashbrook D (2017) Understanding volunteer AT fabricators: opportunities and challenges in DIY-AT for others in e-NABLE. In: Proceedings of the 2017 CHI conference on human factors in computing systems. ACM, pp 6184–6194

Paterson AM, Donnison E, Bibb RJ, Ian Campbell R (2014) Computer-aided design to support fabrication of wrist splints using 3D printing: a feasibility study. Hand Therapy 19(4):102–113

PCMag: The Best 3D Printers of 2018. https://www.pcmag.com/article2/0,2817,2470038,00.asp

Peng H, Guimbretiere F, McCann J, Hudson S (2016) A 3D printer for interactive electromagnetic devices. In: Proceedings of the 29th annual symposium on user interface software and technology. ACM, pp 553–562

Phillips B, Zhao H (1993) Predictors of assistive technology abandonment. Assist Technol 5(1):36–45

Phillips B, Zingalis G, Ritter S, Mehta K (2015) A review of current upper-limb prostheses for resource constrained settings. In: 2015 IEEE global humanitarian technology conference (GHTC), pp 52–58

Ponoko. http://www.ponoko.com

Remondino F (2011) Heritage recording and 3D modeling with photogrammetry and 3D scanning. Remote Sensing 3(6):1104–1138

Replicating Rapid Prototyers: RepRap Wiki. https://www.reprap.org/wiki/RepRap

Sansoni G, Trebeschi M, Docchio F (2009) State-of-the-art and applications of 3D imaging sensors in industry, cultural heritage, medicine, and criminal investigation. Sensors 9(1):568–601

Scandy 3D Scanning. https://www.scandy.co/

Scanect 3D Scanning. http://skanect.occipital.com/

Scherer MJ (1996) Outcomes of assistive technology use on quality of life. Disabil Rehabil 18(9):439–448

Schmidt R, Chen V, Gmeiner T, Ratto M (2015) 3D-printed prosthetics for the developing world. In: SIGGRAPH 2015: Studio. ACM, pp 21:1–21:1

Schmitz M, Steimle J, Huber J, Dezfuli N, Muhlhauser M (2017) Flexibles: deformation-aware 3D-printed tangibles for capacitive touchscreens. In: Proceedings of the 2017 CHI conference on human factors in computing systems. ACM, pp 1001–1014

Schull J (2015) Enabling the future: crowd sourced 3D-printed prosthetics as a model for open source assistive technology innovation and mutual aid. In: Proceedings of the 17th international ACM SIGACCESS conference on computers & accessibility. ACM, pp 1–1

Scripting in Blender with Python. https://docs.blender.org/manual/en/dev/advanced/scripting/index.html

Shapeways Inc. http://www.shapeways.com

Shen H, Edwards O, Miele J, Coughlan JM (2013) CamIO: a 3D computer vision system enabling audio/haptic interaction with physical objects by blind users. In: Proceedings of the 15th international ACM SIGACCESS conference on computers and accessibility. ACM, pp 41:1–41:2

Shi L, McLachlan R, Zhao Y, Azenkot S (2016a) Magic touch: interacting with 3D printed graphics. In: Proceedings of the 18th international ACM SIGACCESS conference on computers and accessibility. ACM, pp 329–330

Shi L, Zelzer I, Feng C, Azenkot S (2016b) Tickers and talker: an accessible labeling toolkit for 3D printed models. In: Proceedings of the 2016 CHI conference on human factors in computing systems. ACM, pp 4896–4907

Single Handed Xbox One Controllers. https://www.benheck.com/controllers

SMA Adaptability Facebook Group: You can build it... we can help! https://www.facebook.com/groups/SMAadaptability

Stangl A, Kim J, Yeh T (2014) 3D printed tactile picture books for children with visual impairments: a design probe. In: Proceedings of the 2014 conference on interaction design and children. ACM, pp 321–324

Stangl A, Hsu C-L, Yeh T (2015) Transcribing across the senses: community efforts to create 3D printable accessible tactile pictures for young children with visual impairments. In: Proceedings of the 17th international ACM SIGACCESS conference on computers & accessibility. ACM, pp 127–137

Taylor B, Dey A, Siewiorek D, Smailagic A (2016) Customizable 3D printed tactile maps as interactive overlays. In: Proceedings of the 18th international ACM SIGACCESS conference on computers and accessibility. ACM, pp 71–79

The Controller Project: Custom Modifications for People with Disabilities. http://thecontrollerproject.com

The Open Prosthetics Project. https://openprosthetics.org

The Trautman Hook on OpenProsthetics.org (Archived). https://web.archive.org/web/20160425230150/http://openprosthetics.org:80/concepts/55/the-trautman-hook

This 3D Printed Adapter Makes Nintendo's Switch Controllers More Accessible. https://makezine.com/2018/01/04/3d-printed-nintendo-switch-controller-adapter/

Tinkercad by Autodesk. https://www.tinkercad.com/

Turk G, Levoy M (1994) Zippered polygon meshes from range images. In: Proceedings of the 21st annual conference on computer graphics and interactive techniques. ACM, pp 311–318

Ultimaker YouMagine. https://www.youmagine.com/

Using Bluefruit BLE to Give Disabled Users Switch Control Access to IOS Devices. https://learn.adafruit.com/ios-switch-control-using-ble?view=all

Von Hippel E (2005) Democratizing innovation. MIT press

Willis K, Brockmeyer E, Hudson S, Poupyrev I (2012) Printed optics: 3D printing of embedded optical elements for interactive devices. In: Proceedings of the 25th annual ACM symposium on user interface software and technology. ACM, pp 589–598

Chapter 39
Internet of Things: An Opportunity for Advancing Universal Access

Federica Cena, Amon Rapp and Ilaria Torre

Abstract IoT enables the worldwide connection of heterogeneous things or objects, which can hence interact with each other and cooperate with their neighbors to reach common goals, by using different communication technologies and communication protocol standards. IoT and related technologies can increase or reduce the gap among people. In this respect, this chapter aims to highlight the virtuose use of the IoT paradigm by providing examples of its application for enhancing universal access in different fields.

39.1 Introduction

Recently, due to the rapid advances in different fields, such as wireless sensor networks and microprocessor, **Internet of Things (IoT)** (Atzori et al. 2010; Li et al. 2015; Whitmore et al. 2015) has become a flourishing research area. IoT enables the worldwide connection of heterogeneous things or objects which, through unique addressing schemes, are able to interact with each other and cooperate with their neighbors to reach common goals, by using different communication technologies and communication protocol standards (Giusto et al. 2010). Moreover, the **Web of Things (WoT)** (Guinard and Triva 2009) paradigm has been introduced to allow real-world objects to be part of the World Wide Web. WoT enables objects interaction at the application layer by using web protocols and technologies.

The number of things that are currently accessing the internet is growing steadily. Things can be simple sensors and actuators, or wireless and mobile devices, or every-

F. Cena · A. Rapp
University of Torino, Turin, Italy
e-mail: federica.cena@unito.it

A. Rapp
e-mail: amon.rapp@unito.it

I. Torre (✉)
University of Genoa, Genoa, Italy
e-mail: ilaria.torre@unige.it

© Springer-Verlag London Ltd., part of Springer Nature 2019   777
Y. Yesilada and S. Harper (eds.), *Web Accessibility*, Human–Computer
Interaction Series, https://doi.org/10.1007/978-1-4471-7440-0_39

day-life objects enhanced with capabilities to interact with the external world through the Internet. When objects, besides connectivity, are augmented with processing capabilities as well, are often called **Smart Objects (SO)**. In (Cena et al. 2017a), we characterize Smart Objects as everyday objects with interacting capabilities, defined as the tight and seamless integration of a physical and a digital counterpart, which augment each other into a unique peculiar entity. The Internet of Things provides a natural environment in which SOs can deploy their abilities. After more than a decade of development (Gubbi et al. 2013; Whitmore et al. 2015; Atzori et al. 2010), the IoT has experimented several forms of smartness, by enhancing the objects or the network (Holler et al. 2014; Atzori et al. 2014).

The IoT/WoT/SO paradigm, allowing to digitally connect everyday objects in the real world, makes possible Wiser's vision of **Ubiquitous Computing** (Weiser 1998), which aims to bring intelligence to our everyday environments making the technology disappear. This idea is also known as **Ambient Intelligence** (Mukherjee et al. 2009). The goal of such technologies is to collect ambient information, through different devices, and to use this information in a wide range of applications. Thus, IoT paradigm can have a high impact on several aspects of everyday life of users. For a private user, domotics, assisted living, e-health, enhanced learning are only a few examples of possible application scenarios. In the business domain, examples of applications are automation and industrial manufacturing, logistics, business/process management, intelligent transportation.

In all the fields mentioned above, the IoT paradigm might be applied to advance universal access, with the aim for all people to have equal opportunity to access to information, health, education, mobility and energy services, and so forth. Accessibility is the term used to indicate whether an object, a service, or an environment can be used by people of all abilities and disabilities. It is a multifaceted concept since accessibility may concern real-world objects and environments as well as web pages, software applications and ICT devices. Accessibility barriers may concern physical and cognitive disability, but also may include logical barriers. For example, an object is not accessible for a user that does not know how to use it but will become accessible after the user receives instructions about it; or an application form that is not accessible to a user who does not comprehend its language, will become accessible if a proper translation is provided (Torre and Celik 2016).

Accessibility is a core theme in the development of smart cities. Like other technologies, the IoT and related technologies can increase or reduce the gap among people. The IoT can offer people with disabilities the assistance and support they need to achieve a good quality of life and allow them to participate in the social and economic life (Nicolau and Montague 2019). Conversely, if IoT devices and applications are designed without taking into account the need of people with special needs they could become more of a disabler than an enabler (Abou-Zahra et al. 2017). In this chapter, we aim to highlight the virtuose use of the IoT paradigm by providing examples of its application for universal access in different fields.

Advancing universal access implies (1) enabling everybody, including people with physical disabilities, to have easy access to all computing resources and sophisticated information services that will soon be made available to the general public and expert users all over the world and (2) providing people with disabilities with advanced assisted living (Nicolau and Montague 2019; Carbonell 2009).

The chapter is organized as follows. First, we provide a background of definitions related to Internet of Things, Web of Things, Smart Objects, and Ambient Intelligence. Then, we present some scenarios that illustrate how these technologies can contribute to support universal access, referring to some relevant state of the art works. Finally, we provide some discussion about how the field can evolve in the future, with open research issues.

39.2 Internet of Things and Universal Access

In this section, we first provide the background definitions of the notions involved in the chapter, and then describe how IoT technology can be used to favor accessibility.

39.2.1 Background and Definitions

Internet of Things. The Internet of Things (IoT) refers to a worldwide network of interconnected heterogeneous objects (RFID, sensors, actuators, wireless devices, smart objects, embedded computers, etc.) uniquely addressable, based on standard communication protocols. All things are seamlessly integrated into the information network (Bandyopadhyay and Sen 2011).

Web of Things. The Web of Things (WoT) exposes Internet of Things (IoT) platforms and devices through the World Wide Web, making them accessible through their virtual representation (Atzori et al. 2014; Guinard et al. 2011). WoT exploits URIs to address things and Web technologies to access them, such as the HTTP protocol, the REST architecture and scripting APIs at the services layer. Moreover, the WoT Interest Group (www.w3.org/WoT) is working to define a framework for the development of standards and services based upon the Web technologies for a combination of the IoT with the Web of Data (Torre and Celik 2015, 2016).

Smart Objects (SO). A SO is an autonomous, physical object augmented with sensing/actuating, processing, storing, and networking capabilities (Kortuem et al. 2010; Fortino et al. 2014). Advanced SOs can show intelligent behavior, due to interacting and problem-solving capabilities. Although a smart object can be seen as an "Intelligent Agent" according to classical definitions (Wooldridge and Jennings 1995), it is different from a mere software agent since it has a physical body and this may impact on cognition and behavior. It is a tight and seamless integration of a physical and a digital counterpart which augment each other into a unique peculiar entity (Cena et al. 2017b).

Ambient Intelligence (AmI). Ambient intelligence refers to a broad research area. AmI research builds upon advances in IoT, sensors and sensor networks, pervasive and ubiquitous computing, and artificial intelligence (Cook et al. 2009). The vision of Ambient Intelligence can be summarized *as* "a digital environment that proactively, but sensibly, supports people in their daily lives" (Augusto 2007). Similarly, **Pervasive computing** (Want and Pering 2005) aims to integrate computation into our daily work practice to enhance our activities without being noticed. In other words, the goal is to allow people living easily in environments in which the objects are sensitive to people's needs, personalized to their requirements, anticipatory of their behavior and responsive to their presence.

In the rest of the chapter, we will use "Internet of Things" as an umbrella term to cover the wider paradigms of IoT, WoT, SO and ambient intelligence.

39.2.2   IoT for Universal Access

The World Health Organization (WHO 2011) strongly defends the use of IoT as a tool that is able to improve the quality of life of people with disabilities. Furthermore, IoT applications have the potential to allow people with disabilities to have the same social and economic opportunities as the rest of the population (Domingo 2012). In this section, we provide examples of different applications domains where it is possible to exploit IoT to increase accessibility, with some relevant state of the art examples.

Smart home/building

Smart home/buildings refer to homes/buildings that have appliances, lighting and/or electronic devices that can be controlled remotely by the owner, often via a mobile app. Smart home-enabled devices can also operate in conjunction with other devices in the home and communicate information to other smart devices. Smart homes enable the automation and control of the home environment using multiple devices such as automatic kitchen equipment, light and door controllers, indoor temperature controllers, water temperature controllers, and home security devices (Piyare 2013, Jyothi et al. 2017, Stefanov et al. 2004).

Smart home automation is very popular due to its numerous benefits, first of all since it reduces the human involvement. Moreover, it can provide various benefits such as greater safety, comfort, and security, a more rational use of energy and other resources thus contributing to a significant savings. This offers very powerful means for supporting and helping people with disabilities and special needs, allowing for independent living. In particular, IoT-related technologies that could be used in Smart Home to help people with disabilities are:

- *Remote controlling*: IoT can help users perform tasks such as controlling appliances, switching lights and being aware of the state of home components. For example, (Welbourne et al. 2009) propose a search engine to find objects, labeling personal objects with RFID tag, especially useful to provide a better quality of life for visually impaired people at home.
- *Head-Tracking Devices*: devices involving facial movements, eyes movements, brain control, gesture recognition, and equipment for navigation that provides

obstacle detection to help people affected by paralysis or similar diseases. In (Rodrigues et al. 2017) there are examples of nonintrusive camera-based system for tracking user movements (face or body) and translating them to pointer movement on the screen; this system enables desktop users with motor disabilities to navigate to all areas of the screen even with very limited physical movement.

- *Voice-controlled interfaces*: for helping people with visual impairments to control household equipment.
- *Touch screen devices*: enable access to graphics information and reading of text content by people with hearing disabilities.

According to Tektonidis and Koumpis (2012) services for home assistance should include: advisory services, monitoring services, dependable services, accessible interfaces, smart interfaces, orchestration services, and third-party services. They proposed the "IOTC4ALL"—Internet of Things and Content for ALL, a framework to help provide smart home solutions for mobile devices to help disabled people perform their activities at home.

Smart economy

Smart economy has been defined as the set and combination of e-business and e-commerce, increased productivity, ICT-enabled and advanced manufacturing and delivery of services, ICT-enabled innovation, as well as new products, new services and business models. It also establishes smart clusters and ecosystems like digital business and entrepreneurship (Manville et al. 2014).

   In this scenario, the main challenge that the IoT paradigm should address toward the increase of universal accessibility is how to counter the current economic system that prioritizes mass production and leads to the sale of high-demand products. According to Treviranus (Treviranus 2016), such economic system is not well-suited to designing for diversity. Mass produced products and pricing depend on scale economies and marginalize unique demands. This represents a barrier to have equal opportunities and accessibility for people with special needs. Big data analyses and social media "likes" risk to increase this trend (Treviranus, 2016). The problem is compounded by the high diversity of disabilities. The use of assistive technologies and the possibility to virtualize services and products offered by the IoT and cloud computing could be a great support. However, assistive technologies have also the problem of maintaining the interoperability with mainstream products, as they are intended to bridge the gap between standard interfaces and the requirements of individuals with disabilities. Personalized manufacturing with 3D printing is one of the directions for a smart economy that goes in the direction of universal accessibility (Lipson and Kurman 2013). The combination of 3D printing with the IoT has the power to enable people to customize their environment making devices connecting one to each other to satisfy individualized needs (Hurst 2019). The 4th industrial revolution is said to implement the collaboration between humans and machines, with processes that are locally controlled and planned (Dombrowski and Wagner 2014). There are still major obstacles in terms of interoperability among IoT silos, but this direction of innovation could move the economy to a market where the consumer plays an active role to get what she/he needs (Rifkin 2014), toward the so-called *mass customization* (Pine 1993).

IoT technologies can also support workers, enabling advanced ergonomics and novel models of work and organization to support universal accessibility. Soldato et al. (Soldatos et al. 2016) identify four major drivers:

(i)   Human-centered production scheduling (notably in terms of workforce allocation), taking into account the (evolving) profile and capabilities of the worker, including his/her knowledge, skills, age, disabilities, and more;

(ii) Workplace adaptation to the user needs, in terms of factory workplace operation and physical configuration (e.g., automation levels and physical world devices' configuration);

(iii) Worker's engagement in the adaptation process (putting aside ethical and privacy considerations, tracking technologies could be adopted to detect workers stress, fatigue, etc.);

(iv) Tracking technologies that are expected to increase workers' safety and well-being.

Smart mobilities

By Smart Mobility we mean ICT supported and integrated transport and logistics systems. IoT has the potential to profoundly transform how transportation systems gather data by bringing together data collected by sensorized objects and devices that can gather and transmit information about real-time activity in the network. These data can then be analyzed by transportation authorities to improve the mobility experience by providing more accurate information, increase safety through more advanced monitoring systems, reduce traffic congestions and improve transportation efficiency by using real-time information. This would result in saving time and improving commuting efficiency, saving costs and reducing CO_2 emissions, as well as improving services. Mobility system users might also provide their own real-time data or contribute to long-term planning (Manville et al. 2014).

IoT may make transportation systems and city environments more accessible by opening a variety of opportunities. Self-driving vehicles, which are enabled by IoT technology, may influence mobility significantly, by making disable population more autonomous and independent. Driverless car technology can reduce the need for special adaptations for disabled users, such as the need for hand controls to operate the accelerator and brake, even though other specific adaptations such as safety belts, or rotating seats which allow people to get in and out more easily will be still required (Kennedys 2017). IoT technology may further enable visually/cognitive/age challenged persons to acquire the necessary guidance to travel across city environments by, e.g., capturing geo-tagged information through their mobile phone, and return information about a pharmacy, the local police station, or points of interest (Tektonidis and Koumpis (2012). TalkingTransit enables visually impaired users to obtain real-time service status and timetables of public transport in Tokyo, also providing in-station information to help them identify a right platform or exit (Kim et al. 2014). In Demand Responsive Transport (DRT) passengers share a vehicle, for instance, a

small bus, which picks up and drops off the passengers at passenger-specified locations and times and can improve the mobility of disabled or elderly people (Broome
et al. 2012; Dikas and Minis 2014). This enables the use of more dynamic and flexible bus routes based on the passengers' preferences. DRT might also lead to reduced
indirect emissions as a direct consequence of enabling more attractive, passenger
adapted, public transport alternatives (Davidsson et al. 2016). Smart wheelchairs,
which typically consist of either a standard power wheelchair base to which a computer and a collection of sensors have been added, or a mobile robot base to which
a seat has been attached, give people with disabilities not only mobility but also the
necessary help and support to handle daily living activities (Leaman and La 2017).

Smart health/wellness

Health care represents one of the most fruitful application domains for the IoT, having
the potential to enable many medical applications such as remote health monitoring,
fitness programs, chronic disease support, and elderly care, as well as compliance
with treatment and medication at home and by healthcare providers (Riazul Islam
et al. 2015). From the users' perspective IoT-based healthcare services could reduce
costs, increase the quality of life, and enrich their experience; whereas from the
healthcare providers' perspective, the IoT may reduce device downtime through the
remote provision and correctly identify optimum times for replenishing supplies
(Riazul Islam et al. 2015).

One of the most promising applications of the IoT in health care is remote health
monitoring, which allows individuals to constantly track physiological parameters
and share data directly with their physicians. This not only does minimize costs,
but also helps people with disabilities, which may have limited mobility, have
autonomously access to a variety of health services. SPHERE, for instance, employs
wearable, environmental, and camera-based sensors for tracking health allowing
elderly and patients with a chronic disease to remain in their own homes while their
health continues to be monitored, as well as caretakers and doctors to promptly
intervene if something happens (Zhu et al. 2015). We-Care is an IoT solution for the
elderly living assistance which is able to monitor and register patients vital information and to provide mechanisms to trigger alarms in emergency situations (Pinto et al.
2017). Pasluosta et al. (2015) explore IoT technologies for increasing independency
of patients with Parkinson's disease, such as wearable sensors for observing gait patterns, tremors, and general activity levels, camera-based technologies positioned in
the patient's home to monitor progression of the illness, as well as machine learning
techniques to define treatment plans. These applications can help people maintain
their independent lifestyle as well as have continuous access to care services, ensuring
their safety and supporting them in their everyday life.

Other examples of IoT technologies in the healthcare domain include RFID tags
that allow medical professionals to track patients and medical equipment, sensors on
the patient and throughout her home to detect falls and wandering, smart pillboxes
tracking patients' adherence to treatment schedules and send reminders, emergency
call pendants to call for help when needed, and telehealth options allowing doctors
to give feedback to patients that cannot move outside their home.

39.3 Discussion

In this section, we provide a discussion about the key factors of IoT technology which favor accessibility. IoT can favor universal information access in several ways:

Remote control. As seen in smart home applications, IoT allows for remote control, such as controlling appliances, switching lights and being aware of the state of home components. This is particularly useful for people with disabilities, as well as for elderly people (Majumder et al. 2017). Moreover, the sensor-based home can be useful for a remote control of the patients themselves, that can be monitored by caregiver and physicians (Ni et al. 2015). In this sense, it is possible to remotely control the health status of the person, increasing her safety through the possibility of intervention in case of danger (falls, illness, etc.).

Multiple and novel interaction modalities. Recent advances in the processing of some input modalities, such as speech, gestures, gaze, or haptics and synergistic combinations of modalities, all of which are currently viewed as appropriate substitutes for direct manipulation when the use of keyboard, mouse, and standard screen is awkward or impossible, are opening new possibilities. The benefits of these advances for users engaged in other manual activities or on the move, or for users with motor or perceptual disabilities, are suggested.

Smartphones can now be used by persons with disabilities thanks to the implementation of a variety of interaction features that are easily accessible by older adults, or people affected by vision or hearing loss or reduced dexterity and mobility. These accessible smartphones are becoming remote means to control a variety of IoT devices, in the context of smart homes and smart mobility, offering a flexible means to interact with a variety of devices.

Moreover, the increasing attention to multimodal and natural forms of interaction makes it possible to compensate for a growing diversity of physical disabilities, and thus to provide a larger community of disabled users with easy access to IoT domain. On the one hand, the great diversity of available new modalities will make it possible to provide physically disabled users with adaptive user interfaces necessary for addressing their specific disabilities, which may evolve in the course of time; on the other hand, flexible synergistic multimodality can be useful for ensuring satisfactory access for users with complex disabilities (e.g., some kinds of palsies or visual deficiencies) or reduced multisensory acuity (e.g., senior users) with sufficient redundancy (Carbonell 2009).

Further, advancements in Brain–Computer Interfaces can empower individuals to directly control objects such as smart home appliances or assistive robots, directly via their thoughts (Zhang et al. 2018).

Web of Things can increase accessibility of real-world objects. Web services and cloud computing enable cyber-physical objects to be available as a service and rapidly provisioned for use in a network to meet the user demands. The Web is an important distribution channel for virtualized systems and smart objects and the Web of Things enables physical objects to be augmented with enhanced services. Thus, it can be exploited to overcome some accessibility barriers. The challenge is to exploit the WoT to make accessible or more usable not only digital devices, but also real-world objects without embedded computing capabilities.

In (Torre and Celik 2015, 2016) we proposed an approach that exploits adaptive and semantic techniques to realize a Web of Things to support especially people with special needs. The approach is primarily based on connecting and sharing data about accessibility requirements and real-world environment data. The approach is also founded on annotating physical objects, and adapting the interaction with the virtual side of cyber-physical objects in order to make physical objects accessible in a smart environment via smart devices.

The basic idea of our approach is that through the virtualization of physical objects, even objects which are not natively accessible and inclusive can become accessible if proper adaptations are performed, for instance, by changing the user interface and the interaction modalities in order to fit the user's special needs. In particular, in (Torre and Celik 2016), we describe how this approach can exploit the Global Public Inclusive Infrastructure (GPII) for the dynamic user interface adaptation. GPII is a project of the Raising the Floor Consortium (raisingthefloor.org), which includes industry, academia, and non-governmental organizations. Cloud4all is a European Commission FP7 project in charge of developing key parts of the GPII, concerning the user interface adaptation. Cloud4all/GPII has developed an infrastructure to automatically launch and customize applications, assistive technologies, and settings on GPII-compatible devices, across different configuration layers (operating system, assistive technologies, applications, cloud-based services, and web sites) to provide an accessible user interface.

39.4   Future Directions

We present here the open issues related to IoT for people with disabilities (Domingo 2012).

Self-management. A significant challenge to the IoT for people with disabilities is self-management. It refers to the process by which the IoT manages its own operation without human intervention. For this purpose, support for self-configuration (automatic configuration of components), self-healing (automatic discovery and correction of faults), self-optimization (automatic monitoring of resources to ensure the optimal functioning with respect to the requirements) and self-protection (proactive identification and protection from arbitrary attacks) capabilities is required (Haller et al. 2008).

Evaluation of usability and accessibility. Using the Internet of Things to make the environment smarter shows the opportunity to provide solutions to help disabled people to become more independent and to perform their daily tasks. However, if such a solution is not effectively provided for them, such goals cannot be accomplished, and those technologies can become yet another barrier (Abascal et al. 2019). For this reason, it would be crucial that the designer of such applications devote time and effort to improve the accessibility of these applications, first designing with users (participatory design) (e.g., Andrews 2014; Spiel et al. 2017) and then evaluating the accessibility of the final solution. Adams and Russell (2006) in a pioneer study attempted to define a methodology for assessing the usability of ambient intelligence applications for users with disabilities.

Standardization and interoperability. It is necessary to create globally accepted standards to avoid interoperability problems. 6LoWPAN provides wireless internet connectivity to low-power devices with limited processing capabilities, so that they can be used in the IoT. As a result, with this standard, interoperability and integration with current heterogeneous Internet-aware devices is accomplished to expand the IoT for including devices specific for disabled people. More effort is still required to achieve interoperability at the level of connectivity but even greater at data and API level or to find new solutions especially in relation to solve semantic interoperability problems (Noura et al. 2018). Using semantics and rich metadata is considered a promising approach (Ganzha et al. 2017) to address the fragmentation problem of IoT platforms often based on closed ecosystems rather than on open models. According to Abou-Zahra and colleagues (Abou-Zahra et al. 2017), interoperability is particularly important for persons with disabilities using assistive technologies and custom solutions. The lack of interoperability makes it hard for assistive technologies to easily tap into IoT systems. For instance, it would be hard for a blind person to use his/her own screen reader to access a variety of IoT systems and services, which might provide their own specific screen reader or even not provide any at all.

Security and privacy. It is essential to guarantee the privacy of the IoT for people with disabilities, who are particularly vulnerable (Zorzi et al. 2010). The IoT should be protected against distributed denial-of-service attacks, which can be defined as the result of any action that prevents any part of the IoT from functioning correctly or in a timely manner. Moreover, a challenge of IoT is to make clear to users how their data will be used (with respect to processing, storage, and sharing), enabling users to take informed decisions on privacy settings of their personal devices (Torre et al. 2018). This is true for all people, but even more for people with disabilities whose health data require special care when they are shared with other entities. Transparency is a strong requirement in the new European GDPR regulation on privacy.

39.5   Authors' Opinion of the Field

In author's opinion, promising future directions of work could be the following ones:

Personalisation. Since each person has peculiar needs it is important to adapt IoT solutions not only to the general disability features, but also to other personal features (such as interests, preferences, aversions) (Brusilovsky 1998, Firmenich et al. 2019). Moreover, it is important to adapt to the context of use, in order to be able to take context-aware decisions based on context information of the environment captured automatically by sensors (Adomavicius and Tuzhilin 2011).

Cooperation among objects. Standardization will allow also the cooperation among smart objects and devices in order to complete tasks (Zorzi et al. 2010). This can enable objects to create communities of social objects, a set of "res social-is" where the object is part of and acts in a social community of objects, with a sort of "social consciousness" and the capability of being proactive in defining new relationships. This can lead to a social internet of things (Atzori et al. 2014).

End user development. End user development is a paradigm that refers to activities and tools that allow end users, i.e., people who are not professional software developers, to program computers and device. This is particularly useful in IoT context, where there is the need to provide nontechnical users with innovative interaction strategies for controlling their behavior (Markopoulus et al. 2017, Ghiani et al. 2017, Lieberman et al. 2017). The idea is to enable nontechnical users to be directly involved in "composing" their smart objects by synchronizing their behavior.

39.6   Conclusion

This chapter aimed at describing and discussing the benefits that can be derived from the implementation of IoT solutions for promoting universal access. We tried to show that IoT has the potential to contribute to the progress of universal access by extending the range of interaction modalities available to users with disabilities, and by providing the necessary technology for implementing enhanced assisted living.

References

Abascal J, Arrue M, Valencia X (2019) Tools for web accessibility evaluation. In: Harper S, Yesilada Y (eds) Web accessibility book, 2nd edn

Abou-Zahra S, Brewer J, Cooper M (2017) Web standards to enable an accessible and inclusive Internet of Things (IoT). In: Proceedings of the 14th Web for All Conference on The Future of Accessible Work. ACM

Adomavicius G, Tuzhilin A (2011) Context-aware recommender systems. In: Recommender systems handbook. Springer, Boston, MA, pp 217–253

Andrews C (2014) Accessible participatory design: engaging and including visually impaired participants. In: Langdon P, Lazar J, Heylighen A, Dong H (eds) Inclusive designing. Springer, Cham

Atzori L, Iera S, Morabito G (2010) The internet of things: a survey. Comput Netw 54:2787–2805

Atzori L, Antonio I, Morabito G (2014) From "smart objects" to "social objects": the next evolutionary step of the internet of things. Commun Mag IEEE 52(1):97–105

Augusto JC (2007) Ambient intelligence: the confluence of ubiquitous/pervasive computing and artificial intelligence. In: Intelligent computing everywhere. Springer, London, pp 213–234

Bandyopadhyay D, Sen J (2011) Internet of things: applications and challenges in technology and standardization. Wirel Pers Commun 58(1), 49–69

Broome K, Worrall L, Fleming J, Boldy D (2012) Evaluation of flexible route bus transport for older people. Transp Policy 21:85–91

Brusilovsky P (1998) Methods and techniques of adaptive hypermedia. In: Adaptive hypertext and hypermedia. Springer, Dordrecht, pp 1–43

Carbonell N (2009) Contributions of "ambient" multimodality to universal access. In: Stephanidis C (ed) The universal access handbook. CRC Press

Cena F, Console L, Matassa A, Torre I (2017a) Principles to design smart physical objects as adaptive recommenders. IEEE Access 5:23532–23549

Cena F, Console L, Matassa A, Torre I (2017b) Multi-dimensional intelligence in smart physical objects. Inf Syst Front 1–22

Cook DJ, Augusto JC, Jakkula VR (2009) Ambient intelligence: technologies, applications, and opportunities. Pervasive Mob Comput 5(4):277–298

Davidsson P, Hajinasab B, Holmgren J, Jevinger Å, Persson JA (2016) The fourth wave of digitalization and public transport: opportunities and challenges. Sustainability 8:1248

Dikas G, Minis I (2014) Scheduled paratransit transport systems. Transp Res B Meth 67:18–34

Dombrowski U, Wagner T (2014) Mental strain as field of action in the 4th industrial revolution. In: Proceedings of the 47th CIRP conference on manufacturing systems, pp 100–105

Domingo MC (2012) An overview of the Internet of Things for people with disabilities. J Netw Comput Appl 35(2):584–596

Firmenich S, Garrido A, Paterno F, Rossi G (2019) User interface adaptation for accessibility. In: Harper S, Yesilada Y (eds) Web accessibility book, 2nd edn

Fortino G, Rovella A, RussoW, Savaglio C (2014) On the classification of cyberphysical smart objects in the internet of things. In Proceedings of the international workshop on networks of cooperating objects for Smart Cities at UBICITEC 2014, vol. 1156, pp. 86–94

Ganzha M, Paprzycki M, Pawłowski W, Szmeja P, Wasielewska K (2017) Semantic interoperability in the internet of things: an overview from the INTER-IoT perspective. J Netw Comput Appl 81:111–124

Ghiani G, Manca M, Paternò F, Santoro C (2017) Personalization of context-dependent applications through trigger-action rules. ACM Trans Comput-Hum Interact 24(2), article no 14

Giusto D, Iera A, Morabito G, Atzori L (eds) (2010) The internet of things: 20th Tyrrhenian workshop on digital communications. Springer Science & Business Media

Gubbi J, Buyya R, Marusic S, Palaniswami M (2013) Internet of Things (IoT): a vision, architectural elements, and future directions. Future Gener Comput Syst 29(7):1645–1660

Guinard D, Trifa V (April 2009) Towards the web of things: web mashups for embedded devices. In: Workshop on mashups, enterprise mashups and lightweight composition on the web (MEM 2009), in proceedings of WWW (International World Wide Web Conferences), vol. 15. Madrid, Spain

Guinard D, Trifa V, Mattern F, Wilde E (2011) From the internet of things to the web of things: resource-oriented architecture and best practices. In: Architecting the internet of things. Springer, Berlin, Heidelberg, pp 97–129. https://doi.org/10.1007/978-3-642-19157-2_5

Haller S, Karnouskos S, Schroth C (Sept 2008) The internet of things in an enterprise context. In: Future internet symposium. Springer, Berlin, Heidelberg, pp 14–28

Holler J, Tsiatsis V, Mulligan C, Avesand S, Karnouskos S, Boyle D (2014) From machine-to-machine to the internet of things: introduction to a new age of intelligence. Academic Press

Hurst A (2019) Fabrication 3D printing and making. In: Harper S, Yesilada Y (eds) Web accessibility book, 2nd edn

Jyothi V, Krishna MG, Raveendranadh B, Rupalin D (Feb 2017) IOT based smart home system technologies. Int J Eng Res Dev 13(2):31–37

Kennedys (2017) Driverless vehicles. Innovation to revolutionise the way we transport modern societies, July 2017. Technical report

Kim J-E, Bessho M, Koshizuka N, Sakamura K (2014). Enhancing public transit accessibility for the visually impaired using IoT and open data infrastructures. In Proceedings of the First International Conference on IoT in Urban Space (URB-IOT '14). ICST (Institute for Computer Sciences, Social-Informatics and Telecommunications Engineering), ICST, Brussels, Belgium, Belgium, pp 80–86

Kortuem G, Kawsar F, Fitton D, Sundramoorthy V (2010) Smart objects as building blocks for the internet of things. Internet Comput IEEE 14(1):44–51

Leaman J, La HM (2017) A comprehensive review of smart wheelchairs: past, present, and future. IEEE Trans Hum-Mach Syst 47(4):486–499

Li S, Da Xu L, Zhao S (2015) The internet of things: a survey. Inf Syst Front 17(2):243–259

Lieberman H, Paternò F, Klann M, Wulf V (2017) "End-user development: an emerging paradigm. In: End-user development. Springer, pp 1–8, 2006

Lipson H, Kurman M (2013) Fabricated: the new world of 3D printing. Wiley, Indianapolis, IN

Majumder S, Aghayi E, Noferesti M, Memarzadeh-Tehran H, Mondal T, Pang Z, Deen M (2017) Smart homes for elderly healthcare—recent advances and research challenges. Sensors 17(11):2496

Manville C, Cochrane G, Cave J, Millard J Pederson JK, Thaarup RK, Liebe A, Wissner M, Massink R, Kotterink B (2014) Mapping smart cities in the EU. http://www.europarl.europa.eu/studies

Markopoulos P, Nichols J, Paternò F, Pipek V (2017) End-user development for the internet of things. ACM Trans Comput-Hum Interact (TOCHI), 24(2):9

Mukherjee S, Aarts E, Doyle T (2009) Special issue on ambient intelligence. Inf Syst Front 11(1):1–5

Ni Q, García-Hernando A, Pau I (2015) The Elderly's independent living in smart homes: a characterization of activities and sensing infrastructure survey to facilitate services development. Sensors

Nicolau H, Montague K (2019) Assistive technologies. In: Harper S, Yesilada Y (eds) Web accessibility book, 2nd edn

Noura M, Atiquzzaman M, Gaedke M (2018) Mobile network application

Pasluosta CF, Gassner H, Winkler J, Klucken J, Eskofier BM (2015) An emerging era in the management of Parkinson's disease: wearable technologies and the internet of things. IEEE J Biomed Health Inform 19(6):1873–1881

Pine BJ (1993) Mass customization: the new frontier in business competition. Harvard Business Press

Pinto S, Cabral J, Gomes T (2017) We-care: an IoT-based health care system for elderly people. In: Conference: 2017 IEEE international conference on industrial technology (ICIT). Toronto, ON, Canada. https://doi.org/10.1109/icit.2017.7915565

Piyare R (2013) Internet of things: ubiquitous home control and monitoring system using android based smart phone. Int J Internet Things 2(1):5–11

Riazul Islam SM, Kwak D, Kabir H, Hossain M, Kyung-Sup Kwak A (2015) The internet of things for health care: a comprehensive survey. IEEE Access 3:678–708

Rifkin J (2014) The zero marginal cost society: The internet of things, the collaborative commons, and the eclipse of capitalism. St. Martin's Press

Rodrigues AS, da Costa VK, Cardoso RC, Machado MB, Machado MB, Tavares TA (June 2017) Evaluation of a head-tracking pointing device for users with motor disabilities. In: Proceedings of the 10th international conference on pervasive technologies related to assistive environments. ACM, pp 156–162

Soldatos J, Gusmeroli S, Malo P, Di Orio G (2016) Internet of things applications in future manufacturing. Digitising industry-internet of things connecting the physical, digital and virtual worlds, pp 153–183

Spiel K, Malinverni L, Good J, Frauenberger C (2017) Participatory evaluation with autistic children. In: Proceedings of the 2017 CHI conference on human factors in computing systems (CHI '17). ACM, New York, NY, USA, pp 5755–5766. https://doi.org/10.1145/3025453.3025851

Stefanov DH, Bien Z, Bang WCh (2004) The smart house for older persons and persons with physical disabilities: structure, technology arrangements, and perspectives. IEEE Trans Neural Syst Rehabil Eng 12(2):228–250

Tektonidis D, Koumpis A (2012). Accessible internet-of-things and internet-of-content services for all in the home or on the move. Int J Interact Mob Technol 6(4)

Torre I, Celik I (2015) User-adapted web of things for accessibility. HT 2015: 341–344

Torre I, Celik I (2016) A model for adaptive accessibility of everyday objects in smart cities. In: 2016 IEEE 27th annual international symposium on personal, indoor, and mobile radio communications (PIMRC), pp 1–6

Torre I, Sanchez OR, Koceva F, Adorni G (2018) Supporting users to take informed decisions on privacy settings of personal devices. Pers Ubiquit Comput 22(2):345–364

Treviranus J (2016). The future challenge of the ADA: shaping humanity's transformation. Inclusion 4(1):30–38

Want R, Pering T (2005) System challenges for ubiquitous & pervasive computing. In: Proceedings of the 27th international conference on software engineering. ACM, pp 9–14

Weiser M (1998) The future of ubiquitous computing on campus. Commun ACM 41(1):41–42

Welbourne E, Battle L, Cole G, Gould, K., Rector, K., Raymer, S., & Borriello, G. (2009). Building the internet of things using RFID: the RFID ecosystem experience. IEEE Internet computing, 13(3)

Whitmore A, Agarwal A, Da Xu L (2015) The internet of things—a survey of topics and trends. Inf Syst Front 17(2):261–274

Wooldridge M, Jennings N (1995) Intelligent agents: theory and practice. Knowl Eng Rev 10:115–152

World Health Organization (2011) World report on disability; June 2011

Zhang X, Yao L, Zhang S, Kanhere S, Sheng QZ, Liu Y (2018) Internet of things meets brain-computer interface: a unified deep learning framework for enabling human-thing cognitive inter-activity

Zhu N, Diethe T, Camplani M, Tao L, Burrows A, Twomey N, Kaleshi D, Mirmehdi M, Flach P, Craddock I (2015) Bridging e-health and the internet of things: the SPHERE project. IEEE Intell Syst 30(4):39–46

Zorzi M, Gluhak A, Lange S, Bassi A (2010) From today's intranet of things to a future internet of things: a wireless-and mobility-related view. IEEE Wireless Commun 17(6):44–51

Chapter 40
Futurama

Yeliz Yesilada and Simon Harper

Abstract Accessibility has, at its heart, the aim of removing developer and content creator preconceptions as to the technology, people, working environment, and use their systems support. The move to mobile has been nothing but positive for the accessibility of people with a visual disability. Similarly in the next 10 years as the Web becomes a utility, imbedded—embedded and invisible—and as wearables, sensors and the Internet of Things (and the Web, IoW) become more prevalent accessibility will be even more crucial. As the Web becomes more seamless, we will need to look for new ways to convey information in many different environments, and here lessons from accessibility will contribute. We have seen over the last 10 years the expansion from physical and sensory disability through cognitive and ageing to inclusion, and situational impairments. Over the next 10 years, our understanding of assistive technology will change because we cannot build for the many combinations of interactions, technologies, environments and users then assistive technology will just become ubiquitous. More attention will be paid to previously under-represented areas such as cognitive and autism spectrum conditions as well as those surrounding comprehension and people with learning difficulties. These groups have often been overlooked in the past; this is changing and will change significantly in the next 10 years. So in 10 years, we predict that new solutions for emerging technologies will be required, that accessibility research will focus more on cognitive and learning spectrum conditions, that access technology will become more ubiquitous, and that this ubiquity will require automated tooling created by experts to assist in the removal of barriers at scale.

Y. Yesilada (✉)
Middle East Technical University, Northern Cyprus Campus, 99738 Kalkanlı,
Güzelyurt, Mersin 10, Turkey
e-mail: yyeliz@metu.edu.tr

S. Harper
University of Manchester, Manchester, UK
e-mail: simon.harper@manchester.ac.uk

© Springer-Verlag London Ltd., part of Springer Nature 2019
Y. Yesilada and S. Harper (eds.), *Web Accessibility*, Human–Computer
Interaction Series, https://doi.org/10.1007/978-1-4471-7440-0_40

40.1 Introduction

Future-gazing is dangerous, and especially dangerous when predicting the Web+10 years, a suite of technologies and uses whose speed of evolution is unmatched. We might also need to define what we mean when we say the 'Web'? The amalgam of technologies which come together to form the traditional browsing experience? We might mean the specific Web technologies which are often used independently of the Web-Browser to facilitate Data Transport, User Interaction, the Internet of Things and the like? Further, there is the Web which is not focused on technology, but on concepts which need to be conveyed Trust, Privacy, Security and Authenticity, for instance. Then again, we might ask to what use will the Web be put? More of the same as today: search, social and shopping or will we see much more activism, individually created content, expansion of platforms or expansion of independent content?

Our ability to trust the Web and the content on it will need to be addressed. In many ways more so than privacy and security. Trust transparency and authenticity of the content will become predominant in an ecosystem of big, small and individual content providers. We will continue to see the Web dominated by big platforms as meta-engines storing, sorting, indexing and providing some structured access to content from Twitch to YouTube and beyond, platforms will be developed for different sections of the Web communities, speaking the language of that specific subculture. The Web will continue the trajectory to utility, present everywhere, but the trajectory of the Web run sensor network as envisioned by the Internet of Things will plateau.

To some degree, future Web Accessibility will be defined by the way the Web itself evolves; however, this is not a simple one-way relationship. Accessibility has, at its heart, the aim of removing developer and content creator preconceptions as to the technology, people, working environment and use their systems support. The move to mobile has been nothing but positive for the accessibility of people with a visual disability because suddenly you could not guarantee everyone would be using a large desktop display with regular dimensions, it is then only a small step, when making Web content and interfaces adaptive, to take the step to accessibility and adapt to no display at all. Similarly in the next 10 years accessibility will be even more crucial as more people will be affected by irregular interaction require-ments regardless of whether they identify as disabled. As the Web becomes a utility, imbedded—embedded and invisible—and as wearables, sensors and the Internet of Things (and the Web, IoW) become more prevalent this will only increase. As the Web becomes more seamless, blending and blurring the divide between the real and virtual worlds we will need to look for new ways to convey information in many different environments, and here lessons from accessibility will contribute. Indeed, as virtual, augmented and mixed reality become increasingly prevalent, Web and therefore accessibility technologies will have a strong influence in making these pri-marily visual displays accessible, and these new kinds of interactive environments will assist accessibility for people with cognitive and learning difficulties including those with affective (emotion) conditions.

What is accessibility? The removal of barriers to interaction and comprehension? If this is so then we may need to redraw the boundaries. We have seen over the last 10 years the expansion from physical and sensory disability through cognitive and ageing to inclusion, and situational impairments. How might this definition expand in the future, what will it include and will this mean that accessibility—which is really just hyper-adaption—will be subsumed into adaptive interfaces. Further, our understanding of assistive technology will change because we cannot build for the many combinations of interactions, technologies, environments and users then assistive technology will just become ubiquitous. Of course, this pre-supposes that developers become experts in accessibility and this is currently unlikely, implying that we will still need expert developers building tools to facilitate accessibility and adaption, but we can see how tooling, corrective technology and automated technology fixing the mistakes of developers and content creators will become increasingly important.

When it comes to addressing specific need and reducing specific barriers, we can see that more attention will be paid to previously under-represented areas such as cognitive and autism spectrum conditions as well as those surrounding comprehension and people with learning difficulties. These groups have often been overlooked in the past because they often occur on a spectrum and we did not have the computational tools to make useful headway. This is changing and will change significantly in the next 10 years.

So in 10 years, we predict that new solutions for emerging technologies will be required, that accessibility research will focus more on cognitive and learning spectrum conditions, that access technology will become more ubiquitous, and that this ubiquity will require automated tooling created by experts to assist in the removal of barriers at scale. Based on these future directions, we organise the rest of this chapter based on the major parts of our book.

40.2 Future Access and Impairments

Understanding the term 'disability' is fundamental to understanding accessibility— the two terms being inextricably linked. The World Health Organisation defines disability as:

> Disabilities is an umbrella term, covering impairments, activity limitations, and participation restrictions. An impairment is a problem in body function or structure; an activity limitation is a difficulty encountered by an individual in executing a task or action; while a participation restriction is a problem experienced by an individual in involvement in life situations. Disability is thus not just a health problem. It is a complex phenomenon, reflecting the interaction between features of a person's body and features of the society in which he or she lives. –World Health Organization, Disabilities[1]

---

[1]Disabilities. World Health Organization. https://www.who.int/topics/disabilities/en/.

In this case, accessibility is an attempt to remove barriers to interaction between features in society and the environment and therefore enable interaction by accommodating features of a person's body (Yesilada et al. 2012). This said, it is fair to characters our implicit focus of attention is on permanent disabilities; with the exclusion of 'Situationally-induced impairments and disabilities (SIID)' (more on this later) (Sears and Young 2003; Sears and Xiao 2003).

We see our understanding of the accessibility domain expanding in the future to encompass impairments that may be transitory or those that are co-related (a co-morbidity) to a condition unrelated to the impairment, and such that treatment of that underlying condition may remove the related impairment. For instance, a person with Lung Cancer may be less able to move, may become breathless and fatigued quicker, may have mobility impairments, but these impairments will normally resolve once the underlying condition is addressed or treated. We have had an implicit focus on permanent disabilities and have been less focused on these seemingly transient impairments, we predict that in the future we will become more inclusive, and begin to address these 'Health-induced impairments and disabilities (HIID)' (Mueller et al. 2017, 2019).

In addition, we predict that certain under-investigated disabilities will have more focus, garnering a better understanding of the accessibility issues surrounding them. Certainly, cognitive impairments such as Autism, which has been under-investigated in the context of accessibility, will become more of a focus area as technology becomes more able to remove barriers, to address and to support this complex disability (see chapter 'Cognitive and Learning Disabilities'). Certain those disabilities which occur on a more pronounced spectrum and those which are more challenging to recruit participants for, or gain understanding about, and access to the community will become increasingly focused upon (Yaneva et al. 2018a).

Further, with the increased use of IoT technology (see chapter 'Internet of Things'), accessibility related to SIIDs will become increasingly important. This is because all users will be impaired by IoT technology, and so by design, the accessibility of these devices will need to be accommodated. Especially those having a Zero UI[2] where the access to those devices must be delivered remotely. This is a great opportunity for accessibility because in the past one of the main barriers to access was the assumption of a keyboard, mouse and screen—ergo a presumption of vision and manual dexterity. As with mobile devices, manufacturers cannot guarantee the access pathway to a technical artefact and so UI flexibility must be in-built. This return to device independence, flexibility and UI agnosticism facilitates powerful accessibility technology.

Finally, we caution researchers to expect the unexpected. With increasing technology and increasing ambient and smart devices barriers to accessibility may arise in areas we are not focused on. If we are to subscribe to the WHO definition 'disability... is a complex phenomenon, reflecting the interaction between features of a person's body and features of the society in which he or she lives' then changes within society

---

[2]https://www.webfx.com/blog/web-design/zero-ui/.

and the environment may indeed produce new 'disabilities' which—as accessibility researchers—will fall to us to understand, address and ultimately solve (Yesilada et al. 2012).

40.3 Evolving Research Methods and Techniques

As the technology evolves, the way we conduct research and also present research will also evolve. The language used for discussing accessibility has changed significantly over the years (see chapter 'Inclusive Writing'). We expect with the new technologies and research methods introduced in the future, the vocabulary used to present the research findings will continue to change. For example, we now widely use SIID (Sears and Young 2003; Sears and Xiao 2003) and this terminology was introduced due to the need of referring particular kinds of disabilities caused by a technological development. This simple example actually showed that we needed to reconsider the definition of web accessibility and how its perception has evolved over the years (Yesilada et al. 2012, 2013a).

Similar to vocabulary used, the way we conduct research will also evolve, and the diversity of the methods used will change. In the past, we have seen and experienced that accessibility research has widely been evaluated and tested in situ (Berkel et al. 2017; Edwards 1995; Harper and Yesilada 2008), however, in the future, we expect to see that context would become more important and therefore methods will also evolve to allow people to conduct experiments more in the wild (i.e. in the real world settings). We will see that more unobtrusive methods and longitudinal studies will be explored and used (Berkel et al. 2017). With the improvement of data science (Cady 2017), we also expect to see that more remote studies will be conducted and their benefits will be facilitated better in the future. In fact, the web itself nicely provides a perfect platform, for remote, longitudinal studies to be conducted in the wild. As it is explained in chapter 'Working with Participants', over the years we have also seen that accessibility and User Experience research has also been started to be considered together. In fact, this is predicted to become even more important in the near future. Furthermore, some of the research methods traditionally have accessibility problems, for example, affinity diagrams are not accessible to visually disabled participants. Therefore, in the future, we expect to see that a variety of techniques will be explored to make these diagrams more accessible.

Guidelines have been a very critical research line for web accessibility. As it is explained in chapter 'Standards, Guidelines and Trends', there has been many changes and improvements over the years. In the future, we expect to see more studies that explore the validity of the proposed guidelines (Brajnik et al. 2011b). As the field has evolved, we have seen that more scientific methods explored and investigated. In the future, we believe better scientific methods will be explored and used. When we compare the first and second edition of our book, in fact, we can see that the techniques, tools and methods arisen from this field have significantly increased (see chapter 'End User Evaluations') and will increase more in the future. The main reason for this is that we believe accessibility scope is going to be broadened even more in the future as more people experience difficulties in using new technologies which mean they can easily experience SIIDs.

Availability of the software developed as part of accessibility research is also critical (Collberg and Proebsting 2016). As it is explained in chapter 'Reproducible and Sustainable Research Software', making collected data and also software developed public is critical for research reproducibility and sustainability; therefore in the future, we expect to see that these two concepts will gain even more importance.

Finally, we have seen a dramatic improvement in artificial Intelligence techniques used for research, especially Machine learning and deep learning algorithms have been phenomenally successfully over the last 5 years (Abou-Zahra et al. 2018). We expect to see more techniques like these to be developed in the near future. However, it is widely known that one of the problems that these algorithms have is the bias (Zou and Schiebinger 2018) mainly due to the bias existing in the data used for training these algorithms. As it was argued by (Zou and Schiebinger 2018) 'Computer scientists must identify sources of bias, de-bias training data and develop artificial intelligence algorithms that are robust to skews in the data'. Therefore, as the accessibility researchers, our role is critical to ensure that there is no bias against disabled users in any AI-based systems developed. We need to ensure that these algorithms are used to improve the lives of disabled people and are not used to exclude them from our society.

40.4   Future in Society and Standards

Due to technology being more integrated into our societies, we will observe many changes and developments in the web accessibility research. As it is highlighted in chapter 'Standards, Guidelines and Trends', with the developments in the Internet of things (IOT) (Sorge and Pearson 2018), the web will continue to be the main interface to the Internet (W3C 2019). We will have smart cities, smart homes and offices, public spaces and living spaces, and therefore, the web interface will be everywhere and it will have more seamless integration with rich applications and media interaction. There is a danger that if the web continues to be inaccessible, with these kinds of developments, unfortunately, it will mean more and more serious exclusion for disabled users. Therefore, as the accessibility research community we need to ensure that as the web evolves, the accessibility technology also evolves. Even though standards and guidelines always have continues improvement, they still need to address these developments carefully and in particular support the development of not only web pages/sites but 'applications/software' that integrates web and back-end software seamlessly. Furthermore, as it is explained in chapter 'Standards, Guidelines and Trends', futuristic guidelines need to address the needs of IOT developments including interoperability, configurability, privacy, security and safety (Sicari et al. 2015).

Compared to the first edition of this book (Harper and Yesilada 2008), we observe that in this second edition we have a better balance in terms of the research conducted addressing different kinds of disabilities. For example, now we see that cognitive disability has more focus than it used to be.[3] In the future, we hope to see even more focus in addressing more variety of disabilities such as cognitive, learning and language disabilities, as well as behavioural disorders and chronic conditions. Especially with the improvements in AI technologies, we hope to see that more automation will be available for supporting these user groups. For instance, automatic image recognition and audio captioning will probably be available in mainstream and aspects of artificial intelligence, such as affective computing will be more widely available. Furthermore, advances in natural language processing (NLP) would also be good for these user groups. As it is explained in chapter 'The policy and standards centred around Cognitive and Learning Disabilities', we will see context analysis, text simplification and adaptation to be more widely integrated into the adaptation and penalisation for these user groups.

In our societies, we will also observe that developments in conversational technologies will be more widely used (Jain et al. 2018). These technologies can have obvious benefits for disabled users but more research needs to be conducted to understand the benefits of these technologies and how they could improve the lives of disabled users. With these technologies, there is also a risk that they can exclude disabled people more if they cannot process conversations with disabled people, especially with the ones who have speech difficulty. Similar to these technologies, as it is explained in chapter 'Inclusion', developments in wearable technologies is also key for inclusion in the future for disabled users (Wentzel et al. 2016).

Further, understanding policy and law requirements for accessibility will be key for ensuring accessibility for all. Especially, in some parts of the world, these policies are key for supporting accessibility. As it is explained in chapter 'Policy and Law', it would be good if every accessibility researcher and practitioner can commit to learning more about the laws and policies that relate to digital accessibility in their own country and state/province. Specialised policies are also important for our societies. For example, in higher education where the views of younger generation could be different from older generations (Karl et al. 2017), specific approaches need to be developed to ensure that we understand the needs and requirements of different roles in a Higher Education Institute. Different countries can approach this problem in different ways but as it is explained in chapter 'Tackling the Inaccessibility of Websites in Post-secondary Education', a more integrated network of countries could be developed to better synthesise research and evidence across countries.

Finally, with all the technology developments explained above, we will need to ensure that *inclusion* is still a priority in our research agenda and we have good

---

[3]We now have four chapters dedicated to cognitive disability: 'Cognitive and Learning Disabilities', 'The policy and standards centred around Cognitive and Learning Disabilities', 'Tools and Applications for Cognitive Accessibility' and 'Technologies for Dyslexia'.

values and ethics integrated into the technologies, especially in AI research, to better support the integration of our societies with the technology developments (Zou and Schiebinger 2018).

40.5   Evolving Techniques and Tools for Web Accessibility

Over the years, we have seen that many tools and techniques developed to address the accessibility of the web for disabled people (Harper and Yesilada 2008). Among these, the most widely researched is the tools for checking accessibility conformance of web pages against guidelines (Brajnik 2004). As it is explained in chapter 'Tools for Web Accessibility Evaluation', even though research has progressed significantly in this area, there still many issues that need to be addressed. For instance, ambiguity in guidelines, personalised accessibility checkers and especially having these tools used after the pages developed rather than during the stages that they were developed (Brajnik et al. 2012). Furthermore, automated accessibility checkers need to be reconsidered as most of them do not consider the context of use during the evaluation process. However, with the developments in IOT, WoT or other similar technologies, we expect to see that the context of use of the web interface will be very critical (Dey et al. 2001). Therefore, as the accessibility research community, we will need to conduct more research to better understand the context and its importance for web accessibility evaluation. Most of the available tools also do not consider user groups or the special needs of users, they tend to do evaluations against a particular set of guidelines that cover different kinds of users and their requirements (Brajnik and Lomuscio 2007). In the future, however, we expect to see that personalised web accessibility evaluation would be key to meet the needs of individuals and their context of use. Besides the context of use, in the future, more research needs to be conducted to understand how new developments, for example, tests conducted for submitting applications to mobile application stores affect the accessibility evaluation of web interfaces (Martin et al. 2017).

In any accessibility evaluation tool developed, regardless of automated or manual, metrics play a key role in the resulting process. As it is discussed in chapter 'Automatic Web Accessibility Metrics: Where We Were and Where We Went', validity, reliability and sensitivity of the evaluation metrics still need to be further researched to understand the impact of the evaluation tools created. Furthermore in the past, proposed metrics are all focused on to be generic metrics; however, metrics could also be personalised and they could be simplified to be better integrated to streamline web interface design and development tools. Similar to metrics, the scope of the web accessibility evaluation is also critical. When only automated evaluation is conducted the presented results are only showing the partial problems (Brajnik et al. 2010, 2011a). However, for full picture, one needs to conduct both automated and manual evaluations with users. Similar to this, when only user evaluation is done one only can see the problems experienced with those particular users or the groups they represent. Therefore, further research needs to be conducted to better understand how the results of these two approaches could be integrated and interpreted (Brajnik and Lomuscio 2007).

Besides the evaluation tools and metrics, over the years we have also observed that a number of specialised tools in diagnosing particular disability (Rello and Ballesteros 2015; Yaneva et al. 2018a; Eraslan et al. 2017; Yaneva et al. 2018b) and also for helping people overcome their disabilities (Rello 2012) are introduced. In the future, we expect to see more research along this line, particularly with different kinds of users. As it is explained in chapter 'Technologies for Dyslexia', even though there are a lot of improvements for cognitive disabilities in terms of tool support, we still need to make sure that social aspects are considered. Especially how these people use these tools or would like to use these tools. Similar to this concern, as it is discussed in chapter 'Tools and Applications for Cognitive Accessibility', personalisation is also key for certain kinds of accessibility, especially for cognitive disabilities.

As it is highlighted in chapter 'Alternative Non-Visual Web Browsing Techniques', it has been almost 30 years since the web was invented but unfortunately, the formatting of web pages is still not separated from the logical structure. In the future, with the new types of documents and standards being introduced, we hope that this will change. Especially, we are envisioning that the automated tools would work better in understanding the visual rendering of pages. This kind of separation would mean that different interaction models could be supported, for instance, it would better support the exploration of haptic interaction or virtual reality interactions. These futuristic, alternative interaction techniques also would allow user interface adaptation and customisation. As it is explained in both 'User Interface Adaptation for Accessibility' and 'Transcoding' chapters, alternative access models are key for accessibility. Variety of document types and structures available on the web are also increasing. For example, we have vector graphics such as SVG, multimedia documents or interactive animations, therefore, we need to have different ways of accessing these types of resources (Duarte et al. 2018). In the future, we think these types of developments would require different types of interaction techniques such as eye and gaze interaction (Yesilada et al. 2013b).

Besides these developments, recently we have also observed that voice-based assistants such as Apple's Siri or Google's assistant are becoming more popular. However, we have still not seen how these assistants could be used for web interaction or any software interaction. In the future, we expect to see more research towards this direction (Jain et al. 2018).

Finally, when we look at the tools and techniques developed for supporting web accessibility, we observe that they are mainly developed for 'catch up'—this means they are developed to address an accessibility problem caused by a particular technology development (Harper and Yesilada 2011). However, in the future, we hope that this will change and we will have accessibility technologies integrated from the beginning so that accessibility does not need to play 'catch up'. For instance, if we have clear separation between content and the presentation, we do not need to have adaptation of the content as it can be directly accessed by Assistive technologies such as screen readers (Yesilada et al. 2008).

40.6 Deeply Ubiquitous Accessibility

Ubiquitous and ambient devices are beginning to proliferate into the general market. With the advent of home automation and the IoT and Zero UI (see earlier) sensors and devices, we are beginning to understand that access must be built-in from the ground up, to facilitate use by anyone, not just those with an impairment (Sicari et al. 2015). Without these accommodations, IoT would be the uber case for SIIDs, a vast swathe of distributed technology made inaccessible to many users by bad development and a lack of foresight. Indeed, thinking about, and building-in access as default, should be an example of best practice for all upcoming technologies.

Home automation is the new domain into which much development effort is being placed (Takayama et al. 2012). With ambient conversational interfaces created to tie together home devices and the adoption of smart heating systems, remote security and intelligent power and lighting, it can be argued that defacto accessibility has arrived (Jain et al. 2018). The smart home, office, an environment is fully accessible, at a cost. We predict that this area will continue to increase and that the lessons learned and the separation of device/functionally/programme logic from the UI will become the standard and not the exception. This kind of development likewise dovetails into the adoption of microservices architectures and supports the move from monolithic systems to microservices which can be easily upgraded and extended (Donham 2018). In large part, this movement was facilitated by prior Web technologies surrounding ReST APIs and Service Oriented Architectures (both covered in the first edition of this book) (Harper and Yesilada 2008).

Critically important is our communities ability to see into the future, to become aware of rapidly developing technologies such that we can make accessibility accommodations from the beginning of the development lifecycle as opposed to forever playing catch up; but to set the rules not purely be reactionary to them. IoT, Industry 4, and deep learning are all with us, but did we see them coming and have we reached out to developers within those domains to contribute access technology? This is particularly important in the ubiquitous world as the associated hardware development costs and the cost of physical deployment can be high. These costs, therefore, affect the product lifecycle and its iteration, possibly leaving us with inaccessible systems for years to come, the cost of the replacement being too high.

Indeed accessibility accommodations at the platform architecture level enable the accessibility expertise to be removed from the general developer and placed where expertise can be best focused. Further, the separation of concerns means bespoke interactive systems and application can be created without affecting the programming logic or associated devices.

Counter-intuitively, the best technical exemplars of this separation in development practices can only be found in the world of ubiquitous and ambient technology; mainly due to the interaction constraints placed on the devices by the environment into which they are deployed. In this version of the book, we have specifically focused on ubiquitous web accessibility: wayfinding, wearables, tangible interfaces, mobile web, fabrication and IoT, these demonstrate a shift from our understanding of what the web is, that the web is ubiquitous, gone are simple use cases such as the networked refrigerator which linked a bar code scanner to a web browser displayed on a monitor on the front. Ubiquity and ambience have become deeper, more embedded, more embedded and much more interactive. The web, society and the environment—life—has become seamless; we need to be working on an accessible life.

40.7 Conclusions

So in 10 years, we predict that new solutions for emerging technologies will be required. These emerging technologies will centre around the Web become a utility within the environment as well as an increased focus on the Web as a publishing mechanism, and an organisational and communication tool.

Accessibility research will focus much more on cognitive and learning spectrum conditions and will move away from the traditional focus of sensory and physical disabilities. Further, the definition of just what accessibility is will change. While we expect the traditional disabilities to keep their preeminent place—they have the greatest impact on the individual, we would also expect to see accessibility work push the bounds of inclusion, and periodic or temporary disabilities too.

We would also expect access technology will become more ubiquitous as the lessons we have learned over the last 25 years have will have direct relevance for the new operating modality of the Web as it moves into the real world. Here interface elements cannot be assumed to exist and types of operation and interaction will mushroom.

This ubiquity will require automated tooling created by experts to assist in the removal of barriers at scale. This means that accessibility research will be of increasing value especially as accessibility and access technology become mainstream.

References

Abou-Zahra S, Brewer J, Cooper M (2018) Artificial intelligence (ai) for web accessibility: is conformance evaluation a way forward? In: Proceedings of the internet of accessible things, W4A '18, pp 20:1–20:4. ACM, New York, USA. https://doi.org/10.1145/3192714.3192834

Berkel NV, Ferreira D, Kostakos V (2017) The experience sampling method on mobile devices. ACM Comput Surv 50(6):93:1–93:40. https://doi.org/10.1145/3123988

Brajnik G (2004) Comparing accessibility evaluation tools: a method for tool effectiveness. Univers Access Inf Soc 3(3):252–263. https://doi.org/10.1007/s10209-004-0105-y

Brajnik G, Lomuscio R (2007) Samba: a semi-automatic method for measuring barriers of accessibility. In: Assets '07: Proceedings of the 9th international ACM SIGACCESS conference on Computers and accessibility, pp 43–50. ACM, New York, USA. https://doi.org/10.1145/1296843.1296853

Brajnik G, Yesilada Y, Harper S (2010) Testability and validity of wcag 2.0: the expertise effect. In: Proceedings of the 12th international ACM SIGACCESS conference on computers and accessibility, ASSETS '10, pp 43–50. ACM, New York, USA. https://doi.org/10.1145/1878803.1878813

Brajnik G, Yesilada Y, Harper S (2011a) The expertise effect on web accessibility evaluation methods. Hum Comput Interact 26(3):1–38. https://doi.org/10.1080/07370024.2011.601670

Brajnik G, Yesilada Y, Harper S (2011b) Web accessibility guideline aggregation for older users and its validation. Univers Access Inf Soc 10(4):403–423

Brajnik G, Yesilada Y, Harper S (2012) Is accessibility conformance an elusive property? A study of validity and reliability of wcag 2.0. ACM Trans Access Comput 4(2):8:1–8:28. https://doi.org/10.1145/2141943.2141946

Cady F (2017) The data science handbook. Wiley, New York

Collberg C, Proebsting TA (2016) Repeatability in computer systems research. Commun ACM 59(3):62–69. https://doi.org/10.1145/2812803

Dey AK, Abowd GD, Salber D (2001) A conceptual framework and a toolkit for supporting the rapid prototyping of context-aware applications. Hum Comput Interact 16(2):97–166. https://doi.org/10.1207/S15327051HCI16234_02

Donham J (2018) A domain-specific language for microservices. In: Proceedings of the 9th ACM SIGPLAN international symposium on scala, Scala 2018, pp 2–12. ACM, New York, USA. https://doi.org/10.1145/3241653.3241654

Duarte C, Salvado A, Akpinar ME, Yeşilada Y, Carriço L (2018) Automatic role detection of visual elements of web pages for automatic accessibility evaluation. In: Proceedings of the Internet of Accessible Things, W4A '18, pp 21:1–21:4. ACM, New York, USA. https://doi.org/10.1145/3192714.3196827

Edwards AD (ed) (1995) Extra-ordinary human-computer interaction. Cambridge university press, Cambridge

Eraslan S, Yaneva V, Yesilada Y, Harper S (2017) Do web users with autism experience barriers when searching for information within web pages? In: Proceedings of the 14th web for all conference on the future of accessible work, W4A '17, pp 20:1–20:4. ACM, New York, USA. https://doi.org/10.1145/3058555.3058566

Harper S, Yesilada Y (eds) (2008) Web accessibility: a foundation for research. Springer, Berlin

Harper S, Yesilada Y (2011) Web accessibility: current trends, IGI global, pp 172–190. Handbook of research on personal autonomy technologies and disability informatics

Jain A, Pecune F, Matsuyama Y, Cassell J (2018) A user simulator architecture for socially-aware conversational agents. In: Proceedings of the 18th international conference on intelligent virtual agents, IVA '18, pp 133–140. ACM, New York, USA. https://doi.org/10.1145/3267851.3267916

Karl KA, Allen RS, White CS, Peluchette JVE, Allen DE (2017) Would you accept a facebook friend request from your boss? Examining generational differences. Int J Virtual Communities Soc Netw 9(1):17–33. https://doi.org/10.4018/IJVCSN.2017010102

Martin W, Sarro F, Jia Y, Zhang Y, Harman M (2017) A survey of app store analysis for software engineering. IEEE Trans Softw Eng 43(9):817–847. https://doi.org/10.1109/TSE.2016.2630689

Mueller J, Jay C, Harper S, Todd C (2017) The role of web-based health information in help-seeking behavior prior to a diagnosis of lung cancer: a mixed-methods study. J Med Internet Res 19(6):e189. https://doi.org/10.2196/jmir.6336, http://www.jmir.org/2017/6/e189/

Mueller J, Davies A, Jay C, Harper S, Blackhall F, Summers Y, Harle A, Todd C (2019) Developing and testing a web-based intervention to encourage early help-seeking in people with symptoms associated with lung cancer. Br J Health Psychol 24(1):31–65. https://doi.org/10.1111/bjhp.12325

Rello L (2012) Dyswebxia: a model to improve accessibility of the textual web for dyslexic users. SIGACCESS Access Comput 102:41–44. https://doi.org/10.1145/2140446.2140455

Rello L, Ballesteros M (2015) Detecting readers with dyslexia using machine learning with eye tracking measures. In: Proceedings of the 12th web for all conference, W4A '15, pp 16:1–16:8. ACM, New York, USA. https://doi.org/10.1145/2745555.2746644

Sears A, Young M (2003) The human-computer interaction handbook. L. Erlbaum Associates Inc., Hillsdale, USA. Physical disabilities and computing technologies: an analysis of impairments, pp 482–503. http://dl.acm.org/citation.cfm?id=772072.772105

Sears LMJJA, Xiao Y (2003) When computers fade... pervasive computing and situationally-induced impairments and disabilities. Proc HCII 2003:1298–1302

Sicari S, Rizzardi A, Grieco L, Coen-Porisini A (2015) Security, privacy and trust in internet of things: the road ahead. Comput Netw 76:146–164. https://doi.org/10.1016/j.comnet.2014.11.008, http://www.sciencedirect.com/science/article/pii/S1389128614003971

Sorge V, Pearson E (eds) (2018) W4A'18: proceedings of the internet of accessible things. ACM, New York, USA

Takayama L, Pantofaru C, Robson D, Soto B, Barry M (2012) Making technology homey: finding sources of satisfaction and meaning in home automation. In: Proceedings of the 2012 ACM conference on ubiquitous computing, UbiComp '12, pp 511–520. ACM, New York, USA. https://doi.org/10.1145/2370216.2370292

W3C (2019) Web of internet, https://www.w3.org/WoT/

Wentzel J, Velleman E, van der Geest T (2016) Wearables for all: development of guidelines to stimulate accessible wearable technology design. In: Proceedings of the 13th web for all conference, W4A '16, pp 34:1–34:4. ACM, New York, USA. https://doi.org/10.1145/2899475.2899496

Yaneva V, Ha LA, Eraslan S, Yesilada Y (2018a) Autism and the web: using web-searching tasks to detect autism and improve web accessibility. SIGACCESS Access Comput (121):2:1–2:1. https://doi.org/10.1145/3264631.3264633

Yaneva V, Ha LA, Eraslan S, Yesilada Y, Mitkov R (2018b) Detecting autism based on eye-tracking data from web searching tasks. In: Proceedings of the internet of accessible things, W4A '18, pp 16:1–16:10. ACM, New York, USA. https://doi.org/10.1145/3192714.3192819

Yesilada Y, Jay C, Stevens R, Harper S (2008) Validating the use and role of visual elements of web pages in navigation with an eye-tracking study. In: 17th international World Wide Web conference, Beijing, China

Yesilada Y, Brajnik G, Vigo M, Harper S (2012) Understanding web accessibility and its drivers. In: Proceedings of the international cross-disciplinary conference on web accessibility, W4A '12, pp 19:1–19:9. ACM, New York, USA. https://doi.org/10.1145/2207016.2207027

Yesilada Y, Brajnik G, Vigo M, Harper S (2013a) Exploring perceptions of web accessibility: a survey approach. Behaviour & Information Technology (just-accepted):1–25

Yesilada Y, Harper S, Eraslan S (2013b) Experiential transcoding: An eyetracking approach. In: Proceedings of the 10th international cross-disciplinary conference on web accessibility, W4A '13, pp 30:1–30:4. ACM, New York, USA. https://doi.org/10.1145/2461121.2461134

Zou J, Schiebinger L (2018) Ai can be sexist and racist - it's time to make it fair. Nature 559(7714):324–326

Index

© Springer-Verlag London Ltd., part of Springer Nature 2019
Y. Yesilada and S. Harper (eds.), *Web Accessibility*, Human–Computer
Interaction Series, https://doi.org/10.1007/978-1-4471-7440-0

Printed in the United States
By Bookmasters